Oxford
Large Print Dictionary, Thesaurus, and Wordpower Guide

Edited by
Sara Hawker

OXFORD
UNIVERSITY PRESS

OXFORD
UNIVERSITY PRESS

Great Clarendon Street, Oxford OX2 6DP

Oxford University Press is a department of the University of Oxford.
It furthers the University's objective of excellence in research, scholarship,
and education by publishing worldwide in

Oxford New York

Auckland Cape Town Dar es Salaam Hong Kong Karachi
Kuala Lumpur Madrid Melbourne Mexico City Nairobi
New Delhi Shanghai Taipei Toronto

With offices in

Argentina Austria Brazil Chile Czech Republic France Greece
Guatemala Hungary Italy Japan Poland Portugal Singapore
South Korea Switzerland Thailand Turkey Ukraine Vietnam

Oxford is a registered trade mark of Oxford University Press
in the UK and in certain other countries

Published in the United States
by Oxford University Press Inc., New York

British Library Cataloguing in Publication Data
Data available

Library of Congress Cataloging in Publication Data
Data available

Designed by George Hammond
Typeset in Stone Serif and Arial by Interactive Sciences Ltd
Printed in Great Britain by
Clays Ltd, Bungay, Suffolk

ISBN 978-0-19-861079-3 (hbk)

Contents

Note on trade marks and proprietary status

This book includes some words which are or are asserted to be proprietary names or trade marks. Their inclusion does not imply that they have acquired for legal purposes a non-proprietary or general significance, nor is any other judgement implied concerning their legal status.

In cases where the editor has some evidence that a word is used as a proprietary name or trade mark this is indicated by the label [trademark], but no judgement concerning the legal status of such words is made or implied thereby.

Preface

The *Oxford Large Print Dictionary, Thesaurus, and Wordpower Guide* is a handy three-in-one resource providing a variety of help with language and vocabulary in a convenient format. It contains separate dictionary and thesaurus sections for ease of reference, and a Wordpower Guide giving many useful lists of information, including confusable words, countries of the world, and a games and puzzles wordbuilder. The Wordpower Guide is located between the dictionary and thesaurus sections, towards the centre of the book.

The large type and generous spacing and margins make this an ideal reference book for adults or children seeking a text that is clear and easy to read. It is especially suitable for people with sight problems.

In producing the *Oxford Large Print Dictionary, Thesaurus, and Wordpower Guide*, the editors have worked closely with the Royal National Institute of the Blind who have approved and made recommendations on all aspects of design and layout.

Abbreviations

ABBREV	abbreviation	inf	informal
ADJ	adjective	PL	plural
ADV	adverb	PREP	preposition
CONJ	conjunction	PRON	pronoun

Labels

Unless otherwise stated, the words and senses in this dictionary are all part of standard English. Some words, however, are appropriate only to certain situations, or are found only in certain contexts or varieties of English, and where this is the case a label (or a combination of labels) is used.

For example, the labels [inf], [old use], and [literary] refer to a particular level of use in the language; in the case of [offensive] or [derogatory], the labels act as warnings that the term in question may cause offence.

The [US] label indicates that a word is used in US English but is not standard in British English.

Subject labels, such as [Music], [Grammar], and [Cricket], indicate that a word is associated with a particular subject field or specialist activity.

Aa

A ABBREV **1** amperes. **2** (Å) angstroms.

a ADJ (called the *indefinite article*) **1** used in mentioning someone or something for the first time; one, any. **2** per.

aardvark NOUN an African animal with a long snout.

aback ADV (**taken aback**) surprised.

abacus NOUN a frame with beads sliding on wires or rods, used for counting.

abandon VERB leave without intending to return; give up. NOUN lack of inhibition.
  abandoned ADJ
  abandonment NOUN

abase VERB humiliate; degrade.

abashed ADJ embarrassed or ashamed.

abate VERB become less intense.

abattoir NOUN a slaughterhouse.

abbey NOUN a building occupied by a community of monks or nuns.

abbot NOUN a man who is the head of a community of monks.

abbreviate VERB shorten a word etc.
  abbreviation NOUN

ABC NOUN **1** the alphabet. **2** the basic facts of a subject.

abdicate VERB **1** renounce the throne. **2** fail to carry out a duty.
  abdication NOUN

abdomen NOUN the part of the body containing the digestive organs.
  abdominal ADJ

abduct VERB kidnap.
  abduction NOUN

aberration NOUN a deviation from what is normal.
  aberrant ADJ

abet VERB (**abetted, abetting**) assist in wrongdoing.

abeyance NOUN (**in abeyance**) in temporary disuse.

abhor VERB (**abhorred, abhorring**) detest.

abhorrent ADJ detestable.
  abhorrence NOUN

abide VERB 1 tolerate.
2 (**abide by**) keep a
promise; obey a rule.
abiding ADJ lasting.
ability NOUN (PL **-ies**) 1 the
power to do something.
2 cleverness.
abject ADJ wretched;
lacking all pride.
abjure VERB renounce;
repudiate.
ablaze ADJ blazing.
able ADJ capable or
competent; clever.
ably ADV
ablutions PLURAL NOUN the
action of washing
yourself.
abnegate VERB renounce.
abnormal ADJ not normal.
abnormality NOUN
abnormally ADV
aboard ADV & PREP on
board.
abode NOUN a house or
home.
abolish VERB put an end to
formally.
abolition NOUN
abominable ADJ causing
revulsion.
abominably ADV
abominate VERB [literary]
detest.
abomination NOUN
aboriginal ADJ existing in
a country from its earliest
times. NOUN (**Aboriginal**)
an aboriginal inhabitant
of Australia.
Aborigine NOUN an
Australian Aboriginal.
abort VERB end a
pregnancy early; end
prematurely and
unsuccessfully.
abortion NOUN an
operation to end a
pregnancy early.
abortive ADJ unsuccessful.
abound VERB be plentiful.
about PREP & ADV
1 concerning.
2 approximately.
3 surrounding.
about-turn a reversal of
direction or policy.
above ADV & PREP at or to a
higher level than; more
than.
above board lawful.
abracadabra NOUN a
magic formula.
abrasion NOUN rubbing or
scraping away; an injury
caused by this.
abrasive ADJ causing
abrasion; harsh.
abreast ADV 1 side by side.
2 informed or up to date.
abridge VERB shorten by
using fewer words.
abridgement NOUN
abroad ADV away from

your home country.

abrupt ADJ **1** sudden.
2 curt. **3** steep.

abscess NOUN a swelling
that contains pus.

abscond VERB leave
secretly or illegally.

abseil VERB descend using
a rope fixed at a higher
point.

absence NOUN **1** the state
of being absent. **2** lack.

absent ADJ not present;
lacking.
absent-minded forgetful;
inattentive. **absent
yourself** stay away.

absentee NOUN a person
who is absent from work
etc.
absenteeism NOUN

absolute ADJ complete;
unrestricted.

absolutely ADV
completely. EXCLAMATION
definitely.

absolution NOUN formal
forgiveness of sins.

absolutism NOUN the
principle that the
government should have
unrestricted powers.

absolve VERB clear of
blame or guilt.

absorb VERB soak up;
assimilate; occupy the
attention of.

absorbent ADJ
absorption NOUN

abstain VERB **1** refrain,
especially from drinking
alcohol. **2** decide not to
vote.
abstention NOUN

abstemious ADJ not self-
indulgent, especially in
eating and drinking.

abstinence NOUN
abstaining, especially
from food or alcohol.

abstract ADJ **1** having no
material existence;
theoretical. **2** (of art) not
representing things
pictorially. VERB remove;
extract. NOUN a summary.
abstraction NOUN

abstruse ADJ hard to
understand.

absurd ADJ ridiculous.
absurdity NOUN

abundant ADJ plentiful.
abundance NOUN

abuse VERB treat badly;
misuse; insult. NOUN cruel
treatment; wrongful use;
insults.
abusive ADJ

abut VERB (**abutted,
abutting**) be next to or
touching.

abysmal ADJ very bad.

abyss NOUN a deep chasm.

AC ABBREV alternating

current.

acacia NOUN a tree or shrub with yellow or white flowers.

academic ADJ **1** of education or study. **2** of theoretical interest only. NOUN a scholar.

academically ADV

academy NOUN (PL **-ies**) **1** a society of scholars or artists. **2** a school.

accede VERB [formal] agree.

accelerate VERB increase in speed.

acceleration NOUN

accelerator NOUN a pedal on a vehicle for increasing speed.

accent NOUN **1** a style of pronunciation. **2** emphasis. **3** a written mark guiding pronunciation. VERB pronounce with an accent; emphasize.

accentuate VERB emphasize; make prominent.

accentuation NOUN

accept VERB say yes to; take as true; resign yourself to.

acceptance NOUN

acceptable ADJ tolerable; satisfactory.

acceptably ADV

access NOUN a way in; the right to see or enter. VERB retrieve computerized data or files.

accessible ADJ able to be reached or obtained.

accessibility NOUN

accession NOUN **1** the reaching of a rank or position. **2** an addition.

accessory NOUN (PL **-ies**) **1** something added as a supplement or decoration. **2** someone who helps in a crime.

accident NOUN **1** an unplanned event causing damage or injury. **2** chance.

accidental ADJ

accidentally ADV

acclaim VERB praise enthusiastically. NOUN enthusiastic praise.

acclamation NOUN

acclimatize (or **-ise**) VERB get used to new conditions.

accolade NOUN praise or honour.

accommodate VERB **1** provide lodging for. **2** adapt to.

accommodation NOUN

accommodating ADJ willing to do as asked.

accompany VERB

(**accompanied,
accompanying**) **1** go with.
2 play an instrumental
part supporting a singer
or instrument.
accompaniment NOUN
accompanist NOUN
accomplice NOUN a
partner in crime.
accomplish VERB succeed
in doing or achieving.
accomplishment NOUN
accomplished ADJ highly
skilled.
accord VERB be consistent
with something. NOUN
agreement.
of your own accord
without being asked.
according ADV (**according
to**) **1** as stated by. **2** in
proportion to.
accordingly ADV
accordion NOUN a
portable musical
instrument with bellows
and keys or buttons.
accost VERB approach and
speak to.
account NOUN **1** a
statement of money paid
or owed; a credit
arrangement with a bank
or firm. **2** a description of
an event. VERB (**account
for**) **1** explain. **2** make up.
accountable ADJ obliged

to account for your
actions.
accountability NOUN
accountant NOUN a
person who keeps or
inspects financial
accounts.
accountancy NOUN
accoutrements ([US]
accouterments) PLURAL
NOUN equipment.
accredited ADJ officially
authorized.
accrue VERB (**accrued,
accruing**) accumulate.
accumulate VERB acquire
more and more of;
increase.
accumulation NOUN
accurate ADJ free from
error.
accuracy NOUN
accuse VERB charge
someone with an offence
or crime.
accusation NOUN
accustom VERB make
used to.
ace NOUN **1** a playing card
with a single spot. **2** [inf] an
expert. **3** an unreturnable
serve in tennis.
acerbic ADJ harsh and
sharp.
acerbity NOUN
acetylene NOUN a
colourless gas, used in

welding.

ache NOUN a dull continuous pain. VERB suffer such a pain.

achieve VERB succeed in doing, reaching, or gaining.
  achievable ADJ
  achievement NOUN
  achiever NOUN

Achilles heel NOUN a vulnerable point.

acid ADJ sour. NOUN any of a class of substances that neutralize alkalis. ADJ containing acid; (of a remark) sharp or unkind.
  acid rain rain made acid by pollution.
  acidic ADJ
  acidity NOUN

acknowledge VERB 1 admit the truth of. 2 confirm receipt of.
  acknowledgement NOUN

acme NOUN the height of perfection.

acne NOUN an eruption of pimples.

acorn NOUN the oval nut of the oak tree.

acoustic ADJ of sound. NOUN (**acoustics**) the qualities of a room that affect the way sound carries.

acquaint VERB 1 make aware of. 2 (**be acquainted with**) know slightly.

acquaintance NOUN a slight knowledge; a person you know slightly.

acquiesce VERB agree.
  acquiescence NOUN
  acquiescent ADJ

acquire VERB gain possession of.
  acquisition NOUN

acquisitive ADJ eager to acquire things.

acquit VERB (**acquitted, acquitting**) 1 declare to be not guilty. 2 (**acquit yourself**) behave or perform.
  acquittal NOUN

acre NOUN a measure of land, 4,840 sq. yds (0.405 hectares).
  acreage NOUN

acrid ADJ bitter.

acrimonious ADJ angry and bitter.
  acrimony NOUN

acrobat NOUN a performer of spectacular gymnastic feats.
  acrobatic ADJ
  acrobatics NOUN

acronym NOUN a word formed from the initial letters of others.

across PREP & ADV from one side to the other of.

acrylic NOUN a synthetic fibre.

act VERB 1 do something; behave. 2 be an actor. NOUN 1 something done. 2 a law made by parliament. 3 a section of a play. 4 an item in a variety show.

acting ADJ serving temporarily.

action NOUN 1 the process of doing; something done. 2 a lawsuit. 3 a battle.

actionable ADJ giving cause for a lawsuit.

activate VERB cause to act or work.
activation NOUN

active ADJ functioning; energetic.
actively ADV

activist NOUN a person who campaigns for change.
activism NOUN

activity NOUN (PL **-ies**) 1 a particular pursuit. 2 lively action.

actor (or **actress**) NOUN a person who performs in a play or film.

actual ADJ 1 existing in fact or reality. 2 current.
actuality NOUN
actually ADV

actuary NOUN (PL **-ies**) an insurance expert who calculates risks and premiums.

actuate VERB activate; motivate.

acumen NOUN shrewdness.

acupuncture NOUN medical treatment involving pricking the skin with needles.

acute ADJ 1 intense; (of an illness) short but severe. 2 sharp-witted. 3 (of an angle) less than 90°.

AD ABBREV Anno Domini (used to indicate that a date comes the specified number of years after the traditional date of Jesus's birth).

adage NOUN a proverb.

adagio ADV [Music] in slow time.

adamant ADJ not changing your mind.

Adam's apple NOUN a projection at the front of the neck.

adapt VERB make or become suitable for new use or conditions.
adaptable ADJ
adaptation NOUN

adaptor NOUN a device for connecting several electric plugs to one socket.

add VERB 1 join to an existing item to increase or enlarge it. 2 say as a further remark. 3 put numbers together to calculate a total.
addition NOUN

addendum NOUN (PL **-da**) a section added to a book.

adder NOUN a poisonous snake.

addict NOUN a person physically dependent on something, especially a drug.
addicted ADJ
addiction NOUN
addictive ADJ

additional ADJ added or extra.
additionally ADV

additive NOUN a substance added.

addle VERB confuse.

addled ADJ (of an egg) rotten.

address NOUN 1 the details of where a person lives or where mail should be delivered. 2 a speech. VERB 1 write the address on mail. 2 speak to. 3 apply yourself to a task.

adenoids PLURAL NOUN the enlarged tissue between the back of the nose and the throat.

adept ADJ very skilful.

adequate ADJ satisfactory.
adequacy NOUN

adhere VERB 1 stick. 2 support a cause or belief.
adherence NOUN
adherent ADJ & NOUN

adhesive ADJ sticking; sticky. NOUN an adhesive substance.
adhesion NOUN

ad hoc ADV & ADJ for a particular occasion or purpose.

adieu EXCLAMATION goodbye.

adjacent ADJ adjoining.

adjective NOUN a word qualifying or describing a noun.

adjoin VERB be next to.

adjourn VERB break off a meeting until later.
adjournment NOUN

adjudge VERB decide judicially.

adjudicate VERB act as judge of.
adjudication NOUN
adjudicator NOUN

adjunct NOUN a non-essential supplement.

adjure VERB urge.

adjust VERB alter slightly; adapt to new conditions.
adjustment NOUN

adjutant NOUN an army officer assisting in

administrative work.

ad lib ADV & ADJ without preparation. VERB (**ad-libbed, ad-libbing**) improvise.

administer VERB 1 manage business affairs. 2 give or hand out.

administration NOUN management of public or business affairs.

administrate VERB

administrative ADJ

administrator NOUN

admirable ADJ worthy of admiration.

admirably ADV

admiral NOUN a naval officer of the highest rank.

admire VERB 1 respect highly. 2 look at with pleasure.

admiration NOUN

admission NOUN 1 a statement admitting something. 2 being allowed to enter.

admissible ADJ

admit VERB (**admitted, admitting**) 1 confess to be true. 2 allow to enter. 3 accept as valid.

admittance NOUN admission.

admonish VERB reprove; warn; exhort.

admonition NOUN

ad nauseam ADV to an excessive extent.

ado NOUN commotion; fuss.

adolescent ADJ & NOUN (a person) between childhood and adulthood.

adolescence NOUN

adopt VERB 1 bring up another's child as your own. 2 choose to follow a course of action.

adoption NOUN

adoptive ADJ

adore VERB love deeply.

adorable ADJ

adoration NOUN

adorn VERB decorate.

adornment NOUN

adrenal ADJ close to the kidneys.

adrenalin (or **adrenaline**) NOUN a stimulant hormone produced by adrenal glands.

adrift ADJ & ADV drifting; no longer fixed in position.

adroit ADJ skilful.

adulation NOUN excessive flattery.

adult ADJ fully grown. NOUN an adult person or animal.

adulterate VERB make impure by adding a substance.

adulteration NOUN

adultery NOUN sexual infidelity to your wife or husband.

adulterer NOUN

adulterous ADJ

advance VERB **1** move forward. **2** suggest. **3** lend money. NOUN **1** a forward movement; an improvement. **2** a loan. **3** (**advances**) a sexual approach.

advancement NOUN

advanced ADJ far on in development or time.

advantage NOUN something putting you in a favourable position.

take advantage of **1** exploit. **2** use.

advantageous ADJ

Advent NOUN **1** the season before Christmas. **2** (**advent**) an arrival.

adventure NOUN an exciting experience or undertaking.

adventurer NOUN

adventurous ADJ

adverb NOUN a word qualifying a verb, adjective, or other adverb.

adversary NOUN (PL **-ies**) an opponent.

adversarial ADJ

adverse ADJ unfavourable; bringing harm.

adversity NOUN (PL **-ies**) hardship.

advertise VERB publicize goods to promote sales, or a vacancy to encourage applications.

advertisement NOUN

advice NOUN a suggestion to someone about their best course of action.

advisable ADJ prudent or sensible.

advise VERB **1** give advice to; recommend. **2** inform.

adviser NOUN

advisory ADJ

advocate NOUN **1** a person who recommends a policy. **2** a person who speaks on behalf of another. VERB recommend.

advocacy NOUN

aegis NOUN protection or support.

aeon ([US] **eon**) NOUN a very long time.

aerate VERB introduce air into.

aerial ADJ **1** existing or taking place in the air. **2** by or from aircraft. NOUN a wire for transmitting or receiving radio waves.

aerobatics NOUN spectacular feats by aircraft in flight.

aerobatic ADJ

aerobics NOUN vigorous exercises designed to increase oxygen intake. **aerobic** ADJ

aerodynamics NOUN the study of moving air and its interaction with objects moving through it. **aerodynamic** ADJ

aeronautics NOUN the study of aircraft flight. **aeronautical** ADJ

aeroplane NOUN a power-driven aircraft with fixed wings.

aerosol NOUN a pressurized can holding a substance for release as a fine spray.

aerospace NOUN the technology and industry concerned with flight.

aesthete ([US] **esthete**) NOUN a person who appreciates art and beauty.

aesthetic ([US] **esthetic**) ADJ to do with beauty or its appreciation. NOUN (**aesthetics**) the study of beauty and artistic taste. **aesthetically** ADV

afar ADV far away.

affable ADJ polite and friendly.

affair NOUN 1 an event or series of events. 2 a person's rightful concerns. 3 a romantic or sexual liaison.

affect VERB 1 have an effect on. 2 pretend to feel or have.

affectation NOUN an artificial and pretentious manner. **affected** ADJ

affection NOUN love or liking. **affectionate** ADJ

affidavit NOUN a written statement sworn on oath.

affiliate VERB connect as a subordinate member or branch. **affiliation** NOUN

affinity NOUN (PL **-ies**) a close resemblance or attraction.

affirm VERB state firmly or publicly. **affirmation** NOUN

affirmative ADJ saying that something is the case. NOUN an affirmative statement.

affix VERB attach; fasten.

afflict VERB cause suffering to. **affliction** NOUN

affluent ADJ wealthy. **affluence** NOUN

afford VERB 1 have enough

affray

money or time for. **2** give or provide.

affray NOUN a public fight or riot.

affront NOUN an open insult. VERB insult or offend.

afloat ADV & ADJ floating; on a boat.

afoot ADV & ADJ going on.

afraid ADJ **1** frightened. **2** regretful.

afresh ADV making a fresh start.

aft ADV at or towards the rear of a ship or aircraft.

after PREP **1** later than. **2** behind; following. CONJ & ADV at a time later than.

after-effect an effect persisting after its cause has gone.

afterbirth NOUN the placenta discharged from the womb after childbirth.

aftermath NOUN the after-effects.

afternoon NOUN the time between noon and evening.

aftershave NOUN an astringent lotion used after shaving.

afterthought NOUN something thought of or added later.

afterwards ADV at a later time.

again ADV **1** once more. **2** besides; too.

against PREP **1** in opposition to. **2** in or into contact with.

agate NOUN a semi-precious stone.

age NOUN **1** the length of life or existence. **2** a historical period. **3** (usually **ages**) a very long time. VERB (**aged**, **ageing**) grow old.

aged ADJ **1** of a specified age. **2** old.

ageism NOUN prejudice on grounds of age. **ageist** NOUN & ADJ

ageless ADJ not growing or seeming to grow old.

agency NOUN (PL **-ies**) **1** an organization providing a particular service. **2** action producing an effect.

agenda NOUN a list of things to be dealt with, especially at a meeting.

agent NOUN **1** a person who acts on behalf of another. **2** a person or thing producing an effect.

aggrandize (or **-ise**) VERB increase the power or reputation of.

aggravate VERB **1** make

worse. **2** [inf] annoy.
aggravation NOUN

aggregate NOUN **1** a whole combining several elements. **2** crushed stone used in making concrete. ADJ formed by combination. VERB combine or unite.

aggression NOUN hostile acts or behaviour.
aggressive ADJ
aggressor NOUN

aggrieved ADJ having a grievance; resentful.

aghast ADJ filled with horror.

agile ADJ nimble or quick-moving.
agility NOUN

agitate VERB **1** worry, disturb; campaign to raise concern. **2** shake briskly.
agitation NOUN
agitator NOUN

AGM ABBREV annual general meeting.

agnostic NOUN a person believing that nothing can be known about God's existence.
agnosticism NOUN

ago ADV in the past.

agog ADJ eager and expectant.

agonize (or **-ise**) VERB **1** worry intensely.

2 (**agonizing**) very painful or worrying.

agony NOUN (PL **-ies**) extreme suffering.

agoraphobia NOUN extreme fear of open spaces.
agoraphobic NOUN & ADJ

agrarian ADJ of land or agriculture.

agree VERB (**agreed**, **agreeing**) **1** hold or express the same opinion. **2** consent. **3** (**agree with**) be good for; approve of.
agreement NOUN

agreeable ADJ pleasant; willing to agree.
agreeably ADV

agriculture NOUN the science or practice of farming.
agricultural ADJ

aground ADV & ADJ (of a ship) touching the sea bottom.

ahead ADV further forward in position or time.

ahoy EXCLAMATION a seaman's shout for attention.

aid VERB & NOUN help.

aide NOUN an assistant.

Aids (or **AIDS**) ABBREV acquired immune deficiency syndrome, a condition developing after infection with the

HIV virus, breaking down a person's immune system.

ail VERB make or become ill.

ailment NOUN a slight illness.

aim VERB point, send, or direct towards a target; intend or try. NOUN aiming; intention.

aimless ADJ without a purpose.
aimlessly ADV

ain't CONTRACTION [inf] am not, is not, are not; has not, have not.

air NOUN 1 a mixture of oxygen, nitrogen, etc., surrounding the earth. 2 a manner; an impression given. 3 (**airs**) an affectation of superiority. 4 a melody. VERB 1 express an opinion publicly. 2 expose to air to dry or ventilate.
air conditioning a system that cools the air in a building or vehicle. **air force** a branch of the armed forces using aircraft.

airborne ADJ carried by air or aircraft; (of aircraft) in flight.

aircraft NOUN (PL **aircraft**) a machine capable of flight in air.

airfield NOUN an area for the take-off and landing of aircraft.

airlift NOUN the large-scale transport of supplies by aircraft. VERB transport in this way.

airline NOUN a company providing an air transport service.

airliner NOUN a passenger aircraft.

airlock NOUN 1 a stoppage of the flow in a pipe, caused by an air bubble. 2 an airtight compartment giving access to a pressurized chamber.

airmail NOUN mail carried by aircraft.

airman NOUN a pilot or crew member in a military aircraft.

airplane NOUN [US] an aeroplane.

airplay NOUN the playing of a recording on radio.

airport NOUN an airfield with facilities for passengers and goods.

airship NOUN a power-driven aircraft that is lighter than air.

airspace NOUN the air and skies above a country.

airstrip NOUN a strip of ground for take-off and landing of aircraft.

airtight ADJ not allowing air to enter or escape.

airwaves PLURAL NOUN the radio frequencies used for broadcasting.

airway NOUN 1 a regular route for aircraft. 2 a passage for air into the lungs.

airworthy ADJ (of aircraft) fit to fly.

airy ADJ (-ier, -iest) 1 well ventilated and spacious. 2 delicate or light. 3 casual or dismissive.
airily ADV

aisle NOUN a passage between rows of seats.

ajar ADV & ADJ (of a door) slightly open.

aka ABBREV also known as.

akimbo ADV with hands on hips.

akin ADJ related; similar.

alabaster NOUN a soft translucent mineral.

à la carte ADJ & ADV ordered as separate items from a menu.

alacrity NOUN eager readiness.

à la mode ADJ & ADV in fashion.

alarm NOUN 1 fear and anxiety. 2 a warning sound or signal; a device to wake someone at a set time. VERB cause alarm to.

alarmist NOUN a person who causes excessive alarm.

alas EXCLAMATION an exclamation of sorrow.

albatross NOUN a large seabird.

albino NOUN (PL -os) a person or animal born with white skin and hair and pink eyes.

album NOUN 1 a blank book for holding photographs, stamps, etc. 2 a collection of recordings issued as a single item.

albumen NOUN egg white.

alchemy NOUN a medieval form of chemistry, seeking to turn other metals into gold.
alchemist NOUN

alcohol NOUN a colourless liquid found in intoxicating drinks such as wine or beer; drink containing this.

alcoholic ADJ containing alcohol. NOUN a person addicted to drinking alcohol.
alcoholism NOUN

alcove NOUN a recess in a

wall.

alderman NOUN [historical] a member of a council below the rank of mayor.

ale NOUN beer.

alert ADJ watchful; observant. VERB warn; make aware.

alfresco ADV & ADJ in the open air.

algae PLURAL NOUN simple water plants with no true stems or leaves.

algebra NOUN a branch of mathematics using letters etc. to represent quantities.

algorithm NOUN a step-by-step procedure for calculation.

alias NOUN a false name. ADV also called.

alibi NOUN evidence that an accused person was elsewhere when a crime was committed.

alien NOUN 1 a foreigner. 2 a being from another world. ADJ 1 foreign; unfamiliar. 2 extraterrestrial.

alienate VERB cause to become unfriendly or unsympathetic.
alienation NOUN

alight¹ VERB get down from a vehicle; land or settle.

alight² ADJ & ADV on fire.

align VERB 1 bring into the correct position. 2 ally yourself.
alignment NOUN

alike ADJ like one another. ADV in the same way.

alimentary ADJ of nourishment.

alimony NOUN money paid by a divorced person to their former spouse.

alive ADJ 1 living; lively. 2 (**alive to**) aware of.

alkali NOUN any of a class of substances that neutralize acids.
alkaline ADJ

all ADJ the whole quantity or extent of. PRON everyone or everything. ADV completely.
all right 1 unhurt. 2 satisfactory.

allay VERB lessen fears.

all-clear NOUN a signal that danger is over.

allege VERB declare without proof.
allegation NOUN
allegedly ADV

allegiance NOUN loyal support.

allegory NOUN (PL **-ies**) a story etc. with a hidden or symbolic meaning.
allegorical ADJ

almond

allegro ADV [Music] briskly.

alleluia (or **hallelujah**) EXCLAMATION & NOUN praise to God.

allergy NOUN (PL **-ies**) an abnormal sensitivity to certain foods, pollens, etc. **allergic** ADJ

alleviate VERB ease pain or distress. **alleviation** NOUN

alley NOUN (PL **-eys**) a narrow street; a long enclosure for skittles or bowling.

alliance NOUN an association formed for mutual benefit.

allied ADJ joined in alliance; working together.

alligator NOUN a reptile of the crocodile family.

alliteration NOUN the occurrence of the same sound at the start of adjacent words.

allocate VERB allot or assign. **allocation** NOUN

allot VERB (**allotted, allotting**) distribute; give as a share.

allotment NOUN 1 a small piece of land rented for cultivation. 2 an allotted share.

allow VERB 1 permit; make possible. 2 set aside for a purpose. 3 admit. 4 (**allow for**) take into account.

allowance NOUN 1 a permitted amount. 2 a sum of money paid regularly. **make allowances** be tolerant or lenient.

alloy NOUN a mixture of chemical elements at least one of which is a metal.

allude VERB refer briefly or indirectly. **allusion** NOUN

allure VERB entice or attract. NOUN attractiveness.

alluvium NOUN a deposit left by a flood. **alluvial** ADJ

ally NOUN (PL **-ies**) a country or person in alliance with another. VERB side with; join or combine.

almanac (or **almanack**) NOUN 1 a calendar giving information on important dates, astronomical data, etc. 2 a book published yearly, containing information about that year.

almighty ADJ 1 all-powerful. 2 [inf] enormous.

almond NOUN an edible

oval-shaped nut.

almost ADV very nearly.

alms PLURAL NOUN [historical] money given to the poor.

aloe NOUN a plant with bitter juice.

aloft ADV high up; upwards.

alone ADJ not with others; without company or help. ADV uniquely.

along PREP & ADV moving over the length of; extending beside.

alongside PREP close to the side of.

aloof ADJ unfriendly and distant.

alopecia NOUN loss of hair.

aloud ADV audibly.

alpaca NOUN a llama with long wool.

alpha NOUN the first letter of the Greek alphabet (A, α).

alphabet NOUN a set of letters in a fixed order representing the sounds of a language.
  alphabetical ADJ
  alphabetically ADV

alpine ADJ of high mountains.

already ADV before this time; as early as this.

Alsatian NOUN a German shepherd dog.

also ADV in addition; besides.

altar NOUN a table used in religious service.

alter VERB make or become different.
  alteration NOUN

altercation NOUN a noisy dispute.

alternate VERB (cause to) occur in turn repeatedly. ADJ **1** every other. **2** (of two things) repeatedly following and replacing each other.

alternative ADJ **1** available as another choice. **2** unconventional. NOUN a choice or option.

although CONJ despite the fact that.

altitude NOUN height above sea or ground level.

alto NOUN (PL **-os**) the highest adult male or lowest female voice.

altogether ADV **1** completely. **2** taking everything into consideration.

altruism NOUN unselfishness.
  altruistic ADJ

aluminium NOUN a lightweight silvery metal.

always ADV at all times; whatever the

circumstances.

Alzheimer's disease
NOUN a brain disorder
which may affect older
people.

AM ABBREV amplitude
modulation.

a.m. ABBREV (Latin *ante
meridiem*) before noon.

amalgam NOUN 1 a blend.
2 an alloy of mercury used
in dentistry.

amalgamate VERB unite
or combine.
amalgamation NOUN

amass VERB heap up;
collect.

amateur NOUN a person
who does something as a
pastime rather than as a
profession.
amateurish ADJ
incompetent or unskilful.

amatory ADJ to do with
love.

amaze VERB overwhelm
with wonder.
amazement NOUN

amazon NOUN a tall, strong
woman.

ambassador NOUN a
senior diplomat
representing their
country abroad.

amber NOUN yellowish
fossilized resin; its colour.

ambidextrous ADJ able to
use either hand equally
well.

ambience NOUN a place's
atmosphere.

ambiguous ADJ having
two or more possible
meanings.
ambiguity NOUN

ambition NOUN a strong
desire to achieve
something.
ambitious ADJ

ambivalent ADJ with
mixed feelings.
ambivalence NOUN

amble VERB & NOUN (walk at)
a leisurely pace.

ambulance NOUN a vehicle
equipped to carry sick or
injured people.

ambush NOUN a surprise
attack by people lying in
wait. VERB attack in this
way.

ameba US spelling of
amoeba.

ameliorate VERB make
better.
amelioration NOUN

amen EXCLAMATION (in
prayers) so be it.

amenable ADJ
1 cooperative.
2 (**amenable to**) able to be
affected by.

amend VERB make minor
alterations in a text etc.

make amends compensate for something.
amendment NOUN
amenity NOUN (PL **-ies**) a pleasant or useful feature of a place.
amethyst NOUN a violet or purple precious stone.
amiable ADJ likeable or friendly.
amiability NOUN
amiably ADV
amicable ADJ friendly.
amicably ADV
amid (or **amidst**) PREP in the middle of.
amino acid NOUN an organic acid found in proteins.
amiss ADV wrongly or badly. ADJ wrong or faulty.
amity NOUN friendly feeling.
ammonia NOUN a strong-smelling gas.
ammonite NOUN a fossil of a spiral shell.
ammunition NOUN a supply of bullets, shells, etc.
amnesia NOUN loss of memory.
amnesty NOUN (PL **-ies**) a general pardon.
amoeba ([US] **ameba**) NOUN (PL **-bae** or **-bas**) a single-celled organism capable of changing shape.
amok (or **amuck**) ADV (**run amok**) be out of control.
among (or **amongst**) PREP **1** surrounded by. **2** included in. **3** shared by; between.
amoral ADJ not based on moral standards.
amorous ADJ showing sexual desire.
amorphous ADJ shapeless.
amount NOUN a total of anything; a quantity. VERB (**amount to**) add up to; be equivalent to.
ampere NOUN a unit of electric current.
ampersand NOUN the sign & (= and).
amphibian NOUN an animal able to live both on land and in water.
amphibious ADJ
amphitheatre ([US] **amphitheater**) NOUN a semicircular unroofed building with tiers of seats round a central arena.
ample ADJ plentiful; quite enough; large.
amply ADV
amplify VERB (**amplified**, **amplifying**), **1** make louder; intensify. **2** add

details to a statement.
amplification NOUN
amplifier NOUN
amplitude NOUN breadth;
abundance.
amputate VERB cut off by
surgical operation.
amputation NOUN
amuck see amok.
amulet NOUN a thing worn
as a charm against
evil.
amuse VERB cause to laugh
or smile; provide with
entertainment.
amusement NOUN
amusing ADJ
an ADJ the form of *a* used
before vowel sounds.
anachronism NOUN
something that seems to
belong to another time.
anachronistic ADJ
anaconda NOUN a large
snake of South America.
anaemia ([US] **anemia**)
NOUN lack of haemoglobin
in the blood.
anaemic ADJ
anaesthetic ([US]
anesthetic) NOUN a
substance stopping you
feeling pain.
anaesthetist NOUN a
medical specialist who
gives patients
anaesthetics.

anaesthetize (or **-ise**) VERB
anagram NOUN a word or
phrase formed by
rearranging the letters of
another.
anal ADJ of the anus.
analgesic NOUN a drug
relieving pain.
analogy NOUN (PL **-ies**) a
comparison; a partial
likeness.
analogous ADJ
analyse ([US] **analyze**)
VERB examine in detail;
psychoanalyse.
analyst NOUN
analysis NOUN (PL **-ses**) a
detailed examination or
study.
analytic (or **analytical**) ADJ
anarchist NOUN a person
who believes that
government should be
abolished.
anarchy NOUN total lack of
organized control;
lawlessness.
anarchic ADJ
anathema NOUN a detested
thing.
anatomy NOUN (PL **-ies**)
bodily structure; the
study of the structure of
the body.
anatomical ADJ
anatomist NOUN
ancestor NOUN a person

from whom you are descended.

ancestral ADJ

ancestry NOUN

anchor NOUN a heavy metal structure for mooring a ship to the sea bottom. VERB moor with an anchor; fix firmly.

anchorage NOUN

anchorman NOUN the compère of a radio or TV programme.

anchovy NOUN (PL **-ies**) a small strong-tasting fish.

ancient ADJ very old.

ancillary ADJ helping in a subsidiary way.

and CONJ **1** together with or added to. **2** then.

andante ADV [Music] in moderately slow time.

androgynous ADJ partly male and partly female in appearance.

anecdote NOUN a short amusing or interesting true story.

anemia US spelling of **anaemia**.

anemone NOUN a plant with white, red, or purple flowers.

anesthetic US spelling of **anaesthetic**.

anew ADV **1** making a new start. **2** again.

angel NOUN **1** a supernatural being, messenger of God. **2** a kind person.

angelic ADJ

angelica NOUN candied stalks of a fragrant plant.

anger NOUN a strong feeling of displeasure. VERB make angry.

angina (or **angina pectoris**) NOUN pain in the chest caused by inadequate supply of blood to the heart.

angle[1] NOUN **1** the space between two lines or surfaces at the point where they meet; a corner. **2** a point of view. VERB present from a particular viewpoint; place obliquely.

angle[2] VERB fish with line and bait; try to obtain something by hinting.

angler NOUN

angling NOUN

Anglican ADJ & NOUN (a member) of the Church of England.

anglicize (or **-ise**) VERB make English in character.

Anglo- COMBINING FORM English or British.

Anglo-Saxon NOUN a

person living in England before the Norman Conquest; the language of the Anglo-Saxons.

angora NOUN fabric made from the hair of a long-haired goat.

angry ADJ (**-ier, -iest**) feeling or showing anger.
angrily ADV

angst NOUN severe anxiety.

anguish NOUN severe physical or mental pain.
anguished ADJ

angular ADJ having angles or sharp corners; forming an angle.

animal NOUN a living being with sense organs, able to move voluntarily.

animate ADJ living. VERB **1** bring to life; make vivacious. **2** make drawings or models into an animated film.
animated ADJ
animation NOUN

animosity NOUN hostility.

animus NOUN animosity.

aniseed NOUN a fragrant flavouring.

ankle NOUN the joint connecting the foot with the leg.

annals PLURAL NOUN a narrative of events year by year.

annex VERB **1** take possession of. **2** add as a subordinate part.
annexation NOUN

annexe NOUN an extension to a building.

annihilate VERB destroy completely.
annihilation NOUN

anniversary NOUN (PL **-ies**) the date on which an event took place in a previous year.

annotate VERB add explanatory notes to.
annotation NOUN

announce VERB make known publicly.
announcement NOUN
announcer NOUN

annoy VERB cause slight anger to.
annoyance NOUN

annual ADJ yearly. NOUN **1** a plant that lives for one year or one season. **2** a book published in yearly issues.
annually ADV

annuity NOUN (PL **-ies**) a yearly allowance.

annul VERB (**annulled, annulling**) cancel or declare invalid.
annulment NOUN

anodyne ADJ inoffensive but dull. NOUN a

painkilling medicine.

anoint VERB apply water or oil to, especially in religious consecration.

anomaly NOUN (PL **-ies**) something that is irregular or inconsistent. **anomalous** ADJ

anon ADV [old use] soon.

anonymous ADJ of unknown or undisclosed name or authorship. **anonymity** NOUN

anorak NOUN a waterproof jacket with a hood.

anorexia (or **anorexia nervosa**) NOUN a condition characterized by an obsessive desire to lose weight. **anorexic** ADJ & NOUN

another ADJ **1** an additional. **2** a different. PRON another one.

answer NOUN **1** something said or written in response to a previous statement. **2** the solution to a problem. VERB **1** speak or act in response. **2** correspond to a description; satisfy a need. **3** (**answer for**) be responsible for.

answerable ADJ having to account for something.

ant NOUN a small insect that lives in highly organized groups.

antagonist NOUN an opponent or enemy. **antagonism** NOUN **antagonize** (or **-ise**) VERB

Antarctic ADJ & NOUN (of) regions round the South Pole.

ante- PREFIX before.

anteater NOUN a mammal that eats ants.

antecedent NOUN something that precedes something else; (**antecedents**) a person's background. ADJ previous.

antedate VERB precede in time.

antediluvian ADJ of the time before Noah's Flood; [inf] antiquated.

antelope NOUN a deer-like wild animal.

antenatal ADJ before birth; of or during pregnancy.

antenna NOUN **1** (PL **-nae**) an insect's feeler. **2** (PL **-nas**) an aerial.

anterior ADJ further forward in position or time.

ante-room NOUN a small room leading to a main one.

anthem NOUN **1** a piece of

music to be sung in a religious service. **2** a song adopted by a country to express patriotic feelings.

anther NOUN a part of a flower's stamen containing pollen.

anthology NOUN (PL **-ies**) a collection of passages from literature, especially poems.

anthracite NOUN a form of coal burning with little flame or smoke.

anthrax NOUN a serious disease of sheep and cattle.

anthropoid ADJ (of apes) resembling a human in form.

anthropology NOUN the study of the origin and customs of human beings.

anthropologist NOUN

anthropomorphic ADJ attributing human form or character to a god or animal.

anti- PREFIX opposed to; counteracting.

antibiotic NOUN a substance that destroys bacteria.

antibody NOUN (PL **-ies**) a protein formed in the blood in reaction to a substance which it then destroys.

anticipate VERB expect or look forward to; deal with in advance.

anticipation NOUN

anticlimax NOUN a dull ending where a climax was expected.

anticlockwise ADJ & ADV in the direction opposite to clockwise.

antics PLURAL NOUN ridiculous behaviour.

antidote NOUN a substance that counteracts the effects of poison.

antifreeze NOUN a substance added to water to prevent freezing.

antihistamine NOUN a drug used to treat allergies.

antimony NOUN a brittle metallic element.

antipathy NOUN (PL **-ies**) strong dislike.

antiperspirant NOUN a substance that prevents or reduces sweating.

Antipodes PLURAL NOUN places on opposite sides of the earth, especially Australia and New Zealand.

Antipodean ADJ

antiquarian ADJ of

antiques and their study. NOUN a person who studies antiques.

antiquated ADJ very old-fashioned.

antique ADJ belonging to the distant past. NOUN an old and usually valuable object.

antiquity NOUN (PL **-ies**) 1 ancient times. 2 great age.

anti-Semitic ADJ hostile to or prejudiced against Jews.

anti-Semitism NOUN

antiseptic ADJ & NOUN (a substance) preventing infection.

antisocial ADJ destructive or hostile to other members of society.

antithesis NOUN (PL **-ses**) an opposite; a contrast.

antler NOUN a branched horn of a deer.

antonym NOUN a word opposite to another in meaning.

anus NOUN the opening through which solid waste matter leaves the body.

anvil NOUN an iron block on which a smith hammers metal into shape.

anxious ADJ 1 troubled and uneasy. 2 (**anxious to**) eager to.

anxiety NOUN

any ADJ 1 one or some of a quantity or amount. 2 an unspecified; expressing indifference as to identity.

anybody PRON any person.

anyhow ADV 1 anyway. 2 in a disorganized or untidy way.

anyone PRON anybody.

anything PRON any item.

anyway ADV 1 used to add a further point. 2 used to dismiss objections or difficulties. 3 used in introducing a new topic.

anywhere ADV & PRON (in or to) any place.

aorta NOUN the main artery carrying blood from the heart.

apace ADV swiftly.

apart ADV separately; to or at a distance; into pieces.

apartheid NOUN a policy of racial segregation, formerly in force in South Africa.

apartment NOUN a flat; a set of rooms.

apathy NOUN lack of interest or concern.

apathetic ADJ

ape NOUN a tailless primate, e.g. a gorilla. VERB imitate or mimic.

aperitif NOUN an alcoholic drink taken as an appetizer.

aperture NOUN an opening, especially one that admits light.

apex NOUN the highest point or level.

aphid NOUN a small insect destructive to plants.

aphorism NOUN a short saying expressing a general truth.

aphrodisiac NOUN a substance arousing sexual desire.

apiary NOUN (PL **-ies**) a place where bees are kept.

apiece ADV to, for, or by each.

aplomb NOUN self-possession or confidence.

apocalypse NOUN a catastrophic event.
apocalyptic ADJ

apocryphal ADJ of doubtful authenticity.

apology NOUN (PL **-ies**) **1** a statement of regret for having done wrong or hurt someone. **2** (**an apology for**) a poor example of.
apologetic ADJ
apologize (or **-ise**) VERB

apoplexy NOUN **1** [dated] a stroke. **2** [inf] extreme anger.
apoplectic ADJ

apostate NOUN a person who renounces a former belief.

Apostle NOUN each of the twelve men sent by Jesus to preach the gospel; (**apostle**) someone who supports and spreads an idea.

apostrophe NOUN the sign ' used to show the possessive case or omission of a letter.

appal ([US] **appall**) VERB (**appalled, appalling**) horrify.
appalling ADJ

apparatus NOUN equipment for scientific or other work.

apparel NOUN [formal] clothing.

apparent ADJ **1** clearly seen or understood. **2** seeming but not real.
apparently ADV

apparition NOUN a ghost.

appeal VERB **1** make an earnest or formal request. **2** refer a decision to a higher court. **3** seem attractive. NOUN **1** an act of appealing. **2** attractiveness.

appear VERB **1** become visible. **2** seem.
appearance NOUN
appease VERB pacify someone by giving what they ask for.
appeasement NOUN
append VERB add at the end.
appendage NOUN
appendicitis NOUN inflammation of the intestinal appendix.
appendix NOUN (PL **-ices** or **-ixes**) **1** a section at the end of a book, giving extra information. **2** a small closed tube of tissue attached to the large intestine.
appertain VERB be relevant.
appetite NOUN desire, especially for food.
appetizing (or **-ising**) ADJ stimulating the appetite.
appetizer NOUN
applaud VERB express approval, especially by clapping.
applause NOUN
apple NOUN a round fruit with firm juicy flesh.
appliance NOUN a piece of equipment for a specific task.
applicable ADJ

appropriate; relevant.
applicability NOUN
application NOUN **1** a formal request. **2** sustained hard work. **3** the action of applying something. **4** a computer program designed for a particular purpose.
applicant NOUN
applicator NOUN
applied ADJ put to practical use.
apply VERB (**applied, applying**) **1** make a formal request. **2** be relevant. **3** spread over a surface. **4** bring into operation. **5** (**apply yourself**) devote your energy and attention.
appoint VERB choose a person for a job; decide on.
appointment NOUN an arrangement to meet; a job.
apportion VERB share out.
apposite ADJ appropriate; relevant.
appraise VERB estimate the value or quality of.
appraisal NOUN
appreciable ADJ considerable.
appreciably ADV
appreciate VERB

1 recognize the good qualities of; understand; be grateful for. **2** increase in value.

appreciation NOUN

appreciative ADJ

apprehend VERB **1** arrest. **2** understand.

apprehension NOUN **1** anxiety. **2** understanding.

apprehensive ADJ

apprentice NOUN a person learning a craft.

apprenticeship NOUN

apprise VERB inform.

approach VERB **1** come nearer to. **2** make a request or suggestion to. **3** start to deal with a task. NOUN an act or manner of approaching; a path leading to a place.

approachable ADJ easy to talk to.

approbation NOUN approval.

appropriate ADJ suitable or proper. VERB take and use; set aside for a special purpose.

appropriation NOUN

approve VERB **1** regard as good or acceptable. **2** formally authorize or accept.

approval NOUN

approx. ABBREV approximate(ly).

approximate ADJ almost but not quite exact. VERB be very similar.

approximation NOUN

après-ski NOUN social activities following a day's skiing.

apricot NOUN an orange-yellow fruit resembling a small peach.

April NOUN the fourth month.

apron NOUN **1** a garment worn over the front of the body to protect clothes. **2** part of a theatre stage in front of the curtain. **3** an area on an airfield for manoeuvring and loading aircraft.

apropos ADV concerning.

apt ADJ **1** appropriate. **2** (**apt to**) having a tendency to.

aptitude NOUN natural ability.

aqualung NOUN a portable underwater breathing apparatus.

aquamarine NOUN a bluish-green gemstone.

aquaplane VERB (of a vehicle) glide uncontrollably on a wet road surface.

aquarium NOUN (PL **-riums**

or **-ria**) a tank for keeping living fish etc.

aquatic ADJ living or taking place in or on water.

aqueduct NOUN a structure carrying a waterway over a valley.

aquiline ADJ like an eagle; curved like an eagle's beak.

arabesque NOUN a ballet position in which one leg is lifted and extended backwards.

arable ADJ (of land) suitable for growing crops.

arachnid NOUN a creature of a class including spiders and scorpions.

arbiter NOUN a person with power to judge in a dispute.

arbitrary ADJ based on random choice.
arbitrarily ADV

arbitrator NOUN an impartial person chosen to settle a dispute.
arbitrate VERB
arbitration NOUN

arbor US spelling of **arbour**.

arboreal ADJ of or living in trees.

arbour ([US] **arbor**) NOUN a shady shelter under trees or a framework with climbing plants.

arc NOUN 1 part of a curve, especially of the circumference of a circle. 2 a luminous electric discharge between two points.

arcade NOUN a covered walk between shops; an enclosed place containing games machines etc.

arcane ADJ mysterious.

arch NOUN a curved structure, especially as a support; a curved shape. VERB form an arch. ADJ affectedly playful.

arch- PREFIX chief or main.

archaeology ([US] **archeology**) NOUN the study of earlier civilizations through their material remains.
archaeologist NOUN

archaic ADJ belonging to former or ancient times.

archaism NOUN an archaic word or phrase.

archangel NOUN an angel of the highest rank.

archbishop NOUN a chief bishop.

archer NOUN a person who shoots with a bow and arrows.

archery NOUN

archetype NOUN a typical example; an original model.
archetypal ADJ

archipelago NOUN (PL **-os** or **-oes**) a group of islands.

architect NOUN a designer of buildings.

architecture NOUN the design and construction of buildings.
architectural ADJ

archive NOUN a collection of historical documents.
archivist NOUN

archway NOUN an arched entrance or passage.

Arctic ADJ 1 of regions round the North Pole. 2 (**arctic**) [inf] very cold.

ardent ADJ passionate; enthusiastic.

ardour ([US] **ardor**) NOUN passion; enthusiasm.

arduous ADJ difficult and tiring.

area NOUN 1 a region; a space for a specific use. 2 the extent of a surface or piece of land.

arena NOUN a level area in the centre of an amphitheatre or sports stadium; an area of activity.

argon NOUN an inert gaseous element.

arguable ADJ 1 able to be asserted or maintained. 2 open to question.
arguably ADV

argue VERB 1 express disagreement; exchange angry words. 2 give reasons for an opinion.

argument NOUN 1 a discussion involving disagreement; a quarrel. 2 a reason put forward.
argumentative ADJ

aria NOUN a solo in an opera.

arid ADJ dry or parched.

arise VERB (**arose, arisen, arising**) 1 start to exist or be noticed. 2 [literary] rise.

aristocracy NOUN (PL **-ies**) the hereditary upper classes.
aristocrat NOUN
aristocratic ADJ

arithmetic NOUN calculating by means of numbers.

ark NOUN 1 (in the Bible) the ship built by Noah to escape the Flood. 2 (**Ark of the Covenant**) a wooden chest in which the writings of Jewish Law were kept.

arm NOUN 1 an upper limb

of the body. **2** a raised side part of a chair. **3** a division of a company or organization. **4** (**arms**) weapons. VERB equip or supply with weapons; make a bomb ready to explode.

armada NOUN a fleet of warships.

armadillo NOUN (PL **-os**) a mammal of South America with a body encased in bony plates.

armament NOUN military weapons.

armchair NOUN an upholstered chair with supports for the arms at the sides.

armistice NOUN an agreement to stop fighting temporarily.

armour ([US] **armor**) NOUN a protective metal covering, especially that formerly worn in battle. **armoured** ADJ

armoury ([US] **armory**) NOUN (PL **-ies**) a place where weapons are kept.

armpit NOUN the hollow under the arm at the shoulder.

army NOUN (PL **-ies**) **1** an organized force for fighting on land. **2** a vast group.

aroma NOUN a pleasant smell. **aromatic** ADJ

aromatherapy NOUN the use of essential plant oils for healing.

arose past of **arise**.

around ADV & PREP **1** on every side of. **2** in or to many places throughout an area. **3** approximately. **4** so as to face in the opposite direction.

arouse VERB waken; stimulate.

arpeggio NOUN (PL **-os**) the notes of a musical chord played in succession.

arraign VERB accuse.

arrange VERB **1** put into order. **2** organize; plan. **3** adapt a piece of music. **arrangement** NOUN

arrant ADJ complete and utter.

array NOUN **1** a display or wide range. **2** an arrangement. **3** [literary] fine clothing. VERB **1** arrange. **2** dress finely.

arrears PLURAL NOUN money owed and overdue for repayment.

arrest VERB **1** seize someone by legal authority. **2** stop. NOUN the legal seizure of an offender.

arrive VERB reach the end of a journey; (of a particular moment) come.
arrival NOUN

arrogant ADJ exaggerating your importance or abilities.
arrogance NOUN

arrogate VERB take or claim for yourself without justification.

arrow NOUN a straight shaft with a sharp point, shot from a bow; a sign shaped like this.

arsenal NOUN a place where weapons are stored or made.

arsenic NOUN a semi-metallic element from which a highly poisonous powder is obtained.

arson NOUN the intentional and unlawful setting on fire of a building.
arsonist NOUN

art NOUN 1 the creation of something beautiful and expressive; paintings and sculptures. 2 (**arts**) subjects other than sciences; creative activities (e.g. painting, music, writing). 3 a skill.

artefact ([US] **artifact**) NOUN a man-made object.

artery NOUN (PL **-ies**) a large blood vessel carrying blood from the heart.
arterial ADJ

artful ADJ crafty.

arthritis NOUN a condition causing pain and stiffness in the joints.
arthritic ADJ

arthropod NOUN an animal with a segmented body and jointed limbs (e.g. a crustacean).

artichoke NOUN a vegetable consisting of the unopened flower head of a thistle-like plant.

article NOUN 1 an individual object. 2 a piece of writing in a newspaper or journal. 3 a clause in an agreement.
definite article the word 'the'. **indefinite article** the word 'a' or 'an'.

articulate ADJ able to express yourself coherently; (of speech) clear and coherent. VERB 1 speak or express clearly. 2 connect by joints.
articulation NOUN

artifact US spelling of **artefact**.

artifice NOUN a clever

deception; skill.

artificial ADJ not originating naturally; man-made.
artificiality NOUN
artificially ADV

artillery NOUN (PL **-ies**) large guns used in fighting on land; a branch of an army using these.

artisan NOUN a skilled manual worker.

artist NOUN **1** a person who creates works of art, especially paintings. **2** a person skilled at a particular task. **3** a professional entertainer.
artistry NOUN

artiste NOUN a professional entertainer.

artistic ADJ of art or artists; skilled in art; aesthetically pleasing.
artistically ADV

artless ADJ simple and natural.

artwork NOUN pictures and diagrams in published material.

arty ADJ [inf] pretentiously displaying your interest in the arts.

as ADV & CONJ **1** used in comparisons to indicate extent or degree; used to indicate manner. **2** while.

3 because. **4** although. PREP in the role or form of.

asbestos NOUN a soft fibrous mineral substance used to make fireproof material.

ascend VERB rise; climb.
ascent NOUN

ascendant ADJ rising.

Ascension NOUN the ascent of Jesus to heaven.

ascertain VERB find out.

ascetic ADJ & NOUN (a person) abstaining from pleasures and luxuries.
asceticism NOUN

ascorbic acid NOUN vitamin C.

ascribe VERB attribute.

asexual ADJ without sex.

ash NOUN **1** a tree with silver-grey bark. **2** powder that remains after something has burnt.

ashamed ADJ feeling shame.

ashen ADJ pale as ashes; grey.

ashore ADV to or on the shore.

aside ADV to or on one side. NOUN a remark made so that only certain people will hear.

asinine ADJ silly.

ask VERB **1** try to obtain an answer or information.

2 make a request. **3** invite someone.

askance ADV (**look askance at**) regard with disapproval.

askew ADV & ADJ crooked or crookedly.

asleep ADV & ADJ in or into a state of sleep.

asp NOUN a small poisonous snake.

asparagus NOUN a plant whose shoots are used as a vegetable.

aspect NOUN **1** a feature or part of something. **2** the appearance of something. **3** the direction in which a building faces.

aspen NOUN a poplar tree.

asperity NOUN harshness.

aspersion NOUN a derogatory remark.

asphalt NOUN a black tar-like substance mixed with gravel for surfacing roads.

asphyxiate VERB suffocate.
asphyxiation NOUN

aspic NOUN a savoury jelly for coating cooked meat, eggs, etc.

aspidistra NOUN a plant with broad tapering leaves.

aspire VERB have a hope or ambition.

aspiration NOUN

aspirin NOUN a drug that relieves pain and reduces fever.

ass NOUN **1** a donkey. **2** [inf] a stupid person.

assail VERB attack violently.
assailant NOUN

assassin NOUN a killer of an important person.

assassinate VERB kill an important person by violent means.
assassination NOUN

assault NOUN & VERB attack.

assemble VERB bring or come together; put together the parts of.

assembly NOUN an assembled group; assembling.

assent NOUN & VERB (express) agreement.

assert VERB **1** state or declare to be true. **2** exercise rights or authority. **3** (**assert yourself**) behave forcefully.
assertion NOUN
assertive ADJ

assess VERB decide the amount or value of; estimate the worth or likelihood of.
assessment NOUN

assessor NOUN

asset NOUN 1 a property with money value. 2 a useful or valuable thing or person.

assiduous ADJ diligent and persevering.

assiduity NOUN

assign VERB allot to a person or purpose; designate to perform a task.

assignment NOUN

assignation NOUN an arrangement to meet.

assimilate VERB absorb or be absorbed into the body, into a larger group, or into the mind as knowledge.

assimilation NOUN

assist VERB help.

assistance NOUN

assistant NOUN a helper; a person who serves customers in a shop.

assizes PLURAL NOUN [historical] a county court.

associate VERB 1 connect in your mind. 2 mix socially. 3 (**associate yourself**) be involved with something. NOUN a work partner or colleague.

association NOUN a group organized for a shared purpose; a link or connection.

assonance NOUN the rhyming of vowel sounds.

assorted ADJ of several sorts.

assortment NOUN

assuage VERB soothe.

assume VERB 1 accept as true without proof. 2 take on a responsibility, quality, etc.

assumption NOUN something assumed to be true.

assurance NOUN 1 an assertion or promise. 2 self-confidence. 3 life insurance.

assure VERB tell confidently or promise.

assured ADJ confident; certain.

assuredly ADV

asterisk NOUN a star-shaped symbol (*).

astern ADV at or towards the stern; backwards.

asteroid NOUN one of many small rocky bodies orbiting the sun between Mars and Jupiter.

asthma NOUN a chronic condition causing difficulty in breathing.

asthmatic ADJ & NOUN

astigmatism NOUN a defect in an eye,

preventing proper focusing.

astonish VERB surprise greatly.

astonishment NOUN

astound VERB amaze.

astral ADJ of or from the stars.

astray ADV & ADJ away from the proper path.

astride ADV & PREP with one leg on each side of.

astringent ADJ 1 causing body tissue to contract. 2 sharp or severe. NOUN an astringent lotion.

astringency NOUN

astrology NOUN the study of the supposed influence of stars on human affairs.

astrologer NOUN

astrological ADJ

astronaut NOUN a person trained to travel in a spacecraft.

astronomical ADJ 1 of astronomy. 2 [inf] very large.

astronomically ADV

astronomy NOUN the study of stars and planets and their movements.

astronomer NOUN

astute ADJ shrewd.

asunder ADV [literary] apart.

asylum NOUN 1 refuge or protection. 2 [dated] a mental institution.

asymmetrical ADJ lacking symmetry.

asymmetry NOUN

at PREP expressing: 1 location, arrival, or time. 2 a value, rate, or point on a scale. 3 a state or condition. 4 direction towards.

ate past of **eat**.

atheist NOUN a person who does not believe in God.

atheism NOUN

athlete NOUN a person who is good at athletics.

athletic ADJ 1 strong, fit, and active. 2 of athletics. NOUN (**athletics**) track and field sports.

athleticism NOUN

atlas NOUN a book of maps.

atmosphere NOUN 1 the mixture of gases surrounding a planet; air. 2 a unit of pressure. 3 the feeling given by a place, situation, etc.

atmospheric ADJ

atoll NOUN a ring-shaped coral reef enclosing a lagoon.

atom NOUN the smallest particle of a chemical element; a very small quantity.

atom bomb a bomb

deriving its power from atomic energy.

atomic ADJ

atomize (or **-ise**) VERB reduce to atoms or fine particles.

atomizer NOUN

atonal ADJ (of music) not written in any key.

atone VERB make amends for a fault.

atonement NOUN

atrocious ADJ very bad.

atrocity NOUN (PL **-ies**) wickedness; a cruel act.

atrophy VERB (**atrophied**, **atrophying**) waste away from lack of use or nourishment. NOUN wasting away.

attach VERB fix to something else; join; ascribe.

attachment NOUN

attaché NOUN a person attached to an ambassador's staff.

attaché case a small case for carrying documents.

attached ADJ (**attached to**) fond of.

attack NOUN a violent attempt to hurt or defeat a person; strong criticism; a sudden onset of illness. VERB make an attack on.

attacker NOUN

attain VERB achieve.

attainable ADJ

attainment NOUN

attempt VERB try. NOUN an effort.

attend VERB **1** be present at; accompany. **2** take notice. **3** (**attend to**) deal with.

attendance NOUN

attendant NOUN an assistant; a person providing service in a particular place. ADJ accompanying.

attention NOUN **1** special care, notice, or attention. **2** a straight standing position in military drill.

attentive ADJ paying attention; considerate and helpful.

attenuate VERB make thin or weaker.

attest VERB provide proof of; declare true or genuine.

attic NOUN a room in the top storey of a house.

attire NOUN [literary] clothes. VERB clothe.

attitude NOUN **1** a fixed way of thinking. **2** a position of the body.

attorney NOUN (PL **-eys**) [US] a lawyer.

attract VERB draw someone in by offering

something appealing; arouse interest or liking in.

attraction NOUN

attractive ADJ pleasing in appearance.

attribute NOUN a characteristic quality. VERB (**attribute to**) regard as belonging to or caused by.

attributable ADJ

attribution NOUN

attrition NOUN wearing away.

attune VERB make receptive or aware.

atypical ADJ not typical.

aubergine NOUN a dark purple vegetable.

auburn ADJ (of hair) reddish brown.

auction NOUN a public sale where articles are sold to the highest bidder. VERB sell by auction.

auctioneer NOUN

audacious ADJ daring.

audacity NOUN

audible ADJ loud enough to be heard.

audibly ADV

audience NOUN 1 a group of listeners or spectators. 2 a formal interview.

audio NOUN sound or the reproduction of sound.

audio-visual using both sight and sound.

audit NOUN & VERB (make) an official examination of accounts.

auditor NOUN

audition NOUN a test of a performer's ability for a particular part. VERB test or be tested in an audition.

auditorium NOUN (**-riums** or **-ria**) the part of a theatre or concert hall where the audience sits.

auditory ADJ of hearing.

auger NOUN a boring tool with a spiral point.

augment VERB add to or increase.

augur VERB be an omen.

augury NOUN

August NOUN the eighth month.

august ADJ majestic.

auk NOUN a northern seabird.

aunt NOUN the sister or sister-in-law of your father or mother.

au pair NOUN a young person from overseas helping with housework in return for board and lodging.

aura NOUN the atmosphere surrounding a person or thing.

aural ADJ of the ear.

au revoir EXCLAMATION goodbye.

auspices PLURAL NOUN (**under the auspices of**) with the support of.

auspicious ADJ being an omen of success.

austere ADJ severely simple and plain.

austerity NOUN

authentic ADJ genuine; known to be true.

authentically ADV

authenticity NOUN

authenticate VERB prove the authenticity of.

authentication NOUN

author NOUN the writer of a book etc.; an originator.

authorship NOUN

authoritarian ADJ demanding strict obedience.

authoritative ADJ **1** reliably accurate or true. **2** commanding obedience and respect.

authority NOUN (PL -ies) **1** power to enforce obedience; a person with this. **2** a person with specialized knowledge.

authorize (or -ise) VERB give official permission for.

authorization NOUN

autistic ADJ suffering from a mental disorder that prevents normal communication and relationships.

autism NOUN

auto- COMBINING FORM self; own.

autobiography NOUN (PL -ies) the story of a person's life written by that person.

autobiographical ADJ

autocrat NOUN a ruler with unrestricted power.

autocracy NOUN

autocratic ADJ

autograph NOUN a person's signature. VERB write your name in or on.

automate VERB convert a machine etc. to automatic operation.

automation NOUN

automatic ADJ functioning without human intervention; done without thinking. NOUN an automatic machine or firearm.

automatically ADV

automaton NOUN (PL -tons or -ta) a robot.

automobile NOUN [US] a car.

automotive ADJ concerned with motor vehicles.

autonomous ADJ independent; self-governing.
autonomy NOUN
autopsy NOUN (PL **-ies**) a post-mortem.
autumn NOUN the season between summer and winter.
autumnal ADJ
auxiliary ADJ giving help or support. NOUN (PL **-ies**) a helper.
avail VERB 1 be of use or help. 2 (**avail yourself of**) make use of.
available ADJ ready to be used; obtainable.
availability NOUN
avalanche NOUN a mass of snow pouring down a mountain.
avant-garde ADJ new and experimental.
avarice NOUN greed for wealth.
avaricious ADJ
avenge VERB take vengeance for.
avenger NOUN
avenue NOUN a wide road, usually tree-lined; a method of approach.
aver VERB (**averred, averring**) state as true.
average NOUN a value arrived at by adding several quantities together and dividing by the number of these; a standard regarded as usual. ADJ found by making an average; ordinary or usual.
averse ADJ having a strong dislike.
aversion NOUN
avert VERB turn away; ward off.
aviary NOUN (PL **-ies**) a large cage or building for keeping birds.
aviation NOUN the practice or science of flying an aircraft.
avid ADJ very interested or enthusiastic.
avocado NOUN (PL **-os**) a pear-shaped tropical fruit.
avoid VERB keep away from; refrain from.
avoidance NOUN
avow VERB declare.
avowal NOUN
avuncular ADJ kind towards a younger person.
await VERB wait for; be in store for.
awake VERB (**awoke, awoken, awaking**) wake. ADJ not asleep.
awaken VERB awake.
award VERB give by official decision as a prize or

penalty. NOUN something awarded; awarding.

aware ADJ having knowledge or realization. **awareness** NOUN

awash ADJ covered or flooded with water.

away ADV to or at a distance; into non-existence.

awe NOUN respect combined with fear or wonder. VERB fill with awe. **awesome** ADJ

awful ADJ 1 extremely bad or unpleasant. 2 very great. **awfully** ADV

awhile ADV for a short time.

awkward ADJ 1 difficult to use, do, or handle; inconvenient; clumsy. 2 uncooperative. 3 embarrassing.

awl NOUN a tool for making holes in leather or wood.

awning NOUN a canvas shelter.

awoke, **awoken** past & past participle of **awake**.

AWOL ABBREV absent without leave.

awry ADV & ADJ twisted to one side; wrong or amiss.

axe ([US] usually **ax**) NOUN a chopping tool with a sharp blade. VERB (**axed**, **axing**) ruthlessly cancel or dismiss.

axiom NOUN an accepted general principle. **axiomatic** ADJ

axis NOUN (PL **axes**) a line through the centre of an object, round which it rotates if spinning.

axle NOUN a rod passing through the centre of a wheel or group of wheels.

ayatollah NOUN a religious leader in Iran.

aye EXCLAMATION [old use or dialect] yes.

azalea NOUN a shrub with brightly coloured flowers.

azure NOUN a deep sky-blue colour.

Bb

BA ABBREV Bachelor of Arts.

babble VERB chatter indistinctly or foolishly. NOUN babbling talk or sound.

babe NOUN a baby.

babel NOUN a confused noise.

baboon NOUN a large monkey.

baby NOUN (PL **-ies**) a very young child or animal; a timid or childish person. ADJ miniature.
babyish ADJ

babysit VERB (**-sat**, **-sitting**) look after a child while its parents are out. **babysitter** NOUN

bachelor NOUN **1** an unmarried man. **2** used in names of university degrees.

bacillus NOUN (PL **-li**) a rod-shaped bacterium.

back NOUN the surface or part furthest from the front; the rear part of the human body from shoulders to hips; the corresponding part of an animal's body; a defensive player positioned near the goal in football etc. ADV **1** at or towards the rear; in or into a previous time, position, or state. **2** in return. VERB **1** support. **2** move backwards. **3** lay a bet on. ADJ **1** situated at the back. **2** of or relating to the past.
back down withdraw a claim or argument. **back out** withdraw from a commitment. **back up** support.
backer NOUN

backbiting NOUN spiteful talk.

backbone NOUN the column of small bones down the centre of the back.

backcloth NOUN a painted cloth at the back of a stage or scene.

backdate VERB declare to be valid from a previous date.

backdrop NOUN a backcloth; a background.

backfire VERB **1** make an explosion in an exhaust

pipe. **2** produce an undesired effect.

backgammon NOUN a board game played with draughts and dice.

background NOUN the back part of a scene or picture; the circumstances surrounding something.

backhand NOUN (in tennis etc.) a backhanded stroke.

backhanded ADJ **1** performed with the back of the hand turned forwards. **2** said with underlying sarcasm.

backlash NOUN a hostile reaction.

backlog NOUN arrears of work.

backpack NOUN a rucksack.

backside NOUN [inf] the buttocks.

backstage ADJ & ADV behind a theatre stage.

backstreet NOUN a side street. ADJ secret and illegal.

backstroke NOUN a swimming stroke performed on the back.

backtrack VERB retrace your route; reverse your opinion.

backup NOUN a support, a reserve; [Computing] a copy of data made in case of loss or damage.

backward ADJ **1** directed to the rear. **2** having made less than normal progress. ADV (also **backwards**) towards the back; with the back foremost; in reverse.

backwash NOUN receding waves created by a ship etc.

backwater NOUN **1** a stretch of stagnant water on a river. **2** a place where change happens very slowly.

backwoods PLURAL NOUN a remote or backward region.

bacon NOUN salted or smoked meat from a pig.

bacterium NOUN (PL **-ia**) a microscopic organism. **bacterial** ADJ

bad ADJ (**worse**, **worst**) **1** of poor quality; having undesirable characteristics. **2** wicked; naughty. **3** harmful; serious. **4** decayed.

bade past of **bid**².

badge NOUN something worn to show membership, rank, etc.

badger NOUN a large burrowing animal with a

black and white striped head. VERB pester.

badly ADV 1 in an unsatisfactory or undesirable way. 2 very intensely.

badminton NOUN a game played with rackets and a shuttlecock over a high net.

baffle VERB be too difficult for; frustrate.
bafflement NOUN

bag NOUN 1 a flexible container; a handbag. 2 (**bags**) [inf] a large amount. VERB (**bagged**, **bagging**) [inf] take or reserve for yourself.

bagatelle NOUN 1 a board game in which balls are struck into holes. 2 something trivial.

baggage NOUN luggage.

baggy ADJ (**-ier, -iest**) hanging in loose folds.

bagpipes PLURAL NOUN a musical instrument with pipes sounded by squeezing air from a bag.

bail (see also **bale**) NOUN 1 money pledged as security that an accused person will return for trial. 2 each of two crosspieces resting on the stumps in cricket. VERB

1 (also **bale**) scoop water out of. 2 (**bail out**) obtain or allow the release of a person on bail; relieve by financial help.

bailiff NOUN a law officer empowered to seize goods for non-payment of fines or debts.

bait NOUN food etc. placed to attract prey; an attraction, an inducement. VERB 1 place bait on or in. 2 torment; taunt.

baize NOUN thick green woollen cloth.

bake VERB cook or harden by dry heat.
baking powder a mixture used to make cakes rise.

baker NOUN a person who bakes or sells bread.
bakery NOUN

balaclava NOUN a woollen cap covering the head and neck.

balalaika NOUN a Russian guitar-like instrument.

balance NOUN 1 an even distribution of weight; stability; proportion. 2 the difference between credits and debits; a remainder. 3 a weighing apparatus. VERB put in a steady position.

balcony NOUN (PL **-ies**) a projecting platform with a rail or parapet; the upper floor of seats in a theatre etc.

bald ADJ **1** having no hair on the head; (of tyres) with the tread worn away. **2** without details.
balding ADJ

bale (see also **bail**) NOUN a large bound bundle of straw etc. VERB make into bales.
bale out (or **bail out**) make an emergency parachute jump from an aircraft.

baleful ADJ menacing.
balefully ADV

balk see **baulk**.

ball NOUN **1** a spherical object used in games; a rounded part or mass; a single delivery of a ball by a bowler. **2** a formal social gathering for dancing.
ball bearing a ring of small steel balls reducing friction between moving parts of a machine; one of these balls.

ballad NOUN a song telling a story.

ballast NOUN heavy material placed in a ship's hold to steady it; coarse stones as the base of a railway or road.

ballet NOUN an artistic dance form performed to music.
ballerina NOUN

ballistics NOUN the study of projectiles and firearms.

balloon NOUN a rubber bag inflated with air or lighter gas. VERB swell outwards.

ballot NOUN a vote recorded on a slip of paper; voting by this. VERB (**balloted**, **balloting**) ask to vote by ballot.

ballpoint NOUN a pen with a tiny ball as its writing point.

ballroom NOUN a large room where dances are held.

balm NOUN a fragrant ointment; a soothing influence.

balmy ADJ (**-ier**, **-iest**) (of air or weather) pleasantly warm.

balsa NOUN lightweight wood from a tropical American tree.

balsam NOUN a scented resinous substance.

baluster NOUN a short pillar in a balustrade.

balustrade NOUN a row of

short pillars supporting a rail or coping.

bamboo NOUN a giant tropical grass with hollow stems.

bamboozle VERB [inf] mystify or trick.

ban VERB (**banned, banning**) forbid officially. NOUN an order banning something.

banal ADJ commonplace or uninteresting.
banality NOUN

banana NOUN a curved yellow fruit.

band¹ NOUN 1 a strip or loop. 2 a range of values or wavelengths.

band² NOUN an organized group of people; a set of musicians. VERB form a band.

bandage NOUN a strip of material for binding a wound. VERB bind with this.

bandanna NOUN a square of cloth tied round the neck.

bandit NOUN a member of a gang of robbers.

bandstand NOUN a covered outdoor platform for a band playing music.

bandwagon NOUN a fashionable or successful

activity or cause.

bandy¹ VERB (**bandied, bandying**) spread gossip; exchange words.

bandy² ADJ (**-ier, -iest**) (of legs) curving apart at the knees.

bane NOUN a cause of annoyance or misfortune.

bang NOUN a sudden loud sharp noise; a sharp blow. VERB strike, especially noisily; close or put down noisily; make a banging noise.

banger NOUN 1 a firework that explodes noisily; [inf] a noisy old car. 2 [inf] a sausage.

bangle NOUN a bracelet of rigid material.

banish VERB condemn to exile; dismiss from your presence or thoughts.
banishment NOUN

banisters (or **bannisters**) PLURAL NOUN the uprights and handrail of a staircase.

banjo NOUN (PL **-os**) a guitar-like musical instrument with a circular body.

bank NOUN 1 a slope, especially at the side of a river; a raised mass of earth etc. 2 a row of lights, switches, etc. **3** an establishment for safe keeping of money; a stock or store. VERB **1** build up into a mound or bank. **2** tilt sideways. **3** place money in a bank. **4** (**bank on**) rely on.

banknote NOUN a piece of paper money.

bankrupt ADJ & NOUN (a person) unable to pay their debts. VERB make bankrupt.

bankruptcy NOUN

banner NOUN a flag; a piece of cloth bearing a slogan.

bannisters see **banisters**.

banns PLURAL NOUN an announcement of a forthcoming marriage.

banquet NOUN an elaborate ceremonial meal.

banshee NOUN a spirit whose wail is said to foretell a death.

bantam NOUN a small chicken.

banter NOUN good-humoured joking. VERB joke in this way.

bap NOUN a large soft bread roll.

baptism NOUN a Christian ceremony of sprinkling with water as a sign of purification, usually with name-giving.

baptize (or **-ise**) VERB

Baptist NOUN a member of a Protestant sect believing in adult baptism by total immersion in water.

bar NOUN **1** a length of solid rigid material. **2** a stripe. **3** a counter or room where alcohol is served. **4** a barrier. **5** one of the short units into which a piece of music is divided. **6** (**the Bar**) barristers or their profession. **7** a unit of atmospheric pressure. VERB (**barred, barring**) **1** fasten with bars. **2** forbid or exclude; obstruct. PREP apart from.

bar code a pattern of printed stripes used as a machine-readable code.

barb NOUN **1** a backward-pointing part of an arrow, fish hook, etc. **2** a wounding remark.

barbarian NOUN an uncivilized person.

barbaric ADJ **1** primitive. **2** savagely cruel.

barbarity NOUN

barbarous ADJ

barbecue NOUN an open-air party where food is cooked on a frame above an open fire; this frame.

VERB cook on a barbecue.

barbed ADJ having barbs; (of a remark) hurtful.

barber NOUN a men's hairdresser.

barbiturate NOUN a sedative drug.

bard NOUN [literary] a poet.

bare ADJ 1 not clothed or covered; not adorned. 2 just sufficient. VERB reveal.
barely ADV

barefaced ADJ shameless or undisguised.

bargain NOUN 1 an agreement where each side does something for the other. 2 something obtained cheaply. VERB 1 discuss the terms of an agreement. 2 (**bargain on/for**) rely on, expect.

barge NOUN a large flat-bottomed boat used on rivers and canals. VERB (**barge in**) intrude.

baritone NOUN a male voice between tenor and bass.

barium NOUN a white metallic element.

bark NOUN 1 a sharp harsh sound made by a dog. 2 the outer layer of a tree. VERB 1 make a barking sound; say in a sharp

commanding voice. 2 scrape skin off a limb accidentally.

barley NOUN a cereal plant; its grain.

barmy ADJ (**-ier, -iest**) [inf] crazy.

barn NOUN a large farm building for storing grain etc.

barnacle NOUN a shellfish that attaches itself to objects under water.

barometer NOUN an instrument measuring atmospheric pressure, used in forecasting weather.
barometric ADJ

baron NOUN 1 a member of the lowest rank of nobility. 2 an influential businessman.
baronial ADJ

baroness NOUN a woman of the rank of baron; a baron's wife or widow.

baronet NOUN the holder of a hereditary title below a baron but above a knight.

baroque ADJ of the ornate architectural or musical style of the 17th–18th centuries; complicated or elaborate.

barque NOUN a sailing ship.

barrack VERB shout protests; jeer at.

barracks PLURAL NOUN buildings for soldiers to live in.

barrage NOUN 1 a heavy bombardment. 2 an artificial barrier across a river.

barrel NOUN 1 a cylindrical container with flat ends. 2 a tube-like part, especially of a gun.

barren ADJ 1 not fertile or fruitful. 2 bleak.

barricade NOUN a barrier. VERB block or defend with a barricade.

barrier NOUN something that prevents advance or access.

barring PREP except for.

barrister NOUN a lawyer representing clients in court.

barrow NOUN 1 a two-wheeled cart pushed or pulled by hand. 2 a prehistoric burial mound.

barter NOUN & VERB (engage in) trade by exchanging goods.

basalt NOUN a dark volcanic rock.

base NOUN 1 the lowest part; a part on which a thing rests or is supported; a starting point. 2 headquarters; a centre of organization. 3 a substance capable of combining with an acid to form a salt. 4 each of four stations to be reached by a batter in baseball. 5 the number on which a system of counting is based. VERB make something the foundation or supporting evidence for. ADJ dishonourable; of inferior value.

baseball NOUN a team game in which the batter has to hit the ball and run round a circuit.

baseless ADJ without foundation.

basement NOUN a storey below ground level.

bash [inf] VERB hit violently. NOUN a violent blow.

bashful ADJ shy.

basic ADJ 1 forming an essential foundation. 2 without elaboration or luxury.
basically ADV

basil NOUN a sweet-smelling herb.

basin NOUN 1 a washbasin. 2 a round open container for food or liquid; a sunken place where water collects; an area drained by a river.

basis NOUN (PL **-ses**) **1** a foundation or support. **2** a system of proceeding: *on a regular basis*.

bask VERB sit or lie comfortably in the sun.

basket NOUN a container for holding or carrying things, made of interwoven cane or wire.

basketball NOUN a team game in which the aim is to throw the ball through a high hooped net.

bass¹ ADJ deep-sounding; of the lowest pitch in music. NOUN the lowest male voice.

bass² NOUN an edible fish.

bassoon NOUN a woodwind instrument with a deep tone.

bastard NOUN **1** [old use] an illegitimate child. **2** [inf] an unpleasant person.

baste VERB **1** moisten with fat during cooking. **2** sew together temporarily with loose stitches.

bastion NOUN a projecting part of a fortified place; a stronghold.

bat NOUN **1** a wooden implement for hitting a ball in games. **2** a flying animal with a mouse-like body. VERB (**batted**, **batting**) perform or strike with the bat in cricket etc.

batch NOUN a set of people or things dealt with as a group.

bated ADJ (**with bated breath**) very anxiously.

bath NOUN a container used for washing the body; a wash in this. VERB wash in a bath.

bathe VERB **1** immerse in or clean with liquid. **2** swim for pleasure. NOUN a swim.

bathroom NOUN a room containing a bath, shower, washbasin, etc.

baton NOUN a short stick, especially one used by a conductor.

batsman NOUN a player batting in cricket etc.

battalion NOUN an army unit of several companies.

batten NOUN a bar of wood or metal, especially holding something in place. VERB fasten with battens.

batter VERB hit hard and often. NOUN **1** a beaten mixture of flour, eggs, and milk, used in cooking. **2** a player batting in baseball.

battery

battery NOUN (PL **-ies**) **1** a device containing and supplying electric power. **2** a group of big guns. **3** a set of similar or connected units of equipment; a series of small cages for intensive rearing of livestock. **4** an unlawful blow or touch.

battle NOUN a fight between large organized forces; a contest. VERB engage in a battle, struggle.

battleaxe NOUN a heavy axe used as a weapon in ancient times; [inf] an aggressive woman.

battlefield NOUN the scene of a battle.

battlements PLURAL NOUN a parapet with openings for firing from.

battleship NOUN a warship of the most heavily armed kind.

batty ADJ (**-ier, -iest**) [inf] crazy.

bauble NOUN a showy trinket or decoration.

baulk (or **balk**) VERB be reluctant; hinder.

bauxite NOUN a mineral from which aluminium is obtained.

bawdy ADJ (**-ier, -iest**) humorously indecent.

bawl VERB shout; weep noisily.

bay NOUN **1** part of the sea within a wide curve of the shore. **2** a recess. **3** a laurel, especially a type used as a herb. VERB (of a dog) give a deep howling cry. ADJ (of a horse) reddish brown. **at bay** forced to face attackers.

bayonet NOUN a stabbing blade fixed to a rifle.

bazaar NOUN **1** a market in an eastern country. **2** a sale of goods to raise funds.

bazooka NOUN a portable weapon firing anti-tank rockets.

BC ABBREV (of a date) before Christ.

be VERB **1** exist; occur; be present. **2** have a specified quality, position, or condition. AUXILIARY VERB used to form tenses of other verbs.

beach NOUN the shore. VERB bring on shore from water.

beacon NOUN a signal fire on a hill.

bead NOUN a small shaped piece of hard material pierced for threading with others on a string; a rounded drop of liquid.

beady ADJ (**-ier, -iest**) (of eyes) small and bright.

beagle NOUN a small hound.

beak NOUN **1** a bird's horny projecting jaws. **2** [inf] a magistrate.

beaker NOUN a tall plastic cup; a glass container used in laboratories.

beam NOUN **1** a long piece of timber or metal carrying the weight of part of a building. **2** a ray of light or other radiation. **3** a ship's breadth. VERB **1** send out radio signals. **2** shine brightly; smile radiantly.

bean NOUN a plant with kidney-shaped seeds in long pods; a seed of this or of coffee.

bear¹ NOUN a large heavy animal with thick fur; a child's toy resembling this.

bear² VERB (**bore, borne**) **1** carry; support a weight. **2** tolerate. **3** (**bear yourself**) behave in a particular way. **4** produce children, young, or fruit. **5** take a specified direction.

beard NOUN the hair around a man's chin. VERB confront boldly.

bearing NOUN **1** a way of standing, moving, or behaving. **2** relevance. **3** a compass direction. **4** a device in a machine reducing friction where a part turns.

beast NOUN **1** a large animal. **2** [inf] an unpleasant person or thing.

beastly ADJ [inf] very unpleasant.

beat VERB (**beat, beaten, beating**) **1** hit repeatedly; move or pulsate rhythmically. **2** defeat; outdo. **3** mix cooking ingredients vigorously. NOUN **1** an accent in music; strong rhythm; throbbing, pulsating. **2** the sound of a drum being struck. **3** an area regularly patrolled by a policeman.

beautician NOUN a person who gives beauty treatments.

beautiful ADJ **1** having beauty. **2** excellent. **beautifully** ADV

beauty NOUN (PL **-ies**) a combination of qualities

giving pleasure to the sight, mind, etc.; a beautiful person; an excellent specimen. **beautify** VERB

beaver NOUN an amphibious rodent that builds dams. VERB (**beaver away**) work hard.

becalmed ADJ unable to move because there is no wind.

because CONJ for the reason that.

beck NOUN (**at someone's beck and call**) doing whatever someone asks.

beckon VERB make a summoning gesture.

become VERB (**became, become, becoming**) 1 turn into; begin to be. 2 suit; befit.

bed NOUN 1 a piece of furniture for sleeping on. 2 a flat base, a foundation; the bottom of a sea or river etc. 3 a garden plot.

bedclothes PLURAL NOUN sheets, blankets, etc.

bedding NOUN bedclothes.

bedevil VERB (**bedevilled, bedevilling**; [US] **bedeviled, bedeviling**) cause continual trouble to.

bedlam NOUN a scene of uproar.

bedraggled ADJ limp and untidy.

bedridden ADJ permanently confined to bed through illness.

bedrock NOUN 1 solid rock beneath loose soil. 2 basic facts or principles.

bedroom NOUN a room for sleeping in.

bedsit (or **bedsitter**) NOUN a room used for both living and sleeping in.

bedsore NOUN a sore developed by lying in bed in one position for a long time.

bedspread NOUN a covering for a bed.

bedstead NOUN the framework of a bed.

bee NOUN an insect that produces honey.

beech NOUN a tree with smooth bark and glossy leaves.

beef NOUN meat from an ox, bull, or cow. VERB [inf] complain.

beefburger NOUN a fried cake of minced beef.

beefy ADJ (**-ier, -iest**) [inf] muscular or strong.

beehive NOUN a structure in which bees live.

beeline NOUN (**make a**

beeline for) hurry straight to.

beep NOUN a high-pitched sound like that of a car horn. VERB make a beep.

beer NOUN an alcoholic drink made from malt and hops.

beeswax NOUN a yellow substance secreted by bees, used as polish.

beet NOUN a plant with a fleshy root used as a vegetable (**beetroot**) or for making sugar (**sugar beet**).

beetle NOUN an insect with hard wing covers.

beetroot NOUN the edible dark red root of a beet.

befall VERB (**befell, befallen, befalling**) [literary] happen; happen to.

befit VERB (**befitted, befitting**) be proper for.

before ADV, PREP, & CONJ at an earlier time than; in front of; rather than.

beforehand ADV in advance.

befriend VERB be supportive and friendly towards.

befuddle VERB confuse.

beg VERB (**begged, begging**) ask earnestly or humbly for; ask for food or money as charity.

beget VERB (**begot, begotten, begetting**) [literary] be the father of; give rise to.

beggar NOUN a person who lives by asking for charity.

begin VERB (**began, begun, beginning**) 1 perform the first or earliest part of an activity; be the first to do a thing. 2 come into existence.
beginner NOUN
beginning NOUN

begonia NOUN a plant with brightly coloured flowers.

begrudge VERB be unwilling to give or allow.

beguile VERB charm or trick.

behalf NOUN (**on behalf of**) as the representative of; in the interests of.

behave VERB 1 act or react in a specified way. 2 (also **behave yourself**) show good manners.

behaviour ([US] **behavior**) NOUN a way of behaving.

behead VERB cut off the head of.

behest NOUN (**at the behest of**) at the request or order of.

behind ADV & PREP 1 at or to

the back of; less advanced than. **2** remaining after. **3** supporting. **4** late; in arrears.

behold VERB (**beheld, beholding**) [old use] see or observe.

beholden ADJ indebted.

beige NOUN a light fawn colour.

being NOUN existence; a living creature.

belated ADJ coming very late or too late.

belch VERB send out wind noisily from the stomach through the mouth. NOUN an act or sound of belching.

beleaguer VERB besiege; harass.

belfry NOUN (PL **-ies**) a space for bells in a tower.

belie VERB (**belied, belying**) contradict, fail to confirm.

belief NOUN something believed; religious faith.

believe VERB **1** accept as true or as speaking truth. **2** (**believe in**) have faith in the truth or existence of. **3** think or suppose.
believer NOUN

belittle VERB disparage.

bell NOUN **1** a cup-shaped metal instrument that makes a ringing sound when struck. **2** a device that buzzes or rings to give a signal.

belle NOUN a beautiful woman.

bellicose ADJ eager to fight.

belligerent ADJ **1** aggressive. **2** engaged in a war.
belligerence NOUN

bellow NOUN a loud deep sound made by a bull; a deep shout. VERB make this sound.

bellows PLURAL NOUN an apparatus for pumping air into something.

belly NOUN (PL **-ies**) the abdomen; the stomach.

belong VERB **1** (**belong to**) be owned by; be a member of. **2** be rightly placed or assigned; fit in a particular environment.

belongings PLURAL NOUN personal possessions.

beloved ADJ dearly loved.

below ADV & PREP at or to a lower level than.

belt NOUN a strip of cloth or leather etc. worn round the waist; a long narrow strip or region. VERB **1** put a belt round. **2** [inf] hit.

bemoan VERB complain

about.

bemused ADJ bewildered.

bench NOUN 1 a long seat of wood or stone; a long work table. 2 the office of judge or magistrate.

benchmark NOUN a standard or criterion.

bend VERB (**bent, bending**) make or become curved; stoop; turn in a new direction; distort rules. NOUN a curve or turn.

beneath ADV & PREP below or underneath; not worthy of.

benefactor NOUN a person who gives financial or other help.

beneficial ADJ favourable or advantageous.

beneficiary NOUN (PL -ies) a person who receives a benefit or legacy.

benefit NOUN 1 an advantage or profit. 2 a state payment to the poor, ill, or unemployed. VERB (**benefited, benefiting**; [US] **benefitted, benefitting**) profit from something; give an advantage to.

benevolent ADJ kind or helpful.
benevolence NOUN

benign ADJ kind; (of a tumour) not malignant.

bent past & past participle of **bend**. NOUN a natural talent. ADJ (**bent on**) determined to do or get.

benzene NOUN a liquid obtained from petroleum and coal tar, used as a solvent, fuel, etc.

bequeath VERB leave in your will.

bequest NOUN a legacy.

berate VERB scold.

bereave VERB deprive, especially of a relative, by death.
bereavement NOUN

bereft ADJ deprived; deserted and lonely.

beret NOUN a round flat cap with no peak.

beriberi NOUN a disease caused by lack of vitamin B.

berry NOUN (PL -ies) a small round juicy fruit with no stone.

berserk ADJ (**go berserk**) go into an uncontrollable destructive rage.

berth NOUN 1 a bunk or sleeping place in a ship or train. 2 a place for a ship to tie up at a wharf. VERB moor at a berth.

beryl NOUN a transparent green gem.

beseech VERB (**besought**, **beseeching**) beg earnestly.

beset VERB (**beset**, **besetting**) trouble persistently.

beside PREP **1** at the side of. **2** compared with. **3** (also **besides**) as well as. ADV (**besides**) as well. **beside yourself** distraught.

besiege VERB lay siege to.

besmirch VERB dishonour.

besotted ADJ infatuated.

bespoke ADJ made to order.

best ADJ most excellent or desirable; most beneficial. ADV **1** better than any others. **2** to the highest degree. NOUN that which is of the highest quality. **best man** a bridegroom's chief attendant.

bestial ADJ of or like a beast, savage. **bestiality** NOUN

bestir VERB (**bestirred**, **bestirring**) (**bestir yourself**) exert yourself.

bestow VERB present as a gift.

bet VERB (**bet** or **betted**, **betting**) **1** stake money on the outcome of a future event. **2** [inf] feel certain.

NOUN an act of betting; the amount staked.

beta NOUN the second letter of the Greek alphabet (B, β).

bête noire NOUN (PL **bêtes noires**) something greatly disliked.

betide VERB [literary] happen to.

betoken VERB be a sign of.

betray VERB hand over to an enemy; be disloyal to; reveal a secret. **betrayal** NOUN

betrothed ADJ engaged to be married. **betrothal** NOUN

better ADJ **1** more excellent. **2** recovered from illness. ADV more excellently or effectively. VERB outdo or surpass.

between PREP & ADV **1** at, across, or in the space or period separating two things. **2** indicating connection or relationship. **3** shared by; together with.

bevel NOUN a sloping edge. VERB (**bevelled**, **bevelling**; [US] **beveled**, **beveling**) give a sloping edge to.

beverage NOUN a drink.

bevy NOUN (PL **-ies**) a large group.

bewail VERB lament a misfortune.

beware VERB be on your guard.

bewilder VERB puzzle or confuse.

bewilderment NOUN

bewitch VERB put under a magic spell; delight greatly.

beyond PREP & ADV at or to the further side of; outside the range or limits of; happening or continuing after.

biannual ADJ happening twice a year.

bias NOUN 1 a prejudice unfairly influencing treatment. 2 a direction diagonal to the weave of a fabric.

biased ADJ prejudiced.

bib NOUN a covering put under a young child's chin to protect its clothes while feeding.

Bible NOUN the Christian or Jewish scriptures.

biblical ADJ

bibliography NOUN (PL -ies) a list of books about a subject or by a specified author.

bibliographer NOUN

bicentenary NOUN (PL -ies) a 200th anniversary.

bicentennial ADJ & NOUN

biceps NOUN the large muscle at the front of the upper arm.

bicker VERB quarrel about unimportant things.

bicycle NOUN a two-wheeled vehicle driven by pedals. VERB ride a bicycle.

bid¹ NOUN 1 an offer of a price, especially at an auction. 2 a statement of the number of tricks a player proposes to win in a card game. 3 an attempt. VERB (**bid, bidding**) 1 offer a price. 2 try to achieve something.

bidder NOUN

bid² VERB (**bid** or **bade, bidden, bidding**) 1 utter a greeting or farewell. 2 [old use] command.

bide VERB (**bide your time**) wait patiently for an opportunity.

biennial ADJ 1 happening every two years. 2 (of a plant) living for two years.

bier NOUN a movable stand for a coffin.

bifocals PLURAL NOUN a pair of glasses with two sections, one for distant and one for close vision.

big ADJ (**bigger, biggest**) of great size, amount, or

intensity; important; serious; grown up.

bigamy NOUN the crime of going through a form of marriage while a previous marriage is still valid.
bigamist ADJ
bigamous ADJ

bigot NOUN a prejudiced and intolerant person.
bigoted ADJ
bigotry NOUN

bijou ADJ small and elegant.

bike NOUN [inf] a bicycle or motorcycle.
biker NOUN

bikini NOUN a woman's two-piece swimming costume.

bilateral ADJ involving two parties.

bile NOUN 1 a bitter yellowish liquid produced by the liver. 2 bad temper.

bilge NOUN a ship's bottom; water collecting there.

bilingual ADJ written in or able to speak two languages.

bilious ADJ feeling sick.

bill NOUN 1 a written statement of charges to be paid. 2 a draft of a proposed law. 3 a programme of entertainment. 4 [US] a banknote. 5 a poster. 6 a bird's beak.

billboard NOUN a hoarding for advertisements.

billet NOUN a lodging for troops. VERB (**billeted**, **billeting**) place in a billet.

billiards NOUN a game played on a table, with three balls which are struck with cues into pockets at the edge of the table.

billion NOUN a thousand million or (less commonly) a million million.

billow NOUN a great wave. VERB rise or move like waves; swell out.

bimbo NOUN (PL **-os**) [inf] an attractive but unintelligent young woman.

bin NOUN a large rigid container or receptacle. VERB (**binned**, **binning**) discard.

binary ADJ of two.

bind VERB (**bound, binding**) 1 tie together; unite a group; secure a cover round a book; cover the edge of cloth. 2 tie up. 3 place under an obligation. NOUN [inf] something irritating or tedious.

binding NOUN **1** a book cover. **2** braid etc. used to bind an edge.

binge NOUN [inf] a bout of excessive eating and drinking.

bingo NOUN a gambling game using cards marked with numbered squares.

binoculars PLURAL NOUN an instrument with lenses for both eyes, for viewing distant objects.

bio- COMBINING FORM of living things.

biochemistry NOUN the chemistry of living organisms.
  biochemist NOUN

biodegradable ADJ able to be decomposed by bacteria.

biodiversity NOUN the variety of living things in an environment.

biography NOUN (PL **-ies**) the story of a person's life.
  biographer NOUN
  biographical ADJ

biology NOUN the study of the life and structure of living things.
  biological ADJ
  biologist NOUN

bionic ADJ having electronically operated artificial body parts.

biopsy NOUN (PL **-ies**) an examination of tissue cut from a living body.

bipartite ADJ consisting of two parts; involving two groups.

biped NOUN an animal that walks on two feet.

biplane NOUN an aeroplane with two pairs of wings.

birch NOUN a tree with thin peeling bark.

bird NOUN **1** a feathered egg-laying animal, usually able to fly. **2** [inf] a young woman.

birdie NOUN [Golf] a score of one stroke under par for a hole.

biro NOUN (PL **-os**) [trademark] a ballpoint pen.

birth NOUN the emergence of young from its mother's body; origin or ancestry.

birthday NOUN the anniversary of the day of your birth.

birthmark NOUN an unusual coloured mark on the skin at birth.

birthright NOUN a right or privilege possessed from birth.

biscuit NOUN a small, flat, crisp cake.

bisect VERB divide into

bisexual

two equal parts.

bisexual ADJ & NOUN (a person) sexually attracted to members of both sexes.

bishop NOUN 1 a senior clergyman. 2 a mitre-shaped chess piece.

bismuth NOUN a metallic element.

bison NOUN (PL **bison**) a wild ox; a buffalo.

bistro NOUN (PL **-os**) a small informal restaurant.

bit¹ NOUN 1 a small piece or quantity; a short time or distance. 2 the mouthpiece of a bridle. 3 a tool for drilling or boring. 4 [Computing] a binary digit.

bit² past of **bite**.

bitch NOUN 1 a female dog. 2 [inf] a spiteful woman; something difficult or unpleasant. VERB [inf] make spiteful comments.

bitchiness NOUN

bitchy ADJ

bite VERB (**bit, bitten, biting**) 1 cut with the teeth to eat or injure. 2 take hold on a surface. 3 cause pain or distress. NOUN 1 an act of biting; a wound made by this. 2 a small meal.

biting ADJ causing a

smarting pain; sharply critical.

bitter ADJ 1 tasting sharp or sour; not sweet. 2 resentful; very distressing. 3 piercingly cold. NOUN beer flavoured with hops and slightly bitter.

bitterness NOUN

bitty ADJ (**-ier, -iest**) lacking unity, disconnected.

bitumen NOUN a black substance made from petroleum.

bivouac NOUN a temporary camp without tents or other cover. VERB (**bivouacked, bivouacking**) camp in a bivouac.

bizarre ADJ strikingly odd in appearance or effect.

blab VERB (**blabbed, blabbing**) talk indiscreetly.

black ADJ 1 of the very darkest colour, like coal; relating to people with dark-coloured skin; (of tea or coffee) without milk. 2 gloomy; hostile; evil; (of humour) macabre. NOUN a black colour or thing; a black person.

black economy unofficial

and untaxed business activity. **black eye** a bruised eye. **black hole** a region in outer space from which matter and radiation cannot escape. **black market** illegal trading in officially controlled goods.

blackberry NOUN an edible dark berry growing on a prickly bush.

blackbird NOUN a European songbird, the male of which is black.

blackboard NOUN a dark board for writing on with chalk, used especially in schools.

blackcurrant NOUN a small round edible black berry.

blacken VERB **1** make or become black. **2** say evil things about.

blackguard NOUN a dishonourable man.

blackhead NOUN a lump of oily matter blocking a pore in the skin.

blackleg NOUN a person who works while fellow workers are on strike.

blacklist NOUN a list of people considered untrustworthy or unacceptable.

blackmail VERB extort money from someone by threatening to reveal compromising information. NOUN the offence of doing this. **blackmailer** NOUN

blackout NOUN a temporary loss of consciousness or memory. VERB (**black out**) **1** lose consciousness. **2** cover windows so that no light can penetrate.

blacksmith NOUN a person who makes and repairs things made of iron.

bladder NOUN the sac in which urine collects in the body.

blade NOUN the flattened cutting part of a knife or sword; the flat part of an oar or propeller; a long narrow leaf of grass.

blame VERB hold responsible for a fault. NOUN responsibility for a fault.

blanch VERB **1** become white or pale. **2** immerse vegetables briefly in boiling water.

blancmange NOUN a jelly-like dessert, made with milk.

bland ADJ **1** dull or

uninteresting. **2** showing no emotion.

blank ADJ **1** not marked or decorated. **2** showing no interest, understanding, or reaction. NOUN a blank space; a cartridge containing no bullet.

blanket NOUN a warm covering made of woollen or similar material. ADJ total and inclusive.

blare VERB & NOUN (make) a loud harsh sound.

blarney NOUN charming and persuasive talk.

blasé ADJ unimpressed through familiarity with something.

blasphemy NOUN (PL **-ies**) irreverent talk about sacred things.
blaspheme VERB
blasphemous ADJ

blast NOUN **1** a wave of air from an explosion; a strong gust. **2** a loud note on a whistle or horn. VERB **1** blow up with explosives. **2** produce a loud sound. **3** [inf] reprimand severely.

blatant ADJ very obvious; shameless.
blatantly ADV

blaze NOUN **1** a bright flame or fire; a bright light; an outburst or display. **2** a white mark on an animal's face. VERB burn or shine brightly.

blazer NOUN a loose-fitting jacket, worn especially by schoolchildren or sports players as part of a uniform.

blazon VERB display or proclaim publicly.

bleach VERB whiten by sunlight or chemicals. NOUN a chemical used to bleach or sterilize.

bleak ADJ cold and cheerless; not hopeful or encouraging.

bleary ADJ (**-ier, -iest**) (of eyes) dull and unfocused.

bleat NOUN the cry of a sheep or goat. VERB utter this cry; speak or complain feebly.

bleed VERB (**bled, bleeding**) leak blood or other fluid; draw blood or fluid from; extort money from.

bleep NOUN a short high-pitched sound. VERB make this sound, especially as a signal.
bleeper NOUN

blemish NOUN a flaw or defect. VERB spoil the appearance of.

blend VERB mix smoothly.

NOUN a mixture.

blender NOUN an appliance for liquidizing food.

bless VERB call God's favour on; consecrate.

blessed ADJ **1** holy. **2** very welcome, much desired.

blessing NOUN **1** (a prayer for) God's favour. **2** approval or support. **3** something you are glad of.

blew past of **blow**.

blight NOUN a disease or fungus that withers plants; a malignant influence. VERB affect with blight; spoil.

blind ADJ **1** unable to see; unreasoning; lacking awareness. **2** (of a road etc.) hidden. VERB make blind or unable to think clearly. NOUN a screen, especially on a roller, for a window.

blindness NOUN

blindfold NOUN a cloth used to cover the eyes and block the sight. VERB cover the eyes of a person with this.

blink VERB open and shut your eyes rapidly; shine unsteadily. NOUN an act of blinking; a quick gleam.

blinker NOUN a leather piece fixed to a bridle to prevent a horse from seeing sideways. VERB obstruct the sight or understanding of.

blip NOUN **1** a slight error or deviation. **2** a short high-pitched sound; a small image on a radar screen.

bliss NOUN perfect happiness.

blissful ADJ

blissfully ADV

blister NOUN a bubble-like swelling on the skin; a raised swelling on a surface. VERB form blisters.

blithe ADJ casual and carefree.

blitz NOUN a sudden intensive attack; an energetic and concerted effort.

blizzard NOUN a severe snowstorm.

bloat VERB swell with fat, gas, or liquid.

bloater NOUN a salted smoked herring.

blob NOUN a drop of liquid; a round mass.

bloc NOUN a group of parties or countries who combine for a purpose.

block NOUN **1** a solid piece of a hard substance, usually with flat sides. **2** a large building divided into flats or offices; a group of buildings enclosed by roads. **4** an obstruction. VERB obstruct or prevent the movement or use of.

block letters plain capital letters.

blockade NOUN the blocking of access to a place, to prevent entry of goods. VERB set up a blockade of.

blockage NOUN an obstruction.

bloke NOUN [inf] a man.

blonde ADJ (also **blond**) fair-haired; (of hair) fair. NOUN a fair-haired woman.

blood NOUN **1** the red liquid circulating in the bodies of animals. **2** family or descent. VERB initiate someone.

blood vessel a tubular structure conveying blood within the body.

bloodhound NOUN a large keen-scented dog, formerly used in tracking.

bloodless ADJ without bloodshed.

bloodshed NOUN killing or wounding.

bloodshot ADJ (of eyes) red from dilated veins.

bloodstream NOUN blood circulating in the body.

bloodthirsty ADJ eager for bloodshed.

bloody ADJ (**-ier, -iest**) **1** covered in blood. **2** involving much bloodshed. VERB stain with blood.

bloody-minded [inf] deliberately uncooperative.

bloom 1 a flower. **2** youthful beauty. VERB **1** bear flowers. **2** be healthy and attractive.

bloomers PLURAL NOUN [historical] women's loose knee-length knickers.

blossom NOUN flowers, especially of a fruit tree. VERB open into flowers; develop and flourish.

blot NOUN a stain of ink etc.; an eyesore. VERB (**blotted, blotting**) **1** make a blot on. **2** soak up with absorbent material. **3** (**blot out**) erase; obscure.

blotch NOUN a large irregular mark.

blotchy ADJ

blouse NOUN a shirt-like garment worn by women.

blow VERB (**blew, blown, blowing**) **1** send out a current of air or breath;

move as a current of air; carry on air or breath. **2** break open with explosives. **3** play a wind instrument. **4** [inf] spend or squander. NOUN **1** a wind; an act of blowing. **2** a stroke with the hand or a weapon; a shock, disappointment, or setback.

blow up 1 explode. **2** inflate; enlarge.

blowfly NOUN (PL **-ies**) a fly that lays its eggs on meat.

blowout NOUN **1** a burst tyre. **2** a melted fuse. **3** [inf] a huge meal.

blowsy ADJ red-faced and slovenly.

blowtorch (or **blowlamp**) NOUN a portable burner with a very hot flame for removing old paint.

blowy ADJ windy.

blubber NOUN whale fat. VERB [inf] sob noisily.

bludgeon NOUN a heavy stick used as a weapon. VERB strike with a bludgeon; coerce.

blue ADJ **1** of a colour like the cloudless sky. **2** [inf] unhappy. **3** [inf] indecent. NOUN **1** a blue colour or thing. **2** (**blues**) melancholy jazz melodies; a state of depression.

blue-blooded of aristocratic descent.

bluish ADJ

bluebell NOUN a plant with blue bell-shaped flowers.

bluebottle NOUN a large bluish fly.

blueprint NOUN a design plan; a model.

bluff VERB pretend; deceive. NOUN **1** bluffing. **2** a broad steep cliff or headland. ADJ abrupt, frank, and hearty.

blunder VERB move clumsily and uncertainly; make a mistake. NOUN a stupid mistake.

blunt ADJ **1** without a sharp edge or point. **2** speaking or expressed plainly. VERB make or become blunt.

blur NOUN something perceived indistinctly. VERB (**blurred, blurring**) make or become indistinct.

blurb NOUN a short description written to promote a book, film, etc.

blurt VERB say abruptly or tactlessly.

blush VERB become red-faced from shame or embarrassment. NOUN blushing.

blusher NOUN a cosmetic giving a rosy colour to cheeks.

bluster VERB 1 blow in gusts. 2 make aggressive but empty threats. NOUN blustering talk.

blustery ADJ

boa NOUN a large snake that crushes its prey.

boar NOUN a wild pig; a male pig.

board NOUN 1 a long piece of sawn wood; a flat piece of wood or stiff material. 2 daily meals supplied in return for payment or services. 3 a committee. VERB 1 get on a ship, aircraft, train, etc. 2 receive or provide accommodation and meals for payment. 3 cover or block with boards.

boarder NOUN a pupil who lives in school during term time.

boardroom NOUN a room where a board of directors meets.

boast VERB 1 talk with pride about your achievements or possessions. 2 possess a desirable feature. NOUN an act of boasting.

boastful ADJ

boat NOUN a vehicle for travelling on water.

boater NOUN a flat-topped straw hat.

boatswain NOUN a ship's officer in charge of equipment, etc.

bob VERB (**bobbed, bobbing**) 1 move quickly up and down. 2 cut hair in a bob. NOUN 1 a bobbing movement. 2 a hairstyle with the hair at the same length just above the shoulders.

bobbin NOUN a small spool holding thread or wire in a machine.

bobble NOUN a small woolly ball as an ornament.

bobsleigh NOUN a mechanically steered sledge with two sets of runners.

bode VERB be a portent of.

bodice NOUN the upper part of a woman's dress; a woman's sleeveless undergarment.

bodily ADJ of the body. ADV by taking hold of the body.

body NOUN (PL **-ies**) 1 the physical form of a person or animal. 2 a corpse. 3 the

main part of something.
4 a collection; a group.

bodyguard NOUN a personal guard for an important person.

bodywork NOUN the outer shell of a motor vehicle.

boffin NOUN [inf] a scientist.

bog NOUN permanently wet spongy ground. VERB (**get bogged down**) become unable to make progress. **boggy** ADJ

bogey NOUN (PL **-eys**) **1** [Golf] a score of one stroke over par at a hole. **2** (also **bogy**) something causing fear.

boggle VERB be amazed or alarmed.

bogus ADJ false.

bohemian ADJ socially unconventional.

boil VERB bubble up with heat; heat liquid until it does this; cook in boiling water. NOUN an inflamed swelling producing pus.

boiler NOUN a container in which water is heated.

boisterous ADJ cheerfully noisy or rough.

bold ADJ **1** confident and courageous. **2** (of a colour or design) strong and vivid.

bole NOUN the trunk of a tree.

bolero NOUN (PL **-os**) **1** a Spanish dance. **2** a woman's short open jacket.

bollard NOUN a short thick post.

bolster NOUN a long pad placed under a pillow. VERB support or prop.

bolt NOUN **1** a sliding bar for fastening a door; a strong metal pin used with a nut to hold things together. **2** a shaft of lightning. **3** a roll of cloth. **4** an arrow from a crossbow. VERB **1** fasten with a bolt. **2** run away. **3** gulp food hastily.

bomb NOUN a device designed to explode and cause damage. VERB **1** attack with bombs. **2** [inf] move quickly. **3** [inf] be a failure.

bombard VERB attack with artillery; attack with questions etc. **bombardment** NOUN

bombastic ADJ using pompous words.

bomber NOUN an aircraft that carries and drops bombs; a person who places bombs.

bombshell NOUN a great shock.

bona fide ADJ genuine.

bonanza NOUN a sudden increase in wealth or luck.

bond NOUN something that unites or restrains; a binding agreement; an emotional link. VERB join or be joined with a bond.

bondage NOUN slavery or captivity.

bone NOUN each of the hard parts making up the vertebrate skeleton. VERB remove bones from. **bony** ADJ

bonfire NOUN a fire built in the open air.

bongo NOUN (PL **-os** or **-oes**) each of a pair of small drums played with the fingers.

bonk VERB [inf] hit.

bonnet NOUN 1 a hat with strings that tie under the chin. 2 a hinged cover over the engine of a motor vehicle.

bonny ADJ (**-ier, -iest**) [Scottish & N. English] good-looking.

bonsai NOUN (PL **bonsai**) an ornamental miniature tree or shrub; the art of growing these.

bonus NOUN an extra payment or benefit.

boo EXCLAMATION an exclamation of disapproval; an exclamation to startle someone. VERB shout 'boo' at.

boob NOUN [inf] 1 a blunder. 2 a breast.

booby trap NOUN a disguised bomb; a trap set as a practical joke.

boogie VERB (**boogied, boogieing**) dance to fast pop music.

book NOUN 1 a literary work consisting of a set of sheets of paper bound in a cover; a main division of a literary work. 2 a record of bets made. VERB 1 reserve, buy, or engage in advance. 2 record details of an offender.

bookkeeping NOUN the systematic recording of business transactions.

booklet NOUN a small thin book.

bookmaker NOUN a person whose business is the taking of bets.

bookworm NOUN [inf] a person fond of reading.

boom VERB 1 make a deep resonant sound. 2 have a period of prosperity. NOUN 1 a booming sound. 2 a period of prosperity. 3 a long pole; a floating barrier.

boomerang NOUN an Australian missile of curved wood that can be thrown so as to return to the thrower.

boon NOUN a benefit.

boor NOUN an ill-mannered person.
boorish ADJ

boost VERB help or encourage. NOUN a source of help or encouragement.
booster NOUN

boot NOUN 1 a shoe covering both foot and ankle. 2 the luggage compartment at the back of a car. VERB 1 [inf] kick. 2 start up a computer.

bootee NOUN a baby's woollen shoe.

booth NOUN a small enclosed compartment; a stall or stand.

bootleg ADJ smuggled or illicit.
bootlegger NOUN

booty NOUN loot.

booze [inf] VERB drink alcohol. NOUN alcoholic drink.

border NOUN a boundary, an edge; a flower bed round part of a garden. VERB 1 form a border to.

2 (**border on**) come close to being.

borderline NOUN a line marking a boundary.

bore¹ past of **bear**.

bore² VERB 1 make weary by being dull. 2 make a hole with a revolving tool. NOUN 1 a tedious person or thing. 2 the hollow inside of a gun barrel.
boredom NOUN

born ADJ 1 existing as a result of birth. 2 having a specified natural ability.

borne past participle of **bear**.

boron NOUN a chemical element used in making steel.

borough NOUN a town or district with rights of local government.

borrow VERB take something from someone, with the intention of returning it.

borstal NOUN the former name of an institution for young offenders.

bosom NOUN the breast.

boss [inf] NOUN an employer; a person in charge. VERB give orders to in a domineering way.

bossy ADJ (**-ier, -iest**) tending to tell people

what to do in an arrogant or annoying way.

bosun, **bo'sun** variants of **boatswain**.

botany NOUN the study of plants.
botanical ADJ
botanist NOUN

botch VERB do a task badly.

both ADJ, PRON, & ADV the two.

bother VERB **1** cause trouble, worry, or annoyance to. **2** take trouble. NOUN **1** (a cause of) inconvenience. **2** trouble; violence.

bottle NOUN a narrow-necked container for liquid. VERB store in bottles or jars.

bottleneck NOUN a narrow point in a road where congestion occurs.

bottom NOUN **1** the lowest part or point; the ground under a stretch of water. **2** the buttocks. ADJ lowest in position, rank, or degree.

botulism NOUN a dangerous form of food poisoning.

boudoir NOUN a woman's bedroom.

bouffant NOUN (of hair) standing out from the head in a rounded shape.

bough NOUN a main branch of a tree.

bought past & past participle of **buy**.

boulder NOUN a large rounded stone.

boulevard NOUN a wide street.

bounce VERB **1** rebound; move up and down; move in a light, lively manner. **2** [inf] (of a cheque) be sent back by a bank as worthless. NOUN an act of bouncing; resilience or liveliness.

bouncer NOUN a person employed to eject troublemakers from a club etc.

bound[1] past and past participle of **bind**.

bound[2] VERB **1** run with a leaping movement. **2** form the boundary of. NOUN **1** a leap. **2** a boundary; a limitation. ADJ **1** heading in a specified direction. **2** (**bound to**) certain to.

boundary NOUN (PL **-ies**) a line marking the limit of an area.

boundless ADJ unlimited.

bounty NOUN (PL **-ies**) generosity; a generous gift.

bounteous ADJ

bountiful ADJ

bouquet NOUN **1** a bunch of flowers. **2** the perfume of wine.

bourbon NOUN an American whisky made from maize.

bourgeois ADJ conventionally middle-class.

bout NOUN **1** a period of exercise, work, or illness. **2** a boxing contest.

boutique NOUN a small shop selling fashionable clothes etc.

bow¹ NOUN **1** a weapon for shooting arrows. **2** a rod with horsehair stretched between its ends, for playing a violin etc. **3** a knot with two loops, for fastening or decoration.

bow² VERB bend the head and upper body as a sign of respect; bend with age or under a weight; submit. NOUN an act of bowing.

bow³ NOUN the front end of a boat or ship.

bowel NOUN the intestine; (**bowels**) the innermost parts.

bowl NOUN **1** a round, deep dish for food or liquid; the hollow rounded part of a spoon etc. **2** a heavy ball weighted to roll in a curve; (**bowls**) a game played with such balls. VERB **1** send rolling along the ground; go fast and smoothly. **2** send a ball to a batsman. **3** (**bowl over**) knock down; overwhelm with surprise or emotion.

bowler NOUN **1** a person who bowls in cricket; a person who plays at bowls. **2** a hard felt hat with a rounded top.

bowling NOUN bowls, skittles, or a similar game.

box NOUN **1** a container with a flat base and sides, usually square and with a lid; a space enclosed by straight lines on a page or screen; a compartment at a theatre. **2** a small evergreen shrub. VERB **1** put into a box. **2** take part in boxing.

box office an office for booking seats at a theatre etc.

boxer NOUN **1** a person who boxes as a sport **2** a breed of dog resembling a bulldog.

boxing NOUN a sport in which contestants fight

each other wearing big padded gloves.

boy NOUN a male child. **boyish** ADJ

boycott VERB refuse to deal with or trade with. NOUN boycotting.

boyfriend NOUN a person's regular male companion or lover.

bra NOUN a woman's undergarment worn to support the breasts.

brace NOUN 1 a device that holds things together or in position; (**braces**) straps to keep trousers up, passing over the shoulders; a wire device worn in the mouth to straighten the teeth. 2 a pair. VERB give support or firmness to.

bracelet NOUN an ornamental band worn on the arm.

bracing ADJ invigorating.

bracken NOUN a large fern.

bracket NOUN 1 any of the marks used in pairs to enclose and separate off words or figures, ( ), [ ], { }; a category of similar people or things. 2 a support for a shelf or lamp, projecting from a wall. VERB enclose in brackets; group together.

brackish ADJ slightly salty.

brag VERB (**bragged, bragging**) boast. **braggart** NOUN

braid NOUN 1 a woven ornamental trimming. 2 a plait of hair. VERB 1 trim with braid. 2 plait.

Braille NOUN a system of representing letters etc. by raised dots which blind people read by touch.

brain NOUN the mass of soft grey matter in the skull, the centre of the nervous system in animals; (also **brains**) intellectual ability. **brainy** ADJ

brainchild NOUN a person's invention or plan.

brainstorm NOUN 1 a sudden mental lapse. 2 a spontaneous discussion in search of new ideas.

brainwash VERB pressurize someone into changing their beliefs by means other than rational argument.

brainwave NOUN a bright idea.

braise VERB cook slowly with little liquid in a closed container.

brake NOUN a device for

bramble NOUN a prickly shrub on which blackberries grow.

bran NOUN the ground inner husks of grain, sifted from flour.

branch NOUN 1 a part of a tree growing out from the trunk; a division of a road, river, etc. 2 a subdivision of a subject. 3 a local shop or office belonging to a large organization. VERB send out or divide into branches.

brand NOUN goods of a particular make; an identifying mark made on skin with hot metal. VERB mark with a brand; stigmatize.

brand new completely new.

brandish VERB wave or flourish.

brandy NOUN (PL **-ies**) a strong alcoholic drink made from wine or fermented fruit juice.

brash ADJ aggressively self-assertive.

brass NOUN a yellow alloy of copper and zinc; musical instruments made of this; a memorial tablet made of this. ADJ made of brass.

brassiere NOUN a bra.

brassy ADJ (**-ier, -iest**) 1 like brass. 2 bold and vulgar.

brat NOUN [derogatory] a child.

bravado NOUN a show of boldness.

brave ADJ able to face and endure danger or pain. VERB face and endure bravely. NOUN [dated] an American Indian warrior. **bravery** NOUN

bravo EXCLAMATION well done!

brawl NOUN a noisy quarrel or fight. VERB take part in a brawl.

brawn NOUN muscular strength. **brawny** ADJ

bray NOUN a donkey's cry. VERB make this cry or sound.

brazen ADJ bold and shameless. VERB (**brazen it out**) behave after doing wrong as if you have no need to be ashamed.

brazier NOUN a portable heater holding burning

coals.

breach NOUN **1** failure to observe a rule or contract. **2** separation or estrangement. **3** a gap in a defence. VERB break through or make a breach in.

bread NOUN food made of baked dough of flour and liquid, usually leavened by yeast.

breadth NOUN width, broadness.

breadwinner NOUN the member of a family who earns money to support the others.

break VERB (**broke**, **broken**, **breaking**) **1** separate into pieces as a result of a blow or strain; interrupt a sequence or habit. **2** fail to keep a promise or law. **3** defeat. **4** reveal bad news. **5** surpass a record. **6** (of a wave) fall on the shore. **7** (of a boy's voice) deepen at puberty. NOUN **1** a pause or gap; a short rest. **2** a fracture. **3** a sudden dash. **4** [inf] an opportunity. **5** points scored consecutively in snooker.

break down stop working; give way to emotion.

break in force your way into a building.

breakable ADJ

breakage NOUN

breakdown NOUN **1** a failure or collapse. **2** an analysis.

breaker NOUN a heavy sea wave that breaks on the shore.

breakfast NOUN the first meal of the day.

breakneck ADJ dangerously fast.

breakthrough NOUN a sudden major advance in an undertaking.

breakwater NOUN a wall built out into the sea to break the force of waves.

breast NOUN the upper front part of the body; either of the two milk-producing organs on a woman's chest.

breaststroke NOUN a swimming stroke performed on your front with circular arm and leg movements.

breath NOUN air drawn into and sent out of the lungs in breathing; a slight movement of wind.

breathless ADJ

breathalyser ([US trademark] **breathalyzer**)

NOUN a device used for measuring the amount of alcohol in a person's breath.

breathalyse ([US] **-yze**) VERB

breathe VERB **1** draw air into the lungs and send it out again. **2** whisper.

breather NOUN a pause for rest.

breathtaking ADJ amazing.

breech NOUN the back part of a gun barrel, where it opens.

breeches PLURAL NOUN trousers reaching to just below the knees.

breed VERB (**bred, breeding**) produce offspring; keep animals for the offspring they produce; give rise to. NOUN a variety of animals within a species; a sort. **breeder** NOUN

breeding NOUN good manners resulting from training or background.

breeze NOUN a light wind. **breezy** ADJ

brethren PLURAL NOUN [old use] brothers.

breve NOUN (in music) a long note.

brevity NOUN briefness; conciseness.

brew VERB **1** make beer; make tea or coffee. **2** (of an unpleasant situation) begin to develop. NOUN a liquid or amount brewed. **brewer** NOUN

brewery NOUN a place where beer is made.

briar see **brier**.

bribe NOUN a gift offered to influence a person to act in favour of the giver. VERB persuade by this. **bribery** NOUN

bric-a-brac NOUN various objects of little value.

brick NOUN a block of baked or dried clay used to build walls. VERB block with a brick structure. **bricklayer** NOUN

bride NOUN a woman at the time of her wedding. **bridal** ADJ

bridegroom NOUN a man at the time of his wedding.

bridesmaid NOUN a girl or woman who accompanies a bride at her wedding.

bridge NOUN **1** a structure providing a way over a gap or other obstacle; a connection between two points or groups. **2** the captain's platform on a ship. **3** the bony upper part of the nose. **4** a card game developed from whist. VERB make or be a bridge over.

bridle NOUN a harness on a horse's head. VERB **1** put a bridle on; restrain. **2** show resentment or anger.

bridleway NOUN a path for riders or walkers.

brief ADJ lasting only for a short time; concise; short. NOUN a set of instructions and information, especially to a barrister about a case. VERB inform or instruct in advance.
briefly ADV

briefcase NOUN a case for carrying documents.

briefs PLURAL NOUN short pants or knickers.

brier (or **briar**) NOUN a prickly shrub.

brigade NOUN an army unit forming part of a division; [inf] a group with a shared purpose or interest.

brigadier NOUN an officer commanding a brigade or of similar status.

brigand NOUN a member of a gang of bandits.

bright ADJ **1** giving out or reflecting much light;

vivid. **2** intelligent. **3** cheerful; encouraging.
brighten VERB
brightness NOUN

brilliant ADJ **1** very bright. **2** very clever.
brilliance NOUN

brim NOUN the edge of a cup or hollow; the projecting edge of a hat. VERB (**brimmed, brimming**) be full to the brim.

brine NOUN salt water.

bring VERB (**brought, bringing**) cause to come or move in a particular direction; accompany; cause to be in a particular state.

bring up look after and educate.

brink NOUN the edge of a steep place or of a stretch of water; the point just before an event or state.

brinkmanship NOUN a policy of pursuing a dangerous course to the brink of catastrophe.

brisk ADJ **1** active and energetic. **2** curt.

brisket NOUN a joint of beef from the breast.

bristle NOUN a short stiff hair. VERB (of hair) stand upright as a result of anger or fear; show indignation.

British ADJ of Britain or its people.

Briton NOUN a British person.

brittle ADJ hard but easily broken.

broach VERB begin discussion of.

broad ADJ 1 large from side to side. 2 in general terms; not precise or detailed. 3 (of an accent) strong. **broad-minded** not easily shocked.

broaden VERB

broadband NOUN a telecommunications technique using a wide range of frequencies, enabling messages to be sent at the same time.

broadcast VERB (**broadcast, broadcasting**) send out by radio or television; make generally known. NOUN a broadcast programme. **broadcaster** NOUN

broadsheet NOUN a large-sized newspaper.

broadside NOUN the firing of all guns on one side of a ship; a strongly worded criticism.

brocade NOUN a fabric woven with raised patterns.

broccoli NOUN a vegetable with tightly packed green or purple flower heads.

brochure NOUN a booklet or leaflet giving information.

brogue NOUN 1 a strong shoe with ornamental perforated bands. 2 a strong regional accent, especially Irish.

broil VERB grill.

broke past of **break**. ADJ [inf] having no money.

broken past participle of **break**. ADJ (of a language) badly spoken by a foreigner.

broker NOUN an agent who buys and sells on behalf of others. VERB arrange a deal.

bromide NOUN a compound used to calm nerves.

bromine NOUN a dark red poisonous liquid element.

bronchial ADJ of the tubes leading into the lungs.

bronchitis NOUN inflammation of the bronchial tubes.

bronco NOUN (PL **-os**) a wild or half-tamed horse of the western US.

brontosaurus NOUN a large plant-eating dinosaur.

bronze NOUN a brown alloy of copper and tin; its colour. VERB make suntanned.

brooch NOUN an ornamental hinged pin fastened with a clasp.

brood NOUN young produced at one hatching or birth. VERB 1 sit on eggs and hatch them. 2 think long, deeply, and sadly.

broody ADJ (**-ier, -iest**) 1 (of a hen) wanting to brood; [inf] (of a woman) wanting children. 2 thoughtful and unhappy.

brook NOUN a small stream. VERB tolerate, allow.

broom NOUN 1 a long-handled brush. 2 a shrub with white, yellow, or red flowers.

broomstick NOUN a broom on which witches are said to fly.

Bros. ABBREV Brothers.

broth NOUN a thin meat or fish soup.

brothel NOUN a house where men visit prostitutes.

brother NOUN 1 the son of the same parents as another person. 2 a male colleague or friend. 3 a monk.

brother-in-law the brother of your husband or wife; the husband of your sister.

brotherly ADJ

brotherhood NOUN comradeship; an association.

brought past and past participle of **bring**.

brow NOUN an eyebrow; a forehead; the summit of a hill.

browbeat VERB (**browbeat, browbeaten, browbeating**) intimidate.

brown ADJ of a colour between orange and black, like earth or wood. VERB make or become brown.

browse VERB 1 read or look at superficially. 2 feed on leaves or grass.

bruise NOUN an injury that discolours skin without breaking it. VERB cause a bruise on.

bruiser NOUN [inf] a tough brutal person.

brunch NOUN a meal combining breakfast and lunch.

brunette NOUN a woman

with brown hair.

brunt NOUN the worst stress or chief impact.

brush NOUN 1 an implement for cleaning, arranging hair, etc., consisting of bristles set into a block; an act of using this; a light touch. 2 a fox's tail. 3 a dangerous or unpleasant encounter. 4 undergrowth. VERB clean, arrange, etc., with a brush; touch lightly in passing.

brusque ADJ curt and offhand.

Brussels sprout NOUN the edible bud of a kind of cabbage.

brutal ADJ savage or cruel. **brutality** NOUN **brutally** ADV

brute NOUN a brutal person or large unmanageable animal. ADJ merely physical. **brutish** ADJ

BSE ABBREV bovine spongiform encephalopathy, a fatal brain disease of cattle.

BST ABBREV British Summer Time.

bubble NOUN a thin sphere of liquid enclosing air or gas; an air-filled cavity.

VERB 1 contain rising bubbles. 2 show great liveliness. **bubbly** ADJ

bubonic plague NOUN a plague characterized by swellings.

buccaneer NOUN a pirate; an adventurer.

buck NOUN 1 the male of a deer, hare, or rabbit. 2 [US & Australian] a dollar. VERB 1 (of a horse) jump with the back arched. 2 (**buck up**) [inf] cheer up.

bucket NOUN an open container with a handle, for carrying liquid.

buckle NOUN a device through which a belt or strap is threaded to secure it. VERB 1 fasten with a buckle. 2 crumple under pressure.

bucolic ADJ rustic.

bud NOUN a leaf or flower not fully open. VERB (**budded**, **budding**) form buds.

Buddhism NOUN an Asian religion based on the teachings of Buddha. **Buddhist** ADJ & NOUN

budding ADJ beginning to develop or be successful.

budge VERB move slightly.

budgerigar NOUN an

Australian parakeet often kept as a pet.

budget NOUN a plan of income and expenditure; the amount of money someone has available. VERB allow or provide for in a budget.

budgie NOUN [inf] a budgerigar.

buff NOUN **1** a fawn colour. **2** [inf] an expert and enthusiast. VERB polish with soft material.

buffalo NOUN (PL **buffaloes** or **buffalo**) a wild ox; a North American bison.

buffer NOUN something that lessens the effect of impact.

buffet[1] NOUN a meal where guests serve themselves; a counter where food and drink are served.

buffet[2] VERB strike repeatedly.

buffoon NOUN a ridiculous but amusing person.

buffoonery NOUN

bug NOUN **1** a small insect; [inf] a germ or an illness caused by one; a fault in a computer system. **2** a hidden microphone. VERB (**bugged, bugging**) **1** install a hidden microphone in. **2** [inf]

annoy.

bugbear NOUN something feared or disliked.

buggery NOUN anal sex.

buggy NOUN (PL **-ies**) a small light vehicle; a lightweight folding pushchair.

bugle NOUN a brass instrument like a small trumpet.

build VERB (**built, building**) **1** construct by putting parts or material together. **2** (**build up**) establish gradually; increase. NOUN bodily shape.

builder NOUN

building NOUN a house or similar structure.

building society an organization that accepts deposits and lends money, especially to people buying houses.

bulb NOUN **1** the rounded base of the stem of certain plants. **2** the glass part giving light in an electric lamp.

bulbous ADJ

bulge NOUN a rounded swelling. VERB form a bulge, swell.

bulimia NOUN an eating disorder marked by bouts of overeating followed by

fasting or vomiting.
bulimic ADJ

bulk NOUN mass; something large and heavy; the majority.

bulkhead NOUN a partition in a ship etc.

bulky ADJ (**-ier, -iest**) large and unwieldy.

bull NOUN 1 the male of the ox, whale, elephant, etc. 2 a pope's official edict.

bulldog NOUN a powerful dog with a short thick neck.

bulldozer NOUN a powerful tractor with a device for clearing ground.

bullet NOUN a small piece of metal fired from a gun.

bulletin NOUN a short official statement of news.

bullfight NOUN the baiting and killing of bulls as an entertainment.

bullion NOUN gold or silver in bulk or bars.

bullock NOUN a castrated bull.

bullseye NOUN the centre of a target.

bully NOUN (PL **-ies**) a person who hurts or intimidates weaker people. VERB (**bullied, bullying**) intimidate.

bulrush NOUN a tall reed-like plant.

bulwark NOUN a defensive wall; a defence.

bum NOUN [inf] the buttocks.

bumble VERB move or act clumsily.

bumblebee NOUN a large bee.

bumf (or **bumph**) NOUN [inf] documents or papers.

bump VERB 1 knock or collide with. 2 travel with a jolting movement. NOUN 1 a knock or collision; the dull sound of this. 2 a swelling or a raised area on a surface. 3 a jolt.
bumpy ADJ

bumper NOUN a horizontal bar at the front or back of a motor vehicle to lessen the damage in collision. ADJ unusually large or successful.

bumpkin NOUN an unsophisticated country person.

bumptious ADJ conceited.

bun NOUN 1 a small sweet cake. 2 hair twisted into a coil at the back of the head.

bunch NOUN a number of things growing or fastened together; a group. VERB form or be formed into a bunch.

bundle NOUN a collection of things loosely fastened or wrapped together. VERB **1** make into a bundle. **2** move or push hurriedly.

bung NOUN a stopper for a jar or barrel. VERB **1** block up. **2** [inf] throw or put.

bungalow NOUN a one-storeyed house.

bungle VERB spoil by lack of skill. NOUN a bungled attempt.

bunion NOUN a painful swelling at the base of the big toe.

bunk NOUN a shelf-like bed.

bunker NOUN **1** a container for fuel. **2** a sandy hollow forming an obstacle on a golf course. **3** a reinforced underground shelter.

bunting NOUN **1** a bird related to the finches. **2** decorative flags.

buoy NOUN an anchored floating object used as a navigation mark.

buoyant ADJ **1** able to float. **2** cheerful.

burden NOUN something carried; an obligation causing hardship. VERB load; oppress.

bureau NOUN (PL **-aux** or **-aus**) **1** a writing desk with drawers. **2** an office or department.

bureaucracy NOUN (PL **-ies**) government by unelected officials; excessive administration. **bureaucrat** NOUN **bureaucratic** ADJ

burgeon VERB grow rapidly.

burglar NOUN a person who breaks into a building in order to steal. **burglary** NOUN **burgle** VERB

burgundy NOUN (PL **-ies**) a red wine; a purplish red colour.

burial NOUN the burying of a corpse.

burlesque NOUN a mocking imitation.

burly ADJ (**-ier, -iest**) with a strong heavy body.

burn VERB (**burned** or **burnt, burning**) be on fire, produce heat or light; damage or destroy by fire, heat, or acid; use fuel; feel hot and painful; feel passionate emotion. NOUN an injury made by burning.

burning ADJ **1** intense. **2** (of an issue) keenly discussed.

burnish VERB polish by rubbing.

burp [inf] NOUN & VERB (make)

a belch.

burr NOUN a strong pronunciation of the letter 'r'.

burrow NOUN a hole dug by an animal as a dwelling. VERB dig a burrow.

bursar NOUN a person who manages the finances of a college or school.

bursary NOUN (PL -ies) a grant.

burst VERB (**burst, bursting**) break suddenly and violently apart; force or be forced open; be very full; appear or come suddenly and forcefully. NOUN an instance of breaking; a brief violent or energetic outbreak.

bury VERB (**buried, burying**) put or hide something underground; cover or conceal; involve yourself deeply.

bus NOUN (PL **buses**; [US] **busses**) a large motor vehicle for public transport by road. VERB (**buses** or **busses, bussed, bussing**) travel or transport by bus.

bush NOUN a shrub; uncultivated land or the vegetation on it.

bushy ADJ (-ier, -iest)

growing thickly.

business NOUN **1** an occupation, profession, or trade; something that is someone's duty or concern. **2** trade or commerce; a commercial establishment.
businessman NOUN
businesswoman NOUN

businesslike ADJ efficient and practical.

busker NOUN a street entertainer performing for donations.

bust NOUN a woman's breasts; a sculptured head, shoulders, and chest. VERB [int] burst or break. ADJ [inf] bankrupt.

bustle VERB make a show of activity or hurry. NOUN excited activity.

busy ADJ (-ier, -iest) having much to do; occupied; full of activity.
busily ADV

busybody NOUN (PL -ies) a nosy, interfering person.

but CONJ introducing contrast; however; except. PREP apart from. ADV merely.

butane NOUN an inflammable gas used in liquid form as fuel.

butch ADJ [inf]

ostentatiously and aggressively masculine.

butcher NOUN a person who cuts up and sells meat as a trade; a savage killer. VERB kill needlessly or brutally.

butchery NOUN

butler NOUN a chief manservant.

butt NOUN 1 the thick end of a tool or weapon; a cigarette stub. 2 a target for ridicule or teasing. VERB 1 push with the head. 2 (**butt in**) interrupt.

butter NOUN a fatty substance made from cream. VERB spread with butter.

buttercup NOUN a wild plant with yellow cup-shaped flowers.

butterfly NOUN (PL -ies) 1 an insect with four large wings. 2 a swimming stroke with both arms lifted at the same time.

butterscotch NOUN a hard toffee-like sweet.

buttock NOUN either of the two fleshy rounded parts at the lower end of the back of the body.

button NOUN a disc or knob sewn to a garment as a fastener or ornament; a knob pressed to operate a device. VERB fasten with buttons.

buttonhole NOUN a slit through which a button is passed to fasten clothing; a flower worn in the buttonhole of a lapel. VERB accost and talk to.

buttress NOUN a support built against a wall; something that supports. VERB reinforce or prop up.

buxom ADJ (of a woman) plump and large-breasted.

buy VERB (**bought, buying**) obtain in exchange for money. NOUN a purchase.

buyer NOUN

buzz NOUN 1 a vibrating humming sound; [inf] a telephone call. 2 [inf] a thrill. VERB 1 make a buzzing sound. 2 be full of activity.

buzzer NOUN

buzzard NOUN a large hawk.

by PREP 1 beside. 2 through the action of. 3 not later than. 4 during. 5 past and beyond. ADV going past.

bye NOUN 1 a run scored from a ball not hit by the batsman. 2 the transfer of a competitor to a higher round in the absence of an opponent.

by-election NOUN an election of an MP to replace one who has died or resigned.

bygone ADJ belonging to the past.

by-law NOUN a regulation made by a local authority or corporation.

bypass NOUN a road taking traffic round a town; an operation providing an alternative passage for blood. VERB go past or round.

by-product NOUN something produced in the process of making something else.

byre NOUN a cowshed.

bystander NOUN a person standing near when something happens.

byte NOUN [Computing] a fixed number of bits (usually eight).

byway NOUN a minor road.

byword NOUN a famous or typical example; a familiar saying.

Cc

C ABBREV Celsius; centigrade. NOUN (as a Roman numeral) 100.

c. ABBREV 1 century. 2 cents. 3 circa.

cab NOUN 1 a taxi. 2 a compartment for the driver of a train, lorry, etc.

cabal NOUN a group involved in a plot.

cabaret NOUN entertainment provided in a nightclub etc.

cabbage NOUN a vegetable with thick green or purple leaves.

cabin NOUN a compartment in a ship or aircraft; a small hut.

cabinet NOUN 1 a cupboard with drawers or shelves. 2 (**the Cabinet**) a committee of senior government ministers.

cable NOUN a thick rope of fibre or wire; a set of insulated wires for carrying electricity or signals.

cable car a vehicle pulled

by a moving cable for carrying passengers up and down mountains.

cache NOUN a hidden store.

cachet NOUN prestige.

cackle NOUN the clucking of hens; a loud laugh. VERB give a cackle.

cacophony NOUN (PL **-ies**) a discordant mixture of sounds.
  cacophonous ADJ

cactus NOUN (PL **-ti** or **-tuses**) a fleshy plant, often with prickles, from a hot dry climate.

cad NOUN [dated] a dishonourable man.

cadaver NOUN a corpse.

cadaverous ADJ very pale and thin.

caddie (or **caddy**) NOUN a golfer's attendant carrying clubs.

caddy NOUN (PL **-ies**) a small box for tea.

cadence NOUN the rise and fall of the voice in speech.

cadenza NOUN a difficult solo passage in a musical work.

cadet NOUN a young trainee in the armed forces or police.

cadge VERB ask for or get by begging.

cadmium NOUN a silvery-white metal.

Caesarean section NOUN an operation to deliver a child by an incision through the walls of the mother's abdomen and womb.

cafe NOUN a small informal restaurant.

cafeteria NOUN a self-service restaurant.

caffeine NOUN a stimulant found in tea and coffee.

caftan see **kaftan**.

cage NOUN a structure of bars or wires, used for confining animals. VERB confine in a cage.

cagey ADJ [inf] secretive or reticent.

cagoule NOUN a light hooded waterproof jacket.

cairn NOUN a mound of stones as a memorial or landmark.

cajole VERB coax.

cake NOUN **1** a sweet food made from a baked mixture of flour, eggs, sugar, and fat. **2** a flat compact mass. VERB form a crust.

calamine NOUN a soothing skin lotion.

calamity NOUN (PL **-ies**) a disaster.
  calamitous ADJ

calcium NOUN a whitish metallic element.

calculate VERB 1 reckon mathematically; estimate. 2 intend or plan.
calculation NOUN
calculator NOUN

calculating ADJ ruthlessly scheming.

caldron US spelling of **cauldron**.

calendar NOUN a chart showing dates of days of the year.

calf NOUN (PL **calves**) 1 the young of cattle, elephants, whales, etc. 2 the fleshy back of the human leg below the knee.

calibrate VERB mark the units of measurement on or check the accuracy of a gauge.
calibration NOUN

calibre ([US] **caliber**) NOUN 1 degree of quality or ability. 2 the diameter of a gun, tube, or bullet.

calico NOUN a cotton cloth.

call VERB 1 shout to attract attention; summon. 2 (of a bird) make its characteristic cry. 3 telephone. 4 name; describe or address in a specified way. NOUN 1 a brief visit. 2 a shout; a bird's cry; a summons. 3 a telephone communication. 4 a need.
call for make necessary.
call off cancel.
caller NOUN

calligraphy NOUN decorative handwriting.

callipers NOUN an instrument for measuring diameters.

callous ADJ feeling no pity or sympathy.

callow ADJ immature and inexperienced.

callus NOUN a patch of hardened skin.

calm ADJ 1 not excited or agitated. 2 not windy or disturbed by wind. NOUN a calm condition. VERB make calm.
calmness NOUN

calorie NOUN a unit of heat; a unit of the energy-producing value of food.
calorific ADJ

calumny NOUN (PL **-ies**) slander.

calve VERB give birth to a calf.

calypso NOUN (PL **-os**) a West Indian song with improvised words on a topical theme.

cam NOUN a projecting part

on a wheel or shaft changing rotary to to-and-fro motion.

camaraderie NOUN comradeship.

camber NOUN a slight convex curve given to a surface, especially of a road.

cambric NOUN thin linen or cotton cloth.

camcorder NOUN a combined video and sound recorder.

came past of **come**.

camel NOUN a large animal either one or two humps on its back.

camellia NOUN an evergreen flowering shrub.

cameo NOUN (PL **-os**) 1 a piece of jewellery with a portrait carved in relief on a background of a different colour. 2 a small part played by a famous actor or actress.

camera NOUN an apparatus for taking photographs or film pictures.

cameraman NOUN

camisole NOUN a woman's bodice-like undergarment with shoulder straps.

camouflage NOUN disguise or concealment by colouring or covering. VERB disguise or conceal in this way.

camp NOUN 1 a place with temporary accommodation in tents; a place where troops are lodged or trained. 2 a group of people with the same ideals. VERB sleep in a tent. ADJ affected or theatrical in style; ostentatiously effeminate.

camp bed a portable folding bed.

camper NOUN

campsite NOUN

campaign NOUN a connected series of military operations; an organized course of action to achieve a goal. VERB conduct or take part in a campaign.

campaigner NOUN

camphor NOUN a strong-smelling white substance used in medicine and mothballs.

campus NOUN the grounds of a university or college.

can[1] NOUN a cylindrical metal container for holding liquid or preserving food. VERB (**canned, canning**) preserve in a can.

can² AUXILIARY VERB (**can, could**) be able or allowed to.

canal NOUN an artificial watercourse; a duct in the body.

canapé NOUN a small piece of bread or pastry with a savoury topping.

canary NOUN (PL **-ies**) a small yellow songbird.

cancan NOUN a lively high-kicking dance performed by women.

cancel VERB (**cancelled, cancelling**; [US] **canceled, canceling**) **1** declare that something arranged will not take place. **2** mark a ticket or stamp to prevent re-use. **3** (**cancel out**) offset or neutralize. **cancellation** NOUN

cancer NOUN a malignant tumour; a disease in which these form. **cancerous** ADJ

candelabrum NOUN (PL **-bra**) a large branched holder for several candles or lamps.

candid ADJ frank.

candidate NOUN a person applying for a job, standing for election, or taking an exam. **candidacy** NOUN

candied ADJ encrusted or preserved in sugar.

candle NOUN a stick of wax enclosing a wick which is burnt to give light.

candlestick NOUN a holder for a candle.

candour ([US] **candor**) NOUN frankness.

candy NOUN (PL **-ies**) [US] sweets.

candyfloss NOUN a fluffy mass of spun sugar.

cane NOUN a stem of a tall reed or grass; a length of cane used as a walking stick, for beating someone, etc. VERB beat with a cane.

canine ADJ of dogs. NOUN a pointed tooth between the incisors and molars.

canister NOUN a small metal container.

canker NOUN a disease of animals or plants.

cannabis NOUN a drug obtained from the hemp plant.

canned past & past participle of **can¹**.

cannelloni PLURAL NOUN rolls of pasta with a savoury filling.

cannibal NOUN a person who eats human flesh. **cannibalism** NOUN

cannibalize (or **-ise**) VERB use parts from a machine to repair another.

cannon NOUN (PL **cannon**) a large gun. VERB bump heavily into.

cannot AUXILIARY VERB the negative form of **can²**.

canny ADJ (**-ier, -iest**) shrewd.

canoe NOUN a light boat propelled by paddling. VERB (**canoed, canoeing**) go in a canoe. **canoeist** NOUN

canon NOUN **1** a member of cathedral clergy. **2** a general rule or principle. **3** a set of writings accepted as genuine. **canonical** ADJ

canonize (or **-ise**) VERB declare officially to be a saint.

canopy NOUN (PL **-ies**) an ornamental cloth held up as a covering.

cant NOUN insincere talk; jargon.

cantankerous ADJ bad-tempered and uncooperative.

cantata NOUN a choral composition.

canteen NOUN **1** a restaurant for employees. **2** a case of cutlery.

canter NOUN a gentle gallop. VERB go at a canter.

cantilever NOUN a projecting beam or girder supporting a structure.

canvas NOUN a strong coarse cloth; a painting on this.

canvass VERB **1** ask for votes. **2** propose a plan for discussion.

canyon NOUN a deep gorge.

cap NOUN **1** a soft, flat hat with a peak; a cover or top; an upper limit. **2** an explosive device for a toy pistol. VERB (**capped, capping**) put a cap on; set an upper limit to.

capable ADJ **1** able or fit to do something. **2** competent or efficient. **capability** NOUN

capacious ADJ roomy.

capacity NOUN (PL **-ies**) **1** the amount that something can contain. **2** ability to do something. **3** a role or function.

cape NOUN **1** a sleeveless cloak. **2** a coastal promontory.

caper VERB jump about friskily. NOUN **1** a frisky movement; [inf] a foolish or illicit activity. **2** a pickled bud of a bramble-like shrub.

capillary NOUN (PL **-ies**) a very fine hair-like tube or blood vessel.

capital NOUN **1** the chief town of a country or region. **2** a capital letter. **3** money with which a business is started. **4** the top part of a pillar. ADJ **1** involving the death penalty. **2** [inf] excellent.

capital letter a large-sized letter used to begin sentences and names.

capitalism NOUN a system in which trade and industry are controlled by private owners for profit. **capitalist** NOUN

capitalize (or **-ise**) VERB **1** convert into or provide with capital. **2** write in capital letters or with a capital first letter. **3** (**capitalize on**) take advantage of.

capitulate VERB surrender or yield.

capon NOUN a domestic cock fattened for eating.

cappuccino NOUN (PL **-os**) coffee made with frothy steamed milk.

caprice NOUN a whim.

capricious ADJ having sudden changes of mood.

capsize VERB (of a boat) overturn.

capstan NOUN a revolving post or spindle on which a cable etc. winds.

capsule NOUN **1** a small gelatin case containing a dose of medicine. **2** a small case or compartment.

captain NOUN a person commanding a ship or aircraft; the leader of a group or team; a naval officer next below rear admiral; an army officer next below major. VERB be captain of. **captaincy** NOUN

caption NOUN a short title or heading; an explanation on an illustration.

captivate VERB attract and hold the interest of.

captive ADJ unable to escape. NOUN a person who has been captured. **captivity** NOUN

captor NOUN a person who takes a captive.

capture VERB **1** gain control of by force; take prisoner. **2** record accurately in words or pictures. **3** cause data to be stored in a computer. NOUN capturing.

car NOUN a motor vehicle for a small number of passengers; a railway carriage or wagon.

carafe NOUN a glass bottle for serving wine or water.

caramel NOUN brown syrup made from heated sugar; toffee tasting like this.

carat NOUN a unit of purity of gold; a unit of weight for precious stones.

caravan NOUN 1 a vehicle equipped for living in, able to be towed by a vehicle. 2 [historical] a group travelling together across a desert.

caraway NOUN a plant with spicy seeds used as flavouring.

carbohydrate NOUN an energy-producing compound (e.g. starch) in food.

carbon NOUN a chemical element occurring as diamond, graphite, and charcoal, and in all living matter. **carbon copy** a copy made with carbon paper; an exact copy. **carbon dating** a method of deciding the age of something by measuring the decay of radiocarbon in it. **carbon dioxide** a gas produced during respiration and by burning carbon. **carbon monoxide** a poisonous gas formed by the incomplete burning of carbon. **carbon paper** paper coated with carbon, used to make copies of documents.

carbonate NOUN a compound releasing carbon dioxide when mixed with acid.

carbonated ADJ (of a drink) fizzy.

carbuncle NOUN 1 a severe abscess. 2 a polished red gem.

carburettor ([US] **carburetor**) NOUN a device mixing air and petrol in a motor engine.

carcass (or **carcase**) NOUN the dead body of an animal.

carcinogen NOUN a cancer-producing substance. **carcinogenic** ADJ

carcinoma NOUN (PL **-mata** or **-mas**) a cancerous tumour.

card NOUN a piece of cardboard or thick paper;

this used to send a message or greeting; this printed with someone's identifying details; a playing card; a credit card; (**cards**) any card game. VERB clean or comb wool with a wire brush or toothed instrument.

cardboard NOUN thin board made from paper pulp.

cardiac ADJ of the heart.

cardigan NOUN a sweater with buttons down the front.

cardinal ADJ most important. NOUN an important RC priest, having the power to elect the Pope.

cardinal number a number denoting quantity rather than order (1, 2, 3, etc.).

cardiograph NOUN an instrument recording heart movements.

cardiology NOUN the branch of medicine concerned with the heart. **cardiologist** NOUN

care NOUN 1 protection and provision of necessities; supervision. 2 serious attention and thought; caution to avoid damage or loss. VERB 1 feel concern or interest. 2 (**care for**) look after; feel affection for; like or enjoy.

career NOUN an occupation undertaken for a long period of a person's life. VERB move swiftly or wildly.

carefree ADJ light-hearted and free from worry.

careful ADJ showing attention or caution. **carefully** ADV

careless ADJ showing insufficient attention or concern. **carelessly** ADV

carer NOUN a person who looks after a sick or disabled person at home.

caress NOUN a gentle loving touch. VERB give a caress to.

caret NOUN a mark (γ) indicating an insertion in text.

caretaker NOUN a person employed to look after a building.

careworn ADJ showing signs of prolonged worry.

cargo NOUN (PL **-oes** or **-os**) goods carried by ship, aircraft, or motor vehicle.

caribou NOUN (PL **caribou**) a North American

reindeer.

caricature NOUN a picture exaggerating someone's characteristics for comic effect. VERB portray in this way.

caries NOUN decay of a tooth or bone.

carmine ADJ vivid crimson.

carnage NOUN great slaughter.

carnal ADJ of the body or flesh.

carnation NOUN a plant with pink, white, or red flowers.

carnival NOUN a festival with processions, music, and dancing.

carnivore NOUN an animal feeding on flesh. **carnivorous** ADJ

carol NOUN a Christmas hymn. VERB (**carolled, carolling**; [US] **caroled, caroling**) sing carols; sing joyfully.

carotid NOUN an artery carrying blood to the head.

carouse VERB drink and be merry.

carousel NOUN 1 [US] a merry-go-round. 2 a rotating conveyor for luggage at an airport.

carp NOUN a freshwater fish. VERB keep finding fault.

carpenter NOUN a person who makes or repairs wooden objects etc. **carpentry** NOUN

carpet NOUN a textile fabric for covering a floor; a covering. VERB (**carpeted, carpeting**) cover with a carpet.

carriage NOUN 1 a section of a train; a horse-drawn vehicle. 2 transport of goods. 3 a person's way of standing and moving. 4 a part of a machine that carries other parts into position. **carriage clock** a small portable clock with a handle on top.

carriageway NOUN the part of the road on which vehicles travel.

carrier NOUN a person or thing carrying something; a company transporting goods; a bag with handles for shopping.

carrion NOUN dead decaying flesh.

carrot NOUN 1 a tapering orange root vegetable. 2 an incentive.

carry VERB (**carried**, **carrying**) 1 transport, support and move; have on your person; transmit a disease. 2 support; assume responsibility. 3 entail a consequence. 4 take a process to a particular point. 5 approve a measure; gain the support of. 6 stock goods. 7 be audible at a distance. **carry on** continue. **carry out** put into practice.

cart NOUN a wheeled vehicle for carrying loads. VERB carry or transport.

carte blanche NOUN full power to do as you think best.

cartel NOUN a manufacturers' or producers' union to control prices.

carthorse NOUN a strong, heavily built horse.

cartilage NOUN the firm elastic tissue in the skeletons of vertebrates.

cartography NOUN map drawing. **cartographer** NOUN

carton NOUN a cardboard or plastic container.

cartoon NOUN 1 a humorous drawing. 2 a film consisting of an animated sequence of drawings. **cartoonist** NOUN

cartridge NOUN 1 a case containing explosive for firearms. 2 a sealed cassette. **cartridge paper** thick strong paper.

cartwheel NOUN a sideways somersault performed with the arms and legs extended.

carve VERB cut hard material to make an object or pattern; cut meat into slices for eating.

cascade NOUN a waterfall. VERB fall like a waterfall.

case NOUN 1 an instance of something's occurring; an instance of a disease. 2 a lawsuit; a set of arguments supporting a position. 3 a container or protective covering; a suitcase. 4 the form of a noun, adjective, or pronoun indicating its grammatical role in a sentence. VERB 1 enclose in a case. 2 [inf] examine a building etc. in preparation for a crime.

casement NOUN a window opening on vertical

hinges.

cash NOUN money in the form of coins or banknotes. VERB **1** give or obtain cash for a cheque etc. **2** (**cash in on**) get profit or advantage from.

cashew NOUN an edible nut.

cashier NOUN a person employed to handle money. VERB dismiss from military service in disgrace.

cashmere NOUN fine soft wool from a breed of goat.

casino NOUN (PL **-os**) a public building or room for gambling.

cask NOUN a barrel for liquids.

casket NOUN a small ornamental box for valuables; [US] a coffin.

casserole NOUN a covered dish in which food is cooked and served; food cooked in this. VERB cook in a casserole.

cassette NOUN a small case containing a reel of magnetic tape or film.

cassock NOUN a long robe worn by clergy and choristers.

cast VERB (**cast**, **casting**) **1** throw; cause to appear on or affect something; direct your eyes or thoughts. **2** shed or discard. **3** register a vote. **4** shape molten metal in a mould. **5** select actors for a play or film; assign a role to. NOUN **1** a set of actors in a play etc. **2** an object made by casting molten metal. **3** a type or quality. **4** a slight squint.

casting vote a deciding vote when those on each side are equal. **cast iron** a hard alloy of iron cast in a mould. **cast-off** a discarded thing.

castanets PLURAL NOUN a pair of shell-shaped pieces of wood clicked in the hand to accompany Spanish dancing.

castaway NOUN a shipwrecked person.

caste NOUN each of the classes of Hindu society.

castigate VERB reprimand severely.

castigation NOUN

castle NOUN a large fortified residence.

castor (or **caster**) NOUN **1** a small swivelling wheel on a leg of furniture. **2** a small container with a perforated top for sprinkling sugar etc.

castor oil an oil from the seeds of a tropical plant, used as a laxative. **castor sugar** finely granulated white sugar.

castrate VERB remove the testicles of.

castration NOUN

casual ADJ 1 relaxed and unconcerned. 2 happening by chance. 3 not regular or permanent: *casual work*. 4 not serious or formal.

casually ADV

casualty NOUN (PL **-ies**) a person killed or injured in a war or accident.

cat NOUN a small furry domesticated animal; a wild animal related to this.

cataclysm NOUN a violent upheaval or disaster.

catacomb NOUN an underground chamber with recesses for tombs.

catalogue ([US] also **catalog**) NOUN a systematic list of items. VERB (**catalogued**, **cataloguing**) list in a catalogue.

catalyst NOUN a substance that aids a chemical reaction while remaining unchanged.

catalytic converter NOUN part of an exhaust system that reduces the harmful effects of pollutant gases.

catamaran NOUN a boat with parallel twin hulls.

catapult NOUN a device with elastic fitted to a forked stick for shooting small stones. VERB hurl from or as if from a catapult.

cataract NOUN 1 a large waterfall. 2 an opaque area clouding the lens of the eye.

catarrh NOUN excessive mucus in the nose or throat.

catastrophe NOUN a sudden great disaster.

catastrophic ADJ

catcall NOUN a whistle of disapproval.

catch VERB 1 grasp and hold a moving object. 2 capture; detect. 3 be in time for a train etc. 4 become infected with. 5 hear; understand. NOUN 1 an act of catching; something caught or worth catching. 2 a fastener for a door or window. 3 a hidden drawback. **catch out** detect in a mistake. **catch up** reach those ahead of you.

catching ADJ infectious.

catchment area NOUN an area from which rainfall drains into a river; an area from which a hospital draws patients or a school draws pupils.

catchphrase NOUN a well-known sentence or phrase.

catchy ADJ (**-ier, -iest**) (of a tune) pleasant and easy to remember.

catechism NOUN a series of questions and answers on the principles of a religion, used for teaching.

categorical ADJ unconditional; absolute. **categorically** ADV

category NOUN (PL **-ies**) a class of things. **categorize** (or **-ise**) VERB

cater VERB supply food; provide what is needed or wanted. **caterer** NOUN

caterpillar NOUN the larva of a butterfly or moth.

caterwaul VERB make a cat's howling cry.

catharsis NOUN (PL **-ses**) a release of strong feeling or tension. **cathartic** ADJ

cathedral NOUN the principal church of a diocese.

Catherine wheel NOUN a rotating firework.

catheter NOUN a tube inserted into the bladder to extract urine.

cathode NOUN an electrode by which current leaves a device.

catholic ADJ **1** all-embracing. **2** (**Catholic**) Roman Catholic. **Catholicism** NOUN

catkin NOUN a hanging flower of willow, hazel, etc.

catnap NOUN a short nap.

catseye NOUN [trademark] a reflector stud on a road.

cattery NOUN (PL **-ies**) a place where cats are boarded.

cattle PLURAL NOUN cows, bulls, and oxen.

catty ADJ (**-ier, -iest**) spiteful.

catwalk NOUN a narrow platform along which models walk to display clothes.

caucus NOUN a group with shared interests within a

political party.

caught past and past participle of **catch**.

cauldron ([US] **caldron**) NOUN a large cooking pot.

cauliflower NOUN a cabbage with a large white flower head.

causal ADJ of or acting as a cause.

cause NOUN 1 something that brings about something else; a reason or motive. 2 a principle or movement supported. VERB make happen. **causation** NOUN

causeway NOUN a raised road across low or wet ground.

caustic ADJ 1 burning by chemical action. 2 sarcastic.

cauterize (or **-ise**) VERB burn tissue to destroy infection or stop bleeding.

caution NOUN 1 care to avoid danger or error. 2 a warning. VERB warn; reprimand.

cautionary ADJ conveying a warning.

cautious ADJ having or showing caution.

cavalcade NOUN a procession.

cavalier ADJ offhand or unconcerned. NOUN (**Cavalier**) a supporter of Charles I in the English Civil War.

cavalry NOUN (PL **-ies**) mounted troops.

cave NOUN a hollow in a cliff or hillside. VERB (**cave in**) collapse; yield.

caveat NOUN a warning.

cavern NOUN a large cave.

cavernous ADJ huge, spacious, or gloomy.

caviar NOUN the pickled roe of sturgeon or other large fish.

cavil VERB (**cavilled, cavilling**; [US] **caviled, caviling**) raise petty objections. NOUN a petty objection.

cavity NOUN (PL **-ies**) a hollow within a solid object.

cavort VERB leap about excitedly.

cayenne NOUN a hot red pepper.

CBE ABBREV Commander of the Order of the British Empire.

cc (or **c.c.**) ABBREV 1 carbon copy or copies. 2 cubic centimetres.

CD ABBREV compact disc.

CD-ROM NOUN a compact

disc holding data for display on a computer screen.

cease VERB come to an end; stop doing something.
ceaseless ADJ

ceasefire NOUN a truce.

cedar NOUN an evergreen tree.

cede VERB surrender territory etc.

cedilla NOUN a mark written under c (ç) to show that it is pronounced as s.

ceilidh NOUN [Scottish & Irish] an informal gathering for traditional music and dancing.

ceiling NOUN the upper interior surface of a room; an upper limit.

celebrate VERB mark or honour with festivities.
celebration NOUN

celebrated ADJ famous.

celebrity NOUN (PL -ies) a famous person; fame.

celery NOUN a plant with edible crisp stems.

celestial ADJ of the sky; of heaven.

celibate ADJ abstaining from sex.
celibacy NOUN

cell NOUN 1 a small room for a prisoner or monk. 2 a microscopic unit of living matter. 3 a device for producing electric current chemically.
cellular ADJ

cellar NOUN an underground room; a stock of wine.

cello NOUN (PL -os) a bass instrument of the violin family.
cellist NOUN

cellophane NOUN [trademark] a thin transparent wrapping material.

cellulite NOUN lumpy fat under the skin, causing a dimpled effect.

Celsius NOUN a scale of temperature on which water freezes at 0° and boils at 100°.

cement NOUN a substance of lime and clay used to make mortar or concrete. VERB join with cement; unite firmly.

cemetery NOUN (PL -ies) a burial ground other than a churchyard.

censor NOUN a person authorized to examine letters, books, films, etc., and suppress any parts regarded as socially or

politically unacceptable. VERB examine and alter in this way.
censorship NOUN

censorious ADJ severely critical.

censure NOUN harsh criticism and rebuke. VERB criticize harshly.

census NOUN an official count of the population.

cent NOUN a 100th of a dollar or other currency.

centaur NOUN a mythical creature, half man, half horse.

centenary NOUN (PL -ies) a 100th anniversary.
centennial ADJ & NOUN

center etc. US spelling of **centre** etc.

centigrade ADJ measured by the centigrade scale of temperature.

centime NOUN a 100th of a franc.

centimetre ([US] **centimeter**) NOUN a 100th of a metre, about 0.4 inch.

centipede NOUN a small crawling creature with many legs.

central ADJ of, at, or forming a centre; most important.
centrally ADV

centralism NOUN a system that centralizes an administration.

centralize (or -ise) VERB bring under the control of a central authority.
centralization NOUN

centre ([US] **center**) NOUN 1 a point or part in the middle of something; a position avoiding extremes. 2 a place where a specified activity takes place; a point where something begins or is most intense. VERB (**centred, centring**) 1 have or cause to have something as a major concern or theme. 2 place in the middle; base at a particular place.

centurion NOUN a commander in the ancient Roman army.

century NOUN (PL -ies) 1 a period of 100 years. 2 100 runs at cricket.

ceramic ADJ made of pottery. NOUN (**ceramics**) the art of making pottery.

cereal NOUN a grass plant with edible grain; this grain; breakfast food made from it.

cerebral ADJ of the brain; intellectual.

cerebral palsy a condition causing jerky, involuntary movements of the muscles.

ceremonial ADJ of or used in ceremonies.

ceremonially ADV

ceremonious ADJ formal and grand.

ceremony NOUN (PL **-ies**) a grand occasion on which special acts are performed; formal politeness.

certain ADJ 1 definite or reliable. 2 feeling sure. 3 specific but not named.

certainly ADV of course; yes.

certainty NOUN (PL **-ies**) conviction; definite truth or reliability; something that is certain.

certifiable ADJ able or needing to be certified.

certificate NOUN an official document attesting certain facts.

certify VERB (**certified, certifying**) declare or confirm formally; declare insane.

certitude NOUN a feeling of certainty.

cervix NOUN (PL **-vices**) a neck-like structure in the womb.

cervical ADJ

cessation NOUN ceasing.

cesspit (or **cesspool**) NOUN a covered pit in which liquid waste or sewage is collected.

cf. ABBREV compare.

chafe VERB 1 warm by rubbing; become sore by rubbing. 2 become irritated or impatient.

chaff NOUN corn husks separated from seed. VERB tease.

chaffinch NOUN a pink-breasted finch.

chagrin NOUN annoyance and embarrassment.

chain NOUN 1 a series of connected metal links; a connected series or sequence; a group of hotels or shops owned by the same company. 2 a unit of measurement (66 feet). VERB fasten with a chain.

chair NOUN 1 a movable seat for one person, usually with a back and four legs. 2 a chairperson; the position of a professor. VERB act as chairperson of.

chairlift NOUN a series of chairs on a cable for carrying people up a mountain.

chairperson NOUN a person who presides over a meeting or board of directors.
chairman NOUN
chairwoman NOUN

chalet NOUN a Swiss hut or cottage; a small cabin in a holiday camp.

chalice NOUN a large goblet.

chalk NOUN white soft limestone; a piece of this or similar coloured substance used for drawing.

challenge NOUN 1 a call to try your skill or strength, especially in a competition; a demanding task. 2 an objection or query. VERB 1 invite to a contest; test the ability of. 2 dispute or query.
challenger NOUN

chamber NOUN a hall used for meetings of a council, parliament, etc.; [old use] a room; (**chambers**) rooms used by a barrister; an enclosed space or cavity.
chamber music music written for a small group of players.

chambermaid NOUN a woman employed to clean hotel bedrooms.

chameleon NOUN a small lizard that changes colour according to its surroundings.

chamois NOUN 1 a small mountain antelope. 2 a piece of soft leather used for cleaning windows, cars, etc.

champ VERB munch noisily.

champagne NOUN a sparkling white French wine.

champion NOUN 1 a person or thing that defeats all others in a competition. 2 a person who fights or speaks in support of another or of a cause. VERB support.
championship NOUN

chance NOUN 1 a possibility or opportunity; a degree of likelihood. 2 development of events without planning or obvious reason. VERB 1 try something uncertain or dangerous. 2 happen; happen to do something. ADJ unplanned.

chancel NOUN the part of a church near the altar.

chancellor NOUN the government minister in

charge of the nation's budget; a state or law official of various other kinds; the non-resident head of a university.

chancy ADJ (**-ier, -iest**) [inf] risky or uncertain.

chandelier NOUN a hanging light with branches for several bulbs or candles.

change VERB make or become different; exchange, substitute, or replace; move from one system, situation, etc. to another; get or give small money or different currency for. NOUN changing; money in small units or returned as balance.
changeable ADJ

changeling NOUN a child or thing believed to have been substituted secretly for another.

channel NOUN 1 a stretch of water connecting two seas; a passage for water. 2 a medium of communication. 3 a band of broadcasting frequencies. VERB (**channelled, channelling**; [US] **channeled, channeling**) direct to a particular end or by a particular route.

chant NOUN a monotonous song; a rhythmic shout of a repeated phrase. VERB say, shout, or sing in a chant.

chaos NOUN great disorder.
chaotic ADJ
chaotically ADV

chap NOUN [inf] a man.

chapatti NOUN a thin flat disc of unleavened bread, used in Indian cookery.

chapel NOUN a small building or room used for prayers; a part of a large church with its own altar.

chaperone NOUN an older woman looking after a young unmarried woman on social occasions. VERB act as chaperone to.

chaplain NOUN a clergyman of an institution, private chapel, ship, or regiment.
chaplaincy NOUN

chapped ADJ (of skin) cracked and sore.

chapter NOUN 1 a division of a book. 2 the canons of a cathedral.

char NOUN a woman employed to clean a private house. VERB (**charred, charring**) become black by burning.

character NOUN 1 the distinctive qualities of someone or something; moral strength. 2 a person in a novel, play, or film; an individual and original person. 3 a printed or written letter or sign.

characteristic NOUN a feature typical of and helping to identify a person or thing. ADJ typical of or distinguishing a person or thing.

characteristically ADV

characterize (or -ise) VERB 1 describe the character of. 2 be a characteristic of.

characterization NOUN

charade NOUN 1 an absurd pretence. 2 (**charades**) a game involving guessing words from acted clues.

charcoal NOUN a black substance made by burning wood slowly.

charge NOUN 1 the price asked for goods or services. 2 an accusation. 3 responsibility and care; someone or something for which you are responsible. 4 a rushing attack. 5 the electricity contained in a substance. 6 a quantity of explosive. VERB 1 ask for a specified price from someone. 2 accuse formally. 3 entrust with a task or responsibility. 4 rush forward in attack. 5 give an electric charge to. 6 load with explosive.

charge card a credit card.

chargé d'affaires NOUN (PL **chargés d'affaires**) an ambassador's deputy.

charger NOUN 1 a cavalry horse. 2 a device for charging a battery.

chariot NOUN a two-wheeled horse-drawn vehicle used in ancient times in battle and in racing.

charioteer NOUN

charisma NOUN the power to inspire devotion and enthusiasm in others.

charismatic ADJ

charitable ADJ 1 of charities. 2 lenient or kind.

charitably ADV

charity NOUN (PL **-ies**) 1 an organization helping the needy; gifts or voluntary work for the needy. 2 kindness and tolerance in judging others.

charlatan NOUN a person falsely claiming to be an expert.

charm NOUN 1 the power to attract, delight, or fascinate. 2 an act, object, or words believed to have magic power; a small ornament worn on a bracelet etc. VERB 1 delight; influence by personal charm. 2 control by magic.

charming ADJ

chart NOUN 1 a table, graph, or diagram; a map for navigators. 2 (**the charts**) a weekly list of the current best-selling pop records. VERB record or show on a chart.

charter NOUN 1 an official document granting rights. 2 hiring an aircraft etc. for a special purpose. VERB 1 grant a charter to. 2 let or hire an aircraft, ship, or vehicle.

charter flight a flight by an aircraft that has been hired for a specific journey.

chartered ADJ (of an accountant, engineer, etc.) qualified according to the rules of an association holding a royal charter.

chary ADJ cautious.

chase VERB go quickly after in order to capture, overtake, or drive away. NOUN a pursuit; hunting.

chasm NOUN a deep cleft.

chassis NOUN (PL **chassis**) the base frame of a vehicle.

chaste ADJ 1 celibate; sexually pure. 2 simple in style.

chastity NOUN

chasten VERB subdue.

chastise VERB reprimand severely.

chat NOUN an informal conversation. VERB (**chatted, chatting**) have a chat.

chateau NOUN (PL **-teaux**) a French castle or large country house.

chattel NOUN a movable possession.

chatter VERB 1 talk quickly and continuously about unimportant matters. 2 (of teeth) rattle together. NOUN chattering talk.

chatterbox NOUN a talkative person.

chatty ADJ (**-ier, -iest**) fond of chatting; (of a letter etc.) informal and lively.

chauffeur NOUN a person

employed to drive a car.

chauvinism NOUN prejudiced belief in the superiority of your own race, sex, etc.
chauvinist NOUN
chauvinistic ADJ

cheap ADJ low in cost or value; poor in quality; contemptible; worthless.
cheapen VERB

cheapskate NOUN [inf] a stingy person.

cheat VERB act dishonestly or unfairly to win profit or advantage; deprive of something by trickery. NOUN a person who cheats; a deception.

check VERB 1 examine, test, or verify. 2 stop or slow the motion of. NOUN 1 an inspection. 2 a hindrance; a control or restraint. 3 the exposure of a chess king to capture. 4 [US] a restaurant bill. 5 a pattern of squares or crossing lines.
check in register at a hotel bill or airport. **check out** pay a hotel bill before leaving.

checker US spelling of **chequer**.

checkmate NOUN the situation in chess where

capture of a king is inevitable. VERB put into checkmate.

checkout NOUN a desk where goods are paid for in a supermarket.

checkpoint NOUN a place where security checks are made on travellers.

cheek NOUN 1 the side of the face below the eye. 2 bold or impudent speech. VERB speak cheekily to.

cheeky ADJ (-ier, -iest) mischievously impudent.
cheekily ADV

cheep NOUN a weak shrill cry like that of a young bird. VERB make this cry.

cheer NOUN 1 a shout of joy, encouragement, or praise. 2 cheerfulness. VERB 1 shout for joy, or in praise or encouragement. 2 make happier.

cheerful ADJ 1 happy and optimistic. 2 bright and pleasant.
cheerfully ADV

cheerless ADJ gloomy or dreary.

cheery ADJ (-ier, -iest) cheerful.

cheese NOUN food made from pressed milk curds.
cheesy ADJ

cheesecake NOUN an open tart filled with flavoured cream cheese.

cheesecloth NOUN a thin loosely-woven cotton fabric.

cheetah NOUN a large, spotted, swift-moving wild cat.

chef NOUN a professional cook.

chemical ADJ of or made by chemistry. NOUN a substance obtained by or used in a chemical process.
chemically ADV

chemist NOUN 1 a person authorized to sell medicine; a shop where medicines, toiletries, etc. are sold. 2 an expert in chemistry.

chemistry NOUN 1 the branch of science concerned with the nature of substances and how they react with each other. 2 complex emotional interaction between people.

chemotherapy NOUN the treatment of cancer with drugs.

chenille NOUN a fabric with a velvety pile.

cheque ([US] **check**) NOUN a written order to a bank to pay out money from an account.

chequer ([US] **checker**) NOUN a pattern of squares of alternating colours.

chequered ADJ 1 marked with a chequer pattern. 2 having frequent changes of fortune.

cherish VERB 1 take loving care of. 2 cling to hopes etc.

cherry NOUN (PL **-ies**) a small soft round fruit with a stone; a bright red colour.

cherub NOUN 1 (PL **-bim**) an angelic being. 2 (in art) a chubby infant with wings.
cherubic ADJ

chess NOUN a game of skill for two players using 32 pieces on a chequered board.

chest NOUN 1 a large strong box. 2 the upper front surface of the body.
chest of drawers a piece of furniture fitted with a set of drawers.

chestnut NOUN 1 a nut which can be roasted and eaten. 2 a reddish-brown colour. 3 an old joke or anecdote.

chevron NOUN a V-shaped symbol.

chew VERB work or grind between the teeth.

chewy ADJ needing much chewing.

chic ADJ stylish and elegant.

chicane NOUN a sharp double bend on a motor-racing track.

chicanery NOUN trickery.

chick NOUN a newly hatched young bird.

chicken NOUN 1 a domestic fowl kept for its eggs or meat. 2 [inf] a coward. ADJ [inf] cowardly.

chickenpox NOUN an infectious illness with a rash of small red blisters.

chicory NOUN a plant whose leaves are eaten in salads and whose root can be used instead of coffee.

chide VERB (**chided** or **chid**, **chidden**, **chiding**) rebuke.

chief NOUN a leader or ruler; the person with the highest rank. ADJ most important; highest in rank.

chiefly ADV mainly.

chieftain NOUN the chief of a clan or tribe.

chiffon NOUN a thin, almost transparent fabric.

chihuahua NOUN a very small smooth-haired dog.

chilblain NOUN a painful swelling caused by exposure to cold.

child NOUN (PL **children**) a young human being; a son or daughter.
childhood NOUN
childless ADJ
childlike ADJ

childbirth NOUN the process of giving birth to a child.

childish ADJ like a child; silly and immature.

chill NOUN 1 an unpleasant coldness. 2 a feverish cold. ADJ chilly. VERB 1 make cold. 2 [inf] relax.

chilli NOUN (PL **-ies**) a small hot-tasting pepper.

chilly ADJ (**-ier, -iest**) rather cold; unfriendly in manner.

chime NOUN the sound of a tuned set of bells; such a set. VERB 1 ring as a chime. 2 (**chime in**) interrupt.

chimney NOUN (PL **-eys**) a structure for carrying off smoke or gases from a fire or furnace.
chimney breast a projecting wall surrounding a chimney.

chimpanzee NOUN an

African ape.

chin NOUN the protruding part of the face below the mouth.

china NOUN fine earthenware; things made of this.

chinchilla NOUN a small squirrel-like South American animal; its grey fur.

chink NOUN 1 a narrow opening, a slit. 2 the sound of glasses or coins striking together. VERB make this sound.

chintz NOUN glazed cotton cloth used for furnishings.

chip NOUN 1 a small piece cut or broken off something hard; a small hole left by breaking off such a piece. 2 a fried oblong strip of potato. 3 a counter used in gambling. VERB (**chipped, chipping**) 1 cut small pieces off hard material. 2 (**chip in**) interrupt; make a contribution.

chipmunk NOUN a striped squirrel-like animal of North America.

chipolata NOUN a small sausage.

chiropody NOUN treatment of minor ailments of the feet.

chiropodist NOUN

chiropractic NOUN treatment of certain physical disorders by manipulation of the joints.

chiropractor NOUN

chirp NOUN a short sharp sound made by a small bird or grasshopper. VERB make this sound.

chirpy ADJ (**-ier, -iest**) [inf] lively and cheerful.

chisel NOUN a tool with a sharp bevelled end for shaping wood, stone, or metal. VERB (**chiselled, chiselling**; [US] **chiseled, chiseling**) cut with this.

chit NOUN a short written note.

chivalry NOUN courteous behaviour by a man towards a woman.

chivalrous ADJ

chive NOUN a herb with onion-flavoured leaves.

chivvy VERB (**chivvied, chivvying**) urge, nag, or pester.

chlorinate VERB treat or sterilize with chlorine.

chlorine NOUN a chemical element in the form of a poisonous gas.

chloroform NOUN a liquid used to dissolve things and formerly as an anaesthetic.

chlorophyll NOUN green pigment in plants.

chock NOUN a block or wedge for preventing a wheel from moving.

chocolate NOUN a dark brown sweet food made from cacao seeds; a drink made with this.

choice NOUN choosing; the right or opportunity to choose; a variety from which to choose; a person or thing chosen. ADJ of especially good quality.

choir NOUN an organized band of singers, especially in church.

choirboy NOUN

choke VERB stop a person breathing by squeezing or blocking the windpipe; have difficulty breathing; clog or smother. NOUN a valve controlling the flow of air into a petrol engine.

choker NOUN a close-fitting necklace.

cholera NOUN a disease causing severe vomiting and diarrhoea.

choleric ADJ easily angered.

cholesterol NOUN a fatty animal substance thought to cause hardening of arteries.

chomp VERB munch noisily.

choose VERB (**chose, chosen, choosing**) select out of a number of things.

choosy ADJ (**-ier, -iest**) [inf] excessively fastidious.

chop VERB (**chopped, chopping**) cut by a blow with an axe or knife; cut into small pieces; hit with a short downward movement. NOUN **1** a downward cutting blow. **2** a thick slice of meat, usually including a rib.

chopper NOUN **1** a chopping tool. **2** [inf] a helicopter.

choppy ADJ (**-ier, -iest**) full of short broken waves.

chopstick NOUN each of a pair of sticks used as eating utensils in China, Japan, etc.

choral ADJ for or sung by a choir.

chorale NOUN a choral composition using the words of a hymn.

chord NOUN a combination of notes sounded together.

chore NOUN a routine or irksome task.

choreography NOUN the composition of stage dances.
choreographer NOUN

chorister NOUN a member of a choir.

chortle NOUN & VERB (give) a loud chuckle.

chorus NOUN 1 a group of singers; a group of singing dancers in a musical etc.; an utterance by many people simultaneously. 2 the refrain of a song. VERB say the same thing as a group.

chose, **chosen** past and past participle of **choose**.

chow NOUN a long-haired dog of a Chinese breed.

christen VERB admit to the Christian Church by baptism; name.

Christian ADJ of or believing in Christianity. NOUN a believer in Christianity.
Christian name a person's first name.

Christianity NOUN the religion based on the teachings of Jesus Christ.

Christmas NOUN a festival held annually on 25 December to celebrate Jesus's birth.

chrome NOUN a hard, bright, metal coating made from chromium.

chromium NOUN a metallic element that does not rust.

chromosome NOUN a thread-like structure carrying genes in animal and plant cells.

chronic ADJ 1 constantly present or recurring; having a chronic disease or habit. 2 [inf] very bad.
chronically ADV

chronicle NOUN a record of events. VERB record in a chronicle.
chronicler NOUN

chronological ADJ following the order in which things happened.
chronologically ADV

chronology NOUN arrangement of events in order of occurrence.

chrysalis NOUN (PL **-lises**) a form of an insect in the stage between larva and adult insect; the case enclosing it.

chrysanthemum NOUN a garden plant flowering in autumn.

chubby ADJ (**-ier, -iest**) round and plump.

chuck VERB 1 [inf] throw carelessly; discard. 2 touch gently under the chin.

chuckle VERB & NOUN (give) a quiet laugh.

chuffed ADJ [inf] pleased.

chug VERB (**chugged, chugging**) (of a boat etc.) move slowly with a loud, regular sound.

chum NOUN [inf] a close friend.

chunk NOUN a thick piece. **chunky** ADJ

church NOUN 1 a building for public Christian worship. 2 (**the Church**) Christians collectively; a particular group of these.

churchyard NOUN an enclosed area round a church.

churlish ADJ ill-mannered or surly.

churn NOUN a machine in which milk is beaten to make butter; a very large milk can. VERB 1 beat milk or make butter in a churn; move and turn violently. 2 (**churn out**) produce large quantities of something without thought or care.

chute NOUN a sloping channel down which things can be slid or dropped.

chutney NOUN (PL -**eys**) a seasoned mixture of fruit, vinegar, spices, etc.

CIA ABBREV (in the US) Central Intelligence Agency.

ciabatta NOUN an Italian bread made with olive oil.

cicada NOUN a chirping insect resembling a grasshopper.

CID ABBREV Criminal Investigation Department.

cider NOUN an alcoholic drink made from apple juice.

cigar NOUN a cylinder of tobacco in tobacco leaves for smoking.

cigarette NOUN a roll of shredded tobacco in thin paper for smoking.

cinch NOUN [inf] a very easy task; a certainty.

cinder NOUN a piece of partly burnt coal or wood.

cinema NOUN a theatre where films are shown; films as an art form or industry.

cinnamon NOUN a spice.

cipher (or **cypher**) NOUN 1 a code. 2 an unimportant person.

circa PREP approximately.

circle NOUN **1** a perfectly round plane figure. **2** a curved tier of seats at a theatre etc. **3** a group with similar interests or shared acquaintances. VERB move in a circle; form a circle round.

circuit NOUN **1** a roughly circular route returning to its starting point. **2** an itinerary regularly followed.

circuitous ADJ long and indirect.

circuitry NOUN electric circuits.

circular ADJ shaped like or moving round a circle. NOUN a letter or leaflet sent to a large number of people.

circulate VERB move around an area; pass from one place or person to another.

circulation NOUN **1** circulating; the movement of blood round the body. **2** the extent to which something is known about or available; the number of copies sold of a newspaper.

circumcise VERB cut off the foreskin of.

circumcision NOUN

circumference NOUN the boundary of a circle; the distance round something.

circumflex NOUN the mark ^ over a letter.

circumnavigate VERB sail completely round.

circumscribe VERB restrict.

circumspect ADJ cautious or wary.

circumstance NOUN an occurrence or fact relevant to an event or situation.

circumstantial ADJ (of evidence) suggesting but not proving something.

circumvent VERB evade a difficulty etc.

circus NOUN a travelling show with performing animals, acrobats, etc.

cirrhosis NOUN a disease of the liver.

cirrus NOUN (PL **-rri**) a high wispy white cloud.

cistern NOUN a tank for storing water.

citadel NOUN a fortress overlooking a city.

cite VERB quote; mention as an example.

citation NOUN

citizen NOUN **1** a person

with full rights in a country. **2** an inhabitant of a city.

citizenship NOUN

citrus NOUN a fruit of a group that includes the lime, lemon, and orange.

city NOUN (PL **-ies**) an important town; a town with special rights given by charter and containing a cathedral.

civic ADJ of a city or citizenship.

civil ADJ **1** of citizens; not of the armed forces or the Church. **2** polite and obliging.

civil engineering the design and construction of roads, bridges, etc. **civil servant** an employee of the **civil service**, government departments other than the armed forces. **civil war** war between citizens of the same country.

civilian NOUN a person not in the armed forces.

civility NOUN (PL **-ies**) politeness.

civilization (or **-isation**) NOUN **1** an advanced stage of social development; progress towards this. **2** the culture and way of life of a particular area or period.

civilize (or **-ise**) VERB **1** bring to an advanced stage of social development. **2** (**civilized**) polite and good-mannered.

cl ABBREV centilitres.

claim VERB **1** demand as your right. **2** assert. NOUN **1** a demand; a right to something. **2** an assertion.

claimant NOUN

clairvoyance NOUN the power of seeing the future.

clairvoyant NOUN & ADJ

clam NOUN a shellfish with a hinged shell.

clamber VERB climb with difficulty.

clammy ADJ (**-ier, -iest**) unpleasantly moist and sticky.

clamour ([US] **clamor**) NOUN a loud confused noise; a loud protest or demand. VERB make a clamour.

clamorous ADJ

clamp NOUN a device for holding things tightly; a device attached to the wheels of an illegally parked car to immobilize it. VERB **1** grip or fasten with a clamp; fit a wheel clamp to a car. **2** (**clamp down on**) suppress or put a stop to.

clan NOUN a group of families with a common ancestor.

clandestine ADJ done secretly.

clang NOUN & VERB (make) a loud ringing sound.

clank NOUN & VERB (make) a sound like metal striking metal.

clap VERB (**clapped**, **clapping**) **1** strike the palms of your hands loudly together, especially in applause. **2** place your hand somewhere quickly; slap someone on the back. NOUN **1** an act of clapping. **2** a sharp noise of thunder.

claret NOUN a dry red wine.

clarify VERB (**clarified**, **clarifying**) **1** make more intelligible. **2** remove impurities from fats by heating.
clarification NOUN

clarinet NOUN a woodwind instrument.
clarinettist NOUN

clarity NOUN clearness.

clash VERB come into conflict; disagree or be at odds; be discordant. NOUN an act or sound of clashing.

clasp NOUN a device for fastening things, with interlocking parts; a grasp or handshake. VERB grasp tightly; embrace closely; fasten with a clasp.

class NOUN **1** a set of people or things with shared characteristics; a standard of quality; a social rank; a set of students taught together. **2** [inf] impressive stylishness. VERB assign to a particular category.

classic ADJ **1** of recognized high quality. **2** typical. **3** simple in style. NOUN **1** a classic author or work etc. **2** (**Classics**) the study of ancient Greek and Roman literature, history, etc.
classicist NOUN

classical ADJ **1** of ancient Greek and Roman civilization. **2** traditional in form and style.

classify VERB (**classified**, **classifying**) **1** arrange systematically. **2** designate as officially secret.
classification NOUN

classroom NOUN a room where a class of students is taught.

classy ADJ (-ier, -iest) [inf] stylish and sophisticated.

clatter NOUN & VERB (make) a rattling sound.

clause NOUN 1 a single part in a treaty, law, or contract. 2 a distinct part of a sentence, with its own verb.

claustrophobia NOUN extreme fear of being in an enclosed space. **claustrophobic** ADJ

clavicle NOUN the collarbone.

claw NOUN a pointed nail on an animal's or bird's foot. VERB scratch or clutch with a claw or hand.

clay NOUN stiff sticky earth, used for making bricks and pottery.

clean ADJ free from dirt or impurities; not soiled or used; not indecent or obscene. VERB make clean. **cleaner** NOUN **cleanliness** NOUN

cleanse VERB make clean or pure.

clear ADJ 1 easily perceived or understood. 2 transparent. 3 free of obstructions. 4 free from blemishes, doubts, or anything undesirable. VERB 1 free or become free from obstacles etc. 2 prove innocent. 3 get past or over. 4 give official approval for. 5 make as net profit. **clearly** ADV

clearance NOUN 1 clearing. 2 official permission. 3 space allowed for one object to pass another.

clearing NOUN a space cleared of trees in a forest.

cleavage NOUN a split or separation; the hollow between full breasts.

cleave[1] VERB (**cleaved** or **cleft** or **clove**, **cleft** or **cloven**, **cleaving**) split or divide.

cleave[2] VERB [literary] stick or cling.

cleaver NOUN a chopping tool.

clef NOUN a symbol on a stave in music, showing the pitch of notes.

cleft ADJ split. NOUN a split. **cleft lip** a congenital split in the upper lip.

clematis NOUN a climbing plant with showy flowers.

clemency NOUN mercy. **clement** ADJ

clementine NOUN a small variety of orange.

clench VERB close the teeth or fingers tightly.

clergy NOUN people ordained for religious duties.
clergyman NOUN

cleric NOUN a member of the clergy.

clerical ADJ 1 of routine office work. 2 of clergy.

clerk NOUN a person employed to do written work in an office.

clever ADJ quick to learn and understand; showing skill.

cliché NOUN an overused phrase or idea.
clichéd ADJ

click NOUN a short sharp sound. VERB make or cause to make such a sound; press a button on a computer mouse.

client NOUN a person using the services of a professional person.

clientele NOUN clients.

cliff NOUN a steep rock face on a coast.

cliffhanger NOUN an ending to an episode of a serial that leaves the audience in suspense.

climate NOUN the regular weather conditions of an area.
climatic ADJ

climax NOUN the most intense or exciting point; the culmination.
climactic ADJ

climb VERB go up to a higher position or level. NOUN an ascent; a route for ascent.
climber NOUN

clinch VERB settle conclusively. NOUN a close hold or embrace.

cling VERB (**clung, clinging**) hold on tightly; stick.

clinic NOUN a place where medical treatment or advice is given.

clinical ADJ 1 of or used in treatment of patients. 2 unemotional and efficient.

clink NOUN & VERB (make) a sharp ringing sound.

clip NOUN 1 a device for holding things together or in place. 2 an act of cutting; an excerpt. 3 [inf] a sharp blow. VERB (**clipped, clipping**) 1 fasten with a clip. 2 cut with shears or scissors. 3 [inf] hit sharply.

clipper NOUN 1 a fast sailing ship. 2 (**clippers**) an instrument for clipping things.

clipping NOUN a newspaper cutting.

clique NOUN a small

exclusive group.

clitoris NOUN the sensitive organ just in front of the vagina.

cloak NOUN a loose sleeveless outer garment. VERB cover or conceal.

cloakroom NOUN **1** a room where outer garments can be left. **2** a toilet.

clobber [inf] NOUN equipment; belongings. VERB hit hard.

clock NOUN an instrument indicating time.

clockwise ADV & ADJ moving in the direction of the hands of a clock.

clockwork NOUN a mechanism with wheels and springs.

clod NOUN a lump of earth.

clog NOUN a wooden-soled shoe. VERB (**clogged**, **clogging**) block or become blocked.

cloister NOUN a covered walk in a monastery etc.

cloistered ADJ sheltered or secluded.

clone NOUN a group of organisms or cells produced asexually from one ancestor; an identical copy. VERB produce a clone; make an identical copy of.

close ADJ **1** near in space or time. **2** very affectionate or intimate. **3** airless or humid. **4** careful and thorough. ADV so as to be very near; leaving little space. VERB **1** shut; cause to cover an opening. **2** bring or come to an end. **3** come nearer together. NOUN **1** an ending. **2** a street closed at one end.

closet NOUN a cupboard; a storeroom. VERB (**closeted**, **closeting**) shut away in private conference or study. ADJ secret or unacknowledged.

closure NOUN closing or being closed.

clot NOUN **1** a thickened mass of liquid. **2** [inf] a stupid person. VERB (**clotted**, **clotting**) form clots.

cloth NOUN woven or felted material; a piece of this for cleaning etc.

clothe VERB put clothes on or provide with clothes.

clothes PLURAL NOUN things worn to cover the body.

clothing NOUN clothes.

cloud NOUN **1** a visible mass of watery vapour floating in the sky; a mass of smoke or dust. **2** a state or cause of gloom. VERB become full of clouds. **cloudy** ADJ

clout [inf] NOUN **1** a blow. **2** influence. VERB hit.

clove[1] past of **cleave**[1].

clove[2] NOUN **1** a dried bud of a tropical tree, used as a spice. **2** any of the small bulbs making up a larger bulb of garlic.

clover NOUN a flowering plant with three-lobed leaves.

clown NOUN a person who does comical tricks. VERB perform or behave as a clown.

club NOUN **1** a group who meet for social or sporting purposes; an organization offering benefits to subscribers; a nightclub. **2** a heavy stick used as a weapon; a stick with a wooden or metal head, used in golf. VERB (**clubbed, clubbing**) **1** strike with a club. **2** (**club together**) combine with others to do something.

cluck NOUN the throaty cry of a hen. VERB make a cluck.

clue NOUN something that helps solve a puzzle or problem.

clump NOUN a cluster or mass. VERB **1** tread heavily. **2** form into a clump.

clumsy ADJ (**-ier, -iest**) awkward and badly coordinated; tactless. **clumsily** ADV **clumsiness** NOUN

clung past and past participle of **cling**.

cluster NOUN & VERB (form) a small close group.

clutch VERB grasp tightly. NOUN **1** a tight grasp. **2** a mechanism that connects a vehicle's engine with the axle and the wheels. **3** a set of eggs laid at one time; chicks hatched from these.

clutter NOUN things lying about untidily. VERB cover with clutter.

cm ABBREV centimetres.

Co. ABBREV **1** Company. **2** County.

co- COMBINING FORM joint; mutual.

c/o ABBREV care of.

coach NOUN **1** a long-distance bus; a railway carriage. **2** a private tutor; an instructor in sports. VERB train or teach.

coagulate VERB change from liquid to semi-solid form.

coal NOUN a hard black mineral burnt as fuel.

coalesce VERB form a single mass; combine.

coalfield NOUN an area where coal is mined.

coalition NOUN a temporary union of political parties.

coarse ADJ **1** composed of large particles; rough in texture. **2** crude or vulgar.

coast NOUN the seashore and land near it. VERB move easily without using power. **coastal** ADJ

coaster NOUN a mat for a glass.

coastguard NOUN an officer of an organization that keeps watch on the coast.

coat NOUN a long outer garment with sleeves; the fur or hair covering an animal's body; a covering layer. VERB cover with a layer.

coating NOUN a covering layer.

coax VERB persuade gently; manipulate carefully or slowly.

cob NOUN **1** a sturdy short-legged horse. **2** a hazelnut. **3** the central part of an ear of maize. **4** a small round loaf. **5** a male swan.

cobalt NOUN a metallic element; a deep blue pigment made from it.

cobble NOUN a rounded stone formerly used for paving roads. VERB mend or assemble roughly.

cobbler NOUN a shoe-mender.

cobra NOUN a poisonous snake of Asia and Africa.

cobweb NOUN a spider's web.

cocaine NOUN a drug used illegally as a stimulant.

cochineal NOUN red food colouring.

cock NOUN a male bird. VERB **1** tilt or bend in a particular direction. **2** set a gun for firing.

cockatoo NOUN a crested parrot.

cockerel NOUN a young male fowl.

cockle NOUN an edible shellfish.

cockpit NOUN the compartment for the pilot in a plane, or for the driver in a racing car.

cockroach NOUN a beetle-like insect.

cocksure ADJ over-confident.

cocktail NOUN a mixed alcoholic drink.

cocky ADJ (**-ier, -iest**) conceited and arrogant.

cocoa NOUN a drink made from powdered cacao seeds and milk.

coconut NOUN a nut of a tropical palm.

cocoon NOUN a silky sheath round a chrysalis; a protective wrapping. VERB wrap in something soft and warm.

cod NOUN a large edible sea fish.

coda NOUN the final part of a musical composition.

code NOUN **1** a system of words or symbols used to represent others for secrecy; a sequence of numbers or letters for identification. **2** a set of laws or rules.

codeine NOUN a painkilling drug.

codify VERB (**codified, codifying**) arrange laws or rules into a code.

coerce VERB compel by threats or force.
coercion NOUN

coexist VERB exist together, especially harmoniously.
coexistence NOUN

coffee NOUN a hot drink made from the bean-like seeds of a tropical shrub; a pale brown colour.

coffer NOUN a large strong box for holding money and valuables.

coffin NOUN a box in which a corpse is placed for burial or cremation.

cog NOUN one of a series of projections on the edge of a wheel, engaging with those of another.

cogent ADJ logical and convincing.
cogency NOUN

cogitate VERB think deeply.
cogitation NOUN

cognac NOUN French brandy.

cognition NOUN gaining knowledge by thought or perception.
cognitive ADJ

cognizant ADJ having knowledge or awareness.
cognizance NOUN

cohabit VERB live together as man and wife.
cohabitation NOUN

cohere VERB stick or hold together.

coherent ADJ logical and consistent; able to speak clearly.

cohesion NOUN the holding together of something.
cohesive ADJ

cohort NOUN a tenth part of a Roman legion; a group or set of people.

coiffure NOUN a hairstyle.

coil VERB wind into rings or a spiral. NOUN 1 something wound in a spiral; one ring or turn in this. 2 a contraceptive device inserted into the womb.

coin NOUN a piece of metal money. VERB 1 make coins by stamping metal. 2 invent a word or phrase.

coinage NOUN 1 coins of a particular type. 2 a coined word or phrase.

coincide VERB happen at the same time or place; be the same or similar.

coincidence NOUN a chance occurrence of events or circumstances at the same time; coinciding.
coincidental ADJ

coke NOUN 1 a solid fuel made by heating coal in the absence of air. 2 [inf] cocaine.

colander NOUN a bowl-shaped perforated container for draining food.

cold ADJ 1 at or having a low temperature. 2 not affectionate or enthusiastic. 3 not prepared or rehearsed. NOUN 1 low temperature; a cold condition. 2 an illness causing catarrh and sneezing.

cold-blooded 1 having a blood temperature varying with that of the surroundings. 2 unfeeling or ruthless. **cold feet** [inf] loss of confidence. **cold-shoulder** treat with deliberate unfriendliness. **cold war** hostility between nations without fighting.

coleslaw NOUN a salad of shredded raw cabbage in mayonnaise.

colic NOUN severe abdominal pain.

collaborate VERB work in partnership.
collaboration NOUN
collaborator NOUN
collaborative ADJ

collage NOUN a picture formed by fixing various items to a backing.

collapse VERB fall down suddenly; fail and come to a sudden end. NOUN collapsing; a sudden failure.

collapsible ADJ

collar NOUN **1** a band round the neck of a garment. **2** a band put round a dog's or cat's neck. VERB [inf] seize.

collate VERB collect and combine.

collateral ADJ additional but subordinate. NOUN security for repayment of a loan.

colleague NOUN a fellow worker in a business or profession.

collect VERB bring or come together; find and keep items of a particular kind as a hobby; fetch.
collectable (or **collectible**) ADJ & NOUN
collector NOUN

collected ADJ calm and controlled.

collection NOUN collecting; a set of objects or money collected.

collective ADJ done by or belonging to all the members of a group.
collectively ADV

college NOUN an educational establishment for higher or professional education; an organized body of professional people.
collegiate ADJ

collide VERB hit when moving.

collie NOUN a breed of dog often used as a sheepdog.

colliery NOUN (PL **-ies**) a coal mine.

collision NOUN an instance when two or more things collide.

colloquial ADJ suitable for informal speech or writing.
colloquialism NOUN
colloquially ADV

collusion NOUN an agreement made for a deceitful or fraudulent purpose.

cologne NOUN a light perfume.

colon NOUN **1** a punctuation mark (:). **2** the lower part of the large intestine.
colonic ADJ

colonel NOUN an army officer next below brigadier.

colonial ADJ of a colony or colonies. NOUN an inhabitant of a colony.

colonialism NOUN a policy of acquiring or maintaining colonies.

colonize (or **-ise**) VERB acquire as a colony;

establish a colony in.
colonist NOUN
colonization NOUN
colonnade NOUN a row of columns.
colony NOUN (PL **-ies**) a country under the control of another and occupied by settlers from there; people of shared nationality or occupation living as a community; a community of animals or plants of one kind.
coloration (or **colouration**) NOUN colouring.
colossal ADJ immense.
colossally ADV
colour ([US] **color**) NOUN the effect on something's appearance of the way it reflects light; pigment or paint; skin pigmentation as an indication of race. VERB put colour on; blush; influence.
colour-blind unable to distinguish between certain colours.
coloured ([US] **colored**) ADJ **1** having a colour. **2** [dated or offensive] of non-white descent.
colourful ([US] **colorful**) ADJ **1** full of colour. **2** vivid or lively.

colourfully ADV
colourless ([US] **colorless**) ADJ without colour; dull.
colt NOUN a young male horse.
column NOUN **1** a round pillar. **2** a vertical division of a page; a regular section in a newspaper or magazine. **3** a line of people or vehicles.
columnist NOUN a journalist who regularly writes a column of comments.
coma NOUN deep unconsciousness.
comatose ADJ in a coma.
comb NOUN **1** an object with a row of teeth, used for tidying hair. **2** a chicken's fleshy crest. VERB tidy with a comb; search thoroughly.
combat NOUN a battle or contest. VERB (**combated**, **combating**) try to stop or destroy.
combatant ADJ & NOUN
combative ADJ
combination NOUN combining or being combined; a set of united but distinct elements.
combine VERB join or unite. NOUN **1** a

combination of people or firms acting together. **2** (in full **combine harvester**) a combined reaping and threshing machine.

combust VERB catch fire or burn.

combustion NOUN

combustible ADJ capable of catching fire.

come VERB (**came, come, coming**) move towards the speaker or a place or point; arrive; occur; pass into a specified state; originate from a specified place; have a specified place in an ordering.

comeback NOUN **1** a return to a former successful position. **2** a retort.

comedian NOUN (FEMININE **comedienne**) a humorous entertainer or actor.

comedown NOUN a fall in status.

comedy NOUN (PL **-ies**) an amusing book, film, or play; the amusing aspect of a series of events etc.

comely ADJ (**-ier, -iest**) [old use] attractive.

comet NOUN a mass of ice and dust with a luminous tail, moving around the solar system.

comeuppance NOUN [inf]

deserved punishment.

comfort NOUN a state of ease and contentment; relief of suffering or grief; a person or thing giving this. VERB make less unhappy.

comforter NOUN

comfortable ADJ **1** providing or enjoying physical or mental ease. **2** financially secure.

comfortably ADV

comic ADJ causing amusement; of comedy. NOUN **1** a comedian. **2** a children's paper with a series of strip cartoons.

comical ADJ

comically ADV

comma NOUN a punctuation mark (,).

command NOUN **1** an order; authority; forces or a district under a commander. **2** the ability to use or control something. VERB give an order to; have authority over.

commandant NOUN an officer in command of a military establishment.

commandeer VERB seize for use.

commander NOUN a person in command; a

naval officer next below captain.

commandment NOUN a rule to be strictly observed.

commando NOUN (PL **-os**) a member of a military unit specially trained for making raids and assaults.

commemorate VERB keep in the memory by a celebration or memorial. **commemoration** NOUN **commemorative** ADJ

commence VERB begin. **commencement** NOUN

commend VERB **1** praise. **2** entrust. **commendable** ADJ **commendation** NOUN

commensurate ADJ corresponding; in proportion.

comment NOUN an expression of opinion. VERB make a comment.

commentary NOUN (PL **-ies**) **1** the making of comments; a set of notes on a text. **2** an account of an event, given as it occurs.

commentator NOUN a person who gives a commentary on an event. **commentate** VERB

commerce NOUN all forms of trade and business.

commercial ADJ of or engaged in commerce; intended to make a profit. **commercially** ADV

commercialize (or **-ise**) VERB operate a business etc. so as to make a profit. **commercialization** NOUN

commiserate VERB express pity or sympathy. **commiseration** NOUN

commission NOUN **1** a task or instruction; an order for a piece of work; a group of people given official authority to do something. **2** a sum paid to an agent selling goods or services. **3** an officer's position in the armed forces. VERB **1** give an instruction to; make someone an officer. **2** place an order for.

commissionaire NOUN a uniformed attendant at the door of a theatre, hotel, etc.

commissioner NOUN a member of a commission; a government official in charge of a district abroad.

commit VERB (**committed**, **committing**) **1** carry out a crime etc. **2** pledge to do something. **3** entrust; send to prison or a psychiatric hospital. **committal** NOUN

commitment NOUN dedication; an obligation; a binding pledge.

committee NOUN a group of people appointed for a particular function by a larger group.

commode NOUN a seat containing a concealed chamber pot.

commodious ADJ roomy.

commodity NOUN (PL **-ies**) an article to be bought and sold; something valuable.

commodore NOUN a naval officer next below rear admiral; a president of a yacht club.

common ADJ **1** found or done often; not rare. **2** generally or widely shared. **3** ordinary or undistinguished. **4** vulgar. NOUN an area of unfenced grassland for public use. **commonly** ADV

commonplace ADJ ordinary. NOUN a trite remark or topic.

commonwealth NOUN an independent state; a federation of states; (**the Commonwealth**) an association of Britain and independent states formerly under British rule.

commotion NOUN confused and noisy disturbance.

communal ADJ shared among a group.

commune VERB communicate mentally or spiritually. NOUN a group of people sharing accommodation and possessions.

communicable ADJ able to be made known or transmitted to others.

communicate VERB **1** exchange news and information; pass on information; transmit or convey. **2** (of two rooms) have a common connecting door. **communicator** NOUN

communication NOUN sharing or imparting information; a letter or message; (**communications**) means of communicating or of travelling.

communicative ADJ talkative or willing to give information.

communion NOUN 1 the sharing of thoughts and feelings. 2 (also **Holy Communion**) a sacrament in which bread and wine are shared.

communiqué NOUN an official announcement or statement.

communism NOUN a political and social system based on common ownership of property. **communist** NOUN & ADJ

community NOUN (PL **-ies**) a body of people living in one place or united by origin, interests, etc.; society or the public.

commute VERB 1 travel regularly between your home and workplace. 2 make a sentence of punishment less severe. **commuter** NOUN

compact ADJ closely or neatly packed together; concise. VERB compress. NOUN 1 a small flat case for face powder. 2 a pact or contract.

compact disc a small disc on which music or other digital information is stored.

companion NOUN a person living or travelling with another; a thing designed to complement another. **companionship** NOUN

company NOUN (PL **-ies**) 1 being with other people; companionship; a group of people. 2 a commercial business. 3 a body of soldiers.

comparable ADJ similar or able to be compared. **comparably** ADV

comparative ADJ involving comparison; based on or judged by comparing; of the grammatical form expressing 'more'. **comparatively** ADV

compare VERB 1 assess the similarity of. 2 declare to be similar. 3 be of equal quality with something. **comparison** NOUN

compartment NOUN a partitioned space.

compass NOUN 1 a device showing the direction of magnetic north. 2 range or scope. 3 (**compasses**) a hinged instrument for drawing circles.

compassion NOUN a feeling of pity. **compassionate** ADJ

compatible ADJ able to exist or be used together;

consistent.

compatibility NOUN

compatriot NOUN a fellow countryman.

compel VERB (**compelled, compelling**) force.

compelling ADJ very interesting; very convincing.

compendium NOUN (PL **-dia** or **-diums**) a collection of information.

compensate VERB make payment to a person in return for loss or damage; counterbalance or offset something.

compensation NOUN

compère NOUN a person who introduces performers in a variety show. VERB act as compère to.

compete VERB try to win something by defeating others; take part in a competition.

competent ADJ **1** skilled and efficient. **2** satisfactory.

competence NOUN

competition NOUN an event in which people compete; competing; the people you are competing with.

competitor NOUN

competitive ADJ involving competition; anxious to win.

compile VERB collect and arrange into a list or book.

compilation NOUN

complacent ADJ smug and self-satisfied.

complacency NOUN

complain VERB express dissatisfaction or pain.

complaint NOUN **1** a declaration of dissatisfaction or annoyance. **2** an illness.

complement NOUN a thing that completes or balances something else; the full number required. VERB form a complement to.

complementary ADJ

complete ADJ having all the necessary parts; finished; total or absolute. VERB make complete; fill in a form.

completely ADV

completion NOUN

complex ADJ made up of many parts; complicated or hard to understand. NOUN **1** a complex whole; a group of buildings. **2** a set of unconscious feelings affecting behaviour.

complexity NOUN

complexion NOUN the condition of the skin of a person's face; the general character of things.

compliant ADJ obedient.

complicate VERB make complicated.

complicated ADJ consisting of many different, intricate, or confusing elements.

complication NOUN being complicated; a factor causing this; a secondary disease aggravating an existing one.

complicity NOUN involvement in wrongdoing.

compliment NOUN a polite expression of praise. VERB pay a compliment to.

complimentary ADJ 1 expressing a compliment. 2 free of charge.

comply VERB (**complied**, **complying**) act in accordance with a request.

component NOUN one of the parts of which a thing is composed.

compose VERB 1 create a work of music or literature. 2 (of parts)

make up a whole. 3 calm.

composer NOUN

composite ADJ made up of parts.

composition NOUN 1 something's elements and the way it is made up; composing. 2 a musical or literary work.

compos mentis ADJ sane.

compost NOUN decayed organic matter used as fertilizer.

composure NOUN calmness.

compound ADJ made up of two or more elements. NOUN 1 a compound substance. 2 a fenced-in enclosure. VERB 1 combine; make by combining. 2 make worse.

comprehend VERB 1 understand. 2 include.

comprehensible ADJ

comprehension NOUN

comprehensive ADJ including much or all. NOUN a school providing secondary education for children of all abilities.

compress VERB squeeze or force into less space. NOUN a pad to stop bleeding or to reduce inflammation.

compression NOUN

compressor NOUN

comprise

comprise VERB consist of.

compromise NOUN a settlement reached by concessions on each side. VERB **1** make a settlement in this way. **2** expose to suspicion, scandal, or danger.

compulsion NOUN forcing or being forced; an irresistible urge.

compulsive ADJ **1** resulting from or driven by an irresistible urge. **2** gripping.

compulsory ADJ required by a law or rule.

compunction NOUN guilt or regret.

compute VERB calculate.

computer NOUN an electronic device for storing and processing data.

computerize (or **-ise**) VERB convert to a system controlled by computer.

comrade NOUN a companion or associate.

comradeship NOUN

con VERB (**conned, conning**) [inf] trick or cheat. NOUN [inf] a confidence trick.

pros and cons see **pro**.

concave ADJ curving inwards like the inner surface of a ball.

conceal VERB hide or keep secret.

concealment NOUN

concede VERB admit to be true; admit defeat in a contest; yield.

conceit NOUN excessive pride in yourself.

conceited ADJ

conceivable ADJ able to be imagined or grasped.

conceive VERB **1** become pregnant. **2** imagine.

concentrate VERB **1** focus all your attention. **2** gather together in a small area; make less dilute. NOUN a concentrated substance.

concentration NOUN

concentric ADJ having the same centre.

concept NOUN an abstract idea.

conceptual ADJ

conception NOUN **1** conceiving. **2** an idea.

concern VERB **1** be about. **2** be relevant to; involve. **3** make anxious. NOUN **1** anxiety. **2** something in which you are interested or involved. **3** a business or firm.

concerned ADJ anxious.

concerning PREP about.

concert NOUN a musical entertainment.

concerted ADJ done in combination.

concertina NOUN a portable musical instrument with bellows and buttons.

concerto NOUN (PL **-tos** or **-ti**) a musical composition for solo instrument and orchestra.

concession NOUN something granted; an allowance or reduced price.

conch NOUN a spiral shell.

conciliate VERB make less hostile or angry. **conciliation** NOUN **conciliatory** ADJ

concise ADJ giving information clearly and briefly.

conclave NOUN a private meeting.

conclude VERB 1 end; settle finally. 2 reach an opinion by reasoning.

conclusion NOUN 1 an ending. 2 an opinion reached.

conclusive ADJ decisive; settling an issue.

concoct VERB prepare from ingredients; invent. **concoction** NOUN

concord NOUN agreement or harmony.

concourse NOUN a large open area at a railway station etc.

concrete NOUN a building material made from gravel, sand, cement, and water. ADJ having a material or physical form; definite. VERB cover or fix with concrete.

concubine NOUN a woman who lives with a man as his wife but is not married to him.

concur VERB (**concurred, concurring**) 1 agree in opinion. 2 happen at the same time. **concurrent** ADJ

concussion NOUN temporary unconsciousness caused by a blow on the head.

condemn VERB 1 express strong disapproval of; declare unfit for use. 2 sentence; doom. **condemnation** NOUN

condensation NOUN 1 droplets of water formed on a cold surface in contact with humid air. 2 condensing.

condense VERB 1 make denser or briefer. 2 change

from gas or vapour to liquid.

condescend VERB behave patronizingly; do something you believe to be beneath you. **condescending** ADJ **condescension** NOUN

condiment NOUN a seasoning for food.

condition NOUN 1 the state something or someone is in; (**conditions**) circumstances. 2 something that is necessary if something else is to exist or occur. VERB 1 influence or determine; train or accustom. 2 bring into the desired condition.

conditional ADJ subject to specified conditions.

conditioner NOUN a substance that improves the condition of hair, fabric, etc.

condole VERB express sympathy. **condolence** NOUN

condom NOUN a contraceptive device worn on a man's penis.

condone VERB forgive or overlook a fault etc.

conducive VERB helping to cause or produce something.

conduct VERB 1 lead or guide; be the conductor of. 2 manage; carry out. 3 transmit heat or electricity. NOUN behaviour; a way of conducting business etc. **conduction** NOUN

conductor NOUN 1 a person who directs an orchestra's or choir's performance. 2 a substance that conducts heat or electricity. 3 a person collecting fares on a bus.

conduit NOUN 1 a channel for liquid. 2 a tube protecting electric wires.

cone NOUN 1 an object with a circular base, tapering to a point. 2 the dry scaly fruit of a pine or fir.

confectionery NOUN sweets and chocolates.

confederate ADJ joined by treaty or agreement. NOUN an accomplice.

confederation NOUN a union of states or groups.

confer VERB (**conferred, conferring**) 1 grant a title etc. 2 have discussions.

conference NOUN a meeting for discussion.

confess VERB acknowledge

or admit; formally declare your sins to a priest.
confession NOUN

confessional NOUN an enclosed stall in a church for hearing confessions.

confessor NOUN a priest who hears confessions.

confetti NOUN bits of coloured paper thrown at a bride and bridegroom.

confidant NOUN a person in whom you confide.

confide VERB tell someone about a secret or private matter.

confidence NOUN trust; certainty; belief in yourself; something told in secret.
confidence trick a swindle achieved by gaining someone's trust.

confident ADJ feeling confidence.

confidential ADJ to be kept secret.
confidentiality NOUN

configuration NOUN an arrangement of parts.

confine VERB keep within limits; shut in.

confinement NOUN 1 being confined. 2 the time of childbirth.

confines PLURAL NOUN boundaries.

confirm VERB 1 establish the truth of; make definite. 2 administer the rite of confirmation to.

confirmation NOUN 1 confirming or being confirmed. 2 a rite admitting a baptized person to full membership of the Christian Church.

confiscate VERB take or seize by authority.
confiscation NOUN

conflict NOUN a fight or struggle; disagreement. VERB clash or disagree.

conform VERB comply with rules, standards, or conventions.

conformist NOUN a person who conforms to rules or conventions.

confound VERB surprise and confuse; prove wrong.

confront VERB meet an enemy etc. face to face; face up to a problem.
confrontation NOUN

confuse VERB 1 bewilder. 2 mix up or identify wrongly. 3 make muddled or unclear.
confusion NOUN

conga NOUN a dance in which people form a long

winding line.

congeal VERB become semi-solid.

congenial ADJ pleasing to your tastes.

congenital ADJ being so from birth.

conger NOUN a large sea eel.

congested ADJ over full; (of the nose) blocked with mucus. **congestion** NOUN

conglomerate NOUN a number of things grouped together; a corporation formed from a merger of firms. **conglomeration** NOUN

congratulate VERB express pleasure at the good fortune of; praise the achievements of. **congratulation** NOUN

congregate VERB flock together.

congregation NOUN people assembled at a church service.

congress NOUN a formal meeting of delegates for discussion; (**Congress**) a law-making assembly, especially in the USA.

conical ADJ cone-shaped.

conifer NOUN a tree bearing cones.

coniferous ADJ

conjecture NOUN & VERB (a) guess.

conjugal ADJ of marriage.

conjugate VERB [Grammar] give the different forms of a verb. **conjugation** NOUN

conjunction NOUN 1 a word such as 'and' or 'if' that connects others. 2 simultaneous occurrence.

conjunctivitis NOUN inflammation of the membrane connecting the eyeball and eyelid.

conjure VERB produce as though by magic; summon or evoke. **conjuror** NOUN

connect VERB join or be joined; associate mentally; put into contact by telephone; (of a train, coach, or flight) arrive so that passengers are in time to catch another.

connection NOUN 1 a link; a place where things connect; connecting trains etc. 2 (**connections**) influential friends or relatives.

connive VERB (**connive at**) secretly allow.

connivance NOUN

connoisseur NOUN an expert, especially in matters of taste.

connote VERB (of a word) imply in addition to its literal meaning.
connotation NOUN

conquer VERB overcome in war or by effort.
conqueror NOUN

conquest NOUN conquering; something won by conquering.

conscience NOUN a sense of right and wrong guiding a person's actions.

conscientious ADJ diligent in your duty.

conscious ADJ 1 awake and alert; aware. 2 intentional.
consciousness NOUN

conscript VERB summon for compulsory military service. NOUN a conscripted person.
conscription NOUN

consecrate VERB make sacred.
consecration NOUN

consecutive ADJ following in unbroken sequence.

consensus NOUN general agreement.

consent VERB agree; give permission. NOUN permission; agreement.

consequence NOUN 1 a result. 2 importance.
consequent ADJ
consequently ADV

consequential ADJ 1 resulting. 2 important.

conservation NOUN conserving; preservation of the natural environment.
conservationist NOUN

conservative ADJ 1 opposed to change. 2 (of an estimate) purposely low. NOUN a conservative person.

conservatory NOUN (PL -ies) a room with a glass roof and walls, built on to a house.

conserve VERB keep from harm, decay, or loss. NOUN jam.

consider VERB 1 think carefully about. 2 believe or think. 3 take into account.

considerable ADJ great in amount or importance.
considerably ADV

considerate ADJ careful not to hurt or inconvenience others.

consideration NOUN

careful thought; a factor taken into account in making a decision; being considerate.

considering PREP taking into account.

consign VERB deliver or send; put for disposal.

consignment NOUN a batch of goods sent to someone.

consist VERB (**consist of**) be composed of.

consistency NOUN (PL -ies) 1 being consistent. 2 the degree of thickness or solidity of semi-liquid matter.

consistent ADJ 1 unchanging. 2 not conflicting.

consistently ADV

console[1] VERB comfort in time of sorrow.

consolation NOUN

console[2] NOUN a panel holding controls for electronic equipment.

consolidate VERB 1 make stronger or more secure. 2 combine.

consolidation NOUN

consommé NOUN clear soup.

consonant NOUN a letter of the alphabet representing a sound made by

obstructing the breath. ADJ in agreement.

consort NOUN a husband or wife, especially of a monarch. VERB associate with someone.

consortium NOUN (PL -ia or -iums) a combination of firms acting together.

conspicuous ADJ easily seen; attracting attention.

conspiracy NOUN (PL -ies) a secret plan made by a group.

conspire VERB 1 plot secretly in a group to do something wrong. 2 (of events) combine to produce an effect as though deliberately.

conspirator NOUN

conspiratorial ADJ

constable NOUN a police officer of the lowest rank.

constabulary NOUN (PL -ies) a police force.

constant ADJ occurring continuously or repeatedly; unchanging; faithful. NOUN an unvarying quantity.

constancy NOUN

constellation NOUN a group of stars.

consternation NOUN great surprise and anxiety or dismay.

constipation NOUN difficulty in emptying the bowels.
  constipated ADJ

constituency NOUN (PL **-ies**) a body of voters who elect a representative.

constituent ADJ forming part of a whole. NOUN **1** a constituent part. **2** a member of a constituency.

constitute VERB be the parts of.

constitution NOUN **1** the principles by which a state is organized. **2** the general condition of the body. **3** the composition of something.

constitutional ADJ of or in accordance with a constitution.

constrain VERB force or compel.

constraint NOUN a limitation or restriction.

constrict VERB make narrower; squeeze; restrict.
  constriction NOUN

construct VERB make by placing parts together. NOUN an idea or theory.

construction NOUN **1** constructing; a thing constructed. **2** an interpretation.

constructive ADJ (of criticism etc.) helpful or useful.

construe VERB interpret.

consul NOUN an official representative of a state in a foreign city.
  consular ADJ
  consulate NOUN

consult VERB seek information or advice from.
  consultation NOUN
  consultative ADJ

consultant NOUN a specialist consulted for professional advice.

consume VERB eat or drink; use up; (of fire) destroy; obsess.

consumer NOUN a person who buys or uses goods or services.

consummate VERB accomplish; complete a marriage by having sex. ADJ highly skilled.
  consummation NOUN

consumption NOUN consuming.

contact NOUN touching; communication; an electrical connection; a person who may be contacted for information or help. VERB get in touch with.

contact lens a small lens worn directly on the eyeball to correct the vision.

contagious NOUN (of a disease) spread by contact.

contain VERB **1** have within itself; include. **2** control or restrain.

container NOUN a receptacle; a metal box of standard design for transporting goods.

contaminate VERB pollute.

contamination NOUN

contemplate VERB **1** gaze at. **2** think about; meditate.

contemplation NOUN

contemplative ADJ

contemporary ADJ **1** living or occurring at the same time. **2** modern. NOUN (PL **-ies**) a person of the same age or living at the same time.

contempt NOUN despising or being despised; disrespectful disobedience.

contemptible ADJ

contemptuous ADJ

contend VERB **1** struggle; compete. **2** assert.

contender NOUN

content¹ ADJ satisfied with what you have. NOUN satisfaction. VERB satisfy.

contented ADJ

contentment NOUN

content² NOUN (also **contents**) what is contained in something; the subject matter of a book etc.

contention NOUN **1** disagreement. **2** an assertion.

contentious ADJ causing disagreement.

contest VERB compete for or in; oppose; argue about. NOUN a struggle for victory; a competition.

contestant NOUN

context NOUN what precedes or follows a word or statement and fixes its meaning; circumstances.

continent¹ NOUN one of the earth's main land masses.

continental ADJ

continent² ADJ able to control the movements of the bowels and bladder.

continence NOUN

contingency NOUN (PL **-ies**) a possible but unpredictable occurrence.

contingent ADJ **1** subject

to chance. **2** depending on other circumstances. NOUN a body of troops contributed to a larger group.

continual ADJ constantly or frequently recurring.
continually ADV

continue VERB **1** not cease; keep existing or happening. **2** resume.
continuation NOUN

continuous ADJ without interruptions.
continuity NOUN

contort VERB force or twist out of normal shape.
contortion NOUN
contortionist NOUN

contour NOUN an outline; a line on a map showing height above sea level.

contra- PREFIX against.

contraband NOUN smuggled goods.

contraceptive ADJ & NOUN (a drug or device) used to prevent a woman becoming pregnant.
contraception NOUN

contract NOUN a formal agreement. VERB **1** make or become smaller or shorter. **2** make a contract. **3** catch an illness.
contractor NOUN
contractual ADJ

contraction NOUN making or becoming smaller; a shortened form of a word or words; a shortening of the womb muscles during childbirth.

contradict VERB say that a statement is untrue or a person is wrong; conflict with.
contradiction NOUN
contradictory ADJ

contraflow NOUN a flow (especially of traffic) in a direction opposite to and alongside the usual flow.

contralto NOUN (PL **-os**) the lowest female voice.

contraption NOUN a strange device or machine.

contrary ADJ **1** opposite in nature, tendency, or direction. **2** deliberately doing the opposite of what is desired. NOUN the opposite.

contrast NOUN a striking difference; a comparison drawing attention to this. VERB be strikingly different; point out the difference between two things.

contravene VERB break a rule etc.
contravention NOUN

contribute VERB give to a common fund or effort; help to cause something. **contribution** NOUN **contributor** NOUN

contrite ADJ remorseful.

contrive VERB skilfully make or bring about; manage to do. **contrivance** NOUN

contrived ADJ artificial; not spontaneous.

control NOUN the power to direct, influence, or restrain something; a means of restraining or regulating; a standard for checking the results of an experiment. VERB (**controlled**, **controlling**) have control of; regulate; restrain.

controversial NOUN causing controversy.

controversy NOUN (PL -ies) a prolonged and heated disagreement.

contusion NOUN a bruise.

conundrum NOUN a riddle or puzzle.

conurbation NOUN a large urban area formed where towns have spread and merged.

convalesce VERB regain health after illness. **convalescence** NOUN

convalescent ADJ & NOUN

convection NOUN the transmission of heat within a liquid or gas by movement of heated particles.

convene VERB call together; assemble. **convener** (or **convenor**) NOUN

convenience NOUN 1 ease or lack of effort; something contributing to this. 2 a toilet.

convenient ADJ involving little trouble or effort; easily accessible.

convent NOUN a community of nuns.

convention NOUN 1 an accepted custom; behaviour generally considered correct. 2 an assembly. 3 a formal agreement. **conventional** ADJ **conventionally** ADV

converge VERB come to or towards the same point.

conversant ADJ (**conversant with**) having knowledge of.

conversation NOUN informal talk between people. **conversational** ADJ

converse¹ VERB hold a

conversation.

converse² ADJ opposite. NOUN the opposite.
conversely ADV

convert VERB change from one form or use to another; cause to change an attitude or belief. NOUN a person persuaded to adopt a new faith or other belief.
conversion NOUN

convertible ADJ able to be converted. NOUN a car with a folding or detachable roof.

convex ADJ curved like the outer surface of a ball.

convey VERB transport or carry; communicate an idea etc.

conveyance NOUN 1 transport; a means of transport. 2 the legal process of transferring ownership of property.
conveyancing NOUN

conveyor belt NOUN a continuous moving belt conveying objects.

convict VERB declare guilty of a criminal offence. NOUN a convicted person in prison.

conviction NOUN 1 a firm belief; confidence. 2 convicting or being convicted.

convince VERB make a person feel certain that something is true.

convivial ADJ sociable and lively; friendly.

convoluted ADJ complicated; intricately coiled.
convolution NOUN

convoy NOUN a group of ships or vehicles travelling together or under escort.

convulse VERB suffer convulsions.

convulsion NOUN 1 a violent involuntary movement of the body. 2 (**convulsions**) uncontrollable laughter.

coo NOUN & VERB (make) a soft murmuring sound like a dove.

cook VERB prepare food by heating; undergo this process. NOUN a person who cooks.
cooker NOUN
cookery NOUN

cookie NOUN [US] a sweet biscuit.

cool ADJ 1 fairly cold. 2 calm; not enthusiastic or friendly. 3 [inf] fashionably attractive. NOUN 1 low temperature. 2 [inf] calmness. VERB make or become cool.

coolly ADV

coop NOUN a cage for poultry. VERB (**coop up**) confine.

cooperate VERB work together for a common end.

cooperation NOUN

cooperative ADJ helpful; involving mutual help; (of a business) owned and run jointly by its members. NOUN a business run on this basis.

co-opt VERB appoint someone as a member of a committee.

coordinate VERB arrange the elements of a complex whole to achieve efficiency; negotiate and work with others. NOUN 1 [Mathematics] any of the numbers used to indicate the position of a point. 2 (**coordinates**) matching items of clothing.

coordination NOUN
coordinator NOUN

coot NOUN a waterbird.

cop NOUN [inf] a police officer.

cope VERB deal successfully with something.

copier NOUN a copying machine.

coping NOUN the sloping top row of masonry of a wall.

copious ADJ plentiful.

copper NOUN 1 a reddish-brown metallic element; a coin containing this; its colour. 2 [inf] a police officer.

coppice (or **copse**) NOUN a group of small trees and undergrowth.

copulate VERB mate or have sex.

copulation NOUN

copy NOUN (PL **-ies**) a thing made to look like another; a specimen of a book etc.; material for a newspaper or magazine article. VERB (**copied, copying**) make a copy of; imitate.

copyright NOUN the sole right to publish a work.

copywriter NOUN a person who writes the text of advertisements.

coquette NOUN a woman who flirts.

coquettish ADJ

coracle NOUN a small wicker boat.

coral NOUN a hard red, pink, or white substance built by tiny sea creatures;

a reddish-pink colour.

cord NOUN **1** long thin flexible material made from twisted strands; a piece of this. **2** corduroy.

cordial ADJ warm and friendly. NOUN a fruit-flavoured drink.
cordially ADV

cordon NOUN a line of police, soldiers, etc. enclosing something. VERB (**cordon off**) enclose with a cordon.

cordon bleu ADJ of the highest class in cookery.

corduroy NOUN cloth with velvety ridges.

core NOUN the central or most important part; the tough central part of an apple etc., containing seeds. VERB remove the core from.

corgi NOUN a small, short-legged breed of dog.

coriander NOUN a fragrant herb.

cork NOUN the light tough bark of a Mediterranean oak; a bottle stopper. VERB stop up with a cork.

corkscrew NOUN a device with a spiral rod for extracting corks from bottles.

corm NOUN a bulb-like underground stem from which buds grow.

cormorant NOUN a large black seabird.

corn NOUN **1** wheat, oats, or maize; grain. **2** a small painful area of hardened skin, especially on the foot.

cornea NOUN the transparent outer covering of the eyeball.

corner NOUN a place or angle where two lines or sides meet; a remote area; a free kick or hit from the corner of the field in football or hockey. VERB **1** force into a position from which there is no escape. **2** drive round a corner. **3** obtain a monopoly of a commodity.

cornerstone NOUN a basis; a vital foundation.

cornet NOUN **1** a brass instrument like a small trumpet. **2** a cone-shaped wafer holding ice cream.

cornflour NOUN fine flour made from maize.

cornflower NOUN a blue-flowered plant.

cornice NOUN an ornamental moulding round the top of an

indoor wall.

cornucopia NOUN a plentiful supply.

corny ADJ (**-ier, -iest**) [inf] sentimental; hackneyed.

corollary NOUN (PL **-ies**) a proposition that follows logically from another.

coronary ADJ of the arteries supplying blood to the heart. NOUN (PL **-ies**) a blockage of the flow of blood to the heart.

coronation NOUN the ceremony of crowning a sovereign.

coroner NOUN an officer holding inquests.

coronet NOUN a small crown.

corpora plural of **corpus**.

corporal NOUN a non-commissioned officer next below sergeant. ADJ of the body.

corporate ADJ shared by members of a group; united in a group.

corporation NOUN a large company or group of companies; a group elected to govern a town.

corps NOUN (PL **corps**) a military unit; an organized body of people.

corpse NOUN a dead body.

corpulent ADJ fat.

corpulence NOUN

corpus NOUN (PL **-pora**) a collection of writings.

corpuscle NOUN a blood cell.

corral NOUN [US] an enclosure for cattle.

correct ADJ **1** true; free from errors. **2** conforming to an accepted standard of behaviour. VERB mark or rectify errors in; put right. **correction** NOUN **correctly** ADV

corrective ADJ correcting what is bad or harmful.

correlate VERB place things together so that one thing affects or depends on another. **correlation** NOUN

correspond VERB **1** be similar, equivalent, or in harmony. **2** write letters to each other.

correspondence NOUN **1** similarity. **2** letters written.

correspondent NOUN **1** a person who writes letters. **2** a person employed by a newspaper or TV news station to gather news and send reports.

corridor NOUN a passage in a building or train giving access to rooms or compartments; a strip of land linking two other areas.

corroborate VERB support or confirm.

corroboration NOUN

corrode VERB destroy a metal etc. gradually by chemical action.

corrosion NOUN

corrosive ADJ

corrugated ADJ shaped into alternate ridges and grooves.

corrupt ADJ 1 able to be bribed; immoral. 2 (of a text or computer data) full of errors. VERB make corrupt.

corruption NOUN

corset NOUN a close-fitting undergarment worn to shape or support the body.

cortège NOUN a funeral procession.

cortex NOUN (PL **-tices**) the outer part of an organ, especially that of the brain.

cortisone NOUN a hormone used in treating allergies.

cosh NOUN a thick heavy bar used as a weapon.

cosine NOUN [Mathematics] the ratio of the side adjacent to an acute angle (in a right-angled triangle) to the hypotenuse.

cosmetic NOUN a substance used to improve a person's appearance. ADJ improving the appearance; superficial.

cosmic ADJ of the universe.

cosmopolitan ADJ free from national prejudices; including people from all parts of the world.

cosmos NOUN the universe.

cosset VERB (**cosseted, cosseting**) pamper.

cost VERB 1 (**cost, costing**) have as its price; involve the sacrifice or loss of. 2 (**costed, costing**) estimate the cost of. NOUN what a thing costs.

costly ADJ expensive.

costume NOUN a style of clothes, especially that of a historical period; garments for a special activity.

cosy ([US] **cozy**) ADJ (**-ier, -iest**) 1 warm and comfortable. 2 not difficult. NOUN (PL **-ies**) a cover to keep a teapot or a boiled egg hot.

cosily ADV

cosiness NOUN

cot NOUN a child's bed with high sides.

coterie NOUN a select group.

cottage NOUN a small simple house, especially in the country.

cottage cheese soft white lumpy cheese made from curds.

cotton NOUN a soft white substance round the seeds of a tropical plant; thread or fabric made from cotton.

couch NOUN a sofa. VERB express in a specified way.

cougar NOUN [US] a puma.

cough VERB expel air etc. from the lungs with a sudden sharp sound. NOUN the act or sound of coughing; an illness causing coughing.

could past of **can²**.

coulomb NOUN a unit of electric charge.

council NOUN a formal group meeting regularly for debate and administration; the body governing a town.

councillor NOUN

counsel NOUN **1** advice.

2 (PL **counsel**) a barrister. VERB (**counselled, counselling**; [US] **counseled, counseling**) advise; give professional psychological help to.

counsellor NOUN

count VERB **1** find the total of; say numbers in order. **2** include. **3** be important. **4** regard in a specified way. **5** (**count on**) rely on. NOUN **1** counting; a total reached by counting. **2** a point to consider; a charge. **3** a foreign nobleman.

countdown NOUN counting seconds backwards to zero; the final period before an important event.

countenance NOUN a person's face or expression. VERB tolerate or allow.

counter NOUN **1** a flat-topped fitment over which goods are sold or business transacted with customers. **2** a small disc used in board games. ADV in the opposite direction; in conflict. VERB speak or act against.

counteract VERB reduce or prevent the effects of.

counter-attack NOUN & VERB (make) an attack in reply to an opponent's attack.

counterbalance NOUN a weight or influence balancing or neutralizing another. VERB act as a counterbalance to.

counterfeit ADJ forged. NOUN a forgery. VERB forge.

counterfoil NOUN a section of a cheque or receipt kept as a record by the person issuing it.

countermand VERB cancel.

counterpane NOUN a bedspread.

counterpart NOUN a person or thing corresponding to another.

counterpoint NOUN [Music] a technique of combining melodies.

counterproductive ADJ having the opposite of the desired effect.

countersign VERB add a second signature to a document already signed by one person.

countersink VERB sink a screw head into a shaped cavity so that the surface is level.

countertenor NOUN a male alto.

countess NOUN a count's or earl's wife or widow; a woman with the rank of count or earl.

countless ADJ too many to be counted.

country NOUN (PL **-ies**) 1 a nation with its own government and territory. 2 land outside large towns.

countryside NOUN

county NOUN (PL **-ies**) a major administrative division of some countries.

coup NOUN 1 (also **coup d'état**) a sudden violent overthrow of a government. 2 a very successful action.

coupe NOUN a sports car with a fixed roof and a sloping back.

couple NOUN two people or things; a married or romantically involved pair. VERB fasten or link together.

couplet NOUN two successive rhyming lines of verse.

coupling NOUN a connecting device.

coupon NOUN a form or ticket entitling the holder

to something.

courage NOUN the ability to control fear when facing danger or pain. **courageous** ADJ

courgette NOUN a small vegetable marrow.

courier NOUN 1 a messenger carrying documents. 2 a person employed to guide and assist tourists.

course NOUN 1 onward progress; a direction taken or intended; a procedure. 2 a series of lessons or treatments. 3 an area on which golf is played or a race takes place. 4 one part of a meal. VERB 1 move or flow freely. 2 pursue hares etc. with greyhounds. **of course** certainly; without doubt.

court NOUN 1 a body of people hearing legal cases; the place where they meet. 2 a courtyard; an area for playing squash, tennis, etc. 3 the home, staff, etc. of a monarch. VERB try to win the love or support of; risk danger etc.

courteous ADJ polite.

courtesy NOUN politeness.

courtier NOUN a sovereign's companion or adviser.

courtly ADJ dignified and polite.

court martial NOUN (PL **courts martial**) a court trying offences against military law; a trial by this.

courtship NOUN a period of wooing.

courtyard NOUN a space enclosed by walls or buildings.

cousin (or **first cousin**) NOUN a child of your uncle or aunt. **second cousin** a child of your parent's cousin.

cove NOUN a small bay.

coven NOUN a gathering of witches.

covenant NOUN a formal agreement or contract. VERB make a covenant.

cover VERB 1 be or place something over; conceal or protect in this way. 2 deal with a subject; report on for a newspaper etc. 3 be enough to pay for; protect by insurance. 4 travel over a distance. 5 keep a gun aimed at. 6 take over someone's job temporarily. 7 (**cover up**) conceal a thing or fact. NOUN 1 a thing that covers;

a wrapper, envelope, or binding of a book; a shelter or protection; a disguise. **2** protection by insurance.
coverage NOUN

coverlet NOUN a bedspread.

covert ADJ done secretly.

covet VERB (**coveted, coveting**) desire a thing belonging to another person.
covetous ADJ

cow NOUN a fully grown female of cattle or certain other large animals (e.g. the elephant or whale). VERB intimidate.

coward NOUN a person who lacks courage.
cowardice NOUN
cowardly ADJ

cowboy NOUN **1** a man in charge of cattle on a ranch. **2** [inf] a dishonest or unqualified tradesman.

cower VERB crouch or shrink in fear.

cowl NOUN a monk's hood or hooded robe; a hood-shaped covering on a chimney.

cowslip NOUN a wild plant with small yellow flowers.

cox NOUN a coxswain.

coxswain NOUN a person who steers a boat.

coy ADJ pretending to be shy or embarrassed.

coyote NOUN a North American wolf-like wild dog.

coypu NOUN a beaver-like aquatic rodent.

cozy US spelling of **cosy**.

crab NOUN a ten-legged shellfish.
crab apple a small sour apple.

crabbed ADJ **1** (or **crabby**) bad-tempered. **2** (of handwriting) hard to read.

crack NOUN **1** a line where a thing is broken but not separated; a narrow opening; a sharp blow. **2** a sudden sharp noise. **3** [inf] a joke. **4** a strong form of cocaine. VERB **1** break without separating; knock sharply; give way under strain; (of a voice) become harsh. **2** make a sudden sharp sound. **3** solve a problem. **4** tell a joke. ADJ excellent.

crackdown NOUN severe measures against something.

cracker NOUN **1** a small explosive firework; a paper tube giving an explosive crack when pulled apart, containing a small gift. **2** a thin dry biscuit.

crackers ADJ [inf] crazy.

crackle VERB make a series of light cracking sounds. NOUN these sounds.

crackpot NOUN [inf] an eccentric person.

cradle NOUN a baby's bed on rockers; a place where something originates. VERB hold or support gently.

craft NOUN **1** a skill; an occupation requiring this. **2** cunning. **3** (PL **craft**) a ship or boat.

craftsman NOUN a worker skilled in a craft. **craftsmanship** NOUN

crafty ADJ (**-ier, -iest**) cunning or using underhand methods. **craftily** ADV

crag NOUN a steep or rugged rock. **craggy** ADJ

cram VERB (**crammed, cramming**) **1** force into too small a space; overfill. **2** study intensively for an exam.

cramp NOUN **1** a painful involuntary tightening of a muscle. **2** a metal bar with bent ends for holding things together. VERB keep within too narrow limits.

crane NOUN **1** a large wading bird. **2** a machine for lifting and moving heavy objects. VERB stretch your neck to see something.

cranium NOUN (**-iums** or **-ia**) the skull.

crank NOUN **1** an L-shaped part for converting to-and-fro into circular motion. **2** an eccentric person. VERB turn a crank to start an engine. **cranky** ADJ

cranny NOUN (PL **-ies**) a crevice.

crash NOUN a loud noise of collision or breakage; a violent collision; a financial collapse. VERB make a crash; be or cause to be involved in a crash. ADJ rapid and concentrated.

crass ADJ very stupid; insensitive.

crate NOUN a packing case made of wooden slats; a container divided into individual units for bottles.

crater NOUN a bowl-shaped cavity; the mouth of a

volcano.

cravat NOUN a strip of fabric worn round the neck and tucked inside a shirt.

crave VERB feel an intense longing for; ask earnestly for.

craving NOUN

craven ADJ cowardly.

crawl VERB 1 move on hands and knees or with the body on the ground; move very slowly. 2 [inf] behave in a servile way. 3 (**crawling with**) very crowded with. NOUN a crawling movement or pace; an overarm swimming stroke.

crayfish NOUN a freshwater shellfish like a small lobster.

crayon NOUN a stick of coloured wax etc. for drawing.

craze NOUN a temporary enthusiasm.

crazy ADJ (-ier, -iest) insane; very foolish; [inf] madly eager.

crazily ADV

creak NOUN a harsh squeak. VERB make this sound.

creaky ADJ

cream NOUN the fatty part of milk; its yellowish-white colour; a thick lotion; the best part. VERB 1 mash with milk or cream. 2 (**cream off**) take the best part of something.

creamy ADJ

crease NOUN 1 a line made in cloth or paper by crushing or pressing. 2 a line marking the limit of the bowler's or batsman's position in cricket. VERB make a crease in; develop creases.

create VERB bring into existence; produce by what you do.

creation NOUN

creator NOUN

creative ADJ involving or showing imagination and originality.

creativity NOUN

creature NOUN an animal; a person.

crèche NOUN a day nursery.

credence NOUN belief.

credentials PLURAL NOUN qualifications, achievements, etc.; documents attesting to these.

credible ADJ believable.

credibility NOUN

credit NOUN 1 a system of

deferring payment for purchases. **2** a record in an account of a sum received; having money in your bank account. **3** acknowledgement or honour for an achievement; a source of honour or pride; (**credits**) acknowledgements of contributors to a film. VERB (**credited, crediting**) **1** attribute. **2** enter in an account. **3** believe.

credit card a plastic card containing machine-readable magnetic code, allowing the holder to make purchases on credit.

creditable ADJ deserving praise.
  creditably ADV

creditor NOUN a person to whom money is owed.

credulous ADJ too ready to believe things.

creed NOUN a set of beliefs or principles.

creek NOUN a narrow inlet of water, especially on a coast.

creep VERB (**crept, creeping**) **1** move slowly, quietly, and stealthily; develop or increase gradually; (of a plant) grow along the ground or

a wall etc. **2** (of skin) have an unpleasant sensation through fear or disgust. NOUN **1** [inf] an unpleasant person. **2** slow and gradual movement. **3** (**the creeps**) [inf] fear or revulsion.

creepy ADJ (**-ier, -iest**) [inf] frightening; disturbing.

cremate VERB burn a corpse to ashes.
  cremation NOUN

crematorium NOUN (PL **-ria** or **-riums**) a place where corpses are cremated.

creole NOUN a hybrid language.

creosote NOUN a brown oily liquid distilled from coal tar, used as a wood preservative.

crêpe NOUN **1** a fabric with a wrinkled surface. **2** a pancake.

crept past and past participle of **creep**.

crescendo NOUN (PL **-dos** or **-di**) a gradual increase in loudness.

crescent NOUN a narrow curved shape tapering to a point at each end; a curved street of houses.

cress NOUN a plant with small leaves used in salads.

crest NOUN **1** a tuft or outgrowth on a bird's or animal's head; a plume on a helmet. **2** the top of a slope or hill; a white top of a large wave. **3** a design above a shield on a coat of arms.

crestfallen ADJ disappointed and sad.

cretin NOUN [inf] a stupid person.

crevasse NOUN a deep open crack especially in a glacier.

crevice NOUN a narrow gap in a surface.

crew¹ NOUN the people working a ship or aircraft; a group working together.

crew cut a very short haircut.

crew² past of **crow**.

crib NOUN **1** a rack for fodder; a cot. **2** [inf] a translation of a text for students' use. VERB (**cribbed**, **cribbing**) [inf] copy dishonestly.

cribbage NOUN a card game.

crick NOUN a sudden painful stiffness in the neck or back.

cricket NOUN **1** an outdoor game for two teams of 11 players with ball, bats, and wickets. **2** a brown insect resembling a grasshopper.

cricketer NOUN

crime NOUN an act that breaks a law; illegal acts.

criminal NOUN a person guilty of a crime. ADJ of or involving crime.

criminality NOUN
criminally ADV

crimp VERB press into ridges.

crimson ADJ & NOUN deep red.

cringe VERB cower; feel embarrassment or disgust.

crinkle NOUN & VERB (a) wrinkle.

crinoline NOUN a light framework formerly worn to make a long skirt stand out.

cripple NOUN a disabled or lame person. VERB make lame; weaken seriously.

crisis NOUN (PL **-ses**) a time of intense danger or difficulty.

crisp ADJ **1** firm, dry, and brittle. **2** cold and bracing. **3** brisk and decisive. NOUN a thin, crisp slice of fried potato.

crispy ADJ

crispbread NOUN a thin, crisp unsweetened biscuit.

criss-cross ADJ & ADV in a pattern of intersecting lines. VERB form a criss-cross pattern.

criterion NOUN (PL **-ria**) a standard of judgement.

critic NOUN **1** a person who points out faults. **2** a person who appraises artistic works and performances.

critical ADJ **1** looking for faults. **2** of literary or artistic criticism. **3** of or at a crisis.

critically ADV

criticize (or **-ise**) VERB **1** find fault with. **2** analyse and evaluate.

criticism NOUN

critique NOUN an analysis and assessment.

croak NOUN a deep hoarse cry or sound like that of a frog. VERB make a croak.

crochet NOUN lacy fabric produced from thread worked with a hooked needle. VERB (**crocheted, crocheting**) make by or do such work.

crock NOUN **1** an earthenware pot. **2** [inf] a weak person.

crockery NOUN household china.

crocodile NOUN **1** a large predatory amphibious tropical reptile. **2** a line of people walking in pairs.

crocus NOUN a small spring-flowering plant.

croft NOUN a small rented farm in Scotland.

crofter NOUN

croissant NOUN a rich crescent-shaped roll.

crone NOUN an old and ugly woman.

crony NOUN (PL **-ies**) a close friend or companion.

crook NOUN **1** a hooked stick; an angle. **2** [inf] a criminal. VERB bend a finger.

crooked ADJ **1** not straight. **2** [inf] dishonest.

croon VERB sing softly.

crop NOUN **1** a plant cultivated on a large scale for its produce; a group or amount produced at one time. **2** a pouch in a bird's gullet where food is broken up for digestion. **3** a very short haircut. VERB (**cropped, cropping**) **1** cut or bite off. **2** (**crop up**) occur unexpectedly.

cropper NOUN (**come a cropper**) [inf] fall heavily; fail badly.

croquet NOUN a game played on a lawn with

crouch

balls driven through hoops with mallets.

croquette NOUN a small ball of potato etc. fried in bread crumbs.

cross NOUN **1** a mark or shape formed by two intersecting lines or pieces; an upright post with a transverse bar, formerly used in crucifixion. **2** an unavoidable affliction. **3** a hybrid; a mixture of two things. **4** a transverse pass of a ball. VERB **1** go or extend across; draw a line across; mark a cheque so that it must be paid into a named account. **2** intersect; mark with a cross. **3** cause to interbreed. **4** oppose the wishes of. ADJ annoyed.

cross-breed an animal produced by interbreeding. **cross-check** verify figures etc. by an alternative method. **cross-examine** question a witness in court to check a testimony already given. **cross-eyed** squinting. **cross-reference** a reference to another place in the same book. **cross-section** a surface or shape revealed by cutting across something; a representative sample.

crossbar NOUN a horizontal bar between uprights.

crossbow NOUN a mechanical bow fixed across a wooden support.

crossfire NOUN gunfire crossing another line of fire.

crossing NOUN a place where things cross; a journey across water; a place to cross a road, border, etc.

crossroads NOUN a place where roads intersect.

crosswise (or **crossways**) ADV in the form of a cross; diagonally.

crossword NOUN a puzzle in which intersecting words have to be inserted into a grid of squares.

crotch NOUN the part of the human body between the legs.

crotchet NOUN a note in music equal to half a minim.

crotchety ADJ irritable.

crouch VERB stoop low with the legs tightly bent. NOUN this position.

croup NOUN an inflammation of the windpipe in children, causing coughing and breathing difficulty.

croupier NOUN a person in charge of a gambling table in a casino.

crouton NOUN a small piece of fried or toasted bread as a garnish.

crow NOUN 1 a large black bird. 2 a cock's cry. VERB (**crowed** or **crew**, **crowing**) (of a cock) make its loud cry; express triumph and glee.

crowbar NOUN an iron bar with a bent end, used as a lever.

crowd NOUN a large group. VERB fill completely or excessively; move or gather in a crowd.

crown NOUN 1 a monarch's ceremonial headdress; (**the Crown**) the supreme governing power in a monarchy. 2 the top of a head, hill, etc. VERB 1 place a crown on a new monarch. 2 form the top of; be the climax of.

crucial ADJ decisive or very important.
crucially ADV

crucible NOUN a container in which metals are melted.

crucifix NOUN a model of a cross with a figure of Jesus on it.

crucify VERB (**crucified**, **crucifying**) put to death by nailing or binding to a cross.
crucifixion NOUN

crude ADJ in a natural or raw state; roughly made; offensively coarse or rude.
crudity NOUN

cruel ADJ (**crueller** or **crueler**, **cruellest** or **cruelest**) deliberately causing pain or suffering.
cruelly ADV
cruelty NOUN

cruet NOUN a set of containers for salt, pepper, etc. at the table.

cruise VERB 1 sail for pleasure or on patrol. 2 travel at a moderate speed. NOUN a voyage on a ship, as a holiday.

cruiser NOUN a fast warship; a motor boat with a cabin.

crumb NOUN a small fragment of bread etc.; a tiny piece.

crumble VERB break into small fragments. NOUN a baked pudding made with fruit and a crumbly topping.

crumbly ADJ

crummy ADJ (**-ier, -iest**) [inf] of poor quality.

crumpet NOUN a flat soft cake eaten toasted.

crumple VERB crush or become crushed into creases; collapse.

crunch VERB crush noisily with the teeth; make a muffled grinding sound. NOUN **1** the sound of crunching. **2** [inf] a crucial point or situation.

crunchy ADJ

crusade NOUN a medieval Christian military expedition to recover the Holy Land from Muslims; a campaign for a cause. VERB take part in a crusade.

crusader NOUN

crush VERB press so as to break, injure, or wrinkle; pound into fragments; defeat or subdue completely. NOUN **1** a crowded mass of people. **2** [inf] an infatuation.

crust NOUN a hard outer layer, especially of bread.

crusty ADJ

crustacean NOUN a creature with a hard shell (e.g. a lobster).

crutch NOUN **1** a support for a lame person. **2** the crotch.

crux NOUN the most important point.

cry NOUN (PL **-ies**) **1** a loud inarticulate shout expressing emotion; a call. **2** a spell of weeping. VERB (**cries, cried, crying**) **1** shed tears. **2** call loudly; scream.

cryogenics NOUN a branch of physics dealing with very low temperatures.

crypt NOUN a room below the floor of a church.

cryptic ADJ mysterious or obscure in meaning.

crystal ADJ a glass-like mineral; high-quality glass; a symmetrical piece of a solidified substance.

crystalline ADJ

crystallize (or **-ise**) VERB form into crystals; become definite in form; preserve fruit in sugar.

cu. ABBREV cubic.

cub NOUN **1** the young of foxes, lions, etc. **2** (also **Cub Scout**) a member of the junior branch of the Scout Association.

cubby hole NOUN a very small room or space.

cube NOUN **1** a solid object with six equal square sides. **2** the product of a number multiplied by itself twice. VERB **1** find the cube of a number. **2** cut into cubes.
cube root a number which produces a given number when cubed.
cubic ADJ

cubicle NOUN a small area partitioned off in a large room.

cubism NOUN a style of painting in which objects are shown as geometrical shapes.
cubist NOUN

cuckoo NOUN a bird that lays its eggs in other birds' nests.

cucumber NOUN a long green-skinned fruit eaten in salads.

cud NOUN food that cattle bring back from the stomach into the mouth and chew again.

cuddle VERB hug lovingly; nestle together. NOUN a gentle hug.
cuddly ADJ

cudgel NOUN a short thick stick used as a weapon. VERB (**cudgelled**, **cudgelling**; [US]

cudgeled, cudgeling) beat with a cudgel.

cue NOUN **1** a signal to do something, especially for an actor to begin a speech. **2** a long rod for striking balls in billiards etc. VERB (**cued, cueing**) give a signal to someone.

cuff NOUN **1** a band of cloth round the edge of a sleeve. **2** a blow with the open hand. VERB strike with the open hand.
off the cuff [inf] without preparation.

cufflink NOUN a device for fastening together the sides of a shirt cuff.

cuisine NOUN a style of cooking.

cul-de-sac NOUN a street closed at one end.

culinary ADJ of or for cooking.

cull VERB gather or select; select and kill animals to reduce numbers.

culminate VERB reach a climax.
culmination NOUN

culottes PLURAL NOUN women's trousers styled to resemble a skirt.

culpable ADJ deserving blame.

culprit NOUN a person who

has committed an offence.

cult NOUN a system of religious worship; excessive admiration of a person or thing.

cultivate VERB **1** prepare and use land for crops; produce crops by tending them. **2** develop a skill etc. by practice. **3** try to win the friendship or support of.
cultivation NOUN

culture NOUN **1** a developed understanding of literature, art, music, etc.; the art, customs, etc. of a particular country or society. **2** artificial rearing of bacteria.
cultural ADJ
culturally ADV

culvert NOUN a drain under a road.

cumbersome ADJ heavy and awkward to carry or use.

cumin NOUN a spice.

cummerbund NOUN a sash for the waist.

cumulative ADJ increasing by additions.

cumulus NOUN (PL **-li**) clouds formed in heaped-up rounded masses.

cunning ADJ skilled at deception; ingenious. NOUN craftiness or ingenuity.

cup NOUN a small bowl-shaped container with a handle for drinking from; a trophy shaped like this. VERB (**cupped, cupping**) form your hands into a cup-like shape.

cupboard NOUN a recess or piece of furniture with a door, in which things may be stored.

cupidity NOUN greed for gain.

cur NOUN a mongrel dog.

curate NOUN a member of the clergy who assists a parish priest.

curator NOUN a person in charge of a museum or other collection.

curb NOUN a means of restraint. VERB restrain.

curdle VERB form or cause to form curds.

curds PLURAL NOUN the thick soft substance formed when milk turns sour.

cure VERB **1** restore to health; get rid of a disease or trouble etc. **2** preserve by salting, drying, etc. NOUN a substance or treatment curing disease; restoration to health.

curfew NOUN a law requiring people to stay indoors after a stated time; this time.

curio NOUN (PL **-os**) an unusual and interesting object.

curious ADJ **1** eager to learn or know something. **2** strange or unusual. **curiosity** NOUN

curl VERB form a curved or spiral shape. NOUN a curled thing or shape; a coiled lock of hair. **curly** ADJ

curler NOUN a small tube round which hair is wound to make it curl.

curlew NOUN a wading bird with a long curved bill.

curmudgeon NOUN a bad-tempered person.

currant NOUN **1** a dried grape used in cookery. **2** a small round edible berry.

currency NOUN (PL **-ies**) **1** money in use in a particular area. **2** being widely used or known.

current ADJ **1** belonging to the present time. **2** in general use. NOUN a body of water or air moving in one direction; a flow of electricity. **currently** ADV

curriculum NOUN (PL **-la**) a course of study.

curriculum vitae NOUN a brief account of your career.

curry NOUN (PL **-ies**) a savoury dish cooked with hot spices.

curse NOUN a call for harm to happen to a person or thing; something causing suffering or annoyance; an offensive word expressing anger. VERB utter a curse; afflict; swear.

cursor NOUN a movable indicator on a computer screen.

cursory ADJ hasty and not thorough.

curt ADJ noticeably or rudely brief.

curtail VERB cut short or reduce. **curtailment** NOUN

curtain NOUN a piece of cloth hung as a screen, especially at a window.

curtsy (or **curtsey**) NOUN (PL **-ies**) a woman's movement of respect made by bending the knees. VERB (**curtsied**, **curtsying**) make a curtsy.

curvaceous ADJ (of a woman) having a shapely

curved figure.

curvature NOUN curving; a curved form.

curve NOUN a line or surface with no part straight or flat. VERB form into a curve.
 curvy ADJ

cushion NOUN a stuffed bag used for sitting or leaning on; a support or protection; a body of air supporting a hovercraft. VERB lessen the impact of.

cushy ADJ (**-ier, -iest**) [inf] pleasant and easy.

cusp NOUN 1 a pointed part where curves meet. 2 a point of transition, especially between astrological signs.

custard NOUN a sweet sauce made with milk and eggs or flavoured cornflour.

custodian NOUN a guardian or keeper.

custody NOUN 1 protective care. 2 imprisonment.

custom NOUN 1 the usual way of behaving or acting. 2 regular dealing by customers. 3 (**customs**) duty on imported goods.

customary ADJ usual.
 customarily ADV

customer NOUN a person buying goods or services from a shop etc.

cut VERB (**cut, cutting**) 1 open, wound, divide, or shape by pressure of a sharp edge; remove or reduce in this way. 2 intersect. 3 divide a pack of cards. 4 avoid or ignore. NOUN 1 cutting; an incision or wound. 2 a piece cut off; [inf] a share. 3 a reduction.

cute ADJ attractive and endearing.

cuticle NOUN the skin at the base of a nail.

cutlass NOUN a short curved sword.

cutlery NOUN table knives, forks, and spoons.

cutlet NOUN a lamb or veal chop from behind the neck; a flat cake of minced meat or nuts and breadcrumbs etc.

cutting ADJ (of remarks) hurtful. NOUN 1 a passage cut through high ground for a railway etc. 2 a piece of a plant for replanting. 3 a piece cut out of a newspaper etc.

cuttlefish NOUN a sea creature that ejects black fluid when attacked.

CV ABBREV curriculum vitae.

cwt ABBREV hundredweight.

cyanide NOUN a strong poison.

cycle NOUN **1** a recurring series of events. **2** a bicycle or motorcycle. VERB ride a bicycle.
  cyclist NOUN

cyclic (or **cyclical**) ADJ recurring regularly.

cyclone NOUN a violent wind rotating around a central area.

cygnet NOUN a young swan.

cylinder NOUN an object with straight sides and circular ends.
  cylindrical ADJ

cymbal NOUN a brass plate struck against another or with a stick as a

percussion instrument.

cynic NOUN a person who believes that people always act from selfish motives.
  cynical ADJ
  cynically ADV
  cynicism NOUN

cypher see **cipher**.

cypress NOUN an evergreen tree.

cyst NOUN a growth on the body containing fluid.

cystic fibrosis NOUN a hereditary disease, often resulting in respiratory infections.

cystitis NOUN inflammation of the bladder.

czar see **tsar**.

Dd

D NOUN (as a Roman numeral) 500.

dab VERB (**dabbed, dabbing**) press lightly with something absorbent; apply with quick strokes. NOUN a quick stroke; a small amount applied.

dabble VERB **1** splash about gently or playfully. **2** work at something in a casual or superficial way.

dachshund NOUN a small dog with a long body and short legs.

dad NOUN [inf] father.

daddy NOUN (PL **-ies**) [inf]

father.

daddy-long-legs [inf] a long-legged flying insect.

daffodil NOUN a yellow flower with a trumpet-shaped central part.

daft ADJ [inf] silly or crazy.

dagger NOUN a short pointed weapon used for stabbing.

dahlia NOUN a plant with brightly coloured flowers.

daily ADJ & ADV every day or every weekday.

dainty ADJ (-ier, -iest) 1 delicate, small, and pretty. 2 fastidious.
daintily ADV
daintiness NOUN

dairy NOUN (PL -ies) a place where milk and its products are processed or sold.

dais NOUN a low, raised platform.

daisy NOUN (PL -ies) a flower with many ray-like petals.

dale NOUN a valley.

dally VERB (**dallied, dallying**) idle or dawdle; flirt.
dalliance NOUN

Dalmatian NOUN a breed of dog with white hair and dark spots.

dam NOUN a barrier built across a river to hold back water. VERB (**dammed, damming**) build a dam across.

damage NOUN 1 harm or injury that reduces something's value, usefulness, or attractiveness. 2 (**damages**) money as compensation for injury. VERB cause damage to.

damask NOUN a fabric woven with a pattern visible on either side.

dame NOUN 1 (**Dame**) the title of a woman with an order of knighthood. 2 [US inf] a woman.

damn VERB condemn to hell; condemn or criticize; swear at. ADJ (also **damned**) said to emphasize anger or frustration.
damnation NOUN

damp ADJ slightly wet. NOUN moistness. VERB 1 make damp. 2 restrain or discourage.
dampen VERB

damper NOUN 1 something that depresses or subdues. 2 a pad silencing a piano string. 3 a metal plate controlling the draught in a flue.

damson NOUN a small purple plum.

dance VERB move with rhythmical steps and gestures, usually to music; move in a quick or lively way. NOUN a spell of dancing; music for this; a social gathering for dancing.
dancer NOUN

dandelion NOUN a wild plant with bright yellow flowers.

dandruff NOUN flakes of dead skin from the scalp.

dandy NOUN (PL **-ies**) a man who pays excessive attention to his appearance. ADJ [inf] excellent.

danger NOUN likelihood of harm or death; something causing this.
dangerous ADJ

dangle VERB hang or swing loosely.

dank ADJ damp and cold.

dapper ADJ neat and precise in dress or movement.

dapple VERB mark with patches of colour or shade.

dare VERB be bold enough to do something; challenge to do something risky. NOUN this challenge.

daredevil NOUN a recklessly daring person.

daring ADJ bold. NOUN boldness.

dark ADJ **1** with little or no light; closer to black than to white. **2** gloomy; evil. NOUN absence of light; night.
dark horse a successful competitor of whom little is known.
darken VERB
darkness NOUN

darkroom NOUN a darkened room for processing photographs.

darling NOUN a loved or lovable person or thing; a favourite. ADJ beloved or lovable.

darn VERB mend a hole in fabric by weaving thread across it.

dart NOUN **1** a small pointed missile; (**darts**) a game in which such missiles are thrown at a target. **2** a sudden run. **3** a tuck shaping a garment. VERB run suddenly.

dash VERB **1** run rapidly. **2** strike or throw violently against something; destroy hopes etc. NOUN **1** a rapid run. **2** a small amount of liquid etc. added to something. **3** a punctuation mark (-) marking a pause or break in the sense or representing omitted letters.

dashboard NOUN the instrument panel of a motor vehicle.

dashing ADJ excitingly stylish and attractive.

dastardly ADJ wicked.

data NOUN facts collected for reference or analysis; facts to be processed by computer.

database NOUN an organized store of computerized data.

date[1] NOUN **1** a specified day of a month or year; the day or year of something's occurrence. **2** [inf] a social or romantic appointment. VERB **1** establish the date of; originate from a specified date; mark with a date; become or show to be old-fashioned. **2** [inf] have a date or regular dates with.

date[2] NOUN a small brown edible fruit.

dated ADJ old-fashioned.

daub VERB smear roughly.

daughter NOUN a female in relation to her parents. **daughter-in-law** a son's wife.

daunt VERB intimidate or discourage. **daunting** ADJ

dawdle VERB walk slowly; idle.

dawn NOUN the first light of day; a beginning. VERB begin; grow light; be realized or understood.

day NOUN **1** a period of 24 hours; the part of this when the sun is above the horizon; the part of this spent working. **2** a time or period.

daybreak NOUN the first light of day.

daydream NOUN & VERB (have) pleasant idle thoughts.

daze VERB cause to feel stunned or bewildered. NOUN a dazed state.

dazzle VERB blind temporarily with bright light; impress with splendour. **dazzling** ADJ

DC ABBREV direct current.

deacon NOUN a Christian minister just below the rank of priest; (in some Christian churches) a person who assists a minister.

dead ADJ **1** no longer alive. **2** lacking sensation or emotion; lacking excitement. **3** no longer functioning. **4** complete. ADV absolutely; exactly.
dead end a cul-de-sac; an occupation with no prospect of development or progress. **dead heat** a race in which two or more competitors finish exactly even.

deaden VERB make less intense; make insensitive or inactive.

deadline NOUN a time limit.

deadlock NOUN a state when no progress can be made.

deadly ADJ (**-lier, -liest**) **1** causing death. **2** [inf] very boring. ADV extremely.

deadpan ADJ expressionless.

deaf ADJ wholly or partly unable to hear; refusing to listen.
deafen VERB
deafness NOUN

deal VERB (**dealt, dealing**) **1** distribute playing cards to players; hand out; inflict a blow or misfortune, etc. **2** engage in trade. **3** (**deal with**) take action about; have as a topic. NOUN **1** a bargain or transaction. **2** treatment received. **3** fir or pine timber.
a great deal a large amount.
dealer NOUN

dean NOUN **1** a clergyman who is head of a cathedral chapter. **2** a university official.

dear ADJ **1** much loved. **2** expensive. NOUN a lovable person.
dearly ADV

dearth NOUN a scarcity or lack.

death NOUN the process of dying; the state of being dead; an end.
deathly ADJ

debacle NOUN an utter and ignominious failure.

debar VERB (**debarred, debarring**) exclude.

debase VERB lower in quality or value.
debasement NOUN

debatable ADJ questionable.

debate NOUN a formal discussion. VERB discuss formally; consider.

debauchery NOUN over-

indulgence in harmful or immoral pleasures.
debauched ADJ
debilitate VERB weaken.
debility NOUN physical weakness.
debit NOUN an entry in an account for a sum owing. VERB (**debited, debiting**) enter as a debit, charge.
debonair ADJ having a carefree, self-confident manner.
debrief VERB question to obtain facts about a completed mission.
debris NOUN scattered broken pieces or rubbish.
debt NOUN something owed; the state of owing something.
debtor NOUN
debut NOUN a first public appearance.
debutante NOUN a young upper-class woman making her first formal appearance in society.
decade NOUN a ten-year period.
decadent ADJ in a state of moral deterioration.
decadence NOUN
decaffeinated ADJ with caffeine removed or reduced.
decamp VERB go away

suddenly or secretly.
decant VERB pour liquid into another container, leaving sediment behind.
decanter NOUN a bottle into which wine may be decanted before serving.
decapitate VERB behead.
decapitation NOUN
decathlon NOUN an athletic contest involving ten events.
decay VERB rot; deteriorate. NOUN rot; deterioration.
decease NOUN death.
deceased ADJ
deceit NOUN deception.
deceitful ADJ
deceive VERB 1 cause to believe something that is not true. 2 be sexually unfaithful to.
decelerate VERB reduce speed.
deceleration NOUN
December NOUN the twelfth month.
decent ADJ 1 conforming to accepted standards of propriety. 2 of an acceptable standard. 3 [inf] kind or generous.
decency NOUN
deception NOUN deceiving; a trick.
deceptive ADJ misleading.

decibel NOUN a unit for measuring the intensity of sound.

decide VERB make up your mind; settle a contest or argument.

decided ADJ having firm opinions; clear or definite.
decidedly ADV

deciduous ADJ (of a tree) shedding its leaves annually.

decimal ADJ reckoned in tens or tenths. NOUN a decimal fraction.
decimal point the dot used in a decimal fraction.

decimate VERB kill or destroy a large proportion of.

decipher VERB make out the meaning of a code or bad handwriting.

decision NOUN a conclusion reached after consideration.

decisive ADJ 1 settling an issue definitively. 2 able to decide quickly and confidently.
decisiveness NOUN

deck NOUN 1 a floor or storey of a ship or bus. 2 the part of a record player that holds and plays the records. VERB decorate.

deckchair NOUN a folding canvas chair.

declaim VERB speak or say impressively.
declamation NOUN
declamatory ADJ

declare VERB announce openly or formally; state firmly.
declaration NOUN

decline VERB 1 decrease in size or number; lose strength or quality. 2 refuse politely. NOUN a gradual decrease or loss of strength.

decode VERB convert from coded form into plain language.

decompose VERB rot or decay.
decomposition NOUN

decompress VERB reduce air pressure in or on.
decompression NOUN

decongestant NOUN a medicinal substance that relieves congestion.

decontaminate VERB free from radioactivity, germs, etc.
decontamination NOUN

decor NOUN the style of decoration used in a room.

decorate VERB 1 make attractive by adding ornaments; paint or paper the walls of. 2 confer a medal or award on.
decoration NOUN
decorative ADJ
decorator NOUN
decorum NOUN correctness and dignity of behaviour.
decorous ADJ
decoy NOUN a person or animal used to lure others into a trap. VERB lure by a decoy.
decrease VERB make or become smaller or fewer. NOUN decreasing; the extent of this.
decree NOUN an order given by a government or other authority. VERB order by decree.
decrepit ADJ made weak by age or use.
decry VERB (**decried, decrying**) denounce publicly.
dedicate VERB devote to a cause or task; address a book etc. to a person as a tribute.
dedication NOUN
dedicated ADJ serious in your commitment to a task; exclusively set aside for a particular purpose.

deduce VERB arrive at a conclusion by reasoning.
deduct VERB subtract.
deduction NOUN 1 deducting; something deducted. 2 deducing; a conclusion deduced.
deed NOUN 1 something done. 2 a legal document.
deem VERB consider to be of a specified character.
deep ADJ 1 extending or situated far down or in from the top or surface. 2 intense or extreme. 3 profound. 4 low-pitched.
deepen VERB
deer NOUN (PL **deer**) a hoofed animal, the male of which usually has antlers.
deface VERB spoil or damage the surface of.
defame VERB attack the good reputation of.
defamation NOUN
defamatory ADJ
default VERB fail to fulfil an obligation, especially to pay debts or appear in court. NOUN 1 failure to fulfil an obligation. 2 a pre-selected option adopted by a computer program unless otherwise instructed.
defeat VERB win victory

over; cause to fail. NOUN
defeating; being defeated.

defeatist NOUN a person
who pessimistically
expects or accepts failure.
defeatism NOUN

defecate VERB discharge
faeces from the body.
defecation NOUN

defect NOUN an
imperfection. VERB desert
your country or cause.
defection NOUN
defector NOUN

defective ADJ imperfect or
faulty.

defence ([US] **defense**)
NOUN protecting;
equipment or resources
for protection; arguments
against an accusation.

defend VERB protect from
attack; uphold by
argument; represent a
defendant.
defender NOUN

defendant NOUN a person
accused or sued in a
lawsuit.

defensible ADJ able to be
defended.

defensive ADJ **1** intended
for defence. **2** sensitive to
criticism.

defer VERB (**deferred,
deferring**) **1** postpone.
2 yield to a person's

wishes or authority.
deferral NOUN

deference NOUN polite
respect.
deferential ADJ

defiance NOUN bold
disobedience.
defiant ADJ

deficiency NOUN (PL **-ies**) a
lack or shortage; an
imperfection.
deficient ADJ

deficit NOUN an amount by
which a total falls short of
what is required.

defile VERB make dirty or
impure.

define VERB state precisely;
give the meaning of; mark
the boundary of.

definite ADJ clearly and
firmly decided or stated;
certain or unambiguous;
with a clear shape or
outline.
definitely ADV

definite article see
article.

definition NOUN a
statement of precise
meaning; distinctness or
clearness of outline.

definitive ADJ settling
something finally and
authoritatively.

deflate VERB cause to
collapse through release

of air; make less confident.

deflect VERB turn aside.
  deflection NOUN

deforest VERB clear of trees.
  deforestation NOUN

deform VERB spoil the shape of.
  deformity NOUN

defraud VERB swindle.

defray VERB provide money to pay costs.

defrost VERB remove ice from a refrigerator; thaw.

deft ADJ skilful and quick.

defunct ADJ no longer existing or functioning.

defuse VERB remove the fuse from an explosive; reduce the tension in a situation.

defy VERB (**defied, defying**) resist or disobey; challenge.

degenerate VERB become worse physically, mentally, or morally. ADJ having degenerated. NOUN a degenerate person.
  degeneracy NOUN
  degeneration NOUN

degrade VERB 1 treat disrespectfully or humiliate. 2 decompose.
  degradation NOUN

degree NOUN 1 the extent to which something is true or present; a stage in a series. 2 a unit of measurement for angles or temperature. 3 an award given by a university or college.

dehumanize (or **-ise**) VERB remove human qualities from.

dehydrate VERB cause to lose a large amount of moisture.
  dehydration NOUN

deify VERB (**deified, deifying**) treat as a god.
  deification NOUN

deign VERB condescend

deity NOUN (PL **-ies**) a divine being.

déjà vu NOUN a feeling of having experienced a present situation before.

dejected ADJ in low spirits.
  dejection NOUN

delay VERB make late; be slow; postpone. NOUN delaying; time lost by delaying.

delectable ADJ delicious or delightful.

delegate NOUN a representative. VERB entrust a task etc. to someone.

delegation NOUN a group

of representatives; delegating.

delete VERB cross out a word etc.

deletion NOUN

deleterious ADJ harmful.

deliberate ADJ **1** intentional. **2** slow and careful. VERB engage in careful discussion or consideration.

deliberately ADV

deliberation NOUN

delicacy NOUN (PL **-ies**) **1** being delicate. **2** a choice food.

delicate ADJ **1** fine or intricate. **2** fragile; prone to illness or injury. **3** requiring tact.

delicatessen NOUN a shop selling unusual or foreign prepared foods.

delicious ADJ delightful, especially to taste or smell.

delight NOUN great pleasure; a source of this. VERB please greatly; feel delight.

delightful ADJ

delineate VERB outline.

delineation NOUN

delinquent ADJ & NOUN (a person) guilty of persistent law-breaking.

delinquency NOUN

delirium NOUN a disordered state of mind, especially during fever; wild excitement.

delirious ADJ

deliver VERB **1** take to an addressee or purchaser; make a speech etc.; aim a blow or attack. **2** rescue or set free. **3** assist in the birth of.

delivery NOUN

dell NOUN a small wooded hollow.

delta NOUN **1** the fourth letter of the Greek alphabet (Δ, δ). **2** an area of land where the mouth of a river has split into several channels.

delude VERB deceive or mislead.

deluge NOUN a flood; a heavy fall of rain; a large quantity of something coming at the same time. VERB flood; overwhelm.

delusion NOUN a false belief or impression.

de luxe ADJ of superior quality; luxurious.

delve VERB search deeply.

demagogue NOUN a political leader who wins support by appealing to popular feelings and prejudices.

demand NOUN a firm or official request; customers' desire for goods or services. VERB make a demand for; need.

demanding ADJ requiring great skill or effort.

demarcation NOUN the marking of a boundary or limits.

demean VERB lower the dignity of.

demeanour ([US] **demeanor**) NOUN the way a person behaves.

demented ADJ mad.

dementia NOUN a mental disorder.

demilitarize (or **-ise**) VERB remove military forces from.

demise NOUN death; failure.

demobilize (or **-ise**) VERB release from military service.

democracy NOUN (PL **-ies**) government by all the people, usually through elected representatives; a country governed in this way.
democratic ADJ

democrat NOUN a person favouring democracy.

demolish VERB pull or knock down; destroy.

demolition NOUN

demon NOUN a devil or evil spirit.
demonic ADJ

demonstrable ADJ able to be proved or shown.
demonstrably ADV

demonstrate VERB **1** prove or show clearly; give an exhibition of. **2** take part in a public protest.
demonstrator NOUN

demonstration NOUN **1** proving; exhibiting. **2** a public protest.

demonstrative ADJ **1** showing feelings openly. **2** demonstrating something.

demoralize (or **-ise**) VERB dishearten.

demote VERB reduce to a lower rank or category.
demotion NOUN

demur VERB (**demurred, demurring**) raise objections.

demure ADJ quiet, modest, and shy.

den NOUN a wild animal's lair; a person's small private room.

denial NOUN the action of denying.

denigrate VERB criticize unfairly.

denim NOUN a strong

cotton fabric; (**denims**) trousers made of this.

denizen NOUN [formal] an inhabitant.

denomination NOUN **1** a branch of a Church or religion. **2** the face value of a coin or bank note. **3** [formal] a name.

denominator NOUN a number below the line in a vulgar fraction.

denote VERB be a sign or symbol of.

denouement NOUN the final outcome of a play or story.

denounce VERB publicly condemn or criticize.

dense ADJ **1** closely packed together. **2** stupid.

density NOUN the degree to which something is full or closely packed.

dent NOUN a hollow left by a blow or pressure. VERB mark with a dent; diminish or discourage.

dental ADJ of teeth or dentistry.

dentist NOUN a person qualified to treat decay and malformations of teeth.
dentistry NOUN

denture NOUN a plate holding an artificial tooth or teeth.

denude VERB strip of covering or property.

denunciation NOUN a public condemnation.

deny VERB (**denied, denying**) **1** say that something is not true. **2** prevent from having. **3** (**deny yourself**) go without something.

deodorant NOUN a substance that prevents unwanted bodily odours.

depart VERB leave.
departure NOUN

departed ADJ dead.

department NOUN a section of an organization with a special function or concern.
department store a large shop selling many kinds of goods.
departmental ADJ

depend VERB (**depend on**) be determined by; rely on.

dependable ADJ reliable.

dependant NOUN a person who depends on another for support.

dependency NOUN (PL **-ies**) being dependent; a country controlled by another.

dependent ADJ depending; controlled by

another.

dependence NOUN

depict VERB represent in a picture or in words.

depiction NOUN

deplete VERB reduce the number of by overuse.

depletion NOUN

deplorable ADJ shockingly bad.

deplorably ADV

deplore VERB strongly disapprove of.

deploy VERB move into position for action; utilize.

deployment NOUN

depopulate VERB reduce the population of.

depopulation NOUN

deport VERB remove a person from a country.

deportation NOUN

deportment NOUN behaviour; bearing.

depose VERB remove from power.

deposit VERB (**deposited, depositing**) 1 put down; leave a layer of earth etc. 2 entrust for safe keeping; pay into a bank or as a guarantee. NOUN 1 a sum paid into a bank; a first instalment of payment. 2 a layer of sediment etc.

deposition NOUN

1 deposing. 2 depositing. 3 a sworn statement.

depository NOUN (PL **-ies**) a storehouse.

depot NOUN a storage area, especially for vehicles; [US] a bus or railway station.

depraved ADJ morally corrupt.

depravity NOUN immoral behaviour or character.

deprecate VERB 1 express disapproval of. 2 disclaim politely.

deprecation NOUN

depreciate VERB diminish in value; belittle.

depreciation NOUN

depredation NOUN plundering or destruction.

depress VERB 1 cause to feel dispirited. 2 press down. 3 reduce the strength or activity of.

depressant ADJ

depression NOUN

1 sadness or gloominess. 2 a long period of inactivity in trading. 3 pressing down; a hollow on a surface; an area of low atmospheric pressure.

depressive ADJ

deprive VERB prevent from using or enjoying

something.

deprivation NOUN

depth NOUN **1** distance downwards or inwards from a surface. **2** detailed treatment; intensity. **3** the deepest or most central part.

deputation NOUN a body of people sent to represent others.

deputize (or **-ise**) VERB act as deputy.

deputy NOUN (PL **-ies**) a person appointed to act as a substitute or representative.

derail VERB cause a train to leave the rails.

derailment NOUN

derange VERB **1** make insane. **2** throw into confusion.

derangement NOUN

derelict ADJ left to fall into ruin.

dereliction NOUN **1** being derelict. **2** failure to do your duty.

deride VERB mock scornfully.

derision NOUN mockery or scorn.

derisive ADJ

derisory ADJ **1** ridiculously or insultingly small. **2** derisive.

derivative ADJ lacking originality. NOUN something derived from another source.

derive VERB obtain from a source; originate.

derivation NOUN

dermatitis NOUN inflammation of the skin.

dermatology NOUN the study of the skin and its diseases.

dermatologist NOUN

derogatory ADJ disparaging.

derv NOUN fuel for diesel engines.

descant NOUN a treble accompaniment to a main melody.

descend VERB **1** go or come down; stoop to unworthy behaviour; make an attack or a sudden visit. **2** (**be descended from**) have as your ancestor(s).

descendant NOUN a person descended from another.

descent NOUN descending; a downward slope; ancestry.

describe VERB give a description of.

description NOUN **1** a spoken or written

account. **2** a kind or sort.

descriptive ADJ describing.

desecrate VERB treat something sacred with violent disrespect.
desecration NOUN

deselect VERB reject an MP as a candidate for re-election.
deselection NOUN

desert[1] NOUN a barren waterless area.

desert[2] VERB abandon; leave your service in the armed forces without permission.
deserter NOUN
desertion NOUN

deserts PLURAL NOUN what you deserve.

deserve VERB be worthy of through your actions or qualities.

deserving ADJ worthy of good treatment.

desiccate VERB dry out moisture from.

design NOUN **1** a drawing that shows how a thing is to be made; a general form or arrangement; a decorative pattern. **2** an intention. VERB prepare a design for; plan or intend.
designer NOUN

designate VERB appoint to a position; officially assign a status to. ADJ appointed but not yet installed.
designation NOUN

desirable ADJ **1** good-looking. **2** advisable or beneficial.
desirability NOUN

desire NOUN a feeling of wanting something strongly; sexual appetite; a thing desired. VERB feel a desire for.

desirous ADJ desiring.

desist VERB stop.

desk NOUN a piece of furniture for reading or writing at; a counter.

desolate ADJ bleak and lonely; very unhappy.
desolation NOUN

desolated ADJ very unhappy.

despair NOUN complete lack of hope. VERB feel despair.

despatch see **dispatch**.

desperado NOUN (PL **-oes** or **-os**) a reckless criminal.

desperate ADJ **1** hopeless; very bad or serious; made reckless by despair. **2** feeling an intense desire or need.
desperation NOUN

despicable ADJ

contemptible.

despise VERB hate.

despite PREP in spite of.

despoil VERB [literary] plunder.

despondent ADJ dejected and discouraged.

  despondency NOUN

despot NOUN a dictator.

  despotic ADJ

  despotism NOUN

dessert NOUN the sweet course of a meal.

destabilize (or -ise) VERB make unstable or insecure.

destination NOUN the place to which a person or thing is going.

destine VERB set apart for a purpose; doom to a particular fate.

destiny NOUN (PL -ies) fate; your future destined by fate.

destitute ADJ extremely poor; without means to live.

  destitution NOUN

destroy VERB pull or break down; ruin; kill an animal.

  destruction NOUN

  destructive ADJ

destroyer NOUN a fast warship.

desultory ADJ without purpose or enthusiasm; moving at random between subjects.

  desultorily ADV

detach VERB separate or unfasten.

detached ADJ 1 separate; not connected. 2 free from bias or emotion.

detachment NOUN 1 objectivity. 2 detaching. 3 a group sent on a military mission.

detail NOUN 1 a small individual fact or item; such items collectively. 2 a small military detachment. VERB 1 describe in detail. 2 assign to a special duty.

detain VERB keep in official custody; delay.

  detainee NOUN

detect VERB discover the presence of.

  detection NOUN

  detector NOUN

detective NOUN a person whose job is to investigate crimes.

détente NOUN an easing of tension between nations.

detention NOUN detaining; imprisonment.

deter VERB (**deterred, deterring**) discourage from action.

detergent NOUN a cleaning substance, especially other than soap.

deteriorate VERB become worse.
  deterioration NOUN

determination NOUN 1 resolution or firmness of purpose. 2 establishing something.

determine VERB 1 be the main factor in establishing something. 2 resolve firmly.

determined ADJ full of determination.

deterrent NOUN something deterring or intended to deter.

detest VERB dislike intensely.
  detestation NOUN

dethrone VERB remove from power.

detonate VERB explode.
  detonation NOUN
  detonator NOUN

detour NOUN a deviation from a direct or intended course.

detract VERB (**detract from**) cause to seem less valuable or impressive.

detractor NOUN a person who criticizes something.

detriment NOUN harm.
  detrimental ADJ

deuce NOUN 1 a score of 40 all in tennis. 2 [inf] (in exclamations) the Devil.

devalue VERB reduce the value of; disparage.
  devaluation NOUN

devastate VERB cause great destruction to.
  devastation NOUN

devastating ADJ very destructive; shocking and distressing.

develop VERB (**developed, developing**) 1 make or become larger, more mature, or more advanced; begin to exist or have. 2 make land etc. usable or profitable. 3 treat a film so as to make a picture visible.
  developer NOUN
  development NOUN

deviant ADJ deviating from accepted standards.

deviate VERB diverge from a route, course of action, etc.
  deviation NOUN

device NOUN a thing made for a particular purpose; a scheme.

devil NOUN an evil spirit; (**the Devil**) the supreme spirit of evil; a cruel person.
  devil's advocate a person

devilment   184

who tests a proposition by arguing against it.
devilish ADJ
devilment NOUN mischief.
devilry NOUN wickedness; mischief.
devious ADJ underhand; (of a route) indirect.
devise VERB plan; invent.
devoid ADJ (**devoid of**) entirely without.
devolution NOUN delegation of power especially from central to local administration.
devolve VERB transfer power to a lower level; (of duties) pass to a deputy.
devote VERB give or use exclusively for a particular purpose.
devoted ADJ showing devotion.
devotee NOUN an enthusiast; a worshipper.
devotion NOUN great love, loyalty, or commitment; religious worship; (**devotions**) prayers.
devotional ADJ
devour VERB eat hungrily or greedily; consume or destroy; take in avidly.
devout ADJ deeply religious; earnestly sincere.
dew NOUN drops of

condensed moisture forming on cool surfaces at night.
dexterity NOUN skill.
dexterous (or **dextrous**) ADJ
diabetes NOUN a disease in which sugar and starch are not properly absorbed by the body.
diabetic ADJ & NOUN
diabolic ADJ of the Devil.
diabolical ADJ very wicked; [inf] extremely bad.
diabolically ADV
diadem NOUN a crown.
diagnose VERB make a diagnosis of.
diagnosis NOUN (PL **-ses**) the identification of a disease or condition after observing its symptoms.
diagnostic ADJ
diagonal ADJ & NOUN (a line) joining opposite corners of a square or rectangle.
diagonally ADV
diagram NOUN a schematic drawing that shows the parts or operation of something.
dial NOUN the face of a clock or watch; a similar plate or disc with a movable pointer; a

movable disc turned to connect one telephone with another. VERB (**dialled, dialling**; [US] **dialed, dialing**) select or operate by using a dial or numbered buttons.

dialect NOUN a local form of a language.

dialogue ([US] **dialog**) NOUN a conversation or discussion.

dialysis NOUN purification of blood by filtering it through a membrane.

diameter NOUN a straight line from side to side through the centre of a circle or sphere.

diametrical ADJ **1** (of opposites) complete. **2** of or along a diameter. **diametrically** ADV

diamond NOUN **1** a very hard clear precious stone. **2** a four-sided figure with equal sides and with angles that are not right angles; a playing card marked with such shapes.

diaphanous ADJ almost transparent.

diaphragm NOUN **1** the muscular partition between the chest and abdomen. **2** a contraceptive cap fitting over the cervix.

diarrhoea ([US] **diarrhea**) NOUN a condition causing frequent fluid bowel movements.

diary NOUN (PL **-ies**) a daily record of events; a book for this or for noting appointments.

diatribe NOUN a violent verbal attack.

dice NOUN (PL **dice**) a small cube marked on each side with 1–6 spots, used in games of chance. VERB cut into small cubes.

dichotomy NOUN (PL **-ies**) a division into two absolutely opposed parts.

dictate VERB **1** say words aloud to be written or recorded. **2** give orders officiously; control or determine. NOUN a command. **dictation** NOUN

dictator NOUN a ruler with unrestricted authority. **dictatorial** ADJ

diction NOUN a manner of uttering or pronouncing words.

dictionary NOUN (PL **-ies**) a book that lists and gives the meaning of the words of a language.

did past of **do**.

didactic ADJ meant or meaning to instruct.

die¹ VERB (**died, dying**) 1 cease to be alive; cease to exist; fade away. 2 (**be dying for** or **to**) [inf] long for or to.

die² NOUN a device for cutting or moulding metal or for stamping a design on coins etc.

diehard NOUN a stubbornly conservative person.

diesel NOUN an oil-burning engine in which ignition is produced by the heat of compressed air; fuel used in this.

diet NOUN a person's usual food; a special restricted course of food adopted to lose weight or for medical reasons. VERB (**dieted, dieting**) restrict what you eat.
dietary ADJ

dietitian (or **dietician**) NOUN an expert in diet and nutrition.

differ VERB be unlike; disagree.

difference NOUN 1 a way in which things are not the same; being different; the remainder when one sum is subtracted from another. 2 a disagreement.

different ADJ not the same; distinct; novel.

differential ADJ of, showing, or depending on a difference; distinctive. NOUN 1 an agreed difference in wage rates. 2 an arrangement of gears allowing a vehicle's wheels to revolve at different speeds when cornering.

differentiate VERB distinguish between; make or become different.
differentiation NOUN

difficult ADJ needing much effort or skill to do, deal with, or understand; hard to please.
difficulty NOUN

diffident ADJ lacking self-confidence.
diffidence NOUN

diffract VERB break up a beam of light into a series of coloured or dark-and-light bands.
diffraction NOUN

diffuse ADJ not concentrated. VERB spread widely or thinly.
diffusion NOUN

dig VERB (**dug, digging**) 1 break up and move soil; extract from the ground in this way. 2 push or

dimension

poke. **3** search for. NOUN **1** digging; an excavation. **2** a sharp push or poke. **3** a cutting remark. **4** (**digs**) [inf] lodgings.
digger NOUN

digest VERB break down food in the body; absorb into the mind. NOUN a methodical summary.
digestible ADJ
digestion NOUN
digestive ADJ

digit NOUN **1** any numeral from 0 to 9. **2** a finger or toe.

digital ADJ of or using digits; (of a clock) showing the time by a row of figures; (of a recording) converting sound into electrical pulses.
digitally ADV

dignify VERB (**dignified**, **dignifying**) treat as important or deserving respect.
dignified ADJ

dignitary NOUN (PL **-ies**) a person holding high rank or position.

dignity NOUN (PL **-ies**) being worthy of respect; a calm and serious manner.

digress VERB depart from the main subject temporarily.
digression NOUN

dike see **dyke**.

dilapidated ADJ in disrepair.
dilapidation NOUN

dilate VERB make or become wider.
dilation NOUN

dilemma NOUN a situation in which a difficult choice has to be made.

dilettante NOUN (PL **-ti** or **-tes**) a person who dabbles in a subject for pleasure.

diligent ADJ working or done with care and effort.
diligence NOUN

dill NOUN a herb.

dilute VERB reduce the strength of fluid by adding water etc. ADJ diluted.
dilution NOUN

dim ADJ (**dimmer**, **dimmest**) **1** not bright or distinct. **2** [inf] stupid. VERB (**dimmed**, **dimming**) make or become less bright or distinct.

dime NOUN a 10-cent coin of the USA.

dimension NOUN **1** an aspect or feature. **2** a measurement such as length or breadth.

dimensional ADJ

diminish VERB make or become less.

diminutive ADJ tiny.

dimple NOUN a small dent, especially in the skin.

din NOUN a loud annoying noise. VERB (**dinned**, **dinning**) impress information on someone by constant repetition.

dine VERB eat dinner.
  diner NOUN

dinghy NOUN (PL **-ies**) a small open boat or inflatable rubber boat.

dingo NOUN (PL **-oes**) an Australian wild dog.

dingy ADJ (**-ier**, **-iest**) dull and drab.

dinner NOUN the chief meal of the day; a formal evening meal.
  dinner jacket a man's jacket for formal evening wear.

dinosaur NOUN an extinct prehistoric reptile, often of enormous size.

dint NOUN (**by dint of**) by means of.

diocese NOUN a district under the care of a bishop.

diode NOUN a semiconductor allowing the flow of current in one direction only and having two terminals.

dip VERB (**dipped**, **dipping**) 1 plunge briefly into liquid. 2 move or slope downwards; lower; lower the beam of headlights. NOUN 1 a short swim; a brief immersion; a liquid in which sheep are dipped to guard against infection; a creamy sauce in which pieces of food are dipped. 2 a hollow.

diphtheria NOUN an infectious disease with inflammation of the throat.

diphthong NOUN a compound vowel sound (as *ou* in *loud*).

diploma NOUN a certificate awarded on completion of a course of study.

diplomacy NOUN handling of international relations; tact.

diplomat NOUN 1 an official representing a country abroad. 2 a tactful person.
  diplomatic ADJ

dipper NOUN 1 a diving bird. 2 a ladle.

dipsomania NOUN an uncontrollable craving for alcohol.
  dipsomaniac NOUN

dire ADJ extremely serious; [inf] very bad.

direct ADJ **1** going straight from one place to another; with nothing or no one in between. **2** frank; clear and explicit. ADV in a direct way or by a direct route. VERB **1** control or manage; order. **2** aim towards; tell someone how to reach a place.

direction NOUN **1** a course along which someone or something moves; the way something faces. **2** control. **3** (**directions**) instructions. **directional** ADJ

directive NOUN an official instruction.

directly ADV **1** in a direct line or manner. **2** immediately.

director NOUN a person in charge of an activity or organization; a member of a board directing a business; a person who supervises acting and filming.

directory NOUN (PL **-ies**) a book listing telephone subscribers etc.; a computer file listing other files.

dirge NOUN a mournful song.

dirt NOUN unclean matter; loose soil.

dirty ADJ (**-ier, -iest**) marked or covered with dirt; obscene; dishonourable or unfair. VERB (**dirtied, dirtying**) make dirty.

disability NOUN (PL **-ies**) a physical or mental incapacity.

disable VERB impair the capacities or activity of; keep from functioning or from doing something.

disabled ADJ having a physical disability.

disabuse VERB disillusion.

disadvantage NOUN an unfavourable condition or position in relation to others; something diminishing your chances of success or effectiveness. **disadvantaged** ADJ **disadvantageous** ADJ

disaffected ADJ discontented and no longer loyal. **disaffection** NOUN

disagree VERB **1** have a different opinion; be inconsistent. **2** (**disagree with**) make ill. **disagreement** NOUN

disagreeable ADJ

unpleasant; bad-tempered.

disallow VERB refuse to sanction.

disappear VERB pass from sight or existence.
disappearance NOUN

disappoint VERB fail to fulfil the hopes or expectations of.
disappointment NOUN

disapprove VERB consider to be bad or immoral.
disapproval NOUN

disarm VERB 1 deprive of weapons; reduce armed forces. 2 make less hostile; win over.
disarmament NOUN

disarrange VERB make untidy.

disarray NOUN disorder or confusion.

disassociate VERB variant of **dissociate**.

disaster NOUN a sudden great misfortune or failure.
disastrous ADJ

disband VERB (of an organized group) break up.

disbelieve VERB refuse or be unable to believe.
disbelief NOUN

disburse VERB pay out money.

disc NOUN 1 a thin, flat round object; a record bearing recorded sound; a layer of cartilage between the vertebrae. 2 (**disk**) a device on which computer data is stored.
disc jockey a person who plays pop records on the radio or at a club.

discard VERB reject as useless or unwanted. NOUN something rejected.

discern VERB perceive with the mind or senses.
discernible ADJ
discernment NOUN

discerning ADJ having good judgement.

discharge VERB 1 dismiss or allow to leave. 2 allow liquid etc. to flow out. 3 pay a debt; fulfil an obligation. NOUN discharging; material flowing from something.

disciple NOUN a pupil or follower; one of the original followers of Jesus.

disciplinarian NOUN a person who enforces strict discipline.

discipline NOUN 1 controlled and obedient behaviour; training and punishment producing this. 2 a branch of learning. VERB train to be orderly; punish.

disciplinary ADJ

disclaim VERB refuse to acknowledge.

disclaimer NOUN a denial of responsibility.

disclose VERB reveal.

disclosure NOUN

disco NOUN (PL **-os**) a place or party where people dance to pop music.

discolour ([US] **discolor**) VERB stain.

discoloration NOUN

discomfit VERB (**discomfited**, **discomfiting**) make uneasy or embarrassed.

discomfiture NOUN

discomfort NOUN slight pain; slight unease or embarrassment.

disconcert VERB unsettle.

disconnect VERB break the connection of; cut off the power supply of.

disconnection NOUN

disconsolate ADJ very unhappy.

discontent NOUN dissatisfaction.

discontented ADJ

discontinue VERB put an end to; cease.

discontinuous ADJ having gaps or breaks.

discord NOUN
1 disagreement or quarrelling.
2 inharmonious sounds.

discordant ADJ

discount NOUN an amount of money taken off something's full price. VERB 1 reduce the price of. 2 disregard as unreliable.

discourage VERB dishearten; deter or dissuade.

discouragement NOUN

discourse NOUN communication or debate; a treatise or lecture. VERB speak or write authoritatively.

discourteous ADJ impolite.

discourtesy NOUN

discover VERB find; learn; be the first to find.

discovery NOUN

discredit VERB (**discredited**, **discrediting**) damage the reputation of; cause to be disbelieved. NOUN damage to a reputation.

discreditable ADJ

discreet ADJ unobtrusive; not giving away secrets.

discrepancy NOUN (PL **-ies**) a difference or failure to match.

discrete ADJ separate and distinct.

discretion NOUN 1 being discreet. 2 freedom to decide something.

discretionary ADJ done or used at a person's discretion.

discriminate VERB distinguish; treat unfairly on the grounds of race, sex, or age.
discrimination NOUN
discriminatory ADJ

discriminating ADJ having good judgement.

discursive ADJ (of writing) flowing and wide-ranging.

discus NOUN a heavy disc thrown in an athletic contest.

discuss VERB talk or write about.
discussion NOUN

disdain VERB & NOUN scorn.
disdainful ADJ

disease NOUN an illness.
diseased ADJ

disembark VERB leave a ship, train, etc.

disembodied ADJ (of a voice) with no obvious physical source.

disembowel VERB (**disembowelled**, **disembowelling**; [US]

disemboweled, **disemboweling**) take out the entrails of.

disenchant VERB disillusion.
disenchantment NOUN

disengage VERB detach; release.

disentangle VERB free from tangles or confusion; separate.

disfavour ([US] **disfavor**) NOUN dislike; disapproval.

disfigure VERB spoil the appearance of.
disfigurement NOUN

disgrace NOUN the loss of other people's respect. VERB bring disgrace on.
disgraceful ADJ
disgracefully ADV

disgruntled ADJ annoyed or resentful.

disguise VERB conceal the identity of. NOUN a means of concealing your identity; being disguised.

disgust NOUN a feeling that something is very offensive or unpleasant. VERB cause disgust in.
disgusting ADJ

dish NOUN a shallow bowl, especially for food; food prepared according to a recipe. VERB (**dish out**) serve food.

dishearten VERB cause to lose hope or confidence.

dishevelled ([US] **disheveled**) ADJ ruffled and untidy.

dishonest ADJ not honest. **dishonesty** NOUN

dishonour ([US] **dishonor**) VERB & NOUN disgrace.

dishonourable ([US] **dishonorable**) ADJ bringing shame or disgrace.

dishwasher NOUN a machine for washing dishes.

disillusion VERB rid of pleasant but mistaken beliefs. **disillusionment** NOUN

disincentive NOUN something that discourages an action or effort.

disinclined ADJ reluctant. **disinclination** NOUN

disinfect VERB clean by destroying harmful bacteria. **disinfectant** NOUN **disinfection** NOUN

disinformation NOUN deliberately misleading information.

disingenuous ADJ insincere.

disinherit VERB deprive of an inheritance.

disintegrate VERB break into small pieces. **disintegration** NOUN

disinterested ADJ impartial.

disjointed ADJ lacking coherent connection.

disk see **disc**.

diskette NOUN [Computing] a small floppy disk.

dislike NOUN distaste or hostility. VERB feel dislike for.

dislocate VERB disturb the arrangement or position of; disrupt. **dislocation** NOUN

dislodge VERB remove from an established position.

disloyal ADJ not loyal. **disloyalty** NOUN

dismal ADJ gloomy; [inf] very bad. **dismally** ADV

dismantle VERB take to pieces.

dismay NOUN a feeling of shock and distress. VERB cause to feel this.

dismember VERB tear or cut the limbs from.

dismiss VERB send away from your presence or employment; disregard.

dismissal NOUN

dismissive ADJ treating something as unworthy of consideration.

dismount VERB get off a thing on which you are riding.

disobedient ADJ not obedient.

disobedience NOUN

disobey VERB disregard orders.

disorder NOUN
1 untidiness. 2 a breakdown of discipline. 3 an ailment.

disorderly ADJ

disorganized (or **-ised**) ADJ not properly planned or arranged; muddled.

disorganization NOUN

disorientate (or **disorient**) VERB cause a person to lose their sense of direction.

disorientation NOUN

disown VERB refuse to have any further connection with.

disparage VERB belittle; criticize.

disparate ADJ very different in kind.

disparity NOUN (PL **-ies**) a great difference.

dispassionate ADJ unemotional and objective.

dispatch (or **despatch**) VERB 1 send off to a destination or for a purpose. 2 complete a task quickly. 3 kill. NOUN 1 sending off. 2 promptness. 3 an official report.

dispel VERB (**dispelled**, **dispelling**) drive or clear away.

dispensable ADJ not essential.

dispensary NOUN (PL **-ies**) a place where medicines are dispensed.

dispensation NOUN 1 exemption. 2 distribution.

dispense VERB 1 deal out; prepare and give out medicine. 2 (**dispense with**) do without; abandon.

disperse VERB go or send in different directions; scatter.

dispersal NOUN

dispirited ADJ dejected.

dispiriting ADJ

displace VERB take the place of; move from its place or home.

displacement NOUN

display VERB show or put on show. NOUN displaying;

something displayed.

displease VERB irritate or annoy.

displeasure NOUN

disposable ADJ **1** designed to be thrown away after use. **2** available for use.

disposal NOUN getting rid of something.

dispose VERB **1** place or arrange. **2** make willing or ready to do something. **3** (**dispose of**) get rid of.

disposition NOUN **1** a person's character; a tendency. **2** arrangement.

disproportionate ADJ relatively too large or too small.

disprove VERB show to be false.

disputable ADJ questionable.

disputant NOUN a person engaged in a dispute.

disputation NOUN an argument or debate.

dispute VERB argue or debate; question the truth of; compete for. NOUN a debate or disagreement.

disqualify VERB (**disqualified**, **disqualifying**) cause or judge to be ineligible or unsuitable.

disqualification NOUN

disquiet NOUN uneasiness or anxiety.

disregard VERB pay no attention to. NOUN lack of attention.

disrepair NOUN bad condition caused by lack of repair.

disreputable ADJ not respectable.

disrepute NOUN a bad reputation.

disrespect NOUN lack of respect.

disrespectful ADJ

disrupt VERB interrupt or disturb an activity or process.

disruption NOUN

disruptive ADJ

dissatisfied ADJ not pleased or contented.

dissatisfaction NOUN

dissect VERB cut apart so as to examine the internal structure.

dissection NOUN

dissemble VERB hide your feelings or motives.

disseminate VERB spread widely.

dissemination NOUN

dissension NOUN disagreement that gives rise to strife.

dissent VERB disagree with a widely or officially held

view. NOUN disagreement.
dissenter NOUN

dissertation NOUN a
lengthy essay.

disservice NOUN an
unhelpful or harmful
action.

dissident NOUN a person
who opposes official
policy.

dissimilar ADJ unlike.

dissimulate VERB conceal
or disguise.

dissipate VERB 1 dispel;
fritter away. 2 (**dissipated**)
living a dissolute life.
dissipation NOUN

dissociate VERB regard as
separate; declare to be
unconnected.
dissociation NOUN

dissolute ADJ lacking
moral restraint or self-
discipline.

dissolution NOUN the
dissolving of an assembly
or partnership.

dissolve VERB (of a solid)
mix with a liquid and
form a solution; disperse
an assembly; end a
partnership or agreement.

dissuade VERB deter by
argument.

distance NOUN the length
of space or time between
two points; being far

away; a far point or part;
the full length of a race
etc. VERB cause to be
separate or dissociated.

distant ADJ far away; at a
specified distance; cool
and aloof.

distaste NOUN dislike or
disapproval.
distasteful ADJ

distemper NOUN 1 a
disease of dogs. 2 a kind of
paint for use on walls.

distend VERB swell from
internal pressure.

distil ([US] **distill**) VERB
(**distilled**, **distilling**)
vaporize and condense a
liquid so as to purify it;
make alcoholic spirits in
this way.
distillation NOUN
distiller NOUN

distillery NOUN a factory
that makes alcoholic
spirits.

distinct ADJ 1 different in
kind. 2 clearly perceptible.
distinctly ADV

distinction NOUN 1 a
contrast or difference;
difference in treatment or
attitude. 2 excellence; an
honour; a high grade in
an exam.

distinctive ADJ
characteristic and

distinguishing.
distinguish VERB
1 perceive a difference; be a differentiating characteristic of.
2 discern.
distinguishable ADJ
distinguished ADJ dignified in appearance; worthy of great respect.
distort VERB pull out of shape; misrepresent.
distortion NOUN
distract VERB draw away the attention of.
distracted ADJ unable to concentrate.
distraction NOUN
1 something that distracts; an entertainment. **2** extreme distress and agitation.
distraught ADJ very worried and upset.
distress NOUN unhappiness; pain; hardship. VERB make unhappy.
distribute VERB divide and share out; spread over an area.
distribution NOUN
distributor NOUN a firm supplying goods to retailers; a device in an engine for passing electric current to the spark plugs.

district NOUN a particular area of a town or region.
distrust NOUN lack of trust. VERB feel distrust in.
distrustful ADJ
disturb VERB **1** interfere with the arrangement of; break the rest or privacy of; **2** make anxious. **3** (**disturbed**) having emotional or mental problems.
disturbance NOUN
disuse NOUN a state of not being used.
disused ADJ
ditch NOUN a long narrow trench for drainage. VERB [inf] abandon.
dither VERB hesitate indecisively.
ditto NOUN (in lists) the same again.
ditty NOUN (PL **-ies**) a short simple song.
divan NOUN a couch without a back or arms; a bed resembling this.
dive VERB plunge head first into water; swim under water using breathing apparatus; move quickly or suddenly downwards. NOUN **1** an act of diving. **2** [inf] a disreputable nightclub or bar.
diver NOUN a person who

dives or swims under water; a diving bird.

diverge VERB separate and go in different directions; be different from.
divergence NOUN
divergent ADJ

diverse ADJ of differing kinds.

diversify VERB (**diversified**, **diversifying**) make or become more varied; (of a company) enlarge its range of products.
diversification NOUN

diversion NOUN **1** diverting; an alternative route avoiding a closed road. **2** a recreation or entertainment.

diversity NOUN (PL **-ies**) being varied; a wide range.

divert VERB **1** turn from a course or route. **2** entertain; distract.

divide VERB **1** separate into parts or from something else. **2** cause to disagree. **3** find how many times one number contains another; be divisible by a number without remainder. NOUN a wide difference between two groups.

dividend NOUN a sum paid to a company's shareholders out of its profits; a benefit from an action.

divider NOUN **1** a thing that divides. **2** (**dividers**) measuring compasses.

divine ADJ **1** of, from, or like God or a god. **2** [inf] wonderful. VERB discover by intuition or magic.
divination NOUN
diviner NOUN

divinity NOUN (PL **-ies**) being divine; a god.

divisible ADJ able to be divided.

division NOUN dividing or being divided; a dividing line or partition; one of the parts into which something is divided.

divisive ADJ tending to cause disagreement.

divorce NOUN the legal ending of a marriage. VERB legally end your marriage with.

divorcee NOUN a divorced person.

divulge VERB reveal information.

DIY ABBREV do-it-yourself.

dizzy ADJ (**-ier, -iest**) feeling giddy.
dizziness NOUN

DJ ABBREV disc jockey.

DNA ABBREV deoxyribonucleic acid, a substance storing genetic information.

do VERB (**does**, **did**, **done**, **doing**) 1 carry out or complete; work at; deal with; provide or make. 2 act or proceed; fare. 3 be suitable or acceptable. AUXILIARY VERB used to form the present or past tense, in questions, for emphasis, or to avoid repeating a verb just used. NOUN (PL **dos** or **do's**) [inf] a party.

docile ADJ submissive or easily managed. **docility** NOUN

dock NOUN 1 an enclosed body of water where ships are loaded, unloaded, or repaired. 2 an enclosure for the prisoner in a criminal court. 3 a weed with broad leaves. VERB 1 (of a ship) come into a dock. 2 (of a spacecraft) join with another craft in space. 3 deduct; cut short.

docker NOUN a labourer who loads and unloads ships in a dockyard.

docket NOUN a document listing goods delivered.

dockyard NOUN the area and buildings round a shipping dock.

doctor NOUN 1 a person qualified to give medical treatment. 2 a person holding a doctorate. VERB 1 tamper with or falsify; adulterate. 2 [inf] castrate or spay an animal.

doctorate NOUN the highest degree at a university. **doctoral** ADJ

doctrinaire ADJ applying theories or principles rigidly.

doctrine NOUN a principle or the beliefs of a religious, political, or other group.

document NOUN a piece of written, printed, or electronic material giving information or evidence. VERB record in written or other form. **documentation** NOUN

documentary ADJ 1 consisting of documents. 2 giving a factual report. NOUN (PL **-ies**) a documentary film.

dodder VERB totter because of age or frailty. **doddery** ADJ

dodge VERB avoid by a quick sideways

movement; evade. NOUN an act of avoiding something.

dodgem NOUN a small electric car driven in an enclosure at a funfair with the aim of bumping into other such cars.

dodo NOUN (PL **-os**) a large extinct bird.

doe NOUN the female of the deer, hare, or rabbit.

does 3rd person singular of **do**.

doff VERB take off your hat.

dog NOUN a four-legged carnivorous wild or domesticated animal; the male of this or of the fox or wolf. VERB (**dogged, dogging**) follow persistently.

dog collar [inf] a white upright collar worn by Christian priests. **dog-eared** with page corners crumpled through use.

dogfight NOUN close combat between military aircraft.

dogfish NOUN a small shark.

dogged ADJ very persistent.

doggerel NOUN bad verse.

dogma NOUN doctrines put forward by authority to be accepted without question.

dogmatic ADJ not admitting doubt or questions.
dogmatically ADV

dogsbody NOUN (PL **-ies**) [inf] a drudge.

doily NOUN (PL **-ies**) a small ornamental lace or paper mat.

doldrums PLURAL NOUN a state of inactivity or depression.

dole NOUN [inf] unemployment benefit. VERB (**dole out**) distribute.

doleful ADJ mournful.
dolefully ADV

doll NOUN a small model of a human figure, used as a child's toy.

dollar NOUN the unit of money in the USA and various other countries.

dollop NOUN [inf] a mass of a soft substance.

dolour ([US] **dolor**) NOUN [literary] sorrow.
dolorous ADJ

dolphin NOUN a small whale with a beak-like snout.

dolt NOUN a stupid person.

domain NOUN an area under a person's control; a field of activity.

dome NOUN a rounded roof with a circular base; something shaped like this.

domestic ADJ of home or household; of your own country; domesticated. **domestically** ADV

domesticate VERB train an animal to live with humans. **domestication** NOUN

domesticity NOUN family life.

domicile NOUN a place of residence.

dominant ADJ most important or powerful. **dominance** NOUN

dominate VERB have a commanding influence over; be most influential or conspicuous in; tower over. **domination** NOUN

domineer VERB control people arrogantly.

dominion NOUN supreme power or control; a ruler's territory.

domino NOUN (PL **-oes**) a small oblong piece marked with 0–6 pips, used in the game of **dominoes**, where the aim is to match pieces with the same value.

don VERB (**donned, donning**) put on. NOUN a university teacher.

donate VERB give as a donation.

donation NOUN a gift (especially of money) to a fund or institution.

done past participle of **do**. ADJ [inf] socially acceptable.

donkey NOUN (PL **-eys**) a long-eared animal of the horse family.

donor NOUN a person who gives or donates something.

donut US spelling of **doughnut**.

doodle VERB scribble idly. NOUN a drawing made in this way.

doom NOUN a grim fate; death or ruin. VERB destine to a grim fate.

doomsday NOUN the day of the Last Judgement.

door NOUN a hinged, sliding, or revolving barrier at the entrance to a room, building, etc.; a doorway.

doorway NOUN an entrance to a room, building, etc.

dope [inf] NOUN **1** an illegal drug. **2** a stupid person. VERB drug.

dopey (or **dopy**) ADJ [inf]

half asleep; stupid.

dormant ADJ temporarily inactive; in a deep sleep.

dormitory NOUN (PL **-ies**) a room with several beds in a school, hostel, etc.

dormouse NOUN (PL **-mice**) a mouse-like animal that hibernates.

dorsal ADJ of or on the back.

dosage NOUN the size of a dose.

dose NOUN an amount of medicine to be taken at one time; an amount of radiation received. VERB give a dose of medicine to.

dossier NOUN a set of documents about a person or event.

dot NOUN a small round mark. VERB (**dotted, dotting**) mark with dots; scatter here and there.

dotage NOUN senility.

dote VERB (**dote on**) be extremely and uncritically fond of. **doting** ADJ

double ADJ consisting of two equal parts; twice the usual size; occurring twice; for two people. ADV twice as much. NOUN **1** a double quantity or thing.

2 a person very like another. VERB **1** make or become twice as much or as many; fold in two; act two parts; have two uses. **2** go back in the direction you came from.

double bass the largest and lowest-pitched instrument of the violin family. **double-breasted** (of a coat) with fronts overlapping. **double chin** a chin with a roll of fat below. **double cream** thick cream with a high fat content. **double-cross** cheat or deceive. **double-decker** a bus with two decks. **double glazing** two sheets of glass in a window, designed to reduce heat loss. **double take** a delayed reaction just after your first reaction.

doubly ADV

double entendre NOUN a phrase with two meanings, one of which is usually indecent.

doublet NOUN [historical] a man's short close-fitting jacket.

doubt NOUN a feeling of uncertainty or disbelief. VERB feel uncertain about;

question whether something is true.

doubtful ADJ feeling doubt; not known for certain; unlikely. **doubtfully** ADV

doubtless ADJ certainly.

dough NOUN **1** a thick mixture of flour and liquid, for baking. **2** [inf] money.

doughnut ([US] **donut**) NOUN a small cake of fried sweetened dough.

doughty ADJ brave and determined.

dour ADJ stern or gloomy-looking.

douse VERB **1** drench with a liquid. **2** extinguish a light.

dove NOUN **1** a bird with a thick body and short legs. **2** a person favouring negotiation rather than violence.

dovetail NOUN a wedge-shaped joint interlocking two pieces of wood. VERB fit together easily and neatly.

dowager NOUN a woman holding a title or property from her dead husband.

dowdy ADJ (**-ier, -iest**) not smart or fashionable.

dowel NOUN a headless wooden or metal pin holding pieces of wood or stone together.

down¹ ADV **1** to, in, or at a lower place or level. **2** to a smaller amount or size. **3** from an earlier to a later point. **4** in or into a worse or weaker position. PREP from a higher to a lower point of; at or to a point further along. ADJ **1** directed or moving downwards. **2** depressed. **3** (of a computer system) out of action. VERB [inf] **1** knock down. **2** swallow.

down and out destitute.

down payment an initial payment when buying something on credit.

down-to-earth sensible and practical. **down under** Australia and New Zealand. **downward** ADJ & ADV **downwards** ADV

down² NOUN **1** very fine soft furry feathers or short hairs. **2** (**downs**) chalk uplands. **downy** ADJ

downbeat ADJ gloomy.

downcast ADJ dejected; (of eyes) looking downwards.

downfall NOUN a loss of

prosperity or power.

downgrade VERB reduce to a lower grade.

downhearted ADJ discouraged and depressed.

downhill ADJ & ADV going downwards; becoming worse.

download VERB transfer data from one computer to another using a direct link.

downmarket ADJ & ADV of or towards lower prices and quality.

downpour NOUN a heavy fall of rain.

downright ADJ & ADV completely; utter.

downside NOUN a negative aspect.

downstairs ADV & ADJ to or on a lower floor.

downstream ADJ & ADV in the direction in which a stream or river flows.

downtown ADJ [US] of the central area of a city.

downtrodden ADJ oppressed.

dowry NOUN (PL **-ies**) property or money brought by a bride to her husband on marriage.

dowse VERB search for underground water or minerals by using a stick which dips when these are present.

doyen NOUN (FEMININE **doyenne**) the most important or highly regarded person in a particular field.

doze VERB sleep lightly. NOUN a short light sleep. **dozy** ADJ

dozen NOUN a set of twelve; (**dozens**) very many.

DPhil ABBREV Doctor of Philosophy.

Dr ABBREV Doctor.

drab ADJ (**drabber**, **drabbest**) dull in colour.

draconian ADJ harsh or strict.

draft NOUN **1** a preliminary written version. **2** a written order to a bank to pay money. **3** [US] military conscription. **4** US spelling of **draught**. VERB **1** prepare a draft of. **2** [US] conscript for military service.

draftsman US spelling of **draughtsman**.

drafty US spelling of **draughty**.

drag VERB (**dragged**, **dragging**) **1** pull or bring with effort; (of time) pass slowly. **2** trail on the ground. **3** search water with nets or hooks. NOUN **1** something that impedes progress; [inf] something irritating or tedious. **2** [inf] women's clothes worn by men. **3** [inf] an act of inhaling on a cigarette.

dragon NOUN a mythical reptile able to breathe out fire.

dragonfly NOUN (PL **-ies**) a long-bodied insect with gauzy wings.

dragoon NOUN a cavalryman or (formerly) mounted infantryman. VERB force into action.

drain VERB **1** draw liquid out of; become dry; draw off liquid by channels or pipes; flow away. **2** gradually deprive of strength or resources. **3** drink all the contents of. NOUN **1** a channel or pipe carrying off water or liquid waste. **2** something that deprives you of energy or resources. **drainage** NOUN

drake NOUN a male duck.

dram NOUN a small drink of spirits.

drama NOUN a play; plays and acting; an exciting series of events.

dramatic ADJ **1** of plays and acting. **2** exciting, striking, or impressive. **dramatically** ADV

dramatist NOUN a writer of plays.

dramatize (or **-ise**) VERB present in dramatic form. **dramatization** NOUN

drank past of **drink**.

drape VERB spread covers loosely over something.

drastic ADJ having an extreme or violent effect.

draught ([US] **draft**) NOUN **1** a current of air in a confined space. **2** an amount of liquid swallowed at one time. **3** (**draughts**) a game played with 24 round pieces on a chessboard. **4** the depth of water needed to float a ship. ADJ used for pulling loads.

draughtsman ([US] **draftsman**) NOUN **1** a person who draws plans or diagrams. **2** a piece used in draughts.

draughty ([US] **drafty**) ADJ (**-ier, -iest**) letting in cold currents of air.

draw VERB (**drew, drawn, drawing**) **1** create a picture or diagram by marking a surface. **2** pull; take out or from a store; take in breath. **3** attract. **4** finish a contest with scores equal. **5** pick lots to decide an outcome. **6** make your way. NOUN **1** a lottery; an act of drawing lots. **2** a contest with equal closing scores. **3** something that attracts.

draw up come to a halt; prepare a contract etc.

drawback NOUN a disadvantage.

drawbridge NOUN a bridge over a moat, hinged for raising.

drawer NOUN **1** a lidless compartment sliding horizontally into and out of a piece of furniture. **2** a person who draws. **3** (**drawers**) knickers or underpants.

drawing NOUN a picture made with a pencil or pen.

drawing pin a pin for fastening paper to a surface. **drawing room** a sitting room.

drawl VERB speak slowly with prolonged vowel sounds. NOUN a drawling manner of speaking.

drawn past participle of **draw**. ADJ looking strained from tiredness or worry.

dread NOUN great fear. VERB fear greatly.

dreadful ADJ very bad or unpleasant.
dreadfully ADV

dream NOUN a series of pictures or events in a sleeping person's mind; something greatly desired; something unreal or impossible. VERB (**dreamed** or **dreamt**, **dreaming**) **1** have a dream while asleep; have an ambition or desire. **2** (**dream up**) invent or imagine something foolish or improbable.

dreamy ADJ absorbed in a daydream.

dreary ADJ (**-ier, -iest**) depressingly dull; gloomy.
drearily ADV

dredge VERB **1** clear an area of water of mud or silt. **2** sprinkle food with flour or sugar.
dredger NOUN

dregs PLURAL NOUN sediment at the bottom of a drink; the least useful, attractive, or valuable part.

drench VERB wet all through.

dress NOUN **1** a woman's or girl's garment with a

bodice and skirt.
2 clothing. VERB 1 put
clothes on. 2 put a
dressing on. 3 decorate.
4 (**dress up**) put on smart
or formal clothes.
dress rehearsal a final
rehearsal, in full costume,
of a dramatic production.
dressage NOUN exercises
to show off a horse's
obedience and
deportment.
dresser NOUN a sideboard
with shelves above it.
dressing NOUN 1 a sauce for
salad. 2 a protective
covering for a wound.
dressing down [inf] a
scolding. **dressing gown**
a loose robe worn when
you are not fully dressed.
dressing table a table
used while dressing or
applying make-up.
dressy ADJ (**-ier, -iest**) (of
clothes) smart or formal.
drew past of **draw**.
dribble VERB 1 flow in
drops; have saliva flowing
from the mouth. 2 (in
football etc.) move the
ball forward with slight
touches. NOUN a thin
stream of liquid; saliva
running from the mouth.
dried ADJ past & past

participle of **dry**.
drier NOUN see **dryer**.
drift VERB be carried by a
current of water or air; go
casually or aimlessly; pass
gradually into a particular
state. NOUN 1 a drifting
movement. 2 a mass of
snow piled up by the
wind. 3 the general
meaning of a speech etc.
drifter NOUN an aimless
person.
driftwood NOUN wood
floating on the sea or
washed ashore.
drill NOUN 1 a tool or
machine for boring holes
or sinking wells.
2 training; repeated
exercises. VERB 1 bore a
hole with a drill 2 train or
be trained.
drily (or **dryly**) ADV in an
ironically humorous way.
drink VERB (**drank, drunk,
drinking**) swallow liquid;
consume alcohol,
especially to excess;
express good wishes in a
toast. NOUN a liquid for
drinking; alcohol.
drinker NOUN
drink-driving NOUN the
crime of driving after
drinking more than the
legal limit of alcohol.

drip VERB (**dripped, dripping**) 1 fall or let fall in drops. 2 (**drip with**) be conspicuously full of or covered in. NOUN 1 a regular fall of drops of liquid; the sound of this; (also **drip-feed**) an apparatus for administering a liquid at a very slow rate into the body, especially intravenously. 2 [inf] an ineffectual person.

dripping NOUN fat melted from roast meat.

drive VERB (**drove, driven, driving**) 1 operate a motor vehicle; travel or convey in a private vehicle. 2 propel or carry forcefully; provide the energy to work a machine; urge onwards; cause to work too hard. NOUN 1 a journey in a private vehicle. 2 an innate urge or motive; determination; an organized effort to achieve something. 3 a short road leading to a house.
driver NOUN

drivel NOUN nonsense.

drizzle NOUN very fine drops of rain. VERB rain very lightly.

droll ADJ strange and amusing.

dromedary NOUN a camel with one hump.

drone NOUN 1 a deep humming sound. 2 a male bee. VERB make a humming sound; speak monotonously.

drool VERB 1 slaver. 2 show great pleasure or desire.

droop VERB bend or hang down limply.
droopy ADJ

drop NOUN 1 a small rounded mass of liquid; a very small amount of liquid. 2 an abrupt fall or slope. VERB (**dropped, dropping**) 1 fall or let fall; make or become lower or less. 2 give up a habit. 3 set down a passenger or load. 4 (**drop off**) fall asleep. 5 (**drop out**) cease to participate.

droplet NOUN small drop of liquid.

dropout NOUN a person who abandons a course of study or rejects conventional society.

droppings PLURAL NOUN animal dung.

dross NOUN rubbish.

drought NOUN a long spell of dry weather; a shortage

of water.

drove[1] past of **drive**.

drove[2] NOUN a flock or herd; a crowd.

drown VERB kill or be killed by immersion in water; (of a sound) be louder than another sound and make it inaudible.

drowsy ADJ (**-ier, -iest**) sleepy.
drowsily ADV
drowsiness NOUN

drub VERB (**drubbed, drubbing**) thrash.

drudge NOUN a person who does laborious or menial work.
drudgery NOUN

drug NOUN a substance used in medicine or as a stimulant or narcotic. VERB (**drugged, drugging**) treat with drugs; add a drug to.

drugstore NOUN [US] a chemist's shop also selling toiletries etc.

Druid NOUN an ancient Celtic priest.

drum NOUN a round frame with a membrane stretched across, used as a percussion instrument; a cylindrical object. VERB (**drummed, drumming**) play a drum; make a continuous rhythmic noise; tap your fingers repeatedly on a surface.
drummer NOUN

drumstick NOUN **1** a stick for beating a drum. **2** the lower part of a cooked chicken's leg.

drunk past participle of **drink**. ADJ unable to think or speak clearly from drinking too much alcohol. NOUN a person who is drunk.
drunkard NOUN
drunken ADJ
drunkenness NOUN

dry ADJ (**-ier, -iest**) **1** without moisture or liquid. **2** uninteresting. **3** (of humour) subtle and understated. **4** (of wine) not sweet. VERB (**dries, dried, drying**) **1** make or become dry; preserve food by removing its moisture. **2** (**dry up**) dry washed dishes; decrease and stop.
dry-clean clean with chemicals without using water. **dry rot** a fungus that causes wood to decay. **dry run** [inf] a rehearsal.

dryer (or **drier**) NOUN a device for drying things.

dryly see **drily**.

dual ADJ composed of two parts; double.

dual carriageway a road with a central strip separating traffic travelling in opposite directions.

dub VERB (**dubbed, dubbing**) 1 give a film a soundtrack in a language other than the original. 2 give a nickname to. 3 confer a knighthood on.

dubious ADJ 1 hesitant; uncertain. 2 suspect or questionable.

duchess NOUN a woman with the rank of duke; a duke's wife or widow.

duchy NOUN (PL **-ies**) the territory of a duke.

duck NOUN 1 a waterbird with a broad blunt bill and webbed feet; the female of this. 2 a batsman's score of 0. 3 a quick dip or lowering of the head. VERB 1 push a person or dip your head under water. 2 lower your head or body to avoid a blow or so as not to be seen; [inf] evade a duty.

duckling NOUN a young duck.

duct NOUN a channel or tube conveying liquid or air; a tube in the body through which fluid passes.

ductile ADJ (of metal) able to be drawn into fine strands.

dud [inf] NOUN something that fails to work.

dudgeon NOUN deep resentment.

due ADJ 1 expected at a particular time. 2 owing. 3 owed or deserving. NOUN 1 what is owed to or deserved by someone. 2 (**dues**) fees. ADV directly: *due north.*

due to because of.

duel NOUN a fight or contest between two people or sides. VERB (**duelled, duelling**; [US] **dueled, dueling**) fight a duel.

duet NOUN a musical composition for two performers.

duffel coat NOUN a heavy woollen coat with a hood.

duffer NOUN [inf] an inefficient or stupid person.

dug[1] past & past participle of **dig**.

dug[2] NOUN an udder or teat.

dugout NOUN 1 an underground shelter. 2 a canoe made from a hollowed tree trunk.

duke NOUN a nobleman of the highest hereditary rank; a ruler of certain small states.
dukedom NOUN

dulcet ADJ sounding sweet.

dulcimer NOUN a musical instrument with strings struck with hand-held hammers.

dull ADJ **1** not interesting or exciting. **2** not bright, resonant, or sharp. **3** stupid. VERB make or become less intense, sharp, or bright.
dully ADV

dullard NOUN a stupid person.

duly ADV as is required or appropriate; as might be expected.

dumb ADJ **1** unable or unwilling to speak; silent. **2** [inf] stupid. VERB (**dumb down**) [inf] make less intellectually challenging.
dumb-bell a short bar with weighted ends, lifted to exercise muscles.

dumbfound VERB astonish.

dummy NOUN (PL **-ies**) **1** a model or replica of a human being; a model of something used as a

substitute. **2** a rubber teat for a baby to suck.
dummy run a trial or rehearsal.

dump VERB deposit as rubbish; put down carelessly; [inf] end a relationship with. NOUN a site for depositing rubbish or waste; a temporary store; [inf] a dull or unpleasant place.

dumpling NOUN a ball of dough cooked in stew or with fruit inside.

dun ADJ & NOUN greyish brown.

dunce NOUN a person slow at learning.

dune NOUN a mound of drifted sand.

dung NOUN animal excrement.

dungarees PLURAL NOUN overalls of coarse cotton cloth.

dungeon NOUN a strong underground cell for prisoners.

dunk VERB dip food into soup or a drink before eating it.

duo NOUN (PL **-os**) a pair of performers; a duet.

duodenum NOUN the part of the intestine next to the stomach.

duodenal ADJ

dupe VERB deceive or trick. NOUN a duped person.

duplicate NOUN an exact copy. ADJ exactly like something specified; having two identical parts. VERB make or be an exact copy of; do something again unnecessarily. **duplication** NOUN

duplicity NOUN deceitfulness.

durable ADJ hard-wearing. PLURAL NOUN (**durables**) goods that can be kept without immediate consumption or replacement. **durability** NOUN

duration NOUN the time during which a thing continues.

duress NOUN the use of force or threats.

during PREP throughout; at a point in the duration of.

dusk NOUN a darker stage of twilight.

dusky ADJ darkish in colour.

dust NOUN fine particles of earth or other matter. VERB **1** wipe dust from the surface of. **2** cover lightly with a powdered substance. **dusty** ADJ

dustbin NOUN a bin for household rubbish.

duster NOUN a cloth for wiping dust from things.

dustman NOUN a man employed to empty dustbins.

dustpan NOUN a container into which dust is brushed from a floor.

Dutch ADJ of the Netherlands. **Dutch courage** false courage obtained by drinking alcohol. **go Dutch** share expenses on an outing.

dutiful ADJ obedient and conscientious. **dutifully** ADV

duty NOUN (PL **-ies**) **1** a moral or legal obligation; a task that you are required to perform. **2** a tax on imports etc.

duvet NOUN a thick soft bed quilt.

DVD ABBREV digital versatile disc.

dwarf NOUN (PL **dwarfs** or **dwarves**) a mythical human-like being of small size and with magic powers; a person or thing much below the usual size. VERB cause to seem small by comparison.

dwell VERB (**dwelt**, **dwelling**) 1 live as an inhabitant. 2 (**dwell on**) write, speak, or think lengthily about.

dwelling NOUN a house etc. to live in.

dwindle VERB gradually become less or smaller.

dye NOUN a substance used to colour something. VERB (**dyed**, **dyeing**) make something a particular colour with dye.

dying present participle of **die**.

dyke (or **dike**) NOUN a wall or embankment to prevent flooding; a drainage ditch.

dynamic ADJ characterized by constant change or activity; energetic or forceful; [Physics] of force producing motion. **dynamically** ADV

dynamics NOUN 1 the study of the forces involved in movement; forces stimulating growth and change. 2 the variations in volume in a musical work.

dynamism NOUN the quality of being dynamic.

dynamite NOUN a powerful explosive. VERB blow up with dynamite.

dynamo NOUN (PL **-os**) a small generator producing electric current.

dynasty NOUN (PL **-ies**) a line of hereditary rulers.

dysentery NOUN a disease causing severe diarrhoea.

dysfunctional ADJ not operating properly; unable to deal with normal social relations.

dyslexia NOUN a condition causing difficulty in reading and spelling. **dyslexic** ADJ & NOUN

dyspepsia NOUN indigestion. **dyspeptic** ADJ & NOUN

Ee

E ABBREV **1** east or eastern.
2 [inf] the drug Ecstasy.

each ADJ & PRON every one of two or more, taken separately. ADV to or for each one individually.

eager ADJ full of desire, interest, or enthusiasm.

eagle NOUN a large, keen-sighted bird of prey.

ear NOUN **1** the organ of hearing; the ability to distinguish sounds accurately. **2** the seed-bearing part of corn.

eardrum NOUN a membrane inside the ear, vibrating when sound waves strike it.

earl NOUN a British nobleman ranking between marquess and viscount.

early ADJ (**-ier, -iest**) & ADV before the usual or expected time; near the beginning of a series, period, etc.

earmark VERB designate for a particular purpose.

earn VERB get or deserve for work or merit; (of invested money) gain as interest.

earnest ADJ showing serious feeling or intention.

earphone PLURAL NOUN device worn on the ears to listen to radio, recorded sound, etc.

earring NOUN a piece of jewellery worn on the ear.

earshot NOUN the distance over which something can be heard.

earth NOUN **1** (also **Earth**) the planet we live on; its surface; soil. **2** a connection of an electrical circuit to ground. VERB connect an electrical circuit to ground.

earthenware NOUN pottery made of coarse baked clay.

earthly ADJ **1** of the earth or human life. **2** remotely possible: *no earthly reason.*

earthquake NOUN a violent movement of part of the earth's crust.

earthworm NOUN a worm

living in the soil.

earthy ADJ (**-ier, -iest**) 1 (of humour etc.) direct and uninhibited. 2 like soil.

ease NOUN lack of difficulty; freedom from anxiety or pain. VERB 1 make or become less severe or intense. 2 move gradually and carefully; make something happen easily.

easel NOUN a frame to support a painting, blackboard, etc.

east NOUN the direction in which the sun rises; the eastern part of a place. ADJ & ADV towards or facing the east; (of wind) from the east.
eastern ADJ
eastward ADJ

Easter NOUN the Christian festival commemorating Jesus's resurrection.

easterly ADJ towards the east; blowing from the east.

easy ADJ (**-ier, -iest**) achieved without great effort; free from worries or problems; not anxious or awkward.
easy-going relaxed in manner.
easily ADV

eat VERB (**ate, eaten, eating**) chew and swallow food; use up resources; erode or destroy.

eau de Cologne NOUN a delicate perfume.

eaves PLURAL NOUN the overhanging edge of a roof.

eavesdrop VERB (**eavesdropped, eavesdropping**) listen secretly to a private conversation.
eavesdropper NOUN

ebb NOUN 1 the movement of the tide out to sea. 2 a decline. VERB 1 flow away. 2 decline.

ebony NOUN the hard black wood of a tropical tree. ADJ black as ebony.

ebullient ADJ full of high spirits.
ebullience NOUN

EC ABBREV European Community.

eccentric ADJ unconventional and strange. NOUN an eccentric person.
eccentrically ADV
eccentricity NOUN

ecclesiastical ADJ of the Christian Church or clergy.

echo NOUN (PL **-oes**) a

repetition of sound caused by reflection of sound waves. VERB (**echoed**, **echoing**) resound, be repeated by echo; repeat someone's words.

éclair NOUN a finger-shaped pastry cake with cream filling.

eclectic ADJ taking ideas from a wide range or sources.

eclipse NOUN the blocking of light from one planet etc. by another; a loss of influence or prominence. VERB cause an eclipse of; outshine.

eco-friendly ADJ not harmful to the environment.

ecology NOUN (the study of) relationships of living things to each other and to their environment. **ecological** ADJ **ecologist** NOUN

economic ADJ **1** of economics or the economy. **2** profitable.

economical ADJ thrifty or avoiding waste. **economically** ADV

economics NOUN the science of the production and use of goods or services; (as PL) the financial aspects of a region or group.

economist NOUN

economize (or **-ise**) VERB reduce your expenses.

economy NOUN (PL **-ies**) **1** a country's system of using its resources to produce wealth. **2** being economical.

ecosystem NOUN a system of interacting organisms and their environment.

ecstasy NOUN (PL **-ies**) **1** intense delight. **2** (**Ecstasy**) a hallucinogenic drug. **ecstatic** ADJ **ecstatically** ADV

eczema NOUN a skin disease causing scaly itching patches.

eddy NOUN (PL **-ies**) a circular movement in water or air etc. VERB swirl in eddies.

edge NOUN **1** the outer limit of an area or object; the area next to a steep drop. **2** the sharpened side of a blade; the narrow side of a thin, flat object. **3** a position of advantage. VERB **1** provide with a border. **2** move slowly and carefully.

edgy ADJ (**-ier, -iest**) tense and irritable.

edible ADJ suitable for eating.

edict NOUN an order issued by someone in authority.

edifice NOUN a large, imposing building.

edify VERB (**edified, edifying**) improve a person's mind or character by teaching.
edification NOUN

edit VERB (**edited, editing**) prepare written material for publication; choose and arrange material for a film etc.

edition NOUN a version of a published text; all the copies of a text etc. issued at one time; one instance of a regular broadcast programme.

editor NOUN a person responsible for the contents of a newspaper etc. or a section of this; a person who edits.

editorial ADJ of an editor. NOUN a newspaper article giving the editor's comments.

educate VERB train the mind, character, and abilities of; teach.
education NOUN

educational ADJ

eel NOUN a snake-like fish.

eerie ADJ (**-ier, -iest**) mysterious and frightening.
eerily ADV

efface VERB rub out or obliterate; make inconspicuous.

effect NOUN **1** a change produced by an action or cause; an impression; (**effects**) lighting, sound, etc. in a film, broadcast, etc. **2** a state of being operative. **3** (**effects**) property. VERB bring about or cause.

effective ADJ **1** achieving the intended result; operative. **2** fulfilling a function in fact though not officially.

effectual ADJ effective.

effeminate ADJ (of a man) feminine in appearance or manner.
effeminacy NOUN

effervescent ADJ fizzy; vivacious or high-spirited.
effervesce VERB
effervescence NOUN

efficacious ADJ producing the desired result.
efficacy NOUN

efficient ADJ working well

with no waste of money or effort.

efficiency NOUN

effigy NOUN (PL **-ies**) a model of a person.

effluent NOUN liquid sewage.

effort NOUN a vigorous attempt; strenuous exertion.

effrontery NOUN bold insolence.

effusive ADJ expressing emotion in an unrestrained way.

e.g. ABBREV (Latin *exempli gratia*) for example.

egalitarian ADJ holding the principle of equal rights for all.

egg NOUN an oval or round object laid by a female bird, reptile, etc., containing an embryo; an ovum; a hen's egg as food. VERB (**egg on**) urge or encourage.

ego NOUN self; self-esteem.

egocentric ADJ self-centred.

egotism NOUN the quality of being too conceited or self-absorbed.

egotist NOUN

egotistic ADJ

egotistical ADJ

egregious ADJ

outstandingly bad.

eider NOUN a large northern duck.

eiderdown NOUN a quilt stuffed with soft material.

eight ADJ & NOUN one more than seven (8, VIII).

eighth ADJ & NOUN

eighteen ADJ & NOUN one more than seventeen (18, XVIII).

eighteenth ADJ & NOUN

eighty ADJ & NOUN ten times eight (80, LXXX).

eightieth ADJ & NOUN

either ADJ & PRON one or other of two; each of two. ADV & CONJ **1** as the first alternative. **2** likewise (used with negatives): *I don't like him and she doesn't either.*

ejaculate VERB **1** eject semen. **2** say suddenly.

ejaculation NOUN

eject VERB throw or force out.

ejection NOUN

ejector NOUN

eke VERB (**eke out**) make a supply etc. last longer by careful use; make a living laboriously.

elaborate ADJ intricate or complicated. VERB develop in detail; add detail to.

elaboration NOUN

elan NOUN energy and flair.

elapse VERB (of time) pass.

elastic ADJ going back to its original length or shape after being stretched or squeezed. NOUN cord or material made elastic by interweaving strands of rubber etc.
elasticity NOUN

elated ADJ very happy and excited.
elation NOUN

elbow NOUN the joint between the forearm and upper arm. VERB strike or push with your elbow.
elbow room enough space to move or work in.

elder ADJ older. NOUN 1 an older person. 2 a tree with small dark berries.

elderly ADJ old.

eldest ADJ first-born; oldest.

elect VERB choose by vote; decide on a course of action. ADJ chosen; elected but not yet in office.

election NOUN an occasion when representatives, office-holders, etc. are chosen by vote; electing or being elected.

electioneer VERB take part in an election campaign.

elective ADJ 1 using or chosen by election. 2 optional.

elector NOUN a person entitled to vote in an election.
electoral ADJ

electorate NOUN the people entitled to vote in an election.

electric ADJ of, producing, or worked by electricity. NOUN (**electrics**) electrical fittings.

electrical ADJ of electricity.
electrically ADV

electrician NOUN a person whose job is to deal with electrical equipment.

electricity NOUN a form of energy occurring in certain particles; a supply of electric current.

electrify VERB (**electrified**, **electrifying**) charge with electricity; convert to the use of electric power.
electrification NOUN

electrocute VERB kill by electric shock.
electrocution NOUN

electrode NOUN a solid conductor through which electricity enters or leaves a vacuum tube etc.

electron NOUN a subatomic particle with a negative electric charge.

electronic ADJ having many small components, e.g. microchips, that control an electric current; concerned with electronic equipment; carried out using a computer.
electronically ADV

electronics PLURAL NOUN the study of the behaviour and movement of electrons; circuits or devices using transistors, microchips, etc.

elegant ADJ graceful and stylish.
elegance NOUN

elegy NOUN (PL **-ies**) a sorrowful poem.
elegiac ADJ

element NOUN **1** a basic part of something; a small amount. **2** a substance that cannot be broken down into other substances; earth, air, fire, and water, formerly thought to make up all matter. **3** (**the elements**) weather. **4** a wire that gives out heat in an electrical appliance.
in your element in a situation or activity that suits you perfectly.
elemental ADJ

elementary ADJ dealing with the simplest facts of a subject.

elephant NOUN a very large animal with a trunk and ivory tusks.

elevate VERB raise to a higher position or level.

elevation NOUN raising or being raised; altitude; a hill.

elevator NOUN [US] a lift.

eleven ADJ & NOUN one more than ten (11, XI).
eleventh ADJ & NOUN

elf NOUN (PL **elves**) an imaginary small being with magic powers.

elicit VERB draw out a response.

eligible ADJ **1** qualified or having the right to something. **2** desirable as a marriage partner.
eligibility NOUN

eliminate VERB get rid of; exclude.
elimination NOUN

elite NOUN a group regarded as superior and favoured.

elitism NOUN favouring of or dominance by a selected group.
elitist NOUN & ADJ

elixir NOUN a liquid used for medicinal or magical purposes.

elk NOUN a large deer.

ellipse NOUN a regular oval shape.
 elliptical ADJ

elm NOUN a tree with rough serrated leaves.

elocution NOUN the art of clear and expressive speech.

elongate VERB lengthen.

elope VERB run away secretly to get married.
 elopement NOUN

eloquence NOUN fluent and persuasive use of language.
 eloquent ADJ

else ADV **1** in addition. **2** instead.
 or else otherwise.

elsewhere ADV in another place.

elucidate VERB explain.

elude VERB skilfully escape from; fail to be understood or achieved by.
 elusive ADJ

emaciated ADJ abnormally thin.
 emaciation NOUN

email NOUN electronic mail, messages sent from one computer user to another and displayed on-screen. VERB send an email to.

emanate VERB originate from a source.
 emanation NOUN

emancipate VERB liberate or free from restrictions.
 emancipation NOUN

emasculate VERB make weaker or less effective.
 emasculation NOUN

embalm VERB preserve a corpse by using spices or chemicals.

embankment NOUN a bank or stone structure to keep a river from spreading or to carry a railway.

embargo NOUN (PL **-oes**) an official ban on trade or another activity. VERB (**embargoed**, **embargoing**) impose an official ban on.

embark VERB **1** board a ship. **2** (**embark on**) begin an undertaking.
 embarkation NOUN

embarrass VERB cause to feel awkward or ashamed; cause financial difficulties to.
 embarrassment NOUN

embassy NOUN (PL **-ies**) the official residence or offices of an ambassador.

embattled ADJ beset by conflicts or problems.

embed (or **imbed**) VERB (**embedded, embedding**) fix firmly in a surrounding mass.

embellish VERB ornament; invent exciting details for a story. **embellishment** NOUN

embers PLURAL NOUN small pieces of live coal or wood in a dying fire.

embezzle VERB take company funds etc. fraudulently for your own use. **embezzlement** NOUN

embittered ADJ resentful or bitter.

emblem NOUN a symbol or design used as a badge of something.

emblematic ADJ representing a particular quality or idea.

embody VERB (**embodied, embodying**) 1 give a tangible or visible form to. 2 include. **embodiment** NOUN

embolism NOUN obstruction of a blood vessel by a clot or air bubble.

emboss VERB carve a raised design on.

embrace VERB 1 hold someone closely in your arms. 2 accept or adopt; include. NOUN an act of embracing.

embrocation NOUN liquid for rubbing on the body to relieve aches.

embroider VERB ornament with needlework; embellish a story. **embroidery** NOUN

embroil VERB involve in an argument or quarrel etc.

embryo NOUN (PL **-os**) an animal developing in a womb or egg; something in an early stage of development. **embryonic** ADJ

emend VERB alter to remove errors.

emerald NOUN a bright green precious stone; its colour.

emerge VERB come up or out into view; become known; recover from a difficult situation. **emergent** ADJ

emergency NOUN (PL **-ies**) a serious situation needing prompt attention.

emery board NOUN a strip of cardboard coated with a rough material, used for filing the nails.

emigrate VERB leave one country and go to settle in another.
emigrant NOUN
emigration NOUN

émigré NOUN an emigrant, especially a political exile.

eminence NOUN fame or superiority; an important person.

eminent ADJ famous or distinguished; outstanding.
eminently ADV

emissary NOUN (PL **-ies**) a person sent to conduct negotiations.

emit VERB (**emitted, emitting**) send out light, heat, fumes, etc.; utter.
emission NOUN

emollient ADJ softening or soothing.

emolument NOUN a fee or salary.

emotion NOUN an intense feeling; feeling contrasted with reason.

emotional ADJ of emotions; arousing or showing emotion.
emotionally ADV

emotive ADJ arousing emotion.

empathize (or **-ise**) VERB share and understand another's feelings.

empathy NOUN the ability to share and understand another's feelings.

emperor NOUN a male ruler of an empire.

emphasis NOUN (PL **-ses**) special importance or prominence; stress on a sound or word; intensity of expression.

emphasize (or **-ise**) VERB stress; treat as important; make more noticeable.

emphatic ADJ using or showing emphasis.
emphatically ADV

emphysema NOUN enlargement of the air sacs in the lungs, causing breathlessness.

empire NOUN a group of countries ruled by a supreme authority; a large organization controlled by one person or group.

empirical ADJ based on observation or experiment rather than theory.
empirically ADV

emplacement NOUN a platform for a gun or battery of guns.

employ VERB give work to; make use of.
employer NOUN

employment NOUN

employee NOUN a person employed by another in return for wages.

empower VERB authorize or enable.

empress NOUN a female ruler of an empire; the wife of an emperor.

empty ADJ (-ier, -iest) 1 containing nothing; without occupants. 2 having no meaning or value. VERB make or become empty.

emptiness NOUN

emu NOUN a large flightless Australian bird resembling an ostrich.

emulate VERB match or surpass; imitate.

emulation NOUN

emulsify VERB (emulsified, emulsifying) convert or be converted into emulsion.

emulsifier NOUN

emulsion NOUN 1 finely dispersed droplets of one liquid in another. 2 a light-sensitive coating on photographic film.

enable VERB give the means or authority to do something.

enact VERB 1 make into a law. 2 play a part or scene.

enactment NOUN

enamel NOUN 1 a glass-like coating for metal or pottery. 2 glossy paint. 3 the hard outer covering of teeth. VERB (**enamelled, enamelling**; [US] **enameled, enameling**) coat with enamel.

enamoured ([US] **enamored**) ADJ fond.

encampment NOUN a camp.

encapsulate VERB 1 symbolize or sum up. 2 summarize.

encase VERB enclose in a case.

enchant VERB delight; bewitch.

enchantment NOUN

encircle VERB surround.

enclave NOUN a small territory wholly within the boundaries of another.

enclose VERB 1 shut in on all sides. 2 include with other contents.

enclosure NOUN 1 an enclosed area; enclosing; fencing off land. 2 something placed in an envelope together with a letter.

encode VERB convert into a coded form.

encompass VERB
1 encircle. 2 include.

encore NOUN an extra performance given in response to calls from the audience.

encounter VERB meet by chance; be faced with. NOUN a chance meeting; a battle.

encourage VERB give hope, confidence, or stimulus to; urge. **encouragement** NOUN

encroach VERB intrude on someone's territory or rights. **encroachment** NOUN

encrust VERB cover with a crust of hard material. **encrustation** NOUN

encumber VERB be a burden to. **encumbrance** NOUN

encyclopedia (or **encyclopaedia**) NOUN a book containing information on many subjects. **encyclopedic** ADJ

end NOUN 1 the point after which something no longer exists or happens; a furthest or final part or point; a remnant. 2 death. 3 a goal. VERB 1 bring or come to an end. 2 (**end up**) eventually reach a particular place or state.

endanger VERB cause danger to.

endear VERB cause to be loved.

endearment NOUN words expressing love.

endeavour ([US] **endeavor**) VERB & NOUN (make) an earnest attempt.

endemic ADJ commonly found in a specified area or people.

ending NOUN the final part.

endless ADJ without end; continual; countless.

endorse VERB 1 declare approval of. 2 sign a cheque on the back. 3 record an offence on a driving licence. **endorsement** NOUN

endow VERB 1 provide with a permanent income or property. 2 (**be endowed with**) possess a desirable quality. **endowment** NOUN

endure VERB experience and survive pain or hardship; tolerate; last. **endurance** NOUN

enema NOUN liquid injected into the rectum to empty the bowels.

enemy NOUN (PL **-ies**) a person who is hostile to and seeks to harm another.

energetic ADJ possessing, showing, or requiring a great deal of energy. **energetically** ADV

energize (or **-ise**) VERB give energy to.

energy NOUN the strength and vitality needed for vigorous activity; the ability of matter or radiation to do work; power derived from physical resources to provide light, heat, etc.

enervate VERB cause to lose vitality.

enfeeble VERB make weak.

enfold VERB surround; embrace.

enforce VERB compel obedience to a law etc.; force to happen or be done. **enforceable** ADJ **enforcement** NOUN

enfranchise VERB give the right to vote.

engage VERB **1** occupy or involve; employ. **2** promise. **3** move part of a machine or engine into position. **4** (**engage in**) occupy yourself with.

engaged ADJ **1** having promised to marry a specified person. **2** occupied; in use.

engagement NOUN **1** a promise to marry a specified person. **2** an appointment. **3** engaging or being engaged. **4** a battle.

engaging ADJ charming.

engender VERB give rise to.

engine NOUN a machine with moving parts that converts energy into motion; a railway locomotive.

engineer NOUN a person skilled in engineering; a person in charge of machines and engines. VERB design and build; contrive to bring about an event.

engineering NOUN the application of science for the design and building of machines and structures.

English NOUN the language of England, used in many varieties throughout the world. ADJ of England or its language.

engrave VERB carve a text or design on a hard

surface.

engraver NOUN

engraving NOUN a print made from an engraved metal plate.

engross VERB absorb the attention of.

engulf VERB swamp.

enhance VERB increase the quality, value, or extent of.

enhancement NOUN

enigma NOUN a mysterious person or thing.

enigmatic ADJ

enjoy VERB 1 take pleasure in. 2 possess and benefit from. 3 (**enjoy yourself**) have a pleasant time.

enjoyable ADJ

enjoyment NOUN

enlarge VERB 1 make or become larger. 2 (**enlarge on**) say more about.

enlargement NOUN

enlighten VERB give greater knowledge or understanding to.

enlightenment NOUN

enlist VERB enrol for military service; secure help or support.

enliven VERB make more interesting or interested.

enmesh VERB entangle.

enmity NOUN hostility.

enormity NOUN (PL -ies)

1 great wickedness. 2 great size.

enormous ADJ very large.

enough ADJ, ADV, & NOUN as much or as many as necessary.

enquire VERB ask.

enquiry NOUN

enrage VERB make furious.

enrich VERB enhance; make more rewarding, nourishing, etc.

enrol ([US] **enroll**) VERB (**enrolled, enrolling**) admit as or become a member.

en route ADV on the way.

ensemble NOUN a thing viewed as a whole; a group of performers.

enshrine VERB preserve and respect.

ensign NOUN a military or naval flag.

enslave VERB take away the freedom of.

ensnare VERB snare; trap.

ensue VERB happen afterwards or as a result.

ensure VERB make certain.

entail VERB involve as a necessary part or consequence.

entangle VERB tangle; entwine and trap.

entanglement NOUN

entente (or **entente**

cordiale) NOUN friendly understanding between countries.

enter VERB **1** go or come in or into; become involved in; register as a competitor. **2** record information in a book, computer, etc.

enterprise NOUN a bold undertaking; a business activity.

enterprising ADJ full of initiative.

entertain VERB **1** amuse. **2** offer hospitality to. **3** consider an idea etc.
entertainer NOUN
entertainment NOUN

enthral ([US] **enthrall**) VERB (**enthralled, enthralling**) hold spellbound.

enthuse VERB fill with or show enthusiasm.

enthusiasm NOUN eager liking or interest.

enthusiast NOUN a person who is full of enthusiasm for something.
enthusiastic ADJ

entice VERB attract by offering something pleasant; tempt.

entire ADJ complete.
entirely ADV

entirety NOUN (**in its entirety**) as a whole.

entitle VERB give a person a right or claim.
entitlement NOUN

entity NOUN (PL **-ies**) a distinct and individual thing.

entomology NOUN the study of insects.
entomologist NOUN

entourage NOUN people accompanying an important person.

entrails PLURAL NOUN intestines.

entrance[1] NOUN a door or passageway into a place; coming in; the right to enter a place.

entrance[2] VERB fill with intense delight.

entreat VERB request earnestly or emotionally.
entreaty NOUN

entrench VERB establish firmly.

entrepreneur NOUN a person who is successful in setting up businesses.
entrepreneurial ADJ

entrust VERB make responsible for; place in a person's care.

entry NOUN (PL **-ies**) **1** entering; an entrance. **2** an item entered in a record. **3** an item entered in a competition.

entwine VERB twist together.

enumerate VERB mention items one by one.

enunciate VERB pronounce; state clearly. **enunciation** NOUN

envelop VERB (**enveloped, enveloping**) wrap up; surround.

envelope NOUN a paper holder for a letter, with a sealable flap.

enviable ADJ desirable enough to arouse envy.

envious ADJ full of envy.

environment NOUN 1 surroundings, setting. 2 the natural world. **environmental** ADJ

environmentalist NOUN a person seeking to protect the natural environment.

environs PLURAL NOUN the surrounding districts, especially of a town.

envisage VERB imagine; foresee.

envoy NOUN a messenger or representative.

envy NOUN discontent aroused by another's possessions or success. VERB (**envied, envying**) feel envy of.

enzyme NOUN a protein formed in living cells and assisting chemical processes.

eon US spelling of **aeon**.

epaulette NOUN an ornamental shoulder piece on a uniform.

ephemeral ADJ lasting only a short time.

epic NOUN a long poem, story, or film about heroic deeds or history. ADJ of or like an epic; on a grand or heroic scale.

epicentre ([US] **epicenter**) NOUN the point on the earth's surface above the focus of an earthquake.

epicure NOUN a person who enjoys fine food and drink. **epicurean** ADJ & NOUN

epidemic NOUN an outbreak of a disease etc. spreading through a community.

epidermis NOUN the outer layer of the skin.

epidural NOUN a spinal anaesthetic affecting the lower part of the body, especially used in childbirth.

epigram NOUN a short witty saying.

epilepsy NOUN a disorder of the nervous system,

causing fits.

epileptic ADJ & NOUN

epilogue NOUN a short concluding section of a book etc.

episcopal ADJ of or governed by bishops.

episode NOUN an event forming one part of a sequence; one part of a serial.

episodic ADJ

epistle NOUN a letter.

epitaph NOUN words inscribed on a tomb in memory of a dead person.

epithet NOUN a descriptive word.

epitome NOUN a perfect example.

epitomize (or **-ise**) VERB be a perfect example of.

epoch NOUN a long and distinct period of time.

equable ADJ **1** calm and even-tempered. **2** free from extremes.

equal ADJ **1** the same in size, amount, value, etc.; having the same rights or status; free from discrimination or disadvantage. **2** (**equal to**) able to deal with. NOUN a person or thing of the same status or quality as another. VERB (**equalled**, equalling; [US] **equaled**, equaling) be the same as in number, amount, or quality.

equality NOUN

equally ADV

equalize (or **-ise**) VERB make equal; match an opponent's score.

equanimity NOUN calmness of mind or temper.

equate VERB consider to be equal or equivalent.

equation NOUN a mathematical statement that two expressions are equal.

equator NOUN an imaginary line round the earth at an equal distance from the North and South Poles.

equatorial ADJ

equestrian ADJ of horse riding.

equilateral ADJ having all sides equal.

equilibrium NOUN (PL **-ria**) a balanced state.

equine ADJ of or like a horse.

equinox NOUN the time of year when night and day are of equal length.

equip VERB (**equipped**, **equipping**) supply with

what is needed.

equipment NOUN the items needed for a particular activity.

equitable ADJ fair and just.

equity NOUN 1 fairness or impartiality. 2 the value of the shares issued by a company.

equivalent ADJ equal in amount, value, meaning, etc. NOUN an equivalent thing.
equivalence NOUN

equivocal ADJ ambiguous.
equivocally ADV

equivocate VERB use words ambiguously.

era NOUN a period of history.

eradicate VERB wipe out.
eradication NOUN

erase VERB rub out.
eraser NOUN

ere PREP & CONJ [literary] before.

erect ADJ upright; (of the penis) enlarged and stiffened. VERB set upright; construct.
erection NOUN

ermine NOUN a stoat; its white winter fur.

erode VERB wear away gradually.
erosion NOUN

erotic ADJ of or arousing sexual desire.
erotically ADV

err VERB (**erred, erring**) make a mistake; do wrong.

errand NOUN a short journey to do a job for someone.

errant ADJ misbehaving.

erratic ADJ irregular or uneven.
erratically ADV

erratum NOUN (PL **-ata**) an error in printing or writing.

erroneous ADJ incorrect.

error NOUN a mistake; being wrong.

erstwhile ADJ former.

erudite ADJ learned.
erudition NOUN

erupt VERB (of a volcano) eject lava; burst out; express an emotion violently.
eruption NOUN

escalate VERB increase in intensity or extent.
escalation NOUN

escalator NOUN a moving staircase.

escapade NOUN a piece of reckless or mischievous conduct.

escape VERB get free; avoid danger; leak from a

container; fail to be remembered by. NOUN an act or means of escaping. **escapee** NOUN

escapism NOUN a tendency to ignore the realities of life.

escapologist NOUN an entertainer whose act involves escaping from ropes and chains.

escarpment NOUN a steep slope at the edge of a plateau etc.

eschew VERB [literary] avoid or abstain from.

escort NOUN a group of people or vehicles accompanying another as a protection or honour; a person accompanying a person of the opposite sex to a social event. VERB act as escort to.

esophagus US spelling of **oesophagus**.

esoteric ADJ intended only for a few people with special knowledge or interest.

ESP ABBREV extrasensory perception.

especial ADJ special; particular.

especially ADV **1** more than any other; particularly, individually.

2 to a great extent.

espionage NOUN spying.

esplanade NOUN a promenade.

espouse VERB support a cause.
espousal NOUN

espy VERB (**espied, espying**) catch sight of.

Esq. ABBREV Esquire, a courtesy title placed after a man's surname.

essay NOUN a short piece of writing. VERB attempt.

essence NOUN **1** the qualities or elements making something what it is. **2** a concentrated extract.

essential ADJ **1** absolutely necessary. **2** central to something's nature. NOUN **1** something absolutely necessary. **2** (**the essentials**) the basic facts.
essentially ADV

establish VERB set up; make permanent or secure; prove.

establishment NOUN **1** establishing or being established. **2** an organization; its staff. **3** (**the Establishment**) the group in society who control policy and resist change.

estate NOUN landed property; a residential or industrial district planned as a unit; property left at someone's death.

esteem VERB think highly of. NOUN respect and admiration.

esthete etc. US spelling of **aesthete** etc.

estimable ADJ worthy of esteem.

estimate VERB make an approximate judgement of something's quantity, value, etc. NOUN such a judgement.
estimation NOUN

estranged VERB no longer friendly or loving.

estrogen US spelling of **oestrogen**.

estuary NOUN (PL **-ies**) the mouth of a large river, affected by tides.

etc. ABBREV et cetera, and other similar things.

etch VERB **1** produce a picture by engraving a metal plate with acid. **2** impress deeply on the mind.
etching NOUN

eternal ADJ existing always; unchanging.
eternally ADV

eternity NOUN (PL **-ies**) unending time; [inf] a very long time.

ether NOUN **1** the upper air. **2** a liquid used as an anaesthetic and solvent.

ethereal ADJ very light and delicate.

ethic NOUN a moral principle or framework; (**ethics**) moral principles.

ethical ADJ of ethics; morally correct.
ethically ADV

ethnic ADJ of a group sharing a common origin, culture, or language.
ethnically ADV
ethnicity NOUN

ethos NOUN the characteristic spirit and beliefs of a community.

etiquette NOUN conventions of behaviour accepted as polite.

étude NOUN a short musical composition.

etymology NOUN (PL **-ies**) an account of a word's origin and development.
etymological ADJ

eucalyptus NOUN an Australian tree whose leaves yield a strong-smelling oil.

Eucharist NOUN the Christian sacrament

commemorating the Last Supper, in which bread and wine are consumed.

eugenics NOUN the science of controlling breeding to produce a population which is healthier, more intelligent, etc.

eulogy NOUN (PL **-ies**) a speech or work praising someone.
eulogize (or **-ise**) VERB

eunuch NOUN a castrated man.

euphemism NOUN a mild expression substituted for an improper or blunt one.
euphemistic ADJ

euphoria NOUN excited happiness.
euphoric ADJ

eureka EXCLAMATION a cry of joy on discovering something.

euro NOUN the single European currency unit, which replaced some national currencies in 2002.

European ADJ of Europe or its people. NOUN a European person.

euthanasia NOUN painless killing, especially of someone with a terminal illness.

evacuate VERB **1** send from a dangerous to a safer place. **2** empty.
evacuation NOUN

evacuee NOUN an evacuated person.

evade VERB escape or avoid.

evaluate VERB find out or state the value of; assess.
evaluation NOUN

evangelical ADJ **1** of the gospel. **2** of a branch of Protestantism emphasizing biblical authority. **3** zealously advocating something.

evangelist NOUN any of the authors of the four Gospels; a person who tries to convert others.
evangelism NOUN
evangelistic ADJ

evaporate VERB turn liquid into vapour; (of something abstract) disappear.
evaporation NOUN

evasion NOUN evading.

evasive ADJ intending to avoid or escape something.

eve NOUN an evening, day, or time just before a special event.

even ADJ **1** level; regular; equally balanced. **2** exactly divisible by two.

3 placid or calm. VERB make or become even. ADV used for emphasis: *even faster.*

evening NOUN the period of time at the end of the day.

event NOUN something that happens; an organized social occasion; an item in a sports programme.

eventful ADJ full of exciting events.

eventual ADJ ultimate or final.

eventuality NOUN (PL **-ies**) a possible event.

eventually ADV in the end; at last.

ever ADV **1** at any time. **2** always.

evergreen ADJ (of a plant) having green leaves throughout the year.

everlasting ADJ lasting forever or for a very long time.

evermore ADV for all the future.

every ADJ each without exception; all possible; happening at specified intervals: *every three months.*

everybody PRON every person.

everyday ADJ used or occurring on ordinary days; ordinary.

everyone PRON everybody.

everything PRON all things; all that is important.

everywhere ADV in every place.

evict VERB expel a tenant by legal process. **eviction** NOUN

evidence NOUN signs of something's truth or existence; statements made in a law court to support a case. VERB be evidence of.

evident ADJ obvious to the eye or mind.

evil ADJ morally bad; harmful; very unpleasant. NOUN wickedness; something wicked.

evoke VERB **1** cause someone to think of. **2** elicit a response. **evocation** NOUN **evocative** ADJ

evolution NOUN the process by which different kinds of animals and plants develop from earlier forms. **evolutionary** ADJ

evolve VERB develop or work out gradually.

ewe NOUN a female sheep.

ex NOUN [inf] a former husband, wife, or partner.

ex- PREFIX **1** out; away. **2** thoroughly. **3** former.

exacerbate VERB make worse.
exacerbation NOUN

exact ADJ completely accurate; giving all details. VERB insist on and obtain.

exacting ADJ requiring great effort.

exactly ADV **1** without vagueness or discrepancy. **2** expressing total agreement.

exaggerate VERB represent as greater than is the case.
exaggeration NOUN

exalt VERB regard or praise highly; raise in rank.

exaltation NOUN **1** extreme happiness. **2** praising; raising in rank.

exam NOUN an examination.

examination NOUN an inspection or investigation; a formal test of knowledge or ability.

examine VERB look at closely; test someone's knowledge or ability.
examiner NOUN

example NOUN something seen as typical of its kind or of a general rule; a person or thing worthy of imitation.

exasperate VERB annoy greatly.
exasperation NOUN

excavate VERB make a hole by digging; dig something out; reveal buried remains by digging a site.
excavation NOUN

exceed VERB be greater than; go beyond the limit of.

exceedingly ADV very.

excel VERB (**excelled, excelling**) **1** be very good at something. **2** (**excel yourself**) do better than you ever have.

excellent ADJ extremely good.
excellence NOUN

except PREP not including. VERB exclude.

excepting PREP except.

exception NOUN something that does not follow a general rule.
take exception to object to.

exceptional ADJ very unusual; outstandingly good.

exceptionally ADV

excerpt NOUN an extract from a book, film, etc.

excess NOUN too large an amount of something; the amount by which one quantity exceeds another; lack of moderation. ADJ exceeding a limit.

excessive ADJ too much.

exchange VERB give or receive in place of another thing. NOUN 1 exchanging; giving money for its equivalent in another currency; a brief conversation. 2 a place for trading a particular commodity. 3 a centre where telephone lines are connected.

exchequer NOUN a national treasury.

excise NOUN duty or tax on certain goods and licences. VERB cut out or away.
excision NOUN

excite VERB cause to feel eager and pleasantly agitated; arouse sexually; cause a feeling or reaction.
excitable ADJ
excitement NOUN

exclaim VERB cry out suddenly.

exclamation NOUN a sudden cry or remark.
exclamatory ADJ

exclude VERB keep out from a place, group, privilege, etc.; omit or ignore as irrelevant.
exclusion NOUN

exclusive ADJ 1 excluding something. 2 limited to one or a few people; catering only for the wealthy. NOUN a story published in only one newspaper.
exclusivity NOUN

excommunicate VERB officially bar from membership of the Christian Church.
excommunication NOUN

excrement NOUN faeces.

excrete VERB expel waste matter from the body.
excretion NOUN
excretory ADJ

excruciating ADJ intensely painful or unpleasant.

excursion NOUN a short journey, especially for pleasure.

excuse VERB 1 justify or defend an action etc.; forgive. 2 exempt. NOUN a reason put forward to justify a fault etc.; a pretext.

excusable ADJ

execrable ADJ very bad or unpleasant.

execute VERB 1 carry out an order; produce or perform a work of art. 2 put a condemned person to death. **execution** NOUN

executioner NOUN an official who executes condemned people.

executive NOUN a person or group with managerial powers, or with authority to put government decisions into effect. ADJ having such power or authority.

executor NOUN a person appointed to carry out the terms of a will.

exemplar NOUN a typical example or good model.

exemplary ADJ 1 serving as a desirable model. 2 serving as a warning to others.

exemplify VERB (**exemplified, exemplifying**) serve as an example of.

exempt ADJ free from an obligation etc. imposed on others. VERB make exempt.

exemption NOUN

exercise NOUN 1 physical activity. 2 a task designed to practise a skill. 3 use of your powers or rights. VERB 1 use a right etc. 2 take physical exercise. 3 occupy the thoughts of.

exert VERB 1 apply a force, influence, etc. 2 (**exert yourself**) make an effort. **exertion** NOUN

exhale VERB breathe out; give off in vapour. **exhalation** NOUN

exhaust VERB 1 tire out. 2 use up completely. NOUN waste gases from an engine etc.; a device through which they are expelled. **exhaustible** ADJ

exhaustion NOUN extreme tiredness.

exhaustive ADJ attending to every detail.

exhibit VERB put on show publicly; display a quality etc. NOUN a thing on public show. **exhibitor** NOUN

exhibition NOUN a public show; a display of a quality etc.

exhibitionism NOUN a tendency to behave in a way designed to attract

attention.
exhibitionist NOUN

exhilarate VERB make joyful or lively.
exhilaration NOUN

exhort VERB urge or advise earnestly.
exhortation NOUN

exhume VERB dig up a buried corpse.

exigent ADJ [formal] pressing or urgent.

exile NOUN banishment or long absence from your country or home, especially as a punishment; an exiled person. VERB send into exile.

exist VERB be present somewhere; live.
existence NOUN
existent ADJ

exit NOUN a way out; a departure. VERB go away.

exodus NOUN a departure of many people.

exonerate VERB show to be blameless.
exoneration NOUN

exorbitant ADJ (of a price) unreasonably high.

exorcize (or **-ise**) VERB free a person or place of an evil spirit.
exorcism NOUN
exorcist NOUN

exotic ADJ belonging to a foreign country; attractively unusual or striking.
exotically ADV

expand VERB 1 make or become larger; give a more detailed account. 2 become less reserved.
expansion NOUN

expanse NOUN a wide area or extent.

expansive ADJ 1 covering a wide area. 2 genial and communicative.

expatiate VERB speak or write at length about a subject.

expatriate NOUN a person living outside their own country.

expect VERB believe that a person or thing will come or a thing will happen; require or see as due; suppose or think.

expectant ADJ 1 filled with anticipation. 2 pregnant.
expectancy NOUN

expectation NOUN a belief that something will happen; a hope.

expedient ADJ advantageous rather than right or just. NOUN a means of achieving something.

expediency NOUN

expedite VERB help or hurry the progress of.

expedition NOUN a journey for a purpose; people and equipment for this.

expeditious ADJ speedy and efficient.

expel VERB (**expelled, expelling**) 1 deprive of membership; force to leave. 2 force out breath etc.

expend VERB spend; use up.

expendable ADJ not causing serious loss if abandoned.

expenditure NOUN the expending of money etc.; an amount expended.

expense NOUN 1 money spent on something; something on which you spend money. 2 (**expenses**) the amount spent doing a job; reimbursement of this.

expensive ADJ costing a great deal of money.

experience NOUN practical involvement in an activity, event, etc.; knowledge or skill gained through this; an event or action from which you learn. VERB undergo or be involved in.

experienced ADJ

experiment NOUN a scientific test to find out or prove something; a trial of something new. VERB conduct an experiment.

experimentation NOUN

experimental ADJ of or used in experiments; still being tested.

experimentally ADV

expert NOUN a person with great knowledge or skill in a particular area.

expertise NOUN expert knowledge or skill.

expiate VERB make amends for.

expiation NOUN

expire VERB 1 die; cease to be valid. 2 breathe out air.

expiry NOUN the end of the period for which something is valid.

explain VERB make clear or understandable; account for.

explanation NOUN
explanatory ADJ

expletive NOUN a swear word.

explicable ADJ able to be explained.

explicit ADJ speaking or

stated plainly.

explode VERB 1 expand and break with a loud noise; show sudden violent emotion; increase suddenly. 2 show a belief to be false. **explosion** NOUN

exploit NOUN a daring act. VERB make full use of; use selfishly and unfairly. **exploitation** NOUN

explore VERB travel into a country etc. in order to learn about it; examine. **exploration** NOUN **exploratory** ADJ **explorer** NOUN

explosive ADJ & NOUN (a substance) able or liable to explode.

exponent NOUN a person who holds and argues for a theory etc.

exponential ADJ (of an increase) more and more rapid.

export VERB send goods etc. to another country for sale. NOUN exporting; an exported item.

expose VERB leave uncovered or unprotected; subject to a risk etc.; allow light to reach film etc. **exposure** NOUN

exposé NOUN a news report revealing shocking information.

exposition NOUN 1 an account and explanation. 2 a large exhibition.

expound VERB explain in detail.

express VERB 1 convey feelings etc. by words or gestures. 2 squeeze out liquid or air. ADJ 1 definitely stated; precisely identified. 2 travelling or operating at high speed. NOUN a fast train or bus making few stops. ADV by express train or special delivery service.

expression NOUN 1 expressing. 2 a look on someone's face conveying feeling. 3 a word or phrase.

expressive ADJ conveying feelings etc. clearly.

expropriate VERB (especially of the state) deprive an owner of property. **expropriation** NOUN

expulsion NOUN expelling or being expelled.

expunge VERB wipe out.

expurgate VERB remove unsuitable matter from a book etc.

exquisite ADJ **1** extremely beautiful and delicate. **2** acute; keenly felt.

extemporize (or **-ise**) VERB speak, perform, or produce without preparation.

extend VERB **1** make longer or larger; stretch and straighten part of the body; reach over an area. **2** offer.

extension NOUN **1** a part added to and enlarging something. **2** extending. **3** a subsidiary telephone.

extensive ADJ large in area or scope.

extent NOUN the area covered by something; scope or scale; the degree to which something is true.

extenuate VERB make an offence seem less serious or more forgivable.
extenuating ADJ

exterior ADJ on or coming from the outside. NOUN an outer surface or appearance.

exterminate VERB destroy completely; kill.
extermination NOUN

external ADJ of or on the outside. NOUN an outward or superficial feature.

externally ADV

externalize (or **-ise**) VERB express, see, or present as existing outside yourself.

extinct ADJ with no living members; no longer active or alight.
extinction NOUN

extinguish VERB put out a light or flame; put an end to.
extinguisher NOUN

extol VERB (**extolled**, **extolling**) praise enthusiastically.

extort VERB obtain by force or threats.
extortion NOUN

extortionate ADJ (of a price) much too high.

extra ADJ additional, more than is usual or expected. ADV more than usually; in addition. NOUN an additional item; a person employed as one of a crowd in a film.

extra- PREFIX outside; beyond.

extract VERB take out or obtain by force or effort; obtain by chemical treatment etc.; select a passage from a book etc. NOUN a passage quoted from a book, film, etc.; the concentrated essence of a substance.

extractor NOUN

extraction NOUN
1 extracting. 2 ancestry or origin.

extradite VERB hand over an accused person for trial in the country where a crime was committed.

extradition NOUN

extramarital ADJ occurring outside marriage.

extramural ADJ for students who are not members of a university.

extraneous ADJ
1 irrelevant. 2 of external origin.

extraordinary ADJ very unusual or surprising.

extraordinarily ADV

extrapolate VERB extend a conclusion etc. beyond what is known, on the basis of available data.

extrapolation NOUN

extrasensory perception NOUN the supposed ability to perceive things by means other than the known senses, e.g. by telepathy.

extraterrestrial ADJ of or from outside the earth or its atmosphere.

extravagant ADJ

spending or using excessively; very expensive; going beyond what is reasonable.

extravagance NOUN

extravaganza NOUN a lavish spectacular display.

extreme ADJ 1 very great or intense; reaching a very high degree; very severe; drastic or immoderate. 2 furthest or outermost. NOUN an extreme point; one end of a scale; a very high degree.

extremely ADV

extremist NOUN a person holding extreme views.

extremism NOUN

extremity NOUN (PL -ies)
1 extreme hardship. 2 the furthest point or limit.
3 (**extremities**) the hands and feet.

extricate VERB free from an entanglement or difficulty.

extrovert NOUN a lively sociable person.

extrude VERB thrust or squeeze out.

exuberant ADJ 1 full of high spirits. 2 growing profusely.

exuberance NOUN

exude VERB ooze; give off

like sweat or a smell.

exult VERB feel or show delight.

exultant ADJ

exultation NOUN

eye NOUN 1 the organ of sight; the power of seeing. 2 something compared to an eye in shape, centrality, etc. VERB (**eyed**, **eyeing**) look at.

eyeball NOUN the whole of the eye within the eyelids.

eyebrow NOUN the fringe of hair on the ridge above the eye socket.

eyelash NOUN one of the hairs fringing the eyelids.

eyelet NOUN a small hole through which a lace can be threaded.

eyelid NOUN either of the two folds of skin that can be moved together to cover the eye.

eyeshadow NOUN a cosmetic applied to the skin round the eyes.

eyesight NOUN the ability to see.

eyesore NOUN an ugly thing.

eyewitness NOUN a person who saw something happen.

eyrie NOUN an eagle's nest.

F

F ABBREV Fahrenheit.

f ABBREV [Music] forte.

fable NOUN a short story, often with a moral.

fabled ADJ famous; legendary.

fabric NOUN 1 woven or knitted cloth. 2 the essential structure of a building etc.

fabricate VERB 1 invent a story etc. 2 construct.

fabrication NOUN

fabulous ADJ
1 extraordinarily great.
2 mythical. 3 [inf] very good.

facade NOUN the front of a building; an outward appearance, especially a misleading one.

face NOUN 1 the front of the head; a person's expression. 2 an aspect. 3 a surface; a side of a mountain. **4** the dial of a clock. VERB **1** have your face or front towards; confront boldly. **2** put a facing on.

lose face become less respected.

facecloth NOUN a small piece of towelling for washing yourself.

faceless ADJ remote and impersonal.

facelift NOUN an operation tightening the skin of the face to remove wrinkles.

facet NOUN one of many sides of a cut stone or jewel; one aspect.

facetious ADJ inappropriately humorous about serious subjects.

facia see **fascia**.

facial ADJ of the face. NOUN a beauty treatment for the face.

facile ADJ misleadingly simple; superficial or glib.

facilitate VERB make easy or easier.

facilitation NOUN

facility NOUN (PL **-ies**) **1** a building, service, or piece of equipment provided for a particular purpose. **2** natural ability.

facing NOUN an outer covering; a layer of material at the edge of a garment for strengthening, etc.

facsimile NOUN an exact copy of a document etc.

fact NOUN something known to be true.

in fact actually.

faction NOUN an organized group within a larger one; dissension between such groups.

factor NOUN **1** a circumstance that contributes towards a result. **2** a number by which a given number can be divided exactly.

factory NOUN (PL **-ies**) a building in which goods are manufactured.

factual ADJ based on or containing facts.

factually ADV

faculty NOUN (PL **-ies**) **1** a mental or physical power. **2** a department teaching a specified subject in a university or college.

fad NOUN a craze.

fade VERB lose colour, freshness, or vigour; disappear gradually.

faeces ([US] **feces**) PLURAL NOUN waste matter

discharged from the bowels.

fag NOUN [inf] **1** a tiring or tedious task. **2** a cigarette.

faggot NOUN **1** a tied bundle of sticks or twigs. **2** a ball of chopped seasoned liver etc., baked or fried.

Fahrenheit NOUN a temperature scale with the freezing point of water at 32° and boiling point at 212°.

fail VERB **1** be unsuccessful; be unable to meet a particular standard. **2** neglect your duty; disappoint someone relying on you. **3** become weak; cease functioning. NOUN a mark too low to pass an exam.

failing NOUN a weakness or fault. PREP if not.

failure NOUN lack of success; a deficiency; a person or thing that fails.

faint ADJ **1** indistinct or slight. **2** about to faint. VERB collapse unconscious. NOUN the act or state of fainting.
faint-hearted timid.

fair NOUN **1** a funfair. **2** a periodic gathering for a sale of goods. ADJ **1** (of hair) blonde. **2** (of weather) fine. **3** just or unbiased. **4** of moderate quality or amount.

fairground NOUN an open space where a fair is held.

fairly ADV **1** justly. **2** moderately; quite.

fairway NOUN the part of a golf course between tee and green.

fairy NOUN (PL **-ies**) an imaginary small being with magical powers.
fairy godmother a person providing help in times of difficulty.

faith NOUN reliance or trust; belief in religious doctrine.
faith healing healing achieved through religious belief rather than medicine.

faithful ADJ **1** loyal. **2** true or accurate.
faithfully ADV

faithless ADJ disloyal.

fake NOUN a person or thing that is not genuine. ADJ counterfeit. VERB make an imitation of; pretend.

falcon NOUN a small long-winged hawk.

falconry NOUN the breeding and training of hawks.

fall VERB (**fell, fallen, falling**) 1 move downwards without control; lose your balance; (of land) slope downwards. 2 decrease. 3 pass into a specified state. 4 lose power; be captured or conquered; die in battle. 5 (of the face) show distress. NOUN 1 falling; something fallen. 2 (**falls**) a waterfall. 3 [US] autumn.
fall out quarrel. **fall through** (of a plan) fail.

fallacy NOUN (PL **-ies**) a mistaken belief; a false argument.
fallacious ADJ

fallible ADJ liable to make mistakes.
fallibility NOUN

fallout NOUN airborne radioactive debris.

fallow ADJ (of land) left unplanted to restore its fertility.

false ADJ 1 not true; incorrect; not genuine. 2 unfaithful.

falsehood NOUN a lie.

falsetto NOUN (PL **-os**) a high-pitched voice.

falsify VERB (**falsified, falsifying**) alter fraudulently.

falsification NOUN

falter VERB lose strength or momentum; move or speak hesitantly.

fame NOUN the state of being famous.
famed ADJ

familiar ADJ 1 well known. 2 having knowledge or experience. 3 friendly or informal.
familiarity NOUN
familiarize (or **-ise**) VERB

family NOUN (PL **-ies**) parents and their children; a person's children; a set of relatives; a group of related plants, animals, or things.

famine NOUN extreme scarcity of food.

famished ADJ extremely hungry.

famous ADJ known to very many people.

fan NOUN 1 a hand-held or mechanical device to create a current of air. 2 an enthusiastic admirer or supporter. VERB (**fanned, fanning**) 1 cool with a fan. 2 spread from a central point.

fanatic NOUN a person with excessive enthusiasm for something.
fanatical ADJ

fanaticism NOUN

fancier NOUN a person with a special interest in something specified.

fanciful ADJ imaginative; imaginary.

fancy NOUN (PL **-ies**) 1 imagination; an unfounded idea. 2 a desire or whim. ADJ (**-ier, -iest**) ornamental, elaborate. VERB (**fancied, fancying**) 1 imagine; suppose. 2 [inf] feel a desire for something; be attracted to someone.

fancy dress an unusual costume or design worn at a party.

fanfare NOUN a short ceremonious sounding of trumpets.

fang NOUN a long sharp tooth; a snake's tooth that injects poison.

fantasize (or **-ise**) VERB daydream.

fantastic ADJ 1 hard to believe; bizarre or exotic. 2 [inf] excellent.
fantastically ADV

fantasy NOUN (PL **-ies**) imagination; a daydream; fiction involving magic and adventure.

far ADV at, to, or by a great distance; by a great deal. ADJ distant.

far-fetched unconvincing or unlikely.

farce NOUN a light comedy; an absurd situation.
farcical ADJ

fare NOUN 1 the price charged for a passenger to travel; a passenger paying this. 2 food provided. VERB get on or be treated in a specified way.

farewell EXCLAMATION goodbye. NOUN a parting.

farm NOUN a unit of land used for raising crops or livestock. VERB make a living by raising crops or livestock.
farmer NOUN

farmhouse NOUN a farmer's house.

farmyard NOUN an enclosed area round farm buildings.

farrier NOUN a person who shoes horses.

farrow VERB give birth to piglets.

fart VERB [inf] send out wind from the anus.

farther, farthest variants of **further, furthest**.

fascia NOUN 1 the instrument panel of a vehicle. 2 a nameplate over a shop front.

fascinate VERB irresistibly interest and attract.
fascination NOUN

fascism NOUN a system of extreme right-wing dictatorship.
fascist NOUN & ADJ

fashion NOUN 1 a manner of doing something. 2 a popular trend; producing and marketing styles of clothing etc. VERB make into a particular shape.

fashionable ADJ currently popular.
fashionably ADV

fast¹ ADJ 1 moving or able to move quickly; working or done quickly. 2 (of a clock etc.) showing a time ahead of the correct one. 3 firmly fixed. ADV 1 quickly. 2 securely or tightly; soundly.

fast² VERB go without food. NOUN a period without eating.

fasten VERB close or do up securely; fix or hold in place.

fastener (or **fastening**) NOUN a device to close or fasten something.

fastidious ADJ attentive to details; very concerned about cleanliness.

fat NOUN an oily substance found in animals; a substance used in cooking made from this, or from plants. ADJ (**fatter**, **fattest**) excessively plump; substantial.
fatten VERB
fatty ADJ

fatal ADJ causing death or disaster.
fatally ADV

fatalist NOUN a person believing that whatever happens is predestined and inescapable.
fatalism NOUN

fatality NOUN (PL **-ies**) a death caused by accident or in war etc.

fate NOUN a power thought to control all events; a person's destiny.

fated ADJ destined by fate.

fateful ADJ leading to great usually unpleasant events.

father NOUN a male parent or ancestor; a founder; a title of certain priests. VERB be the father of.
father-in-law the father of your wife or husband.
fatherhood NOUN
fatherly ADJ

fatherland NOUN your native country.

fathom NOUN a measure (1.82 m) of the depth of water. VERB understand.

fatigue NOUN **1** tiredness. **2** weakness in metal etc., caused by stress. **3** (**fatigues**) soldiers' clothes for specific tasks. VERB tire or weaken.

fatuous ADJ silly.

fault NOUN **1** a defect or imperfection. **2** responsibility for something wrong; a weakness or offence. **3** a break in layers of rock. VERB criticize.
faultless ADJ
faulty ADJ

faun NOUN a Roman god of the countryside with a goat's legs and horns.

fauna NOUN the animals of an area or period.

faux pas NOUN (PL **faux pas**) an embarrassing social blunder.

favour ([US] **favor**) NOUN **1** liking or approval. **2** a kind or helpful act. **3** favouritism. VERB like, approve of, or support.

favourable ([US] **favorable**) ADJ **1** showing approval; giving consent. **2** advantageous.
favourably ADV

favourite ([US] **favorite**) ADJ liked above others. NOUN a favourite person or thing; a competitor expected to win.

favouritism ([US] **favoritism**) NOUN unfairly generous treatment of one person or group.

fawn NOUN **1** a deer in its first year. **2** light yellowish brown. VERB try to win favour by flattery.

fax NOUN a copy of a document which has been scanned and transmitted electronically; a machine for sending and receiving faxes. VERB send someone a fax.

FBI ABBREV (in the USA) Federal Bureau of Investigation.

fear NOUN an unpleasant sensation caused by nearness of danger or pain. VERB be afraid of.
fearless ADJ

fearful ADJ **1** feeling or causing fear. **2** [inf] very great.
fearfully ADV

fearsome ADJ frightening.

feasible ADJ able to be done.
feasibility NOUN

feast NOUN a large elaborate meal; an annual religious celebration. VERB eat heartily.

feat NOUN a remarkable achievement.

feather NOUN each of the structures with a central shaft and fringe of fine strands, growing from a bird's skin. **feathery** ADJ

feature NOUN 1 a distinctive part of the face. 2 a noticeable attribute or aspect. 3 a newspaper article on a particular topic. 4 a full-length cinema film. VERB be a feature of or in.

febrile ADJ feverish; tense and excited.

February NOUN the second month.

feces US spelling of **faeces**.

feckless ADJ idle and irresponsible.

fed past and past participle of **feed**. **fed up** [inf] annoyed or bored.

federal ADJ of a system in which states unite under a central authority but are independent in internal affairs.

federalism NOUN **federalist** NOUN

federate VERB unite on a federal basis.

federation NOUN a federal group of states.

fee NOUN a sum payable for professional advice or services, or for a privilege.

feeble ADJ weak; ineffective. **feebly** ADV

feed VERB (**fed, feeding**) give food to a person or animal; eat; supply with material or information. NOUN food for animals; an act of feeding.

feedback NOUN return of part of a system's output to its source; comments made in response to something done or produced.

feel VERB (**felt, feeling**) 1 perceive or examine by touch; give a specified sensation when touched. 2 experience an emotion or sensation. 3 have an opinion or belief. NOUN the sense of touch; an act of touching; a sensation given by something touched.

feeler NOUN 1 a long slender organ of touch in

certain animals. **2** a tentative suggestion.

feeling NOUN **1** an emotion; (**feelings**) emotional susceptibilities; sympathy or sensitivity. **2** a belief not based on reason.

feet plural of **foot**.

feign VERB pretend.

feint NOUN a sham attack made to divert attention. VERB make a feint.

feisty ADJ (**-ier, -iest**) [inf] spirited and exuberant.

felicitations PLURAL NOUN congratulations.

felicitous ADJ well chosen or apt.

felicity NOUN (PL **-ies**) happiness; a pleasing feature.

feline ADJ of cats; catlike. NOUN an animal of the cat family.

fell¹ past of **fall**.

fell² NOUN a stretch of moor or hilly land, especially in northern England. VERB cut or knock down.

fellow NOUN **1** [inf] a man or boy. **2** an associate or equal; a thing like another. **3** a member of a learned society or governing body of a college.

fellowship NOUN **1** friendly association with others. **2** a society.

felon NOUN a person who has committed a serious violent crime.

felony NOUN

felt¹ past and past participle of **feel**.

felt² NOUN cloth made by matting and pressing wool.

felt-tip pen a pen with a writing point made of fibre.

female ADJ of the sex that can bear offspring or produce eggs; (of plants) fruit-bearing. NOUN a female animal or plant.

feminine ADJ of, like, or traditionally considered suitable for women.

femininity NOUN

feminism NOUN a movement or theory that supports the rights of women.

feminist NOUN

fen NOUN a low-lying marshy or flooded tract of land.

fence NOUN **1** a barrier round the boundary of a field or garden etc. **2** [inf] a person who deals in stolen goods. VERB **1** surround with a fence.

2 engage in the sport of fencing.

fencing NOUN **1** the sport of fighting with blunted swords. **2** fences or material for making fences.

fend VERB **1** (**fend for yourself**) support yourself. **2** (**fend off**) ward off.

fender NOUN **1** a low frame bordering a fireplace. **2** [US] a vehicle's mudguard or bumper.

feng shui NOUN an ancient Chinese system of designing buildings and arranging objects to ensure a favourable flow of energy.

fennel NOUN an aniseed-flavoured plant.

feral ADJ wild.

ferment VERB break down chemically through the action of yeast or bacteria; stir up social unrest. NOUN social unrest.
fermentation NOUN

fern NOUN a flowerless plant with feathery green leaves.

ferocious ADJ fierce or savage.
ferocity NOUN

ferret NOUN a small animal of the weasel family. VERB (**ferreted, ferreting**) rummage.

ferrous ADJ of or containing iron.

ferry NOUN (PL **-ies**) a boat for transporting passengers and goods. VERB (**ferried, ferrying**) convey in a ferry; transport.

fertile ADJ able to produce vegetation, fruit, or young; productive or inventive.
fertility NOUN

fertilize (or **-ise**) VERB **1** introduce pollen or sperm into. **2** add fertilizer to.
fertilization NOUN

fertilizer (or **-iser**) NOUN material added to soil to make it more fertile.

fervent ADJ showing intense feeling.

fervid ADJ fervent.

fervour ([US] **fervor**) NOUN intensity of feeling.

fester VERB **1** make or become septic. **2** (of ill feeling) continue and grow worse.

festival NOUN **1** a day or period of celebration. **2** a series of concerts, plays, etc.

festive ADJ of or suitable for a festival.

festivity NOUN (PL **-ies**) an event or activity celebrating a special occasion; celebration.

festoon NOUN a hanging chain of flowers or ribbons etc. VERB decorate with hanging ornaments.

fetch VERB 1 go for and bring back. 2 be sold for a specified price.

fetching ADJ attractive.

fête NOUN an outdoor event to raise money for something. VERB honour and entertain lavishly.

fetid (or **foetid**) ADJ stinking.

fetish NOUN an object worshipped as having magical powers.

fetlock NOUN a horse's leg above and behind the hoof.

fetter NOUN a shackle for the ankles; a restraint. VERB put into fetters; restrict.

fettle NOUN condition.

fetus (or **foetus**) NOUN (PL **-tuses**) an unborn baby of a mammal.

feud NOUN a state of lasting hostility. VERB be involved in a feud.

fever NOUN an abnormally high body temperature; nervous excitement.
fevered ADJ
feverish ADJ

few ADJ & NOUN not many.

fez NOUN (PL **fezzes**) a high flat-topped red cap worn by some Muslim men.

fiancé NOUN (FEMININE **fiancée**) a person to whom you are engaged to be married.

fiasco NOUN (PL **-os**) a total and ludicrous failure.

fib NOUN a trivial lie. VERB (**fibbed, fibbing**) tell a fib.

fibre ([US] **fiber**) NOUN 1 a thread-like strand; a substance formed of fibres; fibrous material in food that helps it pass through the body. 2 strength of character.
fibrous ADJ

fibreglass ([US] **fiberglass**) NOUN material made of or containing glass fibres.

fickle ADJ not loyal.

fiction NOUN literature describing imaginary events and people; an invented story.
fictional ADJ

fictitious ADJ imaginary

fighter

or invented.

fiddle [inf] NOUN 1 a violin. 2 a swindle. VERB 1 fidget with something. 2 falsify figures etc.

fiddly ADJ [inf] awkward or complicated.

fidelity NOUN faithfulness.

fidget VERB (**fidgeted, fidgeting**) make small restless movements. NOUN a person who fidgets. **fidgety** ADJ

field NOUN 1 an enclosed area of open ground, especially for pasture or cultivation; a sports ground. 2 an area rich in a natural product. 3 a sphere of action or interest. 4 all the competitors in a race or contest. VERB 1 (in cricket etc.) stop and return the ball to prevent scoring. 2 put a team into a contest. **field day** an opportunity for successful unrestrained action. **field events** athletic contests other than races. **field glasses** binoculars. **field marshal** an army officer of the highest rank. **fielder** NOUN

fieldwork NOUN practical research done outside libraries or laboratories.

fiend NOUN 1 an evil spirit; a cruel person. 2 [inf] an enthusiast: *a fitness fiend*.

fiendish ADJ cruel; extremely difficult.

fierce ADJ violent or aggressive; intense or powerful.

fiery ADJ (**-ier, -iest**) 1 consisting of or like fire. 2 passionate.

fiesta NOUN (in Spanish-speaking countries) a festival.

fifteen ADJ & NOUN one more than fourteen (15, XV). **fifteenth** ADJ & NOUN

fifth ADJ & NOUN the next after fourth.

fifty ADJ & NOUN five times ten (50, L). **fiftieth** ADJ & NOUN

fig NOUN a soft, sweet pear-shaped fruit.

fight VERB (**fought, fighting**) struggle, especially in physical combat or war; strive to obtain or accomplish something; argue. NOUN a period of fighting.

fighter NOUN a person who fights; an aircraft designed for attacking others.

figment NOUN something that exists only in the imagination.

figurative ADJ metaphorical.

figure NOUN **1** a number or numerical symbol. **2** bodily shape. **3** a well-known person. **4** a geometric shape; a diagram or drawing. VERB **1** play a part. **2** calculate; [US inf] suppose or think.

figure of speech an expression used for effect rather than literally.

figurehead NOUN a carved image at the prow of a ship; a leader with only nominal power.

figurine NOUN a statuette.

filament NOUN a slender thread; a fine wire giving off light in an electric lamp.

filch VERB [inf] steal.

file NOUN **1** a folder or box for keeping documents. **2** a set of data in a computer. **3** a line of people or things one behind another. **4** a tool with a rough surface for smoothing things. VERB **1** place a document in a file; place on record. **2** march in a long line.

3 shape or smooth a surface with a file.

filial ADJ of or due from a son or daughter.

filibuster NOUN a long speech which delays progress in a parliament etc.

filigree NOUN ornamental work of fine gold or silver wire.

fill VERB **1** make or become full; stop up a cavity. **2** occupy; appoint someone to a vacant post. NOUN (**your fill**) as much as you want or can bear.

fill in 1 complete a form etc. **2** act as someone's substitute. **3** tell someone more details.

filler NOUN a thing or material used to fill a gap or increase bulk.

fillet NOUN a piece of boneless meat or fish. VERB (**filleted, filleting**) remove bones from.

filling NOUN a substance used to fill a cavity etc. ADJ (of food) satisfying hunger.

fillip NOUN a stimulus or incentive.

filly NOUN (PL **-ies**) a young female horse.

film NOUN **1** a thin flexible

strip of light-sensitive material for taking photographs. **2** a story told through a sequence of images projected on a screen. **3** a thin layer. VERB make a film of; record on film.

filmy ADJ (**-ier, -iest**) thin and almost transparent.

filter NOUN a device or substance that lets liquid or gas pass through but holds back solid particles; a device that absorbs some of the light passing through it; an arrangement allowing traffic to filter. VERB pass through a filter; move gradually in or out.

filth NOUN disgusting dirt; obscenity.
filthiness NOUN
filthy ADJ

filtrate NOUN a filtered liquid.

fin NOUN a thin projection from a fish's body, used for propelling and steering itself; a similar projection to improve the stability of aircraft etc.

final ADJ coming at the end of a series or process; allowing no dispute. NOUN the last contest in a series; (**finals**) exams at the end of a degree course.
finally ADV

finale NOUN the closing section of a performance or musical composition.

finalist NOUN a competitor in a final.

finality NOUN the quality or fact of being final.

finalize (or **-ise**) VERB decide on or conclude.

finance NOUN management of money; (**finances**) money resources. VERB fund.
financial ADJ

financier NOUN a person engaged in financing businesses.

finch NOUN a small bird.

find VERB (**found, finding**) **1** discover; learn. **2** work out or confirm by research etc. **3** declare a verdict. **4** (**find out**) detect; learn or discover. NOUN something found, especially something valuable.

fine[1] ADJ **1** of very high quality; satisfactory; in good health. **2** bright and free from rain. **3** thin; in small particles; subtle.

fine[2] NOUN a sum of money to be paid as a penalty.

VERB punish with a fine.

finery NOUN showy clothes etc.

finesse NOUN delicate manipulation; tact.

finger NOUN each of the five parts extending from each hand; any of these other than the thumb; an object compared to a finger; VERB touch or feel with the fingers.

fingerboard NOUN a flat strip on a stringed instrument against which the strings are pressed to produce different notes.

fingerprint NOUN an impression of the ridges on the pad of a finger, used for identification.

finicky ADJ fussy; detailed and fiddly.

finish VERB 1 bring or come to an end; consume the whole or the remains of; reach the end of a race etc. 2 complete; put final touches to. 3 (**finish off**) defeat or kill. NOUN 1 the final part or stage; the end of a race. 2 the way in which something is made; a surface appearance.

finite ADJ limited.

fiord see **fjord**.

fir NOUN an evergreen cone-bearing tree.

fire NOUN 1 combustion; destructive burning; fuel burned to provide heat; a gas or electrical heater. 2 the firing of guns. 3 passionate feeling. VERB 1 send a bullet or shell from a gun. 2 [inf] dismiss from a job. 3 excite. 4 supply fuel to.

fire brigade an organized body of people employed to extinguish fires. **fire engine** a vehicle with equipment for putting out fires. **firing squad** a group ordered to shoot a condemned person.

firearm NOUN a gun, pistol, etc.

firebreak NOUN an obstacle to the spread of fire.

firefly NOUN (PL **-ies**) a phosphorescent beetle.

fireman (or **firefighter**) NOUN a member of a fire brigade.

fireplace NOUN a recess with a chimney for a domestic fire.

firework NOUN a device that is ignited to produce spectacular effects and explosions.

firm ADJ not yielding when

pressed or pushed; securely in place; (of a hold etc.) steady and strong; not giving way to argument, intimidation, etc. ADV firmly. VERB make or become firm. NOUN a business company.

firmament NOUN the sky with the stars etc.

first ADJ coming before all others in time, order, or importance. NOUN **1** the first thing or occurrence; the first day of a month. **2** a top grade in an exam. ADV before all others or another; before doing something else; for the first time.

first aid basic treatment given for an injury etc. before a doctor arrives.

first-class of or in the best quality or category.

first-hand directly from the original source.

firstly ADV

firth NOUN an estuary or narrow sea inlet in Scotland.

fiscal ADJ of government finances.

fish NOUN (PL **fish** or **fishes**) a cold-blooded vertebrate living wholly in water; its flesh as food. VERB try to catch fish; search or feel for something hidden; say something to elicit a compliment etc.

fishery NOUN (PL **-ies**) a place where fish are reared commercially or caught in numbers.

fishmonger NOUN a shopkeeper who sells fish.

fishnet NOUN an open mesh fabric.

fishy ADJ (**-ier, -iest**) **1** like fish. **2** [inf] arousing suspicion.

fission NOUN splitting, especially of an atomic nucleus, with release of energy.

fissure NOUN a cleft.

fist NOUN a tightly closed hand.

fisticuffs PLURAL NOUN fighting with fists.

fit ADJ (**fitter, fittest**) **1** suitable; right and proper; competent or qualified. **2** in good health. VERB (**fitted, fitting**) **1** be the right size and shape for; be small or few enough to get into a space. **2** fix in place; join or be joined. **3** make or be appropriate; make competent. NOUN **1** the way a garment etc. fits. **2** a sudden outburst of emotion, activity, etc.; a sudden attack of convulsions or loss of consciousness.

fitness NOUN

fitful ADJ irregular; occurring in short periods.

fitfully ADV

fitting ADJ right and proper. NOUN **1** the process of having a garment fitted. **2** (**fittings**) items of furniture fixed in a house but removable when the owner moves.

five ADJ & NOUN one more than four (5, V).

fix VERB **1** fasten securely in position; direct the eyes or attention steadily. **2** repair. **3** agree on or settle. **4** [inf] influence a result etc. dishonestly. **5** (**fix up**) organize; provide for. NOUN **1** an awkward situation. **2** [inf] a dose of an addictive drug.

fixation NOUN an obsession.

fixated ADJ

fixative NOUN a substance used to fix or protect something.

fixedly ADV without changing or wavering.

fixture NOUN **1** a piece of equipment or furniture which is fixed in position. **2** a sporting event arranged to take place on a particular date.

fizz VERB (of liquid) produce bubbles of gas with a hissing sound. NOUN the sound of fizzing.

fizzy ADJ

fizzle VERB **1** hiss or splutter feebly. **2** (**fizzle out**) end feebly.

fjord (or **fiord**) NOUN a narrow inlet of sea between cliffs, especially in Norway.

flabbergast VERB [inf] astound.

flabby ADJ (**-ier**, **-iest**) fat and limp.

flabbiness NOUN

flaccid ADJ soft, loose, and limp.

flag NOUN a piece of cloth attached by one edge to a staff or rope as a signal or symbol; a device used as a marker. VERB (**flagged**, **flagging**) **1** mark or signal with a flag. **2** become tired or weak.

flagon NOUN a large bottle for wine or cider.

flagrant ADJ very obvious and unashamed.

flagship NOUN an admiral's ship; the most important product of an organization etc.

flagstone NOUN a large paving stone.

flail NOUN an implement formerly used for threshing grain. VERB thrash or swing about wildly.

flair NOUN natural ability.

flak NOUN 1 anti-aircraft shells. 2 harsh criticism.

flake NOUN a thin, flat piece of something. VERB 1 come off in flakes; break food into flakes. 2 (**flake out**) [inf] fall asleep from exhaustion.
flaky ADJ

flambé ADJ (of food) served covered in flaming alcohol.

flamboyant ADJ showy in appearance or manner.
flamboyance NOUN

flame NOUN a hot, glowing quantity of burning gas coming from something on fire; an orange-red colour. VERB burn with flames; be bright.

flamenco NOUN (PL **-os**) Spanish guitar music with singing and dancing.

flamingo NOUN (PL **-os** or **-oes**) a wading bird with long legs and pink feathers.

flammable ADJ able to be set on fire.

flan NOUN an open pastry or sponge case with filling.

flange NOUN a projecting rim.

flank NOUN a side, especially of the body between ribs and hip; a side of an army etc. VERB be on either side of.

flannel NOUN 1 soft woollen or cotton fabric. 2 a facecloth.

flap VERB (**flapped, flapping**) 1 move wings, arms, etc. up and down; flutter or sway. 2 [inf] panic or be anxious. NOUN 1 a piece of cloth, metal, etc., covering an opening and moving on a hinge. 2 a flapping movement. 3 [inf] a panic.

flapjack NOUN a biscuit made with oats.

flare VERB 1 blaze suddenly; burst into activity or anger. 2 grow wider towards one end. NOUN 1 a sudden blaze; a device producing flame as a signal or illumination. 2 (**flares**) trousers with legs widening from the knee down.

flash VERB give out a sudden bright light; cause to shine briefly; show suddenly, briefly, or ostentatiously; move or send rapidly. NOUN a sudden burst of flame or light; a bright patch; a sudden, brief show of wit, feeling, etc.; a very short time; a device producing a brief bright light in photography. ADJ [inf] ostentatiously expensive, smart, etc.

flashback NOUN a scene in a story, film, etc., set at a time earlier than the main narrative.

flashpoint NOUN a point at which violence flares up.

flashy ADJ (-ier, -iest) ostentatiously smart, expensive, etc.

flask NOUN a narrow-necked bottle; a vacuum flask.

flat ADJ (**flatter, flattest**) **1** having a level, even surface; horizontal. **2** lacking enthusiasm or energy; having lost effervescence; having lost power to generate electric current. **3** firm and definite; (of a price) fixed. **4** [Music] below the correct pitch; (of a note) a semitone lower than a specified note. ADV [inf] absolutely or definitely. NOUN **1** a flat surface or object; level ground. **2** a set of rooms on one floor, forming a home. **3** [Music] (a sign indicating) a note lowered by a semitone.

flat out as fast or as hard as possible.

flatten VERB

flatter VERB compliment insincerely; cause to appear more attractive than is the case.

flattery NOUN

flatulent ADJ suffering from a build-up of gas in the digestive tract.

flatulence NOUN

flaunt VERB display ostentatiously.

flautist NOUN a flute player.

flavour ([US] **flavor**) NOUN a distinctive taste; a special characteristic. VERB give flavour to.

flavouring NOUN

flaw NOUN an imperfection.

flawed ADJ

flawless ADJ

flax NOUN a blue-flowered plant whose stalks are

used to make thread.

flaxen ADJ [literary] pale yellow.

flay VERB 1 strip off the skin or hide of. 2 whip or beat.

flea NOUN a small jumping blood-sucking insect.

fleck NOUN a very small mark; a speck. VERB mark with flecks.

fled past and past participle of **flee**.

fledged ADJ (of a young bird) having large enough wing feathers to fly.

fledgling (or **fledgeling**) NOUN a bird just fledged.

flee VERB (**fled, fleeing**) run away.

fleece NOUN a sheep's woolly hair. VERB [inf] swindle.
  fleecy ADJ

fleet NOUN ships sailing together; vehicles or aircraft under one command or ownership. ADJ [literary] swift and nimble.

fleeting ADJ passing quickly.

flesh NOUN 1 the soft substance of animal bodies; the body as opposed to the mind or soul. 2 the pulpy part of fruits and vegetables. VERB

(**flesh out**) add details to.

fleshy ADJ (-ier, -iest) 1 plump. 2 thick and soft.

flew past of **fly**.

flex NOUN a flexible insulated wire for carrying electric current. VERB bend; move a muscle so that it bends a joint.

flexible ADJ able to bend easily; adaptable.
  flexibility NOUN

flick NOUN 1 a quick, sharp, small movement. 2 [inf] a cinema film. VERB move, strike, or remove with a flick.

flicker VERB burn or shine unsteadily; occur or appear briefly. NOUN an unsteady light; a brief or slight occurrence.

flier see **flyer**.

flight NOUN 1 flying; a journey through air or space; the path of an object moving through the air; a group of birds or aircraft. 2 a series of stairs. 3 feathers etc. on a dart or arrow. 4 running away.

flighty ADJ irresponsible.

flimsy ADJ (-ier, -iest) light and thin; fragile; unconvincing.

flinch VERB make a nervous movement in pain or fear;

shrink from something.

fling VERB (**flung, flinging**) throw or move forcefully. NOUN a period of enjoyment or wild behaviour; a brief sexual relationship.

flint NOUN very hard stone; a piece of a hard alloy producing sparks when struck.

flip VERB (**flipped, flipping**) turn over suddenly and swiftly.

flippant ADJ not showing proper seriousness.

flipper NOUN a sea animal's limb used in swimming; a large flat rubber attachment to the foot for underwater swimming.

flirt VERB behave in a frivolously amorous way. NOUN a person who flirts. **flirtation** NOUN **flirtatious** ADJ

flit VERB (**flitted, flitting**) move swiftly and lightly.

float VERB **1** rest or drift on the surface of liquid; be supported in air. **2** make a suggestion to test reactions. **3** offer the shares of a company for sale. **4** (of currency) have a variable rate of exchange. NOUN **1** a thing designed to float on liquid. **2** money for minor expenditure or giving change. **3** a small vehicle.

floatation see **flotation**.

flock NOUN **1** a number of animals or birds together; a large number of people; a congregation. **2** wool or cotton material as stuffing. VERB gather or go in a group.

floe NOUN a sheet of floating ice.

flog VERB (**flogged, flogging**) **1** beat severely. **2** [inf] sell.

flood NOUN an overflow of water on a place usually dry; an overwhelming quantity or outpouring. VERB cover with flood water; overflow; arrive in great quantities; overwhelm.

floodlight NOUN a lamp producing a broad bright beam. **floodlit** ADJ

floor NOUN **1** the lower surface of a room. **2** a storey. **3** the right to speak in a debate: *have the floor*. VERB **1** provide with a floor. **2** [inf] knock down; baffle.

flooring NOUN material for a floor.

flop VERB (**flopped, flopping**) 1 hang or fall heavily and loosely. 2 [inf] be a failure. NOUN 1 a flopping movement. 2 [inf] a failure.

floppy ADJ (**-ier, -iest**) not firm or stiff.

floppy disk a magnetic disk for storing computer data.

flora NOUN the plants of an area or period.

floral ADJ of flowers.

floret NOUN each of the small flowers of a composite flower.

florid ADJ 1 red or flushed. 2 over-elaborate.

florist NOUN a person who sells flowers.

floss NOUN 1 a mass of silky fibres. 2 soft thread used to clean between the teeth.

flotation (or **floatation**) NOUN floating; the sale of shares in a company for the first time.

flotilla NOUN a small fleet.

flotsam NOUN floating wreckage.

flounce VERB go in an impatient, annoyed manner. NOUN 1 a flouncing movement. 2 a deep frill.

flounder VERB move clumsily in mud or water; be confused or in difficulty. NOUN a small flatfish.

flour NOUN fine powder made from grain, used in cooking.

floury ADJ

flourish VERB 1 grow vigorously; be successful. 2 wave dramatically. NOUN a dramatic gesture; an ornamental curve; a fanfare.

flout VERB disobey a law etc. contemptuously.

flow VERB move steadily and continuously in a current or stream; (of hair etc.) hang loosely. NOUN a steady, continuous stream.

flower NOUN 1 the part of a plant where fruit or seed develops, usually brightly coloured and decorative. 2 the best among a group of people. VERB produce flowers.

flowery ADJ 1 full of flowers. 2 full of ornamental phrases.

flown past participle of **fly**.

flu NOUN influenza.

fluctuate VERB vary irregularly.

fluctuation NOUN

flue NOUN a smoke duct in a chimney; a channel for conveying heat.

fluent ADJ speaking or spoken smoothly and readily.
fluency NOUN

fluff NOUN a soft mass of fibres or down. VERB 1 make something appear fuller and softer. 2 [inf] bungle.
fluffy ADJ

fluid ADJ flowing easily; not fixed or settled. NOUN a liquid.
fluid ounce one-twentieth of a pint (about 28 ml).
fluidity NOUN

fluke NOUN a lucky accident.

flummox VERB [inf] baffle.

flung past and past participle of **fling**.

flunkey (or **flunky**) NOUN (PL **-eys** or **-ies**) a uniformed male servant; a person who does menial work.

fluorescent ADJ giving out bright light when exposed to radiation.
fluorescence NOUN

fluoride NOUN a compound of fluorine with metal.

fluorine NOUN a poisonous pale yellow gas.

flurry NOUN (PL **-ies**) a short rush of wind, rain, or snow; a commotion.

flush VERB 1 make or become red; blush. 2 clean or dispose of with a flow of water. 3 drive out from cover. NOUN 1 a blush. 2 a rush of emotion. 3 an act of cleaning something with a rush of water. ADJ level with another surface.

fluster VERB make agitated and confused. NOUN a flustered state.

flute NOUN 1 a wind instrument consisting of a pipe with holes along it and a mouth hole at the side. 2 an ornamental groove.

flutter VERB move wings hurriedly; wave or flap quickly; (of the heart) beat irregularly. NOUN 1 a fluttering movement; a state of nervous excitement. 2 [inf] a small bet.

fluvial ADJ of or found in rivers.

flux NOUN a flow; continuous change.

fly VERB (**flew, flown, flying**) 1 move through the air on wings or in an aircraft; be thrown through the air; control the flight of; go or move quickly. **2** display a flag. **3** [old use] run away. NOUN (PL **flies**) **1** a two-winged insect. **2** (also **flies**) a fastening down the front of trousers.

flying saucer a disc-shaped flying craft, supposedly piloted by aliens. **flying squad** a group of police etc. organized to reach an incident quickly.

flyer (or **flier**) NOUN **1** a person or thing that flies. **2** a small printed advertisement.

flyover NOUN a bridge carrying one road or railway over another.

flywheel NOUN a heavy wheel revolving on a shaft to regulate machinery.

foal NOUN a young horse or related animal. VERB give birth to a foal.

foam NOUN **1** a mass of small bubbles; a bubbly substance prepared for shaving etc. **2** spongy rubber or plastic. VERB form or produce foam.

fob NOUN a chain for a watch; a tab on a key ring. VERB (**fob off**) (**fobbed**, **fobbing**) give something inferior to someone; deceive into accepting.

focal ADJ of or at a focus.

fo'c's'le see **forecastle**.

focus NOUN (PL **-cuses** or **-ci**) **1** the centre of interest or activity. **2** clear visual definition; an adjustment on a lens to produce a clear image. **3** a point where rays meet. VERB (**focused, focusing** or **focussed, focussing**) **1** adjust the focus of; bring into focus. **2** concentrate.

fodder NOUN food for animals.

foe NOUN an enemy.

foetid see **fetid**.

foetus see **fetus**.

fog NOUN thick mist. VERB (**fogged, fogging**) become covered with steam; make obscure. **foggy** ADJ

fogey NOUN (PL **-eys** or **-ies**) an old-fashioned person.

foghorn NOUN a device making a deep sound to warn ships of hidden rocks etc. in fog.

foible NOUN a minor weakness or eccentricity.

foil NOUN **1** a very thin

flexible sheet of metal. **2** a person or thing emphasizing another's qualities by contrast. VERB thwart or frustrate.

foist VERB cause a person to accept an inferior or unwelcome thing.

fold VERB **1** bend something thin and flat so that one part of it lies over another. **2** wrap; clasp. **3** mix an ingredient gently into a mixture. **4** [inf] (of a business etc.) cease trading. NOUN **1** a shape or line made by folding. **2** a pen for sheep.

folder NOUN a folding cover for loose papers.

foliage NOUN leaves.

folio NOUN (PL **-os**) a folded sheet of paper making two leaves of a book; a book of such pages.

folk NOUN (PL **folk** or **folks**) [inf] people; relatives. ADJ (of music, song, etc.) in the traditional style of a country or region.

folklore NOUN the traditional beliefs and tales of a community.

follicle NOUN a very small cavity containing a hair root.

follow VERB **1** go or come

after; go along a route. **2** act according to instructions etc.; accept the ideas of. **3** pay close attention to. **4** be a consequence or conclusion. **5** (**follow up**) investigate further.

follower NOUN

following NOUN a body of believers or supporters. ADJ next in time or order. PREP as a sequel to.

folly NOUN (PL **-ies**) **1** foolishness; a foolish act. **2** an impractical ornamental building.

foment VERB stir up trouble.

fond ADJ **1** liking someone or something. **2** (of hope) unlikely to be fulfilled.

fondant NOUN a soft sugary sweet.

fondle VERB stroke lovingly.

font NOUN a basin in a church, holding water for baptism.

food NOUN a substance eaten by people or animals to maintain life.

fool NOUN **1** a foolish person. **2** a creamy fruit-flavoured pudding. VERB trick or deceive; behave in a silly or frivolous way.

foolhardy ADJ recklessly bold.

foolish ADJ lacking good sense or judgement; ridiculous.
foolishness NOUN

foolproof ADJ unable to go wrong or be misused.

foolscap NOUN a large size of paper.

foot NOUN (PL **feet**) 1 the part of the leg below the ankle; a lower end; a base. 2 a measure of length = 12 inches (30.48 cm). 3 a unit of rhythm in verse. VERB [inf] pay a bill.
foot-and-mouth disease a contagious viral disease of cattle and sheep.

footage NOUN a length of film.

football NOUN a large round or elliptical inflated ball; a game played with this.
footballer NOUN

foothills PLURAL NOUN low hills near the bottom of a mountain or range.

foothold NOUN a place just wide enough for your foot; a secure position as a basis for progress.

footing NOUN 1 a secure grip with your feet. 2 a position: *put us on an equal footing.*

footlights PLURAL NOUN a row of lights along the front of a stage floor.

footling ADJ trivial.

footloose ADJ without responsibilities.

footman NOUN a manservant.

footnote NOUN a note printed at the bottom of a page.

footprint NOUN an impression left by a foot or shoe.

footstep NOUN a step; the sound of this.

footwear NOUN shoes, socks, etc.

footwork NOUN a manner of moving or using the feet in sports etc.

for PREP 1 in favour or on behalf of. 2 because of. 3 relating to. 4 so as to get, have, or do. 5 in place of. 6 over a period or distance. CONJ [literary] because.

forage VERB search for food. NOUN fodder.

foray NOUN a sudden attack or raid.

forbear VERB (**forbore**, **forborne**, **forbearing**) refrain from.

forbearing ADJ patient or

tolerant.

forbearance NOUN

forbid VERB (**forbade, forbidden, forbidding**) order not to do something; refuse to allow.

forbidding ADJ daunting or uninviting.

force NOUN 1 strength or power; someone or something exerting an influence; [Physics] an influence tending to cause movement. 2 violent compulsion. 3 validity. 4 a body of troops or police. VERB 1 make your way by effort or violence. 2 compel. 3 strain; produce with an effort.

forceful ADJ powerful; assertive.

forcefully ADV

forceps PLURAL NOUN pincers used in surgery etc.

forcible ADJ done by force.

forcibly ADV

ford NOUN a shallow place where a stream may be crossed by wading or driving through. VERB cross a stream etc. in this way.

fore ADJ & ADV in, at, or towards the front. NOUN the front part.

forearm NOUN the arm from the elbow downwards. VERB arm or prepare in advance against possible danger.

forebears PLURAL NOUN ancestors.

foreboding NOUN a feeling that trouble is coming.

forecast VERB (**forecast, forecasting**) predict future weather, events, etc. NOUN a prediction.

forecaster NOUN

forecastle (or **fo'c's'le**) NOUN the forward part of certain ships.

foreclose VERB take possession of property when a loan secured on it is not repaid.

foreclosure NOUN

forecourt NOUN an open area in front of a building.

forefathers PLURAL NOUN ancestors.

forefinger NOUN the finger next to the thumb.

forefront NOUN the very front.

forego see **forgo**.

foregoing ADJ preceding.

foregone conclusion NOUN a predictable result.

foreground NOUN the part

of a scene etc. that is nearest to the observer.

forehand NOUN (in tennis etc.) a stroke played with the palm of the hand turned forwards.

forehead NOUN the part of the face above the eyes.

foreign ADJ of a country or language that is not your own; of other countries; strange or out of place.

foreigner NOUN a person from a foreign country.

foreman NOUN a worker supervising others; the president and spokesman of a jury.

foremost ADJ most advanced in position or rank; most important. ADV first; in the most important position.

forensic ADJ of or used in law courts.

forerunner NOUN a person or thing coming before and foreshadowing another.

foresee VERB (**foresaw, foreseen, foreseeing**) be aware of or realize beforehand.

foreseeable ADJ

foreshadow VERB be an advance sign of a future event etc.

foreshorten VERB show or portray an object as shorter than it is, as an effect of perspective.

foresight NOUN the ability to predict future events and needs.

foreskin NOUN the fold of skin covering the end of the penis.

forest NOUN a large area covered with trees and undergrowth.

forestall VERB prevent or foil by taking action first.

forestry NOUN the science of planting and caring for forests.

forester NOUN

foretaste NOUN a sample or indication of what is to come.

foretell VERB (**foretold, foretelling**) forecast.

forethought NOUN careful planning for the future.

forever ADV **1** for all time. **2** continually.

forewarn VERB warn beforehand.

foreword NOUN an introduction to a book.

forfeit NOUN something that has to be paid or given up as a penalty. VERB give or lose as a forfeit. ADJ forfeited.

forge NOUN a blacksmith's workshop; a furnace where metal is heated. VERB **1** shape metal by heating and hammering. **2** make a fraudulent copy of.

forgery NOUN (PL **-ies**) forging; something forged.

forget VERB (**forgot, forgotten, forgetting**) **1** fail or be unable to remember. **2** (**forget yourself**) behave inappropriately.

forgetful ADJ tending to forget.
forgetfulness NOUN

forget-me-not NOUN a plant with small blue flowers.

forgive VERB (**forgave, forgiven, forgiving**) cease to feel angry or bitter towards or about.
forgiveness NOUN

forgo (or **forego**) VERB (**forwent, forgone, forgoing**) give up; go without.

fork NOUN a pronged implement for holding food or tool for digging; a point where a road, river, etc. divides; one of its branches. VERB **1** (of a road etc.) divide into two branches. **2** lift or dig with a fork. **3** (**fork out**) [inf] give money.
forked ADJ

forlorn ADJ left alone and unhappy.

form NOUN **1** shape, appearance, or structure. **2** the way in which something exists. **3** correct behaviour. **4** a document with blank spaces for information. **5** a school class or year. **6** a bench. VERB create; shape; develop; constitute.

formal ADJ in accordance with rules or conventions; of or for official occasions.
formally ADV

formality NOUN (PL **-ies**) being formal; something done only because required by a rule.

formalize (or **-ise**) VERB make official.

format NOUN the way something is arranged; the shape and size of a book; [Computing] a structure for the processing etc. of data. VERB (**formatted, formatting**) arrange in a format; prepare a disk to receive data.

formation NOUN forming or being formed; a structure or pattern.

formative ADJ influencing development.

former ADJ of an earlier period; mentioned first of two.

formerly ADV in former times.

Formica NOUN [trademark] a hard, plastic material.

formidable ADJ inspiring fear or awe; difficult to achieve.
formidably ADV

formula NOUN (PL **-lae** or **-las**) **1** symbols showing chemical constituents or a mathematical statement. **2** a fixed series of words for use on particular occasions.
formulaic ADJ

formulate VERB **1** create or devise. **2** express precisely.
formulation NOUN

fornicate VERB [formal] have sex outside marriage.
fornication NOUN

forsake VERB (**forsook, forsaken, forsaking**) abandon; give up.

forswear VERB (**forswore, forsworn, forswearing**) renounce.

forsythia NOUN a shrub with yellow flowers.

fort NOUN a fortified building.

forte NOUN something at which a person excels. ADV [Music] loudly.

forth ADV **1** outwards and forwards. **2** onwards from a point in time.

forthcoming ADJ **1** about to occur or appear. **2** communicative.

forthright ADJ frank or outspoken.

forthwith ADV immediately.

fortify VERB (**fortified, fortifying**) **1** strengthen against attack. **2** strengthen or invigorate. **3** increase the alcohol content or nutritive value of.
fortification NOUN

fortitude NOUN courage in bearing pain or trouble.

fortnight NOUN a period of two weeks.

fortress NOUN a fortified building or town.

fortuitous ADJ happening by chance.

fortunate ADJ lucky.
fortunately ADV

fortune NOUN **1** chance seen as affecting people's lives; luck; (**fortunes**) what happens to someone. **2** a large amount of money.

forty ADJ & NOUN four times ten (40, XL).
  fortieth ADJ & NOUN

forum NOUN a place or meeting where a public discussion is held.

forward ADV & ADJ in the direction you are facing or moving; towards a successful end; so as to happen sooner; in or near the front of a ship or aircraft. ADJ bold or over-familiar. NOUN an attacking player in sport. VERB send on a letter etc. to another destination.
  forwards ADV

fossil NOUN the remains of a prehistoric animal or plant that have hardened into rock.
  fossil fuel fuel such as coal or gas, formed from the remains of living organisms.

fossilize (or **-ise**) VERB preserve an animal or plant so that it becomes a fossil.

foster VERB **1** encourage or help the development of. **2** bring up a child that is not your own.

fought past and past participle of **fight**.

foul ADJ **1** causing disgust; very bad; dirty. **2** wicked or obscene. NOUN an action that breaks the rules of a game. VERB **1** make dirty. **2** commit a foul against. **3** (**foul up**) make a mistake with.

found[1] past and past participle of **find**.

found[2] VERB **1** establish an institution etc.; set on a base or basis. **2** melt and mould metal or glass.

foundation NOUN **1** a base or lowest layer; an underlying principle. **2** founding; an institution etc. that is founded.

founder VERB stumble or fall; (of a ship) sink; fail completely. NOUN a person who has founded an institution etc.

foundling NOUN a deserted child of unknown parents.

foundry NOUN (PL **-ies**) a workshop where metal or glass founding is done.

fount NOUN [literary] a fountain; a source.

fountain NOUN an ornamental structure pumping out a jet of water.

fountain pen a pen with a container supplying ink to the nib.

four ADJ & NOUN one more than three (4, IV).

foursome NOUN a party of four people.

fourteen ADJ & NOUN one more than thirteen (14, XIV).

fourteenth ADJ & NOUN

fourth ADJ next after the third. NOUN **1** a fourth thing, class, etc. **2** a quarter.

fowl NOUN a bird kept for its eggs or meat.

fox NOUN **1** a wild animal of the dog family with a bushy tail. **2** a cunning person. VERB [inf] baffle or deceive.

foxglove NOUN a tall plant with flowers shaped like glove-fingers.

foxhound NOUN a hound bred to hunt foxes.

foxtrot NOUN a dance with alternating slow and quick steps; music for this.

foyer NOUN an entrance hall of a theatre, cinema, or hotel.

fracas NOUN (PL **fracas**) a noisy quarrel or

disturbance.

fraction NOUN a number that is not a whole number; a small part or amount.

fractious ADJ irritable; hard to control.

fracture NOUN a break, especially in a bone; breaking. VERB break.

fragile ADJ easily broken or damaged; delicate.

fragility NOUN

fragment NOUN a piece broken off something. VERB (cause to) break into fragments.

fragmentary ADJ

fragmentation NOUN

fragrance NOUN a pleasant smell.

fragrant ADJ

frail ADJ weak; fragile.

frailty NOUN

frame NOUN **1** a rigid structure supporting other parts; a person's body. **2** a rigid structure surrounding a picture, window, etc. **3** a single exposure on a cinema film. VERB **1** put or form a frame round. **2** construct. **3** [inf] arrange false evidence against.

frame of mind a particular mood.

framework NOUN a supporting frame.

franchise NOUN **1** the right to vote in public elections. **2** authorization to sell a company's goods or services in a certain area.

frank ADJ honest in expressing your thoughts and feelings. VERB mark a letter etc. to show that postage has been paid.

frankfurter NOUN a smoked sausage.

frankincense NOUN a sweet-smelling gum burnt as incense.

frantic ADJ wildly agitated or excited.
frantically ADV

fraternal ADJ of a brother or brothers.

fraternity NOUN (PL **-ies**) **1** a group of people with a common interest. **2** brotherhood.

fraternize (or **-ise**) VERB associate with others in a friendly way.

fraud NOUN criminal deception; a dishonest trick; a person carrying this out.
fraudulence NOUN
fraudulent ADJ

fraught ADJ **1** causing or suffering anxiety. **2** (**fraught with**) filled with.

fray VERB (of fabric, rope, etc.) unravel or become worn; (of nerves) be strained. NOUN a fight or conflict.

frazzle NOUN [inf] an exhausted state.
frazzled ADJ

freak NOUN **1** an abnormal person, thing, or event. **2** [inf] an enthusiast for something specified. VERB (**freak out**) [inf] behave wildly and irrationally.

freckle NOUN a light brown spot on the skin.
freckled ADJ

free ADJ (**freer, freest**) **1** not captive, confined, or restricted; not in another's power. **2** not busy or taken up; not in use; not prevented from doing something. **3** not subject to something; without. **4** costing nothing. **5** giving or spending without restraint. ADV at no cost. VERB **1** set free. **2** rid of something undesirable.

free-range referring to farming in which animals are allowed to move around freely in natural conditions.

freely ADV

freedom NOUN **1** being free; independence. **2** unrestricted use. **3** honorary citizenship.

freehand ADJ (of drawing) done by hand without ruler or compasses etc.

freehold NOUN the holding of land or a house etc. in absolute ownership.

freeholder NOUN

freelance ADJ & NOUN (a person) working for various employers rather than permanently employed by one.

freeloader NOUN [inf] a person who lives off others' generosity.

Freemason NOUN a member of a fraternity for mutual help, with elaborate secret rituals.

freesia NOUN a plant with fragrant flowers.

freewheel VERB ride a bicycle without pedalling.

freeze VERB (**froze, frozen, freezing**) **1** change or be changed from liquid to solid by extreme cold; (of weather etc.) be so cold that water turns to ice; feel very cold or die of cold. **2** preserve food etc. at a very low temperature. **3** become motionless; stop a moving image; hold prices or wages at a fixed level; prevent assets from being used. NOUN **1** the freezing of prices etc. **2** [inf] a very cold spell.

freezer NOUN a refrigerated container for preserving and storing food.

freight NOUN goods transported in bulk. VERB transport goods.

freighter NOUN a ship or aircraft carrying mainly freight.

French ADJ & NOUN (the language) of France. **French dressing** a salad dressing of oil and vinegar. **French fries** potato chips. **French horn** a brass wind instrument with a coiled tube. **French window** a window reaching to the ground, used also as a door.

frenetic ADJ wild, agitated, or uncontrolled.

frenetically ADV

frenzy NOUN (PL **-ies**) a state of wild excitement or agitation.

frenzied ADJ

frequency NOUN (PL **-ies**)

the rate at which something occurs or is repeated; frequent occurrence; [Physics] the number of cycles of a carrier wave per second; a band or group of these.

frequent ADJ happening or appearing often. VERB go frequently to, be often in a place.

fresco NOUN (PL **-os** or **-oes**) a picture painted on a wall or ceiling before the plaster is dry.

fresh ADJ **1** new or different; not faded or stale. **2** (of food) recently made or obtained. **3** (of water) not salty. **4** refreshing; vigorous.
freshen VERB

fresher NOUN a first-year university student.

fret VERB (**fretted, fretting**) feel anxious. NOUN each of the ridges on the fingerboard of a guitar etc.

fretful ADJ distressed or irritable.
fretfully ADV

fretwork NOUN woodwork cut in decorative patterns.

friable ADJ easily crumbled.

friar NOUN a member of certain religious orders of men.

fricassée NOUN a dish of pieces of meat served in a thick sauce.

friction NOUN **1** rubbing; resistance of one surface to another that moves over it. **2** conflict of people who disagree.

Friday NOUN the day following Thursday.

fridge NOUN a refrigerator.

fried past and past participle of **fry**.

friend NOUN a person that you know well and like; a supporter of a cause or organization.
friendship NOUN

friendly ADJ (**-ier, -iest**) kind and pleasant; (of people or their relationship) affectionate; (of a game) not part of a serious competition; not harmful to a specified thing.
friendliness NOUN

frieze NOUN a band of decoration round a wall.

frigate NOUN a small fast naval ship.

fright NOUN sudden great fear; a shock; a ridiculous or grotesque person or thing.

frighten VERB make afraid; deter through fear.

frightful ADJ very bad or unpleasant; [inf] terrible. **frightfully** ADV

frigid ADJ intensely cold; sexually unresponsive. **frigidity** NOUN

frill NOUN a gathered or pleated strip of material attached at one edge to a garment etc. for decoration; [inf] an unnecessary extra feature or luxury. **frilled** ADJ **frilly** ADJ

fringe NOUN 1 an ornamental edging of hanging threads; front hair cut short to hang over the forehead. 2 the outer part of an area, group, etc. ADJ (of theatre etc.) unconventional. VERB give or form a fringe to.

frisk VERB 1 leap or skip playfully. 2 feel over or search a person for concealed weapons etc. NOUN a playful leap or skip.

frisky ADJ (-ier, -iest) lively and playful.

frisson NOUN a thrill.

fritter VERB waste money or time on trivial things. NOUN a fried batter-coated slice of fruit or meat etc.

frivolous ADJ not serious; purely for or interested in pleasure. **frivolity** NOUN

frizz VERB (of hair) form into a mass of tight curls. NOUN such curls. **frizzy** ADJ

frock NOUN a woman's or girl's dress.

frog NOUN a small amphibian with long web-footed hind legs.

frogman NOUN a swimmer with a rubber suit and oxygen supply for working under water.

frolic VERB (**frolicked, frolicking**) play about in a lively way. NOUN such play.

from PREP 1 having as the starting point, source, material, or cause. 2 as separated, distinguished, or unlike.

frond NOUN a long leaf or leaf-like part of a fern, palm tree, etc.

front NOUN 1 the side or part normally nearer or towards the spectator or line of motion. 2 a battle line. 3 an outward appearance; a cover for secret activities. 4 a boundary between warm and cold air masses. **5** a promenade at a seaside resort. ADJ of or at the front. VERB **1** have the front towards. **2** lead a group etc. **3** act as a cover for secret activities.

frontage NOUN the front of a building; land bordering this.

frontal ADJ of or on the front.

frontier NOUN a boundary between countries.

frontispiece NOUN an illustration opposite the title page of a book.

frost NOUN small white ice crystals on grass etc.; a period cold enough for these to form. VERB cover or be covered with frost.

frostbite NOUN injury to body tissues due to exposure to extreme cold. **frostbitten** ADJ

frosted ADJ (of glass) having its surface roughened to make it opaque.

frosting NOUN [US] sugar icing.

frosty ADJ (-ier, -iest) **1** cold with frost; covered with frost. **2** unfriendly. **frostiness** NOUN

froth NOUN & VERB foam.

frothy ADJ

frown VERB **1** wrinkle your forehead in thought or disapproval. **2** (**frown on**) disapprove of. NOUN a frowning expression.

froze, **frozen** past and past participle of **freeze**.

fructose NOUN a sugar found in honey and fruit.

frugal ADJ economical; simple and costing little. **frugally** ADV

fruit NOUN **1** the seed-containing part of a plant; this used as food. **2** (**fruits**) the product of labour. VERB produce fruit. **fruit machine** a coin-operated gambling machine.

fruiterer NOUN a shopkeeper selling fruit.

fruitful ADJ producing much fruit or good results. **fruitfully** ADV

fruition NOUN the fulfilment of a hope, plan, or project.

fruitless ADJ producing little or no result.

fruity ADJ (-ier, -iest) like or containing fruit; (of a voice) deep and rich.

frump NOUN a dowdy woman.

frumpy ADJ

frustrate VERB prevent from achieving something or from being achieved. **frustration** NOUN

fry¹ VERB (**fries, fried, frying**) cook or be cooked in very hot fat; be very hot. NOUN a fried meal.

fry² NOUN (PL **fry**) young fish.

ft ABBREV foot or feet (as a measure).

fuchsia NOUN a plant with drooping flowers.

fuddle VERB confuse or stupefy, especially with alcoholic drink.

fuddy-duddy NOUN (PL **-duddies**) [inf] an old-fashioned person.

fudge NOUN **1** a soft sweet made of milk, sugar, and butter. **2** a makeshift way of dealing with a problem. VERB present or deal with inadequately or evasively.

fuel NOUN material burnt as a source of energy; something that increases anger etc. VERB (**fuelled, fuelling**; [US] **fueled, fueling**) supply with fuel.

fugitive NOUN a person who is fleeing or escaping. ADJ passing or vanishing quickly.

fugue NOUN a musical composition using repeated themes in increasingly complex patterns.

fulcrum NOUN (PL **-cra** or **-crums**) the point of support on which a lever pivots.

fulfil ([US] **fulfill**) VERB (**fulfilled, fulfilling**) **1** accomplish; satisfy, do what is required by a contract etc. **2** (**fulfil yourself**) develop and use your abilities fully. **fulfilment** NOUN

full ADJ **1** holding or containing as much as is possible; having a lot of something. **2** complete. **3** plump; (of a garment) using much material in folds or gathers; (of a tone) deep and mellow. ADV directly; very. **full-blooded** vigorous and hearty. **full-blown** fully developed. **full moon** the moon with the whole disc illuminated. **full stop** a dot used as a punctuation mark at the end of a sentence or abbreviation.

fully ADV

fullback NOUN (in football etc.) a defensive player positioned near the goal.

fulminate VERB protest strongly.

fulsome ADJ excessively flattering.

fumble VERB use your hands clumsily; grope about.

fume NOUN pungent smoke or vapour. VERB **1** emit fumes. **2** be very angry.

fumigate VERB disinfect with chemical fumes.
fumigation NOUN

fun NOUN light-hearted amusement.
make fun of cause people to laugh at.

function NOUN **1** the special activity or purpose of a person or thing. **2** an important ceremony. **3** (in mathematics) a relation involving variables; a quantity whose value depends on varying values of others. VERB perform a function; work or operate.

functional ADJ of uses or purposes; practical and useful; working or operating.
functionally ADV

functionary NOUN (PL **-ies**) an official.

fund NOUN a sum of money for a special purpose; (**funds**) financial resources; a stock or supply. VERB provide with money.

fundamental ADJ basic; essential. NOUN a fundamental fact or principle.
fundamentally ADV

fundamentalist NOUN a person who upholds a strict or literal interpretation of traditional religious beliefs.
fundamentalism NOUN

funeral NOUN a ceremony of burial or cremation.

funereal ADJ solemn or dismal.

funfair NOUN a fair consisting of amusements and sideshows.

fungicide NOUN a substance that kills fungus.

fungus NOUN (PL **-gi**) a plant without green colouring matter (e.g. a mushroom or mould).
fungal ADJ

funk NOUN popular dance music with a strong

rhythm.

funky ADJ

funnel NOUN **1** a tube with a wide top for pouring liquid into small openings. **2** a chimney on a steam engine or ship. VERB (**funnelled, funnelling;** [US] **funneled, funneling**) guide through a funnel.

funny ADJ (**-ier, -iest**) **1** causing amusement. **2** puzzling or odd. **funnily** ADV

fur NOUN **1** the short fine hair of certain animals; a skin with this used for clothing. **2** a coating on the inside of a kettle etc. VERB (**furred, furring**) become covered with fur.

furious ADJ very angry; intense or violent.

furl VERB roll up and fasten a piece of fabric.

furlong NOUN an eighth of a mile.

furlough NOUN leave of absence.

furnace NOUN an enclosed fireplace for intense heating or smelting.

furnish VERB **1** provide with furniture. **2** supply someone with something.

furnishings PLURAL NOUN furniture and fitments etc.

furniture NOUN movable articles (e.g. chairs, beds) for use in a room.

furore ([US] **furor**) NOUN an outbreak of public anger or excitement.

furrier NOUN a person who deals in furs.

furrow NOUN a long cut in the ground; a groove. VERB make furrows in.

furry ADJ (**-ier, -iest**) like fur; covered with fur.

further (or **farther**) ADV & ADJ **1** at, to, or over a greater distance; more distant. **2** to a greater extent. **3** additional(ly). VERB help the progress of.

furtherance NOUN assistance or advancement.

furthermore ADV moreover.

furthest (or **farthest**) ADJ most distant. ADV at, to, or by the greatest distance.

furtive ADJ stealthy or secretive.

fury NOUN (PL **-ies**) wild anger; violence.

fuse VERB **1** blend metals etc.; become blended; unite. **2** (of an electrical appliance) stop working

when a fuse melts. **3** fit an appliance with a fuse. NOUN **1** a strip of wire placed in an electric circuit to melt and interrupt the current when the circuit is overloaded. **2** a length of easily burnt material for igniting a bomb or explosive.
fusible ADJ

fuselage NOUN the body of an aeroplane.

fusion NOUN fusing; the union of atomic nuclei, releasing much energy.

fuss NOUN unnecessary excitement or activity; a vigorous protest. VERB show excessive concern about something.

fussy ADJ (**-ier, -iest**) **1** hard to please. **2** full of unnecessary detail.

fusty ADJ **1** smelling stale and stuffy. **2** old-fashioned.

futile ADJ pointless.
futility NOUN

futon NOUN a Japanese padded mattress that can be rolled up.

future NOUN **1** time still to come; what may happen then. **2** a prospect of success. **3** (**futures**) goods or shares bought at an agreed price but paid for later. ADJ of time to come.

futuristic ADJ with very modern technology or design.

fuzz NOUN **1** a fluffy or frizzy mass. **2** [inf] the police.

fuzzy ADJ (**-ier, -iest**) **1** fluffy or frizzy. **2** indistinct.

Gg

g ABBREV grams.

gabble VERB talk quickly and indistinctly.

gable NOUN a triangular upper part of a wall, between sloping roofs.

gad VERB (**gadded**, **gadding**) (**gad about**) go about idly in search of pleasure.

gadget NOUN a small mechanical device or tool.
gadgetry NOUN

gaffe NOUN an embarrassing blunder.

gaffer NOUN [inf] **1** a person in charge of others. **2** an old man.

gag NOUN **1** something put over a person's mouth to silence them. **2** a joke. VERB (**gagged**, **gagging**) **1** put a gag on; deprive of freedom of speech. **2** retch.

gage US spelling of **gauge**.

gaggle NOUN a flock of geese; a disorderly group.

gaiety NOUN light-hearted and cheerful mood or behaviour.

gaily ADV **1** cheerfully. **2** thoughtlessly.

gain VERB **1** obtain or secure. **2** reach a place. **3** increase in speed, value, etc. **4** (of a clock) become fast. **5** (**gain on**) get nearer to someone or something pursued. NOUN an increase in wealth or value; something gained.

gainsay VERB (**gainsaid**, **gainsaying**) deny or contradict.

gait NOUN a manner of walking or running.

gala NOUN an occasion with special entertainments; a sports gathering.

galaxy NOUN (PL **-ies**) a system of stars, especially (**the Galaxy**) the one containing the sun and the earth. **galactic** ADJ

gale NOUN a very strong wind; a noisy outburst.

gall NOUN **1** bold impudence. **2** something very hurtful. **3** a sore made by rubbing. VERB make sore by rubbing; annoy.

gall bladder an organ attached to the liver, storing bile. **galling** ADJ

gallant ADJ brave; chivalrous. **gallantry** NOUN

galleon NOUN a large Spanish sailing ship of the 15th-17th centuries.

gallery NOUN (PL **-ies**) **1** a building for displaying works of art. **2** a balcony in a theatre or hall. **3** a long room or passage.

galley NOUN (PL **-eys**) **1** an ancient ship, usually rowed by slaves. **2** a kitchen on a boat or aircraft.

gallivant VERB [inf] go about looking for fun.

gallon NOUN a measure for liquids = 8 pints (4.546 litres).

gallop NOUN a horse's fastest pace; a ride at this pace. VERB (**galloped, galloping**) go at a gallop; go fast.

gallows NOUN a framework with a noose for hanging criminals.

galore ADV in plenty.

galoshes PLURAL NOUN rubber overshoes.

galvanize (or **-ise**) VERB 1 stimulate into activity. 2 coat iron or steel with zinc.

gambit NOUN an opening move intended to secure an advantage.

gamble VERB play games of chance for money; risk money etc. in hope of gain. NOUN an act of gambling; a risky undertaking. **gambler** NOUN

gambol VERB (**gambolled, gambolling**; [US] **gamboled, gamboling**) jump about playfully.

game NOUN 1 a form of play or sport; a period of play with a closing score. 2 wild animals hunted for sport or food. ADJ willing or eager.

gamekeeper NOUN a person employed to protect and breed game.

gamma NOUN the third letter of the Greek alphabet (Γ, γ).

gammon NOUN cured or smoked ham.

gamut NOUN the whole range or scope.

gander NOUN a male goose.

gang NOUN an organized group, especially of criminals or workers. VERB (**gang up on**) form a group to intimidate someone.

gangling ADJ tall and awkward.

gangplank NOUN a plank for walking to or from a boat.

gangrene NOUN decay of body tissue.

gangster NOUN a member of a gang of violent criminals.

gangway NOUN a passage, especially between rows of seats; a movable bridge from a ship to land.

gannet NOUN a large seabird.

gantry NOUN (PL **-ies**) an overhead framework supporting railway

gaol see **jail**.

gap NOUN a space or opening; an interval. **gappy** ADJ

gape VERB open your mouth wide; be wide open.

garage NOUN a building for storing a vehicle; an establishment selling petrol or repairing and selling vehicles.

garb NOUN clothing. VERB clothe.

garbage NOUN rubbish.

garbled ADJ (of a message or story) distorted or confused.

garden NOUN a piece of cultivated ground by a house; (**gardens**) ornamental public grounds. VERB tend a garden. **gardener** NOUN

gargantuan ADJ gigantic.

gargle VERB wash the throat with liquid held there by breathing out through it. NOUN an act of gargling; a liquid for this.

gargoyle NOUN a waterspout in the form of a grotesque carved face on a building.

signals, road signs, a crane, etc.

garish ADJ too bright and harsh.

garland NOUN a wreath of flowers as a decoration.

garlic NOUN an onion-like plant.

garment NOUN a piece of clothing.

garner VERB gather or collect.

garnet NOUN a red semi-precious stone.

garnish VERB decorate food. NOUN something used for garnishing.

garret NOUN an attic.

garrison NOUN troops stationed in a town or fort. VERB guard a town etc. with a garrison.

garrotte ([US] **garrote**) NOUN a wire or a metal collar used to strangle a victim. VERB strangle with this.

garrulous ADJ talkative.

garter NOUN a band worn round the leg to keep up a stocking.

gas NOUN (PL **-ses**) 1 an airlike substance (not a solid or liquid); such a substance used as fuel. 2 [US] petrol. VERB (**gassed, gassing**) 1 attack or kill with poisonous gas. 2 [inf] talk at length.

gaseous ADJ of or like a gas.

gash NOUN a long deep cut. VERB make a gash in.

gasket NOUN a piece of rubber etc. sealing a joint between metal surfaces.

gasoline NOUN [US] petrol.

gasp VERB draw in breath sharply; speak breathlessly. NOUN a sharp intake of breath.

gastric ADJ of the stomach.

gastroenteritis NOUN inflammation of the stomach and intestines.

gate NOUN **1** a movable barrier in a wall or fence; an entrance. **2** the number of spectators paying to attend a sporting event.

gateau NOUN (PL **-aux** or **-aus**) a large rich cream cake.

gatecrash VERB go to a private party uninvited. **gatecrasher** NOUN

gateway NOUN an opening closed by a gate; a means of entry or access.

gather VERB **1** come or bring together; collect; pick up; summon up: *gather strength*. **2** conclude or infer. **3** draw fabric together in folds by running a thread through it. NOUN a small fold in a garment.

gathering NOUN people assembled.

gauche ADJ socially awkward.

gaudy ADJ (**-ier, -iest**) extravagantly or tastelessly showy or bright. **gaudily** ADV

gauge ([US] **gage**) NOUN **1** a measuring device; a standard measure of thickness etc. **2** the distance between the rails of a railway track. VERB estimate; measure.

gaunt ADJ lean and haggard.

gauntlet NOUN a glove with a long wide cuff. **run the gauntlet** be exposed to something dangerous or unpleasant.

gauze NOUN thin transparent fabric; fine wire mesh.

gave past of **give**.

gavel NOUN a mallet used by an auctioneer or chairman to call for attention.

gay ADJ **1** homosexual. **2** [dated] light-hearted; brightly coloured. NOUN a homosexual person.

gaze VERB look long and steadily. NOUN a long steady look.

gazebo NOUN (PL **-os**) a summer house with a wide view.

gazelle NOUN a small antelope.

gazette NOUN a journal or newspaper.

gazetteer NOUN an index of places, rivers, mountains, etc.

GB ABBREV Great Britain.

GBH ABBREV grievous bodily harm.

GCE ABBREV General Certificate of Education.

GCSE ABBREV General Certificate of Secondary Education.

gear NOUN 1 a set of toothed wheels working together to change the speed of machinery; a particular setting of these. 2 [inf] equipment or clothes. VERB 1 design or adjust the gears in a machine. 2 intend or direct to a particular purpose.

gearbox NOUN a case enclosing a gear mechanism.

geese plural of **goose**.

geisha NOUN a Japanese hostess trained to entertain men.

gel NOUN a jelly-like substance.

gelatin (or **gelatine**) NOUN a clear substance made by boiling bones and used in making jelly etc. **gelatinous** ADJ

geld VERB castrate.

gelding NOUN a castrated horse.

gelignite NOUN an explosive containing nitroglycerine.

gem NOUN a precious stone; something of great beauty or excellence.

gender NOUN being male or female.

gene NOUN each of the factors controlling heredity, carried by a chromosome.

genealogy NOUN (PL **-ies**) a line of descent; the study of family pedigrees. **genealogical** ADJ

genera plural of **genus**.

general ADJ 1 of or involving all or most parts, things, or people; not detailed or specific. 2 (in titles) chief. NOUN an army officer next below field marshal.

general election an

election of parliamentary representatives from the whole country. **general practitioner** a community doctor treating cases of all kinds. **in general 1** mostly. **2** as a whole.
generally ADV

generality NOUN (PL **-ies**) a general statement; being general.

generalize (or **-ise**) VERB **1** speak in general terms. **2** make generally available.
generalization NOUN

generate VERB produce or bring into existence.

generation NOUN **1** all the people born at roughly the same time; one stage in the descent of a family. **2** generating.

generator NOUN a machine converting mechanical energy into electricity.

generic ADJ of a whole genus or group.
generically ADV

generous ADJ giving freely; large, plentiful.
generosity NOUN

genesis NOUN a beginning or origin.

genetic ADJ of genes or genetics. PLURAL NOUN (**genetics**) the science of heredity.

genetic engineering manipulation of DNA to change hereditary features.
genetically ADV
geneticist NOUN

genial ADJ kind and cheerful; (of climate etc.) pleasantly mild.
geniality NOUN
genially ADV

genie NOUN (PL **-ii**) a spirit in Arabian folk lore.

genital ADJ of animal reproduction or sex organs. PLURAL NOUN (**genitals** or **genitalia**) the external sex organs.

genitive NOUN the grammatical case expressing possession or source.

genius NOUN (PL **-ses**) exceptionally great intellectual or creative power; a person with this.

genocide NOUN deliberate extermination of a race of people.

genre NOUN a style of art or literature.

genteel ADJ polite and refined, often affectedly so.
gentility NOUN

Gentile NOUN a non-Jewish person.

gentle ADJ kind and mild; (of climate etc.) moderate. **gentleness** NOUN **gently** ADV

gentleman NOUN a well-mannered man; a man of good social position.

gentry NOUN people of good social position.

genuine ADJ really what it is said to be.

genus NOUN (PL **genera**) a group of similar animals or plants, usually containing several species; a kind.

geography NOUN the study of the earth's physical features, climate, etc.; the features and arrangement of a place. **geographer** NOUN **geographical** ADJ

geology NOUN the study of the earth's structure; the rocks etc. of a district. **geological** ADJ **geologist** NOUN

geometry NOUN the branch of mathematics dealing with lines, angles, surfaces, and solids. **geometric** ADJ **geometrical** ADJ

geranium NOUN a cultivated flowering plant.

gerbil NOUN a rodent with long hind legs, often kept as a pet.

geriatric ADJ of old people. NOUN an old person.

germ NOUN 1 a micro-organism causing disease. 2 a portion of an organism capable of developing into a new organism; a basis from which a thing may develop.

German ADJ & NOUN (a native or the language) of Germany. **German measles** see **rubella**. **German shepherd** a large breed of dog often used as guard dogs; an Alsatian.

germane ADJ relevant.

germinate VERB begin or cause to grow. **germination** NOUN

gestation NOUN the period when a fetus is developing in the womb.

gesticulate VERB make expressive movements with the hands and arms. **gesticulation** NOUN

gesture NOUN 1 a movement designed to convey a meaning.

2 something done to display good intentions etc., with no practical value. VERB make a gesture.

get VERB (**got, getting**) **1** come to possess; receive; succeed in attaining. **2** fetch. **3** experience pain etc.; catch a disease. **4** bring or come into a specified state; arrive or bring somewhere. **5** persuade, induce, or order. **6** capture.
get-together a social gathering.

getaway NOUN an escape after a crime.

geyser NOUN **1** a spring spouting hot water or steam. **2** a water heater.

ghastly ADJ (**-ier, -iest**) **1** causing horror; [inf] very unpleasant. **2** very pale.

gherkin NOUN a small pickled cucumber.

ghetto NOUN (PL **-os**) an area in which members of a minority racial etc. group are segregated.
ghetto blaster a large portable stereo radio etc.

ghost NOUN an apparition of a dead person; a faint trace.

ghostly ADJ like a ghost; eerie.

ghoul NOUN an evil spirit; a person morbidly interested in death and disaster.
ghoulish ADJ

giant NOUN (in fairy tales) a being of superhuman size; an abnormally large person, animal, or thing. ADJ very large.

gibber VERB make meaningless sounds in shock or terror.

gibberish NOUN unintelligible talk; nonsense.

gibbon NOUN a long-armed ape.

gibe see **jibe**.

giblets PLURAL NOUN the liver, heart, etc., of a fowl.

giddy ADJ (**-ier, -iest**) having the feeling that everything is spinning; excitable and silly.

gift NOUN **1** something given or received without payment; a very easy task. **2** a natural talent or ability.

gifted ADJ having great natural ability.

gig NOUN [inf] a live performance by a pop group.

gigantic ADJ very large.

giggle VERB laugh quietly.

NOUN such a laugh.
giggly ADJ

gild VERB cover with a thin layer of gold or gold paint.

gill NOUN one-quarter of a pint.

gills NOUN the organ with which a fish breathes.

gilt ADJ gilded. NOUN gold leaf or paint used in gilding.
gilt-edged (of an investment etc.) very safe.

gimmick NOUN a trick or device to attract attention.
gimmicky ADJ.I

gin NOUN an alcoholic spirit flavoured with juniper berries.

ginger NOUN 1 a hot-tasting root used as a spice. 2 a light reddish-yellow colour.

gingerbread NOUN ginger-flavoured cake.

gingerly ADV cautiously.

gingham NOUN cotton fabric with a checked or striped pattern.

gingivitis NOUN inflammation of the gums.

ginseng NOUN a medicinal plant with a fragrant root.

Gipsy see **Gypsy**.

giraffe NOUN a long-necked African animal.

gird VERB [literary] encircle with a belt or band.

girder NOUN a metal beam supporting a structure.

girdle NOUN a belt; an elastic corset. VERB surround.

girl NOUN a female child; a young woman.

girlfriend NOUN a female friend; a woman with whom someone has a romantic relationship.

giro NOUN (PL **-os**) a banking system in which payment can be made by transferring credit from one account to another; a cheque or payment made by this.

girth NOUN the measurement round something, especially someone's stomach; a band under a horse's belly holding a saddle in place.

gist NOUN the essential points or general sense of a speech etc.

give VERB (**gave, given, giving**) 1 hand over; cause someone to receive something; devote to a cause; cause someone to experience something.

2 do; utter. **3** yield under pressure. NOUN elasticity.

give in acknowledge defeat. **give up** abandon hope or an effort.

glacé ADJ preserved in sugar.

glacial ADJ of or from glaciers; very cold.

glaciation NOUN the formation of glaciers.

glacier NOUN a mass or river of ice moving very slowly.

glad ADJ pleased or joyful.
gladden VERB

glade NOUN an open space in a forest.

gladiator NOUN a man trained to fight at public shows in ancient Rome.

glamour ([US] **glamor**) NOUN an attractive and exciting quality.
glamorize (or **-ise**) VERB
glamorous ADJ

glance VERB **1** look briefly. **2** strike something and bounce off at an angle. NOUN a brief look.

gland NOUN an organ that secretes substances to be used or expelled by the body.
glandular ADJ

glare VERB stare angrily or fiercely; shine with a harsh dazzling light. NOUN a fierce stare; a harsh light.

glaring ADJ conspicuous.

glass NOUN **1** a hard brittle transparent substance; a drinking container made of this; a mirror. **2** (**glasses**) spectacles; binoculars.
glassy ADJ

glasshouse NOUN a greenhouse.

glaucoma NOUN a condition causing gradual loss of sight.

glaze VERB **1** fit or cover with glass. **2** coat with a glossy surface. **3** (of eyes etc.) lose brightness and animation. NOUN a shiny surface or coating.

glazier NOUN a person whose job is to fit glass in windows.

gleam NOUN a briefly shining light; a brief or faint show of a quality. VERB shine brightly.

glean VERB pick up grain left by harvesters; collect.

glee NOUN lively or triumphant joy.
gleeful ADJ

glen NOUN a narrow valley.

glib ADJ articulate but insincere or superficial.

glide VERB move smoothly; fly in a glider. NOUN a gliding movement.

glider NOUN an aeroplane with no engine.

glimmer NOUN a faint gleam. VERB gleam faintly.

glimpse NOUN a brief view of something. VERB catch a glimpse of.

glint NOUN a brief flash of light. VERB send out a glint.

glisten VERB shine like something wet.

glitch NOUN [inf] a sudden problem or fault.

glitter VERB & NOUN sparkle

gloat VERB exult in your own success or another's misfortune.

global ADJ worldwide; of or affecting an entire group.
global warming an increase in the temperature of the earth's atmosphere.
globally ADV

globe NOUN a ball-shaped object, especially one with a map of the earth on it; the world.

globetrotter NOUN [inf] a person who travels widely.

globular ADJ globe-shaped.

globule NOUN a small round drop.

glockenspiel NOUN a musical instrument of metal bars or tubes struck by hammers.

gloom NOUN 1 semi-darkness. 2 depression or sadness.
gloomy ADJ

glorify VERB (**glorified, glorifying**) 1 praise highly; worship. 2 make something seem grander than it is.
glorification NOUN

glorious ADJ having or bringing glory; beautiful or impressive.

glory NOUN (PL **-ies**) fame, honour, and praise; beauty or splendour; a source of fame and pride. VERB take pride or pleasure in something.

gloss NOUN 1 a shine on a smooth surface. 2 a translation or explanation. VERB (**gloss over**) try to conceal a fault etc.
glossy ADJ

glossary NOUN (PL **-ies**) a list of technical or special words with definitions.

glove NOUN a covering for

the hand with separate divisions for fingers and thumb.

glow VERB 1 send out light and heat without flame; have a warm or flushed look or colour. 2 (**glowing**) expressing great praise. NOUN a glowing state.
glow-worm a beetle that can give out a greenish light.

glower VERB scowl.

glucose NOUN a form of sugar found in fruit juice.

glue NOUN a sticky substance used for joining things. VERB (**glued**, **gluing**) fasten with glue; attach closely.

glum ADJ sad and gloomy.

glut VERB (**glutted**, **glutting**) supply or fill to excess. NOUN an excessive supply.

glutinous ADJ sticky.

glutton NOUN a greedy person; a person who is eager for something. **gluttonous** ADJ **gluttony** NOUN

glycerine ([US] **glycerin**) NOUN a thick sweet liquid used in medicines etc.

GMT ABBREV Greenwich Mean Time.

gnarled ADJ knobbly; twisted and misshapen.

gnash VERB grind your teeth.

gnat NOUN a small biting fly.

gnaw VERB bite persistently at something hard.

gnome NOUN a dwarf in fairy tales.

gnu NOUN a large heavy antelope.

go VERB (**goes**, **went**, **gone**, **going**) 1 move or travel. 2 depart; (of time) pass. 3 pass into a specified state; proceed in a specified way: *the party went well.* 4 fit into or be regularly kept in a particular place. 5 function or operate. 6 come to an end; disappear or be used up. NOUN (PL **goes**) 1 an attempt; a turn to do something. 2 energy.
go-ahead [inf] permission to proceed. **go-between** a messenger or negotiator. **go-cart** (or **go-kart**) a miniature racing car. **go off** 1 explode. 2 (of food) become stale or bad.

goad NOUN a pointed stick for driving cattle; a stimulus to activity. VERB provoke to action.

goal NOUN 1 a structure or

area into which players send the ball to score a point in certain games; a point scored. **2** an ambition or aim.

goalkeeper NOUN a player whose job is to keep the ball out of the goal.

goalpost NOUN either of the posts marking the limit of a goal.

goat NOUN a horned animal, often kept for milk.

gobble VERB **1** eat quickly and greedily. **2** (of a turkey) make a throaty sound.

gobbledegook NOUN [inf] unintelligible language.

goblet NOUN a drinking glass with a stem and a foot.

goblin NOUN a mischievous ugly elf.

god NOUN **1** a superhuman being or spirit. **2** (**God**) (in Christianity and some other religions) the creator and supreme ruler of the universe.

goddess NOUN a female deity.

godfather NOUN **1** a male godparent. **2** a head of an illegal organization, especially the Mafia.

godforsaken ADJ with no merit or attractiveness.

godmother NOUN a female godparent.

godparent NOUN a person who represents a child at baptism and takes responsibility for its religious education.

godsend NOUN a very helpful thing, person, or event.

goggle VERB stare with wide-open eyes.

goggles PLURAL NOUN protective glasses.

gold NOUN a yellow metal of high value; coins or articles made of this; its colour; a gold medal (awarded as first prize). ADJ made of or coloured like gold.

gold leaf gold beaten into a very thin sheet. **gold rush** a rush to a newly discovered goldfield.

golden ADJ **1** gold. **2** very happy.

golden jubilee the 50th anniversary of a sovereign's reign. **golden wedding** the 50th anniversary of a wedding.

goldfish NOUN a small reddish carp kept in a bowl or pond.

goldsmith NOUN a person who makes gold articles.

golf NOUN a game in which a ball is struck with clubs into a series of holes. **golfer** NOUN

gondola NOUN a boat with high pointed ends, used on canals in Venice. **gondolier** NOUN

gone past participle of **go**.

gong NOUN a metal plate that resounds when struck.

goo NOUN [inf] a sticky wet substance. **gooey** ADJ

good ADJ (**better, best**) **1** to be desired or approved of; pleasing or welcome. **2** having the right or necessary qualities; performing a particular function well; beneficial. **3** morally correct. **4** well behaved. **5** enjoyable. **6** thorough. NOUN **1** that which is morally right. **2** benefit or advantage. **3** (**goods**) products or possessions; items to be transported. **good-for-nothing** worthless. **Good Friday** the Friday before Easter, commemorating the Crucifixion of Jesus.

goodbye EXCLAMATION & NOUN an expression used when parting.

goodwill NOUN friendly feelings towards other people.

goose NOUN (PL **geese**) a web-footed bird larger than a duck; the female of this. **goose-step** a way of marching in which the legs are kept straight.

gooseberry NOUN an edible berry with a hairy skin.

gopher NOUN an American burrowing rodent.

gore NOUN blood from a wound. VERB pierce with a horn or tusk.

gorge NOUN a narrow steep-sided valley. VERB eat greedily.

gorgeous ADJ beautiful; [inf] very pleasant or attractive.

gorilla NOUN a large powerful ape.

gorse NOUN a wild evergreen thorny shrub with yellow flowers.

gory ADJ covered with blood; involving bloodshed.

gosling NOUN a young goose.

gospel NOUN **1** the teachings of Jesus; (**Gospel**) any of the first four books of the New Testament. **2** something regarded as definitely true.

gossamer NOUN a fine piece of cobweb.

gossip NOUN casual talk about other people's affairs; a person fond of such talk. VERB (**gossiped**, **gossiping**) engage in gossip.

got past and past participle of **get**.

gotten [US] = **got**.

gouge NOUN a chisel with a concave blade. VERB cut out with a gouge; scoop or force out.

goulash NOUN a rich stew of meat and vegetables.

gourd NOUN a hard-skinned fruit whose rind is used as a container.

gourmand NOUN a food lover; a glutton.

gourmet NOUN a connoisseur of good food and drink.

gout NOUN a disease causing inflammation of the joints.

govern VERB conduct the policy etc. of a country, state, etc.; control or influence.

governor NOUN

governance NOUN governing or control.

governess NOUN a woman employed to teach children in a private household.

government NOUN the governing body of a state; the system by which a state is governed.

governmental ADJ

gown NOUN a long dress; a loose overgarment; an official robe.

GP ABBREV general practitioner.

grab VERB (**grabbed**, **grabbing**) grasp suddenly; take greedily. NOUN a sudden clutch or attempt to seize something.

grace NOUN **1** elegance of movement. **2** courtesy; an attractive manner. **3** mercy. **4** a short prayer of thanks for a meal. VERB honour a place etc. with your presence; be an ornament to.

graceful ADJ

gracefully ADV

gracious ADJ kind and pleasant, especially towards inferiors.

gradation NOUN a series of changes; a stage in such a series.

grade NOUN 1 a level of rank or quality; a mark indicating standard of work. 2 [US] a class in school. VERB arrange in grades; assign a grade to.

gradient NOUN a slope; the angle of a slope.

gradual ADJ taking place in stages over a long period.

gradually ADV

graduate NOUN a person who has a university degree. VERB 1 obtain a university degree. 2 change something gradually.

graduation NOUN

graffiti PLURAL NOUN words or drawings scribbled or sprayed on a wall.

graft NOUN 1 a plant shoot fixed into a cut in another plant to form a new growth; living tissue transplanted surgically. 2 [inf] hard work. 3 [inf] bribery. VERB insert a graft in a plant; transplant tissue.

Grail NOUN (in medieval legend) the cup or bowl used by Jesus at the Last Supper.

grain NOUN 1 small seed(s) of a food plant such as wheat or rice; these plants; a small hard particle; a very small amount. 2 the pattern of fibres in wood etc.

gram (or **gramme**) NOUN one-thousandth of a kilogram.

grammar NOUN (the rules governing) the use of words in their correct forms and relationships; a book analysing this.

grammatical ADJ conforming to the rules of grammar.

grammatically ADV

gran NOUN [inf] grandmother.

granary NOUN (PL **-ies**) a storehouse for grain.

grand ADJ large and imposing; ambitious; [inf] excellent. NOUN a grand piano.

grand piano a large piano with horizontal strings.

grandchild NOUN a child of your son or daughter.

granddad NOUN [inf] grandfather.

granddaughter NOUN a female grandchild.

grandeur NOUN splendour.

grandfather NOUN a male grandparent.

grandiloquent ADJ using pompous language.

grandiose ADJ imposing; planned on a large scale.

grandma NOUN [inf] grandmother.

grandmother NOUN a female grandparent.

grandpa NOUN [inf] grandfather.

grandparent NOUN a parent of your father or mother.

grandson NOUN a male grandchild.

grandstand NOUN the principal stand for spectators at a sports ground.

granite NOUN a hard grey stone.

granny (or **grannie**) NOUN (PL **-ies**) [inf] grandmother.

grant VERB 1 give or allow as a privilege. 2 admit to be true. NOUN a sum of money given from public funds for a particular purpose.
take for granted 1 fail to appreciate or be grateful for. 2 assume to be true.

granule NOUN a small grain.
granular ADJ

grape NOUN a green or purple berry growing in clusters, used for making wine.

grapefruit NOUN a large round yellow citrus fruit.

grapevine NOUN a vine bearing grapes.
on the grapevine by a rumour spread unofficially.

graph NOUN a diagram showing the relationship between quantities.

graphic ADJ 1 of drawing, painting, or engraving. 2 giving a vivid description. NOUN (**graphics**) diagrams used in calculation and design; drawings.
graphically ADV

graphite NOUN a form of carbon.

graphology NOUN the study of handwriting.

grapple VERB wrestle; struggle.

grasp VERB 1 seize and hold. 2 understand. NOUN 1 a firm hold or grip. 2 an understanding.

grasping ADJ greedy for money etc.

grass NOUN 1 a plant with green blades; a species of this (e.g. a cereal plant);

ground covered with grass. **2** [inf] marijuana. **3** [inf] an informer.

grass roots the ordinary people in an organization etc., rather than the leaders.

grassy ADJ

grasshopper NOUN a jumping insect that makes a chirping noise.

grate NOUN a metal framework keeping fuel in a fireplace. VERB **1** shred finely by rubbing against a jagged surface. **2** make a harsh noise; have an irritating effect.

grateful ADJ thankful and appreciative.

gratefully ADV

grater NOUN a device for grating food.

gratify VERB (**gratified**, **gratifying**) give pleasure to; satisfy wishes.

gratification NOUN

grating NOUN a screen of spaced bars placed across an opening.

gratis ADJ & ADV free of charge.

gratitude NOUN being grateful.

gratuitous ADJ uncalled for.

gratuity NOUN (PL **-ies**) a small financial reward.

grave[1] NOUN a hole dug to bury a corpse.

grave[2] ADJ **1** causing anxiety or concern. **2** solemn.

gravel NOUN small stones, used for paths etc.

gravelly ADJ **1** like or consisting of gravel. **2** rough-sounding.

graven ADJ carved.

gravestone NOUN a stone placed over a grave.

graveyard NOUN a burial ground.

gravitate VERB be drawn towards.

gravitation NOUN movement towards a centre of gravity.

gravitational ADJ

gravity NOUN **1** the force that attracts bodies towards the centre of the earth. **2** seriousness; solemnity.

gravy NOUN (PL **-ies**) sauce made from the juices from cooked meat.

gray US spelling of **grey**.

graze VERB **1** (of cattle) feed on growing grass; [inf] frequently eat snacks. **2** injure by scraping the skin; touch or scrape lightly in passing. NOUN a grazed place on the skin.

grease NOUN a thick, oily substance used as a lubricant. VERB put grease on.
greasy ADJ

greasepaint NOUN make-up used by actors.

great ADJ much above average in size, amount, or intensity; of outstanding ability or character; important; [inf] very good.
great-aunt (or **great-uncle**) an aunt (or uncle) of your mother or father.

greatly ADV very much.

greed NOUN excessive desire for food, wealth, power, etc.
greedy ADJ

green ADJ 1 of the colour of growing grass; covered with growing grass.
2 concerned with protecting the environment.
3 inexperienced or naive.
NOUN a green colour; a piece of grassy public land; (**greens**) green vegetables.
green belt an area of open land round a town.

greenery NOUN green foliage or plants.

greenfly NOUN a green aphid.

greengrocer NOUN a shopkeeper selling vegetables and fruit.

greenhouse NOUN a glass building for rearing plants.
greenhouse effect the trapping of the sun's radiation by pollution in the atmosphere, causing a rise in temperature.
greenhouse gas a gas contributing to the greenhouse effect.

greet VERB address politely on meeting; welcome; become apparent to sight or hearing.
greeting NOUN

gregarious ADJ sociable.

gremlin NOUN an imaginary mischievous spirit blamed for mechanical faults.

grenade NOUN a small bomb thrown by hand or fired from a rifle.

grew past of **grow**.

grey ([US] **gray**) ADJ of the colour between black and white; dull or depressing. NOUN a grey colour.

greyhound NOUN a swift, slender breed of dog.

grid NOUN a grating; a

system of numbered squares for map references; a network of lines, power cables, etc.

gridiron NOUN a framework of metal bars for cooking on.

gridlock NOUN a traffic jam affecting intersecting streets.

grief NOUN deep sorrow.

grievance NOUN a cause for complaint.

grieve VERB cause grief to; feel grief.

grievous ADJ very serious or distressing.

griffin (or **gryphon**) NOUN a mythological creature with an eagle's head and wings and a lion's body.

griffon NOUN 1 a small terrier-like dog. 2 a vulture.

grill NOUN 1 a device on a cooker for radiating heat downwards; food cooked on this. 2 a grille. VERB 1 cook under a grill or on a gridiron. 2 [inf] question closely and severely.

grille (or **grill**) NOUN a framework of metal bars or wires.

grim ADJ (**grimmer**, **grimmest**) stern or severe; forbidding; disagreeable.

grimace NOUN a contortion of the face in pain or amusement. VERB make a grimace.

grime NOUN ingrained dirt. **grimy** ADJ

grin VERB (**grinned**, **grinning**) smile broadly. NOUN a broad smile.

grind VERB (**ground**, **grinding**) 1 crush into grains or powder. 2 sharpen or smooth by friction; rub together gratingly. 3 oppress. NOUN [inf] hard or tedious work.

grindstone NOUN a revolving disc for sharpening or grinding things.

grip VERB (**gripped**, **gripping**) hold firmly; hold the attention of; affect deeply. NOUN 1 a firm grasp; a method of holding. 2 understanding of or skill in something. 3 a travelling bag.

gripe VERB [inf] grumble. NOUN 1 [inf] a complaint. 2 colic pain.

gripping ADJ very interesting or exciting.

grisly ADJ (**-ier**, **-iest**) causing fear, horror, or disgust.

grist NOUN grain to be

ground.

gristle NOUN tough inedible tissue in meat.

grit NOUN **1** particles of stone or sand. **2** [inf] courage and endurance. VERB (**gritted, gritting**) **1** clench the teeth in determination. **2** spread grit on a road etc. **gritty** ADJ

grizzle VERB [inf] cry fretfully.

grizzled ADJ grey-haired.

groan NOUN & VERB (make) a long deep sound of pain or despair.

grocer NOUN a shopkeeper selling food and household goods.

grocery NOUN (PL **-ies**) a grocer's shop; (**groceries**) a grocer's goods.

grog NOUN a drink of spirits mixed with water.

groggy ADJ (**-ier, -iest**) [inf] weak and unsteady.

groin NOUN **1** the place where the thighs join the abdomen. **2** US spelling of **groyne**.

grommet NOUN **1** a protective metal ring or eyelet. **2** a tube placed through the eardrum to drain the ear.

groom NOUN **1** a person employed to look after horses. **2** a bridegroom. VERB **1** clean and brush an animal; make neat and tidy. **2** prepare a person for a career or position.

groove NOUN a long narrow channel; a fixed routine. VERB cut grooves in.

grope VERB feel about with your hands.

gross ADJ **1** unattractively large or fat. **2** vulgar; [inf] repulsive. **3** (of income etc.) without deductions. NOUN (PL **gross**) twelve dozen. VERB produce or earn as total profit.

grotesque ADJ very odd or ugly.

grotto NOUN (PL **-oes** or **-os**) a picturesque cave.

grouch NOUN [inf] a grumbler; a complaint. **grouchy** ADJ

ground¹ past & past participle of **grind**.

ground² NOUN **1** the solid surface of the earth; an area of this; land of a specified type or used for a specified purpose; (**grounds**) land belonging to a large house. **2** (**grounds**) the reason or justification for a belief or action. **3** (**grounds**) coffee dregs. VERB **1** prevent an aircraft or a pilot from flying. **2** give a basis to. **3** instruct thoroughly in a subject.

ground rent rent paid by the owner of a building to the owner of the land on which it is built.

grounding NOUN basic training.

groundless ADJ without basis or good reason.

groundnut NOUN a peanut.

groundsheet NOUN a waterproof sheet for spreading on the ground.

groundsman NOUN a person employed to look after a sports ground.

groundswell NOUN **1** slow heavy waves. **2** an increasingly forceful public opinion.

groundwork NOUN preliminary or basic work.

group NOUN a number of people or things placed or classed together; a band of pop musicians. VERB form or put into a group; classify.

grouse NOUN **1** a game bird. **2** [inf] a complaint. VERB [inf] grumble.

grout NOUN thin fluid mortar. VERB fill with grout.

grove NOUN a group of trees.

grovel VERB (**grovelled**, **grovelling**; [US] **groveled**, **groveling**) crawl face downwards; behave humbly.

grow VERB (**grew, grown, growing**) **1** (of a living thing) develop and get bigger. **2** become larger or greater over a period of time. **3** become gradually or increasingly: *we grew braver.* **4** (**grow up**) become an adult.

grown-up (an) adult.

growl VERB make a low threatening sound as a dog does. NOUN this sound.

growth NOUN the process of growing; something that has grown; a tumour.

groyne ([US] **groin**) NOUN a solid structure built out into the sea to prevent erosion.

grub NOUN **1** the worm-like larva of certain insects. **2** [inf] food. VERB (**grubbed**, **grubbing**) **1** dig the surface of soil. **2** rummage.

grubby ADJ (**-ier, -iest**) dirty.

grudge NOUN a feeling of

guest

resentment or ill will. VERB begrudge or resent.

gruel NOUN thin oatmeal porridge.

gruelling ([US] **grueling**) ADJ very tiring.

gruesome ADJ horrifying or disgusting.

gruff ADJ (of the voice) low and hoarse; (of a person) appearing bad-tempered.

grumble VERB 1 complain in a bad-tempered way. 2 rumble. NOUN 1 a complaint. 2 a rumbling sound.

grumpy ADJ (**-ier, -iest**) bad-tempered. **grumpily** ADV

grunge NOUN a style of rock music with a raucous guitar sound.

grunt NOUN a gruff snorting sound made or like that made by a pig. VERB make this sound.

gryphon NOUN see **griffin**.

G-string NOUN skimpy knickers consisting of a narrow strip of cloth attached to a waistband.

guarantee NOUN a formal promise to do something or that a thing is of a specified quality; something offered as security. VERB give or be a guarantee.

guarantor NOUN the giver of a guarantee.

guard VERB watch over to protect, prevent escape, etc.; take precautions. NOUN 1 a person guarding someone or something; a railway official in charge of a train; a protective part or device. 2 a state of watchfulness.

guarded ADJ cautious.

guardian NOUN a person who guards or protects; a person legally responsible for someone unable to manage their own affairs.

guava NOUN a tropical fruit.

guerrilla (or **guerilla**) NOUN a member of a small independent group fighting against the government etc.

guess VERB form an opinion without definite knowledge; think likely. NOUN an opinion formed by guessing.

guesswork NOUN guessing.

guest NOUN a person entertained at another's house, or staying at a hotel; a visiting performer.

guest house a private

house offering accommodation to paying guests.

guffaw NOUN a coarse noisy laugh. VERB laugh in this way.

guidance NOUN guiding; advice.

guide NOUN 1 a person who shows others the way; a person employed to point out sights to travellers. 2 a thing helping you to make a decision; a book of information, maps, etc.; a structure marking the correct position or direction of something. VERB act as a guide to.

guidebook NOUN a book of information about a place.

guild NOUN a society for mutual aid or with a common purpose; [historical] an association of craftsmen or merchants.

guile NOUN craftiness.

guillotine NOUN a machine for beheading criminals; a machine for cutting paper or metal. VERB behead or cut with a guillotine.

guilt NOUN the fact of having committed an offence; a feeling that you are to blame.

guilty ADJ (**-ier, -iest**) having committed an offence; feeling or showing guilt.
guiltily ADV

guinea NOUN a former British coin worth 21 shillings (£1.05).

guinea pig NOUN 1 a small domesticated rodent. 2 a person or thing used as a subject for an experiment.

guise NOUN a false outward appearance.

guitar NOUN a stringed musical instrument.
guitarist NOUN

gulf NOUN 1 a large area of sea partly surrounded by land. 2 a deep ravine; a wide difference in opinion.

gull NOUN a seabird with long wings.

gullet NOUN the passage by which food goes from mouth to stomach.

gullible ADJ easily deceived.
gullibility NOUN

gully NOUN (PL **-ies**) a narrow channel cut by water or carrying rainwater from a building.

gulp VERB swallow food etc. hastily or greedily. NOUN the act of gulping; a large

gutsy

mouthful of liquid gulped.

gum NOUN **1** the firm flesh in which teeth are rooted. **2** a sticky substance exuded by certain trees; glue; chewing gum. VERB (**gummed, gumming**) smear or stick together with gum.

gummy ADJ

gumboots PLURAL NOUN wellingtons.

gumption NOUN [inf] resourcefulness or spirit.

gun NOUN a weapon that fires shells or bullets from a metal tube; a device forcing out a substance through a tube. VERB (**gunned, gunning**) shoot someone with a gun.

gunfire NOUN the firing of guns.

gunge NOUN [inf] an unpleasantly sticky and messy substance.

gunman NOUN a person armed with a gun.

gunnel see **gunwale**.

gunner NOUN an artillery soldier; a member of an aircraft crew operating a gun.

gunpowder NOUN an explosive of saltpetre, sulphur, and charcoal.

gunrunning NOUN the smuggling of firearms.

gunwale (or **gunnel**) NOUN the upper edge of a boat's side.

gurgle NOUN & VERB (make) a low bubbling sound.

guru NOUN (PL **-us**) a Hindu spiritual teacher; a revered teacher.

gush VERB **1** flow in a strong, fast stream. **2** express excessive or insincere enthusiasm. VERB a strong, fast flow.

gusset NOUN a piece of cloth inserted to strengthen or enlarge a garment.

gust NOUN a sudden rush of wind, rain, or smoke. VERB blow in gusts.

gusty ADJ

gusto NOUN zest or enthusiasm.

gut NOUN **1** the belly or intestine; (**guts**) the internal parts or essence of something. **2** (**guts**) [inf] courage and determination. VERB (**gutted, gutting**) remove the guts from fish; remove or destroy the internal parts of a building etc.

gutsy ADJ [inf] brave and determined.

gutter NOUN **1** a trough round a roof, or a channel beside a road, for carrying away rainwater. **2** (**the gutter**) a life of poverty. VERB (of a candle) burn unsteadily.

guttural ADJ throaty or harsh-sounding.

guy NOUN **1** [inf] a man. **2** an effigy of Guy Fawkes burnt on 5 Nov. **3** a rope or chain to keep a thing steady or secured.

guzzle VERB eat or drink greedily.

gym NOUN a gymnasium; gymnastics.

gymkhana NOUN a horse-riding competition.

gymnasium NOUN (PL -nasia or -nasiums) a room equipped for physical training and gymnastics.

gymnast NOUN an expert in gymnastics.

gymnastics PLURAL NOUN exercises involving physical agility and coordination.
gymnastic ADJ

gynaecology ([US] **gynecology**) NOUN the study of the physiological functions and diseases of women.
gynaecological ADJ
gynaecologist NOUN

gypsum NOUN a chalk-like mineral used in building etc.

Gypsy (or **Gipsy**) NOUN (PL -ies) a member of a travelling people.

gyrate VERB move in circles or spirals.
gyration NOUN

gyroscope NOUN a device used to keep navigation instruments steady, consisting of a disc rotating on an axis.

ha ABBREV hectares.

haberdasher NOUN a seller of sewing materials etc. **haberdashery** NOUN

habit NOUN 1 a regular way of behaving; [inf] an addiction. 2 a monk's or nun's long dress.

habitable ADJ suitable for living in.

habitat NOUN an animal's or plant's natural environment.

habitation NOUN a place to live in.

habitual ADJ done regularly or constantly; usual. **habitually** ADV

habituate VERB accustom.

hack NOUN 1 a writer producing dull, unoriginal work. 2 a horse for ordinary riding. VERB 1 cut, chop, or hit roughly. 2 gain unauthorized access to computer files. 3 ride a horse for pleasure and exercise. **hacker** NOUN

hacking ADJ (of a cough) dry and frequent.

hackles PLURAL NOUN the hairs on the back of an animal's neck, raised in anger.

hackneyed ADJ (of a phrase etc.) over-used and lacking impact.

hacksaw NOUN a saw for metal.

had past and past participle of **have**.

haddock NOUN an edible sea fish.

haemoglobin ([US] **hemoglobin**) NOUN the red oxygen-carrying substance in blood.

haemophilia ([US] **hemophilia**) NOUN a condition in which blood fails to clot, causing excessive bleeding. **haemophiliac** NOUN

haemorrhage ([US] **hemorrhage**) NOUN heavy bleeding.

haemorrhoid ([US] **hemorrhoid**) NOUN a swollen vein at or near the anus.

hag NOUN an ugly old

woman.

haggard ADJ looking pale and exhausted.

haggis NOUN a Scottish dish made from sheep's offal, oatmeal, etc.

haggle VERB argue about the price or terms of a deal.

hail NOUN a shower of frozen rain; a shower of blows, questions, etc. VERB 1 pour down as or like hail. 2 call out to; welcome or acclaim.

hailstone NOUN a pellet of frozen rain.

hair NOUN one of the fine thread-like strands growing from the skin; these strands on a person's head.

hair-raising terrifying.

haircut NOUN an act of cutting a person's hair; a style of this.

hairdo NOUN (PL **-os**) [inf] the style of someone's hair.

hairdresser NOUN a person who cuts and arranges hair.

hairdressing NOUN

hairgrip NOUN a springy hairpin.

hairpin NOUN a U-shaped pin for keeping hair in place.

hairpin bend a sharp U-shaped bend.

hairy ADJ (**-ier, -iest**) 1 covered with hair. 2 [inf] frightening and difficult.

halcyon ADJ (of a period) happy and peaceful.

hale ADJ strong and healthy.

half NOUN (PL **halves**) 1 each of two equal parts into which something is divided. 2 half a pint, half a pound, etc. 3 [inf] a half-price fare. ADJ & PRON amounting to half of something. ADV to the extent of a half; partly.

half a dozen six. **half board** bed, breakfast, and evening meal at a hotel etc. **half-hearted** not very enthusiastic. **half-term** a short holiday halfway through a school term. **half-time** the interval between two halves of a game.

halfway ADJ & ADV at a point equidistant between two others.

halfwit NOUN a stupid person.

halibut NOUN a large edible flatfish.

halitosis NOUN breath that smells unpleasant.

hall NOUN **1** the room or space inside the front entrance of a house. **2** a large room or building for meetings, concerts, etc.

hallelujah see **alleluia**.

hallmark NOUN an official mark on precious metals to indicate their standard; a distinguishing characteristic.

hallo see **hello**.

hallucinate VERB experience hallucinations.

hallucination NOUN an illusion of seeing or hearing something.

halo NOUN (PL **-oes**) a circle of light, especially one round the head of a sacred figure.

halt VERB come or bring to a stop. NOUN a temporary stop.

halter NOUN a strap round the head of a horse for leading or holding it.

halting ADJ slow and hesitant.

halve VERB divide equally between two; reduce by half.

ham NOUN **1** smoked or salted meat from a pig's thigh. **2** a bad actor. **3** [inf] an amateur radio operator.

ham-fisted clumsy.

hamburger NOUN a flat round cake of minced beef.

hamlet NOUN a small village.

hammer NOUN **1** a tool with a head for hitting nails etc. **2** a metal ball attached to a wire, thrown in an athletic contest. VERB hit or beat with a hammer; hit forcefully; impress an idea etc. on a person's mind.

hammock NOUN a hanging bed of canvas or netting.

hamper NOUN a large lidded basket for carrying food etc. on a picnic. VERB keep from moving or acting freely.

hamster NOUN a small domesticated rodent.

hamstring NOUN a tendon at the back of a knee or hock. VERB (**hamstrung, hamstringing**) cripple by cutting the hamstrings; cripple the activity of.

hand NOUN **1** the part of the arm below the wrist. **2** a pointer on a clock, dial, etc. **3** control or influence; (**a hand**) help. **4** a manual worker. **5** the cards dealt to a player in a card game; a round of a game. **6** a round of applause. **7** a person's handwriting. **8** a unit of measurement of a horse's height. VERB give or pass.

handbag NOUN a small bag to hold a purse and personal articles.

handbook NOUN a small book giving useful facts.

handcuffs PLURAL NOUN a pair of linked metal rings for securing a prisoner's wrists. VERB put handcuffs on.

handful NOUN **1** a few. **2** [inf] a person hard to deal with or control.

handicap NOUN something that makes progress difficult; a disadvantage imposed on a superior competitor to equalize chances; a physical or mental disability. VERB (**handicapped, handicapping**) be a handicap to; place at a disadvantage.

handkerchief NOUN (PL -chiefs or -chieves) a small square of cloth for wiping the nose etc.

handle NOUN a part by which a thing is held, carried, or controlled. VERB touch or move with the hands; deal with; manage.
handler NOUN

handlebar NOUN a steering bar of a bicycle etc.

handout NOUN money etc. given to a needy person; printed information given free of charge.

handsome ADJ **1** good-looking; striking or imposing. **2** (of an amount) large.

handwriting NOUN writing by hand with pen or pencil.

handy ADJ (**-ier, -iest**) **1** ready to hand; convenient; easy to use. **2** skilled with your hands.
handily ADV

handyman NOUN a person who does minor repairs etc.

hang VERB (**hung, hanging;** in sense 2 **hanged, hanging**) **1** support or be supported from above; fasten to a wall; remain static in the air. **2** kill someone by suspending them from a rope tied round the neck. **3** (**hang out**) [inf] spend time relaxing.

hang-glider an unpowered flying device consisting of a frame from which a person hangs in a harness.

hangar NOUN a building for aircraft.

hangdog ADJ shamefaced.

hanger NOUN a shaped piece of wood, metal, etc. to hang a garment on.

hangings PLURAL NOUN draperies hung on walls.

hangman NOUN an executioner who hangs condemned people.

hangover NOUN unpleasant after-effects from drinking too much alcohol.

hanker VERB feel a longing.

hanky NOUN (PL **-ies**) [inf] a handkerchief.

haphazard ADJ done or chosen at random.

hapless ADJ unlucky.

happen VERB **1** take place; occur by chance. **2** (**happen on**) find by chance. **3** (**happen to**) be the fate or experience of.

happy ADJ (**-ier**, **-iest**) **1** pleased or contented. **2** fortunate.

happy-go-lucky cheerfully casual.

happily ADV

happiness NOUN

harangue VERB lecture earnestly and at length.

harass VERB worry or annoy continually; make repeated attacks on.

harassment NOUN

harbour ([US] **harbor**) NOUN a place for ships to moor; a refuge. VERB **1** keep a thought etc. in your mind. **2** shelter.

hard ADJ **1** solid, firm, and rigid; not showing weakness; (of information) reliable. **2** requiring effort; harsh or unpleasant. **3** powerful; (of drinks) strongly alcoholic; (of drugs) strong and addictive. ADV **1** with effort or force. **2** so as to be firm.

hard-hearted unfeeling.

hard shoulder an extra strip of road beside a motorway for use in an emergency.

harden VERB

hardbitten ADJ tough and cynical.

hardboard NOUN stiff board made of compressed wood pulp.

hardly ADV only with difficulty; scarcely.

hardship NOUN suffering or

poverty.

hardware NOUN **1** tools and household implements. **2** machinery used in a computer system.

hardwood NOUN the hard heavy wood of deciduous trees.

hardy ADJ (**-ier, -iest**) capable of enduring cold or harsh conditions.

hare NOUN a field animal like a large rabbit. VERB run rapidly.

hare-brained wild and foolish.

harelip NOUN a cleft lip.

harem NOUN the women's quarters in a Muslim household; the women living in this.

hark VERB **1** [literary] listen. **2** (**hark back**) recall something from the past.

harlequin NOUN a character in traditional pantomime.

harlot NOUN [old use] a prostitute.

harm NOUN damage or injury. VERB cause harm to.

harmful ADJ

harmless ADJ

harmonica NOUN a mouth organ.

harmonium NOUN a musical instrument like a small organ.

harmonize (or **-ise**) VERB **1** add notes to a melody to form chords. **2** make consistent; go well together.

harmony NOUN (PL **-ies**) the combination of musical notes to form chords; pleasing tuneful sound; agreement; consistency.

harmonious ADJ

harness NOUN straps and fittings by which a horse is controlled; fastenings for a parachute etc. VERB put a horse in harness; control and use resources.

harp NOUN a musical instrument with strings in a triangular frame. VERB (**harp on**) talk repeatedly about.

harpoon NOUN a spear-like missile with a rope attached. VERB spear with a harpoon.

harpsichord NOUN a piano-like instrument.

harridan NOUN a bad-tempered old woman.

harrier NOUN **1** a hound used for hunting hares. **2** a falcon.

harrow NOUN a heavy frame with metal spikes

or discs for breaking up soil. VERB draw a harrow over soil.

harrowing ADJ very distressing.

harry VERB (**harried, harrying**) harass.

harsh ADJ disagreeably rough to touch, hear, etc.; severe or cruel; grim.

harvest NOUN the gathering of crop(s); a season's yield of a natural product. VERB gather a crop.

has 3rd person singular of **have**.

has-been [inf] a person who is no longer important.

hash NOUN **1** a dish of chopped recooked meat. **2** [inf] hashish.

hashish NOUN cannabis.

hassle [inf] NOUN annoying inconvenience; harassment. VERB harass; bother.

hassock NOUN a thick firm cushion for kneeling on.

haste NOUN hurry.

hasten VERB hurry; cause to go faster.

hasty ADJ (**-ier, -iest**) hurried; acting or done too quickly.

hastily ADV

hat NOUN a covering for the head.

hat-trick three successes in a row, especially in sports.

hatch[1] NOUN an opening in a deck, ceiling, etc., to allow access.

hatch[2] VERB emerge from an egg; devise a plot.

hatchback NOUN a car with a back door that opens upwards.

hatchet NOUN a small axe.

hate NOUN hatred. VERB dislike greatly.

hateful ADJ arousing hatred.

hatred NOUN intense dislike.

haughty ADJ (**-ier, -iest**) proud and looking down on others.

haughtily ADV

haul VERB **1** pull or drag forcibly. **2** transport by truck etc. NOUN a quantity of goods stolen.

haulage NOUN transport of goods.

haulier NOUN a person or firm transporting goods by road.

haunch NOUN the fleshy part of the buttock and thigh; a leg and loin of meat.

haunt

haunt VERB (of a ghost) appear regularly at or to; linger in the mind of. NOUN a place often visited by a particular person.

haute couture NOUN high fashion.

haute cuisine NOUN high-class cookery.

have VERB (**has, had, having**) **1** possess; hold; contain. **2** experience; suffer from an illness etc. **3** cause to be or be done. **4** be obliged or compelled. **5** give birth to. **6** allow or tolerate. AUXILIARY VERB used with the past participle to form past tenses: *he has gone*.

haven NOUN a refuge.

haversack NOUN a strong bag carried on the back or shoulder.

havoc NOUN great destruction or disorder.

hawk NOUN **1** a bird of prey. **2** a person who favours an aggressive policy. VERB offer items for sale in the street.
hawker NOUN

hawthorn NOUN a thorny tree with small red berries.

hay NOUN grass cut and dried for fodder.

hay fever an allergy caused by pollen and dust.

haystack NOUN a large packed pile of hay.

haywire ADJ out of control.

hazard NOUN a danger; an obstacle. VERB risk; venture.
hazardous ADJ

haze NOUN thin mist.

hazel NOUN **1** a tree with small edible nuts (**hazelnuts**). **2** light brown.

hazy ADJ (**-ier, -iest**) misty; indistinct; vague.
hazily ADV

H-bomb NOUN a hydrogen bomb.

he PRON the male previously mentioned.

head NOUN **1** the part of the body containing the eyes, nose, mouth, and brain. **2** the intellect. **3** the front or top end of something. **4** something shaped like a head. **5** a person in charge. **6** a person considered as a unit: *six pounds a head*. **7** (**heads**) the side of a coin showing a head. VERB **1** be the head of; give a heading to. **2** move in a specified direction. **3** (in football) strike the ball with your head. **4** (**head off**) go in front of someone, forcing them to turn.

come to a head reach a crisis. **head-on** involving the front of a vehicle; involving direct confrontation.

headache NOUN a continuous pain in the head; [inf] a problem.

header NOUN a heading of the ball in football.

headhunt VERB seek to recruit senior staff from another firm.

heading NOUN **1** word(s) at the top of written matter as a title. **2** a direction or bearing.

headlamp NOUN a headlight.

headland NOUN a promontory.

headlight NOUN a powerful light on the front of a vehicle etc.

headline NOUN a heading in a newspaper; (**headlines**) a summary of broadcast news.

headlong ADJ & ADV with the head first; in a rash way.

headmaster (or **headmistress**) NOUN a teacher in charge of a school.

headphones PLURAL NOUN a set of earphones for listening to audio equipment.

headquarters PLURAL NOUN a place from which an organization is controlled.

headstone NOUN a memorial stone set up at the head of a grave.

headstrong ADJ self-willed and obstinate.

headway NOUN progress.

headwind NOUN a wind blowing from directly in front.

heady ADJ (**-ier, -iest**) intoxicating; exciting.

heal VERB make or become healthy again; cure. **healer** NOUN

health NOUN the state of being well and free from illness; mental or physical condition.

health farm an establishment offering controlled regimes of diet, exercise, massage, etc. to improve health.

healthy ADJ (**-ier, -iest**) having or showing good health; producing good

health.
healthily ADV
heap NOUN 1 a number of things or articles lying one on top of another. 2 (**heaps**) [inf] plenty. VERB pile or become piled in a heap; load with large quantities.
hear VERB (**heard, hearing**) 1 perceive sounds with the ear; be informed of; pay attention to; judge a legal case. 2 (**hear from**) be contacted by.
hearing NOUN 1 ability to hear. 2 an opportunity to state your case; a trial in court.
hearsay NOUN rumour or gossip.
hearse NOUN a vehicle carrying the coffin at a funeral.
heart NOUN 1 the muscular organ that keeps blood circulating. 2 the centre of a person's emotions or inner thoughts; courage; enthusiasm. 3 a central or essential part.
heart attack sudden failure of the heart to function normally. **heart-rending** very distressing. **heart-throb** a very good-looking famous man.

heart-to-heart frank and personal.
heartache NOUN deep sorrow.
heartbeat NOUN the pulsation of the heart.
heartbreak NOUN overwhelming grief. **heartbroken** ADJ
heartburn NOUN a burning sensation in the lower part of the chest from indigestion.
hearten VERB encourage.
heartfelt ADJ deeply and strongly felt.
hearth NOUN the floor or surround of a fireplace.
heartless ADJ not feeling pity or sympathy.
hearty ADJ (**-ier, -iest**) 1 vigorous; enthusiastic. 2 (of a meal or an appetite) large. **heartily** ADV
heat NOUN 1 being hot; high temperature; a source of this. 2 intense feeling. 3 a preliminary contest in a sporting competition. VERB make or become hot.
on heat (of female mammals) ready to mate. **heater** NOUN
heated ADJ (of a person or discussion) angry.
heath NOUN flat

uncultivated land with low shrubs.

heathen NOUN a person who does not believe in an established religion.

heather NOUN an evergreen shrub with purple, pink, or white flowers.

heatstroke NOUN an illness caused by overexposure to sun.

heatwave NOUN a long period of hot weather.

heave VERB 1 lift or haul with great effort; [inf] throw. 2 utter a sigh. 3 rise and fall like waves. 4 retch.

heaven NOUN 1 the abode of God or the gods; a place or state of great happiness. 2 (**the heavens**) [literary] the sky.

heavenly ADJ of heaven; of the sky; [inf] very pleasing.

heavy ADJ (-ier, -iest) 1 having great weight; requiring physical effort. 2 unusually great, forceful, or intense. 3 (of food) hard to digest. 4 serious; oppressive.
heavily ADV

heavyweight NOUN the heaviest boxing weight; an influential person.

heckle VERB interrupt a public speaker with aggressive questions or abuse.
heckler NOUN

hectare NOUN a unit of area equal to 10,000 sq. metres (2.471 acres).

hectic ADJ full of frantic activity.
hectically ADV

hedge NOUN a barrier or boundary of bushes or shrubs. VERB 1 surround with a hedge. 2 avoid giving a direct answer or commitment.

hedgehog NOUN a small animal covered in stiff spines.

hedgerow NOUN bushes etc. forming a hedge.

hedonism NOUN the pursuit of pleasure as the chief good.
hedonist NOUN

heed VERB pay attention to. NOUN careful attention.
heedless ADJ

heel NOUN the back part of the human foot; part of a shoe supporting this. VERB 1 renew the heel on a shoe. 2 (of a boat) tilt to one side.

hefty ADJ (-ier, -iest) large, heavy, and powerful.

heifer NOUN a young cow.

height NOUN
1 measurement from base to top or foot to head; distance above ground or sea level. 2 being tall; a high place; the highest degree of something.

heighten VERB make higher or more intense.

heinous ADJ very wicked.

heir NOUN a person entitled to inherit property or a rank.

heiress NOUN a female heir.

heirloom NOUN a possession handed down in a family for several generations.

held past and past participle of **hold**.

helicopter NOUN an aircraft with horizontally rotating overhead rotors.

helium NOUN a light colourless gas that does not burn.

helix NOUN (PL **-ices**) a spiral.

hell NOUN a place of punishment for the wicked after death; a place or state of misery.
hell-bent recklessly determined.
hellish ADJ

hello (or **hallo, hullo**) EXCLAMATION used as a greeting or to attract attention.

helm NOUN the tiller or wheel by which a ship's rudder is controlled.

helmet NOUN a protective head covering.

help VERB 1 make a task etc. easier for someone; improve or ease. 2 serve with food. 3 stop yourself: *I can't help laughing.* 4 (**help yourself**) take what you want. NOUN someone or something that helps.
helper NOUN

helpful ADJ giving help; useful.
helpfully ADV

helping NOUN a portion of food served.

helpless ADJ unable to manage without help; powerless.

helter-skelter ADV in disorderly haste. NOUN a spiral slide at a funfair.

hem NOUN an edge of cloth turned under and sewn down. VERB (**hemmed, hemming**) 1 sew a hem on. 2 (**hem in**) surround and restrict.

hemisphere NOUN half a

sphere; half of the earth.

hemlock NOUN a poisonous plant.

hemoglobin etc. US spelling of **haemoglobin** etc.

hemp NOUN a plant with coarse fibres used in making rope and cloth; cannabis.

hen NOUN a female bird, especially of a domestic fowl.
hen party [inf] a party for women only.

hence ADV **1** for this reason. **2** from this time.

henceforth (or **henceforward**) ADV from this time on.

henchman NOUN a supporter or follower.

henna NOUN a reddish-brown dye.

henpecked ADJ (of a man) nagged by his wife.

hepatitis NOUN inflammation of the liver.

heptagon NOUN a geometric figure with seven sides.

heptathlon NOUN an athletic contest involving seven events.

her PRON the objective case of **she**. ADJ belonging to a female already

mentioned.

herald VERB be a sign of; proclaim the approach of. NOUN a person or thing heralding something.

heraldry NOUN the study of coats of arms.
heraldic ADJ

herb NOUN a plant used as a flavouring or in medicine.
herbal ADJ

herbaceous border NOUN a garden border containing perennial plants.

herbivore NOUN an animal feeding on plants.
herbivorous ADJ

herd NOUN a group of animals feeding or staying together; a mob. VERB cause to move in a group.

herdsman NOUN a man who looks after livestock.

here ADV in, at, or to this place; at this point.

hereabouts ADV near here.

hereafter ADV from now on.
the hereafter life after death.

hereby ADV as a result of this.

hereditary ADJ inherited; holding a position by inheritance.

heredity NOUN inheritance of characteristics from parents.

herein ADV in this document etc.

heresy NOUN (PL **-ies**) a belief, especially a religious one, contrary to orthodox doctrine.

heretic NOUN a person who believes in a heresy.
heretical ADJ

herewith ADV [formal] with this.

heritage NOUN inherited property; a nation's historic buildings etc.

hermaphrodite NOUN a creature with male and female sexual organs.

hermetic ADJ airtight.
hermetically ADV

hermit NOUN a person living in solitude.

hernia NOUN a protrusion of part of an organ through the wall of the cavity containing it.

hero NOUN (PL **-oes**) a man admired for his brave deeds; the chief male character in a story.

heroic ADJ very brave. PLURAL NOUN (**heroics**) over-dramatic behaviour.
heroically ADV

heroin NOUN a powerful addictive drug.

heroine NOUN a woman admired for her brave deeds; the chief female character in a story.

heroism NOUN heroic conduct.

heron NOUN a long-legged wading bird.

herring NOUN an edible North Atlantic fish.

hers POSSESSIVE PRON belonging to her.

herself PRON the emphatic and reflexive form of **she** and **her**.

hertz NOUN (PL **hertz**) [Physics] a unit of frequency of electromagnetic waves.

hesitant ADJ uncertain or reluctant.
hesitancy NOUN

hesitate VERB pause doubtfully; be reluctant.
hesitation NOUN

hessian NOUN a strong coarse fabric.

heterogeneous ADJ made up of people or things of various sorts.
heterogeneity NOUN

heterosexual ADJ & NOUN (a person) sexually attracted to people of the opposite sex.

hew VERB (**hewed, hewn** or

hewed, hewing) chop or cut with an axe etc.

hexagon NOUN a geometric figure with six sides. **hexagonal** ADJ

heyday NOUN the time of someone's or something's greatest success.

HGV ABBREV heavy goods vehicle.

hiatus NOUN (PL **-tuses**) a break or gap in a sequence.

hibernate VERB spend the winter in a sleep-like state. **hibernation** NOUN

hiccup (or **hiccough**) NOUN a sudden stopping of breath with a 'hic' sound; [inf] a temporary setback. VERB (**hiccuped, hiccuping**) suffer from a hiccup.

hide VERB (**hid, hidden, hiding**) put or keep out of sight; keep secret; conceal yourself. NOUN **1** a concealed shelter used to observe wildlife. **2** an animal's skin.

hidebound ADJ rigidly conventional.

hideous ADJ very ugly.

hideout NOUN a hiding place.

hiding NOUN [inf] a severe beating.

hierarchy NOUN a system with grades ranking one above another.

hieroglyphics PLURAL NOUN writing consisting of pictorial symbols.

hi-fi ADJ of high-fidelity sound. NOUN a set of high-fidelity equipment.

higgledy-piggledy ADJ & ADV in complete confusion.

high ADJ **1** extending far upwards or a specified distance upwards; far above ground or sea level. **2** greater or more intense than normal. **3** great in status. **4** (of a sound) not deep or low. **5** (of an opinion) favourable. **6** [inf] under the influence of drugs. NOUN **1** a high level; an area of high pressure. **2** [inf] a euphoric state. ADV in, at, or to a high level. **high fidelity** the reproduction of sound with little distortion. **high-handed** using authority arrogantly. **high-rise** (of a building) with many storeys. **high school** a secondary school. **high-spirited** lively. **high-tech** involving

advanced technology.
high tide the tide at its highest level.

highbrow ADJ very intellectual.

highlands PLURAL NOUN a mountainous region.
highland ADJ
highlander NOUN

highlight NOUN **1** an outstandingly good part of something. **2** a bright area in a picture; a light streak in the hair. VERB emphasize.

highly ADV **1** to a high degree. **2** favourably.
highly strung nervous and easily upset.

highway NOUN a public road; a main route.

highwayman NOUN a person who robbed travellers in former times.

hijack VERB illegally seize control of a vehicle or aircraft in transit. NOUN hijacking.
hijacker NOUN

hike NOUN **1** a long walk. **2** a sharp increase. VERB **1** go for a hike. **2** raise.
hiker NOUN

hilarious ADJ very funny.
hilarity NOUN

hill NOUN a raised part of the earth's surface, lower than a mountain.

hilt NOUN the handle of a sword or dagger.
to the hilt completely.

him PRON the objective case of **he**.

himself PRON the emphatic and reflexive form of **he** and **him**.

hind[1] ADJ situated at the back.

hind[2] NOUN a female deer.

hinder VERB delay or obstruct.

hindrance NOUN a difficulty or obstruction.

hindsight NOUN wisdom about an event after it has occurred.

Hinduism NOUN the principal religion and philosophy of India.
Hindu ADJ & NOUN

hinge NOUN **1** a movable joint such as that on a door or lid. **2** (**hinge on**) depend on. VERB attach or join with a hinge.

hint NOUN a slight or indirect suggestion; a piece of practical information; a slight trace. VERB suggest or indicate.

hinterland NOUN the area away from the coast or around a major town.

hip NOUN 1 the projection of the pelvis on each side of the body. 2 the fruit of a rose.

hippopotamus NOUN (PL **-muses** or **-mi**) a large African river animal with a thick skin.

hippy (or **hippie**) NOUN (PL **-ies**) a young person who rejects conventional clothes and lifestyles.

hire VERB 1 purchase the temporary use of. 2 (**hire out**) grant temporary use of for payment. NOUN hiring.
hire purchase a system of purchase by payment in instalments.

hirsute ADJ hairy.

his ADJ & POSSESSIVE PRON belonging to a male already mentioned.

hiss NOUN a sound like 's'. VERB make this sound; express disapproval with a hiss.

historian NOUN an expert on history.

historic ADJ 1 important in the development of events. 2 of history.

historical ADJ of or concerned with history; belonging to the past.
historically ADV

history NOUN (PL **-ies**) the study of past events; the past; someone's or something's past.

histrionic ADJ excessively theatrical in manner. PLURAL NOUN (**histrionics**) theatrical behaviour.

hit VERB (**hit, hitting**) 1 strike with a blow or missile; strike forcefully against. 2 affect badly. 3 reach a target etc. NOUN 1 a blow; a shot that hits its target. 2 [inf] a success.
hitter NOUN

hitch VERB 1 move something with a jerk. 2 hitch-hike. 3 tether or fasten. NOUN 1 a temporary problem or setback. 2 a kind of knot.
hitch-hike travel by seeking free lifts in passing vehicles.

hither ADV to or towards this place.

hitherto ADV until this time.

HIV ABBREV human immunodeficiency virus (causing Aids).

hive NOUN 1 a structure in which bees live. 2 (**hives**) a red, itchy rash. VERB (**hive off**) separate from a larger group.

HMS ABBREV Her (or His) Majesty's Ship.

hoard VERB save and store away. NOUN a store, especially of valuable things.

hoarding NOUN a large board for displaying advertisements.

hoar frost NOUN white frost.

hoarse ADJ (of a voice) rough and harsh.

hoary ADJ (-ier, -iest) grey with age; old and unoriginal.

hoax VERB deceive jokingly. NOUN a joking deception.

hob NOUN a cooking surface with hotplates.

hobble VERB 1 walk lamely. 2 fasten the legs of a horse to limit its movement. NOUN a hobbling walk.

hobby NOUN (PL -ies) something done for pleasure in your spare time.
hobby horse a stick with a horse's head, used as a toy; [inf] a favourite topic.

hobgoblin NOUN a mischievous imp.

hobnob VERB (hobnobbed, hobnobbing) [inf] mix socially.

hock NOUN 1 the middle joint of an animal's hind leg. 2 a German white wine.

hockey NOUN a field game played with curved sticks and a small hard ball.

hocus-pocus NOUN mystifying and often deceptive talk or behaviour.

hod NOUN 1 a trough on a pole for carrying mortar or bricks. 2 a tall container for coal.

hoe NOUN a tool for loosening soil or scraping up weeds. VERB (hoed, hoeing) dig or scrape with a hoe.

hog NOUN 1 a castrated male pig reared for meat. 2 a greedy person. VERB (hogged, hogging) take greedily.

hoist VERB raise or haul up. NOUN an apparatus for hoisting things.

hoity-toity ADJ haughty.

hold VERB (held, holding) 1 grasp, carry, or support; keep or detain; contain. 2 have, possess, or occupy. 3 stay or keep at a certain level; remain true or valid. 4 consider to be of a particular nature. 5 arrange and take part in.

NOUN **1** an act, manner, or means of holding; a means of exerting influence. **2** a storage cavity below a ship's deck. **hold on** wait; endure. **hold out** resist, survive, or last. **hold-up 1** a delay. **2** a robbery.
holder NOUN

holdall NOUN a large soft travel bag.

holding NOUN **1** land held by lease. **2** (**holdings**) stocks and property owned by someone.

hole NOUN **1** a hollow space or opening in a solid object or surface **2** [inf] an unpleasant or awkward place or situation. VERB make a hole in.
holey ADJ

holiday NOUN a period of recreation. VERB spend a holiday.

holistic ADJ treating the whole person rather than just particular isolated symptoms.

hollow ADJ **1** empty inside; sunken; (of a sound) echoing. **2** worthless. NOUN a cavity; a small valley. VERB make hollow.

holly NOUN an evergreen shrub with prickly leaves and red berries.

hollyhock NOUN a tall plant with large flowers.

holocaust NOUN destruction or slaughter on a mass scale.

hologram NOUN a three-dimensional photographic image.

holster NOUN a leather case holding a pistol or revolver.

holy ADJ (**-ier, -iest**) dedicated to God; pious or virtuous.
holiness NOUN

homage NOUN things said or done as a mark of respect or loyalty.

home NOUN **1** the place where you live. **2** an institution where people needing care may live. ADJ of your home or country; (of a match) played on a team's own ground. ADV at or to your home; to the point aimed at. VERB make its way home or to a target.

home page the main page of an individual's or organization's Internet site.
homeless ADJ
homeward ADJ & ADV
homewards ADV

homely ADJ (-ier, -iest) 1 simple but comfortable. 2 [US] unattractive.

homeopathy (or **homoeopathy**) NOUN treatment of a disease by very small doses of a substance that would produce symptoms of the disease in a healthy person.
homeopathic ADJ

homesick ADJ longing for home.

homework NOUN work set for a pupil to do away from school.

homicide NOUN murder.
homicidal ADJ

homily NOUN (PL -ies) a moralizing lecture.

homogeneous ADJ of the same kind.
homogeneity NOUN

homogenize (or -ise) VERB treat milk so that cream does not separate and rise to the top.

homonym NOUN a word spelt the same way as another.

homosexual ADJ & NOUN (a person) sexually attracted to people of the same sex.
homosexuality NOUN

hone VERB sharpen a tool with a stone.

honest ADJ truthful or trustworthy; fairly earned.
honestly ADV
honesty NOUN

honey NOUN a sweet substance made by bees from nectar.

honeycomb NOUN a bees' six-sided wax structure holding their honey and eggs.

honeyed ADJ (of words) flattering.

honeymoon NOUN a holiday for a newly married couple; an initial period of goodwill. VERB spend a honeymoon.

honeysuckle NOUN a climbing shrub with fragrant pink and yellow flowers.

honk NOUN the cry of a goose; the sound of a car horn. VERB make this noise.

honorary ADJ 1 given as an honour. 2 unpaid.

honour ([US] **honor**) NOUN great respect; a mark of this; privilege; honesty or integrity. VERB 1 regard or treat with great respect. 2 keep an agreement.

honourable ([US] **honorable**) ADJ honest;

deserving honour.
honourably ADV

hood NOUN 1 a covering for the head and neck. 2 a folding roof over a car; [US] a car bonnet.

hoodlum NOUN a hooligan or gangster.

hoodwink VERB deceive.

hoof NOUN (PL **hoofs** or **hooves**) the horny part of a horse's foot.

hook NOUN 1 a curved device for catching hold of or hanging things on; a bent piece of metal for catching fish. 2 a short blow made with the elbow bent. VERB catch or fasten with a hook.

hooked ADJ 1 hook-shaped. 2 [inf] addicted.

hooligan NOUN a violent young troublemaker.

hoop NOUN a circular band of metal or wood; a metal croquet arch.

hooray EXCLAMATION hurrah.

hoot NOUN 1 an owl's cry; the sound of a hooter; a cry of laughter or disapproval. 2 [inf] an amusing person or thing. VERB make a hoot.

hooter NOUN a siren or steam whistle; a car horn.

Hoover NOUN [trademark] a vacuum cleaner. VERB (**hoover**) clean with a vacuum cleaner.

hop[1] VERB (**hopped, hopping**) jump on one foot; (of an animal) jump with all feet together. NOUN a hopping movement; a short journey.

hop[2] NOUN a plant used to flavour beer.

hope NOUN expectation of something desired; something giving grounds for this; something hoped for. VERB feel hope.

hopeful ADJ

hopefully ADV 1 in a hopeful way. 2 it is to be hoped.

hopeless ADJ 1 without hope. 2 inadequate or incompetent.

hopper NOUN a container with an opening at the base for discharging its contents.

hopscotch NOUN a game involving hopping over marked squares.

horde NOUN a large group or crowd.

horizon NOUN 1 the line at which earth and sky appear to meet. 2 the limit of someone's knowledge or interests.

horizontal ADJ parallel to the horizon.

horizontally ADV

hormone NOUN a substance produced by the body that stimulates tissues or cells to action.

hormonal ADJ

horn NOUN **1** a hard pointed growth on the heads of certain animals; the substance of this. **2** a wind instrument with a trumpet-shaped end; a device for sounding a warning signal.

hornet NOUN a large wasp.

hornpipe NOUN a lively solo dance traditionally performed by sailors.

horny ADJ (**-ier, -iest**) **1** of or like horn; hardened and calloused. **2** [inf] sexually excited.

horoscope NOUN a forecast of events based on the positions of stars.

horrendous ADJ horrifying.

horrible ADJ causing horror; very unpleasant.

horribly ADV

horrid ADJ horrible.

horrific ADJ horrifying.

horrifically ADV

horrify VERB (**horrified,**

horrifying) fill with horror.

horror NOUN intense shock and fear or disgust; a terrible event or situation.

hors d'oeuvre NOUN food served as an appetizer.

horse NOUN a four-legged animal with a mane and tail.

horse chestnut a brown shiny nut; the tree bearing this. **on horseback** riding on a horse.

horsefly NOUN a large biting fly.

horseman (or **horsewoman**) NOUN a rider on horseback.

horseplay NOUN boisterous play.

horsepower NOUN (PL **horsepower**) a unit for measuring the power of an engine.

horseradish NOUN a plant with a hot-tasting root used to make sauce.

horseshoe NOUN a U-shaped strip of metal nailed to a horse's hoof.

horticulture NOUN the art of garden cultivation.

horticultural ADJ

hose NOUN **1** (also **hosepipe**) a flexible tube

for conveying water.
2 hosiery. VERB water or spray with a hosepipe.

hosiery NOUN stockings, socks, and tights.

hospice NOUN a hospital or home for the terminally ill.

hospitable ADJ friendly and welcoming.
hospitably ADV

hospital NOUN an institution for treatment of sick or injured people.

hospitality NOUN friendly and generous entertainment of guests.

hospitalize (or **-ise**) VERB send or admit to a hospital.

host NOUN **1** a person entertaining guests; a place providing facilities for visitors. **2** an organism on which another lives as a parasite. **3** a large number of people or things. VERB act as host at an event.

hostage NOUN a person held as security that the holder's demands will be satisfied.

hostel NOUN a place providing cheap accommodation for a particular group.

hostelry NOUN (PL **-ies**) [old use] an inn or pub.

hostess NOUN a woman entertaining guests.

hostile ADJ unfriendly; of an enemy.

hostility NOUN hostile behaviour; (**hostilities**) acts of warfare.

hot ADJ **1** at or having a high temperature. **2** producing a burning sensation when tasted. **3** passionate. **4** [inf] popular. VERB (**hotted, hotting**) (**hot up**) [inf] become more exciting.
hot air [inf] empty or boastful talk. **hot dog** a hot sausage in a bread roll.

hotbed NOUN a place where a particular activity flourishes.

hotchpotch NOUN a confused mixture.

hotel NOUN an establishment providing rooms and meals for tourists and travellers.

hotelier NOUN a hotel keeper.

hotfoot ADV in eager haste.

hothead NOUN an impetuous person.

hothouse NOUN a heated greenhouse.

hotline NOUN a direct telephone line for speedy communication.

hotplate NOUN a heated surface on a cooker or hob.

houmous see **hummus**.

hound NOUN a dog used in hunting. VERB harass.

hour NOUN 1 one twenty-fourth part of a day and night. 2 a point in time. 3 (**hours**) time fixed or set aside for work or an activity.

hourglass NOUN two connected glass globes containing sand that takes an hour to pass from the upper to the lower.

hourly ADJ & ADV done or occurring once an hour; reckoned by the hour.

house NOUN 1 a building for people to live in; a family or dynasty. 2 a legislative assembly; a business firm; a theatre audience. VERB provide accommodation or storage space for; encase.

house-trained (of a pet) trained to be clean in the house. **house-warming** a party to celebrate moving into a new home. **on the house** at the management's expense.

houseboat NOUN a boat used as a home.

housebound ADJ unable to leave your house.

housebreaking NOUN burglary.

household NOUN the occupants of a house regarded as a unit.

householder NOUN a person owning or renting a house or flat.

housekeeper NOUN a person employed to look after a household.

housekeeping NOUN

housewife NOUN a woman managing a household.

housework NOUN cleaning and cooking etc. in a house.

housing NOUN 1 accommodation. 2 a rigid case enclosing machinery.

hove see **heave**.

hovel NOUN a small squalid house.

hover VERB remain in one place in the air; wait about uncertainly.

hovercraft NOUN a vehicle supported by air thrust downwards from its engines.

how ADV 1 by what means

or in what way. **2** to what extent or degree. **3** in what condition.

however ADV **1** nevertheless. **2** in whatever way or to whatever extent.

howl VERB & NOUN (make) a long loud wailing cry or sound.

howler NOUN [inf] a stupid mistake.

h.p. ABBREV **1** hire purchase. **2** horse power.

HQ ABBREV headquarters.

HRH ABBREV Her (or His) Royal Highness.

hub NOUN the central part of a wheel; the centre of activity.

hubbub NOUN a confused noise of voices.

hubris NOUN arrogant pride.

huddle VERB crowd into a small place. NOUN a close group or mass.

hue NOUN a colour or shade.

hue and cry NOUN public outcry.

huff NOUN a bad mood. VERB breathe heavily.
huffy ADJ

hug VERB (**hugged**, **hugging**) hold tightly in your arms; keep close to. NOUN an embrace.

huge ADJ extremely large.

hula hoop NOUN a large hoop for spinning round the body.

hulk NOUN the body of an old ship; a large clumsy-looking person or thing.

hulking ADJ [inf] large and clumsy.

hull NOUN **1** the framework of a ship. **2** the pod of a pea or bean. VERB remove the hulls of beans, peas, etc.

hullabaloo NOUN [inf] an uproar.

hullo see **hello**.

hum VERB (**hummed**, **humming**) **1** make a low continuous sound; sing with closed lips. **2** be in a state of activity. NOUN a humming sound.

human ADJ of people as a whole; not impersonal or insensitive. NOUN (or **human being**) a man, woman, or child.

humane ADJ kind-hearted or merciful.

humanism NOUN a system of thought emphasizing human rather than divine matters and seeking rational solutions to human problems.
humanist NOUN

humanitarian ADJ promoting human welfare and reduction of suffering.

humanity NOUN 1 human nature; the human race. 2 kindness. 3 (**humanities**) arts subjects.

humanize (or **-ise**) VERB make human or humane.

humble ADJ 1 having a low opinion of your importance. 2 of low rank; not large or expensive. VERB make someone seem less important.
humbly ADV

humbug NOUN 1 hypocritical talk or behaviour. 2 a hard peppermint sweet.

humdrum ADJ dull or commonplace.

humerus NOUN (PL **-ri**) the bone in the upper arm.

humid ADJ (of air) warm and damp.
humidity NOUN

humidifier NOUN a device for increasing the moisture in air.

humiliate VERB cause to feel ashamed and foolish.
humiliation NOUN

humility NOUN a humble attitude of mind.

hummock NOUN a hump in the ground.

hummus (or **houmous**) NOUN a dip made from chickpeas and sesame seeds.

humour ([US] **humor**) NOUN 1 the quality of being amusing; the ability to perceive and enjoy this. 2 a state of mind. VERB keep a person contented by doing as they wish.
humorist NOUN
humorous ADJ

hump NOUN a rounded projecting part; a curved deformity of the spine. VERB [inf] hoist and carry.

humus NOUN rich dark organic material in soil, formed by decay of dead leaves and plants.

hunch VERB draw your shoulders up; bend your body forward. NOUN an intuitive feeling.

hunchback NOUN [offensive] a person with a hump on their back.

hundred NOUN ten times ten (100, C).
hundredth ADJ & NOUN

hundredweight NOUN a measure of weight equal to 112 lb (50.802 kg), or in the US 100 lb (45.359 kg).

hung past & past

participle of **hang**. ADJ (of a council, parliament, etc.) with no party having a clear majority.

hung-over [inf] suffering from a hangover.

hunger NOUN 1 discomfort and weakness felt when you have not eaten for some time; lack of food. 2 a strong desire. VERB feel hunger.

hunger strike refusal of food as a form of protest.

hungry ADJ (**-ier, -iest**) feeling hunger.
hungrily ADV

hunk NOUN 1 a large thick chunk. 2 [inf] an attractive man.

hunt VERB pursue wild animals for food or sport; pursue with hostility; search. NOUN an act of hunting; a hunting group.
hunter NOUN

hurdle NOUN a portable fencing panel; a frame to be jumped over in a race; an obstacle or difficulty.

hurl VERB throw violently.

hurly-burly NOUN bustling activity.

hurrah (or **hurray, hooray**) EXCLAMATION used to express joy or approval.

hurricane NOUN a violent storm with a strong wind.

hurried ADJ done with great haste.

hurry VERB (**hurried, hurrying**) move or act with great or excessive haste. NOUN hurrying.

hurt VERB (**hurt, hurt, hurting**) cause pain, injury, or grief to; feel pain; offend. NOUN injury, harm, or distress.

hurtful ADJ causing distress.

hurtle VERB move or hurl rapidly.

husband NOUN the man a woman is married to. VERB use economically.

husbandry NOUN 1 farming. 2 economical management of resources.

hush VERB 1 make or become silent. 2 (**hush up**) stop from becoming known. NOUN silence.

husk NOUN the dry outer covering of certain seeds and fruits. VERB remove the husk from.

husky ADJ (**-ier, -iest**) 1 (of a voice) low and hoarse. 2 big and strong. NOUN (PL **-ies**) an Arctic sledge dog.
huskily ADV

hussy NOUN (PL. **-ies**) a

cheeky or immoral girl or woman.

hustings NOUN a meeting for political candidates to address voters.

hustle VERB push roughly; force to move hurriedly. NOUN hustling.

hut NOUN a small simple or roughly made house or shelter.

hutch NOUN a box-like cage for rabbits.

hyacinth NOUN a plant with fragrant bell-shaped flowers.

hyaena see **hyena**.

hybrid NOUN the offspring of two different species or varieties; something made by combining different elements.

hydrangea NOUN a shrub with clusters of flowers.

hydrant NOUN a water pipe with a nozzle for attaching a fire hose.

hydrate VERB cause to absorb or combine with water.

hydraulic ADJ operated by pressure of fluid conveyed in pipes. NOUN (**hydraulics**) the science of hydraulic operations.

hydrocarbon NOUN a compound of hydrogen and carbon.

hydrochloric acid NOUN a corrosive acid containing hydrogen and chlorine.

hydroelectric ADJ using water power to produce electricity.

hydrofoil NOUN a boat with a structure that raises its hull out of the water when in motion.

hydrogen NOUN an odourless gas.

hydrogen bomb a powerful nuclear bomb.

hydrophobia NOUN extreme fear of water; rabies.

hyena (or **hyaena**) NOUN a doglike African animal.

hygiene NOUN cleanliness as a means of preventing disease.

hygienic ADJ

hymen NOUN the membrane partly closing the opening of the vagina of a virgin girl or woman.

hymn NOUN a song used in religious worship.

hype NOUN [inf] intensive promotion of a product.

hyperactive ADJ abnormally active.

hyperbole NOUN rhetorical exaggeration in speech etc.

hypermarket NOUN a very large supermarket.

hypertension NOUN abnormally high blood pressure.

hypertext NOUN [Computing] a system allowing rapid movement between documents or sections of text.

hyperventilation NOUN abnormally rapid breathing.

hyphen NOUN a sign (-) used to join words together or mark the division of a word at the end of a line.
hyphenate VERB
hyphenation NOUN

hypnosis NOUN an induced sleep-like condition in which a person responds readily to commands or suggestions.
hypnotic ADJ

hypnotism NOUN hypnosis.
hypnotist NOUN

hypnotize (or **-ise**) VERB put into a state of hypnosis.

hypochondria NOUN the state of constantly imagining that you are ill.
hypochondriac NOUN

hypocrisy NOUN falsely pretending to be virtuous; insincerity.

hypocrite NOUN a person guilty of hypocrisy.
hypocritical ADJ

hypodermic ADJ injected beneath the skin. NOUN a hypodermic syringe.

hypotenuse NOUN the longest side of a right-angled triangle.

hypothermia NOUN the condition of having an abnormally low body temperature.

hypothesis NOUN (PL **-ses**) an idea not yet proved to be correct.

hypothetical ADJ supposed but not necessarily true.
hypothetically ADV

hysterectomy NOUN (PL **-ies**) the surgical removal of the womb.

hysteria NOUN wild uncontrollable emotion.
hysterical ADJ

hysterics PLURAL NOUN an outburst of hysteria; [inf] uncontrollable laughter.

Ii

I PRON used by a speaker to refer to himself or herself.

ice NOUN frozen water; an ice cream. VERB **1** cover with icing. **2** (**ice over**) become covered with ice.

ice cream a sweet creamy frozen food.

iceberg NOUN a mass of ice floating in the sea.

icicle NOUN a piece of ice hanging downwards.

icing NOUN a mixture of powdered sugar and liquid or fat used to decorate cakes.

icon NOUN **1** (also **ikon**) a sacred painting or mosaic. **2** [Computing] a graphic symbol on a computer screen.

iconoclast NOUN a person who attacks established traditions.
> **iconoclasm** NOUN

icy ADJ (**-ier, -iest**) covered with ice; very cold; very unfriendly.
> **icily** ADV
> **iciness** NOUN

ID ABBREV identification.

idea NOUN a plan etc.

formed in the mind; an opinion; a mental impression.

ideal ADJ satisfying your idea of what is perfect. NOUN a person or thing regarded as perfect; an aim, principle, or standard.
> **ideally** ADV

idealist NOUN a person with high ideals.
> **idealism** NOUN
> **idealistic** ADJ

idealize (or **-ise**) VERB regard or represent as perfect.

identical ADJ the same; exactly alike.
> **identically** ADV

identification NOUN identifying; something used as a proof of identity.

identify VERB (**identified, identifying**) recognize as being a specified person or thing; associate someone closely with someone or something else; feel sympathy for someone.
> **identifiable** ADJ

identity NOUN (PL **-ies**)
1 who or what someone
or something is. 2 being
the same.
ideology NOUN (PL **-ies**)
ideas that form the basis
of a political or economic
theory.
ideological ADJ
idiocy NOUN (PL **-ies**)
extreme stupidity.
idiom NOUN a phrase whose
meaning cannot be
deduced from the words
in it; an expression
natural to a language.
idiomatic ADJ using
idioms; sounding natural.
idiosyncrasy NOUN (PL
-ies) a way of behaving
distinctive of a particular
person.
idiosyncratic ADJ
idiot NOUN a very stupid
person.
idiotic ADJ
idle ADJ not employed or in
use; lazy; aimless. VERB be
idle; move slowly and
aimlessly; (of an engine)
run slowly in neutral gear.
idleness NOUN
idly ADV
idol NOUN an image
worshipped as a god; an
idolized person or thing.
idolatry NOUN worship of
idols.
idolize (or **-ise**) VERB love
or admire excessively.
idyll NOUN a happy or
peaceful time or situation.
idyllic ADJ
i.e. ABBREV that is.
if CONJ 1 on condition that;
supposing that.
2 whether.
igloo NOUN a dome-shaped
Eskimo snow house.
ignite VERB set fire to; catch
fire.
ignition NOUN igniting; a
mechanism producing a
spark to ignite the fuel in
an engine.
ignoble ADJ not
honourable.
ignobly ADV
ignominy NOUN disgrace or
humiliation.
ignominious ADJ
ignorant ADJ lacking
knowledge; rude or
impolite.
ignorance NOUN
ignore VERB take no
notice of.
iguana NOUN a large
tropical lizard.
ikon see **icon**.
ill ADJ 1 in poor health. 2 of
poor quality. 3 harmful;
unfavourable. ADV badly or
wrongly. NOUN harm; a

misfortune or problem.

ill-gotten gained by evil or unlawful means.

illegal ADJ against the law.
illegality NOUN

illegible ADJ not readable.

illegitimate ADJ **1** born of parents not married to each other. **2** contrary to a law or rule.
illegitimacy NOUN

illicit ADJ unlawful or forbidden.

illiterate ADJ unable to read and write; uneducated.
illiteracy NOUN

illness NOUN the state of being ill; a particular type of ill health.

illogical ADJ not logical.
illogicality NOUN

illuminate VERB light up; explain or clarify.
illumination NOUN

illusion NOUN a false belief; a deceptive appearance.

illusionist NOUN a conjuror.

illusory ADJ based on illusion; not real.

illustrate VERB supply a book etc. with drawings or pictures; make clear by using examples, charts, etc.; serve as an example of.

illustration NOUN
illustrator NOUN

illustrious ADJ well known and respected.

image NOUN a picture or other representation; an optical appearance produced in a mirror or through a lens; a mental picture.

imaginary ADJ existing only in the imagination, not real.

imagination NOUN imagining; the ability to imagine or to plan creatively.
imaginative ADJ

imagine VERB form a mental image of; think or suppose; guess.
imaginable ADJ

imbalance NOUN lack of balance.

imbecile NOUN a stupid person.

imbed see **embed**.

imbibe VERB drink; absorb ideas.

imbue VERB fill with feelings, qualities, or emotions.

imitate VERB try to act or be like; copy.
imitation NOUN

imitative ADJ imitating; not original.

immaculate ADJ spotlessly clean and tidy; free from blemish or fault.

immaterial ADJ 1 having no physical substance. 2 of no importance.

immature ADJ 1 not fully grown. 2 childish or irresponsible.
immaturity NOUN

immeasurable ADJ too large or extreme to measure.
immeasurably ADV

immediate ADJ 1 done or occurring without delay. 2 nearest in time, space, etc.
immediacy NOUN

immediately ADV 1 without delay. 2 very close in time, space, etc. CONJ as soon as.

immemorial ADJ extremely old.

immense ADJ extremely great.
immensity NOUN

immerse VERB put completely into liquid; involve deeply in an activity etc.
immersion NOUN

immigrate VERB come to live permanently in a foreign country.
immigrant ADJ & NOUN

immigration NOUN

imminent ADJ about to occur.
imminence NOUN

immobile ADJ not moving or unable to move.
immobility NOUN
immobilize (or **-ise**) VERB

immolate VERB kill as a sacrifice.

immoral ADJ morally wrong.
immorality NOUN

immortal ADJ living for ever; famous for all time.
immortality NOUN
immortalize (or **-ise**) VERB

immovable ADJ unable to be moved; unyielding.

immune ADJ resistant to infection; exempt from an obligation etc.; not affected.
immunity NOUN
immunize (or **-ise**) VERB

immure VERB confine or imprison.

immutable ADJ unchangeable.

imp NOUN a small devil; a mischievous child.

impact NOUN a collision; a strong effect. VERB 1 collide forcefully with something. 2 press firmly.

impair VERB damage or weaken.

impairment NOUN

impale VERB fix or pierce with a pointed object.

impart VERB make information known; give a quality.

impartial ADJ not favouring one side more than another.
impartiality NOUN

impassable ADJ impossible to travel on or over.

impasse NOUN a deadlock.

impassioned ADJ passionate.

impassive ADJ not feeling or showing emotion.

impatient ADJ **1** intolerant or easily irritated. **2** restlessly eager.
impatience NOUN

impeach VERB charge the holder of a public office with a serious offence.
impeachment NOUN

impeccable ADJ faultless.
impeccably ADV

impede VERB hinder.

impediment NOUN a hindrance or obstruction; a defect in speech, e.g. a lisp or stammer.

impel VERB (**impelled, impelling**) force to do something.

impending ADJ imminent.

impenetrable ADJ **1** impossible to enter or pass through. **2** incomprehensible.

imperative ADJ **1** essential or vital. **2** giving a command. **3** [Grammar] (of a verb) expressing a command. NOUN an essential thing.

imperceptible ADJ too slight to be noticed.

imperfect ADJ **1** flawed or faulty; not complete. **2** [Grammar] (of a tense) referring to a past action not yet completed.
imperfection NOUN

imperial ADJ **1** of an empire or emperor; majestic. **2** (of measures) belonging to the British official non-metric system.
imperially ADV

imperialism NOUN the policy of having or extending an empire.
imperialist NOUN

imperil VERB (**imperilled, imperilling**; [US] **imperiled, imperiling**) endanger.

imperious ADJ arrogantly giving orders.

impersonal ADJ **1** not showing or influenced by

personal feeling. **2** lacking human feelings.

impersonate VERB pretend to be another person. **impersonation** NOUN

impertinent ADJ disrespectful or rude. **impertinence** NOUN

imperturbable ADJ calm and unexcitable.

impervious ADJ **1** impermeable. **2** (**impervious to**) not able to be penetrated or influenced by.

impetuous ADJ acting or done quickly and recklessly.

impetus NOUN a moving or driving force.

impinge VERB make an impact; encroach.

impious ADJ not reverent, especially towards a god.

implacable ADJ unable to be placated; relentless.

implant VERB insert tissue or a device into a living thing; fix an idea in the mind. NOUN something implanted.

implausible ADJ not seeming probable.

implement NOUN a tool. VERB put a decision etc. into effect.

implementation NOUN

implicate VERB show or cause to be involved in a crime etc.

implication NOUN something implied; being implicated.

implicit ADJ **1** implied but not stated. **2** absolute; total and unquestioning.

implore VERB beg earnestly.

imply VERB (**implied**, **implying**) convey without stating directly.

impolite ADJ bad-mannered or rude.

import VERB bring from abroad or from an outside source. NOUN **1** something imported; importing. **2** meaning; importance.

important ADJ having great significance or value; having a high and influential position. **importance** NOUN

importune VERB make insistent requests to.

impose VERB **1** force something unwelcome on someone; put a restriction, tax, etc. into effect. **2** (**impose on**) take unfair advantage of.

imposing ADJ impressive.

imposition NOUN imposing

something; a burden imposed unfairly.

impossible ADJ not able to exist, occur, or be done; very hard to deal with. **impossibility** NOUN **impossibly** ADV

impostor NOUN a person who fraudulently pretends to be someone else.

impotent ADJ powerless; (of a man) unable to achieve an erection. **impotence** NOUN

impound VERB take property into legal custody.

impoverish VERB cause to become poor or weak.

impracticable ADJ not able to be put into practice.

impractical ADJ not showing realism or common sense; not sensible or useful.

imprecise ADJ not precise.

impregnable ADJ safe against attack.

impregnate VERB **1** introduce sperm or pollen into and fertilize. **2** saturate with a substance.

impresario NOUN (PL **-ios**) an organizer of public entertainment.

impress VERB **1** cause or feel admiration. **2** make a mark on something with a seal etc.; fix an idea in the mind.

impression NOUN **1** an idea or opinion about someone or something; an effect produced on the mind. **2** an imitation done for entertainment. **3** a mark impressed on a surface.

impressionable ADJ easily influenced.

impressive ADJ inspiring admiration; grand or awesome.

imprint NOUN **1** a mark made by pressing on a surface. **2** a publisher's name etc. on a title page. VERB impress or stamp a mark on a surface.

imprison VERB put into prison. **imprisonment** NOUN

improbable ADJ not likely to be true or to happen.

impromptu ADJ & ADV without preparation or rehearsal.

improper ADJ not conforming to accepted rules or standards; not decent or modest.

impropriety NOUN

improve VERB make or become better.

improvement NOUN

improvident ADJ not providing for future needs.

improvise VERB perform drama, music etc. without preparation or a script; make from whatever materials are at hand.

improvisation NOUN

impudent ADJ disrespectful.

impudence NOUN

impugn VERB express doubts about the truth or honesty of.

impulse NOUN 1 a sudden urge to do something. 2 a driving force.

impulsive ADJ acting or done without prior thought.

impunity NOUN freedom from punishment or injury.

impure ADJ 1 mixed with unwanted substances. 2 morally wrong.

impurity NOUN

impute VERB attribute a fault to someone.

imputation NOUN

in PREP 1 enclosed or surrounded by; within limits of space or time; contained by. 2 expressing a state or quality. 3 having as a language or medium. 4 into. ADV so as to be enclosed or surrounded; reaching a destination. ADJ 1 at home. 2 [inf] fashionable.

inability NOUN being unable to do something.

inaccessible ADJ hard or impossible to reach or understand.

inaccurate ADJ not accurate.

inaccuracy NOUN

inaction NOUN lack of action.

inactive ADJ not active; not working or taking effect.

inactivity NOUN

inadequate ADJ not of sufficient quantity or quality; incompetent.

inadequacy NOUN

inadmissible ADJ not allowable.

inadvertent ADJ unintentional.

inane ADJ silly.

inanimate ADJ not alive; showing no sign of life.

inappropriate ADJ unsuitable.

inarticulate ADJ not

expressed in words; unable to express ideas clearly.

inattentive ADJ not paying attention.

inaudible ADJ unable to be heard.

inaugurate VERB introduce a policy etc.; admit formally to office. **inaugural** ADJ **inauguration** NOUN

inborn ADJ existing from birth.

inbred ADJ **1** produced by inbreeding. **2** inborn.

inbreeding NOUN breeding from closely related individuals.

incalculable ADJ too great to be calculated or estimated.

incandescent ADJ glowing with heat. **incandescence** NOUN

incantation NOUN words or sounds uttered as a magic spell.

incapable ADJ unable to do something; helpless.

incapacitate VERB prevent from functioning normally.

incarcerate VERB imprison. **incarceration** NOUN

incarnate ADJ embodied, especially in human form.

incarnation NOUN embodiment, especially in human form; (**the Incarnation**) that of God as Jesus.

incendiary ADJ designed to cause fire; tending to provoke conflict. NOUN an incendiary bomb.

incense¹ NOUN a substance burnt to produce fragrant smoke.

incense² VERB make angry.

incentive NOUN something that encourages action or effort.

inception NOUN the beginning of something.

incessant ADJ not ceasing.

incest NOUN sex between very closely related people. **incestuous** ADJ

inch NOUN a measure of length (= 2.54 cm). VERB move gradually.

incidence NOUN the rate at which something occurs.

incident NOUN an event, especially one causing trouble.

incidental ADJ **1** not essential. **2** occurring as a consequence of something else.

incidentally ADV 1 used to introduce a further or unconnected remark. 2 as a chance occurrence.

incinerate VERB burn to ashes.
incinerator NOUN

incipient ADJ beginning to happen or develop.

incise VERB make a cut in.
incision NOUN

incisive ADJ clear and decisive.

incisor NOUN a sharp-edged front tooth.

incite VERB urge on to action; stir up.

incivility NOUN rudeness.

inclement ADJ (of weather) unpleasant.

inclination NOUN 1 a tendency; a liking or preference. 2 a slope or slant.

incline VERB lean; bend. NOUN a slope.
inclined to having a tendency to.

include VERB 1 contain as part of a whole; regard as part of something. 2 put in as part of a group or set.
inclusion NOUN

inclusive ADJ 1 including all charges, services, etc. 2 (**inclusive of**) including.

incognito ADJ & ADV with your identity kept secret.

incoherent ADJ disconnected; unclear or confused.
incoherence NOUN

incombustible ADJ not able to be burnt.

income NOUN money received as wages, interest, etc.

incoming ADJ coming in.

incommunicado ADJ not allowed or not wishing to communicate with others.

incomparable ADJ without an equal.

incompatible ADJ conflicting or inconsistent; unable to exist together.
incompatibility NOUN

incompetent ADJ lacking skill.
incompetence NOUN

incomplete ADJ not complete.

incomprehensible ADJ not able to be understood.
incomprehension NOUN

inconceivable ADJ unable to be imagined; most unlikely.

inconclusive ADJ not fully convincing.

incongruous ADJ out of

place.

incongruity NOUN

inconsequential ADJ unimportant.

inconsiderable ADJ of small size or value.

inconsiderate ADJ not thinking of others' feelings.

inconsistent ADJ not consistent.

inconsistency NOUN

inconstant ADJ
1 frequently changing.
2 disloyal.

incontestable ADJ indisputable.

incontinent ADJ unable to control your bladder or bowels.

incontinence NOUN

incontrovertible ADJ undeniable.

inconvenience NOUN difficulty and discomfort; a cause of this. VERB cause inconvenience to.

inconvenient ADJ difficult or troublesome.

incorporate VERB include as a part.

incorporation NOUN

incorrect ADJ 1 not right or true. 2 not in accordance with standards.

incorrigible ADJ not able

to be reformed or improved.

increase VERB make or become greater. NOUN increasing; the amount by which a thing increases.

increasingly ADV more and more.

incredible ADJ unbelievable; very surprising.

incredulous ADJ feeling or showing disbelief.

incredulity NOUN

increment NOUN an increase in a number or amount.

incriminate VERB cause to appear guilty.

incubate VERB hatch eggs by warmth; cause bacteria etc. to develop.

incubation NOUN

incubator NOUN an apparatus for incubating eggs or bacteria; an enclosed compartment in which a premature baby can be kept.

inculcate VERB fix ideas in someone's mind.

incumbent ADJ forming an obligation or duty. NOUN the holder of an office, especially a rector or a vicar.

incur VERB (**incurred, incurring**) bring something unpleasant on yourself.

incursion NOUN a sudden invasion or raid.

indebted ADJ owing money or gratitude.

indecent ADJ offending against standards of decency; inappropriate. **indecency** NOUN

indecision NOUN inability to decide, hesitation.

indecorous ADJ improper; not in good taste.

indeed ADV in fact; really.

indefatigable ADJ untiring.

indefensible ADJ not able to be justified or defended.

indefinite ADJ not clearly stated or fixed; vague; (of time) not limited. **indefinitely** ADV

indefinite article see article.

indelible ADJ unable to be removed; unable to be forgotten.

indelicate ADJ slightly indecent; tactless. **indelicacy** NOUN

indemnify VERB (**indemnified, indemnifying**) protect or insure a person against penalties that they might incur; compensate. **indemnification** NOUN

indemnity NOUN (PL **-ies**) protection against penalties incurred by your actions; money paid as compensation.

indent VERB **1** start a line of text inwards from a margin; form recesses in a surface. **2** place an official order for goods etc. **indentation** NOUN

indenture NOUN a written contract, especially of apprenticeship.

independent ADJ **1** not ruled or controlled by another. **2** not relying on another; not connected. **independence** NOUN

indescribable ADJ too extreme, unusual, etc., to be described.

indestructible ADJ unable to be destroyed.

indeterminate ADJ not certain; vague.

index NOUN (PL **indexes** or **indices**) **1** an alphabetical list of names, subjects, etc., with references. **2** an indicator of something. VERB record in or provide with an index.

index finger the forefinger.

indicate VERB point out; be a sign of.

indication NOUN

indicative ADJ

indicator NOUN a thing that indicates; a flashing light on a vehicle showing when it is going to turn.

indict VERB make a formal accusation against.

indictment NOUN

indifferent ADJ 1 showing no interest or sympathy. 2 mediocre; not very good.

indifference NOUN

indigenous ADJ native.

indigent ADJ poor.

indigence NOUN

indigestible ADJ difficult or impossible to digest.

indigestion NOUN discomfort caused by difficulty in digesting food.

indignant ADJ feeling or showing indignation.

indignation NOUN anger aroused by something unjust or wicked.

indignity (PL **-ies**) humiliating treatment or circumstances.

indigo NOUN a deep blue dye or colour.

indirect ADJ not direct.

indiscreet ADJ too ready to reveal secrets.

indiscretion NOUN

indiscriminate ADJ done or acting at random; not making a careful choice.

indispensable ADJ essential.

indisposed ADJ 1 slightly ill. 2 unwilling.

indisposition NOUN

indisputable ADJ undeniable.

indissoluble ADJ not able to be destroyed.

indistinct ADJ unclear; obscure.

indistinguishable ADJ unable to be told apart.

individual ADJ single or separate; of or for one person or thing; striking or unusual. NOUN a single person or item as distinct from a group; a person.

individuality NOUN

individualist NOUN a person who is very independent in thought or action.

indoctrinate VERB teach someone to accept a set of beliefs uncritically.

indoctrination NOUN

indolent ADJ lazy.

indolence NOUN

indoor ADJ situated, used, or done inside a building. **indoors** ADV

indubitable ADJ impossible to doubt.

induce VERB 1 persuade. 2 give rise to; bring on childbirth artificially.

inducement NOUN an incentive or bribe.

induct VERB introduce formally to a post or organization.

induction NOUN 1 inducting. 2 inducing childbirth. 3 reasoning by drawing a general rule from individual cases. **inductive** ADJ

indulge VERB 1 satisfy a desire; allow someone to have what they want. 2 (**indulge in**) allow yourself something pleasant. **indulgence** NOUN

indulgent ADJ indulging someone's wishes too freely.

industrial ADJ of, for, or full of industries. **industrial action** a strike or similar protest. **industrial estate** an area of land developed for business and industry.

industrialist NOUN an owner or manager of an industrial business.

industrialized (or **-ised**) ADJ full of industries.

industrious ADJ hardworking.

industry NOUN (PL **-ies**) 1 the manufacture of goods in factories; business activity. 2 hard work.

inebriated ADJ drunk.

inedible ADJ not fit for eating.

ineffable ADJ too great or extreme to be described.

ineffective ADJ not producing the desired effect.

ineffectual ADJ ineffective; unable to deal with a role or situation.

inefficient ADJ wasteful of time or resources.

ineligible ADJ not eligible or qualified.

inept ADJ lacking skill. **ineptitude** NOUN

inequality NOUN (PL **-ies**) lack of equality.

inequitable ADJ unfair or unjust.

inert ADJ without power to move; without active properties; not moving or taking action.

inertia NOUN **1** being inert; slowness to act. **2** the property by which matter continues in its existing state of rest or line of motion unless acted on by a force.

inescapable ADJ unavoidable.

inessential ADJ not essential.

inestimable ADJ too great to be measured.

inevitable ADJ unavoidable.
inevitability NOUN

inexact ADJ not exact.

inexcusable ADJ unable to be excused or justified.

inexorable ADJ impossible to prevent; impossible to persuade.

inexpensive ADJ not expensive.

inexperienced ADJ lacking experience.

inexpert ADJ unskilful.

inexplicable ADJ impossible to explain.

infallible ADJ incapable of failing or being wrong.
infallibility NOUN

infamous ADJ having a bad reputation.
infamy NOUN

infancy NOUN babyhood or early childhood; an early stage of development.

infant NOUN a child during the earliest stage of its life.

infantile ADJ of infants or infancy; very childish.

infantry NOUN troops who fight on foot.

infatuated ADJ filled with intense unreasoning love.
infatuation NOUN

infect VERB affect or contaminate with a disease or its germs; cause to share a particular feeling.

infection NOUN infecting or being infected; a disease spread in this way.

infectious ADJ (of disease) able to spread by air or water; liable to infect others.

infer VERB (**inferred**, **inferring**) work out from evidence.
inference NOUN

inferior ADJ of lower rank, status, or quality. NOUN a person inferior to another.
inferiority NOUN

infernal ADJ **1** of hell. **2** [inf] irritating.

inferno NOUN (PL **-os**) a raging fire; hell.

infertile ADJ unable to have offspring; (of soil)

not producing vegetation.
infertility NOUN

infest VERB be present in a place in large numbers, especially harmfully.
infestation NOUN

infidel NOUN a person who does not believe in a religion.

infidelity NOUN (PL -ies) unfaithfulness to your sexual partner.

infighting NOUN conflict within an organization.

infiltrate VERB make your way into a group etc. secretly and gradually.
infiltration NOUN

infinite ADJ having no end or limit; very great.

infinitesimal ADJ very small.

infinitive NOUN the form of a verb not indicating tense, number, or person (e.g. *to go*).

infinity NOUN (PL -ies) being infinite; an infinite number, space, or time.

infirm ADJ weak from age or illness.
infirmity NOUN

infirmary NOUN (PL -ies) a hospital.

inflame VERB 1 provoke or intensify feelings. 2 cause inflammation in.

inflammable ADJ easily set on fire.

inflammation NOUN redness, heat, and pain in a part of the body.

inflammatory ADJ arousing strong feeling or anger.

inflate VERB 1 cause to swell by filling with air or gas. 2 increase excessively and artificially; exaggerate.
inflatable NOUN

inflation NOUN 1 inflating or being inflated. 2 a general increase in prices and fall in the purchasing power of money.
inflationary ADJ

inflect VERB 1 change the pitch of a voice in speaking. 2 [Grammar] change the ending or form of a word.
inflection NOUN

inflexible ADJ impossible to bend; unwilling to yield or compromise; unable to be changed.
inflexibility NOUN

inflict VERB impose something painful or unpleasant on someone.

influence NOUN power to produce an effect, especially on character, beliefs, or actions; a person or thing with this power. VERB exert influence on.

influential ADJ having great influence.

influenza NOUN a viral disease causing fever, muscular pain, and catarrh.

influx NOUN an arrival of large numbers of people or things.

inform VERB give information to; reveal criminal activities to the authorities.

informal ADJ relaxed; unofficial; casual. **informality** NOUN

informant NOUN a giver of information.

information NOUN facts told or discovered.

informative ADJ giving information.

informed ADJ having a good knowledge of something.

informer NOUN a person who reveals criminal activity to the authorities.

infrared ADJ of or using radiation with a wavelength just greater than that of red light.

infrastructure NOUN the basic structural parts of

something; roads, sewers, etc. regarded as a country's basic facilities.

infrequent ADJ not frequent.

infringe VERB break a rule or agreement; encroach. **infringement** NOUN

infuriate VERB make very angry.

infuse VERB 1 fill with a quality. 2 soak tea or herbs to bring out flavour.

infusion NOUN 1 a drink etc. made by infusing leaves. 2 introducing a new element into something.

ingenious ADJ clever, original, and inventive. **ingenuity** NOUN

ingenuous ADJ innocent and unsuspecting.

inglorious ADJ rather shameful.

ingot NOUN a brick-shaped lump of cast metal.

ingrained ADJ deeply embedded in a surface or in a person's character.

ingratiate VERB act in a way designed to make yourself liked by someone.

ingratitude NOUN lack of gratitude.

ingredient NOUN any of the parts in a mixture.

inhabit VERB live in as your home.
inhabitant NOUN
inhale VERB breathe in air, smoke, gas, etc.
inhalation NOUN
inhaler NOUN a portable device used for inhaling a drug.
inherent ADJ existing in something as a natural or permanent quality.
inherit VERB receive from a predecessor, especially from someone who has died; receive a characteristic from your parents
inheritance NOUN
inhibit VERB restrain or prevent; cause inhibitions in.
inhibited ADJ
inhibition NOUN a feeling that makes you unable to act in a natural or relaxed way.
inhospitable ADJ unwelcoming; (of a place) with a harsh climate or landscape.
inhuman (or **inhumane**) ADJ brutal or cruel.
inhumanity NOUN
inimical ADJ hostile; harmful.
inimitable ADJ impossible

to imitate.
iniquity NOUN (PL **-ies**) great injustice; wickedness.
iniquitous ADJ
initial NOUN the first letter of a word or name. VERB (**initialled, initialling**; [US] **initialed, initialing**) mark or sign with initials. ADJ existing at the beginning.
initiate VERB 1 cause a process etc. to begin. 2 admit to membership of a secret group; introduce to a skill or activity.
initiation NOUN
initiative NOUN 1 the capacity to invent and initiate ideas. 2 a position from which you can act to forestall others. 3 a fresh approach to a problem.
inject VERB 1 force liquid into the body with a syringe. 2 introduce a new element into a situation.
injection NOUN
injunction NOUN an authoritative order, especially one made by a judge.
injure VERB cause injury to.
injury NOUN (PL **-ies**) harm or damage; a wound, broken bone, etc.; unjust treatment.
injustice NOUN lack of

justice; an unjust action.

ink NOUN coloured liquid used in writing, printing, etc. VERB apply ink to.
inky ADJ

inkling NOUN a slight suspicion.

inland ADJ & ADV in or towards the interior of a country.

in-law NOUN a relative by marriage.

inlay VERB (**inlaid, inlaying**) decorate a surface by setting pieces of another material in it so that the surfaces are flush. NOUN inlaid material or design.

inlet NOUN 1 an arm of the sea etc. extending inland. 2 a way in (e.g. for water into a tank).

inmate NOUN a person living in a prison or other institution.

inn NOUN a pub.

innards PLURAL NOUN [inf] the stomach and bowels; the inner parts.

innate ADJ inborn; natural.

inner ADJ inside or nearer to the centre or inside.
innermost ADJ

innings NOUN (in cricket) a batsman's or side's turn at batting.

innocent ADJ 1 not guilty; not intended to cause harm; morally pure. 2 without experience or knowledge, especially of something bad.
innocence NOUN

innocuous ADJ harmless.

innovate VERB introduce something new.
innovation NOUN
innovative ADJ

innumerable ADJ too many to be counted.

inoculate VERB protect against disease with vaccines or serums.
inoculation NOUN

inoperable ADJ unable to be cured by surgical operation.

inoperative ADJ not functioning.

inopportune ADJ happening at an unsuitable time.

inordinate ADJ excessive.

in-patient NOUN a patient staying in a hospital during treatment.

input NOUN something put in or contributed for use or processing; supplying or putting in.

inquest NOUN a judicial investigation, especially of a sudden death.

inquire VERB make an

inquiry.

inquiry NOUN (PL **-ies**) an investigation.

inquisition NOUN an act of detailed or relentless questioning.
inquisitor NOUN

inquisitive ADJ curious; prying.

insalubrious ADJ unwholesome.

insane ADJ mad; extremely foolish.
insanity NOUN

insanitary ADJ dirty and unhygienic.

insatiable ADJ impossible to satisfy.

inscribe VERB write or carve words on a surface; write a dedication on or in.

inscription NOUN words inscribed.

inscrutable ADJ impossible to understand or interpret.

insect NOUN a small creature with six legs, no backbone, and a segmented body.

insecticide NOUN a substance for killing insects.

insecure ADJ **1** not firmly fixed or attached. **2** lacking confidence.

inseminate VERB insert semen into.
insemination NOUN

insensible ADJ unconscious; numb.

insensitive ADJ not sensitive.
insensitivity NOUN

inseparable ADJ impossible to separate or treat separately.

insert VERB place, fit, or incorporate something into something else. NOUN something inserted, especially pages inserted in a magazine etc.
insertion NOUN

inset NOUN a thing inserted. VERB (**inset**, **insetting**) insert.

inshore ADJ & ADV at sea but near or towards the shore.

inside NOUN the inner part of something; the inner side or surface; (**insides**) the stomach and bowels. ADJ on or from the inside. PREP & ADV situated or moving within; within a particular time.
inside out 1 with the inner side turned outwards. **2** thoroughly.

insidious ADJ proceeding in a gradual and harmful way.

insight NOUN intuitive perception and understanding.

insignia PLURAL NOUN symbols of authority or office; an identifying badge.

insignificant ADJ of little importance or value. **insignificance** NOUN

insinuate VERB 1 indirectly suggest something discreditable. 2 gradually move yourself into a favourable position. **insinuation** NOUN

insipid ADJ lacking flavour, interest, or liveliness.

insist VERB demand or state emphatically.

insistent ADJ insisting; forcing itself on your attention. **insistence** NOUN

insolent ADJ disrespectful and rude. **insolence** NOUN

insoluble ADJ 1 impossible to solve. 2 unable to be dissolved.

insolvent ADJ unable to pay your debts. **insolvency** NOUN

insomnia NOUN inability to sleep. **insomniac** NOUN

inspect VERB examine critically or officially. **inspection** NOUN

inspector NOUN 1 a person who inspects. 2 a police officer above sergeant.

inspiration NOUN being inspired; a sudden brilliant idea; someone or something inspiring. **inspirational** ADJ

inspire VERB stimulate to activity; encourage a feeling; cause to feel uplifted.

instability NOUN lack of stability.

install VERB place a person into office ceremonially; set in position and ready for use.

installation NOUN the process of installing; an apparatus etc. installed.

instalment ([US] **installment**) NOUN one of the regular payments made to clear a debt paid over a period of time; one part of a serial.

instance NOUN an example; a particular case. VERB mention as an example.

instant ADJ happening or done immediately; (of food) quickly and easily prepared. NOUN an exact moment; a very short time.

instantaneous ADJ occurring or done instantly.

instead ADV as an alternative.

instep NOUN the middle part of the foot.

instigate VERB bring about an action; urge to act. **instigation** NOUN

instil ([US] **instill**) VERB (**instilled, instilling**) introduce ideas etc. into a person's mind gradually.

instinct NOUN an inborn impulse; a natural tendency or ability. **instinctive** ADJ

institute NOUN an organization for promotion of a specified activity. VERB set up; establish.

institution NOUN **1** an institute. **2** a home in which people with special needs are cared for. **3** an established rule or custom. **institutional** ADJ

instruct VERB **1** teach a subject or skill to. **2** give instructions to. **instructor** NOUN

instruction NOUN **1** the process of teaching. **2** an order. **3** (**instructions**) an explanation of how to do or use something.

instructive ADJ informative.

instrument NOUN **1** a tool for delicate work. **2** a measuring device. **3** a device for producing musical sounds.

instrumental ADJ **1** serving as a means. **2** performed on musical instruments.

instrumentalist NOUN a player of a musical instrument.

insubordinate ADJ disobedient, rebellious. **insubordination** NOUN

insubstantial ADJ lacking reality or solidity.

insufferable ADJ intolerable.

insufficient ADJ not enough.

insular ADJ **1** of an island. **2** narrow-minded. **insularity** NOUN

insulate VERB **1** cover with a substance that prevents the passage of heat, sound, or electricity. **2** protect from something unpleasant. **insulation** NOUN

insulin NOUN a hormone controlling the body's absorption of sugar.

insult VERB speak or act so as to offend someone. NOUN an insulting remark or action.

insuperable ADJ impossible to overcome.

insupportable ADJ unbearable.

insurance NOUN a contract to provide compensation for loss, damage, or death; a sum payable as a premium or in compensation; a safeguard against loss or failure.

insure VERB 1 protect by insurance. 2 ensure.

insurgent ADJ rebellious. NOUN a rebel.

insurmountable ADJ too great to be overcome.

insurrection NOUN a rebellion.

intact ADJ undamaged.

intake NOUN an amount of a substance taken into the body; people entering an establishment at a particular time.

intangible ADJ not solid or real; vague and abstract.

integer NOUN a whole number.

integral ADJ necessary to make a whole complete.

integrate VERB combine parts into a whole; cause to be accepted in a social group.

integration NOUN

integrity NOUN honesty.

intellect NOUN the mind's power of reasoning and acquiring knowledge.

intellectual ADJ of the intellect; having a strong intellect. NOUN an intellectual person.

intelligence NOUN 1 mental ability to learn and understand things. 2 information, especially that of military value; people collecting this.

intelligent ADJ having great mental ability.

intelligentsia NOUN educated and cultured people.

intelligible ADJ able to be understood.

intend VERB have in mind as what you wish to achieve; plan a particular use or destiny for someone or something.

intense ADJ 1 extreme; in a high degree. 2 having strong feelings.

intensity NOUN

intensify VERB (**intensified, intensifying**) make or become more intense.
intensification NOUN

intensive ADJ **1** very thorough or vigorous. **2** intended to achieve the highest level of production possible in an area.

intent NOUN intention. ADJ **1** with concentrated attention. **2** (**intent on**) determined to.

intention NOUN what you intend to do.

intentional ADJ done on purpose.

inter VERB (**interred, interring**) bury a dead body.
interment NOUN

interact VERB have an effect on each other.
interactive ADJ

intercede VERB intervene on someone's behalf.

intercept VERB stop or catch between a starting point and destination.
interception NOUN

interchange VERB **1** (of two people) exchange things. **2** cause to change places. NOUN **1** a process of interchanging. **2** a road junction built on several levels.

intercom NOUN an electrical device allowing one-way or two-way communication.

intercontinental ADJ between continents.

intercourse NOUN **1** dealings between people or countries. **2** sexual intercourse.

interest NOUN **1** wanting to learn about or do something; something about which you feel this; being interesting. **2** money paid for use of money borrowed. **3** advantage: *in my own interest.* **4** a share in an undertaking. VERB arouse the curiosity of.

interested ADJ **1** feeling interest. **2** not impartial.

interesting ADJ arousing interest.

interface NOUN **1** a place where interaction occurs. **2** [Computing] a program or apparatus connecting two machines or enabling a user to use a program.

interfere VERB **1** prevent something's progress or proper functioning. **2** become involved in something without being asked.

interference NOUN interfering; disturbance to radio signals.

interim NOUN an intervening period. ADJ temporary.

interior ADJ inner. NOUN the inner part; the inside.

interject VERB say something suddenly as an interruption.
interjection NOUN

interlock VERB (of two things) fit into each other.

interloper NOUN an intruder.

interlude NOUN 1 an interval. 2 music or other entertainment provided during an interval.

intermarry VERB (**intermarried**, **intermarrying**) (of people of different races or religions) marry each other.
intermarriage NOUN

intermediary NOUN (PL -ies) a person who tries to settle a dispute between others.

intermediate ADJ coming between two things in time, place, or order;

having achieved a basic level in a subject or skill.

interminable ADJ lasting a very long time.

intermission NOUN an interval or pause.

intermittent ADJ occurring at irregular intervals.

intern VERB confine as a prisoner.
internment NOUN

internal ADJ of or in the inside; inside the body; of a country's domestic affairs; applying within an organization.

international ADJ between countries; involving several countries. NOUN a sports contest between players of different countries.

internecine ADJ (of fighting) taking place between members of the same country or group.

Internet NOUN an international information network linking computers.

interplay NOUN interaction.

interpolate VERB interject; add to a text.
interpolation NOUN

interpose VERB 1 place

between one thing and another. **2** intervene between opponents.

interpret VERB explain the meaning of; understand in a particular way; orally translate the words of a person speaking a different language.
interpretation NOUN
interpreter NOUN

interrelated ADJ related to each other.

interrogate VERB question closely.
interrogation NOUN

interrogative ADJ in the form of or used in a question.

interrupt VERB break the continuity of; break the flow of speech etc. by a remark.
interruption NOUN

intersect VERB divide or cross by passing or lying across.
intersection NOUN

intersperse VERB place or scatter between or among other things.

interval NOUN a time between events; a pause or break; the time between acts of a play etc.; a difference in musical pitch.

intervene VERB **1** become involved in a situation to change its course. **2** occur between events.
intervention NOUN

interview NOUN a formal conversation with someone, designed to extract information or assess their suitability for a position. VERB hold an interview with.

intestate ADJ not having made a valid will.

intestine NOUN a long tubular section of the alimentary canal between the stomach and anus.
intestinal ADJ

intimate[1] ADJ **1** closely acquainted or familiar; having a sexual relationship; private and personal. **2** (of knowledge) thorough. NOUN an intimate friend.
intimacy NOUN

intimate[2] VERB suggest or hint.
intimation NOUN

intimidate VERB influence by frightening.
intimidation NOUN

into PREP **1** to a point on or within. **2** resulting in a change of state or condition. **3** concerned with or focusing on.

intolerable ADJ unbearable.

intonation NOUN the rise and fall of the voice in speaking.

intone VERB chant, especially on one note.

intoxicate VERB make drunk; make very excited. **intoxication** NOUN

intractable ADJ hard to deal with or control.

intransigent ADJ stubborn. **intransigence** NOUN

intransitive ADJ (of a verb) not followed by a direct object.

intravenous ADJ within or into a vein.

intrepid ADJ fearless.

intricate ADJ very complicated. **intricacy** NOUN

intrigue VERB 1 arouse the curiosity of. 2 plot secretly. NOUN a plot; a secret love affair. **intriguing** ADJ

intrinsic ADJ existing in a thing as a natural or permanent quality; essential.

introduce VERB 1 make a person known to another; present to an audience.

2 bring into use. 3 insert. 4 occur at the start of.

introduction NOUN introducing; an introductory part.

introductory ADJ introducing a person or thing; preliminary.

introspection NOUN concentration on your own thoughts and feelings. **introspective** ADJ

introvert NOUN an introspective and shy person. **introverted** ADJ

intrude VERB come or join in without being invited or wanted. **intruder** NOUN **intrusion** NOUN **intrusive** ADJ

intuition NOUN the ability to understand or know something without conscious reasoning. **intuitive** ADJ

inundate VERB flood; overwhelm.

inure VERB accustom to something unpleasant.

invade VERB enter territory so as to conquer or occupy it; encroach on; overrun. **invader** NOUN

invalid¹ NOUN a person suffering from ill health.

invalid² ADJ not valid.

invalidate VERB make invalid.

invaluable ADJ extremely useful.

invariable ADJ never changing.

invasion NOUN a hostile or harmful intrusion.

invasive ADJ

invective NOUN abusive language.

inveigh VERB (**inveigh against**) speak or write about with great hostility.

invent VERB make or design something new; make up a false story, name, etc.

inventor NOUN

invention NOUN something invented; inventing.

inventive ADJ creative and original.

inventory NOUN (PL **-ies**) a detailed list of goods or furniture.

inverse ADJ opposite or contrary.

invert VERB turn upside down; reverse the position, order, or relationship of.

inversion NOUN

invertebrate NOUN an animal that has no backbone.

invest VERB 1 use money, time, etc. to earn interest or bring profit. 2 confer rank or office on. 3 endow with a quality.

investment NOUN

investor NOUN

investigate VERB study carefully; inquire into.

investigation NOUN

investigator NOUN

investiture NOUN investing a person with honours or rank.

inveterate ADJ habitual; firmly established.

invidious ADJ liable to cause resentment.

invigilate VERB supervise candidates during an exam.

invigilator NOUN

invigorate VERB give strength or energy to.

invincible ADJ unconquerable.

inviolable ADJ never to be broken or dishonoured.

inviolate ADJ not violated; safe.

invisible ADJ not able to be seen.

invisibility NOUN

invite VERB ask a person politely to come or to do something; risk

provoking.
invitation NOUN

inviting ADJ pleasant and tempting.

invocation NOUN invoking.

invoice NOUN a bill for goods or services. VERB send an invoice to.

invoke VERB call for the help or protection of; summon a spirit.

involuntary ADJ done without intention.

involve VERB have as a part or consequence; cause to participate; require.
involvement ADJ

involved ADJ 1 concerned in something; in a relationship with someone. 2 complicated.

inward (or **inwards**) ADV towards the inside; into or towards the mind, spirit, or soul.

iodine NOUN a chemical used in solution as an antiseptic.

ion NOUN an electrically charged atom that has lost or gained an electron.

iota NOUN a very small amount.

IOU NOUN a signed paper given as a receipt for money borrowed.

IQ ABBREV intelligence quotient, a number showing how a person's intelligence compares with the average.

irascible ADJ hot-tempered.

irate ADJ angry.

ire NOUN anger.

iridescent ADJ shimmering with many colours.
iridescence NOUN

iris NOUN 1 the coloured part of the eyeball, round the pupil. 2 a plant with showy flowers.

Irish ADJ & NOUN (the language of) Ireland.

irk VERB annoy or irritate.

irksome ADJ irritating.

iron NOUN 1 a strong hard metal; a tool made of this. 2 an implement with a heated steel base, used for smoothing clothes etc. 3 (**irons**) fetters. VERB 1 smooth clothes etc. with an iron. 2 (**iron out**) solve problems.

ironmonger NOUN a shopkeeper selling tools and household implements.

irony NOUN (PL **-ies**) the expression of a meaning through words whose literal sense is the

opposite; the development of events in the opposite way to that intended or expected.
ironic ADJ

irradiate VERB 1 expose to radiation. 2 illuminate.
irradiation NOUN

irrational ADJ not guided by reason.

irrefutable ADJ impossible to disprove.

irregular ADJ 1 not even or smooth. 2 contrary to rules or custom.
irregularity NOUN

irrelevant ADJ not relevant.
irrelevance NOUN

irreparable ADJ unable to be repaired.

irreplaceable ADJ impossible to replace.

irrepressible ADJ impossible to control or subdue.

irreproachable ADJ blameless or faultless.

irresistible ADJ too strong or attractive to be resisted.
irresistibility NOUN

irresolute ADJ unable to make up your mind.

irrespective ADJ (irrespective of) regardless of.

irresponsible ADJ not showing a proper sense of responsibility.
irresponsibility NOUN

irretrievable ADJ impossible to retrieve or put right.

irreverent ADJ lacking respect.
irreverence NOUN

irreversible ADJ impossible to alter or undo.

irrevocable ADJ unalterable.

irrigate VERB supply land with water by streams, pipes, etc.
irrigation NOUN

irritable ADJ easily annoyed.
irritability NOUN

irritant NOUN something causing irritation.

irritate VERB 1 annoy. 2 cause to itch.
irritation NOUN

Islam NOUN the Muslim religion.
Islamic ADJ

island NOUN a piece of land surrounded by water.
islander NOUN

isle NOUN an island.

islet NOUN a small island.

isobar NOUN a line on a map connecting places with the same atmospheric pressure.

isolate VERB place apart or alone; separate from others or from a compound.
isolation NOUN

isomer NOUN each of two or more compounds with the same formula but a different arrangement of atoms.

isosceles ADJ (of a triangle) having two sides equal.

isotope NOUN each of two or more forms of a chemical element differing in their atomic weight.

issue NOUN 1 a topic or problem for discussion. 2 the action of supplying something; one edition of a magazine etc. VERB 1 supply or give out. 2 publish.

isthmus NOUN (PL -ses) a narrow strip of land connecting two larger masses of land.

it PRON 1 the thing mentioned or being discussed. 2 used as the subject of an impersonal verb. 3 used to identify someone.

italic ADJ (of type) sloping to the right. PLURAL NOUN (**italics**) italic type.

italicize (or -ise) VERB print in italics.

itch NOUN a tickling sensation in the skin causing a desire to scratch; a restless desire. VERB feel an itch.
itchy ADJ

item NOUN an individual article or unit.

itemize (or -ise) VERB list; state the individual items of.

itinerant ADJ travelling from place to place.

itinerary NOUN (PL -ies) a planned route or journey.

its POSSESSIVE PRON of the thing mentioned; belonging to it.

itself PRON the emphatic and reflexive form of **it**.

ivory NOUN (PL -ies) a hard creamy-white substance forming the tusks of an elephant etc.; its creamy-white colour.

ivy NOUN an evergreen climbing plant.

Jj

jab VERB (**jabbed, jabbing**) poke roughly with something pointed. NOUN a rough poke; [inf] an injection.

jabber VERB talk rapidly, usually unintelligibly.

jack NOUN 1 a portable device for raising heavy weights off the ground. 2 a playing card next below queen. 3 an electrical connection with a single plug. 4 a small ball aimed at in bowls. VERB (**jack up**) raise with a jack.

jackal NOUN a doglike wild animal.

jackass NOUN 1 a male ass. 2 a stupid person.

jackboot NOUN a military boot reaching above the knee.

jackdaw NOUN a bird of the crow family.

jacket NOUN 1 a short coat. 2 an outer covering; the skin of a potato.

jackknife NOUN (PL **-knives**) a large folding knife. VERB (of an

articulated vehicle) fold against itself in an accident.

jackpot NOUN a large prize of money that has accumulated until won.

jacuzzi NOUN [trademark] a large bath with underwater jets of water.

jade NOUN a hard bluish-green precious stone.

jaded ADJ tired and bored.

jagged ADJ having rough sharp projections.

jaguar NOUN a large spotted wild cat.

jail (or **gaol**) NOUN prison. VERB put into jail. **jailer** (or **gaoler**) NOUN

jam NOUN 1 a thick sweet substance made by boiling fruit with sugar. 2 a crowded mass making movement difficult; [inf] a difficult situation. VERB (**jammed, jamming**) 1 pack tightly into a space; block, crowd. 2 become stuck. 3 make a broadcast unintelligible by causing interference.

jamb NOUN the side post of

jamboree

372

a door or window.

jamboree NOUN a large party; a rally.

jangle NOUN a harsh metallic sound. VERB make or cause to make this sound; (of your nerves) be set on edge.

janitor NOUN the caretaker of a building.

January NOUN the first month.

jar¹ NOUN a cylindrical glass or earthenware container.

jar² VERB (**jarred, jarring**) strike with a painful shock; have a painful or disagreeable effect.

jargon NOUN words or expressions developed for use within a particular group of people and hard for others to understand.

jasmine NOUN a shrub with white or yellow flowers.

jaundice NOUN a condition in which the skin becomes abnormally yellow.

jaundiced ADJ **1** affected by jaundice. **2** filled with resentment.

jaunt NOUN a short pleasure trip.

jaunty ADJ (**-ier, -iest**) cheerful and self-confident.

jauntily ADV

javelin NOUN a light spear thrown in sport (formerly as a weapon).

jaw NOUN the bones forming the framework of the mouth.

jay NOUN a noisy bird of the crow family.

jazz NOUN a type of music involving improvisation, strong rhythm, and syncopation.

jealous ADJ envying and resenting another's success; suspiciously protecting possessions or a relationship.

jealousy NOUN

jeans PLURAL NOUN denim trousers.

jeep NOUN [trademark] a small sturdy motor vehicle with four-wheel drive.

jeer VERB laugh or shout rudely or scornfully. NOUN a jeering shout.

jell VERB set as a jelly; [inf] (of plans etc.) become clear and fixed.

jelly NOUN (PL **-ies**) a soft solid food made of liquid set with gelatin; a substance of similar consistency.

jellyfish NOUN a sea animal with a jelly-like body.

jemmy NOUN (PL -ies) a short crowbar.

jeopardize (or -ise) VERB endanger.

jeopardy NOUN danger.

jerk NOUN a sudden sharp movement or pull. VERB move, pull, or stop with a jerk.
jerky ADJ

jerkin NOUN a sleeveless jacket.

jersey NOUN (PL -eys) a knitted woollen pullover with sleeves; machine-knitted fabric.

jest NOUN a joke. VERB make jokes.

jester NOUN a clown at a medieval court.

jet¹ NOUN a hard black mineral; glossy black.

jet² NOUN 1 a stream of water, gas, or flame from a small opening. 2 an engine or aircraft using jet propulsion. VERB (**jetted, jetting**) travel by jet aircraft.
jet lag delayed tiredness etc. after a long flight.

jetsam NOUN goods jettisoned by a ship and washed ashore.

jettison VERB throw overboard; abandon or discard.

jetty NOUN (PL -ies) a landing stage etc. where boats can be moored.

Jew NOUN a person of Hebrew descent or whose religion is Judaism.
Jewish ADJ

jewel NOUN a precious stone cut or set as an ornament; a highly valued person or thing.
jewelled ([US] **jeweled**) ADJ

jeweller ([US] **jeweler**) NOUN a person who makes or sells jewellery.

jewellery ([US] **jewelry**) NOUN necklaces, rings, bracelets, etc.

jib NOUN a triangular sail stretching forward from a mast; a projecting arm of a crane. VERB (**jibbed, jibbing**) 1 refuse to go on. 2 (**jib at**) object to.

jibe (or **gibe**) VERB jeer. NOUN a jeering remark.

jiffy NOUN [inf] a moment.

jig NOUN 1 a lively dance. 2 a device that holds something and guides tools working on it. VERB (**jigged, jigging**) move quickly up and down.

jigsaw NOUN 1 a picture cut into interlocking pieces that have to be fitted together. **2** a machine fretsaw.

jilt VERB abandon a lover.

jingle VERB make a ringing or clinking sound. NOUN **1** this sound. **2** a simple rhyme, especially one used in advertising.

jingoism NOUN excessive patriotism.

jinx NOUN an influence causing bad luck.

jitters PLURAL NOUN [inf] nervousness.
jittery ADJ

jive NOUN a lively dance to jazz music. VERB dance in this style.

job NOUN a paid position of regular employment; a task.

jobcentre NOUN (in the UK) a government office displaying information about available jobs.

jockey NOUN (PL **-eys**) a person who rides in horse races. VERB manoeuvre to gain advantage.

jockstrap NOUN a protective support for the male genitals.

jocular ADJ joking.
jocularity NOUN

jodhpurs PLURAL NOUN trousers worn for horse riding, fitting closely below the knee.

jog VERB (**jogged, jogging**) **1** run at a steady gentle pace; carry on steadily and uneventfully. **2** nudge or knock; stimulate someone's memory. NOUN **1** a steady run. **2** a nudge.
jogger NOUN

joggle VERB shake slightly. NOUN a slight shake.

join VERB **1** connect or be connected. **2** become a member of; come into the company of. **3** (**join up**) enlist in the armed forces. NOUN a place where things join.

joiner NOUN a maker of wooden doors, windows, etc.
joinery NOUN

joint NOUN **1** a join; a structure where bones fit together; a large piece of meat. **2** [inf] a cannabis cigarette. **3** [inf] an establishment for meeting, eating, etc. ADJ shared by two or more people. VERB connect with a joint; cut into joints.
out of joint dislocated.

joist NOUN one of the beams supporting a floor or ceiling.

joke NOUN something said

or done to cause laughter; a ridiculous person or thing. VERB make jokes.

joker NOUN 1 a person who jokes. 2 an extra playing card with no fixed value.

jollification NOUN merrymaking.

jollity NOUN (PL **-ies**) lively celebration.

jolly ADJ (**-ier, -iest**) happy and cheerful; [inf] enjoyable. ADV [inf] very. VERB (**jolly along**) keep a person in good humour.

jolt VERB shake or dislodge with a jerk; move jerkily; surprise or shock into action. NOUN a jolting movement; a shock.

joss stick NOUN a thin stick that burns with a smell of incense.

jostle VERB push roughly.

jot NOUN a very small amount. VERB (**jotted, jotting**) write down briefly.

jotter NOUN a notepad.

joule NOUN a unit of energy.

journal NOUN a daily record of events; a newspaper or periodical.

journalist NOUN a person employed to write for a newspaper or magazine. **journalism** NOUN

journey NOUN (PL **-eys**) an act of travelling from one place to another. VERB make a journey.

journeyman NOUN a reliable but not outstanding workman.

jovial ADJ cheerful and good-humoured. **joviality** NOUN

jowl NOUN the lower part of a person's or animal's cheek.

joy NOUN great pleasure; something causing delight. **joyful** ADJ

joyous ADJ very happy.

joyride NOUN [inf] a fast and dangerous drive in a stolen car. **joyriding** NOUN

joystick NOUN an aircraft's control lever; a device for moving a cursor on a VDU screen.

JP ABBREV Justice of the Peace.

jubilant ADJ happy and triumphant. **jubilation** NOUN

jubilee NOUN a special anniversary.

judder VERB shake noisily or violently. NOUN this movement.

judge NOUN a public officer

appointed to hear and try cases in law courts; a person who decides who has won a contest; a person able to give an authoritative opinion. VERB try a case in a law court; act as judge of.

judgement (or **judgment**) NOUN the ability to make wise decisions; judging; a judge's decision on a case.

judgemental (or **judgmental**) ADJ of judgement; too critical.

judicial ADJ of the administration of justice; of a judge or judgement. **judicially** ADV

judiciary NOUN (PL **-ies**) the whole body of judges in a country.

judicious ADJ showing good judgement.

judo NOUN a Japanese system of unarmed combat.

jug NOUN a container with a handle and a lip, for holding and pouring liquids.

juggernaut NOUN a very large transport vehicle.

juggle VERB toss and catch several objects, keeping at least one in the air at any time; manipulate

skilfully. **juggler** NOUN

jugular vein NOUN either of the two large veins in the neck.

juice NOUN the liquid in fruits and vegetables; fluid secreted by an organ of the body; [inf] electrical energy; petrol.

juicy ADJ (**-ier, -iest**) full of juice; [inf] excitingly scandalous.

ju-jitsu NOUN a Japanese system of unarmed combat.

jukebox NOUN a coin-operated record player.

July NOUN the seventh month.

jumble VERB mix in a confused way. NOUN jumbled articles; items for a jumble sale.

jumble sale a sale of second-hand articles.

jumbo NOUN (PL **-os**) [inf] something that is very large of its kind; (also **jumbo jet**) a very large jet aircraft.

jump VERB **1** move up off the ground etc. by using your legs and feet; make a sudden upward movement; move over something by jumping;

omit or pass over. **2** (**jump at**) seize or accept eagerly. NOUN **1** a jumping movement; a sudden increase or change. **2** an obstacle to be jumped.

jumper NOUN **1** a knitted garment for the upper part of the body; [US] a pinafore dress. **2** a person who jumps.

jumpy ADJ (**-ier, -iest**) [inf] nervous.

junction NOUN a join; a place where roads or railway lines meet.

juncture NOUN **1** a particular point in time or the development of events. **2** a join.

June NOUN the sixth month.

jungle NOUN **1** a tropical forest; a mass of tangled vegetation. **2** a scene of ruthless struggle.

junior ADJ younger in age; lower in rank or authority; of or for younger people. NOUN a junior person.

juniper NOUN an evergreen shrub.

junk NOUN **1** [inf] useless or discarded articles. **2** a flat-bottomed ship with sails, used in the China seas.

junk food food with low nutritional value. **junk mail** unwanted advertising matter sent by post.

junket NOUN a sweet custard-like food made of milk and rennet.

junkie NOUN [inf] a drug addict.

junta NOUN a military or political group ruling a country after seizing power.

jurisdiction NOUN the authority to administer justice or exercise power.

juror NOUN a member of a jury.

jury NOUN (PL **-ies**) a group of people sworn to give a verdict on a case in a court of law.

just ADJ fair to all concerned; morally right; deserved, appropriate. ADV **1** exactly. **2** very recently. **3** barely. **4** only.

justice NOUN **1** just behaviour or treatment; legal proceedings. **2** a judge. **Justice of the Peace** a non-professional magistrate.

justifiable ADJ able to be defended as right or

reasonable.

justifiably ADV

justify VERB (**justified**, **justifying**) **1** show to be right or reasonable; be sufficient reason for. **2** adjust a line of type to fill a space neatly.

justification NOUN

jut VERB (**jutted**, **jutting**) (**jut out**) protrude.

jute NOUN fibre from the bark of certain tropical plants, used to make ropes etc.

juvenile ADJ of or for young people; childish. NOUN a young person or animal.

juvenile delinquent a young person who regularly commits crimes.

juxtapose VERB put things side by side.

juxtaposition NOUN

K ABBREV one thousand; [Computing] kilobytes.

kaftan (or **caftan**) NOUN a long tunic worn by men in the East; a long loose dress.

kale NOUN a green vegetable.

kaleidoscope NOUN a tube containing coloured fragments reflected to produce changing patterns as the tube is rotated.

kaleidoscopic ADJ

kamikaze NOUN (in the Second World War) a Japanese explosive-laden aircraft deliberately crashed on its target. ADJ reckless or suicidal.

kangaroo NOUN an Australian mammal with a pouch to carry its young and strong hind legs for jumping.

kaput ADJ [inf] broken or ruined.

karaoke NOUN entertainment in which people sing popular songs to pre-recorded backing tracks.

karate NOUN a Japanese system of unarmed combat using the hands and feet.

karma NOUN (in Buddhism and Hinduism) a person's actions as affecting their next reincarnation.

kayak NOUN a light covered canoe.

kebab NOUN small pieces of meat etc. cooked on a skewer.

kedgeree NOUN a cooked dish of fish, rice, hard-boiled eggs, etc.

keel NOUN a timber or steel structure along the base of a ship. VERB (**keel over**) capsize; fall over.

keen ADJ **1** eager or enthusiastic. **2** (of eyesight etc.) powerful; (of wind etc.) very cold.

keep VERB (**kept, keeping**) **1** retain possession of; reserve for future use; detain. **2** remain or cause to remain in a specified state or position; continue doing something. **3** provide with food and other necessities; own and look after animals. **4** fulfil a promise. **5** (**keep up**) progress at the same pace as others. NOUN **1** a person's food and other necessities. **2** a strongly

fortified structure in a castle.

keeper NOUN a person who keeps or looks after something.

keeping NOUN custody or charge.
in keeping with appropriate to.

keepsake NOUN something kept in memory of the giver.

keg NOUN a small barrel.

kelp NOUN a type of seaweed.

kennel NOUN a shelter for a dog; (**kennels**) a boarding place for dogs.

kept past and past participle of **keep**.

kerb NOUN a stone edging to a pavement.

kernel NOUN a seed within a husk, nut, or fruit stone; the central or important part.

kerosene NOUN paraffin oil.

kestrel NOUN a small falcon.

ketchup NOUN a thick tomato sauce.

kettle NOUN a container with a spout and handle, for boiling water.

kettledrum NOUN a drum with a membrane

stretched over a large metal bowl.

key NOUN 1 a piece of shaped metal for moving the bolt of a lock, winding a clock, etc.; something giving access or insight; a list explaining the symbols used in a map or table. 2 a button on a panel for operating a typewriter etc.; a lever pressed by the finger on a piano etc. 3 a system of related notes in music.

keyboard NOUN a set of keys on a piano, typewriter, or computer. VERB enter data using a keyboard.

keyboarder NOUN

keyhole NOUN a hole for a key in a lock.

keynote NOUN the prevailing idea of a speech, conference, etc.

keystone NOUN the central stone of an arch, locking others into position.

keyword NOUN a very significant word or concept.

kg ABBREV kilograms.

khaki NOUN a dull brownish-yellow colour.

kibbutz NOUN a communal settlement in Israel.

kick VERB 1 strike or propel with the foot. 2 (of a gun) recoil when fired. 3 [inf] give up an addictive habit. 4 (**kick out**) [inf] expel or dismiss. NOUN 1 an act of kicking; a blow with the foot. 2 [inf] a thrill.

kick-off the start of a football game.

kid NOUN a young goat; [inf] a child. VERB (**kidded, kidding**) [inf] tease or trick.

kidnap VERB (**kidnapped, kidnapping**; [US] **kidnaped, kidnaping**) take someone by force and hold them captive.

kidnapper NOUN

kidney NOUN (PL **-eys**) either of a pair of organs that remove waste products from the blood and secrete urine.

kill VERB 1 cause the death of; put an end to. 2 pass time. NOUN killing; an animal killed by a hunter.

killer NOUN

kiln NOUN an oven for baking or drying things.

kilo NOUN (PL **-os**) a kilogram.

kilogram NOUN a unit of weight or mass in the

metric system (2.205 lb).

kilohertz NOUN a unit of frequency of electromagnetic waves, = 1,000 cycles per second.

kilometre NOUN 1,000 metres (0.62 mile).

kilowatt NOUN 1,000 watts.

kilt NOUN a knee-length skirt of pleated tartan cloth, traditionally worn by Highland men.

kimono NOUN (PL **-os**) a loose Japanese robe worn with a sash.

kin NOUN a person's relatives.

kind NOUN a class of similar people or things. ADJ gentle and considerate towards others.
in kind (of payment) in goods etc., not money.
kindness NOUN

kindergarten NOUN a school for very young children.

kindle VERB light a fire; arouse a feeling.

kindling NOUN small pieces of wood for lighting fires.

kindly ADJ kind. ADV in a kind way; please (used in polite requests).
kindliness NOUN

kindred NOUN a person's relatives. ADJ related; of a similar kind.

kinetic ADJ of movement.

king NOUN 1 a male ruler of a country; a man or thing regarded as supreme. 2 the most important chess piece; a playing card next above queen.

king-size extra large.

kingdom NOUN 1 a country ruled by a king or queen. 2 one of the divisions into which natural objects are classified.

kingfisher NOUN a bird with bright blue feathers that dives to catch fish.

kingpin NOUN an indispensable person or thing.

kink NOUN a sharp twist in something straight; a flaw; a peculiar habit or characteristic. VERB form a kink.

kinky ADJ 1 having kinks. 2 [inf] given to or involving unusual sexual behaviour.

kinsfolk PLURAL NOUN a person's relatives.
kinsman NOUN
kinswoman NOUN

kiosk NOUN a booth where newspapers or refreshments are sold; a public telephone booth.

kip NOUN [inf] a sleep.

kipper NOUN a smoked herring.

kirk NOUN [Scottish] a church.

kismet NOUN destiny or fate.

kiss NOUN & VERB (a) touch or caress with the lips. **the kiss of life** mouth-to-mouth resuscitation.

kit NOUN a set of tools; a set of parts to be assembled; the clothing for a particular activity. VERB (**kitted, kitting**) equip with kit.

kitbag NOUN a bag for holding kit.

kitchen NOUN a room where meals are prepared.

kite NOUN 1 a light framework with fabric stretched over it, attached to a string for flying in the wind. 2 a large hawk.

kith and kin NOUN relatives.

kitsch NOUN objects etc. seen as in poor taste because garish, sentimental, or vulgar.

kitten NOUN a young cat.

kitty NOUN (PL **-ies**) a communal fund.

kiwi NOUN a flightless New Zealand bird.

klaxon NOUN [trademark] an electric horn.

kleptomania NOUN a compulsive desire to steal. **kleptomaniac** NOUN

km ABBREV kilometres.

knack NOUN the ability to do something skilfully.

knacker NOUN a person who buys and slaughters old horses, cattle, etc. VERB [inf] 1 tire out. 2 damage.

knapsack NOUN a bag worn strapped on the back.

knave NOUN 1 [old use] a dishonest man. 2 a jack in playing cards.

knead VERB press and stretch dough with the hands; massage.

knee NOUN the joint between the thigh and the lower leg; a person's lap. VERB (**kneed, kneeing**) hit with the knee. **knee-jerk** (of a reaction) automatic and predictable.

kneecap NOUN the small bone over the front of the knee.

kneel VERB (**knelt** or **kneeled, kneeling**) support yourself on your knees.

knell NOUN the sound of a bell tolled after a death.

knelt past and past participle of **kneel**.

knew past of **know**.

knickers PLURAL NOUN women's underpants.

knick-knack NOUN a small worthless ornament.

knife NOUN (PL **knives**) a cutting or spreading instrument with a blade and handle. VERB stab with a knife.

knight NOUN 1 a man given a rank below baronet, with the title 'Sir'. 2 a chess piece shaped like a horse's head. 3 [historical] a mounted soldier in armour. VERB confer a knighthood on.

knighthood NOUN the rank of knight.

knit VERB (**knitted** or **knit**, **knitting**) 1 make a garment from yarn formed into interlocking loops on long needles. 2 join together; tighten your eyebrows in a frown. **knitting** NOUN

knob NOUN a rounded lump; a round door handle. **knobbly** ADJ

knock VERB 1 hit with an audible sharp blow; strike a door to attract attention. 2 collide with; drive in a particular direction with a blow. 3 [inf] criticize. 4 (**knock out**) strike unconscious; eliminate from a competition. NOUN a sharp blow; the sound of this; a setback.

knock-kneed having knees that bend inwards.

knocker NOUN a hinged device for knocking on a door.

knockout NOUN 1 striking someone unconscious. 2 a tournament in which the loser in each round is eliminated. 3 [inf] an outstanding person or thing.

knoll NOUN a small hill.

knot NOUN 1 a fastening made by tying a piece of thread, rope, etc.; a tangle; a cluster. 2 a hard round spot in timber formed where a branch joins the trunk. 3 a unit of speed used by ships and aircraft, = one nautical mile per hour. VERB (**knotted, knotting**) tie or fasten with a knot; entangle.

knotty ADJ 1 full of knots. 2 very complex.

know VERB (**knew, known, knowing**) **1** have in your mind or memory; feel certain; have learned. **2** be acquainted, familiar, or friendly with a person, place, etc.
know-how practical knowledge or skill.
knowing ADJ showing that you have secret knowledge: *a knowing look*.
knowingly ADV
knowledge NOUN the facts etc. that someone knows; knowing a fact or about a subject; familiarity with someone or something.
knowledgeable ADJ intelligent and well informed.
knuckle NOUN a finger joint; an animal's leg joint as meat. VERB (**knuckle under**) yield or submit.
koala NOUN a bearlike Australian tree-climbing animal with thick grey fur.
Koran NOUN the sacred book of Islam.
kosher ADJ **1** conforming to Jewish dietary laws. **2** [inf] genuine or legitimate.
kowtow VERB behave with exaggerated respect.
krypton NOUN a colourless, odourless gas.
kudos NOUN honour and glory.
kung fu NOUN a Chinese form of unarmed combat.

l ABBREV litres.
lab NOUN [inf] a laboratory.
label NOUN a piece of card, cloth, etc., attached to something and carrying information about it. VERB (**labelled, labelling**; [US] **labeled, labeling**) attach a label to; put in a specified category.
labor etc. US spelling of **labour** etc.
laboratory NOUN (PL **-ies**) a room or building equipped for scientific work.

laborious ADJ needing or showing much effort.

labour ([US] **labor**) NOUN **1** work or exertion; workers. **2** the process of childbirth. VERB work hard; move with effort; explain a point at unnecessary length.

laboured ([US] **labored**) ADJ done with great effort.

labourer ([US] **laborer**) NOUN a person who does manual work.

Labrador NOUN a large dog.

laburnum NOUN a tree with hanging clusters of yellow flowers.

labyrinth NOUN a maze.

lace NOUN **1** decorative fabric made by looping thread in patterns. **2** a cord used to fasten a shoe or garment. VERB **1** fasten with laces. **2** add alcohol to a dish or drink. **lacy** ADJ

lacerate VERB tear flesh.

lachrymose ADJ tearful.

lack NOUN an absence or insufficiency of something. VERB be without something needed or wanted.

lackadaisical ADJ lacking vigour or enthusiasm.

lackey NOUN (PL **-eys**) a servant; a servile follower.

lacklustre ([US] **lackluster**) ADJ lacking brightness, enthusiasm, or conviction.

laconic ADJ using few words.

lacquer NOUN a hard glossy varnish. VERB coat with lacquer.

lacrosse NOUN a game similar to hockey played using sticks with small nets on the ends.

lad NOUN a boy.

ladder NOUN a set of crossbars between uprights, used for climbing up; a series of ascending stages in a career etc.; a strip of unravelled fabric in tights or stockings. VERB cause or develop a ladder.

laden ADJ loaded.

ladle NOUN a deep long-handled spoon for serving soup, etc. VERB serve or transfer with a ladle.

lady NOUN (PL **-ies**) a woman; a well-mannered woman; (**Lady**) the title of wives, widows, or daughters of certain noblemen.

ladybird NOUN a small

flying beetle, usually red with black spots.

ladylike ADJ appropriate to a well-mannered woman.

lag¹ VERB (**lagged, lagging**) fall behind. NOUN a delay.

lag² VERB (**lagged, lagging**) cover a boiler etc. with insulating material.

lager NOUN a light fizzy beer.

laggard NOUN a person who makes slow progress.

lagging NOUN material used to lag a boiler etc.

lagoon NOUN a salt-water lake beside the sea.

laid past & past participle of **lay²**.
laid-back [inf] easy-going and relaxed.

lain past participle of **lie²**.

lair NOUN a place where a wild animal rests; a hiding place.

laissez-faire NOUN a policy of non-interference, especially in politics or economics.

laity NOUN lay people, not clergy.

lake NOUN a large body of water surrounded by land.

lamb NOUN a young sheep. VERB give birth to a lamb.

lambaste (or **lambast**) VERB reprimand severely.

lame ADJ **1** unable to walk normally.
2 unconvincing. VERB make lame.

lamé NOUN a fabric interwoven with gold or silver thread.

lament NOUN an expression of grief; a song or poem expressing grief. VERB feel or express grief or regret.

lamentable ADJ very bad or regrettable.

laminated ADJ made of layers joined one on another.

lamp NOUN a device for giving light.

lampoon NOUN a mocking attack. VERB mock or ridicule.

lance NOUN a long spear. VERB prick or cut open with a lancet.

lancet NOUN a surgeon's pointed two-edged knife.

land NOUN **1** the part of the earth's surface not covered by water; ground or soil; an area of ground as property or for a particular use. **2** a country or state. VERB **1** come or bring ashore; come or bring down from the air.

2 [inf] succeed in obtaining or achieving. **3** [inf] put someone in a difficult situation.

landed ADJ owning land.

landfill NOUN the disposal of waste material by burying it.

landing NOUN **1** coming or bringing ashore or to ground; a place for this. **2** a level area at the top of a flight of stairs.

landlocked ADJ surrounded by land.

landlord (or **landlady**) NOUN a person who rents out property to a tenant; a person who runs a pub.

landmark NOUN a conspicuous feature of a landscape; an event marking an important stage or turning point.

landscape NOUN the scenery of a land area; a picture of this. VERB lay out an area attractively with natural-looking features.

landslide NOUN **1** a fall of earth and rock from a mountain or cliff. **2** an overwhelming majority of votes.

lane NOUN a narrow road, track, or passage; a division of a road for a single line of traffic; one of the parallel strips for runners etc. in a race.

language NOUN words and their use; a system of this used by a nation or group.

languid ADJ lacking vigour or vitality.

languish VERB become weak or faint; live under miserable conditions.

languor NOUN tiredness or laziness. **languorous** ADJ

lank ADJ (of hair) long, limp, and straight.

lanky ADJ tall and thin.

lantern NOUN a lamp protected by a transparent case, carried by a handle.

lap NOUN **1** a flat area over the thighs of a seated person. **2** a single circuit of a racecourse; a section of a journey. VERB (**lapped**, **lapping**) **1** take up liquid with the tongue. **2** (of water) wash against something with a gentle sound. **3** be one or more laps ahead of a competitor.

lapel NOUN a flap folded back at the front of a coat etc.

lapse NOUN **1** a temporary

failure of concentration, memory, etc.; a decline in standard. **2** the passage of time. VERB **1** (of a right or privilege) become invalid. **2** pass into an inferior state.

laptop NOUN a portable computer.

larch NOUN a deciduous tree of the pine family.

lard NOUN a white greasy substance prepared from pig fat.

larder NOUN a storeroom for food.

large ADJ of great size or extent.
at large 1 free to roam about. **2** as a whole.

largely ADV to a great extent.

largesse NOUN money or gifts generously given.

lark NOUN **1** a skylark. **2** [inf] something done for fun. VERB (**lark about**) [inf] behave playfully.

larva NOUN (PL **-vae**) an insect in the first stage of its life.

larynx NOUN the part of the throat containing the vocal cords.

lasagne NOUN a dish of pasta layered with sauces of cheese, meat, tomato, etc.

lascivious ADJ lustful.

laser NOUN a device emitting an intense narrow beam of light.

lash VERB **1** strike with a whip; beat against; (of an animal) move its tail quickly to and fro. **2** tie down. NOUN **1** the flexible part of a whip; a blow with this. **2** an eyelash.

lashings PLURAL NOUN [inf] a lot.

lass (or **lassie**) NOUN [Scottish & N. English] a girl or young woman.

lassitude NOUN lack of energy.

lasso NOUN (PL **-sos** or **-soes**) a rope with a noose for catching cattle.

last¹ ADJ **1** coming after all others; lowest in importance. **2** most recent. ADV **1** most recently. **2** finally. NOUN the last person or thing; all that remains of something. VERB continue; survive or endure; (of resources) be enough for a period of time.
lasting ADJ
lastly ADV

last² NOUN a foot-shaped block used in making and

repairing shoes.

latch NOUN a bar lifted from its catch by a lever, used to fasten a gate etc.; a lock that fastens when a door is closed. VERB fasten with a latch.

late ADJ **1** happening or coming after the proper or expected time. **2** far on in a day or night or period. **3** dead; no longer holding a position. **4** recent. ADV **1** after the proper or expected time. **2** at or until a late time.

lately ADV recently.

latent ADJ existing but not active, developed, or visible.

lateral ADJ of, at, to, or from the side(s).

latex NOUN a milky fluid from certain plants, especially the rubber tree.

lath NOUN (PL **laths**) a narrow, thin strip of wood.

lathe NOUN a machine for holding and turning pieces of wood or metal while they are worked.

lather NOUN froth from soap and water; frothy sweat. VERB cover with or form lather.

Latin NOUN the language of the ancient Romans.

latitude NOUN **1** the distance of a place from the equator, measured in degrees. **2** freedom from restrictions.

latrine NOUN a communal toilet in a camp or barracks.

latter ADJ **1** towards the end or in the final stages; recent. **2** (**the latter**) the second of two things to be mentioned.

latter-day modern or recent.

latterly ADV

lattice NOUN a framework of crossed strips.

laudable ADJ praiseworthy.

laugh VERB make sounds and facial movements expressing amusement. NOUN the act or manner of laughing.

laughing stock a person who is ridiculed.

laughable ADJ ridiculous.

laughter NOUN the act or sound of laughing.

launch VERB send a ship into the water; send a rocket into the air; start an enterprise; introduce a new product. NOUN **1** the process of launching something. **2** a large motor boat.

launder VERB **1** wash and iron clothes etc. **2** transfer illegally obtained money to conceal its origin.

launderette NOUN a place with coin-operated washing machines etc. for public use.

laundry NOUN (PL **-ies**) a place where clothes etc. are washed; clothes etc. for washing.

laurel NOUN an evergreen shrub; (**laurels**) victories or honours gained.

lava NOUN flowing or hardened molten rock from a volcano.

lavatory NOUN (PL **-ies**) a toilet; a room equipped with this.

lavender NOUN a shrub with fragrant purple flowers; light purple.

lavish ADJ generous; luxurious and extravagant. VERB give generously.

law NOUN a rule established by authority; a set of such rules; a statement of what always happens in certain circumstances.

lawful ADJ permitted or recognized by law.

lawless ADJ disregarding the law.

lawn NOUN an area of closely cut grass in a garden or park.

lawsuit NOUN a claim brought to a law court for settlement.

lawyer NOUN a person qualified in legal matters.

lax ADJ not strict or severe. **laxity** NOUN

laxative ADJ & NOUN (a medicine) stimulating the bowels to empty.

lay¹ ADJ not ordained into the clergy; non-professional.

lay² VERB (**laid, laying**) **1** set down carefully; arrange for use; put cutlery etc. on a table for a meal. **2** assign or place. **3** (of a bird) produce eggs.

lay-by an area beside the road where vehicles may stop. **lay into** attack. **lay off** discharge workers temporarily.

lay³ past of **lie²**.

layabout NOUN a lazy person.

layer NOUN one of several sheets or thicknesses of a substance covering a surface. VERB arrange in layers.

layette NOUN an outfit for a newborn baby.

layman NOUN someone not ordained as a clergyman; someone without professional knowledge of a subject.

layout NOUN an arrangement of parts etc. according to a plan.

laze VERB spend time idly.

lazy ADJ (**-ier, -iest**) unwilling to work or use energy; done without effort or care.
lazily ADV

lb ABBREV pounds (in weight).

lea NOUN [literary] an area of grassy land.

leach VERB remove soluble minerals etc. from soil through the action of liquid percolating through it.

lead¹ VERB (**led, leading**) **1** go in front of and cause to follow you; guide. **2** be a reason or motive for someone. **3** be a route or means of access; result or culminate in something. **4** be in command of; be ahead of or superior to. **5** pass your life. NOUN **1** a leading position; being ahead. **2** a clue. **3** the chief part in a play or film. **4** a strap or cord for leading a dog. **5** a wire conveying electric current.

lead² NOUN **1** a heavy grey metal. **2** graphite in a pencil.

leaden ADJ **1** heavy or slow-moving. **2** a dull grey colour.

leader NOUN **1** a person who leads. **2** a newspaper article giving editorial opinions.
leadership NOUN

leaf NOUN (PL **leaves**) **1** a flat green organ growing from the stem or root of a plant. **2** a single sheet of paper in a book; a very thin sheet of metal. VERB (**leaf through**) turn over the leaves of a book.
leafy ADJ

leaflet NOUN **1** a printed sheet of paper giving information. **2** a small leaf of a plant.

league NOUN **1** a group of people or countries united for a purpose; an association of sports clubs that compete against one another. **2** a class or quality of excellence.

leak VERB (of liquid, gas, etc.) pass through a crack;

(of a container) lose contents through a crack or hole; disclose secrets or be disclosed. NOUN a crack or hole through which contents leak; an instance of leaking.

leakage NOUN

leaky ADJ

lean¹ VERB (**leaned** or **lent**, **leaning**) **1** put or be in a sloping position; rest against something for support. **2** (**lean on**) depend on.

lean-to a shed etc. against the side of a building.

lean² ADJ thin; (of meat) with little fat; (of a period) characterized by hardship.

leaning NOUN a tendency or inclination.

leap VERB (**leaped** or **leapt**, **leaping**) **1** jump vigorously. **2** (**leap at**) accept eagerly. NOUN a vigorous jump.

leap year a year with an extra day (29 Feb.), occurring every four years.

leapfrog NOUN a game in which each player vaults over another who is bending down.

learn VERB (**learned** or learnt, **learning**) gain knowledge of or skill in; become aware of; memorize.

learner NOUN

learned ADJ having or showing great learning.

learning NOUN knowledge obtained by study.

lease NOUN a contract allowing the use of land or a building for a specified time. VERB let out or rent by lease.

leasehold NOUN

leash NOUN a dog's lead.

least ADJ smallest in amount or degree; lowest in importance. NOUN the least amount etc. ADV in the least degree.

leather NOUN material made by treating animal skins.

leathery ADJ tough like leather.

leave VERB (**left**, **leaving**) **1** go away from; go away finally or permanently. **2** allow to remain; abandon; deposit or entrust to someone. **3** cause to remain in a specified state. NOUN permission; permission to be absent from duty.

leaven NOUN a substance

such as yeast, causing dough to rise.

lecherous ADJ showing sexual desire in an offensive way.

lechery NOUN

lectern NOUN a stand with a sloping top from which a bible etc. is read.

lecture NOUN a speech giving information about a subject; a lengthy reproof or warning. VERB give a lecture; reprove at length.

lecturer NOUN

led past & past participle of **lead**[1].

ledge NOUN a narrow horizontal projection or shelf.

ledger NOUN a book used for keeping accounts.

lee NOUN shelter from the wind given by a hill, building, etc.

leeward ADJ & ADV

leech NOUN a small blood-sucking worm.

leek NOUN a vegetable with an onion-like flavour.

leer VERB look slyly, maliciously, or lustfully. NOUN a leering look.

lees PLURAL NOUN sediment in wine.

leeway NOUN a degree of

freedom of action.

left[1] past & past participle of **leave**.

left[2] ADJ & ADV of, on, or towards the side of the body which is on the west when you are facing north. NOUN **1** the left side or region; the left hand or foot. **2** people supporting socialism or a more extreme form of socialism than others in their group.

leg NOUN **1** each of the limbs on which a person, animal, etc. stands or moves; a support of a table, chair, etc. **2** one section of a journey or contest.

legacy NOUN (PL **-ies**) something left to someone in a will, or handed down by a predecessor.

legal ADJ of or based on law; authorized or required by law.

legal tender currency that must, by law, be accepted as payment.

legally ADV

legalize (or **-ise**) VERB make permissible by law.

legate NOUN an envoy.

legato ADV [Music]

smoothly and evenly.

legend NOUN **1** a story handed down from the past. **2** a very famous person. **3** an inscription, caption, etc.
legendary ADJ

legible ADJ clear enough to be read.

legion NOUN a division of the ancient Roman army; a huge crowd. ADJ very numerous.

legislate VERB make laws.
legislative ADJ

legislation NOUN laws collectively.

legislature NOUN the group that formulates a country's laws.

legitimate ADJ **1** in accordance with a law or rule; justifiable. **2** born of parents married to each other.
legitimacy NOUN
legitimize (or **-ise**) VERB

legume NOUN a plant of the family bearing seeds in pods.

leisure NOUN time free from work.

leisurely ADJ & ADV without hurry.

lemming NOUN a mouse-like Arctic rodent.

lemon NOUN a yellow citrus fruit with acidic juice; a pale yellow colour.

lemonade NOUN a lemon-flavoured fizzy drink.

lemur NOUN a nocturnal monkey-like animal of Madagascar.

lend VERB (**lent, lending**) give something to someone for temporary use; provide money temporarily in return for payment of interest; add an effect to something.
lender NOUN

length NOUN **1** the measurement or extent from end to end; being long; the full extent; a piece of cloth etc. **2** an extreme effort: *go to great lengths.*

lengthen VERB make or become longer.

lengthways (or **lengthwise**) ADV & ADJ in the direction of a thing's length.

lengthy ADJ (**-ier, -iest**) very long.

lenient ADJ merciful or tolerant.

lens NOUN a piece of glass or similar substance shaped for use in an optical instrument.

Lent NOUN the Christian

period of fasting and repentance before Easter.

lent past and past participle of **lend**.

lentil NOUN a kind of bean.

leopard NOUN a large spotted wild cat.

leotard NOUN a close-fitting stretchy garment worn by dancers, gymnasts, etc.

leper NOUN a person with leprosy.

leprosy NOUN an infectious disease affecting the skin and nerves and causing deformities.

lesbian NOUN a homosexual woman.

lesion NOUN a region in an organ or tissue that is damaged by injury or disease.

less ADJ & PRON not so much; a smaller amount of. ADV to a smaller extent. PREP minus.
lessen VERB

lesser ADJ not so great or important as the other.

lesson NOUN 1 a period of learning or teaching; something to be learnt by a pupil; an experience by which you can learn. 2 a passage from the Bible read aloud.

lest CONJ for fear that.

let VERB (**let, letting**) 1 allow. 2 allow someone to use accommodation in return for payment. 3 used to express an intention, suggestion, or order: *let's go*. NOUN 1 (in tennis etc.) a situation in which a ball is obstructed. 2 a period during which property is let.
let off fire or explode a weapon, firework, etc.; excuse.

lethal ADJ causing death.

lethargy NOUN a lack of energy or vitality.
lethargic ADJ

letter NOUN 1 a symbol representing a speech sound. 2 a written message sent by post. VERB inscribe letters on.

lettuce NOUN a plant whose leaves are eaten in salads.

leukaemia NOUN a disease in which too many white blood cells are produced.

level ADJ 1 flat, even, and horizontal. 2 at the same height or in the same relative position as something. NOUN 1 a position on a scale. 2 a height reached. VERB (**levelled, levelling**; [US]

leveled, leveling) **1** make or become level. **2** aim a gun.

level crossing a place where a road and railway cross at the same level.

level-headed sensible.

lever NOUN a bar pivoted on a fixed point to lift something; a pivoted handle used to operate machinery; a means of power or influence. VERB lift or move with a lever.

leverage NOUN the action or power of a lever; power or influence.

leveret NOUN a young hare.

leviathan NOUN something of enormous size and power.

levitate VERB rise and float in the air.

levity NOUN the flippant treatment of something serious.

levy VERB (**levied, levying**) impose a tax, fee, or fine. NOUN (PL **-ies**) a tax; an act of levying a tax etc.

lewd ADJ treating sexual matters in a crude way.

lexicon NOUN a dictionary; a vocabulary.

liability NOUN (PL **-ies**) **1** being legally responsible. **2** a debt. **3** a person or thing putting you at a disadvantage.

liable ADJ **1** held responsible by law; legally obliged to pay a tax etc. **2** likely to do something.

liaise VERB establish a cooperative link or relationship.

liaison NOUN **1** communication and cooperation. **2** a sexual relationship.

liar NOUN a person who tells lies.

libel NOUN a published false statement that damages a person's reputation. VERB (**libelled, libelling**; [US] **libeled, libeling**) publish a libel against.
libellous ADJ

liberal ADJ **1** tolerant; respecting individual freedom; (in politics) favouring moderate social reform. **2** generous. **3** (of an interpretation) not strict or exact.

liberalize (or **-ise**) VERB make less strict.

liberate VERB set free.
liberator NOUN

libertine NOUN a man who lives an irresponsible immoral life.

liberty NOUN (PL **-ies**)

freedom; a right or privilege.

take liberties behave with undue freedom or familiarity.

libido NOUN (PL **-os**) sexual desire.

librarian NOUN a person who works in a library.

library NOUN (PL **-ies**) a collection of books or records, films, etc. for consulting or borrowing.

libretto NOUN (PL **-rettos** or **-retti**) the words of an opera.

lice plural of **louse**.

licence ([US] **license**) NOUN 1 an official permit to own or do something; permission. 2 freedom to do as you like.

license VERB grant a licence to or for.

licensee NOUN a holder of a licence.

licentious ADJ sexually immoral.

lichen NOUN a low-growing dry plant that grows on rocks etc.

lick VERB 1 pass the tongue over; (of waves or flame) touch lightly. 2 [inf] defeat. NOUN an act of licking; [inf] a quick application of paint etc.

licorice US spelling of **liquorice**.

lid NOUN a hinged or removable cover for a box, pot, etc.; an eyelid.

lie[1] NOUN a statement the speaker knows to be untrue. VERB (**lied, lying**) tell a lie.

lie[2] VERB (**lay, lain, lying**) 1 have or put your body in a flat or resting position; be at rest on something. 2 be in a specified state; be situated. NOUN the pattern or direction in which something lies.

lieu NOUN (**in lieu**) instead.

lieutenant NOUN a rank of officer in the army and navy; a deputy or substitute.

life NOUN (PL **lives**) 1 the ability of animals and plants to function and grow; being alive. 2 the time for which an individual is alive. 3 a way of living. 4 vitality or enthusiasm. 5 a sentence of imprisonment for life.

life jacket a buoyant or inflatable jacket for keeping a person afloat in water.

lifeboat NOUN a boat for rescuing people at sea; a

ship's boat for emergency use.

lifeguard NOUN a person employed to rescue swimmers in difficulty.

lifeless ADJ dead; not animated; without living things.

lifelike ADJ exactly like a real person or thing.

lifeline NOUN a rope thrown to a swimmer in danger; something essential to safety.

lifestyle NOUN a way of spending your life.

lifetime NOUN the duration of a person's life.

lift VERB 1 raise; move upwards; make larger, louder, or higher. 2 pick up and move; remove legal restrictions etc. NOUN 1 an apparatus for moving people and goods from one floor of a building to another. 2 an act or manner of lifting. 3 a free ride in a car etc. 4 a feeling of encouragement.

lift-off vertical take-off of a spacecraft etc.

ligament NOUN a tough flexible tissue holding bones together.

ligature NOUN a thing used for tying; thread used in surgery.

light¹ NOUN 1 the natural energy that makes things visible; a source of light. 2 understanding or enlightenment. 3 a way of regarding something. VERB (**lit** or **lighted, lighting**) 1 provide with light. 2 ignite. 3 (**light up**) become animated. ADJ 1 well lit; not dark. 2 (of a colour) pale.

light-hearted cheerful or carefree. **light year** the distance light travels in one year, about 6 million million miles.

light² ADJ 1 having little weight; easy to lift; of less than usual or average weight. 2 not serious or profound; not solemn, sad, or worried. 3 (of sleep) easily broken. 4 (of food) easy to digest.

lightly ADV

lighten VERB 1 make or become brighter. 2 make or become less heavy.

lighter NOUN 1 a device for lighting cigarettes and cigars. 2 a flat-bottomed boat for carrying ships' cargoes ashore.

lighthouse NOUN a tower with a powerful light to

warn or guide ships.

lighting NOUN a means of providing light; the light itself.

lightning NOUN a flash of bright light produced from cloud by natural electricity.

lightweight NOUN a person of little importance; a boxing weight between featherweight and welterweight.

like[1] PREP resembling; in the same way as; typical of. ADJ similar; the same. CONJ [inf] **1** in the same way that. **2** as if. NOUN a person or thing resembling another.

like[2] VERB **1** enjoy or find pleasant. **2** want or wish for. PLURAL NOUN (**likes**) things you like or prefer.
likeable (or **likable**) ADJ

likelihood NOUN a probability.

likely ADJ (-ier, -iest) **1** probable. **2** promising. ADV probably.

liken VERB point out the likeness of one thing to another.

likeness NOUN resemblance; a copy or portrait.

likewise ADV **1** also. **2** in a similar way.

liking NOUN a fondness.

lilac NOUN a shrub with fragrant purple or white flowers; pale purple.

lilt NOUN **1** a rise and fall of the voice when speaking. **2** a gentle rhythm in a tune.
lilting ADJ

lily NOUN (PL **-ies**) a plant with large flowers on a tall, slender stem.

limb NOUN an arm, leg, or wing; a large branch of a tree.

limber ADJ supple. VERB (**limber up**) exercise in preparation for athletic activity.

limbo[1] NOUN an uncertain period of waiting.

limbo[2] NOUN (PL **-os**) a West Indian dance in which the dancer bends back to pass under a bar.

lime NOUN **1** a white substance used in making cement etc. **2** a green citrus fruit like a lemon; its colour. **3** a tree with heart-shaped leaves.

limelight NOUN the focus of public attention.

limerick NOUN a humorous poem with five lines.

limestone NOUN rock from

which lime is obtained.

limit NOUN a point beyond which something does not continue; a restriction; the greatest amount allowed. VERB set or serve as a limit to. **limitation** NOUN

limousine NOUN a large luxurious car.

limp VERB walk or proceed lamely or with difficulty. NOUN a limping walk. ADJ not stiff or firm.

limpet NOUN a small shellfish that sticks tightly to rocks.

limpid ADJ (of liquids) clear.

linchpin NOUN **1** a pin passed through the end of an axle to secure a wheel. **2** a person or thing vital to an enterprise.

linctus NOUN a soothing cough mixture.

line NOUN **1** a long narrow mark; a wrinkle. **2** a length of cord, rope, wire, etc.; a telephone connection. **3** a row or series of people or things; a row of words; a brief letter; (**lines**) an actor's part. **4** a railway track or route; a company providing ships, aircraft,

or buses on a route. **5** a sphere of activity. VERB **1** stand on either side of a road etc. **2** mark with lines. **3** cover the inside surface of.

lineage NOUN ancestry.

linear ADJ extending along a line; formed with straight lines; proceeding straightforwardly from one stage to another.

linen NOUN cloth made of flax; household articles (e.g. sheets, tablecloths) formerly made of this.

liner NOUN a passenger ship or aircraft.

linesman NOUN an umpire's assistant at the boundary line.

linger VERB stay longer than necessary; take a long time doing something.

lingerie NOUN women's underwear.

linguist NOUN a person who is skilled in languages or linguistics.

linguistic ADJ of language. NOUN (**linguistics**) the study of language.

liniment NOUN an embrocation.

lining NOUN a layer of material or another

substance covering an inner surface.

link NOUN **1** a connection; a means of contact; a person acting as messenger or intermediary. **2** each ring of a chain. VERB connect or join.
linkage NOUN

linoleum NOUN a smooth covering for floors.

linseed NOUN the seed of flax, a source of oil.

lint NOUN a soft fabric for dressing wounds.

lintel NOUN a horizontal timber or stone over a doorway.

lion NOUN a large wild cat.

lip NOUN **1** either of the fleshy edges of the mouth opening. **2** the edge of a container or opening. **3** [inf] impudence.
lip-read understand speech from watching the movements of a speaker's lips.

lipstick NOUN a cosmetic for colouring the lips.

liqueur NOUN a strong sweet alcoholic spirit.

liquid NOUN a flowing substance like water or oil. ADJ **1** in the form of liquid. **2** (of assets) easy to convert into cash.

liquidate VERB **1** close down a business and divide its assets among creditors. **2** convert assets into cash. **3** pay off a debt. **4** kill.

liquidity NOUN a company's possession of liquid assets.

liquidize (or **-ise**) VERB reduce to a liquid.

liquor NOUN **1** alcoholic drink. **2** juice from cooked food.

liquorice ([US] **licorice**) NOUN a black substance used in medicine and as a sweet.

lisp NOUN a speech defect in which s and z are pronounced like th. VERB speak with a lisp.

lissom ADJ slim and supple.

list[1] NOUN a number of connected items or names following one another. VERB make a list of; include in a list.

list[2] VERB (of a ship) lean over to one side.

listen VERB make an effort to hear; pay attention; take notice of and act on what is said.
listener NOUN

listless ADJ without energy or enthusiasm.

lit past & past participle of **light**[1].

litany NOUN (PL **-ies**) a set form of prayer; a long monotonous recital.

liter US spelling of **litre**.

literal ADJ using or interpreting words in their most basic sense. **literally** ADV

literary ADJ of or associated with literature.

literate ADJ able to read and write. **literacy** NOUN

literature NOUN great novels, poetry, and plays; books and printed information on a particular subject.

lithe ADJ supple or agile.

lithium NOUN a light metallic element.

lithography NOUN printing from a plate treated so that ink sticks only to the design. **lithograph** NOUN

litigation NOUN the process of taking a dispute to a law court.

litmus NOUN a substance turned red by acids and blue by alkalis.

litre ([US] **liter**) NOUN a metric unit of capacity (1.76 pints) for measuring liquids.

litter NOUN 1 rubbish left lying about. 2 young animals born at one birth. 3 material used as bedding for animals or to absorb their excrement. VERB make untidy by dropping litter.

little ADJ small in size, amount, or degree; young or younger. NOUN & PRON a small amount; a short time or distance. ADV to a small extent; hardly.

liturgy NOUN (PL **-ies**) a set form of public worship. **liturgical** ADJ

live[1] ADJ 1 alive. 2 burning; unexploded; charged with electricity. 3 (of broadcasts) transmitted while actually happening.

live[2] VERB 1 be or remain alive. 2 have your home in a particular place. 3 spend your life in a particular way.

livelihood NOUN a means of earning or providing the things necessary for life.

lively ADJ (**-ier, -iest**) full of energy or action. **liveliness** NOUN

locale

liven VERB make or become lively.

liver NOUN a large organ in the abdomen, secreting bile.

livery NOUN (PL **-ies**) a distinctive uniform; a colour scheme in which a company's vehicles are painted.

livestock NOUN farm animals.

livid ADJ **1** furiously angry. **2** dark and inflamed.

living ADJ alive. NOUN an income.
  living room a room for general daytime use.

lizard NOUN a reptile with four legs and a long tail.

llama NOUN a South American animal related to the camel.

load NOUN **1** a thing or quantity carried; a weight or source of pressure. **2** the amount of electric current supplied by a source. **3** (**loads**) [inf] a great deal. VERB **1** put a load in or on; burden. **2** put ammunition into a gun or film into a camera; put data into a computer. **3** bias towards a particular outcome.

loaf NOUN (PL **loaves**) a quantity of bread baked as one piece. VERB spend time idly.
  loafer NOUN

loam NOUN rich soil.

loan NOUN a sum of money lent; lending. VERB lend.

loath ADJ unwilling.

loathe VERB feel hatred and disgust for.
  loathing NOUN
  loathsome ADJ

lob VERB (**lobbed, lobbing**) throw or hit a ball slowly in a high arc. NOUN a lobbed ball.

lobby NOUN (PL **-ies**) **1** a porch, entrance hall, or ante-room. **2** a body of people seeking to influence legislation. VERB (**lobbied, lobbying**) seek to persuade an MP etc. to support your cause.
  lobbyist NOUN

lobe NOUN the lower soft part of the ear.

lobster NOUN an edible shellfish with large claws.

local ADJ of or affecting a particular area, or the area where a person lives. NOUN **1** a person living in a particular area. **2** [inf] a person's nearest pub.
  locally ADV

locale NOUN the scene of

an event.

locality NOUN (PL **-ies**) the position of something; an area or neighbourhood.

localize (or **-ise**) VERB confine within an area.

locate VERB discover the position of; situate in a particular place.

location NOUN a place where something is situated; locating something.

loch NOUN [Scottish] a lake; an arm of the sea.

loci plural of **locus**.

lock NOUN **1** a device opened by a key for fastening a door or lid etc. **2** a section of a canal enclosed by gates, where the water level can be changed. **3** a wrestling hold. **4** the extent to which a vehicle's front wheels can be turned using the steering wheel. **5** a piece of hair that hangs together. VERB fasten with a lock; shut into a locked place; make or become rigidly fixed.

lock-up lockable premises; a place where prisoners can be kept temporarily.

locker NOUN a lockable cupboard or compartment.

locket NOUN a small ornamental case worn on a chain round the neck.

lockjaw NOUN tetanus.

lockout NOUN the exclusion of employees from their workplace during a dispute.

locksmith NOUN a maker and mender of locks.

locomotion NOUN the ability to move from place to place.

locomotive NOUN a self-propelled engine for moving trains.

locum NOUN a temporary stand-in for a doctor, clergyman, etc.

locus NOUN (PL **loci**) a particular position.

locust NOUN a tropical grasshopper that devours vegetation.

lodge NOUN **1** a cabin for use by hunters, skiers, etc.; a gatekeeper's house; a porter's room at the entrance to a building. **2** the members or meeting place of a branch of certain societies. **3** a beaver's or otter's lair. VERB **1** live somewhere as a lodger. **2** present a complaint, appeal, etc. to an authority. **3** make or become fixed or embedded.

lodger NOUN a person paying for accommodation in another's house.

lodgings PLURAL NOUN a room or rooms rented for living in.

loft NOUN a space under a roof. VERB hit, throw, or kick a ball in a high arc.

lofty ADJ (**-ier, -iest**) very tall; noble or exalted.

log NOUN **1** a piece cut from a trunk or branch of a tree. **2** a systematic record; a logbook. **3** a device for gauging a ship's speed. **4** a logarithm. VERB (**logged, logging**) **1** enter facts in a logbook. **2** (**log in/on** or **out/off**) begin or finish using a computer system.

loganberry NOUN a large dark red fruit resembling a raspberry.

logarithm NOUN one of a series of numbers set out in tables, used to simplify calculations.

logbook NOUN a book for recording details of a journey.

loggerheads PLURAL NOUN (**at loggerheads**) disagreeing or quarrelling.

logic NOUN a science or method of reasoning; correct reasoning.

logical ADJ of or according to logic; following naturally and sensibly; reasonable.

logistics PLURAL NOUN the detailed organization of a large and complex exercise.

logo NOUN (PL **-os**) a design used as an emblem.

loin NOUN the side and back of the body between the ribs and hip bone.

loincloth NOUN a cloth worn round the body at the hips.

loiter VERB stand about idly.

loll VERB sit, lie, or stand in a relaxed way; hang loosely.

lollipop NOUN a large flat boiled sweet on a small stick.

lolly NOUN [inf] **1** a lollipop. **2** money.

lone ADJ solitary.

lonely ADJ (**-ier, -iest**) **1** solitary; sad because you lack friends. **2** (of a place) remote.

loneliness NOUN

loner NOUN a person who prefers to be alone.

lonesome ADJ lonely.

long[1] ADJ of great length; of a specified length. ADV for a long time; throughout a specified period.

long shot a venture or guess very unlikely to succeed. **long-sighted** able to see clearly only what is at a distance.

long-standing having existed for a long time.

long-suffering bearing provocation patiently.

long-winded talking or writing at tedious length.

long[2] VERB feel an intense desire.

longevity NOUN long life.

longhand NOUN ordinary writing, not shorthand or typing etc.

longing NOUN an intense wish.

longitude NOUN the distance east or west (measured in degrees on a map) from the Greenwich meridian.

longways ADV lengthways.

loo NOUN [inf] a toilet.

look VERB 1 use or direct your eyes in order to see, search, or examine. 2 seem. 3 (**look after**) take care of. NOUN 1 an act of looking. 2 appearance; (**looks**) a person's attractiveness.

lookout NOUN an observation post; a person keeping watch.

loom VERB appear, especially close at hand or threateningly. NOUN an apparatus for weaving cloth.

loop NOUN a curve that is U-shaped or that crosses itself. VERB form into a loop; be loop-shaped.

loophole NOUN a means of evading a rule or contract.

loose ADJ 1 not securely fixed in place; not tethered or shut up. 2 (of a garment) not fitting closely; (of a translation etc.) not exact. VERB set free; unfasten.

loose-leaf with each page removable.

loosen VERB

loot NOUN goods taken from an enemy or by theft. VERB take loot.

lop VERB (**lopped, lopping**) cut off branches from a tree.

lope VERB run with a long

bounding stride.

lopsided ADJ with one side lower, smaller, or heavier than the other.

loquacious ADJ talkative.

lord NOUN a nobleman; the title of certain peers or high officials; a master or ruler. VERB (**lord it over**) behave in an arrogantly superior way towards.

lore NOUN a body of traditions and knowledge.

lorry NOUN (PL **-ies**) a large motor vehicle for transporting heavy loads.

lose VERB (**lost, losing**) **1** cease to have; be deprived of. **2** become unable to find. **3** fail to win a game etc.; waste an opportunity; earn less money than previously. **loser** NOUN

loss NOUN losing or being lost; someone or something lost; someone or something badly missed when lost.

lost past & past participle of **lose**. ADJ unable to find your way; not knowing where you are.

lot PRON & ADV (**a lot** or [inf] **lots**) a large number or amount; a great deal. NOUN **1** [inf] a group or set of people or things. **2** an item for sale at an auction. **3** each of a set of objects drawn at random to make a decision; a person's luck or condition in life. **4** a plot of land.

lotion NOUN a creamy liquid applied to the skin as a cosmetic or medicine.

lottery NOUN (PL **-ies**) a system of raising money by selling numbered tickets and giving prizes to holders of numbers drawn at random.

lotus NOUN a tropical water lily.

loud ADJ **1** making a great deal of noise; easily heard. **2** gaudy or garish. ADV loudly.

loudspeaker NOUN an apparatus that converts electrical impulses into audible sound.

lounge VERB sit or stand about idly. NOUN a sitting room; a waiting room at an airport etc.

lour (or **lower**) VERB frown; (of clouds) look dark and threatening.

louse NOUN (PL **lice**) a small parasitic insect.

lousy ADJ (**-ier, -iest**) [inf] very bad.

lout NOUN a rude or aggressive man or youth.

louvre (or **louver**) NOUN each of a set of overlapping slats arranged to let in air but exclude light or rain.

love NOUN **1** deep, intense affection; sexual passion; a beloved person or thing. **2** (in games) a score of zero. VERB feel love for; like or enjoy greatly.
make love have sex.
lovable ADJ
lover NOUN

lovelorn ADJ pining with unrequited love.

lovely ADJ (**-ier**, **-iest**) beautiful or attractive; delightful.

loving ADJ feeling or showing love.

low¹ ADJ **1** of little height from top to bottom; not far above the ground or sea level; of less than average amount or intensity. **2** inferior. **3** dishonourable. **4** depressed. NOUN a low point; an area of low atmospheric pressure. ADV in, at, or to a low level.
the low-down relevant information. **low-key** not elaborate or ostentatious.

low² VERB (of cattle) make a deep mooing sound.

lowbrow ADJ not intellectual or cultured.

lower¹ VERB let downwards; reduce the height, pitch, or degree of.
lower case letters that are not capitals.

lower² see **lour**.

lowlands PLURAL NOUN low-lying land.

lowly ADJ (**-ier**, **-iest**) of humble rank or condition.

loyal ADJ firm in your allegiance.
loyalty NOUN

loyalist NOUN a person who is loyal, especially while others revolt.

lozenge NOUN **1** a small medicinal tablet that is sucked. **2** a diamond-shaped figure.

LP ABBREV a long-playing record.

LSD NOUN a powerful hallucinogenic drug.

lubricant NOUN a lubricating substance.

lubricate VERB oil or grease machinery etc. to allow smooth movement.

lucid ADJ clearly expressed.
lucidity NOUN

luck NOUN good or bad things apparently happening by chance; good fortune.
luckless ADJ unlucky.
lucky ADJ (-ier, -iest) having, bringing, or resulting from good luck. **luckily** ADV
lucrative ADJ profitable.
ludicrous ADJ ridiculous.
lug VERB (**lugged, lugging**) drag or carry with great effort. NOUN [inf] an ear.
luggage NOUN suitcases and bags holding a traveller's possessions.
lugubrious ADJ sad or gloomy.
lukewarm ADJ only slightly warm; not enthusiastic.
lull VERB send to sleep; cause to feel deceptively confident. NOUN a period of quiet or inactivity.
lullaby NOUN (PL -ies) a soothing song for sending a child to sleep.
lumbago NOUN rheumatic pain in the lower back.
lumber NOUN unwanted furniture; [US] timber sawn into planks. VERB 1 move heavily and awkwardly. 2 burden with something unwanted.

lumberjack NOUN [US] a person who cuts or transports lumber.
luminary NOUN (PL -ies) an eminent person.
luminescent ADJ emitting light without heat.
luminous ADJ shining or glowing, especially in the dark.
lump NOUN a hard or compact mass; a swelling. VERB (**lump together**) group together indiscriminately. **lumpy** ADJ
lunacy NOUN insanity; great stupidity.
lunar ADJ of the moon.
lunatic NOUN an insane person; a very foolish person.
lunch NOUN a midday meal. VERB eat lunch.
luncheon NOUN lunch.
lung NOUN either of the pair of breathing organs in the chest.
lunge NOUN & VERB (make) a sudden forward movement of the body.
lurch VERB & NOUN (make) an unsteady swaying movement.
leave in the lurch leave a person in difficulties.

lure VERB entice. NOUN an enticement; a bait to attract wild animals.

lurid ADJ in glaring colours; vividly shocking or sensational.

lurk VERB wait in hiding to attack someone.

luscious ADJ delicious; voluptuously attractive.

lush ADJ (of grass etc.) growing thickly and strongly; rich or luxurious.

lust NOUN intense sexual desire; any intense desire. VERB feel lust.
lustful ADJ

lustre ([US] **luster**) NOUN a soft glow or shine; prestige or honour.
lustrous ADJ

lusty ADJ (**-ier, -iest**) strong and vigorous.

lute NOUN a guitar-like instrument with a rounded body.

luxuriant ADJ growing profusely.

luxuriate VERB enjoy or indulge in as a luxury.

luxurious ADJ very comfortable and elegant.

luxury NOUN (PL **-ies**) great comfort and extravagance; something unnecessary but very pleasant.

lychee NOUN a sweet white fruit with a brown spiny skin.

Lycra NOUN [trademark] an elastic fabric.

lying present participle of **lie**[1], **lie**[2].

lymph NOUN a colourless fluid containing white blood cells.
lymphatic ADJ

lynch VERB (of a mob) kill someone for an alleged crime without a legal trial.

lynx NOUN a wild animal of the cat family.

lyre NOUN a stringed instrument like a small harp, used in ancient Greece.

lyric ADJ (of poetry) expressing the poet's feelings. NOUN **1** a lyric poem. **2** (**lyrics**) the words of a song.

lyrical ADJ resembling or using language suitable for lyric poetry; [inf] expressing yourself enthusiastically.

lyricist NOUN a person who writes lyrics.

Mm

M ABBREV motorway. NOUN (as a Roman numeral) 1,000.
m ABBREV metres; miles; millions.
MA ABBREV Master of Arts.
mac NOUN [inf] a mackintosh.
macabre ADJ disturbingly interested in or involving death and injury.
macadam NOUN layers of broken stone used in road-making.
macaroni NOUN tube-shaped pasta.
macaroon NOUN a small almond biscuit.
macaw NOUN an American parrot.
mace NOUN **1** a ceremonial staff. **2** a spice.
machete NOUN a broad, heavy knife.
Machiavellian ADJ elaborately cunning or deceitful.
machinations PLURAL NOUN clever scheming.
machine NOUN a mechanical device for performing a particular task; an efficient group of powerful people. VERB produce or work on with a machine.
machine-gun an automatic gun firing bullets in rapid succession. **machine-readable** in a form that a computer can process.
machinery NOUN machines; the parts of a machine; a system or structure.
machinist NOUN a person who works machinery.
machismo NOUN aggressive masculine pride.
macho ADJ aggressively masculine.
mackerel NOUN an edible sea fish.
mackintosh (or **macintosh**) NOUN a raincoat.
macramé NOUN the art of knotting cord in patterns.
macrocosm NOUN the universe; a large complex whole.
mad ADJ (**madder**, **maddest**) **1** not sane;

extremely foolish; frantic or frenzied. **2** [inf] very enthusiastic. **3** [inf] angry.
madness NOUN

madam NOUN a polite form of address to a woman.

madcap ADJ wildly impulsive.

madden VERB make mad or angry.

made past and past participle of **make**.

Madonna NOUN the Virgin Mary.

madrigal NOUN a part-song for unaccompanied voices.

maelstrom NOUN a powerful whirlpool; a scene of confusion.

maestro NOUN (PL **-tri** or **-tros**) a great musical conductor or composer; a master of any art.

magazine **1** an illustrated periodical. **2** a chamber holding cartridges in a gun, slides in a projector, etc. **3** a store for arms or explosives.

magenta ADJ & NOUN purplish red.

maggot NOUN a larva, especially of the bluebottle.

Magi PLURAL NOUN the three wise men from the East who brought gifts to the infant Jesus.

magic NOUN the supposed art of controlling things by supernatural power; an exciting or delightful quality. ADJ using or used in magic.
magical ADJ

magician NOUN a person with magical powers; a conjuror.

magisterial ADJ **1** authoritative. **2** of a magistrate.

magistrate NOUN an official with authority to hold preliminary hearings and judge minor cases.

magma NOUN molten rock under the earth's crust.

magnanimous ADJ noble and generous.
magnanimity NOUN

magnate NOUN a wealthy influential business person.

magnesium NOUN a white metallic element that burns with an intensely bright flame.

magnet NOUN a piece of iron or steel that can attract iron and point north when suspended; a powerful attraction.

magnetic ADJ having the

properties of a magnet.

magnetic tape a strip of plastic coated with magnetic particles, used in recording, computers, etc.

magnetism NOUN the properties and effects of magnetic substances; great charm and attraction.

magnetize (or **-ise**) VERB 1 make magnetic. 2 attract.

magnificent ADJ 1 impressively beautiful, elaborate, or extravagant. 2 very good.

magnificence NOUN

magnify VERB (**magnified**, **magnifying**) make an object seem larger than it is, especially by using a lens; make larger or stronger.

magnification NOUN

magnitude NOUN size; great size or importance.

magnolia NOUN a tree with large white or pink flowers.

magnum NOUN a wine bottle of twice the standard size.

magpie NOUN a black and white bird of the crow family.

maharaja (or **maharajah**) NOUN [historical] an Indian prince.

mahogany NOUN a very hard reddish-brown wood.

maid NOUN a female servant.

maiden NOUN [old use] a young unmarried woman. ADJ first of its kind: *a maiden voyage*.

maiden name a woman's surname before she married.

mail NOUN 1 letters etc. sent by post; the postal system; email. 2 body armour made of metal rings or chains. VERB send by post or email.

maim VERB injure so that a part of the body is useless.

main ADJ chief in size or importance. NOUN a main pipe or channel conveying water, gas, or (usually **mains**) electricity.

mainly ADV

mainframe NOUN a large computer.

mainland NOUN a country or continent without its adjacent islands.

mainstay NOUN a thing on which something else depends.

mainstream NOUN the dominant trend of opinion or style etc.

maintain VERB 1 cause to continue or remain in existence; keep repaired and in good condition; provide with financial support. 2 assert.

maintenance NOUN maintaining something; money paid to a former spouse after a divorce.

maisonette NOUN a flat on two storeys of a larger building.

maize NOUN a tall cereal plant bearing grain on large cobs; its grain.

majestic ADJ stately and dignified, imposing.

majesty NOUN (PL -ies) impressive stateliness; sovereign power; (**Majesty**) the title of a king or queen.

major ADJ 1 important or serious. 2 greater. NOUN an army officer next below lieutenant colonel. VERB [US] specialize in a subject at college.

majority NOUN (PL -ies) 1 the greater number of a group; the number by which votes for one party exceed those for the next. 2 the age at which someone is legally considered adult.

make VERB (**made, making**) 1 form or bring into being; prepare or produce. 2 cause to become of a specified nature; add up to. 3 earn a sum of money. 4 perform a specified action; arrange an agreement. 5 compel to do something. NOUN a brand of goods.

make-believe fantasy or pretence.

maker NOUN

makeshift ADJ temporary and improvised.

maladjusted ADJ unable to cope with normal life.

maladroit ADJ clumsy.

malady NOUN (PL -ies) an illness.

malaise NOUN a feeling of illness, discomfort, or uneasiness.

malapropism NOUN a comical confusion of words.

malaria NOUN a disease causing recurring fever.

malcontent NOUN a dissatisfied and rebellious person.

male ADJ of the sex that can fertilize egg cells

produced by a female; of or characteristic of men; (of a plant) producing pollen, not seeds. NOUN a male person, animal, or plant.

malefactor NOUN a wrongdoer.

malevolent ADJ wishing harm to others.
malevolence NOUN

malformation NOUN a deformity.
malformed ADJ

malfunction VERB function faultily.

malice NOUN a desire to harm others.
malicious ADJ

malign ADJ harmful or evil. VERB say unpleasant and untrue things about.

malignant ADJ 1 (of a tumour) cancerous. 2 malevolent.

malinger VERB pretend illness to avoid work.

mall NOUN a large enclosed shopping precinct.

mallard NOUN a wild duck.

malleable ADJ able to be hammered or pressed into shape; easy to influence.

mallet NOUN a hammer, usually of wood; an instrument for striking the ball in croquet or polo.

malnutrition NOUN weakness resulting from lack of nutrition.

malodorous ADJ stinking.

malpractice NOUN illegal or improper professional behaviour.

malt NOUN barley or other grain prepared for brewing or distilling.

maltreat VERB treat cruelly.
maltreatment NOUN

mammal NOUN a member of the class of animals that bear live young.
mammalian ADJ

mammary ADJ of the breasts.

mammoth NOUN a large extinct elephant. ADJ huge.

man NOUN (PL **men**) 1 an adult male person. 2 a human being; the human race. 3 a small figure used in a board game. VERB (**manned, manning**) provide a place etc. with people to work in or defend it.
manhood NOUN

manacle NOUN a shackle for the wrists or ankles.
manacled ADJ

manage VERB 1 be in

charge of; supervise staff.
2 cope successfully with a
task; succeed in doing or
producing.

manageable ADJ

management NOUN
managing; the people
who manage a business.

manager NOUN a person in
charge of a business etc.

managerial ADJ

manageress NOUN a
woman in charge of a
business etc.

mandarin NOUN 1 a senior
influential official. 2 a
variety of small orange.
3 (**Mandarin**) the literary
and official form of the
Chinese language.

mandate NOUN & VERB (give)
authority to perform
certain tasks.

mandatory ADJ
compulsory.

mandible NOUN a jaw or
jaw-like part.

mandolin NOUN a musical
instrument like a lute.

mane NOUN long hair on
the neck of a horse or
lion.

maneuver US spelling of
manoeuvre.

manful ADJ brave and
resolute.

manganese NOUN a hard

grey metallic element.

mange NOUN a skin disease
affecting hairy animals.

manger NOUN an open
trough for horses or cattle
to feed from.

mangle NOUN a clothes
wringer. VERB damage by
cutting or crushing
roughly.

mango NOUN (PL **-oes** or
-os) a tropical fruit.

mangrove NOUN a tropical
tree growing in swamps.

manhandle VERB 1 move a
heavy object with effort.
2 treat roughly.

manhole NOUN an opening
through which someone
can enter a drain etc. to
inspect it.

mania NOUN violent
madness; an extreme
enthusiasm for
something.

maniac NOUN a person
behaving wildly; a
fanatical enthusiast.

maniacal ADJ

manic ADJ showing wild
excitement; frantically
busy; of or affected by
mania.

manicure NOUN treatment
to improve the
appearance of the hands
and nails. VERB apply such

treatment.

manifest ADJ clear and unmistakable. VERB show clearly; appear.
manifestation NOUN

manifesto NOUN (PL **-os**) a public declaration of policy.

manifold ADJ many and varied. NOUN (in a machine) a pipe or chamber with several openings.

manila NOUN brown paper used for envelopes and wrapping paper.

manipulate VERB 1 handle or control skilfully; treat a part of the body by moving it by hand. 2 control or influence someone unscrupulously.
manipulation NOUN

mankind NOUN human beings in general.

manly ADJ (**-ier, -iest**) brave and strong; considered suitable for a man.

mannequin NOUN a dummy used to display clothes in a shop window.

manner NOUN 1 the way in which something is done or happens; a sort or kind. 2 a person's way of behaving towards others. 3 (**manners**) polite social behaviour.

mannered ADJ 1 having manners of a specified kind. 2 stilted and unnatural.

mannerism NOUN a distinctive personal habit or way of doing something.

manoeuvre ([US] **maneuver**) NOUN 1 a skilful movement; a crafty plan. 2 (**manoeuvres**) large-scale exercises of troops etc. VERB 1 guide or manipulate. 2 perform manoeuvres.
manoeuvrable ADJ

manor NOUN a large country house, usually with lands.
manorial ADJ

manpower NOUN the number of people available for work or service.

manse NOUN a church minister's house, especially in Scotland.

mansion NOUN a large stately house.

manslaughter NOUN the act of killing a person unlawfully but not intentionally.

mantelpiece NOUN the shelf above a fireplace.

mantle NOUN a loose cloak; a covering.

mantra NOUN a phrase repeated to aid concentration during meditation; a statement or slogan frequently repeated.

manual ADJ of the hands; done or operated by the hands. NOUN a handbook.

manufacture VERB make or produce goods on a large scale by machinery; invent a story. NOUN the process of manufacturing. **manufacturer** NOUN

manure NOUN animal dung used as fertilizer.

manuscript NOUN a book or document written by hand or typed.

many ADJ numerous. PRON a large number of something NOUN the majority; most people.

map NOUN a representation of the earth's surface or a part of it; a diagram showing the arrangement of something. VERB (**mapped, mapping**) 1 make a map of. 2 (**map out**) plan in detail.

maple NOUN a tree with broad leaves, and winged fruits.

mar VERB (**marred, marring**) disfigure; spoil.

maracas PLURAL NOUN containers containing beads etc., shaken as a musical instrument.

marathon NOUN a long-distance running race; a long-lasting or gruelling task.

maraud VERB make a raid in search of plunder. **marauder** NOUN

marble NOUN 1 crystalline limestone that can be polished and used in sculpture and building. 2 a small ball of coloured glass used as a toy.

March NOUN the third month.

march VERB walk in a regular rhythm or an organized column; walk purposefully; force to walk somewhere quickly. NOUN the act of marching; a piece of music suitable for marching to.

marchioness NOUN the wife or widow of a marquess; a woman with the rank of marquess.

mare NOUN the female of the horse or a related animal.

margarine NOUN a

substance made from animal or vegetable fat and used like butter.

margin NOUN 1 an edge or border; a blank space around the edges of a page. 2 an amount by which something is won or falls short.

marginal ADJ 1 of or in a margin. 2 slight or unimportant.

marginally ADV

marginalize (or **-ise**) VERB make or treat as insignificant.

marigold NOUN a plant with golden daisy-like flowers.

marijuana NOUN cannabis.

marina NOUN a harbour for yachts and pleasure boats.

marinade NOUN a flavoured liquid in which savoury food is soaked before cooking. VERB soak in a marinade.

marinate VERB marinade.

marine ADJ of the sea or shipping. NOUN a soldier trained to serve on land or sea.

mariner NOUN a sailor.

marionette NOUN a puppet worked by strings.

marital ADJ of marriage.

maritime ADJ living or found near the sea; of seafaring.

mark NOUN 1 a small area on a surface different in colour from the rest; a distinguishing feature. 2 a symbol; an indication of something's presence. 3 a point awarded for a correct answer; the total of such points achieved by someone in a test etc. 4 a target. VERB 1 make a mark or stain on. 2 write a word or symbol on something to indicate ownership, destination, etc.; show the position of; identify, indicate as being of a particular nature. 3 assess the merit of school or college work. 4 pay attention to. 5 (in football etc.) keep close to an opponent to prevent them from gaining the ball.

marked ADJ clearly noticeable.

marker NOUN a person or object that marks something; a broad felt-tipped pen.

market NOUN 1 a place or gathering for the sale of provisions, livestock, etc. 2 demand for a commodity. VERB (**marketed, marketing**) advertise; offer for sale.

market garden a small farm producing vegetables.

marketable ADJ

marking NOUN the colouring of an animal's skin, feathers, or fur.

marksman NOUN a person skilled in shooting.

marmalade NOUN a jam made from oranges.

marmoset NOUN a small bushy-tailed monkey.

maroon NOUN a brownish-red colour. VERB leave stranded in a desolate place.

marquee NOUN a large tent used for a party or exhibition etc.

marquess NOUN a nobleman ranking between duke and earl.

marquetry NOUN inlaid work in wood, ivory, etc.

marquis NOUN a rank in some European nobilities.

marriage NOUN the legal union of a man and woman.

marrow NOUN **1** a soft fatty substance in the cavities of bones. **2** a gourd used as a vegetable.

marry VERB (**married, marrying**) join in marriage; enter into marriage.

marsh NOUN low-lying watery ground.

marshy ADJ

marshal NOUN a high-ranking officer; an official controlling an event or ceremony. VERB (**marshalled, marshalling**; [US] **marshaled, marshaling**) arrange in proper order; assemble.

marshmallow NOUN a soft sweet made from sugar, egg white, and gelatin.

marsupial NOUN a mammal that carries its young in a pouch.

martial ADJ of war.

martinet NOUN a person who exerts strict discipline.

martyr NOUN a person who undergoes death or suffering for their beliefs. VERB make a martyr of.

martyrdom NOUN

marvel NOUN a wonderful thing. VERB (**marvelled, marvelling**; [US] **marveled, marveling**) feel wonder.

marvellous ([US] **marvelous**) ADJ amazing;

very good.

marzipan NOUN an edible paste made from ground almonds.

mascara NOUN a cosmetic for darkening the eyelashes.

mascot NOUN an object believed to bring good luck to its owner.

masculine ADJ of, like, or traditionally considered suitable for men.
masculinity NOUN

mash NOUN a soft pulp of crushed matter; boiled, mashed potatoes. VERB beat into a soft mass.

mask NOUN a covering worn over the face as a disguise or protection. VERB cover with a mask; disguise or conceal.

masochism NOUN pleasure derived from the experience of pain.
masochist NOUN

mason NOUN a person who builds or works with stone.

masonry NOUN stonework.

masquerade NOUN a false show or pretence. VERB pretend to be what you are not.

mass NOUN **1** a coherent body of matter with no definite shape; the quantity of matter a body contains. **2** a large group of people or things; (**masses**) [inf] a large amount. **3** (**the masses**) ordinary people. **4** (usually **Mass**) a celebration of the Eucharist, especially in the RC Church. VERB gather or assemble into a mass.

mass-produced produced in large quantities in a factory.

massacre NOUN a great slaughter. VERB slaughter in large numbers.

massage NOUN rubbing and kneading of the body to reduce pain or stiffness. VERB **1** treat the body in this way. **2** manipulate figures to give a more acceptable result.

masseur NOUN (FEMININE **masseuse**) a person who provides massage professionally.

massive ADJ large and heavy or solid; huge.

mast NOUN a tall pole, especially supporting a ship's sails.

mastectomy NOUN (PL -ies) surgical removal of a

breast.

master NOUN **1** a man who has control of people or things; a male teacher. **2** a person with great skill, a great artist. **3** a recording etc. from which a series of copies is made. ADJ highly skilled. VERB **1** acquire complete knowledge of or expertise in. **2** gain control of.

masterful ADJ **1** powerful and commanding. **2** very skilful.

masterly ADJ very skilful.

mastermind NOUN the person planning and directing an enterprise. VERB plan and direct.

masterpiece NOUN an outstanding piece of work.

mastery NOUN **1** thorough knowledge or great skill. **2** control or supremacy.

masticate VERB chew.

mastiff NOUN a large, strong breed of dog.

masturbate VERB stimulate the genitals with the hand. **masturbation** NOUN

mat NOUN a piece of material placed on a floor or other surface as an ornament or to protect it.

VERB (**matted, matting**) make or become tangled into a thick mass.

matador NOUN a bullfighter.

match NOUN **1** a short stick tipped with material that catches fire when rubbed on a rough surface. **2** a contest in a game or sport. **3** a person or thing exactly like or corresponding or equal to another. VERB **1** correspond or be alike. **2** be equal in ability, extent, etc. **3** set against each other in a contest.

matchmaker NOUN a person who schemes to arrange marriages.

mate NOUN **1** [inf] a friend. **2** the sexual partner of an animal. **3** an assistant to a skilled worker. VERB (of animals) come together for breeding.

material NOUN a substance from which something can be made; facts to be used in a book etc.; cloth, fabric. ADJ **1** of matter; of the physical (not spiritual) world. **2** significant, important.

materialism NOUN concentration on

material possessions rather than spiritual values.
materialistic ADJ
materialize (or **-ise**) VERB appear, become visible; become a fact or happen.
maternal ADJ of a mother; related through your mother.
maternity NOUN motherhood.
mathematics NOUN the science of numbers, quantities, and measurements.
mathematical ADJ
mathematician NOUN
maths ([US] **math**) NOUN mathematics.
matinée NOUN an afternoon performance in a theatre or cinema.
matins NOUN morning prayer.
matriarch NOUN the female head of a family or tribe.
matriarchal ADJ
matrices plural of **matrix**.
matriculate VERB enrol at a college or university.
matrimony NOUN marriage.
matrimonial ADJ
matrix NOUN (PL **-trices** or **-trixes**) an environment

in which something develops; a mould in which something is shaped.
matron NOUN 1 a woman in charge of domestic and medical arrangements at a school etc.; [dated] the woman in charge of nursing in a hospital. 2 a married woman.
matt ADJ not shiny.
matter NOUN 1 physical substance or material. 2 a situation or affair; a problem or issue. VERB be important; be distressing or of concern to someone.
mattress NOUN a fabric case filled with padding or springy material, used on or as a bed.
mature ADJ fully grown or developed; not childish; (of a life assurance policy etc.) due for payment. VERB make or become mature.
maturity NOUN
maudlin ADJ sentimental in a self-pitying way.
maul VERB wound by tearing and scratching.
mausoleum NOUN a magnificent tomb.
mauve ADJ & NOUN pale purple.
maverick NOUN an

unorthodox and independent-minded person.

mawkish ADJ sentimental in a sickly way.

maxim NOUN a sentence giving a general truth or rule of conduct.

maximize (or **-ise**) VERB make as great as possible.

maximum ADJ & NOUN (PL **-mums** or **-ma**) the greatest (amount) possible.

May NOUN the fifth month.

may[1] AUXILIARY VERB used to express a wish, possibility, or permission.

may[2] NOUN hawthorn blossom.

maybe ADV perhaps.

Mayday NOUN an international radio distress signal used by ships and aircraft.

mayhem NOUN violent confusion and disorder.

mayonnaise NOUN a cold creamy sauce made with eggs and oil.

mayor NOUN the head of the municipal corporation of a city or borough.

mayoress NOUN a female mayor; a mayor's wife.

maze NOUN a network of paths etc. through which it is hard to find your way.

MBE ABBREV Member of the Order of the British Empire.

MD ABBREV Doctor of Medicine; Managing Director.

me PRON the objective case of *I*.

mead NOUN an alcoholic drink made from honey and water.

meadow NOUN a field of grass.

meagre ([US] **meager**) ADJ scanty in amount.

meal NOUN **1** an occasion when food is eaten; the food itself. **2** coarsely ground grain.

mealy-mouthed ADJ afraid to speak frankly.

mean[1] ADJ **1** ungenerous; unkind; vicious. **2** of poor quality.

meanness NOUN

mean[2] ADJ & NOUN (something) midway between two extremes; an average.

mean[3] VERB (**meant**, **meaning**) **1** convey or express; signify. **2** intend. **3** result in.

meander VERB follow a winding course; wander

in a leisurely way. NOUN a winding bend in a river or road.

meaning NOUN what is meant.

meaningful ADJ

meaningless ADJ

means NOUN a thing or method used to achieve a result; financial resources.

meantime ADV meanwhile.

meanwhile ADV in the intervening period; at the same time.

measles NOUN an infectious disease producing red spots on the body.

measly ADJ [inf] meagre.

measure VERB find the size, amount, etc. of something by comparison with a known standard; be of a specified size; take or give a measured amount. NOUN 1 a course of action to achieve a purpose; a law. 2 a standard unit used in measuring; a certain quantity or degree.

measurable ADJ

measured ADJ 1 with a slow steady rhythm. 2 carefully considered.

measurement NOUN

measuring; a size etc. found by measuring.

meat NOUN animal flesh as food.

meaty ADJ (**-ier, -iest**) 1 full of meat. 2 substantial or challenging.

mechanic NOUN a skilled workman who uses or repairs machines.

mechanical ADJ of or worked by machinery; done without conscious thought.

mechanics NOUN the study of motion and force; the science of machinery.

mechanism NOUN a piece of machinery; the way something works or happens.

mechanize (or **-ise**) VERB equip with machinery.

medal NOUN a coin-like piece of metal commemorating an event or awarded for an achievement.

medallion NOUN a pendant shaped like a medal.

medallist ([US] **medalist**) NOUN the winner of a medal.

meddle VERB interfere in other people's affairs.

media plural of **medium**.

PLURAL NOUN (**the media**) newspapers and broadcasting as providers or information.

mediaeval see **medieval**.

median ADJ in or passing through the middle. NOUN a median point or line.

mediate VERB act as peacemaker between opposing sides.

medic NOUN [inf] a doctor.

medical ADJ of the science of medicine. NOUN an examination to assess someone's health or fitness.

medicate VERB treat with a medicine or drug.

medication NOUN drugs etc. for medical treatment; treatment with these.

medicinal ADJ having healing properties.

medicine NOUN the science of the prevention and cure of disease; a substance used to treat disease.

medieval (or **mediaeval**) ADJ of the Middle Ages.

mediocre ADJ second-rate. **mediocrity** NOUN

meditate VERB think deeply; focus your mind in silence for relaxation or religious purposes.

Mediterranean ADJ of the Mediterranean Sea or the countries around it.

medium NOUN (PL **-dia**) 1 a means of doing or communicating something; a substance through which something acts or is conveyed; (PL **-diums**) a person claiming to be in contact with the spirits of the dead. 2 a middle quality, state, or size. ADJ roughly halfway between extremes.

medley NOUN (PL **-eys**) an assortment.

meek ADJ quiet and obedient.

meet VERB (**met, meeting**) 1 come into contact with; make the acquaintance of; assemble; wait for and greet on arrival. 2 satisfy a requirement etc. NOUN a gathering or meeting.

meeting NOUN coming together; an assembly for discussion.

megabyte NOUN [Computing] a unit of information equal to one million bytes.

megalith NOUN a large stone, especially as a

prehistoric monument.

megalomania NOUN obsession with power or delusion about your own power.

megalomaniac ADJ & NOUN

megaphone NOUN a funnel-shaped device for amplifying the voice.

melancholy NOUN great sadness or depression. ADJ sad or depressing.

melanin NOUN a dark pigment in the skin, hair, etc.

meld VERB blend.

melee NOUN a confused fight; a disorderly crowd.

mellifluous ADJ sweet-sounding.

mellow ADJ smooth or soft in sound, taste, or colour; relaxed and cheerful. VERB make or become mellow.

melodious ADJ tuneful.

melodrama NOUN a sensational drama.

melodramatic ADJ

melody NOUN (PL **-ies**) sweet music; the main part in a piece of harmonized music.

melodic ADJ

melon NOUN a large sweet fruit.

melt VERB make or become liquid by heating; make

or become less stern; vanish.

member NOUN 1 a person belonging to a particular group or society. 2 [old use] a limb.

membership NOUN

membrane NOUN a thin flexible skin-like tissue.

memento NOUN (PL **-oes** or **-os**) a souvenir.

memo NOUN (PL **-os**) a written message from one colleague to another.

memoir NOUN a written account of events etc. that you remember.

memorable ADJ worth remembering, easy to remember.

memorandum NOUN (PL **-da** or **-dums**) a note written as a reminder; a memo.

memorial NOUN an object or custom etc. established to commemorate an event or person.

memorize (or **-ise**) VERB learn and remember exactly.

memory NOUN (PL **-ies**) the ability to remember things; a thing remembered; the storage capacity of a computer.

men plural of **man**.

menace NOUN something dangerous; a threatening quality. VERB threaten.

menagerie NOUN a small zoo.

mend VERB repair; heal; set right a dispute etc. NOUN a repaired place.

menial ADJ lowly or degrading. NOUN a person who does menial tasks. **menially** ADV

meningitis NOUN inflammation of the membranes covering the brain and spinal cord.

menopause NOUN the time of life when a woman ceases to menstruate.

menstruate VERB (of a woman) discharge blood from the womb each month. **menstrual** ADJ

mental ADJ **1** of, in, or performed by the mind. **2** [inf] mad.

mentality NOUN (PL **-ies**) a characteristic attitude of mind.

menthol NOUN a peppermint-flavoured substance, used medicinally.

mention VERB speak or write about briefly; refer to by name. NOUN a reference to someone or something.

mentor NOUN a trusted adviser.

menu NOUN (PL **-us**) a list of dishes to be served; a list of options displayed on a computer screen.

mercantile ADJ of trade or commerce.

mercenary ADJ working merely for money or reward. NOUN (PL **-ies**) a professional soldier hired by a foreign country.

merchandise NOUN goods bought and sold or for sale.

merchant NOUN a wholesale trader. **merchant navy** shipping employed in commerce.

merciful ADJ showing mercy; giving relief from pain and suffering.

mercurial ADJ liable to sudden changes of mood.

mercury NOUN a heavy silvery liquid metallic element.

mercy NOUN (PL **-ies**) kindness shown to someone in your power; something to be grateful for. **merciless** ADJ

mere ADJ no more or no better than what is specified.
merely ADV
merge VERB combine into a whole; blend gradually.
merger NOUN the combining of two organizations into one.
meridian NOUN any of the great semicircles on the globe, passing through the North and South Poles.
meringue NOUN a small cake made from a mixture of sugar and egg white.
merit NOUN a feature or quality that deserves praise; worthiness. VERB (**merited, meriting**) deserve.
mermaid NOUN an imaginary sea creature, a woman with a fish's tail instead of legs.
merry ADJ (**-ier, -iest**) 1 cheerful and lively. 2 [inf] slightly drunk.
merry-go-round a roundabout at a funfair.
merriment NOUN
mesh NOUN material made of a network of wire or thread; the spacing of the strands in this. VERB (of a gearwheel) engage with another; make or become entangled; be in harmony.
mesmerize (or **-ise**) VERB dominate the attention or will of.
mess NOUN 1 a dirty or untidy condition; a portion of pulpy food; a difficult or confused situation. 2 a room where members of the armed forces have meals. VERB 1 (usually **mess up**) make untidy or dirty; bungle. 2 (**mess about**) behave in a silly or playful way.
message NOUN a spoken or written communication; a significant point or central theme.
messenger NOUN the bearer of a message.
Messiah NOUN a great leader or saviour.
Messrs plural of **Mr**.
messy ADJ (**-ier, -iest**) untidy or dirty; complicated and difficult.
met past and past participle of **meet**.
metabolism NOUN the process by which food is digested and energy supplied.
metabolic ADJ

metal NOUN any of a class of mineral substances such as gold, silver, iron, etc., or an alloy of these.
metallic ADJ

metallurgy NOUN the study of the properties of metals.

metamorphic ADJ (of rock) changed in form or structure by heat, pressure, etc.

metamorphosis NOUN (PL -ses) a change of form or character.
metamorphose VERB

metaphor NOUN the application of a word or phrase to something that it does not apply to literally (e.g. the *evening* of your life, *food* for thought).
metaphorical ADJ

metaphysics NOUN the branch of philosophy dealing with the nature of existence and knowledge.
metaphysical ADJ

mete VERB (**mete out**) dispense justice, punishments, etc.

meteor NOUN a small body of matter entering the earth's atmosphere from outer space and appearing as a streak of light.

meteoric ADJ of meteors; swift and brilliant.

meteorite NOUN a meteor fallen to earth.

meteorology NOUN the study of atmospheric conditions in order to forecast weather.
meteorologist NOUN

meter NOUN 1 a device measuring and indicating the quantity supplied, distance travelled, time elapsed, etc. 2 US spelling of **metre**. VERB measure by a meter.

methane NOUN a colourless inflammable gas.

method NOUN a procedure or way of doing something; orderliness.

methodical ADJ orderly and systematic.

Methodist ADJ & NOUN (a member of) a Protestant religious denomination based on the teachings of John Wesley.

methodology NOUN (PL -ies) a system of methods used in an activity or study.

meths NOUN [inf] methylated spirit.

methylated spirit NOUN a form of alcohol used as a solvent and for heating.

microscope

meticulous ADJ careful and precise.

metre ([US] **meter**) NOUN **1** a metric unit of length (about 39.4 inches). **2** rhythm in poetry.

metric ADJ of or using the decimal system of weights and measures, using the metre, litre, and gram as units.

metrical ADJ of or in poetic metre.

metric ton see ton.

metronome NOUN a device used to indicate tempo while practising music.

metropolis NOUN the chief city of country or region. **metropolitan** ADJ

mettle NOUN courage and strength of character.

mew VERB (of a cat or gull) make a soft, high-pitched sound.

mews NOUN a set of stables converted into houses.

mezzanine NOUN an extra storey set between two others.

mezzo (or **mezzo-soprano**) NOUN a woman's singing voice between soprano and contralto.

mg ABBREV milligrams.

miaow VERB (of a cat) make its characteristic cry.

miasma NOUN an unpleasant or unhealthy atmosphere.

mica NOUN a mineral substance used as an electrical insulator.

mice plural of **mouse**.

microbe NOUN a bacterium or germ.

microchip NOUN a miniature electronic circuit made from a tiny wafer of silicon.

microcosm NOUN a thing that has the features and qualities of something much larger.

microfiche NOUN (PL **-fiche** or **-fiches**) a small sheet of microfilm.

microfilm NOUN a length of film bearing miniature photographs of documents.

microphone NOUN an instrument for picking up sound waves for transmitting or amplifying.

microprocessor NOUN an integrated circuit which can function as the main part of a computer.

microscope NOUN an instrument with lenses that magnify very small things, making them visible.

microscopic ADJ too small to be seen without a microscope.

microwave NOUN an electromagnetic wave of length between about 50 cm and 1 mm; an oven using such waves to heat food quickly.

mid ADJ in the middle.

midday NOUN noon.

middle ADJ occurring at an equal distance from extremes or outer limits; intermediate in rank, quality, etc. NOUN the middle point, position, area, etc. **middle age** the part of life between youth and old age. **middle class** the social group between upper and working classes.

middleman NOUN a trader buying goods from producers and selling them to consumers.

middling ADJ moderately good, large, etc.

midfield NOUN the part of a football pitch away from the goals.

midge NOUN a small biting insect.

midget NOUN a very small person or thing.

midnight NOUN 12 o'clock at night.

midriff NOUN the front part of the body just above the waist.

midst NOUN the middle.

midway ADV halfway.

midwife NOUN a person trained to assist at childbirth.

mien NOUN a person's manner or bearing.

might[1] NOUN great strength or power.

might[2] AUXILIARY VERB 1 used to express possibility or make a suggestion. 2 used politely in questions and requests.

mighty ADJ (**-ier, -iest**) very strong or powerful; very great. ADV [inf] very, extremely.

migraine NOUN a severe form of headache.

migrant ADJ migrating. NOUN a migrant animal; a person travelling in search of work.

migrate VERB (of animals) regularly move from one area to another each season. **migration** NOUN

mike NOUN [inf] a microphone.

mild ADJ gentle; not serious, severe, or harsh; (of weather) moderately warm; not strongly flavoured.

mildew NOUN tiny fungi forming a coating on things exposed to damp.

mile NOUN a measure of length, 1760 yds (about 1.609 km).

mileage NOUN a distance in miles.

milestone NOUN a stone showing the distance to a certain place; a significant event or stage reached.

milieu NOUN (PL **-lieus** or **-lieux**) environment or surroundings.

militant ADJ & NOUN (a person) prepared to take aggressive action. **militancy** NOUN

militarism NOUN support for maintaining and using a military force. **militaristic** ADJ

military ADJ of soldiers or the army or all armed forces. NOUN (**the military**) the armed forces.

militate VERB be a factor preventing something.

militia NOUN a military force, especially of trained civilians available in an emergency.

milk NOUN a white fluid secreted by female mammals as food for their young; cow's milk; a milk-like liquid. VERB draw milk from; gain all possible advantage from; exploit unfairly. **milky** ADJ

mill NOUN machinery for grinding specified material; a building fitted with machinery for manufacturing. VERB **1** grind in a mill. **2** move about as a confused crowd.

millennium NOUN (PL **-iums** or **-ia**) a period of 1,000 years.

miller NOUN someone who owns or works in a mill for grinding corn.

millet NOUN a cereal plant.

milliner NOUN a person who makes or sells women's hats.

million NOUN **1** one thousand thousand (1,000,000). **2** (**millions**) [inf] very many. **millionth** ADJ & NOUN

millionaire NOUN a person who has over a million pounds, dollars, etc.

millipede NOUN a small

crawling creature with many legs.

millstone NOUN a heavy circular stone for grinding corn; a burden of responsibility.

milometer NOUN an instrument measuring the distance in miles travelled by a vehicle.

mime NOUN acting with gestures without words. VERB act in mime.

mimic VERB (**mimicked, mimicking**) imitate, especially playfully or for entertainment. NOUN a person who is clever at mimicking.

mimicry NOUN

mimosa NOUN an acacia tree with yellow flowers.

mince VERB 1 cut meat into very small pieces. 2 walk with short, quick steps and swinging hips. NOUN minced meat.

mincemeat NOUN a mixture of dried fruit, sugar, etc.

mind NOUN 1 the faculty of consciousness and thought; the intellect or memory; sanity: *losing my mind.* 2 attention or concentration. VERB 1 be distressed or worried by.

2 remember to do something; take care. 3 look after temporarily. 4 (**be minded to**) be inclined to.

minded ADJ inclined to think in a particular way.

minder NOUN a person employed to look after someone or something; [inf] a bodyguard.

mindful ADJ conscious or aware of something.

mindless ADJ taking or showing no thought; not requiring thought or intelligence.

mine[1] ADJ & POSSESSIVE PRON belonging to me.

mine[2] NOUN 1 an excavation for extracting metal or coal etc.; an abundant source. 2 an explosive device laid in or on the ground or in water. VERB 1 extract minerals by excavating an area. 2 lay explosive mines under or in.

minefield NOUN an area planted with explosive mines; a situation full unseen dangers.

miner NOUN a person who works in a mine.

mineral NOUN an inorganic natural substance.

mineral water water naturally containing dissolved mineral salts.

minestrone NOUN soup containing vegetables and pasta.

minesweeper NOUN a ship for clearing away mines laid in the sea.

mingle VERB blend together; mix socially.

miniature ADJ very small. NOUN a small-scale portrait, copy, or model.

minibus NOUN a small bus for about twelve people.

minim NOUN a note in music, lasting half as long as a semibreve.

minimal ADJ very small, the least possible; negligible.

minimize (or **-ise**) VERB reduce to a minimum; represent as small or unimportant.

minimum ADJ & NOUN (PL **-ma**) the smallest (amount) possible.

minion NOUN a servant or follower.

minister NOUN 1 the head of a government department; a senior diplomatic representative. 2 a member of the clergy. VERB (**minister to**) attend to the needs of.

ministerial ADJ

ministration NOUN help or service.

ministry NOUN (PL **-ies**) 1 a government department headed by a minister. 2 the work of a minister of religion. 3 a period of government under one Prime Minister.

mink NOUN a small stoat-like animal, farmed for its fur.

minnow NOUN a small fish.

minor ADJ lesser; not very important. NOUN a person not yet legally of adult age.

minority NOUN (PL **-ies**) 1 the smaller part of a group or class; a small group differing from or disagreeing with others. 2 being below the legal age of adulthood.

minster NOUN a large church.

minstrel NOUN a medieval singer and musician.

mint[1] NOUN a place authorized to make a country's coins. VERB make coins.

mint[2] NOUN a fragrant herb; peppermint, a sweet flavoured with this.

minuet NOUN a slow stately dance.

minus PREP with the subtraction of; (of temperature) falling below zero by; [inf] without. ADJ (of a number) less than zero; (of a grade) lower than a specified grade. NOUN the sign (–).

minuscule ADJ very small.

minute[1] NOUN 1 one-sixtieth of an hour or degree; a moment of time. 2 (**minutes**) a written summary of the proceedings of a meeting. VERB record in the minutes.

minute[2] ADJ extremely small; very precise and detailed.

minx NOUN a mischievous girl.

miracle NOUN a welcome event so extraordinary that it is attributed to supernatural causes; an outstanding example or achievement. **miraculous** ADJ

mirage NOUN an optical illusion caused by atmospheric conditions.

mire NOUN swampy ground.

mirror NOUN glass coated so that reflections can be seen in it. VERB reflect in a mirror; correspond to, be the image of.

mirth NOUN amusement.

misadventure NOUN an accident or unlucky occurrence.

misanthrope (or **misanthropist**) NOUN a person who dislikes people in general. **misanthropic** ADJ

misapprehension NOUN a mistaken belief.

misappropriate VERB take dishonestly.

misbehave VERB behave badly.

miscarriage NOUN the birth of a baby or fetus before it can survive independently.

miscarry VERB (**miscarried, miscarrying**) 1 have a miscarriage. 2 (of a plan) fail.

miscellaneous ADJ assorted.

miscellany NOUN (PL **-ies**) a collection of assorted items.

mischief NOUN playful misbehaviour; harm or trouble caused by a person or thing. **mischievous** ADJ

misconception NOUN a

mission

wrong interpretation.

misconduct NOUN bad behaviour.

miscreant NOUN a wrongdoer.

misdemeanour ([US] **misdemeanor**) NOUN a wrongful act.

miser NOUN a person who hoards money and spends as little as possible. **miserly** ADJ

miserable ADJ very unhappy; very small or inadequate.

misery NOUN (PL **-ies**) great unhappiness or discomfort; a cause of this; [inf] someone who is always complaining.

misfire VERB (of a gun or engine) fail to fire correctly; (of a plan etc.) go wrong.

misfit NOUN a person not well suited to their environment.

misfortune NOUN bad luck; an unfortunate event.

misgiving NOUN a slight feeling of doubt, fear, or mistrust.

misguided ADJ badly judged.

mishap NOUN an unlucky accident.

misjudge VERB form a wrong opinion of; estimate wrongly.

mislay VERB (**mislaid, mislaying**) lose temporarily.

mislead VERB (**-led, -leading**) cause to form a wrong impression.

mismanage VERB manage badly or wrongly.

misnomer NOUN a wrongly applied name or description.

misogynist NOUN a man who hates women. **misogyny** NOUN

misprint NOUN an error in printing.

Miss NOUN the title of a girl or unmarried woman.

miss VERB **1** fail to hit, reach, or catch; fail to catch; fail to see or hear; be too late for; fail to take an opportunity. **2** regret the absence of. **3** (**miss out**) omit. NOUN a failure to hit or catch something.

missile NOUN an object thrown or fired at a target.

missing ADJ not present; not in its place.

mission NOUN **1** a task that a person or group is sent to perform; a person's aim or vocation. **2** the headquarters of a group of missionaries.

missionary NOUN (PL **-ies**) a person sent to spread religious faith.

mist NOUN water vapour near the ground or clouding a window etc. VERB cover or become covered with mist.

mistake NOUN an incorrect idea or opinion; an error of judgement. VERB (**mistook, mistaken, mistaking**) misunderstand; identify wrongly.

mistletoe NOUN a plant with white berries, growing on trees.

mistress NOUN a woman who has control of people or things; a female teacher; a married man's female lover.

mistrust VERB feel no trust in. NOUN lack of trust.

misty ADJ (**-ier, -iest**) full of mist; indistinct.

misunderstand VERB (**misunderstood, misunderstanding**) fail to understand correctly. **misunderstanding** NOUN

misuse VERB **1** use wrongly. **2** treat badly. NOUN wrong use.

mite NOUN a very small spider-like animal; a small creature, especially a child.

mitigate VERB make less intense or severe. **mitigation** NOUN

mitre ([US] **miter**) NOUN **1** the pointed headdress of bishops and abbots. **2** a join between pieces of wood that form a right angle.

mitt NOUN a mitten.

mitten NOUN a glove with no partitions between the fingers.

mix VERB **1** combine or be combined to form a whole; prepare by combining ingredients. **2** associate socially. **3** be compatible. **4** (**mix up**) mix thoroughly; confuse. NOUN a mixture.

mixed ADJ composed of various elements; of or for both sexes.

mixture NOUN something made by mixing.

ml ABBREV millilitres.

mm ABBREV millimetres.

mnemonic ADJ & NOUN (a verse etc.) aiding the memory.

moan NOUN a low mournful sound; [inf] a grumble. VERB

give a moan; [inf] complain.

moat NOUN a deep wide water-filled ditch round a castle etc.

mob NOUN a large disorderly crowd; [inf] a group. VERB (**mobbed**, **mobbing**) crowd round in a disorderly or violent way.

mobile ADJ able to move or be moved easily. NOUN 1 an ornamental hanging structure whose parts move in currents of air. 2 (also **mobile phone**) a portable telephone. **mobility** NOUN

mobilize (or **-ise**) VERB assemble troops etc. for active service.

moccasin NOUN a soft flat-soled leather shoe.

mocha NOUN a type of coffee; a drink of coffee and chocolate.

mock VERB tease or ridicule; imitate scornfully. ADJ not genuine or real.

mockery NOUN (PL **-ies**) ridicule; an absurd or unsatisfactory imitation.

mode NOUN 1 a way of doing something. 2 the current fashion.

model NOUN 1 a three-dimensional reproduction, usually on a smaller scale. 2 someone or something seen as an example of excellence. 3 a person employed to pose for an artist or display clothes by wearing them. ADJ exemplary. VERB (**modelled**, **modelling**; [US] **modeled**, **modeling**) 1 make a model of; shape. 2 work as an artist's or fashion model.

modem NOUN a device for transmitting computer data via a telephone line.

moderate ADJ medium; not extreme or excessive. NOUN a holder of moderate views. VERB make or become moderate. **moderation** NOUN

moderator NOUN an arbitrator.

modern ADJ of present or recent times; in current style. **modernity** NOUN

modernize (or **-ise**) VERB adapt to modern ways or needs.

modest ADJ 1 not vain or boastful; not elaborate or ostentatious. 2 small or moderate in size, amount, etc. 3 avoiding indecency.

modesty NOUN

modicum NOUN a small amount.

modify VERB (**modified**, **modifying**) make minor changes to.

modish ADJ fashionable.

modulate VERB regulate or adjust; vary in tone or pitch.

module NOUN a standardized part or independent unit forming part of a complex structure; a unit of training or education. **modular** ADJ

mogul NOUN [inf] an important or influential person.

mohair NOUN yarn made from the fine silky hair of the angora goat.

moist ADJ slightly wet. **moisten** VERB

moisture NOUN tiny droplets of water making something damp.

moisturize (or **-ise**) VERB make skin less dry. **moisturizer** NOUN

molar NOUN a back tooth with a broad top.

molasses NOUN syrup from raw sugar.

mold etc. US spelling of **mould** etc.

mole NOUN 1 a small burrowing animal with dark fur. 2 [inf] a spy within an organization. 3 a small dark spot on human skin.

molecule NOUN a group of atoms forming the smallest unit into which a substance can be divided. **molecular** ADJ

molest VERB pester; assault sexually.

mollify VERB (**mollified**, **mollifying**) soothe the anger of.

mollusc NOUN an animal with a soft body and often a hard shell.

mollycoddle VERB pamper.

molt US spelling of **moult**.

molten ADJ liquefied by heat.

moment NOUN 1 a point or brief portion of time. 2 importance.

momentary ADJ lasting only a moment. **momentarily** ADV

momentous ADJ of great importance.

momentum NOUN impetus gained by movement.

monarch NOUN a king, queen, emperor, or empress.

monarchist NOUN a

supporter of monarchy.

monarchy NOUN (PL **-ies**) a form of government with a monarch as the supreme ruler; a country governed in this way.

monastery NOUN (PL **-ies**) the residence of a community of monks.

monastic ADJ of monks or monasteries.

Monday NOUN the day of the week following Sunday.

monetary ADJ of money or currency.

money NOUN current coins and banknotes; wealth, payment for work.

moneyed ADJ wealthy.

mongoose NOUN (PL **-gooses**) a stoat-like tropical animal that can attack and kill snakes.

mongrel NOUN a dog of no definite breed.

monitor NOUN 1 a device checking or testing the operation of something; a person observing a process to ensure proper procedure. 2 a school pupil with special duties. VERB keep watch over; record and test or control.

monk NOUN a member of a male religious community.

monkey NOUN (PL **-eys**) a small primate, usually long-tailed and tree-dwelling. VERB (**monkeyed**, **monkeying**) behave mischievously; tamper with.

monochrome ADJ done in only one colour or in black and white.

monocle NOUN a single lens worn at one eye.

monogamy NOUN the system of being married to only one person at a time.

monogram NOUN letters (especially a person's initials) combined in a design.

monograph NOUN a scholarly treatise on a single subject.

monolith NOUN a large single upright block of stone.
monolithic ADJ

monologue NOUN a long speech.

monopolize (or **-ise**) VERB have exclusive control or the largest share of; keep to yourself.

monopoly NOUN (PL **-ies**) exclusive control of trade in a commodity; exclusive possession of something.

monotone NOUN a level unchanging tone of voice.

monotonous ADJ dull because lacking in variety or variation.
monotony NOUN

monsoon NOUN a seasonal wind in South Asia; the rainy season accompanying this.

monster NOUN a large, frightening imaginary creature; something very large; a cruel person.

monstrosity NOUN (PL **-ies**) something very large and ugly.

monstrous ADJ outrageous or shocking; huge; ugly and frightening.

month NOUN each of the twelve periods into which the year is divided; a period of 28 days.

monthly ADJ & ADV produced or occurring once a month.

monument NOUN an object commemorating a person or event etc.; a structure of historical importance.

monumental ADJ of great size or importance; of or serving as a monument.

moo NOUN a cow's low deep cry. VERB make this sound.

mooch VERB [inf] pass your time aimlessly.

mood NOUN a temporary state of mind or spirits; a fit of bad temper or depression.

moody ADJ (**-ier, -iest**) given to unpredictable changes of mood; sulky, gloomy.

moon NOUN the earth's satellite, made visible by light it reflects from the sun; a natural satellite of any planet. VERB behave dreamily.

moonlight NOUN light from the moon. VERB (**moonlighted, moonlighting**) [inf] have two paid jobs, one by day and the other in the evening.

moor[1] NOUN a stretch of open uncultivated land with low shrubs.

moor[2] VERB fasten a boat to the shore or to an anchor.

moorhen NOUN a small waterbird.

moorings PLURAL NOUN the cables or a place for mooring a boat.

moose NOUN (PL **moose**) an elk.

moot point NOUN a

debatable or undecided issue.

mop NOUN a pad or bundle of yarn on a stick, used for cleaning things; a thick mass of hair. VERB (**mopped, mopping**) clean with a mop; wipe your eyes, forehead, etc.; soak up liquid by wiping.

mope VERB be unhappy and listless.

moped NOUN a low-powered motorcycle.

moral ADJ concerned with right and wrong conduct; virtuous. NOUN **1** a moral lesson or principle derived from a story etc. **2** (**morals**) a person's standards of behaviour.

morale NOUN the state of a person's or group's spirits and confidence.

morality NOUN (PL **-ies**) moral principles; the extent to which something is right or wrong; a system of values.

moralize (or **-ise**) VERB comment on moral issues, especially self-righteously.

morass NOUN a boggy area; a complicated or confused situation.

moratorium NOUN (PL -riums or -ria) a temporary ban on an activity.

morbid ADJ **1** preoccupied with gloomy or unpleasant things. **2** of disease.

mordant ADJ (of wit) sharply sarcastic.

more NOUN & PRON a greater quantity or degree; an additional quantity. ADV **1** to a greater extent. **2** again.

moreover ADV besides.

mores PLURAL NOUN customs or conventions.

morgue NOUN a mortuary.

moribund ADJ on the point of death.

morning NOUN the part of the day before noon or the midday meal.

moron NOUN [inf] a stupid person.

morose ADJ gloomy and unsociable.

morphine NOUN a painkilling drug made from opium.

Morse code NOUN a code of signals using short and long sounds or flashes of light.

morsel NOUN a small piece of food.

mortal ADJ **1** subject to

death. **2** causing death; lasting until death. NOUN a human being.

mortality NOUN (PL **-ies**) being subject to death; death; the death rate.

mortar NOUN **1** a mixture of lime or cement with sand and water, for joining bricks or stones. **2** a bowl in which substances are pounded with a pestle. **3** a short cannon.

mortgage NOUN a loan for the purchase of property, in which the property itself is pledged as security. VERB pledge property as security in this way.

mortify VERB (**mortified, mortifying**) humiliate or embarrass.

mortise (or **mortice**) NOUN a hole in one part of a framework shaped to receive the end of another part.

mortuary NOUN (PL **-ies**) a place where dead bodies are kept temporarily.

mosaic NOUN a pattern or picture made with small pieces of coloured glass or stone.

Moslem ADJ & NOUN = **Muslim**.

mosque NOUN a Muslim place of worship.

mosquito NOUN (PL **-oes**) a blood-sucking insect.

moss NOUN a small flowerless plant forming a dense growth in moist places. **mossy** ADJ

most NOUN & PRON the greatest amount or number; the majority. ADV **1** to the greatest extent. **2** very.

mostly ADV for the most part.

motel NOUN a roadside hotel for motorists.

moth NOUN an insect like a butterfly but usually flying at night.

mothball NOUN a small ball of a pungent substance for keeping moths away from clothes.

mother NOUN a female parent; the title of the female head of a religious community. VERB look after in a motherly way.

mother-in-law the mother of your wife or husband.

mother-of-pearl an iridescent substance lining the shells of oysters.

motherhood NOUN

motherly ADJ

motif NOUN a pattern; a recurring feature or theme.

motion NOUN 1 moving; movement. 2 a formal proposal put to a meeting for discussion. VERB direct someone with a gesture.

motivate VERB give a motive to; stimulate the interest of.

motive NOUN a person's reason for doing something.

motley ADJ made up of a variety of different things.

motocross NOUN a motorcycle race over rough ground.

motor NOUN a machine supplying power and movement for a vehicle or machine; a car. ADJ 1 driven by a motor. 2 producing motion. VERB [inf] travel by car.

motorbike NOUN a motorcycle.

motorcycle NOUN a two-wheeled motor-driven road vehicle.

motorist NOUN a car driver.

motorway NOUN a road designed for fast long-distance traffic.

mottled NOUN patterned with irregular patches of colour.

motto NOUN (PL **-oes**) a short sentence or phrase expressing an ideal or rule of conduct.

mould ([US] **mold**) NOUN 1 a hollow container into which a liquid is poured to set in a desired shape. 2 a furry growth of tiny fungi on a damp surface. VERB form into a particular shape; influence the development of.

mouldy ADJ

moulder ([US] **molder**) VERB decay, rot away.

moulding ([US] **molding**) NOUN an ornamental strip of plaster or wood.

moult ([US] **molt**) VERB shed old feathers, hair, or skin. NOUN this process.

mound NOUN a pile of earth or stones; a small hill; a large pile.

mount VERB 1 go up stairs, a hill, etc.; get up on to a horse etc. 2 organize and set in process. 3 increase in number, size, or intensity. 4 fix on or in a support or setting. NOUN 1 a support or setting. 2 a mountain.

mountain NOUN a mass of

land rising to a great height; a large heap or pile.

mountaineer NOUN a person who climbs mountains.

mountaineering NOUN

mountainous ADJ **1** full of mountains. **2** huge.

mourn VERB feel or express sorrow about a dead person or lost thing.

mourner NOUN

mournful ADJ sorrowful.

mourning NOUN dark clothes worn as a symbol of bereavement.

mouse NOUN **1** (PL **mice**) a small rodent with a long tail; a quiet timid person. **2** (PL also **mouses**) a small rolling device for moving the cursor on a VDU screen.

mousse NOUN a frothy creamy dish; a soft gel or frothy preparation.

moustache ([US] **mustache**) NOUN hair on the upper lip.

mousy ADJ **1** dull greyish brown. **2** quiet and timid.

mouth NOUN the opening in the face through which food is taken in and sounds uttered; the opening of a bag, cave, cannon, etc; a place where a river enters the sea. VERB form words soundlessly with the lips; say something unoriginal.

mouth organ a small instrument played by blowing and sucking.

mouthpiece NOUN the part of an instrument placed between or near the lips.

move VERB **1** go in a specified direction; change or cause to change position; change your residence. **2** prompt to action; provoke emotion in. **3** make progress. **4** put to a meeting for discussion. NOUN an act of moving; a player's turn during a board game; a calculated action or initiative.

movable ADJ

movement NOUN **1** an act of moving; activity; (**movements**) someone's activities and whereabouts. **2** a group with a common cause. **3** a section of a long piece of music.

movie NOUN [US] a cinema film.

moving ADJ arousing pity

or sympathy.

mow VERB (**mowed, mown, mowing**) cut down grass on an area of ground.

MP ABBREV Member of Parliament.

m.p.h. ABBREV miles per hour.

Mr NOUN (PL **Messrs**) the title prefixed to a man's name.

Mrs NOUN (PL **Mrs**) the title prefixed to a married woman's name.

Ms NOUN the title prefixed to a married or unmarried woman's name.

much PRON a large amount. ADV to a great extent; often.

muck NOUN dirt or mess; manure.

mucky ADJ

mucus NOUN a slimy substance coating the inner surface of hollow organs of the body.

mud NOUN wet soft earth.

muddy ADJ

muddle VERB confuse or mix up; progress in a haphazard way. NOUN a muddled state or collection.

muesli NOUN food of mixed crushed cereals, dried fruit, nuts, etc.

muff NOUN a tube-shaped furry covering for the hands. VERB [inf] bungle.

muffin NOUN a light round yeast cake eaten toasted and buttered.

muffle VERB wrap for warmth or protection, or to deaden sound; make a sound quieter.

muffler NOUN a scarf.

mug NOUN **1** a large drinking cup with a handle. **2** [inf] the face. **3** [inf] a person who is easily outwitted. VERB (**mugged, mugging**) **1** attack and rob someone in a public place. **2** (**mug up**) [inf] revise a subject intensively.

mugger NOUN

muggy ADJ (**-ier, -iest**) (of weather) oppressively damp and warm.

mulberry NOUN a purple or white fruit resembling a blackberry.

mulch NOUN a mixture of wet straw, leaves, etc., spread on ground to protect plants or retain moisture. VERB cover with mulch.

mule NOUN **1** the offspring of a female horse and a male donkey; a stubborn

person. **2** a backless shoe.
mulish ADJ

mull VERB **1** heat wine etc.
with sugar and spices, as a
drink. **2** (**mull over**) think
over.

multicultural ADJ of or
involving several cultural
or ethnic groups.

multifarious ADJ very
varied.

multinational ADJ & NOUN
(a business company)
operating in several
countries.

multiple ADJ having or
involving many parts;
numerous. NOUN a quantity
divisible by another a
number of times without
remainder.

multiplicity NOUN (PL **-ies**)
a large number; a great
variety.

multiply VERB (**multiplied,
multiplying**) add a
number to itself a
specified number of
times; (cause to) become
more numerous.
multiplication NOUN

multitude NOUN a great
number of things or
people.

mum [inf] NOUN mother. ADJ
silent: *keep mum*.

mumble VERB speak

indistinctly.

mummy NOUN (PL **-ies**) **1** [inf]
mother. **2** a corpse
embalmed and wrapped
for burial, especially in
ancient Egypt.

mumps PLURAL NOUN a
disease causing painful
swellings in the neck.

munch VERB chew
vigorously.

mundane ADJ dull or
routine.

municipal ADJ of a
municipality.

municipality NOUN (PL
-ies) a self-governing
town or district.

munificent ADJ very
generous.

munitions PLURAL NOUN
weapons, ammunition,
etc.

mural NOUN a painting on a
wall.

murder NOUN intentional
unlawful killing. VERB kill
intentionally and
unlawfully.
murderer NOUN

murderous ADJ involving
or capable of murder.

murk NOUN darkness or fog.

murky ADJ dark and
gloomy; (of liquid)
cloudy.

murmur NOUN a low

continuous sound; softly spoken words. VERB make a murmur; speak or utter softly.

muscle NOUN a strip of fibrous tissue able to move a part of the body by contracting; power or strength.

muscular ADJ of muscles; having well-developed muscles.

muse VERB be deep in thought. NOUN a poet's source of inspiration.

museum NOUN a place where objects of historical or scientific interest are collected and displayed.

mush NOUN a soft pulp. **mushy** ADJ

mushroom NOUN an edible fungus with a stem and a domed cap. VERB spring up in large numbers.

music NOUN vocal or instrumental sounds arranged in a pleasing way; the written signs representing this.

musical ADJ of or involving music; sweet-sounding. NOUN a play with songs and dancing.

musician NOUN a person who writes or plays music.

musk NOUN a substance secreted by certain animals or produced synthetically, used in perfumes.

musket NOUN a long-barrelled gun formerly used by infantry.

Muslim (or **Moslem**) ADJ of or believing in Muhammad's teaching. NOUN a believer in this faith.

muslin NOUN a thin cotton cloth.

mussel NOUN a bivalve mollusc.

must AUXILIARY VERB **1** used to express necessity, obligation, or insistence. **2** used to express certainty or logical necessity. NOUN [inf] something that should not be missed.

mustache US spelling of **moustache**.

mustard NOUN a hot-tasting yellow paste.

muster VERB gather together; summon your energy or strength. NOUN a formal gathering of troops.

musty ADJ smelling stale or mouldy.

mutant NOUN a living thing differing from its parents

as a result of genetic change.

mutate VERB change in form; undergo genetic change.

mutation NOUN a change in form; a mutant.

mute ADJ silent; dumb. NOUN a device muffling the sound of a musical instrument. VERB deaden or muffle the sound of.

mutilate VERB severely injure or damage.

mutinous ADJ rebellious.

mutiny NOUN (PL **-ies**) a rebellion against authority, especially by members of the armed forces. VERB (**mutinied, mutinying**) engage in mutiny. **mutineer** NOUN

mutter VERB speak or utter in a low unclear tone; grumble privately. NOUN a low indistinct utterance.

mutton NOUN the flesh of sheep as food.

mutual ADJ **1** felt or done by each of two or more people equally. **2** shared by two or more people.

muzzle NOUN the projecting nose and jaws of certain animals; a guard fitted over this to stop an animal biting; the open end of a firearm's barrel. VERB put a muzzle on; prevent from expressing opinions freely.

muzzy ADJ confused or dazed; blurred or indistinct.

my ADJ belonging to me.

myopia NOUN short-sightedness. **myopic** ADJ

myriad NOUN a vast number.

myrrh NOUN a resin used in perfumes and incense.

myself PRON the emphatic and reflexive form of *I* and *me*.

mysterious ADJ difficult or impossible to explain or understand.

mystery NOUN (PL **-ies**) a matter that remains unexplained; a story dealing with a puzzling crime.

mystic NOUN a person who seeks to obtain union with God by spiritual contemplation. **mysticism** NOUN

mystify VERB (**mystified, mystifying**) confuse or baffle.

mystique NOUN an aura of

mystery or mystical power.

myth NOUN a traditional tale containing beliefs about ancient times or natural events and usually involving supernatural beings.

mythical ADJ

mythology NOUN myths; the study of myths.

myxomatosis NOUN an infectious, usually fatal disease of rabbits.

N ABBREV north or northern.

naan see **nan**.

nab VERB (**nabbed**, **nabbing**) [inf] arrest; steal.

nadir NOUN the lowest point.

nag VERB (**nagged**, **nagging**) scold continually; (of pain) be felt persistently. NOUN 1 a person who nags. 2 [inf] a horse.

nail NOUN 1 a thin hard layer over the outer tip of a finger or toe. 2 a small metal spike driven into wood as a fastening. VERB fasten with nails.

naive ADJ lacking experience or judgement. **naivety** NOUN

naked ADJ without clothes; without coverings; (of feelings etc.) undisguised.

namby-pamby ADJ lacking strength or courage.

name NOUN 1 the word(s) by which a person or thing is known. 2 a reputation; a famous person. VERB give a name to; identify or mention; nominate or specify.

namely ADV that is to say.

namesake NOUN a person or thing with the same name as another.

nan (also **naan**) NOUN a soft, flat Indian bread.

nanny NOUN (PL **-ies**) a child's nurse.

nap NOUN 1 a short sleep. 2 short raised fibres on the surface of certain fabrics. VERB (**napped**, **napping**) have a short sleep.

napalm NOUN a highly flammable form of petrol, used in firebombs.

nape NOUN the back of the neck.

naphtha NOUN a flammable oil.

napkin NOUN a piece of cloth or paper used at meals to protect clothes or to wipe the lips.

nappy NOUN (PL **-ies**) a piece of absorbent material worn by a baby to absorb or retain urine and faeces.

narcissism NOUN abnormal self-admiration.
narcissistic ADJ

narcissus NOUN (PL **-cissi**) a flower of the group including the daffodil.

narcotic ADJ & NOUN (a drug) causing drowsiness; (a drug) affecting moods and behaviour.

narrate VERB give an account of.
narration NOUN
narrator NOUN

narrative NOUN a spoken or written account of something.

narrow ADJ **1** small in width. **2** limited in extent or scope; barely achieved; *a narrow escape*. VERB make or become narrow.

narrow-minded intolerant.

nasal ADJ of the nose.

nascent ADJ just coming into existence.

nasturtium NOUN a plant with orange, yellow, or red flowers.

nasty ADJ (**-ier, -iest**) unpleasant; spiteful or unkind; painful or harmful.
nastily ADV
nastiness NOUN

natal ADJ of or from a person's birth.

nation NOUN people of mainly common descent and history usually inhabiting a particular country under one government.

national ADJ **1** of a nation. **2** owned or supported by the state. NOUN a citizen of a particular country.
national curriculum an official curriculum of study to be taught in state schools.
nationally ADV

nationalism NOUN patriotic feeling; a policy of national independence.
nationalist NOUN & ADJ

nationality NOUN (PL **-ies**)

1 the status of belonging to a particular nation. **2** an ethnic group.

nationalize (or **-ise**) VERB convert from private to state ownership.
nationalization NOUN

native ADJ belonging to a place by birth; associated by birth; (of a quality etc.) inborn. NOUN a person born in a specified place; a local inhabitant.

nativity NOUN (PL **-ies**) birth; (**the Nativity**) the birth of Jesus.

NATO ABBREV North Atlantic Treaty Organization.

natter VERB & NOUN [inf] chat.

natural ADJ **1** of or produced by nature; not man-made; having a specified skill or quality from birth. **2** relaxed and unaffected. NOUN **1** a person with a particular gift or talent. **2** [Music] (a sign indicating) a note that is not a sharp or flat.
natural history the study of animals or plants.
naturally ADV

naturalism NOUN realism in art and literature.

naturalist NOUN an expert in natural history.

naturalize (or **-ise**) VERB make a foreigner a citizen of a country; introduce a plant or animal into a region where it is not native.

nature NOUN **1** the physical world with all its features and living things. **2** the typical qualities or character of a person or thing; a type or kind.

naturist NOUN a nudist.
naturism NOUN

naughty ADJ (**-ier, -iest**) **1** disobedient or badly behaved. **2** [inf] slightly indecent.
naughtiness NOUN

nausea NOUN a feeling of sickness; revulsion.

nauseate VERB cause to feel sick or disgusted.

nauseous ADJ suffering from or causing nausea.

nautical ADJ of sailors or seamanship.
nautical mile a unit of 1,852 metres (approx. 2,025 yds).

naval ADJ of a navy.

nave NOUN the main part of a church.

navel NOUN the small hollow in the abdomen where the umbilical cord was attached.

navigable ADJ able to be used by boats and ships.

navigate VERB plan and direct the route of a ship, aircraft, etc.; travel along a planned route.
navigable ADJ
navigation NOUN
navigator NOUN

navy NOUN (PL **-ies**) **1** the branch of a country's armed forces which fights at sea. **2** (also **navy blue**) very dark blue.

Nazi NOUN [historical] a member of the far-right National Socialist German Workers' Party.

NB ABBREV note well (short for Latin *nota bene*).

NE ABBREV north-east; north-eastern.

near ADV **1** at or to a short distance in space or time. **2** almost. PREP **1** a short distance from. **2** on the verge of. ADJ **1** at a short distance away. **2** closely related. **3** close to being: *a near disaster*. VERB draw near.

nearby ADJ & ADV not far away.

nearly ADV almost.

nearside NOUN the side of vehicle nearest the kerb.

neat ADJ **1** tidy or carefully arranged; clever but simple. **2** undiluted.
neaten VERB

nebula NOUN (PL **-lae**) a cloud of gas or dust in space.

nebulous ADJ having no definite form; vague.

necessarily ADV unavoidably.

necessary ADJ **1** needing to be done or achieved, or to be present. **2** unavoidable.

necessitate VERB make necessary.

necessity NOUN (PL **-ies**) being necessary or unavoidable; something essential.

neck NOUN the narrow part connecting the head to the body; the narrow part of a bottle, cavity, etc.
neck and neck level in a race.

necklace NOUN a piece of jewellery worn round the neck.

neckline NOUN the edge of a garment at or below the neck.

necromancy NOUN the supposed art of predicting the future by communicating with the dead.

nectar NOUN a fluid produced by flowers and made into honey by bees.

nectarine NOUN a kind of peach with a smooth skin.

née ADJ born (used in stating a married woman's maiden name).

need VERB 1 require something as essential, not as a luxury. 2 used to express what should or must be done. NOUN 1 something required; requiring something; necessity or reason for something. 2 poverty.

needful ADJ necessary.

needle NOUN a thin pointed piece of metal used in sewing or knitting; a pointer on a compass or dial; the thin leaf of a fir or pine tree. VERB [inf] annoy.

needless ADJ unnecessary.

needlework NOUN sewing or embroidery.

needy ADJ (-ier, -iest) very poor.

nefarious ADJ wicked or criminal.

negate VERB 1 make ineffective. 2 deny the existence of.

negation NOUN

negative ADJ 1 expressing denial, refusal, or prohibition; showing the absence rather than the presence of something. 2 (of a quantity) less than zero. 3 (of a battery terminal) through which electric current leaves. 4 not hopeful or favourable. NOUN 1 a negative statement or word. 2 a photograph with lights and shades or colours reversed, from which positive pictures can be obtained.

neglect VERB fail to give enough care or attention to; fail to do. NOUN neglecting or being neglected.

neglectful ADJ

negligee NOUN a woman's light, thin dressing gown.

negligence NOUN lack of proper care or attention.

negligent ADJ

negligible ADJ too small to be worth taking into account.

negotiate VERB 1 reach agreement by discussion; arrange by such discussion. 2 get past an obstacle successfully.

negotiation NOUN

negotiator NOUN

Negro NOUN (PL **-oes**) [dated or offensive] a black person.

neigh NOUN a horse's high-pitched cry. VERB make this cry.

neighbour ([US] **neighbor**) NOUN a person living next door or near to another. VERB be next or very close to.

neighbourly ADJ

neighbourhood ([US] **neighborhood**) NOUN a district.

neither ADJ & PRON not one nor the other of two. ADV & CONJ **1** not either. **2** also not.

nemesis NOUN something that brings about a person's deserved downfall.

Neolithic ADJ of the later part of the Stone Age.

neologism NOUN a new word.

neon NOUN a gas used in fluorescent lighting.

neonatal ADJ of the newly born.

nephew NOUN a son of your brother or sister.

nepotism NOUN favouritism shown to relatives or friends.

nerve NOUN **1** a fibre in the body along which impulses of sensation pass. **2** (**nerves**) agitation or anxiety. **3** courage and steadiness; [inf] impudence.

nervous ADJ **1** easily alarmed; afraid or anxious. **2** of the nerves.

nervous system the network of nerves which transmits nerve impulses between parts of the body.

nest NOUN **1** a structure or place in which a bird lays eggs and shelters its young; a breeding place or lair. **2** a set of similar articles designed to fit inside each other. VERB **1** build or use a nest. **2** fit an object inside a larger one.

nest egg a sum of money saved for the future.

nestle VERB settle comfortably; (of a place) lie in a sheltered position.

net[1] NOUN **1** open-meshed material of cord, wire, etc.; a piece of this for a particular purpose, e.g. catching fish. **2** (**Net**) the Internet. VERB (**netted**,

netting) catch in a net.

net² (or **nett**) ADJ remaining after all deductions; (of weight) not including packaging. VERB (**netted, netting**) obtain or yield as net profit.

netball NOUN a team game in which a ball has to be thrown into a high net.

nether ADJ lower.

netting NOUN open-meshed fabric.

nettle NOUN a wild plant with leaves that sting when touched. VERB annoy.

network NOUN an arrangement of intersecting lines; a complex system; a group of interconnected people or broadcasting stations, computers, etc. VERB keep in contact with others to exchange ideas and information.

neural ADJ of nerves.

neuralgia NOUN a sharp pain along a nerve.

neurosis NOUN (PL **-oses**) a mental disorder producing depression or abnormal behaviour.

neurotic ADJ of or caused by a neurosis; obsessive or oversensitive.

neuter ADJ 1 (of a noun) neither masculine nor feminine. 2 without developed sexual parts. VERB castrate or spay.

neutral ADJ 1 not supporting either side in a conflict. 2 without distinctive or positive characteristics. NOUN a position of a gear mechanism in which the engine is disconnected from driven parts. **neutrality** NOUN **neutrally** ADV

neutralize (or **-ise**) VERB make neutral or ineffective.

neutron NOUN a subatomic particle with no electric charge.

never ADV 1 not ever. 2 not at all.

nevertheless ADV in spite of this.

new ADJ 1 made, discovered, experienced, etc. recently; not previously owned or used; replacing a former one of the same kind. 2 unfamiliar or different. ADV newly. NOUN (**news**) new information about recent events; a broadcast report of this.

new moon the moon seen as a thin crescent. **New Testament** the books of the Christian Bible telling the life and teachings of Jesus.

newcomer NOUN a person who has arrived recently.

newel NOUN the post at the top or bottom of a stair rail.

newfangled ADJ objectionably new in method or style.

newly ADV recently; afresh.

newsagent NOUN a shopkeeper who sells newspapers.

newsflash NOUN an item of important news, broadcast as an interruption to another programme.

newsgroup NOUN a group of Internet users exchanging emails about a shared interest.

newsletter NOUN a bulletin issued periodically to members of a society etc.

newspaper NOUN a daily or weekly publication containing news and articles on current affairs.

newsprint NOUN cheap, low-quality paper used for newspapers.

newsreader NOUN a person who reads broadcast news reports.

newt NOUN a small lizard-like amphibious animal.

newton NOUN [Physics] a unit of force.

next ADJ nearest in time, space, or order. ADV immediately afterwards. NOUN the next person or thing.

next of kin a person's closest living relative(s).

nib NOUN the metal point of a pen.

nibble VERB take small quick or gentle bites out of. NOUN a small quick bite.

nice ADJ pleasant or enjoyable; good-natured or kind.

nicety NOUN (PL **-ies**) a fine detail; precision.

niche NOUN **1** a small hollow in a wall. **2** a role or job that suits someone.

nick NOUN **1** a small cut. **2** [inf] prison. **3** [inf] condition. VERB **1** make a nick in. **2** [inf] steal.

nickel NOUN **1** a silver-white metallic element. **2** [US] a 5-cent coin.

nickname NOUN another

name by which someone is known. VERB give a nickname to.

nicotine NOUN a poisonous substance found in tobacco.

niece NOUN a daughter of your brother or sister.

niggardly ADJ stingy; meagre.

niggle VERB slightly worry or annoy. VERB a minor worry or criticism.

nigh ADV & PREP [old use] near.

night NOUN the time from sunset to sunrise; an evening.

nightcap NOUN an alcoholic or hot drink taken at bedtime.

nightclub NOUN a club open at night, with a bar and music.

nightdress NOUN a woman's or girl's loose garment worn in bed.

nightfall NOUN dusk.

nightle NOUN [inf] a nightdress.

nightingale NOUN a small bird with a tuneful song.

nightlife NOUN social activities or entertainment available at night.

nightly ADJ & ADV

happening or done every night.

nightmare NOUN a frightening dream; a very unpleasant experience.
  nightmarish ADJ

nightshade NOUN a plant with poisonous berries.

nightshirt NOUN a long shirt worn in bed.

nihilism NOUN the belief that nothing has any value.
  nihilist NOUN

nil NOUN nothing; zero.

nimble ADJ able to move quickly.
  nimbly ADV

nimbus NOUN (PL **-bi** or **-buses**) a raincloud.

nincompoop NOUN a foolish person.

nine ADJ & NOUN one more than eight (9, IX).
  ninth ADJ & NOUN

nineteen ADJ & NOUN one more than eighteen (19, XIX).
  nineteenth ADJ & NOUN

ninety ADJ & NOUN nine times ten (90, XC).
  ninetieth ADJ & NOUN

nip VERB (**nipped**, **nipping**) 1 pinch, squeeze, or bite sharply. 2 [inf] go quickly. NOUN 1 a sharp pinch, squeeze, or bite. 2 a sharp coldness. **3** a small drink of spirits.

nipple NOUN the small projection at the centre of each breast.

nippy ADJ (**-ier, -iest**) [inf] **1** nimble or quick. **2** chilly.

nirvana NOUN (in Buddhism) a state of perfect happiness.

nit NOUN the egg of a human head louse.

nit-picking petty criticism.

nitrate NOUN a substance formed from nitric acid.

nitric acid NOUN a very corrosive acid.

nitrogen NOUN a gas forming about four-fifths of the atmosphere.

nitroglycerine (or **nitroglycerin**) NOUN a powerful explosive.

nitty-gritty NOUN [inf] the most important details.

no ADJ not any. EXCLAMATION used to refuse or disagree with something. ADV not at all. NOUN (PL **noes**) a decision or vote against something.

no. ABBREV number.

nobility NOUN (PL **-ies**) **1** being noble. **2** the aristocracy.

noble ADJ **1** belonging to the aristocracy. **2** having admirable moral qualities, such as courage and honesty. **3** grand and imposing. NOUN a member of the aristocracy.

nobly ADV

nobleman (or **noblewoman**) NOUN a member of the aristocracy.

nobody PRON no person. NOUN (PL **-ies**) a person of no importance.

nocturnal ADJ done or active in the night.

nocturnally ADV

nocturne NOUN a short romantic piece of music.

nod VERB (**nodded, nodding**) **1** move your head down and up quickly to show agreement or as a signal. **2** let your head droop from drowsiness. **3** (**nod off**) [inf] fall asleep. NOUN an act of nodding.

node NOUN **1** a point in a network where lines intersect. **2** a point on a stem where a leaf or bud grows out. **3** a small mass of tissue in the body.

nodule NOUN a small swelling or lump.

nodular ADJ

noise NOUN **1** a sound, especially a loud or unpleasant one. **2** fluctuations accompanying and obscuring an electrical signal.

noisy ADJ (**-ier, -iest**) full of or making much noise.

noisily ADV

nomad NOUN a member of a people that roams to find fresh pasture for its animals.

nomadic ADJ

nom de plume NOUN (PL **noms de plume**) a writer's pseudonym.

nomenclature NOUN a system of names used in a particular subject.

nominal ADJ **1** existing in name only. **2** (of a fee) very small.

nominally ADV

nominate VERB put forward as a candidate for a job or award; arrange a place or date.

nomination NOUN

nominee NOUN

nominative NOUN the grammatical case used for the subject of a verb.

non- PREFIX not: *non-existent.*

nonchalant ADJ calm and casual.

nonchalance NOUN

non-committal ADJ not expressing a definite opinion.

nonconformist NOUN a person who does not follow established practices; (**Nonconformist**) a member of a Protestant Church not conforming to Anglican practices.

nondescript ADJ lacking distinctive characteristics.

none PRON not any; no one. ADV not at all: *none the worse.*

nonentity NOUN (PL **-ies**) an unimportant person.

non-event NOUN a very disappointing or uninteresting event.

non-existent ADJ not real or present.

nonplussed ADJ surprised and confused.

nonsense NOUN words or statements that make no sense; foolish behaviour.

nonsensical ADJ

non sequitur NOUN a statement that does not follow logically from what has just been said.

non-stop ADJ & ADV not ceasing; having no stops

on the way to a destination.

noodles PLURAL NOUN pasta in narrow strips.

nook NOUN a secluded place.

noon NOUN twelve o'clock in the day.

no one NOUN no person.

noose NOUN a loop of rope etc. with a knot that tightens when pulled.

nor CONJ and not; and not either.

norm NOUN a standard type; usual behaviour.

normal ADJ conforming to what is standard or usual. **normality** NOUN **normally** ADV

north NOUN the point or direction to the left of a person facing east; the northern part of a place. ADJ & ADV towards or facing the north; (of wind) from the north. **northward** ADJ & ADV **northwards** ADV

north-east NOUN, ADJ, & ADV (in or towards) the point or direction midway between north and east. **north-easterly** ADJ & NOUN **north-eastern** ADJ

northerly ADJ towards or blowing from the north.

northern ADJ of or in the north.

northerner NOUN a person from the north of a region.

north-west NOUN, ADJ, & ADV (in or towards) the point or direction midway between north and west. **north-westerly** ADJ & NOUN **north-western** ADJ

nose NOUN 1 the organ at the front of the head, used in breathing and smelling; a talent for detecting something. 2 the front end of an aircraft, car, etc. VERB 1 push the nose against something. 2 investigate or pry. 3 move forward slowly.

nosebag NOUN a bag of fodder hung from a horse's head.

nosedive NOUN a steep downward plunge by an aeroplane. VERB make a nosedive.

nosh [inf] NOUN food. VERB eat.

nostalgia NOUN sentimental memory of or longing for things of the past. **nostalgic** ADJ

nostril NOUN either of the

two external openings in the nose.

nosy ADJ (**-ier, -iest**) [inf] inquisitive.

not ADV used to express a negative.

notable ADJ worthy of notice. NOUN an eminent person.

notably ADV

notary NOUN (PL **-ies**) an official authorized to witness the signing of documents.

notation NOUN a system of symbols used in music, mathematics, etc.

notch NOUN **1** a V-shaped cut or indentation. **2** a point or level on a scale. VERB **1** make a notch in. **2** (**notch up**) score or achieve.

note NOUN **1** a brief written record of something; a short or informal letter. **2** a banknote. **3** a musical tone of definite pitch; a symbol representing the pitch and duration of a musical sound. VERB **1** notice; remark on. **2** write down.

notebook NOUN a book with blank pages on which to write notes.

noted ADJ well known.

notepaper NOUN paper for writing letters on.

noteworthy ADJ interesting or important.

nothing NOUN not anything; something unimportant; nought. ADV not at all.

notice NOUN **1** attention or observation. **2** warning or notification; the formal announcement of the termination of a job or an agreement. **3** a sheet of paper displaying information. **4** an announcement or advertisement in a newspaper. VERB become aware of.

noticeable ADJ

noticeably ADV

noticeable ADJ easily seen or noticed.

noticeably ADV

notify VERB (**notified, notifying**) inform about something.

notification NOUN

notion NOUN a belief or idea; an understanding.

notional ADJ

notorious ADJ famous for something bad.

notoriety NOUN

notwithstanding PREP in spite of. ADV nevertheless.

nougat NOUN a chewy sweet.

nought NOUN the figure 0; nothing.

noun NOUN a word that refers to a person, place, or thing.

nourish VERB feed so as to keep alive and healthy.

nourishment NOUN food necessary for life and growth.

nous NOUN [inf] common sense.

nouveau riche NOUN people who have recently become rich and make a display of their wealth.

nova NOUN (PL **-vae** or **-vas**) a star that suddenly becomes much brighter for a short time.

novel NOUN a book-length story. ADJ new or unusual.

novelist NOUN a writer of novels.

novelty NOUN (PL **-ies**) 1 being new, unusual, or original. 2 a small toy or ornament.

November NOUN the eleventh month.

novice NOUN a person new to and inexperienced in an activity; a probationary member of a religious order.

now ADV at the present time; immediately. CONJ as a result of the fact.

nowadays ADV in present times.

nowhere ADV not anywhere.

noxious ADJ unpleasant and harmful.

nozzle NOUN the vent or spout of a hosepipe etc.

nuance NOUN a subtle difference in meaning.

nub NOUN 1 the central point of a problem etc. 2 a small lump.

nubile ADJ (of a young woman) sexually mature and attractive.

nuclear ADJ of the nucleus of an atom or cell; using energy released in nuclear fission or fusion.

nucleic acid NOUN either of two substances, DNA or RNA, present in all living cells.

nucleus NOUN (PL **-clei**) the central part or thing round which others are collected; the central portion of an atom, seed, or cell.

nude ADJ naked. NOUN a naked figure in a picture etc.

nudity NOUN

nudge VERB poke gently with the elbow to attract attention; push slightly or gradually. NOUN a slight push or poke.

nudist NOUN a person who who prefers to wear no clothes. **nudism** NOUN

nugget NOUN a rough lump of gold or platinum found in the earth.

nuisance NOUN an annoying person or thing.

null ADJ having no legal force.

nullify VERB (**nullifiod**, **nullifying**) make legally null; cancel out the effect of. **nullification** NOUN

numb ADJ deprived of the power of sensation. VERB make numb.

number NOUN 1 a quantity or value expressed by a word or symbol; a quantity. 2 a single issue of a magazine; an item in a performance. VERB 1 amount to. 2 assign a number to; count. **number plate** a sign on a vehicle showing its registration number. **numberless** ADJ too many to count.

numeral NOUN a symbol representing a number.

numerate ADJ having a good basic understanding of arithmetic. **numeracy** NOUN

numerator NOUN the number above the line in a vulgar fraction.

numerical ADJ of a number or series of numbers. **numerically** ADV

numerous ADJ great in number.

nun NOUN a member of a female religious community.

nunnery NOUN (PL **-ies**) a community of nuns.

nuptial ADJ of marriage or a wedding. NOUN (**nuptials**) a wedding.

nurse NOUN 1 a person trained to care for sick or injured people. 2 [dated] a person employed to look after young children. VERB 1 look after a sick person. 2 feed a baby from the breast. 3 hold carefully or protectively; harbour a belief or feeling.

nursing home a place providing accommodation and

health care for old people.

nursery NOUN (PL **-ies**) **1** a
room for young children.
2 a place where plants are
grown for sale.
nursery rhyme a
traditional song or poem
for children. **nursery
school** a school for
children below normal
school age.

nurture VERB care for and
promote the growth or
development of; cherish a
hope, belief, etc. NOUN
nurturing.

nut NOUN **1** a fruit with a
hard shell round an
edible kernel; this kernel.
2 a small metal ring with a
threaded hole, for
screwing on to a bolt.
3 [inf] the head. **4** [inf] a mad
person. **5** (**nuts**) [inf] mad.
in a nutshell in the fewest
possible words.

nutty ADJ

nutcase NOUN [inf] a crazy
person.

nutmeg NOUN a spice.

nutrient NOUN a
nourishing substance.

nutriment NOUN
nourishing food.

nutrition NOUN the process
of eating or taking
nourishment.
nutritional ADJ

nutritious ADJ nourishing.

nuzzle VERB press or rub
gently with the nose.

NW ABBREV north-west;
north-western.

nylon NOUN a light, strong
synthetic fibre.

nymph NOUN **1** a
mythological semi-divine
maiden. **2** a young insect.

nymphomania NOUN
excessive sexual desire in
a woman.
nymphomaniac NOUN

Oo

oaf NOUN a stupid or clumsy
man.

oak NOUN a large tree
producing acorns and a
hard wood.

OAP ABBREV old-age
pensioner.

oar NOUN a pole with a flat
blade, used to row a boat.

oasis NOUN (PL **-ses**) a

fertile place in a desert.

oast house NOUN a building containing a kiln for drying hops.

oat NOUN a hardy cereal plant; (**oats**) its grain.

oatcake NOUN an oatmeal biscuit.

oath NOUN 1 a solemn promise. 2 a swear word.

oatmeal NOUN ground oats.

obdurate ADJ stubborn. **obduracy** NOUN

OBE ABBREV Order of the British Empire.

obedient ADJ doing what you are told to do. **obedience** NOUN

obeisance NOUN respect; a bow or curtsy.

obelisk NOUN a tall pillar set up as a monument.

obese ADJ very fat. **obesity** NOUN

obey VERB act in accordance with a person's orders or a rule, law, etc.

obituary NOUN (PL **-ies**) an announcement of someone's death, often with a short biography.

object NOUN 1 something solid that can be seen or touched. 2 a person or thing to which an action or feeling is directed; [Grammar] a noun governed by a transitive verb or a preposition. 3 a goal or purpose. VERB express disapproval or disagreement. **objector** NOUN

objection NOUN a statement of disagreement or disapproval.

objectionable ADJ unpleasant.

objective ADJ not influenced by personal feelings or opinions; having actual existence outside the mind. NOUN a goal or aim. **objectivity** NOUN

objet d'art NOUN (PL **objets d'art**) a small decorative or artistic object.

obligate VERB oblige.

obligation NOUN something you are legally or morally bound to do; the state of being bound in this way.

obligatory ADJ compulsory.

oblige VERB 1 make someone legally or morally bound to do something. 2 do something to help someone.

obliged ADJ grateful.

obliging ADJ polite and helpful.

oblique ADJ 1 slanting. 2 not explicit or direct.

obliterate VERB destroy completely. **obliteration** NOUN

oblivion NOUN the state of being forgotten; the state of being unconscious or unaware.

oblivious ADJ unaware.

oblong NOUN & ADJ (having) a rectangular shape.

obnoxious ADJ very unpleasant.

oboe NOUN a woodwind instrument of treble pitch. **oboist** NOUN

obscene ADJ dealing with sexual matters in an offensive way. **obscenity** NOUN

obscure ADJ not discovered or known about; hard to see or understand. VERB conceal; make unclear. **obscurity** NOUN

obsequious ADJ servile or excessively respectful.

observance NOUN the keeping of a law, custom, or festival.

observant ADJ quick to notice things.

observation NOUN 1 watching carefully; noticing things. 2 a remark.

observatory NOUN (PL -ies) a building equipped for the observation of stars and planets.

observe VERB 1 notice; watch carefully. 2 make a remark. 3 obey a rule; celebrate a festival. **observer** NOUN

obsess VERB preoccupy to a disturbing extent.

obsession NOUN being obsessed; something that a person cannot stop thinking about. **obsessive** ADJ

obsolescent ADJ becoming obsolete.

obsolete ADJ no longer used or of use.

obstacle NOUN something that obstructs progress.

obstetrics NOUN the branch of medicine dealing with childbirth. **obstetrician** NOUN

obstinate ADJ refusing to change your mind; hard to deal with. **obstinacy** NOUN

obstreperous ADJ noisy

and unruly.

obstruct VERB hinder the movement or progress of. **obstruction** NOUN **obstructive** ADJ

obtain VERB 1 get possession of. 2 [formal] be customary.

obtrude VERB be noticeable in an unwelcome way. **obtrusive** ADJ

obtuse ADJ 1 slow to understand. 2 (of an angle) more than 90° but less than 180°; blunt in shape.

obverse NOUN the side of a coin bearing a head or main design; an opposite or counterpart.

obviate VERB remove or prevent a need or difficulty.

obvious ADJ easily seen or understood. **obviously** ADV

occasion NOUN 1 the time at which an event takes place; a special event; a suitable time or opportunity. 2 [formal] reason or cause. VERB [formal] cause.

occasional ADJ happening or done from time to time.

occasionally ADV

occidental ADJ of the countries of the West.

occult NOUN the world of magic and supernatural beliefs and practices.

occupant NOUN a person occupying a place. **occupancy** NOUN

occupation NOUN 1 a job or profession; a way of spending time. 2 occupying or being occupied.

occupational ADJ of or caused by your employment.

occupy VERB (**occupied**, **occupying**) 1 live in; fill a place or space. 2 take control of a country by force. 3 keep busy. **occupier** NOUN

occur VERB (**occurred**, **occurring**) 1 happen. 2 be found or present. 3 (**occur to**) come into the mind of.

occurrence NOUN an incident or event; occurring.

ocean NOUN a very large expanse of sea.

ocelot NOUN a striped and spotted wild cat.

ochre ([US] **ocher**) NOUN pale brownish yellow

earth, used as a pigment.

o'clock ADV used in specifying an hour.

octagon NOUN a geometric figure with eight sides. **octagonal** ADJ

octane NOUN a hydrocarbon present in petrol.

octave NOUN the interval of eight notes between one musical note and the next note of the same name above or below it.

octet NOUN a group of eight voices or instruments; music for these.

October NOUN the tenth month.

octopus NOUN (PL **-puses**) a sea creature with eight tentacles.

ocular ADJ of, for, or by the eyes.

odd ADJ **1** strange or unexpected. **2** (of a number) not exactly divisible by two. **3** occasional. **4** separated from a set or pair.

oddity NOUN (PL **-ies**) an unusual person or thing; being strange.

oddment NOUN an isolated piece or item left over from a larger set.

odds PLURAL NOUN the ratio between the amounts staked by the parties to a bet; the likelihood of something's happening. **at odds** in conflict.

ode NOUN a poem addressed to a person or celebrating an event.

odious ADJ hateful.

odium NOUN widespread hatred or disgust.

odour ([US] **odor**) NOUN a smell. **odorous** ADJ

odyssey NOUN (PL **-eys**) a long eventful journey.

oesophagus ([US] **esophagus**) NOUN the tube from the mouth to the stomach.

oestrogen ([US] **estrogen**) NOUN a hormone responsible for controlling female bodily characteristics.

of PREP **1** helping to form; made up from. **2** belonging to; involving. **3** used in expressions of measurement, value, or age.

off ADV **1** away; so as to be removed or separated. **2** so as to come or bring to an end. **3** not working or connected. PREP away from; leading away from.

ADJ (of food) starting to decay.

off-colour slightly unwell.

off-licence a shop selling alcoholic drinks to be drunk elsewhere. **off-putting** unpleasant or unsettling.

offal NOUN the internal organs of an animal, used as food.

offbeat ADJ [inf] unusual or unconventional.

offcut NOUN a piece of waste material left after cutting off a larger piece.

offence ([US] **offense**) NOUN 1 an illegal act. 2 a feeling of annoyance or resentment.

offend VERB 1 cause to feel indignant or hurt. 2 commit an illegal act. **offender** NOUN

offensive ADJ 1 causing offence; disgusting. 2 used in attacking. NOUN an aggressive action; a campaign.

offer VERB make something available to someone; state what you are willing to do, pay, or give; provide. NOUN an expression of willingness to do, give, or pay something; an amount offered; a reduction in the price of goods.

offering NOUN

offhand ADJ rudely casual or cool in manner ADV without previous thought.

office NOUN 1 a room or building used for clerical and similar work. 2 a position of authority.

officer NOUN a person holding authority, especially in the armed forces; a policeman or policewoman.

official ADJ of or authorized by a public body or authority; formally approved. NOUN a person holding public office.

officially ADV

officiate VERB act as an official in charge of an event; perform a religious ceremony.

officious ADJ bossy.

offload VERB unload.

offset VERB (**offset**, **offsetting**) counterbalance.

offshoot NOUN a thing that develops from something else.

offshore ADJ at sea some distance from land; (of

wind) blowing from the land to the sea.

offside ADJ & ADV in a position where you may not legally play the ball (in football etc.).

offspring NOUN (PL **offspring**) a person's child or children.

often ADV frequently; in many cases.

ogle VERB look lustfully at.

ogre NOUN (in stories) a man-eating giant; a terrifying person.

oh EXCLAMATION expressing surprise, delight, or pain, or used for emphasis.

ohm NOUN a unit of electrical resistance.

oil NOUN 1 a thick, slippery liquid that will not dissolve in water. 2 a thick, sticky liquid obtained from petroleum. 3 (**oils**) oil paints. VERB lubricate or treat with oil. **oily** ADJ

oilfield NOUN an area where mineral oil is found in the ground.

oilskin NOUN cloth waterproofed by treatment with oil.

ointment NOUN a cream rubbed on the skin to heal injuries etc.

OK (or **okay**) ADJ & ADV [inf] all right.

old ADJ 1 having lived or existed for a long time or a specified time. 2 former. **old age** the later part of life. **old-fashioned** no longer fashionable. **Old Testament** the first part of the Christian Bible. **old wives' tale** a traditional but unfounded belief.

olfactory ADJ concerned with the sense of smell.

olive NOUN 1 a small oval fruit from which an oil (**olive oil**) is obtained. 2 a greyish-green colour. ADJ (of the skin) yellowish brown.

olive branch an offer to restore friendly relations.

ombudsman NOUN an official who investigates people's complaints against companies or the government.

omega NOUN the last letter of the Greek alphabet (Ω, ω).

omelette NOUN a dish of beaten eggs cooked in a frying pan.

omen NOUN an event regarded as a prophetic sign.

ominous ADJ giving the

impression that trouble is imminent.

omit VERB (**omitted, omitting**) leave out or exclude; fail to do. **omission** NOUN

omnibus NOUN **1** a volume containing several works originally published separately. **2** [dated] a bus.

omnipotent ADJ having unlimited or very great power. **omnipotence** NOUN

omniscient ADJ knowing everything. **omniscience** NOUN

omnivorous ADJ feeding on both plants and meat.

on PREP **1** into contact with, or aboard. **2** about or concerning. **3** stored in or broadcast by. **4** in the course of. **5** at a point in time. **6** added to. ADV **1** in contact with or covering something. **2** with continued movement or action. **3** taking place or being presented. **4** functioning.

onward ADV & ADJ **onwards** ADV

once ADV **1** on one occasion or for one time only. **2** formerly. **at once 1** immediately.

2 simultaneously. **once-over** a rapid inspection, search, etc.

oncoming ADJ approaching.

one NOUN the smallest whole number (1, I); a single person or thing. ADJ single; a certain: *one day*; the same: *of one mind*. PRON **1** used to refer to the speaker, or to represent people in general. **2** used to refer to a person or thing previously mentioned.

one-sided unfairly biased; very unequal.

onerous ADJ involving effort and difficulty.

oneself PRON the emphatic and reflexive form of *one*.

ongoing ADJ still in progress.

onion NOUN a vegetable with a bulb that has a strong taste and smell.

online ADJ & ADV controlled by or connected to a computer.

onlooker NOUN a spectator.

only ADJ single or solitary. ADV **1** with no one or nothing more besides. **2** no longer ago than. CONJ [inf] except that.

onomatopoeia NOUN the

use of words that imitate the sound of the thing they refer to (e.g. *sizzle*).
onomatopoeic ADJ

onset NOUN a beginning.

onshore ADJ (of wind) blowing from the sea to the land.

onslaught NOUN a fierce attack.

onto PREP on to.

onus NOUN a duty or responsibility.

onyx NOUN a semi-precious stone like marble.

ooze VERB trickle or flow out slowly.

opal NOUN a semi-transparent precious stone.

opalescent ADJ having small points of shifting colour.

opaque ADJ impossible to see through; difficult to understand.
opacity NOUN

open ADJ 1 not closed, fastened, or restricted. 2 not covered; not hidden or disguised. 3 (of a shop etc.) ready to admit customers. 4 spread out or unfolded. 5 not finally settled. VERB 1 make or become open; give access to. 2 establish or begin.

open to subject or vulnerable to. **open house** hospitality to all visitors. **open-plan** having large rooms without dividing walls. **open verdict** a verdict not specifying whether a suspicious death is due to crime.
openness NOUN

opencast ADJ (of mining) on the surface of the ground.

opening NOUN 1 a gap. 2 a beginning. 3 an opportunity.

opera NOUN a play in which words are sung to music.
operatic ADJ

operable ADJ 1 able to be used. 2 suitable for treatment by surgery.

operate VERB 1 use or control a machine; function. 2 perform a surgical operation.

operation NOUN 1 functioning. 2 an act of surgery performed on a patient. 3 an organized action involving a number of people.

operational ADJ 1 in or ready for use. 2 involved in functioning or activity.

operative ADJ
1 functioning. 2 of surgical operations. NOUN a worker.

operator NOUN a person who operates a machine; a person who works at the switchboard of a telephone exchange; a person who runs a business or enterprise.

operetta NOUN a short or light opera.

ophthalmic ADJ of or for the eyes.

opiate NOUN a sedative containing opium.

opine VERB [formal] express or hold as an opinion.

opinion NOUN a personal view not necessarily based on fact or knowledge; the views of people in general; a formal statement of advice by an expert.

opinionated ADJ obstinate in asserting your opinions.

opium NOUN a narcotic drug made from the juice of certain poppies.

opossum NOUN a small tree-living marsupial.

opponent NOUN a person competes with another; a person who disagrees with a proposal etc.

opportune ADJ happening at a good or convenient time.

opportunist NOUN a person who exploits opportunities, especially in an unscrupulous way. **opportunism** NOUN

opportunity NOUN (PL **-ies**) a set of circumstances making it possible to do something.

oppose VERB argue or fight against; compete with.

opposite ADJ 1 facing. 2 totally different. NOUN an opposite person or thing. ADV & PREP in an opposite position to.

opposition NOUN 1 resistance or disagreement; a group of people who oppose something; (**the Opposition**) the main parliamentary party opposing the one in power. 2 a difference or contrast.

oppress VERB govern or treat harshly; distress or make anxious. **oppression** NOUN **oppressor** NOUN

oppressive ADJ harsh and unfair; causing distress or anxiety; (of weather) sultry and tiring.

opt VERB 1 make a choice.
2 (**opt out**) choose not to
participate.

optic ADJ of the eye or
vision.

optical ADJ of vision, light,
or optics.
optical fibre a thin glass
fibre used to transmit
signals. **optical illusion**
something that deceives
the eye by appearing to be
other than it is.

optician NOUN a person
who examines eyes and
prescribes glasses etc.

optics NOUN the study of
vision and the behaviour
of light.

optimal ADJ best or most
favourable.

optimism NOUN a
tendency to take a
hopeful view of things.
optimist NOUN
optimistic ADJ

optimum ADJ & NOUN (PL
-ma or **-mums**) the best or
most favourable
(conditions, amount,
etc.).

option NOUN a thing that
you may choose; the
freedom or right to
choose; a right to buy or
sell something at a
specified price within a
set time.

optional ADJ not
compulsory.
optionally ADV

opulent ADJ ostentatiously
luxurious.
opulence NOUN

opus NOUN (PL **opera**) a
musical composition
numbered as one of a
composer's works.

or CONJ used to link
alternatives; also known
as; otherwise.

oracle NOUN a person or
thing regarded as an
infallible guide; an
ancient shrine where a
god was believed to
answer questions.

oral ADJ 1 spoken not
written. 2 of the mouth;
taken by mouth. NOUN a
spoken exam.
orally ADV

orange NOUN a large round
citrus fruit with a reddish-
yellow rind; its colour.

orang-utan (or **orang-
utang**) NOUN a large ape.

oration NOUN a formal
speech.

orator NOUN a skilful public
speaker.

oratorio NOUN (PL
oratorios) a musical

composition for voices and orchestra, usually with a biblical theme.

oratory NOUN the art of public speaking.
oratorical ADJ

orb NOUN a sphere or globe.

orbit NOUN 1 the curved path of a planet, satellite, or spacecraft round a star or planet. 2 a sphere of activity or influence. VERB (**orbited, orbiting**) move in orbit round.

orbital ADJ 1 of orbits. 2 (of a road) round the outside of a city.

orchard NOUN a piece of land planted with fruit trees.

orchestra NOUN a large group of people playing various musical instruments.
orchestral ADJ

orchestrate VERB 1 arrange music for an orchestra. 2 organize or manipulate a situation etc.
orchestration NOUN

orchid NOUN a showy flower.

ordain VERB 1 appoint ceremonially to the Christian ministry. 2 order or decree officially.

ordeal NOUN a painful or difficult experience.

order NOUN 1 the arrangement of people or things according to a particular sequence or method. 2 a situation in which everything is in its correct place; a state of peace and obedience to law. 3 a command; a request to supply goods etc. 4 a rank, kind, or quality; a group of plants or animals classified as similar. 5 a religious community. VERB 1 give a command; request that something be supplied. 2 arrange methodically.
out of order not functioning.

orderly ADJ neatly arranged; well behaved. NOUN (PL **-ies**) an attendant in a hospital; a soldier assisting an officer.
orderliness NOUN

ordinal number NOUN a number defining a thing's position in a series, such as *first* or *second*.

ordinance NOUN a decree; a religious rite.

ordinary ADJ normal or usual.
ordinarily ADV

ordination NOUN ceremonial appointment to the Christian ministry.

ordnance NOUN mounted guns; military equipment.

ore NOUN solid rock or mineral from which a metal or mineral can be obtained.

oregano NOUN a herb.

organ NOUN 1 a keyboard instrument with pipes supplied with air by bellows. 2 a body part with a specific function. 3 a medium of communication, especially a newspaper. **organist** NOUN

organic ADJ 1 of or derived from living matter. 2 of bodily organs. 3 (of farming methods) using no artificial fertilizers or pesticides. 4 (of development or change) continuous or natural. **organically** ADV

organism NOUN an individual animal, plant, or life form.

organization NOUN organizing; a systematic arrangement; an organized group of people, e.g. a business.

organize (or **-ise**) VERB 1 arrange in an orderly way. 2 make arrangements for.

orgasm NOUN a climax of sexual activity.

orgy NOUN (PL **-ies**) a wild party; unrestrained indulgence in a specified activity. **orgiastic** ADJ

orient NOUN (**the Orient**) the countries of the East. VERB (also **orientate**) 1 position something in relation to the points of a compass. 2 adapt to particular needs or circumstances. 3 (**orient yourself**) find your position in relation to your surroundings. **orientation** NOUN

oriental ADJ of the Far East.

orifice NOUN an opening.

origami NOUN the Japanese decorative art of paper folding.

origin NOUN the point where something begins; a person's ancestry or parentage.

original ADJ 1 existing from the beginning. 2 not copied. 3 new and unusual. NOUN a model on which copies are based.

originality NOUN

originally ADV

originate VERB bring or come into being.

originator NOUN

ornament NOUN an object used as a decoration; decoration.

ornamental ADJ

ornamentation NOUN

ornate ADJ elaborately decorated.

ornithology NOUN the study of birds.

ornithologist NOUN

orphan NOUN a child whose parents are dead. VERB make a child an orphan.

orphanage NOUN a place where orphans are cared for.

orthodox ADJ of or holding conventional or currently accepted beliefs. **Orthodox Church** the Eastern or Greek Church.

orthodoxy NOUN

orthopaedics ([US] **orthopedics**) NOUN the branch of medicine concerned with bones and muscles.

orthopaedic ADJ

oscillate VERB move or swing to and fro.

oscillation NOUN

osier NOUN willow with flexible twigs.

osmosis NOUN the passage of molecules through a membrane from a less concentrated solution into a more concentrated one.

osmotic ADJ

osprey NOUN a large fish-eating bird.

ossify VERB (**ossified**, **ossifying**) turn into bone; stop developing or progressing.

ostensible ADJ apparent, but not necessarily true.

ostensibly ADV

ostentation NOUN a showy display intended to impress.

ostentatious ADJ

osteopathy NOUN the treatment of certain conditions by manipulating bones and muscles.

osteopath NOUN

ostracize (or **-ise**) VERB exclude from a society or group.

ostracism NOUN

ostrich NOUN a large flightless African bird.

other ADJ & PRON **1** used to refer to a person or thing that is different from one already mentioned or known. **2** additional. **3** the alternative of two. **4** those not already mentioned.

otherwise ADV **1** in different circumstances. **2** in other respects. **3** in a different way.

otter NOUN a fish-eating water animal.

ottoman NOUN a low upholstered seat without a back or arms.

ought AUXILIARY VERB **1** expressing duty, desirability, or advisability. **2** expressing strong probability.

ounce NOUN a unit of weight, one-sixteenth of a pound (about 28 grams); a very small amount.

our ADJ of or belonging to us.

ours POSSESSIVE PRON belonging to us.

ourselves PRON the emphatic and reflexive form of *we* and *us*.

oust VERB force out.

out ADV **1** away from a place; in or into the open. **2** away from your home or office. **3** so as to be heard or known. **4** not possible. **5** so as to be extinguished; so as to end or be completed. VERB reveal

that someone is homosexual.

out and out complete. **out of date** no longer current, valid, or fashionable.

outback NOUN a remote or sparsely populated area.

outboard motor NOUN a motor attached to the outside of a boat.

outbreak NOUN a sudden occurrence of war, disease, etc.

outbuilding NOUN an outhouse.

outburst NOUN a sudden release of feeling.

outcast NOUN a person rejected by their social group.

outclass VERB surpass in quality.

outcome NOUN a consequence.

outcrop NOUN a part of a rock formation that is visible on the surface.

outcry NOUN a strong protest.

outdistance VERB get far ahead of.

outdo VERB (**outdid, outdone, outdoing**) do better than.

outdoor ADJ of or for use in the open air.

outdoors ADV

outer ADJ external; further from the centre or inside.
outermost ADJ
outfit NOUN a set of clothes.
outfitter NOUN a supplier of men's clothing.
outgoing ADJ 1 sociable. 2 leaving an office or position. NOUN (**outgoings**) expenditure.
outgrow VERB (**outgrew, outgrown, outgrowing**) grow too large for; stop doing something as you mature.
outhouse NOUN a shed, barn, etc.
outing NOUN a brief journey.
outlandish ADJ bizarre or unfamiliar.
outlast VERB last longer than.
outlaw NOUN a criminal who remains at large. VERB make illegal.
outlay NOUN money spent.
outlet NOUN a way out; a means for giving vent to energy or feelings; a market for goods.
outline NOUN 1 a line showing a thing's shape or boundary. 2 a summary. VERB draw or describe in outline; mark the outline of.

outlook NOUN a person's attitude to life; the prospect for the future.
outlying ADJ situated far from the centre.
outmoded ADJ old-fashioned.
outnumber VERB exceed in number.
outpatient NOUN a person visiting a hospital for treatment but not staying overnight.
outpost NOUN a small military camp at a distance from the main army; a remote settlement.
output NOUN the amount of electrical power, work, etc. produced.
outrage NOUN extreme shock and anger; an extremely immoral or shocking act. VERB cause to feel outrage.
outrageous ADJ shockingly bad or excessive.
outright ADV 1 altogether. 2 frankly. 3 immediately. ADJ 1 total. 2 frank and direct.
outset NOUN the beginning.
outside NOUN the outer side, surface, or part. ADJ

on or near the outside; coming from outside a group. PREP & ADV on or moving beyond the boundaries of; beyond the limits of; not being a member of.

outsider NOUN 1 a non-member of a group. 2 a competitor thought to have no chance in a contest.

outsize ADJ exceptionally large.

outskirts PLURAL NOUN the outer districts.

outspoken ADJ very frank.

outstanding ADJ 1 conspicuous; exceptionally good. 2 not yet paid or dealt with.

outward ADJ & ADV 1 on or from the outside. 2 out or away from a place.
outwardly ADV
outwards ADV

outweigh VERB be more significant than.

outwit VERB (**outwitted, outwitting**) defeat by being cunning or crafty.

ova plural of **ovum**.

oval NOUN & ADJ (having) a rounded elongated shape.

ovary NOUN (PL -ies) a female reproductive organ in which eggs are produced.

ovarian ADJ

ovation NOUN enthusiastic applause.

oven NOUN an enclosed compartment in which things are cooked or heated.

over PREP 1 extending upwards from or above. 2 moving across. 3 so as to cover or protect. 4 greater than. 5 in the course of. ADV 1 moving outwards or downwards. 2 from one side to another. 3 repeatedly. 4 at an end. NOUN [Cricket] a sequence of six balls bowled from one end of the pitch.

overall NOUN (also **overalls**) a loose-fitting garment worn over ordinary clothes for protection. ADJ & ADV including everything; taken as a whole.

overbalance VERB fall due to loss of balance.

overbearing ADJ domineering.

overboard ADV from a ship into the water.

overcast ADJ cloudy.

overcoat NOUN a long, warm coat.

overcome VERB succeed in

dealing with a problem; defeat; overpower.

overdose NOUN & VERB (take) a dangerously large dose of a drug.

overdraft NOUN a deficit in a bank account caused by taking more money than the account holds.

overdrawn ADJ having taken more money from a bank account than it holds.

overdrive NOUN a mechanism providing an extra gear above top gear.

overdue ADJ not paid or arrived etc. by the required or expected time.

overgrown ADJ 1 covered with weeds. 2 having grown too large.

overhaul VERB examine and repair. NOUN an examination and repair.

overhead ADJ & ADV above your head. NOUN (**overheads**) the expenses involved in running a business etc.

overhear VERB (**overheard, overhearing**) hear accidentally.

overjoyed ADJ very happy.

overkill NOUN an excessive amount of something.

overlap VERB (**overlapped, overlapping**) extend over something so as to cover part of it; partially coincide. NOUN a part or amount that overlaps.

overleaf ADV on the other side of a page.

overload VERB put too great a load on or in. NOUN an excessive amount.

overlook VERB 1 fail to notice; disregard. 2 have a view over.

overly ADV excessively.

overnight ADV & ADJ during or for a night.

overpower VERB overcome by greater strength or numbers.

overrate VERB have too high an opinion of.

overreact VERB react more strongly than is justified.

override VERB (**overrode, overridden, overriding**) overrule; be more important than; interrupt the operation of an automatic device.

overrule VERB set aside a decision etc. by using your authority.

overrun VERB (**overran, overrun, overrunning**) 1 occupy in large numbers. 2 exceed a limit.

overseas ADJ & ADV in or to

a foreign country.

oversee VERB (**oversaw, overseen, overseeing**) supervise.

overseer NOUN

overshadow VERB cast a shadow over; be more important or prominent than, distract attention from.

oversight NOUN an unintentional failure to do something.

overspill NOUN people moving from an overcrowded area to live elsewhere.

overstep VERB (**overstepped, overstepping**) go beyond a limit.

overt ADJ done or shown openly.

overtake VERB (**overtook, overtaken, overtaking**) 1 pass while travelling in the same direction. 2 affect suddenly.

overthrow VERB (**overthrew, overthrown, overthrowing**) remove forcibly from power. NOUN a removal from power.

overtime NOUN time worked in addition to normal working hours.

overtone NOUN an

additional quality or implication.

overture NOUN 1 an orchestral piece at the beginning of a musical work. 2 (**overtures**) an initial approach or proposal.

overturn VERB 1 turn upside down or on to its side. 2 reverse a decision etc.

overview NOUN a general survey.

overweening ADJ too proud or confident.

overwhelm VERB 1 bury beneath a huge mass. 2 overcome completely; have a strong emotional effect on.

overwrought ADJ in a state of nervous agitation.

ovulate VERB produce or discharge an egg cell from an ovary.

ovulation NOUN

ovum NOUN (PL **ova**) a reproductive cell produced by a female.

owe VERB be under an obligation to pay or repay money etc. in return for something received; have something through someone else's action.

owing ADJ owed and not

yet paid.

owing to because of.

owl NOUN a bird of prey with large eyes, usually flying at night.

own ADJ belonging to a specified person. VERB **1** possess **2** admit. **3** (**own up**) confess.

owner NOUN

ownership NOUN

ox NOUN (PL **oxen**) a cow or bull; a castrated bull.

oxidation NOUN the process of combining with oxygen.

oxide NOUN a compound of oxygen and one other element.

oxidize (or **-ise**) VERB cause to combine with oxygen.

oxygen NOUN a colourless gas that forms about 20 per cent of the earth's atmosphere.

oxygenate VERB supply or mix with oxygen.

oyster NOUN an edible shellfish with two hinged shells.

oz. ABBREV ounces.

ozone NOUN a colourless toxic gas with a strong odour.

ozone layer a layer of ozone in the stratosphere, absorbing ultraviolet radiation.

Pp

p ABBREV **1** penny or pence. **2** [Music] piano (softly).

PA ABBREV **1** personal assistant. **2** public address.

p.a. ABBREV per annum (yearly).

pace NOUN **1** a single step. **2** a rate of progress. VERB **1** walk steadily; measure a distance by pacing. **2** (**pace yourself**) do something at a steady

rate.

pacemaker NOUN a device for regulating the heartbeat.

pachyderm NOUN an elephant or other very large mammal with thick skin.

pacifist NOUN a person totally opposed to war.

pacifism NOUN

pacify VERB (**pacified,**

pacifying) make calm.
pacification NOUN

pack NOUN **1** a cardboard or paper container and the items in it. **2** a set of playing cards. **3** a group of dogs or wolves. VERB **1** fill a bag with items for travel; put things into a container for storage etc. **2** cram into. **3** cover, surround, or fill.

package NOUN **1** a parcel. **2** a set of proposals or terms. VERB put into a box or wrapping.

packet NOUN a small pack or package.

pact NOUN an agreement or treaty.

pad NOUN **1** a thick piece of soft material. **2** a set of sheets of paper fastened together at one edge. **3** a soft fleshy part under an animal's paw. VERB (**padded, padding**) **1** fill or cover with padding. **2** make larger or longer. **3** walk softly or steadily.

padding NOUN soft material used as a pad.

paddle NOUN a short oar with a broad blade. VERB **1** propel with a paddle. **2** walk with bare feet in shallow water.

paddock NOUN a field or enclosure where horses are kept.

padlock NOUN & VERB (fasten with) a detachable lock attached by a hinged hook.

paediatrics ([US] **pediatrics**) NOUN the branch of medicine which deals with children's diseases. **paediatric** ADJ **paediatrician** NOUN

paedophile ([US] **pedophile**) NOUN a person who is sexually attracted to children.

paella NOUN a Spanish dish of rice, seafood, chicken, etc.

pagan ADJ & NOUN (a person) holding religious beliefs other than those of an established religion.

page NOUN **1** a sheet of paper in a book etc.; one side of this. **2** a young male attendant at a hotel; a boy attending a bride at a wedding. VERB summon over a public address system or with a pager.

pageant NOUN a public entertainment performed by people in costume. **pageantry** NOUN

pager NOUN a small device that bleeps or vibrates to summon the wearer.

pagoda NOUN a Hindu or Buddhist temple or other sacred building.

paid past & past participle of **pay**.

pail NOUN a bucket.

pain NOUN 1 physical discomfort caused by injury or illness; mental suffering. 2 (**pains**) careful effort. VERB cause pain to. **painful** ADJ

painkiller NOUN a drug for reducing pain.

painstaking ADJ very careful and thorough.

paint NOUN colouring matter for applying in liquid form to a surface. VERB apply paint to; depict with paint; describe. **painting** NOUN

painter NOUN 1 a person who paints as an artist or decorator. 2 a rope attached to a boat's bow for tying it up.

pair NOUN a set of two things or people; an article consisting of two joined parts; one member of a pair in relation to the other. VERB arrange or be arranged in a pair or pairs.

paisley NOUN a pattern of curved feather-shaped figures.

pajamas US spelling of **pyjamas**.

pal NOUN [inf] a friend.

palace NOUN the official residence of a king, queen, president, etc.

palaeontology ([US] **paleontology**) NOUN the study of fossil animals and plants.

palatable ADJ pleasant to taste; acceptable.

palate NOUN the roof of the mouth; a person's sense of taste.

palatial ADJ impressively spacious.

palaver NOUN [inf] a fuss.

pale ADJ light in colour; (of a person's face) having less colour than normal. VERB turn pale; seem less important.

palette NOUN a board on which an artist mixes colours; a range of colours used.

palindrome NOUN a word or phrase that reads the same backwards as forwards, e.g. *madam*.

paling NOUN a fence made from pointed stakes; a stake.

pall NOUN a cloth spread over a coffin; a dark cloud of smoke. VERB come to seem less interesting. **pall-bearer** a person helping to carry a coffin at a funeral.

pallet NOUN 1 a straw mattress. 2 a portable platform on which goods can be lifted or stored.

palliate VERB alleviate; make less severe. **palliative** ADJ

pallid ADJ pale. **pallor** NOUN

palm NOUN 1 the inner surface of the hand. 2 an evergreen tree of warm regions, with large leaves and no branches.

palmistry NOUN fortune-telling by examining the lines on the palm of a person's hand.

palomino NOUN (PL **-os**) a golden-coloured horse with a white mane and tail.

palpable ADJ able to be touched or felt; obvious. **palpably** ADV

palpate VERB examine medically by touch.

palpitate VERB (of the heart) throb rapidly. **palpitation** NOUN

palsy NOUN [dated] paralysis. **palsied** ADJ

paltry ADJ (of an amount) very small; petty or trivial.

pampas NOUN vast grassy plains in South America.

pamper VERB treat very indulgently.

pamphlet NOUN a small booklet or leaflet.

pan NOUN a metal container for cooking food in; the bowl of a toilet. VERB (**panned, panning**) 1 [inf] criticize severely. 2 move a camera while filming to give a panoramic effect.

panacea NOUN a remedy for all kinds of diseases or troubles.

panache NOUN a confident stylish manner.

panama NOUN a straw hat.

pancake NOUN a thin, flat cake of fried batter.

pancreas NOUN a digestive gland near the stomach, which also produces insulin.

panda NOUN a bear-like black and white mammal.

pandemonium NOUN uproar.

pander VERB (**pander to**) indulge someone in a bad habit or unreasonable desire.

pane NOUN a sheet of glass in a window or door.

panegyric NOUN a speech or text of praise.

panel NOUN 1 a section in a door, vehicle, garment, etc.; a board on which instruments or controls are fixed. 2 a group of people assembled to discuss or decide something.
panelled ([US] **paneled**) ADJ
panellist ([US] **panelist**) NOUN

pang NOUN a sudden sharp pain.

panic NOUN sudden strong fear. VERB (**panicked**, **panicking**) feel panic.
panicky ADJ

pannier NOUN a large basket carried by a donkey etc.; a bag fitted on a motorcycle or bicycle.

panoply NOUN (PL **-ies**) a splendid display.

panorama NOUN a view of a wide area; a complete survey of a set of events.
panoramic ADJ

pansy NOUN (PL **-ies**) 1 a garden flower. 2 [inf] an effeminate or homosexual man.

pant VERB breathe with short quick breaths.

pantechnicon NOUN [dated] a large van for transporting furniture.

panther NOUN a black leopard.

pantomime NOUN a theatrical show based on a fairy tale, involving slapstick comedy.

pantry NOUN (PL **-ies**) a room or cupboard for storing food.

pants PLURAL NOUN underpants or knickers; [US] trousers.

pap NOUN soft, bland food.

papacy NOUN (PL **-ies**) the position or role of the pope.
papal ADJ

paparazzi PLURAL NOUN photographers who pursue celebrities to get pictures of them.

papaya NOUN a tropical fruit.

paper NOUN 1 a substance manufactured in thin sheets from wood fibre, used for writing on, wrapping, etc. 2 a newspaper. 3 a document; a set of exam questions; an essay or dissertation.

VERB cover a wall with wallpaper.

paperback NOUN a book with flexible paper covers.

paperweight NOUN a small heavy object for holding loose papers down.

paperwork NOUN clerical or administrative work.

papier mâché NOUN a mixture of paper and glue that becomes hard when dry.

paprika NOUN red pepper.

papyrus NOUN (PL **papyri**) a material made in ancient Egypt from the stem of a water plant, used for writing on.

par NOUN [Golf] the number of strokes needed by a first-class player for a hole or course.
  below par not as good or well as usual. **on a par with** equal to in quality or importance.

parable NOUN a story told to illustrate a moral.

paracetamol NOUN a drug that relieves pain and reduces fever.

parachute NOUN a device used to slow the descent of a person or object dropping from a great height. VERB descend or drop by parachute.

parade NOUN a public procession; a formal assembly of troops; an ostentatious display; a promenade or row of shops. VERB march in a parade; display ostentatiously.

paradise NOUN heaven; the Garden of Eden; an ideal place or state.

paradox NOUN a statement that seems self-contradictory but is in fact true.
  paradoxical ADJ

paraffin NOUN an oily liquid obtained from petroleum, used as fuel.

paragon NOUN an apparently perfect person or thing.

paragraph NOUN a distinct section of a piece of writing, begun on a new line.

parakeet NOUN a small parrot.

parallel ADJ **1** (of lines or planes) going continuously at the same distance from each other. **2** existing at the same time and corresponding. NOUN **1** a person or thing similar to another; a comparison. **2** a line of latitude. VERB (**paralleled, paralleling**) be parallel or comparable to.

parallelogram NOUN a figure with four straight sides and opposite sides parallel.

paralyse ([US] **paralyze**) VERB affect with paralysis; prevent from functioning normally.

paralysis NOUN loss of the ability to move part of the body.

paralytic ADJ

paramedic NOUN a person trained to do medical work but not having a doctor's qualifications.

parameter NOUN a thing which decides or limits the way that something can be done.

paramilitary ADJ organized like a military force.

paramount ADJ chief in importance.

paramour NOUN [old use] a lover.

paranoia NOUN a mental condition in which a person has delusions of grandeur or persecution; an abnormal tendency to mistrust others.

paranoid ADJ

paranormal ADJ supernatural.

parapet NOUN a low wall along the edge of a balcony or bridge.

paraphernalia NOUN numerous belongings or pieces of equipment.

paraphrase VERB express in different words.

paraplegia NOUN paralysis of the legs and lower body.

paraplegic ADJ & NOUN

parasite NOUN an animal or plant living on or in another; a person living off someone else but giving nothing in return.

parasitic ADJ

parasol NOUN a light umbrella used to give shade from the sun.

paratroops PLURAL NOUN troops trained to parachute into an attack.

paratrooper NOUN

parboil VERB cook partially by boiling.

parcel NOUN **1** something wrapped in paper to be posted or carried. **2** something considered as a unit. VERB (**parcelled, parcelling**; [US] **parceled**,

parceling) **1** wrap as a parcel. **2** divide into portions.

parched ADJ dried out with heat.

parchment NOUN writing material made from animal skins; paper resembling this.

pardon NOUN forgiveness. VERB (**pardoned, pardoning**) forgive or excuse.

pare VERB trim the edges of; peel; reduce gradually.

parent NOUN a father or mother. VERB be or act as a parent to.
parental ADJ
parenthood NOUN

parentage NOUN ancestry; origin.

parenthesis NOUN (PL **parentheses**) a word or phrase inserted into a passage; a pair of brackets () placed round this.

par excellence ADJ better or more than all others of the same kind.

pariah NOUN an outcast.

parish NOUN **1** an area with its own church and clergyman. **2** a local government area within a county.

parishioner NOUN an inhabitant of a church parish.

parity NOUN equality.

park NOUN **1** a public garden or recreation ground; the enclosed land of a country house. **2** an area for a specified purpose. **3** an area for parking vehicles. VERB temporarily leave a vehicle somewhere.

parka NOUN a hooded windproof jacket.

Parkinson's disease NOUN a disease causing trembling and muscle stiffness.

parlance NOUN a way of speaking.

parley NOUN (PL **-eys**) a discussion to settle a dispute.

parliament NOUN an assembly that makes a country's laws.
parliamentarian ADJ & NOUN
parliamentary ADJ

parlour ([US] **parlor**) NOUN **1** [dated] a sitting room. **2** a shop providing particular goods or services.

parlous ADJ difficult; precarious.

Parmesan NOUN a hard Italian cheese.

parochial ADJ **1** of a

church parish. **2** having a narrow outlook.

parody NOUN (PL **-ies**) an imitation using exaggeration for comic effect. VERB (**parodied, parodying**) make a parody of.

parole NOUN the release of a prisoner before the end of their sentence on condition of good behaviour. VERB release on parole.

paroxysm NOUN an outburst of emotion; a sudden attack of pain, coughing, etc.

parquet NOUN flooring of wooden blocks arranged in a pattern.

parrot NOUN a tropical bird with brightly coloured feathers, able to mimic human speech. VERB (**parroted, parroting**) repeat mechanically.

parry VERB (**parried, parrying**) ward off a blow; avoid answering a question.

parsimonious ADJ mean or stingy.
  parsimony NOUN

parsley NOUN a herb with crinkly leaves.

parsnip NOUN a vegetable with a large yellowish tapering root.

parson NOUN a parish priest.

parsonage NOUN a rectory or vicarage.

part NOUN **1** some but not all of something; a piece or segment combined with others to make a whole. **2** a role played by an actor or actress; a person's contribution to a situation. VERB **1** separate or be separated; divide. **2** (**part with**) give up possession of. ADV partly.
  part of speech a word's grammatical class (e.g. noun, adjective, or verb).
  take part join in.

partake VERB (**partook, partaken, partaking**) **1** join in an activity. **2** eat or drink.

partial ADJ **1** favouring one side in a dispute. **2** not complete or total. **3** (**partial to**) liking something.
  partiality NOUN
  partially ADV

participate VERB take part in something.
  participant NOUN
  participation NOUN

participle NOUN a word

formed from a verb (e.g. *burnt, burning, frightened, frightening*) and used as an adjective or noun (as in *burnt toast*).

particle NOUN a tiny portion of matter.

particular ADJ 1 to with an individual member of a group or class. 2 more than is usual. 3 very careful or concerned about something. NOUN a detail.
in particular especially.
particularly ADV

parting NOUN 1 an act of leaving someone. 2 a line of scalp visible when hair is combed in different directions.

partisan NOUN 1 a strong supporter. 2 a guerrilla. ADJ prejudiced.

partition NOUN division into parts; a structure dividing a space into separate parts. VERB divide into parts or by a partition.

partly ADJ not completely but to some extent.

partner NOUN each of two people sharing with another or others in an activity; each of a pair; the person with whom you have an established relationship. VERB be the partner of.
partnership NOUN

partridge NOUN a game bird.

party NOUN (PL **-ies**) 1 a social gathering. 2 a formally constituted political group; a group taking part in an activity or trip. 3 one side in an agreement or dispute.
party wall a wall between two adjoining houses or rooms.

pass VERB 1 move or go onward, past, through, or across; change from one state to another. 2 transfer to someone else. 3 (of time) elapse; spend time. 4 be successful in an exam; judge to be satisfactory. 5 put a law into effect. NOUN 1 an act of passing. 2 a success in an exam. 3 a permit to enter a place. 4 a route over or through mountains. 5 [inf] a sexual advance.
pass away die. **pass out** become unconscious.

passable ADJ 1 just satisfactory. 2 able to be crossed or travelled on.

passage NOUN 1 the

passing of someone or something; the right to pass through. **2** a way through or across; a journey by sea or air. **3** an extract from a book etc. **passageway** NOUN

passé ADJ old-fashioned.

passenger NOUN a person travelling in a car, bus, train, ship, or aircraft, other than the driver, pilot, or crew.

passer-by NOUN (PL **passers-by**) a person who happens to be going past.

passing ADJ not lasting long; casual.

passion NOUN **1** strong emotion; sexual love; great enthusiasm. **2** (**the Passion**) Jesus's suffering on the cross. **passionate** ADJ

passive ADJ **1** accepting what happens without resistance. **2** [Grammar] (of a verb) having the form used when the subject is affected by the action of the verb. **passivity** NOUN

Passover NOUN a Jewish festival commemorating the escape of the Israelites from slavery in Egypt.

passport NOUN an official document for use by a person travelling abroad, certifying identity and citizenship.

password NOUN a secret word or phrase used to gain admission, prove identity, etc.

past ADJ belonging to the time before the present; no longer existing. NOUN the time before the present; a person's previous experiences. PREP **1** to or on the further side of. **2** in front of; going from one side to the other. **3** beyond the scope or power of. ADV going past or beyond.

pasta NOUN dough formed in various shapes and cooked in boiling water.

paste NOUN **1** a thick, moist substance. **2** an adhesive. **3** a glass-like substance used in imitation gems. VERB fasten or coat with paste.

pastel NOUN **1** a chalk-like crayon. **2** a pale shade of colour.

pasteurize (or **-ise**) VERB sterilize by heating.

pastiche NOUN a work produced to imitate the style of another.

pastille NOUN a small sweet or lozenge.

pastime NOUN a recreational activity.

pastor NOUN a clergyman in charge of a church or congregation.

pastoral ADJ 1 of country life. 2 (of a farm etc.) keeping sheep and cattle. 3 of spiritual and moral guidance.

pastrami NOUN seasoned smoked beef.

pastry NOUN (PL **-ies**) a dough made of flour, fat, and water, used for making pies etc.; an individual item of food made with this.

pasture NOUN grassy land suitable for grazing cattle. VERB put animals to graze.

pasty¹ NOUN (PL **-ies**) a small savoury pie baked without a dish.

pasty² ADJ 1 of or like paste. 2 unhealthily pale.

pat VERB (**patted, patting**) touch gently with the flat of the hand. NOUN 1 an act of patting. 2 a small mass of a soft substance. ADJ & ADV unconvincingly quick and simple.

off pat known by heart.

patch NOUN a piece of cloth etc. put on something to mend or strengthen it; a part or area distinguished from the rest; a plot of land; [inf] a period of time. VERB 1 mend with patches. 2 (**patch up**) repair; settle a quarrel.

patchwork NOUN needlework in which small pieces of cloth are joined to make a pattern.

patchy ADJ (**-ier, -iest**) existing in small isolated areas; uneven in quality.

pâté NOUN a savoury paste made from meat etc.

patella NOUN the kneecap.

patent ADJ 1 obvious. 2 made or sold under a patent. VERB obtain a patent for. NOUN an official right to be the sole maker or user of an invention. **patent leather** glossy varnished leather.

patently ADV

paternal ADJ of or like a father; related through the father.

paternally ADV

paternity NOUN fatherhood.

path NOUN 1 a way by which people pass on foot; a line along which a person or thing moves. 2 a course of

action.
pathetic ADJ arousing pity or sadness; [inf] very inadequate.
pathetically ADV
pathology NOUN the study of disease.
pathological ADJ
pathologist NOUN
pathos NOUN a pathetic quality.
patience NOUN 1 calm endurance. 2 a card game for one player.
patient ADJ showing patience. NOUN a person receiving medical treatment.
patina NOUN a sheen on a surface produced by age or use.
patio NOUN (PL **-os**) a paved area outside a house.
patriarch NOUN the male head of a family or tribe.
patriarchy NOUN (PL **-ies**) a society led or controlled by men.
patriarchal ADJ
patricide NOUN the killing by someone of their own father; someone guilty of this.
patrimony NOUN (PL **-ies**) heritage.
patriot NOUN a person who strongly supports their country.
patriotic ADJ
patriotism NOUN
patrol VERB (**patrolled, patrolling**) walk or travel regularly through an area to see that all is well. NOUN patrolling; a person or group patrolling.
patron NOUN 1 a person giving influential or financial support to a cause. 2 a regular customer.
patron saint a saint regarded as a protector.
patronage NOUN a patron's support; regular custom.
patronize (or **-ise**) VERB 1 treat someone as if they are naive or foolish. 2 be a regular customer of.
patter VERB make a series of quick tapping sounds. NOUN 1 a pattering sound. 2 rapid glib speech.
pattern NOUN 1 a decorative design. 2 a model, design, or set of instructions for making something; an example to follow. 3 a regular sequence of events.
patterned ADJ
paucity NOUN lack or scarcity.
paunch NOUN a large

protruding stomach.

pauper NOUN a very poor person.

pause NOUN & VERB (make) a temporary stop.

pave VERB cover a surface with flat stones.

pavement NOUN a raised path at the side of a road.

pavilion NOUN 1 a building on a sports ground for use by players and spectators. 2 an ornamental building.

paw NOUN a foot of an animal that has claws. VERB touch or scrape with a paw or forefoot; [inf] touch clumsily or improperly.

pawn NOUN a chess piece of the smallest size and value; a person whose actions are controlled by others. VERB leave with a pawnbroker as security for money borrowed.

pawnbroker NOUN a person licensed to lend money on the security of personal property left with them.

pawpaw NOUN a papaya.

pay VERB (**paid, paying**) 1 give someone money for work or goods; give what is owed; suffer a penalty or misfortune on account of your actions. 2 be profitable or worthwhile. 3 give someone or something attention, etc. NOUN wages.

payable ADJ
payment NOUN

payee NOUN a person to whom money is paid or due.

payroll NOUN a list of a firm's employees receiving regular pay.

PC ABBREV 1 police constable. 2 personal computer. 3 politically correct; political correctness.

PE ABBREV physical education.

pea NOUN an edible round seed growing in pods.

peace NOUN freedom from war or disturbance.

peaceable ADJ avoiding conflict; peaceful.

peaceful ADJ free from war or disturbance; not involving violence.
peacefully ADV

peach NOUN a round juicy fruit with a rough stone; a pinkish-yellow colour.

peacock NOUN a large colourful bird with a long fan-like tail.

peahen NOUN the female of

the peacock.

peak NOUN a pointed top, especially of a mountain; a stiff brim at the front of a cap; the point of highest value, intensity, etc. VERB reach a highest point. ADJ maximum.

peaky ADJ looking pale and sickly.

peal NOUN the sound of ringing bells; a set of bells; a loud burst of thunder or laughter. VERB ring or sound loudly.

peanut NOUN 1 an oval edible seed that develops in a pod underground. 2 (**peanuts**) [inf] a small sum of money.

pear NOUN a rounded fruit tapering towards the stalk.

pearl NOUN a round creamy-white gem formed inside the shell of certain oysters.

pearly ADJ

peasant NOUN (especially in the past) a poor smallholder or agricultural labourer.

peasantry NOUN

peat NOUN decomposed plant matter formed in damp areas.

pebble NOUN a small smooth round stone.

pebbly ADJ

pecan NOUN a smooth pinkish-brown nut.

peccadillo NOUN (PL **-os**) a small sin or fault.

peck VERB 1 strike, bite, or pick up with the beak. 2 kiss lightly and hastily. NOUN an act of pecking.

peckish ADJ [inf] hungry.

pectin NOUN a substance found in fruits which makes jam set.

pectoral ADJ of the chest or breast.

peculiar ADJ 1 strange or eccentric. 2 belonging exclusively to one person, place, etc.

peculiarity NOUN

pedal NOUN a lever operated by the foot. VERB (**pedalled, pedalling**; [US] **pedaled, pedaling**) ride a bicycle by using its pedals.

pedant NOUN a person who cares too much about small details or rules.

pedantic NOUN

pedantry NOUN

peddle VERB sell goods by going from house to house.

peddler NOUN see **pedlar**.

pedestal NOUN a base

pedestrian

supporting a column or statue etc.

pedestrian NOUN a person walking, especially in a street. ADJ unimaginative or dull.

pediatrics US spelling of **paediatrics**.

pedicure NOUN cosmetic treatment of the feet and toenails.

pedigree NOUN recorded ancestry; a line of descent. ADJ (of an animal) descended from a known line of animals of the same breed.

pedlar (or **peddler**) NOUN a person peddles goods; a seller of illegal drugs.

peek VERB peep or glance. NOUN a peep.

peel NOUN the skin or rind of a fruit or vegetable. VERB remove the peel from; strip off an outer covering; (of skin etc.) come off in flakes.

peep VERB look quickly or surreptitiously; show slightly. NOUN a brief or surreptitious look.

peephole NOUN a small hole to peep through.

peer¹ VERB look at with difficulty or concentration.

peer² NOUN 1 a member of the nobility. 2 a person who is your equal in age, social status, etc.

peerage NOUN peers as a group; the rank of peer or peeress.

peeress NOUN a female peer; a peer's wife.

peerless ADJ better than all others.

peeved ADJ [inf] annoyed.

peevish ADJ irritable.

peg NOUN a pin or bolt used as a fastening or to hang things on; a clip for holding clothes on a line. VERB (**pegged, pegging**) 1 fix or mark with pegs. 2 keep wages, prices, etc. at a fixed level. **off the peg** (of clothes) ready-made.

pejorative ADJ expressing disapproval.

Pekinese NOUN a small dog with long hair and a snub nose.

pelican NOUN a waterbird with a large pouch in its bill. **pelican crossing** a pedestrian crossing with lights operated by the pedestrians.

pellet NOUN a small round mass of a substance; a

piece of small shot.

pell-mell ADJ & ADV in a confused or rushed way.

pellucid ADJ very clear.

pelmet NOUN a border of cloth or wood above a window.

pelt VERB **1** throw missiles at. **2** [inf] run fast. NOUN an animal skin.

at full pelt as fast as possible.

pelvis NOUN the large bony frame at the base of the spine.

pelvic ADJ

pen NOUN **1** a device for writing with ink. **2** a small enclosure for farm animals. VERB (**penned, penning**) **1** write or compose. **2** shut in a restricted space.

pen name a writer's pseudonym.

penal ADJ of or involving punishment.

penalize (or **-ise**) VERB inflict a penalty on; put at a disadvantage.

penalty NOUN (PL **-ies**) a punishment for breaking a law, rule, etc.

penance NOUN an act performed as an expression of penitence.

pence plural of **penny**.

penchant NOUN a strong liking.

pencil NOUN an instrument containing graphite, used for drawing or writing. VERB (**pencilled, pencilling**; [US] **penciled, penciling**) write or draw with a pencil.

pendant NOUN an ornament hung from a chain round the neck. ADJ (also **pendent**) hanging.

pending ADJ waiting to be decided or settled. PREP until.

pendulous ADJ hanging loosely.

pendulum NOUN a weight hung from a fixed point and swinging freely, used to regulate the mechanism of a clock.

penetrate VERB make a way into or through; see into or through; understand.

penetration NOUN

penetrating ADJ **1** showing great insight. **2** (of sound) piercing.

penfriend NOUN a friend to whom you write regularly without meeting.

penguin NOUN a flightless Antarctic seabird.

penicillin NOUN an

peninsula

antibiotic drug.

peninsula NOUN a piece of land almost surrounded by water.
peninsular ADJ

penis NOUN the male organ used for urinating and having sex.

penitent ADJ feeling or showing regret for having done wrong. NOUN a penitent person.
penitence NOUN
penitential ADJ

pennant NOUN a long tapering flag.

penniless ADJ having no money.

penny NOUN (PL **pennies** for separate coins, **pence** for a sum of money) a British bronze coin worth one hundredth of £1; a former coin worth one twelfth of a shilling.
penny-pinching stingy or mean.

pension NOUN an income paid by the state, an ex-employer, or a private fund to a person who is retired, disabled, etc. VERB (**pension off**) dismiss with a pension.
pensioner NOUN

pensive ADJ deep in thought.

pentagon NOUN a geometric figure with five sides.

pentagram NOUN a five-pointed star.

pentathlon NOUN an athletic event involving five activities.

Pentecost NOUN Whit Sunday.

penthouse NOUN a flat on the top floor of a tall building.

penultimate ADJ last but one.

penumbra NOUN the partially shaded outer part of a shadow.

penury NOUN poverty.
penurious ADJ

people PLURAL NOUN **1** human beings; all those living in a country or society. **2** (PL **peoples**) the members of a nation or ethnic group. VERB populate or fill with people.

pep [inf] NOUN liveliness. VERB (**pepped, pepping**) (**pep up**) make livelier.
pep talk a talk intended to encourage confidence and effort.

pepper NOUN **1** a hot-tasting seasoning powder made from peppercorns.

2 a capsicum. VERB sprinkle with pepper; scatter on or over; hit repeatedly with small missiles.
peppery ADJ
peppercorn NOUN a dried black berry from which pepper is made.
peppermint NOUN a plant producing a strong fragrant oil; a sweet flavoured with this.
peptic ADJ of digestion.
per PREP **1** for each. **2** in accordance with.
perambulate VERB [formal] walk through or round.
per annum ADV for each year.
per capita ADV & ADJ for each person.
perceive VERB become aware of; see, hear, etc.; regard in a particular way.
per cent ADV in or for every hundred.
percentage NOUN a rate or proportion per hundred; a proportion or part.
perceptible ADJ able to be perceived.
perceptibly ADV
perception NOUN perceiving; the ability to perceive.
perceptive ADJ showing insight and understanding.
perch¹ NOUN a branch or bar on which a bird rests or roosts; a high seat. VERB sit or rest somewhere; balance something on a narrow support.
perch² NOUN (PL **perch**) an edible freshwater fish.
percolate VERB filter, especially through small holes; prepare in a percolator.
percolator NOUN a coffee-making pot in which boiling water is circulated through ground coffee in a perforated drum.
percussion NOUN instruments played by being struck or shaken.
peregrinations PLURAL NOUN [old use] travels.
peregrine NOUN a falcon.
peremptory ADJ imperious; insisting on obedience.
perennial ADJ lasting a long or infinite time; (of plants) living for several years. NOUN a perennial plant.
perennially ADV
perestroika NOUN (in the former USSR) reform of the economic and political system.

perfect ADJ **1** without faults or defects. **2** complete or total: *a perfect stranger.* VERB make perfect.
perfection NOUN
perfectly ADV
perfectionist NOUN a person who seeks perfection.
perfidious ADJ treacherous or disloyal.
perfidy NOUN
perforate VERB pierce and make holes in.
perforation NOUN
perform VERB **1** carry out a task etc.; function. **2** entertain an audience by acting, singing, etc.
performance NOUN
performer NOUN
perfume NOUN a sweet smell; a fragrant liquid for applying to the body. VERB give a sweet smell to.
perfunctory ADJ done without thought, effort, or enthusiasm.
pergola NOUN an arched structure covered in climbing plants.
perhaps ADV possibly.
peril NOUN serious danger.
perilous ADJ
perimeter NOUN the boundary or outer edge of an area.

period NOUN **1** a length or portion of time; a lesson in a school **2** an occurrence of menstruation. **3** a full stop. ADJ (of dress or furniture) belonging to a past age.
periodic ADJ happening at intervals.
periodical ADJ periodic. NOUN a magazine etc. published at regular intervals.
periodically ADV
peripatetic ADJ going from place to place.
peripheral ADJ of or on the periphery; of minor importance.
periphery NOUN (PL **-ies**) the outer limits of an area; the fringes of a subject.
periscope NOUN a tube attached to a set of mirrors, enabling you to see things above them and otherwise out of sight.
perish VERB die or be destroyed; (of food, rubber, etc.) rot.
be perished [inf] feel very cold.
perishable ADJ liable to

decay or go bad in a short time.

peritoneum NOUN (PL -neums or -nea) the membrane lining the abdominal cavity.

peritonitis NOUN inflammation of the peritoneum.

perjure VERB (**perjure yourself**) lie under oath.

perjury NOUN the crime of lying under oath.

perk NOUN [inf] a benefit to which an employee is entitled. VERB (**perk up**) make or become more cheerful or lively.

perky ADJ (-ier, -iest) lively and cheerful.

perm NOUN a treatment giving hair a long-lasting artificial wave. VERB treat hair with a perm.

permafrost NOUN permanently frozen subsoil in arctic regions.

permanent ADJ lasting indefinitely.
permanence NOUN

permeable ADJ allowing liquid or gases to pass through.

permeate VERB spread throughout.

permissible ADJ allowable.

permission NOUN consent or authorization.

permissive ADJ tolerant, especially in social and sexual matters.

permit VERB (**permitted, permitting**) allow to do something; make possible. NOUN an official document giving permission.

permutation NOUN each of several possible arrangements of a number of things.

pernicious ADJ harmful.

pernickety ADJ [inf] fussy or over-fastidious.

peroxide NOUN a chemical used as a bleach or disinfectant.

perpendicular ADJ at an angle of 90°to a line or surface. NOUN a perpendicular line.

perpetrate VERB carry out a bad or illegal action.
perpetrator NOUN

perpetual ADJ never ending or changing; very frequent.
perpetually ADV

perpetuate VERB cause to continue indefinitely.

perpetuity NOUN the state of lasting forever.

perplex VERB puzzle or

baffle.

perplexity NOUN

perquisite NOUN [formal] a special privilege or benefit.

per se ADV intrinsically.

persecute VERB treat badly over a long period; harass.

persecution NOUN

persecutor NOUN

persevere VERB continue in spite of difficulties.

perseverance NOUN

persist VERB continue to do something despite difficulty or opposition; continue to exist.

persistence NOUN

persistent ADJ

person NOUN (PL **people** or **persons**) 1 an individual human being. 2 a person's body. 3 [Grammar] one of the three classes of personal pronouns and verb forms, referring to the speaker, the person spoken to, or a third party.

persona NOUN (PL **-nas** or **-nae**) the aspect of someone's character that is presented to others.

personable ADJ attractive in appearance or manner.

personage NOUN a person of importance or high status.

personal ADJ 1 belonging to, affecting, or done by a particular person. 2 concerning a person's private life. 3 of a person's body.

personally ADV

personality NOUN (PL **-ies**) 1 a person's distinctive character; a person with distinctive qualities. 2 a celebrity.

personalize (or **-ise**) VERB 1 design to suit or identify as belonging to a particular individual. 2 cause a discussion etc. to be concerned with personalities rather than abstract topics.

personify VERB (**personified**, **personifying**) represent in human form or as having human characteristics; be an example of a particular quality etc.

personification NOUN

personnel NOUN employees or staff.

perspective NOUN 1 the art of drawing so as to give an effect of solidity and relative position. 2 a particular attitude

towards something;
understanding of the
relative importance of
things.

perspex NOUN [trademark] a
tough transparent plastic.

perspicacious ADJ
showing great insight.
perspicacity NOUN

perspire VERB sweat.
perspiration NOUN

persuade VERB use
reasoning or argument to
make someone believe or
do something.

persuasion NOUN
1 persuading. 2 a belief or
set of beliefs.

persuasive ADJ able to
persuade people.

pert ADJ attractively lively
or cheeky.

pertain VERB be relevant or
related.

pertinacious ADJ
persistent.
pertinacity NOUN

pertinent ADJ relevant.
pertinence NOUN

perturb VERB make
anxious or uneasy.

peruse VERB read carefully.
perusal NOUN

pervade VERB spread
throughout.
pervasive ADJ

perverse ADJ deliberately
behaving unreasonably or
unacceptably; contrary to
reason or expectation.
perversity NOUN

pervert VERB alter, distort,
or misapply; corrupt or
lead astray. NOUN a person
whose sexual behaviour is
abnormal and
unacceptable.
perversion NOUN

pervious ADJ permeable;
penetrable.

pessimism NOUN a
tendency to take a
gloomy view of things.
pessimist NOUN
pessimistic ADJ

pest NOUN an insect or
animal harmful to crops,
stored food, etc.; [inf] an
annoying person or
thing.

pester VERB annoy
continually, especially
with requests or
questions.

pesticide NOUN a
substance used to destroy
harmful insects etc.

pestilence NOUN a deadly
epidemic disease.

pestle NOUN a club-shaped
instrument for grinding
things to powder.

pesto NOUN a sauce of basil,
olive oil, Parmesan

cheese, and pine nuts.

pet NOUN **1** a tame animal kept for company and pleasure. **2** a favourite. ADJ favourite. VERB (**petted, petting**) stroke or pat; kiss and caress.

petal NOUN one of the coloured outer parts of a flower head.

peter VERB (**peter out**) gradually come to an end.

petite ADJ small and dainty.

petition NOUN a formal written request signed by many people. VERB present a petition to.

petrel NOUN a seabird.

petrify VERB (**petrified, petrifying**) **1** change into a stony mass. **2** paralyse with fear.

petrochemical NOUN a chemical obtained from petroleum or natural gas.

petrol NOUN a liquid made from petroleum, used as fuel in motor vehicles.

petroleum NOUN an oil that is refined to produce fuels such as petrol, paraffin, etc.

petticoat NOUN a woman's undergarment in the form of a dress or skirt.

pettifogging ADJ petty or trivial.

petty ADJ (**-ier, -iest**) of little importance; unnecessarily critical of details.

petty cash money kept by an office etc. for spending on small items.

pettiness NOUN

petulant ADJ sulky or irritable.

petulance NOUN

petunia NOUN a plant with white, purple, or red flowers.

pew NOUN a long bench-like seat in a church.

pewter NOUN a grey alloy of tin with lead or other metal.

pH NOUN a measure of acidity or alkalinity.

phallus NOUN (PL **-luses** or **-li**) a penis.

phallic ADJ

phantom NOUN a ghost.

pharaoh NOUN a ruler in ancient Egypt.

pharmaceutical ADJ of medicinal drugs.

pharmacist NOUN a person skilled in pharmacy.

pharmacology NOUN the study of the action of drugs.

pharmacy NOUN (PL **-ies**) a

place where medicinal drugs are prepared or sold; the preparation and dispensing of these drugs.

pharynx NOUN the cavity at the back of the nose and throat.

phase NOUN a distinct period in a process of change or development. VERB 1 carry something out in stages. 2 (**phase in** or **out**) bring gradually into or out of use.

PhD ABBREV Doctor of Philosophy.

pheasant NOUN a large, long-tailed game bird.

phenomenal ADJ extraordinary. **phenomenally** ADV

phenomenon NOUN (PL **-mena**) 1 a fact or situation that is known to exist or happen. 2 a remarkable person or thing.

pheromone NOUN a chemical substance released by an animal and causing a response in others of its species.

phial NOUN a small bottle.

philander VERB (of a man) engage in many casual love affairs. **philanderer** NOUN

philanthropy NOUN the practice of helping people in need. **philanthropic** ADJ **philanthropist** NOUN

philately NOUN stamp collecting. **philatelist** NOUN

philistine NOUN an uncultured person.

philosophical ADJ 1 of philosophy. 2 bearing misfortune calmly. **philosophically** ADV

philosophy NOUN (PL **-ies**) the study of the fundamental nature of knowledge, reality, and existence; a set or system of beliefs. **philosopher** NOUN

phlegm NOUN mucus in the nose and throat.

phlegmatic ADJ not excitable or emotional.

phobia NOUN an extreme or irrational fear or dislike. **phobic** ADJ & NOUN

phoenix NOUN a mythical bird said to have burned itself on a pyre and been born again from its ashes.

phone NOUN a telephone. VERB make a telephone call.

phonecard NOUN a card which can be used instead

of cash in some public telephones.

phonetic ADJ of or representing speech sounds. NOUN (**phonetics**) the study of speech sounds.
phonetically ADV

phoney (or **phony**) [inf] ADJ not genuine. NOUN a phoney person or thing.

phosphate NOUN a compound of phosphorous.

phosphorescent ADJ luminous.
phosphorescence NOUN

phosphorus NOUN a non-metallic element which glows in the dark.

photo NOUN (PL **-os**) a photograph.
photo finish a finish of a race so close that the winner has to be decided from a photograph.

photocopy NOUN (PL **-ies**) a photographic copy of a document. VERB make a photocopy of.
photocopier NOUN

photofit NOUN a picture of a person made up of separate photographs of other people's features.

photogenic ADJ looking attractive in photographs.

photograph NOUN a picture made with a camera. VERB take a photograph of.
photographer NOUN
photographic ADJ
photography NOUN

photosensitive ADJ reacting to light.

photostat NOUN [trademark] a photocopier; a photocopy.

photosynthesis NOUN the process by which green plants use sunlight to convert carbon dioxide and water into nutrients.
photosynthesize (or **-ise**) VERB

phrase NOUN a group of words forming a unit; a unit in a melody. VERB express in words.
phrasal ADJ

phraseology NOUN (PL **-ies**) a form of words used to express something.

physical ADJ **1** of the body; of things perceived by the senses. **2** of physics; of natural forces and laws.
physically ADV

physician NOUN a person qualified to practise medicine.

physics NOUN the study of the nature and properties

of matter and energy.
physicist NOUN
physiognomy NOUN (PL -ies) the features of a person's face.
physiology NOUN the study of the bodily functions of living organisms.
physiological ADJ
physiologist NOUN
physiotherapy NOUN treatment of an injury etc. by massage and exercise.
physiotherapist NOUN
physique NOUN the shape and size of a person's body.
pi NOUN a Greek letter (π) used as a symbol for the ratio of a circle's circumference to its diameter.
pianissimo ADV [Music] very softly.
piano NOUN (PL -os) a musical instrument with strings struck by hammers operated by a keyboard. ADV [Music] softly.
pianist NOUN
pianoforte NOUN [formal] a piano.
piazza NOUN a public square or marketplace.

picador NOUN a mounted bullfighter with a lance.
picaresque ADJ (of fiction) recounting the adventures of a roguish hero.
piccalilli NOUN a pickle of chopped vegetables and hot spices.
piccolo NOUN (PL -os) a small flute.
pick VERB 1 take hold of and remove from its place. 2 select. 3 pull at something repeatedly with the fingers. NOUN 1 an act of selecting; [inf] the best of a group. 2 a pickaxe. 3 a plectrum.
pick on single out for unfair treatment. **pick up** 1 lift. 2 go to collect. 3 improve or increase. 4 casually become acquainted with.
pickaxe NOUN a tool with a pointed iron bar at right angles to its handle, for breaking ground etc.
picket NOUN 1 people stationed outside a workplace to dissuade others from entering during a strike. 2 a pointed stake set in the ground. VERB (**picketed**, **picketing**) 1 form a picket

outside a workplace.

pickings PLURAL NOUN profits or gains.

pickle NOUN **1** vegetables preserved in vinegar or brine. **2** [inf] a difficult situation. VERB preserve in vinegar or brine.

pickpocket NOUN a thief who steals from people's pockets.

pickup NOUN **1** a small van with low sides. **2** an act of picking up a person or goods. **3** a device producing an electrical signal in response to a change, e.g. the stylus holder on a record player.

picnic NOUN an informal outdoor meal. VERB (**picnicked, picnicking**) have a picnic.

picnicker NOUN

pictograph NOUN a pictorial symbol used as a form of writing.

pictorial ADJ of or expressed in pictures.

picture NOUN a painting, drawing, or photograph; a mental image; (**the pictures**) the cinema. VERB represent in a picture; imagine.

picturesque ADJ attractive in a quaint or charming way.

pidgin NOUN a simplified form of a language with elements taken from local language.

pie NOUN a baked dish of ingredients encased in or topped with pastry.

pie chart a diagram representing quantities as sectors of a circle.

piebald ADJ (of a horse) having irregular patches of white and black.

piece NOUN **1** a portion or part; an item in a set. **2** a musical, literary, or artistic work. **3** a small object used in board games.

piece together assemble from individual parts.

piecemeal ADJ & ADV done in stages over a period of time.

piecework NOUN work paid according to the quantity done.

pied ADJ having two or more different colours.

pied-à-terre NOUN (PL **pieds-à-terre**) a small house for occasional use.

pier NOUN **1** a structure built out into the sea, used as a landing stage or a promenade. **2** a pillar supporting an arch or bridge.

pierce VERB make a hole in something with a sharp object; force or cut a way through.

piercing ADJ very sharp, cold, or high-pitched.

piety NOUN being religious or reverent.

pig NOUN 1 an animal with a short, curly tail and a flat snout. 2 [inf] a greedy or unpleasant person.

pig-headed obstinate.

piglet NOUN

pigeon NOUN a bird of the dove family.

pigeonhole NOUN a small compartment where mail can be left for someone; a category in which someone or something is put. VERB put into a particular category.

piggy ADJ like a pig.

piggy bank a money box shaped like a pig.

piggyback NOUN a ride on a person's back.

pigment NOUN colouring matter.

pigmy see **pygmy**.

pigsty NOUN (PL **-ies**) a covered pen for pigs.

pigtail NOUN long hair worn in a plait at the back of the head.

pike NOUN 1 a spear with a long wooden shaft. 2 a large voracious freshwater fish.

pilaster NOUN a rectangular column.

pilchard NOUN a small sea fish.

pile NOUN 1 a number of things lying one on top of another; [inf] a large amount. 2 a large, imposing building. 3 a heavy beam driven into the ground to support foundations. 4 the surface of a carpet or fabric with many small projecting threads. 5 (**piles**) haemorrhoids. VERB 1 lay things on top of one another. 2 get into or out of a vehicle in a disorganized group. 3 (**pile up**) accumulate.

pile-up a collision of several vehicles.

pilfer VERB steal small items of little value.

pilgrim NOUN a person who travels to a sacred place for religious reasons.

pilgrimage NOUN

pill NOUN a small piece of solid medicine for swallowing whole; (**the**

pill) a contraceptive pill.

pillage NOUN & VERB plunder.

pillar NOUN a vertical structure used as a support for a building. **pillar box** a postbox.

pillbox NOUN 1 a small round hat. 2 a small concrete fort.

pillion NOUN a passenger seat behind a motorcyclist.

pillory NOUN (PL -ies) [historical] a wooden frame with holes for the head and hands, in which offenders were locked as a punishment. VERB (**pilloried, pillorying**) ridicule publicly.

pillow NOUN a cushion for supporting the head in bed.

pilot NOUN 1 a person who flies an aircraft; a person qualified to steer ships into or out of a harbour. 2 something done or produced as a test or experiment. VERB (**piloted, piloting**) 1 act as pilot of an aircraft or ship. 2 test a project etc. **pilot light** a small burning jet of gas, used to fire a boiler.

pimiento NOUN a sweet pepper.

pimp NOUN a man who finds clients for a prostitute or brothel.

pimple NOUN a small inflamed spot on the skin. **pimply** ADJ

PIN ABBREV personal identification number.

pin NOUN 1 a thin pointed piece of metal with a round head, used for fastening things together. 2 a peg or stake of wood or metal. VERB (**pinned, pinning**) 1 fasten or attach with pins; hold someone so that they are unable to move. 2 (**pin down**) force to be definite about plans etc. **pins and needles** a tingling sensation. **pin-up** a poster of an attractive person.

pinafore NOUN 1 an apron. 2 a sleeveless dress worn over a blouse or jumper.

pinball NOUN a game in which balls are propelled across a sloping board to strike targets.

pince-nez NOUN a pair of glasses that clip on to the nose.

pincers PLURAL NOUN a tool

for gripping and pulling things; a claw of a lobster etc.

pinch VERB 1 squeeze tightly between your finger and thumb. 2 [inf] steal. NOUN 1 an act of pinching. 2 a small amount.

pine[1] NOUN an evergreen tree with needle-shaped leaves.

pine[2] VERB become weak; miss someone intensely.

pineapple NOUN a large juicy tropical fruit.

ping NOUN & VERB (make) a short sharp ringing sound.

ping-pong table tennis.

pinion NOUN 1 a bird's wing. 2 a small cogwheel. VERB tie or hold someone's arms or legs.

pink ADJ pale red. NOUN 1 a pink colour. 2 a garden plant with fragrant flowers. 3 (**the pink**) [inf] the best condition. VERB cut a zigzag edge on fabric.

pinnacle NOUN a high pointed rock; a small ornamental turret; the most successful moment.

pinpoint VERB locate precisely.

pinstripe NOUN a very narrow stripe in cloth fabric.

pint NOUN a measure for liquids, one-eighth of a gallon (0.568 litre).

pioneer NOUN a person who is one of the first to explore a new region or subject. VERB be the first to explore, use, or develop.

pious ADJ devoutly religious; making a hypocritical display of virtue.

pip NOUN 1 a small seed in fruit. 2 a short high-pitched sound. VERB (**pipped, pipping**) [inf] narrowly defeat.

pipe NOUN 1 a tube through which something can flow. 2 a wind instrument; (**pipes**) bagpipes. 3 a narrow tube with a bowl at one end for smoking tobacco. VERB 1 convey liquid through a pipe. 2 play music on a pipe. 3 utter in a shrill voice. **pipe dream** an unrealistic hope or scheme. **piping hot** very hot.

pipeline NOUN a long pipe for conveying petroleum etc. over a distance.

pipette NOUN a thin tube

for transferring or measuring small amounts of liquid.

piquant ADJ pleasantly sharp in taste or smell. **piquancy** NOUN

pique NOUN a feeling of hurt pride. VERB **1** hurt the pride of. **2** stimulate curiosity etc.

piranha NOUN a fierce tropical freshwater fish.

pirate NOUN a person who attacks and robs ships at sea. VERB reproduce a book, video, etc. without authorization. **piracy** NOUN

pirouette VERB & NOUN (perform) a spin on one leg in ballet.

pistachio NOUN (PL **-os**) a type of nut.

piste NOUN a ski run.

pistil NOUN the seed-producing part of a flower.

pistol NOUN a small gun.

piston NOUN a sliding disc or cylinder inside a tube, especially as part of an engine or pump.

pit NOUN **1** a hole in the ground; a coal mine; a sunken area. **2** a place where racing cars are refuelled etc. during a race. **3** the stone of a fruit. VERB (**pitted, pitting**) **1** make pits or hollows in. **2** set against in competition. **3** remove stones from olives etc.

pitch NOUN **1** an area of ground marked out for an outside game. **2** the degree of highness or lowness of a sound; the level of intensity of something. **3** the steepness of a slope. **4** a form of words used when trying to sell something. **5** a place where a street trader or performer is stationed. **6** a dark tarry substance. VERB **1** throw. **2** set up a tent. **3** set your voice, a piece of music, etc. at a particular pitch; aim at a particular market, level of understanding, etc. **4** (of a ship) plunge forward and back alternately. **5** make a roof slope at a particular angle.

pitch-black (or **pitch-dark**) completely dark.

pitched battle a battle whose time and place are decided beforehand.

pitcher NOUN a large jug.

pitchfork NOUN a long-handled fork for lifting

and tossing hay.

piteous ADJ deserving or arousing pity.

pitfall NOUN an unsuspected danger or difficulty.

pith NOUN **1** spongy tissue in stems or fruits. **2** the essence of something.
pithy ADJ

pitiful ADJ **1** deserving or arousing pity. **2** very small or inadequate.
pitifully ADV

pitta NOUN a flat bread, hollow inside.

pittance NOUN a very small allowance or wage.

pituitary gland NOUN a gland at the base of the brain, influencing growth and development.

pity NOUN (PL **-ies**) a feeling of sorrow for another's suffering; a cause for regret. VERB (**pitied, pitying**) feel pity for.

pivot NOUN a central point or shaft on which a thing turns or swings. VERB (**pivoted, pivoting**) turn on a pivot.

pivotal ADJ vitally important.

pixel NOUN any of the minute illuminated areas making up the image on a VDU screen.

pixie NOUN a small supernatural being in fairy tales.

pizza NOUN a round, flat piece of dough baked with a savoury topping.

pizzeria NOUN a pizza restaurant.

pizzicato ADV plucking the strings of a violin etc. instead of using the bow.

placard NOUN a poster or similar notice.

placate VERB make less angry.
placatory ADJ

place NOUN **1** a particular position or location; a particular town, district, building, etc. **2** a chance to study on a course, belong to a team, etc.; a position in a sequence. VERB **1** put in a particular position or situation; find a home, job, etc. for. **2** identify or classify. **3** make an order for goods. **take place** occur.

placebo NOUN (PL **-os**) a substance prescribed for the patient's psychological benefit rather than for any physical effect.

placement NOUN putting

someone or something in a place or home; posting someone temporarily in a workplace for experience.

placenta NOUN (PL **-tae** or **-tas**) the organ in the womb that nourishes the fetus.

placid ADJ not easily upset. **placidity** NOUN

placket NOUN an opening in a garment for fastenings or access to a pocket.

plagiarize (or **-ise**) VERB copy another person's writings and present them as your own. **plagiarism** NOUN

plague NOUN **1** a deadly contagious disease. **2** an infestation. VERB cause continual trouble to; annoy or pester.

plaice NOUN an edible flatfish.

plaid NOUN fabric woven in a tartan or chequered design.

plain ADJ **1** simple or ordinary; not patterned. **2** easy to perceive or understand; frank or direct. **3** not beautiful or pretty. NOUN a large area of level country.

plain clothes ordinary clothes rather than uniform.

plainness NOUN

plaintiff NOUN a person bringing an action in a court of law.

plaintive ADJ sounding sad.

plait NOUN a length of hair or rope made up of strands woven together. VERB form into a plait.

plan NOUN **1** an intention; a proposed means of achieving something. **2** a map or diagram. VERB (**planned, planning**) **1** intend; work out the details of an intended action. **2** draw a plan of. **planner** NOUN

plane NOUN **1** an aeroplane. **2** a level surface; a level of thought or development. **3** a tool for smoothing wood or metal by paring shavings from it. **4** a tall spreading tree with broad leaves. VERB smooth or pare a surface with a plane. ADJ level.

planet NOUN a large round mass in space orbiting round a star. **planetary** ADJ

planetarium NOUN (PL **-ria** or **-riums**) a room with a domed ceiling on which lights are projected to show the positions of the stars and planets.

plangent ADJ loud and melancholy.

plank NOUN a long flat piece of timber.

plankton NOUN minute life forms floating in the sea, rivers, etc.

plant NOUN 1 a living organism such as a tree, grass, etc., with neither the power of movement nor special organs of digestion. 2 a factory; its machinery. 3 someone placed in a group as an informer. VERB place in soil for growing; place in position.

plantain NOUN 1 a tropical banana-like fruit. 2 a herb.

plantation NOUN an estate on which cotton, tobacco, tea, etc. is cultivated; an area planted with trees.

plaque NOUN 1 a commemorative plate fixed on a wall. 2 a deposit that forms on teeth.

plasma NOUN 1 the colourless fluid part of blood. 2 a kind of gas.

plaster NOUN 1 a mixture of lime, sand, water, etc. used for coating walls. 2 a sticky strip of material for covering cuts. VERB cover with plaster; coat thickly.

plaster of Paris a white paste used for making moulds or casts.

plasterboard NOUN board with a core of plaster, for making partitions etc.

plastic NOUN a synthetic substance that can be moulded to a permanent shape. ADJ 1 made of plastic. 2 easily moulded.

plastic surgery surgery performed to reconstruct or repair parts of the body.

plasticity NOUN

plasticine NOUN [trademark] a soft modelling material.

plate NOUN 1 a flat dish for holding food. 2 articles of gold, silver, or other metal. 3 a flat thin sheet of metal, glass, etc. 4 an illustration on special paper in a book. VERB cover or coat with metal.

plate glass thick glass for windows etc.

plateau NOUN (PL **-teaux** or **-teaus**) 1 an area of level high ground. 2 a state of little change following rapid progress.

platelet NOUN a small disc in the blood, involved in clotting.

platen NOUN a plate in a printing press holding the paper against the type; the roller of a typewriter or printer.

platform NOUN a raised level surface or area on which people or things can stand; a raised structure beside a railway track at a station.

platinum NOUN a precious silvery-white metallic element.

platitude NOUN a commonplace remark. **platitudinous** ADJ

platonic ADJ involving affection but not sexual love.

platoon NOUN a subdivision of a military company.

platter NOUN a large flat serving dish.

platypus NOUN (PL -puses) an Australian animal with a duck-like beak, which lays eggs.

plaudits PLURAL NOUN praise; applause.

plausible ADJ seeming probable; persuasive but deceptive. **plausibility** NOUN **plausibly** ADV

play VERB 1 engage in activity for pleasure and relaxation; take part in a game or sport; compete against another team etc.; move a piece in a game. 2 act the part of. 3 perform on a musical instrument; cause a radio, recording, etc. to produce sound. 4 move or flicker over a surface. NOUN 1 activity for relaxation and enjoyment; playing in a sports match. 2 a dramatic work. 3 freedom of operation.

playing card each of a set of rectangular pieces of card used in games. **player** NOUN

playboy NOUN a rich pleasure-loving man.

playful ADJ full of fun; light-hearted. **playfully** ADV

playgroup NOUN a regular supervised play session for pre-school children.

playhouse NOUN a theatre.

playmate NOUN a child's companion in play.

playpen NOUN a portable enclosure for a young

child to play in.

playwright NOUN a person who writes plays.

plaza NOUN a public square.

plc (or **PLC**) ABBREV public limited company.

plea NOUN 1 an earnest or emotional request. 2 a defendant's answer to a charge in a law court.

plead VERB (**pleaded** [Scottish & US] **pled**, **pleading**) 1 put forward a case in a law court. 2 make an appeal or entreaty. 3 put forward as an excuse.

pleasant ADJ enjoyable; friendly and likeable.

pleasantry NOUN (PL -**ies**) a friendly or humorous remark.

please VERB 1 give pleasure to. 2 wish or desire. 3 (**please yourself**) do as you choose. ADV a polite word of request. **pleased** ADJ

pleasurable ADJ enjoyable. **pleasurably** ADV

pleasure NOUN a feeling of happy satisfaction and enjoyment; a source of this.

pleat NOUN a flat fold of cloth. VERB make pleats in.

plebeian ADJ of the lower social classes; uncultured or vulgar.

plebiscite NOUN a referendum.

plectrum NOUN (PL -**trums** or -**tra**) a small piece of plastic etc. for plucking the strings of a musical instrument.

pledge NOUN a solemn promise; something deposited as a guarantee that a debt will be paid etc.; a token of something. VERB commit by a promise; give as a pledge.

plenary ADJ entire; attended by all members.

plenipotentiary ADJ & NOUN (PL -**ies**) (an envoy) with full powers to take action.

plenitude NOUN abundance; completeness.

plenty PRON enough or more than enough. NOUN a situation where necessities are available in large quantities. **plenteous** ADJ **plentiful** ADJ

plethora NOUN an oversupply or excess.

pleurisy NOUN

inflammation of the membrane round the lungs.

pliable ADJ flexible; easily influenced.
pliability NOUN

pliant ADJ pliable.

pliers PLURAL NOUN pincers with flat surfaces for gripping things.

plight NOUN a predicament.

plimsoll NOUN a canvas sports shoe.

plinth NOUN a slab forming the base of a column or statue etc.

plod VERB (**plodded, plodding**) trudge; work slowly but steadily.

plonk [inf] NOUN cheap wine. VERB set down heavily or carelessly.

plop NOUN a sound like something small dropping into water with no splash.

plot NOUN 1 a secret plan to do something wrong or illegal. 2 the story in a play, novel, or film. 3 a small piece of land. VERB (**plotted, plotting**) 1 secretly plan a wrong or illegal action. 2 mark a route etc. on a map.
plotter NOUN

plough ([US] **plow**) NOUN an implement for turning over soil. VERB 1 turn over earth with a plough. 2 make your way laboriously.

ploy NOUN a cunning manoeuvre.

pluck VERB pull out or off; pick a flower etc.; strip a bird of its feathers. NOUN courage.
plucky ADJ

plug NOUN 1 a piece of solid material that tightly blocks a hole. 2 a device with metal pins that fit into holes in a socket to make an electrical connection. VERB (**plugged, plugging**) 1 block or fill with a plug. 2 (**plug in**) connect an appliance to an electric socket. 3 [inf] promote a product by mentioning it publicly.

plum NOUN 1 an oval fruit with a pointed stone. 2 reddish purple. ADJ [inf] highly desirable.

plumage NOUN a bird's feathers.

plumb NOUN a heavy weight hung on a cord (**plumb line**), used for testing depths or verticality. ADV exactly.

VERB **1** measure the depth of water; get to the bottom of. **2** install a bath, washing machine, etc.

plumber NOUN a person who fits and repairs plumbing.

plumbing NOUN a system of water and drainage pipes etc. in a building.

plume NOUN a long, soft feather; something resembling this.

plummet VERB (**plummeted, plummeting**) fall steeply or rapidly.

plump ADJ full or rounded in shape; rather fat. VERB **1** make more full or rounded. **2** (**plump for**) decide on.

plunder VERB rob. NOUN plundering; goods etc. stolen.

plunge VERB **1** jump or dive; fall suddenly; decrease rapidly. **2** push or go forcefully into something. NOUN an act of plunging.

plunger NOUN a long-handled suction cup used to unblock pipes.

pluperfect ADJ [Grammar] (of a tense) referring to action completed before some past point of time, e.g. *we had arrived*.

plural ADJ more than one in number; [Grammar] (of a word or form) referring to more than one. NOUN [Grammar] a plural word or form.

plurality NOUN

plus PREP with the addition of. ADJ **1** (before a number) above zero. **2** more than the amount indicated. NOUN **1** the sign (+). **2** an advantage.

plush NOUN cloth with a long soft nap. ADJ **1** made of plush. **2** [inf] luxurious.

plutocrat NOUN a wealthy, powerful person.

plutonium NOUN a radioactive metallic element used in nuclear weapons and reactors.

ply[1] NOUN (PL **plies**) a thickness or layer of wood, cloth, etc.

ply[2] VERB (**plied, plying**) **1** use a tool etc.; work at a trade. **2** (of a ship etc.) travel regularly over a route. **3** continually offer food etc. to.

plywood NOUN board consisting of layers of wood glued together.

p.m. ABBREV after noon

(short for Latin *post meridiem*).

pneumatic ADJ filled with or operated by compressed air.

pneumonia NOUN inflammation of the lungs.

poach VERB 1 cook by simmering in a small amount of liquid. 2 take game or fish illegally.

poacher NOUN

pocket NOUN 1 a small bag-like part on a garment; a pouch-like compartment. 2 an isolated group or area. ADJ small. VERB 1 put into your pocket. 2 take dishonestly.

pocket money money given regularly to children.

pock-marked ADJ marked by scars or pits.

pod NOUN a long narrow seed case.

podgy ADJ [inf] short and fat.

podium NOUN (PL **-diums** or **-dia**) a pedestal or platform.

poem NOUN a piece of imaginative writing in verse.

poet NOUN a person who writes poems.

poetic (or **poetical**) ADJ of or like poetry.

poetically ADV

poetry NOUN poems; a poet's work.

po-faced ADJ [inf] serious and disapproving.

pogrom NOUN an organized massacre.

poignant ADJ evoking sadness.

poignancy NOUN

point NOUN 1 a tapered, sharp end; a tip. 2 a particular place or moment. 3 an item, detail, or idea; (**the point**) the most important part. 4 the advantage or purpose of something. 5 a unit of scoring. 6 a dot or other punctuation mark. 7 a promontory. 8 an electrical socket. 9 a junction of two railway lines. VERB 1 direct attention by extending your finger; aim, indicate, or face in a particular direction. 2 fill in joints of brickwork with mortar. **beside the point** irrelevant. **point-blank** at very close range; blunt and direct. **point of view** a way of considering an issue.

pointed ADJ 1 tapering to a point. 2 (of a remark or look) expressing a clear message.

pointer NOUN a thing that points to something; a dog that faces stiffly towards game it has scented.

pointless ADJ having no purpose or meaning.

poise NOUN graceful bearing; self-assurance. VERB cause to be balanced.

poison NOUN a substance that can destroy life or harm health. VERB give poison to; put poison on or in; have a harmful effect on.

poisonous ADJ

poke VERB 1 prod with your finger, a stick, etc. 2 search or pry.

poker NOUN 1 a stiff metal rod for stirring up a fire. 2 a gambling card game.

poky ADJ (-ier, -iest) small and cramped.

polar ADJ 1 of or near the North or South Pole. 2 of magnetic or electrical poles. 3 (of opposites) extreme, absolute.

polar bear a white bear of Arctic regions.

polarize (or -ise) VERB 1 restrict the vibrations of a light wave to one direction. 2 give magnetic poles to. 3 set at opposite extremes of opinion.

Polaroid NOUN [trademark] 1 a material that polarizes light passing through it, used in sunglasses. 2 a camera that prints a photograph as soon as it is taken.

pole NOUN 1 a long rod or post. 2 the north (**North Pole**) or south (**South Pole**) end of the earth's axis. 3 one of the opposite ends of a magnet or terminals of an electric cell or battery.

polecat NOUN a small animal of the weasel family.

polemic NOUN a verbal attack on a belief or opinion.

polemical ADJ

police NOUN a civil force responsible for keeping public order. VERB keep order in a place by means of police.

police state a country where political police control citizens' activities.

policeman NOUN

policewoman NOUN

policy NOUN (PL **-ies**) **1** a general plan of action. **2** an insurance contract.

polio (or **poliomyelitis**) NOUN an infectious disease causing temporary or permanent paralysis.

polish VERB **1** make smooth and shiny by rubbing; refine or perfect. **2** (**polish off**) finish off. NOUN shininess; a substance used to polish something; practised ease and elegance.

polite ADJ having good manners; civilized or well bred.
politeness NOUN

politic ADJ showing good judgement.

political ADJ of the government and public affairs of a country; of or promoting a particular party.
political correctness avoidance of language or behaviour that may be considered discriminatory.
politically ADV

politician NOUN a person holding an elected government post.

politics NOUN the science and art of government; political affairs or life; political principles.

polka NOUN a lively dance for couples.

poll NOUN **1** the votes cast in an election. **2** an estimate of public opinion made by questioning people. VERB record the opinions or votes of; receive a specified number of votes.
poll tax [historical] a tax on each member of the population.

pollard VERB cut off the top and branches of a tree to encourage new growth.

pollen NOUN a fertilizing powder produced by flowers.

pollinate VERB fertilize with pollen.
pollination NOUN

pollster NOUN a person conducting an opinion poll.

pollute VERB make dirty or poisonous.
pollutant NOUN
pollution NOUN

polo NOUN a game like hockey played by teams on horseback.
polo neck a high turned-over collar on a sweater.

poltergeist NOUN a spirit believed to throw things

about noisily.

polyester NOUN a synthetic resin or fibre.

polygamy NOUN a system of having more than one wife or husband at a time. **polygamist** NOUN **polygamous** ADJ

polygon NOUN a geometric figure with many sides.

polygraph NOUN a lie-detecting machine.

polymath NOUN a person with knowledge of many subjects.

polymer NOUN a substance whose molecular structure is formed from many identical small molecules.

polyp NOUN 1 a simple organism with a tube-shaped body. 2 a small growth projecting from a mucous membrane.

polystyrene NOUN a light synthetic material.

polythene NOUN a tough light plastic.

polyunsaturated ADJ (of fat) not associated with the formation of cholesterol in the blood.

polyurethane NOUN a synthetic resin used in paint etc.

pomander NOUN a ball of mixed sweet-smelling substances.

pomegranate NOUN a tropical fruit with many seeds.

pommel NOUN a knob on the hilt of a sword; an upward projection on a saddle.

pomp NOUN the splendid clothes, customs, etc. that are part of a grand ceremony.

pompom NOUN a small woollen ball as a decoration on a hat.

pompous ADJ full of ostentatious dignity and self-importance. **pomposity** NOUN

poncho NOUN (PL -os) a cloak like a blanket with a hole for the head.

pond NOUN a small area of still water.

ponder VERB be deep in thought; think over.

ponderous ADJ heavy or unwieldy; laborious.

pong [inf] NOUN & VERB stink.

pontiff NOUN the Pope.

pontificate VERB speak pompously and at length.

pontoon NOUN 1 a flat-bottomed boat supporting a temporary bridge; such a bridge. 2 a card game.

pony NOUN (PL **-ies**) a small breed of horse.

ponytail NOUN long hair drawn back and tied to hang down.

poodle NOUN a dog with thick curly hair.

pooh-pooh VERB dismiss an idea scornfully.

pool NOUN 1 a small area of still water; a puddle; a swimming pool. 2 a shared fund or supply. 3 a game resembling snooker. 4 (**the pools**) football pools. VERB put into a common fund or supply; share.

poop NOUN a raised deck at the stern of a ship.

poor ADJ 1 having little money or means. 2 of a low quality or standard. 3 deserving sympathy.

poorly ADV badly. ADJ unwell.

pop NOUN 1 a small explosive sound. 2 a fizzy drink. 3 (also **pop music**) modern popular music appealing to young people. VERB (**popped**, **popping**) 1 make a sharp explosive sound; burst with this sound. 2 go or put something

somewhere quickly. ADJ of pop music; made easy for the general public to understand.

popcorn NOUN maize heated to burst and form puffy balls.

Pope NOUN the head of the Roman Catholic Church.

poplar NOUN a tall slender tree.

poplin NOUN a plain woven cotton fabric.

poppadom NOUN a round piece of savoury Indian bread fried until crisp.

poppy NOUN (PL **-ies**) a plant with bright flowers on tall stems.

poppycock NOUN [inf] nonsense.

populace NOUN the general public.

popular ADJ liked, enjoyed, or used by many people; of or for the general public.

popularity NOUN

popularize (or **-ise**) VERB 1 make generally liked. 2 present in an understandable non-technical form.

populate VERB fill with a population.

population NOUN the inhabitants of an area.

populous ADJ thickly populated.

porcelain NOUN fine china.

porch NOUN a roofed shelter over the entrance of a building.

porcupine NOUN an animal covered with protective spines.

pore NOUN a tiny opening on the skin or on a leaf. **pore over** study closely.

pork NOUN the flesh of a pig as food.

pornography NOUN writings or pictures intended to stimulate erotic feelings by portraying sexual activity. **pornographic** ADJ

porous ADJ letting through fluid or air.

porpoise NOUN a small whale.

porridge NOUN a food made by boiling oats or oatmeal in water or milk.

port NOUN 1 a harbour; a town with a harbour. 2 an opening for loading a ship, firing a gun from a tank or ship, etc.; a socket in a computer network into which a device can be plugged. 3 the left-hand side of a ship or aircraft. 4 strong sweet wine.

portable ADJ able to be carried.

portal NOUN a large and impressive doorway or gate.

portcullis NOUN a vertical grating lowered to block the gateway to a castle.

portend VERB foreshadow.

portent NOUN an omen. **portentous** ADJ

porter NOUN 1 a person employed to carry luggage or goods. 2 a doorkeeper of a large building.

portfolio NOUN (PL **-os**) 1 a case for loose sheets of paper. 2 a set of investments. 3 the position and duties of a government minister.

porthole NOUN a window in the side of a ship or aircraft.

portico NOUN (PL **-oes** or **-os**) a roof supported by columns forming a porch or similar structure.

portion NOUN a part or share; an amount of food for one person. VERB divide; distribute portions of.

portly ADJ rather fat.

portmanteau NOUN (PL **-teaus** or **-teaux**) a

travelling bag opening into two equal parts.

portrait NOUN a picture of a person or animal; a description.

portray VERB make a picture of; describe; represent in a play etc. **portrayal** NOUN

pose VERB **1** constitute or present a problem etc. **2** adopt or place in a particular position, especially to be painted, photographed, etc.; pretend to be someone or something. NOUN an attitude in which someone is posed; a pretence.

poser NOUN **1** a puzzling problem. **2** a poseur.

poseur NOUN a person who behaves affectedly.

posh ADJ [inf] very smart or luxurious.

posit VERB assume, especially as the basis of an argument.

position NOUN **1** a place where something is situated. **2** a way in which someone or something stands, is arranged, etc. **3** a situation or set of circumstances; a person's status; a job. **4** a point of view. VERB place or arrange.

positive ADJ **1** indicating agreement or support; hopeful or encouraging; (of the results of a test) showing the presence of something. **2** definite; convinced. **3** (of a battery terminal) through which electric current enters. **4** (of a quantity) greater than zero. NOUN a positive quality.

positive discrimination the policy of favouring members of groups which suffer discrimination when appointing to jobs etc.

positron NOUN a particle with a positive electric charge.

posse NOUN [inf] a group or gang; [historical] a body of law enforcers.

possess VERB **1** have or own. **2** dominate the mind of. **possessor** NOUN

possession NOUN owning; something owned.

possessive ADJ **1** jealously guarding your possessions; demanding someone's total attention. **2** [Grammar] indicating possession.

possible ADJ capable of existing, happening, being done, etc. **possibility** NOUN **possibly** ADV

possum NOUN [inf] an opossum.

post NOUN 1 the official conveyance of letters etc.; the letters etc. conveyed. 2 a piece of timber, metal, etc. set upright to support or mark something. 3 a place of duty; a job; an outpost of soldiers; a trading station. VERB 1 send letters etc. by post. 2 put up a notice. 3 send someone to take up employment in a particular place. **post office** a building where postal business is carried on.

post- PREFIX after.

postage NOUN a charge for sending something by post.

postal ADJ of the post; by post.

postbox NOUN a box into which letters are put for sending by post.

postcard NOUN a card for sending messages by post without an envelope.

postcode NOUN a group of letters and figures in a postal address to assist sorting.

post-date VERB put a date on a cheque etc. that is later than the actual date.

poster NOUN a large picture or notice used for decoration or as an advertisement.

posterior ADJ near or at the back. NOUN the buttocks.

posterity NOUN future generations.

postgraduate NOUN a student studying for a higher degree.

post-haste ADV with great speed.

posthumous ADJ happening, appearing, etc. after a person's death.

postman NOUN a person who delivers or collects letters etc.

postmark NOUN an official mark stamped on a letter etc., giving the date of posting. VERB mark with this.

postmaster (or **postmistress**) NOUN a person in charge of a post office.

post-mortem NOUN an

examination of a body to determine the cause of death; an analysis of something that has happened.

post-natal ADJ after childbirth.

postpone VERB cause an event to take place later than was originally planned.
postponement NOUN

postscript NOUN an additional paragraph at the end of a letter etc.

postulate VERB assume to be true as a basis for reasoning.

posture NOUN the way a person stands, walks, etc. VERB assume a posture, especially for effect.

posy NOUN (PL **-ies**) a small bunch of flowers.

pot NOUN **1** a rounded container used for storage or cooking. **2** [inf] cannabis. VERB (**potted, potting**) **1** plant in a flowerpot. **2** preserve food in a pot. **3** (in billiards or snooker) send a ball into a pocket.
pot belly a large protuberant belly. **pot luck** whatever is available.

potassium NOUN a soft silvery-white metallic element.

potato NOUN (PL **-oes**) a vegetable with starchy white flesh that grows underground as a tuber.

potent ADJ very powerful.
potency NOUN

potentate NOUN a monarch or ruler.

potential ADJ capable of being developed or used. NOUN an ability or capacity for development.
potentiality NOUN
potentially ADV

pothole NOUN a deep underground cave; a hole in a road surface.

potholing NOUN exploring potholes as a pastime.
potholer NOUN

potion NOUN a liquid medicine or drug.

pot-pourri NOUN a scented mixture of dried petals and spices.

potshot NOUN a shot aimed casually.

potted ADJ **1** preserved in a pot. **2** abridged.

potter[1] NOUN a maker of pottery.

potter[2] VERB work on trivial tasks in a leisurely way.

pottery NOUN (PL **-ies**)

articles made of baked clay; a potter's work or workshop.

potty [inf] ADJ **1** mad or stupid. **2** enthusiastic. NOUN (PL **-ies**) a bowl used as a toilet by a young child.

pouch NOUN a small bag or bag-like formation.

pouffe NOUN a padded stool.

poultice NOUN a moist dressing used to reduce inflammation.

poultry NOUN domestic fowls.

pounce VERB swoop down and grasp or attack. NOUN an act of pouncing.

pound¹ NOUN **1** a measure of weight, 16 oz. avoirdupois (0.454 kg) or 12 oz. troy (0.373 kg). **2** a unit of money in Britain and certain other countries.

pound² NOUN an enclosure where stray animals, or illegally parked vehicles, are kept until claimed.

pound³ VERB beat or crush with repeated heavy strokes; (of the heart) beat loudly; run heavily.

pour VERB (cause to) flow; rain heavily; come, go, or send in large quantities.

pout VERB push out your lips. NOUN a pouting expression.

poverty NOUN **1** lack of money and resources; scarcity. **2** inferiority.

powder NOUN a mass of fine dry particles; a medicine or cosmetic in this form. VERB cover or sprinkle with powder. **powdery** ADJ

power NOUN **1** the ability to do something. **2** vigour or strength. **3** control, influence, or authority; an influential person or country etc. **4** a product of a number multiplied by itself a given number of times. **5** mechanical or electrical energy; the electricity supply. VERB supply with mechanical or electrical power. **powerful** ADJ **powerless** ADJ

p.p. ABBREV used when signing a letter on someone else's behalf.

PR ABBREV **1** public relations. **2** proportional representation.

practicable ADJ able to be done. **practicability** NOUN

practical ADJ **1** involving activity rather than study or theory. **2** suitable for use rather than decorative; sensible in approaching problems, doing things, etc.

practical joke a trick played on someone to make them look foolish.

practicality NOUN

practically ADV **1** in a practical way. **2** almost.

practice NOUN **1** repeated exercise to improve skill. **2** action as opposed to theory. **3** a custom or habit. **4** a doctor's or lawyer's business.

practise ([US] **practice**) VERB **1** do something repeatedly or habitually. **2** be working in a particular profession.

practitioner NOUN a professional worker, especially in medicine.

pragmatic ADJ treating things from a practical point of view.

pragmatically ADV

prairie NOUN (in North America) a large treeless area of grassland.

praise VERB express approval or admiration of; express thanks to or respect for God. NOUN approval expressed in words.

praiseworthy ADJ

praline NOUN a sweet substance made by crushing sweetened nuts.

pram NOUN a four-wheeled conveyance for a baby.

prance VERB move springily.

prank NOUN a mischievous act.

prattle VERB chatter in a childish way. NOUN childish chatter.

prawn NOUN an edible shellfish like a large shrimp.

pray VERB say prayers; hope earnestly.

prayer NOUN a solemn request or thanksgiving to God or a god; an earnest hope.

pre- PREFIX before; beforehand.

preach VERB deliver a sermon; recommend a particular way of thinking or behaving; talk in an annoyingly moralizing way.

preacher NOUN

preamble NOUN an opening statement.

pre-arrange VERB arrange beforehand.

precarious ADJ not safe or

secure.

precaution NOUN something done to avoid problems or danger.
precautionary ADJ

precede VERB come or go before in time, order, etc.

precedence NOUN being more important than someone or something else.

precedent NOUN a previous case serving as an example to be followed.

precept NOUN a command or rule of conduct.

precinct NOUN 1 an enclosed area around a place or building. 2 an area closed to traffic in a town.

precious ADJ 1 of great value; beloved. 2 affectedly refined.

precipice NOUN a very steep face of a cliff or rock.

precipitate VERB 1 cause to happen suddenly or prematurely; cause to move suddenly and uncontrollably. 2 cause a substance to be deposited in solid form from a solution. ADJ rash, hasty. NOUN a substance

precipitated from a solution.

precipitation NOUN rain or snow.

precipitous ADJ very steep.

precis NOUN (PL **precis**) a summary. VERB summarize.

precise ADJ exact; accurate over details.
precisely ADV
precision NOUN

preclude VERB prevent from happening.

precocious ADJ having developed earlier than is usual.

preconceived ADJ (of an idea) formed beforehand.
preconception NOUN

precondition NOUN a condition that must be fulfilled beforehand.

precursor NOUN a forerunner.

predator NOUN an animal that hunts and kills others for food.
predatory ADJ

predecessor NOUN a person who held an office, job, etc. before the current holder.

predestination NOUN the doctrine that everything has been determined in advance.

predicament NOUN a difficult situation.

predicate NOUN [Grammar] the part of a sentence that says something about the subject (e.g. *is short* in *life is short*).

predict VERB foretell.
　prediction NOUN
　predictor NOUN

predilection NOUN a special liking.

predispose VERB make likely to do, be, or think something.
　predisposition NOUN

predominate VERB be most numerous or powerful; exert control.
　predominance NOUN
　predominant ADJ

pre-eminent ADJ better than all others.
　pre-eminence NOUN

pre-empt VERB take action to prevent an occurrence; forestall someone.
　pre-emptive ADJ

preen VERB (of a bird) smooth its feathers with its beak.

prefabricated ADJ (of a building) made in sections that can be assembled on site.

preface NOUN an introductory statement. VERB **1** introduce with a preface. **2** lead up to an event.

prefect NOUN **1** a senior school pupil with some authority over younger pupils. **2** an administrative official in certain countries.

prefer VERB (**preferred, preferring**) like one person or thing better than another.
　preferable ADJ
　preferably ADV

preference NOUN preferring; something preferred; favour shown to one person over others.

preferential ADJ favouring a particular person or group.
　preferentially ADV

preferment NOUN promotion.

prefix NOUN a word or syllable placed at the beginning of a word to change its meaning.

pregnant ADJ **1** having a child or young developing in the womb. **2** full of meaning.
　pregnancy NOUN

prehensile ADJ (of an animal's tail) able to grasp

things.

prehistoric ADJ of the period before written records were made.

prehistorically ADV

prejudge VERB form a judgement on before knowing all the facts.

prejudice NOUN a preconceived and irrational opinion; hostility and injustice based on this. VERB 1 cause to have a prejudice. 2 cause harm to.

prejudicial ADJ harmful to rights or interests.

prelate NOUN a clergyman of high rank.

preliminary ADJ preceding a main action or event. NOUN (PL **-ies**) a preliminary action or event.

prelude NOUN an action or event leading up to another; an introductory part or piece of music.

premarital ADJ before marriage.

premature ADJ coming or done before the usual or proper time.

premeditated ADJ planned beforehand.

premenstrual ADJ occurring before a

menstrual period.

premier ADJ first in importance, order, or time. NOUN a prime minister or other head of government.

premiere NOUN the first public performance of a play etc.

premise (or **premiss**) NOUN a statement on which reasoning is based.

premises PLURAL NOUN a house or other building and its grounds.

premium NOUN 1 an amount to be paid for an insurance policy. 2 a sum added to a usual price or charge.

at a premium 1 above the usual price. 2 scarce and in demand.

premonition NOUN a feeling that something will happen.

preoccupation NOUN being preoccupied; something that preoccupies someone.

preoccupy VERB completely fill someone's thoughts.

preparation NOUN preparing; something done to make ready; a substance prepared for

use.
preparatory ADJ
preparing for something.
preparatory school a
private school for pupils
between seven and
thirteen.
prepare VERB make ready
for use; get ready to do or
deal with something.
prepared to willing to.
preponderate VERB be
greater in number, power,
etc.
preponderance NOUN
preponderant ADJ
preposition NOUN a word
used with a noun or
pronoun to show place,
time, or method, e.g.
'*after* dinner' or 'we went
by train'.
prepossessing ADJ
attractive.
preposterous ADJ utterly
absurd or outrageous.
prerequisite NOUN
something that is
required before
something else can
happen.
prerogative NOUN a right
or privilege.
presage VERB be an omen
of. NOUN an omen.
Presbyterian ADJ & NOUN
(a member) of a Church

governed by elders of
equal rank.
prescient ADJ having
knowledge of events
before they happen.
prescience NOUN
prescribe VERB 1 advise
the use of a medicine etc.
2 state officially that
something should be
done.
prescription NOUN
prescribing; a doctor's
written instructions for
the preparation and use
of a medicine.
prescriptive ADJ stating
what should be done.
presence NOUN being
present; a person or thing
that is present without
being seen; an impressive
manner or bearing.
presence of mind ability
to act sensibly in a crisis.
present[1] ADJ 1 being in
the place in question.
2 existing or being dealt
with now. NOUN the time
occurring now.
present[2] NOUN a gift. VERB
1 formally give something
to someone; cause trouble
or difficulty. 2 introduce a
broadcast; represent in a
particular way.
present itself become

apparent.

presentation NOUN

presenter NOUN

presentable ADJ clean or smart enough to be seen in public.

presentiment NOUN a foreboding.

presently ADV **1** soon. **2** now.

preservative NOUN a substance that preserves perishable food.

preserve VERB keep safe, unchanged, or in existence; treat food to prevent it decaying. NOUN **1** interests etc. regarded as one person's domain. **2** (also **preserves**) jam. **preservation** NOUN

preside VERB be in authority or control.

president NOUN the head of an organization; the head of a republic. **presidency** NOUN **presidential** ADJ

press VERB **1** (cause to) move into contact with something by applying force; push downwards or inwards; squeeze or flatten; iron clothes. **2** urge; try hard to persuade or influence; insist on a point. **3** move in a specified direction by pushing. **4** (**press on**) continue with what you are doing. **5** bring into use as a makeshift. NOUN **1** a device for flattening or squeezing. **2** a machine for printing. **3** (**the press**) newspapers or journalists as a whole.

press conference an interview given to a number of journalists.

press-gang force to do something. **press stud** a small fastener with two parts that are pressed together. **press-up** an exercise involving lying on the floor and pressing down with your hands to raise your body.

pressing ADJ urgent.

pressure NOUN **1** steady force applied to an object by something in contact with it. **2** influence or persuasion of an oppressive kind; stress. VERB pressurize a person.

pressure cooker a pan for cooking things quickly by steam under pressure.

pressure group an organized group seeking to exert influence by concerted action.

pressurize (or **-ise**) VERB
1 try to compel into an
action. **2** maintain
constant artificially raised
pressure in an aircraft
cabin etc.

prestige NOUN respect
resulting from good
reputation or
achievements.
prestigious ADJ

presto ADV [Music] very
quickly.

prestressed ADJ (of
concrete) strengthened by
wires within it.

presumably ADV it may be
presumed.

presume VERB **1** suppose to
be true. **2** be
presumptuous.
3 (**presume on**) take
advantage of someone's
kindness etc.
presumption NOUN

presumptuous ADJ
behaving too self-
confidently.

presuppose VERB require
as a precondition; assume
at the beginning of an
argument.
presupposition NOUN

pretence ([US] **pretense**)
NOUN **1** pretending. **2** a
claim to have or be
something.

pretend VERB **1** speak or
behave so as to make
something seem to be the
case when it is not.
2 claim to have a skill,
title, etc.
pretender NOUN

pretension NOUN **1** a claim
to have or be something.
2 pretentiousness.

pretentious ADJ trying to
appear more important,
intelligent, etc., than is
the case.

pretext NOUN a false reason
used to justify an action.

prettify VERB (**prettified**,
prettifying) try to make
something look pretty.

pretty ADJ (**-ier, -iest**)
attractive. ADV [inf] to a
moderate extent.
prettiness NOUN

pretzel NOUN a salty knot-
shaped biscuit.

prevail VERB **1** be stronger.
2 be widespread or
current. **3** (**prevail on**)
persuade.

prevalent ADJ widespread
or common.
prevalence NOUN

prevaricate VERB speak or
act evasively or
misleadingly.
prevarication NOUN

prevent VERB keep from

happening; make unable to do something.
prevention NOUN
preventive (or **preventative**) ADJ designed to prevent something.
previous ADJ coming before in time or order.
previously ADV
prey NOUN an animal hunted or killed by another for food; a victim. **bird of prey** a bird that kills and eats birds and mammals. **prey on 1** kill and eat. **2** distress or worry.
price NOUN the amount of money for which something is bought or sold; an unpleasant experience etc. that is necessary to achieve something. VERB decide the price of.
priceless ADJ invaluable.
prick VERB pierce slightly; feel a pain as from this. NOUN a mark, hole, or pain caused by pricking.
prickle NOUN a small thorn or spine; a tingling sensation. VERB have a tingling sensation.
prickly ADJ **1** having prickles. **2** easily offended.

pride NOUN **1** pleasure or satisfaction felt if you or people close to you have done something well; a source of this; self-respect. **2** a group of lions. **pride of place** the most prominent position. **pride yourself on** be proud of.
priest NOUN **1** a member of the clergy. **2** (also **priestess**) a person who performs ceremonies in a non-Christian religion.
priesthood NOUN
prig NOUN a self-righteous person.
priggish ADJ
prim ADJ very formal or proper and easily shocked or disgusted.
prima ballerina NOUN a chief ballerina.
primacy NOUN pre-eminence.
prima donna NOUN **1** the chief female singer in an opera. **2** a temperamental and self-important person.
prima facie ADJ & ADV accepted as correct until proved otherwise.
primal ADJ **1** primitive or primeval. **2** fundamental.
primary ADJ **1** first in time, order, or importance. **2** (of

primate

542

a school or education) for children below the age of 11. NOUN (PL **-ies**) (in the US) a preliminary election to choose delegates or candidates.

primary colour each of the colours blue, red, and yellow, from which all other colours can be obtained by mixing.

primarily ADV

primate NOUN **1** an animal belonging to the group that includes monkeys, apes, and humans. **2** an archbishop.

prime ADJ **1** most important. **2** excellent. NOUN a state or time of greatest strength, success, excellence, etc. VERB prepare for use or action; provide with information in preparation for something.

prime minister the head of a government. **prime number** a number that can be divided only by itself and one.

primer NOUN **1** a substance painted on a surface as a base coat. **2** an elementary textbook.

primeval ADJ of the earliest times of the

world.

primitive ADJ of or at an early stage of evolution or civilization; simple or crude.

primordial ADJ primeval.

primrose NOUN a pale yellow spring flower.

prince NOUN a son or other close male relative of a king or queen.

princely ADJ of or appropriate to a prince; (of a sum of money) generous.

princess NOUN a daughter or other close female relative of a king or queen; a prince's wife or widow.

principal ADJ first in rank or importance. NOUN **1** the most important person in an organization; the head of a school or college; a leading performer in a play, concert, etc. **2** a sum of money lent or invested, on which interest is paid.

principally ADV

principality NOUN (PL **-ies**) a country ruled by a prince.

principle NOUN a law, rule, or theory that something is based on; (**principles**) beliefs governing your actions and personal behaviour; a scientific law applying across a wide field.

in principle in theory. **on principle** because of your moral principles.

print VERB 1 produce a book etc. by a process involving the transfer of words or pictures to paper. 2 write words without joining the letters. 3 produce a photographic print from a negative. NOUN printed words in a book etc.; a mark where something has pressed a surface; a printed picture or design. **printer** NOUN

printout NOUN printed material produced from a computer printer.

prior ADJ coming before in time, order, or importance. NOUN (FEMININE **prioress**) a person next in rank below an abbot or abbess; a person who is head of a house of friars or nuns.

prioritize (or -ise) VERB treat as more important than other things; arrange in order of importance.

priority NOUN (PL -ies)

something regarded as more important than others; being treated as more important than others; the right to proceed before other traffic.

priory NOUN (PL -ies) a monastery or nunnery governed by a prior or prioress.

prise ([US] **prize**) VERB force something open or apart.

prism NOUN a solid geometric shape with ends that are equal and parallel; a transparent object of this shape that separates white light into colours. **prismatic** ADJ

prison NOUN a building where criminals are kept as a punishment. **prisoner** NOUN

prissy ADJ prim or prudish.

pristine ADJ in its original and unspoilt condition.

privacy NOUN being undisturbed or unobserved.

private ADJ 1 belonging to a particular person or group; confidential; secluded. 2 not provided or owned by the state; not holding public office. NOUN a soldier of the lowest rank.

privation NOUN shortage of food etc.; hardship.

privatize (or **-ise**) VERB transfer from state to private ownership. **privatization** NOUN

privet NOUN a bushy evergreen shrub.

privilege NOUN a special right granted to a person or group; a great honour. **privileged** ADJ

privy NOUN (PL **-ies**) an outside toilet. ADJ (**privy to**) sharing knowledge of a secret.

prize NOUN an award for victory or superiority; something that can be won. ADJ **1** winning a prize. **2** excellent. VERB **1** value highly. **2** US spelling of **prise**.

pro NOUN (PL **pros**) [inf] a professional. **pros and cons** arguments for and against something.

proactive ADJ gaining control by taking the initiative.

probable ADJ likely to happen or be true. **probability** NOUN

probably ADV

probate NOUN the official process of proving that a will is valid.

probation NOUN **1** a period of training and testing on starting a new job. **2** the supervision of an offender by an official as an alternative to imprisonment. **probationer** ADJ

probe NOUN a blunt surgical instrument used to examine the body; an investigation; an unmanned exploratory spacecraft. VERB examine with a probe; conduct an inquiry.

probity NOUN honesty.

problem NOUN something difficult to deal with or understand. **problematic** (or **problematical**) ADJ

proboscis NOUN **1** a mammal's long flexible snout. **2** the long thin mouthpart of some insects.

procedure NOUN a series of actions done to accomplish something, especially an established or official one. **procedural** ADJ

proceed VERB begin or continue a course of action; go on to do.

proceedings PLURAL NOUN an event or series of actions; a lawsuit.

proceeds PLURAL NOUN the profit from a sale, performance, etc.

process NOUN a series of actions to achieve an end; a natural series of events or changes. VERB **1** change or preserve something by a series of mechanical or chemical operations. **2** deal with according to an official procedure. **processor** NOUN

procession NOUN a number of people or vehicles going along in an orderly line.

proclaim VERB announce publicly. **proclamation** NOUN

proclivity NOUN (PL **-ies**) a tendency.

procrastinate VERB postpone action. **procrastination** NOUN

procreate VERB produce young. **procreation** NOUN

procurator fiscal NOUN (in Scotland) a public prosecutor and coroner.

procure VERB obtain. **procurement** NOUN

prod VERB (**prodded, prodding**) **1** poke. **2** stimulate to action. NOUN **1** a poke; a pointed object like a stick. **2** a stimulus.

prodigal ADJ wasteful or extravagant.

prodigious ADJ impressively large.

prodigy NOUN (PL **-ies**) a young person with exceptional abilities.

produce VERB **1** make or manufacture; make happen or exist. **2** present for inspection. **3** administer the staging, financing, etc. of a performance. NOUN things produced or grown. **producer** NOUN **production** NOUN

product NOUN **1** a thing produced. **2** an amount obtained by multiplying one number by another.

productive ADJ producing or achieving a great deal. **productivity** NOUN

profane ADJ **1** not sacred. **2** irreverent or blasphemous. VERB treat with a lack of respect. **profanity** NOUN

profess VERB **1** claim that

something is true.
2 declare your faith in a religion.

profession NOUN 1 a job requiring special training and formal qualifications; the people engaged in this. 2 a claim or declaration.

professional ADJ 1 belonging to a profession. 2 skilful and conscientious. 3 doing something for payment, not as a pastime. NOUN a professional person.

professionally ADV

professor NOUN a university teacher of the highest rank.

proffer VERB offer.

proficient ADJ competent; skilled.

proficiency NOUN

profile NOUN 1 a side view, especially of the face. 2 a short account of a person's character or career. 3 the extent to which someone attracts attention.

profit NOUN financial gain; an advantage or benefit. VERB (**profited, profiting**) make money; benefit someone.

profitable ADJ

profitability NOUN

profitably ADV

profiteering NOUN the making of a large profit in an unfair way.

profligate ADJ wasteful or extravagant; dissolute.

profound ADJ 1 very great. 2 showing or needing great insight.

profundity NOUN

profuse ADJ plentiful.

profusion NOUN

progenitor NOUN an ancestor.

progeny NOUN offspring.

progesterone NOUN a hormone that stimulates the uterus to prepare for pregnancy.

prognosis NOUN (PL -noses) a forecast, especially of the course of a disease.

programme ([US] **program**) NOUN 1 a planned series of future events or actions. 2 a sheet giving details about a play, concert, etc. 3 a radio or television broadcast. 4 (**program**) a series of software instructions for a computer. VERB (**programmed, programming**) 1 (**program**) provide a

computer with a program.
2 make or arrange in a
particular way or
according to a plan.

progress NOUN forward
movement; development.
VERB move forwards;
develop.

progression NOUN

progressive ADJ
1 favouring reform or new
ideas. 2 proceeding
gradually or in stages.

prohibit VERB (**prohibited**,
prohibiting) forbid.

prohibition NOUN

prohibitive ADJ 1 (of a
price) too high.
2 forbidding something.

project NOUN a plan or
undertaking; a piece of
work involving research.
VERB 1 estimate; plan.
2 stick out beyond
something else. 3 cause
light or an image to fall
on a surface or screen;
present yourself to others
in a particular way.

projectile NOUN a missile.

projection NOUN 1 an
estimate of future
situations based on a
study of present ones.
2 the projection of an
image etc. 3 something
sticking out from a

surface.

projector NOUN an
apparatus for projecting
images on to a screen.

prolapse NOUN a condition
in which an organ of the
body slips forward out of
place.

proletariat NOUN working-
class people.

proletarian ADJ & NOUN

proliferate VERB increase
or reproduce rapidly.

proliferation NOUN

prolific ADJ producing
things abundantly.

prolix ADJ (of speech or
writing) long and tedious.

prologue NOUN an
introduction to a play,
poem, etc.

prolong VERB lengthen in
extent or duration.

prolonged ADJ continuing
for a long time.

prom NOUN [inf] 1 a
promenade concert. 2 a
promenade.

promenade NOUN a paved
public walk, especially by
the sea.

promenade concert a
concert of classical music
at which part of the
audience stands.

prominent ADJ famous or
important; sticking out;

conspicuous.

prominence NOUN

promiscuous ADJ having sexual relations with many people.

promiscuity NOUN

promise NOUN a declaration that you will give or do something; signs of future excellence. VERB 1 make a promise. 2 give reason to expect.

promising ADJ likely to turn out well.

promontory NOUN (PL **-ies**) high land jutting out into the sea.

promote VERB 1 raise to a higher rank or office. 2 help the progress of; publicize in order to sell.

promoter NOUN

promotion NOUN

promotional ADJ

prompt ADJ done or acting without delay. VERB 1 cause to happen or do. 2 assist an actor by supplying forgotten words. ADV exactly or punctually.

promulgate VERB make widely known.

prone ADJ 1 lying face downwards. 2 likely to do or suffer something.

prong NOUN each of the pointed parts of a fork.

pronoun NOUN a word used instead of a noun to indicate someone or something already mentioned or known, e.g. *I, this, it.*

pronounce VERB 1 utter a sound or word distinctly or in a certain way. 2 declare or announce.

pronunciation NOUN

pronounced ADJ noticeable.

pronouncement NOUN a declaration.

proof NOUN 1 evidence that something is true or exists. 2 a copy of printed material for correction. ADJ resistant to: *draught-proof.*

proofread VERB read printed proofs and mark any errors.

proofreader NOUN

prop NOUN 1 a support to prevent something from falling, sagging, or failing. 2 [inf] a stage property. VERB (**propped, propping**) support with or as if with a prop.

propaganda NOUN information intended to persuade or convince people.

propagate VERB 1 grow a

new plant from a parent plant. **2** spread or transmit news etc.

propagation NOUN

propane NOUN a hydrocarbon fuel gas.

propel VERB (**propelled, propelling**) push forwards or onwards.

propellant NOUN & ADJ

propeller NOUN a revolving device with blades, for propelling a ship or aircraft.

propensity NOUN (PL -ies) a tendency or inclination.

proper ADJ **1** genuine; in its true form. **2** appropriate or correct.

proper name (or **proper noun**) the name of an individual person, place, or organization.

properly ADV

property NOUN (PL -ies) **1** something owned; a building and its land. **2** a movable object used in a play or film. **3** a quality or characteristic.

prophecy NOUN (PL -ies) a prediction of future events.

prophesy VERB (**prophesied, prophesying**) predict that something will happen.

prophet NOUN **1** a person who foretells events. **2** a religious teacher inspired by God.

prophetic ADJ

prophylactic ADJ intended to prevent disease.

propitiate VERB win or regain the favour of.

propitious ADJ favourable.

proponent NOUN a person putting forward a proposal.

proportion NOUN a part or share of a whole; a ratio; the correct relation in size or degree; (**proportions**) dimensions.

proportional (or **proportionate**) ADJ

proposal NOUN **1** the proposing of something; a plan or suggestion. **2** an offer of marriage.

propose VERB **1** put forward an idea etc. for consideration; nominate for a position. **2** make an offer of marriage to someone.

proposition NOUN **1** a statement or assertion. **2** a suggested plan. **3** a project considered in terms of the likelihood of success. VERB [inf] offer to have sex with someone.

propound VERB put forward an idea etc. for consideration.

proprietary ADJ (of a product) marketed under a registered trade name; of an owner or ownership.

proprietor NOUN the owner of a business. **proprietorial** ADJ

propriety NOUN correctness of behaviour.

propulsion NOUN the process of propelling or being propelled.

pro rata ADJ proportional. ADV proportionally.

prosaic ADJ ordinary and unimaginative. **prosaically** ADV

proscenium NOUN (PL -ums or -ia) the part of a theatre stage in front of the curtain.

proscribe VERB forbid.

prose NOUN ordinary written or spoken language.

prosecute VERB 1 take legal proceedings against someone for a crime. 2 continue a course of action. **prosecution** NOUN **prosecutor** NOUN

proselyte NOUN a recent convert to a religion.

prospect NOUN the likelihood of something's occurring; (**prospects**) chances of success. VERB explore in search of something. **prospector** NOUN

prospective ADJ expected or likely to happen.

prospectus NOUN (PL -tuses) a document giving details of a school, business, etc.

prosper VERB succeed or thrive.

prosperous ADJ financially successful. **prosperity** NOUN

prostate NOUN the gland round the neck of the bladder in male mammals.

prosthesis NOUN (PL -theses) an artificial body part.

prostitute NOUN a person who has sex for money. VERB put your talents to an unworthy use. **prostitution** NOUN

prostrate ADJ 1 face downwards; lying horizontally. 2 overcome or exhausted. VERB cause to be prostrate.

prostration NOUN

protagonist NOUN 1 the chief person in a drama, story, etc. 2 an important person in a real event.

protean ADJ variable; versatile.

protect VERB keep from harm or injury. **protection** NOUN **protector** NOUN

protectionism NOUN a policy of protecting home industries from competition by taxes etc.

protective ADJ giving protection.

protectorate NOUN a country that is controlled and protected by another.

protégé NOUN a person who is guided and supported by another.

protein NOUN an organic compound forming an essential part of humans' and animals' food.

protest NOUN a statement or action indicating disapproval. VERB 1 express disapproval. 2 declare firmly. **protestation** NOUN

Protestant NOUN a member of any of the western Christian Churches that are separate from the Roman Catholic Church.

protocol NOUN the system of rules governing formal occasions; accepted behaviour in a situation.

proton NOUN a subatomic particle with a positive electric charge.

prototype NOUN an original example from which others are developed.

protozoan NOUN (PL **-zoa** or **-zoans**) a one-celled microscopic animal.

protracted ADJ lasting for a long time.

protractor NOUN an instrument for measuring angles.

protrude VERB project or stick out. **protrusion** NOUN

protuberance NOUN a bulging part. **protuberant** ADJ

proud ADJ 1 feeling pride; giving cause for pride; arrogant. 2 slightly sticking out from a surface.

prove VERB (**proved** or **proven, proving**) 1 demonstrate to be true. 2 turn out to be. **proven** ADJ

provenance NOUN a place of origin.

proverb NOUN a short well-known saying.

proverbial ADJ 1 referred to in a proverb. 2 well known.

provide VERB 1 make available to someone. 2 (**provide for**) supply with necessities; make preparations for.

provided (or **providing**) CONJ on condition that.

providence NOUN 1 God's or nature's protection. 2 being provident.

provident ADJ careful in preparing for the future.

providential ADJ happening very luckily.

province NOUN 1 an administrative division of a country. 2 (**the provinces**) all parts of a country outside its capital city.

provincial ADJ 1 of a province or provinces. 2 unsophisticated or narrow-minded. NOUN an inhabitant of a province.

provision NOUN 1 the process of providing things. 2 a stipulation in a treaty or contract etc. 3 (**provisions**) food and drink.

provisional ADJ arranged temporarily.
provisionally ADV

proviso NOUN (PL **-os**) a condition attached to an agreement.

provoke VERB 1 make angry. 2 rouse to action; produce as a reaction.
provocation NOUN
provocative ADJ

provost NOUN the head of a college.

prow NOUN a projecting front part of a ship.

prowess NOUN skill or expertise.

prowl VERB move about restlessly or stealthily.
prowler NOUN

proximity NOUN nearness.

proxy NOUN (PL **-ies**) a person authorized to represent or act for another.

prude NOUN a person who is easily shocked by matters relating to sex.
prudish ADJ

prudent ADJ showing thought for the future.
prudence NOUN

prune NOUN a dried plum. VERB trim a tree etc. by cutting away dead or unwanted parts; reduce.

prurient ADJ having too much interest in sexual matters.
prurience NOUN

pry VERB (**pries, pried, prying**) inquire too inquisitively about someone's private affairs.

PS ABBREV postscript.

psalm NOUN a sacred song.

pseudo ADJ false.

pseudonym NOUN a fictitious name used especially by an author.

psyche NOUN the human soul, mind, or spirit.

psychedelic ADJ **1** (of a drug) producing hallucinations. **2** having vivid colours or abstract patterns.

psychiatry NOUN the study and treatment of mental illness.
psychiatric ADJ
psychiatrist NOUN

psychic ADJ of the soul or mind; of or having apparently supernatural powers. NOUN a person having or claiming psychic powers.

psychoanalyse ([US] **-yze**) VERB treat by psychoanalysis.

psychoanalysis NOUN a method of treating mental disorders by investigating the unconscious elements of the mind.
psychoanalyst NOUN

psychology NOUN the scientific study of the mind; the way in which someone thinks or behaves.
psychological ADJ
psychologically ADV
psychologist NOUN

psychopath NOUN a person suffering from a severe mental illness resulting in antisocial or violent behaviour.
psychopathic ADJ

psychosis NOUN (PL **psychoses**) a severe mental illness in with the sufferer loses contact with reality.
psychotic ADJ

psychosomatic ADJ (of illness) caused or aggravated by mental stress.

psychotherapy NOUN treatment of mental disorders by psychological rather than medical methods.
psychotherapist NOUN

pt. ABBREV **1** pint. **2** part. **3** point.

PTA ABBREV parent-teacher association.

pterodactyl NOUN an extinct reptile with wings.

PTO ABBREV please turn over.

pub NOUN a building in which beer and other drinks are served.

puberty NOUN the period during which adolescents reach sexual maturity.

pubic ADJ of the lower front part of the abdomen.

public ADJ of, for, or known to people in general. NOUN ordinary people in general; people interested in the work of a particular author, performer, etc.

public address system a system of loudspeakers amplifying sound for an audience. **public house** a pub. **public relations** the business of keeping a good public image by an organization or famous person. **public school** (in the UK) a private fee-paying school. **public sector** the part of the economy that is controlled by the state.

publicly ADV

publican NOUN the owner or manager of a pub.

publication NOUN publishing; a published book, newspaper, etc.

publicity NOUN attention given to someone or something by the media; material used in publicizing something.

publicize (or -ise) VERB make widely known; promote or advertise.

publicist NOUN

publish VERB 1 produce a book etc. for public sale. 2 make generally known.

publisher NOUN

puce ADJ & NOUN brownish purple.

puck NOUN a hard rubber disc used in ice hockey.

pucker VERB contract into wrinkles. NOUN a wrinkle.

pudding NOUN 1 a sweet cooked dish; the dessert course of a meal. 2 a savoury dish containing flour, suet, etc.

puddle NOUN a small pool of rainwater or other liquid.

puerile ADJ childish.

puff NOUN 1 a short burst of breath or wind; smoke, etc., blown out by this. 2 a light pastry case with a filling. VERB **1** emit or send out in puffs; breathe heavily. **2** (cause to) swell.

puff pastry light flaky pastry.

puffball NOUN a ball-shaped fungus.

puffin NOUN a seabird with a short striped bill.

puffy ADJ (**-ier, -iest**) puffed out or swollen.

pug NOUN a small breed of dog with a flat nose and wrinkled face.

pugilist NOUN a boxer.

pugnacious ADJ eager to argue or fight.

pugnacity NOUN

puke [inf] VERB & NOUN vomit.

pukka ADJ real or genuine.

pull VERB **1** apply force to something so as to move it towards yourself; attract. **2** move steadily in a specified direction. **3** strain a muscle. NOUN **1** an act of pulling. **2** an attraction; an influence or compulsion. **3** a deep drink. **4** a draw on a pipe etc.

pull out withdraw. **pull through** come or bring through difficulty or danger.

pullet NOUN a young hen.

pulley NOUN (PL **-eys**) a wheel over which a rope etc. passes, used in lifting things.

pullover NOUN a knitted garment for the upper body.

pulmonary ADJ of the lungs.

pulp NOUN a soft, wet mass of crushed material; the soft moist part of fruit. VERB crush to pulp.

pulpy ADJ

pulpit NOUN a raised enclosed platform from which a preacher speaks.

pulsate VERB expand and contract rhythmically.

pulsation NOUN

pulse NOUN **1** the rhythmical beat of the blood as it is pumped around the body. **2** a single beat, throb, or vibration. **3** the edible seed of beans, peas, lentils, etc. VERB pulsate.

pulverize (or **-ise**) VERB crush to powder.

puma NOUN a large brown American wild cat.

pumice NOUN solidified lava used for scouring or polishing.

pummel VERB (**pummelled, pummelling;** [US] **pummeled, pummeling**) strike repeatedly with the fists.

pump NOUN **1** a machine for moving liquid, gas, or air. **2** a plimsoll. VERB **1** force air etc. in a particular direction using a pump; inflate or empty using a pump. **2** move vigorously up and down.

pumpkin NOUN a large round orange-coloured fruit.

pun NOUN a joke that uses a word or words with more than one meaning.

punch VERB **1** strike with the fist. **2** cut a hole in something. **3** press a key on a machine. NOUN **1** a blow with the fist. **2** a device for cutting holes or impressing a design. **3** a drink made of wine or spirits mixed with fruit juices etc.

punchline NOUN the final part of a joke, providing the humour.

punctilious ADJ showing great attention to detail or correct behaviour.

punctual ADJ arriving or doing things at the appointed time.
punctuality NOUN
punctually ADV

punctuate VERB **1** insert the appropriate marks in written material to separate sentences etc. **2** interrupt at intervals.
punctuation NOUN

puncture NOUN a small hole caused by a sharp object. VERB make a puncture in.

pundit NOUN an expert.

pungent ADJ having a strong sharp taste or smell.
pungency NOUN

punish VERB impose a penalty on someone for an offence; treat unfairly.
punishment NOUN

punitive ADJ intended as a punishment.

punk (also **punk rock**) NOUN a loud aggressive form of rock music.

punnet NOUN a small container for fruit etc.

punt[1] NOUN a long narrow, flat-bottomed boat, moved forward with a long pole. VERB travel in a punt.

punt[2] VERB kick a dropped football before it touches the ground.

punter NOUN [inf] **1** a person who gambles. **2** a customer.

puny ADJ (**-ier, -iest**) small and weak.

pup NOUN a young dog; a young wolf, rat, or seal.

pupa NOUN (PL **pupae**) a chrysalis.

pupate VERB become a pupa.

pupil NOUN **1** a person who is taught by another. **2** the opening in the centre of the iris of the eye.

puppet NOUN a kind of doll made to move as an entertainment; a person etc. controlled by another.

puppy NOUN (PL **-ies**) a young dog.

purchase VERB buy. NOUN **1** buying; something bought. **2** a firm hold or grip.

purdah NOUN the Muslim or Hindu system of screening women.

pure ADJ **1** not mixed with any other substances; innocent or morally good. **2** sheer: *pure chance.* **3** (of mathematics or sciences) theoretical rather than practical. **purely** ADV **purity** NOUN

purée NOUN pulped fruit or vegetables etc. VERB make into a purée.

purgative NOUN a laxative.

purgatory NOUN a place or condition of suffering, especially (in RC belief) in which souls undergo purification before going to heaven.

purge VERB **1** empty the bowels by taking a laxative. **2** rid of undesirable people or things. NOUN the process of purging.

purify VERB make pure. **purification** NOUN

purist NOUN a stickler for correctness.

puritan NOUN a person with strong moral beliefs who is critical of others' behaviour. **puritanical** ADJ

purl NOUN a knitting stitch. VERB make this stitch.

purlieus PLURAL NOUN the area around or near a placc.

purloin VERB steal.

purple ADJ & NOUN (of) a colour made by mixing red and blue.

purport NOUN meaning. VERB appear or claim to be or do.

purpose NOUN the intended result of an

action etc.; a feeling of determination. VERB [formal] intend.

on purpose intentionally.

purposeful ADJ

purposely ADV

purr NOUN a low vibrant sound that a cat makes when pleased; any similar sound. VERB make this sound.

purse NOUN 1 a small pouch for carrying money. 2 [US] a handbag. 3 money available for use. VERB pucker the lips.

purser NOUN a ship's officer in charge of accounts.

pursue VERB (**pursued, pursuing**) 1 follow; try to catch or attain. 2 continue along a route; engage in an activity.

pursuit NOUN 1 pursuing. 2 a leisure or sporting activity.

purvey VERB supply food etc. as a business.

purveyor NOUN

pus NOUN thick yellowish matter produced from an infected wound.

push VERB 1 apply force to something so as to move it away from yourself; move forward by exerting force. 2 make your way

forward forcibly. 3 press a button or key. 4 encourage to work hard. 5 [inf] promote the use or acceptance of; sell drugs illegally. NOUN 1 an act of pushing. 2 a vigorous effort.

pusher NOUN

pushchair NOUN a folding chair on wheels, in which a child can be pushed along.

pushy ADJ (**-ier, -iest**) excessively self-assertive or ambitious.

pusillanimous ADJ cowardly.

pussy (or **puss**) NOUN [inf] a cat.

pussyfoot VERB act very cautiously.

pustule NOUN a pimple or blister.

pustular ADJ

put VERB (**put, putting**) 1 cause to be in a certain place, position, state, or relationship. 2 express or phrase. 3 throw a shot or weight as a sport.

put down 1 suppress. 2 kill a sick animal. **put off** 1 postpone. 2 discourage. **put up with** tolerate.

putative ADJ generally considered to be.

putrefy VERB (**putrefied, putrefying**) rot.
putrefaction NOUN
putrid ADJ rotten; stinking.
putt VERB strike a golf ball gently to make it roll along the ground. NOUN this stroke.
putter NOUN
putty NOUN a soft paste that sets hard, used for fixing glass in frames, filling holes, etc.
puzzle NOUN a game, toy, or problem designed to test mental skills or knowledge. VERB cause to feel confused or bewildered; think hard about a problem.
PVC ABBREV polyvinyl chloride, a sort of plastic.
pygmy (or **pigmy**) NOUN (PL **-ies**) a member of a black African people of very short stature; a very small person or thing.
pyjamas ([US] **pajamas**) PLURAL NOUN a loose jacket and trousers for sleeping in.
pylon NOUN a tall metal structure carrying electricity cables.
pyramid NOUN a structure with triangular sloping sides that meet at the top.
pyre NOUN a pile of wood for burning a dead body.
pyromaniac NOUN a person with an uncontrollable impulse to set things on fire.
pyrotechnics PLURAL NOUN a firework display; a brilliant display or performance.
pyrrhic victory NOUN a victory gained at too great a cost to be worthwhile.
python NOUN a large snake that crushes its prey.

Qq

QC ABBREV Queen's Counsel.
quack NOUN **1** a duck's harsh cry. **2** a person who falsely claims to have medical skill. VERB (of a duck) make its harsh cry.
quad NOUN **1** a quadrangle. **2** a quadruplet.
quadrangle NOUN a four-

sided courtyard bordered by large buildings.

quadrant NOUN a quarter of a circle or of its circumference.

quadraphonic (or **quadrophonic**) ADJ (of sound reproduction) using four channels.

quadratic equation NOUN an equation involving the second and no higher power of an unknown quantity.

quadrilateral NOUN a geometric figure with four sides.

quadruped NOUN a four-footed animal.

quadruple ADJ having four parts or members; four times as much as. VERB increase by four times its amount.

quadruplet NOUN one of four children born at one birth.

quaff VERB drink heartily.

quagmire NOUN a bog or marsh.

quail NOUN a small game bird. VERB feel or show fear.

quaint ADJ attractively strange or old-fashioned.

quake VERB shake or tremble, especially with fear.

Quaker NOUN a member of the Society of Friends, a Christian movement rejecting set forms of worship.

qualification NOUN 1 the action of qualifying; a pass in an exam etc. 2 a statement that limits the meaning of another statement.

qualify VERB (**qualified, qualifying**) 1 be entitled to a privilege or eligible for a competition; become officially recognized as able to do a particular job. 2 add something to a statement to limit its meaning. **qualifier** NOUN

qualitative ADJ of or concerned with quality.

quality NOUN (PL **-ies**) 1 a degree of excellence. 2 a distinctive characteristic.

qualm NOUN an uneasy feeling of worry or fear.

quandary NOUN (PL **-ies**) a state of uncertainty.

quango NOUN (PL **-os**) an organization that works independently but with support from the government.

quantify VERB (**quantified,**

quantifying) express or measure the quantity of. **quantifiable** ADJ

quantitative ADJ of or concerned with quantity.

quantity NOUN (PL **-ies**) an amount or number of a substance or things; a large number or amount. **quantity surveyor** a person who measures and prices building work.

quantum leap NOUN a sudden great increase or advance.

quarantine NOUN a period of isolation for people or animals that may have a disease. VERB put into quarantine.

quark NOUN a component of elementary particles.

quarrel NOUN an angry argument; a reason for disagreement. VERB (**quarrelled, quarrelling;** [US] **quarreled, quarreling**) engage in a quarrel.

quarrelsome ADJ liable to quarrel.

quarry NOUN (PL **-ies**) **1** an animal or person that is hunted or chased. **2** a place where stone etc. is dug out of the earth. VERB (**quarried, quarrying**) obtain stone etc. from a quarry.

quart NOUN a quarter of a gallon (two pints or 1.13 litres).

quarter NOUN **1** each of four equal parts of something. **2** three months; a quarter-hour. **3** a US or Canadian coin worth 25 cents. **4** a part of a town. **5** (**quarters**) accommodation. **6** mercy shown to an opponent. VERB **1** divide into quarters. **2** put into lodgings. **quarter-final** a match preceding the semi-final.

quarterdeck NOUN the part of a ship's upper deck nearest the stern.

quarterly ADJ & ADV produced or occurring once in every quarter of a year. NOUN (PL **-ies**) a quarterly periodical.

quartermaster NOUN a regimental officer in charge of accommodation and supplies.

quartet NOUN a group of four instruments or voices; music for these.

quartz NOUN a hard mineral.

quasar NOUN a kind of galaxy which gives off

enormous amounts of energy.

quash VERB reject as invalid; put an end to.

quasi- COMBINING FORM seeming to be but not really so.

quatrain NOUN a stanza or poem of four lines.

quaver VERB (of a voice) tremble. NOUN **1** a trembling sound. **2** a musical note equal to half a crotchet.

quay NOUN a platform in a harbour for loading and unloading ships.
quayside NOUN

queasy ADJ (**-ier, -iest**) feeling sick.
queasiness NOUN

queen NOUN **1** the female ruler of a country; a king's wife; a woman or thing regarded as supreme in some way. **2** a piece in chess; a playing card bearing a picture of a queen. **3** a fertile female bee, ant, etc.
queenly ADJ

queer ADJ **1** strange or odd. **2** [derogatory] (of a man) homosexual. NOUN [derogatory] a homosexual man.

quell VERB suppress.

quench VERB **1** satisfy thirst. **2** put out a fire.

querulous ADJ complaining peevishly.

query NOUN (PL **-ies**) a question. VERB (**queried, querying**) ask a question.

quest NOUN a long search.

question NOUN a sentence requesting information; a matter for discussion or solution; a doubt. VERB ask someone questions; express doubt about. **out of the question** not possible. **question mark** a punctuation mark (?) placed after a question.

questionable ADJ open to doubt.

questionnaire NOUN a list of questions seeking information.

queue NOUN a line of people or vehicles waiting for something. VERB (**queued, queuing** or **queueing**) wait in a queue.

quibble NOUN & VERB (make) a minor objection.

quiche NOUN a baked flan with a savoury filling.

quick ADJ **1** moving or acting fast; taking only a short time. **2** intelligent. **3** (of temper) easily roused. NOUN the sensitive flesh below the nails.

quicken VERB

quickly ADV

quicksand NOUN loose wet sand that sucks in anything resting on it.

quicksilver NOUN mercury.

quickstep NOUN a ballroom dance.

quid NOUN (PL **quid**) [inf] £1.

quid pro quo NOUN (PL **quid pro quos**) a favour etc. given in return for another.

quiet ADJ making little noise; free from disturbance; discreet. NOUN absence of noise or disturbance. VERB make or become quiet.

quieten VERB

quiff NOUN an upright tuft of hair.

quill NOUN **1** a large feather; a pen made from this. **2** a spine of a porcupine or hedgehog.

quilt NOUN a padded bed covering. VERB line with padding and fix with lines of stitching.

quin NOUN [inf] a quintuplet.

quince NOUN a hard yellow fruit.

quinine NOUN a bitter-tasting drug used to treat malaria.

quintessence NOUN a perfect example; an essential characteristic or element.

quintessential ADJ

quintessentially ADV

quintet NOUN a group of five instruments or voices; music for these.

quintuple ADJ having five parts or members; five times as much as. VERB increase by five times its amount.

quintuplet NOUN one of five children born at one birth.

quip NOUN a witty remark. VERB (**quipped**, **quipping**) make a witty remark.

quirk NOUN a peculiar habit; an unexpected twist of fate.

quisling NOUN a traitor who collaborates with occupying forces.

quit VERB (**quitted** or **quit**, **quitting**) **1** leave a place; resign from a job. **2** [US inf] stop or cease.

quite ADV **1** completely. **2** to a certain extent. EXCLAMATION exactly.

quits ADJ on even terms after retaliation or repayment.

quiver VERB slightly shake or vibrate. NOUN **1** a quivering movement or sound. **2** a case for holding arrows.

quixotic ADJ idealistic and impractical.

quiz NOUN (PL **quizzes**) a competition in which people answer questions to test their knowledge. VERB (**quizzed, quizzing**) interrogate.

quizzical ADJ showing mild or amused puzzlement.
quizzically ADV

quoit NOUN a ring thrown to encircle a peg in the game of **quoits**.

quorate ADJ having a quorum present.

quorum NOUN a minimum number of people that must be present for a valid meeting.

quota NOUN a quantity allowed; a share of something that must be done.

quotation NOUN a passage or price quoted.

quotation marks punctuation marks ('' or '' '') enclosing words quoted.

quote VERB **1** repeat a passage or remark from a book or speech; refer to as evidence or authority for a statement. **2** give someone an estimated price.
quotable ADJ

quotidian ADJ daily.

quotient NOUN the result of a division sum.

q.v. ABBREV used to direct a reader to another part of a book.

Rr

R ABBREV Regina or Rex.
rabbi NOUN a Jewish religious leader.
rabbit NOUN a burrowing animal with long ears and a short tail.

rabble NOUN a disorderly crowd.
rabid ADJ having rabies; fanatical.
rabies NOUN a contagious disease of dogs etc., that

can be transmitted to humans.

raccoon (or **racoon**) NOUN a small American mammal with a striped tail.

race NOUN 1 a contest of speed. 2 each of the major divisions of humankind; a subdivision of a species. VERB compete in a race; go at full or excessive speed.

racecourse NOUN a ground where horse races are held.

racetrack NOUN a racecourse; a track for motor racing.

racial ADJ of or based on race.

racially ADV

racism (or **racialism**) NOUN a belief in the superiority of a particular race; hostility to or discrimination against other races.

racist ADJ & NOUN

rack NOUN 1 a framework for hanging or placing things on. 2 [historical] an instrument of torture on which people were tied and stretched. VERB (also **wrack**) cause suffering to.

rack and ruin destruction.

racket NOUN 1 (or **racquet**) a stringed bat used in tennis and similar games. 2 a loud noise. 3 [inf] a fraudulent business or scheme.

racketeer NOUN a person who operates a fraudulent business etc.

raconteur NOUN a skilled storyteller.

racoon see **raccoon**.

racy ADJ lively and exciting.

radar NOUN a system for detecting objects by means of radio waves.

radial ADJ having spokes or lines etc. that radiate from a central point.

radiant ADJ 1 shining or glowing brightly; emitted in rays. 2 looking very happy.

radiance NOUN

radiate VERB 1 (of energy) be emitted in rays or waves. 2 spread out from a central point.

radiation NOUN energy sent out as electromagnetic waves or atomic particles.

radiator NOUN 1 a device for heating a room, usually filled with hot water pumped in through pipes. 2 an engine-cooling device in a vehicle.

radical ADJ fundamental or affecting the basic nature of something; extreme or thorough; advocating extreme political reform. NOUN someone holding radical views.

radically ADV

radii plural of **radius**.

radio NOUN (PL **-os**) the process of sending and receiving messages etc. by electromagnetic waves; a transmitter or receiver for this; sound broadcasting. VERB (**radioed, radioing**) transmit or communicate by radio.

radioactive ADJ giving out harmful radiation or particles.

radioactivity NOUN

radiocarbon NOUN a radioactive form of carbon used in carbon dating.

radiography NOUN the production of X-ray photographs.

radiology NOUN a study of X-rays and similar radiation, especially of their use in medicine.

radiotherapy NOUN the treatment of disease by X-rays or similar radiation.

radish NOUN a plant with a crisp, hot-tasting root, eaten in salads.

radium NOUN a radioactive metallic element.

radius NOUN (PL **-dii** or **-diuses**) **1** a straight line from the centre to the edge of a circle. **2** the thicker long bone of the forearm.

RAF ABBREV Royal Air Force.

raffia NOUN fibre from the leaves of a palm tree, used for making hats, mats, etc.

raffish ADJ slightly disreputable in appearance.

raffle NOUN a lottery with an object as the prize. VERB offer as the prize in a raffle.

raft NOUN a flat structure used as a boat or floating platform.

rafter NOUN one of the sloping beams forming the framework of a roof.

rag NOUN **1** a piece of old cloth; (**rags**) old and torn clothes. **2** a students' carnival in aid of charity.

ragged ADJ

ragamuffin NOUN a person in ragged dirty clothes.

rage NOUN violent anger. VERB **1** show violent anger. **2** continue with great force.
all the rage very popular.

raid NOUN a sudden attack to destroy or seize something; a surprise visit by police to arrest suspects or seize illicit goods. VERB make a raid on.

rail NOUN **1** a horizontal bar. **2** any of the lines of metal bars on which trains or trams run; the railway system. VERB **1** enclose or protect with a rail. **2** complain strongly.

railing NOUN a fence or barrier made of rails.

railway NOUN a set of rails on which trains run; a system of transport using these.

rain NOUN atmospheric moisture falling as drops; a fall of this; a large quantity of things. VERB send down or fall as or like rain.
rainy ADJ

rainbow NOUN an arch of colours formed in rain or spray by the sun's rays.

raincoat NOUN a rain-resistant coat.

rainfall NOUN the amount of rain falling.

rainforest NOUN dense wet tropical forest.

raise VERB **1** move or lift upwards or to an upright position; increase the amount, level, or strength of. **2** express doubts, objections, etc. **3** collect money. **4** bring up a child.

raisin NOUN a dried grape.

rake NOUN **1** a tool with prongs for gathering leaves, smoothing loose soil, etc. **2** a fashionable but dissolute man VERB **1** gather or smooth with a rake; scratch and wound with a set of points; sweep with gunfire etc. **2** search through.

rakish ADJ dashing but slightly disreputable.

rally VERB (**rallied, rallying**) **1** bring or come together (again) for a united effort. **2** revive; recover strength. NOUN (PL **-ies**) **1** a mass meeting held as a protest or in support of a cause. **2** a long-distance driving competition over public roads. **3** a recovery. **4** a series of strokes in tennis etc.

ram NOUN **1** an adult male

sheep. 2 a striking or plunging device. VERB (**rammed, ramming**) strike or push heavily.

Ramadan NOUN the ninth month of the Muslim year, when Muslims fast during daylight hours.

ramble NOUN a walk taken for pleasure. VERB 1 take a ramble. 2 talk at length in a confused way. **rambler** NOUN

ramifications PLURAL NOUN complex results of an action or event.

ramp NOUN a slope joining two levels.

rampage VERB behave or race about violently. NOUN violent behaviour.

rampant ADJ 1 flourishing uncontrollably. 2 (of an animal in heraldry) standing on one hind leg with its forefeet in the air.

rampart NOUN a broad-topped defensive wall.

ramrod NOUN a rod formerly used for ramming a charge into guns.

ramshackle ADJ tumbledown or rickety.

ran past of **run**.

ranch NOUN a large cattle farm in America.

rancid ADJ smelling or tasting like stale fat.

rancour ([US] **rancor**) NOUN bitterness or resentment. **rancorous** ADJ

random ADJ done or occurring without method, planning, etc.

randy ADJ (**-ier, -iest**) [inf] sexually aroused.

rang past of **ring**.

range NOUN 1 a set of similar or related things. 2 the limits between which something operates or varies. 3 the distance over which a thing can travel or be effective. 4 a large open area for grazing or hunting. 5 a place with targets for shooting practice. 6 a series of mountains or hills. VERB 1 vary or extend between specified limits. 2 place in rows or in order. 3 travel over a wide area.

ranger NOUN an official in charge of a park or forest.

rangy ADJ tall, slim, and long-limbed.

rank NOUN 1 a position in a hierarchy, especially in the armed forces; high social position. 2 a line of people or things. 3 (**the**

ranks) ordinary soldiers, not officers. VERB give a rank to; have a specified rank; arrange in ranks. ADJ 1 growing too thickly. 2 foul-smelling; unmistakably bad.

rank and file the ordinary members of an organization.

rankle VERB cause lasting resentment.

ransack VERB go quickly through a place stealing or searching for things.

ransom NOUN a price demanded or paid for the release of a captive. VERB demand or pay a ransom for.

rant VERB make a violent speech.

rap NOUN 1 a quick sharp blow. 2 a type of music in which words are recited over an instrumental backing. VERB (**rapped**, **rapping**) strike with a quick sharp blow.

rapacious ADJ very greedy.

rapacity NOUN

rape[1] VERB have sex with someone against their will. NOUN an act of raping.

rapist NOUN

rape[2] NOUN a plant with oil-rich seeds.

rapid ADJ very quick. PLURAL NOUN (**rapids**) part of a river where the water flows very fast.

rapidity NOUN

rapier NOUN a thin, light sword.

rapport NOUN a harmonious understanding or relationship.

rapprochement NOUN a resumption of friendly relations.

rapt ADJ fascinated.

rapture NOUN intense delight.

rapturous ADJ

rare ADJ 1 very uncommon; exceptionally good. 2 (of meat) only lightly cooked.

rarely ADV

rarity NOUN

rarebit see **Welsh rabbit**.

rarefied ADJ 1 (of air) of lower pressure than usual. 2 esoteric.

raring ADJ [inf] very eager.

rascal NOUN a dishonest or mischievous person.

rash NOUN an eruption of spots or patches on the skin. ADJ acting or done without due consideration of the risks.

rasher NOUN a slice of bacon.

rasp NOUN 1 a coarse file. 2 a grating sound. VERB scrape with a rasp; make a harsh, grating sound.

raspberry NOUN an edible red berry.

Rastafarian (or **Rasta**) NOUN a member of a Jamaican religious movement.

rat NOUN a rodent like a large mouse. VERB (**ratted, ratting**) [inf] desert or betray.
rat race a fiercely competitive struggle for success.

ratatouille NOUN a dish of stewed courgettes, tomatoes, onions, etc.

ratchet NOUN a bar or wheel with notches in which a device engages to prevent backward movement.

rate NOUN 1 a quantity, frequency, etc., measured against another quantity. 2 a fixed price or charge; (**rates**) a tax levied according to the value of buildings and land. 3 a speed. VERB 1 estimate the value of; consider or

regard as. 2 deserve.

rather ADV 1 by preference: *I'd rather not.* 2 to a certain extent. 3 on the contrary; more precisely.

ratify VERB (**ratified, ratifying**) confirm an agreement etc. formally.
ratification NOUN

rating NOUN 1 the level at which a thing is rated. 2 a sailor without a commission.

ratio NOUN (PL **-ios**) the relationship between two amounts, reckoned as the number of times one contains the other.

ration NOUN a fixed allowance of food etc. VERB limit to a ration.

rational ADJ able to think sensibly; based on reasoning.
rationally ADV

rationale NOUN the reasons for an action or belief.

rationalism NOUN treating reason as the basis of belief and knowledge.
rationalist NOUN

rationalize (or **-ise**) VERB 1 invent a rational explanation for. 2 make more efficient.

rattan NOUN thin, pliable stems of a palm, used in

furniture making.

rattle VERB 1 (cause to) make a rapid series of short, hard sounds. 2 [inf] make nervous or irritable. NOUN a rattling sound; a toy that makes this.

rattlesnake NOUN a poisonous American snake.

raucous ADJ loud and harsh.

raunchy ADJ (-ier, -iest) [inf] sexually provocative.

ravage VERB do great damage to. PLURAL NOUN (**ravages**) damage.

rave VERB talk wildly or furiously; speak with rapturous enthusiasm. NOUN a large event with dancing to loud, fast, electronic music.

raven NOUN a large black crow. ADJ (of hair) glossy black.

ravenous ADJ very hungry.

ravine NOUN a deep narrow gorge.

ravioli NOUN small square pasta cases containing a savoury filling.

ravish VERB [dated] rape.

ravishing ADJ very beautiful.

raw ADJ 1 not cooked; not yet processed; inexperienced. 2 (of the skin) red and painful from friction. 3 (of weather) cold and damp. 4 (of an emotion or quality) strong and undisguised.

raw deal unfair treatment.

ray NOUN 1 a line or narrow beam of light or other radiation. 2 a trace of something. 3 a large, flat sea fish.

rayon NOUN a synthetic fabric made from viscose.

raze VERB tear down a building.

razor NOUN a sharp-edged instrument used for shaving.

razzmatazz NOUN [inf] extravagant publicity and display.

RC ABBREV Roman Catholic.

re PREP concerning.

reach VERB 1 stretch out a hand to touch or take something; be able to touch. 2 arrive at; extend as far as; make contact with; achieve. NOUN 1 the distance over which someone or something can reach. 2 a section of a river.

react VERB cause or undergo a reaction.
reactive ADJ
reaction NOUN a response to a stimulus, event, etc.; a chemical change produced by substances acting on each other; an occurrence of one condition after a period of the opposite; a bad physical response to a drug.
reactionary ADJ & NOUN (PL -ies) (a person) opposed to progress and reform.
reactor NOUN an apparatus for the production of nuclear energy.
read VERB (**read, reading**) **1** look at and understand the meaning of written or printed words or symbols; speak such words aloud; study or discover by reading. **2** have a particular wording. **3** (of an instrument) indicate as a measurement. **4** interpret mentally.
reader NOUN
readership NOUN the readers of a newspaper etc.
readily ADV **1** willingly. **2** easily.
readjust VERB adjust again; adapt to a changed situation.
ready ADJ prepared for an activity or situation; available; willing; quick or easy. VERB (**readied, readying**) prepare.
readiness NOUN
reagent NOUN a substance used to produce a chemical reaction.
real ADJ actually existing or occurring; genuine; worthy of the description.
real estate [US] land or housing.
realism NOUN representing or viewing things as they are in reality.
realist NOUN
realistic ADJ showing realism; practical.
realistically ADV
reality NOUN (PL -ies) the quality of being real; something real and not imaginary; life and the world as they really are.
realize (or -ise) VERB **1** become aware of a fact. **2** fulfil a hope or plan. **3** convert an asset into money; be sold for.
realization NOUN
really ADV **1** in fact. **2** thoroughly. EXCLAMATION expressing interest,

surprise, etc.

realm NOUN **1** a kingdom. **2** a field of activity or interest.

ream NOUN **1** 500 sheets of paper. **2** (**reams**) a large quantity.

reap VERB **1** cut grain etc. as harvest. **2** receive as the result of actions.

rear NOUN the back part. ADJ at the back. VERB **1** bring up children; breed animals. **2** (of a horse) raise itself on its hind legs. **3** extend to a great height.

rear admiral the naval rank above commodore.

rearward ADJ & ADV

rearwards ADV

rearguard NOUN troops protecting an army's rear.

rearm VERB arm again.

rearmament NOUN

reason NOUN **1** a motive, cause, or justification. **2** the ability to think and draw logical conclusions; sanity. VERB **1** think and draw logical conclusions. **2** (**reason with**) persuade by logical argument.

reasonable ADJ **1** fair and sensible; appropriate. **2** fairly good.

reasonably ADV

reassure VERB restore confidence to.

reassurance NOUN

rebate NOUN a partial refund.

rebel VERB (**rebelled, rebelling**) refuse to obey the government or ruler; oppose authority or convention. NOUN a person who rebels.

rebellion NOUN

rebellious ADJ

rebound VERB **1** spring back after impact. **2** (**rebound on**) have an unpleasant effect on. NOUN a ball or shot that rebounds.

on the rebound while still upset about a failed relationship.

rebuff VERB reject ungraciously. NOUN a snub.

rebuke VERB reprove. NOUN a reproof.

rebut VERB (**rebutted, rebutting**) declare or show to be false.

rebuttal NOUN

recalcitrant ADJ obstinately disobedient.

recall VERB **1** summon to return. **2** remember; remind someone of. NOUN recalling or being recalled.

recant 574

recant VERB withdraw a former opinion or belief.

recap VERB (**recapped, recapping**) recapitulate.

recapitulate VERB give a summary of.
recapitulation NOUN

recce NOUN [inf] a reconnaissance.

recede VERB move back from a position; diminish; slope backwards.

receipt NOUN the act of receiving; a written acknowledgement that something has been received or paid.

receive VERB **1** acquire, accept, or take in. **2** experience or meet with. **3** greet on arrival.

receiver NOUN **1** a person or thing that receives something. **3** the earpiece of a telephone; an apparatus that converts broadcast electrical signals into sound or images. **4** (also **official receiver**) an official who handles the affairs of a bankrupt company.
receivership NOUN

recent ADJ happening in a time shortly before the present.

recently ADV

receptacle NOUN a container.

reception NOUN **1** an act of receiving; a reaction to something. **2** a formal social occasion to welcome guests. **3** an area in a hotel, office, etc. where guests and visitors are greeted.

receptionist NOUN a person employed to greet and deal with clients or guests.

receptive ADJ quick to receive ideas.

receptor NOUN a nerve ending that responds to a stimulus such as light.

recess NOUN **1** a part or space set back from the line of a wall or room etc. **2** a temporary cessation from business. VERB fit a light etc. in a recess.

recession NOUN a temporary decline in economic activity.

recessive ADJ (of a gene) remaining latent when a dominant gene is present.

recherché ADJ unusual or obscure.

recidivist NOUN a person who constantly commits crimes.

recipe NOUN directions for preparing a dish; something likely to lead to a particular outcome.

recipient NOUN a person who receives something.

reciprocal ADJ given or done in return; affecting two parties equally.

reciprocally ADV

reciprocity NOUN

reciprocate VERB respond to an action or emotion with a similar one.

recital NOUN 1 a musical performance. 2 a long account of a series of facts, events, etc.

recite VERB repeat aloud from memory; state facts, events, etc. in order.

recitation NOUN

reckless ADJ wildly impulsive.

reckon VERB 1 calculate. 2 have as your opinion. 3 (**reckon on**) rely on.

reclaim VERB 1 take action to recover possession of. 2 make land usable.

reclamation NOUN

recline VERB lie back in a relaxed position.

recluse NOUN a person who avoids contact with other people.

recognize (or **-ise**) VERB

1 identify or know again from previous experience; 2 acknowledge as genuine, valid, or worthy.

recognition NOUN

recognizable ADJ

recoil VERB spring or shrink back in fear or disgust; rebound. NOUN the act of recoiling.

recollect VERB remember.

recollection NOUN

recommend VERB suggest as suitable for a purpose or role; (of a quality etc.) make something appealing or desirable.

recommendation NOUN

recompense VERB repay or compensate. NOUN compensation.

reconcile VERB make two people or groups friendly again; persuade to tolerate something unwelcome; make compatible.

reconciliation NOUN

reconnaissance NOUN military observation of an area to gain information.

reconnoitre ([US] **reconnoiter**) VERB (**reconnoitred**, **reconnoitring**) make a reconnaissance of.

reconsider VERB consider again; consider changing.

reconstitute VERB reconstruct; restore dried food to its original form.

reconstruct VERB 1 rebuild after damage. 2 enact a past event.

reconstruction NOUN

record NOUN 1 an account of something kept for evidence or information. 2 a plastic disc carrying recorded sound. 3 facts known about a person's past. 4 the best performance or most remarkable event etc. of its kind. VERB 1 make a record of. 2 convert sound or vision into permanent form for later reproduction.
off the record unofficially.

recorder NOUN 1 a person or thing that records. 2 a simple woodwind instrument.

recount[1] VERB describe in detail.

recount[2] VERB count again. NOUN a second or subsequent counting.

recoup VERB recover a loss.

recourse NOUN a source of help to which someone may turn.

recover VERB 1 regain possession or control of. 2 return to health.

recovery NOUN

recreation NOUN enjoyable leisure activity.

recreational ADJ

recrimination NOUN an accusation in response to another.

recruit NOUN a new member, especially of the armed forces. VERB enlist someone as a recruit.

recruitment NOUN

rectal ADJ of the rectum.

rectangle NOUN a flat shape with four right angles and four sides, two of which are longer than the others.

rectangular ADJ

rectifier NOUN an electrical device converting an alternating current to a direct one.

rectify VERB (**rectified, rectifying**) put right.

rectitude NOUN morally correct behaviour.

rector NOUN 1 a clergyman in charge of a parish. 2 the head of certain schools, colleges, and universities.

rectory NOUN (PL **-ies**) the house of a rector.

rectum NOUN the last section of the large

intestine.

recumbent ADJ lying down.

recuperate VERB recover from illness; regain. **recuperation** NOUN

recur VERB (**recurred, recurring**) happen again or repeatedly. **recurrence** NOUN **recurrent** ADJ

recycle VERB convert waste material for reuse.

red ADJ (**redder, reddest**) 1 of the colour of blood; flushed, especially with embarrassment; (of hair) reddish brown. 2 communist. NOUN 1 a red colour or thing. 2 a communist.

red-blooded virile and healthy. **red carpet** privileged treatment for an important visitor. **red-handed** in the act of doing something wrong. **red herring** a misleading clue. **red-light district** an area with many brothels. **red tape** complicated official rules.

redden VERB

redcurrant NOUN a small edible red berry.

redeem VERB 1 compensate for the faults of; save from

sin. 2 buy back; exchange vouchers etc. for goods. 3 fulfil a promise. **redemption** NOUN

redeploy VERB send to a new place or task. **redeployment** NOUN

redhead NOUN a person with red hair.

redolent ADJ 1 strongly reminiscent of. 2 smelling strongly of.

redouble VERB increase or intensify.

redoubtable ADJ formidable.

redress VERB set right. NOUN reparation or amends.

reduce VERB 1 make or become less. 2 (**reduce to**) bring to a particular state or condition. **reducible** ADJ **reduction** NOUN

redundant ADJ no longer needed or useful; no longer in employment. **redundancy** NOUN

redwood NOUN a very tall evergreen Californian tree.

reed NOUN 1 a water or marsh plant with tall hollow stems. 2 a vibrating part which produces sound in certain wind instruments.

reedy ADJ (of a voice) having a thin high tone.

reef NOUN 1 a ridge of rock or coral just above or below the surface of the sea. 2 a part of a sail that can be drawn in when there is a high wind. VERB shorten a sail.

reek NOUN a strong unpleasant smell. VERB smell strongly.

reel NOUN 1 a cylinder on which something is wound. 2 a lively Scottish or Irish folk dance. VERB 1 wind on or off a reel. 2 stagger. 3 (**reel off**) recite rapidly.

refectory NOUN (PL -ies) the dining room in an educational or religious institution.

refer VERB (**referred, referring**) (**refer to**) mention; turn to for information; pass to someone else for help or decision.
referral NOUN

referee NOUN 1 an umpire, especially in football and boxing. 2 a person willing to provide a reference for someone applying for a job. VERB (**refereed,**

refereeing) be a referee of.

reference NOUN 1 a mention or allusion. 2 the use of a source of information. 3 a letter giving information about someone's suitability for a new job.
with reference to concerning.

referendum NOUN (PL -**dums** or -**da**) a vote by the people of a country on a single political issue.

refine VERB remove impurities or defects from; make small improvements to.

refined ADJ educated, elegant, and having good taste.

refinement NOUN 1 the process of refining. 2 education, elegance, and good taste. 3 an improvement.

refinery NOUN (PL -**ies**) a place where crude substances are refined.

reflect VERB 1 throw back light, heat, or sound; show an image of; bring credit or discredit to. 2 think deeply.
reflector NOUN

reflection NOUN 1 reflecting or being

reflected. **2** a reflected image. **3** serious thought. **4** a sign of something's true nature; a source of discredit.

reflective ADJ **1** reflecting light etc. **2** thoughtful.

reflex NOUN an action done without conscious thought in response to a stimulus. ADJ **1** done as a reflex. **2** (of an angle) more than 180°.

reflexive ADJ [Grammar] referring back to the subject of a clause or verb, e.g. *himself* in *he washed himself*.

reflexology NOUN the massaging of points on the feet as a treatment for stress etc.

reform VERB improve by removing faults; cause to give up bad behaviour. NOUN reforming.
reformation NOUN

refract VERB (of water, air, or glass) make a ray of light change direction when it enters at an angle.
refraction NOUN

refractory ADJ stubborn or unmanageable.

refrain VERB stop yourself from doing something.
NOUN the part of a song repeated at the end of each verse.

refresh VERB give new energy to.

refreshing ADJ **1** relieving tiredness or thirst. **2** new and stimulating.

refreshment NOUN **1** a snack or drink. **2** the giving of new energy.

refrigerate VERB make food or drink cold to keep it fresh.
refrigeration NOUN

refrigerator NOUN an appliance in which food and drink are stored at a low temperature.

refuge NOUN a shelter from danger or trouble.

refugee NOUN a person who has left their country because of war or persecution.

refund VERB pay back money to. NOUN a repayment of money.

refurbish VERB redecorate and improve a building etc.
refurbishment NOUN

refuse[1] VERB say that you are unwilling to do or accept something.
refusal NOUN

refuse[2] NOUN rubbish.

refute VERB prove a statement or person to be wrong.
refutation NOUN
regain VERB obtain again after loss; reach again.
regal ADJ like or fit for a king or queen.
regally ADV
regale VERB feed or entertain well.
regalia PLURAL NOUN emblems of royalty or rank.
regard VERB 1 think of in a particular way. 2 look steadily at. NOUN 1 concern or care. 2 respect or high opinion. 3 a steady gaze. 4 (**regards**) best wishes.
with regard to concerning.
regarding PREP concerning.
regardless ADV 1 despite what is happening. 2 (**regardless of**) without regard for.
regatta NOUN boat races organized as a sporting event.
regency NOUN (PL **-ies**) a period of government by a regent.
regenerate VERB bring new life or strength to; grow new tissue.

regeneration NOUN
regent NOUN a person appointed to rule while the monarch is too young or ill to do so, or is absent.
reggae NOUN a style of popular music originating in Jamaica.
regicide NOUN the killing or killer of a king.
regime NOUN 1 a government. 2 a system of doing things.
regimen NOUN a prescribed course of treatment etc.
regiment NOUN a permanent unit of an army. VERB organize very strictly.
regimental ADJ
Regina NOUN the reigning queen.
region NOUN an area; an administrative division of a country; a part of the body.
regional ADJ
register NOUN 1 an official list. 2 a range of a voice or musical instrument; a level of formality in language. VERB 1 enter in a register; express or convey an opinion or emotion. 2 (of a measuring instrument) show a reading; become aware of.

register office a place where marriages are performed and births, marriages, and deaths are recorded.
registration NOUN
registrar NOUN 1 an official responsible for keeping written records. 2 a hospital doctor training to be a specialist.
registry NOUN (PL **-ies**) 1 a place where registers are kept. 2 registration.
registry office a register office.
regress VERB relapse to an earlier or less advanced state.
regression NOUN
regret NOUN a feeling of sorrow, annoyance, or repentance. VERB (**regretted**, **regretting**) feel regret about.
regretful ADJ
regretfully ADV
regrettable ADJ unfortunate or undesirable.
regrettably ADV
regular ADJ 1 forming or following a definite pattern; occurring at uniform intervals; conforming to an accepted role or pattern.

2 frequent or repeated; doing something frequently. 3 even or symmetrical. 4 forming a country's permanent armed forces. NOUN 1 a regular customer. 2 a regular soldier etc.
regularity NOUN
regulate VERB control the rate or speed of a machine or process; control by rules.
regulator NOUN
regulation NOUN a rule; regulating.
regurgitate VERB bring swallowed food up again to the mouth.
rehabilitate VERB restore to a normal life or good condition.
rehabilitation NOUN
rehash VERB reuse old ideas or material.
rehearse VERB practise a play etc. for later performance; state points again.
rehearsal NOUN
reign NOUN a sovereign's period of rule. VERB rule as a sovereign; be supreme.
reimburse VERB repay money to.
rein NOUN a long strap fastened to a bridle, used

to control a horse; a means of control. VERB control with reins; restrain.

reincarnation NOUN the rebirth of a soul in another body after death.

reindeer NOUN a deer of Arctic regions.

reinforce VERB strengthen with additional people, material, or quantity. **reinforcement** NOUN

reinstate VERB restore to a previous position.

reiterate VERB say again or repeatedly. **reiteration** NOUN

reject VERB refuse to accept. NOUN a person or thing rejected. **rejection** NOUN

rejig VERB (**rejigged**, **rejigging**) rearrange.

rejoice VERB feel or show great joy.

rejoin VERB 1 join again. 2 retort.

rejoinder NOUN a reply or retort.

rejuvenate VERB make more lively or youthful **rejuvenation** NOUN

relapse VERB fall back into a previous state; become worse after improvement. NOUN relapsing.

relate VERB 1 narrate. 2 show to be connected. 3 (**relate to**) have to do with; feel sympathy with.

related ADJ belonging to the same family, group, or type.

relation NOUN 1 the way in which people or things are connected or related. 2 (**relations**) the way in which people or groups behave towards each other. 3 a relative.

relationship NOUN the relation or relations between people or things; an emotional and sexual association between two people.

relative ADJ considered in relation to something else; true only in comparison with something else. NOUN a person connected to another by descent or marriage. **relatively** ADV

relativity NOUN 1 [Physics] a description of matter, energy, space, and time according to Albert Einstein's theories. 2 absence of absolute standards.

relax VERB make or become

less tense; rest; make a rule less strict.

relaxation NOUN

relay NOUN 1 a group of workers etc., relieved after a fixed period by another group; a race between teams in which each person in turn covers part of the total distance. 2 a device activating an electrical circuit. 3 a device which receives and retransmit a signal. VERB receive and pass on or retransmit.

release VERB 1 set free; remove from a fixed position. 2 make information, or a film or recording, available to the public. NOUN 1 releasing. 2 a film or recording released.

relegate VERB consign to a lower rank or position.

relegation NOUN

relent VERB become less severe.

relentless ADJ oppressively constant; harsh or inflexible.

relevant ADJ related to the matter in hand.

relevance NOUN

reliable ADJ able to be relied on.

reliability NOUN

reliably ADV

reliance NOUN dependence on or trust in someone or something.

reliant ADJ

relic NOUN something that survives from earlier times.

relief NOUN 1 reassurance and relaxation after anxiety or stress: alleviation of pain; a break in monotony or tension. 2 assistance to those in need. 3 a person replacing another on duty. 4 a carving etc. in which the design projects from a surface; a similar effect given by colour or shading.

relieve VERB give or bring relief to; release from a task, burden, or duty; raise the siege of.

religion NOUN belief in and worship of a God or gods; a system of faith and worship.

religious ADJ 1 of or believing in a religion. 2 very careful and regular.

relinquish VERB give up.

reliquary NOUN (PL -ies) a receptacle for holy relics.

relish NOUN 1 great enjoyment. 2 a strong-

tasting pickle or sauce.
VERB enjoy greatly.

relocate VERB move to a
different place.
relocation NOUN

reluctant ADJ unwilling.
reluctance NOUN

rely VERB (**relied, relying**)
(**rely on**) have confidence
in; depend on for help
etc.

remain VERB stay; be left or
left behind; continue in
the same condition.

remainder NOUN the
remaining people or
things; a quantity left
after subtraction or
division.

remains PLURAL NOUN things
that remain or are left; a
dead body.

remand VERB send a
defendant to wait for
their trial, either on bail
or in jail.
on remand remanded.

remark NOUN a spoken or
written comment. VERB
1 make a remark. 2 notice.

remarkable ADJ striking
or extraordinary.
remarkably ADV

remedial ADJ 1 providing a
remedy. 2 provided for
children with learning
difficulties.

remedy NOUN (PL **-ies**)
something that cures a
condition or puts a matter
right. VERB (**remedied,
remedying**) set right.

remember VERB keep in
your mind and recall at
will; not fail to do
something necessary.
remembrance NOUN

remind VERB cause to
remember.

reminder NOUN something
that reminds someone.

reminisce VERB think or
talk about the past.
reminiscence NOUN

reminiscent ADJ tending
to remind you of
something.

remiss ADJ negligent.

remission NOUN
1 cancellation of a debt or
penalty. 2 the reduction of
a prison sentence; a
temporary recovery from
an illness.

remit VERB (**remitted,
remitting**) 1 cancel a debt
or punishment. 2 send
money. 3 refer a matter to
an authority. NOUN a task
assigned to someone.

remittance NOUN the
sending of money; money
sent.

remnant NOUN a small

remaining quantity or piece.

remonstrate VERB make a protest.

remorse NOUN deep regret for your wrongdoing. **remorseful** ADJ

remorseless ADJ pitiless; relentless.

remote ADJ 1 far away in place or time; not close; aloof or unfriendly. 2 (of a possibility) very slight.

remove VERB take off or away; dismiss from office; get rid of. NOUN a degree of remoteness or difference. **removable** ADJ **removal** NOUN

remunerate VERB pay or reward for services. **remuneration** NOUN

remunerative ADJ profitable.

Renaissance NOUN a revival of art and learning in Europe in the 14th–16th centuries; (**renaissance**) any similar revival.

renal ADJ of the kidneys.

rend VERB (**rent, rending**) tear.

render VERB 1 provide a service, help, etc.; submit a bill etc. 2 cause to become. 3 interpret or

perform artistically. 4 melt down fat.

rendezvous NOUN (PL **rendezvous**) a prearranged meeting or meeting place.

rendition NOUN the way something is rendered or performed.

renegade NOUN a person who deserts a group, cause, etc.

renege VERB fail to keep a promise or agreement.

renew VERB resume an interrupted activity; replace something broken or worn out; extend the validity of a licence etc.; give fresh life or vigour to. **renewal** NOUN

rennet NOUN curdled milk, used in making cheese.

renounce VERB give up formally; reject.

renovate VERB repair or restore to good condition. **renovation** NOUN

renown NOUN fame. **renowned** ADJ

rent¹ past & past participle of **rend**. NOUN a torn place.

rent² NOUN regular payment made for the use of property or land. VERB pay or receive rent for.

rental NOUN rent; renting.

renunciation NOUN renouncing.

reorganize (or **-ise**) VERB organize in a new way. **reorganization** NOUN

rep NOUN [inf] **1** a representative. **2** repertory.

repair VERB **1** restore to a good condition. **2** [formal] go to a place. NOUN **1** the process of repairing. **2** the condition of an object.

reparation NOUN the making of amends for a wrong; (**reparations**) compensation for war damage paid by a defeated state.

repartee NOUN an exchange of witty remarks.

repast NOUN [formal] a meal.

repatriate VERB send someone back to their own country. **repatriation** NOUN

repay VERB (**repaid**, **repaying**) pay back. **repayment** NOUN

repeal VERB cause a law to be no longer valid. NOUN the repealing of a law.

repeat VERB **1** say or do again. **2** (**repeat yourself**) say the same thing again. **3** (**repeat itself**) occur again in the same way. NOUN something that recurs or is repeated.

repel VERB (**repelled**, **repelling**) drive away or back; disgust.

repellent ADJ causing disgust. NOUN a substance used to keep away pests or to make something impervious to water etc.

repent VERB feel regret about a wrong or unwise action. **repentance** NOUN **repentant** ADJ

repercussion NOUN an unintended consequence.

repertoire NOUN the material known or regularly performed by a person or company.

repertory NOUN (PL **-ies**) **1** the performance by a company of various plays etc. at regular intervals. **2** a repertoire.

repetition NOUN repeating; an instance of this.

repetitious ADJ repetitive.

repetitive ADJ having too much repetition.

replace VERB **1** put back in place. **2** provide or be a substitute for. **replacement** NOUN

replay VERB play a

recording again; play a match again. NOUN something replayed.

replenish VERB refill.

replete ADJ full; well supplied.

replica NOUN an exact copy.

replicate VERB make a replica of.

reply VERB (**replied, replying**) answer. NOUN (PL **-ies**) an answer.

report VERB 1 give an account of. 2 make a formal complaint about. 3 present yourself on arrival; be responsible to a superior. NOUN 1 a spoken or written account; a written assessment of a pupil's progress. 2 an explosive sound.

reporter NOUN a person who reports news for a newspaper or broadcasting company.

repose NOUN a state of rest, peace, or calm VERB rest.

repository NOUN (PL **-ies**) a storage place.

repossess VERB take back goods etc. when payments are not made. **repossession** NOUN

reprehensible ADJ deserving condemnation.

represent VERB 1 speak or act on behalf of. 2 amount to; be an example of. 3 show or describe in a particular way; depict in a work of art; symbolize.

representation NOUN representing or being represented; a picture, diagram, etc.

representative ADJ 1 typical of a group or class. 2 consisting of people chosen to act or speak on behalf of a wider group. NOUN an agent of a firm who visits potential clients to sell its products; a person chosen to represent others.

repress VERB subdue, restrain, or control. **repression** NOUN **repressive** ADJ

reprieve NOUN a postponement or cancellation of punishment; a temporary relief from trouble. VERB give a reprieve to.

reprimand VERB reprove. NOUN a reproof.

reprint VERB print again. NOUN a book reprinted.

reprisal NOUN an act of retaliation.

reproach VERB express

disapproval of. NOUN an act of reproaching.

reproachful ADJ

reprobate NOUN an immoral or unprincipled person.

reproduce VERB produce again; produce a copy of; produce young or offspring.

reproduction NOUN

reproductive ADJ

reproof NOUN an expression of condemnation for a fault.

reprove VERB give a reproof to.

reptile NOUN a cold-blooded animal of a class that includes snakes, lizards, and tortoises.

republic NOUN a country in which the supreme power is held by the people's representatives, not by a monarch.

republican ADJ of or advocating a republic. NOUN a person advocating republican government.

repudiate VERB refuse to accept; deny the truth of.

repudiation NOUN

repugnant ADJ very distasteful.

repulse VERB drive back by force; reject or rebuff.

repulsion NOUN a feeling of extreme distaste.

repulsive ADJ

reputable ADJ having a good reputation.

reputation NOUN what is generally believed about a person or thing.

repute NOUN reputation.

reputed ADJ said or thought to be.

reputedly ADV

request NOUN an act of asking for something; something asked for. VERB ask for; ask someone to do something.

requiem NOUN a Christian Mass for the souls of the dead; music for this.

require VERB 1 need; depend on for success or fulfilment. 2 order or oblige.

requirement NOUN a need.

requisite ADJ required or needed. NOUN something needed.

requisition NOUN an official order laying claim to the use of property or materials. VERB take possession of something by such an order.

rescind VERB repeal or cancel a law etc.

rescue VERB save from

danger or distress. NOUN rescuing.

research NOUN study and investigation to establish facts. VERB carry out research into a subject.

resemble VERB be like.

resemblance NOUN

resent VERB feel bitter towards or about.

resentful ADJ

resentment NOUN

reservation NOUN 1 reserving; reserved accommodation etc.; an area of land set aside for a purpose. 2 doubt.

reserve VERB put aside for future or special use; order or set aside for a particular person; have or keep a right or power. NOUN 1 a supply of something available for use if required; a military force for use in an emergency; a substitute player in a sports team. 2 land set aside for special use, especially the protection of wildlife. 3 lack of friendliness or warmth.

reserved ADJ slow to reveal emotion or opinions.

reservoir NOUN a lake used as a store for a water supply; a container for a supply of fluid.

reshuffle VERB reorganize. NOUN a reorganization.

reside VERB live permanently.

residence NOUN residing; the place where a person lives.

resident NOUN a long-term inhabitant; a guest in a hotel. ADJ living somewhere on a long-term basis.

residential ADJ designed for living in; lived in; providing accommodation.

residue NOUN what is left over.

residual ADJ

resign VERB 1 give up a job or position of office. 2 (**resign yourself**) accept something undesirable but inevitable.

resignation NOUN

resilient ADJ springing back when bent, pressed, etc.; readily recovering from shock or distress.

resilience NOUN

resin NOUN a sticky substance produced by some trees; a similar substance made synthetically, used in plastics.

resist VERB oppose strongly or forcibly; withstand; refrain from accepting or yielding to. **resistance** NOUN **resistant** ADJ

resistor NOUN a device that resists the passage of an electric current.

resolute ADJ determined.

resolution NOUN **1** a firm decision; determination; a formal statement of a committee's opinion. **2** solving a problem etc.

resolve VERB **1** find a solution to. **2** decide firmly on a course of action. **3** separate into constituent parts. NOUN determination.

resonant ADJ (of sound) deep, clear, and ringing. **resonance** NOUN

resonate VERB be filled with a deep, clear, ringing sound.

resort NOUN **1** a popular holiday destination. **2** a strategy or course of action. VERB (**resort to**) turn to for help; adopt as a measure.

resound VERB be filled with a ringing, booming, or echoing sound.

resource NOUN **1** a supply of an asset to be used when needed; (**resources**) available assets. **2** a strategy for dealing with difficulties; the ability to find such strategies.

resourceful ADJ clever at finding ways of doing things.

respect NOUN **1** admiration or esteem; consideration for others' rights and wishes. **2** an aspect of a situation etc. VERB feel or show respect for.

respectable ADJ **1** regarded as conventionally correct. **2** adequate or acceptable; considerable. **respectability** NOUN **respectably** ADV

respective ADJ belonging to each as an individual.

respectively ADV for each separately in the order mentioned.

respiration NOUN breathing.

respirator NOUN a device worn over the nose and mouth to prevent the inhalation of smoke etc.; a device for giving artificial respiration.

respiratory ADJ of respiration.

respite NOUN rest or relief from something difficult or unpleasant.

resplendent ADJ brilliant with colour or decorations.

respond VERB answer or react.

respondent NOUN a defendant in a lawsuit.

response NOUN 1 an answer. 2 an act, feeling, or movement produced by a stimulus or another's action.

responsibility NOUN being responsible; a duty resulting from your job or position.

responsible ADJ 1 obliged to do something or care for someone; being the cause of something and so deserving blame or credit for it. 2 able to be trusted. 3 (of a job) involving important duties etc. 4 (**responsible to**) having to report to a senior person.

responsibly ADV

responsive ADJ responding readily to an influence.

rest VERB 1 stop working or moving in order to relax or recover strength. 2 place or be placed for support; remain or be left in a specified condition. 3 depend or be based on. NOUN 1 a period of resting. 2 a prop or support for an object.

the rest the remaining part, people, or things.

restaurant NOUN a place where meals can be bought and eaten.

restaurateur NOUN a restaurant keeper.

restful ADJ soothing and relaxing.

restitution NOUN 1 the restoring of a thing to its proper owner or original state. 2 compensation.

restive ADJ restless.

restless ADJ unable to rest or relax.

restorative ADJ able to restore health or strength.

restore VERB bring back to a previous condition, place, or owner; repair a building, work of art, etc.; bring back a previous practice, situation, etc.

restoration NOUN

restrain VERB keep under control or within limits.

restraint NOUN

restrict VERB put a limit on or subject to limitations.
restriction NOUN
restrictive ADJ
result NOUN 1 what comes about because of an action etc.; the product of calculation. 2 a final score or mark in a contest or examination. VERB 1 occur as a result. 2 (**result in**) have a particular outcome.
resultant ADJ occurring as a result.
resume VERB begin again or continue after a pause.
resumption NOUN
résumé NOUN a summary.
resurgent ADJ rising or arising again.
resurgence NOUN
resurrect VERB bring back to life or into use.
resurrection NOUN 1 resurrecting. 2 (**Resurrection**) (in Christian belief) the time when Jesus rose from the dead.
resuscitate VERB restore to consciousness.
resuscitation NOUN
retail NOUN the sale of goods to the public. VERB sell or be sold by retail.

retailer NOUN
retain VERB keep possession of; absorb and hold; hold in place.
retainer NOUN a fee paid to a barrister to secure their services.
retaliate VERB repay an injury, insult, etc. by inflicting one in return.
retaliation NOUN
retard VERB cause delay to.
retarded ADJ [offensive] less developed mentally than is usual at a certain age.
retch VERB strain your throat as if vomiting.
retention NOUN retaining.
retentive ADJ able to retain things.
reticent ADJ not revealing your thoughts or feelings.
reticence NOUN
retina NOUN (PL **-nas** or **-nae**) a membrane at the back of the eyeball, sensitive to light.
retinue NOUN attendants accompanying an important person.
retire VERB 1 give up your regular work because of age. 2 withdraw; retreat; go to bed.
retirement NOUN
retiring ADJ shy; avoiding company.

retort VERB make a sharp or witty reply. NOUN **1** a reply of this kind. **2** a glass container used for distilling liquids and heating chemicals.

retrace VERB go back over or repeat a route.

retract VERB pull back; withdraw an allegation. **retractable** ADJ **retraction** NOUN

retreat VERB withdraw after defeat or from an uncomfortable situation; move back. NOUN **1** retreating. **2** a quiet or secluded place.

retrench VERB reduce costs or spending.

retribution NOUN deserved punishment.

retrieve VERB **1** get or bring back; extract information stored in a computer. **2** improve a bad situation. **retrieval** NOUN

retriever NOUN a breed of dog used to retrieve game.

retrograde ADJ going backwards; reverting to an inferior state.

retrospect NOUN (**in retrospect**) when looking back on a past event.

retrospective ADJ looking back on the past;

taking effect from a date in the past.

retsina NOUN a Greek resin-flavoured white wine.

return VERB **1** come or go back; bring, give, put, or send back. **2** yield a profit. **3** elect to office. NOUN **1** an act of returning; a ticket for a journey to a place and back again. **2** a profit.

reunion NOUN a gathering of people who were formerly associated.

reunite VERB bring or come together again.

reuse VERB use again.

Rev. (or **Revd**) ABBREV Reverend.

rev [inf] NOUN a revolution of an engine. VERB (**revved**, **revving**) cause an engine to run faster.

revamp VERB alter so as to improve.

reveal VERB make visible by uncovering; make known.

reveille NOUN a military waking signal.

revel VERB (**revelled**, **revelling**; [US] **reveled**, **reveling**) **1** celebrate in a lively, noisy way. **2** (**revel in**) take great pleasure in. PLURAL NOUN (**revels**) lively, noisy celebrations.

reveller NOUN

revelry NOUN

revelation NOUN revealing; a surprising thing revealed.

revenge NOUN retaliation for an injury or wrong. VERB avenge.

revenue NOUN the income received by an organization, or by a government from taxes.

reverberate VERB be repeated as an echo; continue to have effects.

reverberation NOUN

revere VERB respect or admire deeply.

reverence NOUN deep respect.

reverent ADJ

reverend ADJ a title given to Christian ministers.

reverie NOUN a daydream.

reverse VERB move backwards; cancel; convert to its opposite; turn inside out or upside down etc. ADJ opposite in direction, nature, order, etc. NOUN 1 a change of direction; the opposite side. 2 a setback.

reversal NOUN

reversible ADJ

revert VERB return to a previous state, practice, etc.

reversion NOUN

review NOUN 1 a general survey of events or a subject; revision or reconsideration; a critical report on a book, play, etc. 2 a ceremonial inspection of troops etc. VERB make or write a review of.

reviewer NOUN

revile VERB criticize scornfully.

revise VERB 1 re-examine and alter or correct. 2 reread work already done in preparation for an exam.

revision NOUN

revivalism NOUN the promotion of a return to religious faith.

revivalist NOUN

revive VERB come or bring back to life, consciousness, or strength; restore interest in or use of.

revival NOUN

revoke VERB withdraw a decree, law, etc.

revocation NOUN

revolt VERB 1 rebel against an authority. 2 cause strong disgust in. NOUN rebellion or defiance.

revolting ADJ extremely unpleasant.

revolution NOUN 1 the forcible overthrow of a government and installation of a new one; a complete change in methods etc. 2 a single, complete movement around a central point.

revolutionary ADJ & NOUN

revolutionize (or -ise) VERB change completely.

revolve VERB move in a circle around a central point; be centred on.

revolver NOUN a type of pistol.

revue NOUN a theatrical show consisting of a series of items.

revulsion NOUN strong disgust.

reward NOUN something given or received in return for service or merit. VERB give a reward to.

rewire VERB renew the electrical wiring of.

Rex NOUN a reigning king.

rhapsodize (or -ise) VERB talk or write about something very enthusiastically.

rhapsody NOUN (PL -ies)

1 an expression of great enthusiasm. 2 a romantic musical composition.

rhapsodic ADJ

rheostat NOUN a device for varying the resistance to electric current.

rhesus NOUN a small monkey.

rhesus factor a substance found in human blood.

rhetoric NOUN the art of using words impressively; impressive language.

rhetorical ADJ 1 expressed so as to sound impressive. 2 (of a question) asked for effect rather than to obtain an answer.

rhetorically ADV

rheumatism NOUN a disease causing pain in the joints and muscles.

rheumatic ADJ

rhinestone NOUN an imitation diamond.

rhino NOUN (PL **rhino** or **rhinos**) [inf] a rhinoceros.

rhinoceros NOUN (PL **rhinoceros** or **rhinoceroses**) a large thick-skinned animal with one horn or two on its nose.

rhododendron NOUN an evergreen shrub with large clusters of flowers.

rhombus NOUN a diamond-shaped figure.

rhubarb NOUN a plant with red leaf stalks which are cooked and eaten as fruit.

rhyme NOUN a similarity of sound between words or syllables; a word providing a rhyme to another; a short poem with rhyming lines. VERB have a similar or the same sound.

rhythm NOUN a strong, regular, repeated pattern of movement or sound; a regularly recurring sequence of events. **rhythmic** ADJ **rhythmically** ADV

rib NOUN one of the curved bones round the chest; a structural part resembling this.

ribald ADJ humorous in a coarse or irreverent way.

riband NOUN a ribbon.

ribbon NOUN a decorative narrow strip of fabric; a long, narrow strip.

riboflavin NOUN vitamin B_2.

rice NOUN grains of a cereal plant grown for food on wet land in hot countries.

rich ADJ 1 having much money or many assets. 2 having or producing something in large amounts; abundant. 3 (of soil) fertile. 4 (of food) containing much fat or sugar; (of colour, sound, or smell) pleasantly deep and strong. PLURAL NOUN (**riches**) wealth.

richly ADV fully or thoroughly; elaborately.

Richter scale NOUN a scale for measuring the severity of an earthquake.

rick NOUN 1 a stack of hay etc. 2 a slight sprain or strain. VERB sprain or strain slightly.

rickets NOUN a bone disease caused by vitamin D deficiency.

rickety ADJ shaky or insecure.

rickshaw NOUN a two-wheeled vehicle pulled along by a person.

ricochet VERB (**ricocheted, ricocheting**) rebound from a surface after striking it with a glancing blow. NOUN a rebound of this kind.

rid VERB (**rid, ridding**) 1 free from something unpleasant or unwanted. 2 (**get rid of**) be freed or relieved of.

riddance NOUN (**good riddance**) expressing relief at being rid of a person or thing.

riddle NOUN **1** a cleverly worded question, asked as a game; something puzzling or mysterious. **2** a coarse sieve. VERB make many holes in; permeate.

ride VERB (**rode, ridden, riding**) sit on and control the movements of a horse, bicycle, etc.; travel in a vehicle; be carried or supported by. NOUN a spell of riding; a roller coaster or similar fairground amusement; a path for horse riding.

rider NOUN **1** a person who rides a horse etc. **2** an additional statement or condition.

ridge NOUN a long narrow hilltop; a narrow raised strip; a line where two upward slopes meet. **ridged** ADJ

ridicule NOUN contemptuous mockery. VERB make fun of.

ridiculous ADJ deserving to be laughed at.

rife ADJ widespread; (**rife with**) full of.

riff NOUN a short repeated phrase in jazz etc.

riff-raff NOUN disreputable people.

rifle NOUN a gun with a long barrel. VERB search hurriedly through.

rift NOUN a crack, split, or break; a breach in friendly relations.

rig VERB (**rigged, rigging**) **1** fit sails and rigging on a boat; set up a device or structure. **2** manage or run fraudulently. NOUN **1** an apparatus for a particular purpose. **2** a piece of equipment for extracting oil or gas from the ground.

rigging NOUN the ropes and chains supporting a ship's masts.

right ADJ **1** justified or morally good. **2** factually correct; most appropriate; satisfactory, sound, or normal. **3** of or on the side of the body which is on the east when you are facing north. ADV **1** completely; directly; exactly. **2** correctly. **3** to or on the right-hand side. NOUN **1** that which is morally good. **2** an entitlement to have or do something. **3** the right-

righteous

hand side or direction. **4** a party or group favouring conservative views and capitalist policies. VERB restore to a normal or upright position; rectify.
right angle an angle of 90°.
righteous ADJ virtuous or morally right.
righteousness NOUN
rightful ADJ having a right to something; just or legitimate.
rightfully ADV
rigid ADJ unable to bend; strict or inflexible.
rigidity NOUN
rigmarole NOUN a long complicated procedure.
rigor mortis NOUN stiffening of the body after death.
rigour ([US] **rigor**) NOUN being thorough and accurate; strictness or severity; harshness of weather etc.
rigorous ADJ
rile VERB [inf] annoy.
rill NOUN a small stream.
rim NOUN an edge or border, especially of something circular or round. VERB (**rimmed**, **rimming**) provide with a rim.
rime NOUN frost.

rind NOUN a tough outer layer on fruit, cheese, bacon, etc.
ring¹ NOUN **1** a small circular band worn on a finger; a circular object or mark; a circular device giving out heat on a gas or electric hob. **2** an enclosed area for a sport etc. **3** a group of people with a shared interest etc. VERB surround; draw a circle round.
ring² VERB (**rang, rung, ringing**) **1** make a loud clear resonant sound; echo with a sound; call for attention by sounding a bell. **2** telephone. NOUN **1** an act or sound of ringing. **2** an impression conveyed by words: *a ring of truth*. **3** a telephone call.
ringleader NOUN a person who leads a forbidden activity.
ringlet NOUN a long spiralling curl of hair.
ringworm NOUN a fungal infection producing round scaly patches on the skin.
rink NOUN an enclosed area of ice for skating, ice hockey, etc.
rinse VERB wash out soap etc. from. NOUN an act of

rinsing; a liquid for colouring the hair.

riot NOUN 1 a violent disturbance by a crowd of people. 2 a large and varied display. VERB take part in a riot.
run riot behave in an unrestrained way.

riotous ADJ disorderly or unruly.

RIP ABBREV rest in peace.

rip VERB (**ripped, ripping**) tear or become torn; pull forcibly away. NOUN a torn place.
rip off [inf] cheat; steal.

ripcord NOUN a cord pulled to release a parachute.

ripe ADJ ready for harvesting and eating; matured; (of age) advanced.
ripen VERB

riposte NOUN a quick reply.

ripple NOUN a small wave; a gentle sound that rises and falls. VERB form ripples.

rise VERB (**rose, risen, rising**) 1 come or go up; get up from lying or sitting. 2 increase in quantity, intensity, pitch, etc.; slope upwards. 3 rebel. 4 (of a river) have its source. NOUN an act of

rising; a pay increase; an upward slope.
give rise to cause.

risible ADJ ridiculous.

risk NOUN a possibility of meeting danger or suffering harm; a person or thing that causes this. VERB expose to danger or loss.
risky ADJ

risotto NOUN (PL **-os**) a dish of rice with meat, vegetables, etc.

risqué ADJ slightly indecent.

rissole NOUN a mixture of minced meat formed into a flat shape and fried.

rite NOUN a ritual.

ritual NOUN a set series of actions used in a religious or other ceremony. ADJ done as a ritual.
ritually ADV

rival NOUN a person or thing that competes with or can equal another. VERB (**rivalled, rivalling**; [US] **rivaled, rivaling**) be comparable to.
rivalry NOUN

riven ADJ torn apart.

river NOUN a large natural flow of water.

rivet NOUN a short metal pin or bolt for holding

together two metal plates.
VERB (**riveted, riveting**)
1 fasten with a rivet.
2 attract and hold the
attention of.

rivulet NOUN a small
stream.

RN ABBREV Royal Navy.

RNA ABBREV ribonucleic
acid, a substance in living
cells which carries
instructions from DNA.

road NOUN a prepared track
along which vehicles may
travel; a way to achieving
a particular outcome.
road rage violent anger
caused by conflict with
another driver.

roadworks PLURAL NOUN
construction or repair of
roads.

roadworthy ADJ (of a
vehicle) fit to be used on a
road.

roam VERB wander.

roan ADJ (of a horse)
having a dark coat
sprinkled with white
hairs.

roar NOUN a loud, deep
sound made or like that
made by a lion; a loud
sound of laughter. VERB
give a roar.

roast VERB cook food in an
oven; make or become

very warm. NOUN a joint of
meat that has been
roasted.

rob VERB (**robbed, robbing**)
steal from; deprive
unfairly of something.
robber NOUN
robbery NOUN

robe NOUN a long loose
garment. VERB dress in a
robe.

robin NOUN a small bird
with a red breast.

robot NOUN a machine able
to carry out a complex
series of actions
automatically.
robotic ADJ

robust ADJ sturdy; healthy.

rock NOUN **1** the hard part
of the earth's crust; a
projecting mass of this; a
large stone. **2** a hard sweet
made in sticks. **3** loud
popular music with a
heavy beat. **4** a rocking
movement. VERB **1** move to
and fro or from side to
side. **2** shock greatly.
rock bottom the lowest
possible level. **rock and
roll** rock music with
elements of blues.

rocker NOUN a curved piece
of wood on the bottom of
a rocking chair.

rockery NOUN (PL **-ies**) an

arrangement of rocks in a garden with plants growing between them.

rocket NOUN 1 a missile or spacecraft propelled by a stream of burning gases. 2 a firework that shoots into the air and explodes. VERB (**rocketed, rocketing**) move rapidly upwards or away.

rocky ADJ (**-ier, -iest**) 1 of or like rock; full of rocks. 2 unstable.

rococo ADJ in a highly ornate style of decoration.

rod NOUN a slender straight bar of wood, metal, etc.; a long stick with a line and hook, for catching fish.

rode past of **ride**.

rodent NOUN an animal with strong front teeth for gnawing things.

rodeo NOUN (PL **-eos**) a competition or exhibition of cowboys' skill.

roe[1] NOUN a mass of eggs in a female fish's ovary.

roe[2] NOUN (PL **roe** or **roes**) a small deer.

rogue NOUN 1 a dishonest or mischievous person. 2 an elephant living apart from the herd. **roguish** ADJ

role NOUN an actor's part; a person's or thing's function.

roll VERB 1 move by turning over and over; move on wheels. 2 turn something flexible over on itself to form a ball or cylinder. 3 sway from side to side; (of a deep sound) reverberate. 4 flatten with a roller. NOUN 1 a cylinder formed by rolling flexible material. 2 an act of rolling. 3 a reverberating sound of thunder etc. 4 a small individual loaf of bread. 5 an official list or register.

roll-call the calling of a list of names to check that all are present.

rolling pin a roller for flattening dough. **rolling stock** railway engines, carriages, etc.

roller NOUN 1 a cylinder rolled over things to flatten or spread them, or on which something is wound. 2 a long swelling wave.

roller coaster a switchback at a fair. **roller skate** a boot with wheels, for gliding across a hard surface.

rollicking ADJ full of

boisterous high spirits.

rollmop NOUN a rolled pickled herring.

roly-poly NOUN a pudding of suet pastry spread with jam and rolled up. ADJ plump.

Roman ADJ & NOUN (a native or inhabitant) of Rome or its ancient Empire. **Roman Catholic** (a member of) the Christian Church which has the pope as its head. **Roman numerals** letters representing numbers (I=1, V=5, etc.).

roman NOUN plain upright type.

romance NOUN a feeling of excitement associated with love; a love affair or love story; a feeling of exciting mystery and remoteness from everyday life. VERB try to win the love of.

Romanesque ADJ of or in a style of architecture common in Europe about 900–1200.

romantic ADJ of love; viewing or showing life in an idealized way. NOUN a romantic person. **romantically** ADV

romanticize (or **-ise**) VERB view or represent as better or more beautiful than is the case.

Romany NOUN (PL **-ies**) a Gypsy; the language of the Gypsies.

romp VERB play about in a lively way.

roof NOUN (PL **roofs**) the upper covering of a building, car, cavity, etc. VERB cover with a roof.

rook NOUN 1 a bird of the crow family. 2 a chess piece with a top shaped like battlements.

rookery NOUN (PL **-ies**) a colony of rooks.

room NOUN 1 a division of a building, separated off by walls. 2 space for occupying or moving in; scope to act or happen.

roomy ADJ (**-ier, -iest**) having plenty of space.

roost NOUN a place where birds perch or rest. VERB perch, especially for rest.

rooster NOUN a male domestic fowl.

root NOUN 1 the part of a plant that grows into the earth and absorbs nourishment from the soil; the embedded part of a hair, tooth, etc. 2 the basis or origin of

something. **3** a number in relation to another which it produces when multiplied by itself a specified number of times. **4** (**roots**) a person's family or origins. VERB **1** cause to take root; cause to stand fixed and unmoving. **2** (of an animal) turn up ground with its snout in search of food; rummage.

rope NOUN a strong thick cord. VERB fasten or secure with rope.

rosary NOUN (PL **-ies**) a set series of prayers; a string of beads for keeping count in this.

rose¹ NOUN **1** a fragrant flower with prickly stems. **2** a soft pink colour.

rose² past of **rise**.

rosé NOUN a light pink wine.

rosemary NOUN a shrub with fragrant leaves used as a herb.

rosette NOUN a round badge or ornament made of ribbons.

roster NOUN a list showing people's turns of duty etc.

rostrum NOUN (PL **-tra** or **-trums**) a platform for standing on to make a speech, conduct an orchestra, etc.

rosy ADJ (**-ier, -iest**) **1** deep pink. **2** promising or hopeful.

rot VERB (**rotted, rotting**) gradually decay. NOUN **1** rotting. **2** [inf] nonsense.

rota NOUN a list of duties to be done or people to do them in rotation.

rotate VERB revolve round an axis; arrange, occur, or deal with in a recurrent series.

rotary ADJ

rotation NOUN

rote NOUN regular repetition of something to be learned.

rotisserie NOUN a revolving spit for roasting meat.

rotor NOUN a rotating part of a machine.

rotten ADJ **1** decayed. **2** corrupt; [inf] very bad.

rotund ADJ rounded and plump.

rotunda NOUN a round, domed building or hall.

rouge NOUN a red powder or cream for colouring the cheeks.

rough ADJ **1** not smooth or level; not gentle; difficult and unpleasant. **2** (of

weather or the sea) wild and stormy; harsh in sound or taste; unsophisticated, plain, or basic. **3** not worked out in every detail. NOUN **1** a basic draft. **2** longer grass at the edge of a golf course.

rough-and-ready crude or simple but effective.

roughen VERB

roughly ADV

roughage NOUN dietary fibre.

roughshod ADJ (**ride roughshod over**) treat inconsiderately or arrogantly.

roulette NOUN a gambling game in which a ball is dropped on to a revolving wheel.

round ADJ **1** shaped like a circle, sphere, or cylinder. **2** (of a number) expressed in convenient units rather than exactly. NOUN **1** a circular shape or piece. **2** a tour of visits or inspection; a recurring sequence of activities; one of a sequence of actions or events; one section of a competition. **3** a song for several voices starting the same tune at different times. **4** the amount of

ammunition needed for one shot. ADV **1** in a circle or curve; so as to surround; so as to cover a whole area or group. **2** so as to face in a different direction. **3** so as to reach a new place or position. PREP **1** on every side of. **2** so as to encircle. VERB **1** pass and go round. **2** (**round up** or **down**) alter a number for convenience. **3** make rounded.

round up gather into one place.

roundabout NOUN **1** a revolving platform at a funfair, with model horses etc. to ride on. **2** a road junction at which traffic moves in one direction round a central island. ADJ indirect or circuitous.

rounders NOUN a team game played with bat and ball, in which players have to run round a circuit.

Roundhead NOUN a supporter of the Parliamentary party in the English Civil War.

roundly ADV in a firm or thorough way.

rouse VERB wake; cause to

become active or excited.

rousing ADJ stirring.

rout NOUN a complete defeat; a disorderly retreat. VERB defeat completely and force to retreat.

route NOUN a course or way from a starting point to a destination.

routine NOUN a standard procedure; a set sequence of movements. ADJ in accordance with routine.

roux NOUN (PL **roux**) a mixture of heated fat and flour as a basis for a sauce.

rove VERB wander.

row[1] NOUN people or things in a line.

row[2] VERB propel a boat using oars.

row[3] NOUN a loud noise; an angry argument. VERB quarrel angrily.

rowan NOUN a tree with clusters of red berries.

rowdy ADJ (**-ier, -iest**) noisy and disorderly. **rowdiness** NOUN

rowlock NOUN a device on the side of a boat for holding an oar.

royal ADJ of or suited to a king or queen. **royal blue** deep, vivid blue.

royally ADV

royalist NOUN a person supporting or advocating monarchy.

royalty NOUN (PL **-ies**) **1** the members of a royal family; royal status or power. **2** payment to an author, patentee, etc. for each copy, performance, or use of their work.

RSVP ABBREV please reply (short for French *répondez s'il vous plaît*).

rub VERB (**rubbed, rubbing**) move your hand, a cloth, etc. over a surface while pressing down firmly; polish, clean, dry, or make sore in this way; (**rub out**) erase marks with a rubber. NOUN an act of rubbing; an ointment to be rubbed on.

rubber NOUN a tough elastic substance made from the juice of certain plants or synthetically; a piece of this for erasing pencil marks. **rubbery** ADJ

rubbish NOUN waste or discarded material; nonsense.

rubble NOUN rough fragments of stone, brick, etc.

rubella NOUN a disease with symptoms like mild measles.

rubric NOUN words put as a heading or note of explanation.

ruby NOUN (PL **-ies**) a red precious stone; a deep red colour.

ruby wedding a 40th wedding anniversary.

ruche NOUN a decorative frill of fabric.

ruck VERB crease or wrinkle. NOUN **1** a crease or wrinkle. **2** a tightly packed crowd.

rucksack NOUN a bag carried on the back.

ructions PLURAL NOUN [inf] unpleasant arguments or protests.

rudder NOUN a vertical piece of metal or wood hinged to the stern of a boat, used for steering.

ruddy ADJ (**-ier, -iest**) having a reddish colour.

rude ADJ **1** offensively impolite or bad-mannered. **2** referring to sex etc. in an offensive way. **3** (of health) good.

rudiments PLURAL NOUN the fundamental principles or elements; an undeveloped form of something.

rudimentary ADJ

rue VERB regret deeply.

rueful ADJ

ruff NOUN a pleated frill worn round the neck; a ring of feathers or fur round a bird's or animal's neck.

ruffian NOUN a violent lawless person.

ruffle VERB disturb the calmness or smoothness of; annoy. NOUN a gathered frill.

rug NOUN a small carpet; a thick woollen blanket.

rugby (or **rugby football**) NOUN a team game played with an oval ball which may be kicked or carried.

rugged ADJ **1** having a rocky surface. **2** (of a man) strong-featured.

rugger NOUN [inf] rugby.

ruin VERB completely spoil or destroy; reduce to bankruptcy. NOUN destruction; the complete loss of a person's money or property; the damaged remains of a building etc.

ruination NOUN

ruinous ADJ

rule NOUN **1** a statement or principle governing behaviour or describing a regular occurrence in nature etc.; a dominant custom; government or control. **2** a ruler used by carpenters etc. VERB **1** govern; keep under control; give an authoritative decision. **2** (**rule out**) exclude. **3** draw a line using a ruler.

ruler NOUN **1** a person who rules. **2** a straight strip used in measuring or for drawing straight lines.

ruling NOUN an authoritative decision.

rum NOUN an alcoholic spirit made from sugar cane.

rumba NOUN a ballroom dance.

rumble NOUN & VERB (make) a low continuous sound.

rumbustious ADJ [inf] boisterous.

ruminant NOUN an animal that chews the cud, such as a cow or sheep.

ruminate VERB **1** think deeply. **2** chew the cud.

rummage VERB search clumsily. NOUN an untidy search through a number of things.

rummy NOUN a card game.

rumour ([US] **rumor**) NOUN an unconfirmed story spread among a number of people.
be rumoured be spread as a rumour.

rump NOUN the buttocks.

rumple VERB make less neat and tidy.

rumpus NOUN a noisy disturbance.

run VERB (**ran**, **run**, **running**) **1** move with quick steps with always at least one foot off the ground; move around hurriedly. **2** move smoothly in a particular direction; flow. **3** travel regularly along a route. **4** be in charge of; function; continue, operate, or proceed. **5** stand as a candidate in an election; compete in a race. **6** smuggle drugs. NOUN **1** a spell of running; a running pace; a journey. **2** a point scored in cricket or baseball. **3** a continuous spell or sequence. **4** unrestricted use of a place. **5** an enclosed area where domestic animals can range. **6** a ladder in stockings or tights.
run-down weak or exhausted. **run-of-the-mill** ordinary.

rundown NOUN a brief summary.

rune NOUN a letter of an ancient Germanic alphabet.

rung[1] NOUN a crosspiece of a ladder etc.

rung[2] past participle of **ring**[2].

runner NOUN 1 a person or animal that runs; a messenger. 2 a shoot that grows along the ground and can take root. 3 a groove, strip, or roller etc. for a thing to move on. 4 a long narrow rug.

runner-up a competitor who comes second.

runny ADJ (**-ier, -iest**) semi-liquid; producing mucus.

runt NOUN the smallest animal in a litter.

runway NOUN a prepared surface on which aircraft may take off and land.

rupture NOUN a break or breach; an abdominal hernia. VERB burst or break; cause a hernia in.

rural ADJ of, in, or like the countryside.

ruse NOUN a deception or trick.

rush[1] VERB move or act with great speed; produce, deal with, or transport hurriedly; force into hasty action; make a sudden assault on. NOUN a sudden quick movement; a very busy state or period; a sudden flow or surge.

rush hour one of the times of the day when traffic is busiest.

rush[2] NOUN a water plant with a slender pithy stem.

rusk NOUN a dry biscuit.

russet ADJ soft reddish brown.

rust NOUN a brownish flaky coating forming on iron exposed to moisture. VERB make or become rusty.

rustic ADJ of or like country life; charmingly simple and unsophisticated.

rustle VERB 1 make a sound like paper being crumpled. 2 steal horses or cattle. NOUN a rustling sound.

rustler NOUN

rusty ADJ affected by rust; deteriorating through lack of use.

rut[1] NOUN 1 a deep track made by wheels. 2 a habitual dull pattern of behaviour.

rut[2] NOUN the periodic

sexual excitement of a male deer, goat, etc. VERB (**rutted**, **rutting**) be affected with this.

ruthless ADJ having no pity.

rye NOUN a cereal; whisky made from this.

Ss

S ABBREV south or southern.

sabbath NOUN a day for rest and religious worship.

sabbatical NOUN a period of paid leave for study and travel.

sable ADJ black.

sabotage NOUN wilful damage to machinery, materials, etc. VERB commit sabotage on. **saboteur** NOUN

sabre ([US] **saber**) NOUN a curved sword.

sac NOUN a hollow bag-like structure.

saccharin NOUN an artificial sweetener.

sachet NOUN a small bag or sealed pack.

sack NOUN **1** a large bag made of strong coarse fabric. **2** (**the sack**) [inf] dismissal from employment. VERB **1** [inf] dismiss. **2** plunder a captured town.

sackcloth NOUN coarse fabric for making sacks.

sacrament NOUN any of the symbolic Christian religious ceremonies.

sacred ADJ connected to a god or goddess and greatly revered; to do with religion.

sacrifice NOUN the slaughter of a victim or presenting of a gift to win a god's favour; this victim or gift; the giving up of a valued thing for the sake of something else. VERB offer as a sacrifice. **sacrificial** ADJ

sacrilege NOUN disrespect to a sacred thing. **sacrilegious** ADJ

sacrosanct ADJ too important or precious to be changed.

sacrum NOUN (PL **-crums** or **-cra**) the triangular bone at the base of the spine.

sad ADJ (**sadder, saddest**) feeling, causing, or expressing sorrow.
sadden VERB
saddle NOUN 1 a seat for a rider. 2 a joint of meat from the back of an animal. VERB put a saddle on a horse; burden with a task.
sadism NOUN enjoyment derived from inflicting pain on others.
sadist NOUN
sadistic ADJ
safari NOUN an expedition to observe or hunt wild animals.
safe ADJ protected from risk or danger; not harmed; providing security. NOUN a strong lockable cupboard for valuables.
safely ADV
safeguard NOUN a means of protection. VERB protect.
safety NOUN freedom from risk or danger.
safety pin a pin with a point held in a guard when closed.
saffron NOUN a yellow spice.
sag VERB (**sagged, sagging**) gradually droop or sink.

saga NOUN a long story.
sagacious ADJ wise.
sage NOUN 1 a herb. 2 an old and wise man. ADJ wise.
sago NOUN the starchy pith of the sago palm, used in puddings.
said past and past participle of **say**.
sail NOUN 1 a piece of fabric spread to catch the wind and drive a boat along. 2 a journey by boat. 3 the arm of a windmill. VERB 1 travel by water. 2 move smoothly.
sailor NOUN a member of a ship's crew.
saint NOUN a holy person, especially one venerated by the RC or Orthodox Church; a very good person.
sainthood NOUN
saintly ADJ
sake NOUN (**for the sake of**) in the interest of; out of consideration for.
salacious ADJ containing too much sexual detail.
salad NOUN a cold dish of raw vegetables etc.
salamander NOUN a newt-like animal.
salami NOUN a strongly flavoured sausage, eaten

cold.

salary NOUN (PL **-ies**) a fixed regular payment made to an employee.

salaried ADJ

sale NOUN the exchange of a commodity for money; an event at which goods are sold; the disposal of stock at reduced prices.

saleable ADJ

salesman (or **saleswoman**) NOUN a person employed to sell goods.

salient ADJ most noticeable or important.

saline ADJ containing salt.

saliva NOUN the watery liquid that forms in the mouth.

salivate VERB produce saliva.

sallow ADJ (of the complexion) yellowish.

sally NOUN (PL **-ies**) a sudden charge from a besieged place; a witty remark. VERB (**sallied**, **sallying**) rush out in attack; set out on a journey.

salmon NOUN a large fish with pinkish flesh.

salmonella NOUN a germ causing food poisoning.

salon NOUN a place where a hairdresser, couturier, etc. works; an elegant room for receiving guests.

saloon NOUN 1 a public room, especially on board ship. 2 a car with a separate boot.

salsa NOUN 1 a style of music and dance of Cuban origin. 2 a spicy sauce.

salt NOUN 1 sodium chloride used to season and preserve food. 2 a chemical compound formed by the reaction of an acid with a base. ADJ tasting of salt; preserved in salt. VERB season or preserve with salt.

salt cellar a container for salt.

salty ADJ

salubrious ADJ health-giving.

salutary ADJ producing a beneficial effect.

salutation NOUN a greeting.

salute NOUN a gesture of greeting or acknowledgement; a prescribed movement made in the armed forces etc. to show respect. VERB make a salute to.

salvage NOUN the saving

of a ship or its cargo from loss at sea, or of property from fire etc.; the items saved. VERB save.

salvation NOUN the fact or state of being saved from sin or disaster.

salve NOUN a soothing ointment; something that reduces feelings of guilt. VERB reduce feelings of guilt.

salver NOUN a small tray.

salvo NOUN (PL **-oes** or **-os**) a simultaneous discharge of guns; a sudden series of aggressive statements or acts.

Samaritan NOUN a charitable or helpful person.

samba NOUN a Brazilian dance.

same ADJ exactly alike. PRON the one already mentioned. ADV in the same way.

sample NOUN a small part intended to show the quality of the whole. VERB test by taking a sample of.

sampler NOUN a piece of fabric decorated with many different embroidery stitches.

samurai NOUN (PL **samurai**) (in the past) a Japanese

army officer.

sanatorium NOUN (PL **-riums** or **-ria**) an establishment for treating chronic diseases or convalescents; a room for sick pupils in a school.

sanctify VERB (**sanctified**, **sanctifying**) make holy or sacred.

sanctimonious ADJ ostentatiously pious.

sanction NOUN 1 permission or approval. 2 a penalty imposed on a country or organization. VERB authorize.

sanctity NOUN sacredness or holiness.

sanctuary NOUN (PL **-ies**) 1 a place of refuge; a place where wildlife is protected. 2 a sacred place.

sanctum NOUN a sacred place; a private place.

sand NOUN very fine loose fragments of crushed rock; (**sands**) an expanse of sand. VERB smooth with sandpaper or a sander.

sandal NOUN a light shoe with straps.

sandbag NOUN a bag filled with sand, used to protect a wall or building.

sandbank NOUN a deposit of sand forming a shallow

area in a sea or river.

sandcastle NOUN a model of a castle built out of sand.

sander NOUN a power tool for smoothing surfaces.

sandpaper NOUN paper with a coating of sand, used for smoothing surfaces.

sandstone NOUN rock formed of compressed sand.

sandstorm NOUN a desert storm of wind carrying blown sand.

sandwich NOUN two slices of bread with a filling between. VERB put between two other people or things.

sandy ADJ (**-ier, -iest**) **1** like sand; covered with sand. **2** yellowish brown.

sane ADJ not mad; sensible.

sang past of **sing**.

sanguine ADJ optimistic.

sanitary ADJ of sanitation; hygienic.

sanitary towel a pad worn to absorb menstrual blood.

sanitation NOUN arrangements to protect public health, especially drainage and disposal of sewage.

sanitize (or **-ise**) VERB make hygienic; alter to make more acceptable.

sanity NOUN the condition of being sane.

sank past of **sink**.

sap NOUN the food-carrying liquid in plants. VERB (**sapped, sapping**) exhaust gradually.

sapling NOUN a young tree.

sapper NOUN a military engineer who lays or defuses mines.

sapphire NOUN a blue precious stone; its colour.

sarcasm NOUN ironically scornful language. **sarcastic** ADJ

sarcophagus NOUN (PL **-phagi**) a stone coffin.

sardine NOUN a small herring-like fish.

sardonic ADJ humorous in a mocking way.

sari NOUN a length of cloth draped round the body, worn by Indian women.

sarong NOUN a strip of cloth wrapped round the body and tucked at the waist.

sartorial ADJ of tailoring, clothing, or style of dress.

sash NOUN **1** a strip of cloth worn round the waist or over one shoulder. **2** a frame holding the glass in a window.

sat past and past participle of **sit**.

Satan NOUN the devil.

satanic ADJ

Satanism NOUN the worship of Satan.

satchel NOUN a bag for school books, hung over the shoulder.

sated ADJ fully satisfied.

satellite NOUN **1** a heavenly or artificial body revolving round a planet. **2** a country that is dependent on another.

satellite television television in which the signals are broadcast via satellite.

satiate VERB satisfy fully.

satin NOUN a smooth, glossy fabric.

satire NOUN criticism through the use of humour, irony, exaggeration, or ridicule; a novel or play etc. that uses satire.

satirical ADJ

satirize (or **-ise**) VERB mock or criticize using satire.

satisfactory ADJ acceptable.

satisfactorily ADV

satisfy VERB (**satisfied**, **satisfying**) fulfil the needs or wishes of; make pleased or contented; fulfil a need, requirement, etc.; convince.

satisfaction NOUN

satsuma NOUN a small variety of orange.

saturate VERB make thoroughly wet; fill completely or to excess.

saturation NOUN

Saturday NOUN the day following Friday.

satyr NOUN a woodland god in classical mythology, with a goat's ears, tail, and legs.

sauce NOUN a liquid food added for flavour.

saucepan NOUN a metal cooking pot with a long handle.

saucer NOUN a shallow curved dish on which a cup stands.

saucy ADJ (**-ier**, **-iest**) cheeky; sexually suggestive.

saucily ADV

sauerkraut NOUN chopped pickled cabbage.

sauna NOUN a hot room for cleaning and refreshing the body.

saunter NOUN & VERB (take) a stroll.

sausage NOUN minced seasoned meat in a tubular case of thin skin.

sauté ADJ fried quickly in shallow oil.

savage ADJ wild and fierce; cruel and vicious; primitive and uncivilized. NOUN a primitive or uncivilized person; a brutal person. VERB fiercely attack and maul.

savagery NOUN

savannah NOUN a grassy plain in hot regions.

save VERB 1 rescue or remove from harm or danger. 2 store for future use; avoid wasting. 3 prevent the scoring of a goal. NOUN an act of saving in football etc.

savings PLURAL NOUN money saved.

saviour ([US] **savior**) NOUN a person who rescues people from harm.

savoir faire NOUN the ability to act appropriately in social situations.

savour ([US] **savor**) NOUN flavour; smell. VERB enjoy fully or thoroughly.

savoury ([US] **savory**) ADJ salty or spicy rather than sweet; morally respectable.

saw[1] past of **see**.

saw[2] NOUN a cutting tool with a zigzag edge. VERB (**sawed, sawn, sawing**) cut with a saw.

saw[3] NOUN a saying.

sawdust NOUN powdery fragments of wood, made in sawing timber.

saxophone NOUN a brass wind instrument with finger-operated keys.

say VERB (**said, saying**) 1 utter words; express, convey, or state; have written or shown on the surface. 2 suppose as a possibility. NOUN the opportunity to state your opinion.

saying NOUN a well-known phrase or proverb.

scab NOUN a crust forming over a cut as it heals.

scabbard NOUN the sheath of a sword etc.

scabies NOUN a contagious skin disease.

scaffold NOUN 1 a platform for the execution of criminals. 2 a structure of scaffolding.

scaffolding NOUN poles and planks providing

platforms for people working on buildings etc.

scald VERB burn with hot liquid or steam; clean or peel using boiling water. NOUN an injury by scalding.

scale NOUN 1 a range of values forming a system for measuring or grading something. 2 relative size or extent. 3 (**scales**) an instrument for weighing. 4 a fixed series of notes in a system of music. 5 each of the small overlapping plates protecting the skin of fish and reptiles. 6 a deposit caused in a kettle etc. by hard water; tartar on teeth. VERB 1 climb. 2 represent in proportion to the size of the original. 3 remove scale(s) from. **scaly** ADJ

scallop NOUN 1 an edible shellfish with two hinged fan-shaped shells. 2 (**scallops**) semicircular curves as an ornamental edging. **scalloped** ADJ

scallywag NOUN a rascal.

scalp NOUN the skin of the head excluding the face. VERB cut the scalp from.

scalpel NOUN a small sharp-bladed knife used by a surgeon.

scamp NOUN a rascal.

scamper VERB run with quick, light steps.

scampi PLURAL NOUN large prawns.

scan VERB (**scanned, scanning**) 1 read quickly. 2 pass a radar or electronic beam over; convert a picture or document into digital form for storing or processing on a computer. 3 (of verse) have a regular rhythm. NOUN scanning. **scanner** NOUN

scandal NOUN an action or event causing outrage. **scandalous** ADJ

scandalize (or **-ise**) VERB shock.

scant ADJ barely enough.

scanty ADJ (**-ier, -iest**) too small in size or amount. **scantily** ADV

scapegoat NOUN a person blamed for the wrongdoings of others.

scapula NOUN (PL **-lae** or **-las**) the shoulder blade.

scar NOUN the mark where a wound has healed. VERB (**scarred, scarring**) mark with a scar.

scarce ADJ not enough to supply a demand; rare.

scarcely ADV only just; only a short time before; surely or probably not.

scarcity NOUN a shortage.

scare VERB frighten; be frightened. NOUN a fright; widespread alarm.

scarecrow NOUN a human-like figure set up to scare birds away from crops.

scarf NOUN (PL **scarves** or **scarfs**) a strip of material worn round the neck or tied over the head.

scarlet ADJ & NOUN brilliant red.

scarlet fever an infectious fever producing a scarlet rash.

scarp NOUN a very steep slope.

scary ADJ (**-ier, -iest**) [inf] frightening.

scathing ADJ severely critical.

scatter VERB throw in various random directions; (cause to) move off in different directions.

scatty (or **scatterbrained**) ADJ [inf] disorganized and forgetful.

scavenge VERB search for usable objects among rubbish etc.; (of animals) search for decaying flesh as food.

scavenger NOUN

scenario NOUN (PL **-rios**) 1 the script or summary of a film or play. 2 a possible or hypothetical sequence of events.

scene NOUN 1 the place where something occurs; a view or landscape seen in a particular way; an incident. 2 a piece of continuous action in a play or film. 3 a display of temper or emotion.

scenery NOUN a landscape considered in terms of its appearance; the background used to represent a place on a stage or film set.

scenic ADJ picturesque.

scent NOUN a pleasant smell; liquid perfume; a trail left by an animal, indicated by its smell. VERB 1 make fragrant. 2 discover by smell; suspect or detect the presence of.

sceptical ([US] **skeptical**) ADJ not easily convinced; having doubts.

sceptic NOUN

sceptically ADV

scepticism NOUN

sceptre ([US] **scepter**)

NOUN an ornamental rod carried as a symbol of sovereignty.

schedule NOUN a programme or timetable of events. VERB include in a schedule.

scheduled flight a regular public flight rather than a specially chartered one.

scheme NOUN a plan of work or action; a plot; a system or arrangement. VERB plot.

schism NOUN a disagreement or division between two groups or within an organization.

schizophrenia NOUN a mental disorder whose symptoms include a withdrawal from reality into fantasy.

schizophrenic ADJ & NOUN

schnapps NOUN a strong alcoholic spirit.

scholar NOUN a person studying at an advanced level; a learned person.

scholarly ADJ

scholarship NOUN 1 academic work. 2 a grant made to a student to help pay for their education.

scholastic ADJ of schools or education.

school NOUN 1 an educational institution. 2 a group of people sharing the same ideas or following the same principles. 3 a shoal of whales. VERB train or discipline.

schooner NOUN 1 a sailing ship. 2 a glass for sherry.

science NOUN study or knowledge of the physical or natural world, based on observation and experiment; a particular branch of this.

scientific ADJ

scientist NOUN

scimitar NOUN a short curved oriental sword.

scintillating ADJ sparkling; lively, witty, or exciting.

scissors PLURAL NOUN a cutting instrument with two pivoted blades.

scoff VERB 1 speak scornfully. 2 [inf] eat greedily.

scold VERB rebuke angrily.

sconce NOUN a candle holder attached to a wall.

scone NOUN a soft flat cake, eaten buttered.

scoop NOUN 1 a spoon-like implement; a short-handled deep shovel. 2 [inf] an item of news published by one newspaper before its rivals. VERB lift or hollow with (or as if with) a scoop.

scooter NOUN 1 a lightweight motorcycle. 2 a child's toy consisting of a footboard on wheels, propelled by the foot and steered by a long handle.

scope NOUN the range of a subject, activity, etc.; opportunity.

scorch VERB burn or become burnt on the surface.

scorching ADJ very hot.

score NOUN 1 the number of points, goals, etc. gained in a contest. 2 a set of twenty. 3 the written music for a composition. VERB 1 gain a point, goal, etc. in a contest; keep a record of the score. 2 cut a line or mark into. 3 arrange a piece of music.

scorn NOUN the feeling that someone or something is worthless or despicable. VERB feel or show scorn for.

scornful ADJ

scorpion NOUN a creature related to spiders, with pincers and a sting in its long tail.

Scotch NOUN whisky distilled in Scotland.

scotch VERB put an end to a rumour.

scot-free ADV without injury or punishment.

Scots ADJ Scottish. NOUN the form of English used in Scotland.

Scottish ADJ of Scotland or its people.

scoundrel NOUN a dishonest person.

scour VERB 1 clean by rubbing. 2 search thoroughly.

scourge NOUN 1 a whip. 2 a cause of great suffering. VERB flog.

scout NOUN a person sent to gather information. VERB act as a scout.

scowl NOUN & VERB (make) a bad-tempered frown.

scrabble VERB scratch or search busily with the hands, paws, etc.

scraggy ADJ thin and bony.

scramble VERB 1 move hastily or awkwardly. 2 make a transmission unintelligible except by means of a special receiver; cook beaten eggs in a pan. NOUN 1 an act of scrambling. **2** a motorcycle race over rough ground.

scrap NOUN **1** a small piece or amount; (**scraps**) uneaten food left after a meal. **2** discarded metal suitable for reprocessing. **3** [inf] a fight. VERB (**scrapped, scrapping**) **1** discard as useless. **2** [inf] fight.

scrapbook NOUN a book in which cuttings or pictures may be stuck.

scrape VERB **1** clean, smooth, or damage by passing a hard edge across a surface. **2** just manage to achieve. NOUN **1** a scraping movement or sound. **2** [inf] a difficult situation.

scratch VERB **1** mark or wound with a pointed object; rub or scrape with claws or fingernails. **2** withdraw from a competition. NOUN a mark, wound, or sound made by scratching. **from scratch** from the very beginning. **up to scratch** up to the required standard.

scrawl VERB write in a hurried, untidy way. NOUN scrawled handwriting.

scrawny ADJ thin and bony.

scream VERB give a piercing cry, especially of fear or pain. NOUN a screaming cry or sound.

scree NOUN a mass of loose stones on a mountainside.

screech NOUN & VERB (make) a harsh scream.

screed NOUN a tiresomely long piece of writing or speech.

screen NOUN **1** an upright structure used to divide a room or conceal something. **2** the surface of a television, VDU, etc., on which images and data are displayed; a blank surface on to which an image is projected. VERB **1** conceal or protect with a screen. **2** show or broadcast a film or television programme. **3** examine for the presence or absence of a disease, quality, etc.

screenplay NOUN the script of a film.

screw NOUN **1** a metal pin with a spiral ridge round its length, twisted into a surface to fasten things together. **2** a propeller.

VERB fasten or tighten with screws; rotate something to attach or remove it.

screwdriver NOUN a tool for turning screws.

scribble VERB write or draw hurriedly or carelessly. NOUN something scribbled.

scribe NOUN (in the past) a person who copied out documents.

scrimp VERB economize.

script NOUN 1 handwriting. 2 the text of a play, film, or broadcast.

scripture (or **scriptures**) NOUN sacred writings; those of the Christians or the Jews.

scroll NOUN a roll of paper or parchment; an ornamental design in this shape.

scrotum NOUN (PL **-ta** or **-tums**) the pouch of skin enclosing the testicles.

scrounge VERB cadge. **scrounger** NOUN

scrub VERB (**scrubbed**, **scrubbing**) rub hard to clean, especially with a coarse or bristly implement. NOUN 1 an act of scrubbing. 2 stunted trees and shrubs; land covered with this.

scruff NOUN the back of the neck.

scruffy ADJ (**-ier, -iest**) shabby and untidy.

scrum NOUN a formation in rugby in which players push against each other with their heads down and struggle for possession of the ball; [inf] a disorderly crowd.

scruple NOUN a feeling of doubt as to whether an action is morally right. VERB hesitate because of scruples.

scrupulous ADJ very conscientious or careful.

scrutinize (or **-ise**) VERB examine carefully.

scrutiny NOUN (PL **-ies**) a careful look or examination.

scuba diving NOUN swimming underwater using an aqualung.

scud VERB (**scudded, scudding**) move along fast and smoothly.

scuff VERB scrape the surface of a shoe against something; mark by doing this.

scuffle NOUN & VERB (take part in) a confused struggle or fight.

scull NOUN each of a pair of

small oars used by a single rower; a light boat propelled by a single rower. VERB row with sculls.

scullery NOUN (PL **-ies**) a room for washing dishes and similar work.

sculpt VERB carve or shape.

sculpture NOUN the art of carving or shaping wood, stone, etc.; work made in this way. VERB make or shape by sculpture. **sculptor** NOUN

scum NOUN a layer of dirt or froth on the surface of a liquid; [inf] a worthless person.

scupper VERB sink a ship deliberately; [inf] thwart.

scurf NOUN flakes of dry skin.

scurrilous ADJ insulting or slanderous.

scurry VERB (**scurried**, **scurrying**) run with short, quick steps.

scurvy NOUN a disease caused by lack of vitamin C.

scut NOUN the short tail of a hare, rabbit, or deer.

scuttle NOUN a box or bucket for fetching and holding coal. VERB **1** scurry. **2** sink a ship by letting in water.

scythe NOUN a tool with a curved blade on a long handle, for cutting long grass.

SE ABBREV south-east or south-eastern.

sea NOUN the expanse of salt water surrounding the continents; a section of this; a vast expanse or quantity. **sea horse** a small fish with a horse-like head. **sea lion** a large seal. **sea urchin** a sea animal with a shell covered in spines.

seafaring ADJ & NOUN travelling by sea. **seafarer** NOUN

seafood NOUN shellfish or sea fish as food.

seagull NOUN a gull.

seal[1] NOUN **1** an engraved piece of metal used to stamp a design; its impression. **2** a device used to join things or close something firmly. **3** a confirmation or guarantee. VERB close or fasten securely; mark with a seal; settle an agreement etc.

seal[2] NOUN an amphibious sea animal with flippers.

seam NOUN **1** a line where

two pieces of fabric are sewn together. **2** a layer of coal etc. in the ground.

seaman NOUN a sailor.

seamless ADJ with no obvious joins; smooth and continuous.

seamstress NOUN a woman who sews, especially for a living.

seamy NOUN (**-ier, -iest**) immoral or sordid.

seance NOUN a meeting where people try to make contact with the dead.

seaplane NOUN an aircraft designed to take off from and land on water.

sear VERB scorch or burn.

search VERB hunt through or over in order to find someone or something. NOUN an act of searching.

searching ADJ thorough.

searchlight NOUN an outdoor lamp with a powerful beam.

seasick ADJ made sick by the motion of a ship.
　seasickness NOUN

seaside NOUN the coast as a place for holidays.

season NOUN one of the four divisions of the year; a part of the year when a particular sport or activity takes place. VERB **1** add salt etc. to food. **2** dry or treat timber to prepare it for use.

season ticket a ticket valid for any number of journeys within a particular period.

seasonable ADJ suitable for the season.

seasonal ADJ of a season or seasons; varying with the seasons.
　seasonally ADV

seasoned ADJ experienced.

seasoning NOUN a substance used to enhance the flavour of food.

seat NOUN **1** a thing made or used for sitting on; a place as a member of parliament, a committee, etc.; the site or base of something. **2** a country house. **3** the buttocks. VERB cause to sit; have seats for.

seat belt a strap securing a person to a seat in a vehicle or aircraft.

seaweed NOUN plants growing in the sea.

sebaceous ADJ secreting an oily or greasy substance.

secateurs PLURAL NOUN clippers for pruning

plants.

secede VERB withdraw from membership.
secession NOUN

secluded ADJ (of a place) sheltered and private.

seclusion NOUN privacy.

second[1] ADJ **1** next after the first. **2** inferior or subordinate. NOUN **1** a second highest grade in an exam. **2** an attendant at a duel or boxing match. **3** (**seconds**) goods of inferior quality. VERB formally support a proposal etc.
second-class next or inferior to first class in quality etc. **second-hand** having had a previous owner; heard from another person. **second sight** the supposed ability to foretell the future. **second wind** a renewed capacity for effort.

second[2] NOUN a sixtieth part of a minute.

second[3] VERB transfer temporarily to another job or department.
secondment NOUN

secondary ADJ **1** coming after, or less important than, something else. **2** (of education) for children from the age of 11 to 16 or 18.

secret ADJ kept from the knowledge of most people. NOUN something secret; a means of achieving something.
secrecy NOUN

secretariat NOUN a government office or department.

secretary NOUN (PL **-ies**) a person employed to deal with correspondence and routine office work; the head of a major government department.
secretarial ADJ

secrete VERB **1** hide. **2** (of a cell, gland, etc.) produce and discharge a substance.
secretion NOUN

secretive ADJ inclined to conceal feelings or information.

sect NOUN a group with beliefs, especially religious ones, that differ from those generally accepted.
sectarian ADJ

section NOUN a distinct part; a cross-section; a subdivision. VERB divide into sections.

sector NOUN a distinct area

or part.

secular ADJ not religious or spiritual.

secure ADJ fixed or fastened so as not to slip, come undone, etc.; safe; confident. VERB 1 firmly fix or fasten; protect against danger or threat. 2 obtain.

security NOUN (PL -ies) 1 being secure. 2 precautions taken against espionage, theft, etc. 3 something offered as a guarantee of the repayment of a loan.

sedate ADJ slow and dignified; placid or dull. VERB give a sedative to.

sedative ADJ having a calming effect. NOUN a sedative drug.

sedentary ADJ seated; taking little exercise.

sedge NOUN a grass-like marsh plant.

sediment NOUN solid matter that settles to the bottom of a liquid.

sedition NOUN words or actions inciting rebellion. **seditious** ADJ

seduce VERB persuade to do something unwise; persuade to have sex. **seduction** NOUN **seductive** ADJ

see[1] VERB (**saw, seen, seeing**) 1 perceive with the eyes; experience or witness. 2 understand; deduce. 3 meet; escort. 4 regard in a particular way. 5 consult a specialist or professional.

see[2] NOUN a bishop's or archbishop's district or position.

seed NOUN 1 a plant's fertilized ovule, from which a new plant may grow; semen; the origin of something. 2 one of the stronger competitors in a sports tournament, scheduled to play in a particular order so they do not defeat one another early on. VERB 1 plant with seeds. 2 remove seeds from. 3 give the status of seed to a sports competitor.

seedling NOUN a very young plant.

seedy ADJ (-ier, -iest) sordid or disreputable.

seek VERB (**sought, seeking**) try to find or obtain; try or want to do.

seem VERB give the impression of being. **seemingly** ADV

seemly ADJ in good taste.

seen past participle of **see**[1].

seep VERB ooze slowly through a substance.

seer NOUN a prophet.

see-saw NOUN a long board balanced on a central support, so that children sitting on each end can ride up and down. VERB repeatedly change between two states or positions.

seethe VERB bubble as if boiling; be very angry.

segment NOUN each of the parts into which something is divided.

segmented ADJ

segregate VERB separate from others.

segregation NOUN

seismic ADJ of earthquakes.

seize VERB 1 take hold of forcibly or suddenly; take possession of by force or legal right. 2 take or make use of eagerly. 3 (**seize up**) (of a machine) become jammed.

seizure NOUN seizing; a sudden violent attack of an illness.

seldom ADV not often.

select VERB pick out as the best or most suitable. ADJ carefully chosen; exclusive.

selector NOUN

selection NOUN selecting; things selected; things from which to choose.

selective ADJ choosing carefully.

self NOUN (PL **selves**) a person's essential nature and individuality.

self-assured ADJ confident.

self-centred ADJ thinking only of yourself and your own affairs.

self-confidence NOUN confidence in your own worth and abilities.

self-confident ADJ

self-conscious ADJ nervous or embarrassed because you are very aware of yourself or your actions.

self-contained ADJ 1 complete in itself. 2 not needing or influenced by others.

self-determination NOUN the right or ability of a country to manage its own affairs.

self-evident ADJ obvious.

selfish ADJ concerned primarily with your own needs and wishes.

selfless ADJ unselfish.

self-made ADJ having become successful by your own efforts.

self-possessed ADJ calm and controlled.

self-respect NOUN pride and confidence in yourself.

self-righteous ADJ complacent about your own virtue.

selfsame ADJ the very same.

self-satisfied ADJ smugly pleased with yourself.

self-service ADJ (of a shop etc.) where customers help themselves and pay at a checkout.

self-sufficient ADJ not needing outside help.

sell VERB (**sold, selling**) 1 exchange goods etc. for money; keep goods for sale; (of goods) be sold. 2 persuade someone to accept.
seller NOUN

Sellotape NOUN [trademark] transparent adhesive tape.

selvedge NOUN an edge of cloth woven so that it does not unravel.

semantic ADJ of meaning in language.

semaphore NOUN a system of signalling with the arms.

semblance NOUN an outward appearance or form.

semen NOUN the sperm-bearing fluid produced by men and male animals.

semester NOUN a half-year course or university term.

semibreve NOUN a note in music, equal to two minims or half a breve.

semicircle NOUN half of a circle.
semicircular ADJ

semicolon NOUN a punctuation mark (;).

semiconductor NOUN a substance that conducts electricity in certain conditions.

semi-detached ADJ (of a house) joined to another on one side.

semi-final NOUN a match or round in a contest, preceding the final.

seminal ADJ 1 strongly influencing later developments. 2 of semen.

seminar NOUN a small class for discussion and research.

semi-precious ADJ (of

gems) less valuable than those called precious.

semitone NOUN half a tone in music.

semolina NOUN hard grains left when wheat is ground and sifted, used to make puddings.

senate NOUN the upper house of certain parliaments; the governing body of certain universities.

senator NOUN a member of a senate.

send VERB (**sent, sending**) 1 order or cause to go to a particular destination; propel. 2 bring into a specified state.

senile ADJ losing mental faculties because of old age.

senility NOUN

senior ADJ 1 older; for children above a certain age. 2 holding a higher rank or position. NOUN a senior person.

senior citizen an old-age pensioner.

seniority NOUN

sensation NOUN 1 a feeling produced by stimulation of a sense organ or of the mind. 2 excited interest; a person or thing

producing this.

sensational ADJ causing great public interest or excitement.

sensationalism NOUN deliberate use of sensational stories etc.

sense NOUN 1 any of the powers (sight, hearing, smell, taste, touch) which allow the body to perceive things. 2 a feeling that something is the case; awareness of or sensitivity to. 3 a sane and realistic outlook. 4 a meaning. VERB perceive by a sense or by intuition.

senseless ADJ foolish.

sensibility NOUN (PL **-ies**) sensitivity.

sensible ADJ 1 having or showing common sense. 2 aware.

sensibly ADV

sensitive ADJ 1 quick to detect or be affected by slight changes; appreciating the feelings of others; easily offended or upset. 2 secret or confidential.

sensitivity NOUN

sensitize (or **-ise**) VERB make sensitive or aware.

sensor NOUN a device for detecting a particular

physical property.

sensory ADJ of the senses or sensation.

sensual ADJ of or arousing the physical senses as a source of pleasure.

sensuous ADJ of the senses rather than the intellect; affecting the senses pleasantly.

sent past and past participle of **send**.

sentence NOUN 1 a series of words making a single complete statement. 2 a punishment decided by a law court. VERB pass sentence on an offender.

sentient ADJ able to feel things.

sentiment NOUN 1 an opinion or feeling. 2 sentimentality.

sentimental ADJ full of exaggerated or self-indulgent feelings of tenderness or nostalgia. **sentimentality** NOUN

sentinel NOUN a sentry.

sentry NOUN (PL **-ies**) a soldier keeping watch or guard on something.

separate ADJ not joined or united with others. VERB divide; move or keep apart; stop living together as a couple.

separable ADJ

separation NOUN

sepia NOUN a reddish-brown colour.

September NOUN the ninth month.

septet NOUN a group of seven musicians.

septic ADJ infected with harmful bacteria **septic tank** a tank in which sewage is liquefied by bacterial activity.

septicaemia ([US] **septicemia**) NOUN blood poisoning.

sepulchral ADJ gloomy.

sepulchre ([US] **sepulcher**) NOUN a tomb.

sequel NOUN what follows, especially as a result; a novel or film etc. continuing the story of an earlier one.

sequence NOUN an order in which related items follow one another; a set of things that follow each other in a particular order. **sequential** ADJ

sequestered ADJ isolated or sheltered.

sequin NOUN a small shiny disc sewn on clothes for decoration. **sequinned** ADJ

seraph NOUN (PL **-phim** or **-phs**) a member of the highest order of angels.

serenade NOUN music played for a lover, outdoors and at night. VERB perform a serenade for.

serendipity NOUN the fortunate occurrence of events by chance. **serendipitous** ADJ

serene ADJ calm and peaceful. **serenity** NOUN

serf NOUN a medieval farm labourer tied to working on a particular estate.

serge NOUN strong woollen fabric.

sergeant NOUN a non-commissioned army officer; a police officer ranking just below inspector.

serial NOUN a story presented in a series of instalments. ADJ repeatedly committing the same offence or doing the same thing: *a serial killer.*

serialize (or **-ise**) VERB produce as a serial.

series NOUN (PL **series**) a number of similar things coming one after another; a set of related television or radio programmes.

serious ADJ **1** solemn or thoughtful; sincere. **2** requiring careful thought or action; dangerous or severe.

sermon NOUN a talk on a religious or moral subject.

serpent NOUN a large snake.

serpentine ADJ twisting like a snake.

serrated ADJ having a jagged, saw-like edge.

serried ADJ placed or standing close together.

serum NOUN (PL **-ra** or **-rums**) a thin fluid left when blood has clotted.

servant NOUN a person employed to do domestic work.

serve VERB **1** perform duties or services for; be employed in the armed forces. **2** fulfil a purpose. **3** present food or drink to; (of food or drink) be enough for. **4** attend to a customer. **5** set the ball in play in tennis etc. **6** spend a period in a post or in prison. NOUN an act of serving in tennis etc.

server NOUN a computer or program which controls

or supplies information to a network of computers.

service NOUN **1** the action of serving; a period of employment in an organization; an act of assistance. **2** a system supplying a public need; a department run by the state. **3** (**the services**) the armed forces. **4** a religious ceremony. **5** a matching set of crockery. **6** an act of serving in tennis etc. **7** a routine inspection and maintenance of a vehicle or machine. VERB **1** perform routine maintenance work on. **2** provide services for.

service station a garage selling petrol, oil, etc.

serviceable ADJ functioning; hard-wearing.

serviceman (or **servicewoman**) NOUN a member of the armed forces.

serviette NOUN a table napkin.

servile ADJ excessively willing to serve others.

servitude NOUN slavery; being subject to someone more powerful.

sesame NOUN a tropical plant grown for its oil-rich seeds.

session NOUN a meeting or meetings for discussing something; a period spent in a particular activity.

set VERB (**set, setting**) **1** put, place, or fix in position; bring into a specified state; cause to start doing something. **2** fix or appoint a time or limit; assign a task to; establish as an example or record. **3** adjust a device as required. **4** harden into a solid, semi-solid, or fixed state. **5** (of the sun etc.) appear to move towards and below the earth's horizon. **6** prepare a table for a meal. **7** arrange damp hair into the required style. NOUN **1** a number of people or things grouped together. **2** the way in which something is set. **3** a radio or television receiver. **4** a group of games forming a unit in a tennis match. **5** scenery for a play or film.

set square a right-angled triangular drawing instrument.

setback NOUN something causing a delay in

progress.

sett NOUN a badger's burrow.

settee NOUN a sofa.

setter NOUN a long-haired breed of dog.

setting NOUN 1 the way or place in which something is set. 2 a set of cutlery or crockery laid for one person.

settle[1] VERB 1 resolve a problem or dispute; pay a bill. 2 adopt a more secure or steady lifestyle; become at ease in new surroundings; come to live in a new place; sit or rest comfortably or securely. 3 become quieter or calmer. 4 (**settle for**) accept after negotiation. **settlement** NOUN **settler** NOUN

settle[2] NOUN a wooden seat with a high back and arms.

seven ADJ & NOUN one more than six (7, VII). **seventh** ADJ & NOUN

seventeen ADJ & NOUN one more than sixteen (17, XVII). **seventeenth** ADJ & NOUN

seventy ADJ & NOUN seven times ten (70, LXX). **seventieth** ADJ & NOUN

sever VERB cut or break off.

several PRON more than two but not many. ADJ separate.

severe ADJ 1 strict or harsh; extreme or intense. 2 very plain in style or appearance. **severity** NOUN

sew VERB (**sewed**, **sewn** or **sewed**, **sewing**) make, join, or repair by making stitches with a needle and thread. **sewing** NOUN

sewage NOUN liquid waste drained from houses etc. for disposal.

sewer NOUN an underground channel for carrying sewage.

sex NOUN 1 either of the two main groups (male and female) into which living things are placed; the fact of belonging to one of these. 2 sexual intercourse.

sexism ADJ prejudice or discrimination on the basis of sex. **sexist** ADJ & NOUN

sextant NOUN an instrument for measuring angles and distances.

sextet NOUN a group of six musicians; music for

these.

sexual ADJ **1** of sex; (of reproduction) occurring by fusion of male and female cells. **2** of the two sexes.

sexual intercourse sexual contact involving the insertion of a man's penis into a woman's vagina.

sexually ADV

sexuality NOUN capacity for sexual feelings; a person's sexual preference.

sexy ADJ (**-ier, -iest**) sexually attractive or stimulating.

shabby ADJ (**-ier, -iest**) **1** worn out or scruffy. **2** unfair.

shabbily ADV

shack NOUN a roughly built hut.

shackle NOUN one of a pair of metal rings joined by a chain, for fastening a prisoner's wrists or ankles. VERB put shackles on; restrict or limit.

shade NOUN **1** comparative darkness and coolness caused by shelter from direct sunlight; a screen used to block or moderate light. **2** a colour. VERB block the rays of; screen from direct light; darken parts of a drawing etc.

shadow NOUN **1** a dark area produced by an object coming between light and a surface; partial darkness; a dark patch. **2** a slight trace. VERB **1** cast a shadow over. **2** follow and watch secretly.

shadowy ADJ

shady ADJ (**-ier, -iest**) **1** situated in or giving shade. **2** of doubtful honesty.

shaft NOUN **1** a long, slender, straight handle etc.; an arrow or spear; a ray or beam; a long rotating rod transmitting power in a machine; each of the two poles between which a horse is harnessed to a vehicle. **2** a vertical or sloping passage or opening.

shag NOUN coarse tobacco. ADJ (of a carpet) with a long rough pile.

shaggy ADJ (**-ier, -iest**) (of hair or fur) long, thick, and untidy; having shaggy hair or fur.

shah NOUN a title of the former ruler of Iran.

shake VERB (**shook, shaken, shaking**)

1 tremble or vibrate.
2 move quickly up and down or to and fro.
3 shock or astonish. NOUN an act of shaking.

shaky ADJ (**-ier, -iest**) shaking; not safe or certain.

shakily ADV

shale NOUN stone that splits easily.

shall AUXILIARY VERB used with *I* and *we* to express future tense; expressing a strong statement, intention, or order.

shallot NOUN a small onion-like plant.

shallow ADJ of little depth; superficial. NOUN (**shallows**) a shallow area in a river etc.

sham NOUN a pretence; something that is not genuine. ADJ not genuine. VERB (**shammed, shamming**) pretend.

shaman NOUN (in some societies) a person believed to be able to contact good and evil spirits.

shamble VERB walk in a shuffling or lazy way.

shambles NOUN a state of great disorder.

shame NOUN a painful mental feeling aroused by having done something wrong or foolish; loss of respect; a cause of this; something regrettable. VERB cause to feel shame.

shameful ADJ

shameless ADJ

shamefaced ADJ looking ashamed.

shampoo NOUN a liquid used to wash hair; a preparation for cleaning upholstery etc.; the process of shampooing. VERB wash or clean with shampoo.

shamrock NOUN a clover-like plant.

shandy NOUN (PL **-ies**) beer mixed with lemonade.

shank NOUN the lower part of the leg.

shanty NOUN (PL **-ies**) 1 a shack. 2 a traditional song sung by sailors.

shanty town a settlement where poor people live in roughly built shacks.

shape NOUN 1 an area or form with a definite outline; well-defined structure or arrangement. 2 a particular condition or shape. VERB 1 give a shape to; influence the nature of. 2 (**shape up**) develop or happen in a particular way.

shapely ADJ having an attractive shape.

shard NOUN a broken piece of pottery.

share NOUN 1 a part given to one person out of something divided among several; an amount that someone is entitled to or required to have. 2 one of the equal parts forming a business company's capital and entitling the holder to a proportion of the profits. VERB give or have a share (of).

shareholder NOUN an owner of shares in a company.

shark NOUN 1 a large voracious sea fish. 2 [inf] an unscrupulous swindler.

sharp ADJ 1 having a cutting or piercing edge or point; (of a remark etc.) hurtful. 2 clear and definite. 3 sudden and noticeable. 4 quick to understand, notice, etc. 5 (of a taste or smell) intense and piercing. 6 above the correct or normal pitch in music. ADV precisely. NOUN [Music] (a

sign indicating) a note raised by a semitone.

sharp practice dishonest business dealings.

sharpen VERB

sharpshooter NOUN a skilled marksman.

shatter VERB break violently into small pieces; destroy; distress greatly.

shave VERB 1 remove hair by cutting it off close to the skin with a razor. 2 cut a thin slice from something. NOUN an act of shaving.

shaven ADJ

shaving NOUN a thin strip cut off a surface.

shawl NOUN a large piece of soft fabric worn round the shoulders or wrapped round a baby.

she PRON the female previously mentioned.

sheaf NOUN (PL **sheaves**) a bundle of corn stalks; a similar bundle.

shear VERB (**sheared**, **shorn** or **sheared**, **shearing**) 1 cut or trim with shears. 2 break because of strain. PLURAL NOUN (**shears**) a large cutting instrument shaped like scissors.

sheath NOUN a cover for the blade of a knife or tool; a condom.

sheathe VERB put into a sheath; encase in a tight covering.

shed NOUN a simple building used for storage. VERB (**shed**, **shedding**) 1 lose leaves etc. naturally; discard; accidentally drop or spill. 2 give off light.

sheen NOUN gloss or lustre.

sheep NOUN (PL **sheep**) a grass-eating animal with a thick fleecy coat.

sheepdog NOUN a dog trained to guard and herd sheep.

sheepish ADJ feeling shy or foolish.

sheer ADJ 1 not mixed or qualified. 2 very steep. 3 (of fabric) very thin. VERB swerve from a course.

sheet NOUN 1 a piece of cotton or other fabric used to cover a bed. 2 a large thin piece of glass, metal, paper, etc. 3 an expanse of water, flame, etc.

sheikh NOUN a Muslim or Arab leader.

shelf NOUN (PL **shelves**) a flat piece of wood etc. fastened to a wall etc. for things to be placed on; a ledge of rock.

shell NOUN 1 the hard outer covering of eggs, nut kernels, and of animals such as snails and tortoises; the outer structure or form of something, especially when hollow. 2 a metal case filled with explosive, fired from a large gun. VERB 1 remove the shells of. 2 fire explosive shells at.

shell shock psychological disturbance resulting from exposure to battle conditions.

shellfish NOUN an edible water animal that has a shell.

shelter NOUN a structure that shields against danger, wind, rain, etc.; protection. VERB provide with shelter; take shelter.

shelve VERB 1 put on a shelf. 2 postpone or cancel. 3 slope.

shepherd NOUN a person who tends sheep. VERB guide or direct.

shepherd's pie a pie of minced meat topped with mashed potato.

sherbet NOUN a sweet

powder made into an effervescent drink.

sheriff NOUN the Crown's chief executive officer in a county; a judge in Scotland; [US] the chief law-enforcing officer of a county.

sherry NOUN (PL **-ies**) a fortified wine.

shibboleth NOUN a long-standing belief or principle held by a group of people.

shield NOUN a broad piece of metal etc. carried for protection; any source of protection. VERB protect.

shift VERB move or change from one position to another; transfer blame etc. NOUN **1** a slight change in position etc. **2** a set of workers who start work when another set finishes; the time for which they work.

shiftless ADJ lazy and inefficient.

shifty ADJ [inf] seeming untrustworthy.

shilling NOUN a former British coin worth one twentieth of a pound (12 pence).

shilly-shally VERB (**-shallied, -shallying**) be indecisive.

shimmer VERB & NOUN (shine with) a soft quivering light.

shin NOUN the front of the leg below the knee. VERB (**shinned, shinning**) (**shin up**) climb quickly.

shine VERB **1** (**shone, shining**) give out or reflect light; be excellent or outstanding. **2** (**shined, shining**) polish. NOUN brightness.

shiny ADJ

shingle NOUN **1** a mass of small pebbles on a beach etc. **2** a wooden roof tile. **3** (**shingles**) a disease causing a rash of small blisters.

ship NOUN a large seagoing vessel. VERB (**shipped, shipping**) transport on a ship.

shipment NOUN the shipping of goods; a consignment shipped.

shipping NOUN ships collectively.

shipshape ADJ orderly and neat.

shipwreck NOUN the destruction of a ship at sea.

shipwrecked ADJ

shipyard NOUN a place

where ships are built and repaired.

shire NOUN a county.

shire horse a heavy, powerful breed of horse.

shirk VERB avoid work or a duty.

shirt NOUN a garment for the upper part of the body, with a collar and sleeves.

shirty ADJ [inf] annoyed.

shiver VERB tremble slightly, especially with cold or fear. NOUN a shivering movement. **shivery** ADJ

shoal NOUN 1 a large number of fish swimming together. 2 a shallow place; an underwater sandbank.

shock NOUN 1 a sudden upsetting or surprising event or experience; the feeling caused by this; acute weakness caused by injury, loss of blood, etc. 2 a violent impact or tremor. 3 a thick mass of hair. VERB surprise and distress; scandalize.

shocking ADJ causing shock or disgust; [inf] very bad.

shoddy ADJ badly made or done.

shoe NOUN 1 an outer covering for a person's foot. 2 a horseshoe. VERB (**shod, shoeing**) fit with a shoe or shoes.

shoehorn NOUN a curved implement for easing your heel into a shoe.

shoelace NOUN a cord for lacing up shoes.

shoestring NOUN [inf] a barely adequate amount of money.

shone past and past participle of **shine**.

shoo EXCLAMATION a sound uttered to frighten animals away.

shook past of **shake**.

shoot VERB (**shot, shooting**) 1 fire a gun etc.; kill or wound with a bullet, arrow, etc. 2 move swiftly and suddenly. 3 aim a ball at a goal. 4 film or photograph. 5 (of a plant) put out shoots. NOUN 1 a young branch or new growth of a plant. 2 an occasion when game is shot for sport.

shooting star a small meteor seen to move rapidly. **shooting stick** a walking stick with a handle that unfolds to form a seat.

shop NOUN 1 a building where goods are sold. 2 a workshop. VERB (**shopped, shopping**) buy things from shops.

shop floor the place in a factory where things are made. **shop-soiled** dirty or damaged from being on display in a shop.

shop steward a trade union official elected by workers as their spokesman.

shopper NOUN

shoplifter NOUN a person who steals goods from a shop.

shoplifting NOUN

shore NOUN the land along the edge of the sea or a lake. VERB prop with a length of timber.

shorn past participle of **shear**.

short ADJ 1 of small length in space or time; small in height. 2 not having enough of something; in scarce supply. 3 curt. 4 (of pastry) crumbly. ADV not going far enough. NOUN 1 a small drink of spirits. 2 (**shorts**) trousers reaching only to the knee or thigh. VERB have a short circuit.

short-change cheat, especially by giving insufficient change. **short circuit** a faulty connection in an electrical circuit in which the current flows along a shorter route than normal. **short cut** a quicker route or method. **short-sighted** unable to see things unless they are close to your eyes; lacking foresight.

shorten VERB

shortage NOUN a lack of something.

shortbread (or **shortcake**) NOUN a rich sweet biscuit.

shortcoming NOUN a fault.

shortfall NOUN a deficit.

shorthand NOUN a method of writing rapidly with quickly made symbols.

shortlist NOUN a list of selected candidates from which a final choice will be made. VERB put on a shortlist.

shortly ADV 1 soon. 2 curtly.

shot[1] NOUN 1 a firing of a gun etc.; a person of specified skill in shooting. 2 (in sport) a hit, stroke, or kick of the ball as an attempt to score; [inf] an attempt. **3** a heavy ball used as a missile or thrown as a sport; ammunition. **4** a photograph. **5** [inf] a measure of spirits; an injection.

shot² past & past participle of **shoot**.

shotgun NOUN a gun for firing small bullets at close range.

should AUXILIARY VERB used to express duty or obligation, a possible or expected future event, or (with *I* and *we*) a polite statement or a conditional clause.

shoulder NOUN the joint between the upper arm and the main part of the body. VERB **1** take on a responsibility. **2** push with your shoulder.

shoulder blade the large flat bone of the shoulder.

shout NOUN a loud cry or call. VERB speak or call out loudly.

shove NOUN a rough push. VERB push roughly; place carelessly.

shovel NOUN a spade-like tool for moving sand, snow, etc. VERB (**shovelled**, **shovelling**; [US] **shoveled**, **shoveling**) shift or clear with a shovel.

show VERB (**showed**, **shown**, **showing**) **1** be or make visible; offer for inspection or viewing; present an image of. **2** prove or be evidence of; demonstrate to someone. **3** behave in a particular way towards someone. **4** guide or lead. NOUN a public display or performance; a light entertainment programme; outward appearance, especially when misleading.

show business the entertainment profession.

show off try to impress people.

showdown NOUN a confrontation that settles an argument.

shower NOUN **1** a brief fall of rain or snow. **2** a large number of things that arrive together. **3** a device spraying water over someone's body; a wash in this. VERB **1** (cause to) fall in a shower; give a number of things to. **2** wash in a shower.

showery ADJ

showjumping NOUN the competitive sport of riding horses over a course of obstacles.

shown past participle of **show**.

showroom NOUN a room where goods for sale are displayed.

showy ADJ very bright or colourful; ostentatious or gaudy.

shrank past of **shrink**.

shrapnel NOUN pieces of metal scattered from an exploding bomb.

shred NOUN a small strip torn or cut from something; a very small amount. VERB (**shredded**, **shredding**) tear or cut into shreds.

shrew NOUN a small mouse-like animal.

shrewd ADJ showing good judgement.

shriek NOUN & VERB (make) a piercing cry.

shrill ADJ piercing and high-pitched in sound.

shrimp NOUN a small edible shellfish.

shrine NOUN a sacred or revered place.

shrink VERB (**shrank**, **shrunk**, **shrinking**) 1 make or become smaller. 2 draw back in fear or disgust.

shrinkage NOUN

shrivel VERB (**shrivelled**, **shrivelling** [US] **shriveled**, **shriveling**) shrink and wrinkle from lack of moisture.

shroud NOUN a cloth in which a dead body is wrapped for burial; a thing that conceals. VERB wrap in a shroud; conceal.

shrub NOUN a woody plant smaller than a tree.

shrubbery NOUN (PL **-ies**) an area planted with shrubs.

shrug VERB (**shrugged**, **shrugging**) raise your shoulders as a gesture of indifference or lack of knowledge. NOUN this movement.

shrunken ADJ having shrunk.

shudder VERB shiver or shake violently. NOUN this movement.

shuffle VERB 1 walk without lifting your feet clear of the ground. 2 rearrange. NOUN 1 a shuffling movement or walk. 2 a rearrangement.

shun VERB (**shunned**, **shunning**) avoid.

shunt VERB move a train to a side track; move to a different position.

shut VERB (**shut, shutting**) move something into position to block an opening; keep in or out of a place by blocking an opening; close a book, curtains, etc.; (of a shop etc.) stop operating for business.

shut up [inf] be quiet.

shutter NOUN a screen that can be closed over a window; a device that opens and closes the aperture of a camera.

shuttle NOUN 1 a form of transport travelling frequently between places. 2 a device carrying the weft thread in weaving. VERB move, travel, or send to and fro.

shuttlecock NOUN a small cone-shaped object struck to and fro in badminton.

shy ADJ timid in other people's company. VERB (**shied, shying**) jump in alarm; avoid through nervousness.

SI ABBREV Système International, the international system of units of measurement.

Siamese cat NOUN a cat with pale fur and darker face, paws, and tail.

Siamese twins PLURAL NOUN twins whose bodies are joined at birth.

sibilant ADJ making a hissing sound.

sibling NOUN a brother or sister.

sic ADV written exactly as it stands in the original.

sick ADJ 1 unwell; suffering from nausea. 2 tired of or bored with something. 3 macabre or morbid. **sickness** NOUN

sicken VERB 1 become ill. 2 disgust.

sickle NOUN a curved blade used for cutting corn etc.

sickly ADJ 1 often ill. 2 causing nausea.

side NOUN 1 a surface of an object that is not the top, bottom, front, back, or end; a bounding line of a plane figure; a slope of a hill or ridge. 2 a part near the edge and away from the middle. 3 a position to the left or right of someone or something; either of the halves into which something is divided; an aspect of a problem etc. 4 one of two opposing groups or teams. ADJ at or on the side.

side effect a secondary, usually unwelcome effect.

side-saddle (of a rider) sitting with both feet on the same side of the horse.

sideboard NOUN 1 a piece of furniture with drawers and cupboards for china etc. 2 (**sideboards**) sideburns.

sideburns PLURAL NOUN strips of hair growing on a man's cheeks.

sidelight NOUN one of two small lights on either side of a vehicle.

sideline NOUN 1 something done in addition to your main activity. 2 (**sidelines**) lines bounding the sides of a football pitch etc.; a position etc. apart from the main action.

sidelong ADJ & ADV sideways.

sideshow NOUN a small show at a fair, circus, etc.

sidestep VERB (**sidestepped, sidestepping**) avoid by stepping sideways; evade.

sidetrack VERB distract.

sidewalk NOUN [US] a pavement.

sideways ADV & ADJ to, towards, or from the side.

siding NOUN a short track by the side of a railway, used in shunting.

sidle VERB walk in a furtive or timid way.

siege NOUN the surrounding and blockading of a place by armed forces in order to capture it.

siesta NOUN an afternoon nap or rest.

sieve NOUN a utensil with a mesh through which liquids or fine particles can pass. VERB put through a sieve.

sift VERB 1 sieve. 2 examine carefully and select or analyse.

sigh NOUN & VERB (give) a long deep breath expressing sadness, tiredness, relief, etc.

sight NOUN 1 the ability to see; seeing; the distance within which you can see. 2 something seen or worth seeing; [inf] an unsightly thing. 3 a device looked through to aim or observe with a gun or telescope etc. VERB see.

sightseeing NOUN visiting places of interest.
sightseer NOUN
sign NOUN 1 an indication that something exists, is occurring, or may occur. 2 a signal, gesture, or notice giving information or an instruction. 3 any of the twelve divisions of the zodiac. VERB 1 write your name on a document to authorize it. 2 make a sign.
signal NOUN 1 a sign or gesture giving information or a command; an apparatus indicating whether a railway line is clear. 2 an electrical impulse or radio wave sent or received. VERB (**signalled, signalling**; [US] **signaled, signaling**) make a signal; indicate by means of a signal. ADJ noteworthy.
signatory NOUN (PL **-ies**) a person who has signed an agreement.
signature NOUN a person's name written in a distinctive way, used in signing something.
signature tune a tune announcing a particular radio or television programme.
signet ring NOUN a ring with an engraved design.
significance NOUN 1 importance. 2 meaning.
significant ADJ
signify VERB (**signified, signifying**) indicate; mean; be important.
signpost NOUN a post with arms showing the direction of and distance to certain places.
Sikh NOUN a follower of a religion that developed from Hinduism.
Sikhism NOUN
silage NOUN green fodder stored and fermented in a silo.
silence NOUN complete lack of sound; a situation in which someone refrains from speaking. VERB make silent.
silencer NOUN a device to reduce the noise made by a gun, exhaust, etc.
silent ADJ without sound; not speaking.
silhouette NOUN a dark shadow or outline seen against a light background. VERB show as a silhouette.
silica NOUN a compound of silicon occurring as

quartz and in sandstone.

silicon NOUN a chemical element that is a semiconductor.
silicon chip a microchip.

silicone NOUN a synthetic substance made from silicon.

silk NOUN a fine, soft fibre produced by silkworms, made into thread or fabric.
silken ADJ
silky ADJ

silkworm NOUN a caterpillar which spins a cocoon of silk.

sill NOUN a shelf or slab at the base of a doorway or window.

silly ADJ (**-ier, -iest**) lacking common sense.
silliness NOUN

silo NOUN (PL **silos**) 1 a pit or airtight structure for holding silage. 2 a pit or tower for storing grain. 3 an underground place where a missile is kept ready for firing.

silt NOUN sediment deposited by water in a channel or harbour etc. VERB fill or block with silt.

silver NOUN a shiny, whitish precious metal; articles made of this; coins made of an alloy resembling it; the colour of silver.
silver jubilee the 25th anniversary of a significant event. **silver wedding** a 25th wedding anniversary.
silvery ADJ

simian ADJ of or like a monkey or ape.

similar ADJ alike but not identical.
similarity NOUN
similarly ADV

simile NOUN a figure of speech in which one thing is compared to another.

simmer VERB 1 (cause to) boil very gently. 2 be in a state of barely suppressed anger or excitement.

simper VERB smile in an affected way. NOUN an affected smile.

simple ADJ 1 easily done or understood. 2 plain and basic. 3 having only one element, not compound. 4 of very low intelligence.
simplicity NOUN
simply ADV

simpleton NOUN a person with low intelligence.

simplify VERB (**simplified, simplifying**) make easier

or less complex.
simplification NOUN
simplistic ADJ over-simplified.
simulate VERB imitate; pretend to feel; produce a computer model of.
simulation NOUN
simulator NOUN
simultaneous ADJ occurring at the same time.
sin NOUN an act that breaks a religious or moral law. VERB (**sinned, sinning**) commit a sin.
sinful ADJ
sinner NOUN
since PREP from a specified time or event until the present. CONJ **1** from the time that. **2** because. ADV from that time or event.
sincere ADJ without pretence or deceit.
sincerity NOUN
sine NOUN (in a right-angled triangle) the ratio of the side opposite an angle to the hypotenuse.
sinecure NOUN a paid job which requires little or no effort.
sinew NOUN tough fibrous tissue joining muscle to bone.
sing VERB (**sang, sung,**

singing) make musical sounds with the voice; perform a song; make a whistling sound.
singer NOUN
singe VERB (**singed, singeing**) burn slightly. NOUN a slight burn.
single ADJ **1** only one; designed for one person; not in a romantic or sexual relationship. **2** having only one part; (of a ticket) valid for an outward journey only. NOUN a single person or thing.
single-handed without help. **single-minded** determined to pursue a particular goal. **single out** choose or distinguish from others.
singly ADV
singlet NOUN a sleeveless vest.
singleton NOUN a single person or thing.
singular ADJ **1** exceptional or remarkable. **2** (of a word or form) referring to just one person or thing. NOUN the singular form of a word.
sinister ADJ seeming evil or dangerous.
sink VERB (**sank, sunk,**

sinking) 1 go down below the surface of liquid; move slowly downwards; gradually penetrate the surface of; decline. 2 (**sink in**) be realized or understood. 3 invest money. NOUN a fixed basin with taps and a drainage pipe.

sinuous ADJ curving or undulating.

sinus NOUN a cavity in the bones of the face that connects with the nostrils.

sinusitis NOUN inflammation of a sinus.

sip VERB (**sipped, sipping**) drink in small mouthfuls. NOUN an amount sipped.

siphon NOUN a tube used to move liquid from one container to another. VERB draw off through a siphon.

sir NOUN a polite form of address to a man; used as the title of a knight or baronet.

sire NOUN an animal's male parent. VERB be the sire of.

siren NOUN a device that makes a loud prolonged warning sound.

sirloin NOUN the best part of a loin of beef.

sissy NOUN (PL **-ies**) [inf] a weak or timid person.

sister NOUN 1 a daughter of the same parents as another person. 2 a female colleague. 3 a nun. 4 a senior female nurse.

sister-in-law the sister of your wife or husband; the wife of your brother.

sisterly ADJ

sit VERB (**sat, sitting**) 1 take or be in a position with the body resting on the buttocks; be in a particular position or state; pose for a portrait. 2 serve as a member of a council, jury, etc.; (of a committee etc.) hold a session; take an exam.

sitar NOUN a guitar-like Indian lute.

sitcom NOUN [inf] a situation comedy.

site NOUN the place where something is located or happens. VERB locate.

sitting NOUN a period of posing for a portrait; a session of a committee etc.; a scheduled period for a group to be served in a restaurant.

sitting room a room for sitting and relaxing in.

sitting tenant a tenant

already in occupation.

situated ADJ in a specified position or condition.
situate VERB

situation NOUN the location and surroundings of a place; a set of circumstances; a job.

situation comedy a comedy series in which the same characters are involved in amusing situations.

six ADJ & NOUN one more than five (6, VI).
sixth ADJ & NOUN

sixteen NOUN one more than fifteen (16, XVI).
sixteenth ADJ & NOUN

sixty ADJ & NOUN six times ten (60, LX).
sixtieth ADJ & NOUN

size[1] NOUN the overall measurements or extent of something; one of a series of standard measurements in which things are made and sold. VERB (**size up**) assess.

size[2] NOUN a gluey solution used to glaze paper or stiffen textiles.

sizeable (or **sizable**) ADJ fairly large.

sizzle VERB make a hissing sound like that of frying.

skate NOUN **1** a boot with a blade or wheels attached, for gliding over ice or a hard surface. **2** an edible flatfish. VERB move on skates.

skateboard NOUN a small board with wheels for riding on while standing.

skein NOUN a loosely coiled bundle of yarn.

skeletal ADJ **1** of the skeleton. **2** very thin.

skeleton NOUN the bones and cartilage forming the supporting structure of an animal body; a supporting or basic framework or structure. ADJ referring to a minimum number of people: *a skeleton staff*.

skeleton key a key designed to fit many locks.

skeptical US spelling of **sceptical**.

sketch NOUN a rough drawing or painting; a brief account; a short scene in a comedy show. VERB make a sketch of.

sketchy ADJ not detailed or thorough.

skew VERB change direction; make biased.

skewbald ADJ (of an

animal) having patches of white and brown.

skewer NOUN a pin to hold pieces of food together while cooking. VERB pierce with a skewer.

ski NOUN one of a pair of long narrow strips of wood etc. fixed under the feet for travelling over snow. VERB (**skis, skied, skiing**) travel on skis. **skier** NOUN

skid VERB (**skidded, skidding**) slide uncontrollably off course. NOUN a skidding movement.

skilful ([US] **skillful**) ADJ having or showing skill. **skilfully** ADV

skill NOUN ability to do something well. **skilled** ADJ

skillet NOUN a frying pan.

skim VERB (**skimmed, skimming**) 1 take matter from the surface of a liquid. 2 glide. 3 read quickly. **skimmed milk** milk from which the cream has been removed.

skimp VERB supply or use less than what is necessary.

skimpy ADJ (**-ier, -iest**) scanty.

skin NOUN the tissue forming the outer covering of the body; the skin of a dead animal used for clothing etc.; the outer layer of fruits etc. VERB (**skinned, skinning**) strip the skin from. **skin diving** swimming under water with flippers and an aqualung.

skinflint NOUN [inf] a miser.

skinny ADJ (**-ier, -iest**) very thin.

skint ADJ [inf] very short of money.

skip¹ VERB (**skipped, skipping**) move lightly with a hopping or bouncing step; jump repeatedly over a rope turned over the head and under the feet; omit or move quickly over. NOUN a skipping movement.

skip² NOUN a large open container for builders' rubbish etc.

skipper NOUN [inf] a captain.

skirmish NOUN & VERB (take part in) a minor fight or conflict.

skirt NOUN a woman's garment hanging from the waist and covering the lower body and legs. VERB form or go along the edge of; avoid dealing with.

skirting board NOUN a narrow board round the bottom of the wall of a room.

skit NOUN a short parody or comedy sketch.

skittish ADJ lively and unpredictable.

skittle NOUN one of the wooden pins set up to be bowled down with a ball in the game of skittles.

skive VERB [inf] dodge a duty; play truant.

skivvy NOUN (PL **-ies**) [inf] a female servant.

skulduggery NOUN trickery.

skulk VERB loiter stealthily.

skull NOUN the bony framework of the head.

skullcap NOUN a small close-fitting cap with no peak.

skunk NOUN a black and white animal able to spray a foul-smelling liquid.

sky NOUN (PL **skies**) the region of the upper atmosphere.

skydiving NOUN the sport of jumping from an aircraft and performing acrobatic movements in the sky before landing by parachute.

skylark NOUN a lark that soars while singing.

skylight NOUN a window in a roof.

skyscraper NOUN a very tall building.

slab NOUN a broad flat piece of something solid.

slack ADJ **1** not tight. **2** not busy; lazy or negligent. NOUN **1** a slack piece of rope. **2** (**slacks**) casual trousers. VERB [inf] work slowly or lazily.

slacken VERB make or become slack.

slag NOUN solid waste left when metal has been smelted.
slag off [inf] criticize rudely.

slain past participle of **slay**.

slake VERB satisfy thirst.

slalom NOUN a skiing or canoeing race following a winding course marked out by poles.

slam VERB (**slammed**, **slamming**) shut forcefully and noisily; put or hit forcefully. NOUN a slamming noise.

slander NOUN the crime of making false statements that damage a person's reputation. VERB make such statements about. **slanderous** ADJ

slang NOUN very informal words and phrases used by a particular group of people.

slant VERB 1 slope. 2 present news etc. from a particular point of view. NOUN 1 a slope. 2 a point of view.

slap VERB (**slapped, slapping**) strike with the open hand or a flat object; place forcefully or carelessly. NOUN an act or sound of slapping.

slapdash ADJ hasty and careless.

slapstick NOUN boisterous comedy.

slash VERB cut with a violent sweeping stroke. NOUN 1 a cut made by slashing. 2 an oblique line (/) used between alternatives.

slat NOUN a narrow strip of wood, metal, etc.

slate NOUN rock that splits easily into flat plates; a piece of this used as roofing material.

slattern NOUN [old use] a dirty, untidy woman. **slatternly** ADJ

slaughter VERB kill animals for food; kill ruthlessly or in great numbers. NOUN killing in this way.

slaughterhouse NOUN a place where animals are killed for food.

slave NOUN (in the past) a person owned by and obliged to work for another; a person dependent on or controlled by something. VERB work very hard.

slave-driver a person who makes others work very hard.

slavery NOUN

slaver VERB have saliva flowing from the mouth.

slavish ADJ excessively submissive or imitative.

slay VERB (**slew, slain, slaying**) kill.

sleazy ADJ (**-ier, -iest**) sordid or squalid.

sledge ([US] **sled**) NOUN a cart on runners for travelling over snow. VERB travel or convey in a sledge.

sledgehammer NOUN a large, heavy hammer.

sleek ADJ smooth and glossy; looking well fed and thriving.

sleep NOUN a condition of rest in which the mind is unconscious and the muscles are relaxed. VERB (**slept**, **sleeping**) **1** be asleep. **2** provide with sleeping accommodation. **3** (**sleep with**) have sex with.
sleepy ADJ

sleeper NOUN **1** a railway coach fitted for sleeping in. **2** a beam on which the rails of a railway rest. **3** a ring worn in a pierced ear to keep the hole from closing.

sleepwalk VERB walk about while asleep.

sleet NOUN hail or snow and rain falling together.

sleeve NOUN the part of a garment covering the arm; the cover for a record.

sleigh NOUN a sledge drawn by horses or reindeer.

sleight of hand NOUN skill in using the hands to perform conjuring tricks etc.

slender ADJ **1** slim and graceful. **2** barely enough.

slept past and past participle of **sleep**.

sleuth NOUN [inf] a detective.

slew[1] past of **slay**.

slew[2] VERB turn or swing round.

slice NOUN **1** a thin, broad piece of food cut from a larger portion; a portion. **2** a sliced stroke. VERB **1** cut into slices. **2** strike a ball so that it spins away from the direction intended.

slick ADJ **1** efficient and effortless; glib. **2** smooth and glossy or slippery. NOUN a patch of oil. VERB make sleek.

slide VERB (**slid**, **sliding**) move along a smooth surface, always remaining in contact with it; move or pass smoothly. NOUN **1** a structure with a smooth slope for children to slide down. **2** a piece of glass for holding an object under a microscope. **3** a picture for projecting on to a screen. **4** a hinged clip to hold hair in place.

slight ADJ not great or large; trivial; slender. VERB insult by treating with lack of respect NOUN a snub.
slightly ADV

slim ADJ (**slimmer, slimmest**) attractively thin; of small girth or thickness; very slight. VERB (**slimmed, slimming**) make or become thinner.

slime NOUN an unpleasant thick liquid substance.

slimy ADJ (**-ier, -iest**) 1 like or covered by slime. 2 insincerely flattering.

sling NOUN 1 a loop of fabric used to support or raise a hanging object. 2 a looped strap used to throw a stone etc. VERB (**slung, slinging**) 1 hang or carry with a sling or strap. 2 [inf] throw.

slink VERB (**slunk, slinking**) move in a stealthy way.

slinky ADJ smooth and sinuous.

slip VERB (**slipped, slipping**) slide accidentally; lose your footing; fall or slide out of place; move or place quietly and quickly; get free from; deteriorate gradually. NOUN 1 an act of slipping. 2 a slight mistake. 3 a small piece of paper. 4 a petticoat.

slipped disc a displaced disc in the spine that presses on nerves and causes pain. **slip road** a road for entering or leaving a motorway. **slip up** [inf] make a mistake.

slipper NOUN a light loose shoe for indoor wear.

slippery ADJ difficult to hold or stand on because smooth or wet; untrustworthy.

slipshod ADJ done or doing things carelessly.

slipstream NOUN a current of air driven backward by a revolving propeller or jet engine.

slipway NOUN a sloping structure on which boats are landed or ships built or repaired.

slit NOUN a narrow straight cut or opening. VERB (**slit, slitting**) cut a slit in.

slither VERB slide unsteadily.

sliver NOUN a small thin strip.

slob NOUN [inf] a lazy, untidy person.

slobber VERB slaver.

sloe NOUN a small wild plum.

slog VERB (**slogged, slogging**) 1 work hard. 2 hit hard. NOUN a spell of hard work or tiring walking.

slogan NOUN a word or phrase adopted as a motto or in advertising.

slop VERB (**slopped, slopping**) overflow; spill. NOUN unappetizing liquid food; (**slops**) liquid refuse.

slope NOUN a surface with one end at a higher level than another. VERB slant up or down.

sloppy ADJ (**-ier, -iest**) 1 wet and slushy. 2 careless. 3 too sentimental.

slot NOUN 1 a narrow opening into which something may be inserted. 2 a place in a schedule etc. VERB (**slotted, slotting**) fit into a slot. **slot machine** a machine operated by putting coins into a slot.

sloth NOUN 1 laziness. 2 a slow-moving animal of tropical America. **slothful** ADJ

slouch VERB stand, sit, or move in a lazy way. NOUN a slouching posture.

slough[1] NOUN a swamp.

slough[2] VERB shed old or dead skin.

slovenly ADJ careless and untidy.

slow ADJ not moving or working quickly; not learning quickly or easily; taking a long time; (of a clock) showing an earlier time than the correct one. VERB reduce the speed of. **slow-worm** a snake-like lizard. **slowly** ADV

sludge NOUN thick mud.

slug NOUN 1 a small creature like a snail without a shell. 2 a small amount of a drink; a bullet. VERB (**slugged, slugging**) [inf] hit hard.

sluggish ADJ slow-moving; not energetic or alert.

sluice NOUN a sliding gate controlling a flow of water; a channel carrying off water.

slum NOUN a squalid house or district.

slumber VERB & NOUN sleep.

slump NOUN a sudden great fall in prices or demand. VERB 1 undergo a slump 2 sit down heavily and limply.

slung past and past participle of **sling**.

slunk past and past participle of **slink**.

slur VERB (**slurred,**

slurring) speak in an unclear way. NOUN a damaging allegation.

slurp VERB & NOUN (make) a noisy sucking sound.

slurry NOUN thin liquid cement; fluid manure.

slush NOUN partly melted snow.

slut NOUN a slovenly or immoral woman.

sluttish ADJ

sly ADJ cunning and deceitful.

smack NOUN 1 a slap; the sound of this. 2 a loud kiss. 3 a single-masted boat. VERB 1 slap. 2 close and part the lips noisily. 3 (**smack of**) taste of; suggest.

small ADJ of less than normal size; not great in amount, number, strength, etc. NOUN the narrowest part (of the back).

small hours the period soon after midnight.

small talk polite conversation on unimportant subjects.

smallholding NOUN a small farm.

smallholder NOUN

smallpox NOUN a disease causing blisters that often leave bad scars.

smarmy ADJ [inf] excessively and insincerely friendly.

smart ADJ 1 neat and elegant; well dressed. 2 [inf] intelligent. 3 brisk. VERB give a sharp, stinging pain; feel upset and annoyed.

smarten VERB

smash VERB break noisily into pieces; hit or collide with forcefully; destroy or ruin. NOUN an act or sound of smashing.

smashing ADJ [inf] excellent.

smattering NOUN a slight knowledge; a small amount.

smear VERB 1 spread with a greasy or dirty substance. 2 damage the reputation of. NOUN 1 a mark made by smearing. 2 a slander.

smell NOUN the ability to perceive things with the sense organs of the nose; a quality perceived in this way; an act of smelling. VERB (**smelt** or **smelled**, **smelling**) perceive the smell of; give off a smell.

smelly ADJ

smelt VERB extract metal from its ore by heating

and melting it.

smidgen NOUN [inf] a tiny amount.

smile NOUN a facial expression indicating pleasure or amusement, with lips upturned. VERB give a smile.

smirk NOUN & VERB (give) a smug smile.

smite VERB (**smote, smitten, smiting**) [literary] hit hard.

smith NOUN a person who makes things in metal; a blacksmith.

smithereens PLURAL NOUN [inf] small fragments.

smithy NOUN (PL **-ies**) a blacksmith's workshop.

smitten ADJ strongly attracted to someone.

smock NOUN a loose shirt-like garment; a loose overall.

smog NOUN dense smoky fog.

smoke NOUN visible vapour given off by a burning substance; an act of smoking tobacco. VERB **1** give out smoke; inhale and exhale smoke from a cigarette, pipe, etc. **2** preserve meat or fish by exposure to smoke.

smoker NOUN

smoky ADJ

smokescreen NOUN something intended to disguise or conceal activities.

smooch VERB [inf] kiss and cuddle.

smooth ADJ **1** having an even surface; not harsh in sound or taste; moving evenly without bumping; free from difficulties. **2** charming but perhaps insincere. VERB make smooth.

smote past of **smite**.

smother VERB suffocate or stifle; cover thickly.

smoulder ([US] **smolder**) VERB **1** burn slowly with smoke but no flame. **2** show silent or suppressed anger etc.

smudge NOUN a dirty or blurred mark. VERB make or become blurred or smeared.

smug ADJ (**smugger, smuggest**) irritatingly pleased with yourself.

smuggle VERB convey goods illegally into or out of a country; convey secretly.

smuggler NOUN

smut NOUN **1** a small flake of soot or dirt. **2** indecent

pictures, stories, etc.
smutty ADJ

snack NOUN a small or casual meal.

snag NOUN 1 a problem. 2 a jagged projection; a tear caused by this. VERB (**snagged, snagging**) catch or tear on a snag.

snail NOUN a soft-bodied creature with a shell.

snake NOUN a reptile with a long narrow body and no legs. VERB move in a winding course.

snap VERB (**snapped, snapping**) break with a sharp sound; (of an animal) make a sudden bite; open or close briskly or with a sharp sound; speak suddenly and irritably. NOUN 1 a snapping sound or movement. 2 a snapshot. ADJ done or happening at short notice.

snappy ADJ (**-ier, -iest**) [inf] 1 irritable. 2 neat and stylish. 3 quick.

snapshot NOUN an informal photograph.

snare NOUN a trap, usually with a noose. VERB trap in a snare.

snarl VERB 1 growl with bared teeth; say

aggressively. 2 become entangled. NOUN an act of snarling.

snatch VERB seize quickly or eagerly. NOUN an act of snatching; a fragment of music or talk.

snazzy ADJ (**-ier, -iest**) [inf] stylish.

sneak VERB 1 move, convey, or obtain furtively. 2 [inf] tell tales. NOUN [inf] a telltale.
sneaky ADJ

sneaking ADJ (of a feeling) persistent but not openly acknowledged.

sneer NOUN & VERB (give) a scornful expression or remark.

sneeze NOUN & VERB (give) a sudden involuntary expulsion of air through the nose.

snide ADJ sneering slyly.

sniff VERB draw air audibly through the nose; investigate secretly. NOUN the act or sound of sniffing.

sniffle VERB sniff slightly or repeatedly. NOUN this act or sound.

snigger VERB & NOUN (give) a sly giggle.

snip VERB (**snipped, snipping**) cut with small

quick strokes. NOUN **1** an act of snipping. **2** [inf] a bargain.

snipe NOUN a wading bird. VERB fire shots from a hiding place; make sly critical remarks. **sniper** NOUN

snippet NOUN a small piece.

snivel VERB (**snivelled, snivelling;** [US] **sniveled, sniveling**) cry; complain in a whining way.

snob NOUN a person with an exaggerated respect for social position or wealth. **snobbery** NOUN **snobbish** ADJ

snood NOUN a hairnet worn at the back of a woman's head.

snooker NOUN a game played on a table, with 21 balls to be pocketed in a set order.

snoop VERB [inf] pry.

snooty ADJ (**-ier, -iest**) [inf] snobbishly contemptuous.

snooze [inf] NOUN & VERB (take) a nap.

snore NOUN a snorting sound made during sleep. VERB make such sounds.

snorkel NOUN a tube through which an underwater swimmer can breathe.

snorkelling ([US] **snorkeling**) NOUN

snort NOUN & VERB (make) an explosive sound made by forcing breath through the nose.

snout NOUN an animal's long projecting nose or nose and jaws.

snow NOUN frozen atmospheric vapour falling to earth in white flakes; a fall or layer of snow. VERB **1** fall as or like snow. **2** (**be snowed under**) be overwhelmed with work etc. **snowstorm** NOUN **snowy** ADJ

snowball NOUN a ball of packed snow. VERB increase in size or intensity.

snowdrift NOUN a mass of snow piled up by the wind.

snowdrop NOUN a plant with white flowers blooming in late winter.

snowman NOUN a figure made of snow.

snowplough ([US] **snowplow**) NOUN a device for clearing roads of snow.

snub VERB (**snubbed, snubbing**) reject or ignore

contemptuously. NOUN an act of snubbing. ADJ (of the nose) short and turned up at the end.

snuff NOUN powdered tobacco for sniffing up the nostrils. VERB put out a candle.

snuffle VERB breathe with a noisy sniff. NOUN a snuffling sound.

snug ADJ (**snugger, snuggest**) cosy; close-fitting. NOUN a small cosy room in a pub.

snuggle VERB settle into a warm, comfortable position.

so ADV 1 to such a great extent; to the same extent; extremely. 2 similarly. 3 in this way. CONJ 1 therefore. 2 with the aim or result that. **so-and-so** a person whose name is not known; a disliked person. **so-called** called by a specified name, but perhaps wrongly. **so-so** mediocre.

soak VERB place or lie in liquid so as to become thoroughly wet; (of liquid) penetrate; (**soak up**) absorb.

soap NOUN 1 a substance used for washing things. 2 [inf] a soap opera. VERB wash with soap.

soap opera a television or radio serial dealing with the daily lives of a group of characters.

soapy ADJ

soar VERB rise high, especially in flight.

sob VERB (**sobbed, sobbing**) cry with loud gasps. NOUN a sound of sobbing.

sober ADJ not drunk; serious and realistic; (of colour) not bright. VERB make or become sober.

sobriety NOUN

soccer NOUN football.

sociable ADJ fond of company; friendly and welcoming.

social ADJ 1 of society or its organization. 2 living in or suited to a community; of interaction between friends etc. NOUN a social gathering.

social security money provided by the state for people with little or no income. **social services** welfare services provided by the state. **social worker** a person trained to help people with social problems.

socialism NOUN the theory that a country's resources, industries, and transport should be owned and managed by the state.
socialist NOUN

socialite NOUN a person prominent in fashionable society.

socialize (or **-ise**) VERB mix with other people for pleasure.

society NOUN (PL **-ies**) **1** an ordered community; a particular system of ordering the community. **2** an organization or club. **3** wealthy and fashionable people. **4** company.

sociology NOUN the study of human society.
sociological ADJ
sociologist NOUN

sock NOUN **1** a knitted garment for the foot. **2** [inf] a heavy blow. VERB [inf] hit forcefully.

socket NOUN a hollow into which something fits.

sod NOUN turf; a piece of this.

soda NOUN **1** (also **soda water**) carbonated water. **2** a compound of sodium.

sodden ADJ very wet.

sodium NOUN a soft silver-white metallic element.

sodomy NOUN anal intercourse.

sofa NOUN a long upholstered seat with a back.

soft ADJ **1** easy to mould, cut, compress, or fold; not rough in texture. **2** not loud or harsh; subtle. **3** not strict enough. **4** (of drinks) non-alcoholic; (of a drug) not likely to cause addiction.
soft spot a feeling of affection.
soften VERB

software NOUN computer programs.

soggy ADJ (**-ier, -iest**) very wet and soft.

soil NOUN the upper layer of the earth; a nation's territory. VERB make dirty.

soirée NOUN an evening social gathering.

sojourn NOUN a temporary stay. VERB stay temporarily.

solace VERB & NOUN (give) comfort in distress.

solar ADJ of or from the sun.
solar plexus a network of nerves at the pit of the stomach. **solar system** the sun together with the

planets etc. in orbit around it.

solarium NOUN (PL **-riums** or **-ria**) a room with sunbeds.

sold past and past participle of **sell**.

solder NOUN a soft alloy used for joining metals. VERB join with solder.

soldier NOUN a member of an army. VERB **1** serve as a soldier. **2** (**soldier on**) [inf] persevere doggedly.

sole[1] NOUN **1** the undersurface of a foot; the part of a shoe etc. covering this. **2** an edible flatfish. VERB put a sole on a shoe.

sole[2] ADJ one and only; belonging exclusively to one person or group.

solely ADV

solecism NOUN a grammatical mistake; an instance of bad manners.

solemn ADJ serious; formal and dignified.

solemnity NOUN

solemnize VERB perform a ceremony; mark with a ceremony.

solenoid NOUN a coil of wire magnetized by electric current.

solicit VERB ask someone for something; (of a prostitute) approach someone.

solicitor NOUN a lawyer who advises clients and instructs barristers.

solicitous ADJ anxious about a person's well-being.

solicitude NOUN

solid ADJ **1** firm and stable in shape; not liquid or gas; strongly built. **2** not hollow; of a specified substance throughout: *solid gold*. **3** (of time) uninterrupted. **4** three-dimensional. NOUN a solid substance, object, or food.

solidify VERB

solidity NOUN

solidarity NOUN unity resulting from common aims or interests etc.

soliloquy NOUN (PL **-ies**) a speech made aloud to yourself.

solitaire NOUN **1** a gem set by itself. **2** a game for one person played on a board with pegs.

solitary ADJ alone; isolated; single.

solitude NOUN being solitary.

solo NOUN (PL **-os**) music for a single performer; an

solstice

662

unaccompanied performance etc. ADJ & ADV for or done by one person.
soloist NOUN
solstice NOUN either of the times (about 21 June and 22 Dec.) when the sun reaches its highest or lowest point in the sky at noon.
soluble ADJ 1 able to be dissolved. 2 able to be solved.
solution NOUN 1 a liquid containing something dissolved; the process of dissolving. 2 a way of solving a problem; the answer found.
solve VERB find the answer to.
solvent ADJ having more money than you owe. NOUN a liquid used for dissolving something. **solvency** NOUN
sombre ([US] **somber**) ADJ dark or gloomy.
sombrero NOUN (PL **-os**) a hat with a very wide brim.
some ADJ 1 an unspecified quantity or number of; unknown or unspecified: approximate. 2 considerable.

3 remarkable. PRON some people or things.
somebody PRON 1 an unspecified person. 2 an important person.
somehow ADV in an unspecified or unexplained manner.
someone PRON somebody.
somersault NOUN a leap or roll turning your body upside down and over. VERB move in this way.
something PRON an unspecified or unknown thing or amount.
sometime ADV at an unspecified time. ADJ former.
sometimes ADV occasionally.
somewhat ADV to some extent.
somewhere ADV at, in, or to an unspecified place.
somnolent ADJ sleepy.
son NOUN a male in relation to his parents. **son-in-law** the husband of your daughter.
sonar NOUN a device for detecting objects under water by reflection of sound waves.
sonata NOUN a musical composition for one instrument, usually in

several movements.

song NOUN a set of words to be sung; singing.

songbird NOUN a bird with a musical cry.

sonic ADJ of sound waves.

sonnet NOUN a poem of 14 lines.

sonorous ADJ deep and resonant.

soon ADV 1 after a short time; early. 2 (**sooner**) rather.

soot NOUN a black powdery substance produced by burning. **sooty** ADJ

soothe VERB calm; ease pain or distress. **soothing** ADJ

soothsayer NOUN a prophet.

sop NOUN a concession to pacify an angry person. VERB (**sopped, sopping**) soak up liquid.

sophisticated ADJ 1 experienced in matters of culture or fashion. 2 highly developed and complex. **sophistication** NOUN

sophistry NOUN clever but misleading arguments.

soporific ADJ causing drowsiness or sleep.

sopping ADJ drenched.

soppy ADJ [inf] too sentimental.

soprano NOUN (PL **-os**) the highest singing voice.

sorbet NOUN a water ice.

sorcerer NOUN a magician. **sorcery** NOUN

sordid ADJ dishonest or immoral; dirty.

sore ADJ painful or aching. NOUN a sore place.

sorely ADV very much; severely.

sorrow NOUN deep distress caused by loss, disappointment, etc.; a cause of this. VERB grieve. **sorrowful** ADJ

sorry ADJ (**-ier, -iest**) 1 feeling pity or distress. 2 feeling regret or repentance. 3 wretched or pitiful.

sort NOUN a kind or category; [inf] a person of a specified nature. VERB 1 divide or arrange in classes, categories, etc. 2 (**sort out**) deal with a problem etc.

sortie NOUN an attack by troops from a besieged place; a flight by an aircraft on a military operation.

SOS NOUN an international distress signal; an urgent

appeal for help.

sotto voce ADV in an undertone.

soufflé NOUN a light dish made with beaten egg white.

sought past and past participle of **seek**.

souk NOUN a market in Muslim countries.

soul NOUN 1 the spiritual or immortal element of a person; a person's inner nature; a person. 2 someone embodying a quality: *the soul of discretion*. 3 a kind of music expressing strong emotions, made popular by black Americans.

soulful ADJ showing deep feeling.

soulless ADJ lacking interest or individuality; lacking feeling.

sound[1] NOUN vibrations in the air detectable by the ear; a thing that can be heard. VERB 1 produce or cause to produce sound; say something; give a particular impression. 2 test the depth of water using a line, pole, etc. ADJ 1 in good condition; (of reasoning) valid. 2 (of sleep) deep.

sound barrier the point at which an aircraft approaches the speed of sound. **sound bite** a short, memorable extract from a speech or interview.

soundly ADV

soundproof ADJ

sound[2] NOUN a strait.

soup NOUN liquid food made from meat, vegetables, etc.

sour ADJ 1 tasting sharp; not fresh; tasting or smelling stale. 2 bad-tempered. VERB make or become sour.

source NOUN the place from which something comes or is obtained; a river's starting point; a person or book etc. supplying information.

souse VERB steep in pickle.

south NOUN the point or direction to the right of a person facing east; the southern part of a place. ADJ & ADV towards or facing the south; (of wind) from the south.

southward ADJ & ADV

southwards ADV

south-east NOUN the point or direction midway between south and east.

south-easterly ADJ & NOUN

south-eastern ADJ

southerly ADJ towards or blowing from the south.

southern ADJ of or in the south.

southerner NOUN a person from the south of a region.

south-west NOUN the point or direction midway between south and west.

south-westerly ADJ & NOUN

south-western ADJ

souvenir NOUN a thing kept as a reminder of a person, place, or event.

sou'wester NOUN a waterproof hat with a broad flap at the back.

sovereign NOUN 1 a king or queen who is the supreme ruler of a country. 2 a former British coin worth one pound. ADJ supreme; (of a state) independent.

sovereignty NOUN

sow[1] VERB (**sowed, sown** or **sowed, sowing**) plant seed by scattering it on the earth; plant an area with seed.

sow[2] NOUN an adult female pig.

soya bean NOUN an edible bean that is high in protein.

soy sauce NOUN a sauce made with fermented soya beans.

spa NOUN a place with a health-giving mineral spring.

space NOUN 1 the boundless expanse in which all objects exist and move; the universe beyond the earth's atmosphere. 2 an unoccupied area; room to be or move; a blank patch; an interval of time. VERB arrange with gaps in between.

spacecraft (or **spaceship**) NOUN a vehicle for travelling in outer space.

spacious ADJ providing plenty of space.

spade NOUN a tool for digging, with a broad metal blade on a handle.

spadework NOUN hard preparatory work.

spaghetti NOUN pasta made in long strings.

span NOUN something's extent from end to end; the distance or part between the uprights of an arch or bridge. VERB (**spanned**, **spanning**) extend across or over.

spangle NOUN a small piece of decorative glittering material. VERB cover with spangles.

spaniel NOUN a dog with drooping ears and a silky coat.

spank VERB slap on the buttocks.

spanner NOUN a tool for gripping and turning a nut or bolt.

spar NOUN a strong pole used as a ship's mast, yard, or boom. VERB (**sparred**, **sparring**) box, especially for practice; quarrel.

spare ADJ 1 additional to what is needed; not being used or occupied. 2 thin. NOUN an extra thing kept in reserve. VERB 1 let someone have; be able to do without. 2 refrain from killing or hurting.

sparing ADJ economical.

spark NOUN a fiery particle; a flash of light produced by an electrical discharge; a trace. VERB give off sparks.

spark plug a device that produces a spark to ignite the fuel in a vehicle's engine.

sparkle VERB 1 shine with flashes of light; be lively or witty. 2 (**sparkling**) (of a drink) fizzy. NOUN a sparkling light.

sparkler NOUN a hand-held sparking firework.

sparrow NOUN a small brownish-grey bird.

sparse ADJ thinly scattered.

spartan ADJ not comfortable or luxurious.

spasm NOUN a strong involuntary contraction of a muscle; a sudden brief spell of activity or emotion etc.

spasmodic ADJ occurring in brief irregular bursts. **spasmodically** ADV

spastic [offensive] ADJ affected by cerebral palsy. NOUN a person with cerebral palsy.

spat past & past participle of **spit**.

spate NOUN a number of similar things coming one after another.

spatial ADJ of or existing in space. **spatially** ADV

spatter VERB scatter with or fall in small drops. NOUN a spray or splash.

spatula NOUN a knife-like tool with a broad blunt blade.

spawn NOUN the eggs of fish, frogs, or shellfish. VERB 1 deposit spawn. 2 generate.

spay VERB sterilize a female animal by removing the ovaries.

speak VERB (**spoke, spoken, speaking**) say something; have a conversation; be able to communicate in a particular language.

speaker NOUN 1 a person who speaks. 2 a loudspeaker.

spear NOUN a weapon with a long shaft and pointed tip; a pointed shoot or stem. VERB pierce with a spear or other pointed object.

spearhead NOUN the leader of an attack or movement. VERB lead an attack or movement.

spearmint NOUN a type of mint used in cooking.

special ADJ 1 better than or different from usual. 2 for a particular purpose, recipient, etc. **specially** ADV

specialist NOUN an expert in a particular branch of a subject.

speciality NOUN (PL **-ies**) a skill or subject in which someone is an expert; a product for which a person or region is famous.

specialize (or **-ise**) VERB 1 be or become a specialist. 2 adapt for a particular purpose.

species NOUN (PL **species**) a group of similar animals or plants which can interbreed.

specific ADJ particular; precise and clear. NOUN a precise detail. **specifically** ADV

specification NOUN specifying; details describing a thing to be made or done.

specify VERB (**specified, specifying**) identify precisely; include in specifications.

specimen NOUN a part or individual taken as an example or for examination or testing.

specious ADJ seeming reasonable, but in fact wrong.

speck NOUN a small spot or particle.

speckle NOUN a small patch of colour. **speckled** ADJ

spectacle NOUN **1** a visually striking performance or display. **2** (**spectacles**) a pair of lenses in a frame, worn in front of the eyes to correct vision.

spectacular ADJ very impressive or striking. NOUN a spectacular performance.

spectator NOUN a person who watches a game, incident, etc.

spectre ([US] **specter**) NOUN a ghost; a haunting fear.

spectrum NOUN (PL **-tra**) bands of colour or sound forming a series according to their wavelengths; an entire range of ideas etc.

speculate VERB **1** form opinions by guessing. **2** buy in the hope of making a profit. **speculation** NOUN **speculative** ADJ **speculator** NOUN

sped past and past participle of **speed**.

speech NOUN speaking or the ability to speak; a formal address given to an audience.

speechless ADJ unable to speak because of emotion or shock.

speed NOUN the rate at which someone or something moves or operates; a fast rate. VERB (**sped** or **speeded**, **speeding**) **1** move quickly; (**speed up**) accelerate. **2** drive at an illegal speed. **speedy** ADJ

speedboat NOUN a fast motor boat.

speedometer NOUN a device indicating a vehicle's speed.

speedway NOUN motorcycle racing round an oval dirt track.

spell VERB (**spelled** or **spelt**, **spelling**) **1** give in correct order the letters that form a word. **2** be a sign of. **3** (**spell out**) state explicitly. NOUN **1** words supposed to have magic power; their influence; an ability to control or influence others. **2** a short period of time.

spellbound ADJ entranced.

spend VERB (**spent**, **spending**) **1** pay out money to buy something.

spina bifida

2 use up; pass time etc.

spendthrift NOUN a wasteful spender of money.

sperm NOUN (PL **sperms** or **sperm**) a spermatozoon; semen.

spermatozoon NOUN (PL **-zoa**) the fertilizing cell of a male animal.

spew VERB vomit; pour out in a stream.

sphere NOUN **1** a perfectly round solid figure or object. **2** an area of activity or interest. **spherical** ADJ

sphincter NOUN a ring of muscle controlling an opening in the body.

sphinx NOUN an ancient Egyptian statue with a lion's body and human or animal head.

spice NOUN a flavouring substance with a strong taste or smell; interest or excitement. VERB flavour with spice. **spicy** ADJ

spick and span ADJ neat and clean.

spider NOUN a small creature with a segmented body and eight legs. **spidery** ADJ

spiel NOUN [inf] a glib persuasive speech.

spigot NOUN a small peg or plug.

spike NOUN a thin, pointed piece of metal, wood, etc. VERB **1** impale on a spike. **2** [inf] add alcohol to a drink. **spiky** ADJ

spill VERB (**spilt** or **spilled**, **spilling**) cause or allow to run over the edge of a container; spread outside an allotted space. NOUN **1** an amount spilled. **2** a thin strip of wood or paper for lighting a fire. **spillage** NOUN

spin VERB (**spun**, **spinning**) **1** turn rapidly on an axis. **2** draw out and twist into threads; make yarn in this way. **3** (**spin out**) prolong. NOUN **1** a spinning movement. **2** [inf] a short drive for pleasure.

spin doctor a person employed to give a favourable interpretation of events to the media.

spin-off an incidental benefit.

spina bifida NOUN a condition in which part of the spinal cord is exposed, often causing paralysis.

spinach NOUN a vegetable with green leaves.

spinal ADJ of the spine.

spindle NOUN a rod on which thread is wound in spinning; a revolving pin or axis.

spindly ADJ long or tall and thin.

spine NOUN 1 the backbone; the part of a book where the pages are hinged. 2 a needle-like projection on a plant or animal. **spiny** ADJ

spineless ADJ having no spine; lacking determination.

spinney NOUN (PL -eys) a thicket.

spinster NOUN an unmarried woman.

spiral ADJ forming a continuous curve round a central point or axis. NOUN 1 a spiral line or thing. 2 a continuous, usually harmful, increase or decrease. VERB (**spiralled**, **spiralling**; [US] **spiraled**, **spiraling**) 1 move in a spiral course. 2 increase or decrease continuously.

spire NOUN a tall pointed structure on a church tower.

spirit NOUN 1 a person's mind or soul as distinct from their body; something's characteristic quality; a person's mood. 2 a ghost. 3 courage and determination. 4 the intended meaning of a law etc. 5 a strong distilled alcoholic drink. VERB (**spirited**, **spiriting**) carry off rapidly and secretly.

spirit level a sealed glass tube containing a bubble in liquid, used to test that a surface is level.

spirited ADJ courageous and determined.

spiritual ADJ 1 of the human spirit or soul. 2 of religion or religious belief. NOUN a religious song associated with black Christians of the southern US. **spirituality** NOUN **spiritually** ADV

spiritualism NOUN attempted communication with spirits of the dead. **spiritualist** NOUN

spit VERB (**spat** or **spit**, **spitting**) 1 eject saliva, food, etc. from the mouth. 2 (of rain) fall lightly. NOUN 1 saliva; an act of spitting. **2** a metal spike holding meat while it is roasted. **3** a narrow strip of land projecting into the sea.

spite NOUN malicious desire to hurt or annoy someone. VERB hurt or annoy from spite.
in spite of not being prevented by.
spiteful ADJ

spittle NOUN saliva.

splash VERB **1** cause liquid to fall on something in scattered drops; move or fall with such drops. **2** (**splash out**) spend extravagantly. NOUN **1** splashing. **2** a patch of colour; a small quantity of liquid.

splatter VERB splash or spatter.

splay VERB spread out wide apart.

spleen NOUN **1** an organ involved in maintaining the proper condition of the blood. **2** bad temper.

splendid ADJ very impressive; [inf] excellent.

splendour ([US] **splendor**) NOUN a splendid appearance.

splenetic ADJ bad-tempered.

splice VERB join by interweaving or overlapping the ends.

splint NOUN a rigid support for a broken bone.

splinter NOUN a thin, sharp piece of broken wood etc. VERB break into splinters.
splinter group a small breakaway group.

split VERB (**split**, **splitting**) break into parts by force; divide or share; separate. NOUN a split thing or place; (**splits**) a seated position with the legs stretched fully apart.

splodge NOUN a spot, splash, or smear.

splutter VERB make a rapid series of spitting sounds; speak or utter incoherently. NOUN a spluttering sound.

spoil VERB (**spoilt** or **spoiled**, **spoiling**) **1** make less good or pleasant; (of food) become unfit for eating. **2** harm the character of a child by being indulgent. NOUN (also **spoils**) stolen goods.

spoiler NOUN a device that slows down an aircraft by interrupting the air flow; a similar device on a vehicle, preventing it from being lifted off the road at speed.

spoilsport NOUN a person who spoils others' enjoyment.

spoke[1] NOUN any of the bars connecting the hub to the rim of a wheel.

spoke[2] past of **speak**.

spokesman (or **spokeswoman**) NOUN a person who speaks on behalf of a group.

sponge NOUN 1 a simple sea creature with a soft porous body; a piece of a light absorbent substance used for washing, as padding, etc. 2 a cake with a light, open texture. VERB 1 wipe or wash with a sponge. 2 [inf] live off the generosity of others.

spongy ADJ

sponsor NOUN 1 a person who provides funds for an artistic or sporting event etc.; a person who promises to give money to a charity if another person completes a task or activity. 2 a person who proposes a new law. VERB be a sponsor for.

sponsorship NOUN

spontaneous ADJ not caused by outside influences; not rehearsed.

spontaneity NOUN

spoof NOUN [inf] a parody.

spook NOUN [inf] a ghost.

spooky ADJ

spool NOUN a reel on which something is wound.

spoon NOUN an eating and cooking utensil with a rounded bowl and a handle. VERB transfer with a spoon.

spoon-feed feed with a spoon; give excessive help to.

sporadic ADJ occurring at irregular intervals or in a few places.

sporadically ADV

spore NOUN one of the tiny reproductive cells of fungi, ferns, etc.

sporran NOUN a pouch worn in front of a kilt.

sport NOUN a competitive activity involving physical effort and skill. VERB 1 wear or display prominently. 2 play.

sports car a small, fast car. **sports jacket** a man's jacket for informal wear.

sporting ADJ 1 concerning or interested in sport. 2 fair and generous.

sportsman (or **sportswoman**) NOUN 1 a

person who takes part in sports. **2** a fair and generous person.

spot NOUN **1** a round mark or stain; a pimple. **2** a place. **3** [inf] a small amount. VERB (**spotted**, **spotting**) **1** notice. **2** mark with spots.

on the spot 1 at once. **2** at the scene of an action or event. **spot check** a random check.

spotter NOUN

spotty ADJ

spotless ADJ completely clean or pure.

spotlight NOUN a lamp projecting a strong narrow beam on a small area.

spouse NOUN a husband or wife.

spout NOUN a projecting tube or lip through which liquid is poured or conveyed; a jet of liquid. VERB **1** come or send out in a stream. **2** utter or speak lengthily.

sprain VERB injure by wrenching violently. NOUN this injury.

sprang past of **spring**.

sprat NOUN a small edible fish.

sprawl VERB sit, lie, or fall with arms and legs spread loosely; spread out irregularly. NOUN a sprawling attitude or arrangement.

spray NOUN **1** liquid dispersed in very small drops; a liquid which can be forced out of an aerosol etc. in a spray. **2** a branch with leaves and flowers; a bunch of cut flowers. VERB come or send out in small drops; wet with liquid in this way.

spread VERB (**spread**, **spreading**) **1** open out fully; extend over a wide area or specified period of time. **2** apply in an even layer. **3** (cause to) affect or be known by increasing numbers. NOUN **1** spreading; the extent to which something spreads; a range. **2** a paste for spreading on bread. **3** an article etc. covering several pages of a newspaper. **4** [inf] a lavish meal.

spreadeagled ADJ with arms and legs extended.

spreadsheet NOUN a computer program that manipulates figures in tables for calculation.

spree NOUN a period of unrestrained indulgence.

sprig NOUN a twig or shoot.

sprightly ADJ lively and energetic.

spring VERB (**sprang, sprung, springing**) 1 move suddenly upwards or forwards: appear suddenly. 2 arise or originate. NOUN 1 the season after winter and before summer. 2 a device that reverts to its original shape after being pressed or pulled; elasticity. 3 a jump. 4 a place where water or oil flows naturally from the ground.

spring-clean clean a house etc. thoroughly.

springy ADJ

springboard NOUN a flexible board giving impetus to a gymnast or diver.

sprinkle VERB scatter small drops or particles over a surface; fall in this way.

sprinkler NOUN

sprint VERB run at full speed. NOUN a fast run; a short, fast race.

sprite NOUN an elf or fairy.

sprocket NOUN a projection on a wheel, engaging with links on a chain etc.

sprout VERB begin to grow or appear; produce shoots. NOUN 1 a plant's shoot. 2 a Brussels sprout.

spruce ADJ neat and smart. VERB make smarter. NOUN a fir tree.

sprung past participle of **spring**. ADJ fitted with springs.

spry ADJ active or lively.

spud NOUN [inf] a potato.

spume NOUN froth.

spun past and past participle of **spin**.

spur NOUN 1 a spiked device worn on a horse rider's heel; a stimulus. 2 a projection. VERB (**spurred, spurring**) urge a horse forward with spurs; encourage.

on the spur of the moment on impulse.

spurious ADJ not genuine or authentic.

spurn VERB reject contemptuously.

spurt VERB gush out; increase speed suddenly. NOUN a sudden gush; a sudden burst of activity or speed.

sputum NOUN mixed saliva and mucus.

spy NOUN (PL **spies**) a person who secretly watches or gathers information. VERB (**spied**, **spying**) be a spy; observe; notice.

sq. ABBREV square.

squabble NOUN & VERB (engage in) a noisy and petty quarrel.

squad NOUN a small group working together.

squadron NOUN a unit of an air force; a group of warships.

squalid ADJ dirty and unpleasant; very immoral or dishonest.

squalor NOUN

squall NOUN a sudden storm or wind.

squander VERB spend wastefully.

square NOUN 1 a flat shape with four equal sides and four right angles; an area or object shaped like this. 2 the product of a number multiplied by itself. 3 an instrument for testing right angles. ADJ 1 of square shape. 2 right-angled; level or parallel. 3 of or using units expressing the measure of an area. 4 fair or honest. 5 [inf] old-fashioned. ADV directly; straight. VERB 1 make square. 2 mark with squares. 3 multiply a number by itself. 4 make or be compatible; settle a bill or debt.

square dance a dance in which four couples face inwards from four sides.

squash VERB 1 crush or squeeze until flat or distorted; force into a restricted place. 2 suppress or inhibit. NOUN 1 a crowded place or state. 2 a fruit-flavoured soft drink. 3 a game played with rackets and a small ball in a closed court. 4 a vegetable gourd.

squat VERB (**squatted**, **squatting**) 1 sit on your heels. 2 unlawfully occupy an uninhabited place. NOUN 1 a squatting posture. 2 a place occupied by squatters. ADJ short and stout.

squatter NOUN

squawk NOUN & VERB (make) a loud harsh cry.

squeak NOUN & VERB (make) a short high-pitched cry or sound.

squeaky ADJ

squeal NOUN & VERB (make) a long shrill cry or sound.

squeamish ADJ easily sickened or disgusted.

squeeze VERB **1** press firmly; extract liquid from something by doing this. **2** hug; move or force into or through a tight space. NOUN an act of squeezing; an embrace.

squelch VERB & NOUN (make) a sound like someone treading in thick mud.

squid NOUN a sea creature with ten tentacles.

squiggle NOUN a short curly line.

squiggly ADJ

squint NOUN a condition in which one eye looks in a different direction from the other. VERB have a squint affecting one eye; look with partly closed eyes.

squire NOUN a country gentleman.

squirm VERB wriggle; feel embarrassed.

squirrel NOUN a small tree-climbing animal with a bushy tail.

squirt VERB force liquid out of a small opening in a thin jet; wet with a jet of liquid. NOUN a jet of liquid.

St ABBREV **1** Saint; Street. **2** (**st**) stone (in weight).

stab VERB (**stabbed**, **stabbing**) pierce, wound, or kill with something pointed; poke. NOUN **1** a stabbing thrust; a sudden sharp sensation. **2** [inf] an attempt.

stabilize (or **-ise**) VERB make or become stable.

stabilizer NOUN

stable NOUN a building in which horses are kept; an establishment for training racehorses. VERB put or keep in a stable. ADJ firmly fixed or established.

stability NOUN

staccato ADV [Music] with each sound sharply distinct.

stack NOUN **1** an orderly pile or heap; [inf] a large quantity. **2** a chimney. VERB arrange in a stack; cause aircraft to fly at different levels while waiting to land.

stadium NOUN a sports ground surrounded by tiers of seats for spectators.

staff NOUN **1** a stick used as a support or weapon. **2** the people employed by an organization. **3** a stave in music. VERB provide with a staff of people.

stag NOUN a fully grown male deer.

stag night an all-male party for a man about to marry.

stage NOUN 1 a point reached in a process, journey, etc. 2 a raised platform for theatrical performances etc.; acting as a profession. VERB present on the stage; organize and carry out.

stagecoach NOUN [historical] a large horse-drawn passenger coach running on a regular route.

stagger VERB 1 move or go unsteadily. 2 astonish. 3 arrange so as not to coincide exactly.

stagnant ADJ (of water) not moving and having a stale smell; not active or developing.

stagnate VERB

staid ADJ steady and serious.

stain VERB mark or discolour with dirty patches; dye. NOUN a mark caused by staining; a disgrace or blemish.

stainless steel a steel alloy not liable to rust or tarnish.

stair NOUN each of a set of fixed steps; (**stairs**) a flight of these.

staircase (or **stairway**) NOUN a set of stairs with their supporting structure.

stairwell NOUN the space for a staircase.

stake NOUN 1 a strong stick or post for driving into the ground. 2 a sum of money gambled; a share or interest in an enterprise etc. VERB 1 support on a stake; mark an area with stakes. 2 gamble.

stalactite NOUN a deposit of calcium carbonate hanging like an icicle.

stalagmite NOUN a deposit of calcium carbonate standing like a pillar.

stale ADJ not fresh; no longer new or interesting.

stalemate NOUN a drawn position in chess; a situation where progress is impossible.

stalk NOUN a stem or similar supporting part. VERB 1 pursue stealthily; follow and harass. 2 walk in a stiff or proud manner.

stalker NOUN

stall NOUN 1 a booth or stand for the display and sale of goods. 2 a compartment in a stable or cowshed. 3 a fixed seat in a chancel. 4 (**stalls**) the ground floor seats in a theatre. VERB (of an engine) stop running; (of an aircraft) begin to drop because the speed is too low; stop making progress; be obstructive or evasive.

stallion NOUN an uncastrated male horse.

stalwart ADJ loyal and hard-working. NOUN a stalwart person.

stamen NOUN the pollen-bearing part of a flower.

stamina NOUN the ability to withstand long physical or mental strain.

stammer VERB speak with involuntary pauses or repetitions of a syllable. NOUN this act or tendency.

stamp VERB 1 bring your foot down heavily. 2 press a mark or pattern on a surface. 3 (**stamp out**) suppress by force. NOUN 1 an instrument for stamping a mark; this mark; a characteristic quality. 2 a small adhesive label stuck to a letter or parcel to record payment of postage. 3 an act of stamping the foot.

stampede NOUN a sudden rush of animals or people. VERB take part in a stampede.

stance NOUN a manner of standing.

stanch see **staunch**.

stanchion NOUN an upright post or support.

stand VERB (**stood, standing**) 1 have or take a stationary upright position; set upright; (of a building) be situated. 2 remain in a specified condition; remain undisturbed or unchanged. 3 endure. 4 be a candidate in an election. NOUN 1 an attitude or policy; resistance to attack or pressure. 2 a support or pedestal; a platform; a raised structure for spectators to sit or stand in; a stall for goods.

stand down withdraw. **stand-offish** cold or distant in manner. **stand up for** speak in defence of.

standard NOUN 1 a measure or model used to make

comparisons; a level of quality or achievement. **2** a principle of conduct. **3** a flag. ADJ used or accepted as normal or average.

standard lamp a tall lamp placed on the floor.

standardize (or **-ise**) VERB cause to conform to a standard.

standby NOUN readiness for action; a person or thing ready for use in an emergency; a system of allocating unreserved tickets.

standing NOUN **1** status. **2** duration or length.

standpoint NOUN a point of view.

standstill NOUN inability to proceed.

stank past of **stink**.

stanza NOUN a verse of poetry.

staple NOUN **1** a piece of wire used to fasten papers together; a piece of bent metal used as a fastening. **2** a main or standard food or product etc. ADJ main or important. VERB secure with a staple or staples.
stapler NOUN

star NOUN **1** a large ball of burning gas appearing as a glowing point in the night sky. **2** a mark with points or rays representing a star. **3** a famous actor, performer, etc. VERB (**starred**, **starring**) be a star performer; have as a star.
starry-eyed naively enthusiastic or idealistic.
stardom NOUN
starry ADJ

starboard NOUN the right-hand side of a ship or aircraft.

starch NOUN **1** a carbohydrate occurring in cereals, potatoes, etc. **2** a preparation for stiffening fabrics. VERB stiffen with starch.
starchy ADJ

stare VERB gaze fixedly. NOUN a staring gaze.

starfish NOUN a star-shaped sea creature.

stark NOUN **1** desolate or bare. **2** sharply evident; downright. ADV completely.

starling NOUN a bird with glossy black speckled feathers.

start VERB **1** begin to do or happen; begin to operate or work; make happen or operate; set out on a journey. **2** jump or jerk from surprise. NOUN **1** beginning; the point at which something begins. **2** an advantage given at the beginning of a race etc. **3** a sudden movement of surprise.

starter NOUN the first course of a meal.

startle VERB shock or surprise.

starve VERB die or suffer acutely from lack of food; cause to do this; [inf] feel very hungry.
starvation NOUN

stash VERB [inf] store secretly.

state NOUN **1** the condition that someone or something is in; [inf] an agitated condition. **2** a political community under one government or forming part of a federation; civil government. **3** grandeur or ceremony. VERB express definitely in words.

stately ADJ dignified or grand.

statement NOUN a clear expression of something; an official account of an event; a written report of a financial account.

statesman (or **stateswoman**) NOUN an experienced and respected political leader.

static ADJ **1** not moving or changing. **2** (of an electric charge) acquired by objects that cannot conduct a current. NOUN static electricity; crackling or hissing on a telephone, radio, etc.

station NOUN **1** a place where trains stop for passengers to get on and off. **2** a place where a particular activity is carried on. **3** a broadcasting channel. **4** a place where someone stands, especially on duty; a person's status. VERB assign to a station.

stationary ADJ not moving.

stationer NOUN a seller of stationery.

stationery NOUN paper and other materials needed for writing.

statistic NOUN an item of information obtained by studying numerical data; (**statistics**) the collection and analysis of numerical information.
statistical ADJ

statistician NOUN

statue NOUN a sculptured, cast, or moulded figure.

statuesque ADJ attractively tall and dignified.

statuette NOUN a small statue.

stature NOUN bodily height; importance or reputation.

status NOUN a person's position or rank in relation to others; high rank or prestige.
status quo the existing state of affairs.

statute NOUN a written law.

statutory ADJ required or permitted by law.

staunch ADJ very loyal. VERB (or **stanch**) stop the flow of blood from a wound.

stave NOUN 1 a vertical wooden post; one of the strips of wood forming the side of a cask or tub. 2 a set of five horizontal lines on which music is written. VERB (**stove** or **staved**, **staving**) 1 dent or break a hole in. 2 (**stave off**) ward off.

stay VERB 1 remain in the same place; live temporarily; continue in the same state. 2 stop or postpone. NOUN 1 a period of staying somewhere. 2 a postponement or delay.

stead NOUN (**in someone's/ something's stead**) instead of someone or something.

steadfast ADJ not changing or yielding.

steady ADJ (**-ier, -iest**) 1 firmly fixed; not shaking. 2 regular and even. 3 sensible and reliable. VERB (**steadied, steadying**) make steady.
steadily ADV
steadiness NOUN

steak NOUN a thick slice of meat (especially beef) or fish.

steal VERB (**stole, stolen, stealing**) 1 take dishonestly. 2 move stealthily.

stealth NOUN caution and secrecy.
stealthy ADJ

steam NOUN vapour into which water is changed by boiling; power derived from steam under pressure; momentum. VERB 1 give off steam; become misted over with steam. 2 cook or treat with steam; travel under steam power.

steamer NOUN

steamy ADJ

steamroller NOUN a heavy engine with a large roller, used in road-making.

steed NOUN [literary] a horse.

steel NOUN a very strong alloy of iron and carbon. VERB mentally prepare yourself for something difficult.

steep ADJ 1 sloping sharply. 2 (of a rise or fall) very large or rapid. VERB soak in liquid; permeate thoroughly.

steeple NOUN a church tower and spire.

steeplechase NOUN a race for horses or athletes, with fences to jump.

steeplejack NOUN a person who climbs tall chimneys etc. to do repairs.

steer[1] VERB direct the course of; guide.

steer[2] NOUN a bullock.

stellar ADJ of a star or stars.

stem NOUN 1 the supporting part of a plant; a long, thin supporting section. 2 the root or main part of a word. VERB (**stemmed**,

stemming) 1 stop the flow of. 2 (**stem from**) have as its source.

stench NOUN a foul smell.

stencil NOUN a sheet of card etc. with a cut-out design, painted over to produce the design on the surface below. VERB (**stencilled, stencilling**; [US] **stenciled, stenciling**) decorate with a stencil.

step VERB (**stepped, stepping**) lift and set down a foot or alternate feet. NOUN 1 a movement of a foot and leg in stepping; the distance covered in this way. 2 a level surface to place the foot on in climbing. 3 a level or grade; a measure or action.

step- COMBINING FORM related by remarriage of a parent, as *stepmother, stepson*, etc.

stepladder NOUN a short ladder with a supporting framework.

steppe NOUN a grassy plain, especially in SE Europe and Siberia.

stereo NOUN (PL **-os**) stereophonic sound; a stereophonic hi-fi system.

stereophonic ADJ (of sound reproduction)

using two transmission channels so as to give the effect of sound from more than one source.

stereotype NOUN a standardized conventional idea or character etc. VERB represent as a stereotype.

sterile (or **-ise**) ADJ **1** unable to produce fruit or offspring. **2** free from bacteria.

sterility NOUN

sterilize (or **-ise**) VERB

sterling NOUN British money. ADJ of standard purity; excellent.

stern ADJ strict or severe. NOUN the rear of a ship.

sternum NOUN the breastbone.

steroid NOUN any of a group of organic compounds that includes certain hormones.

stethoscope NOUN a medical instrument for listening to a patient's heart or breathing.

stew VERB cook slowly in a closed pot. NOUN a dish made by stewing meat etc.

steward NOUN **1** a person employed to manage an estate etc. **2** a passengers'

attendant on a ship or aircraft. **3** an official at a race meeting or show etc.

stewardess NOUN a female attendant on a ship or aircraft.

stick VERB (**stuck, sticking**) **1** thrust something sharp into or through something. **2** cling or adhere; become unable to move or work; be unable to make progress. **3** (**stick out**) be prominent or conspicuous. NOUN a thin piece of wood; a similar piece of other material; an implement used to propel the ball in hockey, polo, etc.

sticker NOUN an adhesive label or sign.

stickleback NOUN a small fish with sharp spines on its back.

stickler NOUN a person who insists on something.

sticky ADJ (**-ier, -iest**) **1** sticking to what is touched. **2** humid.

stiff ADJ **1** not bending or moving easily; formal in manner. **2** severe or strong; difficult.

stiffen VERB

stifle VERB feel or cause to

feel unable to breathe; suppress.

stigma NOUN a mark of shame.

stigmata PLURAL NOUN marks corresponding to the marks of the Crucifixion on Christ's body.

stigmatize (or **-ise**) VERB regard or treat as shameful.

stile NOUN steps or bars for people to climb over a fence.

stiletto NOUN (PL **-os**) **1** a thin, high heel on a woman's shoe. **2** a dagger with a narrow blade.

still ADJ **1** not moving. **2** (of drinks) not fizzy. NOUN **1** silence and calm. **2** a photograph taken from a cinema film. **3** a distilling apparatus. ADV **1** continuing the same up to the present or the time mentioned. **2** nevertheless. **3** even. **still life** a picture of inanimate objects.

stillborn ADJ born dead.

stilted ADJ stiffly formal.

stilts PLURAL NOUN a pair of poles with footrests, for walking raised above the ground; posts supporting a building.

stimulant NOUN something that stimulates.

stimulate VERB cause a reaction in the body; motivate or encourage. **stimulation** NOUN

stimulus NOUN (PL **-uli**) something that stimulates.

sting NOUN a sharp wounding part of an insect; a wound made by this; a sharp tingling sensation. VERB (**stung**, **stinging**) wound with a sting; produce a stinging sensation; hurt or upset.

stingy ADJ (**-ier**, **-iest**) mean.

stink NOUN an offensive smell. VERB (**stank** or **stunk**, **stinking**) give off a stink.

stint VERB restrict to a small allowance. NOUN a period of work.

stipend NOUN a salary.

stipulate VERB demand or specify as part of an agreement. **stipulation** NOUN

stir VERB (**stirred**, **stirring**) **1** mix a substance by moving a spoon round in it. **2** move; arouse or

stimulate. NOUN **1** an act of stirring. **2** a commotion.

stirrup NOUN a support for a rider's foot, hanging from the saddle.

stitch NOUN **1** a loop of thread made by a single pass of the needle in sewing or knitting; a method of making a stitch. **2** a sudden pain in the side. VERB make or mend with stitches.

stoat NOUN a weasel-like animal.

stock NOUN **1** a supply of goods or materials available for sale or use. **2** livestock. **3** a business company's capital; a portion of this held by an investor. **4** liquid made by stewing bones etc. **5** ancestry; reputation. **6** the trunk or stem of a tree or shrub. **7** the handle of a rifle. **8** (**stocks**) a wooden structure in which criminals were formerly locked as a public punishment. ADJ common or conventional. VERB keep in stock; provide with a supply.

stock exchange (or **stock market**) a place where stocks and shares are bought and sold.

stockade NOUN a protective fence.

stockbroker NOUN a person who buys and sells shares for clients.

stocking NOUN a close-fitting covering for the foot and leg.

stockist NOUN a firm that stocks certain goods.

stockpile NOUN & VERB (accumulate) a large stock of goods or materials.

stocktaking NOUN making an inventory of stock.

stocky ADJ (**-ier, -iest**) short and sturdy.

stodgy ADJ **1** (of food) heavy and filling. **2** dull.

stoic NOUN a calm and uncomplaining person. **stoical** ADJ **stoicism** NOUN

stoke VERB tend and put fuel on a fire etc.

stole[1] NOUN a woman's long scarf or shawl.

stole[2], **stolen** past and past participle of **steal**.

stolid ADJ not excitable.

stomach NOUN the internal organ in which the first part of digestion occurs; the abdomen; appetite. VERB endure or tolerate.

stomp VERB tread heavily.

stone NOUN **1** a piece of rock; stones or rock as a substance or material. **2** a gem. **3** the hard case round the kernel of certain fruits. **4** (PL **stone**) a unit of weight equal to 14 lb. VERB **1** pelt with stones. **2** remove stones from fruit.

Stone Age the prehistoric period when tools were made of stone.

stonewall VERB obstruct a process by giving evasive replies.

stony ADJ (**-ier, -iest**) **1** full of stones. **2** cold and unfeeling.

stood past and past participle of **stand**.

stooge NOUN a comedian's assistant; a person working for and controlled by others.

stool NOUN **1** a seat without arms or a back. **2** (**stools**) faeces.

stoop VERB bend forwards and down; lower yourself morally. NOUN a stooping posture.

stop VERB (**stopped, stopping**) **1** come or bring to an end; cease doing something; (cause to) cease moving. **2** prevent. **3** block or close. NOUN **1** an act of stopping; a place where a train or bus etc. stops regularly; something that stops or regulates motion. **2** a set of organ pipes.

stop press news added to a newspaper at the last minute.

stopcock NOUN a valve regulating the flow in a pipe etc.

stopgap NOUN a temporary substitute.

stoppage NOUN stopping; an obstruction.

stopper NOUN a plug for closing a bottle etc.

stopwatch NOUN a watch that can be started and stopped, used for timing races etc.

storage NOUN storing; a space for this.

store NOUN **1** a supply of something available for use; a storehouse. **2** a large shop. VERB keep for future use.

storey NOUN (PL **-eys** or **-ies**) a particular level of a building.

stork NOUN a large bird with a long bill.

storm NOUN a disturbance

of the atmosphere with strong winds and rain or snow; an uproar or controversy. VERB **1** move angrily and violently; be angry. **2** suddenly attack and capture.
stormy ADJ

story NOUN (PL **-ies**) an account of an incident (true or invented).

stout ADJ **1** fat; thick and strong. **2** brave and determined. NOUN a strong dark beer.

stove[1] past & past participle of **stave**.

stove[2] NOUN a device for cooking or heating.

stow VERB **1** pack or store away. **2** (**stow away**) hide on a ship, aircraft, etc. to travel secretly.

stowaway NOUN a person who stows away.

straddle VERB sit or stand with one leg on each side of; extend across.

strafe VERB attack with gunfire from the air.

straggle VERB grow or spread untidily; lag behind others.
straggly ADJ

straight ADJ **1** extending or moving in one direction, without a curve or bend; level or even; tidy or orderly. **2** honest and direct. **3** in continuous succession. **4** undiluted. ADV in a straight line or manner; without delay.

straight away immediately.
straighten VERB

straightforward ADJ **1** simple or uncomplicated. **2** frank.

straightjacket see **straitjacket**.

strain VERB **1** make an intense effort; injure a muscle, limb, etc. by overexertion; make great or excessive demands on. **2** sieve to separate solids from liquid. NOUN **1** a force stretching something; an excessive demand on a person's strength etc.; an injury from straining. **2** a variety or breed of animal etc. **3** a tendency in a person's character. **4** the sound of a piece of music.
strainer NOUN

strained ADJ (of manner etc.) not relaxed.

strait NOUN **1** (also **straits**) a narrow stretch of water connecting two seas. **2** (**straits**) trouble or

straitjacket

difficulty.

strait-laced very prim and proper.

straitjacket (or **straightjacket**) NOUN a strong garment used to restrain the arms of a violent person.

strand NOUN **1** a single thread, especially one woven or plaited with others; one element in a complex whole. **2** a shore. VERB run aground; leave in difficulties.

strange ADJ **1** unusual or odd. **2** not known or met before.

stranger NOUN a person you do not know; a person who does not live in or know a place.

strangle VERB kill by squeezing the throat; prevent from developing.

stranglehold NOUN a strangling grip; complete control.

strangulation NOUN strangling.

strap NOUN a strip of flexible material used for fastening, carrying, or holding on to. VERB (**strapped, strapping**) secure or fasten with a strap.

strapping ADJ tall and robust.

stratagem NOUN a cunning plan or scheme.

strategic ADJ **1** of strategy. **2** (of weapons) for use against enemy territory rather than in battle.

strategically ADV

strategy NOUN (PL **-ies**) the planning and directing of military activity in a war etc.; a plan for achieving a major goal.

strategist NOUN

stratify VERB (**stratified, stratifying**) arrange in strata.

stratosphere NOUN a layer of the atmosphere about 10–50 km above the earth's surface.

stratum NOUN (PL **strata**) one of a series of layers or levels.

straw NOUN **1** dry cut stalks of corn etc.; a single piece of this. **2** a narrow tube for sucking up liquid to drink.

straw poll an unofficial test of public opinion.

strawberry NOUN a soft edible red fruit with seeds on the surface.

stray VERB move aimlessly from a group or from the

right course or place. ADJ having strayed. NOUN a stray animal.

streak NOUN 1 a thin line or mark; an element in someone's character. 2 a continuous period of luck etc. VERB 1 mark with streaks. 2 move very rapidly; [inf] run naked in a public place.
streaker NOUN
streaky ADJ

stream NOUN 1 a small river; a flow of liquid, things, or people. 2 a group in which schoolchildren of the same level of ability are placed. VERB 1 move in a continuous flow; float in the wind. 2 run with liquid. 3 arrange schoolchildren in streams.

streamer NOUN a long narrow strip of material used for decoration.

streamline VERB make a car etc. with a smooth shape offering little resistance to movement through water or air; make more efficient by simplifying.

street NOUN a public road lined with buildings.

streetwise ADJ [inf] able to deal well with modern urban life.

strength NOUN 1 being strong. 2 a good or advantageous quality. 3 the total number of people making up a group.
strengthen VERB

strenuous ADJ making or requiring great effort.

stress NOUN 1 pressure; mental or emotional strain. 2 emphasis; extra force given to a syllable or note. VERB 1 emphasize. 2 subject to pressure.
stressful ADJ

stretch VERB 1 pull out tightly or to a greater extent; become longer or wider without breaking; extend part of the body to its full length. 2 extend over an area or period. 3 make demands on. NOUN 1 an act of stretching. 2 the ability to be stretched. 3 a continuous area or period.

stretcher NOUN a long framework used for carrying a sick or injured person.

strew VERB (**strewed, strewn** or **strewed,**

strewing) scatter over a surface; cover with scattered things.

stricken ADJ afflicted by an illness, shock, or grief.

strict ADJ requiring obedience to rules; following rules or beliefs exactly.

stricture NOUN 1 severe criticism. 2 a restriction.

stride VERB (**strode**, **stridden**, **striding**) walk with long steps. NOUN a single long step; (**strides**) progress.

strident ADJ loud and harsh. **stridency** NOUN

strife NOUN quarrelling or conflict.

strike VERB (**struck**, **striking**) 1 hit; come into forcible contact with. 2 attack suddenly; afflict; come suddenly into the mind of. 3 stop work in protest. 4 ignite a match by friction. 5 indicate the hour by chiming. 6 reach an agreement. 7 unexpectedly discover. NOUN 1 a refusal by employees to work. 2 a sudden attack.

striker NOUN 1 a worker on strike. 2 (in football) a forward.

striking ADJ noticeable; impressive.

string NOUN 1 a narrow cord; a length of catgut or wire on a musical instrument, which is vibrated to produce notes; (**strings**) stringed instruments. 2 a sequence of similar items or events. 3 (**strings**) [inf] conditions or requirements. VERB (**strung**, **stringing**) 1 hang up; thread on a string; (**string out**) spread out on a line. 2 fit strings on an instrument etc.

stringent ADJ (of regulations etc.) strict. **stringency** NOUN

stringy ADJ like string; (of food) tough and fibrous.

strip VERB (**stripped**, **stripping**) remove clothes or coverings from; undress; deprive of property, rank, etc. NOUN 1 an act of undressing. 2 a long narrow piece or area.

strip light a tubular fluorescent lamp.

stripe NOUN a long narrow band on a surface, differing in colour or texture from its surroundings.

striped ADJ

stripy ADJ

stripling NOUN a youth.

stripper NOUN 1 a device for stripping something. 2 a striptease performer.

striptease NOUN an entertainment in which a performer gradually undresses.

strive VERB (**strove, striven, striving**) 1 make great efforts. 2 struggle.

strobe NOUN a bright light which shines at rapid intervals.

strode past of **stride**.

stroke VERB gently move your hand over. NOUN 1 an act of hitting; the sound of a striking clock. 2 an act of stroking. 3 a mark made by a movement of a pen, paintbrush, etc. 4 a style of swimming. 5 a loss of consciousness due to an interruption in the supply of blood to the brain.

stroll VERB walk in a leisurely way. NOUN a leisurely walk.

strong ADJ 1 able to move heavy weights or resist great pressure; having skills, qualities, or numbers assisting survival or victory; (of an argument) persuasive; able to bear distress. 2 intense; concentrated; containing much alcohol. 3 indicating the size of a group: *fifty strong*.

strongly ADV

stronghold NOUN a fortified place; the centre of support for a cause.

strongroom NOUN a room designed for safe storage of valuable items.

stroppy ADJ [inf] bad-tempered or awkward.

strove past of **strive**.

struck past & past participle of **strike**.

structure NOUN the way a thing is constructed or organized; a thing's supporting framework or essential parts; a complex whole.

structural ADJ

strudel NOUN flaky pastry filled with apple etc.

struggle VERB move violently to get free; progress with difficulty. NOUN a spell of struggling; a difficult task.

strum VERB (**strummed, strumming**) play a guitar or similar instrument.

strung past and past participle of **string**.

strut NOUN **1** a bar of wood or metal supporting something. **2** a strutting walk. VERB (**strutted, strutting**) walk proudly and confidently.

strychnine NOUN a bitter highly poisonous substance.

stub NOUN **1** a short stump. **2** a counterfoil of a cheque, ticket, etc. VERB (**stubbed, stubbing**) **1** strike your toe against a hard object. **2** extinguish a cigarette by pressure.
stubby ADJ

stubble NOUN the lower ends of corn stalks left in the ground after harvest; short stiff hair or bristles growing after shaving.
stubbly ADJ

stubborn ADJ obstinate or unyielding.
stubbornness NOUN

stucco NOUN plaster used for coating walls or moulding into decorations.
stuccoed ADJ

stuck past & past participle of **stick**.
stuck-up conceited and snobbish.

stud NOUN **1** a piece of metal with a large head that projects from a surface; a fastener consisting of two buttons joined with a bar; a small piece of jewellery pushed through a pierced ear or nose. **2** an establishment where horses etc. are kept for breeding. VERB (**studded, studding**) cover with studs or other small objects.

student NOUN a person studying at a college or university.

studio NOUN (PL **-os**) the workroom of a painter, photographer, etc.; premises where cinema films are made; a room from which television or radio programmes are broadcast.
studio flat a flat containing one main room.

studious ADJ spending much time in study; deliberate and careful.

study NOUN (PL **-ies**) **1** effort and time spent in learning; a detailed investigation into something. **2** a room for reading and writing. **3** a piece of work done for practice or as an experiment. VERB (**studied, studying**) 1 give your attention to acquiring knowledge of a subject; examine attentively. 2 (**studied**) done with careful effort.

stuff NOUN material, articles, etc. of a particular kind, or of a mixed or unspecified kind VERB fill tightly; force into a confined space; fill the skin of a dead animal to make it lifelike.

stuffing NOUN padding used to fill something; a savoury mixture put inside meat etc. before cooking.

stuffy ADJ (**-ier, -iest**) 1 lacking fresh air or ventilation. 2 conventional and narrow-minded.

stultify VERB (**stultified, stultifying**) cause to lose enthusiasm or energy.

stumble VERB trip and lose your balance; walk unsteadily; make mistakes in speaking etc. NOUN an act of stumbling.

stumbling block an obstacle.

stump NOUN 1 the base of a tree left in the ground when the rest has gone; a remaining piece. 2 one of the uprights of a wicket in cricket. VERB baffle.

stumpy ADJ (**-ier, -iest**) short and thick.

stun VERB (**stunned, stunning**) knock unconscious; astonish.

stung past and past participle of **sting**.

stunk past and past participle of **stink**.

stunning ADJ very impressive.

stunt NOUN an action displaying skill and daring; something done to attract attention. VERB hinder the growth or development of.

stupefy VERB (**stupefied, stupefying**) make unable to think properly. **stupefaction** NOUN

stupendous ADJ amazingly large or good.

stupid ADJ lacking intelligence; unable to think clearly. **stupidity** NOUN

stupor NOUN a dazed condition.

sturdy ADJ (**-ier, -iest**) strongly built or made.

sturgeon NOUN a large fish from whose roe caviar is

made.

stutter VERB speak with difficulty; stammer. NOUN a stammer.

sty NOUN (PL **sties**) **1** a pigsty. **2** (also **stye**) an inflamed swelling on the edge of the eyelid.

style NOUN **1** a way of doing something; a particular design, appearance, or arrangement. **2** elegance. VERB design, shape, or arrange in a particular way.

stylish ADJ fashionably elegant.

stylist NOUN a fashion designer; a hairdresser.

stylistic ADJ of literary or artistic style.

stylized (or **-ised**) ADJ represented non-realistically.

stylus NOUN (PL **-luses** or **-li**) a needle-like device for cutting or following a groove in a record.

stymie VERB (**stymied**, **stymieing** or **stymying**) [inf] obstruct or thwart.

suave ADJ charming, confident, and elegant.

sub NOUN [inf] **1** a submarine. **2** a subscription. **3** a substitute.

subatomic ADJ smaller than an atom; occurring in an atom.

subconscious ADJ & NOUN (of) our own mental activities of which we are not aware.

subcontinent NOUN a large land mass forming part of a continent.

subcutaneous ADJ under the skin.

subdivide VERB divide a part into smaller parts. **subdivision** NOUN

subdue VERB bring under control; make quieter or less intense.

subeditor NOUN a person who prepares newspaper etc. text for printing.

subject NOUN **1** a person or thing being discussed or dealt with; a branch of knowledge studied or taught. **2** a citizen in a monarchy. **3** [Grammar] the words in a sentence naming the person or thing performing the action of the verb. ADJ (**subject to**) able to be affected by; conditional on; under the authority of. VERB cause to undergo an experience. **subjection** NOUN

subjective ADJ dependent

on personal taste or views etc.

subjugate VERB bring under control by force. **subjugation** NOUN

subjunctive NOUN [Grammar] (of a verb) expressing what is imagined, wished, or possible.

sublet VERB (**sublet, subletting**) let property etc. that you are already renting to someone else.

sublimate VERB transform into a purer or idealized form. **sublimation** NOUN

sublime ADJ of the highest excellence or beauty.

subliminal ADJ below the level of conscious awareness.

sub-machine gun NOUN a hand-held lightweight machine gun.

submarine NOUN a vessel that can operate under water. ADJ under the surface of the sea.

submerge VERB go or cause to be under water. **submersion** NOUN

submission NOUN the submitting of something; a proposal etc. submitted.

submissive ADJ meek and obedient.

submit VERB (**submitted, submitting**) 1 yield to authority or power; subject to a particular treatment. 2 present for consideration.

subordinate ADJ of lesser importance or rank. NOUN a subordinate person. VERB treat as less important than something else. **subordination** NOUN

subpoena NOUN a writ commanding a person to appear in a law court.

subscribe VERB 1 pay in advance to receive a publication etc. regularly; contribute to a fund. 2 (**subscribe to**) agree with an idea or proposal. **subscriber** NOUN

subscription NOUN a payment to subscribe to something.

subsequent ADJ occurring after something. **subsequently** ADV

subservient ADJ completely obedient. **subservience** NOUN

subside VERB sink to a lower or normal level; become less intense. **subsidence** NOUN

subsidiary

subsidiary ADJ of secondary importance; (of a company) controlled by another. NOUN (PL **-ies**) a subsidiary company.

subsidize (or **-ise**) VERB pay a subsidy to or for.

subsidy NOUN (PL **-ies**) a sum of money given to help keep the price of a product or service low.

subsist VERB keep yourself alive.

subsistence NOUN

subsoil NOUN soil lying below the surface layer.

substance NOUN **1** the matter of which something consists; a particular kind of matter. **2** reality; importance. **3** something's essence or basic meaning.

substantial ADJ **1** strongly built or made; of considerable size, importance, or value. **2** concerning the essence of something.

substantially ADV

substantiate VERB support with evidence.

substitute NOUN a person or thing that acts or serves in place of another. VERB use or serve as a substitute.

substitution NOUN

subsume VERB include or absorb in a larger group.

subterfuge NOUN deceit used to achieve an aim.

subterranean ADJ underground.

subtext NOUN an underlying theme.

subtitle NOUN **1** a caption displayed on a cinema or television screen to translate dialogue. **2** a subordinate title. VERB provide with subtitle(s).

subtle ADJ (**subtler, subtlest**) so slight or delicate as to be hard to analyse or identify; making fine distinctions; ingenious.

subtlety NOUN

subtly ADV

subtotal NOUN the total of part of a group of figures.

subtract VERB remove a part, quantity, or number from a greater one.

subtraction NOUN

suburb NOUN a residential area outside the central part of a town.

suburban ADJ

suburbia NOUN suburbs and their inhabitants.

subvert VERB undermine the authority of a system

	pressure or temptation.

VERB
e with

cal　　　　　l
sugar is　　　

ose for　　　ve
ply;　　　　ke
　　　　　illed
　　　　　er.

asily

　　　　, or

ething
nt trace.
nveying
esting
nt.
ction of　　　after
　　　　　to a
erson　　　　on.
　　　　　wing
　　　　　wing
clothes
er,　　　　erson
and　　　　her.
any of　　se and
which
vide　　　cor) VERB
be r
cl　　icy; (of
　　　hick
　　UN a
　　t.
　SUN
SL give way to

such ADJ **1** of the type previously mentioned or about to be mentioned. **2** to so high a degree.

suck VERB **1** draw liquid or air into the mouth by contracting the lips to create a vacuum; hold in the mouth and roll with the tongue; draw in a particular direction. **2** (**suck up to**) [inf] behave in a servile way to someone to gain advantage. NOUN an act of sucking.

sucker NOUN **1** an organ or device that can adhere to a surface by suction. **2** [inf] a person who is easily deceived.

suckle VERB feed at the breast.

suckling NOUN an unweaned child or animal.

sucrose NOUN sugar.

suction NOUN the force produced when a partial vacuum is created by the removal of air.

sudden ADJ happening or done quickly and unexpectedly.
suddenly ADV
suddenness NOUN

suds

suds PLURAL NOUN a froth of soap and water.

sue VERB (**sued, suing**) take legal proceedings against.

suede NOUN leather with a velvety nap on one side.

suet NOUN hard white fat from round an animal's kidneys, used in cooking.

suffer VERB undergo something unpleasant or harmful; experience pain or distress; tolerate.
suffering NOUN

sufferance NOUN (**on sufferance**) tolerated but only grudgingly.

suffice VERB be enough.

sufficient ADJ enough.
sufficiency NOUN

suffix NOUN a part added on to the end of a word.

suffocate VERB die or cause to die from lack of air.
suffocation NOUN

suffrage NOUN the right to vote in political elections.

suffragette NOUN [historical] a woman who campaigned for the right to vote.

suffuse VERB spread throughout or over.

sugar NOUN a sweet crystalline substance obtained from the juices

of various plants. [...] sweeten or sprinkl[...] sugar

sugar cane a trop[...] plant from which [...] obtained.

sugary ADJ

suggest VERB prop[...] consideration; im[...] cause someone to [...] think of.

suggestible ADJ e[...] influenced.

suggestion NOUN [...] 1 suggesting; som[...] suggested. 2 a sligl[...]

suggestive ADJ c[...] a suggestion; sugg[...] something indece[...]

suicide NOUN the a[...] killing yourself [...] intentionally; a p[...] who does this.
suicidal ADJ

suit NOUN 1 a set of [...] to be worn togeth[...] especially a jacket[...] trousers or skirt. 2 [...] the four sets into [...] pack of cards is di[...] 3 a lawsuit. VERB 1 [...] or good for. 2 (of [...] etc.) enhance the [...] appearance of.

suitable ADJ right [...] purpose or occasi[...]
suitability NOUN

suitably ADV

suitcase NOUN a rectangular case for carrying clothes.

suite NOUN 1 a set of rooms or furniture. 2 a set of musical pieces.

suitor NOUN a man who is seeking to marry a woman.

sulfur etc. US spelling of **sulphur** etc.

sulk VERB be sullen because of resentment or bad temper. NOUN a period of sulking.

sulkily ADV

sulky ADJ

sullen ADJ silent and bad-tempered.

sully VERB (**sullied, sullying**) stain or blemish.

sulphur ([US] **sulfur**) NOUN a pale yellow chemical element.

sulphuric acid a strong corrosive acid.

sulphurous ADJ

sultan NOUN a Muslim king or ruler.

sultana NOUN 1 a seedless raisin. 2 a sultan's wife.

sultry ADJ hot and humid; suggesting passion and sensuality.

sum NOUN 1 an amount of money; a total. 2 an arithmetical problem. VERB (**sum up**) summarize.

summarize (or **-ise**) VERB give a summary of.

summary NOUN (PL **-ies**) a brief statement of the main points of something. ADJ 1 without unnecessary detail. 2 without legal formalities.

summarily ADV

summer NOUN the warmest season of the year.

summery ADJ

summit NOUN 1 the top of a mountain; the highest point. 2 a conference between heads of states.

summon VERB send for; order to appear in a law court; call to a meeting; produce a reaction or quality.

summons NOUN a command summoning a person; a written order to appear in a law court.

sumo NOUN Japanese wrestling.

sumptuous ADJ splendid, lavish, and costly.

sun NOUN the star around which the earth travels; the light or warmth from this; any fixed star. VERB (**sunned, sunning**) expose to the sun.

sunbathe VERB lie in the sun to tan your skin.

sunbeam NOUN a ray of sun.

sunbed NOUN a device with ultraviolet lamps, for acquiring a tan artificially.

sunburn NOUN inflammation of the skin caused by too much exposure to sun.

sundae NOUN a dish of ice cream and fruit, nuts, syrup, etc.

Sunday NOUN the day after Saturday.
Sunday school a class held on Sundays to teach children about Christianity.

sunder VERB [literary] split apart.

sundial NOUN an instrument showing the time by the shadow cast by a pointer.

sundry ADJ various. PLURAL NOUN (**sundries**) various small items.

sunflower NOUN a tall plant with large yellow flowers.

sung past participle of sing.

sunk past participle of sink.

sunken ADJ lying below the level of the surrounding surface.

sunny ADJ (**-ier, -iest**) 1 full of sunshine. 2 cheerful.

sunrise NOUN the rising of the sun.

sunset NOUN the setting of the sun.

sunshine NOUN direct light from the sun.

sunstroke NOUN illness caused by too much exposure to sun.

super ADJ [inf] excellent.

superannuation NOUN an employee's pension.

superb ADJ of the most impressive or splendid kind.

supercharger VERB a device that makes an engine more efficient by forcing extra air or fuel into it.
supercharged ADJ

supercilious ADJ haughty and superior.

superficial ADJ of or on the surface; lacking the ability to think deeply.
superficiality NOUN
superficially ADV

superfluous ADJ more than is required.

superhuman ADJ having exceptional ability or

powers.

superimpose VERB place on top of something else.

superintend VERB oversee.

superintendent NOUN 1 a supervisor. 2 a senior police officer.

superior ADJ 1 higher in status, quality, or power. 2 arrogant and conceited. NOUN a person of higher rank or status.

superiority NOUN

superlative ADJ 1 of the highest quality. 2 of the grammatical form expressing 'most'.

supermarket NOUN a large self-service store selling food and household goods.

supernatural ADJ not able to be explained by the laws of nature.

supernova NOUN (PL -novas or -novae) a star that suddenly increases in brightness because of an explosion.

supernumerary ADJ extra.

superpower NOUN an extremely powerful nation.

superscript ADJ written just above and to the right of a word etc.

supersede VERB take the place of.

supersonic ADJ of or flying at speeds greater than that of sound.

superstition NOUN a belief in magical and similar influences; an idea or practice based on this.

superstitious ADJ

superstore NOUN a large supermarket.

superstructure NOUN a structure that rests on something else; the upper parts of a ship or building.

supervise VERB direct and inspect workers etc.

supervision NOUN

supervisor NOUN

supervisory ADJ

supine ADJ 1 lying face upwards. 2 passive or lazy.

supper NOUN a light or informal evening meal.

supplant VERB take the place of.

supple ADJ bending easily.

supplement NOUN something added as an extra part or to make up for a deficiency. VERB provide or be a supplement to.

supplementary ADJ

supplicate VERB ask

humbly for something.
supplicant NOUN
supplication NOUN
supply VERB (**supplied,
supplying**) provide; make
available to. NOUN (PL **-ies**)
a stock to be used;
supplying; (**supplies**)
necessary goods provided.
support VERB **1** bear the
weight of. **2** assist
financially; encourage,
help, or approve of;
confirm or back up. NOUN
the act of supporting; a
person or thing that
supports.
supporter NOUN
supportive ADJ
suppose VERB assume or
think; take as a
hypothesis; presuppose.
be supposed to be
required or expected to.
supposedly ADV
according to what is
generally believed.
supposition NOUN the
process of supposing;
what is supposed.
suppress VERB **1** put an
end to. **2** keep from being
known.
suppression NOUN
suppurate VERB form pus.
supreme ADJ highest in
authority; greatest or

most important.
supremacy NOUN
supremely ADV
supremo NOUN (PL **-os**) [inf]
a person in overall charge
of something.
surcharge NOUN an
additional charge.
sure ADJ **1** completely
confident. **2** reliable;
certainly true or correct.
3 (**sure to**) certain to
receive, do, etc. ADV [inf]
certainly.
surely ADV
surety NOUN (PL **-ies**) a
guarantee; a guarantor of
a person's promise.
surf NOUN the breaking of
waves on a seashore etc.
VERB ride on the crest of a
wave on a surfboard;
move between sites on
the Internet.
surfer NOUN
surfing NOUN
surface NOUN the outside
or uppermost layer of
something; the top or
upper limit; an outward
appearance. VERB **1** come
to the surface of water
etc.; become apparent.
2 put a specified
surface on.
surfboard NOUN a narrow
board for riding over surf.

surfeit NOUN an excessive amount, especially of food or drink.

surge VERB move forward in or like waves; increase in volume or intensity. NOUN a surging movement or increase.

surgeon NOUN a doctor qualified to perform surgical operations.

surgery NOUN (PL **-ies**) **1** treatment by cutting open the body and repairing or removing parts. **2** a doctor's or dentist's consulting room. **surgical** ADJ

surly ADJ bad-tempered and unfriendly.

surmise VERB guess or suppose. NOUN a guess.

surmount VERB overcome a difficulty or obstacle; be on the top of.

surname NOUN a family name.

surpass VERB outdo; excel.

surplice NOUN a loose white garment worn by clergy and choir members.

surplus NOUN an amount left over.

surprise NOUN an emotion aroused by something sudden or unexpected; something causing this. VERB cause to feel surprise; come on or attack unexpectedly.

surreal ADJ bizarre or dreamlike.

surrender VERB give in to an opponent; hand over. NOUN surrendering.

surreptitious ADJ done stealthily.

surrogate NOUN a deputy. **surrogate mother** a woman who bears a child on behalf of another. **surrogacy** NOUN

surround VERB be all round something. NOUN a border.

surroundings PLURAL NOUN things or conditions around a person or place.

surtax NOUN an additional tax.

surveillance NOUN close observation.

survey VERB look at and take a general view of; examine and report on the condition of a building; measure and map out. NOUN a general view, examination, or description; a report or map produced by surveying. **surveyor** NOUN

survival NOUN surviving; something that has survived from an earlier time.

survive VERB continue to live or exist; not be killed by; remain alive after the death of.
survivor NOUN

susceptible ADJ easily affected or influenced.
susceptibility NOUN

sushi NOUN a Japanese dish of balls of cold rice with raw fish etc.

suspect VERB 1 feel that something may exist or be true. 2 believe someone to be guilty without proof. NOUN a person suspected of a crime etc. ADJ possibly dangerous or false.

suspend VERB 1 hang in the air. 2 stop temporarily; deprive temporarily of a position or right; keep a sentence from being enforced if no further offence is committed.

suspender NOUN an elastic strap to hold up a stocking by its top.

suspense NOUN anxious uncertainty about what may happen.

suspension NOUN

1 suspending. 2 the means by which a vehicle is supported on its axles.
suspension bridge a bridge suspended by cables running between towers.

suspicion NOUN 1 an unconfirmed belief; a feeling that someone is guilty; distrust. 2 a slight trace.
suspicious ADJ

sustain VERB 1 support; give strength to; keep alive or in existence. 2 suffer something unpleasant.

sustainable ADJ (of development etc.) able to be continued without damage to the environment.

sustenance NOUN food or nourishment.

suture NOUN a stitch or thread used in the stitching of a wound or cut.

svelte ADJ slender and graceful.

SW ABBREV south-west or south-western.

swab NOUN a pad for cleaning wounds or taking specimens; a specimen taken with this.

VERB (**swabbed, swabbing**) clean with a swab.

swaddle VERB wrap in garments or a cloth.

swag NOUN [inf] loot.

swagger VERB walk or behave very arrogantly or confidently. NOUN a swaggering walk or manner.

swain NOUN [old use] a young lover or suitor.

swallow VERB cause or allow to go down the throat by using the throat muscles; absorb or engulf; believe. NOUN 1 an act of swallowing. 2 a fast-flying bird with a forked tail.

swam past of **swim**.

swamp NOUN a marsh. VERB flood with water; overwhelm with a mass of things.

swan NOUN a large, white, long-necked waterbird.

swansong NOUN a person's last performance or achievement.

swap (also **swop**) VERB (**swapped, swapping**) exchange or substitute. NOUN an act of swapping.

sward NOUN an expanse of short grass.

swarm NOUN a large cluster of people, insects, etc. VERB 1 move in a swarm; be crowded. 2 (**swarm up**) climb by gripping with the arms and legs.

swarthy ADJ having a dark complexion.

swashbuckling ADJ having daring and romantic adventures.

swastika NOUN a symbol formed by a cross with ends bent at right angles.

swat VERB (**swatted, swatting**) hit hard with something flat.

swatch NOUN a sample of cloth etc.

swathe[1] ([US] **swath**) NOUN a strip cut in one sweep or passage by a scythe or mower.

swathe[2] VERB wrap with layers of coverings.

sway VERB 1 move gently to and fro. 2 influence someone. NOUN 1 a swaying movement. 2 influence or control.

swear VERB (**swore, sworn, swearing**) 1 state or promise on oath; state emphatically. 2 use a swear word.

swear word an offensive or obscene word.

sweat NOUN moisture given off by the body through

the pores as a result of heat, effort, or anxiety. VERB give off sweat; work hard.

sweaty ADJ

sweater NOUN a pullover.

sweatshirt NOUN a loose, warm cotton pullover.

swede NOUN a large variety of turnip.

sweep VERB (**swept, sweeping**) clean by brushing away dirt etc.; move swiftly or forcefully. NOUN **1** an act of sweeping; a sweeping movement or line; a long expanse of land etc. **2** a person who cleans soot out of chimneys.

sweeping ADJ comprehensive; making no exceptions.

sweepstake NOUN a form of gambling in which the money staked is divided among the winners.

sweet ADJ **1** tasting as if containing sugar. **2** having a pleasant smell or sound; pleasant and kind; charming. NOUN a small piece of a sweet substance; a sweet dish forming one course of a meal.

sweet-talk persuade by using flattery or charm.

sweeten VERB

sweetcorn NOUN sweet kernels of maize, eaten as a vegetable.

sweetener NOUN **1** a sweetening substance. **2** [inf] a bribe.

sweetheart NOUN a girlfriend or boyfriend.

swell VERB (**swelled, swollen** or **swelled, swelling**) become larger from pressure within; increase in strength or amount. NOUN **1** a curving shape; a gradual increase. **2** the heaving movement of the sea.

swelling NOUN a swollen place on the body.

swelter VERB be uncomfortably hot.

swept past and past participle of **sweep**.

swerve VERB turn aside from a straight course. NOUN a swerving movement.

swift ADJ quick or prompt. NOUN a fast-flying bird with narrow wings.

swill VERB rinse; (of liquid) swirl round in a container. NOUN kitchen refuse mixed with water and fed to pigs.

swim VERB (**swam, swum, swimming**) **1** move through water using the arms and legs. **2** be covered with liquid. **3** be dizzy. NOUN a period of swimming.

swimmer NOUN

swimmingly ADV easily and satisfactorily.

swindle VERB cheat someone in order to get money. NOUN a piece of swindling.

swine NOUN **1** (PL **swine**) a pig. **2** [inf] a contemptible person.

swing VERB (**swung, swinging**) **1** move to and fro while suspended or on an axis. **2** move by grasping a support and jumping; move in a smooth curve. **3** change from one mood or opinion to another; influence decisively. NOUN **1** a swinging movement; a hanging seat for swinging on. **2** a change in opinion etc.

swingeing ADJ severe; extreme.

swipe VERB [inf] hit with a swinging blow.

swirl VERB move in a spiralling pattern.

swish VERB move with a soft hissing sound. NOUN this sound.

switch NOUN **1** a device operated to turn electric current on or off. **2** a change or exchange. **3** a flexible shoot cut from a tree. VERB **1** change the direction or position of; exchange. **2** turn an electrical device on or off.

switchback NOUN a fairground ride in which an open carriage travels up and down a steep, twisting track; a road with sharp ascents and descents.

switchboard NOUN a panel of switches for connecting incoming telephone calls.

swivel NOUN a link or pivot enabling one part to revolve without turning another. VERB (**swivelled, swivelling**; [US] **swiveled, swiveling**) turn on or as if on a swivel.

swollen past participle of **swell**.

swoon VERB faint.

swoop VERB make a sudden downward rush; make a sudden attack. NOUN an act of swooping.

swop see **swap**.

sword NOUN a weapon with a long blade and a hilt.

swordfish NOUN an edible sea fish with a long sword-like snout.

swore past of **swear**.

sworn past participle of **swear**. ADJ bound by an oath.

swot [inf] VERB (**swotted**, **swotting**) study hard. NOUN a person who studies hard.

swum past participle of **swim**.

swung past and past participle of **swing**.

sycamore NOUN a large tree of the maple family.

sycophant NOUN a person who tries to win favour with someone by flattery. **sycophantic** ADJ

syllable NOUN a unit of sound in a word.

syllabus NOUN (PL **-buses** or **-bi**) the subjects to be covered by a course of study.

syllogism NOUN reasoning in which a conclusion is drawn from two propositions.

sylph NOUN a slender girl or woman.

symbiosis NOUN (PL **-oses**) a relationship between two organisms living in close, mutually beneficial association. **symbiotic** ADJ

symbol NOUN an object, sign etc. used to represent something else; a written character etc. with a special meaning. **symbolic** ADJ **symbolism** NOUN

symbolize (or **-ise**) VERB be a symbol of; represent by means of a symbol.

symmetry NOUN the exact match in size or shape between two halves, parts, or sides of something. **symmetrical** ADJ

sympathetic ADJ feeling or showing sympathy; pleasing or likeable. **sympathetically** ADV

sympathize (or **-ise**) VERB feel or express sympathy.

sympathy NOUN (PL **-ies**) sorrow at someone else's misfortune; understanding between people; support or approval.

symphony NOUN (PL **-ies**) an elaborate musical composition for a full orchestra. **symphonic** ADJ

symposium NOUN (PL -siums or -sia) a meeting for discussing a particular subject.

symptom NOUN a sign of the existence of a condition, especially a disease.

symptomatic ADJ

synagogue NOUN a building for public Jewish worship.

synchronize (or -ise) VERB cause to happen or operate at the same time or the same rate.

syncopate VERB change the accents in music so that weak beats become strong and vice versa.

syncopation NOUN

syndicate NOUN a group of people or firms combining to achieve a common interest. VERB control or manage by a syndicate; arrange publication in many newspapers etc. simultaneously.

syndrome NOUN a set of medical symptoms which tend to occur together.

synergy NOUN cooperation of two or more things to produce a combined effect greater than the sum of their separate parts.

synod NOUN an official meeting of Church ministers and members.

synonym NOUN a word or phrase meaning the same as another in the same language.

synonymous ADJ

synopsis NOUN (PL -opses) a brief summary.

syntax NOUN the way words are arranged to form phrases and sentences.

syntactic ADJ

synthesis NOUN (PL -ses) 1 combining. 2 the production of chemical compounds from simpler substances.

synthesize (or -ise) VERB 1 make by chemical synthesis. 2 combine into a coherent whole.

synthesizer (or -iser) NOUN an electronic musical instrument able to produce a great variety of sounds.

synthetic ADJ made by synthesis; not genuine.

syphilis NOUN a venereal disease.

syringe NOUN a tube with a nozzle and piston, for

sucking in and ejecting liquid. VERB wash out or spray with a syringe.

syrup NOUN a thick sweet liquid.
　syrupy ADJ

system NOUN a set of connected things that form a whole or work together; an organized scheme or method; orderliness.

systematic ADJ methodical.
　systematically ADV

Tt

tab NOUN a small projecting flap or strip.

tabby NOUN (PL -ies) a cat with grey or brown fur and dark stripes.

tabernacle NOUN (in the Bible) a portable shrine; a place of worship for some religions.

table NOUN 1 a piece of furniture with a flat top supported on one or more legs. 2 a list of facts or figures arranged in columns. VERB present for discussion at a meeting.
　table tennis a game played with bats and a small hollow ball on a table.

tableau NOUN (PL -leaux) a silent motionless group arranged to represent a scene.

tablespoon NOUN a large spoon for serving food.

tablet NOUN 1 a slab bearing an inscription etc. 2 a pill in the shape of a disc or cylinder.

tabloid NOUN a small-sized newspaper, often sensational in style.

taboo NOUN a ban or prohibition made by religion or social custom. ADJ prohibited by a taboo.

tabular ADJ arranged in a table or list.

tabulate VERB arrange in tabular form.

tacit ADJ implied or understood but not spoken.

taciturn ADJ saying very little.

tail

tack NOUN **1** a small broad-headed nail. **2** a long stitch as a temporary fastening. **3** a change of course in sailing; an approach to a problem. **4** equipment used in horse riding. VERB **1** fasten or fix with tacks. **2** change course by turning a boat into the wind; do this repeatedly. **3** (**tack on**) casually add.

tackle NOUN **1** a set of ropes and pulleys for lifting etc. **2** equipment for a task or sport. **3** an act of tackling in football etc. VERB **1** start to deal with; confront. **2** try to take the ball from an opponent in football etc.

tacky ADJ (**-ier, -iest**) **1** (of paint, glue, etc.) not quite dry. **2** [inf] tasteless.

tact NOUN sensitivity and skill in dealing with others.
tactful ADJ
tactless ADJ

tactic NOUN an action to achieve a particular end; (**tactics**) the organization of military forces during a war.

tactical ADJ of tactics; (of weapons) for use in a battle or at close quarters.
tactical voting voting for the candidate most likely to defeat the leading candidate.
tactically ADV

tactile ADJ of or using the sense of touch.

tadpole NOUN the larva of a frog or toad, at the stage when it has gills and a tail.

taffeta NOUN a crisp shiny fabric.

tag NOUN **1** a label; an electronic device attached to someone to monitor their movements. **2** a metal point on a shoelace etc. **3** a much-used phrase or quotation. VERB (**tagged, tagging**) **1** attach a tag to. **2** (**tag on**) add at the end. **3** (**tag along**) follow without being invited.

tagliatelle NOUN pasta in ribbon-shaped strips.

tail NOUN **1** an animal's hindmost part, especially when extending beyond its body; the rear or end of something. **2** (**tails**) the side of a coin without the image of a head on it. **3** (**tails**) [inf] a tailcoat. VERB **1** [inf] follow and observe.

2 (**tail off**) gradually become smaller or weaker.

tailback NOUN a long queue of stationary traffic.

tailcoat NOUN a man's formal coat with a long divided flap at the back.

tailgate NOUN a rear door in a car; a hinged flap at the back of a truck.

tailor NOUN a maker of men's clothes. VERB **1** make clothes as a tailor. **2** make or adapt for a special purpose.
tailor-made ADJ

tailplane NOUN a small wing at the tail of an aircraft.

tailspin NOUN an aircraft's spinning dive.

taint NOUN a trace of an undesirable quality. VERB contaminate or spoil.

take VERB (**took, taken, taking**) **1** reach for and hold; accept or receive; steal; capture. **2** carry or bring with you. **3** endure; react to or interpret. **4** require or use up. **5** make a decision, action, etc.; act on an opportunity. **6** study or teach a subject. NOUN **1** a sequence of film or sound recorded at one time. **2** an amount gained or acquired.

take after resemble a parent etc. **take in 1** realize fully. **2** deceive. **take off 1** become airborne. **2** mimic. **take over** take control of. **take part** join in. **take place** occur.

takeaway NOUN a cooked meal bought at a restaurant etc. for eating elsewhere; a place selling this.

takeover NOUN the gaining of control of a business etc.

takings PLURAL NOUN money taken in business.

talc NOUN talcum powder; a soft mineral.

talcum powder NOUN a light powder used to make skin feel smooth and dry.

tale NOUN a story.

talent NOUN a special ability.
talented ADJ

talisman NOUN (PL **-mans**) an object supposed to bring good luck.

talk VERB convey or exchange ideas by spoken words; have the power of speech. NOUN conversation; an address or lecture.

talkative ADJ talking very much.

tall ADJ of great or specified height.

tall order a difficult task.

tall story an unlikely account.

tallow NOUN animal fat used to make candles, lubricants, etc.

tally NOUN (PL **-ies**) a total score etc.; a record of this. VERB (**tallied, tallying**) agree or correspond.

talon NOUN a curved claw.

tambourine NOUN a percussion instrument with jingling metal discs.

tame ADJ (of an animal) not dangerous or frightened of people; unexciting. VERB make tame or manageable.

tamper VERB meddle or interfere.

tampon NOUN a plug of absorbent material inserted into the vagina to absorb menstrual blood.

tan VERB (**tanned, tanning**) **1** make or become brown by exposure to sun. **2** convert animal skin into leather. NOUN yellowish brown; the brown colour of suntanned skin.

tandem NOUN a bicycle for two riders, one behind another.

tandoori NOUN a style of Indian cooking.

tang NOUN a strong taste or smell.

tangy ADJ

tangent NOUN **1** a straight line that touches a curve without intersecting it. **2** [Mathematics] (in a right-angled triangle) the ratio of the sides opposite and adjacent to an angle. **3** a completely different line of thought etc.

tangential ADJ

tangerine NOUN a small orange.

tangible ADJ able to be perceived by touch; real.

tangibly ADV

tangle VERB twist into a knotted mass. NOUN a tangled mass or condition.

tango NOUN (PL **-os**) a ballroom dance.

tank NOUN **1** a large container for liquid or gas. **2** an armoured fighting vehicle moving on a continuous metal track.

tankard NOUN a large beer mug.

tanker NOUN a ship, aircraft, or vehicle for carrying liquid in bulk.

tannin NOUN a bitter-tasting substance found in tea.

tannoy NOUN [trademark] a public address system.

tantalize (or **-ise**) VERB torment by the sight of something desired but kept out of reach or withheld.

tantamount ADJ equivalent.

tantrum NOUN an outburst of bad temper.

tap NOUN **1** a device to regulate the flow of liquid from a pipe or container. **2** a quick, light blow. VERB (**tapped**, **tapping**) **1** strike gently. **2** draw liquid from a cask, barrel, etc.; exploit a resource. **3** fit a device in a telephone, so as to listen to conversations secretly. **on tap** readily available.

tap-dancing dancing performed in shoes with metal pieces on the toes and heels.

tapas PLURAL NOUN small Spanish savoury dishes.

tape NOUN **1** a narrow strip of material for tying, fastening, or labelling things. **2** magnetic tape; a cassette or reel containing this. VERB **1** record on magnetic tape. **2** fasten with tape.

tape measure a strip of tape marked for measuring length. **tape recorder** an apparatus for recording and reproducing sounds on magnetic tape.

taper NOUN a thin candle. VERB **1** reduce in thickness towards one end. **2** (**taper off**) gradually lessen.

tapestry NOUN (PL **-ies**) a piece of thick fabric with a woven or embroidered design.

tapeworm NOUN a ribbon-like worm living as a parasite in the intestines.

tapioca NOUN starchy grains obtained from cassava, used in making puddings.

tapir NOUN a pig-like animal with a flexible snout.

tar NOUN a thick, dark liquid distilled from coal etc.; a similar substance formed by burning tobacco. VERB (**tarred**, **tarring**) coat with tar.

taramasalata NOUN a dip made from fish roe.

tarantula NOUN a very large hairy spider.

tardy ADJ (-ier, -iest) late; slow.

target NOUN a person, object, or place that is the aim of an attack; an objective. VERB (**targeted, targeting**) aim at; direct.

tariff NOUN a list of fixed charges; a tax to be paid.

tarmac NOUN [trademark] broken stone mixed with tar; an area surfaced with this.

tarmacked ADJ

tarnish VERB cause metal to become stained; spoil a reputation. NOUN a stain on metal.

tarot NOUN a pack of cards used for fortune telling.

tarpaulin NOUN a waterproof canvas.

tarragon NOUN an aromatic herb.

tart NOUN 1 a small pie or flan with a sweet filling. 2 [inf] a woman who has many sexual partners. ADJ sour in taste; sharp and sarcastic.

tartan NOUN a checked pattern; cloth marked with this.

tartar NOUN a hard deposit forming on teeth.

tartare sauce NOUN a cold savoury sauce.

task NOUN a piece of work to be done. **task force** a group organized for a special task. **take to task** rebuke.

taskmaster NOUN a person who makes others work hard.

tassel NOUN an ornamental bunch of hanging threads.

taste NOUN 1 the sensation caused in the tongue by things placed on it; the ability to perceive this; a small sample of food or drink; a brief experience. 2 a liking; the ability to perceive beauty or quality. VERB 1 discover or test the flavour of; have a certain flavour. 2 experience.

tasteful ADJ showing good judgement of quality.

tastefully ADV

tasteless ADJ 1 having no flavour. 2 showing poor judgement of quality.

tasty ADJ (-ier, -iest) having a pleasant flavour.

tattered ADJ ragged.

tatters PLURAL NOUN torn pieces.

tattle NOUN & VERB gossip.

tattoo NOUN 1 a permanent

design made on the skin with a needle and ink. **2** a military display. **3** a rhythmic tapping sound. VERB mark skin with a tattoo.

tatty ADJ (**-ier, -iest**) [inf] worn and shabby.

taught past and past participle of **teach**.

taunt VERB jeer at provocatively. NOUN a taunting remark.

taut ADJ stretched tightly.

tautology NOUN saying the same thing again in different words.
tautological ADJ

tavern NOUN [old use] an inn or pub.

tawdry ADJ showy but cheap or tasteless.

tawny ADJ orange-brown.

tax NOUN money compulsorily paid to the state. VERB impose a tax on; make heavy demands on.
tax return a form declaring income for a particular year, used for tax assessment.
taxation NOUN

taxi NOUN a vehicle which transports fare-paying passengers to their chosen destination. VERB

(**taxied, taxiing**) (of an aircraft) move along the ground.

taxidermy NOUN the process of stuffing and mounting the skins of animals in lifelike form.
taxidermist NOUN

TB ABBREV tuberculosis.

tea NOUN **1** a drink made by infusing the dried leaves of a tropical plant in boiling water; these leaves. **2** an afternoon or evening meal at which tea is drunk.
tea bag a small porous sachet of tea leaves.
tea towel a cloth for drying washed crockery etc.

teacake NOUN a flat sweet bun containing currants.

teach VERB (**taught, teaching**) impart information about a particular subject to someone; show someone how to do something.
teacher NOUN

teak NOUN strong heavy wood from an Asian evergreen tree.

team NOUN a group of players forming one side in a competitive sport; a set of people or animals working together. VERB combine into a team or set.

teamwork NOUN organized cooperation.

teapot NOUN a container with a spout, for brewing and pouring tea.

tear[1] VERB (**tore, torn, tearing**) 1 pull forcibly apart or to pieces; make a hole or split in; become torn. 2 [inf] move hurriedly. NOUN a hole etc. made by tearing.

tear[2] NOUN a drop of liquid forming in and falling from the eye.

tear gas a gas causing severe irritation to the eyes.

tearaway NOUN an unruly young person.

tearful ADJ crying or about to cry.

tearfully ADV

tease VERB 1 playfully make fun of or attempt to provoke. 2 pick into separate strands. NOUN a person who teases.

teaspoon NOUN a small spoon for stirring tea etc.

teat NOUN a nipple on an animal's udder; a plastic nipple-shaped device for sucking milk from a bottle.

technical ADJ 1 of a particular subject, craft, etc.; requiring specialized knowledge to be understood. 2 of applied science and mechanical arts. 3 according to a strict legal interpretation.

technically ADV

technicality NOUN (PL -**ies**) a small detail in a set of rules.

technician NOUN 1 an expert in a particular subject or craft. 2 a person employed to look after technical equipment.

Technicolor NOUN [trademark] a process of producing cinema films in colour.

technique NOUN a method of doing something; skill in an activity.

technology NOUN (PL -**ies**) the application of scientific knowledge in industry etc.; equipment developed in this way.

technological ADJ

tectonic ADJ of the earth's crust.

teddy (or **teddy bear**) NOUN (PL -**ies**) a soft toy bear.

tedious ADJ too long, slow, or dull.

tedium NOUN

tee NOUN a place from which a golf ball is struck at the start of play; a small peg for supporting this ball. VERB (**teed, teeing**) place a ball on a tee; (**tee off**) make the first stroke in golf.

teem VERB be full of; (of water or rain) pour.

teenager NOUN a person in their teens.

teenage ADJ

teens PLURAL NOUN the years of age from 13 to 19.

teepee see **tepee**.

tee shirt NOUN a T-shirt.

teeter VERB balance or move unsteadily.

teeth plural of **tooth**.

teethe VERB (of a baby) develop first teeth.

teething troubles problems in the early stages of an enterprise.

teetotal ADJ abstaining completely from alcohol.

teetotaller NOUN

telecommunications PLURAL NOUN communication by telephone, radio, cable, etc.

telegram NOUN a message sent by telegraph.

telegraph NOUN a system or apparatus for sending messages from a distance along wires. VERB send by telegraph.

telekinesis NOUN the supposed ability to move things without touching them.

telepathy NOUN supposed communication by means other than the senses.

telepathic ADJ

telephone NOUN a device for transmitting speech by wire or radio. VERB contact by telephone.

telephonist NOUN an operator of a telephone switchboard.

telephoto lens NOUN a photographic lens producing a large image of a distant object.

teleprinter NOUN a device for transmitting telegraph messages as they are keyed.

telescope NOUN an optical instrument for making distant objects appear larger. VERB make or become shorter by sliding each section inside the next; condense or combine to occupy less space or time.

telescopic ADJ

teletext NOUN an information service transmitted to televisions.

televise VERB transmit by television.

television NOUN a system for transmitting visual images with sound and displaying them electronically on a screen; televised programmes; (also **television set**) an apparatus for receiving these.

televisual ADJ

telex NOUN a system of telegraphy using teleprinters and public transmission lines. VERB send by telex.

tell VERB (**told, telling**) 1 communicate information to; order or instruct; narrate; reveal a secret. 2 perceive or distinguish. 3 have an effect.

tell off [inf] reprimand.

teller NOUN 1 a narrator. 2 a person appointed to count votes. 3 a bank cashier.

telling ADJ having a noticeable effect.

telltale ADJ revealing something. NOUN a person who reveals secrets.

telly NOUN [inf] television.

temerity NOUN audacity or boldness.

temp NOUN [inf] a temporary employee.

temper NOUN 1 a person's state of mind. 2 a fit of anger. VERB 1 reheat and cool metal to increase its strength and elasticity. 2 moderate or neutralize.

temperament NOUN a person's nature as it controls their behaviour.

temperamental ADJ of temperament; liable to unreasonable changes of mood.

temperamentally ADV

temperance NOUN total abstinence from alcohol.

temperate ADJ 1 (of a climate) without extremes. 2 self-restrained.

temperature NOUN the degree of heat or cold; a body temperature above normal.

tempest NOUN a violent storm.

tempestuous ADJ

template NOUN a piece of material used as a pattern for cutting shapes etc.

temple NOUN 1 a building for worship. 2 the flat part between the forehead and the ear.

tempo NOUN (PL **-pos** or **-pi**) the speed of a piece of music; the rate of motion or activity.

temporal ADJ **1** secular. **2** of or denoting time.

temporary ADJ lasting for a limited time.
temporarily ADV

temporize (or **-ise**) VERB delay making a decision.

tempt VERB try to persuade, especially to do something appealing but wrong; arouse a desire in.
temptation NOUN
temptress NOUN

ten ADJ & NOUN one more than nine (10, X).
tenth ADJ & NOUN

tenable ADJ able to be defended or held.

tenacious ADJ determined in holding a position etc.
tenacity NOUN

tenant NOUN a person who rents land or property from a landlord.
tenancy NOUN

tend VERB **1** take care of. **2** have a specified tendency.

tendency NOUN (PL **-ies**) an inclination to act in a particular way.
tendentious ADJ

controversial.

tender ADJ **1** not tough or hard; delicate; painful when touched. **2** gentle and loving. NOUN **1** a formal offer to supply goods or carry out work at a stated price. **2** a boat used to ferry people and supplies to and from a ship. **3** a truck attached to a steam locomotive to carry fuel and water. VERB offer formally; make a tender for a piece of work.
tenderness NOUN

tendon NOUN a strip of strong tissue connecting a muscle to a bone.

tendril NOUN a thread-like part by which a climbing plant clings; a slender curl of hair.

tenement NOUN a building divided into flats.

tenet NOUN a firm belief or principle.

tennis NOUN a game in which players use rackets to strike a soft ball over a net on an open court.

tenor NOUN **1** general meaning or character. **2** the highest ordinary male singing voice.

tense ADJ stretched tightly; nervous and

anxious. VERB make or become tense. NOUN any of the forms of a verb that indicate the time of the action.

tensile ADJ of tension; capable of being stretched.

tension NOUN 1 being stretched tight; strain caused by forces working in opposition; electromagnetic force. 2 mental or emotional strain.

tent NOUN a portable shelter made of canvas etc.

tentacle NOUN a slender flexible part of certain animals, used for feeling or grasping.

tentative ADJ hesitant.

tenterhooks PLURAL NOUN (**on tenterhooks**) in a state of nervous suspense.

tenuous ADJ very slight; very thin.

tenure NOUN the holding of an office or of land or accommodation etc.

tepee (or **teepee**) NOUN a conical tent used by American Indians.

tepid ADJ lukewarm.

tequila NOUN a Mexican liquor.

term NOUN 1 a fixed or limited period; a period of weeks during which a school etc. is open. 2 a word or phrase; each quantity or expression in a mathematical series or ratio etc. 3 (**terms**) conditions offered or accepted; relations between people: *on good terms*.

come to terms with reconcile yourself to.

terminal ADJ 1 of or forming an end. 2 (of a disease) leading to death. NOUN 1 a terminus. 2 a building where air passengers arrive and depart. 3 a point of connection in an electric circuit. 4 a keyboard and screen joined to a central computer system.

terminally ADV

terminate VERB come or bring to an end.

termination NOUN 1 coming or bringing to an end. 2 a medical procedure to end a pregnancy.

terminology NOUN (PL -ies) the technical terms of a subject.

terminological ADJ

terminus NOUN (PL -ini or

-inuses) the end; the last stopping place on a rail or bus route.

termite NOUN a small insect that is destructive to timber.

tern NOUN a seabird.

terrace NOUN **1** a raised level place; a patio. **2** a row of houses built in one block.

terracotta NOUN brownish-red unglazed pottery; its colour.

terrain NOUN land with regard to its natural features.

terrapin NOUN a freshwater turtle.

terrestrial ADJ of the earth; of or living on land; (of television broadcasting) not using a satellite.

terrible ADJ extremely bad, serious, or unpleasant.
terribly ADV

terrier NOUN a small dog.

terrific ADJ **1** very great or intense. **2** [inf] excellent.
terrifically ADV

terrify VERB (**terrified, terrifying**) fill with terror.

terrine NOUN a kind of pâté.

territorial ADJ of territory or its ownership.

territory NOUN (PL **-ies**) an area controlled by a ruler or state; an area with a particular characteristic.

terror NOUN extreme fear; a cause of this.

terrorism NOUN the use of violence and intimidation for political purposes.
terrorist NOUN

terrorize (or **-ise**) VERB threaten and scare over a period of time.

terse ADJ concise or curt.

tertiary ADJ third in order or level.

test NOUN **1** something done to discover a person's or thing's qualities or abilities etc.; a short exam; a procedure to determine the presence or absence of a disease, quality, etc. **2** (also **test match**) an international cricket or rugby match. VERB subject to a test.

test tube a thin glass tube used to hold material in laboratory tests.

testament NOUN **1** a will. **2** evidence or proof. **3** (**Testament**) each of the two divisions of the Bible.

testate ADJ having made a will before dying.

testicle NOUN a male organ that produces sperm.

testify VERB (**testified**, **testifying**) give evidence in court; be evidence or proof of.

testimonial NOUN a formal statement testifying to character, abilities, etc.; a public tribute.

testimony NOUN (PL **-ies**) a declaration (especially under oath); evidence or proof.

testosterone NOUN a hormone responsible for the development of male bodily characteristics.

testy ADJ irritable.

tetanus NOUN a disease causing painful muscular spasms and rigidity.

tetchy ADJ (PL **-ier**, **-iest**) irritable.

tetchily ADV

tête-à-tête NOUN a private conversation between two people.

tether NOUN a rope or chain for tying an animal to a spot. VERB fasten with a tether.

tetrahedron NOUN (PL **-hedra** or **-hedrons**) a solid with four triangular faces.

Teutonic ADJ German.

text NOUN **1** a written work;the main body of a book as distinct from illustrations etc.; written or printed words or computer data. **2** a text message. VERB send someone a text message.

text message an electronic message sent and received via mobile phone.

textual ADJ

textbook NOUN a book used for the study of a subject.

textile NOUN a woven or machine-knitted fabric.

texture NOUN the feel, appearance, or consistency of a substance or fabric.

textural ADJ

thalidomide NOUN a sedative drug, found to cause fetal malformations when taken by pregnant women.

than CONJ & PREP used to introduce the second element in a comparison.

thank VERB express gratitude to. PLURAL NOUN (**thanks**) expressions of gratitude; thank you.

thank you a polite expression of gratitude.

thankful ADJ feeling or expressing gratitude.

thankfully ADV 1 in a thankful way. 2 fortunately.

thankless ADJ unpleasant and unappreciated.

thanksgiving NOUN an expression of gratitude, especially to God.

that ADJ & PRON (PL **those**) a specific (person or thing); the (person or thing) referred to; the further or less obvious (one) of two. ADV to such an extent. PRON used to introduce a clause that defines or identifies something. CONJ introducing a statement or suggestion.

thatch NOUN a roof made of straw or reeds etc. VERB cover with thatch.

thaw VERB make or become unfrozen; become friendlier. NOUN a period of warm weather that melts ice and snow.

the ADJ (called the *definite article*) 1 used to refer to someone or something specific and known; used to refer to something unique. 2 used to refer to something in a general rather than a specific way.

theatre ([US] **theater**) NOUN 1 a place in which plays are performed; the writing and production of plays. 2 a room where surgical operations are performed.

theatrical ADJ of or for the theatre; exaggerated for effect.

thee PRON [old use] the objective case of *thou*.

theft NOUN stealing.

their ADJ of or belonging to them.

theirs POSSESSIVE PRON belonging to them.

them PRON the objective case of *they*.

theme NOUN 1 a subject being discussed or written about. 2 a melody which is repeated in a work. **thematic** ADJ

themselves PRON the emphatic and reflexive form of *they* and *them*.

then ADV 1 at that time. 2 afterwards. 3 in that case.

thence ADV [formal] from that place or source.

theology NOUN (PL **-ies**) the study of God; a system of religious beliefs. **theologian** NOUN **theological** ADJ

theorem NOUN a mathematical statement to be proved by reasoning.

theoretical ADJ concerning or based on theory rather than practice.

theoretically ADV

theorize (or **-ise**) VERB form theories.

theory NOUN (PL **-ies**) a set of ideas formulated to explain something; the principles on which an activity is based.

therapeutic ADJ contributing to the relief or curing of a disease etc.

therapeutically ADV

therapy NOUN (PL **-ies**) a treatment for physical or mental disorders.

therapist NOUN

there ADV in, at, or to that place; on that issue.

thereabouts ADV near there; approximately then.

thereafter ADV after that.

thereby ADV by that means.

therefore ADV for that reason.

thereupon ADV [formal] immediately after that.

thermal ADJ of or using heat; made of a special insulating fabric. NOUN a rising current of hot air.

thermodynamics NOUN the science of the relationship between heat and other forms of energy.

thermometer NOUN an instrument for measuring temperature.

Thermos NOUN [trademark] a vacuum flask.

thermostat NOUN a device that regulates temperature automatically.

thesaurus NOUN a dictionary of synonyms.

these plural of **this**.

thesis NOUN (PL **theses**) 1 a theory put forward and supported by reasoning. 2 a lengthy written essay submitted for a university degree.

thespian ADJ of the theatre. NOUN an actor or actress.

they PRON the people already referred to; people in general; unspecified people.

thiamine (or **thiamin**) NOUN vitamin B_1.

thick ADJ 1 of a great or specified distance

between opposite surfaces. **2** composed of many closely packed elements; fairly stiff in consistency. **3** [inf] stupid. NOUN (**the thick**) the busiest or most intense part.

thicken VERB

thickness NOUN

thicket NOUN a dense group of shrubs or small trees.

thickset ADJ heavily built.

thief NOUN (PL **thieves**) a person who steals.

thieve VERB steal.

thigh NOUN the upper part of the leg.

thimble NOUN a hard cap worn to protect the end of the finger in sewing.

thin ADJ (**thinner, thinnest**) **1** not thick; lean. **2** lacking substance; (of a sound) faint and high-pitched. VERB (**thinned, thinning**) make or become thinner.

thine ADJ & POSSESSIVE PRON [old use] belonging to thee.

thing NOUN **1** an unspecified object, activity, action, etc.; an inanimate object. **2** (**things**) belongings; (**things**) circumstances.

think VERB (**thought, thinking**) **1** have a belief or opinion. **2** use your mind to form ideas, solve problems, etc. NOUN an act of thinking.

think tank a body of experts providing advice and ideas.

third ADJ next after second. NOUN **1** a third thing, class, etc. **2** one of three equal parts.

third-degree burn a burn of the most severe kind. **the third degree** long and severe questioning. **third party** a person besides the two main ones involved in a situation; (of insurance) covering injury suffered by a person other than the insured. **Third World** the developing countries of Asia, Africa, and Latin America.

thirst NOUN the feeling caused by a desire to drink; any strong desire. VERB feel a strong desire.

thirsty ADJ

thirteen ADJ & NOUN one more than twelve (13, XIII).

thirteenth ADJ & NOUN

thirty ADJ three times ten (30, XXX).

thirtieth ADJ & NOUN

this ADJ & PRON (PL **these**) the person or thing near or present or mentioned.

thistle NOUN a prickly plant.

thistledown NOUN the very light fluff on thistle seeds.

thither ADV [old use] to or towards that place.

thong NOUN 1 a strip of leather used as a fastening or lash etc. 2 a G-string.

thorax NOUN (PL **-aces** or **-axes**) the part of the body between the neck and the abdomen. **thoracic** ADJ

thorn NOUN a small sharp projection on a plant; a thorn-bearing tree or shrub. **thorny** ADJ

thorough ADJ complete in every way; detailed and careful. **thoroughly** ADV

thoroughbred NOUN & ADJ (a horse etc.) of pure or pedigree stock.

thoroughfare NOUN a road forming the main route between two places.

those plural of **that**.

thou PRON [old use] you.

though CONJ in spite of the fact that. ADV however.

thought past & past participle of **think**. NOUN an idea; the process of thinking; attention or consideration.

thoughtful ADJ 1 thinking deeply; thought out carefully. 2 considerate. **thoughtfully** ADV

thoughtless ADJ careless; inconsiderate.

thousand ADJ & NOUN ten hundred (1000, M). **thousandth** ADJ & NOUN

thrall NOUN the state of being in another's power.

thrash VERB beat violently and repeatedly; [inf] defeat thoroughly; move wildly or convulsively.

thread NOUN 1 a thin strand of cotton or wool etc. 2 the spiral ridge of a screw. 3 the theme of a story, argument, etc. VERB 1 pass a thread through. 2 move between obstacles.

threadbare ADJ thin and tattered with age.

threat NOUN a stated intention to punish, hurt, or harm; a person or thing thought likely to bring harm or danger.

threaten VERB make or be a threat to.

three ADJ & NOUN one more

than two (3, III).

three-dimensional having or appearing to have length, breadth, and depth.

threesome NOUN a group of three people.

thresh VERB beat out grain from husks of corn; make flailing movements.

threshold NOUN 1 a piece of wood or stone forming the bottom of a doorway. 2 a level or point marking the start of something.

threw past of **throw**.

thrice ADV [old use] three times.

thrift NOUN economical management of resources. **thrifty** ADJ

thrill NOUN a sudden feeling of excitement; something causing this; a wave of emotion. VERB excite.

thriller NOUN an exciting story or film etc.

thrive VERB (**throve** or **thrived**, **thriven** or **thrived**, **thriving**) grow or develop well; prosper.

throat NOUN the passage from the back of the mouth to the oesophagus or lungs; the front of the neck.

throaty ADJ (-ier, -iest)

deep and husky.

throb VERB (**throbbed**, **throbbing**) beat or pulsate with a strong rhythm; feel regular bursts of pain. NOUN a regular pulsation.

throes PLURAL NOUN severe pain.

thrombosis NOUN (PL -oses) the formation of a blood clot in a blood vessel or the heart.

throne NOUN a ceremonial seat for a monarch, bishop, etc.; sovereign power.

throng NOUN a crowded mass of people. VERB gather somewhere in large numbers.

throttle NOUN a device controlling the flow of fuel or power to an engine. VERB strangle.

through PREP & ADV 1 from end to end or side to side of; from start to finish. 2 by means of. ADJ 1 passing straight through a place; (of public transport) continuing to the final destination. 2 having reached the next stage of a competition.

throughout PREP & ADV all the way through.

throughput NOUN the

amount of material processed.

throve past of **thrive**.

throw VERB (**threw, thrown, throwing**) 1 propel through the air from your hand; move or place hurriedly or roughly; send suddenly into a position or condition; project or direct in a particular direction. 2 upset or confuse. NOUN an act of throwing; a small rug or light cover for furniture.

throw away get rid of.

throw up vomit.

throwback NOUN an animal etc. showing characteristics of an earlier ancestor.

thrush NOUN a songbird with a speckled breast.

thrust VERB (**thrust, thrusting**) push suddenly or forcibly. NOUN a thrusting movement or force.

thud NOUN a dull, heavy sound. VERB (**thudded, thudding**) make or fall with a thud.

thug NOUN a violent criminal.

thumb NOUN the short, thick first digit of the hand. VERB 1 turn over pages with the thumb. 2 ask for a lift in a passing vehicle by signalling with the thumb.

thump VERB strike heavily; set down heavily and noisily; thud. NOUN a heavy, dull blow or noise.

thunder NOUN the loud rumbling or crashing noise that accompanies lightning; any similar sound. VERB sound with or like thunder; speak loudly or angrily.

thunderbolt NOUN a lightning flash with a crash of thunder.

thunderclap NOUN a crash of thunder.

thunderous ADJ of or like thunder; threatening.

Thursday NOUN the day after Wednesday.

thus ADV [formal] in this way; as a result of this; to this extent.

thwart VERB prevent from doing what is intended.

thy ADJ [old use] your.

thyme NOUN a fragrant herb.

thyroid NOUN a large gland in the neck, secreting a growth hormone.

tiara NOUN a jewelled

semicircular headdress.

tibia NOUN (PL **tibiae**) the inner shin bone.

tic NOUN an involuntary muscular twitch.

tick NOUN 1 a regular clicking sound, as made by a clock or watch. 2 [inf] a moment. 3 a mark (✓) used to show that an answer is correct or an item on a list has been dealt with. 4 a blood-sucking mite or parasitic insect. VERB 1 make regular ticking sounds. 2 mark with a tick. 3 (**tick over**) (of an engine) run in neutral. 4 (**tick off**) [inf] reprimand.

ticket NOUN 1 a piece of card or paper entitling the holder to enter or travel somewhere etc. 2 a label. 3 notification of a traffic offence.

ticking NOUN strong fabric used for covering mattresses.

tickle VERB touch lightly so as to cause a slight tingling sensation; amuse or appeal to. NOUN the act or sensation of tickling.

ticklish ADJ 1 sensitive to tickling. 2 requiring careful handling.

tidal ADJ of or affected by tides.

tiddler NOUN [inf] a small fish.

tiddlywinks PLURAL NOUN a game involving flicking small counters into a cup.

tide NOUN 1 the sea's regular rise and fall. 2 a trend of feeling or events etc. VERB (**tide over**) help temporarily.

tidings PLURAL NOUN [literary] news.

tidy ADJ (**-ier, -iest**) neat and orderly. VERB (**tidied, tidying**) make tidy.
tidily ADV
tidiness NOUN

tie VERB (**tied, tying**) 1 attach or fasten with cord etc.; form into a knot or bow; link or connect. 2 restrict or limit. 3 make the same score as another competitor. NOUN 1 a thing that ties. 2 a strip of cloth worn round a collar and knotted at the front of the neck. 3 an equal score between competitors. 4 a sports match in which the winners proceed to the next round.
tie-break a means of deciding a winner from competitors who have

tied.

tied ADJ (of a house) for occupation only by a person working for its owner.

tiepin NOUN an ornamental pin for holding a tie in place.

tier NOUN any of a series of rows or levels placed one above the other.

tiff NOUN a petty quarrel.

tiger NOUN a large striped wild cat.

tight ADJ 1 held or fastened firmly; stretched taut; fitting closely or too closely; leaving little room. 2 strict. 3 (of money or time) limited. ADV closely or firmly.
tight-fisted [inf] stingy or mean.
tighten VERB

tightrope NOUN a rope stretched high above the ground, on which acrobats balance.

tights PLURAL NOUN a garment closely covering the legs and lower part of the body.

tigress NOUN a female tiger.

tilde NOUN a mark (˜) put over a letter to mark a change in its pronunciation.

tile NOUN a thin slab of baked clay etc. used for covering roofs, walls, or floors. VERB cover with tiles.

till¹ PREP & CONJ until.

till² NOUN a cash register or drawer for money in a shop etc.

till³ VERB cultivate land for crops.

tiller NOUN a bar by which the rudder of a boat is turned.

tilt VERB slip or move into a sloping position. NOUN a sloping position.
at full tilt at full speed or force.

timber NOUN wood prepared for use in building or carpentry.

timbre NOUN the characteristic quality of the sound of a voice or instrument.

time NOUN 1 the dimension in which events etc. continue or succeed one another; past, present, and future; a period of this; a point of this measured in hours and minutes; an occasion. 2 a person's lifetime or prime. 3 rhythm in music.

4 (**times**) expressing multiplication. VERB **1** arrange when something should happen. **2** measure the time taken by.

time-honoured respected because of antiquity.

timeless ADJ not affected by the passage of time.

timely ADJ occurring at a good time.

timepiece NOUN a clock or watch.

timeshare NOUN an arrangement by which joint owners use a property at different times.

timetable NOUN a list or plan of times at which events are scheduled to take place.

timid ADJ lacking courage or confidence. **timidity** NOUN

timorous ADJ timid.

timpani (or **tympani**) PLURAL NOUN kettledrums.

tin NOUN **1** a silvery-white metal. **2** a metal box or other container; one in which food is sealed for preservation. VERB (**tinned**, **tinning**) seal food in a tin.

tincture NOUN a solution of a medicinal substance in alcohol.

tinder NOUN any dry substance that catches fire easily.

tine NOUN a prong or point of a fork etc.

tinge NOUN a slight trace of a colour, feeling, or quality. VERB (**tinged**, **tingeing**) give a tinge to.

tingle NOUN & VERB (have) a slight prickling or stinging sensation.

tinker NOUN a travelling mender of pots and pans. VERB casually try to repair or improve.

tinkle NOUN a light, clear ringing sound. VERB (cause to) make this sound.

tinnitus NOUN ringing or buzzing in the ears.

tinny ADJ made of thin or inferior metal; having a thin, metallic sound.

tinsel NOUN glittering decorative metallic strips or threads.

tint NOUN a variety or slight trace of a colour. VERB colour slightly.

tiny ADJ (**-ier**, **-iest**) very small.

tip VERB (**tipped**, **tipping**) **1** (cause to) overbalance and fall over; spill contents by doing this.

2 give a small extra amount of money to someone in return for services. **3** name as a likely winner. **4** (**tip off**) [inf] give secret information to. NOUN **1** a small extra amount of money. **2** a useful piece of advice; a prediction of a likely winner. **3** the end of something slender or tapering. **4** a place where rubbish is left.

tipple VERB drink alcohol habitually. NOUN [inf] an alcoholic drink.

tipster NOUN a person who gives tips, especially about likely winners in racing.

tipsy ADJ slightly drunk.

tiptoe VERB (**tiptoed, tiptoeing**) walk very quietly with your heels raised.

tirade NOUN a long angry speech.

tire VERB make or become tired; become bored. NOUN US spelling of **tyre**.

tired ADJ **1** in need of sleep or rest. **2** (**tired of**) bored with.

tireless ADJ not tiring easily.

tiresome ADJ annoying; tedious.

tissue NOUN **1** a substance forming an animal or plant body. **2** tissue paper; a disposable paper handkerchief.

tissue paper very thin, soft paper.

tit NOUN a small songbird.

titanic ADJ enormous.

titanium NOUN a silver-grey metal.

titbit NOUN a small choice bit of food or item of information.

tithe NOUN one-tenth of income or produce, formerly paid to the Church.

titillate VERB excite or stimulate pleasantly.

titivate VERB [inf] make smarter or more attractive.

title NOUN **1** the name of a book, picture, film, etc. **2** a word indicating rank or profession, or used in speaking of or to someone with a particular rank or profession. **3** the position of champion in a sporting contest.

titled ADJ having a title indicating high rank.

titter NOUN & VERB (give) a short, quiet laugh.

tittle-tattle VERB & NOUN gossip.

titular ADJ having a title but no real power.

TNT ABBREV trinitrotoluene, a powerful explosive.

to PREP 1 towards. 2 so as to reach a state. 3 indicating the person or thing affected. 4 indicating that a verb is in the infinitive. ADV into a closed position. **to and fro** backwards and forwards.

toad NOUN a frog-like animal living chiefly on land.

toadstool NOUN a fungus with a rounded cap on a stalk.

toady NOUN (PL **-ies**) a person who is ingratiating or obsequious. VERB (**toadied, toadying**) behave in this way.

toast VERB 1 make bread brown and crisp by holding it against a fire, heated element, etc. 2 (of people at a gathering) drink together in honour of a person or thing. NOUN 1 toasted bread. 2 an act of toasting someone; a person or thing toasted. **toaster** NOUN

tobacco NOUN a preparation of the dried leaves of a plant, used for smoking.

tobacconist NOUN a shopkeeper who sells cigarettes etc.

toboggan NOUN a small sledge used for sliding downhill.

today ADV & NOUN (on) this present day; (at) the present time.

toddle VERB (of a young child) walk with short unsteady steps. **toddler** NOUN

toe NOUN any of the five digits at the end of the foot; the lower end or tip of something. VERB touch with the toe(s).

toehold NOUN a slight foothold.

toffee NOUN a sweet made with heated butter and sugar.

tofu NOUN curd from crushed soya beans.

tog NOUN 1 a unit for measuring the warmth of duvets or clothing. 2 (**togs**) [inf] clothes.

toga NOUN a loose outer garment worn by men in ancient Rome.

together ADV with or near to another person or

thing; at the same time; so as to meet.

toggle NOUN a short piece of wood etc. passed through a loop to fasten a garment.

toil VERB work or move laboriously. NOUN laborious work.

toilet NOUN 1 a bowl for urinating or defecating into. 2 the process of washing and grooming yourself.

toilet water a light perfume.

toiletries PLURAL NOUN articles used in washing and grooming yourself.

token NOUN 1 a thing that represents a feeling, fact, or quality. 2 a voucher that can be exchanged for goods; a disc used to operate a machine. ADJ for the sake of appearances and not effective or important in itself.

told past & past participle of **tell**.

tolerable ADJ 1 endurable. 2 fairly good.

tolerably ADV

tolerance NOUN 1 willingness to tolerate. 2 an allowable variation in the size of machine parts etc.

tolerant ADJ

tolerate VERB permit without protest or interference; endure.

toleration NOUN

toll NOUN 1 a tax paid for the use of certain roads or bridges. 2 loss or damage caused by a disaster. 3 a single ring of a bell. VERB (of a bell) ring with slow strokes, especially to mark a death.

tom (or **tomcat**) NOUN a male domestic cat.

tomahawk NOUN a light axe used in the past by American Indians.

tomato NOUN (PL **-oes**) a red fruit used as a vegetable.

tomb NOUN a grave or other place of burial.

tombola NOUN a game in which tickets for prizes are drawn at random from a revolving drum.

tomboy NOUN a girl who enjoys rough and noisy activities.

tombstone NOUN a memorial stone set up over a grave.

tome NOUN a large book.

tomfoolery NOUN foolish behaviour.

tomorrow ADV & NOUN (on) the day after today; (in) the near future.

tom-tom NOUN a medium-sized cylindrical drum.

ton NOUN a measure of weight, either 2,240 lb **long ton** or 2,000 lb **short ton** or 1,000 kg **metric ton**; a unit of volume in shipping; [inf] a large number or amount.

tone NOUN **1** the quality of a musical sound; the feeling or mood expressed in a person's voice; the general character of something. **2** an interval of a major second in music (e.g. between C and D). **3** a shade of colour. **4** proper firmness of muscles. VERB **1** give firmness to muscles. **2** (**tone down**) make less harsh or extreme.

tone-deaf unable to hear differences in musical pitch.

tonal ADJ

tonality NOUN

toner NOUN **1** a liquid applied to the skin to reduce oiliness. **2** a type of powder or ink used in photocopiers.

tongs PLURAL NOUN a tool with two arms used for grasping things.

tongue NOUN **1** the muscular organ in the mouth, used in tasting and speaking. **2** a language. **3** a strip of leather etc. under the laces of a shoe.

tongue-in-cheek not seriously meant. **tongue-tied** too shy to speak.

tonic NOUN **1** a drink taken to increase energy and well-being; something invigorating. **2** (also **tonic water**) a fizzy soft drink flavoured with quinine.

tonight ADV & NOUN (on) the present evening or night.

tonnage NOUN weight in tons; a ship's carrying capacity expressed in tons.

tonne NOUN a metric ton.

tonsil NOUN either of two small organs near the root of the tongue.

tonsillitis NOUN inflammation of the tonsils.

tonsure NOUN a circular area on a monk's head where the hair is shaved off.

too ADV **1** to a greater extent than is desirable. **2** also.

took past of **take**.

tool NOUN an implement used for a particular task. VERB impress a design on leather.

toot NOUN a short sound made by a horn or whistle. VERB make a toot.

tooth NOUN (PL **teeth**) each of the white bony structures in the jaws, used in biting and chewing; a tooth-like part or projection.

toothpaste NOUN paste for cleaning the teeth.

toothpick NOUN a small pointed instrument for removing food from between the teeth.

top NOUN 1 the highest or uppermost point, part, or surface; something forming the upper part or covering. 2 a garment for the upper part of the body. 3 the highest or most important level etc. 4 a toy that spins on its point when set in motion. ADJ highest in position or rank etc. VERB (**topped**, **topping**) 1 be more than; be at the highest place in a ranking etc.; reach the top of. 2 put a top or cover on.

top hat a man's tall formal black hat. **top-heavy** too heavy at the top and so likely to fall.

topaz NOUN a precious stone of various colours, especially yellow.

topcoat NOUN 1 an overcoat. 2 a final coat of paint.

topiary NOUN the art of clipping shrubs into ornamental shapes.

topic NOUN the subject of a discussion or written work.

topical ADJ having reference to current events. **topically** ADV

topknot NOUN a knot of hair arranged on top of the head.

topless ADJ having the breasts bare.

topography NOUN the arrangement of the physical features of an area of land. **topographical** ADJ

topple VERB overbalance and fall.

topsoil NOUN the top layer of soil.

topsy-turvy ADV & ADJ upside down; in a state of confusion.

tor NOUN a hill or rocky peak.

torch NOUN a small hand-held electric lamp; a burning piece of wood etc. carried as a light.

tore past of **tear**[1].

toreador NOUN a bullfighter.

torment NOUN severe suffering; a cause of this. VERB subject to torment; tease or annoy. **tormentor** NOUN

torn past participle of **tear**[1].

tornado NOUN (PL **-oes** or **-os**) a violent destructive whirlwind.

torpedo NOUN (PL **-oes**) an explosive underwater missile. VERB (**torpedoed, torpedoing**) attack or destroy with a torpedo.

torpid ADJ sluggish and inactive.

torpor NOUN a sluggish condition.

torque NOUN a force causing rotation.

torrent NOUN a fast and powerful stream of liquid; an outpouring. **torrential** ADJ

torrid ADJ intensely hot and dry; passionate.

torsion NOUN the state of being twisted.

torso NOUN (PL **-os**) the trunk of the human body.

tortilla NOUN a Mexican flat maize pancake.

tortoise NOUN a slow-moving reptile with a hard shell.

tortoiseshell NOUN the mottled yellowish-brown shell of certain turtles, used to make jewellery etc.

tortuous ADJ full of twists and turns; complex.

torture NOUN the infliction of pain on someone as a punishment or means of coercion; extreme pain. VERB inflict severe pain on. **torturer** NOUN

Tory NOUN (PL **-ies**) a member or supporter of the British Conservative Party.

toss VERB throw lightly; roll about from side to side; shake or turn food in liquid to coat it lightly. NOUN an act of tossing.

toss-up a situation where two outcomes are equally likely.

tot NOUN 1 a small child. 2 a small drink of spirits. VERB (**totted, totting**) (**tot up**) add up.

tough

total ADJ including everything or everyone; complete. NOUN a total amount. VERB (**totalled, totalling**; [US] **totaled, totaling**) 1 amount to. 2 calculate the total of. **totality** NOUN **totally** ADV

totalitarian ADJ of a regime in which no rival parties or loyalties are permitted.

totalizator (or **totalisator**) NOUN a device that automatically registers bets, so that the total amount can be divided among the winners.

tote [inf] NOUN a system of betting using a totalizator. VERB carry.

totem NOUN a natural object adopted as a tribal emblem. **totem pole** a pole decorated with totems.

totter VERB move in an unsteady way.

toucan NOUN a tropical American bird with a very large beak.

touch VERB 1 be, come, or bring into contact; feel or stroke. 2 harm or interfere with. 3 affect; arouse sympathy or gratitude in. NOUN 1 an act of touching; the ability to perceive things through touching them. 2 a slight trace; a detail. 3 a manner of dealing with something. **touch-and-go** (of an outcome) possible but very uncertain. **touch down** (of an aircraft) land.

touchdown NOUN the moment when an aircraft touches down; (in rugby) an act of scoring by placing the ball down behind the opponents' goal line.

touché EXCLAMATION an acknowledgement of a valid criticism.

touching ADJ arousing pity, affection, or gratitude.

touchline NOUN the side limit of a football field.

touchstone NOUN a standard or criterion.

touchy ADJ easily offended.

tough NOUN 1 strong enough to withstand wear and tear; hard to chew. 2 (of a person) resilient. 3 difficult or unfair; strict; prone to violence. NOUN a rough or violent man.

toughen VERB

toupee NOUN a small wig.

tour NOUN a journey, visiting one place after another. VERB make a tour of.

tourism NOUN the commercial organization of holidays and services for tourists.

tourist NOUN a person visiting a place for pleasure.

tournament NOUN a sporting contest consisting of a series of matches.

tourniquet NOUN a strip of material pulled tightly round a limb to stop the flow of blood from an artery.

tousle VERB ruffle someone's hair.

tout VERB try to sell. NOUN a person who buys tickets for popular events and resells them at high prices.

tow VERB pull another vehicle etc. along behind.

towards (or **toward**) PREP **1** in the direction of. **2** in relation to. **3** as a contribution to.

towel NOUN a piece of absorbent material for drying things. VERB (**towelled**, **towelling**; [US] **toweled**, **toweling**) rub with a towel.

towelling ([US] **toweling**) NOUN fabric for towels.

tower NOUN a tall narrow building; a tall pile or structure. VERB be very tall.
tower block a tall building with many storeys.

town NOUN a collection of houses, shops, etc. larger than a village.
town hall the building containing local government offices.

township NOUN (in South Africa) a suburb or city of mainly black occupation.

towpath NOUN a path beside a canal or river, originally for horses towing barges.

toxic ADJ poisonous; of or caused by poison.
toxicity NOUN

toxin NOUN a poison produced by a living organism.

toy NOUN a thing to play with. ADJ (of a breed of dog) very small. VERB (**toy with**) fiddle with idly; casually consider.
toy boy [inf] a woman's

much younger male lover.

trace NOUN 1 a track or mark left behind; a sign of what has existed or occurred. 2 a very small quantity; a slight indication. VERB 1 find by careful investigation; find the origin or development of. 2 copy a design etc. by drawing over it on transparent paper; give an outline of.

trachea NOUN the windpipe.

track NOUN 1 a rough path or road; a railway line; a racecourse. 2 marks left by a moving person or thing; a course followed. 3 a section on a CD, tape, etc. 4 a continuous band round the wheels of a tank, tractor, etc. VERB follow or find by observing marks left in moving.

tracksuit NOUN a loose warm suit worn for exercise etc.

tract NOUN 1 a stretch of land. 2 a major passage in the body. 3 a pamphlet with a short essay, especially on a religious subject.

tractable ADJ easy to deal with or control.

traction NOUN 1 pulling something over a surface. 2 the grip of wheels on the ground. 3 a way of treating a broken bone by gradually pulling it back into position.

tractor NOUN a powerful vehicle for pulling farm equipment.

trade NOUN 1 the buying and selling of goods and services; an area of commercial activity. 2 a job requiring special skills. VERB engage in trade; exchange goods in trading.

trade-off a compromise.

trade union an organized association of employees formed to protect their rights.

trader NOUN

trademark NOUN a company's registered emblem or name used to identify its goods.

tradesman NOUN a person engaged in trading or a trade.

tradition NOUN a belief or custom handed down from one generation to another; a long-established procedure.

traditional ADJ

traduce VERB misrepresent in an unfavourable way.

traffic NOUN **1** vehicles, ships, or aircraft moving along a route. **2** trading. VERB (**trafficked, trafficking**) trade in something illegal.
trafficker NOUN

tragedian NOUN a writer of tragedies; an actor in tragedy.

tragedy NOUN (PL **-ies**) a serious play with an unhappy ending; a very sad event or situation.

tragic ADJ extremely sad; of dramatic tragedy.
tragically ADV

tragicomedy NOUN (PL **-ies**) a drama with elements of both tragedy and comedy.

trail VERB **1** drag or be dragged behind someone or something; hang loosely; move slowly or wearily. **2** track. NOUN a track left by movement; a line of people or things; a beaten path.

trailer NOUN **1** an unpowered vehicle pulled by another vehicle. **2** a short extract from a film etc., used to advertise it.

train NOUN **1** a joined set of railway vehicles. **2** a line of pack animals or vehicles; a sequence of events. **3** part of a long robe, trailing behind the wearer. VERB **1** teach a particular skill to; practise and exercise to become physically fit. **2** cause a plant to grow in a particular direction. **3** aim a gun etc.

trainee NOUN a person being trained.

trainer NOUN **1** a person who trains people or animals. **2** a soft shoe for sports or casual wear.

traipse VERB walk wearily or reluctantly.

trait NOUN a characteristic.

traitor NOUN a person who betrays their country, organization, etc.
traitorous ADJ

trajectory NOUN (PL **-ies**) the path of a projectile.

tram (or **tramcar**) NOUN a passenger vehicle powered by electricity and running on rails laid in the road.

trammel VERB (**trammelled, trammelling**; [US] **trammeled, trammeling**) hamper or restrain.

tramp VERB walk with heavy footsteps; go on foot across an area. NOUN **1** a vagrant. **2** the sound of heavy footsteps. **3** a long walk.

trample VERB tread on and crush.

trampoline NOUN a sheet of canvas attached by springs to a frame, used for jumping on in acrobatic leaps.

trance NOUN a sleep-like or dreamy state.

tranquil ADJ peaceful and untroubled.
tranquillity NOUN
tranquilly ADV

tranquillize (or -ise; [US] **tranquilize**) VERB give a sedative drug to.

tranquillizer (or -iser; [US] **tranquilizer**) NOUN a drug used to reduce anxiety and tension.

transact VERB perform or carry out business.
transaction NOUN

transcend VERB go beyond the range or limits of; surpass.
transcendence NOUN
transcendent ADJ

transcendental ADJ of a spiritual or non-physical

realm.

transcribe VERB put into written form; write out notes in full.
transcription NOUN

transcript NOUN a written version of a broadcast.

transept NOUN a part lying at right angles to the nave in a church.

transfer VERB (**transferred**, **transferring**) move from one position etc. to another. NOUN transferring; a conveyance of property from one person to another; a design for transferring from one surface to another.
transference NOUN

transfigure VERB transform into something nobler or more beautiful.
transfiguration NOUN

transfix VERB **1** pierce or impale. **2** make motionless with fear or astonishment.

transform VERB change completely or strikingly.
transformation NOUN

transformer NOUN an apparatus for changing the voltage of an electric current.

transfusion NOUN an injection of blood or

other fluid into a blood vessel.

transgress VERB break a rule or law.

transgression NOUN

transgressor NOUN

transient ADJ passing away quickly.

transience NOUN

transistor NOUN a silicon-based device able to amplify or rectify electric currents; a portable radio set using transistors.

transit NOUN the process of travelling or conveying someone or something across an area.

transition NOUN the process of changing from one state to another.

transitional ADJ

transitive ADJ (of a verb) used with a direct object.

transitory ADJ lasting only briefly.

translate VERB express words or text in another language.

translation NOUN

translator NOUN

translucent ADJ partly transparent.

translucence NOUN

transmission NOUN 1 transmitting; a broadcast. 2 the gear transmitting power from engine to axle in a motor vehicle.

transmit VERB (**transmitted, transmitting**) 1 pass on from one person, place, or thing to another. 2 broadcast or send out an electrical signal or a radio or television programme.

transmitter NOUN

transmogrify VERB (**transmogrified, transmogrifying**) change into something else.

transmute VERB change in form or substance.

transmutation NOUN

transparency NOUN (PL -ies) 1 being transparent. 2 a photographic slide.

transparent ADJ 1 able to be seen through. 2 obvious or evident.

transpire VERB 1 become known; take place. 2 (of plants) give off vapour from leaves etc.

transpiration NOUN

transplant VERB transfer to another place or situation; transfer living tissue to another body or part of the body. NOUN transplanting of tissue; something transplanted.

transplantation NOUN

transport VERB convey from one place to another. NOUN **1** a means of conveying people or goods; the process of transporting. **2** (**transports**) extremely strong emotions.

transportation NOUN

transpose VERB **1** cause two or more things to change places. **2** put music into a different key.

transposition NOUN

transverse ADJ crosswise.

transvestite NOUN a person who likes to dress in clothes worn by the opposite sex.

trap NOUN **1** a device for capturing an animal; a scheme for tricking or catching someone. **2** a container or device used to collect a specified thing. **3** a two-wheeled horse-drawn carriage. VERB (**trapped**, **trapping**) catch or hold in a trap.

trapdoor NOUN a door in a floor, ceiling, or roof.

trapeze NOUN a suspended horizontal bar on which acrobatics are performed.

trapezium NOUN a quadrilateral with only two opposite sides parallel.

trapper NOUN a person who traps animals, especially for furs.

trappings PLURAL NOUN accessories; symbols of status.

trash NOUN waste or worthless material.

trashy ADJ

trauma NOUN a physical injury; emotional shock following a stressful event.

traumatic ADJ

traumatize (or **-ise**) VERB

travail NOUN & VERB [old use] labour.

travel VERB (**travelled**, **travelling**; [US] **traveled**, **traveling**) go from one place to another; journey along or through. NOUN travelling; (**travels**) journeys.

traveller ([US] **traveler**) NOUN a person who travels; a Gypsy.

travelogue NOUN a book or film about someone's travels.

traverse VERB travel or extend across.

travesty NOUN (PL **-ies**) a shocking misrepresentation.

trawl NOUN a large wide-mouthed fishing net. VERB fish with a trawl; search thoroughly.

trawler NOUN a boat used in trawling.

tray NOUN a flat board with a rim, used for carrying small articles.

treacherous ADJ guilty of or involving betrayal or deception; having hidden or unpredictable dangers. **treachery** NOUN

treacle NOUN a thick sticky liquid produced when sugar is refined. **treacly** ADJ

tread VERB (**trod, trodden, treading**) walk in a specified way; walk on or along; press or crush with the feet. NOUN **1** the manner or sound of walking. **2** a horizontal surface of a stair. **3** the part of a tyre that touches the ground.

tread water keep upright in water by making treading movements.

treadle NOUN a lever worked by the foot to operate a machine.

treadmill NOUN **1** a large wheel turned by people treading on steps round its edge, used in the past to drive machinery. **2** monotonous routine work.

treason NOUN the crime of betraying your country. **treasonable** ADJ

treasure NOUN a collection of precious metals or gems; a highly valued object or person. VERB value highly; look after carefully.

treasurer NOUN a person in charge of the funds of an institution.

treasury NOUN (PL **-ies**) the revenue of a state, institution, etc.; the government department in charge of the economy.

treat VERB **1** behave towards or deal with in a specified way; give medical treatment to; subject to a chemical or other process. **2** buy something for someone in order to give pleasure. NOUN something special that gives pleasure.

treatise NOUN a written work dealing with one subject.

treatment NOUN **1** a manner of dealing with a person or thing. **2** medical care for an illness or injury.

treaty NOUN (PL **-ies**) a formal agreement between states.

treble ADJ three times as much or as many. NOUN **1** a treble quantity or thing. **2** a high-pitched voice.

tree NOUN a large woody plant with a main stem and a number of branches.

trek NOUN a long arduous journey. VERB (**trekked, trekking**) make a trek.

trellis NOUN a light framework of crossing strips of wood.

tremble VERB shake or shiver; be very frightened. NOUN a trembling movement.

tremendous ADJ immense; [inf] excellent.

tremor NOUN a slight trembling movement; a sudden feeling of fear or excitement.

tremulous ADJ trembling or quivering.

trench NOUN a deep ditch.

trenchant ADJ expressed strongly and clearly.

trend NOUN a general tendency; a fashion.

trendsetter NOUN a person who leads the way in fashion etc.

trendy ADJ (**-ier, -iest**) [inf] fashionable.

trepidation NOUN nervousness.

trespass VERB enter land or property unlawfully; intrude. NOUN the act of trespassing. **trespasser** NOUN

tress NOUN a lock of hair.

trestle table NOUN a board held on a set of supports with sloping legs, forming a table.

triad NOUN a group of three.

trial NOUN **1** a formal examination in a court of law to decide if someone is guilty of a crime. **2** a test of quality or performance. **3** a person or thing that tries your patience.

triangle NOUN a geometric figure with three sides and three angles. **triangular** ADJ

triathlon NOUN an athletic contest involving three different events.

tribe NOUN a community in a traditional society sharing customs and beliefs and led by a chief. **tribal** ADJ

tribulation NOUN trouble

or suffering.

tribunal NOUN a group of people appointed to settle disputes.

tributary NOUN (PL **-ies**) a river or stream flowing into a larger river or lake.

tribute NOUN 1 something said or done as a mark of respect. 2 [historical] payment made by a state to a more powerful one.

trice NOUN (**in a trice**) in a moment.

trick NOUN 1 something done to deceive or outwit someone. 2 a clever act performed for entertainment. 3 a mannerism. VERB deceive or outwit.
trickery NOUN

trickle VERB flow in a thin stream; come or go gradually. NOUN a trickling flow.

tricky ADJ (**-ier, -iest**) difficult.

tricolour ([US] **tricolor**) NOUN a flag with three colours in stripes.

tricycle NOUN a three-wheeled pedal-driven vehicle.

trident NOUN a three-pronged spear.

trifle NOUN 1 something of little value or importance; a very small amount. 2 a cold dessert of sponge cake and fruit with layers of custard, jelly, and cream. VERB (**trifle with**) treat without seriousness or respect.

trifling ADJ trivial.

trigger NOUN a lever for releasing a spring, especially to fire a gun. VERB cause to happen.
trigger-happy apt to shoot on the slightest provocation.

trigonometry NOUN a branch of mathematics dealing with the relationship of sides and angles of triangles.

trilby NOUN (PL **-ies**) a man's soft felt hat.

trill NOUN & VERB (make) a high vibrating sound.

trillion NOUN a million million; [dated] a million million million.

trilobite NOUN a fossil marine creature.

trilogy NOUN (PL **-ies**) a group of three related books, plays, etc.

trim VERB (**trimmed, trimming**) 1 cut untidy edges from; shorten and neaten. 2 decorate.

3 adjust a sail. NOUN **1** decoration. **2** an act of cutting. **3** good condition. ADJ (**trimmer, trimmest**) neat and smart.

trimaran NOUN a boat like a catamaran, with three hulls.

trimming NOUN **1** decoration or accompaniment. **2** (**trimmings**) small pieces trimmed off.

trinity NOUN (PL **-ies**) a group of three; (**the Trinity**) (in Christian belief) the three persons (Father, Son, and Holy Spirit) that make up God.

trinket NOUN a small ornament or piece of jewellery.

trio NOUN (PL **-os**) a group or set of three; a group of three musicians.

trip VERB (**tripped, tripping**) **1** catch your foot on something and fall. **2** (**trip up**) make a mistake. **3** move with quick light steps. **4** activate a mechanism. NOUN **1** a journey or excursion. **2** an act of stumbling. **3** [inf] a hallucinatory experience caused by taking a drug.

tripartite ADJ consisting of three parts.

tripe NOUN **1** the stomach of a cow or sheep as food. **2** [inf] nonsense.

triple ADJ having three parts or members; three times as much or as many. VERB increase by three times its amount.

triplet NOUN each of three children born at one birth; a set of three.

triplicate ADJ existing in three copies or examples.

tripod NOUN a three-legged stand.

tripper NOUN a person who goes on a pleasure trip.

triptych NOUN a picture or carving on three panels.

trite ADJ unoriginal and dull.

triumph NOUN a great victory or achievement; joy resulting from this. VERB be successful or victorious.

triumphal ADJ

triumphant ADJ

triumvirate NOUN a group of three powerful people.

trivet NOUN a metal stand for a kettle or hot dish.

trivia PLURAL NOUN unimportant things.

trivial ADJ of little value or importance.

triviality NOUN

trivially ADV

trod, **trodden** past and past participle of **tread**.

troll NOUN (in stories) an ugly giant or dwarf.

trolley NOUN (PL **-eys**) a basket on wheels for transporting goods; a small table on wheels.

trollop NOUN a promiscuous woman.

trombone NOUN a large brass wind instrument with a sliding tube.

troop NOUN a body of soldiers; a group of people or animals. VERB move in a group.

trooper NOUN a soldier in a cavalry or armoured unit; [US] a state police officer.

trophy NOUN (PL **-ies**) an object awarded as a prize; a souvenir of an achievement.

tropic NOUN a line of latitude 23°27' north or south of the equator; (**the tropics**) the region between these, with a hot climate.

tropical ADJ

trot NOUN a horse's pace faster than a walk; a moderate running pace. VERB (**trotted, trotting**)

move at a trot.

troth NOUN [old use] faithfulness to a promise.

trotter NOUN a pig's foot.

troubadour NOUN a medieval travelling poet.

trouble NOUN **1** difficulty or inconvenience; a cause of this; an unfortunate situation. **2** public unrest. VERB **1** cause distress or inconvenience to. **2** make the effort to do something.

troubleshooter NOUN a person employed to solve problems or faults.

troublesome ADJ causing trouble.

trough NOUN **1** a long, open receptacle for animals' food or water. **2** a region of low atmospheric pressure.

trounce VERB defeat heavily.

troupe NOUN a touring group of entertainers.

trouper NOUN **1** a member of a troupe. **2** a reliable person.

trousers PLURAL NOUN a two-legged outer garment that covers the body from the waist down.

trousseau NOUN (PL **-eaux** or **-eaus**) clothes etc.

collected by a bride for her marriage.

trout NOUN an edible freshwater fish.

trowel NOUN a small garden tool for digging; a similar tool for spreading mortar etc.

troy NOUN a system of weights used for precious metals and gems.

truant NOUN a pupil who stays away from school without permission. VERB (also **play truant**) stay away as a truant. **truancy** NOUN

truce NOUN an agreement to cease hostilities temporarily.

truck NOUN a lorry; an open railway wagon for carrying goods.

truculent ADJ defiant and aggressive.

trudge VERB walk laboriously.

true ADJ 1 in accordance with fact; accurate; genuine. 2 loyal. **truly** ADV

truffle NOUN 1 an underground fungus eaten as a delicacy. 2 a soft chocolate sweet.

trug NOUN a shallow wooden basket.

truism NOUN a statement that is obviously true, especially a hackneyed one.

trump NOUN (in card games) a card of the suit chosen to rank above the others. VERB (**trump up**) invent a false accusation.

trumpet NOUN a brass musical instrument with a flared end; something shaped like this. VERB (**trumpeted, trumpeting**) proclaim loudly; (of an elephant) make a loud sound through its trunk. **trumpeter** NOUN

truncate VERB shorten by cutting off the end. **truncation** NOUN

truncheon NOUN a short thick stick carried as a weapon.

trundle VERB move or roll slowly and unevenly.

trunk NOUN 1 a tree's main stem. 2 the body apart from the head and limbs. 3 a large box for transporting or storing articles. 4 an elephant's long flexible nose. 5 [US] the boot of a car. 6 (**trunks**) men's shorts for swimming.

trunk road an important

main road.

truss NOUN a framework supporting a roof; a surgical support for a hernia. VERB tie up securely.

trust NOUN 1 firm belief in the reliability, strength, or truth of someone or something. 2 responsibility for someone or something. 3 a legal arrangement by which someone manages property for the benefit of others; an organization or company managed by trustees. VERB 1 feel trust in; expect confidently. 2 entrust.
trustful ADJ
trustworthy ADJ

trustee NOUN a person given legal powers to manage property for the benefit of others.

trusty ADJ (-ier, -iest) reliable or faithful.

truth NOUN the quality of being true; something that is true.

truthful ADJ habitually telling the truth; accurate or realistic.
truthfully ADV

try VERB (tries, tried, trying) 1 attempt. 2 (also try out) test something new or different. 3 (try on) put on a garment to see if it fits. 4 be a strain on. 5 subject to a legal trial. NOUN 1 an attempt. 2 a touchdown in rugby, entitling the player's side to a kick at goal.

trying ADJ annoying.

tryst NOUN a secret arrangement to meet.

tsar (or **czar**) NOUN an emperor of Russia before 1917.

tsetse NOUN an African fly that transmits disease by its bite.

T-shirt (or **tee shirt**) NOUN a short-sleeved casual top.

tub NOUN a low, wide, open round container for liquids etc.; a small container for food.

tuba NOUN a large low-pitched brass wind instrument.

tubby ADJ [inf] short and fat.

tube NOUN 1 a long, hollow glass or metal cylinder; a similarly shaped container. 2 (**the Tube**) [trademark] the underground railway system in London.

tuber NOUN a short thick

rounded root or underground stem from which shoots will grow.

tuberculosis NOUN a serious infectious disease, affecting especially the lungs.

tubercular ADJ

tubular ADJ tube-shaped.

tuck NOUN 1 a flat fold stitched in a garment etc. 2 [dated] snacks eaten by children at school. VERB 1 push, fold, or turn between two surfaces; hide or put away neatly. 2 (**tuck in**) [inf] eat heartily.

Tuesday NOUN the day after Monday.

tuft NOUN a bunch of threads, grass, hair, etc., held or growing together at the base.

tug VERB (**tugged, tugging**) pull hard or suddenly. NOUN 1 a vigorous pull. 2 a small, powerful boat for towing others.

tug of war a contest in which two teams pull at opposite ends of a rope.

tuition NOUN teaching or instruction.

tulip NOUN a garden plant with a cup-shaped flower.

tulle NOUN a soft, fine net fabric.

tumble VERB fall headlong; move in an uncontrolled way. NOUN 1 a fall. 2 an untidy mass or state.

tumble dryer a machine for drying washing in a heated rotating drum.

tumbledown ADJ dilapidated.

tumbler NOUN 1 a drinking glass with no handle or stem. 2 an acrobat. 3 a pivoted piece in a lock, holding the bolt.

tumescent ADJ swollen.

tummy NOUN (PL **-ies**) [inf] the stomach.

tumour ([US] **tumor**) NOUN an abnormal growth of tissue in the body.

tumult NOUN a loud, confused noise; confusion or disorder.

tumultuous ADJ

tuna NOUN a large edible sea fish.

tundra NOUN a vast, flat Arctic region where the subsoil is permanently frozen.

tune NOUN a melody; correct musical pitch. VERB 1 adjust a musical instrument to the correct pitch. 2 adjust a radio or television to a particular frequency. 3 adjust an engine to run smoothly.

tuneful ADJ melodious.

tuner NOUN **1** a person who tunes pianos. **2** a radio receiver as part of a hi-fi system.

tungsten NOUN a heavy grey metallic element.

tunic NOUN a close-fitting jacket worn as part of a uniform; a loose garment reaching to the knees.

tunnel NOUN an underground passage. VERB (**tunnelled, tunnelling**; [US] **tunneled, tunneling**) make a passage underground or through something.

tunny NOUN (PL **-ies**) = tuna.

turban NOUN a long length of material worn wound round the head by Muslim and Sikh men.

turbid ADJ (of a liquid) muddy or cloudy.

turbine NOUN a machine or motor driven by a wheel that is turned by a flow of water or gas.

turbo- COMBINING FORM using a turbine; driven by such engines.

turbot NOUN a large edible flatfish.

turbulent ADJ full of disorder or confusion; (of air or water) moving unevenly or violently. **turbulence** NOUN

tureen NOUN a deep covered dish from which soup is served.

turf NOUN (PL **turfs** or **turves**) short grass and the soil just below it; a piece of this. VERB **1** cover with turf. **2** (**turf out**) [inf] force to leave.

turgid ADJ swollen; (of language) pompous.

turkey NOUN (PL **-eys**) a large bird bred for food.

Turkish bath NOUN a hot-air or steam bath followed by massage.

Turkish delight NOUN a sweet of flavoured gelatin coated in powdered sugar.

turmeric NOUN a bright yellow spice.

turmoil NOUN a state of great disturbance or confusion.

turn VERB **1** move around a central point; move so as to face or go in a different direction; aim or direct, **2** make or become. **3** shape wood on a lathe. NOUN **1** an act of turning; a bend in a road; a change of direction; a new development in events.

2 the time when a member of a group is allowed to or must do something. **3** a short performance. **4** a brief feeling of illness. **5** a short walk.
in turn in succession. **turn down** reject. **turn-up** the end of a trouser leg folded upwards.

turncoat NOUN a person who changes sides in a conflict.

turning NOUN a point where a road branches off another.
turning point a moment at which a decisive change takes place.

turnip NOUN a plant with an edible round white root.

turnout NOUN the number of people attending or taking part in an event.

turnover NOUN **1** the amount of money taken in a business. **2** the rate at which employees leave or goods are sold and are replaced. **3** a small pie of pastry folded over a filling.

turnstile NOUN a revolving barrier for admitting people one at a time.

turntable NOUN a circular revolving platform.

turpentine NOUN oil used for thinning paint and as a solvent.

turpitude NOUN [formal] wickedness.

turps NOUN [inf] turpentine.

turquoise NOUN a bluish-green semi-precious stone; its colour.

turret NOUN a small tower; a revolving tower for a gun on a warship or tank. **turreted** ADJ

turtle NOUN a sea creature like a tortoise.
turn turtle capsize. **turtle dove** a small dove with a soft purring call.

turtleneck NOUN a high, round close-fitting neckline.

tusk NOUN a long pointed tooth projecting from the mouth of an elephant, walrus, etc.

tussle NOUN a struggle or scuffle.

tutor NOUN a private teacher; a teacher at a university. VERB act as tutor to.

tutorial ADJ of a tutor. NOUN a student's session with a tutor.

tutu NOUN a dancer's short

skirt made of layers of frills.

tuxedo NOUN (PL **-os** or **-oes**) a dinner jacket.

TV ABBREV television.

twang NOUN **1** a sharp vibrating sound. **2** a nasal intonation. VERB make a twang.

tweak VERB **1** pull or twist sharply. **2** [inf] make fine adjustments to. NOUN a sharp pull.

twee ADJ affectedly pretty or sentimental.

tweed NOUN a thick woollen fabric.

tweet VERB & NOUN (give) a chirp.

tweezers PLURAL NOUN small pincers for handling very small things.

twelve ADJ & NOUN one more than eleven (12, XII).
twelfth ADJ & NOUN

twenty ADJ & NOUN twice ten (20, XX).
twentieth ADJ & NOUN

twice ADV two times; in double amount or degree.

twiddle VERB fiddle with aimlessly.

twig NOUN a small shoot growing from a branch or stem.

twilight NOUN light from the sky after sunset; a period or state of gradual decline.

twill NOUN a fabric with a slightly ridged surface.

twin NOUN each of two children born at the same birth; a thing that is exactly like another. VERB (**twinned, twinning**) link or combine as a pair.

twine NOUN strong thread or string. VERB twist or wind.

twinge NOUN a slight or brief pang.

twinkle VERB shine with a flickering light. NOUN a twinkling light.

twirl VERB spin round lightly or rapidly. NOUN a twirling movement.

twist VERB **1** bend, curl, or distort; force out of the natural position. **2** have a winding course. NOUN an act of twisting; a twisted or spiral shape; an unexpected development in a story etc.

twit NOUN [inf] a stupid person.

twitch VERB make a short jerking movement. NOUN a twitching movement.

twitter VERB & NOUN (make) light chirping sounds.

tyre

two ADJ & NOUN one more than one (2, II).
two-dimensional having or appearing to have length and breadth but no depth. **two-faced** insincere or deceitful. **two-time** be unfaithful to a spouse or lover.
twosome NOUN a pair.
tycoon NOUN a wealthy, influential industrialist.
tying present participle of tie.
tympani see **timpani**.
tympanum NOUN (PL **-pana** or **-panums**) the eardrum.
type NOUN 1 a kind or category; [inf] a person of a specified nature. 2 a perfect example. 3 printed characters or letters. VERB write using a typewriter or computer.
typist NOUN
typecast VERB cast an actor repeatedly in the same type of role.
typeface NOUN a particular design of printed type.
typescript NOUN a typewritten document.
typesetter NOUN a person or machine that arranges type for printing.
typewriter NOUN a machine with keys that

are pressed to produce characters similar to printed ones.
typewritten ADJ
typhoid NOUN a serious infectious fever.
typhoon NOUN a tropical storm.
typhus NOUN an infectious disease transmitted by parasites.
typical ADJ having the distinctive qualities of a particular type of person or thing.
typically ADV
typify VERB (**typified**, **typifying**) be a typical example of.
typography NOUN the art or style of printing.
typographical ADJ
tyrannize (or **-ise**) VERB rule in a cruel way.
tyrannosaurus rex NOUN a large flesh-eating dinosaur.
tyranny NOUN (PL **-ies**) cruel and oppressive government or rule.
tyrannical ADJ
tyrannous ADJ
tyrant NOUN a cruel and oppressive ruler.
tyre ([US] **tire**) NOUN a rubber covering that fits round a wheel.

Uu

U ABBREV universal, a film classification indicating suitability for all ages. **U-turn** the driving of a vehicle in a U-shaped course to reverse its direction; a complete change in policy.

ubiquitous ADJ found everywhere.

udder NOUN a bag-like milk-producing organ of a cow, goat, etc.

UFO ABBREV unidentified flying object.

ugly ADJ (**-ier**, **-iest**) unpleasant to look at; threatening or hostile. **ugliness** NOUN

UK ABBREV United Kingdom.

ukulele NOUN a small four-stringed guitar.

ulcer NOUN an open sore on the body. **ulcerated** ADJ **ulceration** NOUN

ulna NOUN (PL **-nae** or **-nas**) the thinner long bone of the forearm.

ulterior ADJ beyond what is obvious or admitted.

ultimate ADJ final; extreme; fundamental. **ultimately** ADV

ultimatum NOUN (PL **-tums** or **-ta**) a final demand, with a threat of hostile action if this is rejected.

ultramarine NOUN a brilliant deep blue.

ultrasonic ADJ above the range of normal human hearing.

ultrasound NOUN ultrasonic waves.

ultraviolet ADJ of or using radiation with a wavelength shorter than that of visible light rays.

umbilical cord NOUN a flexible tube connecting a fetus to the mother's placenta.

umbrage NOUN (**take umbrage**) be offended.

umbrella NOUN a folding device used as a protection against rain.

umlaut NOUN a mark (¨) over a vowel indicating a change in pronunciation, used especially in Germanic languages.

umpire NOUN a person who supervises a sporting contest to ensure that rules are observed. VERB act as umpire in.

umpteen ADJ [inf] very many.

UN ABBREV United Nations.

unaccountable ADJ 1 not explicable. 2 not having to justify your actions. **unaccountably** ADV

unadulterated ADJ not mixed or diluted.

unanimous ADJ with everyone's agreement. **unanimity** NOUN

unarmed ADJ without weapons.

unassuming ADJ not arrogant or pretentious.

unattended ADJ not supervised or looked after.

unawares ADV unexpectedly.

unbalanced ADJ mentally or emotionally unstable.

unbeknown ADJ (**unbeknown to**) without the knowledge of.

unbelievable ADJ unlikely to be true; extraordinary.

unbending ADJ strict and inflexible.

unbidden ADJ without having been invited.

unbounded ADJ without limits.

unbridled ADJ unrestrained.

unburden VERB (**unburden yourself**) reveal your thoughts and feelings.

uncalled for ADJ undesirable or unnecessary.

uncanny ADJ strange or mysterious. **uncannily** ADV

unceremonious ADJ rude or abrupt.

uncertain ADJ not known, reliable, or definite; not completely sure.

uncle NOUN a brother or brother-in-law of your father or mother.

uncommon ADJ unusual.

uncompromising ADJ inflexible or unwilling to compromise.

unconditional ADJ not subject to conditions.

unconscious ADJ not conscious; not aware; done without you realizing. **unconsciousness** NOUN

uncouth ADJ lacking good manners.

uncover VERB remove a covering from; reveal or expose.

unction NOUN anointing

with oil, especially as a religious rite.

unctuous ADJ excessively polite or flattering.

undecided ADJ not having made a decision; not resolved.

undeniable ADJ undoubtedly true. **undeniably** ADV

under PREP 1 extending below. 2 at a lower level or grade than. 3 controlled by; undergoing. 4 in accordance with rules. ADV in or to a position directly below something. **under way** making progress.

underarm ADJ & ADV done with the arm or hand below shoulder level.

undercarriage NOUN an aircraft's landing wheels and their supports.

underclass NOUN the lowest and poorest social class in a country.

underclothes PLURAL NOUN underwear.

undercoat NOUN a layer of paint used under a finishing coat.

undercover ADJ done or doing things secretly.

undercurrent NOUN an underlying feeling, influence, or trend.

undercut VERB (**undercut,** **undercutting**) 1 offer goods or services for a lower price than a competitor. 2 weaken or undermine.

underdog NOUN a competitor thought unlikely to win.

underdone ADJ not thoroughly cooked.

underestimate VERB make too low an estimate of.

underfoot ADV 1 on the ground. 2 getting in the way.

undergo VERB (**undergoes,** **underwent, undergone,** **undergoing**) experience; be subjected to.

undergraduate NOUN a university student who has not yet taken a degree.

underground ADJ & ADV under the surface of the ground; secretly. NOUN an underground railway.

undergrowth NOUN thick growth of shrubs and bushes under trees.

underhand ADJ done or doing things slyly or secretly.

underlay NOUN material

laid under a carpet.

underlie VERB (**underlay, underlain, underlying**) be the cause or basis of.

underline VERB 1 draw a line under. 2 emphasize.

underling NOUN a subordinate.

undermine VERB weaken gradually; weaken the foundations of.

underneath PREP & ADV below; so as to be concealed by.

underpants PLURAL NOUN an undergarment for the lower part of the body.

underpass NOUN a road passing under another.

underpin VERB (**underpinned, underpinning**) support a structure from below.

underprivileged ADJ not having the normal standard of living or rights.

underrate VERB underestimate.

underscore VERB underline.

undersell VERB (**undersold, underselling**) sell at a lower price than a competitor.

undersigned NOUN the person or people who have signed a particular document.

underskirt NOUN a petticoat.

understand VERB (**understood, understanding**) 1 grasp the meaning, nature, or cause of; see the significance of. 2 infer; assume without being told; interpret in a particular way.

understandable ADJ able to be understood; natural, reasonable, or forgivable. **understandably** ADV

understanding ADJ showing insight or sympathy. NOUN 1 ability to understand; sympathetic insight. 2 an agreement.

understate VERB represent as smaller, less good, etc., than is the case. **understatement** NOUN

understated ADJ pleasingly subtle.

understudy NOUN (PL **-ies**) an actor who studies another's part in order to be able to take their place if necessary. VERB (**understudied, understudying**) be an understudy for.

undertake VERB (**-took,**

-taken, -taking) begin an activity; formally promise to do something.

undertaker NOUN a person whose business is to organize funerals.

undertaking NOUN 1 work etc. undertaken. 2 a formal promise.

undertone NOUN 1 a low or subdued tone. 2 an underlying quality or feeling.

underwear NOUN clothing worn under other clothes, next to the skin.

underwent past of **undergo**.

underworld NOUN 1 a part of society habitually involved in crime. 2 (in mythology) the home of the dead, under the earth.

underwrite VERB (**underwrote, underwritten, underwriting**) accept legal responsibility for an insurance policy; undertake to finance. **underwriter** NOUN

undesirable ADJ harmful or unpleasant.

undo VERB (**undoes, undid, undone, undoing**) 1 unfasten. 2 cancel the effect of. 3 cause

disaster to.

undoubted ADJ not disputed.

undress VERB take clothes off.

undue ADJ excessive. **unduly** ADV

undulate VERB move with a wave-like motion; have a wavy shape. **undulation** NOUN

undying ADJ everlasting.

unearth VERB uncover or bring out from the ground; find by searching.

uneasy ADJ (**-ier, -iest**) troubled or uncomfortable. **unease** NOUN **uneasily** ADV

unemployed ADJ without a paid job. **unemployment** NOUN

unending ADJ endless.

unequalled ([US] **unequaled**) ADJ better or greater than all others.

unequivocal ADJ clear and unambiguous. **unequivocally** ADV

unerring ADJ making no mistake.

uneven ADJ not level or smooth; not regular. **unevenness** NOUN

unexceptionable ADJ

entirely satisfactory.

unexceptional ADJ not unusual or outstanding.

unfailing ADJ constant; never stopping or going wrong.

unfair ADJ not fair or just.

unfaithful ADJ not loyal; having committed adultery.

unfit ADJ 1 unsuitable. 2 not in good physical condition.

unflappable ADJ [inf] calm in a crisis.

unfold VERB 1 open or spread out. 2 reveal or be revealed.

unforeseen ADJ not predicted.

unforgettable ADJ impossible to forget.

unfortunate ADJ having bad luck; regrettable.

unfortunately ADV

unfounded ADJ with no basis.

unfurl VERB unroll or spread out.

ungainly ADJ clumsy or awkward.

unguarded ADJ 1 not guarded. 2 incautious.

unguent NOUN an ointment or lubricant.

ungulate NOUN a hoofed animal.

unhappy ADJ (-ier, -iest)
1 not happy.
2 unfortunate.

unhappily ADV

unhappiness NOUN

unhealthy ADJ (-ier, -iest) not healthy; harmful to health.

unhealthily ADV

unheard-of ADJ previously unknown.

unhinged ADJ mentally unbalanced.

unicorn NOUN a mythical horse-like animal with one straight horn on its forehead.

uniform NOUN distinctive clothing identifying the wearer as a member of an organization or group. ADJ always the same; not differing from one another.

uniformity NOUN

uniformly ADV

unify VERB (**unified**, **unifying**) unite.

unification NOUN

unilateral ADJ done by or affecting only one person or group.

unilaterally ADV

uninterested ADJ not interested or concerned.

uninviting ADJ unattractive or

unpleasant.

union NOUN uniting or being united; a whole formed by uniting parts; an association; a trade union.

Union Jack the national flag of the UK.

unionist NOUN **1** a member of a trade union. **2** a person in Northern Ireland favouring union with Great Britain.

unionize (or **-ise**) VERB make or become members of a trade union.

unique ADJ **1** the only one of its kind; belonging only to one place, person, etc. **2** remarkable.

unisex ADJ suitable for people of either sex.

unison NOUN the fact of two or more things happening or being said at the same time.

unit NOUN **1** an individual thing, person, or group, especially as part of a complex whole. **2** a fixed quantity used as a standard of measurement. **3** a piece of furniture or equipment; part of an institution, having a specialized function.

Unitarian NOUN a person who believes that God is one being and rejects the idea of the Trinity.

unitary ADJ single; of a single whole.

unite VERB join together; make or become one.

unity NOUN (PL **-ies**) the state of being united or coherent; a complex whole.

universal ADJ of, for, or done by all.

universally ADV

universe NOUN the whole of space and everything in it.

university NOUN (PL **-ies**) an educational institution for advanced learning and research.

unkempt ADJ looking untidy or neglected.

unkind ADJ not caring or kind.

unkindness NOUN

unknown ADJ not known. NOUN an unknown person or thing.

unleaded ADJ (of petrol) without added lead.

unleash VERB release or let loose.

unleavened ADJ (of bread) made without yeast.

unless CONJ except when; if not.

unlike ADJ different. PREP different or differently from.

unlikely ADJ not likely to happen or be true.

unlimited ADJ not limited; very great in number.

unmask VERB expose the true nature of.

unmentionable ADJ too shocking to be spoken of.

unmistakable ADJ not able to be mistaken for anything else.

unmistakably ADV

unmitigated ADJ total or absolute.

unmoved ADJ not affected by emotion or excitement.

unnatural ADJ not natural or normal.

unnaturally ADV

unnecessary ADJ not needed; excessive.

unnecessarily ADV

unnerve VERB cause to lose courage or determination.

unobtrusive ADJ not conspicuous or attracting attention.

unpack VERB take things out of a suitcase, bag, etc.

unparalleled ADJ never yet equalled.

unpick VERB undo the stitching of.

unpleasant ADJ causing distaste or distress.

unpopular ADJ not liked or popular.

unpopularity NOUN

unprecedented ADJ never done or known before.

unprepared ADJ not ready or equipped for something.

unprepossessing ADJ unattractive.

unprincipled ADJ without moral principles.

unprofessional ADJ contrary to professional standards of behaviour.

unprofessionally ADV

unprofitable ADJ not profitable; useless.

unprompted ADJ spontaneous.

unqualified ADJ 1 not having the necessary qualifications. 2 complete.

unravel VERB (**unravelled, unravelling**; [US] **unraveled, unraveling**) disentangle or become disentangled; solve.

unreal ADJ strange and not seeming real.

unreasonable ADJ not based on good sense; unfair or excessive.

unreasonably ADV

unrelenting ADJ not becoming less intense, severe, or strict.

unremitting ADJ not ceasing.

unrequited ADJ (of love) not given in return.

unreservedly ADV without any reservations or doubts.

unrest NOUN disturbance or disorder; dissatisfaction.

unrivalled ([US] **unrivaled**) ADJ having no equal.

unruly ADJ disorderly or difficult to control. **unruliness** NOUN

unsaturated ADJ (of organic molecules) containing fewer hydrogen atoms than the maximum possible.

unsavoury ([US] **unsavory**) ADJ disagreeable to the taste or smell; not respectable.

unscathed ADJ without suffering any injury.

unscrupulous ADJ lacking moral scruples or principles.

unseat VERB cause to fall from a saddle; remove from a position of power.

unsettle VERB make anxious or uneasy.

unsettled ADJ changeable; anxious or uneasy; not yet resolved.

unshakeable (or **unshakable**) ADJ firm.

unsightly ADJ ugly.

unskilled ADJ not having or needing special skill or training.

unsociable ADJ disliking company.

unsocial ADJ (of working hours) nor falling within the normal working day.

unsolicited ADJ not requested.

unsophisticated ADJ simple and natural or naive.

unsparing ADJ giving generously.

unspeakable ADJ too bad to be described in words.

unstable ADJ not stable; mentally or emotionally unbalanced.

unstinting ADJ given freely and generously.

unsung ADJ not celebrated or praised.

unswerving ADJ not changing or becoming weaker.

untenable ADJ not able to be maintained or defended against criticism etc.

unthinkable ADJ impossible to imagine or accept.

unthinking ADJ thoughtless.

untidy ADJ (-ier, -iest) in disorder; not keeping things neat.
untidily ADV
untidiness NOUN

until PREP & CONJ up to a specified time, event, etc.

untimely ADJ happening at an unsuitable time; premature.

unto PREP [old use] to.

untold ADJ 1 not told. 2 too much or too many to be counted.

untoward ADJ unexpected and inconvenient.

unusual ADJ not usual; exceptional.
unusually ADV

unveil VERB remove a veil or covering from; reveal or make known.

unwaged ADJ not doing paid work.

unwarranted ADJ not justified.

unwell ADJ ill.

unwieldy ADJ awkward to move or control because of its size, shape, or weight.

unwilling ADJ reluctant.

unwind VERB (**unwound**, **unwinding**) undo something that has been wound or twisted; relax after work or tension.

unwise ADJ foolish.

unwitting ADJ unaware; unintentional.
unwittingly ADV

unwonted ADJ not customary or usual.

unworldly ADJ not aware of the realities of life.

unwritten ADJ (of a rule etc.) based on custom not statute.

up ADV 1 towards a higher place or position; at or to a higher level or value. 2 out of bed. 3 into the desired condition or position. PREP from a lower to a higher point of. ADJ moving or directed upwards. VERB (**upped**, **upping**) increase.
ups and downs alternate good and bad fortune. **up to date** modern or fashionable.
upward ADJ & ADV
upwards ADV

upbeat ADJ [inf] cheerful and optimistic.

upbraid VERB reproach.

upbringing NOUN training and education during

childhood.

update VERB bring up to date.

upend VERB set on end or upside down.

upgrade VERB raise to a higher standard or grade.

upheaval NOUN a sudden violent change or movement.

uphill ADJ & ADV going or sloping upwards.

uphold VERB (**upheld, upholding**) support.

upholster VERB provide furniture with a soft, padded covering. **upholstery** NOUN

upkeep NOUN the process or cost of keeping something in good condition.

uplift VERB cause to feel hopeful or happy.

upmarket ADJ expensive or of high quality.

upon PREP on.

upper ADJ higher in place, position, or rank. NOUN the part of a shoe above the sole.
the upper hand advantage or control.
upper case capital letters.
upper class the social group with the highest status.

uppermost ADJ & ADV highest in place or importance.

uppity ADJ [inf] self-important.

upright ADJ **1** in a vertical position. **2** strictly honest or honourable. NOUN a vertical part or support.

uprising NOUN a rebellion.

uproar NOUN an outburst of noise and excitement or anger.

uproarious ADJ noisy and lively; very funny.

uproot VERB pull a tree etc. out of the ground; force someone to leave their home.

upset VERB (**upset, upsetting**) **1** make unhappy or disappointed. **2** knock over; disrupt or disturb. NOUN a state of being upset. ADJ unhappy, disappointed, or disturbed.

upshot NOUN an outcome.

upside down ADV & ADJ with the upper part where the lower part should be; in or into great disorder.

upstage ADV & ADJ at or towards the back of a theatre stage. VERB draw attention away from someone.

upstairs ADV & ADJ to or on a higher floor.

upstanding ADJ honest and respectable.

upstart NOUN a person newly risen to a high position, especially one who behaves arrogantly.

upstream ADJ & ADV towards the source of a stream or river, against the current.

upsurge NOUN an increase.

uptight ADJ [inf] nervously tense or angry.

upturn NOUN an improvement or upward trend.

upwind ADJ & ADV into the wind.

uranium NOUN a radioactive metallic element used as fuel in nuclear reactors.

urban ADJ of a city or town.

urbane ADJ (of a man) charming, courteous, and refined.

urbanity NOUN

urchin NOUN a poor, raggedly dressed child.

Urdu NOUN a language of Pakistan and India.

ureter NOUN the duct from the kidney to the bladder.

urethra NOUN the duct which carries urine from the body.

urge VERB encourage or advise strongly; recommend strongly. NOUN a strong desire or impulse.

urgent ADJ needing or calling for immediate attention or action.

urgency NOUN

urinal NOUN a receptacle in a public toilet into which men urinate.

urinate VERB pass urine from the body.

urination NOUN

urine NOUN waste liquid which collects in the bladder and is passed out of the body.

urinary ADJ

urn NOUN 1 a container for holding a cremated person's ashes. 2 a large metal container with a tap, for keeping water etc. hot.

us PRON used by a speaker to refer to himself or herself and one or more other people.

USA ABBREV United States of America.

usable ADJ able to be used.

usage NOUN the using of something.

use VERB 1 cause to serve

your purpose or achieve your ends; treat in a specified way; exploit unfairly. 2 (**use up**) consume the whole of. 3 (**used**) second-hand. NOUN the using of something; the power to control and use something; a purpose for which something is used. **used to** 1 was accustomed to. 2 familiar with.

useful ADJ able to be used for a practical purpose. **usefully** ADV

useless ADJ serving no purpose; [inf] hopelessly incompetent.

user NOUN a person who uses something. **user-friendly** easy for people to use or understand.

usher NOUN a person who shows people to their seats in a theatre etc. or in church. VERB lead; escort.

usherette NOUN a woman who ushers people to seats in a theatre etc.

USSR ABBREV [historical] Union of Soviet Socialist Republics.

usual ADJ happening or done typically, regularly, or frequently.

usually ADV

usurp VERB seize power or a position wrongfully or by force.

usury NOUN the lending of money at excessively high rates of interest.

utensil NOUN a tool or container, especially for domestic use.

uterus NOUN the womb. **uterine** ADJ

utilitarian ADJ useful rather than decorative or luxurious.

utility NOUN (PL **-ies**) 1 the state of being useful. 2 a company supplying water, gas, electricity, etc. to the public. **utility room** a room for large domestic appliances.

utilize (or **-ise**) VERB make use of.

utmost ADJ furthest or most extreme. NOUN the furthest point or degree.

Utopia NOUN an imagined place where everything is perfect. **utopian** ADJ

utter[1] ADJ complete or absolute. **utterly** ADV

utter[2] VERB make a sound; say something. **utterance** NOUN

Vv

V (or **v**) NOUN (as a Roman numeral) 5. ABBREV volts; versus.

vacancy NOUN (PL **-ies**) an unoccupied position, job, or hotel room; empty space.

vacant ADJ **1** empty or unoccupied. **2** showing no interest or understanding.

vacate VERB cease to occupy.

vacation NOUN an interval between terms in universities and law courts; [US] a holiday.

vaccinate NOUN inoculate with a vaccine. **vaccination** NOUN

vaccine NOUN a substance used to stimulate the production of antibodies in the body and so give immunity against a disease.

vacillate VERB keep changing your mind. **vacillation** NOUN

vacuous ADJ showing a lack of thought or intelligence.

vacuum NOUN (PL **-cuums** or **-cua**) a space from which air has been removed; a gap.

vacuum cleaner an electrical machine that sucks up dust. **vacuum flask** a container for keeping liquids hot or cold. **vacuum-packed** sealed in a pack with the air removed.

vagabond NOUN a wanderer or vagrant.

vagary NOUN (PL **-ies**) an unpredictable change or action.

vagina NOUN the passage leading from the vulva to the womb. **vaginal** ADJ

vagrant NOUN a person without a settled home. **vagrancy** NOUN

vague ADJ not certain or definite; not expressing yourself clearly.

vain ADJ **1** excessively proud of your appearance, abilities, etc. **2** useless or futile. **in vain** without success.

valance NOUN a short

curtain or hanging frill.

vale NOUN a valley.

valediction NOUN a farewell.

valedictory ADJ

valency (or **valency**) NOUN the combining power of an atom as compared with that of the hydrogen atom.

valentine NOUN a romantic greetings card sent on St Valentine's Day (14 Feb.); a person to whom you send such a card.

valet NOUN a man's personal attendant. VERB (**valeted, valeting**) clean a car.

valiant ADJ brave.

valid ADJ 1 legally binding or acceptable. 2 logically sound.

validity NOUN

validate VERB make or show to be valid.

validation NOUN

valley NOUN (PL **-eys**) a low area between hills.

valour ([US] **valor**) NOUN bravery.

valuable ADJ of great value or worth. PLURAL NOUN (**valuables**) valuable things.

valuation NOUN an estimation of a thing's worth.

value NOUN 1 the amount of money that something is worth; the importance or usefulness of something. 2 (**values**) standards of behaviour. VERB 1 consider precious. 2 estimate the value of.

value added tax a tax on the amount by which goods rise in value at each stage of production.

valve NOUN a device controlling flow through a pipe; a structure allowing blood to flow in one direction only.

vampire NOUN (in stories) a dead person who leaves their grave to drink the blood of living people.

vampire bat a blood-sucking bat.

van NOUN 1 a covered vehicle for transporting goods etc.; a railway carriage for luggage or goods. 2 the leading part; the front.

vandal NOUN a person who damages things wilfully.

vandalism NOUN

vandalize (or **-ise**) VERB

vane NOUN a broad blade forming part of a windmill, propeller, etc.

vanguard NOUN the foremost part of an advancing army etc.

vanilla NOUN a flavouring obtained from the pods of a tropical plant.

vanish VERB disappear completely.

vanity NOUN (PL -ies) 1 conceit. 2 futility.

vanquish VERB conquer.

vantage point NOUN a position giving a good view.

vapid ADJ insipid or uninteresting.

vaporize (or **-ise**) VERB convert or be converted into vapour.

vapour ([US] **vapor**) NOUN moisture suspended in air, into which certain liquids or solids are converted by heating. **vaporous** ADJ

variable ADJ changeable. NOUN a part or element liable to change. **variability** NOUN

variance NOUN (**at variance**) differing; disagreeing.

variant NOUN a form of something differing from others or from a standard.

variation NOUN a change or slight difference; a variant; a repetition of a musical theme with changes and ornamentation.

varicose ADJ (of veins) permanently swollen.

variegated ADJ having irregular patches of colours.

variety NOUN (PL -ies) 1 not being uniform or monotonous; a selection of different things of the same type. 2 a sort or kind. 3 light entertainment involving singing, dancing, and comedy.

various ADJ 1 of different kinds or sorts. 2 several. **variously** ADV

varnish NOUN a liquid that dries to form a shiny transparent coating. VERB coat with varnish.

vary VERB (**varied, varying**) make or be or become different.

vase NOUN a container for holding cut flowers.

vasectomy NOUN (PL -ies) a surgical removal of part of the ducts that carry semen from the testicles, as a means of sterilization.

Vaseline NOUN [trademark] a

thick cream made from petroleum, used as an ointment or lubricant.

vassal NOUN a person or country subordinate to another.

vast ADJ very great in area or size.

VAT ABBREV value added tax.

vat NOUN a large tank for liquids.

vaudeville NOUN a type of entertainment with both musical and comedy acts.

vault NOUN **1** an arched roof. **2** an underground storage room; a burial chamber. **3** an act of vaulting. VERB jump using your hands or a pole.

VCR ABBREV video cassette recorder.

VDU ABBREV visual display unit.

veal NOUN calf's flesh as food.

vector NOUN **1** a quantity (e.g. velocity) that has both magnitude and direction. **2** the carrier of a disease or infection.

veer VERB change direction.

vegan NOUN a person who eats no meat or animal products.

vegetable NOUN a plant grown for food.

vegetarian NOUN a person who does not eat meat. ADJ of or for such people.

vegetate VERB live an uneventful life.

vegetation NOUN plants.

vehement ADJ showing strong feeling.
vehemence NOUN

vehicle NOUN a car, lorry, or other thing used for transporting people or goods.
vehicular ADJ

veil NOUN a piece of fabric concealing or protecting the face; something that conceals. VERB cover with or as if with a veil.

vein NOUN **1** any of the blood vessels conveying blood towards the heart. **2** a narrow streak or stripe; a narrow layer of ore etc. **3** a mood or style.
veined ADJ

Velcro NOUN [trademark] a fastener consisting of two strips of fabric which cling together when pressed.

veld (or **veldt**) NOUN open grassland in southern Africa.

velocity NOUN (PL **-ies**)

speed.

velour NOUN a plush fabric resembling velvet.

velvet NOUN a fabric with a soft, thick, short pile on one side.

venal ADJ susceptible to bribery.

vend VERB sell.

vending machine a slot machine that dispenses small articles

vendor NOUN

vendetta NOUN a feud.

veneer NOUN a thin covering layer of fine wood; a superficial show of a quality.

venerable ADJ given great respect because of age, wisdom, etc.

venerate VERB respect deeply.

veneration NOUN

venereal disease NOUN a disease caught by having sex with an infected person.

venetian blind NOUN a window blind with adjustable horizontal slats.

vengeance NOUN retaliation or revenge.

vengeful ADJ seeking vengeance.

venial ADJ (of a sin) pardonable.

venison NOUN meat from a deer.

venom NOUN 1 a poisonous fluid secreted by snakes etc. 2 bitter feeling or language.

venomous ADJ

vent NOUN 1 an opening allowing gas or liquid to pass through. 2 a slit in a garment.

give vent to express a strong emotion.

ventilate VERB cause air to enter or circulate freely in.

ventilation NOUN

ventilator NOUN 1 a device for ventilating a room etc. 2 a respirator.

ventricle NOUN a cavity, especially in the heart or brain.

ventriloquist NOUN an entertainer who can make their voice seem to come from elsewhere.

ventriloquism NOUN

venture NOUN a risky undertaking. VERB dare to do something risky; dare to say something bold.

venue NOUN an appointed place for a meeting, concert, etc.

veracious ADJ truthful.

veracity NOUN

veranda NOUN a roofed terrace.

verb NOUN a word indicating an action or occurrence.

verbal ADJ 1 of or in words; spoken. 2 of a verb.
verbally ADV

verbatim ADV & ADJ in exactly the same words.

verbiage NOUN excessively long or detailed speech or writing.

verbose ADJ using more words than are needed.

verdant ADJ (of grass etc.) green.

verdict NOUN a decision reached by a jury; a decision or opinion reached after testing something.

verdure NOUN green vegetation.

verge NOUN the extreme edge or brink; a grass edging of a road etc. VERB (**verge on**) come close to being.

verger NOUN a church caretaker.

verify VERB (**verified, verifying**) check the truth or correctness of.
verification NOUN

verisimilitude NOUN the appearance of being true.

veritable ADJ genuine.

vermicelli NOUN pasta made in slender threads.

vermilion ADJ & NOUN bright red.

vermin NOUN (PL **vermin**) an animal or insect regarded as a pest.

vermouth NOUN a red or white wine flavoured with herbs.

vernacular NOUN the ordinary language of a country or district.

vernal ADJ of or occurring in spring.

verruca NOUN an infectious wart on the foot.

versatile ADJ able to do or be used for many different things.
versatility NOUN

verse NOUN poetry; a group of lines forming a unit in a poem or hymn; a numbered division of a Bible chapter.

versed ADJ (**versed in**) skilled or experienced in.

version NOUN a particular form of something, differing from others; an account of events from a particular viewpoint.

verso NOUN (PL **versos**) the

left-hand page of an open book; the back of a loose document.

versus PREP against.

vertebra NOUN (PL **-brae**) any of the small bones forming the backbone.

vertebrate NOUN an animal having a backbone.

vertical ADJ perpendicular to a horizontal line or surface. NOUN a vertical line or surface.

vertically ADV

vertigo NOUN dizziness caused by looking down from a height.

verve NOUN enthusiasm and vigour.

very ADV to a high degree. ADJ **1** actual or precise: *this very moment.* **2** mere: *the very thought.*

vessel NOUN **1** a ship or boat. **2** a tube-like structure conveying fluid in the body, or in a plant. **3** a container for liquids.

vest NOUN an undergarment worn on the upper part of the body. VERB give power or property to.

vested interest a personal reason for wanting something to happen.

vestibule NOUN an entrance hall; a porch.

vestige NOUN a small amount or trace.

vestigial ADJ

vestment NOUN a ceremonial garment worn by clergy or members of a church choir.

vestry NOUN (PL **-ies**) a room in a church, used for changing into ceremonial robes.

vet NOUN **1** a veterinary surgeon. **2** [US] a military veteran. VERB (**vetted, vetting**) examine critically for faults etc.

veteran NOUN a person with long experience, especially in the armed forces.

veterinary ADJ of or for the treatment of diseases and injuries of animals.

veterinary surgeon a person qualified to treat diseased or injured animals.

veto NOUN (PL **-oes**) an authoritative rejection of something proposed; the right to make this. VERB (**vetoed, vetoing**) reject by a veto.

vex VERB annoy.

vexed question a problem

that is much discussed.
vexation NOUN
VHF ABBREV very high frequency.
via PREP by way of; through.
viable ADJ capable of working successfully, or of living or surviving.
viability NOUN
viaduct NOUN a long bridge carrying a road or railway over a valley.
vial NOUN a small bottle.
vibrant ADJ full of energy and enthusiasm; resonant; bright.
vibrate VERB move rapidly and continuously to and fro; (of a sound) resonate.
vibration NOUN
vibrator NOUN
vibrato NOUN (in music) a rapid slight fluctuation in the pitch of a note.
vicar NOUN a member of the clergy in charge of a parish.
vicarage NOUN a vicar's house.
vicarious ADJ experienced in the imagination rather than directly.
vice NOUN 1 wicked or immoral behaviour; criminal activities involving sex or drugs; a

bad habit. 2 ([US] **vise**) a tool with two jaws for holding things firmly.
vice- COMBINING FORM next in rank to.
viceroy NOUN a person governing a colony etc. as the sovereign's representative.
vice versa ADV reversing the order of the items just mentioned.
vicinity NOUN (PL **-ies**) the surrounding district.
vicious ADJ cruel or violent; (of an animal) wild and dangerous.
vicious circle a bad situation producing effects that intensify its original cause.
victim NOUN a person injured or killed or made to suffer.
victimize (or **-ise**) VERB single out for cruel or unfair treatment.
victimization NOUN
victor NOUN a winner.
victorious ADJ having won a victory.
victory NOUN (PL **-ies**) an act of defeating an opponent.
video NOUN (PL **-os**) a recording or broadcasting of pictures; an apparatus

for this; a videotape. VERB (**videoed, videoing**) make a video of.

video game a computer game played on a television screen.

videotape NOUN magnetic tape for recording visual images and sound; a cassette holding this. VERB record on videotape.

vie VERB (**vied, vying**) compete eagerly for something.

view NOUN **1** the ability to see something or to be seen from a particular place; what can be seen from a particular place, especially natural scenery. **2** an attitude or opinion. VERB **1** look at or inspect. **2** regard in a particular way.

viewer NOUN

viewfinder NOUN a device on a camera showing the extent of the area being photographed.

viewpoint NOUN **1** a point of view. **2** a place from which there is a good view.

vigil NOUN a period of staying awake to keep watch or pray.

vigilant ADJ watchful.

vigilance NOUN

vigilante NOUN a member of a self-appointed group trying to prevent crime etc.

vignette NOUN a brief vivid description.

vigour ([US] **vigor**) NOUN physical or mental strength; forcefulness.

vigorous ADJ

Viking NOUN an ancient Scandinavian trader and pirate.

vile ADJ extremely unpleasant or wicked.

vilify VERB (**vilified, vilifying**) speak or write about in an unjust and unpleasant way.

vilification NOUN

villa NOUN a house in a residential district; a rented holiday home.

village NOUN a community of houses and other buildings in a rural area.

villager NOUN

villain NOUN a wicked person.

villainous ADJ

villainy NOUN

villein NOUN [historical] a feudal tenant subject to a lord.

vinaigrette NOUN a salad dressing of oil and

vinegar.

vindicate VERB clear of blame; justify.
vindication NOUN
vindictive ADJ showing a strong or excessive desire for vengeance.
vine NOUN a climbing plant on which grapes grow.
vinegar NOUN a sour liquid made from wine, cider, or beer, used for pickling etc.
vinegary ADJ
vineyard NOUN a plantation of vines for winemaking.
vintage NOUN the year in which a wine was produced; wine of high quality from a particular year; the date of something's origin. ADJ of high quality, especially from a past period.
vintner NOUN a wine merchant.
vinyl NOUN a kind of strong plastic.
viola NOUN an instrument like a violin but of lower pitch.
violate VERB break a rule, promise, etc.; treat with disrespect; rape.
violation NOUN
violent ADJ involving great force or intensity; using excessive physical force.
violence NOUN
violet NOUN a small plant with purple or blue flowers; a bluish-purple colour.
violin NOUN a musical instrument with four strings of treble pitch, played with a bow.
violinist NOUN
violoncello NOUN (PL -cellos) a cello.
VIP ABBREV very important person.
viper NOUN a poisonous snake.
viral ADJ of a virus.
virgin NOUN a person who has never had sex; (**the Virgin**) the Virgin Mary, mother of Jesus. ADJ **1** never having had sex. **2** not yet used.
virginal ADJ
virginity NOUN
virile ADJ (of a man) having strength and a strong sex drive.
virility NOUN
virtual ADJ almost existing or being as described, but not strictly or officially so.
virtual reality a computer-generated simulation of reality.
virtually ADV

virtue NOUN behaviour showing high moral standards; a good or useful quality; [dated] chastity.
virtuous ADJ
virtuoso NOUN (PL **-osos** or **-osi**) an expert performer.
virtuosity NOUN
virulent ADJ (of poison or disease) extremely strong or violent; bitterly hostile.
virulence NOUN
virulently ADV
virus NOUN 1 a minute organism capable of causing disease. 2 a destructive code hidden in a computer program.
visa NOUN an official mark on a passport, permitting the holder to enter a specified country.
visage NOUN [literary] a person's face.
vis-à-vis PREP in relation to.
viscera PLURAL NOUN the internal organs of the body.
visceral ADJ
viscose NOUN a fabric made from cellulose.
viscount NOUN a nobleman ranking between earl and baron.
viscountess NOUN a woman holding the rank of viscount; a viscount's wife or widow.
viscous ADJ thick and sticky.
viscosity NOUN
vise US spelling of **vice** (2).
visibility NOUN the state of being visible; the distance you can see under certain weather conditions etc.
visible ADJ able to be seen or noticed.
visibly ADV
vision NOUN 1 the ability to see; inspired and idealistic ideas about the future. 2 a dream or apparition; an extraordinarily beautiful person.
visionary ADJ idealistic; imaginative. NOUN (PL **-ies**) a visionary person.
visit VERB 1 go or come to see; stay temporarily with or at. 2 inflict harm on someone. NOUN an act of visiting.
visitor NOUN
visitation NOUN 1 an official visit or inspection. 2 trouble regarded as divine punishment.
visor (or **vizor**) NOUN a movable front part of a helmet, covering the face; a screen for protecting the

eyes from light.

vista NOUN a pleasing view.

visual ADJ of or used in seeing.

visual display unit a device displaying information from a computer on a screen.

visually ADV

visualize (or **-ise**) VERB form a mental picture of.

vital ADJ **1** essential for life; absolutely necessary. **2** full of energy.

vitally ADV

vitality NOUN liveliness and vigour.

vitamin NOUN an organic compound present in food and essential for growth and nutrition.

vitiate VERB make imperfect or ineffective.

vitriol NOUN savagely hostile remarks.

vitriolic ADJ

viva EXCLAMATION long live!

vivacious ADJ lively and high-spirited.

vivacity NOUN

vivid ADJ bright or intense; clear; (of imagination) lively.

viviparous ADJ giving birth to live young.

vivisection NOUN performance of experiments on living animals.

vixen NOUN a female fox.

vizor see **visor**.

vocabulary NOUN (PL **-ies**) the words known by a person, or used in a particular language or activity; a list of words and their meanings.

vocal ADJ **1** of or for the voice. **2** expressing opinions freely or loudly. NOUN a piece of sung music.

vocally ADV

vocalist NOUN a singer.

vocalize (or **-ise**) VERB utter.

vocation NOUN a strong desire to pursue a particular career or occupation; a career or occupation.

vocational ADJ

vociferous ADJ vehement or loud.

vodka NOUN a clear Russian alcoholic spirit.

vogue NOUN the current fashion or style.

voice NOUN sounds formed in the larynx and uttered by the mouth; the ability to speak or sing. VERB express in words.

voicemail NOUN an

electronic system which can store messages from telephone callers.

void ADJ **1** empty. **2** not valid. NOUN an empty space. VERB make void; excrete.

voile NOUN a thin, semi-transparent fabric.

volatile ADJ **1** evaporating rapidly. **2** liable to change quickly and unpredictably.
volatility NOUN

vol-au-vent NOUN a small puff pastry case filled with a savoury mixture.

volcano NOUN (PL **-oes**) a mountain with a vent through which lava is forced.
volcanic ADJ

vole NOUN a small rodent.

volition NOUN the exercise of a person's will.

volley NOUN (PL **-eys**) **1** a number of missiles etc. fired at one time; a rapid series of questions, insults, etc. **2** a return of the ball in tennis etc. before it touches the ground. VERB send in a volley.

volleyball NOUN a game for two teams in which a ball is hit by hand over a net.

volt NOUN a unit of electromotive force.

voltage NOUN electromotive force expressed in volts.

volte-face NOUN a complete change of attitude or policy.

voluble ADJ talking easily and at length.

volume NOUN **1** a book. **2** the amount of space held or occupied by a container or object; the amount or quantity of something. **3** the loudness of a sound.

voluminous ADJ (of clothing) loose and full.

voluntary ADJ done, given, or acting by choice; working or done without payment.
voluntarily ADV

volunteer NOUN a person who offers to do something; a person who works for no pay; a person who freely joins the armed forces. VERB offer without being asked.

voluptuous ADJ **1** full of or fond of sensual pleasure. **2** (of a woman) having a full attractive figure.

vomit VERB (**vomited, vomiting**) eject matter

from the stomach through the mouth; emit in vast quantities. NOUN vomited matter.

voodoo NOUN a form of religion based on witchcraft.

voracious ADJ ravenous, greedy, or insatiable. **voracity** NOUN

vortex NOUN (PL **-texes** or **-tices**) a whirlpool or whirlwind.

vote NOUN a formal choice between two or more candidates or courses of action; the right to participate in an election. VERB give or register a vote.

vouch VERB (**vouch for**) guarantee the accuracy or reliability of.

voucher NOUN a document exchangeable for certain goods or services; a receipt.

vouchsafe VERB give or grant.

vow NOUN & VERB (make) a solemn promise.

vowel NOUN a letter or the alphabet representing a speech sound made without audible stopping of the breath, e.g. *a* or *e*.

voyage NOUN a journey by water or in space. VERB make a voyage.

voyeur NOUN a person who gets sexual pleasure from watching others having sex or undressing.

vs. ABBREV versus.

vulcanize (or **-ise**) VERB strengthen rubber by treating it with sulphur.

vulgar ADJ **1** referring inappropriately to sex or bodily functions. **2** lacking refinement or good taste.

vulgar fraction a fraction shown by numbers above and below a line, not decimally. **vulgarity** NOUN

vulnerable ADJ able to be hurt or injured. **vulnerability** NOUN

vulture NOUN a large bird of prey that feeds on dead animals.

vulva NOUN the female external genitals.

vying present participle of **vie**.

Ww

W ABBREV **1** west; western. **2** watts.

wacky ADJ (**-ier, -iest**) [inf] mad or eccentric.

wad NOUN **1** a pad of soft material. **2** a bundle of papers or banknotes. VERB (**wadded, wadding**) compress into a pad.

waddle VERB walk with short swaying steps. NOUN a waddling gait.

wade VERB walk through water or mud; go slowly and laboriously through work etc.

wader NOUN **1** a long-legged waterbird. **2** (**waders**) high waterproof boots.

wafer NOUN a thin, light biscuit.

waffle NOUN **1** [inf] lengthy but vague or trivial talk or writing. **2** a small batter cake eaten hot with butter or syrup. VERB [inf] talk or write waffle.

waft VERB pass gently through the air.

wag VERB (**wagged, wagging**) move briskly to and fro. NOUN **1** a wagging movement. **2** [inf] a witty person.

wage NOUN (also **wages**) a fixed regular payment for work. VERB carry on a war.

wager NOUN & VERB (make) a bet.

waggle VERB wag.

wagon (or **waggon**) NOUN a four-wheeled vehicle for heavy loads; an open railway truck.

waif NOUN a poor, helpless person, especially a child.

wail VERB & NOUN (give) a long sad cry.

waist NOUN the part of the body between ribs and hips; a narrow middle part.

waistcoat NOUN a waist-length sleeveless garment.

waistline NOUN the outline or size of the waist.

wait VERB **1** stay where you are or delay acting until a specified time or event; be delayed or deferred. **2** act as a waiter or waitress. **3** (**wait on**) fetch and carry things for. NOUN an act or period of waiting.

waiter (or **waitress**) NOUN a person who serves customers in a restaurant etc.

waive VERB refrain from insisting on a right etc. **waiver** NOUN

wake[1] VERB (**woke** or **waked, woken** or **waked, waking**) 1 (also **wake up**) stop sleeping. 2 evoke. NOUN a vigil beside the body of a dead person; a party held after a funeral.

wake[2] NOUN a trail of disturbed water left by a ship.

in the wake of following.

waken VERB wake.

walk VERB 1 walk at a fairly slow pace using the legs; travel along a path etc. on foot; accompany on foot. 2 (**walk out**) depart suddenly and angrily. NOUN a journey on foot; a way of walking; a path for walking.

walking stick a stick used for support when walking.

walker NOUN

walkie-talkie NOUN a portable two-way radio.

walkout NOUN a sudden angry departure, especially as a strike.

walkover NOUN an easy victory.

wall NOUN a continuous upright structure forming one side of a building or room or enclosing an area of land; a barrier; something that divides or encloses. VERB surround or enclose with a wall.

wallaby NOUN (PL **-ies**) a marsupial like a small kangaroo.

wallet NOUN a small folding case for money, credit cards, etc.

wallflower NOUN a garden plant.

wallop [inf] VERB (**walloped, walloping**) hit hard. NOUN a heavy blow.

wallow VERB 1 roll in mud or water etc. 2 indulge in. NOUN an act of wallowing.

wallpaper NOUN decorative paper for covering a room's interior walls.

walnut NOUN an edible nut with a wrinkled shell.

walrus NOUN a large sea mammal with long tusks.

waltz NOUN a ballroom dance; the music for this. VERB dance a waltz; [inf] move in a casual, confident way.

wan ADJ pale and ill-looking.

wand NOUN a slender rod, especially used for casting magic spells.

wander VERB go from place to place casually or aimlessly; stray. NOUN wandering.

wanderlust NOUN a strong desire to travel.

wane VERB become weaker; (of the moon) appear to decrease in size.

wangle VERB [inf] obtain by trickery or scheming.

want VERB desire to have or do; lack. NOUN a desire; a lack or need.

wanted ADJ sought by the police.

wanting ADJ lacking or deficient.

wanton ADJ **1** deliberate or unprovoked. **2** sexually immoral.

war NOUN armed conflict, especially between countries; open hostility; a long contest or campaign. VERB (**warred, warring**) engage in war.

warble VERB sing with a gentle trilling note.

ward NOUN **1** a room for patients in a hospital. **2** an administrative division of a city or town. **3** a child under the care of a guardian or court.

ward off keep from being harmful.

warden NOUN an official with supervisory duties.

warder NOUN a prison officer.

wardrobe NOUN a large cupboard for hanging clothes in; a stock of clothes etc.

ware NOUN pottery of a specified type; (**wares**) articles for sale.

warehouse NOUN a building for storing goods or furniture.

warfare NOUN the fighting of a war.

warhead NOUN the explosive head of a missile.

warlike ADJ aggressive or hostile.

warlock NOUN a man who practises witchcraft.

warm ADJ **1** moderately hot; providing warmth. **2** affectionate, kind, or enthusiastic. VERB make or become warm.

warm-blooded having blood that remains at a constant temperature.

warmth NOUN

warmonger NOUN a person who tries to bring about war.

warn VERB inform about a possible danger or problem; advise not to do something; (**warn off**) order to keep away. **warning** NOUN

warp VERB make or become bent or twisted; distort or pervert. NOUN **1** a distortion in shape. **2** the lengthwise threads in a loom.

warrant NOUN a document giving legal authorization for an action; justification. VERB justify; guarantee.

warranty NOUN (PL **-ies**) a guarantee of repair or replacement of a purchased article.

warren NOUN a series of burrows where rabbits live.

warrior NOUN a person who fights in a battle.

wart NOUN a small, hard growth on the skin.

warthog NOUN an African wild pig with wart-like lumps on its face.

wary ADJ (**-ier, -iest**) cautious or suspicious. **warily** ADV **wariness** NOUN

wash VERB **1** clean with water and soap etc. **2** flow past, against, or over. **3** coat thinly with paint. NOUN **1** an act of washing; clothes etc. to be washed; a cleansing solution. **2** water disturbed by a moving ship. **3** a thin coating of paint. **wash up** wash dishes etc. after use.

washbasin NOUN a basin for washing your hands and face.

washed out ADJ pale and tired.

washer NOUN a small flat ring fixed between a nut and bolt.

washing NOUN clothes etc. to be washed or just washed.

washout NOUN [inf] a complete failure.

wasp NOUN a stinging insect with a black and yellow striped body.

waspish ADJ sharply irritable.

wassail [old use] NOUN revelry with a lot of drinking. VERB celebrate in this way; sing carols.

wastage NOUN an amount wasted; loss of employees by retirement or resignation.

waste VERB 1 use carelessly or extravagantly; fail to make use of. 2 become thinner and weaker. ADJ discarded because not wanted; (of land) unfit for use. NOUN 1 an instance of wasting; material that is not wanted. 2 a large expanse of barren land.

wasteful ADJ extravagant.

wastefully ADV

watch VERB look at attentively; observe; be cautious about; look out for; (**watch out**) be careful. NOUN 1 a small timepiece worn on your wrist. 2 an instance or spell of watching. 3 a shift worked by firefighters or police officers.

watchdog NOUN a dog kept to guard property; a guardian of people's rights etc.

watchful ADJ vigilant or alert.

watchman NOUN a man employed to guard an empty building.

watchtower NOUN a tower built as a high observation point.

watchword NOUN a word or phrase expressing a central aim or belief.

water NOUN 1 the liquid which forms the seas, lakes, rivers, and rain. 2 (**waters**) an area of sea controlled by a particular country. 3 a watery secretion. VERB 1 sprinkle water over; provide with water. 2 produce tears or saliva. 3 (**water down**) dilute; make less forceful.

water cannon a device ejecting a powerful jet of water to disperse a crowd.

water closet a toilet flushed by water.

watering can a container with a spout for watering plants. **water lily** a plant that grows in water, with large floating leaves.

water meadow a meadow periodically flooded by a stream. **water table** the level below which the ground is saturated with water.

watery ADJ

watercolour ([US] **watercolor**) NOUN artists' paint thinned with water; a picture painted with this.

watercourse NOUN a stream or artificial water channel.

watercress NOUN a kind of cress that grows in running water.

waterfall NOUN a stream that falls from a height.

waterfront NOUN part of a town alongside a river, lake, or sea.

waterhole NOUN a water-filled hollow where animals drink.

waterline NOUN the level normally reached by water on a ship's side.

waterlogged ADJ saturated with water.

watermark NOUN a faint translucent design in paper.

watermelon NOUN a melon with watery red pulp.

watermill NOUN a mill worked by a waterwheel.

waterproof ADJ unable to be penetrated by water. NOUN a waterproof garment. VERB make waterproof.

watershed NOUN a line of high land separating two river systems; a turning point.

waterskiing NOUN the sport of skimming over water on skis while towed by a motor boat.

waterspout NOUN a rotating column of water formed by a whirlwind over the sea.

watertight ADJ 1 not allowing any water to pass through. 2 impossible to disprove.

waterway NOUN a river, canal, or other navigable channel.

waterworks NOUN a place with machinery for supplying water to a district.

watt NOUN a unit of electric power.

wattage NOUN an amount of electric power expressed in watts.

wattle NOUN 1 interwoven sticks used as material for fences, walls, etc. 2 a fold of skin hanging from the neck of a turkey and some other birds.

wave NOUN 1 a moving ridge of water on the sea's surface. 2 an act of waving your hand. 3 a slight curl in hair. 4 a sudden increase in a phenomenon or emotion. 5 a wave-like motion by which heat, light, sound, or electricity is transmitted. VERB move your hand or arm to and fro as a greeting or signal; move to and fro or up and down.

waveband NOUN a range of wavelengths.

wavelength NOUN 1 the distance between successive crests of a wave of sound, light, radio, etc. 2 a person's way of thinking.

waver VERB be unsteady; be undecided.

wavy ADJ (**-ier, -iest**) having waves or curves.

wax NOUN a soft solid used for polishing, making candles, etc. VERB 1 coat or polish with wax. 2 (of the moon) appear to gradually increase in size; become stronger; [literary] speak or write in the specified way.

waxy ADJ

waxwork NOUN a lifelike dummy made of wax.

way NOUN 1 a method or manner of doing something; someone's characteristic manner. 2 a road or path; progress: *make your way.* 3 a direction. 4 a distance. 5 a respect or aspect.

in the way forming an obstacle. **make way** allow someone to pass.

wayfarer NOUN [literary] a traveller.

waylay VERB (**waylaid, waylaying**) lie in wait for.

wayside NOUN the edge of a road.

wayward ADJ self-willed and unpredictable.

WC ABBREV water closet.

we PRON used by a person referring to himself or herself and another or others; people in general.

weak ADJ lacking strength or energy; lacking power or influence; very diluted.

weaken VERB

weakling NOUN a weak person or animal.

weakness NOUN being weak; a fault; something you cannot resist.

weal NOUN a red swollen mark left on flesh by a blow or pressure.

wealth NOUN a large amount of money, property, etc.; the state of being rich; a large amount.

wealthy ADJ

wean VERB accustom a baby to food other than its mother's milk; cause to give up something gradually.

weapon NOUN a thing used to inflict harm or damage.

wear VERB (**wore, worn, wearing**) 1 have on the body as clothing or ornament. 2 damage by friction or use. 3 (**wear out**) exhaust. 4 (**wear off**) stop being effective or strong. NOUN 1 clothes of a particular type. 2 damage caused by friction or use.

wearisome ADJ causing weariness.

weary ADJ (**-ier, -iest**) very tired; tiring or tedious. VERB (**wearied, wearying**) make or become weary.
wearily ADV
weariness NOUN

weasel NOUN a small, slender carnivorous wild mammal.

weather NOUN the state of the atmosphere in terms of sunshine, rain, wind, etc. VERB 1 wear away or change by exposure to the weather. 2 come safely through.

weathervane (or **weathercock**) NOUN a revolving pointer to show the direction of the wind.

weave VERB (**wove, woven, weaving**) 1 make fabric by interlacing long threads with others. 2 compose a story etc. 3 move from side to side, especially to get round obstacles.

web NOUN 1 a network of fine strands made by a spider etc.; a complex system of interconnected elements. 2 (**the Web**) the World Wide Web. 3 skin between the toes of ducks, frogs, etc.

web page a document that can be accessed via the Internet.

webbed ADJ

website NOUN a collection of web pages with a common theme or source.

wed VERB (**wedded, wedding**) marry; unite or combine.

wedding NOUN a marriage ceremony.

wedge NOUN a piece of wood, metal, etc. with a thick end that tapers to a thin edge. VERB force apart or fix in position with a wedge; force into a narrow space.

wedlock NOUN the married state.

Wednesday NOUN the day after Tuesday.

wee ADJ [Scottish] little.

weed NOUN 1 a wild plant growing where it is not wanted. 2 a thin or weak person. VERB remove weeds from; (**weed out**) remove unwanted items. **weedy** ADJ

week NOUN a period of seven successive days; the five days from Monday to Friday.

weekday NOUN a day other than Sunday or Saturday.

weekend NOUN Saturday and Sunday.

weekly ADJ & ADV happening or produced once a week.

weep VERB (**wept, weeping**) shed tears; (of a sore etc.) exude liquid. NOUN a spell of weeping.

weepy ADJ (**-ier, -iest**) tearful.

weevil NOUN a small beetle.

weft NOUN the crosswise threads in weaving.

weigh VERB 1 find how heavy someone or something is; have a specified weight. 2 assess the nature or importance of; have influence. 3 (**weigh down**) be a burden to.

weight NOUN 1 the heaviness of a person or thing; a unit or system of units for expressing this; a piece of metal of known weight used in weighing; a heavy object or load. 2 influence. VERB 1 make heavier or hold down with a weight. 2 arrange so as to give one party an advantage.

weighting NOUN extra pay or allowances given in special cases.

weighty ADJ (**-ier, -iest**) heavy; serious, important, or influential.

weir NOUN a small dam built to regulate the flow of a river.

weird ADJ uncanny or bizarre.

welcome NOUN an instance or way of greeting someone; a pleased reaction. VERB greet in a polite or friendly way; be glad to receive. ADJ gladly received; much wanted or needed.

weld VERB unite pieces of metal by heating or pressure; unite into a whole. NOUN a welded joint.

welder NOUN

welfare NOUN well-being; organized help given to people in need.
welfare state a system under which the state provides pensions, health care, etc.
well¹ ADV (**better, best**) 1 in a good, appropriate, or advantageous way. 2 kindly or favourably. 3 thoroughly; extremely. 4 very probably; with good reason. ADJ in good health; satisfactory. EXCLAMATION used to express surprise, anger, resignation, etc.
well-being good health, happiness, and security.
well disposed having a sympathetic or friendly attitude. **well off** wealthy. **well read** having read much literature. **well spoken** having an educated and refined voice. **well-to-do** wealthy.
well² NOUN a shaft sunk into the ground to obtain water, oil, etc.; an enclosed shaft-like space. VERB (of liquid) rise to the surface.
wellington NOUN a knee-length waterproof boot.
Welsh ADJ & NOUN (the language) of Wales.
Welsh rabbit (or **rarebit**) melted cheese on toast.
welt NOUN 1 a leather rim to which the sole of a shoe is attached. 2 a weal.
welter NOUN a large disordered number of items.
welterweight NOUN a boxing weight between lightweight and middleweight.
wench NOUN [old use] a girl or young woman.
wend VERB (**wend your way**) go.
went past of **go**.
wept past and past participle of **weep**.
werewolf NOUN (in myths) a person who at times turns into a wolf.
west NOUN the direction in which the sun sets; the western part of a place. ADJ & ADV towards or facing the west; (of a wind) from the west.
westward ADJ & ADV
westwards ADV
westerly ADJ towards or facing the west; blowing from the west.
western ADJ of or in the west. NOUN a film or novel about cowboys in western

North America.

westerner NOUN a person from the west of a region.

westernize (or **-ise**) VERB bring under the influence of Europe and North America.

wet ADJ (**wetter, wettest**) soaked or covered with liquid; rainy; (of paint etc.) not yet dry. VERB (**wetted, wetting**) make wet. NOUN wet weather; wetness.

wet blanket someone who spoils other people's pleasure by being gloomy.

wet nurse a woman employed to breastfeed another's child.

wether NOUN a castrated ram.

wetsuit NOUN a close-fitting rubber garment worn by divers etc.

whack [inf] VERB strike forcefully. NOUN a sharp blow.

whale NOUN a very large sea mammal.

whalebone NOUN a hard substance growing in the upper jaw of some whales.

whaler NOUN a whaling ship; a sailor engaged in whaling.

whaling NOUN the hunting and killing of whales.

wharf NOUN (PL **wharfs** or **wharves**) a landing stage where ships load and unload.

what PRON & ADJ **1** asking for information about something. **2** used to emphasize something great or remarkable. PRON the thing that. ADV to what extent?

whatever (or **whatsoever**) PRON anything or everything that. ADJ of any kind or number.

wheat NOUN a cereal crop whose grain is ground to make flour.

wheedle VERB coax.

wheel NOUN a disc or circular frame that revolves on a shaft passing through its centre, used to move a vehicle, as part of a machine, etc.; a turn or rotation. VERB **1** push or pull a vehicle with wheels. **2** turn; move in circles or curves.

wheelbarrow NOUN a three-wheeled cart with two handles at the rear.

wheelbase NOUN the distance between a

vehicle's front and rear axles.

wheelchair NOUN a chair on wheels for a person who cannot walk.

wheeze VERB breathe with a hoarse whistling sound. NOUN this sound.
wheezy ADJ

whelk NOUN a shellfish with a spiral shell.

whelp NOUN a puppy. VERB give birth to puppies.

when ADV **1** at what time? on what occasion? **2** on the occasion on which. CONJ **1** at the time that; whenever; as soon as. **2** although.

whence ADV & CONJ [formal] from which or from where.

whenever CONJ & ADV at whatever time; every time that.

where ADV in or to which place? in what direction or respect? at, in, or to which; in or to a place or situation in which.

whereabouts ADV in or near what place? NOUN a person's or thing's approximate location.

whereas CONJ in contrast with the fact that.

whereby CONJ by which.

whereupon CONJ immediately after which.

wherever ADV & CONJ at or to whatever place.

wherewithal NOUN the money etc. needed for something.

whet VERB (**whetted, whetting**) sharpen a knife etc.; stimulate appetite or interest.

whether CONJ introducing a choice between alternatives.

whetstone NOUN a stone used for sharpening cutting tools.

whey NOUN the watery liquid left when milk forms curds.

which ADJ & PRON specifying a particular member or members of a set; introducing further information about something just referred to.

whichever ADJ & PRON no matter which.

whiff NOUN a puff of air or odour.

while CONJ **1** during the time that; at the same time as. **2** although; whereas. NOUN a period of time.

while away pass time in

an interesting way.

whilst CONJ while.

whim NOUN a sudden desire.

whimper VERB & NOUN (make) a feeble crying sound.

whimsical ADJ playfully fanciful; capricious.
whimsically ADV

whine NOUN a long, high complaining cry or similar shrill sound. VERB give or make a whine; complain peevishly.

whinge VERB [inf] complain peevishly.

whinny NOUN (PL **-ies**) a gentle neigh. VERB (**whinnied, whinnying**) neigh gently.

whip NOUN 1 a cord or strip of leather on a handle, used for striking a person or animal. 2 a dessert made from cream etc. beaten into a frothy mass. 3 an official maintaining discipline in a political party. VERB (**whipped, whipping**) 1 strike with a whip. 2 beat into a froth. 3 move or take out quickly.

whiplash NOUN injury caused by a jerk to the head.

whippet NOUN a small, slender breed of dog.

whirl VERB spin round and round; move with bewildering speed. NOUN a whirling movement; busy or confused activity.

whirlpool NOUN a current of water whirling in a circle.

whirlwind NOUN a mass of air whirling rapidly about a central point. ADJ very rapid.

whirr NOUN & VERB (make) a low, continuous regular sound.

whisk VERB 1 move or take out suddenly and quickly. 2 beat into a froth. NOUN 1 a utensil for beating eggs etc. 2 a bunch of twigs etc. for brushing or flicking things.

whisker NOUN a long stiff hair growing from the face of a cat etc.; (**whiskers**) hairs growing on a man's cheek.

whisky ([Irish & US] **whiskey**) NOUN a spirit distilled from malted grain.

whisper VERB speak very softly. NOUN a very soft tone; a whispered remark.

whist NOUN a card game

usually for two pairs of players.

whistle NOUN a shrill sound made by forcing breath between the lips or teeth; a similar sound; a device for producing this. VERB make such a sound; produce a tune in this way.

whistle-stop very fast and with only brief pauses.

Whit ADJ Whitsun.

Whit Sunday the seventh Sunday after Easter.

white ADJ 1 of the colour of milk or fresh snow; relating to people with light-coloured skin; very pale. 2 (of coffee or tea) with milk. NOUN 1 a white colour or thing; a white person. 2 the transparent substance round egg yolk; the pale part of the eyeball around the iris.

white-collar of work in an office. **white elephant** a useless possession. **white lie** a harmless lie told to avoid hurting someone's feelings. **white spirit** light petroleum used as paint thinner or solvent.

whiten VERB

whitebait NOUN very small fish used as food.

whitewash NOUN 1 a liquid containing lime or powdered chalk, used for painting walls white. 2 deliberate concealment of mistakes. VERB 1 paint with whitewash. 2 conceal mistakes.

whither ADV [old use] to what place.

whiting NOUN a small sea fish used as food.

Whitsun (or **Whitsuntide**) NOUN the weekend or week including Whit Sunday.

whittle VERB carve wood by cutting thin slices from it; gradually reduce.

whizz VERB (**whizzed**, **whizzing**) move quickly through the air with a hissing sound; move or go fast.

who PRON 1 what or which person or people? 2 introducing more information about someone just mentioned.

whodunnit ([US] **whodunit**) NOUN [inf] a detective story or play.

whoever PRON any or every person who.

whole ADJ complete or entire; in one piece. NOUN the full amount; a complete system made up of parts.

on the whole considering everything; in general.

wholefood NOUN food which has not been unnecessarily processed.

wholehearted ADJ without doubts or reservations.

wholeheartedly ADV

wholemeal ADJ made from whole grains of wheat including the husk.

wholesale NOUN the selling of goods in large quantities to be sold to the public by others. ADJ & ADV **1** being sold in such a way. **2** on a large scale.

wholesaler NOUN

wholesome ADJ good for health or well-being.

wholly ADV entirely or fully.

whom PRON used instead of *who* as the object of a verb or preposition.

whoop VERB & NOUN (make) a loud cry of excitement.

whooping cough an infectious disease marked by violent convulsive coughs.

whopper NOUN [inf] something very large; a blatant lie.

whore NOUN a prostitute.

whorl NOUN each of the turns of a spiral or coil; a spiral or coil; a ring of leaves or petals.

whose PRON & ADJ belonging to whom or to which.

why ADV for what reason or purpose; on account of which. EXCLAMATION expressing surprise, annoyance, etc.

wick NOUN a length of thread in a candle or lamp etc. which carries liquid fuel to the flame.

wicked ADJ **1** morally bad; evil or sinful. **2** playfully mischievous.

wickedness NOUN

wicker NOUN twigs interwoven to make furniture, baskets, etc.

wickerwork NOUN

wicket NOUN a set of three stumps with two bails across the top, used in cricket; a small door or gate.

wide ADJ **1** of great width; having a particular width. **2** including a variety of people or things. **3** far from the target. ADV to the full extent; far from the target.

widen VERB

widespread ADJ found or distributed over a wide area.

widow NOUN a woman whose husband has died and who has not remarried.

widowed ADJ made a widow or widower.

widower NOUN a man whose wife has died and who has not remarried.

width NOUN the extent of something from side to side; wide range or extent.

wield VERB hold and use a tool etc.; have and use power.

wife NOUN (PL **wives**) the woman a man is married to.

wig NOUN a covering of hair worn on the head.

wiggle VERB move repeatedly from side to side. NOUN an act of wiggling.
wiggly ADJ

wigwam NOUN a conical tent formerly lived in by some North American Indian peoples.

wild ADJ **1** not domesticated or tame; not cultivated or inhabited. **2** uncontrolled; [inf] very enthusiastic; [inf] very angry. **3** random: *a wild guess.* NOUN (**the wilds**) desolate places.

wild goose chase a useless search.

wildcat ADJ (of a strike) sudden and unofficial.

wildebeest NOUN a gnu (a kind of antelope).

wilderness NOUN an uncultivated, uninhabited area.

wildfire NOUN (**spread like wildfire**) spread very fast.

wildfowl PLURAL NOUN birds hunted as game.

wildlife NOUN wild animals and plants.

wiles PLURAL NOUN cunning plans.

wilful ([US] **willful**) ADJ **1** deliberate. **2** stubbornly self-willed.
wilfully ADV

will¹ AUXILIARY VERB used with *I* and *we* to express promises or obligations, and with other words to express a future tense.

will² NOUN **1** your power to decide on something and take action; a desire or intention. **2** (also **will power**) determination used to achieve something. **3** a legal document with instructions for the disposal of someone's property after their death. VERB **1** exercise your will; influence by doing this. **2** bequeath in a will. **at will** whenever you like.

willing ADJ ready to do what is asked; given or done readily.

willingly ADV

willingness NOUN

will-o'-the-wisp NOUN **1** a faint flickering light seen on marshy ground. **2** a hope or aim that can never be fulfilled.

willow NOUN a tree with flexible branches and narrow leaves.

willowy ADJ tall and slim.

willy-nilly ADV whether you like it or not.

wilt VERB droop through heat or lack of water; feel tired and weak.

wily ADJ cunning.

wimp NOUN [inf] a feeble or timid person.

win VERB (**won, winning**) **1** defeat an opponent in a contest; gain as the result of a contest etc., or by effort. **2** (**win over**) gain someone's agreement. NOUN a victory in a game or contest.

winner NOUN

wince VERB & NOUN (make) a slight movement from pain or embarrassment etc.

winch NOUN a hauling or lifting device consisting of a cable winding round a rotating drum. VERB hoist or haul with a winch.

wind[1] NOUN **1** a natural current of air; breath as needed for exertion. **2** gas in the stomach or intestines. **3** an orchestra's wind instruments. VERB cause to be out of breath.

wind instrument a musical instrument played by blowing a current of air into it.

wind[2] VERB (**wound, winding**) move in a twisting or spiral course; wrap something repeatedly around something else or round on itself; operate by turning a key, handle, etc. **wind up** bring or come to an end.

windbag NOUN [inf] a person who talks too much.

windbreak NOUN a screen giving shelter from the

wind.

windfall NOUN **1** fruit blown off a tree by the wind. **2** an unexpected financial gain.

windmill NOUN a building with projecting sails or vanes that turn in the wind and produce energy for grinding corn etc.

window NOUN **1** an opening in a wall, filled with glass to let in light. **2** a framed area on a computer screen for viewing information.

window-shop spend time looking at goods in shop windows.

windpipe NOUN the tube carrying air down the throat to the lungs.

windscreen ([US] **windshield**) NOUN the glass screen at the front of a vehicle.

windsock NOUN a canvas cylinder flown at an airfield to show the direction of the wind.

windsurfing NOUN the sport of surfing on a board to which a sail is fixed.

windswept ADJ exposed to strong winds.

windward ADJ & ADV (on the side) facing the wind.

wine NOUN an alcoholic drink made from fermented grape juice.

wing NOUN **1** a kind of limb used by a bird, bat, or insect for flying; a projection on both sides of an aircraft, supporting it in the air. **2** a part of a large building; the bodywork above the wheel of a car; (**wings**) the sides of a theatre stage. **3** the part of a football or rugby field close to the sidelines; a group or faction within an organization. VERB **1** fly; move very quickly. **2** wound in the wing or arm.

winged ADJ

winger NOUN an attacking player on the wing in football etc.

wingspan NOUN the measurement across wings from one tip to the other.

wink VERB rapidly close and open one eye as a signal; shine intermittently. NOUN an act of winking.

winkle NOUN an edible sea snail.

winkle out extract or prise

out.

winning ADJ charming. PLURAL NOUN (**winnings**) money won by gambling etc.

winnow VERB fan or toss grain to free it of chaff.

winsome ADJ appealing.

winter NOUN the coldest season of the year. VERB spend the winter in a particular place.

wintry ADJ

wipe VERB 1 rub a surface to clean or dry it; remove dirt etc. in this way. 2 (**wipe out**) destroy completely. NOUN an act of wiping; a piece of material for wiping.

wiper NOUN

wire NOUN a strand of metal; a length of this used for fencing, conducting electric current, etc. VERB 1 install electric wires in. 2 fasten or strengthen with wire.

wireless NOUN [dated] a radio.

wiring NOUN a system of electric wires in a building, vehicle, etc.

wiry ADJ like wire; thin but strong.

wisdom NOUN the quality of being wise; knowledge and experience.

wisdom tooth a molar tooth at the back of the mouth, usually appearing at about the age of 20.

wise ADJ having or showing experience, knowledge, and good judgement.

wisecrack [inf] NOUN & VERB (make) a witty remark.

wish NOUN a desire or hope; a thing desired or hoped for; (**wishes**) expressions of friendly feeling. VERB feel a desire; desire or express a desire for something to happen to someone.

wishbone NOUN a forked bone between a bird's neck and breast.

wishful thinking NOUN over-optimistic expectations.

wishy-washy ADJ feeble or bland.

wisp NOUN a small, thin bunch or strand.

wispy ADJ

wisteria NOUN a climbing shrub with fragrant bluish-lilac flowers.

wistful ADJ full of sad or vague longing.

wistfully ADV

wit NOUN amusing

witch

ingenuity in expressing words or ideas; a person who has this; intelligence. **at your wits' end** worried and not knowing what to do.

witch NOUN a woman who practises witchcraft. **witch doctor** a person believed to have magic powers that cure illness. **witch hazel** a shrub used to make an astringent lotion. **witch-hunt** a campaign against a person who holds unpopular views.

witchcraft NOUN the use of magic powers.

with PREP 1 accompanied by; in the same direction as. 2 having. 3 using. 4 in relation to. 5 indicating opposition or separation. 6 affected by.

withdraw VERB (**withdrew, withdrawn, withdrawing**) 1 remove or take away; take money from a bank account; take back a statement etc. 2 go away from a place. **withdrawal** NOUN

withdrawn ADJ very shy or reserved.

wither VERB 1 become dry and shrivelled. 2 decline.

withering ADJ scornful.

withhold VERB (**withheld, withholding**) refuse to give; suppress a reaction etc.

within PREP inside; not beyond the limit or scope of; in a time no longer than. ADV inside.

without PREP not having; in the absence of; not doing a specified action.

withstand VERB (**withstood, withstanding**) endure successfully.

witless ADJ stupid.

witness NOUN a person who sees or hears something; a person who gives evidence in a law court; a person who watches the signing of a document and signs to confirm this. VERB be a witness of.

witticism NOUN a witty remark.

witty ADJ (**-ier, -iest**) clever, inventive, and funny. **wittily** ADV

wives plural of **wife**.

wizard NOUN a man with magical powers; a person with great skill in a particular field. **wizardry** NOUN

wizened ADJ shrivelled or

wooded

wrinkled with age.

woad NOUN a plant whose leaves were formerly used to make blue dye.

wobble VERB stand or move unsteadily; (of the voice) quiver. NOUN a wobbling movement or sound.
wobbly ADJ

woe NOUN sorrow or distress; (**woes**) troubles.
woeful ADJ

woebegone ADJ looking unhappy.

wok NOUN a large bowl-shaped frying pan used in Chinese cookery.

woke, woken past and past participle of **wake**.

wold NOUN an area of high, open country.

wolf NOUN (PL **wolves**) a wild animal of the dog family. VERB eat quickly and greedily.
cry wolf raise false alarms.
wolfish ADJ

woman NOUN (PL **women**) an adult female person.
womanhood NOUN
womanly ADJ

womanize (or **-ise**) VERB (of a man) have many casual affairs with women.
womanizer NOUN

womankind NOUN women in general.

womb NOUN the organ in female mammals in which the young develop before birth.

wombat NOUN a burrowing Australian marsupial like a small bear.

women plural of **woman**.

won past and past participle of **win**.

wonder NOUN a feeling of surprise and admiration; a person or thing that evokes this. VERB **1** feel curiosity. **2** feel surprise and admiration.

wonderful ADJ extremely good or remarkable.
wonderfully ADV

wont [formal] ADJ accustomed to do something. NOUN your usual behaviour.

woo VERB seek to marry; seek the favour of.

wood NOUN **1** the tough fibrous substance of a tree. **2** (also **woods**) a small forest.
woody ADJ

woodcut NOUN a print made from a design cut in wood.

wooded ADJ covered with trees.

wooden ADJ 1 made of wood. 2 showing no emotion.

woodland NOUN wooded country.

woodlouse NOUN (PL **-lice**) a small insect-like creature with a grey segmented body.

woodpecker NOUN a bird that taps tree trunks with its beak to find insects.

woodwind NOUN wind instruments other than brass instruments.

woodwork NOUN the art or practice of making things from wood; wooden parts of a room.

woodworm NOUN the larva of a kind of beetle that bores into wood.

woof NOUN a dog's gruff bark. VERB bark.

wool NOUN the soft hair forming the coat of a sheep or goat; yarn or fabric made from this.

woollen ([US] **woolen**) ADJ made of wool. PLURAL NOUN (**woollens**) woollen garments.

woolly ADJ (**-ier, -iest**) 1 covered with wool; made of or like wool. 2 vague or confused. NOUN (PL **-ies**) [inf] a woollen garment.

word NOUN a unit of language which has meaning and is used with others to form sentences; a remark; news or a message; a promise; a command. VERB express in a particular style.

word processor a computer or program for producing and storing text.

wording NOUN the way something is worded.

wordy ADJ using too many words.

wore past of **wear**.

work NOUN 1 activity involving mental or physical effort; such activity as a means of earning money; a task to be done. 2 a thing or things done or made. 3 (**works**) a factory; the mechanism of a clock or other machine. VERB 1 do work as your job. 2 function properly; operate a machine etc. 3 have the desired result; bring about or accomplish. 4 shape or produce.

work-to-rule a refusal to do extra work or overtime

as a form of protest.

workaday ADJ ordinary.

worker NOUN a person who works; a neuter bee or ant etc. that does the basic work of the hive or colony.

workhouse NOUN a former public institution where poor people were housed in return for work.

working ADJ 1 having paid employment; doing manual work. 2 used as a basis for work or discussion. NOUN 1 a mine or part of a mine. 2 (**workings**) the way in which a system operates.

working class the social group consisting largely of people who do manual or industrial work.

workman NOUN a man employed to do manual work.

workmanlike ADJ efficient; practical.

workmanship NOUN the skill with which a product is made.

workout NOUN a session of physical exercise.

workshop NOUN 1 a room or building in which things are made or repaired. 2 a meeting for discussion or practice of a particular subject or activity.

workstation NOUN a desktop computer that is part of a network.

worktop NOUN a flat surface for working on in a kitchen.

world NOUN 1 the earth with all its countries and peoples. 2 all that belongs to a particular region, period, or area of activity. **World Wide Web** a system of linked and cross-referenced documents for accessing information on the Internet.

worldly ADJ of or concerned with material rather than spiritual things; sophisticated.

worldwide ADJ throughout the world.

worm NOUN a creature with a long soft body and no backbone or limbs; (**worms**) internal parasites. VERB 1 move by crawling or wriggling; insinuate yourself; obtain by clever persistence. 2 rid an animal of parasitic worms.

wormwood NOUN a plant with a bitter flavour.

worn past participle of **wear**. ADJ thin or damaged as a result of wear.
worn out exhausted; damaged by use.
worry VERB (**worried, worrying**) 1 feel or cause to feel anxious; annoy or disturb. 2 (of a dog) repeatedly push at and bite something. NOUN (PL **-ies**) anxiety or unease; a source of anxiety.
worse ADJ & ADV less good or well. NOUN something worse.
worsen VERB
worship NOUN reverence and respect paid to a god; adoration of or devotion to a person or thing. VERB (**worshipped, worshipping**; [US] **worshiped, worshiping**) honour as a god; take part in an act of worship; idolize.
worshipper NOUN
worst ADJ & ADV most bad or badly. NOUN the worst part, feature, event, etc.
worth ADJ having a specified value; deserving to be treated in a particular way. NOUN value or merit; the amount that a specified sum will buy.

worthless ADJ
worthwhile ADJ worth the time or effort spent.
worthy ADJ (**-ier, -iest**) having great merit; deserving. NOUN (PL **-ies**) a worthy or important person.
would AUXILIARY VERB used in senses corresponding to **will**[1] in the past tense, conditional statements, questions, polite requests and statements, and to express probability.
wound[1] NOUN an injury to the body caused by a cut, blow, etc.; injury to feelings. VERB inflict a wound on.
wound[2] past & past participle of **wind**[2].
wove, woven past and past participle of **weave**.
wow [inf] EXCLAMATION expressing astonishment.
WPC ABBREV woman police constable.
wrack NOUN seaweed. VERB see **rack**.
wraith NOUN a ghost.
wrangle NOUN a long dispute or argument. VERB engage in a wrangle.
wrap VERB (**wrapped, wrapping**) enclose in paper or soft material;

encircle or wind round.
NOUN a shawl.
wrapped up in absorbed
by.
wrapper NOUN
wrapping NOUN
wrath NOUN anger.
wrathful ADJ
wreak VERB cause damage;
exact revenge.
wreath NOUN a decorative
ring of flowers or leaves.
wreathe VERB encircle;
twist into a wreath; wind
or curve.
wreck NOUN the
destruction of a ship at
sea; a ship that has
suffered this; something
destroyed or dilapidated;
a person in a very bad
state. VERB cause a ship to
sink; destroy or ruin.
wreckage NOUN the
remains of something
wrecked.
Wren NOUN (in the UK) a
member of the former
Women's Royal Naval
Service.
wren NOUN a very small
bird.
wrench VERB twist or pull
violently round; damage
or injure by twisting. NOUN
1 a violent twist or pull.
2 an adjustable spanner-
like tool.
wrest VERB wrench away;
obtain by force or effort.
wrestle VERB fight
(especially as a sport) by
grappling with and trying
to throw down an
opponent; struggle with a
task or problem.
wrestler NOUN
wretch NOUN an
unfortunate person; a
despicable person.
wretched ADJ **1** very
unhappy. **2** of poor
quality. **3** infuriating.
wriggle VERB **1** move with
short twisting
movements. **2** (**wriggle
out of**) avoid doing. NOUN
a wriggling movement.
wring VERB (**wrung,
wringing**) twist and
squeeze, especially to
remove liquid; squeeze
someone's hand firmly or
forcibly; obtain with
effort or difficulty.
wrinkle NOUN a small line
or fold, especially in
fabric or a person's skin.
VERB make or cause
wrinkles on.
wrinkly ADJ
wrist NOUN the joint
connecting the hand and
forearm.

writ NOUN a formal command issued by a court etc.

write VERB (**wrote, written, writing**) make letters or other symbols on a surface with a pen, pencil, etc.; compose a text or musical work; write and send a letter to someone; write the necessary details on a cheque etc.

write-off a vehicle too damaged to be worth repairing. **write-up** a newspaper review.

writer NOUN

writhe VERB twist or squirm in pain or embarrassment.

writing NOUN handwriting; literary works.

wrong ADJ **1** not true or correct; mistaken. **2** unjust, dishonest, or immoral. **3** unsuitable or undesirable. ADV **1** mistakenly or incorrectly. **2** unjustly. NOUN an immoral or unjust action. VERB treat unjustly.

wrongly ADV

wrongdoing NOUN illegal or dishonest behaviour.

wrongdoer NOUN

wrongful ADJ not fair, just, or legal.

wrongfully ADV

wrote past of **write**.

wrought ADJ (of metals) shaped by hammering.

wrought iron tough iron suitable for forging or rolling.

wrung past and past participle of **wring**.

wry ADJ (**wryer, wryest** or **wrier, wriest**) **1** (of humour) dry or mocking. **2** (of the face) contorted in disgust or disappointment.

WWW ABBREV World Wide Web.

Xx

X NOUN (as a Roman numeral) ten.
X-ray a photograph made by using electromagnetic radiation (**X-rays**) that can penetrate solids.
xenon NOUN a gaseous element, present in air.
xenophobia NOUN a strong dislike or fear of foreigners.

Xerox NOUN [trademark] a machine for producing photocopies; a photocopy. VERB (**xerox**) photocopy.
Xmas NOUN [inf] Christmas.
xylophone NOUN a musical instrument with flat wooden bars struck with small hammers.

Yy

yacht NOUN a medium-sized sailing boat; a powered boat equipped for cruising.
yachting NOUN
yak NOUN a long-haired Asian ox.
yam NOUN the edible tuber of a tropical plant.
yang NOUN (in Chinese philosophy) the active male force in the universe.
yank [inf] VERB pull sharply. NOUN **1** a sharp pull.

2 (**Yank**) an American.
yap NOUN a shrill bark. VERB (**yapped, yapping**) bark shrilly.
yard NOUN **1** a unit of length equal to 3 feet (0.9144 metre). **2** a piece of enclosed ground next to a building. **3** a pole slung from a mast to support a sail.
yardstick NOUN a standard of comparison.
yarmulke (or **yarmulka**) NOUN a skullcap worn by

Jewish men.

yarn NOUN **1** any spun thread. **2** [inf] a story.

yashmak NOUN a veil worn by Muslim women in certain countries.

yawn VERB involuntarily open your mouth wide and draw in breath, usually when tired or bored; have a wide opening. NOUN an act of yawning.

yd ABBREV yard.

year NOUN the period of 365 days (or 366 in leap years) from 1 Jan. to 31 Dec; any consecutive period of twelve months; the time taken by the earth to go round the sun.

yearling NOUN an animal between one and two years old.

yearly ADJ & ADV happening or produced once a year or every year.

yearn VERB feel great longing.

yeast NOUN a fungus used to cause fermentation in making beer and wine and as a raising agent in making bread.

yell NOUN & VERB (give) a shout or scream.

yellow ADJ **1** of the colour of egg yolks or ripe lemons. **2** [inf] cowardly. NOUN a yellow colour. VERB turn yellow.
yellowish ADJ

yelp NOUN & VERB (make) a shrill bark or cry.

yen NOUN **1** (PL **yen**) the basic monetary unit in Japan. **2** [inf] a longing or yearning.

yeoman NOUN [historical] a man who owned and farmed a small estate.

yes EXCLAMATION & NOUN an affirmative reply; used as a response to someone who is addressing you.

yesterday ADV on the day before today. NOUN the day before today; the recent past.

yet ADV **1** up until now or then; this soon; from now into the future. **2** still; even. CONJ nevertheless.

yeti NOUN a large manlike animal said to live in the Himalayas.

yew NOUN an evergreen tree with dark needle-like leaves.

Y-fronts PLURAL NOUN [trademark] men's underpants with a Y-shaped seam at the front.

Yiddish NOUN the language used by Jews from eastern Europe.

yield VERB 1 produce or provide a natural or industrial product. 2 surrender; hand over to another; move or give way when pushed or pressed. NOUN an amount yielded or produced.

yin NOUN (in Chinese philosophy) the passive female presence in the universe.

yob NOUN [inf] a rude, aggressive young man.

yodel VERB (**yodelled, yodelling**; [US] **yodeled, yodeling**) sing with a quickly alternating change of pitch. NOUN a yodelling cry. **yodeller** NOUN

yoga NOUN a Hindu system of meditation and self-control; exercises used in this.

yogurt (or **yoghurt**) NOUN food made from milk that has been thickened by the action of bacteria.

yoke NOUN a wooden crosspiece fastened over the necks of two oxen pulling a plough etc.; a frame fitting over someone's shoulders and holding a load at each end; part of a garment fitting over the shoulders. VERB harness with a yoke; join or link.

yokel NOUN an unsophisticated country person.

yolk NOUN the yellow part in the middle of an egg.

yonder ADJ & ADV [old use] over there.

yonks PLURAL NOUN [inf] a long time.

yore NOUN (**of yore**) [literary] long ago.

Yorkshire pudding NOUN a baked batter pudding eaten with roast beef.

you PRON 1 the person or people addressed. 2 any person in general.

young ADJ having lived or existed for only a short time. NOUN an animal's offspring.

youngster NOUN a young person.

your ADJ of or belonging to you.

yours POSSESSIVE PRON belonging to you.

yourself PRON (PL **-selves**) the emphatic and reflexive form of *you*.

youth NOUN 1 the state or

period of being young. **2** a young man; young people.

youth hostel a place providing cheap accommodation for young people.

youthful ADJ young; characteristic of young people.

yowl VERB & NOUN (make) a loud wailing cry.

yo-yo NOUN (PL **-yos**) [trademark] a disc-shaped toy that can be made to rise and fall on a string that winds round it in a groove. VERB (**yo-yoed, yo-yoing**) move up and down rapidly.

yucca NOUN a plant with sword-like leaves.

yuck (or **yuk**) EXCLAMATION [inf] an expression of disgust.

Yuletide NOUN [old use] Christmas.

yummy ADJ (**-ier, -iest**) [inf] delicious.

yuppie (or **yuppy**) NOUN [inf] a young middle-class professional person who earns a great deal of money.

Zz

zany ADJ (**-ier, -iest**) crazily funny.

zap [inf] VERB (**zapped, zapping**) **1** destroy. **2** move or propel suddenly.

zeal NOUN great energy, enthusiasm, and commitment.
zealous ADJ

zealot NOUN a person who is fanatical in support of a cause.

zebra NOUN an African horse-like animal with black and white stripes.
zebra crossing a pedestrian road crossing marked with broad white stripes.

Zen NOUN a form of Buddhism.

zenith NOUN the part of the sky directly overhead; the highest point.

zephyr NOUN [literary] a soft gentle wind.

zero NOUN (PL **-os**) the figure 0; a point marked 0

on a graduated scale or a temperature corresponding to this.

zest NOUN 1 keen enjoyment or interest. 2 orange or lemon peel as flavouring.

zigzag NOUN a line having sharp alternate right and left turns. ADJ & ADV in a zigzag. VERB (**zigzagged**, **zigzagging**) move in a zigzag.

zilch NOUN [inf] nothing.

zinc NOUN a white metallic element.

zing [inf] NOUN vigour. VERB move swiftly.

Zionism NOUN a movement for the development of a Jewish nation in Israel. **Zionist** NOUN

zip NOUN (also **zipper**) a fastener with teeth that interlock when brought together by a sliding tab. VERB (**zipped**, **zipping**) 1 fasten with a zip. 2 [inf] move at high speed.

zircon NOUN a brown or semi-transparent mineral.

zit NOUN [inf] a pimple.

zither NOUN a stringed instrument played with the fingers.

zodiac NOUN (in astrology) a band of the sky divided into twelve equal parts (**signs of the zodiac**) each named after a constellation.

zombie NOUN 1 (in stories) a corpse that has been brought back to life by magic. 2 [inf] a completely unresponsive person.

zone NOUN an area having particular characteristics or a particular use. VERB divide into zones. **zonal** ADJ

zoo NOUN a place where wild animals are kept for display, conservation, and study.

zoology NOUN the scientific study of animals. **zoological** ADJ **zoologist** NOUN

zoom VERB 1 move very quickly. 2 (of a camera) change smoothly from a long shot to a close-up or vice versa.

zucchini NOUN (PL **-ini** or **-inis**) [US] a courgette.

zygote NOUN a cell formed by the union of two gametes.

Wordpower Guide

The Wordpower Guide is made up of four separate sections providing a range of useful extra information. The lists of countries of the world and wedding anniversaries may come in handy for crossword solvers, while the games and puzzles wordbuilder should prove a useful resource for players of word games. The final section explains the difference between pairs of words which are similar in sound and spelling and which are consequently easy to confuse, such as **counsel** and **council** or **stationary** and **stationery**.

Countries of the world

Country	Related adjective/noun
Afghanistan	Afghan
Albania	Albanian
Algeria	Algerian
Andorra	Andorran
Angola	Angolan
Antigua and Barbuda	Antiguan, Barbudan
Argentina	Argentinian
Armenia	Armenian
Australia	Australian
Austria	Austrian
Azerbaijan	Azerbaijani
Bahamas	Bahamian
Bahrain	Bahraini
Bangladesh	Bangladeshi
Barbados	Barbadian
Belarus	Belarussian
Belgium	Belgian
Belize	Belizian
Benin	Beninese
Bhutan	Bhutanese
Bolivia	Bolivian
Bosnia–Herzegovina	Bosnian
Botswana	Botswanan/Tswana
Brazil	Brazilian
Brunei	Bruneian
Bulgaria	Bulgarian
Burkina Faso	Burkinese
Burma (officially called Myanmar)	Burmese
Burundi	Burundian
Cambodia	Cambodian

Country	Related adjective/noun
Cameroon	Cameroonian
Canada	Canadian
Cape Verde Islands	Cape Verdean
Central African Republic	–
Chad	Chadian
Chile	Chilean
China	Chinese
Colombia	Colombian
Comoros	Comoran
Congo	Congolese
Congo, Democratic Republic of (formerly **Zaire**)	Congolese
Costa Rica	Costa Rican
Croatia	Croat or Croatian
Cuba	Cuban
Cyprus	Cypriot
Czech Republic	Czech
Denmark	Danish/Dane
Djibouti	Djiboutian
Dominica	Dominican
Dominican Republic	Dominican
Ecuador	Ecuadorean
Egypt	Egyptian
El Salvador	Salvadorean
Equatorial Guinea	Equatorial Guinean
Eritrea	Eritrean
Estonia	Estonian
Ethiopia	Ethiopian
Fiji	Fijian
Finland	Finn
France	French
Gabon	Gabonese
Gambia, the	Gambian

Country	Related adjective/noun
Georgia	Georgian
Germany	German
Ghana	Ghanaian
Greece	Greek
Grenada	Grenadian
Guatemala	Guatemalan
Guinea	Guinean
Guinea-Bissau	–
Guyana	Guyanese
Haiti	Haitian
Holland (see **Netherlands**)	
Honduras	Honduran
Hungary	Hungarian
Iceland	Icelandic/Icelander
India	Indian
Indonesia	Indonesian
Iran	Iranian
Iraq	Iraqi
Ireland, Republic of	Irish
Israel	Israeli
Italy	Italian
Ivory Coast	Ivorian
Jamaica	Jamaican
Japan	Japanese
Jordan	Jordanian
Kazakhstan	Kazakh
Kenya	Kenyan
Kuwait	Kuwaiti
Kyrgyzstan	Kyrgyz
Laos	Laotian
Latvia	Latvian
Lebanon	Lebanese
Lesotho	Lesothan/Mosotho, pl.Basotho

Country	Related adjective/noun
Liberia	Liberian
Libya	Libyan
Liechtenstein	–/Liechtensteiner
Lithuania	Lithuanian
Luxembourg	–/Luxembourger
Macedonia	Macedonian
Madagascar	Malagasay or Madagascan
Malawi	Malawian
Malaysia	Malaysian
Maldives	Maldivian
Mali	Malian
Malta	Maltese
Mauritania	Mauritanian
Mauritius	Mauritian
Mexico	Mexican
Micronesia, Federated States of	Micronesian
Moldova	Moldovan
Monaco	Monegasque or Monacan
Mongolia	Mongolian
Morocco	Moroccan
Mozambique	Mozambican
Myanmar (see **Burma**)	
Namibia	Namibian
Nauru	Nauruan
Nepal	Nepalese
Netherlands, the	Dutch
New Zealand	–/New Zealander
Nicaragua	Nicaraguan
Niger	Nigerien
Nigeria	Nigerian
North Korea	North Korean
Norway	Norwegian

Country	Related adjective/noun
Oman	Omani
Pakistan	Pakistani
Panama	Panamanian
Papua New Guinea	Papua New Guinean or Guinean
Paraguay	Paraguayan
Peru	Peruvian
Philippines	Filipino or Philippine
Poland	Polish/Pole
Portugal	Portuguese
Qatar	Qatari
Romania	Romanian
Russia	Russian
Rwanda	Rwandan
St Lucia	St Lucian
Samoa	Samoan
San Marino	–
São Tomé and Principe	–
Saudi Arabia	Saudi Arabian or Saudi
Senegal	Senegalese
Seychelles, the	Seychellois
Sierra Leone	Sierra Leonean
Singapore	Singaporean
Slovakia	Slovak or Slovakian
Slovenia	Slovene or Slovenian
Solomon Islands	–/Solomon Islander
Somalia	Somali or Somalian
South Africa	South African
South Korea	South Korean
Spain	Spanish/Spaniard
Sri Lanka	Sri Lankan
Sudan	Sudanese
Suriname	Surinamese

Country	Related adjec
Swaziland	Swazi
Sweden	Swedish/Sw
Switzerland	Swiss
Syria	Syrian
Taiwan	Taiwanese
Tajikistan	Tajik or Ta
Tanzania	Tanzaniar
Thailand	Thai
Togo	Togolese
Tonga	Tongan
Trinidad and Tobago	Trinidadi
Tunisia	Tunisian
Turkey	Turkish/
Turkmenistan	Turkmen
Tuvalu	Tuvaluar
Uganda	Ugandar
Ukraine	Ukrainia
Union of Serbia and Montenegro	Serbian,
United Arab Emirates	—
United Kingdom	British/
United States of America	Americ
Uruguay	Urugua
Uzbekistan	Uzbek
Vanuatu	Vanua
Vatican City	—
Venezuela	Venez
Vietnam	Vietna
Yemen	Yemer
Zambia	Zamb
Zimbabwe	Zimba

Gar wor

Players
have a
unusua
a *q* not
be part
the foll
which
Dr or *M*
allowed

Two-l

aa: roug
ab: an a
ad: an a
ag: [S. A
various
irritati
pleasu
ah: expre
sympa
ai: the th
am: the
an: a forr
article
as: used
extent
at: expre
time
aw: expre
protest,

...nes and puzzles
...dbuilder

...of word games may be at an advantage if they
...cess to a supply of short words or words with
...l spellings. Two-letter words, words containing
...followed by a *u*, and words beginning with *x* can
...cularly useful and a wide selection is included in
...owing lists. Proper names and abbreviations
...re not pronounced as they are spelt (such as
...*r*) are excluded from the lists as they are not
...in most word games.

...tter words

...h cindery lava

...odominal muscle

...dvertisement

...rican] expressing

... emotions, e.g.

...on, grief, or

...e

...ssing surprise,

...hy, pleasure, etc.

...ree-toed sloth

...resent tense of *be*

...n of the indefinite

...o confer relative

...r degree

...sing location or

...ssing mild

...entreaty, etc.

ba: (in Egyptian mythology) the soul

be: exist

bi: bisexual

bo: a kind of fig tree

by: beside

da: one's father

DJ: a disc jockey

do: perform (an action)

dy: a type of sediment

eh: seeking explanation or agreement

El: an elevated railway or section of railway

em: a measuring unit in printing

en: a measuring unit in printing

er: expressing doubt or hesitation

ex: a former spouse or partner

fa: a musical note

Ga: a member of a people living in Ghana

GI: a soldier in the US army

go: move or travel

ha: expressing surprise, triumph, etc.

he: a male person or animal previously mentioned

hi: used as a greeting

ho: expressing surprise, triumph, etc.

id: a part of the mind

if: introducing a conditional clause

in: within

io: a North American moth

is: the present tense of *be*

it: a thing previously mentioned

ja: [S. African] yes

jo: [Scottish, old use] a sweetheart

Ju: used to designate a kind of Chinese pottery

ka: (in Egyptian mythology) the spirit

ki: a plant of the lily family

KO: a knockout in a boxing match

la: a musical note

li: a Chinese unit of distance

lo: [old use] used to draw attention to something

ma: one's mother

MD: [Brit.] a managing director

me: the objective case of 'I'

mi: a musical note

mo: a moment

MP: a Member of Parliament

mu: the 12th letter of the Greek alphabet

my: belonging to me

no: not any

nu: the 13th letter of the Greek alphabet

ob: a type of gene

od: a power once thought to pervade the natural world

of: belonging to

og: [Australian, old use] a shilling

oh: expressing surprise, anger, disappointment, etc.

oi: used to attract attention

OK: used to express assent, agreement, etc.

om: a mystic syllable

which constitutes a sacred mantra

on: supported by or covering

op: an operation

or: used to link alternatives

os: a bone

ou: a Hawaiian bird

ow: expressing pain

ox: a cow or bull

oy: = oi

Oz: Australia

pa: one's father

pi: the 16th letter of the Greek alphabet

po: a chamber pot

qi: (in Chinese philosophy) the life force

ra: (in Norway and Sweden) a moraine

re: a musical note

ri: a Japanese unit of length

se: a Chinese musical instrument

si: = te

so: therefore

ta: thank you

te: a musical note

ti: = te

TV: a television

uh: expressing hesitation

um: expressing hesitation

up: towards a higher position

us: the objective case of 'we'

Wa: a member of a people living on the borders of China and Burma

we: one's self and others

Wu: a dialect of Chinese

xi: the 14th letter of the Greek alphabet

xu: a monetary unit of Vietnam

ye: [old use] the plural form of 'thou'

Yi: a people living in parts of China

yo: used as a greeting

yu: an ancient Chinese wine container

Words with a *q* not followed by a *u*

qadi: a Muslim judge

qanat: an irrigation tunnel

qasida: an Arabic or Persian poem

qawwal: a qawwali singer

qawwali: Muslim devotional music

qi: (in Chinese

philosophy) the life force

qibla: the direction towards Mecca

qigong: a Chinese system of physical exercises

qin: a Chinese musical instrument

qintar: a monetary unit of Albania

qiviut: wool from the musk ox

qwerty: the standard layout of typewriters and keyboards

tariqa: the Sufi method of spiritual learning

Words beginning with *x*

xanthan: a polysaccharide

xanthate: a chemical compound

xanthene: a chemical compound

xanthic: yellowish

xanthin: a yellow colouring matter

xanthine: a biochemical compound

xanthoma: a yellow patch on the skin

xebec: a sailing ship

xeme: a fork-tailed gull

xenia: gifts to a guest or guests

xenial: relating to hospitality

xenon: a noble gas

xeric: very dry

xeroma: abnormal dryness of a body part

xerox: to photocopy

Xhosa: a South African people or their language

xi: the 14th letter of the Greek alphabet

xiphoid: sword-shaped

Xmas: Christmas

xoanon: a wooden image of a god

xography: a photographic process

xu: a monetary unit of Vietnam

xylan: a compound found in wood

xylary: of or relating to xylem

xylem: plant tissue

xylene: a liquid hydrocarbon

xylite: a volatile liquid

xylol: = xylene

xylose: a plant sugar

xyrid: a sedge-like herb

xyster: a surgical instrument

xyston: an ancient Greek spear

xystus: an ancient Greek portico

Wedding anniversaries

References to golden and silver weddings date from the middle of the 19th century, with diamond weddings following soon afterwards. From these there developed a tradition of associating significant anniversaries with particular materials, and then to the giving of gifts made from these materials.

Year	Name	Year	Name
1st	Paper	13th	Lace
2nd	Cotton	14th	Ivory
3rd	Leather	15th	Crystal
4th	Linen (or Silk)	20th	China
5th	Wood	25th	Silver
6th	Iron	30th	Pearl
7th	Wool (or Copper)	35th	Coral (or Jade)
8th	Bronze	40th	Ruby
9th	Pottery (or China)	45th	Sapphire
10th	Tin (or Aluminium)	50th	Gold
11th	Steel	55th	Emerald
12th	Silk	60th	Diamond

Commonly confused words

There are many words in the English language which look or sound alike but have quite different meanings. Such words are very easy to confuse and the following list explains the differences between many pairs of words that commonly cause problems.

accept agree to do or receive
except not including

access a way of entering a place
excess too much of something

adverse unfavourable
averse opposed

affect cause a change in
effect bring about; (*as noun*) a result

allusion an indirect reference
illusion a false belief

alternate one after another
alternative available instead

amoral having no moral sense
immoral not conforming to moral standards

ante before
anti against

appraise assess the quality of
apprise inform

assent approval or agreement
ascent an act of going up something

balmy pleasantly warm
barmy mad or crazy

biannual twice a year
biennial every two years

censor act as censor of
censure criticize harshly

chord a group of musical notes
cord a length of string

climactic forming a climax
climatic relating to climate

complement add to in a way that improves
compliment politely praise

compose make up a whole
comprise consist of

confident self-assured; certain
confidant a person in whom one confides

council an administrative body
counsel advice or guidance

credible believable
credulous too ready to believe

definite clear and distinct
definitive conclusive; authoritative

defuse remove the fuse from; reduce tension in
diffuse spread out; (*as adjective*) not clear or concise

deprecate disapprove of
depreciate decrease in value

desert a waterless area; (*as verb*) abandon
dessert a pudding

discreet careful to avoid attention
discrete separate

disinterested impartial
uninterested not interested

draw make a picture of; pull; have an equal score
drawer a sliding storage compartment

ensure make sure
insure take out insurance on

equable even-tempered
equitable fair

especially in particular; above all
specially for a special purpose

exceptionable causing disapproval
exceptional unusually good

faint hard to see or hear; temporarily lose consciousness
feint paper with faint lines; a movement in boxing
 or fencing

flair a natural ability
flare a burst of flame or light; (*as verb*) become angry

flaunt display ostentatiously
flout disregard a rule or custom

flounder (of a person) struggle or be in difficulties
founder (of an undertaking) fail or come to nothing

forego (*old use*) go before
forgo go without

forever continually
for ever eternally

fortuitous happening by chance
fortunate happening by good chance; lucky

gourmand a glutton
gourmet a food connoisseur

grisly horrific or revolting
grizzly as in *grizzly bear*

hangar a building for aircraft
hanger as in *clothes hanger*

hoard a store of valuables
horde a large group of people

illicit not allowed
elicit produce a response or reaction

imply suggest strongly
infer deduce or conclude

impracticable not able to be done
impractical not sensible or realistic

incredible not believable
incredulous unable to believe

ingenious well thought out
ingenuous innocent or honest

interment burial
internment confinement

its belonging to it
it's it is, or it has

loath reluctant or unwilling
loathe dislike greatly

loose not fixed; (*as verb*) unfasten or relax
lose be deprived of or no longer have

luxuriant lush
luxurious comfortable and rich

masterful powerful or domineering
masterly highly skilful

militate be a powerful factor in preventing
mitigate make less severe

naught (*old use*) nothing (as in *come to naught*)
nought the digit 0; nothing

naval relating to a navy
navel the place where a person's umbilical cord was cut

occupant a person in a vehicle, seat, etc.
occupier the person living in a property

official having authorized status
officious aggressive in asserting authority

ordinance an authoritative order
ordnance mounted guns; military stores

palate the roof of the mouth; the sense of taste
palette an artist's mixing board

pedal a lever that powers a bicycle
peddle sell goods

pitiable deserving pity
pitiful causing pity

pole a piece of wood
poll voting in an election

pore (*pore over*) read closely
pour flow or cause to flow

practicable able to be done
practical effective or realistic; skilled at manual tasks

precipitate hasty or headlong
precipitous abruptly steep

prescribe recommend with authority; issue a
  prescription
proscribe forbid or condemn

prevaricate avoid giving a direct answer
procrastinate delay or postpone action

principal most important or main; (*as noun*) the chief
  person
principle a basis of belief or action

purposely intentionally
purposefully resolutely

regrettable causing regret; undesirable
regretful feeling regret

shear cut wool off; cut
sheer utter or complete (as in *sheer delight*); swerve
  or avoid

site a place where something happens
sight the ability to see

sociable friendly and willing to mix with people
social relating to society

stationary not moving
stationery materials for writing

storey a part of a building on one level
story an account of imaginary events

straight extending without a curve
strait a narrow passage of water

titillate excite pleasantly
titivate adorn or smarten

tortuous twisting or devious
torturous causing torture; tormenting

triumphal done or made to celebrate a victory
triumphant victorious; jubilant after a victory

unsociable not willing to mix with people
unsocial socially inconvenient

venal open to bribery; corrupt
venial (of a sin) minor

who's who is
whose belonging to which person

Aa

abandon VERB 1 = **desert**, leave, forsake, jilt. 2 = **give up**, renounce, relinquish, forswear.

abashed ADJ = **embarrassed**, ashamed, shamefaced, mortified, humiliated.

abbey NOUN = **monastery**, convent, priory, cloister, friary, nunnery.

abbreviate VERB = **shorten**, reduce, cut, condense, abridge, summarize, precis.

abdicate VERB 1 = **resign**, stand down, retire, quit. 2 = **give up**, renounce, relinquish, waive, forgo, abandon, surrender.

abduct VERB = **kidnap**, carry off, run/make off with, seize.

aberration NOUN = **deviation**, anomaly, abnormality, irregularity, freak.

abide VERB (**abide by**) = **keep to**, comply with, observe, follow, obey, hold to, adhere to, stick to.

ability NOUN 1 = **capacity**, capability, potential, power, facility, faculty. 2 = **talent**, competence, proficiency, skill, expertise, aptitude, dexterity, knack; [inf] know-how.

able ADJ = **competent**, capable, talented, skilful, skilled, clever, accomplished, gifted, proficient, expert, adept, efficient, adroit.

abnormal ADJ = **unusual**, strange, odd, peculiar, uncommon, curious, queer, weird, unexpected, exceptional, irregular, atypical, anomalous, deviant, aberrant.

abolish VERB = **do away with**, put an end to, end, stop, terminate, axe, scrap, quash, annul, cancel, invalidate, nullify, void, rescind, repeal, revoke.

abominable ADJ = **hateful**, loathsome, detestable, odious, obnoxious, despicable, contemptible, disgusting, revolting, repellent, repulsive, offensive, repugnant, abhorrent, foul, vile, horrible, nasty.

abortive ADJ = **failed**, unsuccessful, vain, futile, useless, fruitless.

abrasive ADJ = **caustic**, cutting, harsh, acerbic, biting, sharp.

abridge VERB = **shorten**, cut down, condense, abbreviate, truncate, summarize, precis.

abrupt ADJ **1** = **sudden**, quick, hurried, hasty, swift, rapid, precipitate, unexpected. **2** = **curt**, blunt, brusque, short, terse, brisk, gruff, unceremonious, rude.

abscond VERB = **run away**, decamp, bolt, flee, make off, take flight, take to your heels.

absent ADJ = **away**, off, out, elsewhere, unavailable, lacking, gone, missing, truant.

absent-minded ADJ = **forgetful**, inattentive, scatterbrained, distracted, preoccupied, absorbed, oblivious.

absolute ADJ **1** = **complete**, total, utter, out and out, outright, unqualified, unadulterated, unalloyed, downright, undiluted, consummate, unmitigated. **2** = **unlimited**, unrestricted, supreme, unconditional, full, sovereign.

absorb VERB **1** = **soak up**, suck up, sop up. **2** = **take in**, assimilate, digest. **3** = **occupy**, engage, fascinate, captivate, engross, immerse, rivet.

absorbing ADJ = **fascinating**, gripping, interesting, captivating, engrossing, riveting, spellbinding, intriguing.

abstain VERB = **refrain**, decline, forbear, desist, avoid, eschew.

abstemious ADJ = **self-denying**, self-restrained, moderate, temperate, abstinent, ascetic, puritanical.

abstract ADJ = **theoretical**, conceptual, notional, intellectual, metaphysical, philosophical.

absurd ADJ = **ridiculous**, foolish, silly, idiotic, stupid, nonsensical, senseless, inane, crazy, ludicrous, laughable, preposterous, farcical, hare-brained, asinine; [inf] daft.

abundant ADJ = **plentiful**, ample, large, huge, copious, lavish, rich, profuse, teeming, overflowing, galore.

abuse VERB 1 = **mistreat**, ill-treat, maltreat, ill-use, injure, hurt, harm, damage. 2 = **misuse**, misapply, mishandle, misemploy, exploit. 3 = **insult**, swear at, curse, vilify, malign, defame, slander, libel. NOUN 1 = **mistreatment**, ill-treatment, maltreatment, injury, hurt, harm, damage. 2 = **misuse**, misapplication, mishandling, exploitation. 3 = **swearing**, cursing, invective, vilification, vituperation, defamation, slander, insults, curses, expletives, swear words.

abusive ADJ = **insulting**, rude, offensive, slanderous, libellous, derogatory, defamatory.

academic ADJ 1 = **educational**, scholastic, instructional. 2 = **theoretical**, hypothetical, abstract, conjectural, notional, speculative. 3 = **scholarly**, studious, literary, well read, intellectual, erudite, learned, cultured, highbrow, bookish, cerebral. NOUN = **scholar**, lecturer, don, teacher, tutor, professor, fellow.

accelerate VERB = **speed up**, pick up speed, hasten, hurry, quicken.

accent NOUN 1 = **pronunciation**, intonation, enunciation, articulation, inflection, tone, brogue. 2 = **stress**, emphasis, accentuation, force, beat, prominence.

accentuate VERB = **stress**, highlight, emphasize, underline, draw attention to, heighten, point up, underscore, accent.

accept VERB 1 = **receive**, take, get, gain, obtain, acquire. 2 = **agree to**, accede to, consent to, acquiesce in, concur with, comply with, go along with; recognize, acknowledge. 3 = **believe**, trust, credit, have faith in; [inf] swallow.

acceptable ADJ = **satisfactory**, adequate,

passable, admissible, tolerable.

access NOUN = **entry**, entrance, way in, admittance, admission, approach, means of approach.

accident NOUN 1 = **mishap**, misfortune, misadventure, disaster, tragedy, catastrophe, calamity. 2 = **crash**, collision; [inf] smash, pile-up. 3 = **chance**, fate, fortune, luck; [inf] fluke.

accidental ADJ = **chance**, unintentional, unintended, inadvertent, unexpected, unforeseen, unlooked-for, fortuitous, unplanned, unpremeditated.

acclaim VERB = **praise**, applaud, cheer, celebrate, salute, honour, commend, hail, extol, laud. NOUN = **praise**, commendation, honour, tribute, congratulations, applause, plaudits, bouquets.

accommodate VERB = **house**, put up, cater for, lodge, board, billet.

accommodating ADJ = **obliging**, cooperative, helpful, considerate, unselfish, willing, hospitable, kind, agreeable.

accommodation NOUN = **housing**, lodging, shelter, residence, house, billet, lodgings, quarters, digs.

accompany VERB = **escort**, go with, keep company, attend, usher, conduct, chaperone.

accomplice NOUN = **partner-in-crime**, accessory, collaborator, abetter, associate, helper, henchman; [inf] sidekick.

accomplish VERB = **achieve**, carry out, fulfil, perform, attain, realize, succeed in, bring about/off, effect, execute.

accomplished ADJ = **skilled**, skilful, expert, gifted, talented, proficient, adept, masterly, polished, practised, capable, able, competent, experienced, professional, consummate.

account NOUN 1 = **statement**, report, description, record, narration, narrative, story, recital, explanation, tale, version. 2 = **bill**, invoice, reckoning, tally, charges, debts.

accumulate VERB = **gather**, collect, increase, accrue; amass, collect, stockpile, pile/heap up, store, hoard.

accurate ADJ = **correct**, right, true, exact, precise, factual, truthful, faultless, reliable, faithful, sound, authentic; [inf] spot-on, bang-on.

accuse VERB = **charge**, indict, arraign, summons; blame, hold responsible, condemn, denounce; [US] impeach; [inf] point the finger at.

accustomed ADJ **1** = **usual**, customary, habitual, regular, established, normal, conventional, expected, familiar, common, traditional, ordinary, set, wonted. **2** = **used**, given, in the habit, habituated.

ache NOUN = **pain**, soreness, discomfort, throbbing, twinge, pang. VERB = **hurt**, smart, sting, be sore/painful, pound, throb.

achieve VERB = **succeed**, accomplish, manage, carry out, complete, attain, gain, obtain, get, reach, win, bring off, effect, perform, fulfil.

acknowledge VERB = **accept**, admit, concede, agree, allow, recognize, confess, grant, own up to, acquiesce to, accede to.

acquaintance NOUN **1** = **friend**, contact, colleague. **2** = **knowledge**, awareness, familiarity, understanding.

acquire VERB = **get**, obtain, gain, buy, purchase, come by, pick up.

acquit VERB = **clear**, exonerate, set free, free, release, discharge, let off.

acrid ADJ = **bitter**, sharp, pungent, harsh, caustic.

acrimonious ADJ = **angry**, bitter, bad-tempered, hostile, rancorous, spiteful, acerbic, acid, sharp, vitriolic, caustic.

act NOUN **1** = **action**, deed, feat, exploit, undertaking, achievement, step, move, operation. **2** = **law**, statute, bill, decree, enactment, edict. **3** = **routine**, performance, number, turn, item. VERB **1** = **behave**, conduct yourself, carry on. **2** = **take action**, take steps, move. **3** = **function**, work, operate, serve.

4 = perform, play, appear as, portray, represent.

acting ADJ **= temporary**, interim, provisional, stopgap, stand-in, fill-in, deputy, pro tem.

action NOUN **1 = activity**, movement, exertion, work; drama, liveliness, excitement; vigour, energy, vitality, initiative, enterprise. **2** see **act (1)**.

activate VERB **1 = set off**, start, trigger, initiate. **2 = stimulate**, prompt, stir, energize, rouse, arouse, galvanize, fire, motivate.

active ADJ **= energetic**, lively, busy, dynamic, enthusiastic, vigorous, brisk, bustling, vivacious, sprightly, spry, animated, enterprising, spirited; industrious, tireless, hard-working, committed.

activity NOUN **1 = hobby**, pastime, pursuit, interest, recreation, diversion, project, enterprise, undertaking. **2 = movement**, action, bustle, excitement, liveliness, commotion, hurly-burly, animation, life, stir.

actual ADJ **= real**, genuine, true, authentic, indisputable, factual, verified, confirmed, bona fide, definite, unquestionable, tangible, in existence, living.

acute ADJ **1 = sharp**, intense, piercing, severe, extreme, fierce, sudden, excruciating, violent, shooting, keen, racking. **2 = serious**, urgent, pressing, grave, critical.

adamant ADJ **= determined**, resolute, resolved, firm, unyielding, unshakeable, stubborn, intransigent.

adapt VERB **1 = get used**, adjust, get accustomed, habituate yourself, get acclimatized, reconcile yourself, accommodate yourself. **2 = alter**, change, modify, adjust, tailor, convert, remodel, restyle.

add VERB **1 = attach**, append, affix, include, incorporate, tack on. **2 = total**, count (up), reckon up, tot up.

addiction NOUN **= dependency**, craving, habit, compulsion, obsession, enslavement.

addition NOUN **= increase**, supplement, increment, adjunct, accessory, addendum, appendage, appendix, postscript, afterthought, attachment, extra.

additional ADJ = **extra**, added, more, further, supplementary, other, new, fresh.

address NOUN **1** = **location**, place, residence, home, house; [formal] abode, domicile, dwelling. **2** = **speech**, talk, lecture, oration, disquisition, discourse.

adequate ADJ = **satisfactory**, passable, all right, average, competent, unexceptional, acceptable, unexceptionable, tolerable.

adhere VERB = **stick**, cohere, cling, bond; be fixed, be glued.

adjacent ADJ = **neighbouring**, adjoining, bordering, next, close, next door, touching, abutting.

adjourn VERB = **break off**, interrupt, suspend, discontinue, postpone, put off, delay, defer, prorogue.

adjust VERB **1** = **adapt**, get accustomed, get used, reconcile yourself, accommodate yourself, get acclimatized, habituate yourself. **2** = **alter**, modify, adapt, regulate, tailor, customize, tune, change, rearrange, remodel, rejig, fix, repair.

administer VERB **1** = **manage**, direct, run, control, organize, supervise, oversee, preside over, superintend, regulate, govern, conduct. **2** = **give**, dispense, provide, supply, distribute, hand out, mete out, dole out.

admirable ADJ = **commendable**, creditable, worthy, praiseworthy, laudable, meritorious, deserving, estimable, good, excellent, fine, exemplary, wonderful, marvellous.

admiration NOUN = **approval**, regard, respect, praise, appreciation, commendation, approbation, esteem.

admire VERB = **respect**, look up to, think highly of, esteem, applaud, commend.

admission NOUN
1 = **admittance**, entry, entrance, access.
2 = **acknowledgement**, confession, acceptance, disclosure.

admit VERB = **acknowledge**, confess, own up, concede, grant, accept, recognize, allow, reveal, disclose.

adolescent ADJ = **teenage**, young, pubescent, immature, childish, juvenile, puerile.

adopt VERB = **accept**, espouse, embrace, take on, assume, choose, approve, follow, support, back.

adore VERB = **love**, dote on, be devoted to, cherish, treasure, think the world of, worship, hero-worship, idolize.

adorn VERB = **decorate**, embellish, ornament, enhance, beautify, deck, bedeck, trim.

adult ADJ = **fully grown**, grown-up, mature, of age, nubile.

adulterate VERB = **contaminate**, taint, pollute, debase, doctor, corrupt, defile, dilute, water down, weaken.

advance VERB 1 = **move forward**, move ahead, proceed, forge ahead, gain ground, make headway, approach, press on, push on. 2 = **speed up**, bring forward, accelerate, step up, expedite. 3 = **suggest**, put forward, present, submit, propose, offer, proffer. 4 = **lend**, loan, provide, put up. NOUN = **development**, breakthrough, discovery, finding, progress, improvement, invention.

advanced ADJ = **sophisticated**, modern, latest, up to date; progressive, innovative, original, new, forward-looking, experimental, avant-garde, pioneering, trend-setting, ahead of the times.

advantage NOUN 1 = **benefit**, good point, value, asset, plus, bonus, virtue, boon, blessing. 2 = **superiority**, upper hand, edge, trump card.

advantageous ADJ = **beneficial**, helpful, useful, of use, profitable, worthwhile.

adventure NOUN = **exploit**, deed, feat, escapade, venture, undertaking.

adventurous ADJ = **daring**, brave, bold, courageous, heroic, enterprising, intrepid, daredevil.

adverse ADJ
1 = **unfavourable**, disadvantageous, inauspicious, unpropitious, unfortunate, untoward, unlucky, harmful, detrimental, deleterious.
2 = **hostile**, unfriendly, antagonistic, negative, uncomplimentary, unfavourable.

adversity NOUN
= **misfortune**, bad luck, trouble, woe, affliction, disaster, sorrow, misery, hard times, tribulation.

advertise VERB = **publicize**, promote, market, tout, announce, broadcast; [inf] plug, hype.

advertisement NOUN
= **commercial**, blurb; flyer, poster; [inf] ad, advert.

advice NOUN = **guidance**, help, counsel, suggestions, recommendations, hints, tips, ideas; warning, caution.

advisable ADJ = **prudent**, sensible, wise, recommended,

appropriate, expedient, judicious, politic.

advise VERB = **give guidance**, counsel, offer suggestions; advocate, recommend, urge, suggest, encourage, enjoin.

advocate VERB
= **recommend**, advise, urge; support, back, argue for, favour, endorse, champion. NOUN
= **supporter**, champion, proponent, backer, spokesman, exponent, apologist.

affable ADJ = **friendly**, agreeable, pleasant, amiable, good-natured, polite, civil, courteous.

affair NOUN 1 = **event**, incident, occurrence, episode, happening, case.
2 = **business**, concern, responsibility, matter, problem. 3 = **relationship**, love affair, romance, fling, involvement, liaison, intrigue.

affect VERB 1 = **act on**, influence, have an effect/ impact on, change, modify, transform.
2 = **move**, touch, upset, trouble, disturb, concern, perturb, stir, hit. 3 = **adopt**,

assume, feign, sham,
simulate; [inf] put on.

affectation NOUN
= **pretentiousness**,
pretence, artificiality,
affectedness, pretension,
posturing.

affected ADJ = **unnatural**,
contrived, artificial,
pretentious, mannered,
insincere, studied; [inf]
put-on.

affection NOUN
= **fondness**, liking, love,
soft spot, warmth,
attachment, tenderness,
friendship.

affectionate ADJ = **fond**,
loving, caring, devoted,
tender, doting, warm,
friendly.

affinity NOUN 1 = **similarity**,
resemblance, likeness,
correspondence,
similitude. 2 = **liking**,
fondness, closeness,
kinship, like-mindedness,
rapport.

affirm VERB = **state**, assert,
declare, proclaim,
maintain, confirm, attest,
avow, swear, pronounce.

afflict VERB = **trouble**,
burden, distress, worry,
bother, oppress, torture,
plague, rack, torment,
beset, harass, bedevil,
curse.

afraid ADJ 1 = **frightened**,
scared, terrified, petrified,
fearful, intimidated,
nervous, alarmed,
panicky. 2 = **sorry**,
apologetic, regretful.

aftermath NOUN = **effects**,
after-effects,
consequences,
repercussions, results.

age NOUN 1 = **maturity**, old
age, advancing years,
seniority, elderliness.
2 = **era**, epoch, period,
time, generation. VERB
= **grow old**, mature, ripen,
develop.

aged ADJ = **old**, elderly,
senior, in your dotage,
long in the tooth.

agent NOUN
= **representative**,
middleman, go-between,
broker, negotiator,
intermediary, proxy,
trustee, spokesman,
spokeswoman.

aggravate VERB = **make
worse**, worsen,
exacerbate, intensify,
inflame, compound,
increase, heighten,
magnify, add to.

aggressive ADJ = **hostile**,
belligerent, combative,
violent, argumentative,

quarrelsome, warlike, antagonistic, provocative, pugnacious, bellicose, bullying.

aggrieved ADJ = **resentful**, indignant, affronted, offended, put out, piqued, annoyed.

agile ADJ = **nimble**, lithe, limber, fit, supple, graceful, acrobatic, light-footed, quick-moving.

agitated ADJ = **upset**, worried, flustered, ruffled, disconcerted, perturbed, disturbed, unsettled, worked up, tense, nervous, on edge, edgy, jumpy.

agonizing ADJ = **excruciating**, racking, very painful, acute, harrowing, searing.

agony NOUN = **suffering**, anguish, pain, torment, torture.

agree VERB 1 = **concur**, be of the same mind, see eye to eye. 2 = **match**, correspond, accord, coincide, fit, tally. 3 = **consent**, accept, assent, accede, acquiesce; allow, admit.

agreement NOUN 1 = **accord**, concurrence, harmony, accordance,

conco
2 = **con**
settler
treaty,

ailme
illness
comp
infirr

aim NO
objec
goal,
inten
aspir
desig
direc
focus
inter
wan
seek
ende

air NO
atm
2 = **a**
imp
aura
feel
flav
3 (**a**
pre
gra
aer
2 = (
voi
cor
sta

airl
sti

mugg
aisle
passa
walkv

alarm
appre
uneas
const
fright
2 = **sire**
warni
VERB = 1
panic,
disma
shock

alcoho
drink,
the ha

alcoho
= **drun**
dipson
drinke

alert A
vigilan
on you
circum
lookou
quick-v
percep
the bal
advise,
notify,

alibi NOU
defence
explana

alien AD
unfami

y, oppressive, sultry.
|OUN = **passageway**,
e, gangway,
ay.
NOUN 1 = **fear**,
hension, anxiety,
ness, dismay,
rnation, panic,
trepidation.
n, alert, alarm bell,
ng, tocsin, whistle.
righten**, scare,
terrify, unnerve,
, disturb, startle,
upset, worry.
NOUN = **liquor**,
spirits; [inf] booze,
rd stuff.
lic NOUN
ard**, drunk,
aniac, problem
, sot; [inf] lush.
J 1 = **watchful**,
t, observant, wary,
r guard/toes,
spect, on the
t. 2 = **sharp**, quick,
vitted, bright,
ive, keen; [inf] on
. VERB = **warn**,
forewarn, inform,
ip off.
N = **excuse**,
, justification,
tion, story.
) = **foreign**, strange,
iar, outlandish,

exotic.
alike ADJ = **similar**, the same, indistinguishable, identical, interchangeable, matching, twin.
alive ADJ 1 = **living**, breathing, live, sentient; [old use] quick. 2 (**alive to**) = **aware of**, conscious of, mindful of, sensitive to.
allay VERB = **lessen**, diminish, reduce, alleviate, calm, assuage, ease, quell, relieve, subdue, soothe, quieten, quiet.
allegation NOUN = **charge**, accusation, claim, assertion, contention, declaration.
allege VERB = **claim**, assert, maintain, contend, declare, state, attest.
alleged ADJ = **supposed**, claimed, declared, so-called, professed, stated.
allegiance NOUN = **loyalty**, faithfulness, fidelity, devotion, obedience; [historical] fealty.
alleviate VERB = **reduce**, ease, lessen, diminish, relieve, allay, assuage, palliate, lighten, soothe, subdue, temper, soften.
alliance NOUN

= **association**, union, coalition, partnership, affiliation, league, confederation, federation, syndicate, cartel, consortium.

allot VERB = **allocate**, assign, give out, share out, distribute, award, apportion, grant, divide up, mete out, dole out, dish out.

allow VERB = **permit**, let, give permission, authorize, consent, sanction, approve, license, give the go-ahead.

allowance NOUN **1** = **quota**, allocation, ration, portion, share. **2** = **payment**, subsidy, remittance, grant.

allude VERB = **refer to**, mention, touch on, suggest, hint at.

ally NOUN = **partner**, associate, colleague, friend, confederate, supporter. VERB = **join**, unite, join forces, combine, band together, team up, collaborate, side, align yourself.

alone ADJ = **by yourself**, on your own, solo, solitary, unaccompanied, unaided, unassisted, single-handed; isolated, separate, apart; lonely, friendless, forlorn.

aloof ADJ = **distant**, unfriendly, unapproachable, remote, stand-offish, unsociable, reserved, stiff, cold, undemonstrative, unforthcoming.

also ADV = **as well**, too, in addition, additionally, moreover, besides, to boot.

alter VERB = **change**, adjust, adapt, modify, revise, reshape, remodel, vary, convert, transform, amend, emend.

alteration NOUN = **change**, adjustment, modification, adaptation, revision, amendment, reorganization, conversion, transformation.

amalgamate VERB = **combine**, merge, unite, join, blend, integrate, fuse, join forces, link up.

amass VERB = **collect**, gather, accumulate, pile up, store up, hoard.

amateur NOUN = **non-professional**, layman, dabbler, dilettante.

amateurish ADJ

= **unprofessional**,
unskilful, untrained,
incompetent, inexpert,
clumsy, crude, rough and
ready.
amaze VERB = **astonish**,
surprise, astound, startle,
dumbfound, flabbergast,
shock, stagger, stun,
stupefy; [inf] bowl over.
amazement NOUN
= **astonishment**, surprise,
shock, stupefaction,
incredulity, disbelief.
amazing ADJ
= **astonishing**,
astounding, stunning,
extraordinary, incredible,
remarkable, sensational,
fantastic, phenomenal,
staggering, stupendous,
unbelievable.
ambassador NOUN
= **diplomat**, consul, envoy,
emissary, representative,
plenipotentiary.
ambiguous ADJ
= **ambivalent**, equivocal,
double-edged; obscure,
unclear, vague, uncertain,
enigmatic.
ambition NOUN **1** = **drive**,
enterprise, initiative,
eagerness, determination;
[inf] get-up-and-go.
2 = **goal**, aim, objective,
desire, object, intent,

purpose, design, target,
wish, aspiration, dream.
ambitious ADJ = **forceful**,
enterprising, determined,
aspiring, motivated,
enthusiastic, committed,
eager.
ambivalent ADJ
= **equivocal**, ambiguous,
uncertain, doubtful,
inconclusive, unclear,
irresolute, in two minds,
undecided.
amenable ADJ
1 = **agreeable**,
accommodating,
cooperative, compliant,
tractable, willing,
acquiescent, biddable,
complaisant.
2 = **susceptible**, receptive,
responsive.
amend VERB = **revise**, alter,
change, modify, adapt,
adjust; edit, rephrase,
reword.
amenity NOUN = **facility**,
service, convenience,
resource, advantage.
amiable ADJ = **friendly**,
agreeable, pleasant,
charming, likeable,
sociable, genial,
congenial, good-natured.
amnesty NOUN = **pardon**,
reprieve, pardoning;
release.

amorous ADJ = **loving**, passionate, sexual, lustful, ardent.

amorphous ADJ = **shapeless**, formless, unstructured, nebulous, vague, indeterminate.

amount NOUN = **quantity**, number, total, aggregate, sum, mass, weight, volume, bulk. VERB (**amount to**) = **add up to**, total, come to, equal, make, correspond to.

ample ADJ = **enough**, sufficient, plenty, plentiful, enough and to spare, abundant, copious, lavish, bountiful, profuse, liberal, generous.

amplify VERB **1** = **boost**, increase, intensify, heighten, magnify. **2** = **expand**, enlarge on, add to, elaborate on, fill out, flesh out, develop.

amuse VERB **1** = **entertain**, divert, make laugh, regale with, delight, cheer, please. **2** = **occupy**, engage, entertain, busy, absorb, engross.

amusement NOUN **1** = **laughter**, merriment, mirth, hilarity, fun, gaiety, pleasure, delight, enjoyment.

2 = **entertainment**, interest, diversion, pleasure, recreation, pastime, hobby, sport, game.

amusing ADJ see **funny**.

analyse VERB = **study**, examine, investigate, review, evaluate, interpret, scrutinize, enquire into, dissect.

analysis NOUN = **study**, examination, investigation, scrutiny, enquiry, review, evaluation, interpretation.

anarchy NOUN = **lawlessness**, revolution, insurrection, chaos, disorder, mob rule.

ancestor NOUN = **forebear**, forerunner, forefather, progenitor, predecessor, antecedent.

anchor VERB **1** = **moor**, berth, make fast, tie up. **2** = **secure**, fix, fasten, attach.

ancient ADJ = **very old**, age-old, time-worn, time-honoured, archaic, antediluvian; early, prehistoric, primeval, primordial, immemorial, bygone, of yore.

ancillary ADJ = **secondary**,

auxiliary, subsidiary,
supplementary,
additional, subordinate,
extra.

angelic ADJ 1 = **heavenly**,
divine, ethereal, holy.
2 = **innocent**, pure,
virtuous, saintly, good.

anger NOUN = **rage**, fury,
wrath, temper,
annoyance, vexation, ire,
exasperation, outrage,
indignation, irritation,
aggravation. VERB
= **infuriate**, enrage,
incense, outrage, annoy,
exasperate, antagonize,
vex, irritate, aggravate.

angle NOUN 1 = **corner**,
intersection, bend, fork.
2 = **point of view**,
viewpoint, standpoint,
opinion, position, slant.

angry ADJ = **furious**,
enraged, incensed,
outraged, wrathful,
seething, raging,
annoyed, irritated,
exasperated, fuming,
irate, indignant, vexed,
heated; [inf] apoplectic,
mad, up in arms.

anguish NOUN = **agony**,
suffering, pain, distress,
torment, torture, misery,
sorrow, grief, woe,
heartache, tribulation.

animal NOUN = **creature**,
beast, brute; (**animals**)
wildlife, fauna.

animated ADJ = **lively**,
energetic, excited,
enthusiastic, spirited,
exuberant, vivacious,
vibrant, cheerful, bright,
ebullient, bubbly, eager,
zestful, active, alive,
sprightly, vigorous.

animation NOUN
= **liveliness**, vitality,
vivacity, high spirits,
energy, excitement,
enthusiasm, ebullience,
zest, exuberance, life,
spirit, verve, sparkle.

animosity NOUN = **hostility**,
dislike, enmity,
unfriendliness,
resentment, antagonism,
hate, hatred, loathing,
antipathy, bitterness,
spite, bad blood, rancour,
ill will, acrimony, malice,
animus.

annals PLURAL NOUN
= **records**, archives,
history, chronicles,
accounts, registers.

annex VERB = **seize**, take
over, conquer,
appropriate, occupy.

annihilate VERB = **destroy**,
wipe out, exterminate,
obliterate, eliminate,

eradicate, liquidate, slaughter.

announce VERB = **make known**, make public, publish, put out, report, state, reveal, declare, disclose, broadcast, proclaim, advertise, blazon.

announcement NOUN = **statement**, report, bulletin; declaration, proclamation, disclosure, publication, notification.

announcer NOUN = **presenter**, newsreader, broadcaster, anchorman, anchorwoman, master of ceremonies, MC, compère.

annoy VERB = **irritate**, exasperate, infuriate, anger, vex, provoke, put out, antagonize, get on someone's nerves, peeve, irk, gall, pique; [inf] aggravate, bug, nettle.

annoyance NOUN 1 = **irritation**, exasperation, anger, ire, vexation, pique. 2 = **nuisance**, pest, bother, irritant, trial; [inf] pain, hassle, bind, bore.

annoyed ADJ = **irritated**, exasperated, cross, vexed, peeved, riled, put out, disgruntled; [inf] miffed, shirty.

annoying ADJ = **irritating**, infuriating, exasperating, maddening, trying, galling, troublesome, tiresome, irksome, bothersome, vexatious.

annul VERB = **cancel**, nullify, declare null and void, invalidate, void, rescind, revoke, repeal.

anomalous ADJ = **abnormal**, irregular, atypical, aberrant, exceptional, unusual, odd, eccentric, bizarre, peculiar.

anonymous ADJ = **unnamed**, unidentified, nameless, unknown, incognito, unattributed, unsigned.

answer NOUN 1 = **reply**, response, rejoinder, retort, riposte, comeback. 2 = **solution**, remedy. VERB 1 = **reply**, respond, react, come back, retort, rejoin. 2 = **solve**, remedy. 3 = **meet**, satisfy, fulfil, suit, measure up to, serve. 4 = **correspond to**, fit, match, conform to.

answerable ADJ = **responsible**, accountable, liable.

antagonism NOUN

= **animosity**, hostility, enmity, antipathy, rivalry, friction, conflict.

antagonize VERB = **annoy**, anger, irritate, alienate, offend, provoke.

anthem NOUN = **hymn**, psalm, song of praise, chant, chorale.

anthology NOUN = **collection**, compilation, miscellany, selection, treasury, compendium.

anticipate VERB 1 = **expect**, foresee, predict, forecast, be prepared for; look forward to. 2 = **prevent**, pre-empt, forestall, second-guess.

anticipation NOUN 1 = **expectation**, prediction, forecast. 2 = **expectancy**, excitement, suspense.

anticlimax NOUN = **disappointment**, let-down, bathos, comedown; [inf] damp squib.

antics PLURAL NOUN = **pranks**, capers, escapades, high jinks, horseplay.

antipathy NOUN = **dislike**, hostility, enmity, opposition, animosity, antagonism, aversion.

antiquated ADJ = **old-fashioned**, out of date, outmoded, outdated, behind the times, antediluvian, passé.

antiseptic ADJ = **disinfected**, disinfectant, sterile, sterilized, sanitized.

antisocial ADJ 1 = **unsociable**, unfriendly, uncommunicative, misanthropic, reclusive. 2 = **disruptive**, disorderly, rude, unruly, objectionable, unacceptable.

antithesis NOUN = **opposite**, reverse, converse, inverse, other extreme.

anxiety NOUN = **worry**, concern, apprehension, disquiet, uneasiness, nervousness, stress, tension, strain, misgiving, fear, fretfulness, angst.

anxious ADJ = **worried**, concerned, apprehensive, fearful, nervous, uneasy, disturbed, afraid, perturbed, agitated, edgy, troubled, upset, tense, overwrought, fretful; [inf] nervy, jittery, on edge.

apathetic ADJ

= **uninterested**,
indifferent,
unenthusiastic,
unconcerned, impassive,
half-hearted, uninvolved,
lukewarm.
aperture NOUN = **opening**,
gap, hole, crack, slit,
orifice, fissure.
apex NOUN 1 = **top**, peak,
summit, tip, head, crest,
crown, pinnacle.
2 = **height**, zenith, climax,
culmination, acme.
apologetic ADJ = **regretful**,
sorry, remorseful,
contrite, repentant,
penitent, ashamed,
rueful.
apostle NOUN = **evangelist**,
missionary, disciple,
follower; advocate,
proponent, propagandist,
supporter.
appal VERB = **shock**,
horrify, dismay, sicken,
disgust, outrage, alarm,
nauseate, revolt.
appalling ADJ = **shocking**,
horrific, horrifying,
disgusting, terrible,
dreadful, awful, ghastly,
frightful, atrocious,
hideous.
apparatus NOUN = **device**,
instrument, contraption,
mechanism, appliance,
machine, gadget, tool;
equipment, gear, tackle.
apparent ADJ 1 = **clear**,
plain, obvious, evident,
recognizable, noticeable,
manifest, visible,
unmistakable, patent.
2 = **seeming**, ostensible,
superficial, outward.
apparition NOUN = **ghost**,
phantom, spirit, spectre,
wraith; [inf] spook.
appeal NOUN 1 = **request**,
plea, call, application,
entreaty, petition, cri de
cœur, supplication.
2 = **attraction**, interest,
allure, temptation,
charm, fascination,
seductiveness. VERB 1 = **ask**,
request, beg, plead,
implore, entreat, call,
beseech, petition.
2 = **interest**, tempt,
fascinate, charm, engage,
entice, enchant, beguile.
appear VERB 1 = **turn up**,
show up, come into view,
materialize, arrive.
2 = **occur**, materialize, be
revealed, be seen, emerge,
come to light, crop up.
3 = **seem**, look, come
across as. 4 = **perform**, act,
take part, play.
appearance NOUN 1 = **look**,
air, manner, demeanour,

aspect, mien.
2 = semblance,
impression, guise, image.

appease VERB **= placate,**
pacify, conciliate, mollify,
soothe, propitiate.

appendage NOUN
1 = addition, attachment,
addendum, adjunct,
appurtenance. **2 = limb,**
member, projection,
protuberance.

appendix NOUN
= supplement, addition,
addendum, postscript,
codicil, coda, epilogue.

appetite NOUN **1 = hunger;**
taste, palate. **2 = keenness,**
eagerness, passion, desire,
lust, hunger, thirst,
yearning, longing,
craving, relish; [inf] yen.

appetizing ADJ
= delicious, mouth-
watering, tasty, succulent,
palatable; inviting,
tempting, appealing.

applaud VERB **1 = clap,**
cheer, give a standing
ovation; [inf] bring the
house down. **2 = praise,**
admire, commend,
congratulate, salute,
acclaim, hail.

applause NOUN **= clapping,**
ovation, a big hand,
cheering, bravos, encores,

curtain calls.

appliance NOUN **= device,**
gadget, instrument,
apparatus, machine,
mechanism, tool,
implement, contraption.

applicable ADJ **= relevant,**
appropriate, pertinent,
apposite, apropos.

applicant NOUN
= candidate, interviewee,
job-seeker, competitor,
claimant, petitioner,
supplicant.

apply VERB **1 = put in for,** try
for; request, seek,
petition, appeal. **2 = be
relevant,** relate, have a
bearing, pertain,
appertain. **3 = put on,** rub
on/in, cover with, spread,
smear. **4 = use,** employ,
exercise, bring to bear,
utilize. **5 (apply yourself)**
= make an effort, be
industrious, work hard,
devote yourself, persevere.

appoint VERB **1 = select,**
name, choose, designate,
elect, install. **2 = set,** fix,
decide on, arrange,
establish, settle on,
determine, designate.

appointment NOUN
1 = meeting, engagement,
date, arrangement,
interview, rendezvous,

assignation, fixture;
[literary] tryst. **2** = **job**, post,
position, office, situation.
appreciate VERB **1** = **value**,
rate highly, prize, admire,
respect, treasure, think a
lot of. **2** = **recognize**,
realize, acknowledge, be
aware of, know,
understand, comprehend.
appreciative ADJ
= **grateful**, thankful,
obliged, indebted,
beholden.
apprehensive ADJ
= **worried**, anxious,
uneasy, on edge, nervous,
frightened, afraid, fearful,
concerned.
apprentice NOUN = **trainee**,
learner, pupil, student,
beginner, novice,
probationer, tyro.
approach VERB **1** = **move
towards**, come/draw
nearer, near, bear down
on; reach. **2** = **appeal to**,
make overtures to,
proposition, sound out.
3 = **set about**, tackle, make
a start on, embark on,
undertake. NOUN
1 = **method**, procedure,
way, style, manner,
technique, means, modus
operandi. **2** = **appeal**,
application, proposal,

overture, proposition.
appropriate ADJ
= **suitable**, fitting, proper,
right, apt, timely,
opportune, seemly,
becoming, correct,
relevant, pertinent,
apposite. VERB = **take over**,
take possession of, seize,
confiscate, requisition,
annex, commandeer;
steal, misappropriate.
approval NOUN
1 = **admiration**,
appreciation, liking,
favour, respect, esteem,
approbation.
2 = **acceptance**,
agreement, endorsement,
authorization, assent,
consent, ratification,
sanction, permission,
mandate; [inf] OK, go-
ahead.
approve VERB **1** = **be
pleased with**, think well
of, like, hold with,
admire, respect. **2** = **agree
to**, accept, consent to,
permit, pass, allow,
sanction, authorize,
endorse, ratify; [inf]
rubber-stamp.
approximate ADJ
= **estimated**, rough,
inexact, imprecise.
approximately ADV

= **roughly**, about, around, circa, more or less, nearly, close/near to, in the region of, approaching, almost, not far off.

apt ADJ 1 = **suitable**, appropriate, fitting, apposite, felicitous. 2 = **likely**, inclined, prone, liable, given, disposed.

aptitude NOUN = **talent**, ability, gift, skill, flair, knack, capability, faculty.

arbitrary ADJ = **capricious**, random, chance, whimsical, unpredictable, irrational, illogical.

arbitrate VERB = **adjudicate**, judge, referee, umpire, mediate, negotiate.

arbitrator NOUN = **adjudicator**, judge, mediator, referee, umpire, arbiter, negotiator, intermediary, go-between.

arc NOUN = **curve**, crescent, semicircle, half-moon, arch, curvature.

arcane ADJ = **secret**, mysterious, recondite, enigmatic, abstruse, esoteric, cryptic.

arch NOUN = **archway**, vault, span, bridge. ADJ = **playful**, mischievous, roguish, saucy, knowing.

archetype NOUN = **prototype**, essence, quintessence, model, embodiment, pattern, original, standard, paradigm.

ardent ADJ = **passionate**, fervent, impassioned, eager, enthusiastic, intense, keen, zealous, vehement, fierce.

arduous ADJ = **hard**, difficult, demanding, exhausting, laborious, strenuous, tiring, gruelling, punishing, tough, onerous, heavy, rigorous, back-breaking, taxing.

area NOUN 1 = **size**, extent, expanse, measurement, space, square footage, acreage. 2 = **region**, district, environment, vicinity, locality, zone, territory, neighbourhood, environs, terrain, sector, quarter, province, precinct.

argue VERB 1 = **quarrel**, row, disagree, bicker, fight, squabble, dispute, wrangle, fall out, have words. 2 = **claim**, maintain, hold, reason, insist, contend, declare, assert.

argument NOUN
1 = quarrel, row, disagreement, fight, squabble, dispute, difference of opinion, altercation, falling-out, wrangle, clash; [inf] tiff.
2 = case, reasoning, reasons, grounds, evidence.

argumentative ADJ
= quarrelsome, disputatious, combative, belligerent, litigious.

arid ADJ **= dry**, dried up, waterless, parched, scorched, desiccated, barren, infertile, desert, lifeless, sterile.

arise VERB **= come to light**, appear, turn/crop up, emerge, occur.

aristocracy NOUN
= nobility, peerage, upper class, gentry, high society, elite, ruling class.

aristocratic ADJ **= noble**, titled, blue-blooded, upper class, well bred, refined, gracious, dignified.

arm NOUN **1 = limb**, appendage, forelimb, member. **2 = branch**, department, section, offshoot, division, sector.

VERB **= equip**, supply, provide, issue with, furnish.

armaments PLURAL NOUN
= weapons, guns, arms, firearms, weaponry, munitions, ordnance.

armistice NOUN see **truce**.

army NOUN **1 = armed force**, troops, soldiers, infantry, soldiery. **2 = crowd**, horde, throng, swarm, pack, host, multitude, mob.

aroma NOUN **= smell**, scent, odour, fragrance, perfume, bouquet.

arouse VERB **1 = wake (up)**, awaken, waken, rouse.
2 = cause, stimulate, stir up, inspire, induce, provoke, whip up, foster, kindle.

arrange VERB **1 = put in order**, set out, sort, lay out, array, organize, position, group, tidy.
2 = fix, organize, plan, set up, schedule, settle on, determine.

arrangement NOUN
1 = order, ordering, organization, positioning, grouping. **2 = agreement**, plan, deal, contract, bargain, pact, understanding, settlement.

array NOUN = **range**, collection, selection, assortment, arrangement, line-up, display, presentation.

arrest VERB 1 = **take into custody**, apprehend, take prisoner, detain, seize; [inf] nick. 2 = **stop**, halt, block, prevent, obstruct, hinder, impede, delay, slow down, check, stem.

arrive VERB = **come**, appear, enter, show/turn up, make an appearance; [inf] roll in/up.

arrogant ADJ = **haughty**, proud, conceited, self-important, pompous, bumptious, overbearing, superior, high-handed, imperious, overweening; [inf] high and mighty, cocky.

art NOUN 1 = **painting**, drawing, fine art, design. 2 = **skill**, craft, talent, flair, aptitude, knack, facility, technique.

artful ADJ = **cunning**, crafty, sly, devious, tricky, scheming, wily, clever, shrewd, canny, calculating.

article NOUN 1 = **thing**, object, item, commodity, artefact. 2 = **story**, piece, item, report, feature.

articulate ADJ = **fluent**, eloquent, lucid, silver-tongued, expressive, clear, coherent. VERB = **express**, voice, put into words, vocalize, say, utter.

artificial ADJ 1 = **synthetic**, imitation, fake, mock, ersatz, man-made, manufactured, fabricated. 2 = **false**, feigned, affected, fake, unnatural, insincere, forced, sham, contrived, put-on, bogus, pseudo; [inf] phoney.

artist NOUN 1 = **painter**, sculptor, old master. 2 = **craftsman**, craftswoman, expert, master, past master, genius, virtuoso.

artistic ADJ 1 = **creative**, imaginative, talented, gifted, sensitive, cultured, cultivated; [inf] arty. 2 = **attractive**, tasteful, in good taste, aesthetic, decorative, exquisite, beautiful, stylish, elegant, graceful.

artistry NOUN = **skill**, art, talent, ability, flair, expertise, creativity, proficiency, craftsmanship.

artless ADJ = **innocent**,

naive, simple, childlike, ingenuous, guileless.

ascend VERB = **climb**, go up, rise, mount, scale; take off, lift off, fly up.

ascendancy NOUN = **domination**, dominance, control, authority, power, rule, command, supremacy, sway, mastery, sovereignty, the upper hand.

ascent NOUN = **climb**, rise; slope, incline, gradient, acclivity.

ascertain VERB = **find out**, establish, discover, work out, learn, determine, identify, confirm, verify.

ascetic ADJ = **abstemious**, spartan, self-denying, frugal, austere, self-disciplined, strict, puritanical, monastic.

ascribe VERB = **attribute**, put down, assign, chalk up, impute, credit, accredit; lay at the door of, blame.

ashamed ADJ = **shamefaced**, sorry, apologetic, embarrassed, sheepish, guilty, remorseful, mortified, contrite, penitent, repentant, rueful, chagrined.

ashen ADJ = **pale**, white, pallid, wan, colourless, grey, ghostly.

ask VERB 1 = **enquire**, query; question, interrogate, quiz. 2 = **request**, seek, solicit, demand, call, appeal, apply; beg, implore, plead, beseech, supplicate. 3 = **invite**, summon, bid.

asleep ADJ = **sleeping**, dozing, snoozing; [inf] dead to the world, in the land of Nod.

aspect NOUN 1 = **feature**, facet, side, part, characteristic, element, detail, angle, slant. 2 = **appearance**, look, expression, air, demeanour, cast, mien.

aspiration NOUN = **aim**, desire, objective, ambition, goal, wish, hope, dream, longing, yearning.

aspire VERB = **desire**, hope, long, wish, dream, yearn, aim, seek.

aspiring ADJ = **would-be**, aspirant, potential, hopeful, expectant, ambitious; [inf] wannabe.

assail VERB see **attack**.

assassin NOUN = **murderer**, killer, gunman; [inf] hit

man.

assassinate VERB
= **murder**, kill, execute,
slay, eliminate.

assault VERB 1 = **attack**,
strike, hit, punch, beat
up, thump; [inf] lay into,
rough up. 2 = **molest**, rape,
sexually assault, interfere
with.

assemble VERB 1 = **gather**,
collect, congregate, meet,
rally, convene; round up,
summon, muster,
mobilize, marshal.
2 = **construct**, build, erect,
set up, piece/fit together,
fabricate, manufacture,
connect, join.

assembly NOUN
= **gathering**, meeting,
crowd, group,
congregation, throng,
rally, convention.

assent NOUN = **agreement**,
consent, acceptance,
approval, permission,
sanction, acquiescence,
approbation. VERB = **agree**,
accept, consent, comply,
approve, acquiesce,
concede, concur, accede.

assert VERB = **declare**,
state, maintain, contend,
pronounce, insist,
proclaim, claim, swear,
affirm, aver.

assertive ADJ = **confident**,
self-assured, assured,
forceful, strong-willed,
authoritative, dominant,
pushy, decisive,
determined.

assess VERB = **judge**,
evaluate, estimate, gauge,
rate, determine, work out,
appraise, weigh up,
reckon.

asset NOUN 1 = **advantage**,
benefit, strength, strong
point, forte, resource,
blessing, boon, godsend.
2 (**assets**) = **wealth**,
money, resources, capital,
property, possessions,
belongings, holdings,
goods, valuables, estate,
effects, chattels.

assign VERB 1 = **allocate**,
allot, give, distribute,
share out, apportion,
consign. 2 = **appoint**,
select, nominate,
designate, name,
delegate, commission.

assignation NOUN
= **rendezvous**, date,
meeting, tryst,
appointment.

assignment NOUN 1 = **task**,
job, duty, mission,
undertaking.
2 = **allocation**,
distribution, allotment,

apportionment.

assimilate VERB = **absorb**, take in, digest, grasp, understand; incorporate, integrate.

assist VERB 1 = **help**, aid, support, lend a hand, play a part, abet, cooperate, collaborate, support, back.
2 = **facilitate**, make easier, boost, further, promote, expedite.

assistance NOUN = **help**, aid, a helping hand, support, backing, cooperation, collaboration.

assistant NOUN = **helper**, subordinate, second-in-command, aide, deputy, number two, right-hand man/woman, man/girl Friday; [inf] sidekick.

associate VERB 1 = **link**, connect, relate, join.
2 = **mix**, socialize, keep company, fraternize, rub shoulders; [inf] hobnob, hang out.

association NOUN = **federation**, alliance, partnership, union, confederation, syndicate, coalition, league, cartel, consortium, club.

assorted ADJ = **various**, miscellaneous, mixed, varied, diverse, sundry, multifarious; [old use] divers.

assortment NOUN = **mixture**, mixed bag, selection, variety, collection, jumble, miscellany.

assume VERB 1 = **suppose**, presume, think, take it, take for granted, believe, surmise, conclude, imagine, guess, gather.
2 = **adopt**, acquire, put on, affect. 3 = **undertake**, accept, take on, shoulder.

assumption NOUN = **supposition**, presumption, belief, hypothesis, theory, conjecture, surmise, conclusion, guess, expectation, premise.

assurance NOUN 1 = **self-confidence**, self-assurance, poise, confidence. 2 = **promise**, guarantee, word, oath, pledge, bond.

assure VERB = **promise**, guarantee, give your word, swear, pledge, vow, declare, affirm, attest.

assured ADJ 1 = **confident**, self-confident, self-assured, self-reliant,

astonish

poised. **2 = certain**, definite, guaranteed, sure, confirmed.

astonish VERB **= amaze**, astound, stagger, stun, surprise, dumbfound, take aback, startle, stupefy, flabbergast.

astute ADJ **= shrewd**, clever, quick, quick-witted, acute, canny, wily, cunning, artful; intelligent, perceptive, insightful, sagacious, wise.

asylum NOUN **= refuge**, sanctuary, shelter, safety, protection, safe haven.

asymmetrical ADJ **= uneven**, lopsided, askew, crooked, unbalanced, irregular, awry.

athletic ADJ **1 = muscular**, strong, well built, powerful, sturdy, robust, strapping, brawny; fit, in trim. **2 = sporting**, sports, gymnastic.

atmosphere NOUN **1 = air**, sky, heavens, stratosphere, ether. **2 = ambience**, air, mood, feeling, spirit, character, tone, quality, flavour, aura, tenor.

atom NOUN **= bit**, particle, scrap, shred, speck, fragment, jot, trace, iota, crumb, grain.

atone VERB **= make amends**, compensate, make up for, pay, do penance, make good, expiate.

atrocious ADJ **= appalling**, abominable, terrible, dreadful, vile, outrageous, wicked, horrific, horrifying, sickening, revolting, ghastly, heinous, despicable, monstrous, inhuman, hideous, fiendish, diabolical.

atrocity NOUN **= outrage**, crime, offence, horror, abomination, monstrosity, violation, evil.

atrophy VERB **= waste away**, wither, shrivel, decay, wilt, deteriorate, decline, degenerate.

attach VERB **= fasten**, stick, affix, join, connect, link, tie, couple, pin, add, append.

attack VERB **1 = assault**, assail, set on, beat up, strike, hit, punch; charge, pounce; [inf] lay into, do over, rough up. **2 = criticize**, censure, condemn, denounce, pillory. NOUN 1 = **assault**, offensive, raid, ambush, sortie, onslaught, charge, strike, invasion, foray, incursion. 2 = **criticism**, censure, condemnation, denunciation, tirade, diatribe. 3 = **fit**, seizure, bout, spasm, convulsion, paroxysm.

attain VERB = **achieve**, accomplish, gain, obtain, get, win, earn, acquire, reach, realize, fulfil, succeed in, bring off, secure, procure.

attempt VERB = **try**, strive, endeavour, seek, aim, undertake, make an effort, have a go; [inf] have a shot/crack. NOUN = **try**, go, effort, endeavour.

attend VERB 1 = **be present**, appear, put in an appearance, turn up, visit, go to; [inf] show up. 2 = **look after**, take care of, care for, nurse, tend, see to, minister to. 3 = **escort**, accompany, chaperone, guide, conduct, usher, shepherd. 4 = **pay attention**, take notice/ note, listen, concentrate, heed.

attention NOUN 1 = **consideration**, contemplation, deliberation, observation, scrutiny, thought, study, investigation. 2 = **notice**, awareness, observation, heed, recognition, regard. 3 = **care**, treatment, therapy, ministration.

attentive ADJ 1 = **alert**, aware, watchful, awake, observant, vigilant, intent, focused, committed, heedful. 2 = **considerate**, thoughtful, helpful, conscientious, polite, kind, obliging.

attitude NOUN = **view**, point of view, opinion, viewpoint, outlook, belief, standpoint, frame of mind, position, perspective, stance, thoughts, ideas.

attract VERB = **appeal to**, interest, fascinate, charm, captivate, entice, tempt, engage, bewitch, seduce, beguile, lure.

attractive ADJ = **good-looking**, beautiful, handsome, pretty, lovely, stunning, striking, gorgeous, desirable, appealing, seductive, fetching, comely, prepossessing; [inf] cute.

attribute NOUN = **quality**, feature, characteristic, property, mark, sign, trait. VERB = **ascribe**, assign, put down to, credit, impute, chalk up.

audacious ADJ = **bold**, daring, fearless, brave, courageous, intrepid, valiant, plucky, reckless, daredevil.

audacity NOUN 1 = **boldness**, daring, fearlessness, bravery, courage, valour, pluck. 2 = **effrontery**, cheek, impudence, impertinence, gall.

audience NOUN 1 = **spectators**, listeners, viewers, crowd, house, turnout, congregation. 2 = **interview**, meeting, hearing, consultation.

augment VERB = **increase**, add to, top up, supplement, enlarge, expand, multiply, extend, boost, amplify, swell, magnify.

augury NOUN = **sign**, omen, portent, warning, prophecy.

august ADJ = **dignified**, stately, majestic, noble, imposing, impressive, exalted, grand.

auspicious ADJ = **favourable**, promising, hopeful, encouraging, bright, rosy, fortunate, propitious, timely.

austere ADJ 1 = **plain**, severe, simple, unadorned, unornamented, stark. 2 = **abstemious**, spartan, self-disciplined, puritanical, frugal, ascetic, self-denying.

authentic ADJ 1 = **genuine**, real, true, bona fide, actual, legitimate, valid; [inf] the real McCoy. 2 = **true**, accurate, honest, reliable, dependable.

authenticate VERB = **verify**, validate, prove, confirm, substantiate, corroborate.

author NOUN = **writer**, novelist, dramatist, playwright, poet, essayist, journalist.

authoritarian ADJ = **dictatorial**, domineering, tyrannical, strict, despotic, autocratic, imperious, high-handed, bossy.

authoritative ADJ 1 = **reliable**, accurate, authentic, sound, dependable, definitive, valid. **2** = **confident**, self-assured, assertive, commanding, masterful, lordly.

authority NOUN **1** = **right**, power, authorization, prerogative; jurisdiction, influence, rule, command, charge, sovereignty, supremacy; [inf] say-so. **2** (**authorities**) = **government**, administration, officialdom, establishment; [inf] powers that be. **3** = **expert**, specialist, master, pundit.

authorize VERB = **permit**, allow, agree to, consent to, approve, sanction, endorse, license.

automatic ADJ **1** = **automated**, mechanical, mechanized, electronic, computerized, robotic. **2** = **instinctive**, spontaneous, involuntary, unconscious, reflex, knee-jerk, unthinking, mechanical.

autonomy NOUN = **independence**, freedom, self-government, self-determination, self-sufficiency, individualism.

auxiliary ADJ = **additional**, supplementary, ancillary, extra, reserve, spare, back-up.

available ADJ = **obtainable**, to hand, handy, unoccupied, vacant, at your disposal, ready, convenient, accessible.

avaricious ADJ = **greedy**, grasping, covetous, acquisitive, rapacious.

average ADJ **1** = **ordinary**, usual, standard, normal, typical, regular. **2** = **mediocre**, unexceptional, middling, run-of-the-mill, undistinguished, ordinary, unremarkable. NOUN = **mean**, median.

averse ADJ = **opposed**, hostile, antipathetic, unwilling, disinclined, reluctant, loath.

aversion NOUN = **dislike**, distaste, hatred, repugnance, antipathy; reluctance, unwillingness.

avert VERB = **deflect**, ward off, fend off, turn aside/away, parry, stave off, prevent.

avid ADJ = **keen**, eager, enthusiastic, fervent, ardent, fanatical, zealous, passionate.

avoid VERB 1 = **evade**, keep away from, steer clear of, dodge, give a wide berth to, sidestep; [inf] duck, get out of. 2 = **abstain from**, refrain from, eschew.

await VERB = **wait for**, expect, anticipate.

award NOUN 1 = **prize**, trophy, decoration, medal, reward. 2 = **grant**, scholarship, bursary. VERB = **confer**, give, grant, bestow, present, endow.

aware ADJ = **conscious**, mindful, familiar, informed, acquainted, cognizant.

awareness NOUN = **consciousness**, perception, realization, knowledge, sense, understanding, appreciation.

awe NOUN = **wonder**, wonderment, amazement, admiration, respect.

awesome ADJ = **sublime**, awe-inspiring, stupendous, breathtaking, magnificent, impressive, imposing, dramatic, grand, marvellous, amazing, stunning.

awful ADJ see **bad**.

awkward ADJ 1 = **inconvenient**, difficult, troublesome, problematic. 2 = **unwieldy**, cumbersome, unmanageable, bulky. 3 = **clumsy**, ungainly, uncoordinated, graceless, gawky. 4 = **uncooperative**, unhelpful, disobliging, contrary, obstructive, perverse; [inf] bloody-minded. 5 = **embarrassing**, uncomfortable, tricky, difficult.

Bb

babble VERB = **chatter**, prattle, gabble, jabber.

baby NOUN = **infant**, newborn, child, babe. ADJ = **miniature**, tiny, little, mini, dwarf.

babyish ADJ = **childish**, infantile, immature, juvenile, puerile.

back NOUN 1 = **rear**, stern,

tail end, end. **2** = **reverse**, other side. ADJ = **rear**, hind, end, hindmost, last. VERB **1** = **support**, uphold, sanction, endorse, champion; sponsor, finance, underwrite. **2** = **reverse**, back off, retreat, withdraw, backtrack.

backer NOUN = **supporter**, champion; sponsor, promoter, patron, underwriter; [inf] angel.

background NOUN = **surroundings**, setting, context, circumstances, conditions, framework, environment.

backing NOUN see **support**.

backslide VERB = **relapse**, lapse, regress, revert, weaken, slip.

bad ADJ **1** = **poor**, inadequate, unsatisfactory, substandard, inferior, defective, deficient, faulty, incompetent, second-rate, inept, shoddy, awful, terrible, dreadful, frightful; [inf] hopeless, lousy. **2** = **unpleasant**, disagreeable, nasty, horrid, horrible, foul, appalling, atrocious.

3 = **serious**, severe, grave, dangerous, disastrous, calamitous, dire. **4** = **immoral**, wicked, evil, corrupt, sinful, criminal, depraved, villainous, dishonest, dishonourable, base. **5** = **mischievous**, naughty, unruly, wayward, disobedient. **6** = **rotten**, decayed, mouldy, off, rancid, sour, putrid.

badge NOUN = **emblem**, crest, insignia; sign, mark, symbol.

badger VERB = **pester**, bother, plague, nag, harass, torment, persecute.

baffle VERB = **bewilder**, bemuse, mystify, perplex, puzzle, confuse, confound, nonplus, floor, bamboozle; [inf] flummox, stump.

bag NOUN = **handbag**, shoulder bag; case, suitcase, grip, satchel, holdall, rucksack. VERB **1** = **catch**, capture, shoot, kill, trap, snare, land. **2** = **get**, gain, acquire, obtain, reserve, secure, get hold of.

baggage NOUN = **luggage**, bags, cases, belongings,

things.
bait NOUN = **lure**, decoy,
attraction, enticement,
temptation, incentive,
inducement, carrot. VERB
= **tease**, taunt, torment,
provoke, annoy, harass,
plague, persecute.
balance NOUN 1 = **stability**,
poise, steadiness,
equilibrium.
2 = **correspondence**,
equivalence, symmetry,
equality, parity,
proportion, equipoise,
evenness. 3 = **remainder**,
rest, difference, residue.
VERB 1 = **steady**, stabilize,
poise. 2 = **offset**, cancel
out, counterbalance,
compensate for, even up.
bald ADJ 1 = **hairless**, bare,
smooth. 2 = **plain**, simple,
unadorned,
straightforward,
forthright, frank, direct,
blunt, stark.
ball NOUN = **sphere**, globe,
orb, globule.
ballot NOUN = **vote**, poll,
election, referendum,
plebiscite.
ban VERB = **prohibit**, forbid,
veto, outlaw, proscribe,
interdict, bar, debar,
exclude, banish. NOUN
= **prohibition**, veto,

embargo, moratorium,
boycott, bar, proscription.
banal ADJ = **trite**, clichéd,
hackneyed,
commonplace,
unoriginal,
unimaginative, stale,
boring, dull, stock,
stereotyped,
platitudinous; [inf] corny,
old hat.
band NOUN 1 = **group**, troop,
troupe, crowd, crew, gang,
company, body, pack,
bunch. 2 = **group**,
orchestra, ensemble.
3 = **stripe**, strip, line, belt,
bar, streak, swathe.
bandit NOUN = **brigand**,
outlaw, robber, thief,
highwayman, footpad,
desperado, gangster,
hijacker.
bandy VERB 1 = **exchange**,
swap, trade. 2 = **spread**,
circulate, pass on,
disseminate. ADJ = **bowed**,
curved, bent, bow-legged.
bang NOUN 1 = **boom**, crash,
thud, slam, clash, clap,
report, explosion.
2 = **blow**, bump, knock,
slap, punch, stroke, cuff,
smack, rap; [inf] whack. ADV
= **exactly**, precisely,
absolutely, right.
banish VERB 1 = **exile**, expel,

exclude, deport, expatriate, ostracize, eject, evict, outlaw, oust. **2** = **dismiss**, drive away, dispel, get rid of, suppress.

bank NOUN **1** = **slope**, mound, embankment, hillock, incline, ridge, rise, pile, mass. **2** = **edge**, shore, brink, side, margin, embankment. **3** = **store**, reserve, supply, fund, stock, hoard, repository, pool, reservoir. **4** = **row**, array, panel, tier.

bankrupt ADJ = **insolvent**, ruined, in liquidation, destitute, penniless; [inf] broke, bust.

banner NOUN = **flag**, standard, pennant, pennon, colours, ensign, streamer.

banquet NOUN = **feast**, repast, dinner; [inf] blow-out, spread.

banter NOUN = **repartee**, badinage, raillery, teasing, joking.

bar NOUN **1** = **beam**, rod, pole, shaft, stake, stick, spar, rail. **2** = **barrier**, obstacle, obstruction, impediment, hindrance, check, deterrent, problem, difficulty.

3 = **band**, stripe, belt, strip, streak, line. **4** = **cake**, slab, block, brick, wedge; ingot. **5** = **pub**, public house, inn, tavern. VERB **1** = **exclude**, ban, banish, keep out, prohibit, forbid, outlaw, ostracize, proscribe. **2** = **block**, obstruct, check, impede, prevent.

barbarian NOUN = **savage**, brute, ruffian, hooligan, lout; [inf] yob.

barbaric ADJ **1** = **uncivilized**, primitive, wild, unsophisticated, crude, brutish. **2** = **cruel**, brutal, savage, bestial, barbarous, vicious, ferocious.

bare ADJ **1** = **naked**, nude, undressed, stripped; [inf] starkers, in the buff. **2** = **empty**, unfurnished, plain, undecorated, austere. **3** = **plain**, simple, unadorned, unvarnished, unembellished, basic, essential, bald, stark. **4** = **mere**, minimum, paltry, meagre, scanty. VERB = **reveal**, uncover, expose, lay bare; strip.

barely ADV = **hardly**, scarcely, just, narrowly, by the skin of your teeth.

bargain NOUN = **agreement**,

deal, pact, contract, arrangement, understanding, promise, pledge. VERB 1 = **negotiate**, haggle, barter, argue.
2 (**bargain on/for**) = **expect**, allow for, anticipate, be prepared for, take into account.

barrage NOUN
1 = **broadside**, bombardment, fusillade, salvo, volley, battery, shelling, cannonade.
2 = **onslaught**, deluge, torrent, stream, storm.

barrel NOUN = **cask**, keg, vat, butt, tun, hogshead.

barren ADJ 1 = **infertile**, unproductive, unfruitful, waste, desert, arid, bare, bleak, desolate, lifeless, empty. 2 = **sterile**, infertile, childless.

barricade NOUN see **barrier**. VERB = **block off**, blockade, bar, obstruct; fortify, defend.

barrier NOUN 1 = **bar**, fence, railing, barricade, blockade, roadblock.
2 = **obstacle**, obstruction, hurdle, hindrance, impediment, bar, stumbling block.

barter VERB = **haggle**, bargain, negotiate, discuss terms.

base NOUN 1 = **foundation**, foot, bottom, support, stand, pedestal, plinth, rest, substructure.
2 = **basis**, core, fundamentals, essence, essentials, root, heart, source, origin, mainspring.
3 = **headquarters**, centre, camp, station, post, starting point. VERB
1 = **found**, build, support, rest, ground, construct, establish. 2 = **locate**, station, centre, situate, place. ADJ = **ignoble**, dishonourable, mean, low, sordid, contemptible, shameful, shabby, despicable, unworthy, disreputable, unprincipled, immoral, evil, wicked, sinful.

basic ADJ 1 = **fundamental**, essential, intrinsic, underlying, primary, central, key, indispensable, vital.
2 = **plain**, simple, austere, spartan, unadorned, stark, minimal.

basin NOUN = **bowl**, dish, pan, container, receptacle.

basis NOUN 1 = **foundation**,

base, grounding, support.
2 = **starting point**,
beginning, point of
departure, cornerstone,
core, essence, heart,
thrust. 3 = **footing**,
position, arrangement,
condition, status; system,
way, method.

bask VERB = **lie**, laze, relax,
sunbathe, lounge, loll;
wallow, luxuriate, revel,
delight, relish, lap up.

batch NOUN = **set**, group,
lot, collection, bunch,
quantity, pack.

bathe VERB 1 = **wash**, clean,
cleanse, rinse, soak, steep,
wet, immerse. 2 = **swim**, go
swimming, take a dip.

baton NOUN = **stick**, rod,
staff, wand.

batter VERB = **beat**, hit,
strike, bash, bludgeon,
belabour, pound.

battle NOUN = **conflict**,
fight, fighting, clash,
engagement, skirmish,
affray, confrontation,
combat, encounter,
campaign, war, action,
hostilities, fray, struggle,
crusade.

battlefield NOUN
= **battleground**, front,
combat zone, theatre of
war.

bawdy ADJ = **ribald**,
indecent, salacious,
earthy, suggestive,
naughty, racy, raunchy,
risqué, erotic, titillating.

bawl VERB 1 = **shout**, cry,
yell, roar, bellow, holler.
2 = **sob**, wail, cry, howl,
weep, blubber.

bay NOUN 1 = **cove**, inlet,
gulf, basin, arm, bight,
creek, fjord, estuary.
2 = **alcove**, recess, niche,
opening, nook.

bazaar NOUN 1 = **market**,
mart, souk. 2 = **fête**, fair,
bring-and-buy sale.

beach NOUN = **shore**,
strand, seashore, sands,
seaside.

beached ADJ = **stranded**,
high and dry, aground,
stuck, marooned.

bead NOUN = **drop**, droplet,
globule, drip, blob, dot,
dewdrop.

beaker NOUN = **cup**, mug,
glass, tumbler.

beam NOUN 1 = **bar**, spar,
rafter, girder, support,
boom, plank, board, joist,
timber. 2 = **ray**, shaft,
stream, streak, pencil,
gleam. VERB 1 = **emit**,
radiate, shine, broadcast,
transmit, direct. 2 = **smile**,
grin.

bear VERB 1 = **hold**, support, carry, sustain, prop up, shoulder. 2 = **bring**, carry, transport, convey, fetch, deliver, move, take. 3 = **endure**, tolerate, abide, stand, cope with, brook, stomach, put up with. 4 = **produce**, yield, give, supply, provide.

bearable ADJ = **endurable**, tolerable, supportable, sustainable.

bearing NOUN 1 = **carriage**, deportment, posture, stance, gait, demeanour, air, behaviour, manner. 2 = **relevance**, pertinence, connection, significance, relation, application.

beast NOUN 1 = **animal**, creature, brute. 2 = **brute**, monster, fiend, devil, ogre.

beat VERB 1 = **hit**, strike, batter, thrash, slap, whip, cuff, cane, smack, thump, pound, drub, flog; [inf] bash, whack, clout, wallop. 2 = **pulsate**, throb, pound, palpitate, thump, vibrate. 3 = **defeat**, outdo, conquer, trounce, vanquish, overcome, subdue, outclass. 4 = **whisk**, whip, stir, blend, mix. NOUN

1 = **pulsation**, vibration, throbbing, pounding, palpitation. 2 = **rhythm**, tempo, metre, measure, time.

beautiful ADJ = **lovely**, attractive, pretty, gorgeous, ravishing, stunning, good-looking, exquisite; picturesque, scenic; [Scottish] bonny; [old use] fair, comely.

beautify VERB = **adorn**, embellish, decorate, prettify; [inf] do up, titivate.

beauty NOUN = **attractiveness**, loveliness, prettiness, good looks, glamour; [old use] comeliness.

because CONJ = **since**, as, for the reason that, seeing that/as.

beckon VERB = **gesture**, signal, gesticulate, motion.

become VERB 1 = **turn into**, grow into, develop into; grow, get, come to be. 2 = **suit**, flatter, look good on. 3 = **befit**, suit, behove.

becoming ADJ = **flattering**, fetching, attractive, elegant, stylish, chic, tasteful.

bedraggled ADJ

= **dishevelled**, untidy, unkempt, messy, disarranged.

befall VERB = **happen (to)**, occur, take place, come about, come to pass, transpire; [literary] betide.

before PREP 1 = **prior to**, previous to, earlier than, in advance of, leading up to. 2 = **in front of**, in the presence of, in the sight of. 3 = **rather than**, in preference to, sooner than. ADV = **earlier**, previously, beforehand, in advance, formerly, ahead.

befuddled ADJ = **confused**, bemused, dazed, bewildered, muddled, groggy.

beg VERB 1 = **ask for money**, cadge; [inf] scrounge. 2 = **plead**, entreat, ask, seek, crave, beseech, implore, pray, supplicate.

beget VERB 1 = **father**, sire, spawn. 2 = **produce**, give rise to, bring about, cause, result in, lead to.

beggar NOUN = **vagrant**, tramp, down-and-out, mendicant, sponger; [inf] scrounger.

begin VERB 1 = **start**, commence, set about, embark on, initiate, establish, institute, inaugurate, found, pioneer. 2 = **arise**, emerge, appear, occur, happen, originate, materialize, spring up.

beginner NOUN = **novice**, learner, trainee, apprentice, new recruit.

beginning NOUN 1 = **start**, origin, commencement, outset, dawn, rise, birth, inception, emergence, genesis. 2 = **prelude**, introduction, preface, opening.

beguile VERB = **charm**, attract, delight, enchant, bewitch, please; lure, seduce, tempt, deceive, trick.

behave VERB 1 = **act**, conduct yourself, perform, function, acquit yourself. 2 = **be good**, be polite, mind your manners.

behaviour NOUN = **conduct**, actions, deportment, manners, ways.

being NOUN 1 = **creature**, living thing, animal, person, individual, human, mortal. 2 = **existence**, life, actuality, reality.

belated ADJ = **late**, overdue, delayed, tardy, behind time.

belief NOUN 1 = **opinion**, judgement, view, thought, feeling, conviction, way of thinking, theory, notion, impression. 2 = **faith**, creed, credo, doctrine, dogma, persuasion, tenet, teaching, ideology.

believe VERB 1 = **accept**, be convinced by, trust; [inf] swallow, buy, fall for. 2 = **think**, hold, suppose, reckon, be of the opinion, imagine, conjecture, understand, surmise, guess, hypothesize.

belittle NOUN = **disparage**, slight, deprecate, make light of, detract from, denigrate, scoff at.

belligerent ADJ see **aggressive**.

belong VERB 1 = **be owned by**, be the property of. 2 = **be a member of**, be in, be associated with, be affiliated to. 3 = **be at home**, be suited, fit in, be accepted.

belongings PLURAL NOUN = **property**, possessions, effects, goods, chattels; [inf] stuff, things.

beloved ADJ = **loved**, adored, dear, dearest, cherished, treasured, prized, precious, darling.

belt NOUN 1 = **girdle**, sash, waistband, cummerbund. 2 = **strip**, stretch, band, region, zone, area, tract.

bemused ADJ = **bewildered**, confused, puzzled, perplexed, baffled, befuddled, disconcerted.

bend VERB 1 = **turn**, curve, twist, curl, veer, swerve, loop, wind. 2 = **stoop**, lean, crouch, bow, hunch. NOUN = **curve**, corner, turn, twist, arc, loop, crook.

benefactor NOUN = **helper**, supporter, sponsor, patron, backer, donor; [inf] angel.

beneficial ADJ = **advantageous**, favourable, profitable, helpful, useful, worthwhile, valuable, rewarding.

benefit NOUN 1 = **advantage**, asset; [inf] plus. 2 = **good**, welfare, well-being, advantage, convenience; aid, assistance, help, service. VERB 1 = **help**, serve, aid, assist, advance, further, forward, boost, improve, better. **2** = **gain**, profit, do well.

benevolent ADJ = **kind**, kind-hearted, kindly, benign, generous, beneficent, magnanimous, humanitarian, altruistic, philanthropic, caring, compassionate.

benign ADJ see **benevolent**.

bent ADJ = **determined**, resolved, set, committed, fixated, insistent. NOUN = **tendency**, inclination, leaning, talent, gift, flair, ability, aptitude, predilection, propensity, proclivity.

bequeath VERB = **leave**, will, make over, pass on, hand down, transfer, donate, give.

bequest NOUN = **legacy**, inheritance, endowment.

berth NOUN **1** = **bunk**, bed, cot. **2** = **mooring**, dock, quay, pier.

beseech VERB = **implore**, beg, entreat, plead with, appeal to, call on.

best ADJ = **finest**, greatest, top, foremost, leading, pre-eminent, premier, prime, first, supreme, superlative, unrivalled, second to none, unsurpassed, peerless, matchless, unparalleled, ideal, perfect.

bestial ADJ = **savage**, brutish, brutal, barbaric, cruel, vicious, violent.

bestow VERB = **confer**, grant, endow with, vest in, present, award.

bet VERB = **wager**, gamble, stake, risk, put/lay money, speculate. NOUN = **wager**, stake; [inf] flutter.

betray VERB = **be disloyal to**, break your promise to, be unfaithful to, inform on, stab in the back; [inf] do the dirty on, grass on, shop.

bias NOUN = **prejudice**, partiality, partisanship, favouritism, unfairness, one-sidedness, bigotry, discrimination.

bid NOUN **1** = **offer**, tender, proposal. **2** = **attempt**, effort, endeavour, try; [inf] crack, stab.

big ADJ **1** = **large**, great, tall, high, huge, immense, enormous, colossal, massive, mammoth, vast, prodigious, gigantic, giant, monumental, gargantuan, king-size;

[inf] whopping, mega.
2 = **important**, significant, major, momentous, weighty, far-reaching, critical.

bigoted ADJ = **prejudiced**, biased, one-sided, narrow-minded, discriminatory, intolerant, blinkered.

bill NOUN = **invoice**, account, statement; [US] check; [inf] tab.

bind VERB = **tie (up)**, fasten, secure, make fast, attach, strap, lash, tether.

birth NOUN **1** = **childbirth**, delivery, nativity, confinement. **2** = **ancestry**, lineage, blood, descent, parentage, family, extraction, origin, stock.

bit NOUN **1** = **piece**, fragment, scrap, shred, crumb, grain, speck, snippet, spot, drop, pinch, dash, iota, jot, whit, atom, particle; [inf] smidgen, tad. **2** = **moment**, minute, second; [inf] jiffy, tick.

bitter ADJ **1** = **acrid**, tart, sour, sharp, harsh, unsweetened.
2 = **resentful**, embittered, rancorous, begrudging, spiteful, sour, jaundiced.
3 = **painful**, distressing, upsetting, grievous, sad, tragic, harrowing, agonizing. **4** = **cold**, icy, freezing, biting, piercing, penetrating.

bizarre ADJ see **weird (2)**.

black ADJ **1** = **jet**, ebony, sable, inky, sooty, pitch-black, pitch-dark, raven.
2 = **evil**, wicked, sinful, bad, cruel, depraved, vile, corrupt. **3** = **disastrous**, bad, tragic, calamitous, fateful, grievous. **4** see **gloomy**.

blame VERB **1** = **accuse**, hold responsible, condemn. **2** = **attribute**, ascribe, impute. NOUN = **responsibility**, accountability, guilt, fault, culpability, liability.

blameless ADJ = **innocent**, faultless, guiltless, irreproachable, unimpeachable, above reproach.

bland ADJ **1** = **tasteless**, insipid, flavourless.
2 = **dull**, boring, uninteresting, uninspired, uninspiring, unoriginal, unexciting, tedious, vapid.

blank ADJ **1** = **bare**, plain, clean, unmarked, clear.
2 = **expressionless**,

inscrutable, impassive, unresponsive, vacant, empty, uncomprehending, glazed, vacuous, emotionless, uninterested. **3** = **confused**, baffled, bewildered, at a loss, uncomprehending, puzzled, perplexed.

blasphemous ADJ = **profane**, sacrilegious, irreligious, impious, irreverent, disrespectful.

blasphemy NOUN = **sacrilege**, profanity, impiety, impiousness, irreverence.

blast NOUN **1** = **gust**, gale, wind, squall. **2** = **explosion**, detonation, discharge, burst. **3** = **blare**, roar, wail, hoot. VERB = **blow up**, bomb, dynamite, explode.

blatant ADJ = **flagrant**, glaring, obvious, undisguised, overt, brazen, shameless, bare-faced, naked, sheer, stark, unmistakable, out-and-out.

blaze NOUN **1** = **fire**, conflagration, flames, inferno. **2** = **beam**, gleam, shine, radiance, dazzle, flash, flare. VERB **1** = **burn**, be on fire, flame, catch fire. **2** = **shine**, dazzle, beam, flare, flash, glitter.

bleak ADJ **1** = **desolate**, bare, barren, exposed, cold, unwelcoming, waste, desert, stark, windswept. **2** = **dismal**, dreary, gloomy, depressing, discouraging, disheartening, miserable, hopeless.

blemish NOUN = **defect**, flaw, fault, imperfection, blot, stain, mark, blotch. VERB = **spoil**, mar, damage, injure, mark, stain, taint, disfigure, discolour, tarnish, blot.

blend VERB = **mix**, combine, mingle, amalgamate, unite, merge, compound, fuse, coalesce, meld. NOUN = **mixture**, mix, combination, amalgam, fusion, union, amalgamation, synthesis.

bless VERB = **sanctify**, consecrate, dedicate, make sacred.

blessed ADJ **1** = **sacred**, holy, consecrated, hallowed, sanctified. **2** = **welcome**, gratifying, much needed, wonderful, marvellous. **3** (**blessed**

with) = **favoured with**, endowed with, having, lucky to have.

blessing NOUN
1 = **benediction**, dedication, prayer, invocation. **2** = **approval**, permission, consent, sanction, backing, endorsement, assent, support, approbation; [inf] go-ahead. **3** = **godsend**, boon, benefit, bonus, help, stroke of luck.

blight NOUN **1** = **disease**, fungus, infestation, canker. **2** = **affliction**, scourge, bane, curse, plague, misfortune, trouble. VERB = **ruin**, destroy, spoil, wreck.

blind ADJ **1** = **sightless**, unseeing, unsighted. **2** = **obtuse**, blinkered, imperceptive, unaware, insensitive, heedless, careless, unobservant, oblivious, uncritical, unthinking, unreasoning, irrational. NOUN **1** = **shutter**, shade, curtain, screen. **2** = **cover**, pretext, camouflage, smokescreen, front, facade.

bliss NOUN see **ecstasy**.

bloated ADJ = **swollen**, distended, puffy, inflated, enlarged.

blob NOUN = **drop**, droplet, globule, ball, bead, spot, splash, blotch.

block VERB **1** = **clog**, choke, jam, close, obstruct, constrict, stop up, plug, dam, barricade, bar. **2** = **hinder**, prevent, obstruct, hamper, impede, frustrate, thwart, check, stop, halt. NOUN **1** = **blockade**, barrier, barricade, obstacle, bar, hindrance, impediment, obstruction, deterrent, check, stumbling block. **2** = **bar**, piece, chunk, hunk, cake, lump, slab.

blood NOUN = **ancestry**, lineage, family, descent, birth, extraction, pedigree, origin, stock.

bloodshed NOUN = **killing**, carnage, slaughter, murder, massacre, butchery, bloodletting, bloodbath.

bloodthirsty ADJ = **savage**, cruel, murderous, ferocious, homicidal, vicious, brutal, barbaric, barbarous, violent.

bloom NOUN **1** = **blossom**, flower. **2** = **freshness**, radiance, glow,

perfection, beauty. VERB
1 = **flower**, blossom,
burgeon, bud. 2 = **flourish**,
prosper, thrive, be
healthy, be happy, do
well.

blot NOUN 1 = **spot**, smudge,
blotch, stain, mark, blob,
smear, splodge.
2 = **blemish**, imperfection,
eyesore, defect, fault, flaw.
VERB 1 = **mark**, stain,
smudge, blotch, spatter.
2 (**blot out**) = **obliterate**,
erase, efface, wipe out,
delete; obscure, conceal,
hide.

blow VERB 1 = **puff**, blast,
gust, roar, bluster. 2 = **waft**,
buffet, whirl, whisk,
sweep, drive, carry,
convey. 3 = **sound**, play,
toot. NOUN 1 = **hit**, bang,
knock, slap, smack,
punch, rap; [inf] whack,
wallop, clout, bash.
2 = **shock**, bombshell,
upset, disaster, calamity,
catastrophe,
disappointment, setback.

blow up 1 = **explode**,
detonate, burst, blast.
2 = **inflate**, pump up, swell,
distend, puff up.

blueprint NOUN = **design**,
plan, diagram, prototype,
model, pattern,
representation.

bluff VERB = **pretend**, sham,
feign, fake, lie; trick,
deceive, mislead,
hoodwink, hoax, dupe,
fool. ADJ = **blunt**,
straightforward, frank,
candid, outspoken, direct,
forthright.

blunder VERB = **make a
mistake**, slip up, err,
miscalculate, bungle. NOUN
= **error**, mistake, slip,
miscalculation, faux pas,
oversight, gaffe.

blunt ADJ 1 = **dull**,
unsharpened, rounded.
2 = **direct**, frank,
straightforward, candid,
forthright, bluff,
outspoken, brusque,
abrupt, undiplomatic,
tactless. VERB = **dull**, take
the edge off, deaden,
numb, dampen, lessen,
reduce.

blurred ADJ = **indistinct**,
blurry, hazy, misty,
cloudy, foggy, fuzzy,
vague, unfocused,
unclear, obscure, ill-
defined, nebulous, dim,
faint.

blurt VERB (**blurt out**) = **let
slip**, blab, disclose, reveal,
let out, divulge; [inf] spill
the beans, let on.

blush VERB = **redden**, flush, colour, go red.

blustery ADJ = **stormy**, windy, gusty, squally, wild, tempestuous, violent.

board NOUN 1 = **plank**, beam, panel, slat, timber. 2 = **food**, meals, provisions, keep. 3 = **panel**, committee, council, directorate. VERB 1 = **get on**, go aboard, enter, embark, mount. 2 = **lodge**, stay, live, room.

boast VERB 1 = **brag**, crow, swagger, show off; [inf] blow your own trumpet. 2 = **possess**, have, own, pride itself on, enjoy, benefit from.

boastful ADJ = **conceited**, bragging, arrogant, swollen-headed, full of yourself; [inf] cocky, big-headed.

bodily ADJ = **corporeal**, physical, corporal, fleshly; material, tangible.

body NOUN 1 = **figure**, frame, form, physique, build; trunk, torso. 2 = **corpse**, cadaver, carcass, remains. 3 = **set**, group, band, party, company, crowd, number. 4 = **accumulation**, collection, quantity, mass, corpus.

bog NOUN = **marsh**, swamp, fen, quagmire, morass, mire.

bogged down = **stuck**, mired, hampered, hindered, obstructed, swamped, overwhelmed.

bohemian ADJ = **unconventional**, eccentric, unorthodox, original, avant-garde, artistic, alternative; [inf] offbeat, way-out.

boisterous ADJ = **lively**, spirited, animated, playful, exuberant, frisky, unruly, rough, wild, irrepressible, undisciplined, rumbustious, uproarious, rowdy, noisy.

bold ADJ 1 = **daring**, brave, adventurous, dauntless, courageous; plucky, intrepid, audacious, confident, fearless, valiant, heroic, valorous, undaunted, daredevil. 2 = **striking**, eye-catching, prominent, conspicuous, noticeable, vivid, bright, strong.

bolster VERB = **support**, prop up, shore up, hold up, reinforce, buttress, strengthen, aid, help.

bolt NOUN = **bar**, latch, lock, catch, fastening, pin, peg, rivet. VERB 1 = **lock**, latch, bar, fasten, secure. 2 = **run**, dash, sprint, dart, rush, hurtle, hurry, fly, flee, escape; [inf] scarper. 3 = **gobble**, guzzle, wolf, gulp, devour.

bombard VERB = **attack**, shell, bomb, blitz, strafe, blast, pound, fire at, assault, assail, batter.

bonanza NOUN = **windfall**, godsend, bonus, jackpot.

bond NOUN 1 = **chain**, fetter, shackle, manacle, restraint. 2 = **link**, connection, tie, attachment, relationship, friendship, association. 3 = **contract**, agreement, deal, pledge, promise, guarantee, word. VERB = **unite**, join, bind, connect, attach, fasten, fix, secure, stick, glue, fuse.

bonus NOUN = **gain**, benefit, advantage, extra, plus, boon.

bony ADJ = **thin**, angular, lean, skeletal, emaciated, cadaverous, gaunt; [inf] scrawny.

book NOUN = **volume**, tome, work, title, publication.

VERB = **reserve**, charter, order, pre-arrange.

booklet NOUN = **leaflet**, pamphlet, brochure.

boom VERB = **resound**, reverberate, rumble, thunder, bang, roar, crash. NOUN 1 = **crash**, bang, blast, rumble, roar, thunder, reverberation. 2 = **upturn**, upsurge, improvement, growth, surge, increase, boost.

boorish ADJ = **rude**, crude, loutish, coarse, ill-mannered, uncivilized, uncouth, oafish, vulgar; [inf] yobbish.

boost VERB = **encourage**, help, support, uplift, increase, raise, heighten, promote, further, advance, improve, assist. NOUN = **impetus**, encouragement, stimulus, spur; increase, upturn, rise, improvement, advance; [inf] shot in the arm.

booth NOUN 1 = **stall**, stand, kiosk. 2 = **cubicle**, compartment, cabin.

booty NOUN = **loot**, plunder, haul, spoils, gains, pickings; [inf] swag.

border NOUN = **edge**, perimeter, verge,

boundary, frontier, borderline, limit, margin, periphery, brink, fringe, rim. VERB 1 = **adjoin**, abut, touch, join, be next to. 2 = **surround**, enclose, encircle, circle, edge, fringe, bound. 3 (**border on**) = **verge on**, approach, come close to, approximate, resemble.

bore VERB 1 = **stultify**, weary, tire, pall on, leave cold. 2 = **pierce**, drill, cut; tunnel, mine, dig, sink.

boring ADJ = **tedious**, dull, uninteresting, monotonous, dreary, humdrum, uninspiring, soporific, unvaried, tiresome, wearisome.

boss NOUN = **head**, chief, leader, manager, director, employer, supervisor, foreman, overseer; [inf] gaffer.

bossy ADJ = **domineering**, overbearing, dictatorial, high-handed, authoritarian, imperious, officious.

botch VERB = **bungle**, make a mess of, do badly, mismanage; [inf] mess up, screw up.

bother VERB 1 = **disturb**, inconvenience, pester, harass, annoy, irritate, vex, plague, hound; [inf] hassle. 2 = **take the time**, make the effort, go to the trouble. 3 = **trouble**, worry, concern, distress, perturb. NOUN 1 = **nuisance**, annoyance, irritation, pest, trouble, worry. 2 = **trouble**, disturbance, commotion, disorder, uproar, fighting, brouhaha.

bottom NOUN 1 = **base**, foundation, basis, substructure, underpinning. 2 = **lowest point**, nadir. 3 = **underneath**, underside, lower side, underbelly.

bounce VERB = **jump**, leap, spring, bob, rebound, skip, recoil, ricochet.

bound VERB = **leap**, jump, spring, skip, hop, vault, bounce. ADJ 1 = **certain**, sure, destined, fated. 2 (**bound for**) = **heading for**, going to, travelling towards, making for.

boundary NOUN = **frontier**, border, borderline, limit, edge, dividing line, perimeter, margin, bounds, periphery, fringe.

boundless ADJ = **unlimited**, infinite,

unbounded, unending,
untold, inexhaustible,
immeasurable, vast.

bounty NOUN = **generosity**,
munificence, altruism,
largesse, benevolence,
kindness, philanthropy.

bouquet NOUN 1 = **bunch of flowers**, spray, posy,
nosegay, corsage.
2 = **smell**, aroma,
fragrance, scent, perfume,
nose.

bout NOUN 1 = **attack**, spell,
fit, period, paroxysm.
2 = **match**, contest, fight,
round, competition,
encounter.

bow VERB 1 = **curtsy**, bob,
bend your knee, salaam.
2 = **submit**, yield, give in,
surrender, accept,
capitulate.

bowels PLURAL NOUN
1 = **intestines**, entrails,
guts, viscera, insides.
2 = **interior**, depths, inside,
core, belly.

bowl NOUN = **basin**, dish,
pan, container, vessel.

box NOUN = **container**,
receptacle, crate, case,
carton, pack, package,
chest, trunk, coffer,
casket.

boy NOUN = **youth**, lad,
youngster, schoolboy, kid,
stripling.

boycott NOUN = **ban**,
embargo, veto, bar,
prohibition, sanction,
restriction.

brace VERB 1 = **strengthen**,
support, reinforce, shore
up, prop up, buttress.
2 = **steady**, secure,
stabilize. 3 = **prepare**,
(get) ready, nerve.

bracing ADJ = **invigorating**,
refreshing, stimulating,
energizing, reviving,
restorative, fresh, brisk,
crisp.

brag VERB see **boast**.

brains PLURAL NOUN
= **intelligence**, intellect,
mind, cleverness, wit,
brainpower, shrewdness,
acumen.

branch NOUN 1 = **bough**,
limb, stem, arm.
2 = **department**, division,
subdivision, section,
subsection, part, wing.
VERB = **fork**, divide,
separate, bifurcate, split,
subdivide.

brand NOUN = **make**, type,
kind, sort, variety, line,
trade name, trademark.
VERB 1 = **stamp**, mark,
burn, sear. 2 = **stigmatize**,
mark out, label.

brandish VERB = **flourish**,

wave, wield, raise, swing, display, shake.

bravado NOUN = **bluster**, swaggering, boldness, machismo, bragging, boasting.

brave ADJ = **courageous**, valiant, fearless, intrepid, plucky, heroic, bold, daring, undaunted, lion-hearted, spirited, dauntless, valorous.

bravery NOUN = **courage**, courageousness, fearlessness, pluck, boldness, intrepidity, daring, nerve, valour; [inf] guts.

brawl NOUN = **fight**, scuffle, affray, fracas, skirmish, free-for-all, tussle, brouhaha.

brawny ADJ = **muscular**, powerful, burly, strong, robust, sturdy, strapping.

brazen ADJ = **bold**, shameless, unashamed, unabashed, defiant, barefaced, blatant, impudent, insolent, cheeky.

breach NOUN 1 = **violation**, infringement, contravention, transgression. 2 = **rift**, split, break, schism, estrangement, separation, division. 3 = **break**, rupture, split, opening, crack, gap, hole, fissure, fracture. VERB 1 = **break through**, burst, rupture. 2 = **break**, contravene, violate, infringe, defy, disobey, flout.

break VERB 1 = **smash**, crack, shatter, split, burst, fracture, fragment, splinter, snap, disintegrate. 2 = **violate**, contravene, infringe, breach, disobey, defy, flout. 3 = **stop**, pause, rest, discontinue, give up. 4 = **beat**, surpass, outdo, better, exceed, top, cap. 5 = **tell**, announce, reveal, impart, disclose, divulge. NOUN 1 = **interval**, pause, stop, halt, intermission, rest, respite, breathing space; [inf] breather. 2 = **breach**, split, rupture, rift, discontinuation.

breakdown NOUN 1 = **stoppage**, failure, malfunctioning. 2 = **collapse**, failure, disintegration, foundering. 3 = **analysis**, classification, examination, categorization.

breakthrough NOUN

= **advance**, leap forward, quantum leap, discovery, find, innovation, development, improvement, revolution.

breathe VERB 1 = **inhale**, exhale, respire; puff, pant, gasp, wheeze. 2 = **whisper**, murmur, sigh, say.

breathtaking ADJ = **spectacular**, magnificent, awesome, awe-inspiring, amazing, astounding, exciting, thrilling, stunning.

breed VERB 1 = **reproduce**, procreate, multiply, give birth. 2 = **produce**, bring about, give rise to, create, generate, stir up, engender, foster, arouse. NOUN 1 = **variety**, type, kind, strain, stock, line. 2 = **stock**, species, race, lineage, extraction, pedigree.

breezy ADJ = **windy**, blowy, blustery, gusty, fresh.

brevity NOUN = **conciseness**, concision, pithiness, succinctness, incisiveness.

brew VERB 1 = **make**, prepare, infuse, ferment. 2 = **be imminent**, loom, develop, be impending.

bribe VERB = **buy off**, pay off, suborn. NOUN = **inducement**, incentive; [inf] backhander, sweetener.

bridge NOUN 1 = **viaduct**, overpass, flyover. 2 = **bond**, link, tie, connection. VERB = **span**, cross, go over, pass over, traverse, extend across.

bridle VERB 1 = **restrain**, curb, check, keep control of, govern, master, subdue. 2 = **bristle**, take offence, take umbrage, be affronted.

brief ADJ = **short**, concise, succinct, to the point, terse, pithy; quick, fleeting, momentary, passing. VERB = **instruct**, inform, tell, prepare, prime; [inf] fill in.

bright ADJ 1 = **shining**, brilliant, vivid, dazzling, sparkling, glittering, gleaming, radiant, glowing, shimmering, luminous. 2 = **intelligent**, clever, smart, brainy, quick-witted. 3 = **promising**, encouraging, favourable, hopeful, auspicious, propitious.

brighten VERB 1 = **light up**, lighten, illuminate,

irradiate. **2** = **cheer up**, gladden, enliven, animate; [inf] perk up, buck up.

brilliant ADJ **1** = **bright**, shining, intense, radiant, beaming, gleaming, sparkling, dazzling, lustrous. **2** see **clever**.

brim NOUN = **rim**, lip, edge, brink.

bring VERB **1** = **fetch**, carry, bear, take, convey, transport, deliver; lead, guide, conduct, usher, escort. **2** = **cause**, create, produce, result in, engender, occasion, wreak.

brink NOUN **1** = **edge**, margin, limit, rim, boundary, fringe. **2** = **verge**, threshold, point.

brisk ADJ **1** = **quick**, rapid, fast, swift, speedy, energetic, lively, vigorous, sprightly, spirited. **2** = **abrupt**, curt, brusque, sharp, crisp.

bristle NOUN = **hair**, stubble, whisker, prickle, spine, quill, barb.

brittle ADJ = **breakable**, hard, crisp, fragile, delicate.

broach VERB = **introduce**, raise, bring up, mention, touch on.

broad ADJ **1** = **wide**, large, extensive, vast, expansive, sweeping. **2** = **wide-ranging**, comprehensive, inclusive, encyclopedic, all-embracing. **3** = **general**, non-specific, rough, approximate; loose, vague.

broadcast VERB **1** = **transmit**, relay, put on air, televise. **2** = **announce**, make public, report, publicize, air, spread, circulate, disseminate. NOUN = **programme**, show, transmission.

broad-minded ADJ = **open-minded**, liberal, tolerant, fair, free-thinking, enlightened, permissive.

brochure NOUN = **booklet**, leaflet, pamphlet, handout, circular.

brood NOUN = **offspring**, young, family, clutch, litter. VERB = **worry**, agonize, fret, dwell on.

brook NOUN = **stream**, burn, beck, rivulet, runnel. VERB = **tolerate**, stand, bear, allow.

browse VERB = **look through**, skim, scan,

glance at, thumb through, leaf through, peruse.

brush NOUN 1 = **broom**, sweeper, besom, whisk. 2 = **encounter**, clash, confrontation, conflict, skirmish, tussle. VERB 1 = **sweep**, clean, groom, buff. 2 = **touch**, graze, kiss, glance.

brusque ADJ = **abrupt**, curt, blunt, short, terse, gruff, offhand, discourteous.

brutal ADJ = **savage**, cruel, vicious, sadistic, violent, bloodthirsty, callous, murderous, heartless, merciless, inhuman, barbarous, barbaric, ferocious.

brute NOUN 1 = **animal**, beast, creature. 2 = **savage**, monster, sadist, fiend, devil.

bubble VERB = **fizz**, foam, froth, effervesce, boil, simmer.

bubbly ADJ 1 = **fizzy**, foamy, frothy, effervescent, sparkling. 2 = **vivacious**, lively, animated, excited, bouncy, ebullient.

bucket NOUN = **pail**, pitcher, scuttle.

buckle NOUN = **clasp**, fastener, clip, catch, hasp. VERB 1 = **fasten**, do up, strap, hook, clasp, clip. 2 = **bend**, twist, contort, warp, crumple, distort.

bud NOUN = **shoot**, sprout, floret. VERB = **sprout**, shoot, germinate.

budget NOUN = **financial plan**, forecast, statement, account, allowance, allocation, quota.

buff NOUN = **fan**, enthusiast, aficionado, devotee, expert. VERB = **polish**, shine, rub, burnish.

buffet[1] NOUN = **cafe**, cafeteria, snack bar.

buffet[2] VERB = **batter**, strike, pound, hit, lash, strike.

bug NOUN 1 = **insect**; [inf] creepy-crawly. 2 = **germ**, virus, microbe, micro-organism. 3 = **fault**, flaw, defect, gremlin, error, imperfection.

build VERB = **construct**, make, erect, put up, assemble, set up, create, form. NOUN = **physique**, body, frame, shape.

building NOUN = **structure**, construction, edifice, pile, erection.

build-up NOUN = **growth**, increase, expansion, enlargement, accumulation, escalation, development.

bulge VERB = **swell**, project, protrude, stick out, balloon, distend. NOUN = **swelling**, bump, protuberance, protrusion, lump.

bulk NOUN 1 = **size**, volume, quantity, weight, mass, magnitude, dimensions. 2 = **majority**, preponderance, greater part, body.

bulky ADJ = **unwieldy**, awkward, large, big, massive, hulking, weighty.

bulletin NOUN = **report**, announcement, statement, newsflash, message, communiqué, communication, dispatch.

bully VERB = **intimidate**, coerce, browbeat, oppress, persecute, torment, terrorize, tyrannize, cow.

bulwark NOUN 1 = **rampart**, embankment, fortification, bastion. 2 = **support**, defence, guard, protection, safeguard.

bump VERB 1 = **hit**, bang, strike, knock, crash into, collide with. 2 = **bounce**, jolt, shake, jerk, rattle. NOUN 1 = **bang**, crash, thud, thump, knock, smash, collision. 2 = **lump**, swelling, contusion, injury, bulge, protuberance.

bumpy ADJ = **rough**, uneven, rutted, potholed, pitted, lumpy.

bunch NOUN 1 = **collection**, cluster, batch, set, bundle, sheaf, clump. 2 = **bouquet**, spray, posy, nosegay. 3 = **group**, crowd, band, gang, flock, knot, cluster.

bundle NOUN = **bunch**, collection, heap, stack, parcel, bale, sheaf. VERB 1 = **tie**, wrap, pack, parcel, roll. 2 = **push**, shove, hurry, hustle, manhandle.

bungle VERB = **botch**, mess up, make a mess of, mismanage, spoil, muff; [inf] screw up.

burden NOUN 1 = **load**, weight, cargo, freight. 2 = **responsibility**, duty, obligation, onus, charge, care, worry, problem, trouble, difficulty, encumbrance. VERB 1 = **load**, overload, be laden, weigh down, encumber, hamper. 2 = **trouble**, worry, oppress, distress, afflict, torment, strain, tax, overwhelm.

bureau NOUN 1 = **agency**, office, department, service. 2 = **desk**, writing desk.

bureaucracy NOUN = **officialdom**, administration, civil service, government; regulations, paperwork, red tape.

burglar NOUN = **housebreaker**, intruder, thief, robber.

burglary NOUN = **break-in**, housebreaking, breaking and entering, theft, robbery.

burial NOUN = **funeral**, interment, entombment, obsequies.

burlesque NOUN = **parody**, caricature, mockery, travesty, satire, lampoon; [inf] send-up, spoof.

burly ADJ = **well built**, muscular, brawny, thickset, stocky, beefy, sturdy, big, strong, strapping, hefty.

burn VERB 1 = **be on fire**, be alight, blaze, smoulder, flare, flicker. 2 = **set fire to**, set alight, ignite, light, kindle, incinerate, sear, char, scorch. 3 = **long**,

yearn, crave, hunger, lust, hanker.

burning ADJ 1 = **on fire**, blazing, ablaze, alight, smouldering. 2 = **intense**, eager, passionate, fervent, ardent, fervid. 3 = **important**, crucial, significant, urgent, pressing, critical, vital, essential, pivotal.

burrow NOUN = **tunnel**, hole, hollow, lair, den, earth, warren, set. VERB = **dig**, tunnel, excavate, mine, hollow out.

burst VERB 1 = **split**, break open, rupture, shatter, explode, fracture, disintegrate, fragment. 2 = **rush**, charge, dash, career, plough, hurtle.

bury VERB 1 = **inter**, lay to rest, entomb. 2 = **conceal**, hide, cover, engulf.

bush NOUN 1 = **shrub**, plant; undergrowth, shrubbery. 2 = **scrub**, brush, the wild, backwoods.

bushy ADJ = **thick**, shaggy, dense, luxuriant, spreading.

business NOUN 1 = **trade**, commerce, traffic, industry, buying and selling. 2 = **company**, firm, enterprise, corporation, concern, organization, venture. **3 = occupation**, profession, line, career, job, trade, vocation, work, employment. **4 = concern**, affair, responsibility, duty, function, obligation, problem.

businesslike ADJ **= professional**, efficient, organized, methodical, systematic, well ordered, practical.

bustle NOUN **= activity**, flurry, stir, movement, hustle, hurly-burly, commotion, excitement. VERB **= hurry**, rush, dash, scurry, scramble, run.

busy ADJ **1 = hectic**, active, full, eventful, energetic, tiring. **2 = unavailable**, otherwise engaged; [inf] tied up. **3 = engaged**, occupied, involved, working, hard at work, absorbed, engrossed; [inf] on the go.

busybody NOUN **= meddler**, troublemaker, mischief-maker, gossip; [inf] nosy parker.

butt NOUN **1 = handle**, shaft, hilt, haft. **2 = stub**, end, remnant; [inf] dog end. **3 = target**, victim, object, subject. VERB **1 = knock**, shove, bump, push. **2 = interrupt**, intrude, interfere.

buttocks NOUN **= bottom**, posterior, rump, backside, behind, hindquarters; [inf] bum.

buttonhole VERB **= accost**, waylay, detain, take aside.

buttress NOUN **= support**, prop, reinforcement, strut, stanchion, pier. VERB **= strengthen**, support, reinforce, prop up, shore up, brace, underpin.

buy VERB **= purchase**, pay for, procure, get, acquire, obtain, come by. NOUN **= purchase**, acquisition, bargain, deal.

bygone ADJ **= past**, former, previous, earlier, one-time, of old, antiquated, ancient, obsolete, outmoded.

bystander NOUN **= onlooker**, spectator, eyewitness, witness, watcher, passer-by.

Cc

cabin NOUN 1 = **hut**, shack, shed, chalet, lodge. 2 = **berth**, compartment.

cable NOUN = **rope**, cord, hawser, line, guy; wire, lead.

cadaverous ADJ = **gaunt**, haggard, emaciated, skeletal, ashen, pale, wan, ghostly.

cadence NOUN = **rhythm**, beat, tempo, lilt, intonation, modulation.

cafe NOUN = **cafeteria**, snack bar, bistro, buffet, brasserie.

cage NOUN = **pen**, enclosure, pound, coop, hutch, aviary.

cajole VERB = **coax**, wheedle, persuade, prevail on, inveigle; [inf] sweet-talk.

cake NOUN 1 = **bun**, gateau, pastry. 2 = **block**, bar, slab, lump, cube. VERB 1 = **clot**, harden, solidify, congeal, coagulate. 2 = **cover**, coat, plaster, encrust.

calamitous ADJ = **disastrous**, catastrophic, devastating, cataclysmic, dire, tragic.

calamity NOUN = **disaster**, catastrophe, tragedy, misfortune, cataclysm.

calculate VERB 1 = **work out**, compute, determine, count up, figure, reckon up, total. 2 = **estimate**, gauge, judge. 3 = **design**, plan, aim, intend.

calculating ADJ see **crafty**.

calibre NOUN 1 = **bore**, gauge, diameter, size. 2 = **quality**, worth, stature, distinction, ability, merit, talent, capability, expertise.

call VERB 1 = **cry (out)**, shout, exclaim, yell, scream, roar. 2 = **telephone**, phone, ring. 3 = **convene**, summon, order, convoke. 4 = **name**, christen, baptize, dub, designate, describe as, label, term. NOUN 1 = **cry**, shout, exclamation, yell, scream, roar. 2 = **need**, occasion, reason, cause, justification, grounds, excuse.

callous ADJ = **insensitive**, unfeeling, hard, heartless, hard-hearted, cold, uncaring, unsympathetic, merciless, pitiless.

callow ADJ = **immature**, inexperienced, naive, unsophisticated; [inf] wet behind the ears.

calm ADJ **1** = **composed**, relaxed, collected, cool, controlled, self-controlled, self-possessed, tranquil, unruffled, serene, unflappable, imperturbable, poised, level-headed, equable; [inf] laid-back. **2** = **still**, windless, tranquil, quiet, peaceful. VERB **1** = **soothe**, quieten, pacify, placate. **2** = **compose yourself**, control yourself, cool down, get a grip. NOUN = **composure**, self-control, tranquillity, serenity, sangfroid, quietness, peace, peacefulness.

camouflage NOUN = **disguise**, concealment, mask, screen, cover-up, front, facade, blind. VERB = **disguise**, hide, conceal, mask, screen, cloak, cover.

camp NOUN = **encampment**, settlement, campsite, camping ground, bivouac.

campaign NOUN **1** = **battle**, war, offensive, attack. **2** = **crusade**, drive, push, struggle, battle plan, strategy. VERB = **fight**, battle, work, crusade, strive, struggle.

cancel VERB **1** = **call off**, abandon, scrap, drop, axe. **2** = **annul**, invalidate, nullify, revoke, rescind, countermand, withdraw, quash. **3** (**cancel out**) = **counterbalance**, offset, counteract, neutralize.

cancer NOUN = **carcinoma**, tumour, malignancy, growth.

candid ADJ = **frank**, open, honest, truthful, direct, plain-spoken, blunt, straightforward, sincere, forthright.

candidate NOUN = **applicant**, interviewee; contender, nominee, aspirant, possibility.

candour NOUN = **frankness**, honesty, truthfulness, openness, directness, sincerity.

canvass VERB **1** = **campaign**, electioneer, drum up support. **2** = **propose**, suggest, discuss, debate.

canyon NOUN = **ravine**, gorge, gully, defile.

capable ADJ = **able**, competent, effective, efficient, proficient, accomplished, talented, adept, skilful, experienced, practised, qualified.

capacity NOUN **1** = **volume**, size, magnitude, dimensions, measurements, proportions. **2** = **ability**, capability, competence, proficiency, skill, talent. **3** = **position**, post, job, office; role, function.

caper VERB = **frolic**, romp, skip, gambol, prance, dance.

capital NOUN = **assets**, wealth, finance, funds, principal, cash, savings, resources, means, reserves, property, wherewithal.

capitulate VERB = **surrender**, yield, give in/up, back down, submit, cave in, relent.

capricious ADJ = **fickle**, unpredictable, unreliable, impulsive, changeable, mercurial, volatile, erratic, wayward.

capsize VERB = **overturn**, turn over, keel over, turn turtle.

capsule NOUN = **pill**, tablet, lozenge.

captain NOUN
1 = **commander**, master; [inf] skipper. **2** = **chief**, head, leader; [inf] boss.

captivate VERB = **charm**, delight, enchant, bewitch, fascinate, beguile, entrance, mesmerize, enthral, enrapture.

captive ADJ = **imprisoned**, caged, incarcerated, confined, detained, interned; [inf] under lock and key. NOUN = **prisoner**, detainee, internee.

captivity NOUN
= **imprisonment**, detention, confinement, internment, incarceration.

capture VERB = **catch**, arrest, apprehend, take prisoner, take captive, seize.

carafe NOUN = **flask**, decanter, jug, pitcher, bottle, flagon.

carcass NOUN = **body**, corpse, remains, cadaver.

care NOUN **1** = **safe keeping**, supervision, custody, charge, protection, control, responsibility; guardianship.

2 = **carefulness**, caution, heed, attention; thought, regard, consideration, concern, solicitude.

3 = **worry**, anxiety, trouble, stress, pressure, strain; sorrow, woe, hardship. VERB = **mind**, be concerned, worry/trouble yourself, bother.

career NOUN = **profession**, occupation, job, vocation, calling, employment, line of work, métier.

carefree ADJ = **unworried**, untroubled, blithe, airy, nonchalant, insouciant, happy-go-lucky, free and easy, easy-going, relaxed; [inf] laid back.

careful ADJ 1 = **cautious**, alert, attentive, watchful, vigilant, wary, on your guard, heedful.

2 = **conscientious**, painstaking, meticulous, diligent, scrupulous, punctilious, methodical.

careless ADJ
1 = **inattentive**, thoughtless, negligent, unthinking, heedless, irresponsible, remiss.

2 = **slapdash**, shoddy, slipshod; [inf] sloppy.

caress VERB = **fondle**, stroke, touch, pet.

caretaker NOUN = **janitor**, concierge.

cargo NOUN = **freight**, load, consignment, goods, merchandise, shipment.

caricature NOUN
= **cartoon**, parody, lampoon, burlesque, satire.

carnage NOUN = **slaughter**, massacre, butchery, blood bath, holocaust, pogrom.

carnal ADJ = **sexual**, sensual, erotic, lustful, lascivious, fleshly, bodily, physical.

carnival NOUN = **festival**, celebration, fiesta, gala, festivity.

carriage NOUN 1 = **coach**, vehicle. 2 = **bearing**, deportment, posture, stance, comportment.

carry VERB 1 = **convey**, transport, move, transfer, take, bring, fetch, bear, haul, lug. 2 = **support**, bear, sustain, hold up, shoulder. 3 = **involve**, lead to, result in, entail.

carton NOUN = **box**, container, package, packet, pack.

cartoon NOUN
1 = **animation**, comic strip.

2 = **caricature**, parody, lampoon, burlesque, satire.

carve VERB **1** = **sculpt**, sculpture, chisel, cut, hew, whittle, form, shape, fashion, mould. **2** = **engrave**, etch, incise. **3** = **slice**, cut up.

cascade NOUN = **waterfall**, falls, cataract. VERB = **gush**, pour, surge, spill, overflow, stream.

case NOUN **1** = **instance**, occurrence, manifestation, demonstration, example, illustration, specimen. **2** = **situation**, position, state of affairs, circumstances, conditions, facts. **3** = **trial**, proceedings, lawsuit, action, suit. **4** = **container**, box, receptacle, canister, crate, carton, pack, suitcase, trunk.

cash NOUN = **money**, change, notes, coins; currency.

cask NOUN = **barrel**, keg, vat, butt, tun.

cast VERB **1** = **throw**, toss, fling, pitch, hurl, sling, lob, launch. **2** = **emit**, give off, send out, shed, radiate, diffuse, spread.

3 = **mould**, form, fashion, sculpt, model.

castigate VERB = **rebuke**, reprimand, scold, censure, upbraid, berate, admonish, chide, take to task, chastise.

castle NOUN = **fortress**, citadel, stronghold, keep.

castrate VERB = **neuter**, geld, sterilize, cut.

casual ADJ **1** = **indifferent**, unconcerned, lackadaisical, blasé, nonchalant, insouciant, offhand; easy-going, free and easy, blithe, carefree, devil-may-care; [inf] laid-back. **2** = **chance**, accidental, unplanned, unexpected, unforeseen, serendipitous. **3** = **relaxed**, informal, friendly, unceremonious.

casualty NOUN = **fatality**, victim, loss.

catacomb NOUN = **crypt**, tomb, vault, sepulchre.

catalogue NOUN = **list**, record, register, inventory, index, directory, archive.

cataract NOUN = **waterfall**, falls, cascade, rapids.

catastrophe NOUN = **disaster**, calamity, cataclysm, tragedy.

catch VERB **1** = **grasp**, seize,

grab, clutch, grip, hold; receive, intercept.
2 = **capture**, apprehend, arrest, take prisoner; trap, snare; [inf] nab. **3** = **hear**, make out, discern, perceive, understand, follow, grasp. **4** = **surprise**, come across, discover, find. **5** = **contract**, get, develop, go down with.
NOUN **1** = **bolt**, lock, fastening, fastener, clasp, hasp, hook, latch.
2 = **snag**, disadvantage, drawback, difficulty, hitch, stumbling block.

catching ADJ = **contagious**, infectious, communicable, transmittable, transmissible.

categorical ADJ = **unqualified**, unconditional, unequivocal, unambiguous, definite, absolute, emphatic, positive, direct, conclusive, unreserved.

category NOUN = **class**, group, classification, type, sort, kind, variety, grade, order, rank.

catholic ADJ = **wide**, broad, wide-ranging, all-embracing, comprehensive, all-inclusive, eclectic, diverse.

cause NOUN **1** = **origin**, source, root, beginning, mainspring, author, originator, creator, agent. **2** = **reason**, basis, grounds, justification, call, need. **3** = **principle**, ideal, belief, conviction. VERB = **bring about**, produce, create, give rise to, lead to, result in, provoke, generate, engender, arouse, occasion, precipitate.

caustic ADJ **1** = **corrosive**, acid. **2** = **cutting**, sarcastic, scathing, mordant, sharp, bitter, acerbic.

caution NOUN **1** = **care**, wariness, circumspection, vigilance, heed, attention. **2** = **warning**, reprimand. VERB **1** = **warn**, advise, urge, counsel. **2** = **reprimand**, admonish, rebuke.

cautious ADJ = **careful**, wary, guarded, circumspect, chary, watchful, vigilant, attentive, heedful.

cavalcade NOUN = **parade**, procession, cortège, march past.

cavalier ADJ = **offhand**, indifferent, casual,

dismissive, insouciant, unconcerned.

cave NOUN = **cavern**, grotto, pothole, cavity.

cavity NOUN = **hole**, hollow, crater, pit, gap, space.

cease VERB = **stop**, finish, quit, end, discontinue, suspend, terminate; desist, leave off, refrain from.

ceaseless ADJ = **endless**, constant, continual, continuous, non-stop, perpetual, never-ending, incessant, relentless, unremitting, interminable, everlasting.

celebrate VERB 1 = **enjoy yourself**, make merry, revel, party.
2 = **commemorate**, honour, observe, keep, toast, drink to.

celebration NOUN
1 = **party**, festival, festivity, revelry, merrymaking, jollification.
2 = **commemoration**, remembrance, observance.

celebrity NOUN = **star**, superstar, personality, household name.

celibate ADJ = **chaste**, pure, virginal, abstinent, self-denying.

cemetery NOUN
= **graveyard**, burial ground, churchyard, necropolis.

censor VERB = **expurgate**, bowdlerize, cut, delete, edit.

censorious ADJ = **critical**, disapproving, judgemental, moralistic, fault-finding, captious.

censure NOUN = **criticism**, blame, condemnation, denunciation, castigation, disapproval, reproof, reproach, rebuke, reprimand. VERB see **criticize**.

central ADJ 1 = **middle**, mid, mean. 2 = **main**, chief, principal, foremost, basic, fundamental, key, essential, primary, pivotal, core, cardinal.

centre NOUN = **middle**, heart, core, nucleus, mid point, hub, kernel, focus, focal point.

ceremonial ADJ = **formal**, official, state, public; ritual, stately, courtly, solemn.

ceremony NOUN 1 = **rite**, ritual, observance; service, sacrament, liturgy. 2 = **pomp**, protocol, formalities, decorum, etiquette.

certain ADJ 1 = **sure**, confident, convinced, satisfied, persuaded. 2 = **assured**, inevitable, destined, inescapable, inexorable, unarguable. 3 = **definite**, unquestionable, undisputed, reliable, dependable, infallible, foolproof.

certainty NOUN 1 = **confidence**, assurance, conviction, certitude. 2 = **inevitability**, foregone conclusion.

certificate NOUN = **certification**, authorization, document, credentials, guarantee; licence, diploma.

certify VERB = **verify**, guarantee, attest, validate, confirm, substantiate, endorse, vouch for, testify to, prove, demonstrate.

cessation NOUN = **end**, finish, termination, conclusion, discontinuation.

chagrin NOUN = **annoyance**, irritation, dissatisfaction, anger, vexation, displeasure; embarrassment, mortification, shame.

chain NOUN 1 = **shackle**, fetter, manacle, bonds, coupling, link. 2 = **series**, succession, sequence, string, train, course.

challenge VERB 1 = **dare**, invite, throw down the gauntlet to, defy. 2 = **question**, dispute, call into question, protest against, object to, disagree with. 3 = **stimulate**, inspire, stretch, test, tax.

challenging ADJ = **stimulating**, inspiring, testing, demanding, taxing.

champion NOUN 1 = **winner**, prizewinner, medallist, victor, title-holder. 2 = **supporter**, defender, upholder, backer, advocate, proponent. VERB = **advocate**, promote, defend, support, uphold, stand up for, back.

chance NOUN 1 = **accident**, coincidence, luck, fate, destiny, fluke, providence, serendipity, fortuity. 2 = **possibility**, likelihood, prospect, probability, odds. 3 = **opportunity**, time, occasion, turn. ADJ = **accidental**, fortuitous, adventitious, fluky, coincidental, serendipitous; unintentional, unintended, inadvertent, unplanned.

change VERB 1 = **alter**, adjust, transform, modify, convert, vary, fluctuate, amend, rearrange, reorganize, reform, reconstruct, transmute, metamorphose, transmogrify, mutate. 2 = **exchange**, swap, switch, substitute; transpose. NOUN 1 = **alteration**, modification, adaptation, difference, transformation, conversion, variation, reorganization, rearrangement, reconstruction, shift, transition, metamorphosis, transmutation, mutation, transmogrification. 2 = **coins**, silver, cash.

changeable ADJ = **variable**, shifting, fluctuating, unstable, unsteady, irregular, erratic, unreliable, inconsistent, unpredictable, volatile, capricious, fickle, inconstant, mercurial.

channel NOUN 1 = **passage**, strait, waterway, fjord. 2 = **gutter**, conduit, culvert, ditch, gully, trough. 3 = **medium**, means, agency, route. VERB = **convey**, conduct, transmit, transport, guide, direct.

chaos NOUN = **disorder**, disarray, disorganization, confusion, mayhem, bedlam, pandemonium, turmoil, tumult, uproar, disruption, upheaval, anarchy.

chaotic ADJ = **disorderly**, in disarray, disorganized, confused, topsy-turvy; tumultuous, anarchic.

character NOUN 1 = **personality**, nature, disposition, temperament, temper, make-up. 2 = **strength**, honour, integrity, moral fibre, fortitude, backbone. 3 = **eccentric**, original, individual, one-off. 4 = **letter**, sign, symbol, figure.

characteristic NOUN = **quality**, attribute, feature, trait, property, peculiarity, quirk, mannerism, idiosyncrasy, hallmark. ADJ = **typical**, distinctive, particular, special, peculiar, specific, idiosyncratic.

characterize VERB = **portray**, depict, describe, present, identify, categorize; typify, mark, distinguish.

charade NOUN = **pretence**, travesty, mockery, farce, parody, pantomime.

charge VERB 1 = **ask**, levy, demand, exact; invoice. 2 = **accuse**, arraign, indict, prosecute, try. 3 = **attack**, storm, assault, rush, assail. 4 = **entrust**, tax, burden, encumber, saddle. NOUN 1 = **cost**, rate, price, fee, payment, levy, toll. 2 = **accusation**, allegation, indictment, arraignment. 3 = **attack**, assault, offensive, raid, strike, onslaught. 4 = **care**, custody, responsibility, protection, safe keeping, guardianship.

charitable ADJ = **generous**, philanthropic, magnanimous, munificent, bountiful, open-handed; liberal, lenient, tolerant, kind, understanding, broad-minded, sympathetic.

charity NOUN 1 = **aid**, welfare, handouts, largesse, philanthropy. 2 = **compassion**, humanity, goodwill, sympathy, tolerance, generosity, kindness, altruism, humanitarianism, benevolence.

charm NOUN 1 = **attraction**, appeal, allure, fascination, charisma. 2 = **amulet**, trinket, talisman, mascot. VERB = **delight**, please, attract, captivate, fascinate, win over, bewitch, beguile, enchant, seduce, enthral, intrigue.

chart NOUN = **graph**, table, diagram, map, plan.

chase VERB = **pursue**, run after; hunt, track, trail, tail.

chasm NOUN = **abyss**, ravine, gorge, canyon, crevasse, fissure, rift.

chaste ADJ = **virginal**, celibate, abstinent, self-restrained, self-denying; innocent, virtuous, pure, undefiled, unsullied.

chasten VERB = **subdue**, humble, deflate, put someone in their place.

chastity NOUN = **celibacy**,

abstinence, virginity, self-restraint, self-denial, virtue, purity, innocence.

chat VERB = **talk**, gossip, chatter; [inf] natter. NOUN = **talk**, gossip, conversation, heart-to-heart.

chatty ADJ = **talkative**, garrulous, loquacious, voluble.

chauvinism NOUN = **jingoism**, xenophobia, racism, sexism, prejudice, bigotry.

cheap ADJ 1 = **inexpensive**, low-cost, economical, affordable, reasonable; cut-price, reduced, discounted. 2 = **poor-quality**, inferior, shoddy, tawdry, second-rate; [inf] tacky.

cheat VERB 1 = **deceive**, trick, swindle, defraud, dupe, hoodwink, double-cross; [inf] con. 2 = **avoid**, elude, evade, dodge, escape. NOUN = **swindler**, fraud, fake, charlatan, mountebank; [inf] con-man, phoney.

check VERB 1 = **examine**, inspect, look over, scrutinize, test, monitor, investigate, study, vet. 2 = **stop**, halt, arrest, slow down; obstruct, inhibit, bar, impede, block, curb, delay, thwart. NOUN = **examination**, inspection, scrutiny, test, investigation, study.

cheeky ADJ = **impudent**, impertinent, insolent, disrespectful, impolite, irreverent, forward; [inf] saucy.

cheer VERB 1 = **acclaim**, applaud, hail, clap. 2 = **brighten**, hearten, gladden, buoy up, enliven, uplift, perk up. NOUN 1 = **acclaim**, acclamation, applause, ovation; hooray, hurrah. 2 = **cheerfulness**, happiness, gladness, merriment, gaiety, joy, pleasure, jubilation, rejoicing, festivity, revelry.

cheerful ADJ 1 = **happy**, glad, merry, joyful, jolly, jovial, animated, buoyant, light-hearted, carefree, gleeful, cheery, jaunty, optimistic, in good spirits, sparkling, exuberant, blithe, happy-go-lucky. 2 = **bright**, sunny, pleasant, agreeable.

cherish VERB 1 = **treasure**, prize, hold dear, love,

adore, dote on, idolize, nurture, protect. **2** = **have**, entertain, harbour, cling to.

chest NOUN **1** = **breast**, thorax, sternum. **2** = **box**, crate, case, trunk, container, coffer, casket.

chew VERB = **bite**, crunch, gnaw, masticate, champ.

chic ADJ = **stylish**, fashionable, smart, elegant, sophisticated.

chief NOUN **1** = **chieftain**, headman, ruler, leader, overlord. **2** = **head**, principal, director, manager, chairman, governor; [inf] boss. ADJ **1** = **head**, leading, principal, premier, highest, foremost, supreme, arch. **2** = **main**, principal, cardinal, key, primary, prime, central, fundamental, predominant, pre-eminent, overriding.

child NOUN = **boy**, girl, youngster, infant, baby, toddler, tot, adolescent, juvenile, minor; [Scottish] bairn; son, daughter; [inf] kid, nipper.

childbirth NOUN = **labour**, delivery, confinement, parturition.

childhood NOUN = **youth**, infancy, babyhood, boyhood, girlhood, adolescence, minority.

childish ADJ = **immature**, infantile, juvenile, puerile, irresponsible, foolish, silly.

childlike ADJ = **innocent**, unsophisticated, trusting, gullible, naive, ingenuous, guileless, artless, credulous.

chilly ADJ **1** = **cold**, cool, wintry, frosty, icy, raw, freezing. **2** = **unfriendly**, aloof, unwelcoming, hostile.

chime VERB = **ring**, peal, toll.

chink NOUN = **crack**, gap, cleft, rift, slit, fissure, crevice, split, opening, aperture, cranny.

chip NOUN **1** = **shard**, flake, fragment, splinter, paring, sliver. **2** = **nick**, scratch, fault, flaw.

chivalrous ADJ = **courteous**, polite, gallant, gentlemanly, gracious, considerate, well mannered.

choice NOUN **1** = **selection**, election, choosing. **2** = **alternative**, option, possibility. **3** = **range**,

variety, assortment. ADJ
= **best**, excellent, superior,
first-rate, first-class, prize,
prime, select, special,
exclusive.

choke VERB 1 = **strangle**,
asphyxiate, throttle,
suffocate, smother, stifle.
2 = **clog**, bung up, block,
obstruct, plug, stop up.

choose VERB = **select**, pick,
decide on, opt for, plump
for, settle on, agree on,
elect; name, nominate,
vote for.

choosy ADJ = **fussy**,
particular, finicky,
pernickety, fastidious,
hard to please.

chop VERB 1 = **cut down**,
fell, hack down, hew, lop.
2 = **cut up**, dice, cube.

choppy ADJ = **rough**,
turbulent, stormy, squally.

chorus NOUN 1 = **choir**,
ensemble, choristers.
2 = **refrain**.

christen VERB = **baptize**,
name, call; dub,
designate, style, term.

chronic ADJ 1 = **persistent**,
long-lasting, long-
standing, constant,
continuing. 2 = **inveterate**,
confirmed, hardened.

chronicle NOUN = **record**,
account, history, story,
description, annals,
narrative, journal,
archive, log.

chubby ADJ = **plump**,
tubby, fat, dumpy, stout,
portly, rotund, roly-poly,
podgy.

chunk NOUN = **lump**, piece,
block, hunk, slab, wedge.

church NOUN = **house of
God**, cathedral, chapel,
abbey, minster.

churlish ADJ = **rude**,
impolite, boorish,
ungracious, ill-mannered,
discourteous, surly,
sullen.

cinema NOUN = **films**,
movies, motion pictures,
the silver screen.

circle NOUN 1 = **ring**, disc,
hoop, band. 2 = **group**, set,
crowd, ring, coterie,
clique. VERB 1 = **revolve**,
rotate, orbit,
circumnavigate, wheel,
whirl, swivel.
2 = **surround**, ring,
encircle, enclose.

circuitous ADJ = **winding**,
indirect, meandering,
roundabout, twisting,
tortuous, rambling,
zigzag.

circular ADJ = **round**,
annular. NOUN = **pamphlet**,
leaflet, flyer,

advertisement.

circulate VERB = **spread**, communicate, broadcast, disseminate, publicize, advertise, put about.

circumference NOUN = **perimeter**, border, boundary, edge, rim, verge, margin.

circumspect ADJ = **cautious**, wary, careful, chary, guarded, on your guard.

circumstances PLURAL NOUN = **situation**, state of affairs, conditions, position, context, background, factors, occurrences, events, happenings; facts.

citadel NOUN = **fortress**, fort, fortification, stronghold, bastion.

citation NOUN = **quotation**, quote, extract, excerpt, passage.

cite VERB = **quote**, mention, refer to, name, adduce, specify.

citizen NOUN = **subject**, national, native, passport-holder; inhabitant, resident, denizen.

city NOUN = **town**, conurbation, metropolis, municipality.

civil ADJ = **polite**, courteous, well mannered, well bred; cordial, pleasant, helpful, obliging.

civilization NOUN 1 = **development**, advancement, progress, enlightenment, culture, refinement, sophistication. 2 = **society**, community, nation, people.

civilized ADJ = **enlightened**, advanced, developed, cultured, cultivated, educated, sophisticated, refined, polished.

claim VERB 1 = **request**, ask for, apply for; demand, insist on. 2 = **profess**, maintain, assert, state, declare, allege, contend, hold, avow, affirm.

clairvoyance NOUN = **second sight**, ESP, extrasensory perception, telepathy, sixth sense.

clamber VERB = **scramble**, climb, scrabble, shin.

clamour NOUN = **noise**, uproar, racket, row, din, shouting, yelling, commotion, hubbub, hullabaloo, brouhaha.

clandestine ADJ = **secret**, covert, surreptitious,

furtive, cloak-and-dagger.
clarify VERB = **explain**, clear
up, throw light on,
simplify, elucidate.
clash VERB = **fight**, contend,
skirmish, come to blows;
quarrel, wrangle, dispute,
cross swords, lock horns.
clasp NOUN = **catch**,
fastener, fastening, clip,
hook, buckle, pin, hasp.
VERB = **embrace**, hug,
squeeze, clutch, grip,
grasp, hold.
class NOUN 1 = **category**,
group, sort, type, kind,
variety, classification,
grade, denomination,
species, genus, genre.
2 = **rank**, social stratum,
level, echelon. 3 = **quality**,
excellence stylishness,
elegance, chic,
sophistication. VERB see
classify.
classic ADJ 1 = **definitive**,
authoritative;
outstanding, first-rate,
first-class, best, finest,
excellent, superior,
masterly. 2 = **typical**,
archetypal,
quintessential, vintage;
model, representative,
perfect, prime, textbook.
3 = **simple**, elegant,
understated; traditional,

timeless, ageless.
classify VERB = **categorize**,
class, group, grade, rank,
order, sort, organize,
codify, catalogue,
systematize, bracket.
clause NOUN = **section**,
subsection, paragraph,
article; proviso,
stipulation.
claw NOUN = **nail**, talon,
pincer. VERB = **scratch**, tear,
scrape, lacerate, rip, maul.
clean ADJ 1 = **unstained**,
spotless, unsoiled,
hygienic, sanitary,
disinfected, sterile,
sterilized, washed,
scrubbed. 2 = **pure**, clear,
unpolluted,
uncontaminated,
untainted. 3 = **good**,
upright, virtuous, decent,
respectable, moral,
upstanding, honourable.
4 = **unused**, unmarked,
blank, new. VERB = **wash**,
cleanse, wipe, sponge,
scour, swab, launder, dust,
mop, sweep.
clear ADJ 1 = **bright**,
cloudless, fine, sunny.
2 = **transparent**, limpid,
translucent, pellucid,
crystalline. 3 = **obvious**,
plain, evident, apparent,
definite, indisputable,

patent, manifest, incontrovertible.
4 = **comprehensible**, plain, intelligible, understandable, lucid, coherent. **5** = **open**, empty, unobstructed, unimpeded, free. VERB **1** = **empty**, vacate, evacuate. **2** = **acquit**, absolve, exonerate. **3** = **jump**, vault, leap, hurdle. **4** = **earn**, gain, make, net. **5** = **authorize**, sanction, permit, allow, pass, accept.

clearance NOUN = **authorization**, permission, consent, sanction, approval, endorsement.

clear-cut ADJ = **definite**, clear, specific, precise, explicit, unambiguous.

cleft NOUN = **split**, crack, fissure, gap, crevice, rift.

clemency NOUN = **mercy**, leniency, compassion, kindness, humanity, pity, sympathy.

clergyman NOUN = **priest**, cleric, minister, chaplain, ecclesiastic, bishop, pastor, vicar, rector, parson, curate, deacon.

clerical ADJ **1** = **office**, secretarial.

2 = **ecclesiastical**, spiritual, priestly, pastoral, canonical.

clever ADJ = **intelligent**, bright, sharp, quick-witted, smart, gifted, talented, skilled, brilliant, able, capable, knowledgeable, educated; shrewd, ingenious, astute, wily, canny.

cliché NOUN = **platitude**, commonplace, banality, truism, old chestnut.

client NOUN = **customer**, buyer, purchaser, shopper, consumer, user, patron, regular.

cliff NOUN = **precipice**, crag, bluff, escarpment, scarp, promontory, tor.

climax NOUN = **culmination**, high point, height, peak, pinnacle, summit, top, acme, zenith.

climb VERB **1** = **go up**, ascend, mount, scale, clamber up, shin up. **2** = **rise**, increase, shoot up, soar.

clinch VERB = **settle**, secure, conclude, seal, complete, confirm, wrap up.

cling VERB **1** = **clutch**, hold on to, grasp, grip, clasp. **2** = **stick**, adhere, cohere.

clip VERB **1** = **cut**, crop, trim,

snip, shear, prune. **2** = **pin**, staple, fasten, fix, attach. NOUN **1** = **fastener**, clasp, pin. **2** = **excerpt**, cutting, snippet; trailer.

clique NOUN = **coterie**, in-crowd, set, group, gang, faction, ring.

clog VERB = **obstruct**, block, jam, stop up, plug, bung up.

cloistered ADJ = **secluded**, sheltered, protected, sequestered; solitary, reclusive.

close ADJ **1** = **near**, adjacent, neighbouring, adjoining. **2** = **strong**, marked, distinct, pronounced. **3** = **intimate**, dear, bosom, devoted, inseparable. **4** = **careful**, rigorous, thorough, minute, detailed, assiduous, meticulous, painstaking, conscientious. **5** = **humid**, muggy, airless, stuffy, sticky, oppressive. VERB **1** = **shut**, slam, fasten, secure, lock, bolt, latch. **2** = **seal off**, stop up, obstruct, block. **3** = **end**, conclude, finish, terminate, wind up.

closet VERB = **shut away**, sequester, cloister, seclude, confine, isolate. ADJ = **secret**, unacknowledged, covert, clandestine, surreptitious, furtive.

clot VERB = **coagulate**, set, congeal, solidify, thicken, curdle.

cloth NOUN = **fabric**, material, textile, stuff.

clothe VERB = **dress**, attire, garb, robe.

clothes PLURAL NOUN = **garments**, clothing, dress, attire, garb, apparel.

cloudy ADJ **1** = **overcast**, dark, grey, leaden, sunless. **2** = **opaque**, murky, muddy, milky, turbid.

club NOUN **1** = **cudgel**, baton, truncheon, cosh, staff. **2** = **society**, group, association, organization, circle, league.

clue NOUN = **sign**, lead, hint, indication, indicator, pointer, evidence, information, tip, tip-off.

clump NOUN = **cluster**, thicket, group, bunch, mass.

clumsy ADJ **1** = **awkward**, uncoordinated, ungainly, inept, maladroit, heavy-handed, inexpert, graceless, ungraceful.

2 = **tactless**, insensitive, undiplomatic, gauche, crass, ill-judged.

cluster NOUN = **bunch**, clump, group, crowd, knot, huddle. VERB = **gather**, collect, assemble, congregate, group, huddle, crowd.

clutch VERB = **grip**, grasp, clasp, cling to, hang on to, grab, seize.

coach NOUN **1** = **bus**; [dated] charabanc. **2** = **instructor**, trainer; teacher, tutor. VERB = **instruct**, teach, tutor, school drill, train.

coagulate VERB = **congeal**, clot, thicken, set, solidify, stiffen.

coalition NOUN = **union**, alliance, league, association, federation, bloc.

coarse ADJ **1** = **rough**, bristly, prickly, scratchy. **2** = **rude**, ill-mannered, impolite, boorish, loutish, uncouth, crass. **3** = **vulgar**, indecent, obscene, crude, smutty, dirty, indelicate.

coast NOUN = **shore**, seashore, coastline, seaside, seaboard.

coat NOUN **1** = **jacket**, overcoat. **2** = **fur**, hair, wool, fleece, hide, pelt.

3 = **layer**, covering, coating, overlay, film, patina, veneer.

coax VERB = **cajole**, persuade, wheedle, inveigle, talk into, induce, prevail on.

cocky ADJ = **arrogant**, conceited, vain, swollen-headed, cocksure.

code NOUN **1** = **cipher**, cryptogram. **2** = **system**, laws, rules, regulations.

coerce VERB = **force**, compel, pressure, pressurize, drive, bully, intimidate, terrorize, browbeat.

cogent ADJ = **convincing**, persuasive, compelling, forceful, effective, sound, powerful, strong, weighty, potent, influential, telling.

coherent ADJ = **logical**, reasoned, reasonable, rational, consistent; clear, lucid, articulate; intelligible, comprehensible.

coil VERB = **loop**, wind, spiral, curl, twist, snake, wreathe, entwine, twine.

coincide VERB **1** = **occur simultaneously**; clash. **2** = **agree**, tally, match, correspond, concur.

coincidence NOUN
= **chance**, accident, luck, fluke, fortuity, serendipity.

coincidental ADJ
= **accidental**, chance, fluky, unintentional, unplanned; fortuitous, serendipitous.

cold ADJ 1 = **chilly**, cool, freezing, bitter, icy, chill, wintry, frosty, raw, perishing, biting, glacial, arctic; [inf] nippy.
2 = **unfriendly**, inhospitable, unwelcoming, forbidding, frigid, formal, stiff.

cold-blooded ADJ
= **ruthless**, callous, inhuman, brutal, barbaric, heartless, merciless, hard-hearted.

collaborate VERB
= **cooperate**, join forces, unite, combine.

collapse VERB 1 = **fall down**, cave in, give way, crumple, subside. 2 = **faint**, pass out, black out, swoon. 3 = **break down**, fail, fold, fall through, founder, disintegrate.

colleague NOUN = **co-worker**, associate, workmate, partner.

collect VERB 1 = **gather**, accumulate, pile up, stockpile, amass, store, hoard, save. 2 = **assemble**, congregate, converge, mass, flock together.
3 = **fetch**, call for, pick up.

collection NOUN
1 = **accumulation**, pile, stockpile, store, stock, supply, heap, hoard.
2 = **donations**, contributions, gifts, offerings, alms.

collective ADJ = **joint**, united, combined, shared, common, cooperative, collaborative.

college NOUN = **university**, institute, school, academy; [historical] polytechnic.

collide VERB = **crash**; hit, bang into, smash into, cannon into, plough into.

collision NOUN = **crash**, impact, accident, smash, pile-up.

colloquial ADJ
= **conversational**, informal, everyday; idiomatic, demotic, vernacular.

colonize VERB = **occupy**, settle, populate, people; take over.

colony NOUN
1 = **dependency**, territory,

protectorate, satellite.
2 = **community**, group, ghetto, quarter.

colour NOUN = **hue**, tint, shade, tone, coloration, colouring, pigmentation, pigment. VERB **1** = **tint**, dye, paint, stain. **2** = **influence**, affect, prejudice, bias, warp, distort.

colourful ADJ **1** = **bright**, vivid, vibrant, rich, multi-coloured, iridescent, psychedelic; gaudy. **2** = **graphic**, lively, animated, dramatic, fascinating, stimulating.

column NOUN **1** = **pillar**, post, support, upright, pilaster, obelisk. **2** = **line**, file, queue, procession, train, cavalcade. **3** = **article**, piece, item, feature.

comb VERB = **search**, hunt through, scour, go over with a fine-tooth comb.

combat NOUN = **battle**, fighting, conflict, hostilities, action. VERB = **fight**, battle, tackle, attack, counter, resist, grapple with, struggle against, withstand.

combative ADJ = **aggressive**, belligerent, pugnacious, bellicose, quarrelsome, argumentative, truculent.

combination NOUN **1** = **amalgamation**, amalgam, blend, mixture, mix, fusion, marriage, integration, synthesis, composite. **2** = **cooperation**, collaboration, association, union, partnership, league.

combine VERB **1** = **join forces**, unite, cooperate, get together, team up. **2** = **mix**, blend, fuse, merge, amalgamate, integrate, synthesize, join, marry.

combustible ADJ = **flammable**, inflammable, incendiary, explosive.

come VERB **1** = **approach**, advance, draw near, bear down on, close in on. **2** = **arrive**, appear, turn up, materialize; [inf] show up.

comedian NOUN **1** = **comic**, humorist. **2** = **wit**, wag, joker, clown.

comedy NOUN = **humour**, wit, wittiness, fun, funny side.

comfort NOUN **1** = **ease**, well being, contentment, relaxation, cosiness;

luxury, opulence.
2 = **solace**, consolation,
support, reassurance. VERB
= **console**, support, solace,
reassure, cheer, soothe,
hearten, uplift.

comfortable ADJ 1 = **cosy**,
snug, homely, pleasant;
[inf] comfy. 2 = **affluent**,
prosperous, well-to-do,
luxurious; untroubled,
contented, happy.

comic ADJ = **funny**,
humorous, amusing,
droll, entertaining,
hilarious.

command VERB 1 = **order**,
tell, direct, instruct,
charge, require. 2 = **be in
charge of**, control, lead,
head. NOUN 1 = **order**,
instruction, decree,
directive, edict, dictate,
injunction, fiat,
commandment.
2 = **charge**, control,
authority, power,
direction, leadership,
rule. 3 = **knowledge**,
grasp, mastery.

commemorate VERB
= **celebrate**, remember,
honour, pay tribute to,
salute, mark.

commence VERB = **begin**,
start, initiate, inaugurate,
embark on.

commendable ADJ
= **admirable**, praiseworthy,
laudable, creditable,
worthy, meritorious,
deserving.

comment VERB = **say**,
observe, state, declare,
remark, opine. NOUN
= **remark**, observation,
statement.

commentary NOUN
1 = **narration**, description,
account, report.
2 = **explanation**,
interpretation, analysis,
critique, exegesis.

commerce NOUN
= **business**, trade, trading,
dealing, buying and
selling, traffic.

commission NOUN
1 = **task**, job, project,
mission, assignment.
2 = **percentage**, brokerage,
share, fee; [inf] cut. VERB
1 = **engage**, employ, hire,
appoint, contract, book.
2 = **order**, pay for,
authorize.

commit VERB 1 = **carry out**,
perpetrate, enact, do.
2 = **entrust**, trust, deliver,
hand over, give, consign.

commitment NOUN
1 = **dedication**, devotion,
loyalty, allegiance.
2 = **promise**, pledge,

undertaking, vow.
3 = **obligation**, duty,
responsibility, tie; task,
engagement.
committed ADJ
= **dedicated**, enthusiastic,
devoted, keen, passionate,
single-minded,
wholehearted,
unwavering, ardent.
common ADJ **1** = **ordinary**,
average, normal,
conventional, typical,
unexceptional,
commonplace, run-of-
the-mill, undistinguished,
unsurprising, everyday,
customary.
2 = **widespread**, general,
universal, popular,
accepted, prevalent,
prevailing, shared, public,
communal, collective.
3 = **vulgar**, coarse,
uncouth, unrefined,
plebeian.
commotion NOUN
= **disturbance**, uproar,
disorder, tumult,
pandemonium, rumpus,
hubbub, fracas,
hullabaloo, row, furore,
brouhaha, confusion,
upheaval, disruption,
turmoil, fuss; [inf] to-do.
communal ADJ = **common**,
collective, shared, joint,

general, cooperative.
communicate VERB
1 = **convey**, tell, impart,
relay, transmit, pass on,
announce, report,
recount, relate, present;
spread, disseminate,
promulgate, broadcast.
2 = **talk**, be in touch,
converse, liaise.
communicative ADJ
= **talkative**, chatty, open,
frank, candid, expansive,
forthcoming.
compact ADJ **1** = **dense**,
compressed, tightly
packed, solid, firm, close.
2 = **concise**, succinct,
terse, brief, pithy.
3 = **small**, neat, portable,
handy.
companion NOUN = **escort**,
friend, partner,
confederate, colleague,
associate, crony, comrade.
companionship NOUN
= **friendship**, company,
fellowship, camaraderie,
intimacy, rapport.
company NOUN
1 = **business**, firm,
organization,
corporation,
conglomerate,
consortium, concern,
enterprise, house,
establishment,

partnership. 2 = **group**, band, party, body, troupe.

comparable ADJ = **similar**, alike, analogous, related, equivalent.

compare VERB 1 = **contrast**, measure against, juxtapose; liken, equate. 2 = **bear comparison**, be comparable, be on a par.

comparison NOUN 1 = **contrast**, juxtaposition. 2 = **resemblance**, likeness, similarity, analogy.

compassionate ADJ = **sympathetic**, empathetic, understanding, caring, warm; merciful, lenient, considerate, kind, humane.

compatible ADJ 1 = **well suited**, like-minded, in tune. 2 = **consistent**, in keeping, consonant.

compel VERB = **force**, make, coerce, pressure, pressurize, constrain, oblige.

compelling ADJ 1 = **fascinating**, gripping, enthralling, mesmerizing. 2 = **convincing**, forceful, powerful, weighty, conclusive, cogent.

compensate VERB

1 = **recompense**, repay, reimburse, make good. 2 = **offset**, counterbalance, counteract, make up for, balance, cancel out, neutralize.

compensation NOUN = **recompense**, repayment, reimbursement, indemnification.

compete VERB 1 = **take part**, participate, go in for. 2 = **contend**, struggle, fight, vie, strive.

competent ADJ = **capable**, able, proficient, skilful, skilled, adept, accomplished, expert, efficient.

competition NOUN = **contest**, match, game, tournament, championship, event, race, rally, trial.

competitive ADJ = **ambitious**, combative, keen; ruthless, cut-throat.

competitor NOUN 1 = **contestant**, contender, challenger, participant, candidate. 2 = **rival**, opponent, adversary.

compile VERB = **collect**, gather, accumulate, amass, assemble, put together, collate.

complain VERB = **grumble**, moan, grouse, gripe, carp, whine.

complaint NOUN
1 = **grievance**, criticism, protest, objection, grouse, grumble. 2 = **illness**, disease, sickness, ailment, disorder, malady, infection.

complete ADJ 1 = **entire**, whole, full, total; uncut, unabridged, unexpurgated.
2 = **finished**, done, concluded, ended, finalized. 3 = **absolute**, utter, out-and-out, downright, thorough, unmitigated, unqualified, sheer. VERB 1 = **finish**, conclude, end, finalize; [inf] wrap up. 2 = **round off**, finish off, crown, cap.

completely ADV = **totally**, utterly, absolutely, quite, thoroughly, wholly, altogether.

complex ADJ
= **complicated**, difficult, intricate, convoluted, involved, elaborate, labyrinthine.

complicated ADJ see **complex**.

complication NOUN
= **difficulty**, problem, obstacle, snag, catch, drawback, setback.

compliment NOUN
= **praise**, tributes, flattery, commendation, congratulations, accolades, plaudits, bouquets. VERB
= **congratulate**, praise, commend, flatter, pay tribute to, salute, extol, laud.

complimentary ADJ
= **congratulatory**, admiring, approving, appreciative, flattering, laudatory.

comply VERB = **obey**, conform to, observe, abide by, keep to, adhere to, follow, respect.

component NOUN = **part**, piece, element, bit, section, constituent, ingredient, unit.

compose VERB 1 = **write**, make up, create, think up, produce; pen. 2 = **form**, make up, constitute, comprise.

composition NOUN
1 = **structure**, make-up, organization, configuration, constitution, form, framework. 2 = **work**, piece, opus.

compound NOUN = **blend**, mixture, amalgam, combination, alloy, synthesis. VERB = **worsen**, add to, exacerbate, aggravate, intensify, heighten.

comprehend VERB = **understand**, grasp, take in, follow, fathom.

comprehensible ADJ = **understandable**, clear, straightforward, intelligible, lucid.

comprehensive ADJ = **complete**, all-inclusive, full, all-embracing, total, encyclopedic, wholesale, universal, exhaustive, detailed, thorough, broad, wide-ranging.

compress VERB = **compact**, squeeze, press together, crush, squash, flatten, cram, tamp.

comprise VERB 1 = **consist of**, contain, be composed of, encompass, include. 2 = **make up**, form, constitute, compose.

compromise VERB 1 = **meet halfway**, give and take. 2 = **damage**, harm, injure, undermine, discredit; endanger, jeopardize. NOUN = **understanding**, deal, agreement; happy medium.

compulsion NOUN 1 = **obligation**, constraint, duress, coercion, pressure. 2 = **urge**, need, desire, drive; fixation, addiction, obsession.

compulsive ADJ = **obsessive**, uncontrollable, irresistible, overwhelming, urgent; obsessional, addicted, incorrigible, incurable.

compulsory ADJ = **obligatory**, mandatory, required, requisite, essential, statutory.

comrade NOUN = **friend**, companion, colleague, partner, associate, co-worker.

conceal VERB = **hide**, cover, obscure, screen, mask, disguise, camouflage.

concede VERB = **admit**, acknowledge, accept, allow, grant, confess, recognize, own.

conceit NOUN = **pride**, vanity, egotism, self-importance, self-satisfaction, narcissism.

conceited ADJ = **proud**, vain, narcissistic, self-important, egotistical,

self-satisfied, smug,
boastful, arrogant; [inf]
cocky, big-headed.

conceivable ADJ
= **credible**, believable,
thinkable, imaginable,
possible.

concentrate VERB
1 = **focus on**, put your
mind to. 2 = **collect**,
gather, crowd, mass,
congregate.

concern NOUN 1 = **worry**,
anxiety, disquiet, distress,
apprehension,
perturbation.
2 = **responsibility**, duty,
job, task. 3 = **business**,
company, firm,
enterprise, organization,
establishment. VERB
1 = **affect**, involve, apply
to, touch. 2 = **worry**,
disturb, trouble, bother,
perturb, distress.

concerning PREP = **about**,
relating to, regarding, as
regards, involving, with
reference/respect to, re,
apropos.

concerted ADJ = **joint**,
combined, united,
collective, collaborative,
cooperative.

concise ADJ = **succinct**,
brief, short, compact,
condensed, terse,
compressed, to the point,
pithy, laconic.

conclude VERB 1 = **end**,
finish, cease, terminate,
discontinue; [inf] wind up.
2 = **deduce**, infer, gather,
judge, conjecture,
surmise.

conclusion NOUN 1 = **end**,
finish, close, completion,
termination, cessation.
2 = **deduction**, inference,
opinion, judgement,
verdict.

conclusive ADJ = **decisive**,
definitive, certain,
incontrovertible,
unquestionable,
categorical, irrefutable,
convincing.

concoct VERB = **invent**,
devise, think up,
formulate, hatch,
dream up.

concrete ADJ = **actual**,
real, definite, genuine,
factual, substantial, solid,
physical, visible, material,
tangible, palpable.

condemn VERB
1 = **denounce**, criticize,
censure, deplore,
castigate, revile.
2 = **sentence**, pass
sentence on, convict.
3 = **damn**, doom, destine.

condescend VERB = **deign**,

lower yourself, demean yourself, stoop, descend; patronize, talk down to.

condescending ADJ = **patronizing**, supercilious, disdainful, superior, lofty; [inf] snooty.

condition NOUN 1 = **state of affairs**, situation, circumstances, position. 2 = **shape**, fitness, health, order, trim, fettle. 3 = **proviso**, stipulation, prerequisite, requirement. 4 = **disease**, illness, disorder, complaint, problem, ailment, malady.

conditional ADJ = **provisional**, dependent, contingent, qualified, limited, restricted, provisory.

condone VERB = **allow**, tolerate, excuse, pardon, forgive, overlook, disregard.

conducive ADJ = **contributory**, helpful, favourable, useful, instrumental, advantageous, beneficial.

conduct NOUN = **behaviour**, actions, performance. VERB 1 = **direct**, run, manage, administer, lead, organize, control,

supervise, regulate. 2 = **show**, guide, lead, escort, accompany, take.

confer VERB 1 = **bestow**, present, award, grant, give. 2 = **talk**, consult, debate, deliberate, discuss, converse.

conference NOUN = **meeting**, seminar, discussion, convention, forum, symposium.

confess VERB = **admit**, acknowledge, own up, disclose, reveal, divulge, unburden yourself, confide, come clean.

confide VERB = **confess**, reveal, disclose, tell, divulge; open your heart.

confidence NOUN 1 = **belief**, faith, conviction, trust, credence. 2 = **self-assurance**, poise, self-confidence, self-possession, aplomb.

confident ADJ 1 = **certain**, sure, convinced, positive, optimistic, sanguine. 2 = **self-assured**, self-possessed, self-confident, poised; [inf] together.

confidential ADJ = **secret**, private, classified, off the record.

confine VERB 1 = **enclose**,

cage, lock up, imprison, detain, jail, shut up, intern, incarcerate, coop up. **2 = restrict**, limit.

confirm VERB **1 = verify**, prove, bear out, corroborate, validate, authenticate, substantiate. **2 = ratify**, endorse, approve, sanction. **3 = guarantee**, assure, affirm, promise.

confiscate VERB **= seize**, impound, take away, appropriate, commandeer.

conflict NOUN **1 = war**, campaign, battle, fighting, confrontation, engagement, encounter, hostilities; warfare, combat. **2 = dispute**, disagreement, dissension, clash; discord, friction, strife, antagonism, hostility, feud, schism. VERB **= clash**, differ, disagree, be at odds/variance.

conform VERB **= comply with**, abide by, obey, observe, follow, keep to, stick to.

confront VERB **= face (up to)**, tackle, stand up to, challenge, take on, brave.

confuse VERB **1 = bewilder**, puzzle, perplex, bemuse, baffle, mystify, befuddle, disorientate, nonplus; [inf] flummox. **2 = muddle**, mix up, obscure, cloud, complicate.

confusion NOUN **1 = bewilderment**, perplexity, bafflement, puzzlement, mystification, bemusement, disorientation. **2 = disorder**, disarray, disorganization, untidiness, chaos; turmoil, disruption, upheaval, muddle, mess.

congeal VERB **= solidify**, coagulate, thicken, clot, harden, jell.

congenial ADJ **= agreeable**, pleasant, pleasing, genial, convivial, companionable, like-minded, friendly, sympathetic.

congenital ADJ **1 = hereditary**, inherited, innate, inborn. **2 = inveterate**, compulsive, chronic, incurable, incorrigible.

congratulate VERB **= praise**, commend, applaud, salute, pay tribute to.

congregate VERB = **gather**, assemble, collect, mass, group, convene, converge, meet, crowd, cluster, throng.

conjecture NOUN = **guess**, speculation, theory, surmise, inference.

conjugal ADJ = **matrimonial**, nuptial, marital.

connect VERB 1 = **attach**, link, fix, couple, secure, tie. 2 = **associate**, link, equate, bracket.

connection NOUN 1 = **attachment**, fastening, coupling. 2 = **link**, relationship, association, relation.

connive VERB (**connive at**) = **overlook**, disregard, condone, turn a blind eye to.

connotation NOUN = **nuance**, undertone, overtone, suggestion, implication.

conquer VERB 1 = **defeat**, beat, vanquish, overpower, overthrow, subdue, rout, trounce, subjugate, triumph over, overwhelm, crush, quell, worst. 2 = **seize**, occupy, invade, annex, overrun.

conquest NOUN 1 = **victory**, triumph; defeat, overthrow, subjugation, rout. 2 = **occupation**, seizure, possession, annexation, invasion.

conscience NOUN = **morals**, principles, ethics, standards, scruples, qualms, compunction.

conscientious ADJ = **diligent**, industrious, hard-working, painstaking, careful, meticulous, thorough, punctilious, dedicated, scrupulous, assiduous.

conscious ADJ 1 = **awake**, aware, alert, sentient. 2 = **deliberate**, premeditated, intentional, intended, on purpose, calculated, voluntary.

consecrate VERB = **sanctify**, bless, hallow.

consecutive ADJ = **successive**, succeeding, following, in succession, in a row, running.

consent NOUN = **agreement**, assent, acceptance, approval, permission, sanction; [inf] go-ahead. VERB = **agree**, assent, acquiesce, accede, allow, approve.

consequence NOUN
= **result**, effect, outcome, aftermath, repercussion, upshot.

consequent ADJ
= **resulting**, resultant, subsequent, following, attendant.

conservation NOUN
= **preservation**, protection, safe keeping, safeguarding, care, husbandry, upkeep, maintenance; ecology, environmentalism.

conservative ADJ
= **conventional**, traditional, orthodox; cautious, unadventurous, old-fashioned, hidebound, reactionary.

conserve VERB = **preserve**, save, safeguard, keep, protect, take care of, husband.

consider VERB 1 = **think about**, reflect on, weigh up, ponder, contemplate, deliberate over, mull over.
2 = **believe**, regard as, deem, hold to be, judge, rate.

considerable ADJ
= **substantial**, sizeable, appreciable, fair, significant, handsome, decent, generous, large, ample.

considerate ADJ
= **thoughtful**, kind, helpful, attentive, solicitous, unselfish, compassionate, sympathetic, charitable, patient, generous, obliging, accommodating.

consignment NOUN = **load**, batch, delivery, shipment, cargo.

consist VERB = **be composed of**, be made up of, comprise, contain, include, incorporate.

consistent ADJ
1 = **constant**, regular, unchanging, unvarying, steady, stable, uniform.
2 = **compatible**, consonant.

consolation NOUN
= **comfort**, sympathy, solace, compassion, pity, commiseration, relief, help, support, encouragement, reassurance.

conspicuous ADJ = **clear**, visible, obvious, evident, apparent, prominent, notable, noticeable, marked, plain, unmistakable, manifest, patent, striking, glaring, blatant, flagrant; obtrusive, showy, ostentatious.

conspiracy NOUN = **plot**, scheme, machinations, intrigue, collusion.

constant ADJ 1 = **even**, regular, uniform, stable, steady, unchanging, fixed, consistent, unvarying. 2 = **continual**, unending, non-stop, sustained, incessant, endless, unceasing, persistent, interminable, unremitting, relentless.

consternation NOUN = **dismay**, distress, anxiety, perturbation, alarm, surprise, astonishment, amazement.

construct VERB = **build**, make, assemble, erect, put up, manufacture, produce, fabricate, fashion.

construction NOUN = **building**, structure, edifice, framework.

constructive ADJ = **useful**, helpful, productive, practical, valuable, worthwhile, beneficial.

consult VERB 1 = **confer**, discuss, talk, deliberate.

2 = **ask**, call in, turn to.

consume VERB 1 = **eat**, drink, devour, swallow, ingest, gobble, guzzle. 2 = **use**, utilize, expend, deplete.

contact VERB = **communicate with**, get in touch with, approach, write to, phone, call, ring up, speak to. NOUN = **touch**, proximity, exposure; communication, association, dealings.

contagious ADJ = **catching**, communicable, transmittable, transmissible, infectious.

contain VERB 1 = **hold**, carry, accommodate, seat. 2 = **include**, comprise, take in, incorporate, involve. 3 = **restrain**, hold in, control, keep in check, suppress, repress, curb, stifle.

container NOUN = **receptacle**, vessel, holder, repository.

contaminate VERB = **pollute**, defile, corrupt, poison, taint, infect, sully.

contemplate VERB 1 = **think about**, meditate on, consider, ponder, reflect on, muse on, dwell on, deliberate over, ruminate over. **2 = have in mind**, intend, plan, propose, envisage. **3 = look at**, view, regard, examine, inspect, observe, scrutinize, survey, eye.

contemplative ADJ = **thoughtful**, pensive, reflective, meditative, ruminative.

contemporary ADJ = **current**, modern, present-day, up to date, latest, fashionable; [inf] trendy.

contempt NOUN = **scorn**, disdain, disgust, loathing, abhorrence, detestation, hatred.

contemptible ADJ = **despicable**, detestable, deplorable, disgraceful, loathsome, odious, discreditable, mean, shameful, base, vile, shabby, sordid.

contemptuous ADJ = **scornful**, disdainful, insulting, disrespectful, derisive, insolent, mocking, condescending, patronizing, superior, supercilious, snide.

contented ADJ = **satisfied**, content, pleased, happy, glad, gratified, at ease/

peace, relaxed, serene, tranquil, unworried, untroubled; complacent.

contentment NOUN = **satisfaction**, contentedness, happiness, pleasure, gratification, ease, comfort, peace, serenity, equanimity, tranquillity; complacency.

contest NOUN **1** see **competition**. **2 = struggle**, battle, fight, tussle. VERB **1 = compete for**, contend for, fight for, vie for, battle for, go for. **2 = challenge**, question, oppose, object to.

contestant NOUN = **competitor**, entrant, candidate, contender, participant, rival, opponent, adversary.

context NOUN = **circumstances**, situation, conditions, state of affairs, background, setting, frame of reference, framework.

continual ADJ **1 = constant**, continuous, unending, never-ending, unremitting, relentless, unrelenting, unrelieved. **2 = frequent**, repeated, recurrent, recurring, regular.

continue VERB 1 = **carry on**, go on, keep on, persist, persevere; stay, remain. 2 = **resume**, recommence, restart, return to, take up. 3 = **prolong**, extend, sustain, maintain, preserve, perpetuate.

continuous ADJ = **constant**, uninterrupted, non-stop, perpetual, sustained, ceaseless, incessant, relentless, unceasing, unremitting, endless, never-ending, interminable, unbroken.

contour NOUN = **outline**, silhouette, profile, figure, shape, form, line, curve.

contract NOUN = **agreement**, arrangement, settlement, covenant, compact, understanding, bargain, deal. VERB 1 = **shrink**, reduce, diminish, decrease, decline. 2 = **tense**, tighten, flex. 3 = **catch**, develop, get, go down with.

contradictory ADJ = **opposing**, opposite, opposed, conflicting, incompatible, inconsistent, irreconcilable, contrary.

contraption NOUN = **device**, machine, mechanism, gadget, contrivance; [inf] gizmo.

contrary ADJ 1 = **opposing**, opposite, contradictory, conflicting, contrasting, incompatible, irreconcilable, inconsistent, antithetical. 2 = **awkward**, wilful, perverse, obstinate, stubborn, headstrong, wayward, recalcitrant, refractory.

contrast NOUN = **difference**, dissimilarity, disparity, distinction, dissimilitude. VERB 1 = **compare**, juxtapose. 2 = **differ**, conflict, be at odds/variance.

contribute VERB 1 = **give**, donate, provide, present, supply, bestow. 2 = **lead to**, be conducive to, help, play a part in.

contribution NOUN 1 = **donation**, gift, offering, present, handout. 2 = **participation**, input.

contrite ADJ = **penitent**, repentant, remorseful, regretful, sorry, conscience-stricken, rueful.

control NOUN 1 = **authority**, power, charge, management, command, direction, rule, government, supervision, jurisdiction, dominance, mastery, leadership, reign, supremacy.
2 = **limitation**, restriction, regulation, check, restraint, curb, brake. VERB
1 = **be in charge of**, manage, head, direct, command, rule, govern, oversee, preside over.
2 = **regulate**, restrain, keep in check, restrict, curb, hold back, contain, subdue, bridle.

controversial ADJ
= **disputed**, contentious, tendentious, at issue, debatable, moot, vexed.

controversy NOUN
= **dispute**, argument, debate, disagreement, dissension, contention, altercation, wrangle, war of words.

convene VERB = **call**, summon, convoke; assemble, gather, meet.

convenient ADJ
1 = **suitable**, appropriate, fitting, favourable, advantageous, opportune,

timely, well timed, expedient. 2 = **accessible**, nearby, handy, at hand.

convention NOUN
= **custom**, usage, practice, tradition, way, habit, norm; propriety, etiquette, protocol.

conventional ADJ
1 = **orthodox**, traditional, established, accepted, mainstream, accustomed, customary; normal, standard, ordinary, usual.
2 = **conservative**, traditionalist, conformist, bourgeois, old-fashioned, unadventurous.

converge VERB = **meet**, intersect, join.

conversation NOUN = **talk**, discussion, chat, dialogue, gossip, heart-to-heart, palaver; [inf] natter.

convert VERB = **change**, turn, transform, metamorphose, transfigure, transmogrify, transmute; alter, modify, adapt.

convey VERB 1 = **transport**, carry, bring, fetch, take, move, bear, shift, transfer.
2 = **transmit**, communicate, pass on, tell, relate, impart, reveal, disclose.

convict NOUN = **prisoner**, criminal, offender, felon, lawbreaker. VERB = **find guilty**, sentence.

conviction NOUN 1 = **confidence**, assurance, belief, certainty, certitude. 2 = **belief**, view, principle, opinion, thought, idea.

convince VERB = **persuade**, satisfy, assure; induce, prevail on, talk round, win over.

convincing ADJ = **persuasive**, powerful, strong, compelling, conclusive, cogent.

convivial ADJ = **friendly**, genial, cordial, sociable, affable, amiable, congenial, agreeable, jolly, cheerful.

convoy NOUN = **group**, line, fleet, cortège, cavalcade, motorcade.

cool ADJ 1 = **chilly**, fresh, refreshing, breezy, draughty; [inf] nippy. 2 = **calm**, relaxed, composed, collected, self-possessed, level-headed, self-controlled, unperturbed, unruffled, serene. 3 = **aloof**, distant, reserved, stand-offish, unfriendly, offhand, undemonstrative, unwelcoming, uncommunicative, impassive. VERB 1 = **chill**, refrigerate. 2 = **lessen**, diminish, reduce, dampen.

cooperate VERB = **join forces**, unite, combine, collaborate, coordinate, pull together.

cooperative ADJ 1 = **joint**, united, shared, combined, concerted, collective, collaborative. 2 = **helpful**, obliging, accommodating, willing.

coordinate VERB = **arrange**, organize, order, synchronize, harmonize; cooperate, liaise, collaborate.

cope VERB 1 = **manage**, succeed, survive, get by. 2 (**cope with**) = **handle**, deal with, take care of.

copious ADJ = **abundant**, plentiful, ample, profuse, extensive, generous, lavish.

copy NOUN 1 = **reproduction**, imitation, replica, likeness; counterfeit, forgery, fake. 2 = **duplicate**, facsimile, carbon copy, photocopy. VERB

1 = **imitate**, mimic, emulate, mirror, echo, ape, parrot; plagiarize.
2 = **reproduce**, replicate, forge, counterfeit.

cord NOUN = **string**, rope, twine, cable, line, ligature.

core NOUN = **centre**, heart, nucleus, nub, kernel, crux, essence, gist; [inf] nitty-gritty.

corner NOUN = **bend**, angle, curve, turn, crook; junction, intersection, crossroads, fork. VERB = **trap**, capture, run to earth.

corpse NOUN = **body**, remains, cadaver, carcass.

correct ADJ 1 = **right**, accurate, true, exact, precise, unerring, faithful, strict, faultless, flawless; [inf] spot on. 2 = **proper**, suitable, appropriate, fit, fitting, seemly. VERB = **rectify**, amend, remedy, repair, emend.

correspond VERB = **agree**, concur, coincide, match, tally, correlate.

correspondence NOUN = **letters**, mail, post.

corroborate VERB = **confirm**, verify, bear out, authenticate, validate, substantiate, uphold, back up.

corrupt ADJ 1 = **dishonest**, unscrupulous, dishonourable, untrustworthy, unprincipled, venal, fraudulent. 2 = **immoral**, depraved, wicked, evil, sinful, degenerate, perverted, dissolute, debauched, decadent. VERB 1 = **bribe**, buy (off), suborn. 2 = **deprave**, pervert.

cosmopolitan ADJ 1 = **international**, global, universal; multicultural, multiracial. 2 = **sophisticated**, urbane, worldly, worldly-wise, well travelled.

cost NOUN = **price**, charge, rate, value, quotation; payment, expense, outlay.

costly ADJ = **expensive**, dear; exorbitant, extortionate; [inf] steep.

cosy ADJ = **comfortable**, snug, warm, relaxed, homely; [inf] comfy.

coterie NOUN = **clique**, set, crowd, circle, gang, club.

count VERB 1 = **add up**, calculate, total, reckon up, tally, compute, tot up. 2 = **regard**, consider,

think, hold, judge, deem.
3 = **matter**, be of account,
signify.

countenance NOUN = **face**,
features, expression, look,
visage, mien.

counteract VERB = **offset**,
balance, counterbalance,
neutralize, cancel out;
prevent, thwart, frustrate,
impede, hinder, hamper.

counterfeit ADJ = **fake**,
forged, imitation, bogus,
spurious, ersatz; [inf]
phoney. NOUN = **fake**, copy,
forgery.

counterpart NOUN
= **equivalent**, equal,
opposite number, peer.

countless ADJ
= **innumerable**,
incalculable, infinite,
limitless, untold, myriad.

country NOUN 1 = **state**,
nation, realm, kingdom,
province, principality.
2 = **land**, territory, terrain;
landscape, scenery,
setting; countryside.

courage NOUN = **bravery**,
fearlessness, pluck,
boldness, valour, daring,
nerve, intrepidity; [inf]
guts.

courageous ADJ = **brave**,
valiant, fearless, intrepid,
plucky, bold, daring,

undaunted, dauntless,
lion-hearted, valorous.

course NOUN 1 = **route**, way,
track, direction, path,
line, tack, trajectory,
orbit. 2 = **way**, method,
approach, policy, plan,
strategy. 3 = **duration**,
passage, period, term,
span. 4 = **classes**,
lectures, curriculum,
syllabus.

court NOUN 1 = **law court**,
court of law, tribunal,
bench, chancery, assizes.
2 = **attendants**, household,
retinue, entourage, train,
suite.

courteous ADJ = **polite**,
well mannered, civil,
gracious, mannerly, well
bred, civilized.

cove NOUN = **bay**, inlet,
fjord.

cover VERB 1 = **protect**,
shield, shelter, hide,
conceal, veil; cake, coat,
plaster, smother, daub,
blanket, overlay, carpet,
mantle, shroud. 2 = **deal
with**, involve, take in,
contain, encompass,
embrace, incorporate,
treat. 3 = **report**, write up,
describe. NOUN 1 = **covering**,
sleeve, wrapper, envelope,
sheath, jacket, casing;

awning, canopy,
tarpaulin; lid, top, cap,
veneer, coating, coat,
covering, layer, carpet,
blanket, mantle, veil.
2 = **disguise**, front,
camouflage, pretence,
facade, smokescreen,
pretext. **3** = **insurance**,
protection, indemnity,
indemnification.
covert ADJ = **secret**,
surreptitious, furtive,
stealthy, cloak-and-
dagger, clandestine.
covet VERB = **desire**, want,
wish for, long for, hanker
after.
cowardly ADJ = **fearful**,
timorous, faint-hearted,
spineless, lily-livered,
craven, pusillanimous; [inf]
chicken, yellow.
cower VERB = **cringe**,
shrink, flinch, recoil,
blench.
coy ADJ = **coquettish**, arch,
kittenish, shy, modest,
demure, bashful.
crack NOUN **1** = **fracture**,
break, chip, split; fissure,
crevice, breach, chink,
gap, cleft, cranny.
2 = **attempt**, try; [inf] go,
shot, stab. VERB = **fracture**,
break, fragment, split,
splinter, snap.

cradle NOUN **1** = **crib**, cot,
bassinet. **2** = **birthplace**,
source, fount, wellspring.
VERB = **hold**, shelter,
support, protect.
craft NOUN **1** = **skill**,
expertise, mastery,
artistry, art, technique,
aptitude, dexterity, talent,
flair. **2** = **trade**, occupation,
pursuit, profession, line of
work. **3** = **vessel**, ship,
boat.
crafty ADJ = **cunning**,
artful, calculating,
scheming, wily, shrewd,
astute, canny, sharp,
guileful, sly, devious.
cram VERB = **stuff**, push,
force, pack, ram, press,
squeeze.
crash VERB = **collide with**,
bump into, smash into,
plough into; hit, strike.
NOUN = **collision**, accident,
smash, pile-up.
crate NOUN = **box**, case,
chest.
crater NOUN = **hole**, hollow,
pit, cavity, depression.
crawl VERB = **creep**, slither,
squirm, wriggle, worm
your way.
craze NOUN = **trend**,
fashion, fad, vogue,
enthusiasm, passion,
obsession, mania.

crazy ADJ 1 = **mad**, insane, deranged, demented, lunatic, unbalanced, unhinged; [inf] out of your mind, nuts, round the bend, barmy, bonkers. 2 = **foolish**, stupid, foolhardy, idiotic, irrational, unreasonable, illogical, senseless, absurd, impractical, silly, asinine, ludicrous.

cream NOUN = **lotion**, ointment, salve, unguent, liniment; moisturizer, emollient.

crease NOUN = **wrinkle**, furrow, line, fold, crinkle, ridge, corrugation. VERB = **crumple**, wrinkle, rumple, crinkle, ruck up, pucker.

create VERB 1 = **produce**, originate, design, establish, set up, invent, make, build, construct, develop, fabricate, found, form, mould, forge. 2 = **bring about**, engender, generate, lead to, result in, cause.

creative ADJ = **inventive**, imaginative, original, artistic, resourceful, ingenious.

creature NOUN 1 = **animal**, beast; [US] critter.

2 = **person**, human being, individual.

credentials PLURAL NOUN = **documents**, documentation, papers; references, certificates, diplomas.

credible ADJ = **believable**, plausible, convincing, likely, conceivable.

credit NOUN = **praise**, acclaim, commendation, acknowledgement, tribute, kudos, glory, recognition, esteem, respect, admiration. VERB 1 = **believe**, accept, trust; [inf] fall for, swallow, buy. 2 = **ascribe**, attribute, assign, accredit, chalk up, put down.

creditable ADJ = **praiseworthy**, commendable, laudable, meritorious, admirable, deserving.

credulous ADJ = **gullible**, over-trusting, naive, unsuspicious; [inf] born yesterday.

creed NOUN = **belief**, faith; principles, teaching, doctrine, ideology, dogma, tenets, credo.

creek NOUN = **inlet**, bay, estuary, bight; [Scottish] firth.

creep VERB = **tiptoe**, sneak, steal, slip, slink, sidle, edge, inch.

crest NOUN 1 = **comb**, tuft, plume. 2 = **summit**, top, peak, crown, brow. 3 = **badge**, emblem, regalia, insignia, device, coat of arms.

crestfallen ADJ = **downcast**, dejected, glum, downhearted, disheartened, dispirited, despondent, disconsolate, disappointed, sad.

crevice NOUN = **fissure**, cleft, crack, cranny, split, rift, slit, opening, gap, hole, interstice.

crime NOUN 1 = **offence**, felony, misdemeanour, misdeed, wrong. 2 = **lawbreaking**, wrongdoing, delinquency, criminality.

criminal ADJ 1 = **unlawful**, illegal, illicit, lawless, felonious, delinquent, villainous, wicked, nefarious; [inf] crooked, bent. 2 = **deplorable**, scandalous, shameful, reprehensible. NOUN = **offender**, lawbreaker, wrongdoer, felon, delinquent, malefactor, miscreant, culprit, villain; [inf] crook.

cringe VERB = **cower**, shrink, flinch, recoil, shy away.

cripple VERB = **disable**, incapacitate, lame, paralyse, immobilize.

crisis NOUN = **emergency**, disaster, catastrophe, calamity, predicament, plight, extremity.

crisp ADJ 1 = **crunchy**, crispy, brittle. 2 = **invigorating**, bracing, fresh, refreshing. 3 = **brisk**, decisive, no-nonsense, brusque.

criterion NOUN = **measure**, standard, benchmark, yardstick, scale, touchstone, barometer.

critic NOUN 1 = **reviewer**, commentator, judge, pundit. 2 = **attacker**, detractor.

critical ADJ 1 = **censorious**, disapproving, disparaging, derogatory, uncomplimentary, unfavourable, negative. 2 = **crucial**, decisive, pivotal, key, all-important, vital. 3 = **dangerous**, grave, serious, risky, perilous, hazardous, precarious.

criticism NOUN

= **condemnation**, censure, disapproval; attack, broadside; [inf] flak.

criticize VERB = **find fault with**, censure, denounce, condemn, attack, lambaste, pillory, denigrate, cast aspersions on; [inf] knock, pan.

crooked ADJ = **bent**, twisted, warped, contorted, misshapen; winding, twisting, zigzag; lopsided, askew, off-centre.

crop NOUN = **harvest**, yield, produce, vintage, fruits. VERB **1** = **cut**, trim, clip, shear, lop. **2** (**crop up**) = **happen**, arise, occur, emerge, materialize.

cross NOUN **1** = **affliction**, trouble, worry, burden, trial, tribulation, curse. **2** = **hybrid**, mixture, crossbreed; mongrel. VERB **1** = **span**, pass over, bridge, traverse. **2** = **intersect**, meet, join, connect, crisscross. **3** = **oppose**, resist, defy; obstruct, impede, hinder, hamper. ADJ = **annoyed**, irritated, vexed, angry, irate, irascible, fractious, crotchety, querulous.

crossing NOUN **1** = **junction**, crossroads, intersection. **2** = **journey**, passage, voyage.

crouch VERB = **squat**, bend, duck, stoop, hunch, hunker down.

crowd NOUN **1** = **horde**, throng, mob, mass, multitude, host, rabble, army, herd, flock, drove, swarm, troupe, troop, pack; assembly, gathering, congregation. **2** = **audience**, house, turnout, gate, spectators. VERB **1** = **gather**, cluster, flock, swarm, throng, huddle. **2** = **surge**, push/elbow your way, jostle; squeeze, pile, throng, cram, jam.

crowded ADJ = **full**, busy, packed, teeming, swarming, crammed, thronged, populous.

crown NOUN **1** = **coronet**, diadem, circlet. **2** = **top**, crest, summit, apex, tip, peak. VERB **1** = **enthrone**, install. **2** = **cap**, round off, complete, perfect.

crucial ADJ = **vital**, essential, all-important, critical; decisive, pivotal, key.

crude ADJ **1** = **unrefined**, unprocessed, natural, raw.

2 = **rough**, primitive, simple, basic, rudimentary, makeshift, rough-and-ready.

cruel ADJ = **brutal**, savage, inhuman, barbaric, barbarous, brutish, bloodthirsty, murderous, sadistic, wicked, evil, monstrous; callous, ruthless, merciless, pitiless, remorseless, uncaring, heartless, cold-blooded, unfeeling, unkind, inhumane.

crumble VERB = **disintegrate**, fall apart, fall to pieces, collapse, fragment, break up.

crumple VERB = **crush**, scrunch, squash, screw up, mangle; crease, rumple, wrinkle, crinkle.

crunch VERB = **bite into**, gnaw, champ, chomp, munch.

crusade NOUN = **campaign**, drive, movement, push, struggle, battle, war.

crush VERB **1** = **squash**, squeeze, press, mash, compress, mangle, pound, pulverize, grind, pulp; crease, crumple. **2** = **put down**, defeat, suppress, subdue, overpower, quash, stamp out, extinguish. **3** = **humiliate**, mortify, chagrin.

cry VERB **1** = **weep**, sob, wail, snivel, whimper, bawl, howl; [inf] blubber. **2** = **call out**, exclaim, yell, shout, bellow, roar. NOUN = **call**, exclamation, yell, shout, bellow, roar.

crypt NOUN = **tomb**, vault, burial chamber, sepulchre, catacomb, mausoleum.

cryptic ADJ = **mysterious**, enigmatic, puzzling, perplexing, mystifying, obscure, arcane; ambiguous, elliptical.

cuddle VERB = **hug**, embrace, clasp, hold tight; snuggle, nestle.

cudgel NOUN = **club**, cosh, stick, truncheon, baton.

cue NOUN = **signal**, sign, indication, reminder, prompt.

culpable ADJ = **guilty**, in the wrong, at fault, blameworthy, to blame.

culprit NOUN = **guilty party**, offender, wrongdoer, miscreant, lawbreaker, criminal, malefactor.

cult NOUN **1** = **sect**, denomination, group, movement, church, persuasion. **2** = **obsession**, fixation, mania, passion.

cultivate VERB **1** = **till**, farm, work, plough, dig. **2** = **woo**, court, pay court to, ingratiate yourself with, curry favour with.

cultural ADJ = **artistic**, aesthetic, intellectual.

culture NOUN **1** = **artistic awareness**, intellectual awareness, education, enlightenment, discernment, discrimination, taste, refinement, polish, sophistication. **2** = **civilization**, way of life, lifestyle; customs, traditions, heritage.

cultured ADJ = **artistic**, enlightened, civilized, educated, well read, learned, knowledgeable, discerning, discriminating, refined, polished, sophisticated.

cunning ADJ = **crafty**, wily, artful, guileful, devious, sly, scheming, calculating; shrewd, astute, clever, canny; deceitful, deceptive, duplicitous.

curator NOUN = **keeper**, caretaker, custodian, guardian, steward.

curb VERB = **restrain**, check, control, contain, hold back, repress, suppress, moderate, dampen, subdue.

cure NOUN = **remedy**, antidote, treatment, therapy; panacea, nostrum. VERB **1** = **heal**, remedy, rectify, put right, repair, fix. **2** = **preserve**, smoke, salt, dry.

curious ADJ **1** = **inquisitive**; intrigued, interested, dying to know, agog. **2** see **strange**.

curl VERB **1** = **spiral**, coil, bend, twist, wind, loop, twirl, wreathe; meander, snake. **2** = **crimp**, perm. NOUN = **ringlet**, kink, wave, corkscrew.

curly ADJ = **curled**, crimped, kinky, wavy, frizzy, permed.

current ADJ = **present**, present-day, contemporary, modern; popular, prevailing, prevalent, accepted, common, widespread. NOUN = **flow**, stream, tide, undercurrent, undertow; backdraught, slipstream, thermal.

curse NOUN **1** = **malediction**, the evil eye; [inf] jinx.

2 = **swear word**, expletive, obscenity, oath, profanity, blasphemy.

cursory ADJ = **hasty**, rapid, hurried, quick, perfunctory, casual, superficial, desultory.

curt ADJ = **terse**, brusque, abrupt, clipped, monosyllabic, short; ungracious, rude, impolite, discourteous.

curtail VERB = **reduce**, cut, decrease, lessen, trim; restrict, limit, curb; shorten, truncate.

curtain VERB = **screen off**, separate off, mask, shield, conceal, hide, isolate.

curve NOUN = **bend**, turn, loop, curl, twist, hook; arc, arch, bow, undulation, curvature.

cushion VERB 1 = **pillow**, cradle, support, prop, rest. 2 = **soften**, lessen, diminish, decrease, mitigate, dull, deaden.

custody NOUN 1 = **care**, charge, guardianship, keeping, safe keeping, protection. 2 = **detention**, imprisonment, incarceration, confinement.

custom NOUN 1 = **tradition**, practice, usage, way, convention, habit, wont; mores. 2 = **trade**, business, patronage.

customary ADJ = **usual**, traditional, normal, conventional, familiar, accepted, routine, established, time-honoured, regular; accustomed, habitual, wonted.

customer NOUN = **buyer**, purchaser, shopper, consumer, patron, client.

cut VERB 1 = **gash**, slash, lacerate, slit, nick; lance. 2 = **carve**, slice, chop, sever, cleave. 3 = **trim**, clip, crop, snip, shear, dock, shave, pare, mow. 4 = **reduce**, decrease, lessen, retrench, slash. 5 = **shorten**, abridge, abbreviate, precis, summarize. NOUN 1 = **gash**, laceration, slash, incision. 2 = **cutback**, decrease, reduction. 3 = **share**, portion, percentage.

cutting ADJ = **wounding**, hurtful, caustic, barbed, pointed, sarcastic, sardonic, sharp, mordant, snide, spiteful.

cycle NOUN = **series**, sequence, succession, run; round, rotation.

dare

cyclical ADJ = **recurring**, recurrent, regular, repeated.
cynical ADJ = **sceptical**, doubtful, distrustful, suspicious, pessimistic, negative; disenchanted, disillusioned, jaundiced.

Dd

daily ADJ = **everyday**, quotidian, diurnal.
dainty ADJ 1 = **petite**, delicate, neat, exquisite, graceful, elegant, pretty, fine. 2 = **particular**, fastidious, fussy, choosy, finicky.
dally VERB = **dawdle**, loiter, delay, linger, procrastinate, waste time; [inf] dilly-dally.
damage NOUN 1 = **harm**, injury, destruction, impairment, vandalism, ruin, devastation. 2 (**damages**) = **compensation**, recompense, restitution, redress. VERB = **harm**, injure, spoil, vandalize, destroy, wreck, ruin, mar, deface, mutilate, impair, sabotage.
damaging ADJ see **harmful**.
damp ADJ 1 = **moist**, clammy, sweaty, dank. 2 = **rainy**, drizzly, humid, misty, foggy.
dance VERB = **caper**, skip, prance, frolic, gambol.
danger NOUN 1 = **risk**, peril, hazard, jeopardy, precariousness, insecurity, instability. 2 = **chance**, possibility, threat.
dangerous ADJ 1 = **risky**, perilous, unsafe, hazardous, precarious; exposed, defenceless; [inf] hairy. 2 = **menacing**, threatening, ruthless, violent, desperate, wild, fierce, ferocious.
dangle VERB = **hang**, swing, sway, trail, droop, flap, wave.
dappled ADJ = **spotted**, mottled, flecked variegated; piebald, pied, brindled.
dare VERB 1 = **risk**, hazard, venture. 2 = **challenge**,

defy, invite.

daring ADJ = **bold**, adventurous, brave, courageous, intrepid, fearless, undaunted.

dark ADJ 1 = **black**, pitch-black, jet-black, inky; shadowy, shady, murky, dim, cloudy, overcast. 2 = **sallow**, swarthy, black, olive, tanned.

dart VERB = **rush**, dash, bolt, sprint, race, run, tear, fly, shoot, scuttle.

dash VERB 1 = **rush**, run, hurry, race, sprint, tear, speed, fly, dart, bolt, shoot. 2 = **shatter**, destroy, ruin, wreck. NOUN = **bit**, pinch, drop, sprinkling, touch.

dashing ADJ = **debonair**, stylish, smart, elegant, attractive.

data PLURAL NOUN = **information**, facts, figures, details, statistics.

date NOUN 1 = **day**, point in time. 2 = **meeting**, appointment, engagement, rendezvous, assignation, tryst. 3 = **partner**, escort, girlfriend, boyfriend.

dated ADJ = **out of date**, out-dated, old-fashioned, outmoded, antiquated; [inf] old hat.

daunt VERB = **intimidate**, frighten, overawe, scare, dismay, unnerve, cow, dishearten, dispirit.

dawdle VERB = **loiter**, delay, linger, take your time, waste time, idle, dally, straggle.

dawn NOUN = **daybreak**, break of day, sunrise, cockcrow; [US] sunup.

day NOUN 1 = **daytime**, daylight. 2 = **period**, time, epoch, age, era, generation.

daze VERB = **stun**, stupefy, confuse, bewilder, dumbfound.

dead ADJ 1 = **deceased**, lifeless, gone, passed on/away, departed, defunct, extinct. 2 = **dull**, boring, tedious, uneventful, flat, uninspiring. 3 = **complete**, total, absolute, utter.

deaden VERB = **desensitize**, numb, anaesthetize; reduce, moderate, blunt, dull, diminish, mitigate, alleviate.

deadlock NOUN = **stalemate**, impasse, stand-off.

deadly ADJ = **fatal**, lethal, mortal; toxic, poisonous.

deal NOUN = **agreement**, transaction, arrangement, contract, bargain, understanding, settlement, pact. VERB 1 = **trade**, buy and sell, traffic. 2 = **distribute**, share out, allocate, hand out, dole out, apportion. 3 = **administer**, deliver, give, inflict.
deal with = **attend to**, see to, take care of, cope with, handle, manage, tackle.
dealer NOUN = **trader**, broker, retailer, wholesaler, supplier, distributor, merchant, trafficker.
dear ADJ 1 = **beloved**, loved, adored, cherished. 2 = **expensive**, costly, overpriced, pricey.
dearth NOUN = **lack**, scarcity, shortage, deficiency, insufficiency, paucity.
death NOUN 1 = **dying**, demise, end. 2 = **killing**, murder, massacre, slaughter.
debacle NOUN = **fiasco**, disaster, catastrophe, failure, collapse.
debase VERB = **degrade**, devalue, demean, disgrace, dishonour, shame, discredit, cheapen.
debatable ADJ = **arguable**, questionable, open to question, moot, disputable.
debate NOUN = **discussion**, dialogue, talk; argument, dispute, wrangle, conflict.
debauched ADJ = **degenerate**, dissipated, dissolute, immoral, decadent.
debris NOUN = **rubble**, wreckage, detritus, rubbish, litter, waste, remains, ruins.
debt NOUN 1 = **bill**, account, dues, arrears. 2 = **obligation**, indebtedness.
decay VERB 1 = **rot**, decompose, putrefy, spoil, perish, corrode. 2 = **degenerate**, decline, deteriorate, crumble, disintegrate, die, wither, atrophy.
deceit NOUN = **deception**, dishonesty, duplicity, double-dealing, fraud, treachery.
deceitful ADJ = **dishonest**, untruthful, insincere, false, untrustworthy, unscrupulous, unprincipled, two-faced,

duplicitous, double-dealing, treacherous.

deceive VERB = **take in**, fool, delude, trick, hoodwink, dupe, swindle, cheat, double-cross; [inf] con.

decent ADJ 1 = **proper**, correct, appropriate, seemly, fitting, suitable, tasteful, decorous, respectable. 2 = **honest**, trustworthy, dependable, kind, thoughtful, obliging, helpful, generous, courteous, civil. 3 = **sufficient**, acceptable, reasonable, adequate, ample.

deception NOUN see **deceit**.

deceptive ADJ = **misleading**, illusory, wrong, deceiving, unreliable.

decide VERB = **make up your mind**, resolve, determine, commit yourself; choose, opt, elect.

decided ADJ = **clear**, distinct, definite, obvious, marked, pronounced, unmistakable.

decision NOUN = **conclusion**, resolution, judgement, verdict, pronouncement, findings.

decisive ADJ 1 = **determined**, resolute, firm, strong-minded, purposeful, unhesitating, unwavering. 2 = **deciding**, determining, conclusive, critical, crucial, significant, influential.

declaration NOUN 1 = **statement**, announcement, proclamation, pronouncement, edict. 2 = **assertion**, profession, affirmation, attestation, avowal.

declare VERB = **proclaim**, announce, state, express; assert, maintain, affirm, profess, avow, swear.

decline VERB 1 = **refuse**, turn down, reject, rebuff. 2 = **lessen**, decrease, dwindle, wane, fade, ebb, taper off, flag, deteriorate, diminish. NOUN = **decrease**, reduction, downturn, downswing, slump, deterioration.

decorate VERB 1 = **adorn**, ornament, festoon, beautify, embellish, garnish, trim. 2 = **renovate**, refurbish; [inf] do up.

decoration NOUN
1 = **adornment**,
ornamentation,
embellishment.
2 = **ornament**, trinket,
bauble, knick-knack.
3 = **medal**, award, ribbon.
decorous ADJ = **proper**,
seemly, decent,
becoming, fitting,
tasteful, correct,
appropriate, suitable,
polite, well mannered,
refined, genteel,
respectable.
decorum NOUN = **propriety**,
decency, correctness,
seemliness, respectability,
good taste, politeness,
courtesy.
decrease VERB = **lessen**,
reduce, drop, diminish,
decline, dwindle, fall off;
die down, abate, subside,
tail off, ebb, wane. NOUN
= **reduction**, drop, decline,
downturn, diminution.
decree NOUN 1 = **order**,
edict, command,
commandment, mandate,
proclamation, dictum,
fiat. 2 = **judgement**,
verdict, adjudication,
ruling. VERB = **order**,
command, rule, dictate,
pronounce, proclaim,
ordain.

decrepit ADJ = **dilapidated**,
ramshackle, derelict,
tumbledown, run-down.
dedicate VERB = **devote**,
commit, give, pledge.
dedicated ADJ
= **committed**, devoted,
wholehearted,
enthusiastic, keen,
zealous, single-minded.
deduce VERB = **conclude**,
infer, work out, reason,
surmise.
deduction NOUN
1 = **conclusion**, inference,
supposition, surmise.
2 = **subtraction**, removal.
deed NOUN = **act**, action,
feat, exploit,
performance,
undertaking,
accomplishment, stunt,
achievement.
deep ADJ 1 = **fathomless**,
bottomless, yawning,
cavernous. 2 = **profound**,
extreme, intense, great,
heartfelt, fervent, ardent,
impassioned. 3 = **low**,
bass, rich, resonant,
sonorous. 4 = **engrossed**,
absorbed, preoccupied,
rapt, immersed.
deface VERB = **spoil**,
disfigure, mar, damage,
mutilate, vandalize.
defame VERB = **slander**,

libel, cast aspersions on, malign, insult, vilify, traduce, besmirch, defile.

defeat VERB **1** = **beat**, conquer, get the better of, vanquish, trounce, overcome, overpower, overwhelm, crush, subjugate, subdue, quell. **2** = **baffle**, puzzle, perplex, confound, frustrate. NOUN = **conquest**, rout, overthrow, subjugation.

defect NOUN = **fault**, flaw, imperfection, deficiency, shortcoming, weakness.

defective ADJ = **faulty**, flawed, imperfect, malfunctioning.

defence NOUN **1** = **protection**, guard, shield, safeguard, shelter, fortification. **2** = **justification**, vindication, plea, explanation, excuse.

defenceless ADJ = **vulnerable**, helpless, exposed, weak, powerless, unguarded, unprotected.

defend VERB **1** = **protect**, guard, safeguard, preserve, secure, shelter, screen, shield. **2** = **justify**, vindicate, argue for; support, back, stand by, stand up for.

defer VERB = **postpone**, put off/back, delay.

defiant ADJ = **intransigent**, obstinate, uncooperative, recalcitrant; obstreperous, truculent, disobedient, insubordinate, rebellious, mutinous.

deficiency NOUN **1** = **lack**, shortage, scarcity, want, dearth, insufficiency, paucity. **2** see **defect**.

define VERB = **explain**, spell out, elucidate, describe, interpret, expound, clarify.

definite ADJ **1** = **specific**, precise, particular, exact, clear, clear-cut, explicit, fixed, established, settled, confirmed. **2** = **certain**, sure, decided, positive, guaranteed, assured, conclusive.

definitive ADJ = **conclusive**, final, ultimate; positive, definite, authoritative.

deflect VERB = **turn aside**, divert, parry, fend off, ward off, avert.

deformed ADJ = **misshapen**, malformed, distorted, contorted, twisted, crooked; maimed, disfigured, mutilated.

defraud VERB = **cheat**, swindle, rob; [inf] rip off.

deft ADJ = **dexterous**, adroit, skilful, skilled, adept, proficient, able, clever, expert, quick.

defy VERB 1 = **disobey**, disregard, ignore, flout, contravene. 2 = **resist**, stand up to, confront, face, meet head-on.

degenerate VERB = **deteriorate**, decline, worsen, regress, slide.

degrade VERB = **debase**, cheapen, demean, devalue, shame, disgrace, dishonour, humiliate, mortify.

degree NOUN = **level**, standard, grade, mark; amount, extent, measure; magnitude, intensity, strength; proportion, ratio.

deign VERB = **condescend**, lower yourself, stoop, demean yourself.

deity NOUN = **god**, goddess, divinity.

dejected ADJ see **sad**.

delay VERB 1 = **postpone**, put off/back, defer, hold over. 2 = **hold up**, detain, hinder, obstruct, hamper, impede. 3 = **linger**, loiter, dawdle, dally, tarry; [inf]

dilly-dally. NOUN = **hold-up**, wait; hindrance, obstruction, impediment.

delegate VERB = **pass on**, hand over, transfer, entrust, assign, devolve. NOUN = **representative**, agent, envoy, emissary.

delegation NOUN = **deputation**, legation, mission, commission.

delete VERB = **erase**, cross out, rub out, remove, take out, obliterate, efface.

deliberate ADJ 1 = **intentional**, planned, calculated, studied, conscious, purposeful, wilful, premeditated. 2 = **careful**, unhurried, cautious, steady, regular, measured.

deliberately ADV = **intentionally**, on purpose, by design, knowingly.

delicate ADJ 1 = **fine**, fragile, dainty, exquisite, slender, graceful, flimsy, wispy, gossamer. 2 = **frail**, sickly, weak, unwell, infirm, ailing. 3 = **careful**, sensitive, tactful, discreet, considerate, diplomatic, politic. 4 = **difficult**, awkward, tricky, sensitive, critical, precarious; [inf]

ticklish, touchy.

delicious ADJ = **appetizing**, tasty, delectable, mouth-watering, savoury, palatable, luscious.

delight NOUN = **joy**, pleasure, happiness, bliss, ecstasy, elation, jubilation.

delighted ADJ see **happy**.

deliver VERB 1 = **distribute**, carry, bring, take, transport, convey, send, dispatch, remit. 2 = **set free**, save, liberate, free, release, rescue. 3 = **aim**, give, deal, administer, inflict.

deluge NOUN = **flood**, downpour, inundation, spate, rush. VERB = **flood**, inundate, swamp, engulf, drown, overwhelm.

delusion NOUN = **misconception**, illusion, fallacy, misapprehension, mistake, fantasy.

delve VERB = **search**, rummage, hunt through, investigate, probe, examine.

demand VERB 1 = **ask for**, request, insist on, claim. 2 = **require**, need, necessitate, call for, involve. NOUN = **request**, requirement, claim.

demanding ADJ see **difficult (1)**.

demeanour NOUN = **air**, attitude, appearance, manner; bearing, conduct, behaviour.

demolish VERB = **knock down**, flatten, raze, level, bulldoze, destroy.

demonstrate VERB = **show**, indicate, establish, prove, confirm, verify; reveal, display, exhibit, illustrate.

demonstration NOUN 1 = **exhibition**, exposition, presentation, display. 2 = **proof**, confirmation, substantiation, verification. 3 = **protest**, march, rally, lobby, picket.

demoralize VERB = **discourage**, dishearten, dispirit, depress.

demur VERB = **object**, take exception, protest, dissent, cavil.

demure ADJ = **modest**, unassuming, quiet, reticent, bashful, shy, diffident, coy.

denigrate VERB = **disparage**, belittle, deprecate, decry, cast aspersions on, malign.

denote VERB = **indicate**,

mean, stand for, signify, designate, represent, symbolize.

denounce VERB = **condemn**, attack, criticize, censure, castigate, decry, inveigh against.

dense ADJ = **close-packed**, crowded, compressed, compact, thick, solid.

deny VERB = **repudiate**, reject, contradict, gainsay, refute, rebut.

depart VERB = **leave**, go, withdraw, decamp, retire, retreat, set off/out, be on your way.

department NOUN = **section**, division, unit, branch, office, bureau, agency.

depend VERB (**depend on**) 1 = **be dependent on**, hinge on, rest on, be contingent on. 2 = **rely on**, count on, bank on, trust in.

dependable ADJ = **reliable**, trustworthy, trusty, faithful, steadfast, steady, responsible.

dependent ADJ 1 = **conditional on**, contingent on, subject to, determined by. 2 = **reliant on**, supported by, sustained by.

depict VERB = **portray**, represent, illustrate, delineate, picture; describe, relate, detail.

deplete VERB = **exhaust**, use up, consume, expend, drain, empty.

deplorable ADJ = **disgraceful**, shameful, reprehensible, scandalous, shocking, despicable, contemptible, abominable, lamentable, dire.

deploy VERB 1 = **arrange**, position, dispose, distribute, station. 2 = **use**, utilize, bring into play, have recourse to.

deport VERB = **expel**, banish, exile, expatriate, extradite.

deposit NOUN 1 = **down payment**, instalment, retainer. 2 = **sediment**, silt, alluvium. VERB 1 = **bank**, lodge, consign, entrust, store, stow. 2 = **put**, place, lay, set.

depot NOUN = **station**, garage, terminus, terminal.

depression NOUN 1 = **sadness**, unhappiness, despair, gloom, dejection, despondency,

melancholy, desolation.
2 = **recession**, slump,
slowdown.

deprive VERB
= **dispossess**, strip, deny,
divest, rob.

deputy NOUN = **substitute**,
representative, stand-in,
delegate, envoy, proxy,
agent.

derelict ADJ = **abandoned**,
deserted, neglected,
dilapidated, ramshackle,
tumbledown, run-down,
in disrepair.

deride VERB = **mock**,
ridicule, jeer at, scoff at,
sneer at, make fun of,
laugh at, scorn.

derogatory ADJ
= **disparaging**, critical,
disapproving,
unflattering, insulting,
defamatory.

descend VERB 1 = **go/come
down**, fall, drop, sink,
subside, plunge,
plummet. 2 = **get down/
off**, alight, disembark.

descent NOUN 1 = **slope**,
incline, dip, drop,
gradient, declivity.
2 = **ancestry**, parentage,
origins, lineage,
extraction, heredity,
stock, line, pedigree,
blood.

describe VERB = **recount**,
relate, report, detail, tell,
narrate, set out, portray,
depict.

description NOUN
= **account**, report,
chronicle, narration,
commentary, portrayal,
depiction.

desert NOUN = **wasteland**,
wilderness. VERB
= **abandon**, forsake, leave,
jilt, walk out on, leave in
the lurch, throw over.

deserted ADJ
= **abandoned**, empty,
neglected, vacant,
uninhabited, desolate,
lonely, godforsaken.

deserve VERB = **merit**,
warrant, rate, justify,
earn.

design NOUN 1 = **plan**,
blueprint, drawing,
sketch, outline, map,
diagram. 2 = **pattern**,
motif, style. 3 = **intention**,
aim, purpose, plan,
objective, goal, end,
target, hope, desire, wish,
aspiration. VERB 1 = **plan**,
outline, map out, draft.
2 = **create**, invent,
originate, conceive.
3 = **intend**, aim, plan,
tailor, mean.

desire VERB = **wish for**,

want, long for, yearn for, crave, ache for, set your heart on, hanker after, covet, aspire to. NOUN
1 = **wish**, want, fancy, longing, yearning, craving, hankering, aspiration. 2 = **lust**, passion.

desolate ADJ
1 = **abandoned**, deserted, barren, uninhabited, lonely, isolated, remote, cheerless, dismal, godforsaken. 2 = **sad**, unhappy, miserable, wretched, downcast, dejected, downhearted, melancholy, depressed, forlorn, despondent, distressed, bereft.

despair NOUN
= **hopelessness**, depression, despondency, pessimism, melancholy, misery, wretchedness.

desperate ADJ = **urgent**, pressing, acute, critical, crucial, drastic, serious, grave, dire, extreme, great.

despise VERB = **hate**, detest, loathe, abhor, abominate, look down on, disdain, scorn.

despondent ADJ
= **downcast**, miserable,

sad, disheartened, discouraged, disconsolate, dispirited, downhearted, despairing, melancholy, woebegone.

despotic ADJ = **autocratic**, dictatorial, tyrannical, authoritarian, totalitarian.

destined ADJ = **fated**, ordained, predestined, doomed, certain, sure, bound.

destiny NOUN = **fate**, providence, kismet; fortune, luck, chance, karma; future, lot.

destitute ADJ = **penniless**, impoverished, poverty-stricken, poor, impecunious, penurious, indigent.

destroy VERB 1 = **demolish**, wreck, annihilate, knock down, tear down, level, raze, wipe out, ruin, devastate, lay waste to, ravage, wreak havoc on.
2 = **kill**, put down, put to sleep.

destructive ADJ
= **ruinous**, devastating, disastrous, catastrophic, calamitous; injurious, harmful, damaging.

detach VERB = **disconnect**, unfasten, remove, undo,

separate, uncouple, loosen, free, disengage.

detached ADJ
= **dispassionate**, disinterested, uninvolved, objective, unbiased, unprejudiced, impersonal, indifferent, aloof.

detail NOUN = **item**, point, particular, factor, nicety, fact, element, aspect, circumstance, feature, respect, attribute, component, part, unit.

detailed ADJ = **full**, comprehensive, exhaustive, thorough, itemized, precise, exact, specific, meticulous, painstaking.

detain VERB **1** = **delay**, hold up, keep, slow down, hinder, impede. **2** = **confine**, imprison, lock up, jail, incarcerate, hold.

detect VERB **1** = **notice**, note, perceive, discern, make out, observe, spot, recognize, distinguish, identify, sense. **2** = **find out**, discover, uncover, bring to light, expose, reveal.

detention NOUN = **custody**, confinement, imprisonment, incarceration, internment, arrest.

deter VERB = **discourage**, dissuade, put off, scare off; prevent, stop.

deteriorate VERB
= **worsen**, decline, degenerate, sink, slip, go downhill.

determination NOUN
= **resolution**, resolve, will power, persistence, tenacity, perseverance, single-mindedness, fortitude, dedication, doggedness.

determine VERB
1 = **decide**, resolve, make up your mind. **2** = **find out**, discover, learn, establish, work out, ascertain. **3** = **affect**, influence, regulate, control, dictate, govern, shape.

determined ADJ = **firm**, resolute, single-minded, steadfast, tenacious, strong-willed, dedicated, persistent, persevering, dogged, unwavering, stubborn, obdurate, intransigent.

deterrent NOUN
= **disincentive**, discouragement, restraint, curb, check.

detest VERB = **loathe**, hate,

abhor, despise, abominate, abhor.

detract VERB = **take away from**, diminish, reduce, lessen, lower, devalue.

detrimental ADJ = **harmful**, damaging, injurious, hurtful, destructive, deleterious, inimical, unfavourable.

devastate VERB = **destroy**, ruin, lay waste to, ravage, demolish, wreck, flatten, obliterate.

develop VERB 1 = **grow**, evolve, mature, improve, expand, spread, enlarge, advance, progress, flourish, prosper, make headway. 2 = **begin**, start, come about, result, ensue, break out.

development NOUN 1 = **growth**, evolution, advance, improvement, expansion, spread, progress. 2 = **event**, occurrence, happening, incident, circumstance, situation. 3 = **estate**, complex.

deviate VERB = **diverge**, branch off, turn aside, veer, swerve, drift, stray; digress.

device NOUN = **appliance**, gadget, implement, tool, utensil, apparatus, instrument, machine, contraption; [inf] gizmo.

devil NOUN 1 = **demon**, fiend, evil spirit. 2 = **Satan**, Lucifer, the Prince of Darkness, Beelzebub.

devious ADJ = **cunning**, underhand, sly, crafty, wily, artful, scheming, calculating, deceitful, dishonest.

devise VERB = **create**, invent, concoct, conceive, work out, formulate, compose, frame, think up, hatch.

devoted ADJ = **committed**, faithful, loyal, true, dedicated, staunch, devout, steadfast.

devotee NOUN = **fan**, enthusiast, admirer, follower, adherent, disciple, supporter, fanatic.

devotion NOUN = **love**, loyalty, commitment, allegiance, dedication, faithfulness, fidelity.

devour VERB = **consume**, gobble, guzzle, wolf down.

devout ADJ = **pious**, religious, godly, churchgoing, reverent, God-fearing.

diagonal ADJ = **crossways**, crosswise, slanting, slanted, sloping, oblique.

diagram NOUN = **plan**, picture, representation, drawing, sketch, outline, figure.

dialect NOUN = **vernacular**, patois.

dialogue NOUN = **conversation**, talk, debate, discussion, discourse, parley, colloquy.

diary NOUN = **journal**, chronicle, record, log, history, annals.

dictate VERB = **order**, command, decree, ordain, direct, decide, control, govern.

dictator NOUN = **despot**, autocrat, tyrant, oppressor.

dictatorial ADJ = **tyrannical**, despotic, overbearing, domineering, imperious, high-handed, authoritarian, peremptory, bossy.

die VERB 1 = **expire**, perish, pass on/away; [inf] kick the bucket, snuff it. 2 = **come to an end**, disappear, vanish, fade, decline, ebb, dwindle, melt away, wane, wither.

differ VERB 1 = **vary**, contrast, diverge, deviate. 2 = **disagree**, conflict, clash, quarrel, argue.

difference NOUN = **dissimilarity**, contrast, distinction, variance, variation, divergence, deviation, contradiction, disparity, imbalance, dissimilitude, differentiation.

different ADJ = **dissimilar**, contrasting, diverse, disparate, divergent, incompatible, inconsistent, at variance, at odds, clashing, conflicting.

difficult ADJ 1 = **hard**, demanding, laborious, onerous, burdensome, tough, strenuous, arduous, exhausting, exacting, tiring, wearisome, back-breaking. 2 = **complex**, complicated, problematic, puzzling, baffling, perplexing, knotty, thorny, hard. 3 = **troublesome**, demanding, unmanageable, intractable, perverse, recalcitrant, obstreperous, refractory, fractious, uncooperative.

difficulty NOUN
1 = **problem**, complication, snag, hitch, obstacle, hindrance, hurdle, pitfall, impediment, barrier.
2 = **predicament**, quandary, dilemma, plight.

diffident ADJ = **shy**, modest, bashful, unconfident, timid, timorous, self-effacing, unassuming, humble, meek.

dig VERB **1** = **cultivate**, turn over, work, till, harrow.
2 = **excavate**, burrow, mine, quarry, hollow out, scoop out, tunnel, gouge.
3 = **poke**, nudge, prod, jab.

dignified ADJ = **formal**, grave, solemn, stately, noble, decorous, ceremonious, majestic, august, lofty, regal, lordly, imposing, grand, impressive.

dignitary NOUN = **luminary**, worthy, notable, VIP, big name, leading light.

dignity NOUN = **stateliness**, nobility, solemnity, gravity, gravitas, decorum, propriety, majesty, regality,

grandeur.

dilapidated ADJ
= **run-down**, ramshackle, in ruins, ruined, tumbledown, shabby, in disrepair, decrepit, neglected.

dilemma NOUN = **difficulty**, problem, quandary, predicament, catch-22.

diligent ADJ = **assiduous**, industrious, conscientious, hard-working, painstaking, sedulous, meticulous, thorough, careful.

dim ADJ **1** = **faint**, weak, feeble, dull; subdued, muted. **2** = **vague**, ill-defined, indistinct, unclear, shadowy, blurred, hazy, nebulous.

dimension NOUN **1** = **size**, extent, length, width, area, volume, capacity, proportions. **2** = **aspect**, facet, side, feature, element.

diminish VERB = **decrease**, lessen, decline, reduce, subside, die down, abate, dwindle, fade, moderate, let up, ebb, wane, recede.

diminutive ADJ = **small**, tiny, little, petite.

din NOUN = **noise**, uproar, row, racket, commotion,

hullabaloo, hubbub,
clamour, cacophony.
dingy ADJ = **dark**, dull, dim,
gloomy, drab, dismal,
dreary, cheerless, murky,
dirty, grimy, shabby,
seedy.
dip VERB 1 = **descend**, sink,
subside, fall, drop,
decline. 2 = **immerse**,
plunge, submerge, duck,
dunk. NOUN = **hollow**, basin,
concavity, depression,
slope, incline.
diplomatic ADJ = **tactful**,
sensitive, discreet, polite,
careful, delicate,
thoughtful, considerate,
prudent, judicious,
politic.
dire ADJ = **terrible**, dreadful,
awful, appalling,
frightful, horrible,
atrocious, grim, cruel,
disastrous, ruinous,
calamitous, catastrophic.
direct ADJ 1 = **straight**,
undeviating; non-stop,
uninterrupted, unbroken.
2 = **frank**, straightforward,
candid, open, honest,
sincere, outspoken,
forthright, matter-of-fact,
blunt. 3 = **exact**, complete,
absolute, diametrical. VERB
1 = **guide**, steer, lead,
conduct, usher.

2 = **manage**, lead, run,
control, supervise,
oversee. 3 = **aim**, point,
train.
dirt NOUN 1 = **grime**, dust,
soot, muck, mud, filth,
sludge, slime. 2 = **earth**,
soil, clay, loam.
dirty ADJ 1 = **unclean**, filthy,
stained, grimy, soiled,
grubby, dusty, mucky,
sooty, muddy, polluted,
foul, tarnished.
2 = **obscene**, indecent,
vulgar, smutty, coarse,
rude. VERB = **soil**, stain,
muddy, blacken, smudge,
smear, sully, pollute.
disability NOUN
= **handicap**, infirmity,
impairment, affliction,
disablement, incapacity.
disadvantage NOUN
= **drawback**, snag,
downside, weakness, flaw,
defect, fault, handicap,
liability.
disagree VERB 1 = **take
issue**, dissent, be at
variance, quarrel, argue,
wrangle, dispute, debate.
2 = **differ**, vary, conflict,
clash, contrast, diverge.
disagreeable ADJ
= **unpleasant**,
objectionable, horrible,
nasty, offensive,

obnoxious, off-putting.

disappear VERB = **vanish**, be lost to view, fade away, melt away, evaporate.

disappoint VERB = **let down**, fail, dash someone's hopes, upset, sadden.

disappointed ADJ = **saddened**, upset, disheartened, downhearted, downcast, depressed, despondent, dispirited, crestfallen.

disapprove VERB = **object to**, dislike, deplore, frown on, criticize, censure, condemn, denounce.

disarray NOUN = **disorder**, confusion, chaos, mess, muddle, shambles.

disaster NOUN = **catastrophe**, calamity, cataclysm, tragedy; accident, misfortune, misadventure.

disastrous ADJ = **catastrophic**, cataclysmic, calamitous, devastating, tragic, ruinous.

discard VERB = **throw out/away**, dispose of, get rid of, jettison, dispense with, scrap, reject.

discern VERB = **see**, notice, observe, perceive, make out, distinguish, detect, recognize.

discerning ADJ = **discriminating**, astute, shrewd, perceptive, penetrating, judicious, sensitive, sophisticated.

discharge VERB 1 = **emit**, exude, release, leak. 2 = **dismiss**, eject, expel; [inf] fire, sack. 3 = **set free**, release, liberate. 4 = **carry out**, perform, do, accomplish, fulfil, execute.

disciple NOUN = **apostle**, follower, acolyte, adherent, devotee, believer, advocate, proponent.

disciplinarian NOUN = **martinet**, hard taskmaster, tyrant, slave-driver.

discipline NOUN = **control**, self-control, self-restraint, strictness, regulation, direction, order, authority; training, teaching. VERB 1 = **control**, restrain, regulate, govern, check, curb. 2 = **punish**, penalize; chastise, castigate, reprimand.

disclose VERB = **reveal**, divulge, tell, impart, let slip.

discomfort NOUN 1 = **pain**, ache, soreness, tenderness, irritation. 2 = **unease**, embarrassment, discomfiture.

disconcert VERB = **unsettle**, take aback, perturb, discomfit, discompose, nonplus, throw.

disconnect VERB = **undo**, detach, disengage, uncouple, unfasten, unplug.

discontented ADJ = **dissatisfied**, displeased, disgruntled, unhappy, disaffected, fed up.

discord NOUN = **disagreement**, conflict, friction, strife, hostility, antagonism.

discordant ADJ = **dissonant**, cacophonous, inharmonious, off-key, tuneless.

discount NOUN = **reduction**, rebate. VERB = **disregard**, ignore, dismiss, overlook, pass over, take no notice of.

discourage VERB 1 = **dishearten**, dispirit, demoralize, cast down, unnerve, daunt, intimidate. 2 = **dissuade**, put off, deter, talk out of.

discourse NOUN = **address**, speech, lecture, oration, sermon, homily; essay, treatise, dissertation, paper.

discover VERB 1 = **find**, come across, locate, stumble on, bring to light, unearth. 2 = **find out**, learn, realize, ascertain.

discredit VERB 1 = **disgrace**, dishonour, compromise, stigmatize, smear, tarnish, taint. 2 = **disprove**, invalidate, refute.

discreet ADJ = **careful**, circumspect, cautious, wary, guarded, sensitive, prudent, judicious, chary, tactful, reserved, diplomatic, muted, understated, delicate, considerate, politic, wise, sensible, sagacious.

discrepancy NOUN = **inconsistency**, disparity, deviation, variance, variation, difference, divergence, disagreement, dissimilarity, conflict.

discriminate VERB = **distinguish**, differentiate, tell apart.

discrimination NOUN
1 = **discernment**, (good) taste, judgement, perception, acumen, insight, refinement, sensitivity. 2 = **prejudice**, bias, intolerance, bigotry, favouritism; chauvinism, racism, sexism.

discuss VERB = **talk over**, debate, consider, confer about; examine, explore, analyse.

discussion NOUN = **conversation**, talk, dialogue, chat, debate, discourse, consultation; explanation, exploration, analysis.

disdainful ADJ = **scornful**, contemptuous, derisive, condescending, arrogant, proud, supercilious, haughty, superior.

disease NOUN see **illness**.

diseased ADJ = **unhealthy**, infected, septic.

disfigure VERB = **mutilate**, deface, deform, scar, spoil, mar, damage, injure, maim.

disgrace NOUN = **shame**, humiliation, dishonour, disrepute, disrespect, scandal, ignominy, degradation, discredit, stigma.

disgraceful ADJ = **scandalous**, outrageous, shocking, shameful, contemptible, despicable, ignominious, reprehensible.

disgruntled ADJ = **dissatisfied**, displeased, discontented, annoyed, irritated, vexed, fed up.

disguise VERB = **camouflage**, cover up, conceal, dissemble, hide, screen, mask, veil, cloak.

disgust NOUN = **revulsion**, repugnance, abhorrence, loathing, detestation. VERB = **sicken**, nauseate, revolt, repel; outrage, shock, appal, scandalize.

dish NOUN = **plate**, platter, bowl, basin, tureen, salver.

dishevelled ADJ = **untidy**, rumpled, messy, scruffy, bedraggled, tousled, unkempt.

dishonest ADJ = **untruthful**, deceitful, lying, two-faced; fraudulent, corrupt, treacherous, cunning, devious, underhand, dishonourable, unscrupulous, unprincipled, unfair, unjust.

dishonour NOUN see
  disgrace.
dishonourable ADJ
  = **shameful**, disreputable,
  discreditable,
  ignominious, ignoble,
  blameworthy,
  contemptible, despicable,
  reprehensible, shabby,
  unseemly, unprincipled,
  unscrupulous.
disinfect VERB = **sterilize**,
  sanitize, clean, cleanse,
  purify, fumigate,
  decontaminate.
disintegrate VERB = **fall
  apart**, fall to pieces, break
  up, fragment, shatter,
  crumble.
disinterested ADJ
  = **unbiased**, unprejudiced,
  impartial, detached,
  objective, dispassionate,
  impersonal, neutral.
disjointed ADJ
  = **incoherent**, rambling,
  disconnected,
  disorganized, confused,
  muddled.
dislike NOUN = **aversion**,
  distaste, disapproval,
  disfavour, animosity,
  hostility, antipathy.
disloyal ADJ = **unfaithful**,
  faithless, false,
  inconstant,
  untrustworthy,

treacherous, traitorous,
  perfidious, double-
  dealing, deceitful, two-
  faced.
dismal ADJ = **gloomy**,
  bleak, miserable,
  wretched, drab, dreary,
  dingy, cheerless,
  depressing, uninviting.
dismay NOUN
  = **consternation**, distress,
  anxiety, alarm, concern.
  VERB = **shock**, take aback,
  startle, alarm, disturb,
  perturb, upset, unsettle,
  unnerve.
dismiss VERB = **discharge**,
  get rid of, lay off, make
  redundant; [inf] sack, fire.
disobedient ADJ
  = **insubordinate**,
  rebellious, defiant,
  unruly, wayward,
  mutinous, wilful,
  uncooperative, naughty,
  obstreperous.
disobey VERB = **defy**,
  disregard, ignore,
  contravene, flout,
  infringe, violate.
disorder NOUN 1 = **mess**,
  untidiness, chaos,
  muddle, clutter,
  confusion, disarray,
  disorganization,
  shambles. 2 = **disturbance**,
  disruption, rioting,

unrest. 3 = **disease**, complaint, affliction, illness, sickness, malady.

disorganized ADJ = **confused**, disorderly, untidy, chaotic, jumbled, muddled, in disarray, unsystematic, haphazard, slapdash, careless; [inf] hit-or-miss.

disown VERB = **renounce**, repudiate, reject, abandon, forsake, deny, turn your back on.

disparity NOUN = **discrepancy**, difference, dissimilarity, contrast, gap, inequality.

dispatch VERB = **send**, post, mail, forward, transmit.

disperse VERB = **break up**, disband, separate, scatter, leave; dissipate, dissolve, vanish, melt away.

displace VERB = **dislodge**, dislocate, move; replace, supplant.

display VERB 1 = **show**, exhibit, present, lay/set out, array. 2 = **manifest**, evince, betray, reveal. NOUN = **show**, exhibition, exhibit, presentation, demonstration; spectacle, parade, pageant.

displease VERB = **annoy**, irritate, anger, put out, irk, vex, offend, pique, gall, exasperate.

disposed ADJ = **inclined**, willing, predisposed, minded, prepared, ready.

disprove VERB = **refute**, rebut, give the lie to, discredit, invalidate.

dispute NOUN = **argument**, quarrel, row, altercation, wrangle, squabble; debate. VERB 1 = **debate**, argue, disagree, quarrel, wrangle, squabble. 2 = **question**, challenge, contest, take issue with, impugn.

disquiet NOUN = **unease**, anxiety, agitation, worry, concern.

disregard VERB = **ignore**, take no notice of, discount, overlook, turn a blind eye to.

disreputable ADJ = **infamous**, notorious, louche, dishonourable, dishonest, unprincipled, unsavoury, untrustworthy.

disrespectful ADJ = **impolite**, discourteous, ill-mannered, rude, uncivil, insolent, impertinent, impudent, cheeky.

disrupt VERB = **upset**, interrupt, disturb, interfere with, obstruct, impede, play havoc with.

dissatisfied ADJ = **discontented**, displeased, disgruntled, disappointed, frustrated, unhappy, vexed, irritated, annoyed, fed up.

disseminate VERB = **spread**, circulate, distribute, disperse, communicate, publicize, promulgate, propagate.

dissident NOUN = **dissenter**, rebel, non-conformist.

dissimilar ADJ = **different**, distinct, disparate, contrasting, mismatched.

dissipate VERB 1 = **disperse**, disappear, vanish, evaporate, dissolve. 2 = **squander**, waste, fritter away, run through.

dissociate VERB = **separate**, set apart, isolate, detach, disconnect, divorce.

dissolve VERB 1 = **liquefy**, melt, deliquesce. 2 = **end**, bring to an end, terminate, discontinue, wind up, disband.

dissuade VERB = **talk out of**, discourage from, deter from, put off.

distance NOUN = **interval**, space, span, gap, extent; length, width, breadth, depth; range, reach.

distant ADJ 1 = **faraway**, far-off, remote, out of the way, outlying, far-flung. 2 = **reserved**, aloof, uncommunicative, remote, withdrawn, unapproachable, reticent, unfriendly, unresponsive; [inf] stand-offish.

distasteful ADJ = **disagreeable**, unpleasant, displeasing, undesirable, off-putting, objectionable, offensive, obnoxious, unsavoury.

distinct ADJ 1 = **discrete**, separate, different, unconnected, contrasting. 2 = **clear**, well defined, unmistakable, recognizable, visible, obvious, pronounced, prominent, striking.

distinction NOUN 1 = **contrast**, difference, dissimilarity, differentiation, division. 2 = **renown**, fame, celebrity, prominence, eminence, pre-eminence, merit, worth, greatness,

diverse

excellence.

distinctive ADJ
= **distinguishing**,
characteristic, typical,
particular, special.

distinguish VERB 1 = **tell
apart**, differentiate,
discriminate. 2 = **set apart**,
separate, characterize.
3 = **make out**, see, perceive,
discern, pick out.

distinguished ADJ
= **eminent**, renowned, well
known, prominent,
noted, famous, illustrious,
celebrated, famed,
respected, acclaimed,
esteemed.

distort VERB
= **misrepresent**, pervert,
twist, falsify, misreport.

distraught ADJ
= **distressed**, desperate,
overwrought, frantic,
hysterical, beside yourself.

distress NOUN 1 = **anguish**,
suffering, pain, agony,
torment, heartache,
heartbreak; misery,
wretchedness, sorrow,
grief, woe, sadness,
unhappiness, despair.
2 = **hardship**, poverty,
deprivation, privation,
destitution, indigence,
penury, need. VERB = **upset**,
pain, trouble, worry,
disturb, sadden.

distribute VERB = **give out**,
deal out, dole out, hand
out/round; allocate, allot,
apportion, share out,
divide up, parcel out;
circulate, pass around,
deliver.

district NOUN = **area**,
region, locality,
neighbourhood, sector,
quarter, territory, zone,
ward, parish.

distrust NOUN = **mistrust**,
doubt, suspicion,
scepticism, wariness.

disturb VERB 1 = **interrupt**,
distract, bother, trouble,
intrude on, pester, harass,
plague; [inf] hassle.
2 = **concern**, trouble,
worry, perturb, upset,
agitate, alarm, dismay,
distress, unsettle.

ditch NOUN = **trench**,
trough, channel, dyke,
drain, gutter, gully, moat.

dive VERB = **plunge**,
plummet, nosedive, fall,
drop, swoop, pitch.

diverge VERB = **separate**,
fork, branch off, bifurcate,
divide, split, part.

diverse ADJ = **assorted**,
various, miscellaneous,
mixed, varied,
heterogeneous, different,

differing.

diverting ADJ = **amusing**, entertaining, fun, enjoyable, pleasurable, interesting.

divide VERB 1 = **split**, cut up, separate, halve, bisect; segregate, partition, separate. 2 = **branch**, fork, diverge, split in two. 3 = **share out**, allocate, allot, apportion, distribute, hand out, dole out.

divine ADJ = **heavenly**, celestial, holy, angelic, saintly, seraphic, sacred.

division NOUN 1 = **dividing line**, divide, boundary, borderline. 2 = **section**, subsection, subdivision, category, class, group, grouping, set. 3 = **branch**, department, unit.

dizzy ADJ = **light-headed**, giddy, faint, shaky, weak at the knees, woozy.

do VERB 1 = **perform**, carry out, undertake, execute, accomplish, discharge, achieve, implement. 2 = **suffice**, be sufficient, serve the purpose, fit/fill the bill. 3 = **grant**, render, pay, give.

docile ADJ = **amenable**, compliant, tractable, manageable, accommodating, obedient, pliant, biddable, submissive.

dock NOUN = **pier**, quay, wharf, jetty, harbour, port, marina. VERB = **deduct**, subtract, remove, take off; cut.

doctor NOUN = **physician**, GP, consultant, registrar.

doctrine NOUN = **creed**, credo, dogma, belief, teaching, ideology; tenet, maxim, canon, principle, precept.

document NOUN = **paper**, certificate, deed, contract, record; licence, visa, warrant.

dodge VERB = **evade**, avoid, elude, escape, give someone the slip; sidestep, get out of. NOUN = **ruse**, ploy, scheme, stratagem, trick.

dog NOUN = **hound**, canine, mongrel, puppy; [inf] pooch, mutt.

dogged ADJ = **determined**, tenacious, single-minded, unflagging, persistent, persevering, tireless.

dogmatic ADJ = **assertive**, insistent, emphatic, adamant, authoritarian, opinionated, peremptory, domineering, overbearing, dictatorial.

doleful ADJ = **mournful**, sad, sorrowful, dejected, depressed, miserable, disconsolate, woebegone.

dominant ADJ
1 = **assertive**, authoritative, forceful, domineering, commanding, controlling, pushy.
2 = **chief**, main, leading, principal, predominant, paramount, primary.

dominate VERB 1 = **rule**, govern, control, command, direct, preside over; tyrannize, intimidate. 2 = **overlook**, tower above, loom over.

domineering ADJ = **overbearing**, authoritarian, autocratic, imperious, high-handed, peremptory, bossy, arrogant, dictatorial, tyrannical.

donate VERB = **give**, contribute, present, grant, bestow.

donation NOUN = **contribution**, gift, present, grant, offering, handout.

doom NOUN = **destruction**, downfall, ruin, ruination,

death. VERB = **destine**, fate, condemn, predestine.

door NOUN = **doorway**, opening, portal, entrance, entry, exit.

dormant ADJ = **sleeping**, asleep, inactive, inert, latent, quiescent.

dot NOUN = **spot**, speck, fleck, speckle.

dote VERB (**dote on**) = **adore**, love, idolize, worship, treasure.

double-cross VERB = **betray**, cheat, trick, deceive, hoodwink.

doubt VERB = **distrust**, mistrust, suspect, question, query. NOUN = **distrust**, mistrust, suspicion, scepticism, uncertainty; reservations, misgivings.

doubtful ADJ 1 = **in doubt**, uncertain, unsure.
2 = **suspicious**, distrustful, mistrustful, sceptical.
3 = **dubious**, uncertain, questionable, debatable.

dowdy ADJ = **frumpy**, unfashionable, inelegant; [inf] mumsy.

downcast ADJ = **downhearted**, dispirited, depressed, dejected, disconsolate, crestfallen, despondent, sad, unhappy, miserable, gloomy, glum.

downright ADJ = **complete**, total, absolute, utter, thorough, out-and-out.

drab ADJ = **dull**, colourless, grey, dingy, dreary, cheerless, dismal, gloomy.

draft NOUN = **outline**, plan, skeleton, abstract, bare bones.

drag VERB = **pull**, haul, draw, tug, yank, trail, tow, lug.

drain VERB 1 = **draw off**, extract, remove, siphon off, pump out, bleed. 2 = **flow**, pour, run; seep, leak, trickle, ooze. 3 = **use up**, exhaust, deplete, sap. NOUN = **channel**, pipe, sewer, conduit.

dramatic ADJ 1 = **theatrical**, stage, thespian. 2 = **exciting**, action-packed, sensational, spectacular, thrilling, suspenseful, electrifying, stirring.

dramatist NOUN = **playwright**, scriptwriter, screenwriter.

drastic ADJ = **extreme**, serious, desperate, radical; heavy, severe, harsh, draconian.

draw VERB 1 = **sketch**, delineate, design, trace, portray, depict. 2 = **pull**, haul, drag, tug, yank, tow, trail, lug. 3 = **attract**, interest, win, capture, lure, entice. 4 = **drain**, siphon off, pump out. NOUN 1 = **lure**, attraction, pull, appeal, allure. 2 = **lottery**, raffle, sweepstake. 3 = **tie**, dead heat, stalemate.

drawback NOUN = **disadvantage**, catch, problem, snag, difficulty, trouble, flaw, hitch, stumbling block.

drawing NOUN = **picture**, sketch, illustration, portrayal, representation, depiction; diagram.

dread NOUN = **fear**, fright, terror, trepidation, foreboding.

dreadful ADJ 1 = **terrible**, frightful, horrible, grim, awful, dire; horrifying, alarming, shocking, distressing, appalling, harrowing; ghastly, fearful, horrendous. 2 = **nasty**, unpleasant, disagreeable, repugnant, revolting, distasteful, odious.

dream NOUN 1 = **vision**, nightmare, hallucination,

fantasy; daydream,
reverie. **2** = **ambition**,
aspiration, hope, goal,
aim, objective, desire,
wish.

dreary ADJ = **dull**,
uninteresting, uneventful,
tedious, boring,
humdrum, monotonous,
wearisome.

drench VERB = **soak**,
saturate, wet through.

dress NOUN **1** = **frock**, gown,
robe. **2** = **clothes**, clothing,
garments, attire, costume,
outfit, ensemble. VERB
= **clothe**, attire, garb.

dribble VERB = **drool**, slaver,
slobber.

drink VERB **1** = **swallow**, sip,
swill, swig, quaff.
2 = **imbibe**, tipple. NOUN
= **alcohol**, liquor, spirits;
[inf] booze.

drip VERB = **dribble**, trickle,
drop, drizzle, leak.

drive VERB **1** = **operate**,
steer, handle, guide,
direct, manage. **2** = **force**,
compel, coerce, oblige,
impel, pressure, goad,
spur, prod. NOUN **1** = **trip**,
run, outing, journey,
jaunt, spin. **2** = **energy**,
determination,
enthusiasm, vigour,
motivation, keenness,

enterprise, initiative; [inf]
get-up-and-go.

drop VERB = **fall**, descend,
plunge, dive, plummet,
tumble, dip, sink, pitch.
NOUN **1** = **droplet**, globule,
bead, bubble, blob.
2 = **decrease**, fall,
decline, reduction, cut,
slump. **3** = **incline**, slope,
descent, declivity.

drown VERB = **flood**,
submerge, inundate,
deluge, swamp, engulf.

drug NOUN **1** = **medicine**,
medication, medicament.
2 = **narcotic**, stimulant; [inf]
dope.

drunk ADJ = **intoxicated**,
inebriated, merry, tipsy;
[inf] tiddly, plastered,
paralytic, sloshed, tight.
NOUN = **drunkard**,
alcoholic, dipsomaniac.

dry ADJ = **arid**, parched,
dehydrated, desiccated,
withered, shrivelled.

dubious ADJ = **doubtful**,
sceptical, uncertain,
unsure, hesitant,
undecided, irresolute;
suspicious, questionable,
suspect.

duct NOUN = **pipe**, tube,
conduit, channel,
passage, canal, culvert.

due ADJ **1** = **owing**, owed,

dull

payable, unpaid,
outstanding. 2 = **deserved**,
merited, justified.
3 = **proper**, correct,
rightful, fitting,
appropriate, apt.

dull ADJ 1 = **uninteresting**,
boring, tedious, tiresome,
wearisome, monotonous,
flat, unimaginative,
uninspired, uninspiring,
lacklustre. 2 = **drab**,
dreary, sombre, faded,
washed-out. 3 = **overcast**,
cloudy, gloomy, dreary,
dark, leaden, murky,
lowering. 4 = **muted**,
muffled, indistinct.

dumbfound VERB
= **astound**, amaze,
astonish, startle, stun,
stagger.

dump VERB = **dispose of**,
get rid of, discard, throw
away/out, scrap, jettison.
NOUN = **tip**, rubbish dump,
scrapyard.

duplicate NOUN = **copy**,
photocopy, carbon copy;
replica, reproduction. ADJ
= **matching**, twin,

identical, corresponding.

duplicity NOUN = **deceit**,
deception, dishonesty,
double-dealing,
chicanery, guile.

durable ADJ = **long-lasting**,
hard-wearing, strong,
sturdy, tough.

dusk NOUN = **twilight**,
sunset, sundown,
nightfall, gloaming.

dutiful ADJ
= **conscientious**,
obedient, deferential,
respectful, filial.

duty NOUN
1 = **responsibility**,
obligation, commitment.
2 = **job**, task, assignment,
mission, function, charge,
role.

dwindle VERB = **diminish**,
decrease, lessen, shrink,
fade, wane.

dye NOUN = **colour**, shade,
tint, pigment.

dynamic ADJ = **energetic**,
active, lively, spirited,
enthusiastic, motivated,
vigorous, strong, forceful,
powerful.

Ee

eager ADJ 1 = **keen**, enthusiastic, avid; [inf] raring. 2 = **longing**, yearning, anxious, intent, agog, impatient.

early ADV = **ahead of time**, beforehand, in good time. ADJ 1 = **advanced**, forward; premature, untimely. 2 = **primitive**, prehistoric, ancient.

earn VERB 1 = **get**, make, clear, bring in, take home, gross, net. 2 = **gain**, win, achieve, secure, obtain, merit, deserve.

earnest ADJ 1 = **serious**, solemn, sober, studious, staid. 2 = **sincere**, fervent, ardent, heartfelt, wholehearted.

earth NOUN = **soil**, clay, loam, turf, clod, sod, ground.

earthly ADJ = **worldly**, temporal, secular, mortal, human, material, mundane, carnal, fleshly, physical, corporeal.

ease NOUN 1 = **effortlessness**, simplicity, facility.

2 = **comfort**, contentment, affluence, wealth, prosperity, luxury. VERB = **lessen**, mitigate, reduce, lighten, diminish, moderate, ameliorate, relieve, assuage, allay, soothe, palliate.

easy ADJ = **simple**, uncomplicated, straightforward, undemanding, effortless, painless, trouble-free; [inf] child's play.

easy-going ADJ = **even-tempered**, relaxed, carefree, happy-go-lucky, placid, serene, tolerant, undemanding, amiable, good-natured, patient, understanding; [inf] laid-back.

eat VERB 1 = **consume**, devour, swallow, chew, munch, bolt, wolf, tuck into, ingest; [inf] scoff. 2 = **erode**, wear away, corrode; damage, destroy.

ebb VERB = **recede**, retreat, fall back, subside.

eccentric ADJ = **odd**, strange, queer, peculiar,

unconventional, idiosyncratic, quirky, weird, bizarre, outlandish; [inf] offbeat.

echo VERB = **reverberate**, resonate, resound.

eclipse VERB 1 = **block**, cover, blot out, obscure, conceal, darken, shade. 2 = **outshine**, overshadow, surpass, exceed, transcend.

economical ADJ 1 = **thrifty**, sparing, careful, prudent, frugal, penny-pinching, parsimonious. 2 = **cheap**, inexpensive, low-cost.

economize VERB = **cut back**, cut costs, scrimp, save, retrench, tighten your belt.

ecstasy NOUN = **bliss**, delight, rapture, joy, elation, euphoria, jubilation.

ecstatic ADJ = **blissful**, enraptured, rapturous, euphoric, joyful, overjoyed, jubilant, elated, in transports of delight, delirious, on cloud nine, in seventh heaven.

edge NOUN 1 = **border**, boundary, extremity, fringe, margin, side; lip, rim, brim, brink, verge; perimeter, circumference, periphery, limits, bounds. 2 = **advantage**, superiority, upper hand, ascendancy, whip hand. VERB = **creep**, inch; sidle, steal, slink.

edgy ADJ = **nervous**, tense, anxious, apprehensive, on tenterhooks, uneasy, jumpy; [inf] uptight.

edit VERB = **correct**, emend, revise, rewrite, reword; shorten, condense, cut, abridge.

educate VERB = **teach**, instruct, tutor, school, coach, train; inform, enlighten.

educated ADJ = **well read**, informed, knowledgeable, learned, enlightened, cultivated, cultured.

eerie ADJ = **uncanny**, unearthly, ghostly, mysterious, strange, odd, weird, frightening; [inf] spooky, scary.

effect NOUN 1 = **result**, outcome, consequence, upshot, repercussions, ramifications, impact, aftermath. 2 = **effectiveness**, success, influence, efficacy, power.

effective ADJ = **successful**, effectual, efficacious, potent,

powerful; helpful,
beneficial, advantageous,
valuable, useful.

effervescent ADJ
= **bubbly**, fizzy, frothy,
foamy, sparkling,
carbonated.

efficient ADJ = **well
organized**, methodical,
systematic, capable,
competent, productive,
businesslike; streamlined,
cost-effective.

effigy NOUN = **statue**,
statuette, figurine, model,
likeness, image.

effort NOUN 1 = **exertion**,
power, energy, work,
application, labour, toil,
struggle, strain.
2 = **attempt**, try,
endeavour; [inf] go, shot,
crack, stab.

effusive ADJ = **gushing**,
unrestrained, extravagant,
fulsome, lavish,
enthusiastic.

egg VERB (**egg on**)
= **encourage**, urge, push,
drive, goad, spur, prod.

egotistic ADJ = **egocentric**,
self-absorbed, self-
centred, selfish, self-
obsessed; narcissistic,
vain.

eject VERB = **evict**, expel,
throw out, force out,

remove.

elaborate ADJ
1 = **complicated**, detailed,
complex, involved,
intricate, convoluted.
2 = **ornate**, fancy, showy,
fussy, ostentatious,
extravagant, baroque,
rococo. VERB = **expand on**,
enlarge on, flesh out,
add to.

elastic ADJ = **stretchy**,
stretchable, flexible,
springy, pliant, pliable,
supple.

elderly ADJ = **old**, aged,
ageing, ancient, long in
the tooth, past your
prime.

elect VERB = **vote for**,
choose, pick, select; opt,
decide.

election NOUN = **ballot**,
poll, vote, referendum,
plebiscite.

elegant ADJ = **stylish**,
graceful, tasteful, artistic,
fashionable,
sophisticated, chic, smart,
dashing, debonair.

element NOUN = **part**,
piece, ingredient, factor,
feature, component,
constituent, segment,
unit, module.

elementary ADJ 1 = **basic**,
introductory, preparatory,

fundamental, rudimentary. **2** = **easy**, simple, straightforward, uncomplicated.

elf NOUN = **fairy**, pixie, sprite, goblin, hobgoblin, imp, puck.

elicit VERB = **bring out**, draw out, obtain, evoke, call forth.

eligible ADJ **1** = **entitled**, permitted, allowed, qualified, able. **2** = **desirable**, suitable; available, single, unmarried, unattached.

eloquent ADJ = **articulate**, fluent, silver-tongued, expressive, persuasive, effective, lucid, vivid, graphic.

elude VERB = **avoid**, dodge, evade, escape from, shake off, give someone the slip.

embargo NOUN = **ban**, bar, prohibition, proscription, veto, moratorium; boycott.

embarrassed ADJ = **mortified**, red-faced, abashed, ashamed, shamefaced, humiliated, chagrined, awkward, self-conscious, sheepish.

embellish VERB = **decorate**, adorn, ornament, beautify, enhance, trim, gild, festoon, deck.

embezzle VERB = **steal**, pilfer, misappropriate, filch, purloin.

emblem NOUN = **crest**, insignia, badge, symbol, sign, representation, token, image, figure, mark.

embody VERB **1** = **personify**, represent, symbolize, stand for, typify, exemplify. **2** = **incorporate**, include, contain, encompass.

embrace VERB = **hug**, hold, cuddle, clasp, squeeze, enfold.

emend VERB = **alter**, change, edit, correct, revise, rewrite, improve, polish, refine.

emerge VERB **1** = **appear**, surface, come out, materialize. **2** = **come to light**, transpire.

emergency NOUN = **crisis**, accident, disaster, catastrophe, calamity.

eminent ADJ = **important**, great, distinguished, well known, celebrated, famous, renowned, noted, prominent, respected, esteemed, pre-eminent, outstanding.

emit VERB = **discharge**, give out/off, issue, disgorge, vent, send forth, eject, spew out, emanate, radiate, exude, ooze, leak, excrete.

emotional ADJ = **moving**, touching, affecting, poignant, emotive, impassioned, heart-rending, tear-jerking, powerful.

emphasis NOUN = **prominence**, importance, significance; stress, weight, accent, attention, priority.

emphasize VERB = **stress**, underline, highlight, point up, spotlight; accent, accentuate, underscore.

emphatic ADJ = **forceful**, vehement, firm, vigorous, forcible, categorical, unequivocal, definite, decided.

employ VERB 1 = **hire**, engage, take on, recruit, appoint. 2 = **use**, make use of, utilize, apply, exercise, bring to bear.

employee NOUN = **worker**, member of staff, hand; (**employees**) personnel, staff, workforce.

empower VERB = **authorize**, entitle, permit, allow, enable, license, qualify.

empty ADJ 1 = **unfilled**, vacant, unoccupied, uninhabited, hollow, void, bare, unadorned, blank. 2 = **meaningless**, futile, ineffective, ineffectual, useless, insubstantial, idle, purposeless, aimless, worthless, valueless. VERB = **vacate**, clear, evacuate; unload, void.

enable VERB = **allow**, permit, equip, empower, facilitate, entitle, authorize, license.

enchanting ADJ = **bewitching**, charming, delightful, attractive, appealing, captivating, irresistible, fascinating, engaging, endearing, alluring, winsome.

enclose VERB 1 = **surround**, circle, encircle, ring; shut in, confine, fence in, wall in. 2 = **include**, put in, insert.

enclosure NOUN = **compound**, yard, pen, ring, fold, paddock, stockade, corral.

encounter VERB 1 = **meet**, run into; [inf] bump into.

2 = **be faced with**, come up against, experience. NOUN = **fight**, battle, clash, confrontation, engagement, skirmish.

encourage VERB **1** = **cheer**, rally, stimulate, motivate, inspire, stir, hearten, animate, invigorate, embolden. **2** = **urge**, persuade, exhort, spur on, egg on. **3** = **promote**, foster, help, assist, support, aid, back, boost, strengthen.

encroach VERB = **trespass**, intrude, invade, infringe, infiltrate, impinge.

encyclopedic ADJ = **comprehensive**, complete, wide-ranging, all-inclusive, all-embracing, all-encompassing, thorough, compendious, vast.

end NOUN **1** = **ending**, finish, close, conclusion, cessation, termination, completion, resolution, climax, finale, culmination; denouement, epilogue. **2** = **edge**, border, boundary, limit, extremity, margin, tip. **3** = **butt**, stub, remnant. **4** = **aim**, goal, purpose,

intention, objective, design, aspiration, ambition, object. **5** = **death**, demise, expiry, decease. NOUN = **finish**, stop, close, cease, conclude, terminate, discontinue, break off; [inf] wind up.

endanger VERB = **threaten**, put at risk, jeopardize, imperil, risk.

endearing ADJ = **charming**, adorable, lovable, engaging, disarming, appealing, winning, sweet, enchanting, winsome.

endeavour VERB = **try**, attempt, strive, venture, struggle, essay.

endless ADJ = **unlimited**, infinite, limitless, boundless, inexhaustible; continual, constant, continuous, everlasting, unceasing, ceaseless, unending, interminable, incessant.

endorse VERB = **support**, back, agree with, approve, favour, subscribe to, recommend, champion, uphold, affirm, sanction.

endurance NOUN = **stamina**, staying power, perseverance, tenacity, fortitude, determination.

endure VERB 1 = **undergo**, go/live through, survive, withstand, weather. 2 = **last**, live on, continue, persist, remain.

enemy NOUN = **adversary**, opponent, foe, rival, antagonist.

energetic ADJ = **active**, lively, vigorous, dynamic, brisk, spirited, animated, vibrant, sprightly, spry, tireless, indefatigable.

energy NOUN = **vigour**, strength, stamina, power, forcefulness, drive, enthusiasm, life, animation, liveliness, vivacity, vitality, spirit, fire, zest, exuberance, verve, effervescence, brio.

enforce VERB 1 = **apply**, implement, bring to bear, impose. 2 = **force**, compel, coerce, extort, exact.

engage VERB 1 = **employ**, hire, take on. 2 = **capture**, catch, grab, attract, win; occupy, absorb, hold, engross, grip. 3 = **take part**, participate in, join in, enter into, embark on, set about, tackle.

engender VERB = **cause**, produce, create, bring about, give rise to, lead to, arouse, generate, occasion.

enhance VERB = **add to**, increase, heighten, improve, strengthen, boost, intensify, enrich, complement.

enjoy VERB 1 = **take pleasure in**, delight in, appreciate, like, love, relish, revel in, savour, luxuriate in. 2 = **have**, possess, benefit from, be blessed with.

enjoyable ADJ = **entertaining**, amusing, diverting, satisfying, pleasant, lovely, agreeable, pleasurable, fine, great.

enlarge VERB = **expand**, extend, add to, augment, amplify, supplement, magnify, widen, broaden, lengthen; distend, dilate, swell, inflate.

enlighten VERB = **inform**, tell, notify, advise, apprise, update.

enlist VERB 1 = **enrol**, join up, sign up for, volunteer for. 2 = **obtain**, secure, get, procure, win.

enliven VERB = **brighten up**, cheer up, hearten, stimulate, uplift, invigorate, revitalize, buoy up, revive, refresh.

enormous ADJ = **huge**, immense, massive, vast, gigantic, colossal, mammoth, gargantuan, mountainous, prodigious, tremendous, stupendous, titanic, vast.

enough ADJ = **sufficient**, adequate, ample.

enquire VERB see **inquire**.

enrage VERB = **madden**, infuriate, incense, exasperate, provoke, anger.

ensue VERB = **follow**, result, develop, proceed, succeed, emerge; occur, happen, transpire, supervene.

ensure VERB = **guarantee**, secure, assure, confirm, establish, verify.

entail VERB = **involve**, require, call for, necessitate, demand, cause, produce, result in, lead to, give rise to, occasion.

enter VERB 1 = **go in**, set foot in, gain access to. 2 = **penetrate**, pierce, puncture. 3 = **begin**, start, commence, embark on, engage in. 4 = **take part in**, participate in, go in for. 5 = **record**, register, put down, note, file, log.

enterprise NOUN 1 = **venture**, undertaking, project, operation, endeavour, scheme, plan. 2 = **business**, company, firm, concern, organization, corporation, establishment.

enterprising ADJ = **resourceful**, entrepreneurial, imaginative, ingenious, inventive, creative; quick-witted, clever, bright, sharp; enthusiastic, dynamic, ambitious, energetic.

entertain VERB 1 = **amuse**, divert, delight, please, charm, interest, beguile, engage, occupy, absorb. 2 = **consider**, contemplate, countenance.

entertainment NOUN 1 = **amusement**, fun, enjoyment, recreation, diversion, pleasure. 2 = **show**, performance, production, spectacle, extravaganza.

enthralling ADJ = **captivating**, enchanting, fascinating, bewitching, gripping, riveting, charming, intriguing, mesmerizing.

enthusiasm NOUN
= **eagerness**, keenness,
fervour, ardour, passion,
zeal, gusto, zest;
commitment, devotion.

enthusiast NOUN = **fan**,
devotee, aficionado, lover,
fanatic; [inf] nut, freak,
addict.

enthusiastic ADJ = **eager**,
keen, avid, fervent,
ardent, passionate,
zealous, vehement;
wholehearted,
committed, devoted,
fanatical; [inf] mad.

entice VERB = **tempt**, lure,
seduce, inveigle, beguile,
persuade, coax.

entire ADJ = **whole**,
complete, total, full.

entirely ADV = **completely**,
absolutely, totally, wholly,
altogether, utterly, in
every respect, thoroughly.

entitle VERB 1 = **qualify**,
authorize, allow, permit,
enable, empower. 2 = **call**,
name, dub, designate.

entourage NOUN = **retinue**,
escort, attendants,
companions, followers;
[inf] groupies.

entrance NOUN 1 = **way in**,
entry, door, portal, gate;
foyer, lobby, porch.

2 = **admission**,
admittance, right of
entry, access, ingress.

entreat VERB = **beg**,
implore, beseech, plead
with, appeal to, petition.

envelop VERB = **enfold**,
cover, wrap, swathe,
swaddle, cloak, surround.

envious ADJ = **jealous**,
covetous, green-eyed,
grudging, begrudging,
resentful.

environment NOUN
= **surroundings**, habitat,
territory, domain, milieu,
situation, location, locale,
background, conditions,
circumstances, setting,
context, framework.

envisage VERB = **predict**,
foresee, anticipate,
expect; imagine, visualize,
picture, conceive of, think
of, dream of.

envy NOUN = **jealousy**,
covetousness, resentment,
bitterness. VERB = **covet**;
begrudge, grudge, resent.

ephemeral ADJ = **fleeting**,
transitory, transient,
momentary, brief,
passing, fugitive.

episode NOUN 1 = **part**,
instalment, chapter.
2 = **incident**, occurrence,
event, happening,

experience, adventure, matter, affair.

epitome NOUN = **personification**, embodiment, incarnation, essence, quintessence, archetype, model.

epoch NOUN = **era**, age, period, time.

equal ADJ = **identical**, alike, like, the same, matching, equivalent, corresponding. NOUN = **equivalent**, peer; match, parallel, twin, counterpart. VERB = **match**, measure up to, equate with, rival, emulate.

equanimity NOUN = **composure**, self-control, self-possession, level-headedness, equilibrium, poise, aplomb, sangfroid, calmness, serenity, tranquillity, phlegm, imperturbability.

equip VERB = **provide**, supply, furnish, issue, fit, kit, arm.

equivalent ADJ = **equal**, identical, the same; similar, comparable, corresponding, commensurate.

equivocal ADJ = **ambiguous**, indefinite, non-committal, vague, unclear; ambivalent, uncertain, unsure, indecisive.

era NOUN = **age**, epoch, period, time, aeon; generation.

eradicate VERB = **eliminate**, get rid of, remove, obliterate; exterminate, destroy, annihilate, wipe out, stamp out, extinguish.

erase VERB = **delete**, rub out, remove, blot out, efface, obliterate.

erode VERB = **wear away/down**, eat away, corrode, abrade, destroy.

erotic ADJ = **arousing**, stimulating, exciting, titillating, seductive, sexy, raunchy.

err VERB = **make a mistake**, blunder, miscalculate, slip up; misbehave, transgress.

errand NOUN = **task**, job, chore, assignment.

erratic ADJ = **unpredictable**, inconsistent, changeable, inconstant, irregular, fitful, changing, varying, fluctuating, uneven; unreliable, mercurial, capricious.

error NOUN = **mistake**,

inaccuracy, miscalculation, blunder, slip-up, oversight; misprint; fallacy, misconception.

escalate VERB = **increase**, soar, shoot up, rocket; intensify, heighten, accelerate.

escapade NOUN = **exploit**, stunt, adventure, caper, antics.

escape VERB 1 = **get away/out**, run away, break free, break out, bolt, flee; [inf] do a bunk. 2 = **avoid**, evade, dodge, elude; circumvent, sidestep. NOUN = **breakout**, getaway, flight.

escort NOUN 1 = **entourage**, retinue, attendants, cortège, convoy; guard. 2 = **partner**, date, companion. VERB = **accompany**, guide, conduct, lead, usher.

esoteric ADJ = **abstruse**, obscure, arcane, recondite, mysterious.

essence NOUN 1 = **quintessence**, soul, heart, core, substance, lifeblood. 2 = **extract**, concentrate, tincture, elixir.

essential ADJ 1 = **necessary**, important, indispensable, vital, crucial. 2 = **basic**, fundamental, intrinsic, inherent, innate, elemental.

establish VERB 1 = **set up**, found, institute, form, start, begin, create, inaugurate, organize. 2 = **prove**, show, demonstrate, confirm, attest to, verify.

establishment NOUN = **firm**, business, company, concern, organization, enterprise, corporation, operation.

estate NOUN 1 = **property**, lands, grounds. 2 = **assets**, holdings, capital, effects, possessions, wealth, fortune.

esteem VERB = **respect**, admire, value, look up to, revere.

estimate VERB = **work out**, calculate, assess, gauge, reckon, evaluate, judge.

eternal ADJ = **endless**, everlasting, never-ending, immortal, deathless, undying, permanent; ceaseless, incessant, constant, continuous, unremitting, interminable, relentless, perpetual.

eternity NOUN
= **immortality**, the afterlife, the hereafter, heaven, paradise.

ethical ADJ = **moral**, honourable, upright, righteous, good, virtuous, decent, principled, honest, just.

euphoric ADJ = **elated**, joyful, ecstatic, jubilant, rapturous, blissful, intoxicated, on cloud nine, in seventh heaven.

evacuate VERB = **leave**, abandon, vacate, quit, withdraw from.

evade VERB = **avoid**, dodge, escape from, elude, shake off; circumvent, sidestep; [inf] give someone the slip.

evaluate VERB = **assess**, appraise, weigh up, gauge, judge, rate, estimate.

evasive ADJ = **equivocal**, prevaricating, elusive, ambiguous, non-committal, vague.

even ADJ 1 = **flat**, level, smooth, plane.
2 = **constant**, steady, uniform, consistent, stable, regular. 3 = **tied**, level, all square, neck and neck.

evening NOUN = **night**, twilight, dusk, nightfall, sunset, sundown.

event NOUN 1 = **occasion**, affair, occurrence, happening, episode, circumstance, phenomenon.
2 = **competition**, contest, fixture, game, tournament, race.

eventful ADJ = **busy**, action-packed, full, active, hectic, exciting.

everlasting ADJ = **never-ending**, endless, eternal, perpetual, undying, immortal, deathless, indestructible, abiding, enduring.

evict VERB = **turn out**, throw out, eject, expel, remove, oust; [inf] kick/turf out.

evidence NOUN 1 = **proof**, verification, confirmation, substantiation, corroboration.
2 = **testimony**, statement, deposition, affidavit, attestation.

evident ADJ = **obvious**, clear, apparent, plain, noticeable, visible, conspicuous, manifest, patent.

evil ADJ 1 = **wicked**, wrong, bad, immoral, sinful,

corrupt, nefarious, vile, base, iniquitous, heinous, villainous, malicious, malevolent. **2 = bad**, harmful, injurious, destructive, deleterious, pernicious. NOUN **= wickedness**, wrong, wrongdoing, sin, immorality, vice, corruption, depravity, villainy.

evoke VERB **= bring to mind**, conjure up, summon (up), elicit, kindle, stimulate, stir up, awaken, arouse.

evolution NOUN **= development**, progress, growth, rise; natural selection, Darwinism.

evolve VERB **= develop**, grow, progress, advance, mature.

exacerbate VERB **= aggravate**, worsen, intensify, heighten, inflame.

exact ADJ **= precise**, accurate, correct, faithful, true, literal, strict. VERB **= require**, demand, insist on, impose; extract, wring, wrest.

exaggerate VERB **= overstate**, overemphasize, overestimate, embellish, amplify, embroider, elaborate.

examination NOUN **1 = study**, inspection, scrutiny, investigation, analysis, observation, consideration, appraisal. **2 = exam**, test, paper.

examine VERB **= study**, investigate, survey, analyse, review, consider, assess, appraise, weigh up, inspect.

example NOUN **1 = sample**, specimen, instance, case, illustration. **2 = model**, pattern, ideal, standard, precedent.

exasperate VERB **= anger**, infuriate, annoy, irritate, madden, provoke, irk, vex, gall.

exceed VERB **= surpass**, beat, outdo, outstrip, outshine, transcend, better, top, cap, overshadow, eclipse.

excellent ADJ **= very good**, first-rate, first-class, high-quality, great, fine, superior, superb, outstanding, marvellous, splendid, brilliant, supreme, superlative, exemplary, consummate; [inf] terrific, tremendous, fantastic.

exceptional ADJ
1 = **unusual**, uncommon, out of the ordinary, atypical, rare, anomalous, abnormal.
2 = **outstanding**, extraordinary, remarkable, phenomenal, prodigious.

excerpt NOUN = **extract**, quote, citation, quotation, passage, piece, clip.

excess NOUN = **surplus**, glut, overabundance, surfeit, superfluity. ADJ = **surplus**, superfluous, redundant, unwanted.

excessive ADJ = **immoderate**, intemperate, overindulgent, unrestrained, uncontrolled, lavish, extravagant; superfluous; unreasonable, disproportionate, exorbitant, extortionate.

exchange VERB = **trade**, swap, barter, interchange.

excitable ADJ = **temperamental**, emotional, highly strung, nervous, volatile, mercurial, tempestuous.

excite VERB **1** = **stimulate**, animate, thrill, exhilarate, electrify, intoxicate, titillate.
2 = **arouse**, awaken, provoke, kindle, stir up, engender.

excitement NOUN
1 = **animation**, enthusiasm, exhilaration, anticipation. **2** = **thrill**, pleasure, delight, joy; [inf] kick, buzz.

exciting ADJ = **thrilling**, exhilarating, stimulating, gripping, dramatic, intoxicating, electrifying, riveting; provocative, titillating.

exclaim VERB = **call**, cry, shout, yell.

exclamation NOUN = **call**, cry, shout, yell, interjection.

exclude VERB **1** = **bar**, debar, keep out, shut out, prohibit, ban.
2 = **eliminate**, rule out, preclude.

exclusive ADJ = **select**, upmarket, elite, fashionable, chic, elegant, stylish.

excruciating ADJ = **agonizing**, unbearable, acute, searing, severe, intense.

excuse NOUN

1 = **explanation**, reason, grounds, justification, defence, mitigation. **2** = **pretext**, pretence. VERB **1** = **forgive**, pardon, exonerate. **2** = **let off**, exempt, release, relieve, free.

execute VERB **1** = **put to death**, kill. **2** = **carry out**, accomplish, bring off, achieve, complete.

exemplary ADJ = **model**, ideal, perfect, faultless, impeccable; excellent, outstanding, admirable, commendable, laudable.

exemplify VERB = **typify**, epitomize, symbolize, represent, illustrate, demonstrate.

exempt VERB = **free**, release, exclude, excuse, absolve, spare; [inf] let off.

exercise NOUN = **activity**, exertion, training; gymnastics, sports, games, aerobics. VERB **1** = **work out**, train. **2** = **employ**, use, make use of, utilize, apply.

exert VERB **1** = **employ**, exercise, use, make use of, utilize, apply, bring to bear. **2** (**exert yourself**) = **make an effort**, try hard, strive, endeavour, struggle, do your best.

exhaust VERB **1** = **tire**, wear out, fatigue, drain, weary, sap, debilitate; [inf] knacker. **2** = **use up**, deplete, consume, finish, run through.

exhausting ADJ = **tiring**, wearing, enervating; gruelling, punishing, strenuous, arduous, back-breaking.

exhaustive ADJ = **comprehensive**, all-inclusive, complete, full, encyclopedic, thorough, in-depth; detailed, meticulous, painstaking.

exhibit VERB **1** = **(put on) display**, show, present, model, unveil. **2** = **show**, indicate, reveal, display, demonstrate, manifest, evince.

exhibition NOUN = **display**, show, demonstration, presentation, exposition.

exhilaration NOUN = **elation**, euphoria, joy, happiness, delight; excitement, gaiety, animation, vivacity.

exhort VERB = **urge**, persuade, press, encourage, advise, counsel, entreat, enjoin.

exile VERB = **banish**, deport,

expatriate, expel, drive out. NOUN = **expatriate**, deportee, refugee, displaced person.

exist VERB = **live**, breathe, draw breath, subsist, survive.

existing ADJ = **in existence**, existent, extant, living, surviving, remaining.

exit NOUN 1 = **way out**, egress, door, doorway, gate, gateway. 2 = **departure**, withdrawal, leaving, retreat.

exorbitant ADJ = **excessive**, unreasonable, extortionate, excessive, prohibitive, outrageous.

exotic ADJ 1 = **foreign**, non-native, tropical. 2 = **striking**, colourful, unusual, eye-catching, unconventional.

expand VERB = **grow**, enlarge, swell; extend, augment, broaden, widen, develop, diversify, build up; branch out, spread, proliferate.

expanse NOUN = **area**, stretch, tract, sweep, region.

expect VERB 1 = **suppose**, assume, believe, imagine, think, presume, surmise, reckon. 2 = **anticipate**, envisage, predict, forecast, hope for, look for, await. 3 = **demand**, insist on, require, ask for.

expectant ADJ = **hopeful**, eager, excited, agog, in suspense, on tenterhooks.

expectation NOUN = **assumption**, belief, supposition, surmise, calculation, prediction; anticipation, expectancy.

expedient ADJ = **convenient**, useful, pragmatic, advantageous, beneficial, helpful, politic, judicious, prudent. NOUN = **means**, measure, stratagem, scheme, plan, contrivance.

expel VERB = **evict**, banish, drive out, exile, throw out, expatriate, deport; [inf] kick out.

expense NOUN = **cost**, price, outlay, payment, expenditure, outgoings, charge, bill, overheads.

expensive ADJ = **overpriced**, exorbitant, steep, costly, dear, extortionate.

experience NOUN 1 = **familiarity**, knowledge,

involvement, participation, contact, acquaintance, exposure, observation, understanding. 2 = **event**, incident, occurrence, happening, episode, adventure. VERB = **undergo**, encounter, meet, come across, go through, face, sustain.

experienced ADJ = **practised**, proficient, accomplished, skilful, seasoned, trained, expert, adept, capable, knowledgeable, qualified, well versed, professional, veteran.

experiment NOUN = **test**, trial, examination, observation, investigation, assessment, evaluation, appraisal.

experimental ADJ = **trial**, exploratory, pilot, tentative, preliminary.

expert NOUN = **authority**, specialist, master, pundit, maestro, virtuoso, connoisseur; [inf] buff.

expire VERB 1 = **run out**, lapse, finish, end, terminate. 2 see **die**.

explain VERB 1 = **describe**, spell out, clarify, elucidate, explicate,

interpret. 2 = **account for**, justify, vindicate, legitimize.

explanation NOUN 1 = **description**, elucidation, clarification; interpretation, exegesis. 2 = **account**, justification, reason, excuse, defence, alibi.

expletive NOUN = **swear word**, oath, curse, obscenity, profanity.

explicit ADJ = **(crystal) clear**, understandable, plain, precise, exact, straightforward, detailed, specific, unambiguous.

explode VERB 1 = **blow up**, detonate, go off, erupt, burst. 2 = **disprove**, invalidate, refute, discredit, debunk, give the lie to.

exploit VERB 1 = **make use of**, use, utilize, turn to account, capitalize on; [inf] cash in on. 2 = **take advantage of**, abuse, misuse. NOUN = **feat**, deed, adventure, stunt, achievement.

explore VERB 1 = **travel over**, traverse, survey, inspect, reconnoitre. 2 = **investigate**, look into, consider, research, study, review.

exponent NOUN = **advocate**, supporter, upholder, defender, champion, promoter, proponent, propagandist.

expose VERB 1 = **subject**, lay open, put at risk, put in jeopardy. 2 = **uncover**, reveal, unveil, unmask, lay bare; discover, bring to light.

expression NOUN 1 = **utterance**, articulation, voicing. 2 = **(turn of) phrase**, term, idiom, saying. 3 = **look**, countenance, appearance, air, mien.

extend VERB 1 = **expand**, increase, enlarge, lengthen, widen, broaden; add to, augment, enhance, develop, supplement. 2 = **prolong**, protract, draw out, spin out. 3 = **offer**, give, proffer, hold out. 4 = **continue**, stretch, carry on, reach, lead.

extensive ADJ 1 = **large**, sizeable, substantial, spacious, considerable, vast. 2 = **broad**, wide, wide-ranging, comprehensive, thorough, inclusive.

extent NOUN 1 = **area**, size, expanse, length; proportions, dimensions. 2 = **degree**, scale, level, magnitude, scope; breadth, reach, range.

exterior ADJ = **outer**, outside, outermost, outward, external, surface.

extinguish VERB 1 = **put out**, blow out, quench, smother, douse, snuff out. 2 = **destroy**, end, remove, annihilate, wipe out, eliminate, eradicate.

extra ADJ = **additional**, more, further, supplementary, added, other.

extract VERB 1 = **pull out**, prise out, remove, withdraw. 2 = **extort**, exact, wring, wrest. NOUN = **excerpt**, passage, citation, quotation.

extraordinary ADJ = **remarkable**, exceptional, amazing, astonishing, incredible, unbelievable, phenomenal; out of the ordinary, unusual, uncommon, rare, surprising.

extravagant ADJ 1 = **spendthrift**, profligate, wasteful, lavish, imprudent, improvident, prodigal; expensive, costly, high-priced. **2 = excessive**, unreasonable, immoderate, unrestrained; effusive, fulsome.

extreme ADJ **1 = utmost**, maximum, supreme, great, acute, intense, severe, high, exceptional, extraordinary. **2 = drastic**, serious, desperate, dire, harsh, tough, strict, rigorous, draconian. **3 = radical**, extremist, immoderate, fanatical, revolutionary.

extremely ADV **= very**, exceedingly, exceptionally, uncommonly, unusually, decidedly, particularly, eminently, remarkably, really, awfully, terribly.

exuberant ADJ **= elated**, exhilarated, cheerful, animated, lively, high-spirited, spirited, buoyant, effervescent, vivacious, excited, ebullient, enthusiastic, irrepressible, energetic.

exultant ADJ **= joyful**, overjoyed, jubilant, triumphant, delighted, cock-a-hoop.

eyewitness NOUN **= witness**, observer, spectator, onlooker, bystander, passer-by.

Ff

fabric NOUN **= cloth**, material, textile, stuff.

fabricate VERB **= make up**, invent, concoct, think up, hatch, trump up.

fabulous ADJ **1 = mythical**, legendary, fairy-tale, fabled; imaginary, made-up. **2** see **marvellous**.

face NOUN **1 = countenance**, visage, physiognomy, features; [inf] mug. **2 = expression**, look, appearance, air, mien. VERB **1 = look on to**, overlook, give on to. **2 = encounter**, meet, come up against, confront, withstand, cope with, deal with, brave.

facet NOUN = **aspect**, feature, characteristic, element, side, point, part.

facetious ADJ = **flippant**, frivolous, tongue-in-cheek, glib.

facility NOUN 1 = **aptitude**, talent, gift, flair, skill, knack, genius, ability, capability. 2 = **amenity**, resource, service, convenience.

fact NOUN 1 = **truth**, actuality, reality, certainty. 2 = **detail**, particular, point, item, piece of information.

faction NOUN = **group**, section, set, wing, branch, arm, contingent, camp, clique, coterie, caucus, cabal, splinter group.

factor NOUN = **element**, part, component, ingredient, constituent, point, detail, item, facet, aspect, feature, characteristic, consideration.

factual ADJ = **truthful**, true, accurate, authentic, historical, genuine; true-to-life, correct, exact, honest, faithful, unbiased, objective, unvarnished.

fad NOUN = **craze**, mania, enthusiasm, vogue, fashion, trend.

fade VERB = **dwindle**, diminish, die away, disappear, vanish, peter out, dissolve, melt away, wane.

fail VERB = **be unsuccessful**, fall through, founder, misfire, come to grief; [inf] come a cropper.

failing NOUN = **fault**, shortcoming, weakness, imperfection, defect, flaw, foible.

failure NOUN = **fiasco**, debacle; [inf] flop, washout, dead loss.

faint ADJ 1 = **indistinct**, unclear, vague, ill-defined, pale, faded. 2 = **soft**, quiet, muted, low, weak, feeble, muffled. 3 = **slight**, small, slim, slender, remote, unlikely. 4 = **dizzy**, giddy, light-headed; [inf] woozy. VERB = **black out**, pass out, keel over, swoon.

fair ADJ 1 = **just**, impartial, unbiased, unprejudiced, objective, even-handed, equitable, lawful, legal, legitimate. 2 = **blond(e)**, light, yellow, golden, flaxen. 3 = **fine**, dry, bright, clear, sunny. NOUN

1 = **exhibition**, display, show, exposition, expo. 2 = **festival**, carnival, fête, gala, funfair.

fairly ADV = **reasonably**, quite, pretty, passably, moderately, rather, somewhat.

faith NOUN 1 = **trust**, belief, confidence, conviction, credence, reliance; optimism, hopefulness. 2 = **religion**, church, denomination, belief, creed, persuasion, teaching, doctrine.

faithful ADJ 1 = **loyal**, devoted, constant, dependable, true, reliable, trustworthy, staunch, unswerving, unwavering, steadfast, dedicated, committed. 2 = **accurate**, true, exact, precise, strict.

fake ADJ = **counterfeit**, forged, fraudulent, bogus, sham, imitation, false, pseudo, mock, simulated, artificial, synthetic, reproduction, ersatz; assumed, affected, put-on, feigned, insincere; [inf] phoney. NOUN 1 = **forgery**, counterfeit, copy. 2 = **fraud**, charlatan, impostor, sham, mountebank, quack; [inf] phoney.

fall VERB 1 = **drop**, descend, come/go down, sink, dive, plummet, cascade. 2 = **fall down/over**, trip, stumble, slip, tumble, topple over, keel over, collapse, go head over heels. 3 = **decrease**, decline, go down, diminish, dwindle, plummet, slump. NOUN 1 = **downfall**, demise, collapse, ruin, failure, decline, deterioration. 2 = **decrease**, cut, dip, reduction, downswing, slump.

fallacy NOUN = **misconception**, mistake, misapprehension, delusion, misinterpretation.

false ADJ = **incorrect**, wrong, erroneous, untrue, untruthful, fictitious, inaccurate, misleading, fallacious, fabricated, spurious.

falsify VERB = **alter**, doctor, tamper with, forge, distort.

fame NOUN = **renown**, celebrity, stardom, popularity, prominence, eminence, stature; notoriety, infamy.

familiar ADJ 1 = **well**

known, recognized, accustomed, common, customary, everyday, ordinary, commonplace, habitual, usual, stock, routine, mundane, run-of-the-mill, conventional. 2 = **acquainted**, knowledgeable, informed, conversant, well up, au fait.

family NOUN 1 = **relatives**, relations, (next of) kin, kinsfolk, kindred, people; [inf] folks. 2 = **children**, offspring, progeny; [inf] kids. 3 = **ancestry**, parentage, pedigree, birth, descent, lineage, bloodline, stock, forebears, forefathers.

famous ADJ = **well known**, renowned, celebrated, famed, noted, prominent, eminent, great, illustrious, acclaimed; popular, legendary; notorious, infamous.

fan NOUN = **admirer**, follower, devotee, enthusiast, aficionado, supporter; [inf] groupie.

fanatic NOUN = **extremist**, zealot, militant, activist, partisan, bigot, radical; [inf] maniac.

fanatical ADJ 1 = **extremist**, extreme, zealous, militant, sectarian, bigoted, dogmatic, radical, intolerant, partisan, rabid. 2 = **enthusiastic**, eager, keen, fervent, passionate, obsessive.

fancy NOUN = **desire**, urge, wish; inclination, whim, impulse, notion; yearning, longing, hankering; [inf] yen. VERB 1 = **think**, believe, suppose, imagine, reckon. 2 = **wish for**, want, desire, hanker after. ADJ = **ornate**, elaborate, ornamental, decorative, ostentatious, showy, flamboyant; [inf] flash, snazzy.

fantasy NOUN 1 = **imagination**, fancy, creativity, invention, make-believe. 2 = **dream**, daydream, pipe dream.

far ADJ = **faraway**, far-flung, distant, remote, out of the way, outlying.

farcical ADJ = **ridiculous**, ludicrous, absurd, laughable, preposterous, nonsensical, idiotic, foolish, asinine.

far-fetched ADJ = **improbable**, unlikely, implausible, incredible, unbelievable; [inf] hard to take/swallow.

fascinate VERB = **captivate**, enchant, bewitch, enthral, entrance, hold spellbound, rivet, transfix, mesmerize, charm, intrigue, absorb, engross.

fashion NOUN **1** = **style**, vogue, trend, mode, taste, craze, rage, fad. **2** = **clothes**, couture; [inf] rag trade. **3** = **way**, manner, method, system, mode, approach.

fashionable ADJ = **stylish**, up to date, contemporary, modern, in vogue, modish, popular, all the rage, trendsetting, smart, chic, elegant; [inf] trendy, with it.

fast ADJ **1** = **quick**, rapid, swift, speedy, brisk, hurried, breakneck, hasty, express, fleet; [inf] nippy. **2** = **secure**, fastened, tight, firm, closed, shut; immovable. ADV = **quickly**, rapidly, swiftly, speedily, briskly, post-haste; [inf] hell for leather, at a rate of knots.

fasten VERB **1** = **attach**, fix, affix, clip, pin, tie, bind, tether, hitch, anchor. **2** = **bolt**, lock, secure, chain, seal; do up.

fastidious ADJ = **fussy**, over-particular, finicky; scrupulous, painstaking, punctilious; [inf] choosy, picky, pernickety.

fat ADJ = **plump**, stout, overweight, obese, heavy, chubby, portly, corpulent, rotund, flabby, pot-bellied, paunchy, fleshy; [inf] tubby, beefy, podgy, roly-poly.

fatal ADJ **1** = **mortal**, deadly, lethal; terminal, incurable. **2** = **ruinous**, disastrous, catastrophic, calamitous, cataclysmic.

fate NOUN = **destiny**, providence, kismet, chance, the stars; future, lot, end.

fated ADJ = **predestined**, preordained, destined, inevitable, inescapable, sure, ineluctable, doomed.

father NOUN = **parent**, paterfamilias, patriarch; [inf] dad, daddy, pop, pa, pater. VERB = **sire**, beget.

fatigue NOUN = **tiredness**, weariness, exhaustion, lethargy, lassitude, listlessness, enervation.

fatuous ADJ = **silly**, foolish,

stupid, senseless, inane, idiotic, ridiculous, asinine, vacuous, witless.

fault NOUN 1 = **defect**, flaw, imperfection, blemish, failing, weakness, weak point, shortcoming. 2 = **misdeed**, wrongdoing, offence, misdemeanour, indiscretion, transgression, peccadillo. **at fault** = **to blame**, in the wrong, culpable, responsible, guilty, blameworthy.

faulty ADJ = **defective**, malfunctioning, broken, out of order, damaged.

favour NOUN 1 = **service**, good turn/deed, kindness, courtesy. 2 = **approval**, approbation, goodwill, kindness, benevolence. 3 = **backing**, support, patronage. VERB 1 = **approve of**, advocate, recommend, support, back, be in favour of. 2 = **prefer**, like, be partial to, go for.

favourable ADJ 1 = **approving**, complimentary, commendatory, enthusiastic, positive. 2 = **advantageous**, in your favour, beneficial, helpful, good, promising, encouraging, auspicious, opportune, propitious.

favourite ADJ = **best-loved**, most-liked, favoured, preferred, chosen, pet. NOUN = **first choice**, pick; darling, pet; [inf] blue-eyed boy.

fear NOUN = **fearfulness**, fright, terror, alarm, panic, trepidation, dread, nervousness, anxiety, worry, unease, foreboding.

fearful ADJ = **afraid**, frightened, scared, terrified, apprehensive, alarmed, uneasy, nervous, panicky, anxious, worried.

feasible ADJ = **practicable**, possible, achievable, attainable, workable, viable, reasonable, realistic, within reason.

feast NOUN = **banquet**, dinner, repast; [inf] blow-out, spread.

feat NOUN = **deed**, act, action, exploit, achievement, accomplishment, performance, attainment.

feature NOUN 1 = **characteristic**, property, attribute, quality, property, trait, mark, peculiarity, idiosyncrasy; aspect, facet, side. **2** (**features**) = **face**, countenance, visage, physiognomy; [inf] mug. **3** = **article**, piece, item, report, story, column.

federation NOUN = **confederation**, league, alliance, coalition, union, syndicate, consortium, association.

feeble ADJ **1** = **weak**, frail, infirm, sickly, puny, delicate, ailing, helpless, debilitated, decrepit, incapacitated, enfeebled. **2** = **ineffectual**, unsuccessful, ineffective, unconvincing, implausible, flimsy.

feed VERB **1** = **nourish**, sustain, cater for, provide for. **2** = **eat**, graze, browse.

feel VERB **1** = **touch**, stroke, caress, fondle, handle, finger; paw, grope. **2** = **be aware of**, notice, be conscious of, perceive, sense. **3** = **experience**, undergo, have, go through, bear, endure, suffer. **4** = **think**, believe, consider, hold, judge, reckon.

feeling NOUN **1** = **sensation**, sense, awareness, consciousness; emotion, sentiment. **2** = **idea**, suspicion, notion, inkling, hunch; presentiment, premonition. **3** = **sympathy**, pity, compassion, understanding, concern, sensitivity, empathy, fellow-feeling. **4** = **atmosphere**, air, aura, feel, ambience, impression.

fence NOUN = **barrier**, railing, rail, paling, barricade, stockade, palisade. VERB **1** = **enclose**, surround, encircle. **2** = **shut in**, confine, pen, coop up, separate off.

fend VERB **1** (**fend for yourself**) = **take care of yourself**, support yourself get by, cope, manage. **2** (**fend off**) = **ward off**, stave off, parry, turn aside, divert, deflect.

ferocious ADJ = **fierce**, savage, brutal, ruthless, cruel, merciless, vicious, barbarous, violent, barbaric, inhuman, bloodthirsty, murderous; wild, untamed, predatory, rapacious.

fertile ADJ 1 = **fruitful**, productive, rich, fecund. 2 = **inventive**, creative, original, ingenious, resourceful, productive.

fervent ADJ = **passionate**, ardent, impassioned, intense, vehement, heartfelt, emotional, fervid; zealous, fanatical, enthusiastic, avid.

festival NOUN = **carnival**, gala, fête, fiesta, celebrations, festivities.

festive ADJ = **jolly**, merry, joyous, joyful, happy, jovial, light-hearted, cheerful, jubilant, high-spirited.

festoon VERB = **decorate**, hang, drape, wreathe, garland, adorn, ornament, deck.

fetch VERB 1 = **(go and) get**, bring, carry, convey, transport. 2 = **sell for**, realize, go for, bring in, yield.

feud NOUN = **vendetta**, conflict, rivalry, quarrel, argument, hostility, enmity, strife, discord, bad blood.

feverish ADJ 1 = **fevered**, febrile, hot, burning. 2 = **frenzied**, excited, frenetic, agitated, nervous, overwrought, frantic, worked up, wild.

few ADJ 1 = **not many**, hardly any, scarcely any, one or two, a handful of, a couple of. 2 = **scarce**, rare, in short supply, scant, thin on the ground.

fiasco NOUN = **failure**, disaster, debacle, catastrophe; [inf] flop, washout.

fibre NOUN = **thread**, strand, filament.

fickle ADJ = **capricious**, changeable, volatile, mercurial; inconstant, undependable, disloyal, unfaithful, faithless, flighty, giddy, skittish.

fiction NOUN 1 = **novels**, stories, creative writing. 2 = **fabrication**, lie, untruth, falsehood, invention, fib.

fictional ADJ = **fictitious**, invented, made-up, imaginary, unreal, make-believe, mythical.

fidelity NOUN = **faithfulness**, loyalty, commitment, constancy, trustworthiness, dependability, reliability; allegiance, obedience.

fidgety ADJ = **restless**, restive, on edge, jumpy, uneasy, nervous, nervy, twitchy; [inf] jittery.

field NOUN 1 = **pasture**, meadow, paddock; [literary] glebe, lea, mead. 2 = **area**, sphere, province, department, subject, domain, territory. 3 = **range**, scope, extent; limits.

fiend NOUN 1 = **devil**, demon. 2 = **brute**, monster, beast, barbarian, sadist, ogre.

fiendish ADJ = **wicked**, cruel, vicious, evil, villainous; brutal, savage, barbaric, barbarous, inhuman, murderous, ruthless, merciless, dastardly.

fierce ADJ 1 = **ferocious**, savage, wild, vicious, bloodthirsty, dangerous, aggressive, violent. 2 = **passionate**, intense, powerful, ardent, strong, impassioned, fervent, fiery, fervid.

fight VERB 1 = **come to blows**, grapple, scuffle, brawl, tussle, spar, joust, clash, wrestle; battle, war, wage war, take up arms; [inf] scrap. 2 = **quarrel**, argue, feud, bicker, squabble, fall out, wrangle, dispute. 3 = **oppose**, contest, take a stand against, object to, challenge, defy. NOUN 1 = **brawl**, scuffle, tussle, skirmish, struggle, affray; battle, engagement, clash, conflict, combat, contest, encounter; [inf] scrap, punch-up. 2 = **quarrel**, dispute, argument, altercation, feud.

figure NOUN 1 = **number**, numeral, digit, integer, symbol. 2 = **cost**, price, amount, value, total, sum. 3 = **shape**, form, outline, silhouette. 4 = **body**, physique, build, frame, proportions. 5 = **diagram**, illustration, picture, drawing.

file NOUN 1 = **folder**, portfolio, document case. 2 = **dossier**, information, documents, records, data. 3 = **line**, column, row, string, chain, crocodile. VERB 1 = **record**, categorize, classify, organize, store, archive. 2 = **march**, parade, troop.

fill VERB 1 = **crowd into**, throng, squeeze into, cram into. 2 = **pack**, load, stack, supply, stock; replenish, top up. **3** = **stop up**, block up, plug, seal, close, clog.

film NOUN **1** = **movie**, (motion) picture, video; [inf] flick. **2** = **layer**, coat, coating, covering, patina, skin.

filter VERB = **strain**, sieve, sift, filtrate, purify, refine.

filth NOUN = **dirt**, muck, grime, mud, mire, slime, excrement, ordure, pollution.

filthy ADJ = **dirty**, mucky, grubby, grimy, soiled, muddy, squalid, foul, polluted, contaminated, unwashed.

final ADJ **1** = **last**, closing, concluding, finishing, terminal, end, ultimate. **2** = **absolute**, conclusive, irrevocable, indisputable, decisive, definite, binding.

finale NOUN = **climax**, culmination; end, ending, finish, close, conclusion, termination; denouement.

finalize VERB = **complete**, conclude, settle, work out, tie up, wrap up, put the finishing touches to, clinch, sew up.

finance NOUN (**finances**) = **money**, funds, cash, resources, assets, capital, revenue, income. VERB = **pay for**, fund, subsidize, invest in, underwrite.

financial ADJ = **monetary**, fiscal, pecuniary, economic.

find VERB **1** = **discover**, come across, chance on, stumble on; come up with, hit on, bring to light, uncover, ferret out, locate, pinpoint, track down. **2** = **recover**, get back, retrieve. **3** = **get**, obtain, achieve, attain, acquire, gain, earn. **4** = **learn**, realize, discover, observe, notice, note, perceive. **5** = **judge**, adjudge, declare, pronounce.

finding NOUN = **decision**, conclusion, verdict, judgement, pronouncement, decree, order, ruling.

fine ADJ **1** = **excellent**, first-class, first-rate, great, exceptional, outstanding, superior, magnificent, splendid, choice, select, prime, superb, rare; [inf] top-notch. **2** = **all right**, satisfactory, acceptable, agreeable, convenient, suitable; [inf] OK. **3 = well**, healthy, fit, thriving, in the pink. **4 = fair**, dry, bright, clear, cloudless, sunny. **5 = sheer**, light, lightweight, thin, flimsy, diaphanous, filmy, gauzy, transparent, translucent.

finish VERB **1 = complete**, conclude, end, close, finalize, terminate, round off; accomplish, carry out, discharge, do, get done; stop, cease, discontinue; [inf] wind up, wrap up, sew up. **2 = use up**, consume, exhaust, empty, drain, get through; [inf] polish off. NOUN **= end**, completion, conclusion, close, cessation, termination, finale.

finite ADJ **= limited**, restricted, delimited, fixed.

fire NOUN **1 = blaze**, conflagration, inferno, flames, combustion. **2 = gunfire**, sniping, bombardment, flak, shelling. **3 = passion**, intensity, ardour, zeal, energy, spirit, vigour, fervour, enthusiasm. VERB **1 = shoot**, let off, discharge. **2 = stimulate**, animate, arouse, rouse, stir up, excite, inflame, inspire, galvanize, electrify.

firm ADJ **1 = hard**, hardened, stiff, rigid, unyielding, solid, solidified, compacted, compressed, dense, set. **2 = secure**, stable, steady, strong, fixed, fast, immovable. **3 = settled**, fixed, decided, definite, established, confirmed. **4 = constant**, enduring, abiding, long-standing, long-lasting, steadfast, devoted, staunch. **5 = determined**, resolute, resolved, unfaltering, unwavering, adamant, emphatic, insistent. NOUN **= business**, company, concern, establishment, organization, corporation, conglomerate.

first ADJ **1 = initial**, earliest, original, introductory, opening. **2 = basic**, fundamental, rudimentary, key, cardinal, primary. **3 = foremost**, principal, paramount, top, prime, chief, leading, main, major.

fit

fit ADJ **1** = **well**, healthy, in good health/shape, strong, robust, hale and hearty. **2** = **capable**, able, competent, prepared, qualified, trained, equipped, eligible. **3** = **fitting**, proper, suitable, apt, appropriate. VERB **1** = **agree with**, accord with, concur with, correspond with, match, tally with, suit, go with. **2** = **join**, connect, put together, fix, insert, attach. NOUN **1** = **convulsion**, spasm, paroxysm, seizure, attack. **2** = **bout**, outburst, outbreak.

fix VERB **1** = **fasten**, secure, attach, connect, join, couple, stick, glue, pin, nail, screw, bolt, implant, embed. **2** = **decide on**, settle, set, agree on, arrange, determine, establish, name, specify. **3** = **repair**, mend, put right, patch up.

fixation NOUN = **obsession**, preoccupation, compulsion, mania; [inf] thing.

fizzy ADJ = **bubbly**, bubbling, sparkling, effervescent, carbonated, gassy.

flag NOUN = **standard**, ensign, banner, pennant, streamer, colours. VERB **1** = **tire**, weaken, wilt, droop. **2** = **fade**, decline, wane, diminish, ebb, decrease, dwindle.

flagrant ADJ = **obvious**, glaring, blatant, overt, shameless, barefaced, undisguised; shocking, scandalous, outrageous.

flair NOUN **1** = **ability**, aptitude, facility, skill, talent, gift, knack, instinct. **2** = **style**, panache, dash, élan, good taste, discrimination, discernment.

flash VERB **1** = **glare**, gleam, shine, glint, sparkle, flicker, shimmer, twinkle, glimmer, glisten. **2** = **show off**, flaunt, flourish, display, parade.

flat ADJ **1** = **level**, horizontal, even, smooth, plane. **2** = **stretched out**, prone, spreadeagled, prostrate, supine, recumbent. **3** = **deflated**, punctured, burst. **4** = **monotonous**, boring, dull, tedious, uninteresting, lifeless, dead, lacklustre, bland, insipid, dreary.

5 = **outright**, direct, definite, positive, explicit, firm, conclusive, complete, categorical, unconditional.

flatter VERB = **compliment**, praise, fawn on; [inf] sweet-talk, butter up, play up to.

flattery NOUN = **praise**, adulation, compliments, blandishments, blarney; [inf] sweet talk.

flaunt VERB = **show off**, parade, display; [inf] flash.

flavour NOUN **1** = **taste**, savour. **2** = **flavouring**, seasoning, tastiness, tang, piquancy, spiciness, zest. **3** = **atmosphere**, spirit, essence, nature, character, quality, feel, feeling, ambience.

flaw NOUN = **fault**, defect, imperfection, failing, shortcoming, blemish, weakness, weak spot, foible.

flawless ADJ = **perfect**, unblemished, unmarked, undamaged, pristine, impeccable, immaculate, faultless.

flee VERB = **run away/off**, make off, take flight, bolt, take to your heels, decamp; [inf] scarper, skedaddle, vamoose.

fleeting ADJ = **brief**, short-lived, transient, momentary, rapid, swift, transitory, ephemeral, evanescent, passing, fugitive.

flexible ADJ **1** = **bendable**, pliable, pliant, elastic, plastic, springy, supple. **2** = **adaptable**, adjustable, open-ended. **3** = **cooperative**, accommodating, amenable, easy-going.

flight NOUN **1** = **aviation**, flying, aeronautics. **2** = **escape**, departure, exit, getaway, exodus.

flimsy ADJ **1** = **insubstantial**, fragile, frail, makeshift, rickety, shaky, gimcrack. **2** = **thin**, light, fine, delicate, sheer, filmy, diaphanous, transparent, gauzy. **3** = **feeble**, weak, poor, inadequate, unconvincing, implausible.

flinch VERB = **wince**, start, shy away, recoil, draw back, blench.

flippant ADJ = **frivolous**, facetious, glib, tongue-in-cheek, irreverent, cheeky, disrespectful.

flirt VERB = **chat up**, toy

with, lead on, tease. NOUN
= **coquette**, tease, vamp.
flirtatious ADJ
= **coquettish**, flirty,
kittenish, teasing, come-
hither.
flock NOUN 1 = **herd**, drove.
2 = **flight**, gaggle, skein.
3 = **crowd**, group, throng,
mass, host, multitude,
swarm, horde.
flood NOUN = **deluge**,
torrent, inundation,
spate, overflow. VERB
1 = **inundate**, deluge,
immerse, submerge,
swamp, drown, engulf.
2 = **oversupply**, saturate,
glut, overwhelm.
floor NOUN = **storey**, level,
tier, deck.
flop VERB 1 = **collapse**,
slump, drop, sink; droop,
sag, dangle. 2 = **fail**, fall
flat; [inf] bomb.
florid ADJ = **red**, ruddy,
flushed, high-coloured,
rubicund.
flourish VERB 1 = **brandish**,
wave, wield, swing;
display, exhibit, flaunt,
show off. 2 = **thrive**,
develop, burgeon, bloom,
blossom; succeed,
prosper.
flout VERB = **defy**, break,
disobey, violate, breach,

ignore, disregard.
flow VERB = **run**, course,
glide, drift, circulate;
trickle, seep, ooze,
dribble, drip, spill;
stream, swirl, surge,
sweep, gush, cascade,
pour, roll, rush. NOUN
= **current**, course, stream,
tide, spate; gush, outflow,
outpouring.
flower NOUN 1 = **bloom**,
blossom, floweret, floret;
annual, perennial.
2 = **best**, finest, pick,
cream, elite.
fluctuate VERB = **vary**,
change, alter, swing,
oscillate, alternate, rise
and fall, go up and down,
see-saw, yo-yo.
fluent ADJ = **articulate**,
eloquent, silver-tongued,
smooth-spoken.
fluffy ADJ = **fleecy**, woolly,
fuzzy, downy, furry, soft.
fluid ADJ 1 = **liquid**,
liquefied, melted, molten,
running, flowing.
2 = **smooth**, graceful,
elegant, effortless, easy.
3 = **flexible**, open to
change, adaptable,
adjustable; unstable,
fluctuating, shifting. NOUN
= **liquid**, solution.
flush VERB 1 = **blush**, turn

red, redden, colour.
2 = **wash**, rinse, sluice, cleanse, clean.

fluster VERB = **agitate**, unnerve, ruffle, unsettle, upset, disconcert, perturb, confuse, nonplus; [inf] rattle, faze.

fly VERB = **soar**, glide, wheel, hover; take wing, wing its way.

foam NOUN = **froth**, bubbles, fizz, head, spume, lather, effervescence, suds.

focus NOUN = **centre (of attention)**, central point, focal point, hub, pivot, nucleus, heart; cynosure. VERB = **aim**, point, turn; concentrate on, zero in on, centre on, pinpoint.

fog NOUN = **mist**, smog, haze; [inf] pea-souper.

foggy ADJ = **misty**, smoggy, dark, murky, hazy.

foible NOUN = **weakness**, weak point, failing, shortcoming, flaw, quirk, idiosyncrasy, eccentricity.

foil VERB = **thwart**, frustrate, stop, defeat, block, baulk, prevent, impede, obstruct, hamper, hinder.

fold NOUN = **layer**, pleat, crease, wrinkle, pucker, furrow, crinkle. VERB **1** = **double up**, turn under/ up, bend, tuck, crease, gather, pleat. **2** = **wrap**, enfold, clasp, embrace, envelop, hug, squeeze. **3** = **fail**, collapse, go out of business, go bankrupt, go to the wall; [inf] go bust, go under.

folk NOUN = **people**, populace, population, citizenry, public.

follow VERB **1** = **go/come behind**, trail, pursue, shadow, stalk, track, dog, hound; [inf] tail. **2** = **obey**, observe, comply with, heed, keep, conform to, stick to, adhere to, accept. **3** = **result**, arise, develop, ensue, emanate, issue, proceed, spring. **4** = **understand**, comprehend, take in, grasp, fathom. **5** (**follow up**) = **investigate**, research, look into, check out, pursue.

following ADJ = **next**, ensuing, succeeding, subsequent. NOUN = **supporters**, fans, admirers, devotees, public, audience, patrons.

foment VERB = **incite**, instigate, stir up, provoke, arouse, encourage, whip up, agitate.

fond

978

fond ADJ **1** = **adoring**, devoted, loving, affectionate, caring, warm, tender, doting, indulgent. **2** = **unrealistic**, foolish, naive, deluded, vain.

fondle VERB = **caress**, stroke, pat, pet; [inf] paw.

food NOUN = **nourishment**, sustenance, nutriment, diet, fare, (daily) bread, board, provender, foodstuffs, refreshments, edibles, meals, provisions, rations, victuals, comestibles; [inf] grub.

fool NOUN **1** = **idiot**, ass, halfwit, blockhead, dunce, ignoramus, dolt, simpleton; [inf] numbskull, nincompoop, ninny, nit, dope, clot, chump, dimwit, moron, twit. **2** = **dupe**, laughing stock; [inf] sucker, mug. VERB = **trick**, deceive, hoax, dupe, take in, hoodwink, delude, bamboozle; [inf] con, kid, have on.

foolish ADJ = **stupid**, silly, idiotic, mad, crazy, unintelligent, dense, brainless, mindless, obtuse, half-witted, moronic, inane, absurd, ludicrous, ridiculous, laughable, fatuous, asinine, senseless, irresponsible, ill-advised; [inf] thick, dim, dumb, dopey.

foolproof ADJ = **infallible**, certain, sure, guaranteed, safe, dependable, trustworthy, reliable.

forbid VERB = **prohibit**, ban, bar, debar, outlaw, veto, proscribe, disallow.

forbidding ADJ **1** = **stern**, grim, hard, hostile, unfriendly, unwelcoming, off-putting. **2** = **frightening**, ominous, threatening, menacing, sinister, daunting.

force NOUN **1** = **power**, strength, vigour, energy, muscle, might; effort, impact, exertion, pressure. **2** = **coercion**, duress, compulsion, pressure, constraint. **3** = **persuasiveness**, validity, weight, effectiveness, influence, cogency. **4** = **detachment**, unit, squad, group, patrol. VERB **1** = **compel**, coerce, make, pressure, pressurize, impel, oblige, constrain, press-gang, dragoon. **2** = **drive**, push, thrust, shove, press.

3 = **wrest**, extract, extort, wring.

forceful ADJ **1** = **powerful**, vigorous, strong, dynamic, energetic, assertive. **2** = **persuasive**, telling, convincing, compelling, effective, potent, cogent, valid.

forecast VERB = **predict**, foretell, foresee, prophesy, forewarn of, divine. NOUN = **prediction**, prophecy, prognostication, augury, prognosis.

foreign ADJ **1** = **overseas**, distant, remote, alien, exotic. **2** = **strange**, unfamiliar, unknown, unheard of, odd, peculiar, curious.

foremost ADJ = **leading**, principal, premier, top, prime, primary, paramount, chief, main, supreme, highest.

forerunner NOUN = **predecessor**, precursor, antecedent, ancestor, forefather; harbinger, herald.

foreshadow VERB = **presage**, bode, augur, portend, prefigure, indicate, mean, signal, signify, point to.

forest NOUN = **woodland**, wood(s), trees, plantation.

forestall VERB = **pre-empt**, anticipate, intercept, thwart, frustrate, stave off, ward off, fend off, prevent, avert, foil.

forethought NOUN = **foresight**, far-sightedness, anticipation, (forward) planning; prudence, care, caution.

forever ADV = **always**, evermore, ever, for all time, until the end of time, eternally, until kingdom come.

forge VERB = **fake**, falsify, counterfeit, copy, imitate.

forgery NOUN = **fake**, counterfeit, fraud, imitation, replica; [inf] phoney.

forget VERB **1** = **fail to remember**, lose track of, overlook. **2** = **disregard**, put out of your mind, ignore. **3** = **neglect**, omit, fail.

forgetful ADJ = **absent-minded**, vague, disorganized; [inf] scatterbrained, scatty.

forgive VERB = **pardon**, absolve, exonerate, let off, excuse, let bygones be bygones, bury the hatchet.

forgiveness NOUN
= **pardon**, amnesty,
reprieve, absolution,
exoneration, remission,
clemency, mercy.

forgiving ADJ = **merciful**,
lenient, magnanimous,
understanding,
compassionate, humane,
soft-hearted, forbearing,
tolerant, indulgent.

forgo VERB = **do/go without**,
waive, renounce, sacrifice,
relinquish, surrender,
abstain from, refrain
from, eschew, give up.

fork VERB = **branch**, diverge,
bifurcate, divide, split,
separate.

forlorn ADJ = **unhappy**, sad,
miserable, wretched,
woebegone, disconsolate,
dejected, despondent,
downcast.

form NOUN 1 = **shape**,
formation, configuration,
structure, construction,
arrangement, appearance,
layout. 2 = **type**, kind, sort,
variety, style, genre.
3 = **condition**, fitness,
health, shape, trim, fettle.
4 = **manners**, polite
behaviour, etiquette; [inf]
the done thing. VERB
1 = **make**, fashion, shape,
model, mould, construct,
build, assemble, produce,
create. 2 = **devise**,
formulate, think up, plan,
draw up, hatch, develop,
conceive, dream up.
3 = **set up**, establish,
found, institute,
inaugurate. 4 = **take
shape**, appear,
materialize, emerge.
5 = **comprise**, make up,
constitute.

formal ADJ = **official**, set,
fixed, conventional,
standard, regular,
customary, approved,
prescribed, pro forma,
legal; stately, ceremonial,
ritual, solemn, dignified.

formation NOUN
1 = **arrangement**, pattern,
order, grouping,
configuration, structure,
format, layout,
disposition, design.
2 = **establishment**,
institution, founding,
creation, inauguration.

former ADJ 1 = **previous**,
ex-, preceding, late,
sometime, erstwhile;
prior, foregoing.
2 = **earlier**, past, bygone, of
yore.

formidable ADJ
1 = **intimidating**, daunting,
alarming, frightening,

fearsome, forbidding; [inf] scary. **2 = strong**, powerful, impressive, mighty, great, redoubtable, terrific, indomitable, invincible. **3 = difficult**, arduous, onerous, tough, stiff, challenging.

formulate VERB **1 = draw up**, work out, plan, map out, compose, devise, think up, conceive, create, invent, design. **2 = define**, set down, specify, itemize, detail.

forsake VERB **1 = desert**, abandon, leave, jilt, throw over, cast aside, reject. **2 = give up**, renounce, relinquish, repudiate.

forthcoming ADJ **1 = future**, coming, expected, imminent, impending. **2 = communicative**, talkative, expansive, voluble, chatty, loquacious, open.

forthright ADJ **= direct**, frank, open, candid, blunt, outspoken, plain-spoken, straightforward, honest.

fortify VERB **1 = protect**, secure, strengthen; buttress, shore up. **2 = invigorate**, energize, revive, refresh, restore.

fortitude NOUN **= strength**, courage, bravery, backbone, mettle, spirit, strong-mindedness, tenacity, resilience, determination.

fortunate ADJ **= lucky**, blessed, favoured, in luck; favourable, advantageous, happy, felicitous.

fortune NOUN **1 = chance**, accident, luck, coincidence, serendipity, providence; fate, destiny. **2 = wealth**, riches, property, assets, means, possessions. **3 = huge amount**, mint, king's ransom; [inf] packet, bomb.

foster VERB **1 = encourage**, promote, further, stimulate, boost, advance, cultivate, help, aid, assist, support. **2 = bring up**, rear, raise, care for, look after, take care of, parent.

foul ADJ **1 = disgusting**, revolting, repulsive, nauseating, sickening, loathsome, odious, abominable, offensive, nasty. **2 = dirty**, contaminated, polluted, adulterated, tainted, defiled, filthy, unclean.

3 = **blasphemous**, profane, obscene, vulgar, offensive, coarse, filthy, dirty, indecent, smutty.

4 = **abhorrent**, detestable, hateful, despicable, contemptible, dishonourable, disgraceful, base, low, mean, sordid, vile, wicked, heinous, iniquitous, nefarious.

found VERB = **establish**, set up, institute, originate, initiate, create, start, inaugurate, endow.

foundation NOUN **1** = **base**, bottom, substructure, bedrock, underpinning. **2** = **basis**, groundwork, principles, fundamentals, rudiments.

fountain NOUN = **spray**, jet, spout, well, fount.

fracas NOUN = **disturbance**, altercation, fight, brawl, affray, rumpus, scuffle, skirmish, free-for-all.

fracture NOUN = **break**, rupture, split, crack, fissure, cleft, rift, chink, crevice.

fragile ADJ = **flimsy**, breakable, frail, delicate, insubstantial, brittle, dainty, fine.

fragment NOUN = **piece**, part, particle, shred, chip, shard, sliver, splinter, scrap, bit, snip, snippet, wisp.

fragmentary ADJ = **incomplete**, partial, piecemeal, disjointed, discontinuous, uneven, bitty, sketchy, patchy.

fragrance NOUN = **scent**, smell, perfume, aroma, bouquet.

frail ADJ = **weak**, infirm, ill, unwell, sickly, ailing, delicate, fragile.

frame NOUN **1** = **structure**, framework, foundation, bodywork, chassis, skeleton, shell, casing, support. **2** = **body**, physique, build, figure, shape, size.

frank ADJ = **candid**, direct, straightforward, plain, plain-spoken, outspoken, blunt, open, sincere, honest, truthful, explicit.

frantic ADJ = **distraught**, overwrought, panic-stricken, panicky, beside yourself, at your wits' end, frenzied, wild, hysterical, frenetic, worked up, fraught, agitated.

fraud NOUN **1** = **fraudulence**, sharp practice, cheating, swindling, embezzlement, deceit, double-dealing, duplicity, chicanery. **2 = ruse**, trick, deception, swindle, hoax. **3 = impostor**, fake, cheat, swindler, trickster, charlatan, quack, mountebank; [inf] phoney, con man.

fraudulent ADJ = **dishonest**, criminal, illegal, unlawful; unscrupulous, dishonourable; [inf] crooked, shady.

freak NOUN = **aberration**, abnormality, oddity, irregularity, anomaly; malformation, monstrosity, mutant. ADJ = **abnormal**, unusual, aberrant, anomalous, atypical, exceptional, unaccountable, unpredictable, unforeseeable, bizarre, queer, odd.

free ADJ **1 = free of charge**, complimentary, for nothing, gratis, on the house. **2 = without**, devoid of, lacking in, exempt from. **3 = available**, unoccupied, at leisure, with time to spare. **4 = empty**, vacant, available, spare. **5 = independent**, self-governing, autonomous, sovereign, democratic. **6 = at liberty**, at large, loose, unconfined, unfettered. VERB = **set free**, release, let go, liberate, turn loose, untie, unleash; rescue, extricate.

freedom NOUN **1 = liberty**, emancipation, independence, autonomy, sovereignty, self-government. **2 = scope**, latitude, flexibility, margin, elbow room, licence, free rein.

freezing ADJ = **bitter**, icy, frosty, glacial, arctic, wintry, raw, biting, piercing, penetrating.

freight NOUN = **cargo**, load, consignment, lading, merchandise, goods.

frenzy NOUN = **madness**, mania, wildness, hysteria, delirium, dementedness, fever, tumult.

frequent ADJ **1 = many**, numerous, recurring, repeated, recurrent, persistent, continual. **2 = regular**, habitual. VERB = **visit**, haunt, patronize.

fresh ADJ **1 = natural**, unprocessed, raw. **2 = new**, brand-new, recent, latest, up to date, modern, innovative, different, original, novel, unusual, unconventional, unorthodox. **3** = **energetic**, vigorous, invigorated, lively, spry, sprightly; refreshed, rested, revived. **4** = **additional**, more, further, extra, supplementary. **5** = **clear**, bright, cool, crisp, pure, clean, refreshing, bracing, invigorating.

friction NOUN **1** = **abrasion**, attrition, rubbing, chafing, scraping, rasping. **2** = **dissension**, dissent, disagreement, discord, strife, conflict, hostility, rivalry, animosity, antagonism, bad feeling.

friend NOUN = **companion**, comrade, playmate, intimate, confidante, alter ego, familiar; [inf] mate, pal, chum; [US inf] buddy.

friendly ADJ = **amiable**, affable, warm, genial, agreeable, companionable, cordial, convivial, sociable, hospitable, neighbourly, outgoing, approachable, accessible, communicative, open, good-natured, kindly, benign; [inf] matey.

friendship NOUN = **companionship**, intimacy, rapport, affinity, attachment, harmony, camaraderie, fellowship.

fright NOUN **1** = **fear**, terror, alarm, horror, dread, fearfulness, trepidation. **2** = **scare**, shock.

frighten VERB = **scare**, terrify, startle, petrify, terrorize, shock, panic, put the fear of God into; [inf] spook.

frightful ADJ = **dreadful**, terrible, awful, horrible, horrific, hideous, ghastly, gruesome, grisly, macabre, shocking, harrowing, appalling.

fringe NOUN **1** = **border**, frill, ruffle, trimming, tassels, edging. **2** = **edge**, border, perimeter, periphery, margin, rim, limits, outskirts.

frisky ADJ = **lively**, bouncy, playful, in high spirits, high-spirited, exuberant, perky, skittish; [inf] full of beans.

frivolous ADJ **1** = **silly**,

flighty, foolish, dizzy, empty-headed, feather-brained, giddy, superficial, shallow. **2 = flippant**, facetious, glib; jokey, light-hearted.

front NOUN **1 = facade**, face, frontage, fore, forefront, foreground, anterior; prow. **2 = head**, top, lead, beginning. **3 = front line**, vanguard, van. **4 = show**, act, pretence. **5 = cover**, blind, screen, disguise, pretext.

frontier NOUN **= border**, boundary, limit, edge, rim, bounds.

frosty ADJ **1 = freezing**, frozen, icy, glacial, frigid, arctic, wintry, bitter. **2 = unfriendly**, cold, unwelcoming, hostile.

froth NOUN **= foam**, fizz, lather, head, scum, effervescence, bubbles, suds, spume.

frown VERB **1 = scowl**, glare, glower, knit your brows, lour, look daggers. **2 = disapprove of**, not take kindly to, take a dim view of, look askance at.

frugal ADJ **= thrifty**, economical, sparing, careful, cautious, prudent, abstemious.

fruitful ADJ **1 = fertile**, fecund, prolific. **2 = useful**, worthwhile, productive, well spent, profitable, advantageous, beneficial, rewarding, gainful.

fruition NOUN **= fulfilment**, realization, materialization, achievement, attainment, success, completion, consummation, maturation, maturity, ripening.

fruitless ADJ **= futile**, useless, vain, in vain, to no avail, worthless, pointless, ineffective, unproductive, profitless, unrewarding, unsuccessful, unavailing.

frustrate VERB **1 = discourage**, dishearten, dispirit, depress, dissatisfy, anger, annoy, vex, irritate, exasperate. **2 = defeat**, thwart, obstruct, impede, hamper, hinder, check, block, foil, baulk, stymie, stop.

fugitive NOUN **= escapee**, runaway, deserter, refugee, renegade.

fulfil VERB **1 = accomplish**, carry out, execute, perform, discharge, complete. **2** = **achieve**, realize, attain, consummate. **3** = **satisfy**, conform to, fill, answer, meet, comply with.

full ADJ **1** = **filled**, filled to the brim, brimming, overflowing, filled to capacity. **2** = **crowded**, packed, crammed; [inf] chock-a-block, jam-packed. **3** = **satisfied**, sated, gorged, replete. **4** = **complete**, entire, whole, comprehensive, thorough, exhaustive, detailed, all-inclusive, all-encompassing, extensive, unabridged. **5** = **well rounded**, plump, buxom, shapely, curvaceous, voluptuous. **6** = **baggy**, voluminous, loose-fitting, capacious.

fun NOUN = **amusement**, entertainment, recreation, relaxation, enjoyment, pleasure, diversion, play, playfulness, jollification, merrymaking.

function NOUN **1** = **role**, capacity, responsibility, duty, task, job, post, situation, office, occupation, employment, business, charge, concern, activity. **2** = **social event**, gathering, reception, party. VERB = **work**, go, run, operate.

functional ADJ **1** = **practical**, useful, serviceable, utilitarian, workaday. **2** = **working**, in working order, operative, in commission, in service.

fund NOUN **1** = **reserve**, collection, pool, kitty, endowment, foundation, grant. **2** (**funds**) = **money**, cash, capital, means, resources, savings. VERB = **finance**, pay for, sponsor, subsidize, endow.

fundamental ADJ = **basic**, rudimentary, elemental, underlying, primary, cardinal, prime, first, principal, chief, key, central, structural, organic, inherent, intrinsic, vital, essential, important, pivotal, indispensable, necessary.

funny ADJ **1** = **amusing**, comical, comic, humorous, hilarious, entertaining, diverting, hysterical, witty, riotous, droll, facetious, farcical, waggish. **2** = **peculiar**, odd, strange, curious, weird, queer, bizarre, mysterious, suspicious, dubious.

furious ADJ 1 = **enraged**, raging, infuriated, livid, fuming, incensed, beside yourself; [inf] mad, apoplectic. 2 = **violent**, fierce, wild, intense, vehement, tumultuous, tempestuous, stormy, turbulent.

furniture NOUN = **furnishings**, fittings, effects, movables, chattels.

furrow NOUN 1 = **groove**, trench, channel, rut, trough, ditch, hollow. 2 see **wrinkle**.

further ADJ = **additional**, more, extra, supplementary, other, new, fresh. VERB = **advance**, facilitate, aid, assist, help, promote, encourage, foster.

furtive ADJ = **secretive**, secret, stealthy, surreptitious, clandestine, sneaky, shifty, covert, conspiratorial, sly.

fury NOUN 1 = **anger**, rage, wrath, ire. 2 = **fierceness**, violence, ferocity, intensity, force, power.

fuss NOUN = **fluster**, agitation, excitement, bother, palaver, commotion, ado, worry; [inf] to-do, flap, tizzy.

fussy ADJ = **particular**, over-particular, finicky, pernickety, fastidious, hard to please, difficult, demanding; [inf] faddy, choosy, picky.

futile ADJ = **useless**, vain, in vain, to no avail, pointless, fruitless, unsuccessful, unprofitable, unavailing, uneffective.

future ADJ = **forthcoming**, coming; prospective, intended, planned, destined.

fuzzy ADJ 1 = **downy**, frizzy, woolly, furry, fleecy, fluffy. 2 = **out of focus**, unfocused, blurred, blurry, indistinct, unclear, ill-defined, misty, bleary.

gadget

Gg

gadget NOUN = **appliance**, apparatus, device, mechanism, instrument, tool, implement, invention, contraption; [inf] widget, gizmo.

gaiety NOUN = **cheerfulness**, light-heartedness, merriment, glee, happiness, high spirits, joyfulness, exuberance, liveliness, animation, vivacity.

gain VERB 1 = **obtain**, get, acquire, secure, procure, attain, achieve, win. 2 = **reach**, arrive at, make. NOUN 1 = **increase**, addition, rise, increment. 2 = **profit**, earnings, advantage, benefit, reward, yield, return, winnings, proceeds, dividend, interest; [inf] pickings.

gainful ADJ = **profitable**, rewarding, remunerative, lucrative, productive, beneficial, fruitful, advantageous, worthwhile, useful.

gallant ADJ 1 = **chivalrous**, gentlemanly, courteous, polite, attentive, gracious, considerate, thoughtful. 2 = **brave**, courageous, valiant, bold, daring, fearless, intrepid, heroic.

galvanize VERB = **electrify**, shock, stir, startle, jolt, spur, prod, stimulate, fire, energize, inspire.

gamble VERB = **bet**, wager, stake money, lay money; [inf] have a flutter.

game NOUN 1 = **pastime**, diversion, recreation, entertainment, amusement, sport, play. 2 = **match**, contest, fixture, round, bout.

gang NOUN = **group**, band, company, crowd, pack, horde, mob.

gangster NOUN = **racketeer**, crook, criminal, hoodlum, robber; [US inf] hood, mobster.

gap NOUN 1 = **opening**, hole, aperture, cavity, space, breach, break, rift, fissure, cleft, chink, crack, crevice, cranny, orifice, interstice. 2 = **pause**, break, intermission, interval, interlude, lull, respite, breathing space. **3** = **difference**, disparity; chasm, gulf.

gape VERB = **stare**, gaze, goggle; [inf] gawk, rubberneck.

garbage NOUN = **waste**, rubbish, refuse, litter, debris, junk, detritus; [US] trash.

garbled ADJ = **distorted**, confused, muddled, mixed up; misquoted, misreported.

garish ADJ = **gaudy**, showy, loud, lurid, brassy, tawdry, tasteless; [inf] flashy, flash.

garrison NOUN **1** = **troops**, soldiers, force, detachment, unit, brigade, platoon, squadron. **2** = **barracks**, base, fort, fortress, fortification, stronghold, camp, encampment.

gash VERB = **cut**, slash, tear, lacerate, wound, gouge, slit.

gasp VERB = **pant**, puff, puff and blow, gulp, choke, catch your breath, fight for breath, wheeze.

gate NOUN = **barrier**, turnstile; gateway, doorway, entrance, exit, opening.

gather VERB **1** = **come together**, collect, assemble, congregate, meet, cluster, mass, convene, foregather, converge; summon, round up, muster, marshal. **2** = **accumulate**, amass, store, garner, stockpile, hoard; [inf] stash away. **3** = **understand**, believe, hear, learn, infer, deduce, conclude, surmise.

gathering NOUN = **assembly**, congregation, group, crowd, throng, horde, meeting, convention, rally.

gauche ADJ = **awkward**, maladroit, inept, inelegant, graceless, unsophisticated, uncultured.

gaudy ADJ see **garish**.

gauge NOUN **1** = **meter**, dial, scale. **2** = **size**, diameter, width, thickness, breadth; bore, calibre.

gaunt ADJ = **haggard**, drawn, cadaverous, skeletal, emaciated, skinny, bony, lean, scrawny.

gaze VERB = **stare**, gape,

goggle; [inf] gawk, gawp, rubberneck.

gear NOUN 1 = **equipment**, tools, kit, apparatus, implements, tackle, appliances, utensils, supplies, accessories, paraphernalia, accoutrements.
2 = **belongings**, possessions, things, luggage, baggage, effects; [inf] stuff.

genealogy NOUN = **family tree**, ancestry, pedigree, line, lineage, descent, parentage, birth, extraction, family, stock, bloodline, heritage.

general ADJ 1 = **usual**, customary, common, ordinary, normal, standard, regular, everyday, typical, conventional, habitual.
2 = **common**, accepted, widespread, shared, broad, prevalent, prevailing, popular, public. 3 = **universal**, blanket, comprehensive, all-inclusive, across-the-board, sweeping, catholic, encyclopedic.
4 = **miscellaneous**, assorted, diversified, composite, mixed,

heterogeneous. 5 = **broad**, loose, rough, approximate, vague, inexact, imprecise.

generally ADV = **usually**, in general, as a rule, normally, ordinarily, typically, for the most part, mainly, by and large, on average, on the whole.

generate VERB = **cause**, give rise to, produce, create, engender, bring about, lead to.

generous ADJ 1 = **liberal**, magnanimous, benevolent, munificent, beneficent, bountiful, bounteous, open-handed, charitable, unstinting, free-handed; princely.
2 = **abundant**, plentiful, lavish, ample, rich, copious.

genial ADJ = **amiable**, affable, friendly, congenial, amicable, convivial, agreeable, good-humoured, good-natured, pleasant, cordial, cheerful, cheery, kind, kindly, benign.

genius NOUN
1 = **mastermind**, prodigy, virtuoso, master, maestro.
2 = **brilliance**, intelligence, cleverness, brains, fine mind.

genteel ADJ = **refined**, respectable, decorous, well mannered, courteous, polite, proper, correct, seemly, well bred, ladylike, gentlemanly, dignified, gracious.

gentle ADJ 1 = **tender**, kind, kindly, humane, benign, lenient, compassionate, tender-hearted, placid, sweet-tempered, mild, quiet, peaceful. 2 = **moderate**, light, temperate, soft.

genuine ADJ 1 = **real**, authentic, true, pure, actual, bona fide, veritable, pukka; legitimate, lawful, legal, valid; [inf] kosher. 2 = **sincere**, truthful, honest, frank, candid, open, natural, unaffected, artless, ingenuous; [inf] upfront.

germ NOUN = **microbe**, micro-organism, bacillus, bacterium, virus; [inf] bug.

gesture NOUN = **signal**, sign, wave, indication, gesticulation. VERB = **gesticulate**, signal, motion, wave, indicate.

get VERB 1 = **acquire**, obtain, come by, secure, procure; buy, purchase. 2 = **receive**, be sent, be given. 3 = **fetch**, collect, carry, transport, convey. 4 = **earn**, make, bring in, clear, take home. 5 = **become**, grow, turn.

ghastly ADJ = **terrible**, horrible, frightful, dreadful, awful, horrific, horrendous, hideous, shocking, appalling, grim, gruesome.

ghost NOUN 1 = **apparition**, spectre, spirit, phantom, wraith; [inf] spook. 2 = **suggestion**, hint, trace, glimmer, shadow.

ghostly ADJ = **spectral**, phantom, unearthly, supernatural, eerie, weird, uncanny; [inf] spooky, scary.

giant ADJ = **gigantic**, enormous, huge, colossal, immense, vast, mammoth, gargantuan, titanic, towering.

giddy ADJ = **dizzy**, faint, light-headed, unsteady; [inf] woozy.

gift NOUN 1 = **present**, offering, donation, bonus; gratuity, tip; bequest, legacy. 2 = **talent**, aptitude, flair, facility, knack, ability, faculty, capacity, skill, expertise, genius.

gifted ADJ = **talented**, brilliant, clever, intelligent, able, accomplished, masterly, skilled, expert, adept.

giggle VERB = **titter**, snigger, chuckle, chortle, laugh.

girl NOUN = **young woman**, young lady, miss; [Scottish] lass, lassie; [inf] bird, chick; [literary] maid, maiden, damsel.

girth NOUN = **circumference**, perimeter, width, breadth.

gist NOUN = **essence**, substance, core, nub, crux, sense, meaning, significance, thrust, import.

give VERB 1 = **present**, hand (over), bestow, donate, contribute, confer, award, grant, accord, leave, will, bequeath, entrust, consign, vouchsafe. 2 = **allow**, permit. 3 = **provide**, supply, furnish, proffer, offer.

give in = **give up**, surrender, yield, capitulate, submit, succumb. **give up** = **stop**, cease, desist from, abandon, discontinue; [inf] quit. **give way** = **cave in**, collapse, break, fall apart, bend, buckle.

glad ADJ 1 = **happy**, pleased, delighted, thrilled, overjoyed; gratified, thankful; [inf] chuffed, tickled pink. 2 = **willing**, eager, ready, prepared. 3 = **joyful**, pleasing, welcome, cheering, gratifying.

glamorous ADJ 1 = **beautiful**, elegant, chic, stylish, fashionable; charming, charismatic, appealing, alluring, seductive; [inf] classy. 2 = **exciting**, thrilling, glittering, colourful, exotic, cosmopolitan; [inf] ritzy, glitzy, jet-setting.

glamour NOUN 1 = **beauty**, elegance, style, charisma. 2 = **excitement**, allure, fascination, magic, romance, mystique.

glance VERB = **glimpse**, catch a glimpse, peek, peep.

glare VERB 1 = **scowl**, glower, frown, look daggers, lour, stare. 2 = **dazzle**, beam, blaze.

glaring ADJ = **obvious**, conspicuous, unmistakable, manifest, overt, patent, visible, flagrant, blatant, outrageous.

glass NOUN = **tumbler**, flute, schooner, goblet, beaker, chalice.

glasses PLURAL NOUN = **spectacles**, bifocals, sunglasses, lorgnette, pince-nez.

glassy ADJ 1 = **shiny**, glossy, smooth, clear, transparent, translucent. 2 = **glazed**, blank, expressionless, empty, vacant.

glaze NOUN = **gloss**, varnish, lacquer, enamel, finish, lustre, shine, gloss.

gleam VERB = **shine**, flash, glint, glisten, glitter, flicker, shimmer, glimmer, sparkle, twinkle.

glee NOUN = **mirth**, merriment, gaiety, delight, joy, happiness, pleasure, excitement, exhilaration, elation, exuberance, triumph, jubilation.

glib ADJ = **smooth-talking**, slick, smooth, smooth-tongued, silver-tongued, articulate; insincere, disingenuous, facile, flippant; [inf] flip.

glimpse VERB = **catch sight of**, spot, spy, make out, notice, discern. NOUN = **glance**, peek, peep.

glisten VERB = **shine**, shimmer, sparkle, twinkle, flicker, glint, glitter, gleam, glimmer.

glitter VERB = **sparkle**, twinkle, wink, glint, flash, gleam, shimmer, glimmer.

gloat VERB = **relish**, revel, glory, rejoice, exult, triumph, crow; [inf] rub it in.

global ADJ 1 = **worldwide**, international. 2 = **general**, overall, comprehensive, universal, all-encompassing, all-inclusive; thorough, total, across the board.

globule NOUN = **bead**, drop, ball, droplet.

gloomy ADJ 1 = **dark**, sunless, dim, shadowy, black, murky. 2 = **sad**, melancholy, unhappy, miserable, sorrowful, despondent, woebegone, disconsolate, dejected, downcast, downhearted, glum, dispirited, desolate, depressed, blue, pessimistic, morose.

glorious ADJ 1 = **illustrious**, celebrated, famous, acclaimed, distinguished,

honoured; outstanding, great, magnificent, noble, triumphant.
2 = **wonderful**, marvellous, superb, sublime, lovely, beautiful; [inf] super, great, fantastic, terrific, tremendous, heavenly, divine, fabulous.

glory NOUN **1** = **distinction**, fame, kudos, renown, honour, prestige, acclaim, praise, eminence, recognition.
2 = **splendour**, magnificence, grandeur, majesty, beauty. VERB = **exult**, rejoice, delight, revel; boast, crow, gloat.

gloss VERB (**gloss over**) = **conceal**, hide, cover up, disguise, mask, veil, whitewash.

glossy ADJ = **shiny**, gleaming, bright, smooth, lustrous, glistening, polished, burnished, silky, silken, sleek.

glow VERB **1** = **gleam**, shine, glimmer, flicker. **2** = **blush**, flush, redden, colour (up); burn. NOUN **1** = **gleam**, glimmer, shine, radiance, light. **2** = **blush**, rosiness, flush, pinkness, redness; bloom.

glower VERB = **scowl**, glare, frown, look daggers, lour.

glowing ADJ = **favourable**, enthusiastic, complimentary, ecstatic, rapturous; [inf] rave.

glue NOUN = **adhesive**, gum, fixative, paste. VERB = **stick**, paste, gum, fix, affix, seal.

glum ADJ = **gloomy**, melancholy, sad, despondent, miserable, dejected, downcast, downhearted, dispirited, depressed.

glut NOUN = **surplus**, excess, surfeit, overabundance, oversupply, saturation, superfluity.

glutinous ADJ = **sticky**, viscous, viscid, tacky, gluey.

gluttonous ADJ = **greedy**, voracious, insatiable.

gnarled ADJ = **knotty**, lumpy, bumpy, knobbly, twisted, crooked, distorted, misshapen, nodular.

gnaw VERB = **chew**, munch, bite, champ, chomp, worry.

go VERB **1** = **move**, proceed, progress, walk, travel, journey. **2** = **leave**, depart, withdraw, retire, set off/out. **3** = **work**, function, operate, run. **4** = **become**, grow, get, turn. **5** = **stop**, cease, disappear, vanish, fade away, melt away. NOUN = **try**, attempt, turn, bid, endeavour, essay; [inf] shot, stab, crack.

goad NOUN = **stimulus**, incentive, inducement, impetus, encouragement, spur. VERB = **prompt**, stimulate, induce, motivate, spur, provoke, prod, rouse.

goal NOUN = **aim**, objective, end, purpose, ambition, target, design, intention, intent, aspiration.

go-between NOUN = **intermediary**, mediator, middleman, negotiator, messenger, agent, broker.

godforsaken ADJ = **desolate**, dismal, dreary, bleak, wretched, miserable, gloomy, deserted, neglected, remote, isolated.

godsend NOUN = **blessing**, boon, bonus, plus, benefit, stroke of luck.

good ADJ **1** = **virtuous**, moral, ethical, righteous, right-minded, honourable, upright, honest, noble, worthy, admirable, exemplary. **2** = **fine**, superior, excellent, superb, marvellous, wonderful, first-rate, first-class, great; satisfactory, acceptable. **3** = **well behaved**, well mannered, obedient, dutiful. **4** = **competent**, capable, able, accomplished, skilful, efficient, adept, proficient, expert. **5** = **reliable**, dependable, trustworthy, loyal, faithful, staunch; close, intimate, bosom. **6** = **fine**, healthy, sound, robust, strong. **7** = **wholesome**, healthy, nutritious, nutritional, beneficial. **8** = **valid**, legitimate, genuine, authentic, sound, bona fide. **9** = **enjoyable**, pleasant, agreeable, pleasurable, delightful, nice, lovely; [inf] super, fantastic, fabulous, terrific. NOUN **1** = **benefit**, advantage, gain, profit, interest, well-being, welfare. **2** = **virtue**, morality, rectitude, honesty, integrity, probity. **3** (**goods**) = **property**, belongings, possessions, effects, chattels; merchandise, wares, products.

goodbye EXCLAMATION
= **farewell**, adieu, au
revoir, ciao; [inf] bye,
cheerio, cheers, see you.

good-natured ADJ = **kind**,
kind-hearted, kindly,
warm-hearted, generous,
benevolent, charitable,
friendly, helpful,
accommodating, amiable,
tolerant.

gorge NOUN = **chasm**,
canyon, ravine, defile,
pass.

gorgeous ADJ 1 = **beautiful**,
attractive, lovely, good-
looking, sexy; [inf]
stunning. 2 = **splendid**,
magnificent, superb,
impressive, wonderful,
imposing, dazzling,
breathtaking.

gory ADJ = **bloody**,
bloodstained, grisly;
violent, brutal, savage,
sanguinary.

gossip NOUN = **rumours**,
scandal, tittle-tattle,
hearsay, whispering
campaign. VERB = **tittle-
tattle**, talk, whisper, tell
tales.

govern VERB 1 = **rule**,
preside over, reign over,
control, be in charge of,
command, lead, run,
head. 2 = **determine**,

decide, regulate, direct,
dictate, shape; affect,
influence, sway.

government NOUN
= **administration**, regime,
parliament, ministry,
executive, rule,
leadership, command,
control.

gown NOUN = **dress**, frock,
robe.

grab VERB = **grasp**, seize,
snatch, clutch, grip, clasp,
take hold of.

grace NOUN 1 = **elegance**,
poise, gracefulness,
finesse; suppleness,
agility, nimbleness, light-
footedness. 2 = **courtesy**,
decency, (good) manners,
politeness, decorum,
respect, tact. 3 = **blessing**,
prayer, thanksgiving,
benediction. VERB = **adorn**,
decorate, ornament,
embellish, enhance,
beautify.

graceful ADJ = **elegant**,
fluid, fluent, natural,
neat; agile, supple,
nimble, light-footed.

gracious ADJ = **courteous**,
cordial, kindly,
benevolent, friendly,
amiable, considerate,
pleasant, polite, civil, well
mannered, chivalrous,

grate

charitable, obliging, accommodating, beneficent.

grade NOUN = **level**, degree, stage, echelon, rank, standing, station, position, order, class, category, group. VERB = **classify**, class, categorize, sort, group, rank, evaluate, rate, value.

gradient NOUN = **slope**, incline, hill, rise, bank, acclivity, declivity.

gradual ADJ = **progressive**, steady, even, measured, unhurried, step-by-step, successive, continuous, systematic.

grain NOUN 1 = **particle**, granule, bit, piece, scrap, crumb, fragment, speck, trace, mite, iota. 2 = **texture**, weave, pattern, nap.

grand ADJ 1 = **impressive**, imposing, magnificent, splendid, superb, palatial, stately, majestic, luxurious, lavish, opulent. 2 = **great**, noble, aristocratic, distinguished, august, illustrious, eminent, esteemed, venerable, pre-eminent, prominent, notable, renowned.

grandiose ADJ 1 = **grand**, impressive, magnificent, imposing, splendid, superb, stately, majestic. 2 = **ambitious**, extravagant, bold, overambitious.

grant VERB 1 = **allow**, consent, permit; give, allow, award, accord, bestow, confer, endow. 2 = **acknowledge**, concede, accept, admit. NOUN = **award**, endowment, allowance, subsidy, bursary; scholarship.

graphic ADJ = **vivid**, explicit, striking, expressive, descriptive, colourful, lively, detailed.

grapple VERB 1 = **fight**, wrestle, struggle, tussle, battle, brawl. 2 = **tackle**, face, cope with, deal with, handle, confront, get to grips with.

grasp VERB 1 = **grip**, clutch, hold, clasp, grab, snatch, take hold of, seize. 2 = **understand**, comprehend, follow, take in, perceive; [inf] get.

grate VERB 1 = **shred**, mince, grind, granulate. 2 = **rasp**, scrape, jar, scratch. 3 = **irritate**, annoy, rile, exasperate, chafe, set someone's teeth on edge.

grateful ADJ = **thankful**, appreciative, obliged, indebted, obligated, beholden.

gratify VERB = **please**, delight, gladden, satisfy.

gratitude NOUN = **gratefulness**, thankfulness, thanks, appreciation, indebtedness.

gratuitous ADJ = **unprovoked**, unjustified, uncalled for, unwarranted, unjustifiable, needless, unnecessary, superfluous.

gratuity NOUN = **tip**, bonus, present, gift.

grave ADJ 1 = **solemn**, serious, sober, sombre, unsmiling, grim, severe, stern. 2 = **serious**, important, significant, weighty, momentous, urgent, pressing, critical.

graveyard NOUN = **cemetery**, burial ground, churchyard, necropolis.

gravity NOUN = **solemnity**, seriousness, sombreness; importance, significance, momentousness, weightiness.

graze VERB = **scrape**, abrade, skin, scratch, chafe, bark.

greasy ADJ = **fatty**, oily, buttery, oleaginous; slippery, slippy, slimy.

great ADJ 1 = **large**, big, extensive, vast, immense, huge, spacious, enormous, gigantic, colossal, mammoth, prodigious, tremendous, substantial, sizeable. 2 = **impressive**, grand, magnificent, imposing, splendid, majestic, glorious, sumptuous. 3 = **prominent**, eminent, pre-eminent, distinguished, illustrious, august, celebrated, renowned, noted, notable, famous, famed, leading. 4 = **gifted**, talented, outstanding, remarkable, exceptional, first-rate, expert, skilful, skilled, masterly, adept, proficient, adroit. 5 see **excellent**.

greed NOUN 1 = **gluttony**, voracity. 2 = **avarice**, acquisitiveness, rapacity, covetousness, cupidity. 3 = **desire**, hunger, craving, longing, eagerness.

greedy ADJ 1 = **gluttonous**, voracious, ravenous,

insatiable. **2 = avaricious**, acquisitive, grasping, rapacious, covetous.
3 = eager, hungry, avid, longing, craving.

green ADJ **1 = grassy**, verdant, leafy.
2 = inexperienced, untrained, new, raw, immature, inexpert; naive, unsophisticated, callow; [inf] wet behind the ears.

greenhouse NOUN **= hothouse**, glasshouse, conservatory.

greet VERB **= salute**, hail, acknowledge, address, receive, meet, welcome.

greeting NOUN **1 = hello**, salute, salutation, acknowledgement, welcome. **2 (greetings) = good wishes**, best wishes, regards, congratulations, compliments, respects.

grey ADJ **= cloudy**, overcast, dull, sunless, gloomy, dreary, dismal, cheerless, depressing.

grief NOUN **= sorrow**, mourning, lamentation, misery, sadness, anguish, distress, heartache, heartbreak, desolation.

grievance NOUN **1 = complaint**, grumble, axe to grind, bone to pick; [inf] grouse, gripe.
2 = injustice, wrong, unfairness, injury, affront, insult.

grieve VERB **1 = mourn**, lament, sorrow, weep and wail, cry, sob. **2 = hurt**, wound, pain, sadden, upset, distress.

grim ADJ **1 = stern**, forbidding, unsmiling, dour, formidable, harsh, stony; cross, surly, sour, ill-tempered; threatening, menacing. **2 = resolute**, determined, firm, adamant, unyielding, unshakeable, obdurate, stubborn, unrelenting, relentless. **3 = dreadful**, horrible, horrendous, terrible, horrific, dire, ghastly, awful, appalling, frightful, shocking, unspeakable, grisly, hideous, gruesome.

grimy ADJ **= dirty**, grubby, mucky, stained, soiled, filthy.

grind VERB **1 = crush**, pound, pulverize, mill, powder, granulate.
2 = sharpen, file, whet, hone; smooth, polish, sand.

grip VERB 1 = **grasp**, clutch, hold, clasp, clench, take hold of, grab, seize.
2 = **absorb**, engross, rivet, hold spellbound, entrance, fascinate, enthral, mesmerize. NOUN
1 = **grasp**, hold; purchase.
2 = **understanding**, comprehension, awareness, perception, grasp.

grisly ADJ see **gruesome**.

groan VERB = **moan**, cry, call out, whimper.

grope VERB = **feel**, fumble, scrabble, search, hunt, rummage.

gross ADJ 1 = **obese**, corpulent, overweight, fat, bloated, fleshy, flabby.
2 = **coarse**, crude, vulgar, obscene, rude, lewd, dirty, filthy, smutty, blue, risqué, indecent, indelicate, offensive.

grotesque ADJ
= **malformed**, deformed, misshapen, distorted, twisted, gnarled; ugly, unsightly, monstrous, hideous, freakish, unnatural, abnormal, strange, odd, peculiar.

ground NOUN 1 = **soil**, earth, turf, loam; land, terrain; floor, terra firma. 2 = **pitch**, stadium, field, arena.

groundless ADJ
= **unfounded**, unsubstantiated, unwarranted, unjustified, unjustifiable; irrational, illogical, unreasonable.

grounds PLURAL NOUN
1 = **surroundings**, land, property, estate, gardens, park, parkland.
2 = **reason**, cause, basis, base, foundation, justification, rationale, premise, occasion, pretext. 3 = **dregs**, deposit, lees, sediment.

groundwork NOUN
= **preliminaries**, preparations, spadework, planning.

group NOUN 1 = **set**, lot, category, classification, class, batch, family, species, genus, bracket.
2 = **company**, band, party, body, gathering, congregation, assembly, collection, bunch, cluster, crowd, flock, pack, troop, gang, batch. 3 = **faction**, set, coterie, clique.
4 = **society**, association, league, guild, circle, club.
VERB 1 = **classify**, class, categorize, sort, grade, rank, bracket.

2 = **assemble**, collect, gather together, arrange, organize, marshal, range, line up, dispose.

grovel VERB = **abase yourself**, toady, fawn, curry favour, kowtow, lick someone's boots; [inf] crawl.

grow VERB **1** = **lengthen**, extend, expand, stretch, spread, thicken, widen, fill out, swell, increase, multiply, proliferate. **2** = **develop**, sprout, shoot up, germinate, bud, burgeon. **3** = **flourish**, thrive, prosper, succeed, develop. **4** = **become**, get, turn, wax. **5** = **produce**, cultivate, farm, propagate, raise.

growth NOUN **1** = **increase**, expansion, enlargement, development, proliferation, multiplication, extension. **2** = **tumour**, cancer, malignancy; lump, swelling, excrescence.

grubby ADJ = **dirty**, filthy, grimy, soiled, mucky, stained.

grudge NOUN = **resentment**, bitterness, ill will, pique, grievance, hard feelings, rancour, animosity, antipathy, disgruntlement. VERB = **begrudge**, resent, envy, be jealous of.

gruelling ADJ = **exhausting**, tiring, wearying, taxing, demanding, arduous, laborious, back-breaking, strenuous, punishing, hard, difficult, harsh, severe.

gruesome ADJ = **grisly**, ghastly, frightful, horrible, horrifying, horrific, horrendous, awful, dreadful, grim, terrible, hideous, disgusting, repulsive, revolting, repugnant, repellent, macabre, sickening, appalling, shocking, loathsome, abhorrent, odious.

grumble VERB = **complain**, moan, protest, carp; [inf] grouse, gripe, bellyache, whinge.

grumpy ADJ = **bad-tempered**, surly, churlish, crotchety, tetchy, testy, crabby, cantankerous, curmudgeonly; [inf] grouchy.

guarantee NOUN **1** = **warranty**, warrant, covenant, bond, contract, guaranty. **2** = **pledge**, promise, assurance, word (of honour), oath, bond. VERB **1** = **underwrite**, sponsor, support, vouch for. **2** = **promise**, pledge, give your word, swear.

guard VERB = **defend**, shield, safeguard, protect, watch over; patrol, police, defend, keep safe. NOUN **1** = **sentry**, sentinel, nightwatchman, lookout, watch; guardian, custodian. **2** = **warder**, jailer, keeper.

guarded ADJ = **careful**, cautious, circumspect, wary, chary; [inf] cagey.

guess NOUN = **conjecture**, surmise, hypothesis, theory, supposition, speculation, estimate, prediction; [inf] guesstimate. VERB **1** = **conjecture**, surmise, estimate, hypothesize, postulate, predict, speculate. **2** = **suppose**, believe, think, imagine, suspect, dare say, reckon.

guest NOUN **1** = **visitor**, caller, company. **2** = **resident**, boarder, lodger, patron.

guidance NOUN **1** = **advice**, counsel, recommendations, suggestions, tips, hints, pointers. **2** = **direction**, control, leadership, management, supervision, charge.

guide VERB **1** = **lead**, conduct, show, usher, shepherd, direct, pilot, steer, escort, accompany, attend. **2** = **control**, direct, manage, command, be in charge of, govern, preside over, superintend, supervise, oversee. **3** = **advise**, counsel. NOUN **1** = **escort**, chaperone, courier, usher, attendant. **2** = **adviser**, counsellor, mentor, guru. **3** = **guidebook**, handbook, vade mecum.

guilty ADJ **1** = **to blame**, blameworthy, culpable, at fault, responsible, errant, delinquent, offending. **2** = **remorseful**, ashamed, conscience-stricken, shamefaced, regretful, contrite, repentant, penitent, rueful, sheepish, hangdog.

guise NOUN = **likeness**, semblance, form; pretence, disguise, facade, front, screen.

gulf NOUN **1** = **bay**, cove,

inlet, bight. **2** = **divide**, division, separation, gap, breach, rift, chasm, abyss.

gullible ADJ = **credulous**, over-trustful, unsuspecting, ingenuous, naive, innocent, inexperienced, green; [inf] born yesterday.

gulp VERB **1** = **swallow**, quaff, swill, swig. **2** = **bolt**, wolf, gobble, guzzle, devour, tuck into. NOUN = **swallow**, mouthful, draught, swig.

gunman NOUN = **armed robber**, sniper, terrorist, assassin, murderer, killer; [inf] hit man, hired gun.

gush VERB **1** = **stream**, rush, spout, spurt, surge, jet, well, pour, burst, cascade, flood, flow, run, issue. **2** = **enthuse**, wax lyrical, rave. NOUN = **stream**, outpouring, spurt, jet, spout, rush, burst, surge, cascade, flood, torrent, spate.

gusto NOUN = **zest**, enthusiasm, relish, zeal, fervour, verve, enjoyment, delight, pleasure, appreciation, appetite.

gut NOUN = **stomach**, belly, abdomen, bowels; intestines, entrails, viscera; [inf] insides, innards. VERB = **eviscerate**, disembowel.

gutter NOUN = **drain**, sewer, sluice, culvert, conduit, pipe, channel, trench, trough, ditch, furrow.

guttural ADJ = **husky**, throaty, gruff, gravelly, harsh, croaky, rasping, deep, low, rough, thick.

gyrate VERB = **rotate**, revolve, wheel round, turn round, circle, whirl, pirouette, twirl, swirl, spin, swivel.

Hh

habit NOUN 1 = **custom**, practice, wont, way, routine, matter of course, pattern, convention, norm, usage. 2 = **addiction**, dependence, weakness, obsession, fixation. 3 = **costume**, dress, garb, attire, clothes, clothing, garments.

habitual ADJ 1 = **usual**, customary, accustomed, regular, normal, set, fixed, established, routine, wonted, common, ordinary, familiar, traditional. 2 = **confirmed**, addicted, chronic, inveterate, hardened, ingrained.

habituate VERB = **accustom**, make used to, acclimatize, condition, break in, inure, harden.

hackneyed ADJ = **banal**, trite, overused, tired, worn-out, stale, clichéd, platitudinous, unoriginal, unimaginative, stock; [inf] corny.

haggard ADJ = **gaunt**, drawn, pinched, hollow-cheeked, exhausted, drained, careworn, wan, pale.

hail VERB 1 = **greet**, salute, call out to, address. 2 see **acclaim**.

hair NOUN 1 = **locks**, tresses. 2 = **coat**, fur, pelt, wool, fleece, mane.

hair-raising ADJ = **terrifying**, blood-curdling, spine-chilling, frightening; [inf] scary.

hairy ADJ = **hirsute**, woolly, shaggy, bushy, fuzzy, fleecy; bristly, bearded, unshaven.

half-hearted ADJ = **lukewarm**, unenthusiastic, apathetic, uninterested, lacklustre, cursory, perfunctory, superficial, desultory.

hallmark NOUN = **mark**, trademark, stamp, sign, badge, symbol, characteristic, indicator, indication.

hallucination NOUN = **illusion**, delusion, figment of the imagination, vision, fantasy, apparition, mirage, chimera.

halt VERB = **stop**, terminate, block, end, finish, suspend, break off, impede, check, curb, stem. NOUN = **stop**, stoppage, cessation, end, standstill, pause, interval, interlude, intermission, break, hiatus.

hammer VERB = **beat**, batter, pound, hit, strike, bang.

hamper VERB = **hinder**, obstruct, impede, hold back/up, inhibit, delay, retard, slow down, block, check, frustrate, thwart, foil, curb, interfere with, restrict, handicap.

hand NOUN 1 = **fist**, palm; [inf] mitt. 2 = **pointer**, indicator, needle. 3 = **worker**, employee, operative, labourer. VERB = **give**, pass, deliver, present; distribute, dole out, mete out, dispense, apportion; [inf] dish out.

handicap NOUN = **impediment**, disadvantage, hindrance, obstruction, obstacle, encumbrance, check, block, barrier, stumbling block, constraint, restriction, limitation, drawback, shortcoming.

handle VERB 1 = **touch**, feel, hold, finger, pat, caress, stroke, fondle. 2 = **cope with**, deal with, manage, tackle. 3 = **be in charge of**, control, administer, direct, conduct, supervise, take care of. 4 = **drive**, steer, operate, manoeuvre. 5 = **deal in**, trade in, traffic in, market, sell, stock, carry. NOUN = **shaft**, grip, handgrip, hilt, haft, knob, stock.

handsome ADJ 1 = **good-looking**, attractive, personable; [inf] dishy. 2 = **substantial**, sizeable, princely, large, big, considerable.

handy ADJ 1 = **to hand**, at hand, within reach, available, accessible, near, nearby, close. 2 = **useful**, convenient, practical, serviceable, functional, user-friendly. 3 = **deft**, dexterous, nimble-fingered, adroit, adept, skilful, skilled.

hang VERB 1 = **be suspended**, dangle, swing, sway; hover, float, drift. 2 = **adorn**, decorate, deck, ornament, drape, cover.

hang-up NOUN = **fixation**, preoccupation, obsession, phobia, neurosis.

hanker VERB = **long**, yearn, crave, desire, hunger, thirst, covet, want, wish, set your heart on, pine.

haphazard ADJ = **unplanned**, random, indiscriminate, chaotic, unsystematic, disorganized, slapdash, careless, casual, hit-or-miss, arbitrary.

happen VERB = **take place**, occur, come about, come to pass, present itself, arise, materialize, transpire, crop up.

happening NOUN = **occurrence**, event, incident, occasion, affair, circumstance, phenomenon, eventuality, episode, experience.

happy ADJ 1 = **cheerful**, cheery, merry, in good/high spirits, joyful, light-hearted, jovial, gleeful, buoyant, carefree, blithe, smiling, glad, pleased, delighted, elated, ecstatic, blissful, euphoric, overjoyed, exuberant, in seventh heaven. 2 = **lucky**, fortunate, advantageous, favourable, beneficial, opportune, timely, convenient, welcome, propitious, auspicious, fortuitous.

harass VERB 1 = **bother**, pester, annoy, provoke, badger, hound, torment, plague, persecute, nag, bedevil; [inf] hassle. 2 = **harry**, attack, assail, beleaguer, set upon.

harbour NOUN 1 = **port**, anchorage, dock, marina. 2 = **refuge**, shelter, haven, sanctuary, retreat, asylum. VERB 1 = **shelter**, shield, protect, conceal, hide. 2 = **nurse**, nurture, cherish, cling to, entertain, bear.

hard ADJ 1 = **firm**, solid, compact, compacted, compressed, dense, rigid, stiff, stony. 2 = **strenuous**, arduous, tiring, exhausting, back-breaking, laborious, gruelling, tough, difficult, uphill. 3 = **complicated**, complex, involved, puzzling, perplexing, baffling, knotty, thorny. 4 = **harsh**, strict, rigorous, severe, stern, hard-hearted, unfeeling, unsympathetic, intransigent, unrelenting, unsparing, callous, implacable, obdurate, unyielding, unjust, unfair. **5 = forceful**, violent, heavy, strong, powerful, sharp.

harden VERB **= solidify**, set, stiffen, cake, congeal, clot, coagulate.

hardly ADV **= scarcely**, barely, (only) just.

hardship NOUN **= adversity**, deprivation, privation, want, need, destitution, poverty, penury, austerity, suffering, affliction, pain, misery, wretchedness, tribulation, trials.

hardy ADJ **= healthy**, fit, strong, robust, sturdy, tough, rugged, vigorous.

harm NOUN **= hurt**, injury, pain, suffering, trauma; damage, impairment. VERB **= hurt**, injure, wound, maltreat, ill-treat, ill-use, abuse; damage, impair, spoil, mar.

harmful ADJ **= hurtful**, injurious, detrimental, damaging, deleterious, disadvantageous, destructive, dangerous, pernicious, bad.

harmless ADJ **= innocuous**, safe, non-toxic; inoffensive, unoffending, innocent, blameless.

harmonious ADJ **1 = melodious**, tuneful, musical, sweet-sounding, mellifluous, dulcet. **2 = peaceful**, friendly, amicable, cordial, amiable, congenial, united, cooperative, in tune, in accord, compatible, sympathetic.

harmony NOUN **1 = agreement**, accord, unanimity, cooperation, unity, unison, good will, amity, affinity, rapport, sympathy, friendship, fellowship, peace, peacefulness. **2 = compatibility**, congruity, consonance, coordination, balance, symmetry. **3 = tunefulness**, melodiousness, mellifluousness.

harrowing ADJ **= distressing**, agonizing, traumatic, heart-rending, heart-breaking, painful.

harsh ADJ **1 = grating**, jarring, rasping, strident, raucous, discordant, dissonant; rough,

guttural, hoarse.
2 = **garish**, gaudy, glaring, loud, bright, lurid.
3 = **cruel**, brutal, savage, barbarous, despotic, tyrannical, ruthless, merciless, pitiless, relentless, unrelenting, inhuman, hard-hearted.
4 = **severe**, stringent, stern, rigorous, uncompromising, punitive, draconian.
5 = **austere**, grim, hard, inhospitable, bleak, spartan.
harvest NOUN = **crop**, yield, produce, vintage. VERB = **gather**, reap, glean, pick.
haste NOUN = **speed**, swiftness, rapidity, briskness.
hasty ADJ **1** = **swift**, rapid, quick, fast, speedy, hurried, brisk.
2 = **impetuous**, reckless, rash, precipitate, impulsive, unthinking.
hatch VERB = **devise**, concoct, contrive, plan, invent, formulate, conceive, dream up, think up.
hate VERB = **loathe**, detest, abhor, dislike, despise, abominate.
hatred NOUN = **hate**, loathing, detestation, abhorrence, dislike, aversion, hostility, ill will, enmity, animosity, antipathy, revulsion, repugnance.
haughty ADJ = **arrogant**, proud, conceited, self-important, vain, pompous, condescending, supercilious, patronizing, snobbish, disdainful; [inf] snooty, high and mighty, stuck-up, hoity-toity.
haul VERB = **drag**, pull, tug, draw, heave, lug, tow.
haunt VERB **1** = **frequent**, patronize. **2** = **torment**, plague, disturb, trouble, worry, prey on someone's mind, weigh on, obsess.
have VERB **1** = **own**, possess, keep, use. **2** = **get**, receive; obtain, acquire, procure, secure, gain. **3** = **contain**, include, comprise, consist of. **4** = **experience**, undergo, encounter, meet, face, go through. **5** = **feel**, entertain, harbour, foster, nurse, cherish.
haven NOUN = **refuge**, shelter, sanctuary, asylum.
havoc NOUN
1 = **devastation**,

destruction, damage, rack and ruin. **2** = **chaos**, disorder, confusion, disruption, mayhem, disorganization.

hazard NOUN = **danger**, peril, risk, jeopardy, threat, menace.

hazardous ADJ = **dangerous**, risky, perilous, precarious, unsafe, insecure; [inf] dicey.

haze NOUN = **mist**, mistiness, fog, cloud, smog, vapour.

hazy ADJ **1** = **misty**, foggy, cloudy, smoggy. **2** = **vague**, indefinite, fuzzy, faint, unclear, dim, indistinct.

head NOUN **1** = **skull**, cranium. **2** = **mind**, intelligence, intellect, brain(s), wit, reasoning, understanding. **3** = **leader**, chief, commander, director, manager, superintendent, supervisor, principal, captain. **4** = **front**, fore, forefront, van, vanguard. VERB **1** = **lead**, be in charge of, command, control, run, supervise, rule, govern, guide. **2** (**head off**) = **divert**, intercept, deflect, turn aside, block

off, cut off.

headquarters NOUN = **head office**, base, HQ, command post, mission control.

heal VERB **1** = **cure**, remedy, treat. **2** = **reconcile**, patch up, settle, mend, resolve.

healthy ADJ **1** = **fit**, robust, strong, vigorous, flourishing, blooming, hale and hearty, in fine fettle; [inf] in the pink. **2** = **beneficial**, nutritious, nourishing, wholesome.

heap NOUN = **pile**, stack, mound, mountain, mass, accumulation, collection; hoard, store, stock. VERB = **pile up**, stack, collect, assemble; hoard, store, stock up.

hear VERB **1** = **discover**, learn, find out, gather, pick up, get wind of. **2** = **try**, judge, adjudge, adjudicate.

hearing NOUN = **inquiry**, trial, inquest, investigation, tribunal.

heart NOUN **1** = **passion**, love, affection, emotions, feelings. **2** = **tenderness**, compassion, sympathy, empathy, humanity, fellow feeling, goodwill, kindness. **3** = **spirit**,

enthusiasm, keenness,
eagerness, liveliness.
4 = **essence**, crux,
substance, core,
quintessence.

heartache NOUN = **sorrow**,
grief, sadness, anguish,
pain, agony, suffering,
misery, wretchedness,
despair, desolation.

heartbreaking ADJ = **sad**,
pitiful, tragic, poignant,
painful, agonizing,
distressing, upsetting,
heart-rending, bitter,
harrowing, traumatic.

heartfelt ADJ = **deep**,
profound, wholehearted,
sincere, earnest, genuine,
ardent, fervent,
passionate, enthusiastic,
eager.

heartless ADJ = **unfeeling**,
unsympathetic, unkind,
uncaring, cold, cold-
blooded, hard-hearted,
cruel, callous, hard,
merciless, pitiless,
inhuman.

heat NOUN 1 = **hotness**,
warmth, warmness.
2 = **passion**, warmth,
intensity, vehemence,
ardour, fervour, zeal,
eagerness, enthusiasm.
VERB = **warm (up)**, reheat,
cook.

heated ADJ = **vehement**,
passionate, fierce, angry,
furious, stormy, intense,
impassioned, animated,
spirited.

heathen NOUN = **pagan**,
infidel, idolater;
unbeliever, atheist;
heretic.

heave VERB = **lift**, haul, tug,
raise, hoist.

heaven NOUN 1 = **paradise**,
nirvana, the hereafter.
2 = **ecstasy**, bliss, rapture,
joy.

heavenly ADJ = **celestial**,
divine, holy, angelic,
seraphic.

heavy ADJ 1 = **weighty**,
hefty, substantial;
unwieldy, cumbersome.
2 = **hard**, forceful, strong,
powerful, violent, sharp.
3 = **arduous**, laborious,
strenuous, onerous,
demanding, difficult,
tough.

hectic ADJ = **busy**, active,
frantic, frenetic, frenzied,
manic, fast and furious.

hedge VERB 1 = **surround**,
enclose, encircle, border.
2 = **equivocate**,
prevaricate, temporize,
beat about the bush, hum
and haw.

heed NOUN = **attention**,

notice, note, regard; consideration, thought, care. VERB = **pay attention to**, attend to, take notice/note of, note, listen to, bear in mind, mind, mark, take into account.

hefty ADJ 1 = **heavy**, burly, big, large, muscular, brawny, strapping, sturdy, beefy, strong, powerful, well built. 2 = **substantial**, sizeable, huge, extortionate, stiff.

height NOUN 1 = **altitude**, elevation; tallness, stature. 2 = **top**, summit, peak, crest, crown, apex. 3 = **peak**, zenith, apex, climax, pinnacle, apogee.

heighten VERB 1 = **raise**, lift, elevate. 2 = **intensify**, increase, add to, augment, boost, strengthen, amplify, magnify, enhance.

help VERB 1 = **assist**, aid, lend a hand, be of service. 2 = **support**, back, contribute to, promote, boost. 3 = **soothe**, relieve, ameliorate, alleviate, assuage, ease. NOUN 1 = **assistance**, aid, service, support, benefit, use, advantage; guidance, advice, backing. 2 = **relief**,

alleviation, remedy, cure.

helper NOUN = **assistant**, aide, deputy, auxiliary, right-hand man/woman, henchman, colleague, associate, co-worker, partner, ally.

helpful ADJ 1 = **useful**, of use/service, beneficial, valuable, advantageous, practical, constructive, productive, instrumental. 2 = **supportive**, kind, obliging, accommodating, cooperative, neighbourly, charitable.

helping NOUN = **portion**, serving, ration, piece, plateful, share.

helpless ADJ = **defenceless**, unprotected, vulnerable, exposed; weak, incapable, powerless, impotent, dependent.

hem VERB (**hem in**) = **shut in**, fence in, confine, constrain, restrict, limit, trap; surround, enclose.

herd NOUN = **flock**, pack, mob, crowd, throng, horde. VERB = **drive**, round up, shepherd, guide, lead.

hereditary ADJ = **genetic**, congenital, inherited, innate, inborn, inbred.

heretic NOUN = **dissenter**, apostate, non-believer, agnostic, atheist, nonconformist, free thinker, iconoclast; pagan, heathen.

heritage NOUN = **history**, tradition, background, past; culture, customs.

hermit NOUN = **recluse**, solitary, anchorite.

heroic ADJ = **brave**, courageous, valiant, intrepid, fearless, gallant, valorous, stout-hearted, bold, daring, undaunted, dauntless, doughty.

hesitant ADJ **1** = **uncertain**, unsure, undecided, doubtful, dubious, sceptical, irresolute, indecisive, vacillating, wavering; diffident, timid, shy. **2** = **reluctant**, unwilling, disinclined.

hesitate VERB **1** = **delay**, pause, hang back, wait, vacillate, waver, dither, shilly-shally, stall, temporize. **2** = **demur**, scruple, have misgivings, think twice.

hew VERB = **chop**, hack, cut, saw, lop; carve, sculpt, shape, fashion.

hidden ADJ **1** = **concealed**, secret, unseen, out of sight, camouflaged, disguised. **2** = **obscure**, indefinite, unclear, vague, cryptic, mysterious, abstruse, arcane.

hide VERB **1** = **go into hiding**, take cover, lie low, go to ground, go underground. **2** = **conceal**, secrete; [inf] stash. **3** = **obscure**, block, veil, eclipse, cloud, shroud. **4** = **keep secret**, cover up, mask, camouflage, disguise.

hideous ADJ = **ugly**, unsightly, grotesque, monstrous, repulsive, repellent, revolting, gruesome, disgusting, ghastly.

hierarchy NOUN = **ranking**, grading, ladder, pecking order.

high ADJ **1** = **tall**, lofty, soaring, towering, steep. **2** = **high-ranking**, leading, top, powerful, important, prominent, eminent, influential, distinguished, illustrious. **3** = **good**, favourable, approving, admiring, flattering, complimentary. **4** see **excellent**.

highbrow ADJ = **intellectual**, scholarly, bookish, academic, cultured.

high-handed ADJ
= **autocratic**, tyrannical,
domineering,
overbearing, imperious,
peremptory, arrogant,
bossy.

hilarious ADJ = **hysterical**,
uproarious, side-splitting.

hill NOUN 1 = **hillock**, knoll,
hummock, tor, mound,
mount. 2 = **slope**, incline,
gradient, bank.

hinder VERB = **hamper**,
obstruct, impede, inhibit,
curb, delay, interfere with,
set back, slow down, hold
up; restrict, constrain,
block, check, curtail,
frustrate, handicap.

hindrance NOUN
= **impediment**, obstacle,
obstruction, hurdle,
handicap, block, bar,
barrier, drawback, snag,
difficulty, stumbling
block.

hint NOUN 1 = **clue**, inkling,
indication, intimation,
mention; tip-off. 2 = **tip**,
pointer, advice, help,
suggestion. 3 = **touch**,
trace, dash, soupçon,
tinge, taste. VERB
= **suggest**, insinuate,
imply, indicate, allude to,
intimate, suggest.

hire VERB 1 = **rent**, lease,
charter. 2 = **appoint**, sign
on, take on, engage,
employ.

historic ADJ = **famed**,
notable, famous,
celebrated, renowned,
momentous, significant,
important, consequential,
memorable, remarkable,
epoch-making, red-letter.

historical ADJ
= **documented**, recorded,
chronicled, archival,
authentic, factual, actual;
past, bygone.

history NOUN 1 = **annal**,
record, chronicle,
account, narrative, report,
memoir. 2 = **background**,
past, experiences,
antecedents. 3 = **the past**,
former times, bygone
days, time gone by,
antiquity.

hit VERB 1 = **strike**, smack,
slap, punch, box, cuff,
buffet, thump, batter,
pound, pummel, thrash,
hammer, bang, knock,
club, swat; [inf] whack,
wallop, bash, belt, clout,
clobber. 2 = **run into**,
collide with, bang into,
bump into.

hoard VERB = **store (up)**,
stock up, stockpile, put

hoarse

by, lay in, set aside, save, accumulate, amass, collect, gather, squirrel away; [inf] stash away. NOUN = **store**, stockpile, supply, reserve, fund, cache, reservoir, accumulation; [inf] stash.

hoarse ADJ = **croaky**, gruff, rough, throaty, harsh, husky, gravelly, rasping, guttural.

hoax NOUN = **practical joke**, prank, trick; fraud; [inf] scam. VERB = **trick**, fool, deceive, hoodwink, delude, dupe, take in; [inf] con.

hobble VERB = **limp**, stumble, totter, stagger.

hobby NOUN = **interest**, pursuit, pastime, diversion, recreation.

hobnob VERB = **associate**, fraternize, socialize, mingle, mix, consort.

hold VERB 1 = **clasp**, clutch, grasp, grip, clench, seize, cling to. 2 = **bear**, carry, take, support, hold up, sustain. 3 = **detain**, confine, lock up, imprison, incarcerate. 4 = **keep**, occupy, engage, absorb, engross, catch, capture. 5 = **contain**, take, accommodate. 6 = **stand**, apply, be in force, exist, be the case. NOUN 1 = **grip**, grasp, clutch, clasp. 2 = **control**, power, influence, mastery, authority, sway.

holder NOUN 1 = **owner**, possessor, bearer, keeper, custodian. 2 = **container**, case, casing, receptacle, stand, cover, covering, housing, sheath.

hole NOUN 1 = **opening**, aperture, gap, orifice, space, breach, break, fissure, crack, rift, puncture, perforation, cut, split, gash, slit, vent. 2 = **pit**, crater, cavity, pothole, depression, hollow.

holiness NOUN = **sanctity**, sanctitude, saintliness, divinity, spirituality, piety, virtue, purity.

hollow ADJ 1 = **empty**, vacant, unfilled, void. 2 = **sunken**, deep-set, concave. 3 = **worthless**, empty, pointless, meaningless, useless, futile, pyrrhic. NOUN = **indentation**, depression, dip, hole, crater, cavern, pit, cavity, trough.

holocaust NOUN = **genocide**, mass murder,

honourable

annihilation, massacre, slaughter, extermination, butchery, ethnic cleansing.

holy ADJ **1** = **devout**, God-fearing, pious, spiritual, religious, good, virtuous, pure, saintly. **2** = **sacred**, blessed, sanctified, consecrated, hallowed, divine.

home NOUN **1** = **house**, abode, residence, domicile, dwelling, habitation. **2** = **homeland**, birthplace, fatherland, motherland. VERB (**home in on**) = **aim at**, focus on, concentrate on, pinpoint, zero in on.

homeless ADJ = **of no fixed abode**, down-and-out, vagrant, itinerant, on the streets.

homely ADJ = **comfortable**, cosy, snug, welcoming, friendly, relaxed, informal.

homily NOUN = **sermon**, lecture, speech, address, discourse, lesson, talk, oration.

honest ADJ **1** = **principled**, upright, honourable, ethical, moral, righteous, virtuous, good, worthy, decent, law-abiding,

upstanding, incorruptible, trustworthy, reliable, scrupulous, reputable. **2** = **truthful**, frank, candid, forthright, straightforward, open, straight; [inf] upfront.

honorary ADJ = **nominal**, titular, in name only; unpaid, unsalaried.

honour NOUN **1** = **honesty**, integrity, ethics, morals, high principles, virtue, rectitude, decency, probity, truthfulness, trustworthiness, reliability. **2** = **glory**, prestige, privilege, kudos, cachet, distinction, merit, credit; esteem, respect. VERB **1** = **esteem**, respect, admire, defer to; revere, venerate, worship. **2** = **acclaim**, applaud, salute, lionize, pay homage/tribute to, praise, eulogize. **3** = **fulfil**, discharge, carry out, observe, keep (to), be true to.

honourable ADJ = **honest**, upright, ethical, moral, principled, upstanding, righteous, right-minded, virtuous, good, decent, fair, just, truthful, trustworthy, reliable, dependable.

hooligan NOUN = **thug**, vandal, lout, delinquent, ruffian, tearaway, hoodlum; [inf] yob.

hoop NOUN = **ring**, band, circle, loop.

hop VERB = **jump**, leap, bound, spring, skip, caper, dance.

hope NOUN = **expectation**, hopefulness, expectancy, anticipation, desire, wish, aspiration, ambition, dream; belief, assurance, confidence, conviction, faith, trust, optimism. VERB = **expect**, anticipate, wish for, aspire to, dream of.

hopeful ADJ 1 = **optimistic**, confident, positive, buoyant, sanguine; [inf] upbeat. 2 = **encouraging**, promising, heartening, reassuring, favourable, auspicious, propitious.

hopeless ADJ = **despairing**, in despair, desperate, pessimistic, despondent, demoralized, wretched, defeatist.

horde NOUN = **crowd**, throng, mob, mass, multitude, host, army, pack, gang, troop, drove, swarm, flock.

horrible ADJ 1 = **awful**, dreadful, terrible, horrific, horrifying, frightful, fearful, horrendous, shocking, gruesome, hideous, grim, ghastly, harrowing, abominable, appalling. 2 = **disagreeable**, nasty, unpleasant, obnoxious, odious, revolting, repulsive, loathsome, abhorrent, hateful, vile, insufferable.

horrify VERB = **shock**, appal, outrage, scandalize, disgust, revolt, repel, nauseate, sicken, offend.

horror NOUN 1 = **terror**, fear, alarm, fright, dread, panic, trepidation; loathing, disgust, revulsion, abhorrence. 2 = **atrocity**, outrage.

horse NOUN = **pony**, foal, colt, stallion, mare, steed, mount, hack, nag, filly.

hospitable ADJ = **welcoming**, sociable, friendly, convivial, neighbourly, kind, warm, helpful, obliging, generous.

hospital NOUN = **clinic**, infirmary, sanatorium,

hospice.

host NOUN = **presenter**, compère, master of ceremonies, MC, anchorman, anchorwoman.

hostile ADJ = **unfriendly**, unkind, bitter, unsympathetic, malicious, vicious, rancorous, venomous; antagonistic, aggressive, confrontational, belligerent, truculent.

hostility NOUN = **antagonism**, unfriendliness, malevolence, malice, ill will, rancour, venom, hatred, enmity, animosity; aggression, belligerence.

hot ADJ 1 = **heated**, boiling, piping hot, scalding, sizzling; scorching, roasting, searing, sweltering, baking, torrid, sultry, humid, muggy. 2 = **spicy**, peppery, piquant, pungent.

house NOUN 1 = **residence**, abode, home, domicile, habitation. 2 = **family**, clan, line, dynasty, lineage, ancestry. VERB = **accommodate**, lodge, put up, take in; shelter,

harbour.

household NOUN = **family**, house, ménage, establishment.

hover VERB 1 = **float**, be suspended, hang. 2 = **linger**, loiter, wait, hang about.

howl VERB = **bay**, yowl, yelp, bark; cry, wail, bellow.

hub NOUN = **centre**, middle, core, heart, focus, focal point.

huddle VERB = **crowd**, throng, press, pack, cluster, herd, squeeze, gather, congregate.

hue NOUN = **colour**, tone, shade, tint, tinge.

hug VERB = **embrace**, cuddle, hold close/tight, cling to, squeeze.

huge ADJ = **enormous**, immense, great, massive, colossal, vast, prodigious, gigantic, giant, gargantuan, mammoth, monumental, mountainous, titanic.

hull NOUN = **framework**, body, frame, skeleton, structure.

hum VERB = **murmur**, drone, vibrate, thrum, buzz, whirr, purr.

human ADJ 1 = **mortal**, flesh and blood, fallible, weak, vulnerable, erring, imperfect. **2 = kind**, kindly, considerate, understanding, sympathetic, compassionate, humane, tolerant.

humane ADJ **= kind**, compassionate, understanding, considerate, sympathetic, forgiving, merciful, lenient, forbearing, gentle, tender, benign, benevolent, charitable, humanitarian.

humble ADJ **1 = meek**, deferential, respectful, submissive, self-effacing, unassertive, modest. **2 = lowly**, poor, undistinguished, mean, ignoble, low-born; common, ordinary, simple, inferior, unremarkable, unpretentious. VERB **= humiliate**, mortify, subdue, demean, shame.

humdrum ADJ **= commonplace**, routine, run-of-the-mill, unvaried, uneventful, ordinary, everyday, mundane, monotonous, dull, uninteresting, boring, tedious, prosaic.

humiliate VERB **= mortify**, shame, humble, disgrace, embarrass, discomfit, chasten, subdue, deflate, abash, abase, degrade, crush, demean.

humility NOUN **= humbleness**, modesty, meekness, diffidence, lack of vanity/pride.

humorous ADJ **= funny**, amusing, entertaining, witty, comical, jocular, hilarious, droll.

humour NOUN **1 = comedy**, jokes, gags, wit, witticisms. **2 = mood**, temper, temperament, state of mind, disposition, spirits.

hump NOUN **= protrusion**, protuberance, projection, bulge, swelling, lump, bump, knob.

hunch NOUN **= feeling**, intuition, suspicion, inkling, impression, idea.

hunger NOUN **1 = lack of food**, starvation, ravenousness. **2 = longing**, craving, yearning, desire, thirst, appetite, hankering, lust.

hungry ADJ **1 = famished**, ravenous, starving, starved, empty. **2 = longing**, yearning, craving, eager, keen, desirous, greedy, covetous.

hunt VERB 1 = **chase**, pursue, stalk, track, trail, follow, shadow; [inf] tail. 2 = **search for**, look for, seek, try to find.

hurdle NOUN 1 = **fence**, barrier, railing, rail, bar. 2 = **obstacle**, hindrance, impediment, obstruction, stumbling block, snag, complication, difficulty, problem, handicap.

hurried ADJ = **quick**, rapid, fast, swift, speedy, hasty, rushed, cursory, superficial, perfunctory.

hurry VERB = **be quick**, make haste, hasten, speed, run, dash, rush, sprint, scurry; [inf] get a move on, step on it, hotfoot it.

hurt VERB 1 = **ache**, smart, sting, throb, burn. 2 = **injure**, wound, bruise, cut, scratch, lacerate, maim, damage, mutilate. 3 = **upset**, sadden, grieve, distress, pain, cut to the quick. 4 = **harm**, damage, spoil, blight, mar, impair.

hurtful ADJ = **upsetting**, wounding, distressing, unkind, nasty, mean, spiteful, malicious, cutting, cruel.

husband NOUN = **spouse**, partner, consort; groom, bridegroom.

hush VERB = **silence**, quieten, shush, shut up. NOUN = **quiet**, quietness, silence, stillness, peace, calm, tranquillity.

hustle VERB = **push**, shove, jostle, elbow, nudge, shoulder; thrust, manhandle, frogmarch.

hut NOUN = **shed**, lean-to, shack, cabin, shanty, hovel; [Scottish] bothy.

hygienic ADJ = **sanitary**, clean, germ-free, disinfected, sterilized, sterile, aseptic, uncontaminated.

hypnotize VERB = **mesmerize**, entrance, enthral, spellbind, transfix, bewitch, captivate.

hypocrisy NOUN = **insincerity**, falseness, sanctimoniousness, dishonesty, cant, pietism.

hypocritical ADJ = **sanctimonious**, pious, false, insincere, dishonest, two-faced; [inf] phoney.

hypothesis NOUN = **theory**, thesis, theorem,

proposition, premise,
postulate, supposition,
assumption, conjecture,
speculation.
hypothetical ADJ
= **theoretical**, speculative,
notional, academic,
suppositional.
hysteria NOUN = **hysterics**,

frenzy, madness,
delirium, derangement,
mania.
hysterical ADJ = **frenzied**,
frantic, wild, out of
control, berserk, beside
yourself, distraught;
deranged, delirious,
raving.

icy ADJ 1 = **freezing**, chilly,
frigid, frosty, biting, raw,
bitter, arctic, glacial.
2 = **frozen**, glassy, slippery,
slippy.
idea NOUN 1 = **concept**,
thought, conception,
image, notion. 2 = **theory**,
view, viewpoint, opinion,
belief. 3 = **impression**,
feeling, sense, suspicion,
inkling, hunch. 4 = **plan**,
design, aim, scheme,
intention, objective,
object, goal, target.
ideal ADJ 1 = **perfect**,
consummate, supreme,
flawless, exemplary,
classic, archetypal, model.
2 = **unattainable**, Utopian,
impracticable, ivory-

towered, imaginary,
romantic, fairy-tale. NOUN
1 = **archetype**, model,
pattern, exemplar,
paradigm, yardstick.
2 = **principle**, standard,
value; morals, ethics.
idealistic ADJ
= **impractical**, Utopian,
visionary, romantic,
quixotic, unrealistic; [inf]
starry-eyed.
identical ADJ 1 = **the same**,
the very same, one and
the same, selfsame.
2 = **alike**,
indistinguishable,
corresponding, matching,
twin.
identify VERB 1 = **recognize**,
single out, pick out, spot,

point out, pinpoint, discern, distinguish, name. 2 = **establish**, find out, ascertain, diagnose. 3 = **relate to**, empathize with, sympathize with, feel for.

identity NOUN 1 = **name**, specification.
2 = **personality**, self, selfhood, individuality.

ideology NOUN = **doctrine**, creed, credo, teaching, dogma, theory, tenets, beliefs, ideas, principles, convictions.

idiom NOUN 1 = **phrase**, expression, turn of phrase. 2 = **language**, speech, usage, vocabulary, parlance, jargon; [inf] lingo.

idiomatic ADJ = **colloquial**, informal, vernacular, conversational, natural.

idiosyncrasy NOUN = **peculiarity**, oddity, eccentricity, trait, mannerism, quirk, habit, characteristic, foible.

idiot NOUN = **fool**, ass, halfwit, blockhead, dunce, ignoramus, dolt, simpleton; [inf] numbskull, nincompoop, ninny, nit, dope, clot, chump, dimwit, moron, twit.

idiotic ADJ = **stupid**, foolish, senseless, absurd, fatuous, inane, asinine, half-witted, hare-brained, lunatic, crazy, insane, mad, moronic, nonsensical, ridiculous.

idle ADJ 1 = **lazy**, indolent, slothful, sluggish, shiftless. 2 = **inoperative**, out of action, inactive, unused. 3 = **empty**, unoccupied, vacant, spare, aimless.

idol NOUN 1 = **icon**, effigy, graven image, fetish, totem. 2 = **hero**, heroine, star, celebrity, favourite, darling; [inf] blue-eyed boy.

idolize VERB = **hero-worship**, worship, adore, dote on, lionize, revere, venerate.

ignite VERB 1 = **set fire to**, light, set on fire, kindle, touch off. 2 = **catch fire**, burn, burst into flames.

ignominious ADJ = **humiliating**, mortifying, undignified, ignoble, inglorious, embarrassing, undignified; shameful, dishonourable, disgraceful, discreditable.

ignorant ADJ 1 = **uneducated**, unschooled, illiterate,

ignore

benighted. **2** = **unaware**, unfamiliar, unconscious, unacquainted, uninformed, unenlightened; [inf] in the dark.

ignore VERB **1** = **disregard**, pay no attention to, take no notice of, brush aside, shrug off, turn a blind eye to, turn a deaf ear to.
2 = **slight**, spurn, cold-shoulder, send to Coventry, cut.

ill ADJ = **sick**, unwell, poorly, ailing, sickly, infirm, off-colour, indisposed; nauseous, queasy.

ill-advised ADJ = **unwise**, imprudent, injudicious, misguided, foolish, foolhardy, rash, short-sighted.

illegal ADJ = **unlawful**, illegitimate, illicit, criminal, felonious, unauthorized, banned, forbidden, prohibited, proscribed, contraband, black-market, bootleg.

illness NOUN = **sickness**, ailment, disease, complaint, malady, disorder, affliction, indisposition, infection.

illogical ADJ = **irrational**, unreasonable, unsound, incorrect, invalid, erroneous, fallacious, faulty, flawed, specious, unscientific.

ill-treat VERB = **mistreat**, abuse, harm, injure, damage, maltreat, misuse.

illuminating ADJ = **instructive**, informative, enlightening, explanatory, revealing, helpful.

illusion NOUN **1** = **delusion**, misapprehension, misconception, fantasy.
2 = **hallucination**, figment of the imagination, mirage.

illusory ADJ = **imagined**, imaginary, fanciful, fancied, unreal; false, mistaken, misleading.

illustrate VERB
1 = **decorate**, adorn, ornament, embellish.
2 = **demonstrate**, exemplify, show, display; explain, elucidate, clarify.

illustration NOUN = **picture**, drawing, sketch, figure, plate, artwork.

image NOUN = **likeness**, representation, depiction, portrayal, painting, picture, portrait, effigy, figure, statue, sculpture, bust.

imaginary ADJ = **unreal**, non-existent, illusory, fanciful, chimerical; fictitious, fictional, mythical, made-up, invented.

imagination NOUN = **creativity**, vision, inspiration, inventiveness, originality, innovation, ingenuity.

imaginative ADJ = **creative**, inventive, original, innovative, visionary, inspired, resourceful, ingenious.

imagine VERB 1 = **picture**, visualize, see in your mind's eye, envision, envisage, conjure up. 2 = **assume**, presume, expect, suppose, think, believe, take it, dare say, surmise, guess, reckon.

imitate VERB 1 = **copy**, emulate, mirror, echo. 2 = **mimic**, ape, impersonate, parody, mock, caricature; [inf] send up, take off.

imitation NOUN 1 = **copy**, reproduction, replica, simulation. 2 = **mimicry**, impersonation, impression, parody, caricature, burlesque; [inf]

send-up, take-off, spoof. ADJ = **artificial**, simulated, synthetic, man-made, mock, fake, ersatz.

immature ADJ = **childish**, juvenile, infantile, babyish, puerile, callow, jejune, inexperienced, unsophisticated.

immediate ADJ = **instant**, instantaneous, prompt, swift, speedy; sudden, abrupt, precipitate.

immediately ADV = **right away**, right now, straight away, at once, instantly, now, this minute, directly, promptly, without delay.

immense ADJ = **huge**, vast, massive, enormous, gigantic, colossal, giant, great, extensive, monumental, tremendous, prodigious, elephantine, titanic.

immerse VERB 1 = **submerge**, plunge, dip, dunk, duck, sink. 2 = **absorb**, engross, occupy, engage, preoccupy, involve, bury.

immigrant NOUN = **settler**, newcomer, incomer, migrant, emigrant.

imminent ADJ = **impending**,

approaching, close at hand, near, coming, forthcoming, in the offing, on the horizon, on the way, brewing, looming.

immobile ADJ = **unmoving**, motionless, still, static, stationary, at a standstill, stock-still, rooted to the spot.

immoral ADJ = **bad**, wicked, evil, unprincipled, dishonest, unethical, sinful, corrupt, depraved, vile, base, degenerate, debauched, dissolute, indecent, lewd, licentious.

immortal ADJ = **undying**, eternal, deathless, everlasting, never-ending, endless, imperishable, indestructible, lasting, enduring, immutable.

impact NOUN 1 = **collision**, crash, smash, bump, knock, bang. 2 = **influence**, effect; results, consequences, repercussions.

impair VERB = **weaken**, lessen, decrease, reduce, diminish, damage, mar, spoil, injure, harm, hinder, impede, undermine.

impart VERB = **pass on**, convey, communicate, transmit, relate, tell, make known, report; disclose, reveal, divulge.

impartial ADJ = **unbiased**, unprejudiced, disinterested, objective, detached, neutral, equitable, even-handed, fair, just, open-minded.

impatient ADJ 1 = **restless**, restive, agitated, nervous, edgy. 2 = **eager**, anxious, keen, yearning, longing. 3 = **irritable**, testy, tetchy, snappy, querulous, peevish, short-tempered, intolerant.

impede VERB = **hinder**, obstruct, hamper, handicap, block, check, curb, bar, hold up/back, delay, interfere with, disrupt, slow down, thwart, frustrate, baulk, stop.

impediment NOUN = **hindrance**, obstruction, obstacle, handicap, block, stumbling block, check, bar, barrier, drawback, difficulty, snag, setback.

imperceptible ADJ = **unnoticeable**, indiscernible, invisible; slight, small, subtle, faint, fine, negligible, microscopic, minute.

imperfect ADJ 1 = **faulty**, flawed, defective, blemished, damaged, broken. 2 = **deficient**, inadequate, insufficient, rudimentary, limited, patchy, sketchy.

imperfection NOUN 1 = **fault**, flaw, defect, blemish, deformity; crack, scratch, stain, spot, mark. 2 = **failing**, foible, deficiency, weakness, shortcoming, limitation.

imperious ADJ = **overbearing**, overweening, domineering, peremptory, arrogant, high-handed, assertive, commanding, authoritarian, dictatorial, bossy.

impersonal ADJ = **aloof**, distant, remote, unemotional, formal, stiff, businesslike.

impersonate VERB = **imitate**, mimic, ape, mock, parody, caricature, masquerade as, pose as, pass yourself off as.

impertinent ADJ = **insolent**, impudent, cheeky, rude, impolite, discourteous, disrespectful, bold, brazen, forward.

imperturbable ADJ = **self-possessed**, composed, collected, calm, serene, unexcitable, unflappable, cool, placid, even-tempered, phlegmatic.

impetuous ADJ = **impulsive**, hasty, hot-headed, rash, reckless, precipitate, foolhardy, incautious; spontaneous, impromptu, spur-of-the-moment, unthinking, unplanned.

impetus NOUN 1 = **momentum**, energy, force, drive, power, propulsion. 2 = **stimulus**, motivation, incentive, inducement, inspiration, encouragement, push, boost.

implausible ADJ = **unlikely**, improbable, hard to believe, unconvincing, far-fetched, incredible, unbelievable.

implement NOUN = **tool**, utensil, appliance, instrument, gadget, device, apparatus, contrivance. VERB = **carry out**, fulfil, execute, perform, discharge, accomplish, achieve, realize, bring about, enact.

implication NOUN
= **suggestion**, inference, insinuation, innuendo, hint, intimation, imputation.

implicit ADJ 1 = **implied**, indirect, unspoken, unstated, tacit, understood. 2 = **absolute**, complete, total, wholehearted, utter, unqualified, unconditional, unreserved, unquestioning.

implore VERB = **beg**, appeal to, entreat, plead with, beseech, ask, request, importune.

imply VERB = **insinuate**, hint, suggest, intimate, make out.

important ADJ
1 = **significant**, crucial, far-reaching, critical, vital, pivotal, momentous, weighty, serious, grave, urgent, consequential; salient, chief, main, principal, major, paramount; necessary, essential, indispensable.
2 = **eminent**, prominent, pre-eminent, leading, foremost, outstanding, distinguished, esteemed, notable, influential, powerful, high-ranking, prestigious.

imposing ADJ
= **impressive**, striking, grand, splendid, majestic, spectacular.

impossible ADJ = **out of the question**, inconceivable, unthinkable, unimaginable, impracticable, unattainable, unworkable.

impostor NOUN = **fake**, fraud, charlatan, mountebank, trickster, cheat; [inf] con man.

impractical ADJ
= **unrealistic**, unworkable, unfeasible, impracticable, non-viable; unsuitable, inappropriate.

imprecise ADJ = **inexact**, approximate, estimated, rough, inaccurate, incorrect.

impress VERB = **make an impact on**, move, stir, sway, influence, affect, rouse, inspire, galvanize.

impression NOUN
1 = **effect**, influence,

impact. **2** = **mark**, indentation, dent, outline, imprint.
3 = **feeling**, sense, perception, notion, idea, belief, opinion, suspicion, inkling, intuition, hunch.
4 = **impersonation**, imitation, mimicry, parody, caricature; [inf] take-off, send-up.

impressionable ADJ = **suggestible**, susceptible, pliable, malleable, gullible, ingenuous, naive.

impressive ADJ = **imposing**, striking, magnificent, splendid, spectacular, stirring, rousing, exciting, powerful, inspiring.

imprison VERB = **put in prison**, jail, lock up, put under lock and key, incarcerate, confine, intern.

imprisonment NOUN = **custody**, incarceration, internment, confinement, detention.

improbable ADJ = **unlikely**, doubtful, questionable, dubious, implausible, far-fetched, unconvincing, unbelievable, incredible.

impromptu ADJ = **unrehearsed**, ad lib, unprepared, extempore, spontaneous, improvised, unscripted; [inf] off-the-cuff.

improper ADJ
1 = **unseemly**, unbecoming, inappropriate, unsuitable, unethical. **2** = **indecent**, off-colour, risqué, suggestive, smutty, obscene, lewd.

improve VERB = **ameliorate**, amend, reform, rehabilitate, set/put right, correct, rectify, upgrade, revamp, modernize; progress, make progress, pick up, rally, look up.

improvement NOUN = **amelioration**, reform, reformation, rehabilitation, rectification, upgrade, revamp, progress, rally, recovery, upswing.

impudent ADJ see **impertinent**.

impulse NOUN **1** = **urge**, instinct, compulsion, drive. **2** = **stimulus**, inspiration, stimulation, incentive, spur, motivation.

impulsive ADJ = **impetuous**,

spontaneous, instinctive, unplanned, spur-of-the-moment; hasty, precipitate, rash, reckless, foolhardy, madcap, devil-may-care.

inaccurate ADJ = **inexact**, imprecise, incorrect, wrong, erroneous, faulty, imperfect, flawed, defective, unreliable; fallacious, false, mistaken, untrue.

inadequate ADJ = **insufficient**, lacking, wanting, deficient, in short supply, meagre, scanty, scant, niggardly, scarce, sparse.

inadvertent ADJ = **accidental**, unintentional, unpremeditated, unplanned, unconscious, unwitting, unthinking.

inanimate ADJ = **lifeless**, insentient, insensate, dead, defunct.

inappropriate ADJ = **unsuitable**, unfitting, out of place, unseemly, unbecoming, improper, indecorous, inapposite, incongruous, out of keeping.

inarticulate ADJ 1 = **unintelligible**, incomprehensible, incoherent, unclear, indistinct, mumbled. 2 = **tongue-tied**, lost for words.

inauspicious ADJ = **unpropitious**, unpromising, unfortunate, unfavourable, ill-omened, ominous.

incapable ADJ = **incompetent**, ineffective, ineffectual, inadequate, inept, useless, feeble.

incessant ADJ = **unceasing**, ceaseless, non-stop, endless, unending, never-ending, everlasting, eternal, constant, continual, perpetual, continuous, uninterrupted, unbroken, unremitting.

incident NOUN 1 = **event**, happening, occurrence, episode, experience, proceeding, occasion. 2 = **disturbance**, commotion, scene, row, fracas, contretemps, skirmish, clash, conflict, confrontation.

incidental ADJ = **secondary**, subsidiary, subordinate, minor, peripheral, inessential, non-essential, inconsequential, tangential.

incite VERB **1** = **instigate**, provoke, foment, whip up, stir up. **2** = **encourage**, urge, egg on, goad, spur, prod, stimulate, drive.

inclination NOUN = **tendency**, leaning, propensity, proclivity, predisposition, weakness, penchant, predilection, partiality, preference, affinity.

incline VERB **1** = **tend**, lean, swing, veer. **2** = **bend**, slope, slant, bank, cant, tilt, lean, tip, list. NOUN = **slope**, gradient, hill, declivity, descent, ascent, ramp, rise.

include VERB **1** = **contain**, take in, incorporate, cover, embrace, encompass, comprise. **2** = **add**, allow for, count, take into account.

incoherent ADJ = **disconnected**, disjointed, disordered, confused, unclear, mixed up, muddled, jumbled, garbled, rambling, unintelligible, inarticulate.

income NOUN = **salary**, pay, earnings, wages, remuneration; takings, profits, revenue, proceeds.

incomparable ADJ = **inimitable**, unequalled, matchless, nonpareil, unrivalled, peerless, unparalleled, unsurpassed, superlative, supreme.

incompatible ADJ = **unsuited**, mismatched, ill-matched; irreconcilable, conflicting, discordant.

incompetent ADJ = **incapable**, inept, inefficient, unqualified, useless, inadequate, deficient, inexpert, unskilful, bungling, amateurish.

incomprehensible ADJ = **unintelligible**, impenetrable, indecipherable, over your head, unfathomable, baffling, bewildering, mystifying, arcane, abstruse, recondite.

inconceivable ADJ = **unimaginable**, unthinkable, incredible, unbelievable, impossible, out of the question.

inconclusive ADJ

incongruous

= **indefinite**, indeterminate, indecisive, undetermined, unsettled, unresolved, ambiguous.

incongruous ADJ = **out of place**, inappropriate, discordant, jarring, out of keeping, at odds, strange, odd, unsuitable.

inconsiderate ADJ = **thoughtless**, unthinking, uncaring, insensitive, tactless, uncharitable, unkind, ungracious, selfish.

inconsistent ADJ = **incompatible**, out of keeping, contrary, at odds, at variance, in opposition, conflicting, in conflict.

inconspicuous ADJ = **unobtrusive**, unnoticeable, ordinary, plain, unremarkable, undistinguished, unexceptional.

inconvenience NOUN = **trouble**, bother, disruption, disturbance, problems, annoyance, difficulty; [inf] hassle.

inconvenient ADJ = **awkward**, unsuitable, inappropriate, inopportune, inexpedient, troublesome, bothersome, tiresome, vexatious, annoying, ill-timed, untimely.

incorporate VERB = **include**, embrace, absorb, integrate, assimilate, subsume, embody, encompass.

incorrect ADJ = **wrong**, inaccurate, erroneous, mistaken, wide of the mark, inexact, false, fallacious.

incorrigible ADJ = **inveterate**, habitual, hardened, incurable, hopeless, unrepentant.

increase VERB = **grow**, expand, extend, multiply, intensify, heighten, mount, escalate, mushroom, snowball, spread; add to, enhance, build up, enlarge, augment, raise, strengthen, step up. NOUN = **growth**, rise, enlargement, expansion, extension, increment, addition, intensification, escalation.

incredible ADJ 1 = **unbelievable**, hard to believe, far-fetched, unconvincing, inconceivable,

unimaginable,
unthinkable, impossible.
2 = **extraordinary**,
wonderful, great,
supreme, tremendous,
marvellous, amazing,
magnificent,
phenomenal, spectacular.

incredulous ADJ
= **disbelieving**, sceptical,
cynical, distrustful,
mistrustful, doubtful,
dubious, unconvinced,
suspicious.

incriminate VERB
= **implicate**, involve,
inculpate, inform against,
blame, accuse, pin the
blame on, point the
finger at.

indecent ADJ = **improper**,
indelicate, risqué, off-
colour, ribald, bawdy,
vulgar, crude, obscene,
dirty, smutty, coarse,
lewd, lascivious,
salacious, pornographic,
raunchy.

indecisive ADJ
= **irresolute**, hesitant, in
two minds, wavering,
vacillating, ambivalent,
undecided, uncertain.

indefatigable ADJ
= **tireless**, untiring,
unflagging, persistent,
tenacious, dogged,

assiduous, industrious,
indomitable, relentless.

indefinite ADJ = **vague**,
unclear, imprecise,
inexact, ambiguous,
ambivalent, equivocal,
evasive; indeterminate,
unspecified.

independence NOUN
1 = **self-government**,
autonomy, self-
determination,
sovereignty, freedom,
home rule. **2** = **freedom**,
liberty, self-sufficiency,
self-reliance.

independent ADJ **1** = **self-
governing**, autonomous,
free, sovereign, self-
determining, non-
aligned. **2** = **self-sufficient**,
self-reliant, self-
supporting, standing on
your own two feet.
3 = **separate**,
unconnected, unrelated,
distinct, different.

indestructible ADJ
= **unbreakable**, durable,
imperishable, enduring,
perennial, deathless,
undying, immortal,
everlasting.

indicate VERB = **show**,
demonstrate, point to,
signal, signify, denote,
betoken, suggest, imply;

indication

display, manifest, reveal, betray; make known, state, declare.

indication NOUN = **sign**, symptom, mark, manifestation, demonstration, evidence, signal; omen, augury, portent, warning.

indifferent ADJ = **unconcerned**, apathetic, uninterested, unenthusiastic, unimpressed, detached, impassive, dispassionate, unresponsive, unmoved.

indigenous ADJ = **native**, original, aboriginal.

indignant ADJ = **angry**, irate, annoyed, cross, aggrieved, affronted, irritated, vexed, riled, exasperated, piqued, disgruntled.

indirect ADJ **1** = **circuitous**, roundabout, meandering, winding, zigzag; tortuous. **2** = **oblique**, inexplicit, implicit, implied.

indiscreet ADJ = **imprudent**, unwise, incautious, injudicious, ill-advised, ill-judged, foolish, impolitic, careless, tactless, insensitive, undiplomatic.

indiscriminate ADJ = **non-selective**, unselective, undiscriminating, aimless, hit-or-miss, haphazard, random, arbitrary, unsystematic, unthinking, casual, careless.

indispensable ADJ = **essential**, vital, all-important, crucial, imperative, key, necessary, requisite.

indisputable ADJ = **incontestable**, incontrovertible, undeniable, irrefutable, unquestionable, indubitable, certain, sure, definite, conclusive.

indistinct ADJ **1** = **blurred**, fuzzy, out of focus, bleary, hazy, misty, shadowy, dim, obscure, indefinite. **2** = **muffled**, muted, low, muttered, mumbled.

individual ADJ **1** = **single**, separate, discrete; lone, sole, solitary. **2** = **characteristic**, distinctive, distinct, particular, peculiar, personal, personalized, special.

induce VERB **1** = **persuade**, convince, talk into, prevail on, move, prompt, inspire, influence,

encourage, motivate.
2 = **bring about**, cause, produce, create, give rise to, generate, engender, occasion, lead to.

indulge VERB = **pamper**, spoil, mollycoddle, pander to, humour, go along with.

indulgent ADJ = **permissive**, easy-going, compliant, fond, doting, soft-hearted, kind, sympathetic, liberal, forgiving, lenient, tolerant.

industrious ADJ = **hard-working**, diligent, assiduous, conscientious, painstaking, indefatigable, tireless, unflagging; busy, active, energetic, vigorous.

ineffective ADJ = **unsuccessful**, unproductive, fruitless, unprofitable, abortive, futile, useless, ineffectual, inefficient, inadequate; feeble, inept, lame.

inept ADJ = **incompetent**, incapable, unskilled, inexpert, clumsy, awkward, maladroit, heavy-handed.

inequality NOUN = **disparity**, imbalance, variation, variability, difference, discrepancy, dissimilarity; unfairness, discrimination, bias, prejudice.

inert ADJ = **unmoving**, motionless, immobile, inanimate, still, stationary, static; dormant, sleeping; unconscious, comatose, lifeless, insentient; idle, inactive, sluggish, lethargic, torpid.

inertia NOUN = **inactivity**, inaction, immobility, stagnation, stasis, idleness, indolence, laziness, sloth, sluggishness, lethargy, torpor.

inevitable ADJ = **unavoidable**, inexorable, inescapable, ineluctable, fated, destined, predestined; assured, certain, sure.

inexperienced ADJ = **unpractised**, untrained, unschooled, unqualified, unskilled, amateur, unseasoned; naive, unsophisticated, callow, immature, green; [inf] wet behind the ears.

inexplicable ADJ = **unaccountable**,

incomprehensible,
unfathomable, insoluble;
baffling, puzzling,
mysterious, strange,
mystifying.

infallible ADJ **1** = **unfailing**,
foolproof, dependable,
trustworthy, reliable, sure,
certain, guaranteed.
2 = **unerring**, faultless,
flawless, impeccable,
perfect.

infamous ADJ = **notorious**,
ill-famed, of ill-repute.

infant NOUN = **baby**, child,
toddler; [Scottish] bairn.

infantile ADJ = **childish**,
babyish, puerile,
immature, juvenile.

infatuated ADJ = **besotted**,
obsessed, head over heels,
smitten; enamoured,
captivated, bewitched.

infatuation NOUN
= **obsession**, fixation,
crush, passion, love.

infect VERB = **contaminate**,
pollute, taint, blight,
poison.

infectious ADJ
= **contagious**,
communicable,
transmissible, catching.

infer VERB = **deduce**,
conclude, work out,
reason, surmise.

inferior ADJ **1** = **lower**,

lesser, subordinate,
junior, ancillary, minor,
lowly, humble, menial.
2 = **second-rate**, poor, bad,
defective, substandard,
low-quality, shoddy,
cheap.

infest VERB = **overrun**,
spread through, invade,
swarm over, beset, plague.

infidelity NOUN
= **unfaithfulness**, adultery,
faithlessness, disloyalty,
treachery, duplicity,
deceit.

infinite ADJ **1** = **boundless**,
unbounded, unlimited,
limitless, without end.
2 = **countless**, numberless,
innumerable,
immeasurable,
incalculable, untold,
inestimable,
indeterminable.

infinitesimal ADJ = **tiny**,
minute, microscopic,
minuscule, inappreciable,
imperceptible.

infirm ADJ = **feeble**,
enfeebled, weak, frail,
debilitated, decrepit,
ailing, ill, unwell, sick,
poorly.

inflame VERB = **incite**,
excite, arouse, stir up,
whip up, ignite, kindle,
foment, provoke,

stimulate.

inflate VERB = **blow up**, pump up, puff up/out, dilate, distend, swell.

inflexible ADJ

1 = **unchangeable**, unalterable, immutable, unvarying, firm, fixed, hard and fast, entrenched, stringent, strict. **2** = **adamant**, stubborn, obdurate, obstinate, intractable, intransigent, unbending, uncompromising, inexorable, steely, iron-willed.

inflict VERB = **administer**, deal out, mete out, deliver; impose, exact, wreak; foist.

influence NOUN = **effect**, impact, control, sway, power, hold, authority; leverage; [inf] clout. VERB = **affect**, have an effect on, sway, determine, guide, control, shape.

inform VERB **1** = **tell**, advise, apprise, notify, acquaint, brief, enlighten; [inf] fill in. **2** (**inform on**) = **betray**, incriminate, inculpate; [inf] grass on, rat on.

informal ADJ = **casual**, unceremonious, unofficial, simple, unpretentious, everyday, relaxed, easy.

information NOUN = **details**, particulars, facts, figures, statistics, data; knowledge, intelligence, news; [inf] the low-down.

informative ADJ = **instructive**, illuminating, enlightening, edifying, educational, revealing; newsy.

infrequent ADJ = **rare**, occasional, irregular, sporadic, unusual, few and far between, intermittent; [inf] once in a blue moon.

infringe VERB = **break**, disobey, violate, contravene, transgress, breach, disregard, defy, flout.

ingenious ADJ = **clever**, intelligent, smart, sharp, talented, brilliant, resourceful, inventive, imaginative, creative, original, subtle; crafty, wily, cunning.

ingenuous ADJ = **naive**, innocent, trusting, trustful, wide-eyed, inexperienced, green; open, sincere, honest, candid, artless, guileless.

ingratiating ADJ
= **sycophantic**, toadying,
fawning, unctuous,
obsequious, servile.

inhabit VERB = **live in**, dwell
in, reside in, occupy;
people, populate.

inhabitant NOUN
= **resident**, dweller,
occupier, occupant; local,
native.

inherent ADJ 1 = **intrinsic**,
built-in, essential, basic,
fundamental. 2 = **innate**,
inborn, congenital,
natural.

inheritance NOUN
= **legacy**, bequest,
endowment, birthright,
heritage, patrimony.

inhibit VERB = **impede**, hold
back, prevent, stop,
hamper, hinder, obstruct,
interfere with, curb,
restrict, restrain,
constrain.

inhibited ADJ = **shy**,
reticent, self-conscious,
reserved, repressed,
insecure, unconfident,
withdrawn.

inhospitable ADJ
1 = **unwelcoming**,
unfriendly, unsociable,
discourteous, ungracious,
cool, cold, aloof, unkind,
unsympathetic, hostile,
inimical. 2 = **bleak**, bare,
uninviting, desolate,
lonely, empty.

inimical ADJ 1 = **hostile**,
unfriendly, unwelcoming,
antagonistic. 2 = **harmful**,
injurious, detrimental,
deleterious, damaging.

initial ADJ = **first**, opening,
early, primary,
preliminary, introductory,
inaugural.

initiate VERB = **begin**, start,
commence, open,
institute, inaugurate, get
under way, launch,
originate, pioneer.

initiative NOUN
= **enterprise**,
resourcefulness,
inventiveness, originality,
creativity, drive,
dynamism, ambition.

injunction NOUN
= **command**, instruction,
order, ruling, direction,
directive, dictate, decree.

injure VERB = **hurt**, harm,
damage, wound; impair,
spoil, mar, blight.

injurious ADJ = **harmful**,
hurtful, damaging,
deleterious, detrimental,
disadvantageous,
unfavourable, destructive,
inimical.

injury NOUN = **harm**, hurt, damage; wound, sore, cut, bruise, gash, laceration, abrasion, lesion, contusion, trauma.

injustice NOUN = **unfairness**, unjustness, inequity; bias, prejudice, discrimination.

inkling NOUN = **idea**, notion, sense, impression, suggestion, indication, suspicion, hunch; hint, clue.

innate ADJ = **inborn**, inbred, congenital, hereditary, inherited, inherent, intrinsic, ingrained, natural.

inner ADJ = **interior**, inside, central, middle.

innocent ADJ 1 = **not guilty**, guiltless, blameless, in the clear, above suspicion, irreproachable. 2 = **naive**, ingenuous, unsophisticated, artless, guileless, childlike, trustful, trusting, credulous, inexperienced, unworldly, gullible; [inf] wet behind the ears.

innocuous ADJ = **safe**, harmless, inoffensive.

innuendo NOUN = **insinuation**, implication, intimation, suggestion, hint, overtone, undertone.

inquire VERB = **ask**, investigate, question, query, research, look into, examine, explore, probe, scrutinize, study.

inquiry NOUN 1 = **investigation**, examination, exploration, probe, scrutiny, study. 2 = **question**, query.

inquisitive ADJ = **inquiring**, questioning, curious, interested; intrusive, meddlesome, prying; [inf] nosy.

inscrutable ADJ = **enigmatic**, impenetrable, unreadable, cryptic.

insensitive ADJ 1 = **heartless**, uncaring, unfeeling, callous, tactless, thick-skinned, inconsiderate, thoughtless. 2 = **impervious**, immune, oblivious, unaffected.

insidious ADJ = **stealthy**, subtle, surreptitious, cunning, crafty, sly, wily.

insignificant ADJ = **unimportant**, trivial, trifling, negligible, inconsequential, petty.

insincere ADJ = **untruthful**,

dishonest, deceptive, disingenuous, hypocritical, deceitful, duplicitous, double-dealing, two-faced, mendacious, false, fake, put-on, feigned.

insinuate VERB = **imply**, hint, suggest, indicate, intimate.

insist VERB = **maintain**, assert, declare, contend, protest, swear, stress, reiterate.

insistent ADJ = **persistent**, determined, adamant, importunate, tenacious, dogged, unrelenting; urgent; emphatic, firm, assertive.

insolent ADJ = **impertinent**, impudent, cheeky, rude, ill-mannered, impolite, disrespectful, insulting.

insolvent ADJ = **bankrupt**, penniless, impoverished, penurious, impecunious; [inf] broke.

inspect VERB = **examine**, check, look over, survey, scrutinize, vet, study, view, investigate, assess, appraise.

inspection NOUN = **examination**, check, check-up, survey, scrutiny, view, observation, investigation, probe, assessment, appraisal.

inspiration NOUN 1 = **stimulus**, stimulation, motivation, fillip, encouragement, goad, spur; muse, influence. 2 = **creativity**, originality, inventiveness, genius, vision.

inspire VERB 1 = **stimulate**, motivate, encourage, influence, rouse, stir, energize, galvanize. 2 = **arouse**, awaken, prompt, kindle, produce.

instance NOUN = **case (in point)**, example, illustration, occasion, occurrence.

instant ADJ = **instantaneous**, immediate, prompt, rapid, swift, speedy; sudden, abrupt. NOUN = **moment**, minute, second; juncture, point.

instigate VERB 1 = **set in motion**, start, commence, begin, initiate, launch, institute, organize. 2 = **incite**, encourage, urge, goad, provoke, spur on, push, motivate, persuade.

instinct NOUN 1 = **natural feeling**, tendency,

inclination, intuition, sixth sense. **2 = talent**, gift, ability, flair, aptitude, knack, bent.

instinctive ADJ **= intuitive**, natural, innate, inborn, inherent; unconscious, subconscious, automatic, reflex, knee-jerk spontaneous, involuntary; [inf] gut.

institute NOUN **= institution**, establishment, organization, foundation, society, association, league, guild, consortium.

instruct VERB **1 = tell**, order, direct, command, charge, enjoin. **2 = teach**, educate, tutor, coach, train, school, drill, prime.

instruction NOUN **1 = teaching**, education, coaching, training, schooling. **2 = directive**, direction, order, command, injunction, dictate, bidding.

instructive ADJ **= informative**, educational, enlightening, illuminating, revealing, useful, helpful, edifying.

instructor NOUN **= teacher**, tutor, coach, trainer.

instrument NOUN **= implement**, tool, appliance, apparatus, mechanism, utensil, gadget, contrivance, device.

instrumental ADJ **= helpful**, useful, of service, contributory, active, involved, influential, significant, important.

insubordinate ADJ **= defiant**, rebellious, mutinous, disobedient, refractory, recalcitrant, undisciplined, unruly, disorderly, wayward.

insufficient ADJ **= inadequate**, deficient, in short supply, scarce, meagre, scant, scanty, at a premium.

insular ADJ **= narrow-minded**, provincial, parochial, blinkered; intolerant, prejudiced, biased, bigoted.

insult NOUN **= slight**, affront, jibe, snub, slur, dig. VERB **= abuse**, slight, disparage, libel, slander, malign, defame, denigrate, cast aspersions on; offend, affront.

insure VERB **= indemnify**, cover, underwrite,

guarantee.

intact ADJ = **whole**, complete, entire, perfect, in one piece, unbroken, undamaged.

intangible ADJ
1 = **impalpable**, incorporeal, ethereal.
2 = **indefinable**, indescribable, vague, subtle, elusive.

integral ADJ = **essential**, necessary, indispensable, basic, fundamental, inherent, intrinsic, innate.

integrate VERB = **combine**, amalgamate, merge, unite, blend, consolidate, intermingle, mix; incorporate, unify, assimilate.

integrity NOUN = **honesty**, rectitude, virtue, probity, principle, morality, honour, decency.

intellect NOUN = **mind**, brain, intelligence, understanding, reason, thought, sense, judgement.

intellectual ADJ
1 = **mental**, cerebral, cognitive. 2 = **intelligent**, academic, educated, well read, erudite, learned, bookish, highbrow,

scholarly, studious.

intelligence NOUN = **intellect**, mind, brain, brain-power, reason, understanding, acumen, wit, cleverness; [inf] nous.

intelligent ADJ = **clever**, bright, sharp, quick-witted, smart, perceptive, educated, knowledgeable.

intelligible ADJ = **understandable**, comprehensible, clear, lucid, plain, straightforward, legible, decipherable.

intend VERB = **mean**, plan, propose, aim, be resolved, be determined.

intense ADJ 1 = **acute**, fierce, severe, extreme, strong, powerful, potent, vigorous, great, profound, deep, concentrated.
2 = **earnest**, ardent, eager, keen, enthusiastic, zealous, impassioned, passionate, fervent, fervid, vehement.

intensify VERB = **strengthen**, increase, deepen, heighten, add to, fuel, fan, escalate, step up, raise.

intensive ADJ = **concentrated**, in-depth, thorough, exhaustive, thoroughgoing; vigorous, all-out, strenuous.

intent ADJ 1 = **attentive**, absorbed, engrossed, focused, enthralled, fascinated, rapt; fixed, steady, earnest, intense. 2 (**intent on**) = **set on**, bent on, determined to.

intention NOUN = **aim**, purpose, objective, goal, intent, end, target, aspiration, wish, ambition, plan, design.

intentional ADJ = **deliberate**, wilful, purposeful, planned, calculated, conscious, premeditated, pre-arranged.

intercept VERB = **cut off**, stop, head off, block, obstruct, impede, interrupt, waylay.

interest NOUN 1 = **attentiveness**, attention, absorption; curiosity, inquisitiveness. 2 = **attraction**, appeal, fascination, charm, allure. 3 = **concern**, consequence, importance, import, moment, significance, note, relevance. 4 = **pastime**, hobby, diversion, amusement, pursuit, relaxation. VERB = **appeal to**, attract, intrigue, absorb, engross, fascinate, rivet, grip, captivate, amuse, entertain.

interested ADJ = **attentive**, intent, absorbed, engrossed, curious, fascinated, riveted, gripped, captivated, intrigued.

interesting ADJ = **absorbing**, intriguing, engrossing, fascinating, riveting, gripping, compelling, compulsive, spellbinding, captivating, appealing, amusing, entertaining, stimulating, thought-provoking.

interfere VERB 1 = **hinder**, inhibit, impede, obstruct, check, block, hamper, handicap. 2 = **meddle**, butt in, intervene; [inf] poke your nose in.

interim ADJ = **temporary**, provisional, stopgap, caretaker, acting.

interlude NOUN = **interval**, intermission, break, pause, rest, respite, breathing space, hiatus.

intermediary NOUN = **mediator**, go-between,

broker, agent,
middleman, arbitrator,
negotiator.

intermediate ADJ
= **halfway**, in-between,
middle, mid, midway,
intervening, transitional,
intermediary.

interminable ADJ
= **endless**, never-ending,
everlasting, incessant,
ceaseless, non-stop.

intermittent ADJ = **fitful**,
spasmodic, irregular,
sporadic, occasional,
periodic, on and off.

internal ADJ 1 = **inner**,
inside, inward, interior.
2 = **domestic**, home, civil.

international ADJ
= **worldwide**, global,
intercontinental,
universal; cosmopolitan.

interpret VERB 1 = **explain**,
elucidate, clarify,
illuminate, shed light on.
2 = **decode**, decipher,
solve, crack.
3 = **understand**, take (to
mean), construe, read.

interrogate VERB
= **question**, cross-
examine, cross-question,
quiz, grill.

interrogation NOUN
= **questioning**, cross-
examination, inquisition,

investigation, grilling; [inf]
the third degree.

interrupt VERB 1 = **cut in**,
barge in, interfere, butt
in. 2 = **suspend**, adjourn,
discontinue, break off,
stop, halt, end.

intersect VERB 1 = **bisect**,
cut in two, divide.
2 = **cross**, criss-cross,
meet.

interval NOUN = **interlude**,
intermission, break;
interim, meantime,
meanwhile.

intervene VERB 1 = **occur**,
happen, take place; ensue,
result, follow.
2 = **intercede**, mediate,
arbitrate, step in;
interfere.

intimate ADJ 1 = **close**,
dear, cherished, bosom.
2 = **informal**, friendly,
welcoming, warm, cosy,
snug. 3 = **personal**,
private, confidential,
secret. VERB = **imply**,
suggest, hint, insinuate,
indicate.

intimidate VERB = **frighten**,
terrify, scare, terrorize,
cow, subdue, daunt,
browbeat, bully, coerce,
pressure, pressurize,
threaten.

intolerable ADJ

= **unbearable**, unendurable, insufferable, insupportable.

intolerant ADJ = **bigoted**, illiberal, narrow-minded, parochial, provincial, insular, small-minded, prejudiced, biased, partisan.

intonation NOUN = **pitch**, tone, timbre, cadence, lilt, inflection.

intricate ADJ = **complex**, complicated, convoluted, tangled, entangled, twisted; elaborate, ornate, detailed.

intrigue VERB = **interest**, fascinate, attract, draw. NOUN = **plot**, conspiracy, scheme, machination.

intrinsic ADJ = **inherent**, innate, inborn, inbred, congenital, natural, basic, fundamental, integral.

introduce VERB 1 = **present**, make acquainted. 2 = **preface**, precede, lead into, start, begin. 3 = **bring in**, originate, launch, inaugurate, institute, initiate, establish, found, set in motion, usher in, pioneer.

introduction NOUN = **foreword**, preface, preamble, prologue, prelude.

introductory ADJ = **prefatory**, preliminary, opening, initial, starting, first.

introspective ADJ = **inward-looking**, introverted, contemplative, reflective, meditative.

intrude VERB = **encroach**, impinge, trespass, infringe, obtrude, invade, violate.

intruder NOUN = **burglar**, housebreaker, thief, trespasser, interloper.

intuition NOUN = **instinct**, sixth sense, presentiment, feeling, hunch, inkling.

inundate VERB 1 = **flood**, deluge, swamp, submerge, engulf. 2 = **overwhelm**, overload, snow under, bog down.

inure VERB = **harden**, toughen, season, condition, habituate, familiarize, accustom, acclimatize.

invade VERB = **occupy**, conquer, capture, seize, take (over), annex; march into, overrun, overwhelm, storm, attack.

invalid ADJ = **false**, untrue, inaccurate, faulty, fallacious, spurious; unsubstantiated, untenable, baseless, ill-founded, groundless.

invaluable ADJ = **indispensable**, vital, irreplaceable, all-important, priceless, worth its weight in gold.

invasion NOUN **1** = **occupation**, capture, seizure, annexation, takeover. **2** = **intrusion**, encroachment, infringement, violation.

inveigle VERB = **persuade**, talk into, cajole, wheedle, coax, sweet-talk, beguile, tempt, entice, seduce.

invent VERB **1** = **originate**, create, design, devise, contrive, formulate, think up, conceive; coin. **2** = **make up**, fabricate, concoct, hatch, trump up.

invention NOUN = **creation**, innovation, design, contrivance, construction, device; [inf] brainchild.

inventive ADJ = **original**, creative, innovative, imaginative, inspired, ingenious, resourceful.

invest VERB **1** = **put money** into, fund, subsidize. **2** = **spend**, expend, put in, devote, contribute, donate, give.

investigate VERB = **inquire** into, research, probe, explore, scrutinize, study, examine.

investigation NOUN = **inquiry**, scrutiny, research, probe, exploration, study, survey, review, examination.

inveterate ADJ = **confirmed**, habitual, hardened, chronic, addicted, incorrigible.

invigorate VERB = **revitalize**, energize, refresh, revive, vivify, rejuvenate, enliven, perk up, animate, galvanize, fortify, stimulate, exhilarate.

invisible ADJ = **undetectable**, imperceptible, indiscernible, unseen, unnoticed, hidden, concealed.

invite VERB = **ask for**, request, call for, solicit, look for, seek, appeal for, summon.

inviting ADJ = **attractive**, appealing, pleasant,

agreeable, delightful, engaging, tempting, enticing, alluring, appetizing.

involuntary ADJ
1 = **reflexive**, reflex, automatic, mechanical, spontaneous, instinctive, unconscious, unthinking, unintentional.
2 = **unwilling**, against your will, forced, compulsory, obligatory.

involve VERB 1 = **entail**, imply, mean, require, necessitate. 2 = **include**, count in, cover, embrace, take in, incorporate, encompass, comprise, contain.

involved ADJ
= **complicated**, intricate, complex, elaborate, convoluted, knotty, tortuous, labyrinthine.

iota NOUN = **bit**, mite, speck, atom, jot, whit, particle.

ironic ADJ 1 = **sarcastic**, sardonic, wry, mocking, scornful, satirical.
2 = **paradoxical**, incongruous.

irrational ADJ = **illogical**, unreasonable, groundless, unfounded, unjustifiable; ridiculous, silly, foolish, senseless.

irregular ADJ
1 = **asymmetric**, lopsided, crooked. 2 = **uneven**, unsteady, shaky, fitful, variable, erratic, spasmodic, fluctuating, inconsistent. 3 = **improper**, unethical, unprofessional, unacceptable, illegitimate.

irrelevant ADJ
= **immaterial**, unrelated, unconnected, extraneous, beside the point.

irresistible ADJ
1 = **overwhelming**, overpowering, compelling, uncontrollable.
2 = **tempting**, alluring, enticing, seductive, captivating, enchanting, tantalizing.

irresponsible ADJ
= **undependable**, unreliable, untrustworthy, careless, reckless, rash, flighty, scatterbrained, thoughtless, incautious.

irreverent ADJ
= **disrespectful**, impertinent, cheeky, flippant, rude, discourteous, impolite.

irrevocable ADJ
= **unalterable**,

unchangeable, fixed, settled, irreversible, immutable.

irritable ADJ = **bad-tempered**, irascible, cross, snappy, testy, tetchy, touchy, crabbed, peevish, petulant, cantankerous, grumpy, grouchy, crotchety.

irritate VERB = **annoy**, vex, provoke, irk, nettle, peeve, get on someone's nerves, exasperate, anger; [inf] aggravate.

irritation NOUN
1 = **annoyance**, vexation, exasperation, indignation. 2 = **irritant**, nuisance, inconvenience.

isolate VERB = **set apart**, segregate, cut off, separate, quarantine.

isolated ADJ 1 = **remote**, out of the way, off the beaten track, secluded, unfrequented, desolate, godforsaken, inaccessible, cut-off. 2 = **solitary**, lonely, cloistered.

issue NOUN 1 = **matter**, question, point, subject, topic; problem. 2 = **edition**, number, copy, impression. VERB 1 = **put out**, send out, release, announce, publish, distribute, circulate, broadcast. 2 = **emanate**, emerge, pour, flow. 3 = **supply**, provide, furnish, equip.

item NOUN 1 = **article**, thing, object; element, constituent, component, ingredient. 2 = **point**, detail, matter, particular, issue.

Jj

jab NOUN = **poke**, prod, dig, nudge, elbow, butt.

jabber VERB = **chatter**, prattle, babble, gabble, prate, blather, rattle on.

jacket NOUN = **casing**, case, sheath, cover, covering, sleeve, wrapping, wrapper.

jagged ADJ = **serrated**, toothed, indented; spiky, barbed, uneven, rough, craggy.

jam VERB = **wedge**, force,

ram, thrust, push, stick, press, cram, pack, crowd, squeeze, sandwich.

jar VERB 1 = **jolt**, jerk, shake, vibrate. 2 = **grate on**, irritate, set someone's teeth on edge.

jargon NOUN = **slang**, idiom, cant, argot.

jaundiced ADJ = **bitter**, resentful, cynical, pessimistic, sceptical, distrustful, suspicious, misanthropic.

jaunt NOUN = **trip**, outing, excursion, expedition, mini break, tour, drive.

jaunty ADJ = **cheerful**, cheery, happy, merry, lively, perky, bubbly, buoyant, carefree, blithe.

jealous ADJ 1 = **envious**, covetous, begrudging, grudging, resentful, green-eyed.
2 = **suspicious**, possessive, distrustful, mistrustful.

jeer VERB = **taunt**, mock, ridicule, deride, jibe at, barrack, boo, scoff at, laugh at, sneer at.

jell VERB 1 = **set**, stiffen, solidify, thicken, congeal, coagulate. 2 = **take shape**, form, crystallize.

jeopardy NOUN = **risk**, danger, peril.

jerk VERB 1 = **pull**, yank, tug, wrench, tweak, pluck.
2 = **jolt**, lurch, bump, jump, bounce.

jerky ADJ 1 = **spasmodic**, fitful, convulsive, twitchy, shaky, tremulous.
2 = **jolting**, lurching, bumpy, bouncy, rough.

jet NOUN = **stream**, gush, spurt, spout, spray, rush, fountain.

jetty NOUN = **pier**, wharf, quay, dock, breakwater, groyne.

jewel NOUN = **gem**, gemstone, precious stone.

jib VERB = **baulk at**, recoil from, shrink from, fight shy of.

jibe, **gibe** NOUN = **taunt**, sneer, jeer, insult, barb; [inf] dig.

jilt VERB = **abandon**, walk out on, throw over, leave, forsake.

jingle VERB = **clink**, chink, jangle, rattle, tinkle, ding, ring, chime. NOUN = **ditty**, rhyme, refrain, limerick, tune.

job NOUN 1 = **occupation**, profession, trade, employment, vocation, career, métier, position, post, situation, appointment. 2 = **duty**,

jocular 1048

jocular ADJ = **humorous**, funny, amusing, witty, comic, comical, facetious, joking, playful, droll, entertaining.

jog VERB 1 = **run**, trot, lope. 2 = **nudge**, prod, poke, push, elbow. 3 = **stimulate**, activate, stir, prompt.

join VERB 1 = **fasten**, attach, tie, bind, couple, connect, unite, link, splice, yoke, glue, cement, fuse, weld, solder. 2 = **team up**, band together, cooperate, collaborate. 3 = **enlist**, sign up, enrol, become a member. NOUN = **junction**, intersection, connection, joint, seam.

joint NOUN see **join**. ADJ = **common**, shared, mutual, combined, collective, cooperative, united, concerted.

joke NOUN 1 = **jest**, witticism, quip, gag, pun, wisecrack; [inf] crack. 2 = **practical joke**, prank, trick, jape. VERB 1 = **crack jokes**, jest, banter, quip. 2 = **fool around**, tease, pull someone's leg; [inf] kid.

jolly ADJ = **happy**, merry, gay, joyful, joyous, jovial, glad, gleeful, cheerful, cheery, good-humoured, genial, carefree, buoyant, light-hearted, blithe, exuberant.

jolt VERB 1 = **push**, thrust, jar, shake, joggle, jog. 2 = **bump**, bounce, jerk, lurch, judder. 3 = **startle**, surprise, shock, shake, stun.

jostle VERB = **push**, shove, elbow, barge, bump/bang into.

journal NOUN 1 = **diary**, notebook, log, logbook, chronicle, record. 2 = **periodical**, magazine, gazette, digest, newspaper, paper.

journalist NOUN = **reporter**, columnist, correspondent, reviewer; [inf] hack.

journey NOUN = **trip**, expedition, tour, trek, voyage, cruise, passage, odyssey, pilgrimage; travels, globetrotting.

jovial ADJ see **jolly**.

joy NOUN = **delight**, pleasure, gladness, happiness, rapture, glee, bliss, ecstasy, elation, rejoicing, exultation, jubilation, euphoria, transports.

joyful ADJ = **overjoyed**, elated, thrilled, delighted, pleased, happy, glad, blithe, gleeful, jubilant, ecstatic, exultant, euphoric, enraptured; [inf] over the moon, in seventh heaven, on cloud nine.

judge VERB 1 = **try**, hear, adjudicate, adjudge. 2 = **assess**, appraise, evaluate, examine, review. 3 = **consider**, believe, think, deduce, surmise, conclude, decide. NOUN 1 = **magistrate**, justice, sheriff; [inf] beak. 2 = **adjudicator**, arbiter, assessor, examiner.

judgement NOUN 1 = **discernment**, acumen, shrewdness, common sense, perception, perspicacity, discrimination, wisdom, judiciousness, prudence; [inf] nous. 2 = **verdict**, decision, adjudication, ruling, finding, decree, sentence.

judicial ADJ 1 = **judiciary**, juridical, judicatory, legal. 2 = **judge-like**, impartial, unbiased, critical, analytical, discriminating, discerning, perceptive.

judicious ADJ = **wise**, prudent, politic, sagacious, shrewd, astute, sensible, sound, discerning, intelligent, smart, clever.

jug NOUN = **pitcher**, carafe, decanter, jar, crock, ewer.

juggle VERB = **change**, alter, manipulate, tamper with, falsify; [inf] fix, doctor.

juice NOUN = **extract**, sap, secretion, liquid, liquor, fluid, serum.

juicy ADJ 1 = **succulent**, moist; ripe. 2 = **racy**, risqué, spicy, sensational, scandalous, fascinating.

jumble VERB = **disorganize**, muddle, disarrange, disorder, mix up. NOUN = **clutter**, muddle, mess, disarray, hotchpotch, mishmash.

jump VERB 1 = **leap**, spring, bound, vault, hurdle, hop; skip, caper, dance, prance. 2 = **start**, flinch, jerk, recoil. NOUN 1 = **leap**, spring, vault, bound, hop. 2 = **hurdle**, fence, obstacle, barrier. 3 = **rise**, increase, upsurge; [inf] hike. 4 = **start**, jerk.

junction NOUN 1 = **join**, joint, juncture, link,

connection, seam, union.
2 = **crossroads**, crossing,
intersection, interchange.

juncture NOUN = **point**,
point in time, time, stage,
period, critical point,
crucial moment, moment
of truth, turning point,
crisis, crux, extremity.

junior ADJ = **younger**,
subordinate, lesser, lower,
minor, secondary.

junk NOUN see **rubbish**.

just ADJ 1 = **fair**, equitable,
even-handed, impartial,
unbiased, objective,
neutral, disinterested,
unprejudiced, open-
minded. 2 = **valid**, sound,
well founded, justified,
justifiable, defensible,
reasonable.

justice NOUN = **justness**,

fairness, fair play, fair-
mindedness, equity, even-
handedness, impartiality,
objectivity, neutrality.

justifiable ADJ = **valid**,
sound, well founded,
legitimate, tenable,
defensible, sustainable,
warranted, reasonable,
within reason, justified.

justify VERB 1 = **give
grounds for**, give reasons
for, explain, account for,
defend, vindicate.
2 = **warrant**, be good
reason for, substantiate.

jut VERB = **stick out**, project,
protrude, bulge out,
overhang.

juvenile ADJ = **childish**,
puerile, infantile,
immature; callow, green,
unsophisticated, naive.

Kk

kaleidoscopic ADJ
= **many-coloured**,
variegated, motley,
rainbow-like, psychedelic.

keen ADJ 1 = **eager**,
enthusiastic, ardent,
passionate, zealous,
fervent, committed,

dedicated, conscientious;
impatient, itching, dying,
raring. 2 = **sharp**, acute,
powerful; discerning,
perceptive, sensitive,
discriminating, astute,
shrewd, penetrating,
perspicacious.

keep VERB 1 = **carry on**, continue, maintain, persist, persevere. 2 = **hold on to**, keep hold of, retain; [inf] hang on to. 3 = **save up**, store, hoard, pile up, collect. 4 = **provide for**, support, maintain, sustain, feed; look after, nurture. 5 = **abide by**, comply with, adhere to, fulfil, honour, obey, observe.

keeper NOUN = **curator**, custodian, caretaker, steward, guardian, administrator.

keepsake NOUN = **memento**, souvenir, remembrance, reminder, token.

kernel NOUN = **nub**, nucleus, core, centre, heart, essence; [inf] nitty-gritty.

key NOUN 1 = **answer**, solution, explanation, guide, clue, pointer. 2 = **tone**, pitch, timbre, tonality.

kick VERB 1 = **boot**, punt. 2 = **give up**, stop, abandon, quit, desist from.

kill VERB 1 = **murder**, slay, do away with, slaughter, butcher, massacre, assassinate, liquidate, exterminate, dispatch, put to death, execute; [inf] bump off, do in. 2 = **destroy**, put an end to, ruin, wreck, extinguish, dash, shatter.

killer NOUN = **murderer**, butcher, slayer, assassin, executioner, gunman; [inf] hit man.

killing NOUN = **murder**, manslaughter, homicide, slaughter, butchery, massacre, bloodshed, carnage, extermination, execution.

killjoy NOUN = **spoilsport**; [inf] wet blanket, party-pooper.

kin NOUN = **relatives**, relations, family, folks, people, kindred, kith and kin, kinsfolk.

kind ADJ = **kindly**, good-natured, kind-hearted, warm-hearted, caring, affectionate, warm, considerate, helpful, thoughtful, obliging, unselfish, selfless, altruistic, compassionate, sympathetic, understanding, benevolent, benign, friendly, neighbourly, hospitable, public-spirited, well meaning,

generous, bountiful. NOUN
= **sort**, type, variety,
brand, class, category,
genus, species.

kindle VERB 1 = **light**, set
alight, set on fire, set fire
to, ignite. 2 = **stimulate**,
rouse, arouse, excite, stir,
awaken, inspire, trigger,
provoke.

kindred ADJ = **related**,
connected, allied; like,
similar, corresponding,
comparable, analogous.

kink NOUN 1 = **twist**,
corkscrew, curl, twirl,
knot, tangle. 2 = **flaw**,
defect, problem, snag,
hitch. 3 = **quirk**,
eccentricity, foible,
idiosyncrasy.

kinky ADJ = **perverted**,
warped, deviant,
abnormal, unnatural.

kit NOUN 1 = **equipment**,
apparatus, tools,
implements, instruments,
utensils, gear, tackle,
paraphernalia. 2 = **clothes**,
clothing, garments, dress,
outfit; strip. VERB = **equip**,
supply, provide, fit out,
furnish.

knack NOUN = **talent**, skill,
aptitude, gift, flair, ability,
capability, capacity,
expertise, genius, facility.

knit VERB = **unite**, unify,
draw/join together, bond,
fuse.

knob NOUN = **bump**, lump,
protuberance, bulge,
swelling, knot, node,
nodule.

knock VERB 1 = **bang**, tap,
rap, pound, hammer.
2 = **hit**, strike, bump, crack;
[inf] bash. 3 = **collide with**,
bang into, bump into, run
into, crash into.

knoll NOUN = **hillock**, hill,
hummock, mound,
hump, barrow.

knot NOUN 1 = **cluster**,
group, huddle, bunch,
gathering, band. 2 = **node**,
nodule. VERB = **tie**, fasten,
secure, do up.

know VERB 1 = **be aware**,
realize, be conscious,
sense, notice, perceive.
2 = **be familiar with**, be
conversant with, be
acquainted with,
understand, comprehend,
have a grasp of, be versed
in. 3 = **have met**, be
acquainted with,
associate with, be friends
with, socialize with, be on
good terms with.

knowledge NOUN
1 = **learning**, erudition,
scholarship, education,

wisdom, enlightenment.
2 = **understanding**, grasp,
comprehension,
command, mastery, skill,
expertise, proficiency,
know-how. **3** = **familiarity**,
acquaintance.
knowledgeable ADJ

1 = **well informed**,
educated, learned,
erudite, scholarly, well
read, cultured, cultivated,
enlightened.
2 = **acquainted**, familiar,
au fait, conversant,
experienced.

label NOUN = **tag**, ticket, tab,
sticker, marker. VERB
= **categorize**, classify,
describe, designate,
brand, call, name, dub.
laborious ADJ = **hard**,
heavy, difficult, arduous,
strenuous, onerous,
gruelling, tiring,
wearying, wearisome.
labour NOUN **1** = **(hard)
work**, toil, exertion,
effort, industry, travail,
drudgery, donkey work.
2 = **employees**, workers,
workmen, workforce,
hands, labourers.
3 = **childbirth**, birth,
delivery, contractions,
labour pains; [formal]
parturition. VERB = **work**,
toil, slave away, drudge,
struggle, exert yourself,

travail.
labyrinth NOUN = **maze**,
warren, network, web,
entanglement.
labyrinthine ADJ
= **intricate**, complicated,
complex, involved,
tortuous, convoluted,
tangled, elaborate.
lacerate VERB = **cut (open)**,
tear, gash, slash, rip,
mutilate, hurt, wound,
injure, maim.
lack NOUN = **absence**, want,
need, deprivation,
deficiency, privation,
dearth, insufficiency,
shortage, scarcity,
paucity.
laconic ADJ = **brief**,
concise, terse, succinct,
short, elliptical, crisp,
pithy, to the point.

laden ADJ = **loaded**, burdened, weighed down, weighted, encumbered.

lady NOUN 1 = **woman**, female. 2 = **noblewoman**, gentlewoman, aristocrat.

ladylike ADJ = **genteel**, refined, well bred, decorous, proper, correct, respectable, well mannered, courteous, polite, gracious.

lag VERB = **fall behind**, fall back, trail, bring up the rear, dally, straggle, hang back, drag your feet.

laid-back ADJ = **relaxed**, at ease, easy, easy-going, free and easy, unexcitable, imperturbable, unflappable.

lair NOUN = **den**, burrow, hole.

lake NOUN = **pond**, tarn, pool, reservoir, lagoon; [Scottish] loch.

lame ADJ 1 = **limping**, hobbling, halting, crippled; [inf] gammy. 2 = **weak**, feeble, thin, flimsy, unconvincing, unsatisfactory.

lament VERB 1 = **mourn**, grieve, sorrow, wail, moan, weep, cry, sob, keen, beat your breast. 2 = **complain about**, bemoan, bewail, deplore.

lamentable ADJ = **deplorable**, regrettable, tragic, terrible, wretched, woeful, sorrowful, distressing, grievous.

lamp NOUN = **light**, lantern.

land NOUN 1 = **dry land**, solid ground, earth, terra firma. 2 = **soil**, earth, loam. 3 = **grounds**, fields, open space; property, estate, real estate. 4 = **country**, nation, state, realm, province, kingdom. VERB = **touch down**, come down, alight, come to rest; berth, dock, come ashore, disembark.

landscape NOUN = **countryside**, scenery, country, panorama, perspective.

language NOUN 1 = **speech**, communication, speaking, talking, words, vocabulary, conversation, discourse. 2 = **tongue**, mother/native tongue; [inf] lingo.

languid ADJ = **languorous**, unhurried, indolent, lazy, idle, listless, lethargic, inert, sluggish.

languor NOUN = **lassitude**, lethargy, torpor, tiredness, weariness, idleness, inertia, indolence, laziness, sluggishness.

lank ADJ = **limp**, lifeless, dull, straggling, straight, long.

lanky ADJ = **tall**, thin, spindly, gangling, gangly, lean, scrawny, gawky.

lap NOUN = **circuit**, circle, leg, orbit, round.

lapse NOUN 1 = **slip**, error, mistake, blunder, failing, fault, failure, omission, oversight; [inf] slip-up. 2 = **interval**, gap, pause, intermission, interlude, hiatus, break. VERB 1 = **decline**, deteriorate, worsen, degenerate; [inf] go downhill. 2 = **expire**, run out, become void, become invalid.

large ADJ 1 = **big**, great, sizeable, substantial, considerable, goodly, tall, high, huge, immense, enormous, colossal, massive, mammoth, vast, prodigious, gigantic, giant, monumental, gargantuan. 2 = **burly**, heavy, thickset, strapping, hulking, hefty, fat, stout, corpulent. 3 = **abundant**, copious, plentiful, ample, liberal, generous.

at large = **at liberty**, free, unconfined, unrestrained; on the loose, on the run, fugitive.

lascivious ADJ = **lewd**, lecherous, lustful, licentious, libidinous, salacious, ribald.

last ADJ 1 = **final**, closing, concluding, ending, finishing, ultimate, terminal. 2 = **hindmost**, rearmost, at the end/back. 3 = **previous**, preceding. VERB 1 = **continue**, go on, carry on, remain, persist, keep on. 2 = **survive**, endure, hold on/out, hang on.

late ADJ 1 = **behind schedule**, behind, not on time, tardy, overdue, delayed. 2 = **deceased**, dead, departed. 3 = **former**, recent, previous, preceding, past, prior.

latent ADJ = **dormant**, quiescent, inactive, hidden, concealed, undeveloped, unrealized, potential, possible.

lateral ADJ = **sideways**, sidelong, edgeways, indirect, oblique, slanting.

latitude NOUN = **scope**, freedom, liberty,

independence, leeway, free rein, licence.

laudable ADJ
= **praiseworthy**, commendable, admirable, meritorious, deserving, creditable, worthy.

laugh VERB = **chuckle**, chortle, guffaw, giggle, titter, snigger, be doubled up; [inf] be in stitches, be creased up, fall about, crack up.

laughter NOUN = **laughing**, chuckling, chortling, guffawing, giggling, tittering, sniggering; [inf] hysterics.

launch VERB 1 = **fire**, discharge, propel, throw, cast, hurl, let fly, blast off. 2 = **set in motion**, get going, begin, start, embark on, initiate, instigate, institute, inaugurate, establish, set up, introduce.

lavish ADJ 1 = **generous**, liberal, bountiful, open-handed, unstinting, unsparing, free. 2 = **sumptuous**, luxurious, extravagant, expensive, opulent, grand, splendid. 3 = **abundant**, copious, plentiful, liberal, prolific. VERB = **heap**, shower, pour,

give, bestow.

law NOUN 1 = **rule**, regulation, statute, enactment, act, decree, edict, command, order, ruling, directive; legislation, constitution. 2 = **principle**, precept, credo, tenet, canon.

law-abiding ADJ = **honest**, honourable, upright, upstanding, good, virtuous, dutiful, obedient, compliant.

lawful ADJ = **legal**, legitimate, licit, valid, permissible, allowable, rightful, proper, constitutional, legalized, authorized.

lawless ADJ 1 = **anarchic**, disorderly, unruly, insurgent, rebellious, insubordinate, riotous, mutinous. 2 = **unlawful**, illegal, law-breaking, illicit, illegitimate, criminal, felonious.

lawyer NOUN = **solicitor**, barrister, advocate, counsel, Queen's Counsel, QC; [US] attorney.

lax ADJ = **slack**, slipshod, negligent, remiss, careless, heedless, slapdash, casual; easy-going, lenient, permissive, indulgent, overindulgent.

lay VERB 1 = **set**, deposit, plant, settle, position; set out, arrange, dispose. 2 = **attribute**, assign, ascribe, impute. 3 = **impose**, inflict, encumber, saddle, charge, burden.

laze VERB = **idle**, loaf, lounge, loll, take it easy, relax, unwind.

lazy ADJ = **idle**, indolent, slothful, work-shy, sluggish, lethargic, languorous.

lead VERB 1 = **guide**, show the way, conduct, usher, escort, steer, shepherd. 2 = **cause**, make, induce, prompt, move, incline, dispose, predispose. 3 = **result in**, give rise to, bring on, provoke, contribute to. 4 = **command**, direct, govern, rule, manage, be in charge of, preside over, head, oversee. NOUN 1 = **leading position**, first place, van, vanguard. 2 = **clue**, tip-off, pointer. 3 = **leash**, strap, cord, rope.

leader NOUN 1 = **ruler**, head, chief, commander, director, governor, principal, captain, skipper, manager, overseer; [inf] boss. 2 = **pioneer**, trendsetter, front runner, innovator, trailblazer, originator.

leading ADJ 1 = **chief**, main, principal, foremost, key, central. 2 = **greatest**, best, pre-eminent, top, star.

leaflet NOUN = **pamphlet**, booklet, brochure, handbill, circular, flyer.

league NOUN = **alliance**, confederation, federation, union, association, coalition, consortium, guild, corporation, cooperative, syndicate, group.

leak VERB 1 = **seep out**, escape, drip, ooze out; exude, discharge, emit, issue. 2 = **disclose**, divulge, reveal, make known, impart, pass on, give away, let slip; [inf] blab, spill the beans. NOUN 1 = **drip**, leakage, escape, seepage, discharge. 2 = **hole**, opening, puncture, crack, fissure, gash, slit.

lean VERB 1 = **be supported**, be propped, recline. 2 = **incline**, bend, slant,

tilt, slope, bank, list.
3 = depend, be dependent, rely, count, trust. ADJ see **thin**.

leaning NOUN = **tendency**, inclination, bent, proclivity, propensity, penchant, predisposition, predilection, partiality, preference, bias, liking, fondness, taste.

leap VERB = **jump**, bound, hop, skip, spring, vault, hurdle.

learn VERB **1 = master**, grasp, take in, absorb, assimilate, pick up.
2 = memorize, learn by heart, get off pat.
3 = discover, find out, gather, hear, be informed, understand, ascertain, get word/wind of.

learned ADJ = **erudite**, scholarly, well educated, knowledgeable, well read, cultured, intellectual, academic, literary, bookish.

learner NOUN = **beginner**, trainee, apprentice, pupil, student, novice, tyro, neophyte, greenhorn.

lease VERB = **rent (out)**, hire (out), charter; let out, sublet.

leash NOUN = **lead**, rope, cord, strap.

leave VERB **1 = depart**, go, withdraw, retire, exit, make off, pull out, decamp; [inf] push off, do a bunk, vamoose.
2 = abandon, desert, forsake, leave in the lurch.
3 = give up, quit, resign from, retire from.
4 = bequeath, will, endow, hand down, transfer.
5 = cause, produce, generate, result in. NOUN
1 = permission, consent, authorization, sanction, warrant, dispensation.
2 = holiday, vacation, break, time off, furlough, sabbatical.

lecherous ADJ = **lustful**, licentious, lascivious, lewd, salacious, debauched.

lecture NOUN **1 = talk**, speech, address, discourse, disquisition.
2 = scolding, reprimand, rebuke, reproof, reproach, tirade, diatribe; [inf] dressing-down, telling-off. VERB **1 = speak**, talk, hold forth, declaim.
2 = scold, reprimand, rebuke, reprove, reproach, remonstrate with, upbraid, berate, chide.

lecturer NOUN = **teacher**, tutor, scholar, academic, don.

ledge NOUN = **shelf**, sill, mantel, mantelpiece, projection, overhang, ridge, step.

left ADJ 1 = **left-hand**; port. 2 = **left-wing**, socialist, communist, radical, progressive.

leg NOUN 1 = **limb**, member, shank; [inf] peg, pin. 2 = **part**, portion, segment, section, bit, stretch, stage, lap.

legal ADJ = **lawful**, legitimate, licit, legalized, valid, right, permissible, permitted, allowed, authorized, sanctioned, licensed.

legalize VERB = **make legal**, decriminalize, legitimize, legitimatize, validate, permit, allow, authorize, sanction, license.

legend NOUN = **myth**, saga, epic, (folk) story, (folk) tale, fable.

legendary ADJ 1 = **mythical**, traditional, fabled, storybook, fairy-tale. 2 = **famous**, celebrated, acclaimed, illustrious, famed, renowned.

legitimate ADJ 1 = **legal**, lawful, licit, rightful, real, true, proper, authorized, permitted, allowed, sanctioned, licensed. 2 = **valid**, justifiable, reasonable, sound, admissible, well founded, sensible, bona fide.

leisure NOUN = **free time**, spare time, time off, relaxation, recreation, inactivity.

leisurely ADJ = **unhurried**, relaxed, easy, easy-going, gentle, comfortable, restful, slow, lazy, lingering.

lend VERB 1 = **loan**; advance. 2 = **impart**, add, give, bestow, confer, provide, supply.

length NOUN 1 = **distance**, extent, span, reach. 2 = **period**, stretch, duration, term, span. 3 = **piece**, section, measure, segment, swatch.

lengthen VERB = **draw out**, prolong, protract, stretch out, elongate.

lengthy ADJ = **long**, long-lasting, prolonged, extended, protracted, long-drawn-out.

lenient ADJ = **merciful**,

forgiving, sparing, compassionate, humane, forbearing, tolerant, indulgent, kind, easy-going.

lessen VERB 1 = **grow less**, abate, decrease, diminish, subside, moderate, slacken, die down, let up, ease off, tail off, ebb, wane. 2 = **relieve**, soothe, allay, assuage, alleviate, ease, dull, deaden, blunt, take the edge off.

lesson NOUN 1 = **class**, seminar, tutorial, lecture. 2 = **example**, warning, deterrent, message, moral.

let VERB 1 = **allow**, permit, authorize, sanction, grant, license, assent to, consent to, agree to, give the go-ahead. 2 = **let out**, rent (out), lease, hire out, sublet.

let-down NOUN = **disappointment**, disillusionment, anticlimax; [inf] washout.

lethal ADJ = **fatal**, deadly, mortal, death-dealing, murderous, killing; poisonous, toxic, virulent, destructive.

lethargic ADJ = **sluggish**, inactive, slow, torpid, listless, languid, lazy, slothful, indolent, weary, enervated, fatigued.

letter NOUN 1 = **character**, sign, symbol. 2 = **message**, note, line, missive, epistle, dispatch.

level ADJ 1 = **flat**, smooth, even, plane, flush, horizontal. 2 = **even**, uniform, regular, consistent, constant, stable, steady, unchanging, unvarying. 3 = **equal**, on a level, neck and neck, level-pegging, side by side. NOUN = **position**, rank, standing, status, degree, grade, stage, standard.

liable ADJ 1 = **responsible**, accountable, answerable; blameworthy, at fault. 2 = **apt**, likely, inclined, disposed, predisposed, prone. 3 = **exposed**, subject, susceptible, vulnerable, in danger of.

liar NOUN = **fibber**, perjurer, false witness, deceiver.

libel NOUN = **defamation**, denigration, vilification, disparagement, aspersions, calumny, slander, false report, slur, smear. VERB = **defame**, vilify, blacken someone's name, denigrate, disparage, cast aspersions on, slander, traduce, slur, smear.

libellous ADJ = **defamatory**, denigratory, disparaging, derogatory, slanderous, false, misrepresentative, scurrilous.

liberal ADJ 1 = **tolerant**, broad-minded, open-minded, enlightened, unprejudiced, indulgent, permissive. 2 = **generous**, magnanimous, open-handed, unsparing, unstinting, munificent, bountiful. 3 = **copious**, ample, abundant, lavish, plentiful, profuse.

liberate VERB = **set free**, free, release, let out, let go, discharge, set loose, rescue, emancipate.

liberty NOUN = **freedom**, independence; autonomy, sovereignty, self-government, self-rule.
at liberty = **free**, loose, on the loose, at large, unconfined.

licence NOUN 1 = **permit**, certificate, credentials, document, documentation, pass. 2 = **permission**, authority, right, authorization, leave, entitlement; liberty, freedom.

license VERB = **permit**, allow, authorize, sanction, entitle, let, empower.

lid NOUN = **cover**, top, cap, covering.

lie¹ NOUN = **untruth**, falsehood, fib, white lie, fabrication, invention, fairy story; [inf] whopper. VERB = **tell a lie**, perjure yourself, fib, bear false witness.

lie² VERB 1 = **recline**, be recumbent, be prostrate, be supine, be prone, sprawl, rest, repose, lounge, loll. 2 = **be situated**, be located, be placed, be positioned.

life NOUN 1 = **existence**, being, living, animation. 2 = **living things**, living creatures, fauna, flora. 3 = **lifetime**, days, lifespan, time on earth, existence.

lifelike ADJ = **true-to-life**, realistic, photographic, faithful, authentic; vivid, graphic.

lift VERB = **pick up**, uplift, hoist, heave up, raise (up), heft.

light¹ NOUN 1 = **illumination**,

luminescence,
luminosity, brightness,
brilliance, radiance,
incandescence, blaze,
glare, glow, lustre.
2 = **lamp**, lantern.
3 = **aspect**, angle, slant,
approach, viewpoint,
standpoint. VERB 1 = **set fire
to**, ignite, kindle.
2 = **illuminate**, brighten,
lighten, irradiate. ADJ
1 = **bright**, well lit, sunny.
2 = **pale**, pastel, faded,
bleached; fair, blonde.

light² ADJ 1 = **lightweight**,
easy to lift/carry,
portable. 2 = **flimsy**, thin,
delicate, floaty, gossamer.
3 = **easy**, simple,
undemanding; [inf] cushy.
4 = **entertaining**,
diverting, amusing,
humorous, funny;
frivolous, superficial,
trivial.

lighten VERB 1 = **brighten**,
light up, illuminate, shed
light on, irradiate.
2 = **lessen**, reduce, ease,
alleviate, relieve.

like ADJ = **similar**, the same,
comparable,
corresponding,
analogous, parallel,
equivalent, of a kind,
identical, matching, akin.

NOUN = **equal**, match,
counterpart, fellow, twin,
parallel, peer. VERB 1 = **be
fond of**, be attracted to, be
keen on, love, have a soft
spot for. 2 = **enjoy**, be keen
on, be partial to, love,
adore, delight in, relish,
revel in. 3 = **wish**, want,
desire, prefer.

likeable ADJ = **pleasant**,
nice, friendly, agreeable,
amiable, genial,
charming, engaging,
pleasing, appealing,
lovable.

likelihood NOUN
= **probability**, chance,
prospect, possibility.

likely ADJ 1 = **probable**,
possible, to be expected,
on the cards, odds-on.
2 = **apt**, inclined, tending,
liable, prone.
3 = **promising**, talented,
gifted; [inf] up-and-
coming.

liken VERB = **compare**,
equate, correlate, link,
associate.

likeness NOUN
1 = **resemblance**,
similarity, sameness,
similitude,
correspondence, analogy.
2 = **picture**, drawing,
sketch, painting, portrait,

photograph, study, representation, image.

liking NOUN = **fondness**, love, affection, desire, preference, partiality, penchant, bias, weakness, soft spot, taste, predilection, inclination, proclivity.

limb NOUN 1 = **arm**, leg, wing, member, extremity, appendage. 2 = **branch**, bough.

limit NOUN 1 = **boundary**, border, bound, frontier, edge, perimeter, confines, periphery. 2 = **maximum**, ceiling, limitation, restriction, check, restraint. VERB = **restrict**, curb, check, restrain, constrain, freeze, peg.

limitation NOUN = **restriction**, curb, restraint, constraint, control, check, impediment, obstacle, obstruction, bar, barrier, block, deterrent.

limp ADJ = **floppy**, droopy, soft, flaccid, flabby, loose, slack.

line NOUN 1 = **rule**, bar, underline, underscore, stroke, slash. 2 = **band**, stripe, strip, belt, seam. 3 = **furrow**, wrinkle, crease,

crow's-foot. 4 = **outline**, contour, configuration, shape, delineation, silhouette, profile. 5 = **row**, queue, procession, column, file, string, chain, crocodile. 6 = **business**, field, trade, occupation, employment, profession, work, job, career. 7 = **lineage**, descent, ancestry, parentage, family, extraction, heritage, stock.

linger VERB = **stay**, remain, wait/hang around, dawdle, loiter, dally, take your time, tarry, dilly-dally.

link NOUN 1 = **ring**, loop, connection, coupling, joint. 2 = **connection**, relationship, association; bond, tie, attachment, affiliation. VERB = **connect**, join, fasten, attach, bind, unite, couple, yoke; associate, relate.

lip NOUN = **edge**, rim, brim, verge, brink.

liquid NOUN = **fluid**, liquor, solution, juice, sap.

liquidize VERB = **purée**, liquefy, blend.

list NOUN = **catalogue**, inventory, record, register,

roll, file, index, directory, listing, enumeration. VERB = **record**, register, enter, itemize, enumerate, catalogue, file, classify, alphabetize.

listen VERB = **pay attention**, hear, attend, hark, give ear, lend an ear, prick up your ears, be all ears.

listless ADJ = **lethargic**, enervated, spiritless, lifeless, inactive, inert, languid, apathetic, sluggish, torpid.

literal ADJ = **word-for-word**, verbatim, exact, precise, faithful, strict.

literary ADJ = **well read**, learned, well educated, intellectual, cultured, highbrow, erudite, bookish.

literature NOUN **1** = **written works**, writings, published works. **2** = **brochures**, leaflets, pamphlets, circulars, information, data.

lithe ADJ = **agile**, flexible, supple, limber, loose-limbed, lissom.

litter NOUN **1** = **rubbish**, debris, refuse, junk, detritus, waste; [US] trash, garbage. **2** = **brood**, young, offspring.

little ADJ **1** = **small**, short, slight, petite, tiny, wee, miniature, diminutive; [inf] pint-sized. **2** = **unimportant**, insignificant, minor, trivial, trifling, petty, paltry, inconsequential, negligible.

liturgy NOUN = **ritual**, worship, service, ceremony, rite, observance, celebration, sacrament.

live ADJ **1** = **alive**, living, breathing, animate, vital. **2** = **glowing**, aglow, burning, alight, flaming, aflame, blazing, smouldering.

livelihood NOUN = **living**, subsistence, means of support, income, keep, sustenance; work, employment, occupation, job.

lively ADJ **1** = **full of life**, active, animated, energetic, vigorous, spirited, high-spirited, vivacious, exuberant, enthusiastic, buoyant, bouncy, perky, spry, sprightly. **2** = **animated**, spirited, stimulating, heated. **3** = **busy**, crowded, bustling, hectic.

living ADJ 1 = **alive**, live, breathing, animate, vital. 2 = **current**, in use, extant, existing, surviving. NOUN see **livelihood**.

load NOUN 1 = **cargo**, freight, consignment, shipment, lorryload. 2 = **burden**, onus, encumbrance, weight, responsibility, duty, charge, obligation; strain, trouble, worry, pressure; cross, millstone, albatross. VERB 1 = **fill (up)**, charge, pack, stock; heap, stack, stuff, cram. 2 = **burden**, weigh down, saddle, charge, tax, encumber, overburden, overwhelm, trouble, worry.

loaf VERB = **laze**, lounge, loll, idle, hang about, waste time.

loan VERB = **lend**, advance.

loath ADJ = **reluctant**, unwilling, disinclined, averse, opposed, resistant.

loathe VERB = **hate**, detest, abhor, despise, abominate, dislike.

loathing NOUN = **hatred**, hate, detestation, abhorrence, aversion, repugnance, disgust, revulsion, antipathy, dislike.

loathsome ADJ = **hateful**, detestable, abhorrent, odious, repugnant, disgusting, repulsive, revolting, nauseating, abominable, vile, nasty, obnoxious, horrible, offensive.

local NOUN 1 = **inhabitant**, resident, parishioner. 2 = **pub**, public house, bar, inn, tavern.

locality NOUN = **vicinity**, area, neighbourhood, district, region.

locate VERB 1 = **find**, discover, identify, pinpoint, detect, track down, run to earth. 2 = **situate**, site, position, place, put, build, base, establish, station, settle.

location NOUN = **position**, place, situation, whereabouts, bearings, site, spot, point, scene, setting, venue, locale; [formal] locus.

lock VERB = **bolt**, fasten, bar, secure, padlock. NOUN 1 = **bolt**, catch, fastener, clasp, bar, hasp. 2 = **tress**, strand, hank, curl, ringlet.

locker NOUN = **cupboard**, compartment, cabinet, chest, safe.

lodge VERB 1 = **board**, have

digs/lodgings, put up, reside, dwell. **2 = register**, submit, present, put forward, place, file, lay.

lofty ADJ **1 = towering**, soaring, tall, high. **2 = noble**, exalted, grand, sublime, fine, high-minded.

log NOUN **= logbook**, record, register, journal, diary, ledger, account.

logic NOUN **= reason**, reasoning, judgement, wisdom, sense, good sense, common sense, rationality, rationale.

logical ADJ **1 = reasoned**, well reasoned, rational, sound, cogent, coherent, clear. **2 = reasonable**, natural, understandable, predictable, unsurprising, likely.

loiter VERB **= hang around**, linger, wait, skulk; loaf, lounge, idle, waste time.

lone ADJ **= single**, solitary, sole, unaccompanied.

lonely ADJ **1 = friendless**, alone, isolated, lonesome, forlorn, unloved, with no one to turn to. **2 = remote**, desolate, isolated, out of the way, off the beaten track, deserted, uninhabited, unfrequented, godforsaken.

long ADJ **= lengthy**, extended, extensive, prolonged, protracted, long-lasting, long-drawn-out, interminable. VERB **= wish**, desire, want, yearn, crave, hunger, thirst, itch, lust, pine, hanker.

longing NOUN **= wish**, desire, yearning, craving, hunger, thirst, itch, lust, hankering; [inf] yen.

look VERB **1 = glance**, gaze, stare, gape, peer, peep, peek; watch, observe, view, regard, eye, examine, study, inspect, scan, scrutinize, survey, contemplate, ogle; [inf] gawp. **2 = seem**, appear, give the appearance of being, strike someone as. **3 = face**, overlook, front, give on to. NOUN **1 = glance**, view, examination, inspection, scan, survey, peep, peek, glimpse, gaze, stare; [inf] dekko. **2 = expression**, face, countenance, features, mien, appearance.

look after = take care of, care for, minister to, attend to, tend, mind, keep an eye on, protect.

lookalike NOUN = **double**, twin, living image, clone, doppelgänger; [inf] spitting image, dead ringer.

loom VERB = **appear**, emerge, take shape, materialize, be imminent, be on the horizon.

loop NOUN = **coil**, hoop, noose, circle, ring, oval, spiral, curl, twirl, whorl, twist, convolution.

loose ADJ 1 = **at large**, at liberty, free, on the loose, unconfined, untied. 2 = **wobbly**, insecure, rickety, unsteady. 3 = **loose-fitting**, roomy, baggy, slack, shapeless, sloppy. 4 = **inexact**, imprecise, vague, indefinite, broad, general, approximate. VERB = **set free**, turn/let loose, untie, unchain, unleash, let go, release, free.

loosen VERB = **slacken**, relax, loose, let go, lessen, weaken.

loot NOUN = **booty**, spoils, plunder, haul; [inf] swag. VERB = **plunder**, pillage, rob, burgle, steal, ransack, sack, despoil.

lop VERB = **cut**, chop, hack, prune, sever, dock, clip, crop.

lose VERB 1 = **mislay**, misplace, drop, forget. 2 = **be defeated**, be beaten, be trounced.

lost ADJ 1 = **missing**, gone missing/astray, mislaid, misplaced. 2 = **astray**, off course, disorientated, having lost your bearings.

lotion NOUN = **cream**, salve, ointment, moisturizer, balm, emollient, lubricant, unguent, liniment, embrocation.

lottery NOUN = **draw**, raffle, sweepstake, tombola.

loud ADJ 1 = **blaring**, booming, noisy, deafening, resounding, reverberant, sonorous, stentorian, thunderous, tumultuous, clamorous, ear-splitting, piercing, strident, harsh, raucous. 2 = **garish**, gaudy, flashy, flamboyant, lurid, glaring, showy, obtrusive, vulgar, tasteless; [inf] flash.

lounge VERB = **laze**, lie, recline, relax, take it easy, sprawl, slump, loll, repose, loaf, idle, loiter, hang about. NOUN = **sitting room**, drawing room, living room, parlour.

lout NOUN = **hooligan**, boor,

oaf, ruffian; [inf] yob.

lovable ADJ = **adorable**, dear, sweet, cute, charming, lovely, delightful, captivating, enchanting, engaging, appealing, winsome, winning, endearing.

love VERB **1** = **be in love with**, adore, dote on, worship, idolize, treasure, prize, cherish, be devoted to, care for, hold dear. **2** = **like**, be addicted to, enjoy greatly, relish, delight in, be partial to, have a soft spot for. NOUN **1** = **affection**, fondness, care, attachment, intimacy, devotion, adoration, passion, ardour, infatuation. **2** = **liking**, appetite, penchant, weakness, partiality, enjoyment, relish.

love affair NOUN = **affair**, romance, relationship, liaison, fling, intrigue.

lovely ADJ **1** = **beautiful**, pretty, attractive, good-looking, comely, sweet, charming, adorable, enchanting, engaging, seductive, ravishing. **2** = **delightful**, pleasant, nice, pleasing, marvellous, wonderful, terrific, fabulous.

lover NOUN **1** = **boyfriend**, girlfriend, mistress, beau, beloved, sweetheart. **2** = **admirer**, devotee, fan, enthusiast, aficionado; [inf] buff.

loving ADJ = **affectionate**, fond, devoted, caring, adoring, doting, demonstrative, tender, warm; amorous, ardent, passionate.

low ADJ **1** = **short**, small, little, squat, stunted. **2** = **scarce**, scanty, scant, sparse, meagre, few, inadequate, depleted. **3** = **soft**, quiet, muted, subdued, muffled, gentle, indistinct. **4** = **depressed**, dejected, despondent, downhearted, downcast, gloomy, glum, unhappy, sad, miserable, blue, fed up. **5** = **unfavourable**, poor, bad, adverse, negative.

low-down NOUN = **information**, data, facts, facts and figures; [inf] info, gen.

lower ADJ = **lesser**, subordinate, junior, inferior. VERB **1** = **let down**, take down, haul down.

2 = soften, quieten, hush, tone down, muffle, turn down, mute. **3 = reduce**, bring down, lessen, cut, slash.

lowly ADJ = **humble**, low-born, plebeian; simple, plain, ordinary, modest, common.

loyal ADJ = **faithful**, true, trusted, trustworthy, trusty, steadfast, staunch, dependable, reliable, devoted, dutiful, constant, unchanging, unwavering, unswerving; patriotic.

loyalty NOUN = **faithfulness**, fidelity, allegiance, devotion; patriotism.

lucid ADJ = **clear**, crystal-clear, comprehensible, intelligible, understandable, plain, simple, direct, vivid, graphic.

luck NOUN **1 = fate**, fortune, destiny, chance, accident, hazard, serendipity. **2 = good luck**, good fortune, success, prosperity.

lucky ADJ **1 = fortunate**, in luck, favoured, charmed, successful, prosperous. **2 = providential**, fortuitous, fortunate, advantageous, timely, opportune, expedient, auspicious, propitious.

lucrative ADJ = **profitable**, profit-making, money-making, well paid, gainful, remunerative.

ludicrous ADJ = **absurd**, ridiculous, stupid, laughable, risible, farcical, silly, nonsensical, preposterous, idiotic.

lull VERB = **soothe**, quiet, hush, silence, calm, still, quell, assuage, allay, ease. NOUN = **respite**, interval, break, hiatus, let-up, calm, quiet, quietness, tranquillity.

luminous ADJ = **bright**, shining, brilliant, radiant, dazzling, glowing, luminescent, phosphorescent.

lump NOUN **1 = chunk**, wedge, hunk, piece, mass, cake, nugget, clod, gobbet, wad. **2 = bump**, swelling, bruise, bulge, protuberance, growth, tumour.

lunatic NOUN = **maniac**, madman, madwoman, psychopath; [inf] loony, nut, nutter, nutcase.

lunge VERB = **thrust**, spring, launch yourself, rush,

dive.

lurch VERB = **stagger**, sway, reel, weave, stumble, totter.

lure VERB = **entice**, attract, inveigle, draw, allure, tempt, seduce, beguile.

lurid ADJ **1** = **bright**, glaring, dazzling, fluorescent, vivid, showy, gaudy.
2 = **sensational**, exaggerated, graphic, explicit, unrestrained, shocking, startling; [inf] juicy.

lurk VERB = **skulk**, lie in wait, hide, conceal yourself, loiter.

luscious ADJ = **juicy**, sweet, succulent, mouth-watering, tasty, appetizing, delicious, delectable; [inf] scrumptious.

lush ADJ **1** = **luxuriant**, abundant, rich, profuse, dense, thick, overgrown, prolific, rank.
2 = **luxurious**, sumptuous, grand, palatial, opulent, lavish, elaborate, extravagant; [inf] plush.

lustful ADJ = **lecherous**, lascivious, lewd, libidinous, licentious, hot-blooded, passionate.

luxuriant ADJ = **lush**, rich, abundant, profuse, dense, thick, riotous, overgrown, prolific.

luxurious ADJ = **opulent**, sumptuous, expensive, costly, de luxe, grand, splendid, magnificent, palatial, well appointed, extravagant, fancy; [inf] plush.

luxury NOUN **1** = **opulence**, sumptuousness, grandeur, splendour, magnificence.
2 = **extra**, non-essential, frill, extravagance, indulgence, treat.

lying ADJ = **untruthful**, mendacious, false, dishonest, deceitful, double-dealing, two-faced.

lyrical ADJ = **effusive**, rapturous, ecstatic, euphoric, carried away, impassioned.

Mm

macabre ADJ = **gruesome**, grisly, gory, morbid, horrific, horrible, frightful.

machine NOUN = **appliance**, apparatus, instrument, tool, device, contraption, gadget, mechanism.

machismo NOUN = **masculinity**, manliness, virility, chauvinism.

mad ADJ **1** = **insane**, deranged, crazy, demented, lunatic, non compos mentis, unbalanced, unhinged, manic; [inf] out of your mind, nuts, round the bend, barmy, batty, bonkers. **2** = **foolish**, stupid, foolhardy, idiotic, irrational, unreasonable, illogical, senseless, absurd, impractical, silly, asinine, ludicrous. **3** see **enthusiastic**.

madden VERB = **anger**, infuriate, enrage, incense, exasperate, irritate, annoy, provoke.

madman NOUN = **maniac**, lunatic, psychopath; [inf] loony, nutter, psycho.

madness NOUN = **insanity**, craziness, dementia, mental illness, derangement, lunacy, mania, psychosis.

magazine NOUN = **periodical**, journal, supplement.

magic NOUN **1** = **sorcery**, witchcraft, wizardry, enchantment, the occult, voodoo. **2** = **sleight of hand**, conjuring, illusion, trickery.

magician NOUN = **sorcerer**, witch, wizard, warlock, enchanter, enchantress.

magnanimous ADJ = **generous**, charitable, benevolent, kind, indulgent, bountiful, noble, altruistic, philanthropic, unselfish, selfless, self-sacrificing, merciful, forgiving.

magnificent ADJ **1** = **splendid**, grand, impressive, resplendent, grandiose, imposing, striking, glorious, majestic, noble, stately, awe-inspiring, sumptuous, opulent, luxurious, lavish. **2 = excellent**, masterly, skilful, impressive, fine.

magnify VERB **1 = augment**, enlarge, expand, amplify, intensify, heighten, boost, enhance. **2 = exaggerate**, overstate, overemphasize, dramatize, embellish, enhance.

magnitude NOUN **= size**, extent, measure, proportions, dimensions, amplitude.

mail NOUN **= post**, letters, parcels, correspondence.

main ADJ **= chief**, principal, head, leading, foremost, central, prime, premier, primary, supreme, predominant, pre-eminent, paramount, pivotal.

mainly ADV **= mostly**, on the whole, largely, by and large, predominantly, chiefly, principally, overall, generally, usually, as a rule.

maintain VERB **1 = continue**, keep up, carry on, preserve, prolong, sustain. **2 = care for**, look after, keep up, conserve, preserve. **3 = support**, provide for, keep, finance, feed, nurture. **4 = insist**, hold, declare, assert, state, affirm, claim, contend.

maintenance NOUN **1 = upkeep**, repairs, preservation, conservation, care. **2 = alimony**, support, allowance, keep.

majestic ADJ **= regal**, royal, princely, noble, stately, awesome, lofty, distinguished, magnificent, grand, splendid, resplendent, glorious, impressive, imposing, proud.

major ADJ **1 = greatest**, best, leading, foremost, chief, outstanding, notable, eminent. **2 = important**, significant, crucial, vital, weighty.

majority NOUN **1 = larger part**, most, bulk, mass, preponderance, lion's share. **2 = coming-of-age**, age of consent, adulthood, manhood, womanhood, maturity.

make VERB **1 = build**, construct, assemble, erect, manufacture, fabricate, create, form, fashion, model, compose, formulate. **2** = **force**, compel, pressurize, oblige, require. **3** = **cause**, create, bring about, generate, engender, effect. **4** = **appoint**, designate, name, nominate, select, elect, install, invest, ordain. **5** = **gain**, acquire, obtain, get, secure, win, earn, net, gross. NOUN = **brand**, label, sort, type, variety, mark.

make believe = pretend, fantasize, daydream, imagine, play-act. **make do** = **get along**, scrape by, manage, cope, muddle through.

make-believe NOUN = **pretence**, fantasy, daydreaming, play-acting, charade. ADJ = **pretended**, feigned, made-up, fantasy, imaginary, unreal, fictitious, mock, pretend.

makeshift ADJ = **stopgap**, make-do, provisional, temporary, substitute, improvised.

malice NOUN = **malevolence**, ill will, animosity, hostility, enmity, hatred, hate, spite, vindictiveness, rancour, bitterness.

malicious ADJ = **malevolent**, malign, hostile, spiteful, vindictive, rancorous, bitter, venomous, hurtful, defamatory.

malign VERB = **slander**, libel, defame, smear, vilify, cast aspersions on, denigrate.

maltreat VERB = **treat badly**, mistreat, abuse, bully, harm, hurt, molest.

manage VERB **1** = **be in charge of**, run, head, direct, control, preside over, lead, govern, rule, command, supervise, oversee, administer, organize, handle. **2** = **cope**, get along, survive, make do.

manageable ADJ **1** = **easy**, doable, practicable, possible, feasible, viable. **2** = **controllable**, tractable, compliant, docile, accommodating, amenable, submissive.

management NOUN **1** = **managers**, employers, bosses, owners, proprietors, directors, directorate, administration. **2** = **running**, charge, care, leadership, control, command, administration.

mandatory ADJ = **obligatory**, compulsory, required, requisite, essential, imperative, necessary.

mangle VERB = **mutilate**, maul, butcher, disfigure, deform.

manhandle VERB 1 = **maul**, mistreat, abuse, injure, damage, treat roughly. 2 = **heave**, haul, shove, tug; [inf] hump.

mania NOUN 1 = **frenzy**, violence, hysteria, derangement, dementia. 2 = **obsession**, compulsion, fixation, fetish, preoccupation, passion, enthusiasm.

maniac NOUN see **madman**.

manifest ADJ = **obvious**, clear, plain, apparent, patent, noticeable, conspicuous, unmistakable, distinct, blatant.

manifestation NOUN 1 = **display**, demonstration, illustration, exemplification, indication, expression.

2 = **evidence**, proof, testimony, substantiation, sign, indication, symptom.

manipulate VERB 1 = **handle**, wield, ply, work. 2 = **influence**, control, exploit, manoeuvre, direct, guide. 3 = **juggle**, falsify, doctor, fiddle, tamper with.

mankind NOUN = **man**, homo sapiens, the human race, humans, people.

manly ADJ = **masculine**, macho, virile, muscular, strapping, rugged, tough.

manner NOUN 1 = **way**, means, method, approach, technique, procedure, methodology, fashion, mode. 2 = **air**, appearance, demeanour, bearing, behaviour, conduct. 3 = **kind**, sort, type, variety, form, nature, category.

mannered ADJ = **affected**, unnatural, artificial, stilted, theatrical, pretentious.

mannerism NOUN = **habit**, characteristic, trait, idiosyncrasy, quirk, foible.

manoeuvre NOUN 1 = **movement**, move. 2 = **trick**, stratagem, tactic, subterfuge, device, dodge, ploy, ruse, scheme. VERB = **move**, work, steer, guide, direct, manipulate.

manufacture VERB = **make**, produce, build, construct, assemble, create, fabricate, fashion, model, forge.

many ADJ = **a lot**, lots, numerous, innumerable, countless, scores, multiple, copious.

mar VERB see **spoil (1)**.

march VERB = **walk**, parade, process, step, pace, stride.

margin NOUN 1 = **edge**, side, verge, border, perimeter, boundary, periphery. 2 = **leeway**, latitude, scope, allowance, extra, surplus.

marginal ADJ = **slight**, small, tiny, minute, minor, insignificant, negligible.

maritime ADJ = **naval**, marine, nautical, seafaring.

mark NOUN 1 = **stain**, blemish, spot, blotch, smudge, scratch, scar, dent, chip, nick, line, score, cut. 2 = **marker**, guide, pointer, landmark, signpost. 3 = **sign**, symbol, indication, symptom, feature, token, evidence, proof. VERB 1 = **stain**, scratch, scar, dent, chip, score, cut. 2 = **initial**, label, stamp, brand. 3 = **correct**, assess, evaluate, appraise, grade. 4 = **celebrate**, commemorate, honour, observe.

marked ADJ = **pronounced**, striking, clear, glaring, blatant, unmistakable, conspicuous, noticeable.

maroon VERB = **abandon**, desert, strand.

marriage NOUN 1 = **married state**, matrimony, wedlock, union, match. 2 = **wedding**, nuptials.

marry VERB = **wed**, become man and wife; [inf] tie the knot, get hitched.

marsh NOUN = **marshland**, bog, swamp, mire, quagmire, fen.

marshal VERB = **assemble**, gather, collect, muster, arrange, deploy.

martial ADJ = **militant**, warlike, combative, belligerent, pugnacious.

marvel VERB = **be amazed**, be awed, wonder. NOUN = **wonder**, sensation, spectacle, phenomenon, miracle.

marvellous ADJ = **amazing**, astounding,

astonishing, awesome, breathtaking, sensational, remarkable, spectacular, phenomenal, excellent, splendid, wonderful, magnificent, superb, super, great, smashing, fantastic, terrific, fabulous; [inf] ace, wicked.

masculine ADJ = **male**, manly, virile, macho, muscular, rugged.

mash VERB = **crush**, pulp, purée, squash.

mask NOUN = **disguise**, cover, camouflage, veil, front, facade. VERB = **disguise**, hide, conceal, cover up, camouflage, veil, screen.

mass NOUN
1 = **concentration**, conglomeration, assemblage, collection.
2 = **majority**, greater part, most, bulk, preponderance. ADJ = **wholesale**, universal, widespread, general, extensive. VERB = **amass**, accumulate, assemble, gather, collect.

massacre VERB see **kill**.

massage VERB = **rub**, knead, pummel, manipulate.

master NOUN = **lord**, ruler, governor, commander, captain, chief, head; [inf] boss. VERB 1 = **conquer**, vanquish, defeat, overcome, overpower, subdue, quash, suppress, control, curb. 2 = **learn**, grasp; [inf] get the hang of.

masterful ADJ = **authoritative**, powerful, controlling, domineering, dictatorial, overbearing, peremptory, high-handed.

mastermind VERB = **direct**, manage, plan, organize, arrange, engineer, conceive, devise, think up.

match VERB
1 = **complement**, blend, harmonize, coordinate, team, tally, correspond.
2 = **be equal to**, rival, vie with, compare with.
3 = **pair up**, mate, unite, join, combine, link, ally.

matching ADJ = **corresponding**, equivalent, parallel, analogous, complementary, the same, twin, identical, like.

material NOUN 1 = **matter**, substance, stuff, medium.
2 = **fabric**, cloth, textile.
3 = **data**, information,

facts, details.

materialize VERB
1 = **happen**, occur, come about, take place.
2 = **appear**, turn up, become visible, come to light, emerge.

matrimonial ADJ = **marital**, conjugal, nuptial.

matter NOUN 1 = **material**, substance, stuff. 2 = **affair**, business, situation, circumstance, event, occurrence, incident. 3 = **subject**, topic, issue, point. VERB = **be important**, signify, count, be relevant.

mature ADJ 1 = **adult**, grown-up, full-grown, of age. 2 = **ripe**, ready.

maudlin ADJ = **mawkish**, sentimental; [inf] soppy.

maverick NOUN = **nonconformist**, rebel, dissenter, dissident, eccentric.

maxim NOUN = **aphorism**, proverb, adage, saying, axiom.

maximum ADJ = **highest**, greatest, biggest, largest, topmost, most, utmost.

mayhem NOUN = **havoc**, disorder, confusion, chaos, bedlam.

meadow NOUN = **field**, pasture, paddock; [literary] lea, mead, glebe.

meagre ADJ = **paltry**, sparse, scant, inadequate, insufficient, insubstantial, skimpy, miserly, stingy.

mean¹ ADJ 1 = **miserly**, niggardly, parsimonious, penny-pinching, tight-fisted, stingy. 2 = **nasty**, disagreeable, unpleasant, unfriendly, offensive, obnoxious, bad-tempered, churlish, cantankerous.

mean² VERB 1 = **indicate**, signify, express, convey, denote, designate, represent, symbolize, connote, imply, suggest. 2 = **intend**, aim, set out, contemplate, desire, want, wish. 3 = **involve**, entail, lead to, result in.

meander VERB = **wind**, zigzag, snake, curve.

meaning NOUN
1 = **definition**, explanation, interpretation.
2 = **significance**, point, value, worth, importance.

means PLURAL NOUN = **way**, method, expedient, manner, medium, channel, avenue, course.

measure NOUN 1 = **size**, dimension, proportions, magnitude, amplitude,

mass, bulk, quantity.
2 = **share**, portion,
division, quota, ration,
percentage. 3 = **action**,
act, procedure, step,
means, expedient. VERB
= **calculate**, compute,
estimate, quantify,
evaluate, rate, assess,
appraise, gauge,
determine, judge.

mechanical ADJ
1 = **automated**, automatic,
motorized. 2 = **automatic**,
unthinking, unconscious,
involuntary, instinctive.

mechanism NOUN
1 = **machine**, apparatus,
appliance, tool, device,
instrument, contraption.
2 = **process**, procedure,
system, method, means,
medium.

meddle VERB see **interfere**
(2).

mediate VERB = **arbitrate**,
negotiate, conciliate,
intervene, intercede,
umpire, referee.

medicinal ADJ = **medical**,
therapeutic, curative,
healing, remedial,
restorative.

medicine NOUN
= **medication**, drug,
remedy, cure.

mediocre ADJ

= **indifferent**, average,
ordinary, commonplace,
run-of-the-mill, tolerable,
passable, adequate,
unexceptional, inferior,
second-rate, poor; [inf]
so-so.

meditate VERB
= **contemplate**, think,
muse, ponder, consider,
concentrate, reflect,
deliberate, ruminate.

medium NOUN 1 = **median**,
mid-point, middle,
centre, average, norm,
standard. 2 = **means**,
agency, channel, avenue,
instrument. ADJ = **middle**,
mean, median, midway,
intermediate.

meek ADJ = **docile**,
humble, submissive,
compliant, amenable,
dutiful, deferential, weak,
timid.

meet VERB 1 = **encounter**,
contact, come across,
chance on, happen on;
[inf] bump into. 2 = **come
together**, abut, adjoin,
join, connect, touch,
converge, intersect.
3 = **gather**, assemble,
congregate, convene,
muster. 4 = **treat**, handle,
approach, answer.
5 = **satisfy**, fulfil, comply

with. **6** = **carry out**, perform, execute, discharge. **7** = **face**, encounter, undergo, experience, bear, suffer, endure.

meeting NOUN
1 = **encounter**, contact, rendezvous, tryst.
2 = **gathering**, assembly, conference, congregation, convention; [inf] get-together.

melancholy ADJ see **sad** (1).

mellow ADJ = **gentle**, easy-going, pleasant, amicable, amiable, good-natured, affable, genial, jovial, cheerful, happy.

melodious ADJ = **melodic**, musical, tuneful, harmonious, lyrical, dulcet, sweet.

melodramatic ADJ = **theatrical**, overdramatic, histrionic, extravagant, overdone.

melody NOUN = **tune**, air, music, refrain, theme, song.

melt VERB = **dissolve**, thaw, defrost, soften.

member NOUN
1 = **adherent**, associate, fellow. **2** = **limb**, appendage.

memorable ADJ = **unforgettable**, momentous, significant, notable, noteworthy, important, consequential, remarkable, outstanding, striking, impressive.

memorial NOUN = **monument**, statue, shrine.

memory NOUN
1 = **remembrance**, recollection, recall.
2 = **commemoration**, honour, tribute.

menace NOUN = **threat**, danger, hazard, jeopardy.

mend VERB **1** = **repair**, fix, restore, rehabilitate, renovate, cure, heal.
2 = **put right**, rectify, correct, amend, improve.

menial ADJ = **lowly**, humble, unskilled, routine, humdrum, boring. NOUN = **servant**, domestic, drudge, underling; [inf] dogsbody, skivvy.

mentality NOUN **1** = **frame of mind**, attitude, outlook, character, disposition, make-up.
2 = **intellect**, intelligence, IQ, brains, mind, understanding.

mention VERB **1** = **refer to**,

allude to, touch on; cite, quote. **2** = **say**, state, remark. **3** = **tell**, communicate, disclose, divulge, reveal. NOUN = **reference**, allusion, remark, indication.

mentor NOUN = **adviser**, counsellor, guide, guru, teacher, tutor, coach, instructor.

mercenary ADJ = **grasping**, greedy, acquisitive, avaricious, covetous.

merchandise NOUN = **goods**, wares, stock, commodities, produce.

merchant NOUN = **trader**, dealer, wholesaler, seller, vendor, retailer.

merciful ADJ = **lenient**, clement, compassionate, forgiving, forbearing, humane, tender-hearted, kind, tolerant, generous, beneficent.

merciless ADJ = **ruthless**, relentless, harsh, pitiless, unforgiving, unsparing, barbarous, inhumane, inhuman, heartless, callous, cruel, unsympathetic.

mercy NOUN = **leniency**, clemency, compassion, pity, charity, forgiveness, humanity, kindness, tolerance.

merge VERB = **join**, amalgamate, unite, combine, incorporate, blend, fuse, mingle, mix, intermix.

merit NOUN **1** = **excellence**, quality, worth, value. **2** = **good point**, advantage, asset, plus. VERB = **deserve**, earn, be worth, be entitled to, warrant, rate, incur.

meritorious ADJ = **praiseworthy**, laudable, commendable, admirable, estimable, creditable, excellent, exemplary, good, worthy, deserving.

merry ADJ = **cheerful**, cheery, gay, high-spirited, light-hearted, buoyant, carefree, joyful, jolly, convivial, happy.

mesh NOUN = **netting**, net, lattice, latticework, lacework.

mesmerize VERB = **hypnotize**, spellbind, entrance, enthral, bewitch, captivate, enchant, fascinate, hypnotize.

mess NOUN **1** = **disorder**, untidiness, disarray, clutter, shambles, litter, jumble, muddle, chaos, confusion. **2 = plight**, predicament, difficulty, trouble, quandary, dilemma, muddle, mix-up, confusion.

message NOUN **1 = communication**, news, word, tidings, note, memorandum, letter, missive, bulletin, communiqué, memo. **2 = meaning**, idea, point, theme, moral.

messenger NOUN **= courier**, envoy, emissary, agent, go-between.

messy ADJ **= untidy**, disordered, dirty, slovenly, cluttered, littered, muddled, chaotic, disorganized, in disarray.

metamorphosis NOUN **= transformation**, transfiguration, change, alteration, conversion, mutation.

method NOUN **1 = procedure**, technique, system, practice, modus operandi, process, approach, way, manner, mode. **2 = order**, organization, structure, plan, design, purpose, pattern.

methodical ADJ **= orderly**, organized, systematic, structured, logical, efficient.

meticulous ADJ **= conscientious**, careful, scrupulous, punctilious, painstaking, exacting, thorough, perfectionist, fastidious.

microscopic ADJ **= infinitesimal**, minuscule, tiny, minute.

middle ADJ **= mid**, medium, midway, halfway, central, intermediate, median. NOUN **= mean**, median, mid-point, centre.

middling ADJ **= average**, medium, ordinary, fair, moderate, adequate, passable, mediocre, indifferent, unremarkable; [inf] so-so, fair-to-middling.

might NOUN **= force**, power, strength, potency, toughness.

mighty ADJ **1 = forceful**, powerful, strong, potent, tough, robust, vigorous. **2 = huge**, massive, vast, enormous, colossal, gigantic.

migrant ADJ **= migratory**, wandering, nomadic, itinerant.

mild ADJ **1** = **tender**, gentle, sensitive, sympathetic, warm, humane, forgiving, placid, meek, docile, calm, tranquil, mellow. **2** = **gentle**, soft, warm, balmy. **3** = **bland**, insipid, tasteless.

milieu NOUN = **environment**, surroundings, setting, location.

militant NOUN = **activist**, extremist, partisan.

military NOUN = **army**, armed forces, services, militia, navy, air force.

milky ADJ = **white**, creamy, pearly, ivory, alabaster, cloudy.

mill NOUN = **factory**, plant, foundry, works, workshop. VERB = **grind**, pulverize, crush, powder.

mimic VERB **1** = **impersonate**, imitate, copy, ape, parody; [inf] take off. **2** = **resemble**, look like, mirror, simulate.

mind NOUN **1** = **brain**, psyche, ego, subconscious. **2** = **brainpower**, intellect, mentality, intelligence, brains, wits, understanding, comprehension, sense.

3 = **memory**, recollection, remembrance. **4** = **opinion**, outlook, (point of) view, belief, judgement, attitude, feeling. VERB **1** = **object to**, care about, be bothered by, resent, dislike, disapprove of. **2** = **heed**, attend to, listen to, note, mark, observe, respect, obey, follow, comply with. **3** = **look after**, take care of, attend to, tend, watch.

mindful ADJ = **paying attention to**, heedful of, watchful of, careful of, wary of, chary of, cognizant of, aware of, conscious of, alert to, alive to, sensible of.

mine NOUN **1** = **colliery**, pit, quarry, workings. **2** = **source**, repository, store. VERB = **excavate**, quarry, dig, extract.

mingle VERB **1** = **mix**, blend, combine, merge, unite, amalgamate, fuse. **2** = **circulate**, socialize, hobnob, fraternize.

miniature ADJ = **small-scale**, mini, midget, baby, dwarf; [inf] pint-sized.

minimal ADJ = **minimum**, least, smallest, slightest, nominal, token.

minimize VERB 1 = **reduce**, decrease, curtail, cut back. 2 = **belittle**, play down, deprecate, underestimate.

minimum ADJ = **minimal**, lowest, smallest, least, slightest.

minion NOUN = **lackey**, flunkey, henchman, underling, servant.

minor ADJ = **lesser**, insignificant, unimportant, inconsequential, inferior, trivial, negligible, trifling, slight.

minute ADJ = **tiny**, minuscule, microscopic, miniature, little, small.

miracle NOUN = **wonder**, marvel, phenomenon.

miraculous ADJ = **supernatural**, fantastic, magical, inexplicable, unaccountable, phenomenal, wonderful, wondrous, remarkable.

mirror VERB = **reflect**, imitate, emulate, copy, follow, mimic, echo, ape, impersonate.

mirth NOUN = **gaiety**, merriment, cheerfulness, hilarity, glee, laughter.

misapprehension NOUN see **misunderstanding**.

misbehave VERB = **behave badly**, be naughty, be disobedient, get up to mischief; [inf] act up.

miscellaneous ADJ = **varied**, assorted, mixed, diverse, sundry, motley, indiscriminate, heterogeneous.

miscellany NOUN = **assortment**, mixture, variety, collection, medley, pot-pourri, mix, mishmash.

mischief NOUN = **mischievousness**, naughtiness, bad behaviour, misconduct, wrongdoing, delinquency.

mischievous ADJ 1 = **naughty**, bad, badly behaved, disobedient, troublesome, delinquent. 2 = **playful**, teasing, impish, roguish, arch.

miserable ADJ = **unhappy**, dejected, depressed, downcast, downhearted, despondent, desolate, gloomy, dismal, blue, melancholy, sad, forlorn.

miserly ADJ see **mean**[1] (1).

misery NOUN 1 = **distress**, wretchedness, suffering, anguish, grief, sorrow, heartbreak, despair, depression, melancholy,

woe, sadness,
unhappiness. **2 = trouble**,
misfortune, adversity,
hardship, affliction,
ordeal, pain, burden, trial,
tribulation.

misfortune NOUN **= bad luck**, setback, adversity,
misadventure, mishap,
blow, accident, disaster,
affliction, trial,
tribulation.

misgiving NOUN **= qualm**,
doubt, reservation,
apprehension, unease,
uncertainty.

misguided ADJ
= mistaken, deluded,
erroneous, wrong, ill-
advised, unwise,
injudicious, imprudent,
foolish.

mishap NOUN **= accident**,
trouble, setback, reverse,
misadventure,
misfortune.

mislay VERB **= lose**,
misplace, miss.

mislead VERB **= misinform**,
misdirect, delude, take in,
deceive, fool, hoodwink,
pull the wool over
someone's eyes.

misleading ADJ see
deceptive.

miss VERB **1 = skip**, play
truant from. **2 = let slip**,
pass up, overlook,
disregard. **3 = long for**,
pine for, yearn for, ache
for.

misshapen ADJ
= deformed, distorted,
warped, crooked.

missing ADJ **= lost**, mislaid,
misplaced, absent, gone
astray.

mission NOUN
1 = assignment, task, job,
errand, work, duty,
charge. **2 = vocation**,
calling, pursuit, quest.
3 = delegation,
deputation, task force.

missive NOUN
= communication,
message, letter, memo,
note, memorandum,
bulletin, communiqué,
dispatch.

mistake NOUN **= error**,
fault, inaccuracy, slip,
blunder, miscalculation,
misunderstanding,
oversight, faux pas,
slip-up.

mistreat VERB **= maltreat**,
ill-treat, ill-use, abuse,
mishandle, harm, hurt,
molest.

mistrust VERB **= distrust**,
suspect, have reservations
about, have misgivings,
be wary, question, doubt.

misty ADJ = **hazy**, foggy, cloudy, blurred, indistinct, vague.

misunderstand VERB = **misinterpret**, misconstrue, misread; [inf] get the wrong end of the stick.

misunderstanding NOUN = **misapprehension**, mistake, error, mix-up, misinterpretation, misconception, misbelief.

misuse VERB **1** = **abuse**, squander, waste, dissipate. **2** = **maltreat**, mistreat, ill-treat, abuse, manhandle, harm, hurt, bully, molest.

mitigate VERB = **alleviate**, reduce, diminish, lessen, attenuate, allay, assuage, palliate, soothe, relieve, ease, soften, temper, mollify, moderate.

mix VERB **1** = **blend**, combine, mingle, merge, unite, join, amalgamate, fuse. **2** = **socialize**, mingle, meet people. NOUN = **mixture**, blend, combination, union, amalgamation, fusion.

mixed ADJ **1** = **assorted**, varied, miscellaneous, diverse, heterogeneous. **2** = **hybrid**, cross-bred,

interbred, mongrel. **3** = **ambivalent**, equivocal, unsure, uncertain.

mixture NOUN **1** = **compound**, blend, mix, brew, concoction. **2** = **assortment**, variety, mélange, collection, medley, pot-pourri, conglomeration, jumble, mix, mishmash.

moan NOUN = **groan**, lament, lamentation, wail, whimper, whine. VERB **1** = **groan**, wail, whimper, whine. **2** = **complain**, whine, carp; [inf] grouse, gripe, whinge.

mob NOUN = **crowd**, horde, multitude, rabble, mass, throng, host, gang. VERB = **crowd around**, surround, besiege, jostle.

mobilize VERB = **muster**, rally, marshal, assemble, organize, prepare, ready.

mock VERB = **ridicule**, jeer, sneer, deride, scorn, make fun of, tease, taunt, insult. ADJ = **imitation**, artificial, simulated, synthetic, fake, sham, false, bogus, pseudo.

mockery NOUN **1** = **ridicule**, jeering, derision, contempt, scorn, disdain, gibe, insult. **2** = **parody**, travesty, caricature, lampoon.

model NOUN 1 = **replica**, representation, mock-up, copy, dummy, imitation. 2 = **prototype**, archetype, original, pattern, paradigm, sample, example. 3 = **style**, design, form, mark, version, type, variety, kind, sort. 4 = **ideal**, paragon, perfect example, exemplar, epitome.

moderate ADJ 1 = **middle-of-the-road**, average, middling, ordinary, fair, modest, tolerable, passable, adequate. 2 = **restrained**, controlled, sober. VERB = **abate**, let up, die down, calm down, lessen, decrease, diminish, mitigate, alleviate, ease.

moderately ADV = **quite**, rather, somewhat, fairly, reasonably, to some extent.

modern ADJ 1 = **contemporary**, present-day, present, current, 21st-century. 2 = **fashionable**, in style, in vogue, modish, new, newfangled, fresh; [inf] trendy, with it.

modernize VERB = **update**, renovate, refresh, revamp, rejuvenate.

modest ADJ 1 = **self-effacing**, self-deprecating, unassuming; shy, bashful, self-conscious, diffident, reserved, reticent. 2 = **small**, ordinary, simple, plain, humble, inexpensive, unostentatious, unpretentious.

modicum NOUN = **little (bit)**, iota, jot, atom, scrap, crumb, shred, mite, drop.

modify VERB = **alter**, change, adjust, adapt, revise, recast, reform, rework, redo, refine.

moist ADJ = **wet**, damp, clammy, humid, dank, dewy, soggy, juicy.

moisture NOUN = **water**, liquid, wetness, damp, humidity, dew.

molest VERB = **pester**, annoy, plague, torment, harass, badger, harry, persecute, bother; [inf] hassle, bug.

mollify VERB = **calm**, pacify, placate, appease, soothe, quiet.

moment NOUN = **minute**, second, instant, point, time, juncture; [inf] tick, jiffy.

momentary ADJ = **brief**, short-lived, fleeting, passing, transient, transitory, ephemeral, temporary.

momentous ADJ = **crucial**, critical, vital, decisive, pivotal, important, significant, consequential, fateful, historic.

momentum NOUN = **impetus**, impulse, thrust, drive, power, energy, force.

money NOUN = **cash**, finance, capital, funds, banknotes, currency, coins, coinage; [inf] dough, lolly, bread, dosh.

monitor NOUN = **detector**, scanner, recorder, observer, watchdog, overseer, supervisor, invigilator. VERB = **observe**, scan, record, survey, follow, check, oversee, supervise, invigilate.

monopolize VERB = **corner**, control, take over, dominate.

monotonous ADJ = **unvarying**, unchanging, repetitious, uniform, routine, humdrum, uninteresting, unexciting, dull, boring, tedious.

monster NOUN = **fiend**, beast, brute, barbarian, savage, villain, ogre.

monstrous ADJ
1 = **malformed**, abnormal, grotesque, freakish, mutant. 2 see **outrageous**.

monument NOUN = **memorial**, statue, shrine, mausoleum, obelisk.

mood NOUN = **humour**, temper, disposition, frame of mind.

moody ADJ = **temperamental**, changeable, unpredictable, volatile, mercurial, unstable, impulsive, capricious.

moot ADJ = **debatable**, open to question, doubtful, disputable, arguable, controversial, unresolved, undecided.

moral NOUN = **lesson**, teaching, message, meaning, significance, point.

morale NOUN = **confidence**, heart, spirit, hope, hopefulness, optimism.

morality NOUN = **morals**, standards, ethics, principles.

morbid ADJ = **gruesome**,

grisly, macabre, hideous, horrible.

more ADV = **to a greater extent**, further, longer. PRON = **extra**, addition, supplement, increase, increment.

moreover ADV = **besides**, furthermore, further, what is more, in addition, also, as well, into the bargain, to boot.

moron NOUN see **fool (1)**.

morsel NOUN = **bite**, nibble, bit, crumb, grain, piece, scrap, taste.

mortal ADJ 1 = **temporal**, transient, ephemeral, impermanent, perishable, human, earthly, worldly, corporeal. 2 = **deadly**, sworn, irreconcilable, bitter, implacable.

mortify VERB = **humiliate**, humble, disgrace, shame, abash, chasten, crush, discomfit, embarrass.

mostly ADV = **on the whole**, largely, mainly, chiefly, predominantly.

motherly ADJ = **maternal**, protective, comforting, caring, loving, affectionate, fond, warm, tender.

motion NOUN = **mobility**, locomotion, movement, travel, flow, action, activity.

motionless ADJ = **unmoving**, still, stationary, immobile, static, frozen.

motivate VERB = **move**, cause, lead, persuade, prompt, drive, impel, spur, induce, provoke, incite, inspire.

motive NOUN = **motivation**, reason, rationale, grounds, cause, basis, occasion, incentive, inducement, influence, stimulus, spur.

mottled ADJ = **blotched**, blotchy, speckled, spotted, marbled, flecked, dappled.

motto NOUN = **maxim**, aphorism, adage, saying, axiom, precept.

mould VERB = **shape**, form, fashion, model, create, design, carve, sculpt.

mouldy ADJ = **mildewed**, decaying, rotting, rotten, bad.

mound NOUN = **hillock**, knoll, rise, hummock, tump, embankment, bank, dune.

mount VERB 1 = **ascend**, go up, climb, scale. 2 = **increase**, grow,

escalate, intensify.
3 = **stage**, put on, prepare, organize, arrange.
mountain NOUN = **peak**, height, pinnacle, fell, alp; [Scottish] ben; [literary] mount.
mourn VERB = **grieve**, sorrow, lament, bewail, bemoan.
mournful ADJ see **sad (1)**.
mouth NOUN **1** = **lips**, jaws; [inf] gob, trap. **2** = **opening**, entrance, entry, inlet, aperture.
move VERB **1** = **go**, walk, march, proceed, progress, advance. **2** = **carry**, transport, transfer, shift.
3 = **take action**, act, do something, get moving.
4 = **move house**, relocate, leave, go away. **5** = **affect**, touch, impress, upset, disturb, disquiet.
6 = **provoke**, incite, rouse, excite, stimulate, motivate, influence, prompt, cause, induce.
7 = **propose**, put forward, advocate, recommend, suggest. NOUN
1 = **movement**, motion, action, activity, gesture, gesticulation. **2** = **action**, act, deed, measure, step, manoeuvre, tactic,

stratagem. **3** = **turn**, go.
movement NOUN **1** = **move**, motion, action, gesture, gesticulation.
2 = **campaign**, crusade, drive, group, party, organization, coalition, front.
moving ADJ **1** = **affecting**, touching, emotive, emotional, poignant, stirring, arousing, upsetting, disturbing.
2 = **movable**, mobile, motile, unfixed.
3 = **driving**, dynamic, impelling, motivating, stimulating, inspirational.
muck NOUN **1** = **dirt**, grime, filth, mud, slime, sludge; [inf] gunk, gunge. **2** = **dung**, manure, excrement, faeces.
muddle VERB **1** = **confuse**, mix up, jumble, scramble, mess up. **2** = **confuse**, disorientate, bewilder, perplex, puzzle, baffle, nonplus, confound.
muddy VERB **1** = **dirty**, begrime, soil. **2** = **make unclear**, cloud, confuse, mix up, jumble, scramble, get into a tangle.
muffle VERB **1** = **wrap up**, swathe, swaddle, envelop.
2 = **deaden**, dull, dampen,

stifle, smother, suppress, soften, quieten, mute.

mug VERB = **assault**, attack, rob.

muggy ADJ = **close**, stuffy, sultry, oppressive, airless, humid.

multiple ADJ = **several**, many, numerous, various.

multiply VERB **1** = **breed**, reproduce. **2** = **increase**, grow, accumulate, augment, proliferate.

multitude NOUN = **crowd**, assembly, throng, host, horde, mass, mob.

munch VERB = **chew**, chomp, masticate, crunch, eat.

mundane ADJ = **common**, ordinary, everyday, workaday, usual, prosaic, pedestrian, routine, customary, normal, typical, commonplace.

murder NOUN = **killing**, slaying, manslaughter, homicide, slaughter, assassination, butchery, carnage, massacre. VERB see **kill** (1).

murderer NOUN = **killer**, slayer, cut-throat, assassin, butcher.

murderous ADJ = **fatal**, lethal, deadly, mortal, homicidal, bloodthirsty.

murky ADJ = **dark**, dim, gloomy, dirty, muddy, dingy, dull, cloudy.

murmur NOUN = **whisper**, undertone, mutter, mumble, burble, drone. VERB = **whisper**, speak sotto voce, mutter, mumble, burble, drone.

muscular ADJ = **brawny**, strapping, well built, hefty, rugged, beefy, burly.

muse VERB = **think**, meditate, ruminate, contemplate, reflect, deliberate, daydream.

musical ADJ = **tuneful**, melodic, melodious, harmonious, dulcet.

muster VERB = **assemble**, rally, mobilize, round up, marshal, collect.

musty ADJ = **fusty**, mouldy, stale, stuffy, airless, damp, dank.

mutation NOUN = **change**, variation, alteration, transformation, metamorphosis, transmogrification, transfiguration.

mute ADJ = **silent**, speechless, wordless, taciturn, uncommunicative; [inf] mum.

muted ADJ = **soft**, subdued, subtle, discreet, quiet, understated.

mutinous ADJ = **rebellious**, insurgent, revolutionary, subversive, traitorous, insubordinate, disobedient, riotous, unruly.

mutiny NOUN = **rebellion**, revolt, insurrection, insurgence, uprising, revolution.

mysterious ADJ = **enigmatic**, impenetrable, inscrutable, incomprehensible, inexplicable, unfathomable, obscure, arcane, cryptic, supernatural, uncanny, mystical, peculiar, strange, weird, curious, bizarre, mystifying, perplexing, puzzling.

mystery NOUN = **enigma**, puzzle, secret, riddle, conundrum.

mystic, **mystical** ADJ = **spiritual**, paranormal, transcendental, other-worldly, supernatural, occult, metaphysical.

mystify VERB = **confuse**, bewilder, confound, perplex, baffle, nonplus, puzzle; [inf] stump, bamboozle.

myth NOUN 1 = **legend**, saga, (folk) tale, story, fable, allegory, parable, fairy story. 2 = **fantasy**, delusion, invention, fabrication, untruth, lie.

mythical ADJ 1 = **legendary**, mythological, fabled, fabulous, fairy-tale, fictitious. 2 = **imagined**, imaginary, pretend, make-believe, unreal, invented, fabricated, non-existent, made-up, untrue.

Nn

nadir NOUN = **the lowest point**, rock-bottom, the depths.

nag VERB = **scold**, carp, pick on, keep on at, harp on at, henpeck, bully, chivvy. NOUN = **shrew**, scold, harpy, termagant.

naive ADJ = **innocent**, artless, childlike, ingenuous, guileless, unsophisticated, unworldly.

naked ADJ = **nude**, bare, stripped, unclothed, undressed; [inf] starkers, in the buff.

name NOUN = **appellation**, designation, cognomen, denomination, sobriquet, title, label, epithet; [inf] moniker, handle. VERB = **christen**, baptize, call, entitle, label, term, title, dub.

nameless ADJ = **unnamed**, untitled, anonymous, unidentified, unspecified.

nap NOUN = **catnap**, doze, rest, lie-down; [inf] snooze, kip.

narrate VERB = **tell**, relate, recount, recite, describe, detail.

narrator NOUN = **reporter**, storyteller, chronicler.

narrow ADJ 1 = **slender**, thin, slim, slight, attenuated. 2 = **limited**, restricted, select, exclusive.

narrow-minded ADJ = **intolerant**, illiberal, reactionary, prejudiced, bigoted, biased, discriminatory, provincial, insular, small-minded.

nasty ADJ = **unpleasant**, disagreeable, distasteful, horrible, vile, foul, hateful, loathsome, revolting, disgusting, odious, obnoxious, repellent, repugnant, offensive, objectionable, unsavoury.

nation NOUN = **country**, land, state, kingdom, empire, realm, republic, commonwealth, people, race, society.

national ADJ = **nationwide**, countrywide, state,

widespread. NOUN = **citizen**, subject, native.

native ADJ **1** = **inborn**, inherent, innate, intrinsic, instinctive, natural, congenital, hereditary. **2** = **indigenous**, domestic, local.

natural ADJ **1** = **organic**, pure, unrefined, whole, plain. **2** = **native**, inborn, inherent, innate, intrinsic, instinctive, congenital, hereditary, ingrained. **3** = **genuine**, real, authentic, unaffected, unpretentious, candid, open, frank, ingenuous, artless, guileless.

nature NOUN **1** = **natural forces**, creation, the environment, the earth. **2** = **kind**, sort, type, variety, category, class. **3** = **temperament**, personality, disposition, humour.

naughty ADJ = **mischievous**, badly behaved, disobedient, defiant, unruly, wayward, delinquent, undisciplined, errant.

nauseous ADJ = **sick**, queasy, bilious, nauseated, green about the gills.

nautical ADJ = **maritime**, naval, marine, seagoing, seafaring.

near ADJ **1** = **close**, nearby, in the vicinity, alongside, at close range/quarters, accessible, within reach, adjacent, adjoining, bordering. **2** = **approaching**, coming, imminent, forthcoming, in the offing, impending, looming.

nearly ADV = **almost**, virtually, well-nigh, about, practically, roughly, approximately.

neat ADJ **1** = **tidy**, orderly, spick and span, shipshape. **2** = **smart**, spruce, trim, dapper, well groomed. **3** = **adroit**, skilful, dexterous, deft, nimble, agile.

necessary ADJ = **needed**, essential, required, requisite, vital, indispensable, imperative, mandatory, obligatory, compulsory.

need VERB = **require**, necessitate, demand, call for, want, lack. NOUN = **requirement**, want, prerequisite, requisite, essential.

needless ADJ
= **unnecessary**, uncalled-for, gratuitous, pointless, dispensable, expendable, inessential.

negative ADJ
= **pessimistic**, defeatist, gloomy, cynical, jaundiced, critical, unhelpful.

neglect VERB 1 = **fail to look after**, abandon, forsake, leave alone. 2 = **let slide**, shirk, be remiss/lax about. NOUN = **negligence**, neglectfulness, carelessness, heedlessness, laxity.

negligent ADJ = **neglectful**, remiss, lax, careless, inattentive, heedless, thoughtless, unmindful, slack, sloppy, slapdash, slipshod.

negligible ADJ = **trivial**, trifling, insignificant, paltry, petty, tiny, small, minor, inconsequential.

negotiate VERB = **bargain**, debate, parley, haggle.

neighbourhood NOUN = **district**, area, region, locality, quarter, precinct.

neighbouring ADJ = **adjacent**, adjoining, bordering, nearby, near, in the vicinity.

nemesis NOUN = **downfall**, undoing, ruin, Waterloo.

nervous ADJ = **on edge**, edgy, tense, anxious, agitated, worried, fretful, uneasy, jumpy, on tenterhooks, apprehensive, frightened, scared; [inf] jittery, uptight.

nestle VERB = **snuggle**, curl up, cuddle up.

net NOUN = **netting**, fishnet, mesh, lattice, webbing. VERB = **catch**, trap, snare, ensnare, bag.

neurotic ADJ = **unstable**, obsessive, fixated, over-sensitive, hysterical, irrational.

neuter ADJ = **asexual**, sexless. VERB = **castrate**, geld, emasculate, spay.

neutral ADJ = **impartial**, unbiased, unprejudiced, open-minded, non-partisan, disinterested, objective.

neutralize VERB = **counteract**, cancel, nullify, negate, annul, invalidate.

new ADJ = **modern**, recent, state-of-the-art, contemporary, current, latest, up-to-date, modish, avant-garde, futuristic, newfangled.

newcomer NOUN = **arrival**, incomer, immigrant, settler, stranger, outsider, foreigner, alien.

news PLURAL NOUN = **information**, facts, data, report, story, statement, announcement, press release, communiqué, bulletin, dispatch, the latest; [inf] gen, info.

newspaper NOUN = **paper**, gazette, journal, tabloid, broadsheet.

next ADJ 1 = **following**, succeeding, successive, subsequent, later, ensuing. 2 = **neighbouring**, adjacent, adjoining, bordering.

nice ADJ 1 = **good**, pleasant, enjoyable, pleasurable, agreeable, delightful, charming. 2 = **fine**, dry, sunny, warm.

niggardly ADJ = **mean**, miserly, stingy, tight-fisted, parsimonious.

nimble ADJ = **agile**, sprightly, spry, skilful, deft.

nippy ADJ = **icy**, chilly, bitter, raw.

noble ADJ 1 = **aristocratic**, blue-blooded, titled. 2 = **generous**, magnanimous, self-sacrificing, honourable. 3 = **impressive**, imposing, magnificent, awesome, stately, grand.

nod VERB = **incline**, bob, bow, dip.

noise NOUN = **sound**, din, hubbub, racket, row, uproar, commotion, rumpus, pandemonium.

nomad NOUN = **itinerant**, traveller, migrant, wanderer, vagabond, vagrant, tramp.

nominal ADJ 1 = **in name only**, titular, theoretical, self-styled. 2 = **token**, symbolic, minimal.

nominate VERB = **name**, propose, submit, recommend.

nonchalant ADJ = **self-possessed**, calm, cool, unconcerned, blasé, casual, easy-going; [inf] laid-back.

nonplus VERB = **take aback**, stun, dumbfound, confound, astound, astonish, amaze, surprise, disconcert, bewilder.

nonsense NOUN = **rubbish**, balderdash, drivel, gibberish, twaddle, bunkum, tripe, tosh, gobbledegook, mumbo-jumbo, poppycock, claptrap, bilge.

nonsensical ADJ
= **meaningless**,
incomprehensible,
unintelligible, senseless,
foolish, absurd, silly,
inane, stupid, ridiculous,
ludicrous.

non-stop ADJ = **incessant**,
ceaseless, constant,
continuous, continual,
unbroken, relentless,
persistent, endless,
interminable.

nook NOUN = **corner**,
cranny, recess, alcove,
niche, crevice.

normal ADJ **1** = **usual**,
ordinary, standard,
average, common,
commonplace,
conventional, typical,
regular, run-of-the-mill,
everyday. **2** = **well
adjusted**, rational, sane.

normally ADV = **usually**,
ordinarily, as a rule,
generally, commonly,
habitually.

nose NOUN = **proboscis**,
snout, muzzle; [inf] conk,
hooter. VERB = **pry**, snoop,
search, investigate.

nosy ADJ = **inquisitive**,
curious, interfering,
meddlesome, intrusive.

notable ADJ = **noteworthy**,

remarkable, outstanding,
important, significant,
momentous, memorable,
striking, impressive,
uncommon, unusual,
special, extraordinary.

note NOUN **1** = **record**,
account, notation,
comment, jotting,
footnote, annotation.
2 = **letter**, message,
memorandum, memo,
epistle, communication.
VERB **1** = **observe**, perceive,
behold, detect. **2** = **write
down**, record, register.

noted ADJ = **notable**,
distinguished, eminent,
prominent, illustrious,
famous, renowned,
celebrated, acclaimed.

notice NOUN **1** = **attention**,
heed, note, regard,
consideration, vigilance.
2 = **bulletin**, poster, leaflet,
advertisement. VERB = **see**,
note, observe, perceive,
spy, detect, behold, spot,
heed, mark.

noticeable ADJ
= **observable**, visible,
discernible, perceptible,
distinct, evident, obvious,
apparent, manifest,
patent, plain, clear,
conspicuous.

notify VERB = **inform**, tell,

advise, apprise, warn,
alert.

notion NOUN = **idea**, belief,
opinion, thought,
impression, view,
conviction, hypothesis,
theory.

notorious ADJ = **infamous**,
disreputable,
dishonourable,
scandalous.

nourishing ADJ
= **nutritious**, wholesome,
healthy, beneficial.

nourishment NOUN = **food**,
nutriment, nutrition,
sustenance, provisions.

novel ADJ = **new**, fresh,
different, original,
unusual, imaginative,
inventive,
unconventional,
innovative, ground-
breaking.

novice NOUN = **beginner**,
newcomer, apprentice,
trainee, learner, student,
pupil, recruit.

now ADV = **at present**, at the
moment, for the time
being, currently.

noxious ADJ
= **unwholesome**,
unhealthy, poisonous,
toxic, harmful.

nucleus NOUN = **core**,
kernel, centre, heart, nub.

nude ADJ see **naked**.

nudge VERB = **poke**, jab,
prod, elbow, push, shove.

nuisance NOUN = **pest**,
bother, irritant,
annoyance, trouble,
problem, difficulty.

numb ADJ = **without
feeling**, insensible,
anaesthetized, paralysed,
immobilized, frozen,
dazed, stunned. VERB
= **deaden**, anaesthetize,
paralyse, immobilize,
freeze, daze, stun.

number NOUN = **figure**,
digit, numeral, unit,
integer.

numerous ADJ = **many**,
lots, innumerable,
myriad, several, various.

nurse VERB 1 = **take care of**,
look after, tend, minister
to. 2 = **suckle**, breast-feed,
feed.

nurture VERB = **feed**,
nourish, take care of,
provide for, tend, bring
up, rear.

nutritious ADJ see
nourishing.

nuzzle VERB = **nose**, nudge,
prod, push.

Oo

oaf NOUN = **lout**, boor, brute, clodhopper.

oath NOUN 1 = **vow**, promise, pledge, word (of honour). 2 = **curse**, swear word, expletive, blasphemy, profanity, obscenity.

obedient ADJ = **compliant**, acquiescent, dutiful, deferential, respectful, submissive, docile, meek.

obese ADJ see **fat**.

obey VERB = **abide by**, comply with, adhere to, observe, conform to, respect, follow.

object NOUN 1 = **thing**, article, entity, item. 2 = **objective**, aim, goal, target, end, purpose, design, intention, point. VERB = **protest**, demur, take exception, oppose, complain.

objection NOUN = **protest**, protestation, complaint, opposition, disapproval, grievance, qualm.

objectionable ADJ = **offensive**, obnoxious, unpleasant, disagreeable, unacceptable, nasty, disgusting, loathsome, hateful, detestable, deplorable, intolerable, contemptible, odious.

objective ADJ = **unbiased**, unprejudiced, impartial, neutral, disinterested, detached, fair, open-minded. NOUN see **object (2)**.

obligate VERB = **oblige**, compel, require, necessitate, impel, force.

obligatory ADJ = **compulsory**, mandatory, necessary, essential, required, requisite, imperative, unavoidable.

oblige VERB 1 see **obligate**. 2 = **do someone a favour**, help, accommodate, assist.

obliging ADJ see **helpful**.

oblique ADJ 1 = **slanting**, sloping, inclined, angled, tilted, diagonal. 2 = **indirect**, implied, ambiguous, evasive, backhanded.

obliterate VERB = **erase**, eradicate, efface, blot out, rub out, wipe out, delete, destroy, annihilate, eliminate.

oblivious ADJ = **heedless**, unaware, ignorant, blind, deaf, inattentive, absent-minded, unconcerned, preoccupied.

obscene ADJ = **indecent**, pornographic, blue, off-colour, risqué, lewd, smutty, suggestive, vulgar, dirty, filthy, coarse, offensive, immoral, improper.

obscure ADJ **1** = **unclear**, indeterminate, opaque, abstruse, arcane, cryptic, mysterious, puzzling, confusing, unfathomable, incomprehensible, impenetrable, vague, indefinite, indistinct, hazy, ambiguous, blurred, fuzzy. **2** = **unknown**, unheard-of, insignificant, minor, unimportant, unsung.

obsequious ADJ = **servile**, subservient, submissive, slavish, fawning, grovelling, sycophantic, ingratiating.

observant ADJ = **alert**, sharp, eagle-eyed, attentive, vigilant, watchful, on guard, intent, aware.

observation NOUN **1** = **scrutiny**, monitoring, surveillance, attention, consideration, study, examination. **2** = **remark**, comment, statement, pronouncement.

observe VERB **1** = **see**, notice, perceive, discern, detect, espy, behold, watch, view, spot, witness. **2** = **keep**, obey, adhere to, abide by, heed, follow, comply with, respect. **3** = **celebrate**, commemorate, mark, remember, solemnize.

observer NOUN = **watcher**, onlooker, witness, eyewitness, spectator, bystander, viewer.

obsess VERB = **preoccupy**, haunt, possess, consume, engross, dominate, control, prey on, plague, torment.

obsession NOUN = **preoccupation**, fixation, passion, mania, enthusiasm, infatuation, compulsion, fetish, craze; [inf] hang-up.

obsolete ADJ = **discontinued**, extinct, bygone, outmoded, antiquated, out of date, old-fashioned, dated, antique, archaic, ancient.

obstacle NOUN = **bar**, barrier, obstruction, impediment, hindrance, hurdle, stumbling block, snag, difficulty.

obstinate ADJ = **stubborn**, mulish, pig-headed, wilful, strong-minded, perverse, recalcitrant, unyielding, inflexible, immovable, intransigent, uncompromising, persistent, tenacious.

obstreperous ADJ = **unruly**, disorderly, rowdy, boisterous, rough, riotous, out of control, wild, undisciplined.

obstruct VERB = **block**, barricade, bar, shut off, choke, clog, stop, hinder, impede, hamper, frustrate, thwart, curb.

obtain VERB **1** = **get**, acquire, come by, procure, secure, gain, pick up. **2** = **be in force**, be effective, exist, stand, prevail, hold.

obtuse ADJ see **stupid**.

obvious ADJ = **clear**, plain, visible, noticeable, perceptible, evident, apparent, manifest, patent, conspicuous, pronounced, transparent, prominent, unmistakable.

occasion NOUN **1** = **time**, juncture, point, instance, case, circumstance. **2** = **event**, incident, occurrence, happening, episode, affair.

occasional ADJ = **infrequent**, intermittent, irregular, sporadic.

occasionally ADV = **now and then**, from time to time, sometimes, once in a while, periodically, sporadically.

occupation NOUN **1** = **job**, profession, business, employment, career, vocation, trade, craft, line, field. **2** = **occupancy**, tenancy, tenure, residence, inhabitancy, possession. **3** = **invasion**, seizure, takeover, conquest, capture.

occupy VERB **1** = **live in**, inhabit, reside in, dwell in. **2** = **fill**, take up, utilize. **3** = **invade**, overrun, seize, take over.

occur VERB **1** = **happen**, take place, come about, materialize, transpire, arise, crop up. **2** = **be found**, be present, exist, appear.

occurrence NOUN

1 = happening, event, incident, circumstance, affair, episode.
2 = existence, appearance, manifestation.

odd ADJ **1 = strange**, eccentric, queer, peculiar, weird, bizarre, offbeat, freaky. **2 = occasional**, random, irregular, periodic, haphazard, seasonal, irregular.

odious ADJ **= abhorrent**, hateful, offensive, disgusting, repulsive, vile, unpleasant, disagreeable, loathsome, despicable, contemptible.

odour NOUN **= aroma**, smell, scent, perfume, fragrance, bouquet; stench, stink.

offence NOUN **1 = crime**, wrongdoing, misdemeanour, misdeed, sin, transgression.
2 = annoyance, anger, indignation, wrath, displeasure, disapproval, resentment.

offend VERB **1 = affront**, upset, displease, annoy, anger, irritate, outrage, insult. **2 = commit a crime**, break the law, do wrong, sin, err, transgress.

offender NOUN
= wrongdoer, culprit, criminal, lawbreaker, miscreant, delinquent, sinner.

offensive ADJ **= hurtful**, wounding, abusive, objectionable, outrageous, insulting, rude, discourteous, impolite.

offer VERB **1 = put forward**, propose, submit, suggest, recommend. **2 = volunteer**.

offering NOUN
= contribution, donation, gift, present, handout.

offhand ADJ **= casual**, unceremonious, cavalier, careless, cursory, abrupt, brusque, impolite, rude.

office NOUN **1 = place of business**, workplace.
2 = post, position, role, function, responsibility.

official ADJ **= authorized**, accredited, approved, certified, endorsed, sanctioned, recognized, accepted, legitimate, bona fide, proper.

officiate VERB **= take charge**, preside, oversee, superintend, chair.

officious ADJ **= self-important**, dictatorial, domineering, interfering, intrusive, meddlesome; [inf] pushy.

offset VERB
= **counterbalance**,
counteract, cancel out,
compensate for, make up
for.

offspring NOUN = **children**,
family, progeny, young,
descendants, heirs,
successors; [inf] kids.

often ADV = **frequently**, a
lot, repeatedly, time and
again, over and over;
[literary] oft.

oily ADJ 1 = **greasy**, fatty.
2 = **smooth-talking**,
flattering, glib, unctuous.

ointment NOUN = **cream**,
lotion, salve, balm,
liniment.

old ADJ 1 = **older**, elderly,
aged, mature, getting on,
ancient, decrepit, senile,
senior; [inf] over the hill.
2 = **dilapidated**, run-down,
tumbledown, ramshackle.
3 = **out-of-date**, outdated,
old-fashioned, outmoded,
passé, archaic, obsolete
antiquated. 4 = **bygone**,
past, early, earlier,
primeval, prehistoric.

old-fashioned ADJ see **old**
(3).

omen NOUN = **portent**, sign,
premonition, warning,
prediction, forecast,
prophecy.

ominous ADJ
= **threatening**, menacing,
gloomy, sinister, bad,
unpromising,
inauspicious,
unfavourable, unlucky.

omit VERB 1 = **leave out**,
exclude, except, miss, pass
over, drop. 2 = **forget**,
neglect, overlook, skip.

omnipotent ADJ = **all-
powerful**, almighty,
supreme, invincible.

onerous ADJ = **arduous**,
strenuous, difficult, hard,
taxing, demanding,
exacting, wearisome.

ongoing ADJ = **in progress**,
current, developing,
growing.

onset NOUN = **start**,
beginning,
commencement,
inception.

onslaught NOUN = **assault**,
attack, raid, foray, push,
thrust, blitz.

onus NOUN = **burden**,
responsibility, liability,
obligation, duty.

open ADJ 1 = **ajar**, unlocked,
unbolted, unfastened,
gaping, yawning.
2 = **exposed**, extensive,
broad, sweeping, airy,
uncluttered. 3 = **frank**,
candid, honest,

forthright, direct, blunt.
4 = obvious, clear,
noticeable, visible,
apparent, evident, overt,
conspicuous, patent,
unconcealed,
undisguised, blatant.
5 = unbiased,
unprejudiced, impartial,
objective, disinterested,
dispassionate. VERB
= unlock, unbolt, unlatch;
unwrap, undo, untie.

opening NOUN **1 = gap**,
aperture, space, hole,
orifice, vent. **2 = vacancy**,
position, job,
opportunity, chance.

operate VERB **1 = work**,
function, go, run,
perform, act. **2 = use**,
utilize, employ, handle.

operational ADJ
= operative, workable,
working, functioning, in
use, usable.

opinion NOUN **= view**, belief,
thought, standpoint,
judgement, estimation,
feeling, impression,
notion, conviction.

opponent NOUN
= opposition, rival,
adversary, contestant,
competitor, enemy, foe,
contender, antagonist.

opportune ADJ see

favourable (2).

opportunity NOUN
= chance, favourable time;
[inf] break.

oppose VERB **= be hostile
to**, stand up to,
contradict, counter,
confront, resist,
withstand, defy, fight.

opposite ADJ **1 = facing**,
face-to-face. **2 = opposing**,
differing, different,
contrary, contradictory,
conflicting, discordant,
incompatible.

opposition NOUN
1 = hostility, resistance,
defiance. **2 = opponent**,
rival, adversary,
competition, antagonist,
enemy, foe.

oppress VERB **= subjugate**,
suppress, crush, subdue,
tyrannize, repress,
persecute.

oppressive ADJ
1 = tyrannical, despotic,
draconian, repressive,
domineering, harsh,
cruel, ruthless, merciless.
2 = muggy, close, airless,
stuffy, stifling, sultry.

oppressor NOUN **= tyrant**,
despot, autocrat,
persecutor, bully, dictator.

optimistic ADJ **= positive**,
sanguine, hopeful,

optimum

confident, cheerful, buoyant; [inf] upbeat.

optimum ADJ = **best**, ideal, perfect, peak, top, optimal.

option NOUN = **choice**, alternative, possibility, preference.

optional ADJ = **voluntary**, discretionary, elective.

opulent ADJ = **luxurious**, sumptuous; [inf] plush, ritzy.

orbit NOUN 1 = **revolution**, circle, circuit, cycle, rotation. 2 = **sphere**, range, scope, domain.

ordeal NOUN = **trial**, test, tribulation, suffering, affliction, torment, trouble.

order NOUN 1 = **orderliness**, neatness, tidiness, harmony, organization, uniformity, regularity, symmetry, pattern. 2 = **condition**, state, shape. 3 = **arrangement**, grouping, system, organization, structure, classification, categorization, sequence. 4 = **command**, directive, instruction, decree, edict, injunction. VERB 1 = **command**, instruct, direct, bid. 2 = **request**,

call for, requisition, book, reserve.

orderly ADJ 1 = **neat**, tidy, shipshape, organized, methodical, systematic, efficient, businesslike. 2 = **well behaved**, disciplined, controlled, restrained.

ordinary ADJ = **usual**, normal, standard, conventional, typical, common, commonplace, customary, habitual, everyday, regular, routine, established, run-of-the-mill, unremarkable, unexceptional.

organization NOUN 1 = **arrangement**, regulation, coordination, categorization, administration, management. 2 see **company (1)**.

organize VERB 1 = **arrange**, regulate, marshal, coordinate, systematize, standardize, sort, classify, categorize, catalogue. 2 = **administrate**, run, manage.

orientate VERB 1 = **adapt**, adjust, accommodate, familiarize, acclimatize. 2 = **direct**, guide, lead.

origin NOUN 1 = **source**,

basis, derivation, root, provenance, genesis, spring. 2 = **descent**, ancestry, pedigree, lineage, heritage, parentage, extraction.

original ADJ 1 = **aboriginal**, indigenous, early, first, primitive. 2 = **innovative**, inventive, new, novel, creative, imaginative, individual, unusual, unconventional, unprecedented.

originate VERB 1 = **arise**, stem, spring, result, derive, start, begin, commence. 2 = **invent**, dream up, conceive, initiate, create, formulate, inaugurate, pioneer, introduce, establish, found, develop.

ornament NOUN = **knick-knack**, trinket, bauble, accessory, decoration, adornment, embellishment, trimming.

ornamental ADJ = **decorative**, attractive, showy.

ornate ADJ = **elaborate**, decorated, embellished, fancy, ostentatious, showy.

orthodox ADJ

1 = **conservative**, faithful, strict, devout, observant. 2 = **conventional**, accepted, mainstream, conformist, established, traditional, usual.

ostensible ADJ = **apparent**, seeming, outward, alleged, claimed, supposed.

ostentation NOUN = **showiness**, extravagance, flamboyance, pretentiousness, affectation.

ostentatious ADJ = **showy**, loud, extravagant, flamboyant, flashy, pretentious, affected, overdone; [inf] flash, swanky.

ostracize VERB = **cold-shoulder**, exclude, shun, spurn, avoid, boycott, reject, blackball, blacklist.

other ADJ 1 = **different**, unlike, dissimilar, distinct, separate. 2 = **more**, additional, further, extra, alternative.

outbreak NOUN = **eruption**, upsurge, outburst, start.

outburst NOUN = **eruption**, explosion, attack, fit, paroxysm.

outclass VERB = **surpass**,

outshine, eclipse,
overshadow, outstrip,
outdo, defeat.

outcome NOUN = **result**,
upshot, issue, conclusion,
after-effect, aftermath.

outdated ADJ = **old-fashioned**, outmoded,
dated, passé, antiquated,
archaic.

outdo VERB = **surpass**, top,
exceed, outstrip,
outshine, eclipse,
outclass, defeat.

outer ADJ 1 = **outside**,
outermost, outward,
exterior, external, surface,
superficial. 2 = **outlying**,
distant, remote.

outgoing ADJ 1 = **extrovert**,
demonstrative, friendly,
affable, sociable, open,
expansive, talkative,
gregarious. 2 = **retiring**,
departing, leaving.

outgoings PLURAL NOUN
= **costs**, expenses,
expenditure, outlay,
overheads.

outlandish ADJ = **strange**,
unfamiliar, odd, unusual,
extraordinary, peculiar,
queer, curious, eccentric,
bizarre, weird; [inf] wacky.

outline NOUN 1 = **sketch**,
rundown, summary,
synopsis. 2 = **contour**,

silhouette, profile,
perimeter.

outlook NOUN 1 = **view**,
viewpoint, perspective,
attitude, standpoint,
interpretation, opinion.
2 = **view**, vista, panorama,
aspect.

outlying ADJ = **out-of-the-way**, remote, distant, far-flung, isolated.

output NOUN = **production**,
productivity, yield,
harvest.

outrage NOUN 1 = **atrocity**,
crime, horror, enormity.
2 = **offence**, affront, insult,
injury, abuse, scandal.
3 = **anger**, fury, rage,
indignation, wrath,
annoyance, resentment,
horror.

outrageous ADJ
= **shocking**, scandalous,
monstrous, appalling,
atrocious, abominable,
wicked, dreadful, terrible,
horrendous, unspeakable.

outside ADJ 1 = **outer**,
outermost, outward,
exterior, external;
outdoor, out-of-doors.
2 = **slight**, small, faint,
remote, vague.

outsider NOUN = **alien**,
stranger, foreigner,
immigrant, incomer,

intruder, outcast, misfit.

outskirts PLURAL NOUN
= **edges**, fringes, suburbs, environs, outlying districts, borders.

outspoken ADJ = **candid**, frank, forthright, direct, blunt, plain-spoken.

outstanding ADJ
= **excellent**, exceptional, superlative, pre-eminent, notable, noteworthy, distinguished, important, great.

outwit VERB = **get the better of**, outsmart, trick, dupe, fool.

overall ADJ
= **comprehensive**, universal, all-embracing, inclusive, general, sweeping, blanket, global. ADV = **on the whole**, in general.

overawe VERB = **intimidate**, daunt, disconcert, frighten, alarm, scare.

overcome VERB = **conquer**, defeat, vanquish, beat, master, get the better of, overpower, overwhelm, overthrow, subdue, quash, crush. ADJ
= **overwhelmed**, moved, emotional, speechless.

overdue ADJ 1 = **late**, behind, delayed, belated, tardy. 2 = **unpaid**, owing, outstanding, in arrears.

overhang VERB = **stick out**, extend, project, protrude, jut out.

overhead ADV = **above**, high up, on high, in the sky, aloft.

overlook VERB 1 = **fail to notice**, miss, neglect, ignore, disregard, omit, forget. 2 = **look over**, have a view of.

overpowering ADJ
= **overwhelming**, unbearable, intolerable, unendurable.

overriding ADJ = **most important**, predominant, principal, primary, paramount, chief, main, major, foremost, central.

oversight NOUN
1 = **carelessness**, inattention, neglect, laxity, dereliction, omission. 2 = **mistake**, error, blunder, gaffe, fault, omission, slip, lapse.

overt ADJ = **obvious**, noticeable, undisguised, apparent, manifest, patent, open, blatant, conspicuous.

overtake VERB = **pass**, go past, leave behind, outstrip.

overthrow VERB see
overcome.

overtone NOUN
= **implication**, innuendo,
hint, suggestion,
insinuation, connotation.

overwhelm VERB
1 = **overcome**, move,
dumbfound, stagger, take
aback. 2 = **inundate**, flood,
engulf, swamp, overload,

snow under.

overwhelming ADJ
= **uncontrollable**,
irrepressible, irresistible,
overpowering.

owe VERB = **be in debt**, be
obligated, be indebted, be
beholden.

own VERB = **possess**, have,
keep, retain, hold.

own up see **confess**.

pace NOUN 1 = **step**, stride.
2 = **speed**, swiftness,
rapidity, velocity.

pacify VERB = **calm down**,
placate, appease, mollify,
soothe, quieten.

pack NOUN 1 = **packet**,
package, carton. 2 = **gang**,
crowd, mob, group, band,
company, troop; [inf]
bunch. VERB 1 = **fill**, store,
stow, load, stuff, cram.
2 = **fill**, crowd, throng,
mob, jam. 3 (**pack up**)
= **finish**, halt, stop, cease.

packed ADJ = **full**, crowded,
crammed, jammed,
brimful, chock-full.

pact NOUN = **agreement**,
treaty, deal, contract,

settlement, bargain,
covenant, bond.

pad NOUN 1 = **padding**,
wadding, stuffing,
cushion. 2 = **notepad**,
notebook, jotter. VERB
= **pack**, stuff, cushion.

paddock NOUN = **field**,
meadow, pen, corral.

pagan NOUN = **unbeliever**,
heathen, infidel. ADJ
= **heathen**, infidel,
idolatrous.

pageant NOUN = **display**,
spectacle, extravaganza,
show, parade.

pain NOUN 1 = **soreness**,
hurt, ache, agony, throb,
twinge, pang, spasm,
cramp, discomfort.

2 = **suffering**, hurt, sorrow, grief, heartache, sadness, unhappiness, distress, misery, anguish.

pained ADJ = **hurt**, aggrieved, reproachful, offended, insulted, upset, unhappy.

painful ADJ = **sore**, hurting, aching, throbbing, smarting, tender, agonizing, excruciating.

painless ADJ = **easy**, simple, effortless, plain sailing; [inf] child's play, a cinch.

painstaking ADJ = **careful**, thorough, assiduous, conscientious, meticulous, punctilious, scrupulous.

painting NOUN = **picture**, illustration, representation, likeness.

pair NOUN = **couple**, duo, brace, two, twosome.

palatable ADJ = **agreeable**, acceptable, satisfactory, pleasant, pleasing, nice.

palatial ADJ = **luxurious**, splendid, grand, magnificent, majestic, opulent, sumptuous; [inf] plush.

pale ADJ **1** = **white**, colourless, anaemic, wan, drained, pallid, pasty, peaky, ashen, waxen. **2** = **light**, pastel, muted, faded, bleached, washed-out. **3** = **dim**, faint, weak, feeble.

palliate VERB see **alleviate**.

pallid ADJ see **pale (1)**.

palpable ADJ = **tangible**, touchable, solid, concrete.

paltry ADJ **1** = **small**, meagre, trifling, minor, insignificant, derisory. **2** = **worthless**, sorry, puny, petty, trivial.

pamper VERB = **spoil**, cosset, indulge, mollycoddle.

pamphlet NOUN = **leaflet**, booklet, brochure, circular.

panache NOUN = **style**, verve, flamboyance, zest, brio.

pander VERB (**pander to**) = **gratify**, indulge, humour, please, satisfy.

panic NOUN = **alarm**, fright, fear, terror, horror, agitation, hysteria. VERB = **be alarmed**, take fright, be hysterical, lose your nerve, overreact.

panic-stricken ADJ = **panicky**, alarmed, frightened, scared, terrified, horrified, agitated, hysterical.

panoramic ADJ = **wide**, extensive, sweeping, comprehensive.

pant VERB = **puff**, huff, blow, gasp, wheeze.

paper NOUN 1 = **newspaper**, journal, gazette, broadsheet, tabloid; [inf] rag. 2 = **essay**, article, dissertation, treatise, thesis, monograph, report, study.

parade NOUN = **procession**, cavalcade, spectacle, pageant. VERB 1 = **march**, process. 2 = **display**, show off, exhibit, flaunt.

paradox NOUN = **contradiction**, inconsistency, incongruity, anomaly, self-contradiction.

parallel ADJ 1 = **side by side**, equidistant. 2 = **similar**, like, analogous, comparable, equivalent, corresponding, matching. NOUN = **counterpart**, equivalent, analogue, match, duplicate, equal. VERB = **be similar to**, resemble, correspond to, compare with.

paralyse VERB = **immobilize**, numb, incapacitate, debilitate, disable, cripple.

parameter NOUN = **limit**, limitation, restriction, specification, guidelines.

parched ADJ = **dry**, baked, scorched, desiccated, dehydrated, arid.

pardon NOUN 1 = **forgiveness**, forbearance, indulgence, clemency, leniency, mercy. 2 = **free pardon**, reprieve, acquittal, absolution, amnesty, exoneration. VERB 1 = **excuse**, condone, let off. 2 = **reprieve**, release, acquit, absolve, exonerate.

pardonable ADJ = **forgivable**, excusable, allowable, understandable, minor, venial.

parentage NOUN = **family**, birth, ancestry, lineage, descent, heritage.

pariah NOUN = **outcast**, leper, persona non grata, untouchable, undesirable.

parliament NOUN = **legislative assembly**, congress, senate, chamber, house.

parody NOUN = **lampoon**, spoof, send-up, satire, pastiche, caricature, take-off. VERB = **lampoon**, satirize, caricature, mimic, take off, send up.

parry VERB = **ward off**, fend off, avert, deflect, block, rebuff, repel, repulse.

part NOUN 1 = **portion**, division, section, segment, bit, piece, fragment, scrap, fraction, sector, area, region. 2 = **role**, function, job, task, work, responsibility. VERB 1 = **divide**, separate, split, break up. 2 = **leave**, go away, say goodbye, separate.

partial ADJ 1 = **part**, limited, incomplete, fragmentary. 2 = **biased**, prejudiced, partisan, one-sided, discriminatory, preferential, unfair.

participate VERB = **take part**, join in, engage, contribute, share.

particle NOUN = **bit**, piece, speck, spot, atom, molecule.

particular ADJ 1 = **specific**, individual, precise. 2 = **special**, especial, exceptional, unusual, uncommon, remarkable. 3 = **fastidious**, discriminating, selective, fussy, painstaking, meticulous, punctilious, demanding, finicky; [inf] pernickety, picky.

particularly ADV 1 = **especially**, specially, singularly, peculiarly, distinctly, exceptionally, unusually, uncommonly. 2 = **in particular**, specifically, explicitly, expressly, specially.

partisan NOUN 1 = **guerrilla**, resistance fighter. 2 = **supporter**, adherent, devotee, backer, follower, disciple.

partition VERB = **divide**, subdivide, separate, screen off, fence off.

partly ADV = **in part**, partially, half, somewhat, fractionally, slightly.

partnership NOUN = **association**, cooperation, collaboration, alliance, union, fellowship.

party NOUN 1 = **gathering**, function, reception, celebration, festivity, soirée; [inf] shindig, rave-up. 2 = **alliance**, association, group, faction, camp.

pass VERB 1 = **go**, move, proceed, progress, travel. 2 = **go past**, go by,

overtake, outstrip.
3 = **hand over**, reach, give,
transfer. **4** = **go by**,
proceed, advance, elapse.
5 = **spend**, occupy, fill,
use, employ, while away.
6 = **succeed in**, get
through. **7** = **vote for**,
accept, approve, adopt,
authorize, ratify. NOUN
= **permit**, warrant, licence.
pass for = **be taken for**,
be accepted as, be
mistaken for. **pass out**
see **faint**.

passable ADJ
1 = **adequate**, all right,
tolerable, fair, acceptable,
satisfactory, mediocre,
average, unexceptional.
2 = **open**, clear, navigable.

passage NOUN **1** = **passing**,
progress, course.
2 = **journey**, voyage, trek,
crossing, trip, tour.
3 = **passageway**, corridor,
hall, hallway. **4** = **extract**,
excerpt, quotation,
citation, verse.

passer-by NOUN *see*
bystander.

passion NOUN **1** = **intensity**,
fervour, ardour, zeal,
vehemence, emotion,
feeling, zest, eagerness.
2 = **fascination**, interest,
obsession, fixation, craze,

mania.

passionate ADJ
1 = **impassioned**, intense,
fervent, fervid, ardent,
zealous, vehement, fiery,
emotional, heartfelt.
2 = **ardent**, desirous, sexy,
amorous, sensual, erotic,
lustful.

passive ADJ = **inactive**,
unassertive, submissive,
compliant, pliant,
acquiescent, tractable.

past ADJ **1** = **gone**, bygone,
elapsed, over, former,
long ago. **2** = **former**,
previous, prior, erstwhile,
one-time, sometime.

pastel ADJ = **pale**, soft,
delicate, muted.

pastime NOUN = **hobby**,
leisure activity,
recreation, diversion,
amusement,
entertainment,
distraction, relaxation.

pastoral ADJ see **rural**.

pasture NOUN = **field**,
meadow, grazing.

patch NOUN **1** = **cover**,
covering, shield. **2** = **plot**,
area, piece, tract. VERB
= **cover**, mend, repair, fix.

patent ADJ see **obvious**.

path NOUN **1** = **pathway**,
footpath, footway, track,
trail. **2** = **course**, route,

circuit, track, orbit, trajectory.

pathetic ADJ 1 = **pitiful**, moving, touching, poignant, heartbreaking, sad, mournful.
2 = **lamentable**, deplorable, miserable, feeble, poor, inadequate, unsatisfactory.

patience NOUN 1 = **calm**, composure, equanimity, serenity, tranquillity, restraint, tolerance, forbearance, stoicism, fortitude.
2 = **perseverance**, persistence, endurance, tenacity, assiduity, staying power.

patient ADJ = **uncomplaining**, serene, calm, composed, tranquil, tolerant, accommodating, forbearing, stoical.

patriotic ADJ = **nationalist**, nationalistic, flag-waving.

patrol VERB = **police**, guard, monitor. NOUN 1 = **watch**, guard, monitoring.
2 = **sentry**, guard, watchman, watch.

patron NOUN 1 = **sponsor**, backer, benefactor, promoter. 2 = **customer**, client, shopper, regular.

patronize VERB 1 = **look down on**, condescend to, treat contemptuously.
2 = **frequent**, shop at, buy from, do business with, trade with.

patronizing ADJ = **condescending**, supercilious, superior, haughty, snobbish; [inf] snooty.

pattern NOUN 1 = **design**, decoration, motif, ornamentation.
2 = **design**, guide, blueprint, model, plan, template.

pause VERB = **stop**, halt, cease, desist, rest, delay, hesitate. NOUN = **break**, halt, stoppage, cessation, interruption, lull, respite, gap, interval, rest; [inf] breather.

pay VERB 1 = **settle up**, remunerate, reimburse, recompense, reward.
2 = **spend**, expend, lay out, disburse, hand over, remit, render; [inf] fork out, cough up. 3 = **make money**, be profitable.
4 = **repay**, be beneficial, be advantageous, be worthwhile. NOUN = **payment**, salary, wages, earnings, fee, remuneration, stipend.

payment

payment NOUN
1 = **settlement**, discharge, clearance. 2 see **pay**.
3 = **instalment**, premium, amount, remittance.

peace NOUN
1 = **peacefulness**, tranquillity, serenity, calm, rest, restfulness, quiet, calmness, repose.
2 = **peacefulness**, peaceableness, accord, harmony, concord.
3 = **treaty**, truce, ceasefire, armistice, agreement.

peaceable ADJ = **peace-loving**, non-violent, placid, mild, good-natured, even-tempered, amiable, pacific, pacifist.

peaceful ADJ = **tranquil**, restful, quiet, calm, still, undisturbed, serene, composed, placid, untroubled.

peacemaker NOUN
= **conciliator**, mediator, arbitrator, appeaser, pacifier.

peak NOUN 1 = **top**, summit, crest, pinnacle. 2 = **height**, climax, culmination, zenith, acme.

peculiar ADJ = **strange**, odd, queer, funny, curious, unusual, abnormal, eccentric, unconventional, bizarre, weird, outlandish.

peculiarity NOUN
= **characteristic**, feature, quality, property, trait, attribute.

pedantic ADJ = **precise**, exact, scrupulous, overscrupulous, punctilious, meticulous, over-nice, perfectionist, quibbling, hair-splitting, casuistical, pettifogging; [informal] nit-picking.

pedestal NOUN = **base**, support, stand, pillar, plinth.

pedestrian ADJ
= **plodding**, unimaginative, uninspired, dull, flat, prosaic, mundane, humdrum, run-of-the-mill, mediocre.

peer NOUN 1 = **noble**, nobleman, noblewoman, aristocrat, lord, lady.
2 = **equal**, co-equal, fellow.

peerless ADJ
= **incomparable**, matchless, unrivalled, unsurpassed, unparalleled, superlative, second to none.

penalize VERB = **punish**, discipline, fine.

penalty NOUN

= **punishment**, fine, forfeit.

penance NOUN = **atonement**, reparation, amends.

penchant NOUN = **liking**, fondness, preference, taste, partiality, predilection.

penetrate VERB 1 = **pierce**, perforate, stab, prick, gore, spike. 2 = **permeate**, pervade, fill, suffuse.

penitent ADJ = **repentant**, contrite, regretful, remorseful, sorry, apologetic, rueful, ashamed.

penniless ADJ = **impecunious**, penurious, impoverished, indigent, poor, poverty-stricken, destitute.

pensive ADJ = **thoughtful**, reflective, contemplative, meditative, ruminative.

penury NOUN = **poverty**, impoverishment, indigence, destitution.

people NOUN 1 = **human beings**, humans, mortals, {men, women, and children}. 2 = **race**, ethnic group, tribe. 3 = **citizens**, subjects, inhabitants, nation; the public, the populace.

perceive VERB = **see**, catch sight of, spot, observe, glimpse, notice, make out, discern; recognize, realize, grasp, understand, apprehend.

perception NOUN 1 = **discernment**, appreciation, awareness, recognition, consciousness, knowledge, grasp, understanding, comprehension, apprehension, notion, conception, idea, sense. 2 = **perspicacity**, discernment, understanding, discrimination, insight.

perceptive ADJ = **penetrating**, astute, shrewd, discerning, perspicacious, discriminating, intuitive, sensitive.

peremptory ADJ = **imperious**, high-handed, overbearing, autocratic, dictatorial, domineering.

perfect ADJ 1 = **flawless**, faultless, impeccable, immaculate, pristine; exemplary, ideal. 2 = **exact**, precise, accurate, faithful.

perform VERB 1 = **do**, carry

out, execute, discharge, conduct, effect, bring about, bring off, accomplish, achieve, fulfil, complete. **2 = act**, play, appear. **3 = function**, work, operate, run, go.

performance NOUN = **show**, production, entertainment, act; [inf] gig.

performer NOUN = **actor/ actress**, player, entertainer, artist, artiste, musician, singer, dancer.

perfume NOUN = **scent**, fragrance, aroma, smell, bouquet; cologne.

perfunctory ADJ = **cursory**, superficial, desultory, brief, hasty, hurried, rapid, casual.

peril NOUN = **danger**, jeopardy, risk, hazard, menace, threat.

perilous ADJ = **dangerous**, risky, precarious, hazardous.

perimeter NOUN = **boundary**, border, limits, edge, margin, periphery.

period NOUN = **time**, spell, interval, term, stretch, span, age, era, epoch, aeon.

periodic ADJ = **periodical**, recurrent, recurring, repeated, regular; intermittent, occasional, infrequent, sporadic.

peripheral ADJ **1 = outer**, outlying, surrounding. **2 = minor**, lesser, secondary, subsidiary, unimportant, irrelevant.

permanent ADJ = **lasting**, enduring, continuing, perpetual, everlasting, eternal, abiding, constant, irreparable, irreversible, lifelong, indissoluble, indelible.

permeate VERB = **spread through**, pervade, saturate, fill, perfuse, steep, charge.

permissible ADJ = **permitted**, allowable, acceptable, authorized, sanctioned, legal, lawful, legitimate.

permission NOUN = **authorization**, sanction, leave, licence, dispensation, consent, assent, go-ahead, agreement, approval, approbation.

permissive ADJ = **liberal**, tolerant, broad-minded, open-minded, easy-going, indulgent, lenient.

permit VERB = **allow**, let, authorize, sanction,

grant, license, consent to, assent to, agree to; tolerate, stand for.

perpetual ADJ
1 = **everlasting**, eternal, never-ending, unending, endless, undying, permanent, lasting, abiding, enduring.
2 = **incessant**, unceasing, ceaseless, non-stop, continuous, unbroken, unremitting, interminable.

perpetuate VERB
= **preserve**, conserve, sustain, maintain, continue.

perplex VERB = **puzzle**, baffle, mystify, stump, bewilder, confuse, nonplus, disconcert.

persecute VERB = **oppress**, tyrannize, abuse, mistreat, maltreat, ill-treat, torment, victimize.

persevere VERB = **persist**, keep on, keep going, continue, carry on, press on.

persist VERB see **persevere**.

persistent ADJ
1 = **determined**, pertinacious, dogged, indefatigable, resolute, steadfast, unyielding, stubborn, obstinate.
2 = **constant**, continual, continuous, interminable, incessant, unceasing, relentless.

person NOUN = **individual**, human (being), creature, living soul, mortal.

personable ADJ
= **pleasant**, agreeable, amiable, affable, likeable, charming; attractive, good-looking.

personal ADJ
1 = **individual**, private, confidential, secret.
2 = **personalized**, individual, idiosyncratic, characteristic, unique.

personality NOUN
1 = **nature**, disposition, character, temperament, make-up. 2 = **celebrity**, household name, star, luminary, leading light.

personification NOUN
= **embodiment**, incarnation, epitome, quintessence, essence.

personnel NOUN = **staff**, employees, workers, workforce, manpower.

perspective NOUN
= **outlook**, view, viewpoint, point of view, standpoint, stance, angle, slant, attitude.

persuade VERB = **prevail on**, induce, convince, win over, talk into, bring round, influence, sway, inveigle, cajole, wheedle.

persuasive ADJ = **convincing**, cogent, compelling, forceful, weighty, telling.

perturb VERB = **disturb**, worry, trouble, upset, disquiet, disconcert, unsettle.

pervade VERB = **permeate**, spread through, fill, suffuse, perfuse, infuse.

pervasive ADJ = **prevalent**, extensive, ubiquitous, omnipresent, rife, widespread, universal.

perverse ADJ = **awkward**, contrary, uncooperative, unhelpful, obstructive, disobliging, recalcitrant, stubborn, obstinate.

pervert VERB 1 = **distort**, twist, bend, abuse, misapply, falsify. 2 = **corrupt**, warp, deprave, debauch, debase, degrade.

perverted ADJ = **depraved**, corrupt, deviant, abnormal, warped, twisted, sick, unhealthy, immoral, evil.

pessimist NOUN = **prophet of doom**, cynic, defeatist, fatalist.

pessimistic ADJ = **gloomy**, negative, cynical, defeatist, fatalistic, bleak, despairing.

pester VERB = **badger**, bother, nag, harass, torment, plague, bedevil, hound, persecute; [inf] hassle.

pet NOUN = **favourite**, darling, idol, apple of your eye; [inf] blue-eyed boy/girl. VERB = **stroke**, caress, fondle, pat.

peter VERB (**peter out**) = **fade**, wane, ebb, diminish, taper off, die out, fizzle out.

petrify VERB = **terrify**, frighten, horrify, scare to death.

petulant ADJ = **querulous**, peevish, fretful, cross, irritable, fractious, grumpy, sulky.

phantom NOUN = **ghost**, apparition, spectre, wraith; [inf] spook.

phenomenal ADJ = **extraordinary**, remarkable, exceptional, singular, unparalleled, unprecedented, amazing, astonishing, astounding, prodigious, sensational.

phenomenon NOUN

1 = **fact**, experience, occurrence, happening, event, incident.
2 = **marvel**, prodigy, rarity, wonder, sensation, miracle.

philanderer NOUN = **womanizer**, ladies' man, flirt, Lothario, Casanova, Don Juan.

philanthropic ADJ = **public-spirited**, charitable, benevolent, magnanimous, generous, kind, munificent, bountiful, open-handed.

philistine ADJ = **uncultured**, uneducated, unenlightened, ignorant, boorish.

philosophical ADJ = **calm**, composed, cool, collected, self-possessed, stoical, impassive, phlegmatic, imperturbable, dispassionate, unruffled, patient, resigned.

philosophy NOUN 1 = **thought**, thinking, reasoning. 2 = **beliefs**, credo, convictions, ideology, ideas, doctrine, tenets, principles.

phlegmatic ADJ = **calm**, composed, serene, tranquil, placid, impassive, stolid, imperturbable.

phobia NOUN = **aversion**, fear, dread, horror, terror, hatred, loathing, detestation, antipathy, revulsion, dislike.

photograph NOUN = **photo**, snap, snapshot, picture, shot, print, slide, transparency.

phrase NOUN = **expression**, term, idiom, saying.

physical ADJ = **bodily**, corporeal, corporal, carnal, fleshly; material, concrete, tangible, palpable, visible, real.

physician NOUN = **doctor**, GP, specialist, consultant.

physique NOUN = **body**, build, shape, frame, figure.

pick VERB 1 = **choose**, select, opt for, plump for, single out, decide on, settle on, fix on, elect.
2 = **harvest**, gather, collect, pluck. NOUN 1 = **choice**, selection, option, preference. 2 = **best**, choicest, prime, cream, flower.

picture NOUN = **painting**, drawing, sketch, watercolour, print, canvas, portrait,

illustration, likeness. VERB
1 = **imagine**, call to mind,
visualize, see. **2** = **paint**,
draw, depict, portray,
illustrate.

picturesque ADJ
= **beautiful**, pretty, lovely,
attractive, scenic,
charming, quaint,
pleasing, delightful.

piece NOUN **1** = **part**, bit,
section, segment, unit;
fragment, shard, shred,
slice, chunk, lump, hunk,
wedge. **2** = **share**, slice,
portion, quota,
percentage.

pier NOUN = **jetty**, quay,
wharf, dock, landing
stage.

pierce VERB = **penetrate**,
puncture, perforate, prick,
stab, spike.

piercing ADJ **1** = **shrill**, ear-
splitting, high-pitched,
loud. **2** = **bitter**, biting,
cutting, raw, cold,
freezing, glacial, arctic.
3 = **searching**, probing,
penetrating, shrewd,
sharp, keen.

pig NOUN = **hog**, boar, sow,
porker, swine, piglet.

pile NOUN = **heap**, stack,
mound, mass, quantity;
collection, accumulation,
store, stockpile, hoard.

VERB **1** = **heap**, stack. **2** (**pile
up**) = **increase**, grow,
mount up, escalate,
accumulate, accrue,
build up.

pile-up NOUN = **crash**,
collision, smash,
accident.

pill NOUN = **tablet**, capsule,
lozenge.

pillage VERB = **plunder**, rob,
raid, loot, sack, ransack,
ravage, lay waste.

pilot NOUN **1** = **airman**/
airwoman, aviator, flier.
2 = **navigator**, steersman,
helmsman. VERB = **fly**,
drive, navigate, steer,
manoeuvre.

pimple NOUN = **spot**,
pustule; [inf] zit.

pin VERB **1** = **attach**, fasten,
fix, tack, nail. **2** = **pinion**,
hold, restrain,
immobilize.

pinnacle NOUN = **peak**,
height, culmination, high
point, acme, zenith,
climax, summit, apex,
apogee.

pinpoint VERB = **identify**,
discover, distinguish,
locate, home in on, put
your finger on.

pioneer NOUN **1** = **settler**,
colonist, explorer.
2 = **developer**, innovator,

ground-breaker, trailblazer. VERB = **develop**, introduce, launch, initiate, institute, originate, create, break new ground.

pious ADJ 1 = **religious**, holy, godly, churchgoing, devout, reverent, God-fearing, righteous. 2 = **sanctimonious**, hypocritical, self-righteous, holier-than-thou, goody-goody.

pipe NOUN = **tube**, cylinder, conduit, main, duct, channel, pipeline, drainpipe.

piquant ADJ = **spicy**, peppery, tangy, tasty, savoury, sharp.

pit NOUN = **hole**, trench, trough, hollow, excavation, cavity, crater, pothole; shaft, mineshaft; colliery, quarry, mine.

pitch VERB 1 = **throw**, fling, hurl, toss, lob; [inf] chuck, bung. 2 = **put up**, set up, erect, raise. 3 = **fall**, tumble, topple, plunge. NOUN 1 = **field**, ground, stadium, arena, playing field. 2 = **level**, point, degree, height, extent, intensity.

piteous ADJ = **pitiful**, pathetic, distressing, moving, sad, heart-rending, plaintive, poignant, touching.

pitfall NOUN = **trap**, hazard, peril, danger, difficulty, snag, catch, stumbling block.

pitiful ADJ see **piteous**.

pity NOUN 1 = **commiseration**, condolence, sympathy, compassion, fellow feeling, understanding, sorrow, sadness. 2 = **(crying) shame**, misfortune. VERB = **feel sorry for**, commiserate with, sympathize with, feel for.

pivot NOUN = **axis**, fulcrum, axle, swivel.

placate VERB = **calm**, pacify, soothe, appease, conciliate, mollify.

place NOUN = **location**, site, spot, setting, position, situation, area, region, locale, venue; country, state, region, locality, district. VERB 1 = **put**, position, set, deposit, rest, settle, station, situate. 2 = **order**, rank, grade, class, classify, categorize, bracket.

placid ADJ = **calm**,

composed, self-possessed, serene, tranquil, equable, even-tempered, peaceable, easy-going, unperturbed, imperturbable, stolid, phlegmatic.

plague VERB = **afflict**, torment, bedevil, trouble, beset; pester, harass, badger, bother, persecute, hound.

plain ADJ 1 = **clear**, obvious, evident, apparent, manifest, transparent, patent, unmistakable. 2 = **straightforward**, uncomplicated, comprehensible, intelligible, understandable, lucid. 3 = **simple**, basic, ordinary, unsophisticated. 4 = **unattractive**, ugly, unprepossessing, ill-favoured.

plaintive ADJ = **mournful**, doleful, melancholy, sad, sorrowful, wistful, pitiful.

plan NOUN 1 = **scheme**, proposal, proposition; system, method, procedure, strategy, stratagem, formula; way, means, measure, tactic. 2 = **blueprint**, drawing, diagram, sketch, layout.

VERB 1 = **arrange**, organize, work out, map out, schedule. 2 = **intend**, aim, propose, mean; contemplate, envisage.

plane ADJ = **flat**, level, horizontal, even, flush, smooth.

plant NOUN 1 = **flower**, vegetable, herb, shrub, weed. 2 = **factory**, works, foundry, mill, workshop.

plaster VERB = **cover thickly**, smother, spread, coat, smear.

plate NOUN 1 = **dish**, platter, salver. 2 = **sheet**, panel, layer, pane, slab. 3 = **illustration**, picture, photograph, print, lithograph.

platform NOUN = **dais**, rostrum, podium, stage, stand.

platitude NOUN = **truism**, commonplace, banality.

plausible ADJ = **believable**, credible, persuasive, likely, feasible, conceivable.

play VERB 1 = **amuse yourself**, entertain yourself, enjoy yourself, have fun; frisk, gambol, romp, cavort. 2 = **act**, perform, portray, represent. 3 = **take part in**,

participate in, engage in.
4 = compete against,
oppose, take on,
challenge. NOUN
= amusement,
entertainment,
recreation, diversion,
leisure, enjoyment, fun,
merrymaking, revelry.
player NOUN **1 = competitor**,
contestant, participant.
2 = performer, actor/
actress, entertainer,
artist(e), thespian.
3 = performer, musician,
instrumentalist.
playful ADJ **1 = fun-loving**,
high-spirited, frisky,
lively, exuberant,
mischievous, impish.
2 = light-hearted, joking,
humorous, jocular,
facetious, tongue-in-
cheek.
plea NOUN **= appeal**,
entreaty, supplication,
petition.
plead VERB **= appeal to**,
beg, entreat, beseech,
implore, request.
pleasant ADJ **1 = pleasing**,
pleasurable, agreeable,
enjoyable, entertaining,
amusing, delightful.
2 = friendly, amiable,
affable, genial, likeable,
charming, engaging.

please VERB **1 = gladden**,
delight, charm, divert,
entertain, amuse.
2 = want, wish, see fit,
like, desire, be inclined.
pleased ADJ **= happy**, glad,
cheerful, delighted,
thrilled; contented,
satisfied, gratified,
fulfilled.
pleasure NOUN
= happiness, delight, joy,
enjoyment,
entertainment,
amusement, diversion,
satisfaction, gratification,
fulfilment, contentment.
pledge NOUN **1 = promise**,
word of honour, vow,
assurance, commitment,
undertaking, oath.
2 = security, surety,
guarantee, collateral. VERB
= promise, give your word,
vow, undertake, swear.
plentiful ADJ **= abundant**,
copious, ample, profuse,
lavish, liberal, generous.
plenty NOUN (**plenty of**)
= enough, sufficient, a
great/good deal of, masses
of; [inf] lots of, heaps of,
stacks of, piles of.
plethora NOUN
= overabundance, excess,
superfluity, surplus,
surfeit, glut.

pliable ADJ 1 = **flexible**, bendable, bendy, pliant, elastic, supple. 2 = **malleable**, compliant, biddable, tractable.

plot NOUN 1 = **conspiracy**, intrigue, machinations. 2 = **storyline**, story, scenario. VERB 1 = **plan**, scheme, conspire, intrigue. 2 = **map**, chart, mark.

ploy NOUN = **ruse**, tactic, scheme, trick, stratagem, gambit, manoeuvre, move.

plucky ADJ see **brave**.

plummet VERB = **fall** (headlong), plunge, hurtle, nosedive, dive, drop.

plump ADJ = **chubby**, rotund, buxom, stout, fat, fleshy, portly, roly-poly; [inf] tubby, podgy.

plunder VERB = **rob**, pillage, loot, raid, ransack, strip. NOUN = **loot**, booty, spoils; [inf] swag.

plunge VERB 1 = **thrust**, stick, jab, push, drive. 2 = **dive**, nosedive, plummet, drop, fall, pitch.

poet NOUN = **bard**, troubadour, minstrel.

poignant ADJ = **touching**, moving, sad, pitiful, piteous, heart-rending, tear-jerking, plaintive.

point NOUN 1 = **tip**, top, extremity, prong, spike, tine. 2 = **promontory**, headland, head, cape. 3 = **place**, position, location, situation, site, spot, area, locality. 4 = **time**, juncture, stage, period, moment, instant. 5 = **heart of the matter**, essence, nub, core, pith, crux. 6 = **characteristic**, trait, attribute, quality, feature, property. VERB = **direct**, aim, level, train.

pointless ADJ = **futile**, useless, in vain, unavailing, fruitless, senseless.

poise NOUN = **composure**, equanimity, self-possession, aplomb, self-assurance, calmness, serenity, dignity.

poison NOUN = **venom**, toxin. VERB = **contaminate**, pollute, blight, taint.

poisonous ADJ = **venomous**, deadly, lethal, toxic, noxious.

poke VERB = **jab**, prod, dig, elbow, nudge, push, thrust.

poky ADJ = **cramped**,

narrow, small, tiny, confined.

pole NOUN = **post**, pillar, stanchion, stake, stick, support, prop, rail, rod.

policy NOUN = **plans**, strategy, stratagem, approach, system, programme, procedure.

polish VERB 1 = **buff**, rub, burnish, shine. 2 = **perfect**, refine, improve, hone.

polished ADJ 1 = **burnished**, shining, shiny, glossy, gleaming, lustrous. 2 = **refined**, cultivated, civilized, well bred, polite, well mannered, urbane, suave, sophisticated. 3 = **expert**, accomplished, masterly, skilful, proficient, adept.

polite ADJ 1 = **well mannered**, courteous, civil, respectful, deferential, well behaved, well bred; tactful, diplomatic. 2 = **civilized**, refined, cultured, genteel, urbane, sophisticated.

politic ADJ = **wise**, prudent, sensible, advisable, judicious, expedient, shrewd, astute.

poll NOUN = **vote**, ballot, referendum, plebiscite.

pollute VERB = **contaminate**, infect, taint, poison, dirty, foul.

pomp NOUN = **ceremony**, pageantry, show, spectacle, splendour, grandeur, magnificence, majesty.

pompous ADJ = **self-important**, puffed up, imperious, overbearing, arrogant, haughty, proud.

ponder VERB = **think about**, consider, reflect on, mull over, contemplate, meditate on, ruminate on, muse on.

poor ADJ 1 = **penniless**, hard up, badly off, poverty-stricken, needy, indigent, impoverished, impecunious, destitute, penurious. 2 = **inadequate**, deficient, unsatisfactory, below par, inferior, substandard, imperfect, bad. 3 = **wretched**, unfortunate, unlucky, luckless, hapless, ill-fated, ill-starred.

populace NOUN = **the (general) public**, the (common) people, the population, the masses.

popular ADJ 1 = **well liked**, liked, favoured, in demand, sought-after, all the rage. 2 = **current**, prevalent, prevailing, widespread, general, common.

population NOUN = **inhabitants**, residents, community, people, citizenry, populace, society.

pore NOUN = **opening**, orifice, hole, outlet.

port NOUN = **harbour**, anchorage, dock, mooring, marina.

portent NOUN see **omen**.

portion NOUN = **share**, quota, part, allocation, slice; piece, bit, section; helping, serving.

portrait NOUN = **painting**, picture, drawing, likeness.

portray VERB 1 = **paint**, draw, sketch, depict, represent. 2 = **describe**, characterize.

pose VERB 1 = **constitute**, present, create, cause, produce, give rise to. 2 = **strike a pose**, attitudinize, put on airs; [inf] show off. NOUN 1 = **posture**, stance, position, attitude. 2 = **act**, pretence, facade, front, masquerade, affectation.

position NOUN 1 = **situation**, location, site, place, spot, area, locality, setting. 2 = **posture**, stance, attitude, pose. 3 = **state**, condition, circumstances, situation. 4 = **post**, job, appointment. 5 = **level**, grade, grading, rank, status, standing. VERB = **place**, locate, situate, put, set, station.

positive ADJ 1 = **confident**, optimistic, cheerful, hopeful, sanguine; [inf] upbeat. 2 = **good**, favourable, promising, encouraging, heartening. 3 = **definite**, conclusive, incontrovertible, indisputable, irrefutable. 4 = **certain**, sure, convinced, satisfied.

possess VERB = **own**, have, be blessed with, enjoy.

possessions PLURAL NOUN = **belongings**, things, property, effects, worldly goods.

possibility NOUN = **chance**, likelihood, probability; risk, danger.

possible ADJ 1 = **feasible**, practicable, doable, attainable, achievable. 2 = **likely**, potential, conceivable, probable.

post NOUN = **pole**, stake, upright, prop, support, picket, strut, pillar,

paling, stanchion. VERB
= **put up**, stick up, pin, pin
up, attach, fix, fasten.

poster NOUN = **placard**,
notice, bill,
advertisement.

postpone VERB = **defer**, put
off/back, delay, hold over,
adjourn.

posture NOUN = **position**,
pose, attitude, stance;
bearing, carriage.

potent ADJ = **powerful**,
strong, mighty,
formidable, influential,
forceful; convincing,
cogent, compelling,
persuasive.

potential ADJ = **possible**,
likely, probable,
prospective; latent. NOUN
= **promise**, possibilities,
potentiality, prospects,
ability, capability.

potion NOUN = **drink**, brew,
concoction, mixture.

pounce VERB = **swoop on**,
spring on, jump at/on,
ambush, take by surprise,
take unawares.

pound[1] NOUN = **compound**,
enclosure, pen, yard.

pound[2] VERB 1 = **beat**, strike,
hit, batter, thump,
pummel, punch. 2 = **throb**,
pulsate, pulse, palpitate,
race.

pour VERB = **gush**, rush,
stream, flow, course,
spout, spurt.

poverty NOUN
= **pennilessness**,
hardship, deprivation,
indigence,
impoverishment,
destitution, penury,
privation.

power NOUN 1 = **ability**,
capability, capacity,
potential; faculty.
2 = **strength**, force, might,
weight. 3 = **control**,
authority, mastery,
domination, dominance,
rule, command,
ascendancy, supremacy,
dominion, sway.

powerful ADJ 1 = **strong**,
sturdy, strapping, stout,
robust, vigorous, tough.
2 = **influential**, dominant,
authoritative,
commanding, forceful,
strong, vigorous, potent.
3 = **cogent**, compelling,
convincing, persuasive,
eloquent.

powerless ADJ = **weak**,
feeble, impotent, helpless,
defenceless.

practicable ADJ
= **feasible**, realistic,
possible, viable, workable,
doable.

practical ADJ 1 = **applied**, empirical, hands-on.
2 = **functional**, useful, utilitarian.
3 = **businesslike**, sensible, down-to-earth, pragmatic, realistic, hard-headed.

practice NOUN 1 = **action**, operation, application, effect, exercise, use.
2 = **training**, preparation, study, exercise, drill, work-out, rehearsal.
3 = **procedure**, method, system, usage, tradition, convention.

practise VERB 1 = **carry out**, perform, do, execute, follow, pursue, observe.
2 = **work at**, run through, go over, rehearse, polish.

praise VERB 1 = **applaud**, acclaim, compliment, congratulate, pay tribute to, laud, eulogize.
2 = **worship**, glorify, honour, exalt. NOUN = **approbation**, applause, acclaim, compliments, congratulations, commendation, tributes, accolades, plaudits.

praiseworthy ADJ = **commendable**, laudable, admirable, meritorious, worthy, excellent, exemplary, sterling, fine.

prance VERB = **leap**, spring, jump, skip, cavort, caper, gambol.

prank NOUN = **trick**, practical joke, hoax, caper, stunt.

precarious ADJ = **risky**, hazardous, perilous, dangerous, touch-and-go.

precaution NOUN = **safeguard**, preventative/preventive measure, provision.

precious ADJ 1 = **valuable**, costly, expensive, dear, priceless, rare. 2 = **valued**, cherished, prized, treasured, beloved.

precipitate VERB = **hasten**, accelerate, expedite, speed up, push forward, bring on, trigger.

precise ADJ = **exact**, accurate, correct, specific, detailed, explicit, unambiguous, definite.

preclude VERB = **prevent**, prohibit, rule out, debar, bar, hinder, impede.

preconception NOUN = **preconceived idea**, assumption, presupposition, presumption, prejudgement, prejudice.

predecessor NOUN

= **precursor**, forerunner, antecedent, ancestor, forefather, forebear.

predicament NOUN = **difficult situation**, plight, tight corner, mess, emergency, crisis, dilemma, quandary, trouble; [inf] jam, hole, fix, pickle, scrape, tight spot.

predict VERB = **forecast**, foretell, prophesy, foresee, anticipate.

predilection NOUN = **liking**, fondness, preference, partiality, taste, penchant.

pre-eminent ADJ = **outstanding**, leading, foremost, chief, excellent, distinguished, prominent, eminent, important.

preface NOUN = **introduction**, foreword, preamble, prologue, prelude.

prefer VERB favour, incline towards, choose, select, pick, opt for, go for.

preference NOUN = **liking**, partiality, predilection, fondness, taste, inclination, penchant.

pregnant ADJ
1 = **expecting**, in the family way, with child; [inf] in the club.

2 = **meaningful**, eloquent, significant, expressive.

prejudice NOUN = **bias**, discrimination, partisanship, partiality, chauvinism, bigotry, intolerance, racism, sexism.

prejudiced ADJ = **biased**, discriminatory, partisan, chauvinistic, bigoted, intolerant, narrow-minded, racist, sexist.

prejudicial ADJ = **detrimental**, deleterious, unfavourable, damaging, injurious, harmful, hurtful, inimical.

preliminary ADJ = **introductory**, prefatory, prior, precursory, opening, initial, preparatory.

prelude NOUN 1 = **overture**, opening, introduction, start, beginning.
2 = **introduction**, preface, prologue, preamble.

premature ADJ = **early**, untimely, unseasonable.

premeditated ADJ = **planned**, prearranged, intentional, intended, deliberate, calculated, wilful.

premonition NOUN = **foreboding**,

presentiment, intuition, feeling, hunch.

preoccupy VERB = **engross**, absorb, distract, obsess, occupy, prey on someone's mind.

preparation NOUN 1 = **arrangements**, plans, provisions; groundwork, spadework. 2 = **mixture**, compound, concoction, potion.

prepare VERB = **get ready**, arrange, develop, put together, draw up, produce, construct, compose, concoct.

preposterous ADJ = **absurd**, ridiculous, ludicrous, farcical, laughable, outrageous.

prerequisite ADJ = **necessary**, required, essential, requisite, vital, obligatory, mandatory, compulsory.

presence NOUN 1 = **existence**, being; attendance, appearance. 2 = **magnetism**, aura, charisma, personality.

present[1] ADJ 1 = **existing**, existent, extant. 2 = **present-day**, current, contemporary. 3 = **in attendance**, available, at hand. NOUN = **today**, now,

here and now.

present[2] VERB 1 = **give**, hand over, confer, bestow, award, grant, accord. 2 = **introduce**, announce. NOUN = **gift**, donation, offering, contribution, gratuity.

presentiment NOUN = **foreboding**, premonition, intuition, feeling, hunch.

preserve VERB = **conserve**, protect, safeguard, defend, guard, care for, keep, save, maintain, uphold, keep alive.

preside VERB = **be in charge of**, control, direct, run, conduct, supervise, govern, rule.

press VERB 1 = **depress**, push down. 2 = **iron**, smooth out, flatten. 3 = **urge**, entreat, exhort, implore, pressurize, force, compel, coerce. NOUN = **newspapers**, the media, Fleet Street.

pressure NOUN 1 = **force**, weight, compression. 2 = **compulsion**, coercion, constraint, duress. 3 = **strain**, stress, tension, burden, load.

prestige NOUN = **status**, standing, stature,

reputation, repute, fame, renown, honour, esteem, importance, influence, eminence; kudos, cachet.

prestigious ADJ = **important**, prominent, impressive, high-ranking, reputable, respected, esteemed, eminent, distinguished, well known, celebrated, illustrious, renowned, famous.

presume VERB = **assume**, take it, suppose, believe, think, imagine, judge, guess, surmise, conjecture.

presumptuous ADJ = **overconfident**, cocksure, arrogant, bold, forward, impertinent, impudent, cocky.

pretence NOUN = **show**, semblance, appearance, false front, guise, facade, masquerade.

pretend VERB = **put on an act**, act, play-act, put it on, dissemble, sham, feign, fake, dissimulate, dissemble, make believe.

pretentious ADJ = **affected**, ostentatious, showy, grandiose, elaborate, extravagant.

pretty ADJ = **lovely**, attractive, good-looking, personable, appealing, cute; [Scottish] bonny.

prevail VERB = **win**, triumph, carry the day, conquer, overcome.

prevalent ADJ = **widespread**, prevailing, frequent, usual, common, current, popular, general, universal; endemic, rampant, rife.

prevaricate VERB = **equivocate**, shilly-shally, hum and haw, hedge, beat about the bush, play for time.

prevent VERB = **put a stop to**, halt, arrest, avert, fend off, stave off, ward off, hinder, impede, hamper, obstruct, baulk, foil, thwart, frustrate, forestall, prohibit, bar.

previous ADJ 1 = **former**, ex-, past, erstwhile. 2 = **preceding**, foregoing, earlier, prior.

price NOUN = **cost**, charge, fee, levy; amount, figure, sum.

prick VERB = **pierce**, puncture, perforate, stab, nick, spike.

pride NOUN 1 = **self-esteem**, dignity, self-respect, self-worth. 2 = **conceit**, vanity,

priggish

arrogance, self-importance, hubris, narcissism.

3 = **satisfaction**, gratification, pleasure, joy, delight.

pride yourself on = **be proud of**, take pride in, revel in, glory in.

priggish ADJ = **prudish**, puritanical, prim, strait-laced, starchy, self-righteous, sanctimonious, narrow-minded, holier-than-thou.

prim ADJ = **proper**, demure, starchy, strait-laced, prudish, prissy, old-maidish, priggish, puritanical.

primary ADJ **1** = **prime**, chief, main, principal, leading, predominant, paramount, basic, fundamental, essential. **2** = **earliest**, original, initial, first, opening.

prime ADJ **1** see **primary (1)**. **2** = **top-quality**, best, first-class, choice, select.

primitive ADJ **1** = **ancient**, earliest, primeval, primordial, primal. **2** = **crude**, simple, rudimentary, rough, unsophisticated. **3** = **uncivilized**, barbarian,

barbaric, savage.

principal ADJ = **main**, chief, primary, leading, foremost, first, dominant, key, crucial, vital, essential, basic, prime, central; premier, paramount, major, overriding.

principle NOUN = **doctrine**, belief, creed, credo, rule, criterion, tenet, code, ethic, dictum, canon, law.

prison NOUN = **jail**, gaol, lock-up; [inf] nick.

prisoner NOUN = **convict**, captive, detainee, internee; [inf] jailbird.

pristine ADJ = **unmarked**, unblemished, spotless, immaculate, clean, in mint condition.

private ADJ **1** = **confidential**, secret, unofficial, off-the-record, hush-hush. **2** = **personal**, intimate, secret. **3** = **reserved**, retiring, self-contained, uncommunicative, secretive.

privation NOUN = **deprivation**, disadvantage, poverty, hardship, indigence, destitution.

privilege NOUN

= **advantage**, benefit; prerogative, entitlement, right.

prize NOUN = **trophy**, medal, award, accolade, reward, honour. VERB = **value**, treasure, cherish, hold dear.

probable ADJ = **likely**, odds-on, expected, anticipated, predictable, on the cards.

probe NOUN = **investigate**, scrutinize, inquire into, examine, study, research, analyse.

problem NOUN = **difficulty**, complication, trouble, mess, predicament, plight, dilemma, quandary.

problematic ADJ = **difficult**, hard, troublesome, complicated, puzzling, knotty, thorny, ticklish, tricky.

procedure NOUN = **course/ plan of action**, policy, system, method, methodology, modus operandi, technique, means, practice, strategy.

proceed VERB = **make your way**, go, advance; carry on, press on, progress, continue.

proceedings PLURAL NOUN 1 = **activities**, events, goings-on, doings, happenings. 2 = **case**, lawsuit, litigation, trial.

proceeds PLURAL NOUN = **takings**, profits, returns, receipts, income, earnings.

process NOUN = **method**, system, technique, means, practice, approach, way, procedure, operation.

procession NOUN = **parade**, march, column, file, train, cortège, cavalcade, motorcade.

proclaim VERB = **announce**, declare, pronounce, advertise, publish, broadcast, promulgate.

proclivity NOUN = **tendency**, inclination, leaning, propensity, bent, penchant, predisposition, weakness.

procrastinate VERB = **delay**, stall, temporize, play for time, drag your feet.

procure VERB = **obtain**, acquire, get, secure.

prod VERB = **poke**, jab, dig, elbow, butt, push, shove.

prodigy NOUN = **genius**,

wonder, marvel, sensation.

produce VERB 1 = **make**, manufacture, create, construct, build, fabricate, put together, assemble, fashion. 2 = **present**, offer, provide, furnish, advance.

product NOUN = **commodity**, artefact; goods, wares, merchandise.

productive ADJ = **fertile**, fruitful, rich, high-yielding, prolific.

profess VERB = **declare**, maintain, announce, proclaim, assert, state, affirm, avow.

profession NOUN 1 = **career**, job, calling, business, vocation, occupation, line of work, métier. 2 = **declaration**, announcement, proclamation, assertion, statement, affirmation.

professional ADJ = **skilled**, skilful, proficient, expert, masterly, adept, competent, efficient, experienced.

proffer VERB = **offer**, tender, present, give, submit, volunteer, suggest, propose.

profile NOUN 1 = **outline**, silhouette, contour, lines, shape, form, figure. 2 = **short biography**, sketch, thumbnail sketch, portrait, vignette.

profit NOUN 1 = **takings**, proceeds, gain, yield, return, receipts, income, earnings, winnings. 2 = **gain**, benefit, advantage, good, value, use, avail.

profitable ADJ 1 = **money-making**, commercial, remunerative, lucrative. 2 = **beneficial**, advantageous, rewarding, helpful, productive, useful, worthwhile, valuable.

profound ADJ 1 = **deep**, intense, great, extreme, sincere, earnest, heartfelt, wholehearted, fervent. 2 = **intelligent**, discerning, penetrating, perceptive, astute, thoughtful, insightful.

profuse ADJ = **abundant**, copious, plentiful, prolific.

programme NOUN 1 = **agenda**, calendar, schedule, timetable; syllabus, curriculum. 2 = **production**, show, performance, broadcast.

progress NOUN = **headway**, advance, advancement, progression, development, growth. VERB = **make your way**, advance, go, continue, proceed, forge ahead.

progressive ADJ = **modern**, advanced, radical, innovative, revolutionary, forward-looking, avant-garde.

prohibit VERB = **forbid**, ban, bar, proscribe, veto, interdict, outlaw; rule out, preclude.

prohibitive ADJ = **exorbitant**, steep, extortionate, excessive, preposterous.

project NOUN = **scheme**, plan, programme, enterprise, undertaking, venture, campaign. VERB = **jut out**, protrude, extend, stick out, stand out.

proliferate VERB = **increase**, multiply, extend, expand, burgeon, accelerate, escalate, rocket, snowball, mushroom.

prolong VERB = **lengthen**, draw out, drag out, protract, spin out.

prominent ADJ 1 = **protruding**, protuberant, jutting out. 2 = **conspicuous**, noticeable, eye-catching, obtrusive. 3 = **eminent**, important, distinguished, illustrious, celebrated, well known, famous, renowned.

promise VERB = **give your word**, swear, vow, pledge, undertake, commit yourself, guarantee. NOUN 1 = **word (of honour)**, undertaking, assurance, guarantee, commitment, vow, oath, pledge. 2 = **potential**, talent, ability, aptitude.

promising ADJ = **encouraging**, hopeful, favourable, auspicious, propitious, optimistic, bright.

promontory NOUN = **headland**, head, point, cape; cliff.

promote VERB 1 = **elevate**, upgrade. 2 = **advance**, further, aid, help, contribute to, foster, boost. 3 = **advertise**, publicize, push; [inf] plug, hype.

prompt ADJ = **immediate**, instant, swift, rapid,

speedy, quick, fast, early.
VERB = **cause**, make, move,
induce, impel, spur on,
motivate, stimulate,
inspire, provoke.
pronounced ADJ
1 = **marked**, noticeable,
obvious, evident,
conspicuous, striking,
distinct, unmistakable.
2 = **decided**, definite,
clear, strong, distinct.
proof NOUN = **evidence**,
substantiation,
corroboration,
confirmation,
verification,
authentication,
validation.
prop NOUN = **support**,
upright, buttress, bolster,
stanchion, truss, column,
post, pole, shaft. VERB
(**prop up**) = **hold up**, shore
up, bolster up, buttress,
support, brace, underpin.
propel VERB = **move**, push,
drive, thrust, force, impel.
propensity NOUN see
proclivity.
proper ADJ 1 = **right**,
correct, suitable, fitting,
appropriate, accepted,
established, orthodox,
conventional. 2 = **seemly**,
decorous, respectable,
decent, refined, genteel.

property NOUN
1 = **possessions**,
belongings, goods, effects,
chattels; real estate, land.
2 = **quality**, attribute,
characteristic, feature,
power.
prophecy NOUN
= **prediction**, forecast,
prognostication.
prophesy VERB = **predict**,
foretell, forecast, foresee.
prophet NOUN = **seer**,
soothsayer, oracle.
proponent NOUN
= **advocate**, supporter,
backer, promoter,
champion.
proportion NOUN 1 = **ratio**,
distribution. 2 = **portion**,
part, segment, amount,
quantity, share,
percentage.
proposal NOUN = **scheme**,
plan, idea, project,
motion, proposition,
suggestion,
recommendation.
propose VERB 1 = **put
forward**, advance, offer,
present, submit, suggest.
2 = **intend**, mean, plan,
have in mind, aim.
prosaic ADJ
= **unimaginative**, ordinary,
uninspired,
commonplace, dull,

tedious, boring, humdrum, mundane, pedestrian.

prospect NOUN = **likelihood**, odds, chance(s), probability, possibility.

prospective ADJ = **future**, to-be, intended, expected, potential, possible, likely.

prosper VERB = **do well**, thrive, flourish, succeed, get ahead, make good.

prosperous ADJ = **well off**, well-to-do, affluent, wealthy, rich, successful.

prostrate ADJ = **prone**, lying down, flat, stretched out, horizontal.

protect VERB 1 = **keep safe**, save, safeguard, shield, preserve, defend, shelter, secure. 2 = **guard**, defend, watch over, look after, take care of.

protection NOUN 1 = **safe keeping**, safety, care, charge, keeping, preservation, defence, security. 2 = **safeguard**, shield, barrier, buffer, screen, cover.

protest VERB = **object**, take exception, complain, demur, remonstrate, make a fuss, inveigh against; [inf] kick up a fuss. NOUN

= **objection**, complaint, remonstration, fuss, outcry.

protocol NOUN = **etiquette**, conventions, formalities, customs, proprieties.

protuberant ADJ = **bulging**, bulbous, jutting out, sticking out, protruding, prominent.

proud ADJ 1 = **pleased**, glad, happy, satisfied, gratified. 2 = **arrogant**, conceited, vain, self-important, haughty, disdainful, supercilious; [inf] high-and-mighty.

prove VERB = **establish**, demonstrate, substantiate, corroborate, verify, validate, authenticate, confirm.

proverb NOUN = **saying**, adage, maxim, saw, axiom, aphorism.

provide VERB = **supply**, give, furnish, equip, issue, come up with, contribute.

provincial ADJ 1 = **local**, small-town, rural. 2 = **unsophisticated**, parochial, small-minded, insular, inward-looking, narrow-minded.

provisional ADJ = **temporary**, interim, stopgap, transitional; to be confirmed, tentative.

provisions PLURAL NOUN
= **supplies**, stores,
groceries, food and drink,
foodstuffs, provender.

proviso NOUN = **condition**,
stipulation, provision,
rider, qualification,
restriction.

provoke VERB 1 = **annoy**,
anger, incense, enrage,
irritate, exasperate,
infuriate, vex, gall.
2 = **arouse**, produce, cause,
give rise to, engender,
result in, lead to, trigger.

prowess NOUN = **skill**,
expertise, ability, talent,
genius, aptitude,
proficiency, know-how.

prowl VERB = **slink**, skulk,
steal, sneak, creep.

proxy NOUN
= **representative**, deputy,
substitute, agent,
delegate, surrogate.

prudent ADJ = **wise**,
judicious, sage, shrewd,
sensible, far sighted,
politic, circumspect,
cautious, careful.

prudish ADJ = **priggish**,
prim, strait-laced, prissy,
puritanical.

pry VERB = **interfere**,
meddle, intrude; [inf] poke
your nose in, snoop.

pub NOUN = **public house**,
bar, tavern, inn.

public ADJ 1 = **popular**,
general, common,
universal, widespread.
2 = **prominent**, well
known, important,
eminent, respected,
influential, prestigious,
famous. NOUN = **people**,
population, country,
nation, community,
citizens, citizenry,
populace, the masses.

publication NOUN = **book**,
newspaper, magazine,
periodical, journal,
booklet, brochure, leaflet,
pamphlet.

publicize VERB 1 = **make
public**, announce,
broadcast, publish,
spread, distribute,
promulgate. 2 promote,
advertise, push; [inf] hype,
plug.

puff NOUN = **gust**, waft,
breath, flurry, breeze,
draught. VERB 1 = **pant**,
blow, gasp. 2 = **swell**,
distend, inflate, dilate,
bloat.

pugnacious ADJ
= **belligerent**, bellicose,
combative, aggressive,
antagonistic,
argumentative,

quarrelsome.

pull VERB 1 = **haul**, drag, draw, trail, tow, tug, heave, yank. 2 = **strain**, sprain, wrench.

pulsate VERB = **beat**, throb, pulse, palpitate, pound, thud, thump, drum.

punch VERB = **strike**, hit, thump, pummel; [inf] wallop, whack, clout.

punctual ADJ = **on time**, on the dot, prompt, in good time.

puncture VERB = **perforate**, pierce, prick, penetrate.

pungent ADJ = **sharp**, strong, acid, sour, bitter, tart; spicy, piquant.

punish VERB = **discipline**, teach someone a lesson, penalize.

puny ADJ = **weak**, weakly, frail, feeble, undersized, stunted, small, slight, little.

purchase VERB see **buy**. NOUN 1 = **buy**, acquisition, investment. 2 = **grip**, hold, foothold, footing, toehold, leverage.

pure ADJ 1 = **unalloyed**, unmixed, unadulterated, flawless, perfect, genuine, real, true. 2 = **clean**, clear, fresh, unpolluted, untainted, uncontaminated. 3 = **virginal**, chaste, virtuous, undefiled, unsullied, unblemished, blameless. 4 = **sheer**, utter, absolute, downright, out-and-out, complete, total.

purify VERB = **clean**, cleanse, decontaminate, disinfect, sterilize, sanitize, fumigate.

puritanical ADJ = **prudish**, prim, priggish, prissy, ascetic, abstemious, austere, strait-laced, moralistic.

purpose NOUN 1 = **reason**, point, basis, motivation, cause, justification. 2 = **aim**, intention, object, objective, goal, end, target, ambition, aspiration, desire, wish, hope.

purposeful ADJ = **determined**, resolute, firm, steadfast, single-minded, persistent, tenacious, dogged, committed, dedicated.

pursue VERB 1 = **go after**, follow, chase, hunt, stalk, track, trail, shadow; [inf] tail. 2 = **engage in**, work at, practise.

push VERB 1 = **shove**, thrust, propel, drive, ram, butt, elbow, jostle. **2** = **press**, depress. **3** = **press**, urge, egg on, spur on, prod, goad, incite; dragoon, force, coerce.

pushy ADJ = **assertive**, self-assertive, overbearing, domineering, aggressive, forceful.

put VERB **1** = **place**, lay, set, deposit, position, rest, stand, situate, settle. **2** = **attribute to**, impute to, assign to, pin on.

3 = **set before**, present, submit, offer, put forward, set forth.

puzzle VERB = **perplex**, baffle, mystify, confuse, bewilder; [inf] flummox, stump.

puzzling ADJ = **baffling**, perplexing, bewildering, confusing, complicated, mysterious, obscure, abstruse, incomprehensible, impenetrable, cryptic.

quagmire NOUN = **bog**, marsh, swamp, morass, mire, fen.

quail VERB = **flinch**, shrink, recoil, cower, cringe, shiver, tremble, quake, blanch.

qualification NOUN **1** = **certificate**, diploma, degree, licence; eligibility, proficiency, capability, aptitude, skill, ability. **2** = **modification**, limitation, reservation, stipulation; condition, proviso, caveat.

qualified ADJ = **trained**, certificated, chartered, professional; proficient, skilled, experienced, expert.

quality NOUN **1** = **degree of excellence**, standard, grade, calibre, sort, type, kind, variety. **2** = **feature**, trait, attribute, characteristic, aspect, point.

qualm NOUN = **doubt**, misgiving, scruple, hesitation, reluctance, anxiety, apprehension, disquiet, uneasiness, concern.

quantity NOUN = **number**, amount, total, aggregate, sum, quota, weight, mass, volume, bulk.

quarrel NOUN = **argument**, row, fight, disagreement, dispute, squabble, altercation, wrangle, tiff. VERB = **argue**, row, fight, squabble, bicker, wrangle, fall out.

quarrelsome ADJ see **argumentative**.

quarry NOUN = **prey**, victim.

quarter NOUN 1 = **district**, area, region, part, neighbourhood, locality, zone. 2 (**quarters**) = **accommodation**, lodgings, rooms; [inf] digs.

quash VERB 1 = **cancel**, reverse, revoke, rescind, repeal, annul, nullify, invalidate, overrule, overturn, reject. 2 = **put an end to**, crush, stamp out, squash, quell, suppress.

quaver VERB = **quiver**, tremble, shake.

queasy ADJ = **sick**, nauseous, nauseated, bilious, ill.

queer ADJ = **odd**, strange, peculiar, unusual, extraordinary, funny, curious, weird, bizarre, uncanny; unconventional, unorthodox, atypical, anomalous, abnormal.

quench VERB 1 = **satisfy**, slake, sate, satiate. 2 = **extinguish**, put out, blow out, douse.

question NOUN 1 = **query**, enquiry. 2 = **issue**, problem, matter, concern, subject, topic, theme. VERB 1 = **interrogate**, cross-examine, quiz, interview; [inf] grill, pump. 2 = **call into question**, query, doubt, suspect.

queue NOUN = **line**, row, column, file, chain, string.

quibble NOUN = **criticism**, complaint, objection, niggle. VERB = **object**, complain, cavil, split hairs; [inf] nit-pick.

quick ADJ 1 = **fast**, rapid, speedy, swift, fleet. 2 = **prompt**, without delay, immediate, instantaneous. 3 = **brief**, fleeting, momentary, hasty, hurried, cursory, perfunctory.

quicken VERB = **speed up**, accelerate, hurry, hasten.

quiet ADJ 1 = **silent**, hushed, noiseless, soundless. 2 = **soft**, low,

muted, inaudible.
3 = **peaceful**, sleepy,
tranquil, calm, restful,
undisturbed. **4** = **discreet**,
confidential, private,
secret.

quintessence NOUN
= **essence**, core, heart,
soul, spirit.

quit VERB **1** = **give up**, stop,
cease, leave off, refrain
from, desist from.
2 = **leave**, depart, resign,
walk out.

quite ADV **1** = **completely**,
entirely, totally, wholly,
absolutely. **2** = **fairly**,
relatively, moderately,
reasonably, to some
extent, rather, somewhat.

quiver VERB = **tremble**,

shiver, vibrate, quaver,
quake, shudder, pulsate.

quizzical ADJ
= **questioning**, puzzled,
perplexed, baffled,
mystified; amused,
teasing.

quota NOUN = **share**,
allowance, allocation,
portion, ration, slice; [inf]
cut, whack.

quotation NOUN
1 = **citation**, quote,
excerpt, extract, selection,
passage, line. **2** = **estimate**,
quote, price, charge,
figure.

quote VERB **1** = **repeat**,
recite. **2** = **cite**, name,
instance, mention, refer
to, allude to.

Rr

race NOUN = **contest**,
competition, chase,
pursuit, relay. VERB = **run**,
sprint, dash, dart, bolt,
speed, hare, fly, tear,
zoom.

racism NOUN = **racial
discrimination**, racialism,
chauvinism, xenophobia,
bigotry.

radiant ADJ **1** = **shining**,
glowing, bright,
illuminated, brilliant,
luminous, lustrous.
2 = **joyful**, happy, elated,
ecstatic, delighted,
euphoric.

radiate VERB = **send out**,
give off/out, emit,
emanate, scatter, diffuse,

cast, shed.

radical ADJ
1 = **fundamental**, basic, essential, deep-seated, intrinsic. 2 = **thorough**, complete, total, comprehensive, exhaustive, sweeping, far-reaching, profound, drastic. 3 = **extremist**, extreme, militant; revolutionary, progressive.

raffle NOUN = **lottery**, draw, sweepstake, tombola.

rage NOUN = **fury**, anger, wrath, ire. VERB = **be furious**, be enraged, seethe, be beside yourself, rant, rave, storm, fume.

ragged ADJ = **tattered**, threadbare, frayed, torn, ripped, in holes.

raid NOUN = **attack**, assault, onslaught, invasion, incursion, sortie, sally. VERB 1 = **attack**, assault, invade, assail, storm, rush, set upon. 2 = **plunder**, pillage, loot, ransack.

rain NOUN = **rainfall**, precipitation, drizzle, shower, cloudburst, torrent, downpour, deluge. VERB = **pour**, teem, pelt down, tip down;

drizzle.

raise VERB 1 = **lift**, hoist, uplift, hold aloft, elevate. 2 = **increase**, put up; heighten, augment, amplify, intensify; [inf] hike, jack up. 3 = **put forward**, bring up, advance, suggest, present, moot, broach. 4 = **bring up**, rear, nurture, educate.

rally VERB 1 = **come together**, assemble, group, convene; summon, round up, muster, marshal, mobilize. 2 = **recover**, recuperate, revive, get better, improve, perk up. NOUN = **meeting**, gathering, assembly, convention, convocation.

ram VERB 1 = **force**, thrust, plunge, push, cram, stuff, jam. 2 = **strike**, hit, run into, crash into, collide with.

ramble VERB = **walk**, hike, wander, stroll, amble, roam, rove.

rambling ADJ = **long-winded**, verbose, wordy, prolix; wandering, roundabout, circuitous, disconnected, disjointed.

ramifications PLURAL NOUN = **consequences**, results,

effects, outcome, upshot, aftermath.

rampage VERB = **run riot**, run amok, go berserk.

rampant ADJ = **out of control**, unrestrained, unchecked, unbridled, widespread, rife.

random ADJ = **haphazard**, arbitrary, indiscriminate, sporadic, casual, unsystematic, disorganized, unplanned; chance, accidental.

range NOUN 1 = **scope**, compass, limits, bounds, confines, span, gamut, reach, sweep, extent, area, field, orbit. 2 = **assortment**, variety, selection, array, collection. VERB = **extend**, stretch, reach, cover, go, run; fluctuate, vary.

rank NOUN = **grade**, level, echelon, stratum, class, status, position, station.

rapacious ADJ = **grasping**, greedy, acquisitive, avaricious, covetous.

rapid ADJ = **quick**, fast, swift, speedy, fleet, hurried, hasty, prompt, precipitate.

rapport NOUN = **affinity**, bond, empathy, sympathy, understanding.

rapture NOUN see **ecstasy**.

rare ADJ 1 = **infrequent**, few and far between, scarce, sporadic, scattered. 2 = **unusual**, uncommon, out of the ordinary, exceptional, atypical, singular, remarkable, unique.

rascal NOUN 1 = **scallywag**, imp, scamp, mischief-maker. 2 = **villain**, scoundrel, rogue, blackguard, ne'er-do-well.

rash ADJ = **reckless**, impetuous, hasty, impulsive, madcap, audacious, foolhardy, foolish, incautious, headstrong, careless, heedless, thoughtless, imprudent, hare-brained.

rate NOUN 1 = **percentage**, ratio, proportion, scale, degree, standard. 2 = **charge**, price, cost, tariff. 3 = **pace**, speed, tempo, velocity. VERB 1 = **judge**, assess, appraise, evaluate, measure, weigh up, grade, rank. 2 = **regard as**, consider, deem, reckon.

ratify VERB = **confirm**, endorse, sign, sanction, authorize, validate.

ratio NOUN = **proportion**, correlation, relationship, percentage, fraction, quotient.

ration NOUN = **allowance**, quota, allocation, portion, share, amount, helping, proportion, percentage. VERB = **limit**, restrict, control.

rational ADJ = **sensible**, reasonable, reasoned, logical, sound, intelligent, judicious, prudent, astute, shrewd.

rationalize VERB 1 = **explain**, account for, justify, defend, excuse. 2 = **streamline**, reorganize, modernize.

rattle VERB = **clatter**, clank, jangle, clink, clang.

raucous ADJ = **strident**, piercing, shrill, screeching, harsh, grating, discordant; loud, noisy.

ravage VERB = **devastate**, lay waste, ruin, destroy, despoil.

rave VERB 1 = **rant and rave**, rage, storm, fulminate, shout. 2 = **rhapsodize**, enthuse, gush, wax lyrical.

ravenous ADJ = **starving**, starved, famished, voracious.

raw ADJ 1 = **uncooked**, fresh. 2 = **unrefined**, crude, unprocessed, untreated. 3 = **cold**, chilly, freezing, bitter, bleak.

ray NOUN = **beam**, shaft, streak, stream, gleam.

reach VERB 1 = **stretch**, extend, hold out, thrust out, stick out. 2 = **get to**, arrive at, come to. NOUN = **scope**, range, compass, ambit.

react VERB = **respond**, behave, act, conduct yourself.

reactionary ADJ = **conservative**, right-wing, traditionalist, diehard.

read VERB 1 = **peruse**, study, scan, pore over, scrutinize. 2 = **interpret**, construe, take to mean.

readable ADJ 1 = **legible**, clear, intelligible, comprehensible. 2 = **enjoyable**, entertaining, interesting, gripping, enthralling.

readily ADV = **willingly**, gladly, happily, cheerfully, eagerly.

ready ADJ 1 = **prepared**, (all) set, organized, arranged; completed,

finished, done; [inf] psyched up, geared up.
2 = **willing**, eager, pleased, disposed, happy, glad.

real ADJ **1** = **actual**, existent, unimaginary; factual. **2** = **authentic**, genuine, bona fide. **3** = **sincere**, heartfelt, earnest, unfeigned.

realistic ADJ **1** = **practical**, pragmatic, rational, down-to-earth, matter-of-fact, sensible, commonsensical, level-headed. **2** = **lifelike**, true-to-life, true, faithful, naturalistic.

reality NOUN = **fact**, actuality, truth.

realize VERB **1** = **understand**, grasp, take in, comprehend, apprehend, recognize, see, perceive, discern. **2** = **fulfil**, achieve, accomplish, bring off, actualize.

realm NOUN = **kingdom**, country, land, dominion, nation.

reap VERB **1** = **cut**, harvest, gather in. **2** = **receive**, obtain, get, acquire, secure, realize.

rear NOUN = **back**, back part, hind part, tail, tail end.

VERB = **bring up**, raise, care for, nurture, parent.

reason NOUN **1** = **grounds**, cause, basis, motive, motivation, rationale; explanation, justification, argument, defence, vindication, excuse. **2** = **reasoning**, rationality, logic, cognition; good sense, judgement, wisdom, sagacity. VERB = **think**, cogitate; calculate, conclude, deduce, judge.

reasonable ADJ **1** = **sensible**, fair, fair-minded, rational, logical, just, equitable; level-headed, realistic, practical, commonsensical. **2** = **within reason**, practicable, appropriate, suitable. **3** = **tolerable**, passable, acceptable, average; [inf] OK.

reassure VERB = **put someone's mind at rest**, put at ease, encourage, hearten, cheer up.

rebel NOUN = **revolutionary**, insurgent, mutineer. VERB = **mutiny**, riot, revolt, rise up.

rebellion NOUN = **revolt**, revolution, insurrection, uprising, mutiny, insurgence.

rebellious ADJ = **defiant**, disobedient, unruly, insubordinate, mutinous, unmanageable, recalcitrant.

rebound VERB 1 = **bounce back**, recoil, ricochet, boomerang. 2 = **misfire**, backfire.

rebuff NOUN = **snub**, rejection, slight; [inf] brush-off. VERB = **reject**, refuse, turn down, spurn, snub, slight.

rebuke VERB = **reprimand**, tell off, scold, chide, admonish, reproach, reprove, berate, upbraid, castigate, take to task; [inf] tick off.

recalcitrant ADJ = **intractable**, refractory, unmanageable, disobedient, insubordinate, defiant, rebellious, wayward.

receive VERB 1 = **be given**, get, gain, acquire; be sent, accept. 2 = **undergo**, experience, meet with, sustain, be subjected to.

recent ADJ = **new**, fresh, latest, modern, contemporary, current, up to date.

recess NOUN 1 = **alcove**, niche, nook, corner, bay. 2 = **break**, interval, rest, holiday, vacation.

reciprocal ADJ = **mutual**, shared, common, joint, give-and-take, corresponding.

recital NOUN 1 = **performance**, concert, show. 2 = **account**, report, description; litany, list, catalogue.

recite VERB = **say**, repeat, declaim; enumerate, list, reel off, recount, relate, describe.

reckless ADJ = **rash**, impulsive, careless, thoughtless, heedless, madcap, wild, precipitate, headlong, hasty, irresponsible, harebrained, foolhardy, imprudent, unwise.

reckon VERB 1 = **think**, be of the opinion, believe, suppose, dare say. 2 = **count**, calculate, work out, add up, compute.

recline VERB = **lie**, rest, repose, loll, lounge, sprawl, stretch out.

recluse NOUN = **hermit**, lone wolf, loner.

recognize VERB 1 = **know**, identify, place, remember, recall. 2 = **acknowledge**, accept, admit, concede; be aware of, perceive, discern, appreciate.

recoil VERB = **draw back**, spring back, shrink, shy away, flinch.

recommend VERB = **advocate**, commend, put in a good word for, speak well of, endorse, vouch for; suggest, put forward, propose.

reconcile VERB = **reunite**, make peace between, bring to terms; pacify, appease, placate, mollify.

reconnaissance NOUN = **survey**, exploration, inspection, observation; [inf] recce.

reconnoitre VERB = **survey**, explore, investigate, scrutinize, inspect, observe; [inf] check out.

record NOUN 1 = **document**, account, register, report, log, logbook, file, documentation, minutes; chronicle, annals, archives. 2 = **disc**, album, CD, single, recording. VERB 1 = **write down**, take down, put in writing, note, enter, document. 2 = **register**, read, indicate, show, display.

recover VERB 1 = **get back**, regain, recoup, retrieve, reclaim. 2 = **recuperate**, get better/well, convalesce, improve, rally, revive, pull through.

recreation NOUN 1 = **relaxation**, leisure, amusement, entertainment, enjoyment. 2 = **activity**, pastime, hobby.

recruit NOUN = **new member**, initiate, beginner, learner, trainee, novice. VERB = **enlist**, call up, draft, conscript.

rectify VERB = **put right**, right, correct, amend, remedy, repair, fix, make good.

rectitude NOUN = **righteousness**, virtue, honour, integrity, principle, probity, honesty.

recurrent ADJ = **recurring**, repeated, periodic, cyclical, regular, perennial, frequent.

red ADJ 1 = **scarlet**, ruby, vermilion, crimson, rosy, carmine. 2 = **flushed**, blushing; florid, ruddy.

redolent ADJ 1 = **evocative**, suggestive, reminiscent. 2 = **sweet-smelling**, fragrant, scented, aromatic.

reduce VERB = **lessen**, lower, bring down, decrease, cut, curtail, contract, shorten, abbreviate; moderate, alleviate, ease.

redundant ADJ = **unnecessary**, inessential, unwanted, surplus, superfluous.

reel VERB = **stagger**, lurch, sway, stumble, totter, wobble.

refer VERB (**refer to**) 1 = **consult**, turn to, look at, have recourse to. 2 = **pass**, hand on, send, transfer. 3 = **mention**, allude to, touch on, speak of, cite.

referee NOUN = **umpire**, judge, adjudicator.

reference NOUN 1 = **mention**, allusion, citation. 2 = **testimonial**, recommendation, good word, credentials.

refine VERB 1 = **purify**, clean, cleanse, filter. 2 = **improve**, perfect, polish.

refined ADJ = **cultivated**, cultured, polished, gracious, stylish, elegant, sophisticated, urbane, well mannered, well bred,

gentlemanly, ladylike, genteel.

refinement NOUN = **cultivation**, taste, discrimination, grace, graciousness, style, elegance, finesse, sophistication, urbanity, good breeding, good manners, gentility.

reflect VERB = **think**, contemplate, mull over, ponder, meditate, muse, ruminate, cogitate, brood.

reflection NOUN 1 = **image**, mirror image, likeness. 2 = **thought**, thinking, consideration, contemplation, meditation, rumination, cogitation.

reflex ADJ = **automatic**, involuntary, knee-jerk, spontaneous.

reform VERB 1 = **improve**, make better, ameliorate, amend, rectify, correct, rehabilitate. 2 = **mend your ways**, turn over a new leaf; [inf] go straight.

refrain VERB = **desist**, abstain, forbear, avoid, eschew, stop, give up, quit.

refresh VERB = **invigorate**, revitalize, revive, restore, fortify, enliven, stimulate, energize, rejuvenate.

refreshing ADJ
= **invigorating**, reviving,
bracing, stimulating,
exhilarating, energizing.

refuge NOUN = **shelter**,
safety, security,
protection, asylum,
sanctuary; haven, retreat.

refund VERB = **repay**,
return, pay back;
reimburse, compensate.

refuse VERB = **turn down**,
decline, pass up; reject,
spurn, rebuff.

refute VERB = **prove wrong**,
disprove, rebut,
invalidate.

regain VERB = **get back**,
win back, recover, recoup,
retrieve, reclaim,
repossess.

regard VERB 1 = **watch**, look
at, gaze at, stare at,
observe, study, scrutinize,
eye. 2 = **look on**, view,
consider, see, think of,
deem, judge. NOUN 1 = **look**,
gaze, stare, observation,
scrutiny. 2 = **care**,
consideration, heed,
attention, thought.
3 = **respect**, esteem,
admiration, approval,
approbation.

regenerate VERB = **renew**,
restore, revitalize, revive,

revivify, rejuvenate.

region NOUN = **area**,
province, territory,
division, section, sector,
zone, quarter, part.

register NOUN = **list**, roll,
roster, index, directory,
catalogue. VERB 1 = **record**,
enter, write down, put in
writing, note, log.
2 = **read**, record, indicate,
show. 3 = **display**, exhibit,
express, evince, betray,
reveal, reflect.

regress VERB = **revert**,
relapse, lapse, backslide,
degenerate, retrogress.

regret VERB 1 = **feel sorry
about**, feel contrite about,
repent, rue. 2 = **lament**,
bemoan, mourn, grieve
over; deplore. NOUN
= **sorrow**, remorse,
contrition, repentance,
compunction, ruefulness,
penitence.

regretful ADJ = **sorry**,
apologetic, remorseful,
contrite, repentant,
conscience-stricken,
rueful, penitent.

regrettable ADJ
= **deplorable**,
reprehensible,
blameworthy, disgraceful;
unfortunate, unwelcome,
ill-advised.

regular ADJ 1 = **usual**, normal, customary, habitual, routine, typical, accustomed. 2 = **rhythmic**, steady, even, constant, unchanging. 3 = **even**, uniform, consistent, fixed, symmetrical. 4 = **official**, established, conventional, proper, orthodox, standard, usual, traditional.

regulate VERB 1 = **control**, adjust. 2 = **supervise**, police, monitor; manage, direct, guide, govern.

regulation NOUN = **rule**, ruling, order, directive, act, law, decree, statute, edict.

rehearsal NOUN = **practice**, run-through; [inf] dry run.

rehearse VERB = **practise**, try out, run through, go over.

reinforce VERB = **strengthen**, fortify, bolster up, shore up, buttress, prop up, support; augment, increase, add to, supplement.

reject VERB 1 = **refuse**, turn down, decline. 2 = **rebuff**, spurn, snub, discard, abandon, desert, forsake, cast aside.

relapse VERB = **lapse**, regress, retrogress, revert, backslide, degenerate.

relate VERB 1 = **recount**, tell, narrate, report, impart, communicate, recite, chronicle. 2 = **connect**, associate, link, correlate. 3 (**relate to**) = **apply to**, be relevant to, concern, refer to, pertain to.

related ADJ = **connected**, associated, linked, allied, affiliated, concomitant; akin, kindred.

relation NOUN 1 = **connection**, association, link, tie in, correlation, alliance, bond, relationship, interrelation. 2 = **relative**, kinsman, kinswoman.

relative ADJ 1 = **comparative**, comparable, respective, correlative, parallel, corresponding. 2 = **proportionate**, in proportion, commensurate. NOUN see **relation** (2).

relax VERB 1 = **loosen**, slacken, weaken, lessen. 2 = **unwind**, loosen up, ease up/off, take it easy; rest, unbend; [inf] chill out.

relaxation NOUN = **leisure**, recreation, enjoyment, amusement, entertainment, pleasure, rest, refreshment.

relay VERB = **pass on**, communicate, send, transmit, spread, circulate.

release VERB 1 = **set free**, free, let go/out, liberate; deliver, emancipate; untie, loose, unleash. 2 = **make public**, make known, issue, break, announce, reveal, divulge, disclose, publish, broadcast, circulate, disseminate.

relent VERB = **soften**, capitulate, yield, give way/in, come round.

relentless ADJ 1 = **harsh**, ruthless, merciless, pitiless, implacable, cruel, hard, strict, severe, obdurate, unyielding, inflexible, unbending. 2 = **unrelenting**, unremitting, persistent, incessant, constant, ceaseless, non-stop.

relevant ADJ = **applicable**, pertinent, apposite, material, to the point, germane.

reliable ADJ = **dependable**, trustworthy, trusty, true, faithful, devoted, steadfast, staunch, constant, unfailing.

relief NOUN 1 = **alleviation**, mitigation, reduction, lessening. 2 = **aid**, help, assistance, succour. 3 = **respite**, break; [inf] let-up.

relieve VERB 1 = **alleviate**, mitigate, assuage, allay, soothe, soften, ease, dull, reduce, lessen, diminish. 2 = **aid**, help, assist, rescue, save, succour.

religious ADJ 1 = **holy**, divine, theological, scriptural, spiritual. 2 = **churchgoing**, godly, God-fearing, pious, devout.

relinquish VERB = **give up**, renounce, resign, abdicate, surrender.

relish NOUN = **enjoyment**, delight, pleasure, satisfaction, gratification, zest, gusto. VERB = **enjoy**, delight in, love, adore, revel in, savour.

reluctant ADJ = **unwilling**, disinclined, unenthusiastic, grudging, loath, averse.

rely VERB = **depend on**,

count on, bank on, trust in, swear by.

remain VERB = **stay**, continue, carry on, last, persist, endure, prevail.

remainder NOUN = **remnant**, residue, rest, balance; surplus, excess.

remains PLURAL NOUN 1 = **remnants**, leftovers, leavings; residue, rest. 2 = **relics**, antiquities. 3 = **corpse**, body, cadaver, carcass.

remark VERB = **mention**, comment, say, state, declare, pronounce, observe. NOUN = **comment**, observation, statement, utterance, declaration, pronouncement.

remarkable ADJ = **extraordinary**, unusual, singular, notable, noteworthy, memorable, exceptional, outstanding, striking, impressive, phenomenal, wonderful, marvellous.

remedy NOUN 1 = **cure**, treatment, medicine, medication, medicament, antidote. 2 = **solution**, answer, panacea. VERB 1 = **cure**, heal, treat, counteract. 2 = **rectify**, solve, put right, redress, fix, sort out.

remember VERB = **recall**, call to mind, recollect, think of, bear in mind; reminisce about, look back on.

remiss ADJ = **negligent**, neglectful, irresponsible, lax, slack, slipshod, careless.

remnant NOUN 1 = **remainder**, residue, rest, remains, leftovers. 2 = **piece**, fragment, scrap.

remorse NOUN = **regret**, sorrow, contrition, penitence, repentance, guilt, ruefulness, compunction.

remorseful ADJ = **sorry**, regretful, contrite, penitent, repentant, guilt-ridden, chastened, rueful.

remote ADJ 1 = **distant**, far (off), out of the way, outlying, inaccessible, off the beaten track, isolated, secluded, lonely. 2 = **unlikely**, improbable, implausible, doubtful, dubious, slight, slim, small. 3 = **aloof**, distant, detached, withdrawn, reserved, uncommunicative.

remove VERB 1 = **take away**, move, shift, transfer, carry away. **2 = dismiss,** discharge, oust, dislodge, depose; [inf] sack, fire. **3 = take off,** pull off, doff. **4 = get rid of,** abolish, eliminate, axe, do away with, eradicate.

remunerative ADJ = **profitable,** well paid, lucrative, gainful.

rendezvous NOUN = **appointment,** date, meeting, assignation.

renegade NOUN = **defector,** deserter, turncoat, traitor.

renege VERB = **go back on your word,** break your promise, default, back out, pull out.

renounce VERB = **give up,** relinquish, abandon, abdicate, surrender, waive, forego.

renovate VERB = **modernize,** refurbish, overhaul, restore, revamp, repair, redecorate; [inf] do up.

repair VERB = **mend,** fix, put right, restore, patch up.

repay VERB = **pay back,** refund, reimburse, recompense, compensate.

repeal VERB = **revoke,** rescind, abrogate, annul, nullify, set aside, cancel, reverse.

repeat VERB = **say again,** restate, reiterate, recapitulate, recap; recite, quote, parrot, duplicate, replicate.

repel VERB **1 = repulse,** fight off, drive back, force back, ward off, fend off, keep at bay. **2 = revolt,** disgust, sicken, nauseate, turn someone's stomach.

repellent ADJ = **repulsive,** revolting, disgusting, sickening, nauseating, repugnant, abhorrent, offensive, obnoxious, loathsome, vile, nasty, abominable, horrible, horrid, foul.

repentant ADJ = **penitent,** remorseful, apologetic, regretful, contrite, rueful, ashamed, guilt-ridden.

repercussion NOUN = **effect,** result, consequence, reverberation, backlash.

repetitive ADJ = **recurrent,** unchanging, unvaried, monotonous, dreary, tedious, boring, mechanical, automatic.

replace VERB **1 = put back,** return, restore. **2 = take the place of,** succeed, supersede, supplant; substitute for, stand in for,

fill in for, cover for.
replete ADJ = **full (up)**,
satiated, sated, glutted,
gorged, stuffed, well fed.
replica NOUN = **copy**,
duplicate, facsimile,
model, reproduction,
imitation.
reply VERB = **answer**,
respond, rejoin, retort,
come back, counter. NOUN
= **answer**, response,
rejoinder, retort, riposte,
comeback.
report NOUN 1 = **account**,
statement, record.
2 = **article**, piece, story,
communiqué, dispatch,
bulletin. VERB
1 = **announce**,
communicate, give an
account of, describe,
outline, detail, reveal,
divulge, disclose. 2 = **tell
on**, inform on; [inf] grass
on, rat on. 3 = **present
yourself**, arrive, turn up,
clock on/in.
reporter NOUN = **journalist**,
correspondent,
columnist; [inf] hack.
repose NOUN = **rest**,
relaxation, ease, peace,
inactivity; sleep, slumber.
reprehensible ADJ
= **deplorable**, disgraceful,
despicable, culpable,

blameworthy, bad,
shameful, discreditable,
dishonourable,
indefensible,
unjustifiable, inexcusable.
represent VERB 1 = **stand
for**, symbolize, personify,
epitomize, typify,
embody. 2 = **depict**,
portray, render, delineate,
illustrate, picture.
representation NOUN
= **depiction**, portrayal,
portrait, illustration,
picture, painting,
drawing, sketch, image,
model.
representative ADJ
1 = **typical**, archetypal,
characteristic, illustrative,
indicative. 2 = **elected**,
elective, democratic. NOUN
= **spokesman**,
spokeswoman, agent;
mouthpiece.
repress VERB = **restrain**,
hold back, subdue,
control, suppress, keep in
check, bottle up, stifle,
curb.
reprieve NOUN = **stay of
execution**, remission,
pardon, amnesty.
reprimand VERB see
rebuke.
reprisal NOUN = **retaliation**,
revenge, vengeance,

retribution, an eye for an eye.

reproachful ADJ = **disapproving**, critical, censorious, reproving, accusatory.

reproduce VERB 1 = **copy**, duplicate, replicate, recreate, imitate, emulate, mirror, simulate. 2 = **breed**, procreate, bear young, multiply, propagate.

reproduction NOUN = **copy**, duplicate, replica, facsimile, print.

reprove VERB see **rebuke**.

repudiate VERB = **disown**, reject, abandon, forsake, desert, renounce, turn your back on, wash your hands of.

reputable ADJ = **respectable**, respected, of good repute, well thought of, prestigious; reliable, dependable, trustworthy.

reputation NOUN = **repute**, standing, name, character, position, status.

request NOUN = **appeal**, entreaty, petition, plea, application, call. VERB = **ask for**, appeal for, call for, solicit, seek, apply for, put in for; beg, entreat.

require VERB 1 = **need**, be in need of. 2 = **call for**, demand, necessitate, involve, entail.

requirement NOUN = **need**, wish, demand, want, necessity, prerequisite, stipulation.

rescue VERB = **save**, come to the aid of; free, set free, release, liberate.

research NOUN = **experimentation**, study, tests, investigation, fact-finding, testing, exploration. VERB = **investigate**, inquire into, look into, probe, explore, analyse, study, examine.

resemblance NOUN = **likeness**, similarity, similitude, sameness, correspondence, comparability.

resemble VERB = **be like**, look like, be similar to, take after, remind you of.

resent VERB = **begrudge**, grudge, be annoyed/angry at, dislike.

resentful ADJ = **aggrieved**, offended, indignant, irritated, disgruntled, annoyed, piqued, grudging, bitter, embittered.

resentment NOUN

= **bitterness**, indignation, irritation, annoyance, pique, disgruntlement, ill will, animosity.

reservation NOUN
1 = **booking**, engagement.
2 = **doubt**, qualm, scruple, misgivings, scepticism, unease, hesitation.

reserve VERB 1 = **put aside**, put away, keep, save, retain. 2 = **book**, engage, charter, hire. NOUN
1 = **store**, stock, supply, pool, cache, stockpile, hoard. 2 = **reticence**, detachment, distance, remoteness, formality, coolness.

reserved ADJ = **reticent**, aloof, detached, remote, formal, undemonstrative, cool, uncommunicative, unsociable, unfriendly, unresponsive, quiet, unforthcoming, private.

residence NOUN = **house**, home, dwelling, domicile, quarters, lodgings.

resident NOUN
= **inhabitant**, occupant, occupier, householder, denizen.

residue NOUN = **remainder**, remnant, rest, surplus, extra, excess, remains, leftovers.

resign VERB = **give notice**, hand in your notice, leave, quit.

resilient ADJ 1 = **elastic**, springy, flexible, pliant, supple, pliable. 2 = **tough**, strong, hardy.

resist VERB 1 = **withstand**, be proof against, weather.
2 = **oppose**, fight against, defy; obstruct, impede, hinder, block, thwart, frustrate. 3 = **refrain**, forbear, stop/restrain yourself.

resolute ADJ
= **determined**, resolved, decided, single-minded, purposeful, firm, staunch, steadfast, unwavering, unfaltering, unswerving, tenacious, dogged, persevering, persistent, unshakeable, strong-willed.

resolution NOUN
1 = **determination**, resolve, will power, firmness, purposefulness, doggedness, perseverance, persistence, tenacity, staying power.
2 = **decision**, resolve, commitment, promise, pledge.

resolve VERB 1 = **decide**, make up your mind,

determine. 2 = **solve**, settle, sort out, fix, deal with, put right, rectify.

resort VERB = **fall back on**, turn to, have recourse to, make use of, use, avail yourself of. NOUN = **recourse**, expedient, course (of action), alternative, option, possibility, hope.

resourceful ADJ see **enterprising**.

respect NOUN 1 = **esteem**, regard, high opinion, admiration, veneration, reverence, deference, honour. 2 = **aspect**, facet, feature, way, sense, particular, point, detail. VERB = **esteem**, think highly of, admire, look up to, revere, honour.

respectable ADJ = **reputable**, of good repute, upright, honest, honourable, trustworthy, good, well bred, proper.

respective ADJ = **individual**, separate, personal, own, particular, specific.

respite NOUN = **rest**, break, breathing space, lull, relief; [inf] breather, let-up.

response NOUN = **answer**, reply, rejoinder, retort, comeback.

responsibility NOUN 1 = **duty**, task, role, job. 2 = **blame**, fault, guilt, culpability, liability, accountability.

responsible ADJ 1 = **in charge**, in control, accountable, liable, answerable; to blame, at fault, guilty, culpable. 2 = **trustworthy**, sensible, level-headed, reliable, dependable.

rest NOUN 1 = **repose**, relaxation, leisure, time off; sleep, slumber. 2 = **break**, interval, interlude, intermission, lull, respite, breathing space. VERB = **relax**, unwind, put your feet up, take it easy; sleep, take a nap, catnap, doze.

restful ADJ = **quiet**, calm, tranquil, relaxing, peaceful, soothing.

restless ADJ 1 = **sleepless**, wakeful, tossing and turning, fitful. 2 = **uneasy**, ill at ease, on edge, fidgety, agitated.

restore VERB 1 = **renovate**, repair, fix, mend, refurbish, rebuild, revamp, redecorate; [inf] do up. 2 = **return**, give back, hand back.

restrain VERB = **control**, hold in check, check, curb, subdue, suppress, repress, contain, smother, stifle, bottle up, rein in.

restraint NOUN
1 = **constraint**, check, curb, control, restriction, limitation, rein. **2** = **self-restraint**, self-control, self-discipline, moderation.

restrict VERB **1** = **hinder**, impede, hamper, handicap, obstruct. **2** = **limit**, keep under control, regulate, control, moderate.

restriction NOUN
= **constraint**, limitation, control, check, curb; condition, proviso, stipulation, qualification.

result NOUN = **outcome**, consequence, upshot, sequel, effect, repercussion, ramification. VERB **1** = **follow**, ensue, develop, stem, spring, evolve, occur, happen, come about. **2** (**result in**) = **end in**, culminate in, finish in, terminate in.

resume VERB = **carry on**, continue, recommence, begin again, reopen.

retain VERB = **keep**, keep hold of, hold/hang on to, preserve, maintain.

retiring ADJ = **shy**, diffident, self-effacing, unassuming, reserved, reticent, quiet, timid.

retract VERB **1** = **draw in**, pull in/back. **2** = **take back**, withdraw, disavow, recant, disclaim, backtrack on.

retreat VERB **1** = **withdraw**, pull back, back off, give way/ground, retire, turn tail. **2** = **go back**, recede, ebb. NOUN **1** = **withdrawal**, evacuation. **2** = **refuge**, haven, shelter, sanctuary, hideaway, hideout.

retribution NOUN
= **reprisal**, retaliation, revenge, vengeance, punishment, justice, requital, an eye for an eye, tit for tat.

retrieve VERB = **get back**, recover, regain, recoup, salvage, rescue.

return VERB **1** = **go back**, come back, recur, reoccur, reappear. **2** = **give back**, repay, pay back; put back, replace, restore, reinstall. NOUN **1** = **homecoming**; reappearance, recurrence.

2 = **profit**, yield, gain, interest, dividend.

reveal VERB 1 = **show**, bring to light, uncover, lay bare, expose, unveil.
2 = **disclose**, divulge, tell, let slip, give away, release, leak, make known/public, broadcast, publicize.

revel VERB 1 = **celebrate**, make merry, party, carouse. 2 (**revel in**) = **delight in**, love, adore, relish, savour, lap up.

revelry NOUN = **celebrations**, festivities, jollification, merrymaking, revels.

revenge NOUN = **vengeance**, retaliation, retribution, reprisal, an eye for an eye.

revenue NOUN = **income**, profits, returns, receipts, proceeds, takings.

reverberate VERB = **resound**, echo, ring, resonate.

revere VERB = **respect**, admire, esteem, think highly of, look up to.

reverse VERB = **change**, alter; set aside, cancel, overturn, revoke, repeal, rescind, annul, nullify, invalidate. NOUN 1 = **opposite**, contrary,

converse, antithesis.
2 = **other side**, back, underside, flip side.
3 = **setback**, upset, failure, misfortune, mishap, blow, disappointment.

review NOUN 1 = **study**, analysis, evaluation, survey, examination, assessment, appraisal.
2 = **criticism**, critique, notice. VERB = **analyse**, examine, study, survey, scrutinize, assess, appraise, evaluate.

revise VERB 1 = **amend**, emend, correct, alter, change, edit, rewrite.
2 = **go over**, reread; [inf] swot/mug up on.

revival NOUN = **renaissance**, restoration, resurrection, rebirth, regeneration.

revive VERB 1 = **bring round**, resuscitate.
2 = **refresh**, restore, energize, regenerate, enliven, revitalize.

revolt VERB 1 = **rise up**, take up arms, rebel, mutiny.
2 = **repel**, disgust, sicken, nauseate, turn someone's stomach.

revolting ADJ see **repellent**.

revolution NOUN

= **rebellion**, revolt, insurrection, uprising, rising, insurgence, coup.

revolutionary ADJ
1 = **rebellious**, rebel, mutinous, seditious, subversive, extremist.
2 = **progressive**, radical, innovative, new, avant-garde, experimental.

revolve VERB = **go round**, turn round, rotate, spin, circle, orbit.

reward NOUN
= **recompense**, award, payment, bonus, present, gift.

rewarding ADJ
= **satisfying**, gratifying, fulfilling, beneficial, profitable, worthwhile, valuable.

rhetorical ADJ = **pompous**, grandiose, high-flown, oratorical, bombastic, grandiloquent, turgid.

rhythm NOUN = **beat**, cadence, tempo, time, metre.

ribald ADJ = **bawdy**, risqué, coarse, earthy, rude, naughty, racy, suggestive.

rich ADJ 1 = **wealthy**, affluent, well off, well-to-do, prosperous, moneyed; [inf] well heeled, loaded, rolling in it. 2 = **plentiful**, abundant, ample, profuse, copious, lavish.
3 = **fertile**, productive, fecund, fruitful. NOUN
(**riches**) = **wealth**, affluence, money, capital, property, assets, resources.

rid VERB 1 = **clear**, free, scourge. 2 (**get rid of**)
= **dispose of**, throw away/out, clear out, discard, do away with; destroy, eliminate.

riddle NOUN = **puzzle**, poser, conundrum, brain-teaser, problem, enigma, mystery.

ridicule NOUN = **derision**, mockery, scorn, jeering, jeers, taunts, satire, sarcasm. VERB = **deride**, mock, laugh at, scoff at, scorn, jeer at, jibe at, make fun of, taunt.

ridiculous ADJ = **absurd**, laughable, farcical, ludicrous, risible, stupid, foolish, half-baked, inane, fatuous, senseless, silly; preposterous, outrageous.

rife ADJ = **widespread**, common, prevalent, general, extensive, ubiquitous, universal, endemic.

rifle VERB = **rummage**, search, hunt; ransack.

rift NOUN 1 = **split**, crack, break, fissure, cleft, crevice, cranny.
2 = **disagreement**, breach, split, division, schism, estrangement, fight, row, quarrel, conflict, feud.

rig VERB = **manipulate**, engineer, tamper with, misrepresent, distort, falsify.

right ADJ 1 = **just**, fair, equitable, good, proper, moral, ethical, honourable, honest, lawful, legal. 2 = **correct**, accurate, unerring, exact, precise; [inf] spot on.
3 = **suitable**, appropriate, fitting, proper, desirable, ideal; opportune, favourable, convenient. NOUN = **prerogative**, privilege, authority, power, licence, permission, entitlement. VERB = **rectify**, put to rights, sort out, fix, remedy, repair.

righteous ADJ = **good**, virtuous, upright, moral, ethical, law-abiding, honest, honourable, high-minded.

rigid ADJ 1 = **stiff**, hard, taut, unbendable, inelastic. 2 = **strict**, severe, stern, stringent, rigorous, inflexible, uncompromising.

rigorous ADJ = **meticulous**, painstaking, thorough, scrupulous, conscientious, punctilious, careful, accurate, precise.

rim NOUN = **brim**, edge, lip, border, margin, brink.

rind NOUN = **peel**, skin.

ring[1] NOUN 1 = **band**, circle, halo, disc. 2 = **arena**, enclosure, stadium.
3 = **gang**, syndicate, cartel, association, league. VERB = **circle**, encircle, surround, enclose, hem in, fence in, seal off.

ring[2] VERB 1 = **toll**, peal, chime, ding, clang, tinkle.
2 = **call**, telephone, phone.

rinse VERB = **wash**, clean, sluice, flush.

riot NOUN = **uproar**, commotion, disturbance, tumult, melée, fracas, fray, brawl; violence, fighting. VERB = **run riot**, go on the rampage, run wild/ amok.

riotous ADJ 1 = **disorderly**, uncontrollable, unruly, unmanageable, rowdy, wild, violent, lawless, anarchic. 2 = **loud**, noisy, boisterous, uproarious.

ripe ADJ = **mature**, full grown, mellow, juicy, luscious, tender, sweet.

rise VERB 1 = **move up**, arise, ascend, climb. 2 = **rise up**, tower, soar, rear up. 3 = **increase**, soar, rocket, escalate, shoot up. NOUN = **increase**, hike, escalation, upsurge, upswing.

risk NOUN = **danger**, possibility, chance, peril, threat, jeopardy. VERB = **endanger**, imperil, jeopardize, hazard, put at risk, gamble with.

risky ADJ = **dangerous**, hazardous, perilous, precarious, uncertain; [inf] dicey.

rite NOUN = **ritual**, ceremony, service, sacrament, liturgy, tradition.

rival NOUN = **opponent**, adversary, antagonist, competitor, challenger, contender. VERB = **compete with**, vie with, match, equal, measure up to, compare with.

road NOUN = **street**, thoroughfare, highway.

roam VERB see **wander**.

roar VERB = **bellow**, yell, bawl, shout, howl; [inf]
holler.

rob VERB = **steal from**, burgle, hold up, break into, mug, defraud, swindle, cheat; [inf] rip off.

robber NOUN = **burglar**, thief, mugger, housebreaker; bandit, highwayman.

robbery NOUN = **theft**, burglary, stealing, housebreaking, larceny, misappropriation, embezzlement, fraud; mugging, hold-up, break-in, raid.

robot NOUN = **automaton**, android, machine.

robust ADJ = **healthy**, strong, vigorous, muscular, powerful, tough, rugged, sturdy, strapping, brawny, burly.

rock NOUN = **boulder**, stone. VERB = **move to and fro**, swing, sway, roll, lurch, pitch.

rocky ADJ 1 = **stony**, pebbly. 2 = **unsteady**, unstable, shaky, teetering, wobbly.

rod NOUN = **bar**, stick, pole, baton, staff.

rogue NOUN = **villain**, scoundrel, rascal, reprobate, wretch, cad, blackguard, ne'er-do-well; [inf] rotter, bounder.

role NOUN 1 = **part**, character. 2 = **capacity**, function, position, job, post, office.

roll VERB 1 = **go round**, turn, rotate, revolve, spin, whirl, wheel. 2 = **furl**, coil, fold. 3 = **toss**, rock, pitch, lurch, sway, reel.

romance NOUN 1 = (**love**) **affair**, liaison, courtship. 2 = **mystery**, glamour, excitement, exoticism, mystique.

romantic ADJ 1 = **loving**, amorous, affectionate, tender, sentimental. 2 = **unrealistic**, idealistic, impractical, starry-eyed, fairy-tale. NOUN = **dreamer**, idealist, sentimentalist.

room NOUN 1 = **space**, elbow room; area, expanse, extent. 2 = **scope**, capacity, margin, leeway, latitude, freedom, opportunity.

roomy ADJ see **spacious**.

root NOUN 1 = **radicle**, rhizome, tuber. 2 = **source**, origin, genesis, starting point, basis, foundation, beginnings. VERB (**root out**) = **eradicate**, get rid of, weed out, do away with, eliminate, abolish, destroy.

rope NOUN = **cord**, cable, line, strand, hawser.

rot VERB 1 = **decompose**, decay, crumble, disintegrate, perish. 2 = **go bad**, go off, spoil, putrefy, fester. NOUN = **decay**, decomposition, putrefaction, mould, blight.

rotate VERB = **revolve**, go round, turn, spin, whirl, swivel, wheel, gyrate.

rotten ADJ 1 = **decaying**, bad, off, mouldy, rancid, decomposing, putrid, putrescent, festering. 2 = **corrupt**, immoral, dishonourable, bad, contemptible, despicable, wicked, villainous, evil.

rough ADJ 1 = **uneven**, irregular, bumpy, rutted, rocky, stony, rugged, craggy. 2 = **coarse**, bristly, scratchy; shaggy, hairy, bushy. 3 = **stormy**, squally, wild, tempestuous, turbulent, choppy. 4 = **harsh**, severe, hard, tough, difficult, unpleasant, arduous. 5 = **preliminary**, hasty, quick, cursory, incomplete, rudimentary, basic. 6 = **approximate**, inexact, imprecise, vague.

round ADJ = **circular**, ring-shaped, cylindrical, spherical, globular, bulbous, convex, curved. NOUN **1** = **succession**, sequence, series, cycle. **2** = **stage**, level; heat, game.

roundabout ADJ = **indirect**, circuitous, meandering, tortuous; oblique, circumlocutory, periphrastic.

rouse VERB **1** = **wake (up)**, awaken. **2** = **stir up**, excite, electrify, galvanize, stimulate, inspire, arouse.

route NOUN = **course**, way, itinerary, road, path.

routine NOUN = **pattern**, procedure, practice, custom, habit, programme, schedule, formula, method, system. ADJ = **usual**, normal, everyday, common, ordinary, typical, customary, habitual, conventional, standard.

row[1] NOUN = **line**, column, queue, procession, chain, string, crocodile.

row[2] NOUN see **argument**.

rowdy ADJ = **unruly**, disorderly, noisy, boisterous, loud, wild, rough, unrestrained, riotous.

royal ADJ = **regal**, kingly, queenly, princely, sovereign.

rub VERB **1** = **massage**, knead, stroke. **2** = **scrub**, scour, polish, clean. **3** (**rub out**) = **erase**, efface, obliterate, expunge, remove.

rubbish NOUN **1** = **waste**, refuse, litter, lumber, junk, debris, detritus; [US] garbage, trash. **2** see **nonsense**.

rude ADJ **1** = **ill-mannered**, bad-mannered, impolite, discourteous, impertinent, insolent, impudent, cheeky, disrespectful, curt, brusque, blunt, offhand. **2** = **vulgar**, coarse, indelicate, smutty, dirty, naughty, risqué, blue, ribald, bawdy.

rudimentary ADJ **1** = **elementary**, basic, fundamental. **2** = **undeveloped**, immature, incomplete, vestigial. **3** = **primitive**, crude, rough-and-ready, simple.

rudiments PLURAL NOUN = **basics**, fundamentals, essentials, foundation; [inf]

nuts and bolts.

ruffle VERB = **rumple**, dishevel, tousle, disarrange, disorder, mess up; [inf] muss up.

rugged ADJ 1 = **rough**, uneven, bumpy, rocky, stony, craggy. 2 = **strong-featured**, rough-hewn; strong, tough, sturdy, vigorous, brawny, robust, muscular; [inf] hunky.

ruin VERB = **destroy**, devastate, lay waste, demolish, wreck, spoil. NOUN = **destruction**, devastation, wreckage, demolition, disintegration.

ruined ADJ = **derelict**, in ruins, dilapidated, in disrepair, ramshackle, tumbledown.

rule NOUN 1 = **ruling**, law, regulation, statute, order, decree, edict, commandment, directive, act. 2 = **principle**, precept, standard, axiom, maxim. 3 = **government**, administration, jurisdiction, reign, authority, command, power, dominion. VERB 1 = **preside over**, govern, control, run, administer, manage. 2 = **order**, decree,

pronounce, ordain, lay down; decide, determine, resolve.

ruling NOUN = **judgement**, decision, adjudication, finding, verdict, decree, pronouncement.

rumour NOUN = **gossip**, hearsay, talk; report, story, whisper.

run VERB 1 = **race**, rush, hasten, hurry, dash, sprint, bolt, dart, career, tear, charge, speed; jog, lope; [inf] hare. 2 = **move**, glide, slide, roll, flow, course. 3 = **continue**, extend, stretch, reach. 4 = **manage**, be in charge of, control, head, lead, direct, administer, supervise, superintend, oversee. NOUN 1 = **jog**, sprint, dash. 2 = **spell**, spate; sequence, series, succession; streak, chain, string.

run-of-the-mill ADJ = **ordinary**, average, undistinguished, unexceptional, unremarkable, commonplace, everyday, conventional, routine.

rupture NOUN = **break**, fracture, crack, split, burst, fissure.

rural ADJ = **pastoral**, rustic, bucolic; agricultural, agrarian.

rush VERB = **hurry**, hasten, run, race, dash, sprint, bolt, dart, career, tear, charge, speed, scurry, scamper. NOUN 1 = **surge**, flow, gush, spurt, stream, flood. 2 = **hurry**, haste, speed, urgency, rapidity.

rut NOUN 1 = **furrow**, groove, track, trough, ditch, hole, pothole. 2 = **treadmill**, dead end, boring routine.

ruthless ADJ = **merciless**, pitiless, cruel, heartless, hard-hearted, cold-blooded, harsh, callous, remorseless, implacable; barbarous, inhuman, brutal, savage, sadistic.

Ss

sabotage NOUN = **damage**, destruction, vandalism, disruption. VERB = **damage**, destroy, wreck, ruin, incapacitate, cripple, vandalize, disrupt.

sack VERB = **dismiss**, discharge; [inf] fire, kick out, give someone their cards, boot out.

sacred ADJ = **holy**, blessed, hallowed, consecrated, sanctified; religious, spiritual.

sacrifice NOUN = **offering**, gift, oblation. VERB 1 = **give up**, forgo, renounce, abandon, surrender, relinquish. 2 = **offer (up)**, immolate.

sacrilege NOUN = **desecration**, profanity, blasphemy, impiety, irreverence, disrespect.

sad ADJ 1 = **unhappy**, miserable, sorrowful, gloomy, melancholy, mournful, woebegone, wretched, dejected, downcast, despondent, depressed, doleful, glum, dispirited, disconsolate, heartbroken; [inf] blue, down in the mouth/ dumps. 2 = **unfortunate**, sorry, distressing, heartbreaking, heart-rending, pitiful, tragic.

safe ADJ 1 = **secure**, protected, sheltered,

guarded, defended, free from harm/danger, out of harm's way; impregnable, unassailable.
2 = **unharmed**, alive and well, unhurt, unscathed, out of danger; [inf] OK.
NOUN = **strongbox**, safety-deposit box.
safeguard NOUN = **protection**, defence, precaution, security; surety. VERB = **protect**, preserve, guard, secure.
safety NOUN = **protection**, security, shelter, sanctuary, refuge.
sag VERB = **sink**, droop, subside, slump.
saga NOUN = **epic**, chronicle, legend, history.
sailor NOUN = **seaman**, seafarer, mariner, boatman; [inf] salt, sea dog.
saintly ADJ = **holy**, godly, pious, religious, devout, God-fearing, virtuous, righteous, innocent, pure, angelic.
salary NOUN = **pay**, wages, earnings, remuneration, fee, emolument, stipend.
sally NOUN = **sortie**, foray, thrust, offensive, drive, attack, raid, assault.
salute NOUN = **greeting**, salutation, address, welcome. VERB 1 = **greet**, address, hail, acknowledge, welcome.
2 = **pay tribute to**, pay homage to, honour.
salvage VERB = **rescue**, save, recover, retrieve, reclaim.
same ADJ 1 = **identical**, selfsame, one and the same, very same.
2 = **matching**, alike, duplicate, twin, interchangeable, indistinguishable, corresponding, equivalent.
3 = **unchanging**, unvarying, invariable, consistent, uniform.
sample NOUN = **specimen**, example, bit, taste, taster.
sanctify VERB = **consecrate**, bless, hallow.
sanctimonious ADJ = **self-righteous**, smug, holier-than-thou, pious, hypocritical; [inf] goody-goody.
sanction NOUN
1 = **authorization**, permission, consent, approval, endorsement, backing, support, go-ahead; [inf] thumbs up,

green light, OK.
2 = penalty, punishment.
sanctuary NOUN **1 = refuge**,
haven, shelter, retreat,
hideout, hideaway.
2 = holy place, temple,
shrine, sanctum.
sane ADJ **1 = of sound
mind**, in your right mind,
compos mentis, rational,
lucid. **2 = sensible**,
reasonable, judicious,
prudent, wise, advisable.
sap VERB **= drain**, enervate,
exhaust, weaken,
enfeeble, debilitate.
sarcasm NOUN **= derision**,
scorn, mockery, ridicule;
irony.
sarcastic ADJ **= derisive**,
scornful, mocking,
sneering, jeering; ironic,
sardonic, satirical, caustic,
trenchant; [inf] sarky.
satanic ADJ **= diabolical**,
fiendish, devilish,
demonic, wicked, evil,
vile, foul, iniquitous.
satire NOUN **= parody**,
burlesque, caricature,
lampoon; [inf] spoof,
send-up.
satirical ADJ **= mocking**,
ironic, sarcastic, sardonic,
caustic, trenchant,
mordant.
satirize VERB **= mock**,

ridicule, deride, make fun
of, parody, lampoon,
caricature; [inf] send up.
satisfaction NOUN
= fulfilment, gratification,
pleasure, enjoyment,
delight, happiness, pride,
content, contentment.
satisfactory ADJ
= adequate, all right,
acceptable, fine,
sufficient, competent,
passable; [inf] OK.
satisfy VERB **= fulfil**, gratify,
appease, assuage, meet;
satiate, sate, slake,
quench.
saturate VERB **= soak**,
drench, waterlog, steep,
douse; permeate, imbue,
pervade, suffuse.
saunter VERB **= stroll**,
amble, wander, meander,
walk, promenade; [inf]
mosey.
savage ADJ **1 = vicious**,
brutal, cruel, sadistic,
violent, murderous,
bloodthirsty, barbarous.
2 = fierce, ferocious, wild,
untamed,
undomesticated, feral.
3 = primitive, uncivilized.
VERB **= maul**, lacerate, tear
to pieces, attack.
save VERB **1 = rescue**; free,
set free, liberate, deliver,

bail out, salvage.
2 = **protect**, safeguard, keep safe, preserve.
3 = **put/set aside**, put by, keep, reserve, conserve, stockpile, store, hoard.
savings PLURAL NOUN = **capital**, assets, reserves, funds, nest egg.
saviour NOUN = **rescuer**, knight in shining armour, good Samaritan, friend in need.
savour VERB = **enjoy**, appreciate, delight in, relish, revel in.
say VERB **1** = **speak**, utter, voice, pronounce.
2 = **state**, declare, remark, announce, observe, comment, mention, opine; claim, maintain, assert. **3** = **estimate**, judge, guess, predict, speculate, conjecture, surmise.
saying NOUN = **proverb**, maxim, aphorism, axiom, adage, epigram, saw; platitude, cliché.
scaffold NOUN
1 = **scaffolding**, framework, gantry.
2 = **gallows**, gibbet.
scale NOUN **1** = **succession**, sequence, series, ranking, ladder, hierarchy, pecking order. **2** = **extent**, scope,

size, magnitude, dimensions. VERB = **climb**, ascend, shin up, mount.
scan VERB = **scrutinize**, examine, study, survey, inspect, look through, cast your eye over, leaf through, thumb through.
scandal NOUN
1 = **wrongdoing**, impropriety, misconduct.
2 = **disgrace**, shame, outrage, injustice.
scandalous ADJ = **disgraceful**, shameful, outrageous, shocking, monstrous, deplorable, wicked, criminal.
scant ADJ = **little**, minimal, limited, insufficient, inadequate, deficient.
scanty ADJ = **meagre**, scant, sparse, minimal, small, paltry, negligible, insufficient, inadequate, deficient, limited, restricted.
scar NOUN = **mark**, blemish, discoloration, disfigurement, cicatrix.
scarce ADJ = **in short supply**, meagre, scant, scanty, sparse, insufficient, deficient, inadequate, lacking, at a premium, rare, few and far between, uncommon,

unusual.

scare VERB = **frighten**, alarm, startle, terrify, terrorize, petrify, put the fear of God into.

scathing ADJ = **withering**, searing, savage, fierce, stinging, biting, mordant, trenchant, caustic, scornful, harsh, sharp.

scatter VERB
1 = **disseminate**, spread, sow, sprinkle, strew, broadcast, fling, toss, throw. **2** = **break up**, disperse, disband, separate.

scenario NOUN = **plot**, outline, synopsis, storyline, plan, sequence of events.

scene NOUN **1** = **place**, location, site, position, spot, locale. **2** = **event**, incident, happening, episode. **3** = **fuss**, exhibition, commotion, to-do, tantrum, furore, brouhaha.

scenery NOUN = **landscape**, countryside, country; view, vista, panorama.

scenic ADJ = **picturesque**, pretty, beautiful, pleasing.

scent NOUN **1** = **aroma**, perfume, fragrance, smell, bouquet. **2** = **track**, trail, spoor.

sceptical ADJ = **doubting**, doubtful, dubious, distrustful, mistrustful, suspicious, disbelieving, incredulous, unconvinced, cynical.

schedule NOUN = **plan**, programme, timetable, diary, calendar, itinerary, agenda.

scheme NOUN **1** = **plan**, programme, project, course of action, procedure, strategy, formula, tactic. **2** = **arrangement**, system, organization. **3** = **plot**, ruse, ploy, machinations, intrigue, conspiracy. VERB = **plot**, conspire, intrigue, manoeuvre, plan.

scholar NOUN = **academic**, intellectual; authority, expert; [inf] egghead.

scholarly ADJ = **learned**, erudite, academic, well read, intellectual, literary, studious, bookish, highbrow.

school NOUN = **academy**, college, seminary. VERB = **train**, coach, drill, discipline, educate, teach, instruct, prepare, prime.

scintillating ADJ

= **sparkling**, dazzling, effervescent, lively, vivacious, animated, brilliant, witty, clever.

scoff VERB = **mock**, ridicule, deride, jeer, sneer, jibe, taunt, laugh, belittle, scorn.

scold VERB see **rebuke**.

scope NOUN 1 = **extent**, range, sphere, area, realm, compass, orbit, reach, span, sweep. 2 = **opportunity**, freedom, latitude, capacity.

scorch VERB = **burn**, singe, char, sear, blacken.

score NOUN = **result**, outcome, total, tally. VERB 1 = **win**, gain, achieve, chalk up, notch up. 2 = **scratch**, cut, notch, scrape, nick, chip, gouge.

scorn NOUN = **contempt**, disdain, derision, mockery. VERB 1 = **deride**, look down on, look down your nose at, disdain, mock, scoff at, sneer at. 2 = **rebuff**, spurn, shun, reject.

scornful ADJ = **contemptuous**, disdainful, supercilious, withering, scathing, derisive, mocking, snide.

scoundrel NOUN see **rogue**.

scour VERB 1 = **scrub**, rub, clean, cleanse, abrade, wash, polish. 2 = **search**, comb, hunt through, leave no stone unturned.

scowl VERB = **frown**, glower, glare, lour, look daggers.

scramble VERB 1 = **clamber**, climb, crawl, scrabble. 2 = **hurry**, hasten, rush, race, scurry.

scrap NOUN 1 = **fragment**, piece, bit, snippet, shred, remnant. 2 = **waste**, junk, rubbish, scrap metal. 3 (**scraps**) = **leftovers**, leavings, remains, remnants. VERB = **throw away/out**, get rid of, discard, dispose of, abandon, jettison; [inf] chuck out, ditch.

scrape VERB 1 = **scour**, rub, scrub, file, rasp. 2 = **graze**, scratch, abrade, skin, cut, bark.

scratch VERB = **scrape**, abrade, graze, skin, cut, lacerate, bark. NOUN = **graze**, abrasion, cut, laceration, wound.

scream VERB = **shriek**, howl, shout, cry out, yell, screech, bawl; [inf] holler.

screen NOUN = **partition**, divider; protection, shield, safeguard, shelter,

guard, buffer. VERB
1 = **partition off**, divide off;
conceal, hide; protect,
shelter, shield, guard.
2 = **vet**, check, test,
examine, investigate.
scrimp VERB = **skimp**,
economize, tighten your
belt, draw in your horns.
script NOUN
1 = **handwriting**, writing,
hand, calligraphy. **2** = **text**,
screenplay, lines, words.
scrounge VERB = **cadge**,
beg, borrow; [inf] sponge,
freeload.
scrub VERB = **rub**, scour,
clean, cleanse, wash.
scruffy ADJ = **untidy**,
unkempt, dishevelled,
shabby, down at heel,
ragged, tattered, messy,
tatty.
scruples PLURAL NOUN
= **qualms**, compunction,
hesitation, misgivings,
second thoughts, doubt,
uneasiness, reluctance.
scrupulous ADJ
= **meticulous**, careful,
painstaking, thorough,
rigorous, strict,
conscientious,
punctilious, strict.
scrutinize VERB = **examine**,
study, inspect, survey,
peruse; investigate, probe,

inquire into.
scrutiny NOUN
= **examination**, study,
inspection, survey,
perusal; investigation,
exploration, check,
inquiry.
sculpture NOUN = **statue**,
statuette, bust, figure,
figurine.
seal NOUN = **emblem**,
symbol, insignia, badge,
crest, monogram. VERB
1 = **fasten**, secure, shut,
close. **2** = **close off**, cordon
off, fence off. **3** = **clinch**,
settle, conclude,
complete.
seam NOUN **1** = **join**,
stitching. **2** = **layer**,
stratum, vein, lode.
sear VERB = **burn**, singe,
scorch, char.
search VERB = **hunt**
through, look through,
rummage through, rifle
through, scour, ransack,
comb, turn upside down;
seek, look high and low,
leave no stone unturned.
NOUN = **hunt**, quest.
seasoned ADJ
= **experienced**, practised,
well versed, established;
veteran.
seat NOUN **1** = **chair**, bench,
settle, stool, stall.

2 = headquarters, base, centre, hub, heart; location, site. VERB **1 = place**, position, put; ensconce, install. **2 = hold**, take, have room for, accommodate.

secede VERB **= withdraw**, break away, split, pull out, disaffiliate, resign.

secluded ADJ **= sheltered**, concealed, hidden, private, unfrequented, off the beaten track.

seclusion NOUN **= privacy**, solitude, retreat, retirement, withdrawal, isolation, concealment, hiding, secrecy.

second ADJ **= next**, following, subsequent. VERB **= support**, back, approve, endorse.

secondary ADJ **= lesser**, subordinate, ancillary, subsidiary, peripheral, minor, incidental.

secret ADJ **1 = confidential**, private, classified, under wraps; [inf] hush-hush. **2 = hidden**, concealed, disguised; clandestine, furtive, undercover, underground, surreptitious, stealthy, cloak-and-dagger, covert.

secrete VERB

1 = discharge, produce, emit, excrete. **2 = hide**, conceal, cover up, stow away; [inf] stash away.

secretive ADJ **= reticent**, uncommunicative, unforthcoming, reserved, silent, quiet; [inf] cagey.

sectarian ADJ **= partisan**, separatist; extreme, fanatical, doctrinaire.

section NOUN **= part**, segment, division, component, piece, portion, bit, unit.

sector NOUN **1 = part**, division, branch, department, arm, field. **2 = zone**, quarter, district, area, region.

secular ADJ **= lay**, non-religious; temporal, worldly, earthly.

secure ADJ **1 = safe**, out of harm's way, sheltered, protected, invulnerable; unworried, at ease, confident, relaxed. **2 = fastened**, fixed, closed, shut, locked. VERB **1 = fasten**, close, shut, lock, bolt, chain, seal; fortify, strengthen, protect. **2 = acquire**, obtain, gain, get, get hold of.

sedate ADJ **1 = slow**,

unhurried, steady, dignified, relaxed, leisurely. **2** = **calm**, placid, quiet, uneventful, dull.

sedative NOUN = **tranquillizer**, sleeping pill, narcotic, opiate.

sediment NOUN = **dregs**, lees, grounds, deposit, residue, precipitate.

seduce VERB = **attract**, lure, tempt, entice, beguile, inveigle.

seductive ADJ = **attractive**, alluring, tempting, provocative, exciting, sultry, sexy.

see VERB **1** = **make out**, catch sight of, glimpse, spot, notice, perceive, discern, espy. **2** = **understand**, grasp, comprehend, follow, take in, realize, fathom. **3** = **escort**, accompany, show, usher, lead.

seek VERB **1** = **search for**, look for, be after, hunt for. **2** = **ask for**, request, solicit, appeal for, beg for.

seem VERB = **appear (to be)**, look, look like, look to be; come across as.

seep VERB = **ooze**, leak, exude, drip, trickle, percolate.

segment NOUN = **section**, part, division, piece, portion, slice.

segregate VERB = **separate**, set apart, isolate, cut off.

seize VERB **1** = **grab**, snatch, take hold of, grasp, grip, clutch. **2** = **confiscate**, impound, commandeer, appropriate. **3** = **abduct**, take captive, kidnap.

seldom ADV = **rarely**, hardly ever, infrequently; [inf] once in a blue moon.

select VERB = **choose**, pick, single out, opt for, decide on, settle on. ADJ **1** = **choice**, prime, first class, finest, best, top quality. **2** = **exclusive**, elite, privileged.

selection NOUN **1** = **choice**, pick, option. **2** = **variety**, range, array; assortment, anthology, miscellany, collection.

selective ADJ = **particular**, discriminating, discerning; fussy, fastidious; [inf] choosy.

self-confidence NOUN = **self-assurance**, self-possession, poise, aplomb.

self-conscious ADJ = **awkward**, shy, bashful, blushing, nervous,

embarrassed,
uncomfortable.

self-important ADJ
= **pompous**, vain,
conceited, arrogant, full
of yourself, swollen-
headed, egotistical,
presumptuous,
overbearing.

self-indulgent ADJ
= **hedonistic**, pleasure-
seeking, sybaritic,
extravagant, indulgent.

selfish ADJ = **egocentric**,
egotistic, egotistical, self-
seeking, self-centred, self-
absorbed.

self-respect NOUN = **self-
esteem**, pride/faith in
yourself, amour propre.

self-righteous ADJ
= **sanctimonious**, self-
satisfied, holier-than-
thou, smug, pious,
complacent; [inf] goody-
goody.

sell VERB 1 = **put up for sale**,
put on sale, vend, auction
off, barter. 2 = **trade in**,
deal in, traffic in, stock,
peddle, hawk.

seller NOUN = **vendor**,
retailer, shopkeeper,
trader, merchant, dealer,
rep; pedlar, hawker.

semblance NOUN
= **appearance**, show, air,
guise, pretence, facade,
front, veneer.

send VERB 1 = **dispatch**,
forward, mail, post, remit.
2 = **propel**, project, eject,
discharge, shoot out.

sensation NOUN 1 = **feeling**,
sense, awareness,
consciousness,
perception, impression.
2 = **stir**, excitement,
commotion, furore,
scandal.

sensational ADJ
= **spectacular**, exciting,
thrilling, startling,
staggering, dramatic,
amazing, shocking,
scandalous, lurid.

sense NOUN 1 = **feeling**,
sensation, faculty,
sensibility.
2 = **appreciation**,
awareness,
understanding,
comprehension.
3 = **common sense**,
wisdom, sagacity,
discernment, perception,
wit, intelligence,
shrewdness, brains, nous.
4 = **meaning**, definition;
import, signification,
implication, nuance,
drift, gist. VERB = **feel**, be
aware/conscious of,
perceive, discern, pick up,

suspect, intuit.
sensible ADJ = **practical**, realistic, down-to-earth, wise, prudent, judicious, sagacious, shrewd, intelligent, rational, logical, reasonable.
sensitive ADJ 1 = **delicate**, fine, soft, fragile.
2 = **responsive**, receptive, perceptive, understanding, empathetic, intuitive.
3 = **touchy**, oversensitive, thin-skinned, defensive, temperamental.
sensual ADJ = **physical**, carnal, bodily, fleshly, sensuous; hedonistic, sybaritic.
sentiment NOUN = **feeling**, view, thought, attitude, opinion, belief.
sentimental ADJ = **emotional**, romantic, nostalgic, affectionate, loving, tender; mawkish; [inf] soppy.
sentry NOUN = **guard**, lookout, watch, watchman, sentinel.
separate ADJ = **unconnected**, unrelated, distinct, different, detached, discrete, independent, autonomous. VERB

1 = **disconnect**, detach, disengage; sever, sunder.
2 = **divide**, come between, keep apart, partition.
3 = **break up**, split up, part, divorce.
septic ADJ = **infected**, festering, putrefying, putrid.
sequel NOUN = **follow-up**, development, result, consequence, outcome, upshot.
sequence NOUN = **chain**, course, cycle, series, progression, succession, order, pattern.
serendipity NOUN = **chance**, luck, good fortune, fortuitousness, happy accident.
serene ADJ = **calm**, composed, tranquil, peaceful, placid, still, quiet, unperturbed, unruffled, unflappable.
series NOUN = **succession**, sequence, chain, course, string, run, cycle, set, row; spate, wave.
serious ADJ 1 = **solemn**, earnest, unsmiling, thoughtful, preoccupied, pensive, grave, sombre, sober, dour, poker-faced.
2 = **important**, significant, momentous, weighty, far-

reaching, urgent, pressing, crucial, vital, life-and-death. **3** = **acute**, grave, severe, bad, critical, grievous, dangerous.

sermon NOUN = **homily**, address, oration, lecture.

servant NOUN = **attendant**, retainer, domestic, maid, charwoman, cleaner; menial, drudge, lackey; [inf] skivvy.

serve VERB **1** = **work for**, be employed by. **2** = **carry out**, complete, fulfil, perform; spend. **3** = **dish up**, give out, distribute; supply, provide. **4** = **attend to**, deal with, see to; help, assist.

service NOUN **1** = **good turn**, favour, kindness. **2** = **work**, employment, labour. **3** = **ceremony**, ritual, rite, sacrament.

serviceable ADJ **1** = **functional**, utilitarian, practical, durable, hard-wearing, tough, strong. **2** = **functioning**, usable, operational, working.

servile ADJ = **subservient**, obsequious, sycophantic, fawning, submissive, toadying.

session NOUN **1** = **period**, time, spell, stretch.

2 = **meeting**, sitting, assembly, conference, discussion.

set VERB **1** = **put**, place, lay, deposit, position, rest; [inf] stick, park, plonk. **2** = **fix**, embed, insert, mount. **3** = **adjust**, regulate, synchronize, calibrate, programme. **4** = **lay**, prepare, arrange. **5** = **solidify**, harden, stiffen, thicken, jell, cake, congeal, coagulate. **6** = **establish**, create, institute. **7** = **fix**, agree on, appoint, decide on, name, specify, stipulate, determine, designate, select, choose, arrange, schedule. NOUN = **collection**, group, series, batch, array, assortment, selection.

setback NOUN = **problem**, difficulty, complication, obstruction, hold-up, hitch, delay, disappointment, misfortune, blow.

setting NOUN = **environment**, surroundings, milieu, background, location, situation, place, position, site.

settle VERB **1** = **resolve**,

clear up, patch up, sort out, work out, put right, rectify, remedy, reconcile. 2 = **make your home**, set up home, put down roots; move to, emigrate to. 3 = **calm down**, quieten down, be quiet, be still. 4 = **land**, alight, come to rest, perch; sit down.

settlement NOUN 1 = **community**, colony, encampment, outpost, post. 2 = **resolution**, agreement, deal, pact.

sever VERB 1 = **cut off**, chop off, hack off, detach, sunder; amputate, dock. 2 = **break off**, discontinue, suspend, end, terminate, cease.

severe ADJ 1 = **harsh**, strict, rigorous, unsparing, relentless, merciless, ruthless; sharp, caustic, biting, cutting, scathing, withering. 2 = **acute**, serious, grave, critical, dire, dangerous. 3 = **fierce**, strong, violent, intense, powerful. 4 = **demanding**, taxing, exacting, tough, difficult, hard, arduous, punishing. 5 = **stern**, grim, austere, forbidding, dour, unsmiling, sombre, sober. 6 = **austere**, stark, spartan, ascetic, plain, simple, unadorned, unembellished.

sew VERB = **stitch**, embroider, mend, darn.

sexy ADJ 1 = **erotic**, titillating, arousing, exciting. 2 = **seductive**, desirable, alluring, provocative, sultry, nubile, voluptuous.

shabby ADJ = **worn**, worn-out, threadbare, ragged, frayed, tattered, scruffy, tatty, the worse for wear.

shade NOUN 1 = **shadiness**, shadow(s), shelter, cover. 2 = **colour**, hue, tone, tint. 3 = **nuance**, degree, gradation, difference, variety. VERB = **screen**, cover, shelter; darken, dim.

shadow NOUN 1 see **shade** (1). 2 = **silhouette**, outline, shape.

shady ADJ 1 = **shaded**, shadowy, dark, dim; leafy. 2 = **suspicious**, suspect, questionable, dubious, untrustworthy, disreputable, dishonest, shifty.

shaft NOUN 1 = **pole**, stick, rod, staff, stem, handle, hilt. 2 = **ray**, beam, gleam, streak, pencil.

3 = **passage**, duct, tunnel, well, flue.

shake VERB **1** = **vibrate**, tremble, quiver, quake, shudder, shiver, judder, wobble, rock, sway.
2 = **jiggle**, joggle, agitate, waggle; brandish.
3 = **shock**, alarm, worry, distress, upset.

shaky ADJ **1** = **trembling**, tremulous, quivering, unsteady, wobbly, weak, tottering, teetering.
2 = **faint**, dizzy, giddy, light-headed.
3 = **unreliable**, questionable, dubious, doubtful, tenuous, flimsy.

shallow ADJ = **superficial**, facile, simplistic; lightweight, trifling, trivial, empty, frivolous, foolish, silly.

sham NOUN = **pretence**, fake, forgery, counterfeit, simulation. ADJ = **pretend**, feigned, fake, artificial, put-on, simulated, affected, insincere, false, bogus; [inf] phoney, pseudo.

shambles PLURAL NOUN = **chaos**, muddle, mess, confusion, disorder, disarray, disorganization.

shame NOUN

1 = **humiliation**, ignominy, mortification, chagrin, embarrassment; guilt, remorse, contrition.
2 = **disgrace**, dishonour, discredit, degradation, disrepute, infamy, opprobrium. **3** = **pity**, misfortune, bad luck.

shamefaced ADJ = **ashamed**, embarrassed, guilty, conscience-stricken, remorseful, contrite, penitent, sheepish.

shameful ADJ = **disgraceful**, dishonourable, discreditable, deplorable, despicable, contemptible, ignoble, shabby, reprehensible, scandalous, outrageous, shocking.

shameless ADJ see **brazen**.

shape NOUN **1** = **form**, figure, configuration, formation, structure, contour, outline, silhouette, profile.
2 = **condition**, state, health, trim, fettle.

shapely ADJ = **well proportioned**, curvy, curvaceous, voluptuous.

share NOUN = **allowance**,

ration, allocation, quota, portion, part, measure, helping; [inf] cut, slice, whack. VERB **1** = **divide**, split, go halves; [inf] go fifty-fifty, go Dutch. **2** = **divide up**, allocate, apportion, parcel out, ration out.

sharp ADJ **1** = **razor-edged**, keen, cutting, sharpened, honed. **2** = **intense**, acute, severe, stabbing, shooting, excruciating. **3** = **harsh**, bitter, hard, cutting, scathing, caustic, barbed, acrimonious, trenchant, venomous, malicious, vitriolic, hurtful, cruel. **4** = **sudden**, abrupt, rapid, steep, unexpected. **5** = **intelligent**, bright, clever, smart, shrewd, astute, canny, discerning, perceptive, quick-witted.

sharpen VERB = **hone**, whet, strop, grind.

shatter VERB **1** = **smash**, break, splinter, fracture, pulverize, crush, crack. **2** = **destroy**, wreck, ruin, dash, devastate.

sheath NOUN = **scabbard**; cover, covering, case, casing, envelope, sleeve.

shed NOUN = **hut**, outhouse, lean-to, shack. VERB **1** = **drop**, spill, let fall. **2** = **slough off**, cast off, moult.

sheen NOUN = **shine**, lustre, gloss, polish, patina.

sheepish ADJ = **embarrassed**, ashamed, shamefaced, abashed, hangdog, mortified, chastened.

sheer ADJ **1** = **utter**, complete, total, pure, absolute, downright, out-and-out. **2** = **steep**, abrupt, precipitous, perpendicular. **3** = **diaphanous**, gauzy, transparent, see-through

sheet NOUN **1** = **pane**, panel, plate. **2** = **leaf**, page, folio. **3** = **expanse**, area, stretch, sweep.

shell NOUN **1** = **carapace**, case, casing, husk, pod, integument. **2** = **bullet**, cartridge, shot; shrapnel. VERB = **bomb**, bombard, strafe, fire on.

shelter NOUN = **protection**, cover, screen; safety, security, refuge, sanctuary, asylum. VERB = **protect**, shield, screen, cover, save, guard, defend.

sheltered ADJ = **quiet**, withdrawn, secluded,

isolated, protected, cloistered, reclusive.

shepherd VERB = **escort**, conduct, usher, guide, direct, steer.

shift VERB = **move**, carry, transfer, switch, reposition, rearrange.

shine VERB 1 = **gleam**, glow, glint, sparkle, twinkle, glitter, glisten, shimmer, flash, beam, radiate. 2 = **polish**, burnish, buff, wax, gloss. NOUN 1 = **light**, brightness, gleam, glow, glint, sparkle, twinkle, glitter, shimmer, flash, glare, beam, radiance, illumination. 2 see **sheen**.

shiny ADJ = **shining**, polished, burnished, gleaming, glossy, satiny, lustrous.

shirk VERB = **avoid**, evade, dodge, get out of; [inf] skive off.

shiver VERB = **tremble**, quiver, shake, shudder, quaver, quake.

shock NOUN = **blow**, upset, revelation, bolt from the blue, bombshell, thunderbolt, eye-opener. VERB = **appal**, horrify, scandalize, outrage, revolt, disgust, nauseate, sicken, traumatize; distress, upset; astound, dumbfound, stagger, amaze, astonish, stun.

shoddy ADJ = **poor-quality**, inferior, second-rate, trashy, cheap, cheapjack; [inf] tacky.

shoot VERB 1 = **gun down**, mow down, hit, pick off, bag, fell, kill. 2 = **fire**, discharge, launch, let fly. 3 = **race**, dash, sprint, charge, dart, fly, hurtle, bolt, streak, run, speed. NOUN = **bud**, offshoot, scion, sucker, sprout, tendril, sprig.

shop NOUN = **store**, boutique, emporium; supermarket, superstore.

shore NOUN = **seashore**, seaside, beach, coast, strand.

short ADJ 1 = **small**, little, tiny, squat, diminutive; [Scottish] wee; [inf] pint-sized. 2 = **brief**, concise, succinct, to the point, pithy, abridged, summarized, curtailed, truncated. 3 = **brief**, momentary, temporary, short-lived, cursory, fleeting, passing, transitory, transient.

shortage NOUN = **dearth**, scarcity, lack, deficiency,

paucity, deficit, shortfall, want.

shortcoming NOUN = **defect**, fault, flaw, imperfection, failing, drawback, weakness.

short-sighted ADJ 1 = **myopic**, near-sighted. 2 = **imprudent**, injudicious, unwise, ill-advised; unimaginative, narrow-minded.

shot NOUN 1 = **crack**, bang, blast, explosion, gunfire. 2 = **pellet**, bullet, slug, projectile; ammunition.

shout VERB = **cry out**, call out, yell, roar, bellow, scream, bawl; [inf] holler.

shove VERB = **push**, thrust, force, ram, shoulder, elbow.

show VERB 1 = **exhibit**, display, present, uncover. 2 = **manifest**, express, reveal, make known, convey; betray. 3 = **demonstrate**, explain, describe, teach, instruct. 4 = **escort**, accompany, usher, conduct, attend, guide, lead, direct, steer. NOUN 1 = **display**, exhibition, presentation, exposition, spectacle. 2 = **performance**, production.

3 = **appearance**, guise, semblance, pretence, pose, affectation.

show-off NOUN = **exhibitionist**, extrovert, braggart, boaster.

showy ADJ = **ostentatious**, ornate, flamboyant, elaborate, fancy, gaudy, garish, flashy.

shred NOUN 1 = **tatter**, fragment, strip, ribbon, rag. 2 = **scrap**, bit, iota, whit, particle, jot, trace.

shrewd ADJ = **astute**, sharp, clever, intelligent, smart, perceptive, wise, sagacious, canny; cunning, crafty, wily.

shriek VERB = **scream**, screech, squeal, squawk.

shrill ADJ = **high-pitched**, high, sharp, piercing, penetrating, ear-splitting.

shrink VERB 1 = **get smaller**, contract, diminish, lessen, reduce, dwindle, decline, shrivel. 2 = **draw back**, recoil, retreat, flinch, cringe.

shrivel VERB = **wither**, wilt, dry up, shrink, wrinkle.

shroud VERB = **cover**, envelop, cloak, blanket, veil, screen, conceal, hide.

shun VERB = **avoid**, evade, steer clear of, shy away

from, keep your distance
from, cold-shoulder.

shut VERB = **close**, pull to,
fasten, lock, secure, seal.

shy ADJ = **bashful**, diffident,
reserved, reticent, self-
effacing, withdrawn,
timid, timorous, nervous,
introverted, self-
conscious.

sick ADJ **1** = **unwell**, ill,
ailing, indisposed, poorly,
under the weather.
2 = **nauseous**, nauseated,
queasy, bilious, green
about the gills. **3** = **tired**,
weary, bored, fed up.
4 = **morbid**, macabre,
ghoulish, perverted.

sicken VERB = **nauseate**,
turn someone's stomach,
revolt, disgust, repulse.

sickly ADJ = **unhealthy**, in
poor health, delicate,
frail, weak.

sickness NOUN **1** = **illness**,
disease, ailment,
complaint, malady,
infirmity, indisposition,
disorder; [inf] bug.
2 = **nausea**, queasiness,
biliousness.

side NOUN **1** = **edge**, border,
verge, boundary, margin,
fringe(s), flank, bank,
perimeter, periphery.
2 = **district**, quarter, area,

sector, neighbourhood.
3 = **aspect**, angle, point of
view, viewpoint, opinion,
standpoint. **4** = **camp**,
faction, caucus, party,
wing.

sieve NOUN = **strainer**, filter,
colander, riddle.

sight NOUN **1** = **eyesight**,
vision. **2** = **view**, glimpse,
look. **3** = **landmark**,
monument, spectacle.

sign NOUN **1** = **indication**,
symptom, mark, pointer,
manifestation, token,
evidence. **2** = **signpost**,
notice, placard.
3 = **gesture**, signal, wave,
gesticulation. **4** = **symbol**,
mark, cipher, hieroglyph.
5 = **omen**, portent,
warning, forewarning,
augury, presage.

signal NOUN = **sign**, gesture,
cue; indication, evidence,
pointer. VERB = **gesture**,
indicate, beckon, motion,
gesticulate, nod, sign.

significance NOUN
1 = **importance**,
consequence, magnitude,
seriousness. **2** = **meaning**,
sense, import,
signification, point, gist,
essence.

significant ADJ
1 = **important**, of

consequence, weighty, momentous, serious, notable, noteworthy.
2 = meaningful, eloquent, expressive, pregnant, knowing.

signify VERB **1 = indicate**, be a sign of, be evidence of, point to, betoken.
2 = mean, denote, represent, symbolize, stand for.

silence NOUN **= quiet**, quietness, hush, still, stillness, peace, peacefulness, tranquillity. VERB **= quiet**, quieten, hush; muffle, deaden, mute.

silent ADJ **1 = quiet**, hushed, still, peaceful, noiseless, soundless.
2 = speechless dumb, mute, tongue-tied; taciturn, tight-lipped, uncommunicative, mum.
3 = unspoken, wordless, tacit, implicit.

silhouette NOUN **= outline**, contour, profile, form, shape.

silky ADJ **= silken**, smooth, sleek, glossy, satiny.

silly ADJ **= foolish**, stupid, idiotic, mindless, brainless, senseless, misguided, unwise,

imprudent, thoughtless, foolhardy, irresponsible, mad, hare-brained, absurd, fatuous, vacuous, inane, asinine, immature, childish; [inf] daft, crazy.

similar ADJ **= like**, alike, comparable, corresponding, analogous, parallel, equivalent; kindred.

similarity NOUN **= resemblance**, likeness, similitude, comparability, correspondence, parallel, equivalence.

simple ADJ **1 = easy**, uncomplicated, straightforward, effortless, elementary; [inf] a piece of cake. **2 = clear**, plain, intelligible, comprehensible, understandable, lucid.
3 = plain, classic, understated, unadorned, undecorated.

simplistic ADJ **= oversimplified**, facile, shallow, superficial, naive.

simultaneous ADJ **= concurrent**, contemporaneous, concomitant, coinciding, coincident, synchronous.

sin NOUN **= wrong**, wrongdoing, crime,

offence, misdeed,
transgression; trespass.
VERB = **transgress**, trespass,
fall from grace.

sincere ADJ = **genuine**,
real, true, honest,
unfeigned, unaffected,
bona fide, wholehearted,
heartfelt, earnest,
profound.

sinful ADJ = **wrong**, evil,
wicked, bad, iniquitous,
immoral, corrupt;
profane, blasphemous,
sacrilegious.

sing VERB = **carol**, croon,
chant; trill, warble.

singe VERB = **scorch**, burn,
sear, char.

single ADJ 1 = **one**, sole,
lone, solitary, unique,
isolated. 2 = **individual**,
particular, separate,
distinct. 3 = **unmarried**,
unwed, unattached,
(fancy) free. VERB (**single
out**) = **pick**, choose, select,
decide on, earmark.

singular ADJ
= **extraordinary**,
exceptional, rare,
unusual, remarkable,
unique, outstanding,
notable, noteworthy,
striking, signal.

sinister ADJ 1 = **menacing**,
ominous, threatening,

forbidding, frightening;
[inf] scary. 2 = **evil**, wicked,
bad, criminal, corrupt,
nefarious, villainous.

sink VERB 1 = **go under**,
submerge, founder,
capsize; scuttle, scupper.
2 = **fall**, drop, descend, go
down, plunge, plummet.

sinuous ADJ = **winding**,
curving, twisting,
meandering, undulating,
serpentine.

sit VERB = **sit down**, take a
seat, settle down, be
seated, take a pew.

site NOUN = **location**,
situation, position, place,
locality, setting.

situate VERB = **place**,
position, locate, site,
station, establish.

situation NOUN 1 = **place**,
position, location, site,
setting, environment.
2 = **circumstances**, affairs,
condition, state. 3 = **post**,
position, place, job,
employment.

size NOUN = **dimensions**,
measurements,
proportions, magnitude,
bulk, area, expanse,
extent.

sketch NOUN 1 = **drawing**,
outline, diagram, plan.
2 = **outline**, rundown,

summary, synopsis.
3 = **skit**, act, scene. VERB
= **draw**, rough out,
outline.
sketchy ADJ = **incomplete**,
patchy, rough, cursory,
perfunctory, superficial,
vague, imprecise, hurried,
hasty.
skilful ADJ = **skilled**, able,
good, accomplished,
adept, competent,
efficient, adroit, deft,
dexterous, masterly,
expert, experienced,
trained, practised,
professional, proficient,
talented.
skill NOUN = **expertise**,
skilfulness, ability,
adeptness, competence,
adroitness, deftness,
dexterity, aptitude,
finesse, prowess,
proficiency, talent.
skin NOUN **1** = **epidermis**,
cuticle, derma.
2 = **complexion**, colouring.
3 = **hide**, pelt, fleece.
4 = **peel**, rind. **5** = **film**,
coating, coat, layer.
skinny ADJ = **thin**, lean,
scraggy, scrawny,
emaciated, skeletal, skin
and bone.
skip VERB **1** = **bound**, jump,
leap, spring, hop, bounce,

dance, caper, prance,
gambol, frisk. **2** = **omit**,
leave out, miss out, pass
over.
skirmish NOUN = **battle**,
fight, clash, conflict,
encounter, confrontation,
tussle, fracas.
slab NOUN = **hunk**, piece,
chunk, lump, slice,
wedge.
slack ADJ **1** = **loose**, limp;
flaccid, sagging, saggy.
2 = **slow**, quiet, sluggish.
3 = **lax**, negligent, remiss,
careless, slapdash,
slipshod, sloppy,
lackadaisical.
slake VERB = **satisfy**,
quench, assuage, relieve.
slam VERB = **bang**, crash,
smash, dash, fling, throw.
slander NOUN
= **defamation**,
misrepresentation, libel,
vilification,
disparagement,
denigration. VERB
= **defame**, libel, cast
aspersions on, malign,
vilify, smear, denigrate,
run down.
slanderous ADJ
= **defamatory**, libellous,
damaging, malicious,
disparaging, pejorative,
scurrilous.

slang NOUN
= **colloquialisms**, jargon, patois, argot, cant; [inf] lingo.

slant VERB 1 = **slope**, tilt, lean, dip, shelve, list.
2 = **bias**, distort, twist, skew. NOUN 1 = **slope**, tilt, gradient, incline. 2 = **point of view**, viewpoint, standpoint, stance, angle, perspective.

slap VERB = **smack**, strike, hit, cuff, spank; [inf] wallop, clout, whack.

slaughter VERB = **kill**, butcher, massacre, murder, slay. NOUN
= **massacre**, murder, butchery, killing, carnage.

slave NOUN = **serf**, vassal.
VERB = **toil**, drudge, slog, graft, labour, work your fingers to the bone.

slaver VERB = **slobber**, drool, dribble, salivate.

slavery NOUN
= **enslavement**, bondage, servitude, subjugation, thrall.

slavish ADJ = **servile**, subservient, obsequious, sycophantic, fawning.

sleek ADJ = **smooth**, glossy, shiny, lustrous, silken, silky, satiny.

sleep VERB = **be asleep**, slumber, doze, drowse; [inf] snooze, kip. NOUN = **nap**, catnap, doze, siesta; [inf] snooze, kip, forty winks, shut-eye.

sleepy ADJ = **drowsy**, tired, somnolent, languorous, lethargic, sluggish, comatose.

slender ADJ = **slim**, thin, slight, lean, svelte, willowy, sylphlike.

slice NOUN = **piece**, portion, wedge, chunk, slab.

slick ADJ 1 = **smooth**, well organized, efficient, effortless, polished.
2 = **glib**, fluent, plausible, smooth-talking.

slide VERB = **slip**, skid, slither, skate, skim, glide.

slight ADJ 1 = **small**, tiny, minute, modest, negligible, insignificant, minimal, trivial. 2 = **slim**, slender, petite, diminutive. VERB = **snub**, insult, rebuff, cold-shoulder, scorn. NOUN
= **insult**, snub, affront, rebuff.

slim ADJ = **slender**, thin, slight, lean, svelte, willowy, sylphlike.

slimy ADJ = **slippery**, greasy, mucky, wet, sticky.

slink VERB = **sidle**, sneak,

creep, steal, slip, slide.

slip VERB 1 = **skid**, slither, slide, lose your footing/balance. 2 = **steal**, creep, sneak, slink. = **decline**, deteriorate, degenerate, worsen, go downhill. NOUN = **mistake**, slip-up, error, blunder, miscalculation, oversight.

slippery ADJ = **greasy**, oily, slimy, icy, glassy, smooth.

slit NOUN = **cut**, split, slash, gash, rip, incision, tear, rent, fissure, opening.

slogan NOUN = **motto**, catchphrase, jingle.

slope VERB = **slant**, incline, lean, tilt, dip, drop. NOUN = **gradient**, slant, incline, angle, pitch, tilt; hill, hillock, bank.

sloping ADJ = **slanting**, oblique, at an angle, aslant, angled, tilting, leaning.

slot NOUN = **slit**, crack, hole, opening, aperture.

slovenly ADJ = **scruffy**, untidy, messy, unkempt, dishevelled, bedraggled.

slow ADJ 1 = **unhurried**, leisurely, sedate, measured; ponderous, plodding, dawdling, sluggish. 2 = **time-consuming**, protracted, long-drawn-out, prolonged, lengthy, interminable. VERB 1 = **reduce speed**, decelerate, brake. 2 = **hold back/up**, delay, retard, set back.

sluggish ADJ = **inactive**, inert, lifeless, listless, lethargic, torpid, indolent, lazy, slothful, drowsy, sleepy, enervated.

slump NOUN = **drop**, fall, nosedive, collapse, downturn, slide, decline, decrease. VERB 1 = **plummet**, nosedive, fall, drop, go down, slide. 2 = **collapse**, sink, fall, flop.

slur NOUN = **insult**, slight, slander, libel, allegation, smear, stain.

sly ADJ = **cunning**, crafty, wily, artful, conniving, scheming, devious, underhand, deceitful.

smack VERB see **slap**.

small ADJ 1 = **little**, tiny, petite, slight, minute, miniature, minuscule, diminutive; [Scottish] wee; [inf] pint-sized. 2 = **slight**, minor, unimportant, trifling, trivial, insignificant, inconsequential.

smart ADJ = **well dressed**,

fashionable, stylish, elegant, chic, neat, spruce, trim, dapper; [inf] natty.

smash VERB 1 = **break**, shatter, splinter, crack. 2 = **collide with**, crash into, hit, strike, run into. 3 = **destroy**, ruin, shatter, devastate, wreck, dash.

smear VERB 1 = **spread**, daub, rub, slather, plaster. 2 = **smudge**, streak, mark, soil. 3 = **sully**, tarnish, blacken, taint, stain, defame, slander, libel.

smell NOUN 1 = **odour**, scent, aroma, perfume, fragrance, bouquet. 2 = **stink**, stench, reek; [inf] pong. VERB 1 = **scent**, sniff. 2 = **stink**, reek; [inf] pong.

smelly ADJ = **foul-smelling**, stinking, rank, malodorous, fetid; [literary] noisome.

smile VERB = **beam**, grin; smirk, simper.

smog NOUN = **fog**, haze, fumes, smoke, pollution.

smooth ADJ 1 = **even**, level, flat, plane, unwrinkled; glossy, sleek, silky, polished. 2 = **calm**, still, tranquil, glassy, undisturbed. 3 = **steady**, regular, rhythmic, uninterrupted, unbroken, fluid; easy, effortless, trouble-free. 4 = **suave**, urbane, sophisticated, debonair, courteous, gracious; glib, slick; [inf] smarmy.

smother VERB 1 = **suffocate**, stifle, asphyxiate, choke. 2 = **smear**, spread, cover, plaster.

smudge NOUN = **mark**, spot, smear, streak, stain, blotch, splotch.

smug ADJ = **self-satisfied**, complacent, pleased with yourself, superior.

snag NOUN = **catch**, drawback, hitch, stumbling block, obstacle, disadvantage, inconvenience, problem, complication.

snap VERB 1 = **break**, fracture, splinter, crack. 2 = **bark**, snarl, growl; [inf] jump down someone's throat.

snare VERB = **trap**, ensnare, catch, capture. NOUN = **trap**, gin, springe, net.

snatch VERB = **seize**, grab, take hold of, pluck, clutch at.

sneak VERB 1 = **creep**, steal, tiptoe, slip, slide, slink, sidle. **2** = **tell tales**, inform; [inf] tell, rat, grass.

sneaking ADJ = **secret**, private, hidden, concealed, unexpressed, undisclosed.

sneer VERB = **scoff at**, scorn, disdain, mock, jeer at, ridicule, taunt, deride, insult.

snigger VERB = **titter**, giggle; sneer, smirk.

snippet NOUN = **bit**, piece, scrap, fragment, particle, shred; excerpt, extract.

snivel VERB = **whimper**, whine, weep, cry, sob; [inf] grizzle, blub, blubber.

snobbish ADJ = **pretentious**, superior; arrogant, condescending, haughty, disdainful, supercilious, patronizing; [inf] snooty, stuck-up, high and mighty, hoity-toity, toffee-nosed.

snub VERB = **ignore**, shun, rebuff, spurn, cut, slight, cold-shoulder, insult.

snug ADJ = **cosy**, comfortable, warm, homely; [inf] comfy.

snuggle VERB = **nestle**, cuddle, curl up, nuzzle.

soak VERB **1** = **drench**, wet through, saturate. **2** = **steep**, immerse, souse, marinate. **3** = **permeate**, penetrate, seep into.

soaking ADJ = **soaked**, drenched, sodden, saturated, sopping, wringing wet.

soar VERB **1** = **fly**, take flight, take off, ascend, climb, rise. **2** = **rise**, increase, rocket, spiral.

sob VERB = **weep**, cry, snivel, howl, bawl; [inf] blub, blubber.

sober ADJ **1** = **teetotal**, abstinent; [inf] on the wagon. **2** = **serious**, solemn, thoughtful, sombre, grave, earnest, staid, level-headed, realistic, rational, matter-of-fact.

sociable ADJ = **friendly**, affable, cordial, neighbourly, companionable, gregarious, convivial, communicative, genial, outgoing.

socialize VERB = **mix**, mingle, fraternize, consort, hobnob.

society NOUN **1** = **mankind**, humanity, civilization, the public, the people, the population, the community. **2** = **community**, culture,

soft

civilization. **3** = **high
society**, aristocracy,
gentry, nobility, upper
classes, elite, beau monde;
[inf] upper crust.
4 = **association**, club,
group, circle, fraternity,
league, union, alliance.
soft ADJ **1** = **pliable**, pliant,
supple, malleable;
squashy, spongy, pulpy,
doughy. **2** = **smooth**,
velvety, fleecy, downy,
furry, silky, silken, satiny.
3 = **gentle**, light, mild,
moderate. **4** = **low**, dim,
faint, subdued, muted;
hushed, whispered,
murmured, quiet.
soften VERB = **ease**,
cushion, temper,
mitigate, assuage.
soil NOUN = **earth**, ground,
loam, sod, turf. VERB
= **dirty**, stain, muddy,
smear, splash, smudge,
sully.
solemn ADJ **1** = **serious**,
grave, sober, sombre,
unsmiling; pensive,
thoughtful. **2** = **dignified**,
ceremonious, stately,
formal, majestic,
imposing, grand.
3 = **sincere**, genuine,
earnest, honest, heartfelt.
solicitous ADJ

= **concerned**, caring,
attentive, considerate;
anxious, worried.
solid ADJ **1** = **firm**, hard,
compacted, solidified, set.
2 = **sound**, substantial,
strong, sturdy, stout,
durable, well built, stable.
3 = **sound**, well founded,
valid, reasonable, logical,
cogent, convincing,
reliable. **4** = **continuous**,
uninterrupted, unbroken.
solidarity NOUN = **unity**,
unanimity, like-
mindedness, camaraderie,
team spirit, harmony.
solidify VERB = **harden**, set,
jell, congeal, cake.
solitary ADJ **1** = **lonely**,
friendless, alone, on your
own; reclusive, cloistered.
2 = **remote**, out of the way,
isolated, cut-off,
unfrequented, in the
middle of nowhere.
solution NOUN = **answer**,
result, resolution,
panacea, way out, key,
explanation.
solve VERB = **resolve**,
answer, find the key to,
work out, fathom,
decipher, clear up, get to
the bottom of, unravel.
sombre ADJ **1** = **dark**, dull,
drab, sober, funereal.

2 = gloomy, depressed, sad, melancholy, doleful, mournful, lugubrious, solemn, serious, sober.

sometimes ADV = **occasionally**, now and then/again, from time to time, once in a while, every so often.

sonorous ADJ = **deep**, rich, full, resonant, clear, ringing.

soon ADV = **shortly**, before long, in a minute/moment, any minute, in the near future; [inf] pronto, in two shakes.

soothe VERB = **ease**, assuage, alleviate, allay, moderate, mitigate, palliate, soften, lessen, reduce.

sophisticated ADJ **1 = worldly-wise**, worldly, experienced, suave, urbane, cultured, cultivated, polished, refined, elegant, stylish, cosmopolitan. **2 = advanced**, modern, state-of-the-art.

sorcerer NOUN = **magician**, wizard, warlock, necromancer, magus.

sorcery NOUN = **magic**, witchcraft, necromancy, black arts.

sordid ADJ = **sleazy**, seedy, unsavoury, tawdry, cheap, degenerate, disreputable, dishonourable, discreditable, contemptible, ignominious, shameful, immoral.

sore ADJ = **painful**, aching, hurting, tender, inflamed, raw, smarting, throbbing, bruised, wounded, injured. NOUN = **wound**, scrape, abrasion, cut, laceration, graze, boil, abscess, lesion, swelling.

sorrow NOUN **1 = sadness**, unhappiness, grief, misery, distress, heartache, heartbreak, anguish, wretchedness, dejection, depression, mourning. **2 = trouble**, woe, misfortune, affliction, trial, tribulation.

sorry ADJ **1 = regretful**, apologetic, repentant, penitent, remorseful, contrite, ashamed, shamefaced, conscience-stricken, rueful, guilt-ridden. **2 = sympathetic**, compassionate, moved. **3 = sad**, unhappy, distressed, grieved, sorrowful, upset.

sort NOUN = **kind**, type, variety, class, category, style, group, set, genre, order, breed, make, brand, stamp, ilk. VERB **1** = **classify**, class, categorize, catalogue, grade, rank, group, arrange, order, organize, systematize. **2** = **resolve**, settle, clear up, solve, fix, deal with.

sortie NOUN = **sally**, foray, charge, raid, attack.

soul NOUN **1** = **spirit**, psyche, inner self. **2** = **personification**, embodiment, incarnation, essence, epitome. **3** = **person**, human being, individual, creature.

sound NOUN = **noise**; utterance, cry. VERB **1** = **resound**, reverberate, resonate. **2** = **operate**, set off, ring. ADJ **1** = **healthy**, fit, in good shape. **2** = **solid**, substantial, sturdy, well built, undamaged. **3** = **well founded**, valid, reasonable, logical, cogent, weighty, convincing, reliable.

sour ADJ **1** = **acid**, tart, bitter, sharp, vinegary. **2** = **bad**, off, stale, rancid, curdled. **3** = **embittered**, bitter, resentful, rancorous, spiteful, jaundiced, irritable, bad-tempered.

source NOUN **1** = **origin**, genesis, root, fount, derivation, beginning, start, rise, cause, provenance, author, originator. **2** = **wellspring**, well head.

sovereign NOUN = **ruler**, monarch, king, queen, emperor, empress, tsar, potentate. ADJ **1** = **supreme**, absolute, unlimited; chief, principal, dominant, predominant, ruling. **2** = **independent**, self-ruling, self-governing, autonomous.

sow VERB = **scatter**, spread, broadcast, disperse, strew, disseminate, distribute.

space NOUN **1** = **room**, expanse, extent, capacity, area, volume, scope, latitude, margin, leeway. **2** = **gap**, opening, interstice, break. **3** = **time**, duration, period, span, stretch, interval.

spacious ADJ = **roomy**, commodious, capacious,

sizable, large, big, ample.
span NOUN 1 = **length**, extent, reach, stretch, spread, distance. 2 = **time**, duration, period, space, stretch, interval. VERB = **bridge**, cross, traverse, pass over.
spare ADJ = **extra**, additional, reserve, supplementary, auxiliary; surplus, superfluous. VERB 1 = **afford**, part with, give, provide, do without. 2 = **let off**, reprieve, release, have mercy/pity on.
sparing ADJ = **economical**, frugal, thrifty, careful, prudent, parsimonious.
sparkle VERB & NOUN = **twinkle**, flicker, shimmer, flash, glitter, glint, shine, gleam, glisten.
sparse ADJ = **scanty**, scattered, meagre, scarce, few and far between, in short supply.
spartan ADJ = **austere**, harsh, frugal, stringent, rigorous, strict, severe, ascetic, abstemious.
spasm NOUN 1 = **contraction**, convulsion, cramp, twitch. 2 = **fit**, paroxysm, attack, bout, seizure, burst.
spasmodic ADJ = **intermittent**, fitful, irregular, sporadic, erratic, periodic.
spate NOUN = **series**, succession, run, string, epidemic, outbreak, wave.
speak VERB 1 = **utter**, voice, express, say, pronounce, articulate, enunciate, vocalize, state, tell. 2 = **talk**, chat, gossip, converse, communicate.
speaker NOUN = **speech-maker**, lecturer, orator, demagogue.
spear NOUN = **javelin**, lance, pike, assegai, harpoon.
special ADJ 1 = **exceptional**, remarkable, unusual, rare, out of the ordinary, extraordinary, singular, notable, outstanding, unique. 2 = **significant**, momentous, memorable, red-letter.
specialist NOUN = **expert**, authority, professional, connoisseur, master.
species NOUN = **sort**, kind, type, variety, class, category, group, genus, breed, genre.
specific ADJ 1 = **particular**, specified, fixed, set,

distinct, definite. **2** = **clear-cut**, unambiguous, unequivocal, exact, precise, explicit, express.

specify VERB = **state**, name, stipulate, identify, define, set out, itemize, detail, list, spell out, enumerate.

specimen NOUN = **sample**, example, illustration, instance; model, prototype, pilot.

speck NOUN = **spot**, fleck, dot, speckle; particle, bit, atom, iota, grain, trace.

speckled ADJ = **mottled**, flecked, spotted, dappled, brindled.

spectacle NOUN **1** = **sight**, vision, scene, picture. **2** = **display**, show, exhibition, pageant, parade, extravaganza.

spectacular ADJ = **impressive**, magnificent, splendid, breathtaking, glorious, dazzling, sensational, stunning, dramatic, remarkable; striking, picturesque.

spectator NOUN = **viewer**, observer, onlooker, watcher, witness.

speculate VERB = **conjecture**, theorize, hypothesize, guess, surmise; reflect, think, wonder, muse.

speculative ADJ = **conjectural**, theoretical, hypothetical, suppositional, academic; tentative, unproven.

speech NOUN **1** = **communication**, talk, conversation, discussion, dialogue. **2** = **diction**, articulation, enunciation, elocution, pronunciation. **3** = **talk**, lecture, address, discourse, oration, sermon.

speed NOUN = **rate**, tempo, momentum, pace; rapidity, swiftness, haste, hurry, alacrity, promptness, velocity.

spell NOUN **1** = **incantation**, charm, abracadabra, magic formula. **2** = **period**, interval, stretch, run, patch.

spellbound ADJ = **riveted**, entranced, enthralled, rapt, bewitched, fascinated, captivated, mesmerized.

spend VERB **1** = **pay out**, expend, disburse; [inf] fork out, shell out, splurge. **2** = **occupy**, pass, fill, take up, while away.

spendthrift NOUN

= **prodigal**, profligate, wastrel.

sphere NOUN 1 = **globe**, ball, orb, globule. 2 = **area**, field, range, scope, extent, compass.

spice NOUN = **flavouring**, seasoning, condiment.

spicy ADJ = **piquant**, tangy, hot, peppery, spiced, seasoned, tasty.

spill VERB = **pour**, flow, overflow, run, slop, slosh.

spin VERB = **revolve**, rotate, turn, circle, whirl, gyrate.

spine NOUN 1 = **backbone**, spinal column, vertebrae. 2 - **needle**, spike, barb, quill.

spiral NOUN = **coil**, twist, whorl, corkscrew, helix.

spirit NOUN 1 = **soul**, psyche, inner self, ego. 2 = **apparition**, ghost, phantom, spectre, wraith, shade; [inf] spook. 3 = **courage**, bravery, valour, mettle, pluck, grit, backbone, determination; [inf] guts. 4 = **ethos**, essence, quintessence; atmosphere, mood, feeling.

spirited ADJ = **courageous**, brave, valiant, heroic, plucky, determined, resolute, vigorous, lively, vivacious, animated, energetic.

spiritual ADJ 1 = **non-material**, incorporeal, ethereal, intangible, other-worldly. 2 = **religious**, sacred, divine, holy, ecclesiastic.

spit VERB = **expectorate**, hawk. NOUN = **spittle**, saliva, sputum.

spite NOUN = **malice**, ill-will, malevolence, venom, hostility, resentment, rancour, vengefulness, vindictiveness.

spiteful ADJ = **malicious**, malevolent, venomous, malign, hostile, resentful, snide, rancorous, vengeful, vindictive; [inf] bitchy, catty.

splash VERB = **spatter**, sprinkle, spray, shower, splatter, squirt, slosh, slop.

splendid ADJ = **magnificent**, imposing, superb, grand, sumptuous, resplendent, opulent, luxurious, plush, de luxe, palatial, rich, costly, lavish, ornate, gorgeous, glorious, dazzling, elegant, handsome.

splendour NOUN

= **magnificence**, grandeur, sumptuousness, opulence, luxury, luxuriousness, richness, elegance.

splinter NOUN = **sliver**, fragment, shiver, shard, chip, shred, piece, bit.

split VERB 1 = **break**, chop, hew, lop, cleave, splinter; rend, rip, tear, slash, slit. 2 = **divide**, separate. 3 = **share (out)**, divide up, apportion, distribute, dole out, parcel out, allot, allocate; [inf] divvy up. 4 = **break up**, separate, part; divorce. NOUN 1 = **break**, cut, rent, rip, tear, slash, slit, crack, fissure, breach. 2 = **division**, rift, schism, rupture, separation, break-up, alienation, estrangement.

spoil VERB 1 = **damage**, impair, mar, blemish, disfigure, deface, injure, harm, ruin, destroy, wreck. 2 = **pamper**, overindulge, mollycoddle, cosset, coddle, baby. 3 = **go bad/off**, turn, rot, decompose, perish, decay.

spoilsport NOUN = **killjoy**, dog in the manger, misery; [inf] wet blanket, party-pooper.

spongy ADJ = **soft**, cushiony, squashy, springy, resilient, elastic; porous, absorbent.

sponsor NOUN = **patron**, backer, promoter, guarantor, supporter, angel. VERB = **finance**, back, fund, subsidize; promote, support; [inf] bankroll.

spontaneous ADJ = **unplanned**, unpremeditated, unrehearsed, impromptu, extempore, spur-of-the-moment; voluntary, unforced, unprompted; [inf] off-the-cuff.

sporadic ADJ = **irregular**, intermittent, scattered, random, infrequent, occasional, isolated, spasmodic.

sport NOUN 1 = **games**, physical exercise. 2 = **amusement**, entertainment, diversion, fun, pleasure, enjoyment.

spot NOUN 1 = **mark**, dot, speck, fleck, smudge, stain, blotch, splotch, patch. 2 = **pimple**, pustule, boil, blackhead. 3 = **area**, place, site, location, scene, setting, situation. VERB = **catch sight of**, see, notice, observe, espy, discern, detect, make out, pick out, recognize.

spotless ADJ 1 = **clean**, pristine, immaculate, shining, gleaming. 2 = **pure**, flawless, faultless, unsullied, untainted, blameless, above reproach.

spotlight NOUN = **limelight**, public eye, glare of publicity, public attention/interest.

spout VERB = **spurt**, gush, spew, squirt, jet, spray, emit, erupt, disgorge, pour, stream, flow.

sprawl VERB = **stretch out**, lounge, lie, recline, slump, flop, loll.

spray NOUN 1 = **shower**, jet, mist, drizzle; spume, spindrift, foam, froth. 2 = **atomizer**, vaporizer, aerosol, sprinkler. 3 = **sprig**, posy, bouquet, nosegay, corsage. VERB = **jet**, spout, gush; sprinkle, shower.

spread VERB 1 = **stretch**, extend, open out, unfurl, unroll, fan out. 2 = **cover**, coat, daub, apply, smear, plaster, slather. 3 = **disseminate**, circulate, put about, make public,

broadcast, publicize, propagate, promulgate. NOUN = **extent**, stretch, span, reach, compass, sweep.

spree NOUN = **fling**, orgy; [inf] binge, splurge.

spring VERB 1 = **jump**, leap, bound, vault, hop. 2 = **appear**, materialize, shoot up, pop up; mushroom, proliferate. 3 = **originate**, derive, stem, arise, emanate, proceed, start. NOUN = **jump**, leap, bound, vault, hop.

sprinkle VERB = **spray**, shower, splash, spatter, scatter, strew.

sprout VERB = **bud**, germinate, burgeon; shoot up, spring up, grow, develop, appear.

spruce ADJ = **neat**, well groomed, smart, trim, dapper, elegant; [inf] natty.

spur NOUN = **goad**, prod, stimulus, incentive, inducement, encouragement, impetus. VERB = **stimulate**, encourage, prod, goad, induce, motivate, prompt, urge, impel.

spurious ADJ = **bogus**, fake, fraudulent, sham, feigned, specious; [inf]

phoney, pseudo.

spurn VERB = **reject**, turn down, rebuff, snub, slight, cold-shoulder, disdain, scorn.

spurt VERB = **gush**, squirt, shoot, surge, jet, spring, pour, stream, spray, spout.

spy NOUN = **secret agent**, double agent, mole. VERB = **keep under surveillance**, watch, keep watch on, keep an eye on, keep under observation.

squabble NOUN = **row**, quarrel, dispute, argument, wrangle, tiff. VERB = **row**, quarrel, argue, bicker, have words, wrangle, fall out.

squalid ADJ 1 = **dirty**, filthy, dingy, grubby, grimy, seedy, sordid, sleazy; [inf] grotty. 2 = **sordid**, unsavoury, base, corrupt, dishonest, dishonourable, disgraceful, contemptible, shameful.

squander VERB = **waste**, dissipate, fritter away, run through; [inf] blow.

square NOUN 1 = **piazza**, plaza, quadrangle. 2 = **fogey**, conservative, traditionalist; [inf] stick-in-the-mud, fuddy-duddy. ADJ 1 = **equal**, even, level

pegging, drawn. 2 = **fair**, just, equitable, honest, straight, upright, above board, ethical; [inf] on the level. 3 = **old-fashioned**, behind the times, conservative, traditionalist, conventional, conformist, bourgeois, strait-laced, stuffy; [inf] fuddy-duddy.

squash VERB 1 = **crush**, squeeze, flatten, compress, press, pulp, mash, pulverize. 2 = **crowd**, cram, pack, force, jam, squeeze, wedge.

squat ADJ = **dumpy**, stubby, thickset, stocky, short.

squeak NOUN & VERB = **squeal**, peep, cheep, yelp, whimper.

squeeze VERB 1 = **compress**, crush, squash, mash, pulp. 2 = **grip**, clutch, pinch, press. 3 = **crowd**, cram, pack, jam, squash, wedge.

squirm VERB = **wriggle**, wiggle, writhe, twist, turn.

stab VERB = **knife**, run through, skewer, impale, spear, slash. NOUN 1 = **puncture**, gash, slash, incision. 2 = **pang**, twinge, ache, throb, spasm.

stable ADJ **1** = **firm**, solid, steady, secure, fixed, fast, immovable. **2** = **strong**, steadfast, established, long-lasting, long-term, unwavering, abiding, durable, enduring, lasting. **3** = **well balanced**, balanced, steady, sensible, responsible, down-to-earth, sane.

stack NOUN = **heap**, pile, tower, mound, mountain.

staff NOUN **1** = **stick**, cane, crook, rod, pole, baton, mace, sceptre.
2 = **employees**, workers, workforce, personnel.

stage NOUN **1** = **point**, period, step, juncture, time, phase, level. **2** = **lap**, leg, stretch. **3** = **platform**, dais, rostrum, podium. VERB = **put on**, produce, direct, perform, mount, present.

stagger VERB **1** = **reel**, sway, teeter, totter, wobble, lurch. **2** = **amaze**, astound, dumbfound, astonish, flabbergast, shock, stupefy, stun.

stagnant ADJ = **still**, motionless, standing; stale, dirty, brackish.

staid ADJ = **sedate**, quiet, serious, solemn, sober, respectable, proper, decorous, stiff, stuffy.

stain VERB = **soil**, mark, discolour, dirty, smudge, smear, spatter, splatter. NOUN **1** = **mark**, spot, blotch, smudge, smear.
2 = **blemish**, injury, taint, blot, stigma, disgrace.

stake NOUN **1** = **post**, pole, stick, upright, spike, paling. **2** = **wager**, bet, ante. **3** = **share**, interest, investment, involvement.

stale ADJ **1** = **old**, off, dry, hard, mouldy, musty, rancid. **2** = **stuffy**, musty, fusty. **3** = **hackneyed**, tired, worn-out, banal, trite, unoriginal; [inf] corny, old hat.

stalemate NOUN = **deadlock**, impasse, stand-off.

stalk NOUN = **stem**, shoot, twig, branch, trunk. VERB **1** = **pursue**, follow, shadow, trail, hunt; [inf] tail. **2** = **stride**, march, flounce, strut.

stall VERB = **play for time**, temporize, delay, drag your feet, beat about the bush, hedge, stonewall. NOUN = **booth**, stand, table, counter, kiosk.

stamina NOUN = **endurance**, staying power, resilience, fortitude, strength, energy, determination, grit.

stamp VERB 1 = **trample**, step, tread; crush, squash, flatten. 2 = **imprint**, inscribe, engrave, emboss, mark. 3 (**stamp out**) = **quash**, suppress, put down, quell, crush, extinguish, put an end to, eradicate, eliminate. NOUN = **mark**, hallmark, indication, sign, characteristic, quality.

stance NOUN 1 = **posture**, pose. 2 see **standpoint**.

stand VERB 1 = **rise**, get to your feet, get up. 2 = **remain in force**, remain valid, hold (good), apply, be the case. 3 = **put up with**, tolerate, stomach, bear, take, endure, abide, brook.

standard NOUN 1 = **quality**, level, grade, calibre. 2 = **yardstick**, benchmark, measure, criterion, guide, guideline, norm, touchstone, model, pattern, example, exemplar. 3 = **principle**, ideal; (**standards**) code of behaviour, morals, ethics. 4 = **flag**, banner, pennant, streamer, ensign, colours. ADJ = **usual**, ordinary, average, normal, common, regular, stock, typical, set, fixed, conventional.

standing NOUN = **status**, rank, social station, footing, place.

standpoint NOUN = **point of view**, viewpoint, opinion, perspective, angle, attitude, stance, stand.

staple ADJ = **chief**, primary, main, principal, basic, fundamental, essential.

star NOUN 1 = **heavenly body**, celestial body. 2 = **celebrity**, superstar, name, leading light, personality, somebody, VIP.

stare VERB = **gaze**, gape, goggle, glare; [inf] gawp.

stark ADJ = **desolate**, bare, barren, arid, empty, godforsaken, bleak, depressing, grim.

start VERB 1 = **begin**, commence, get going, get under way; [inf] get the ball rolling, get down to it, get cracking, kick off. 2 = **set out/off**, depart, leave; [inf] hit the road.

3 = **establish**, set up, found, create, institute, initiate, inaugurate, launch, organize, mastermind. **4** = **jump**, jerk, twitch, recoil, flinch. NOUN = **beginning**, commencement, opening, inception, inauguration, dawn, birth; [inf] kick-off.

startle VERB = **shock**, scare, frighten, alarm, surprise, astonish.

starving ADJ = **starved**, famished, ravenous; undernourished, malnourished.

state NOUN **1** = **condition**, shape, situation, circumstances, state of affairs, position. **2** = **country**, nation, land, realm, kingdom, republic. VERB = **express**, voice, utter, say, declare, set out, assert, announce, make known, air, reveal, disclose, divulge.

stately ADJ = **ceremonial**, dignified, solemn, majestic, royal, regal, magnificent, grand, glorious, splendid, elegant, imposing, impressive, august.

statement NOUN = **declaration**, affirmation, assertion, announcement, utterance, communication, proclamation; account, testimony, report.

static ADJ = **unmoving**, unchanging, constant, stable, steady, invariable; unmoving, motionless, immobile.

station NOUN **1** = **terminus**, terminal, depot. **2** = **base**, office, headquarters. **3** = **post**, place, position.

stationary ADJ = **unmoving**, motionless, immobile, at a standstill.

statue NOUN = **statuette**, sculpture, effigy, figure, figurine, bust, head.

statuesque ADJ = **dignified**, stately, majestic, imposing, impressive, regal.

stature NOUN **1** = **height**, tallness, size. **2** = **status**, reputation, importance, standing, eminence, prominence, note, renown.

status NOUN = **standing**, rank, level, position, place; importance, stature, prominence, prestige.

staunch ADJ = **loyal**,

faithful, committed, devoted, dedicated, dependable, reliable, stalwart, constant, steadfast, unwavering.

stay VERB 1 = **remain**, wait, stay put, continue, linger, tarry. 2 = **lodge**, room; visit, sojourn, holiday. 3 = **check**, curb, arrest, stop, delay, hold, prevent, hinder, impede, obstruct. NOUN 1 = **visit**, sojourn, stop, stopover, holiday, vacation. 2 = **postponement**, suspension, adjournment, deferment, delay.

steadfast ADJ 1 see **staunch**. 2 = **firm**, determined, resolute, unchanging, unyielding, uncompromising.

steady ADJ 1 = **firm**, fixed, stable, secure, immovable. 2 = **still**, motionless, unmoving, unwavering. 3 = **uniform**, even, regular, rhythmic, consistent. 4 = **well balanced**, sensible, level-headed, rational, down-to-earth, calm, reliable, dependable, responsible. VERB 1 = **stabilize**, secure, balance, brace, support. 2 = **calm**, settle, compose,

quieten, control, get a grip on.

steal VERB 1 = **thieve**, take, misappropriate, pilfer, purloin, filch, embezzle; plagiarize; [inf] pinch, nick, swipe, rip off. 2 = **slip**, slide, tiptoe, sneak, creep, slink, sidle.

stealing NOUN = **theft**, robbery, larceny, burglary, embezzlement.

stealthy ADJ = **secret**, furtive, surreptitious, sly, clandestine, covert.

steep ADJ = **sheer**, abrupt, precipitous, perpendicular, vertical.

steeple NOUN = **spire**, tower, belfry, minaret.

steer VERB = **guide**, navigate, drive, pilot, manoeuvre; lead, direct, conduct, usher, shepherd.

step NOUN 1 = **stride**, pace, footstep, footfall, tread. 2 = **walk**, gait. 3 = **rung**, stair, tread. 4 = **course of action**, move, act, action, measure, manoeuvre, procedure. 5 = **stage**, level, grade, rank, degree. VERB = **walk**, tread, stride, pace, move.

stereotyped ADJ = **typecast**, conventional, stock, standard,

formulaic, hackneyed, clichéd, banal, trite.
sterile ADJ 1 = **infertile**, barren, unproductive. 2 = **sterilized**, antiseptic, disinfected, aseptic, sanitary, hygienic.
sterilize VERB 1 = **disinfect**, fumigate, decontaminate, purify. 2 = **neuter**, castrate, geld, spay.
stern ADJ 1 = **strict**, harsh, hard, rigorous, stringent, rigid, exacting, demanding, unsparing, inflexible, authoritarian. 2 = **severe**, forbidding, frowning, serious, unsmiling, sombre, sober, dour, austere.
stew NOUN = **casserole**, hotpot, ragout, fricassée, goulash.
stick NOUN = **cane**, staff, crook, pole, post, upright; club. VERB 1 = **push**, insert, jab, poke. 2 = **pierce**, penetrate, puncture, prick, spear, stab, run through, impale. 3 = **glue**, paste, gum, tape, fasten, attach, fix; cling, adhere. 4 (**stick out**) = **protrude**, jut out, project, stand out.
sticky ADJ 1 = **adhesive**; gummy, gluey, glutinous, viscous, tacky. 2 = **humid**,

close, muggy, sultry, oppressive.
stiff ADJ 1 = **rigid**, inflexible, inelastic, firm, hard. 2 = **difficult**, hard, arduous, tough, laborious, exacting, demanding, formidable, challenging, tiring, exhausting. 3 = **formal**, reserved, unfriendly, cold, austere; [inf] starchy, stand-offish.
stifle VERB 1 = **suffocate**, smother, asphyxiate, choke. 2 = **suppress**, check, restrain, hold back, choke back, muffle, curb.
stigma NOUN = **shame**, disgrace, dishonour, stain, taint.
still ADJ 1 = **motionless**, unmoving, immobile, inert, stock-still, stationary, static. 2 = **quiet**, silent, hushed, soundless, noiseless, tranquil, undisturbed.
stilted ADJ = **stiff**, unnatural, wooden, strained, forced, laboured, constrained, awkward.
stimulant NOUN 1 = **tonic**, restorative; [inf] pick-me-up. 2 see **stimulus**.
stimulate VERB = **encourage**, spur on, prompt, motivate, move,

activate, galvanize, kindle, fire, trigger.

stimulating ADJ
1 = **restorative**, reviving, energizing, invigorating.
2 = **interesting**, exciting, stirring, thought-provoking, inspiring, intriguing, provocative.

stimulus NOUN = **incentive**, fillip, spur, boost, encouragement, impetus, stimulant; [inf] shot in the arm.

sting VERB **1** = **smart**, burn, hurt. **2** = **hurt**, wound, distress, grieve, upset, pain, mortify.

stingy ADJ = **mean**, miserly, parsimonious, niggardly, tight-fisted, cheese-paring, penny-pinching.

stipulate VERB = **specify**, set down, set out, lay down, demand, require, insist.

stipulation NOUN
= **specification**, demand, requirement, condition, precondition, provision, proviso, prerequisite.

stir VERB **1** = **mix**, blend, beat, whip. **2** = **move**, disturb, agitate, rustle.
3 = **stimulate**, excite, arouse, awaken, waken, kindle, quicken, inspire.

4 = **rouse**, spur, prompt, encourage, motivate, drive; incite, provoke, inflame, goad. NOUN
= **excitement**, commotion, disturbance, fuss, uproar, to-do, brouhaha.

stirring ADJ = **exciting**, thrilling, stimulating, moving, inspiring, heady, passionate, impassioned.

stock NOUN **1** = **store**, supply, stockpile, reserve, reservoir, accumulation, hoard, cache. **2** = **supplies**, goods, merchandise, wares. **3** = **animals**, livestock, cattle, sheep.
4 = **shares**, investment, holding, money.
5 = **descent**, lineage, ancestry, extraction, family, parentage, pedigree. ADJ **1** = **standard**, regular, average. **2** = **usual**, routine, conventional, traditional, stereotyped, clichéd, hackneyed, formulaic.

stockpile VERB = **collect**, accumulate, amass, store, put away/by, hoard, save; [inf] salt away, stash away.

stocky ADJ = **thickset**, sturdy, chunky, burly, brawny, solid, strapping, hefty.

stoical ADJ = **long-suffering**, philosophical, uncomplaining, patient, forbearing, tolerant, resigned, phlegmatic.

stolid ADJ = **impassive**, phlegmatic, unemotional, cool, calm, placid, unexcitable.

stomach NOUN = **abdomen**, belly, paunch, pot belly; [inf] tummy, gut. VERB = **stand**, put up with, bear, take, tolerate, abide, endure.

stone NOUN 1 = **pebble**, rock, boulder. 2 = **kernel**, pit, seed, pip.

stony ADJ 1 = **rocky**, pebbly, gravelly, shingly. 2 = **cold**, chilly, frosty, hard, stern, severe, unfriendly, unfeeling, uncaring, unsympathetic.

stooge NOUN = **underling**, lackey, henchman, minion; [inf] dogsbody, sidekick.

stoop VERB 1 = **bend**, lean, crouch. 2 = **sink**, descend, lower yourself, resort.

stop VERB 1 = **bring/come to an end**, halt, end, put an end to, finish, terminate, bring to a standstill, wind up, conclude, discontinue, cut short,

interrupt. 2 = **cease**, refrain from, desist from, give up, forbear from; [inf] quit, leave off, knock off, pack in. 3 = **prevent**, hinder, obstruct, impede, block, bar. 4 = **plug**, seal, block, close; staunch, stem. NOUN 1 = **halt**, end, finish, close, cessation, conclusion, termination, standstill, stoppage, discontinuation. 2 = **break**, stopover, stay, sojourn, visit.

stopgap ADJ = **temporary**, provisional, interim, fill-in, makeshift, short-term.

store NOUN 1 = **supply**, stock, stockpile, reserve, bank, cache, reservoir. 2 = **storeroom**, storehouse, warehouse, repository, depository. 3 = **shop**, supermarket, retail outlet, emporium. VERB = **stockpile**, collect, accumulate, amass, put aside/away, hoard, keep; [inf] squirrel away, salt away, stash away.

storm NOUN = **gale**, hurricane, cyclone, tempest, squall, typhoon.

stormy ADJ = **blustery**, windy, gusty, squally, rainy, wild, tempestuous, turbulent.

story NOUN **1 = tale**, narrative, anecdote; fable, myth, legend; [inf] yarn. **2 = news item**, article, feature, scoop.

stout ADJ **1 = fat**, plump, portly, tubby, dumpy, corpulent, rotund, stocky, thickset, burly. **2 = strong**, heavy, solid, substantial, sturdy, durable, robust, tough. **3 = brave**, courageous, valiant, valorous, gallant, fearless, intrepid, bold, doughty, determined, resolute, staunch, steadfast.

stow VERB **= place**, put, pack, store, load; [inf] stash.

straight ADJ **1 = direct**, undeviating. **2 = successive**, consecutive, in a row, running. **3 = in order**, orderly, neat, tidy, shipshape, spick and span. **4 = honest**, sincere, frank, candid, truthful, forthright, straightforward; [inf] upfront.

straightforward ADJ **1 = uncomplicated**, easy, simple, elementary, effortless, undemanding,

plain sailing. **2 = frank**, honest, candid, direct, forthright, plain-speaking; [inf] upfront.

strain VERB **= tax**, overtax, overwork, tire, overextend; overdo it. NOUN **= stress**, pressure, demands; overwork, exhaustion, fatigue.

strained ADJ **1 = forced**, artificial, unnatural, false, constrained, stiff. **2 = awkward**, uneasy, uncomfortable, tense, edgy, embarrassed.

strand NOUN **1 = thread**, fibre, filament, length. **2 = element**, component, theme.

stranded ADJ **1 = helpless**, high and dry, abandoned, left in the lurch. **2 = grounded**, beached, shipwrecked, wrecked, marooned.

strange ADJ **= peculiar**, odd, bizarre, unusual, atypical, abnormal, curious, weird, funny, unfamiliar, out of the ordinary, queer, extraordinary, uncanny.

strangle VERB **1 = throttle**, choke, strangulate, garrotte. **2 = suppress**, inhibit, repress, check, restrain, hold back, curb, stifle.

strap NOUN = **band**, belt, thong, cord, tie. VERB = **fasten**, secure, tie, bind, lash.

stratagem NOUN = **plan**, scheme, manoeuvre, tactic, ploy, trick, ruse, plot, machination, subterfuge.

strategy NOUN = **master plan**, game plan, policy, programme, plan of action, scheme, tactics.

stratum NOUN = **layer**, seam, vein, lode.

stray VERB 1 = **wander**, go astray, drift. 2 = **digress**, deviate, get sidetracked, go off at a tangent. ADJ 1 = **homeless**, lost, abandoned. 2 = **random**, chance, freak, unexpected, isolated, lone, single.

streak NOUN 1 = **line**, band, strip, stripe, bar; smear, smudge, mark. 2 = **element**, vein, trace, touch; trait, characteristic. 3 = **spell**, period, run, stretch.

stream NOUN 1 = **river**, brook, rivulet, rill, beck; [Scottish] burn; [US] creek. 2 = **flow**, rush, gush, surge, jet, current, cascade. VERB = **flow**, run, pour, course, spill, gush, surge, flood, cascade, well.

streamlined ADJ 1 = **aerodynamic**, smooth, sleek. 2 = **efficient**, smooth-running, well run, slick.

street NOUN = **road**, thoroughfare, avenue, boulevard.

strength NOUN 1 = **power**, might, force, brawn, muscle, muscularity, sturdiness, robustness, vigour, toughness, stamina. 2 = **fortitude**, courage, bravery, pluck, backbone; [inf] grit, guts. 3 = **advantage**, asset, strong point, forte.

strenuous ADJ 1 = **arduous**, laborious, taxing, demanding, difficult, hard, tough, uphill, heavy, exhausting, tiring. 2 = **vigorous**, energetic, zealous, forceful, strong, spirited, determined, resolute, tenacious, tireless, dogged.

stress NOUN 1 = **strain**, pressure, tension, worry, anxiety. 2 = **emphasis**, priority, importance,

weight; accent,
accentuation. VERB
= **emphasize**, accentuate,
underline, underscore,
point up, highlight, press
home.

stretch VERB 1 = **extend**,
elongate, lengthen,
expand, draw out, pull
out. 2 = **strain**, overtax,
overextend, drain, sap.
NOUN 1 = **expanse**, area,
tract, belt, extent, sweep.
2 = **period**, time, spell,
term, run, stint.

strict ADJ 1 = **precise**,
exact, literal, faithful.
2 = **stern**, severe, harsh,
uncompromising,
authoritarian, firm,
austere, rigorous, hard,
tough.

stride VERB = **step**, pace,
walk, stalk, march.

strident ADJ = **harsh**,
raucous, rough, grating,
jarring, shrill, loud.

strike VERB 1 = **hit**, slap,
smack, beat, thrash,
thump, punch, cuff, rap,
cane; [inf] wallop, belt,
clout, whack, bash,
clobber. 2 = **run into**,
knock into, bang into,
bump into, collide with.
3 = **attack**, afflict, affect,
hit. 4 = **go on strike**, take

industrial action, down
tools, walk out. NOUN
= **industrial action**,
walkout.

striking ADJ 1 = **noticeable**,
obvious, conspicuous,
distinct, marked,
unmistakable,
remarkable,
extraordinary, incredible,
amazing. 2 = **impressive**,
imposing, grand,
splendid, magnificent,
superb, marvellous,
wonderful.

stringent ADJ = **strict**, firm,
rigid, rigorous, severe,
harsh, tough, exacting,
inflexible, hard and fast.

strip VERB 1 = **undress**,
disrobe. 2 = **take away**,
dispossess of, deprive of,
confiscate. NOUN = **piece**,
bit, band, belt, ribbon,
slip, shred.

stripe NOUN = **strip**, band,
belt, bar, streak.

strive VERB = **try**, attempt,
endeavour, make an
effort, exert yourself,
labour, strain, struggle.

stroke NOUN = **thrombosis**,
embolism, seizure. VERB
= **caress**, fondle, pat, pet,
touch, rub, massage.

stroll VERB = **saunter**,
amble, wander, meander,

ramble, promenade, take the air; [inf] mosey.

strong ADJ **1** = **powerful**, brawny, muscular, strapping, sturdy, burly, robust, vigorous, tough, hardy, lusty. **2** = **determined**, forceful, assertive, tough, tenacious, formidable, redoubtable. **3** = **solid**, well built, secure, well fortified, impregnable; heavy-duty, sturdy, durable, hard-wearing, long-lasting. **4** = **intense**, vehement, passionate, fervent, fervid. **5** = **keen**, eager, enthusiastic, dedicated, staunch, loyal, steadfast. **6** = **persuasive**, cogent, compelling, convincing, potent, weighty, sound, valid, well founded.

structure NOUN **1** = **building**, edifice, construction, erection, pile. **2** = **construction**, form, configuration, shape, constitution, composition, make-up, organization, system, arrangement, design, framework.

struggle VERB **1** = **strive**, try, endeavour, exert yourself, battle, labour, toil, strain. **2** = **fight**, grapple, wrestle, scuffle.

strut VERB = **swagger**, swank, parade, flounce; [US inf] sashay.

stubborn ADJ = **obstinate**, mulish, pig-headed, wilful, strong-minded, perverse, recalcitrant, unyielding, inflexible, immovable, intransigent, uncompromising, persistent, tenacious.

student NOUN = **undergraduate**, pupil, schoolboy, schoolgirl, trainee, apprentice, probationer.

studied ADJ = **deliberate**, careful, conscious, calculated, intentional; affected, forced, strained, artificial.

studious ADJ = **scholarly**, academic, intellectual, bookish, serious, earnest.

study VERB **1** = **work**, revise; [inf] swot, cram, mug up. **2** = **investigate**, inquire into, research, look into, examine, analyse, review.

stuff NOUN **1** = **material**, fabric, matter, substance. **2** = **things**, objects, articles, items, luggage, baggage, belongings, possessions,

goods, paraphernalia. VERB
= **fill**, pad, pack, load,
cram, squeeze, press,
force, compress, jam,
thrust, shove.

stuffy ADJ = **airless**, close,
muggy, fuggy, musty,
stale.

stumble VERB 1 = **trip**, slip,
lose your balance; stagger,
totter, teeter. 2 = **stammer**,
stutter, hesitate, falter.

stun VERB 1 = **daze**, stupefy,
knock out, lay out. 2 see
astonish.

stunning ADJ
= **sensational**, wonderful,
marvellous, magnificent,
glorious, impressive,
splendid, beautiful,
lovely, gorgeous.

stupid ADJ = **foolish**, silly,
idiotic, mad, crazy,
insane, unintelligent,
dense, brainless,
mindless, obtuse, slow-
witted, simple-minded,
half-witted, moronic,
inane, absurd, ludicrous,
ridiculous, laughable,
fatuous, asinine,
crackbrained, senseless,
irresponsible, ill-advised;
[inf] thick, dim, dumb,
dopey.

sturdy ADJ = **well built**,
muscular, athletic, strong,
strapping, powerful,
robust, tough, hardy,
lusty; solid, substantial,
well made, durable.

style NOUN 1 = **technique**,
method, methodology,
approach, manner, way,
mode, system. 2 = **kind**,
type, variety, sort, genre.
3 = **stylishness**, elegance,
poise, sophistication,
chic, flair, dash, panache.
4 = **fashion**, trend, vogue,
mode.

stylish ADJ = **fashionable**,
smart, sophisticated,
elegant, chic, modern, up
to date; [inf] trendy, natty,
classy.

subdue VERB 1 = **conquer**,
defeat, vanquish,
overcome, subjugate,
triumph over, crush,
quash. 2 = **control**, curb,
restrain, check, hold back,
repress, suppress, stifle,
quell.

subdued ADJ 1 = **dim**,
muted, soft, subtle,
unobtrusive. 2 = **low-
spirited**, downcast,
dejected, depressed,
gloomy, despondent,
dispirited, sombre.

subject NOUN 1 = **topic**,
theme, question, subject
matter; substance, gist.

2 = **branch of knowledge**, discipline. **3** = **citizen**, national. ADJ (**subject to**) **1** = **conditional on**, contingent on, dependent on. **2** = **susceptible to**, liable to, prone to, vulnerable to.

sublime ADJ = **exalted**, noble, lofty, awe-inspiring, majestic, magnificent, glorious, supreme, superb, perfect, ideal, wonderful, marvellous, splendid.

submerge VERB **1** = **dive**, sink, plummet. **2** = **immerse**, dip, plunge, duck, dunk. **3** = **flood**, inundate, deluge, engulf, swamp.

submissive ADJ = **compliant**, yielding, acquiescent, unassertive, passive, obedient, biddable, dutiful, docile, meek; [inf] under someone's thumb.

submit VERB **1** = **yield**, give way/in, capitulate, surrender; accept, accede, acquiesce, comply, conform. **2** = **put forward**, present, offer, proffer, tender, propose, suggest.

subordinate ADJ = **lower-**ranking, junior, lower; lesser, minor, secondary, subsidiary, ancillary, auxiliary. NOUN = **junior**, assistant, second, deputy, aide.

subscribe VERB (**subscribe to**) = **agree with**, accept, believe in, endorse, back, support.

subsequent ADJ = **following**, ensuing, succeeding, later, future, next.

subservient ADJ = **submissive**, deferential, compliant, obedient, meek, biddable, docile, passive, downtrodden; [inf] under someone's thumb.

subside VERB = **abate**, let up, moderate, ease, quieten, calm, slacken, die out, peter out, lessen, dwindle, recede.

subsidize VERB = **contribute to**, back, support, invest in, sponsor, finance, fund, underwrite.

subsidy NOUN = **grant**, contribution, backing, support, sponsorship, finance, funding.

substance NOUN **1** = **matter**, material, stuff, mass. **2** = **solidity**, body,

corporeality, reality.
3 = **importance**,
significance, weight,
meaningfulness, validity.
substantial ADJ **1** = **solid**,
sturdy, strong, well built,
durable. **2** = **considerable**,
real, significant,
important, notable,
major, valuable, useful;
sizeable, significant, large,
appreciable.
substitute NOUN
= **replacement**, deputy,
relief, proxy, reserve,
surrogate, stand-in,
locum.
subterfuge NOUN
= **trickery**, guile, cunning,
intrigue, deviousness,
deceit, duplicity,
deception.
subtle ADJ **1** = **delicate**,
faint, understated, low-
key, muted. **2** = **fine**, fine-
drawn, nice, slight.
subversive ADJ
= **disruptive**,
troublemaking,
inflammatory, seditious,
revolutionary.
subvert VERB = **undermine**,
destabilize, disrupt,
destroy, damage, weaken,
sabotage.
succeed VERB **1** = **triumph**,
achieve success, do well,

thrive, make it. **2** = **be**
successful, work (out),
come off; [inf] do the trick.
3 = **follow**, replace, take the
place of, supersede.
success NOUN
= **prosperity**, affluence,
wealth, fame, eminence.
successful ADJ
1 = **victorious**,
triumphant.
2 = **prosperous**, affluent,
wealthy, well-to-do,
famous, eminent.
3 = **flourishing**, thriving,
booming, profitable,
moneymaking, lucrative.
succession NOUN
= **sequence**, series,
progression, course, run,
cycle, chain, train.
successor NOUN = **heir**,
next-in-line, replacement.
succulent ADJ = **juicy**,
moist, luscious, mouth-
watering.
succumb VERB = **yield**, give
in/way, submit, surrender,
capitulate.
sudden ADJ = **unexpected**,
unforeseen, unlooked-for;
immediate,
instantaneous, instant,
abrupt, rapid, swift.
suffer VERB **1** = **be in pain**,
hurt, ache, be in distress.
2 = **experience**, undergo,

sustain, encounter, meet with, endure.

sufficient ADJ = **enough**, adequate, plenty of, ample.

suffocate VERB = **smother**, stifle, asphyxiate.

suffuse VERB = **permeate**, pervade, cover, spread over, imbue, bathe.

suggest VERB 1 = **propose**, put forward, submit, recommend, advocate. 2 = **indicate**, hint, imply, intimate, insinuate.

suggestion NOUN 1 = **proposal**, proposition, motion, submission, recommendation. 2 = **hint**, trace, touch, suspicion. 3 = **insinuation**, hint, implication, intimation.

suggestive ADJ = **provocative**, titillating, indecent, indelicate, improper, ribald, risqué, vulgar, smutty, lewd, salacious.

suit NOUN 1 = **outfit**, ensemble. 2 = **lawsuit**, court case, action, proceedings.

suitable ADJ = **appropriate**, acceptable, satisfactory, fitting, fit, right, befitting, in keeping.

sulky ADJ = **sullen**, moody, piqued, petulant, disgruntled, grumpy, ill-humoured, in a bad mood, bad-tempered, churlish, surly.

sullen ADJ = **surly**, sulky, sour, morose, resentful, moody, gloomy, grumpy, bad-tempered.

sultry ADJ 1 = **close**, airless, stuffy, stifling, oppressive, muggy, humid, sticky, hot. 2 = **sensual**, sexy, voluptuous, seductive.

sum NOUN = **amount**, (sum) total, grand total, tally, aggregate.

summarize VERB = **sum up**, give a synopsis of, precis, encapsulate, abridge, condense, outline, put in a nutshell.

summary NOUN = **synopsis**, precis, résumé, abstract, abridgement, digest, outline. ADJ = **immediate**, instant, instantaneous, prompt, rapid, sudden, abrupt, peremptory.

summerhouse NOUN = **gazebo**, pavilion, arbour, bower.

summit NOUN 1 = **top**, peak, crest, crown, apex. 2 = **peak**, height, pinnacle, zenith, acme, culmination, climax.

summon VERB 1 = **send for**, call for. 2 = **order**, convene, assemble, convoke, muster, rally.

summons NOUN = **writ**, subpoena.

sumptuous ADJ = **lavish**, luxurious, de luxe, opulent, magnificent, splendid.

sunrise NOUN = **dawn**, crack of dawn, daybreak, cockcrow; [US] sunup.

sunset NOUN = **nightfall**, twilight, dusk; [US] sundown.

superb ADJ = **superlative**, excellent, first-rate, first-class, outstanding, remarkable, brilliant, marvellous, magnificent, wonderful, splendid, fantastic, fabulous.

supercilious ADJ = **arrogant**, haughty, conceited, proud, disdainful, scornful, condescending, superior, patronizing, imperious, snobbish, snobby; [inf] high and mighty, hoity-toity, snooty, stuck-up.

superficial ADJ 1 = **surface**, exterior, external, outer; slight. 2 = **cursory**, perfunctory, hasty, hurried, casual, sketchy, desultory. 3 = **shallow**, empty-headed, trivial, frivolous, silly, lightweight, trivial.

superfluous ADJ = **spare**, surplus, extra, unneeded, excess, unnecessary, redundant.

superior ADJ 1 = **higher**, higher-ranking, senior. 2 = **better**, finer, greater. 3 see **supercilious**.

superlative ADJ = **excellent**, magnificent, wonderful, marvellous, supreme, best, consummate, outstanding, remarkable, first-rate, first-class, premier, prime, unsurpassed, unparalleled, unrivalled.

supernatural ADJ = **unearthly**, otherworldly, spectral, ghostly, phantom; mystic, occult, paranormal, psychic.

supersede VERB = **take the place of**, replace, take over from, displace, succeed, supplant.

supervise VERB = **oversee**, be in charge of, direct, manage, run, superintend, keep an eye on, watch, observe.

supervisor NOUN
= **manager**, director, overseer, controller, superintendent, governor, chief, head; foreman.

supplant VERB = **take the place of**, replace, displace, supersede, oust, usurp, overthrow, remove, unseat.

supple ADJ 1 = **lithe**, lissom, loose-limbed, limber. 2 = **pliant**, pliable, soft, flexible, malleable, elastic.

supplement NOUN 1 = **addition**, extra, add-on, adjunct. 2 = **surcharge**, increase. VERB = **add to**, augment, increase, top up, boost.

supplementary ADJ = **additional**, extra, add-on, further.

supply VERB 1 = **provide**, give, furnish, contribute, donate, grant; [inf] fork out, shell out. 2 = **satisfy**, meet, fulfil. NOUN 1 = **stock**, store, reserve, reservoir, stockpile, hoard, cache. 2 (**supplies**) = **provisions**, stores, rations, food, foodstuffs, produce.

support VERB 1 = **bear**, carry, hold up, prop up, brace, shore up, underpin, buttress.

2 = **maintain**, provide for, sustain, take care of, look after. 3 = **comfort**, encourage, buoy up, hearten, fortify. 4 = **back up**, substantiate, bear out, corroborate, confirm, verify, validate, authenticate, endorse, ratify. 5 = **back**, champion, help, assist, aid, side with, vote for, stand up for; advocate, promote, champion, espouse, defend; subsidize, finance, fund; [inf] stick up for. NOUN 1 = **base**, foundations, pillar, post, prop, underpinning, substructure, brace, buttress. 2 = **encouragement**, succour, comfort, help, assistance, backing; tower of strength, prop, mainstay.

supporter NOUN 1 = **contributor**, donor, sponsor, patron, benefactor, well-wisher. 2 = **advocate**, backer, adherent, promoter, champion, defender, apologist; helper, ally, voter. 3 = **fan**, follower.

supportive ADJ = **helpful**, encouraging, caring,

sympathetic, understanding, loyal, concerned, reassuring.

suppose VERB 1 = **assume**, dare say, take as read, presume, expect, imagine, believe, think, fancy, suspect, guess, surmise, reckon, conjecture.
2 = **hypothesize**, postulate, posit.

supposition NOUN = **assumption**, presumption, suspicion, surmise, conjecture, speculation, theory, hypothesis.

suppress VERB 1 = **crush**, quash, conquer, stamp out, extinguish, put down, put an end to.
2 = **restrain**, stifle, hold back, control, keep in check, curb, bottle up.
3 = **keep secret**, conceal, hide, hush up, withhold, cover up.

supremacy NOUN = **ascendancy**, dominance, superiority, predominance, dominion, authority, mastery, control, power, rule, sovereignty.

supreme ADJ 1 = **highest-ranking**, highest, leading, chief, foremost, principal.

2 = **extreme**, greatest, utmost, uttermost, maximum.

sure ADJ 1 = **certain**, definite, positive, convinced, confident, assured; unhesitating, unwavering.
2 = **guaranteed**, unfailing, infallible, unerring, tested, tried and tested, foolproof; [inf] sure-fire.

surface NOUN 1 = **outside**, exterior, top.
2 = **appearance**, facade. ADJ = **superficial**, external, exterior, outward, skin deep. VERB = **appear**, come to light, emerge, materialize, arise, crop up.

surge VERB = **gush**, rush, stream, flow, pour, cascade.

surly ADJ = **bad-tempered**, grumpy, crotchety, grouchy, cantankerous, irascible, testy, gruff, abrupt, brusque, churlish, morose, sullen, sulky.

surmise VERB = **guess**, conjecture, suspect, deduce, assume, presume, gather, suppose, think, believe, imagine.

surmount VERB = **get over**, overcome, conquer,

triumph over, beat, get the better of.

surpass VERB = **excel**, exceed, transcend, outdo, outshine, outstrip, beat, overshadow, eclipse.

surplus NOUN = **excess**, surfeit, glut; remainder, residue. ADJ = **excess**, superfluous, unwanted, leftover, unused, remaining, extra, spare.

surprise VERB 1 = **astonish**, amaze, take aback, startle, astound, stun, flabbergast, stagger, take someone's breath away; [inf] bowl over. 2 = **take by surprise**, catch unawares, catch off guard, catch red-handed. NOUN 1 = **astonishment**, amazement, incredulity, wonder. 2 = **shock**, bolt from the blue, bombshell, eye-opener.

surprising ADJ = **astonishing**, amazing, startling, astounding, staggering, incredible, extraordinary; unexpected, unforeseen.

surrender VERB 1 = **give in**, give yourself up, yield, submit, capitulate, lay down your arms, raise the white flag, throw in the towel. 2 = **relinquish**, renounce, forgo, cede, waive, hand over, deliver up, sacrifice.

surreptitious ADJ = **stealthy**, clandestine, secret, sneaky, sly, furtive, covert.

surround VERB = **encircle**, enclose, encompass, ring, fence in, hem in, confine.

surroundings PLURAL NOUN = **environment**, setting, background, milieu, vicinity, locality, habitat.

surveillance NOUN = **observation**, watch, scrutiny, reconnaissance, spying, espionage.

survey VERB = **look at/over**, observe, view, contemplate, regard, examine, inspect, scan, study, consider, inspect, scrutinize, take stock of, size up. NOUN 1 = **study**, consideration, review, overview, examination, inspection, scrutiny. 2 = **investigation**, inquiry, probe, questionnaire, census.

survive VERB = **live on**, continue, remain, last, persist, endure, go on, carry on.

susceptible ADJ 1 = **impressionable**,

credulous, gullible, naive, innocent, ingenuous.
2 (susceptible to) = **open to**, receptive to, vulnerable to, defenceless against.

suspect VERB **1** = **feel**, have a feeling, be inclined to think, fancy, surmise, guess, conjecture, have a hunch, suppose, believe, think, conclude.
2 = **doubt**, have misgivings about, distrust, mistrust.

suspend VERB = **adjourn**, interrupt, cut short, break off, postpone, delay, defer, prorogue.

suspense NOUN = **uncertainty**, tension, doubt, anticipation, expectation, expectancy, excitement, anxiety, nervousness.

suspicion NOUN **1** = **doubt**, misgiving, qualm, scepticism, distrust, mistrust. **2** = **feeling**, intuition, impression, inkling, hunch, fancy, belief, notion, idea.

suspicious ADJ **1** = **doubtful**, unsure, wary, sceptical, distrustful, mistrustful, disbelieving.
2 = **questionable**, dubious, suspect, odd, strange,

queer, funny; [inf] fishy, shady.

sustain VERB **1** = **bear**, support, carry, prop up, shore up. **2** = **comfort**, help, assist, encourage, buoy up, cheer up, hearten, succour. **3** = **keep alive**, maintain, preserve, feed, nourish.

sustained ADJ = **continuous**, steady, persistent, constant, prolonged, perpetual, unremitting.

sustenance NOUN = **food**, nourishment, nutriment, provisions, victuals, rations, provender.

swallow VERB = **gulp down**, eat, drink, consume, devour, ingest; [inf] scoff, swill, swig.

swamp NOUN = **marsh**, bog, quagmire, mire, morass, fen. VERB **1** = **flood**, inundate, deluge, soak, drench, saturate.
2 = **overwhelm**, engulf, snow under, overload, besiege, beset.

swap VERB = **exchange**, trade, barter, switch, change, replace.

swarm NOUN = **crowd**, multitude, horde, host, mob, throng, army, flock, herd, pack, drove. VERB = **flock**, crowd, throng, stream, surge.

sway VERB 1 = **swing**, shake, undulate, rock. 2 = **influence**, affect, persuade, prevail on, bring round, win over, manipulate. NOUN = **jurisdiction**, rule, government, sovereignty, dominion, control, command, power, authority, ascendancy, domination, mastery.

swear VERB 1 = **promise**, pledge, vow, give your word. 2 = **insist**, avow, declare, assert, maintain. 3 = **curse**, blaspheme.

swear word NOUN = **expletive**, oath, curse, obscenity, profanity.

sweet ADJ 1 = **sweetened**, sugary, sugared, syrupy, saccharine. 2 = **fragrant**, aromatic, perfumed, scented. 3 = **melodious**, musical, tuneful, dulcet, mellifluous, harmonious, silvery. 4 = **good-natured**, amiable, pleasant, agreeable, friendly, kindly, charming, likeable, appealing, engaging, winning, winsome. NOUN 1 = **dessert**, pudding; [inf] afters. 2 = **bonbon**, sweetmeat; [US] candy.

sweetheart NOUN = **girlfriend**, boyfriend, lover, suitor, admirer, beau; [literary] swain.

swell VERB 1 = **expand**, bulge, distend, inflate, dilate, bloat, puff up, balloon. 2 = **increase**, grow, rise, mount, escalate, multiply, proliferate, snowball, mushroom.

swelling NOUN = **bump**, lump, bulge, blister, inflammation, protuberance.

sweltering ADJ = **hot**, torrid, tropical, stifling, humid, sultry, sticky; [inf] boiling, baking.

swerve VERB = **veer**, skew, deviate, sheer, go off course.

swift ADJ = **fast**, rapid, quick, fleet, brisk, prompt, immediate, instantaneous, speedy, sudden, abrupt, hasty.

swindle VERB = **defraud**, cheat, trick, dupe, deceive, fleece; [inf] do, con, diddle, rip off, pull a fast one on.

swing VERB 1 = **sway**, move

to and fro, flutter, flap;
hang, dangle. 2 = **curve**,
veer, turn, bend, wind,
twist. 3 = **change**,
fluctuate, oscillate, shift,
waver, see-saw, yo-yo.

swirl VERB = **whirl**, eddy,
circulate, revolve, spin,
twist, churn.

switch NOUN = **change**,
move, shift, transition,
reversal, turnaround,
about turn, U-turn. VERB
1 = **change**, shift, reverse.
2 = **exchange**,
interchange, trade, swap.

swollen ADJ = **distended**,
bulging, inflated, dilated,
bloated, puffy, tumescent.

sycophantic ADJ
= **servile**, subservient,
obsequious, toadying,
ingratiating, unctuous,
oily; [inf] smarmy.

symbol NOUN 1 = **emblem**,
token, sign, figure,
representation, image.
2 = **logo**, badge, crest,
insignia, monogram.

symbolic ADJ
= **emblematic**,
representative, typical;
figurative, allegorical,
metaphorical.

symbolize VERB = **stand
for**, represent, exemplify,
denote, signify, mean;

typify, personify,
epitomize.

symmetrical ADJ
= **balanced**, proportional,
regular, even, uniform,
harmonious, consistent.

sympathetic ADJ
1 = **compassionate**,
caring, concerned,
solicitous, empathetic,
understanding, sensitive;
comforting, supportive,
considerate, kind.
2 = **likeable**, pleasant,
pleasing, agreeable,
congenial, friendly,
genial.

sympathize VERB
= **commiserate with**, pity,
offer your condolences,
feel (sorry) for, identify
with, empathize with.

sympathy NOUN
1 = **compassion**, caring,
concern, solicitude;
commiseration, pity,
condolence, comfort,
solace, support, kindness.
2 = **rapport**, fellow feeling,
affinity, empathy,
harmony, accord,
compatibility, fellowship.

symptom NOUN = **sign**,
indication, signal, mark,
characteristic, feature,
token, evidence.

synthesis NOUN

= **combination**, union, blend, amalgam, fusion, composite, mixture, compound.

synthetic ADJ = **imitation**, man-made, fake, artificial, mock, ersatz.

system NOUN 1 = **structure**, organization, network, arrangement, set-up.

2 = **method**, methodology, technique, process, procedure, approach, practice, means, way, modus operandi.

systematic ADJ = **methodical**, organized, orderly, planned, systematized, logical, efficient, businesslike.

table NOUN = **chart**, diagram, figure, graph, plan; list, index. VERB = **submit**, put forward, propose, suggest.

tablet NOUN 1 = **slab**, panel, stone. 2 = **pill**, capsule, lozenge.

taboo ADJ = **forbidden**, prohibited, banned, proscribed.

tacit ADJ = **implicit**, understood, implied, unstated, unspoken, silent, wordless.

taciturn ADJ = **unforthcoming**, uncommunicative, reticent, tight-lipped, quiet, silent.

tackle NOUN = **gear**,

equipment, apparatus, tools, implements, accoutrements, paraphernalia, trappings. VERB = **undertake**, address, apply yourself to, get to grips with, embark on, take on; confront, face up to.

tact NOUN = **diplomacy**, discretion, sensitivity, thoughtfulness, consideration, delicacy, finesse.

tactful ADJ = **diplomatic**, politic, discreet, sensitive, thoughtful, considerate, delicate, subtle, perceptive.

tactic NOUN = **manoeuvre**, expedient, stratagem,

trick, scheme, plan, ploy, course of action, method, approach, tack.

tactical ADJ = **strategic**, politic, shrewd, skilful, adroit, clever, cunning.

tailor NOUN = **outfitter**, dressmaker, couturier, clothier, costumier. VERB = **customize**, adapt, adjust, modify, change, alter, mould, fit, cut, shape.

take VERB **1** = **get/lay hold of**, grasp, grip, clutch. **2** = **get**, receive, obtain, gain, acquire, secure, procure, come by, win. **3** = **seize**, capture, arrest, abduct. **4** = **steal**, appropriate, filch, pilfer, purloin; [inf] pinch, nick. **5** = **require**, need, necessitate. **6** = **carry**, bring, transport, convey. **7** = **escort**, accompany, conduct, guide, lead, usher. **8** = **hold**, contain, accommodate.

takings PLURAL NOUN = **proceeds**, receipts, earnings, winnings, profit, gain, income, revenue.

tale NOUN = **story**, narrative, anecdote, legend, fable, myth, parable, allegory, saga; [inf] yarn.

talent NOUN = **gift**, flair, aptitude, facility, knack, bent, ability, faculty.

talented ADJ = **gifted**, skilled, skilful, accomplished, able, capable, deft, adept, proficient, brilliant, expert.

talk VERB = **speak**, chat, chatter, gossip, natter; communicate, converse, discourse, confer, consult, parley. NOUN **1** = **conversation**, chat, discussion, dialogue, parley. **2** = **lecture**, speech, address, discourse, oration.

talkative ADJ = **loquacious**, garrulous, voluble, chatty.

tall ADJ = **big**, high, lofty, towering, soaring, sky-high.

tally NOUN = **count**, record, total, reckoning. VERB = **agree**, correspond, accord, concur, coincide, conform, match.

tame ADJ **1** = **domesticated**, domestic, docile. **2** = **unexciting**, uninteresting, uninspired, dull, bland, insipid, pedestrian, humdrum,

boring, tedious. VERB
1 = **domesticate**, break in,
train. 2 = **subdue**,
discipline, curb, control,
master, overcome,
suppress, repress.
tamper VERB = **meddle**,
interfere, mess about,
tinker, fiddle.
tangible ADJ 1 = **touchable**,
palpable, corporeal,
physical. 2 = **concrete**,
real, actual, definite, clear.
tangled ADJ = **entangled**,
twisted, snarled, ravelled,
knotted, knotty, matted,
messy.
tantalize VERB - **tease**,
torment, torture, tempt,
entice; excite, titillate.
target NOUN 1 = **objective**,
goal, object, aim, end,
intention. 2 = **butt**, victim,
object, subject.
tariff NOUN = **tax**, duty, toll,
excise, levy.
tarnish VERB = **sully**,
besmirch, blacken, stain,
blemish, blot, taint.
tart NOUN = **pastry**, tartlet,
pie, strudel. ADJ = **sharp**,
sour, acid, tangy, piquant.
task NOUN = **job**, duty,
chore, assignment,
commission, mission,
undertaking.
taste NOUN 1 = **flavour**,
savour, tang. 2 = **morsel**,
bite, mouthful, spoonful,
sample, sip, soupçon.
3 = **liking**, love, fondness,
fancy, preference,
penchant, predilection,
inclination, partiality,
appetite.
4 = **discrimination**,
discernment, judgement;
finesse, elegance, grace,
style. VERB = **sample**, test,
try, nibble, sip.
tasteful ADJ = **in good
taste**, aesthetic, artistic,
elegant, graceful, refined,
stylish, chic.
tasteless ADJ
1 = **flavourless**, bland,
insipid, watery,
unappetizing,
uninteresting. 2 = **vulgar**,
crude, tawdry, garish,
gaudy, loud, flashy,
showy, cheap.
tasty ADJ = **delicious**,
appetizing, palatable,
delectable, mouth-
watering.
taunt VERB = **jeer at**, sneer
at, insult, tease, torment,
provoke, goad, ridicule,
deride, mock, poke fun at.
taut ADJ = **tight**, stretched,
rigid, flexed, tensed.
tawdry ADJ = **showy**,
gaudy, flashy, garish,

loud, tasteless.

tax NOUN = **levy**, charge, duty, toll, excise, tariff. VERB = **strain**, stretch, overburden, try, wear out, exhaust, sap, drain.

teach VERB = **instruct**, educate, school, tutor, coach, train, drill.

teacher NOUN = **tutor**, instructor, governess, coach, trainer, lecturer, professor, don; mentor, guru.

team NOUN = **group**, band, company, gang, crew, troupe, squad, side, line-up.

tear NOUN = **rip**, split, hole, rent, run, rupture. VERB = **rip**, split, rend, rupture.

tease VERB = **make fun of**, poke fun at, taunt, bait, goad; mock, ridicule, deride; [inf] pull someone's leg, wind up.

technique NOUN 1 = **method**, system, procedure, approach, way, strategy, means. 2 = **skill**, proficiency, expertise, mastery, artistry, ability.

tedious ADJ = **wearisome**, tiresome, tiring, dull, boring, uninteresting, soporific, dreary, uninspired, flat, monotonous, humdrum.

tell VERB 1 = **relate**, recount, narrate, report, recite, describe; utter, voice, state, declare, communicate, impart, divulge. 2 = **inform**, apprise, notify, brief, fill in. 3 = **instruct**, order, command, direct, bid, enjoin, call on, require.

telling ADJ = **revealing**, significant, important, meaningful, influential, striking, potent, powerful, compelling.

temper NOUN 1 = **mood**, humour, frame of mind. 2 = **bad mood**, fury, rage, tantrum, pet; [inf] paddy, strop. VERB = **moderate**, soften, modify, mitigate, alleviate, allay, lessen, weaken.

temperament NOUN = **disposition**, nature, character, personality, make-up, constitution, mind.

temperamental ADJ = **excitable**, emotional, volatile, mercurial, capricious, erratic, unpredictable, touchy, moody, highly strung, neurotic.

temperate ADJ

= **moderate**, mild, gentle, clement, balmy.

temple NOUN = **place of worship**, shrine, sanctuary, house of God.

tempo NOUN = **beat**, rhythm, cadence, time, speed.

temporal ADJ = **secular**, worldly, material, earthly.

temporary ADJ 1 = **short-term**, interim, provisional. 2 = **brief**, fleeting, passing, momentary, short-lived.

tempt VERB = **entice**, lure, attract, appeal to, seduce, tantalize, persuade, induce, inveigle, cajole, coax.

tenable ADJ = **justifiable**, defensible, defendable, supportable, credible, reasonable, rational, sound, viable.

tend VERB = **look after**, take care of, care for, attend to, minister to.

tendency NOUN = **inclination**, disposition, predisposition, proclivity, propensity, penchant.

tender ADJ 1 = **fragile**, frail, delicate, sensitive. 2 = **loving**, affectionate, warm, compassionate, soft-hearted, kind, warm, caring, gentle, solicitous, generous.

tense ADJ 1 = **tight**, taut, rigid, stretched. 2 = **nervous**, keyed up, worked up, overwrought, anxious, uneasy, worried, apprehensive, agitated, jumpy, edgy, on edge; [inf] uptight.

tension NOUN 1 = **tightness**, tautness, rigidity. 2 = **strain**, stress, pressure, anxiety, worry, suspense, uncertainty.

tentative ADJ 1 = **speculative**, conjectural, exploratory, trial, provisional. 2 = **hesitant**, faltering, uncertain, unsure, cautious.

tenuous ADJ = **slight**, flimsy, weak, insubstantial, shaky, doubtful, dubious.

term NOUN 1 = **word**, expression, phrase, name, title, denomination, designation. 2 = **period**, time, spell, interval, stretch.

terminal ADJ = **fatal**, deadly, mortal, lethal; incurable. NOUN 1 = **terminus**, depot. 2 = **workstation**, visual display unit, VDU.

terminate VERB = **end**, conclude, finish, stop, wind up, discontinue.

terminology NOUN = **language**, phraseology, vocabulary, nomenclature, jargon, terms, words; [inf] lingo.

terrible ADJ **1** = **bad**, poor, incompetent, useless, hopeless, atrocious. **2** = **dreadful**, terrifying, frightening, frightful, horrifying, horrible, horrific, horrendous, harrowing, hideous, grim, unspeakable, appalling, awful, gruesome, ghastly.

terrific ADJ **1** = **tremendous**, great, huge, massive, colossal, mighty, prodigious, considerable, intense, extreme. **2** see **excellent**.

terrify VERB = **frighten**, scare, petrify, horrify, make someone's blood run cold.

territory NOUN **1** = **region**, area, terrain, tract. **2** = **sphere**, province, field, sector, domain.

terror NOUN = **fright**, fear, dread, horror.

terrorize VERB = **persecute**, victimize, torment, tyrannize, menace, threaten, bully; scare, frighten, terrify, petrify.

terse ADJ **1** = **concise**, succinct, compact, brief, short, crisp, pithy. **2** = **abrupt**, curt, brusque, laconic, clipped.

test NOUN = **trial**, experiment, examination, check, assessment, evaluation, appraisal, investigation, analysis, study. VERB = **trial**, pilot; examine, check, assess, evaluate, appraise, investigate, analyse, study.

testimony NOUN = **evidence**, attestation, sworn statement, deposition, affidavit.

texture NOUN = **feel**, touch, appearance, surface, grain.

thanks PLURAL NOUN = **gratitude**, gratefulness, acknowledgement, appreciation, recognition.

thaw VERB = **melt**, defrost, soften, liquefy.

theatrical ADJ **1** = **dramatic**, stage, thespian. **2** = **melodramatic**, histrionic, exaggerated, overdone, ostentatious, showy, affected.

theft NOUN = **stealing**, robbery, burglary, larceny, embezzlement.

theme NOUN 1 = **topic**, subject (matter), thesis, text, argument. 2 = **melody**, motif, leitmotif.

theoretical ADJ = **hypothetical**, conjectural, speculative, suppositional, notional.

theory NOUN = **hypothesis**, thesis, conjecture, supposition, speculation, postulation; opinion, view, belief.

therefore ADV = **so**, thus, accordingly, as a result, consequently, hence.

thesis NOUN 1 = **theory**, hypothesis, contention, argument, proposition, premise, postulation. 2 = **dissertation**, paper, treatise, disquisition, essay, monograph.

thick ADJ 1 = **broad**, wide, large, big, bulky, sturdy, chunky, solid, substantial. 2 = **semi-solid**; clotted, coagulated, viscid, viscous. 3 = **dense**, heavy, opaque, soupy, murky, impenetrable.

thicken VERB = **set**, solidify, congeal, clot, coagulate.

thief NOUN = **robber**, burglar, housebreaker, shoplifter, pickpocket, mugger.

thin ADJ 1 = **slim**, slender, lean, slight; skinny, spindly, gaunt, scrawny, scraggy, bony, skeletal, wasted, emaciated, undernourished, underweight. 2 = **fine**, light, delicate, flimsy, diaphanous, sheer, gauzy, filmy, translucent. 3 = **insubstantial**, weak, feeble, lame, poor, unconvincing, tenuous.

thing NOUN 1 = **object**, article, item, artefact. 2 = **action**, act, deed, exploit, feat, undertaking, task, job, chore. 3 = **event**, happening, occurrence, incident, episode. 4 = **quality**, characteristic, attribute, property, trait, feature.

think VERB 1 = **believe**, suppose, expect, imagine, surmise, conjecture, guess, fancy. 2 = **consider**, deem, hold, reckon, assume, presume. 3 = **ponder**, meditate, deliberate, contemplate, muse, cogitate, ruminate, concentrate, brood, reflect.

thirsty ADJ = **parched**, dehydrated, dry; [inf] gasping.

thorny ADJ 1 = **prickly**, spiky, barbed, spiny, sharp. 2 see **difficult (2)**.

thorough ADJ = **in-depth**, exhaustive, complete, comprehensive, thoroughgoing, intensive, extensive, widespread, sweeping, all-embracing, all-inclusive, detailed, meticulous, scrupulous, assiduous, conscientious, painstaking, punctilious, methodical, careful.

thought NOUN 1 = **idea**, notion, view, theory, opinion. 2 = **thinking**, contemplation, consideration, reflection, meditation, rumination, introspection.

thoughtful ADJ 1 = **pensive**, reflective, introspective, meditative, contemplative, ruminative. 2 = **considerate**, attentive, caring, solicitous, helpful, kind, neighbourly, compassionate, charitable, unselfish.

thoughtless ADJ 1 = **inconsiderate**, insensitive, tactless, undiplomatic, unkind. 2 = **unthinking**, heedless, absent-minded, careless, imprudent, unwise, foolish, silly, reckless, rash, precipitate.

thread NOUN = **yarn**, cotton, filament, fibre.

threadbare ADJ = **worn**, old, thin, frayed, tattered, ragged, shabby.

threat NOUN 1 = **warning**, ultimatum. 2 = **danger**, risk, hazard.

threaten VERB 1 = **menace**, intimidate, browbeat, bully, terrorize. 2 = **endanger**, imperil, jeopardize, put at risk.

threatening ADJ = **menacing**, intimidating, minatory; ominous, sinister, inauspicious, foreboding.

threshold NOUN 1 = **doorway**, doorstep, entrance. 2 = **beginning**, inception, opening, dawn, brink, verge.

thrifty ADJ see **economical**.

thrill NOUN = **excitement**, exhilaration, pleasure, delight, joy; [inf] buzz, kick. VERB = **excite**, stimulate, arouse, stir, electrify, intoxicate.

thrilling ADJ = **exciting**, stirring, electrifying, gripping, riveting, action-packed.

thrive VERB = **flourish**, prosper, bloom, burgeon, succeed, boom.

throb VERB = **beat**, pulse, pulsate, palpitate, pound.

throng NOUN = **crowd**, horde, mob, mass, host, multitude, swarm, flock, pack, herd, drove.

throttle VERB = **choke**, strangle, strangulate, garrotte.

throw VERB 1 = **hurl**, toss, sling, fling, pitch, lob, propel, launch, cast; [inf] heave, chuck. 2 = **disconcert**, discomfit, disturb, astonish, surprise, dumbfound.

thrust VERB = **push**, shove, ram, drive, force, propel.

thug NOUN = **ruffian**, hoodlum, bully boy, hooligan, villain, gangster.

thwart VERB = **frustrate**, foil, baulk, check, block, stop, prevent, defeat, impede, obstruct, hinder, hamper, stymie.

tidy ADJ 1 = **neat**, trim, orderly, in order, spruce, shipshape, spick and span. 2 = **organized**, well organized, methodical, systematic, businesslike. VERB = **clear up**, put in order, straighten, spruce up, neaten.

tie VERB 1 = **fasten**, attach, fix, bind, secure, tether, moor, lash, couple, rope, chain. 2 = **draw**, be equal, be neck and neck.

tier NOUN = **row**, rank, bank, line, layer, level, storey.

tight ADJ 1 = **fast**, secure, fixed. 2 = **taut**, rigid, stiff, tense, stretched. 3 = **cramped**, restricted, limited, constricted.

till VERB = **cultivate**, work, farm, plough, dig.

tilt VERB = **lean**, list, slope, slant, incline, tip.

time NOUN 1 = **age**, era, epoch, period. 2 = **while**, spell, stretch, stint, term. 3 = **moment**, point, instant, occasion, juncture. 4 = **beat**, measure, tempo, rhythm, metre. VERB = **schedule**, arrange, fix, set, timetable, organize.

timely ADJ = **opportune**, well timed, convenient, appropriate, seasonable, felicitous.

timetable NOUN
= **schedule**, programme,
calendar, agenda.

timid ADJ = **fearful**, afraid,
faint-hearted, timorous,
nervous, scared,
frightened, cowardly; shy,
diffident, self-effacing.

tinker VERB = **fiddle**, toy,
tamper, mess about.

tint NOUN = **shade**, colour,
tone, tinge, hue.

tiny ADJ = **minute**, small,
little, diminutive,
miniature, minuscule,
infinitesimal,
microscopic;
insignificant, trifling,
negligible,
inconsequential.

tip NOUN 1 = **point**, peak, top,
summit, apex, crown.
2 = **end**, extremity, point.
VERB 1 = **tilt**, lean, list, cant,
slant, topple, overturn,
fall over, capsize. 2 = **pour**,
empty, unload, dump.

tirade NOUN = **diatribe**,
harangue, rant, lecture.

tire VERB = **wear out**, weary,
exhaust, drain, enervate,
debilitate; flag, droop.

tired ADJ = **worn out**, weary,
fatigued, exhausted,
drained, enervated; [inf]
done in, all in, knackered.

tireless ADJ = **untiring**,
unflagging, indefatigable,
energetic, industrious,
vigorous, determined,
resolute, dogged.

tiresome ADJ
1 = **wearisome**, laborious,
tedious, boring,
monotonous, dull,
uninteresting, unexciting,
humdrum, routine.
2 = **troublesome**, irksome,
vexatious, irritating,
annoying, exasperating,
trying.

tiring ADJ = **wearying**,
wearing, fatiguing,
exhausting, enervating,
arduous, laborious,
strenuous, onerous.

titillate VERB = **excite**,
arouse, stimulate, thrill,
tantalize.

title NOUN = **name**,
designation,
denomination, epithet,
sobriquet; [inf] moniker.

token NOUN 1 = **symbol**,
sign, emblem, badge,
representation,
indication, mark.
2 = **memento**, souvenir,
keepsake, remembrance,
reminder. ADJ
= **perfunctory**, superficial,
nominal, slight, minimal.

tolerable ADJ = **passable**,
adequate, satisfactory,

fair, average, mediocre, ordinary, indifferent, unexceptional; [inf] OK.

tolerant ADJ = **open-minded**, unprejudiced, unbiased, unbigoted, broad-minded, liberal, forbearing, long-suffering, charitable, lenient, indulgent, permissive, easy-going.

tolerate VERB 1 = **permit**, allow, sanction, condone, accept. 2 = **endure**, bear, take, stand, put up with, abide, stomach.

toll NOUN 1 = **charge**, fee, payment, levy, tariff. 2 = **cost**, damage, loss.

tomb NOUN = **grave**, sepulchre, vault, crypt, catacomb, mausoleum.

tone NOUN 1 = **sound**, pitch, timbre, tonality. 2 = **mood**, air, attitude, character, spirit, tenor, vein.

tonic NOUN = **restorative**, stimulant; [inf] pick-me-up.

tool NOUN = **implement**, instrument, utensil, device, apparatus, gadget, appliance, machine, contrivance, contraption.

top NOUN 1 = **summit**, peak, pinnacle, crest, crown, tip, apex, vertex, apogee. 2 = **cap**, lid, stopper, cork, cover. ADJ 1 = **topmost**, uppermost, highest. 2 = **foremost**, leading, principal, pre-eminent, greatest, finest. 3 = **maximum**, maximal, greatest, utmost.

topic NOUN = **subject**, theme, issue, question, argument, thesis.

topical ADJ = **current**, up to date, contemporary, recent, relevant.

topple VERB 1 = **fall over**, tip over, keel over, overturn, overbalance. 2 = **overthrow**, oust, unseat, bring down.

torment NOUN = **agony**, suffering, torture, pain, anguish, misery, distress, affliction, wretchedness. VERB = **torture**, rack, afflict, harrow, plague.

torrent NOUN = **flood**, deluge, inundation, spate, cascade, stream, rush, current.

tortuous ADJ = **twisting**, winding, serpentine, zigzag, convoluted, complicated, complex.

torture NOUN 1 = **abuse**, ill-treatment. 2 = **agony**, suffering, pain, torment,

anguish, misery, distress.
VERB **1** abuse, ill-treat.
2 = **torment**, rack, afflict,
harrow, plague.

toss VERB = **throw**, hurl,
cast, sling, pitch, lob,
propel, launch; [inf] chuck.

total NOUN = **sum**,
aggregate, whole, entirety,
totality. ADJ **1** = **complete**,
entire, whole, full,
comprehensive,
combined, aggregate,
overall. **2** = **utter**, absolute,
complete, downright, out
and out, outright,
unmitigated, unqualified.
VERB **1** = **add up to**, come
to, amount to. **2** = **add up**,
count, tot up.

totalitarian ADJ
= **autocratic**,
authoritarian, despotic,
dictatorial, tyrannical,
undemocratic, oppressive.

totter VERB = **teeter**,
wobble, stagger, stumble,
reel, sway, lurch.

touch VERB **1** = **meet**,
converge, adjoin, abut.
2 = **tap**, brush, graze, feel,
stroke, pat, fondle, caress.
3 = **affect**, move, influence,
have an effect on. NOUN
= **bit**, trace, suggestion,
hint, tinge; dash, taste,
spot, drop, pinch, speck,
soupçon.

touching ADJ = **moving**,
affecting, heartwarming,
emotional, emotive,
poignant.

touchy ADJ = **sensitive**,
hypersensitive,
oversensitive, thin-
skinned, tetchy, testy,
irritable, peevish,
querulous, bad-tempered,
short-tempered.

tough ADJ **1** = **strong**,
durable, resilient, sturdy,
robust, solid, stout, hard-
wearing. **2** = **chewy**,
leathery, gristly, stringy,
fibrous. **3** = **difficult**, hard,
arduous, onerous,
laborious, strenuous,
exacting, taxing,
gruelling, demanding.
4 = **strict**, stern, severe,
rigorous, harsh, hard-
hitting, unsentimental.

tour NOUN = **trip**, excursion,
journey, expedition,
jaunt, outing,
peregrination. VERB = **travel
round/through**, explore,
holiday in, visit.

tourist NOUN = **visitor**,
sightseer, holidaymaker,
tripper.

tournament NOUN
= **competition**, contest,
meeting, event, fixture.

tout VERB = **ask for**, solicit, seek, appeal for, beg for.

tow VERB = **pull**, draw, drag, haul, tug, lug.

toxic ADJ = **poisonous**, virulent, noxious; dangerous, harmful.

trace NOUN 1 = **mark**, sign, vestige, indication, evidence, remains, remnant. 2 = **bit**, touch, hint, suggestion, suspicion, tinge. VERB = **find**, discover, detect, unearth, track down.

track NOUN 1 = **path**, pathway, footpath, way. 2 = **mark**, trace, footprint, trail, spoor. 3 = **course**, orbit, route, trajectory. VERB = **follow**, pursue, trail, trace, tail, stalk.

trade NOUN 1 = **commerce**, buying and selling, dealing, traffic, business. 2 = **line of work**, occupation, job, career, profession, craft, vocation, calling, work, employment. VERB 1 = **buy and sell**, deal, traffic. 2 = **swap**, exchange, barter, switch.

trader NOUN = **merchant**, dealer, buyer, seller.

tradition NOUN = **custom**, practice, convention, ritual, observance, habit, institution, usage.

traditional ADJ = **customary**, conventional, established, accustomed, ritual, habitual, set, routine, usual, wonted, time-honoured, age-old.

tragedy NOUN = **disaster**, calamity, catastrophe, misfortune, affliction, adversity.

tragic ADJ 1 = **disastrous**, calamitous, catastrophic, devastating, fatal, terrible, dreadful, appalling, awful. 2 = **sad**, unhappy, pathetic, moving, distressing, heart-rending, pitiful, piteous.

trail NOUN 1 = **track**, scent, spoor, traces, marks, signs, footprints. 2 = **path**, pathway, footpath, way, route. VERB 1 = **drag**, sweep, dangle, hang down, droop. 2 see **track**.

train NOUN = **procession**, line, file, column, convoy, cavalcade, caravan. VERB 1 = **instruct**, teach, coach, tutor, school, ground, drill. 2 = **exercise**, work out. 3 = **aim**, point, focus, direct, level.

trait NOUN = **characteristic**,

attribute, feature, quality, property, idiosyncrasy, peculiarity, quirk.

traitor NOUN = **turncoat**, renegade, defector, deserter, double agent, quisling, fifth columnist.

trample VERB = **tread on**, step on, stamp on, squash, crush, flatten.

trance NOUN = **daze**, stupor, dream.

tranquil ADJ = **peaceful**, restful, calm, quiet, still, serene, placid, undisturbed.

transaction NOUN = **deal**, undertaking, arrangement, bargain, negotiation.

transcend VERB = **exceed**, surpass, outdo, outstrip, outclass, outshine, eclipse.

transfer VERB **1** = **convey**, move, shift, remove, take, carry, transport. **2** = **make over**, sign over, hand over, pass on, consign.

transform VERB = **change**, alter, convert, transfigure, transmogrify; revolutionize, reconstruct, rebuild, reorganize, rework.

transformation NOUN = **change**, alteration, conversion, metamorphosis, transfiguration, transmogrification.

transgress VERB = **break**, infringe, breach, contravene, violate, defy, disobey.

transient ADJ = **transitory**, brief, short-lived, impermanent, momentary, ephemeral, fleeting, passing.

transit NOUN = **movement**, transport, transportation, haulage, conveyance; travel, passage.

transition NOUN = **change**, transformation, conversion, metamorphosis, shift, switch, progression, progress, passage.

transmit VERB **1** = **transfer**, pass on, communicate, convey, impart, dispatch, relay, disseminate, spread, circulate. **2** = **broadcast**, relay, send out, air, televise.

transparent ADJ = **clear**, see-through, translucent, pellucid, crystalline, limpid, glassy.

transpire VERB = **come about**, happen, occur, take place, befall.

transport VERB = **convey**, take, transfer, move, shift, carry, send, deliver; ship, ferry. NOUN = **conveyance**, transportation; transit, carriage, freight.

trap NOUN = **snare**, net, gin; pitfall, booby trap. VERB **1** = **snare**, ensnare, entrap; capture, catch, corner. **2** = **trick**, dupe, deceive, lure, inveigle, beguile.

trappings PLURAL NOUN = **accessories**, accoutrements, appurtenances, appointments, trimmings, paraphernalia, equipment, apparatus, gear.

traumatic ADJ = **painful**, agonizing, shocking, disturbing, distressing, hurtful, upsetting.

travel VERB = **journey**, tour, voyage, wander, ramble, roam, rove.

traveller NOUN = **tripper**, tourist, holidaymaker, sightseer, globetrotter.

treacherous ADJ **1** = **traitorous**, double-crossing, renegade, perfidious; duplicitous, disloyal, faithless. **2** = **hazardous**, dangerous, perilous, risky.

tread VERB = **walk**, step, stride, pace, march, tramp; trample, crush, squash, flatten.

treason NOUN treachery, betrayal, disloyalty, faithlessness, sedition, subversion, mutiny, rebellion.

treasure NOUN = **riches**, valuables, wealth, fortune, jewels, gems, gold, silver. VERB = **value**, prize, hold dear, cherish.

treat VERB **1** = **deal with**, handle, tackle. **2** = **regard**, consider, view, look on. **3** = **medicate**, nurse, care for, attend to, tend; cure, heal, remedy. NOUN = **luxury**, indulgence, extravagance; titbit, delicacy; present, gift.

treatise NOUN = **discourse**, exposition, disquisition, dissertation, thesis, study, essay, paper, monograph, tract, pamphlet.

treatment NOUN **1** = **conduct**, handling, use, dealings. **2** = **medication**, therapy, nursing, care, ministration.

treaty NOUN = **agreement**, settlement, pact, deal,

covenant, contract, concordat, entente.

trek VERB = **tramp**, hike, trudge, march, slog, footslog. NOUN = **expedition**, trip, journey, hike, march.

tremble VERB = **shake**, quiver, quaver; shudder, judder, teeter, totter, wobble, rock.

tremendous ADJ 1 = **great**, huge, enormous, immense, massive, vast, colossal, prodigious, stupendous, gigantic, gargantuan, mammoth. 2 see **excellent**.

trend NOUN 1 = **tendency**, drift, course, direction, current, inclination. 2 = **fashion**, vogue, style, mode, look, craze.

trespass VERB = **intrude**, encroach, infringe, invade.

trial NOUN 1 = **court case**, hearing, inquiry, tribunal. 2 = **test**, dry run, try-out, check, experiment. 3 = **nuisance**, pest, bother, annoyance, irritant.

tribute NOUN = **accolade**, commendation, testimonial, paean, eulogy, panegyric, praise, homage, congratulations, compliments, bouquets.

trick NOUN 1 = **stratagem**, ploy, ruse, dodge, wile, manoeuvre, deceit, deception, subterfuge. 2 = **knack**, art, technique, skill. 3 = **hoax**, (practical) joke, prank, jape. VERB = **deceive**, delude, mislead, take in, cheat, hoodwink, fool, dupe, hoax, defraud, swindle; [inf] con.

trickle VERB = **drip**, dribble, leak, ooze, seep.

tricky ADJ = **difficult**, problematic, awkward, delicate, sensitive, ticklish, thorny, knotty.

trim VERB = **cut**, clip, snip, shear, prune, pare.

trip NOUN = **excursion**, tour, expedition, voyage, jaunt, outing. VERB = **stumble**, lose your footing, stagger, slip, fall, tumble.

triumph NOUN 1 = **conquest**, victory, win, success, achievement. 2 = **exultation**, jubilation, elation, delight, joy, glee, pride. VERB = **win**, succeed, come first, carry the day.

triumphant ADJ 1 = **victorious**, successful, undefeated, unbeaten. 2 = **exultant**, jubilant, elated, joyful, gleeful, proud, cock-a-hoop.

trivial ADJ = **unimportant**, insignificant, negligible, inconsequential, petty, minor, paltry, trifling.

troops PLURAL NOUN = **armed forces**, army, military, services, soldiers.

trouble NOUN 1 = **problems**, bother, inconvenience, worry, anxiety, distress, stress, harassment, unpleasantness; [inf] hassle. 2 = **misfortune**, difficulty, trial, tribulation, burden, pain, woe, grief, heartache, misery, affliction, suffering. 3 = **disturbance**, disorder, unrest, fighting, fracas. VERB = **worry**, bother, concern, disturb, upset, agitate, distress, perturb, annoy, irritate, vex, irk; inconvenience.

troublemaker NOUN = **mischief-maker**, agitator, rabble-rouser, firebrand.

troublesome ADJ = **annoying**, irritating, exasperating, maddening, infuriating, irksome, bothersome, tiresome, worrying, upsetting; difficult, awkward, problematic, taxing.

trounce VERB = **defeat**, beat hollow, rout, thrash, crush, overwhelm.

truant VERB = **play truant**, malinger; [inf] skive, play hookey, bunk off.

truce NOUN = **ceasefire**, armistice, peace, respite.

true ADJ 1 = **correct**, accurate, right, verifiable; literal, factual, unvarnished. 2 = **real**, genuine, authentic, actual, bona fide, proper. 3 = **loyal**, faithful, trustworthy, reliable, dependable, staunch, steadfast, constant, devoted, dedicated.

trust NOUN 1 = **faith**, confidence, belief, conviction, credence, assurance, certainty, reliance. 2 = **responsibility**, duty, obligation.

trustworthy ADJ = **reliable**, dependable, staunch, loyal, faithful, trusty, responsible, sensible, level-headed, honest, honourable, upright, ethical, principled.

truth NOUN = **veracity**, truthfulness, sincerity, candour, honesty;

accuracy, correctness.

truthful ADJ **1** = **honest**, sincere, trustworthy, genuine; candid, frank, open, forthright, straight. **2** = **true**, accurate, correct, factual, faithful, reliable; unvarnished, unembellished, veracious.

try VERB **1** = **attempt**, aim, endeavour, exert yourself, strive, seek. **2** = **try out**, test, put to the test, appraise, evaluate, assess; sample.

trying ADJ = **troublesome**, bothersome, tiresome, irksome, vexatious, annoying, irritating, exasperating.

tug VERB = **pull**, drag, lug, draw, haul, heave, tow.

tumble VERB = **fall**, topple, lose your footing, stumble, trip up.

tumbledown ADJ = **dilapidated**, ramshackle, decrepit, derelict, ruined, in ruins, rickety.

tumult NOUN = **din**, uproar, commotion, racket, hubbub, hullabaloo, clamour, shouting, yelling, pandemonium, babel, bedlam.

tumultuous ADJ = **loud**, noisy, clamorous, deafening, thunderous, uproarious; rowdy, unruly, disorderly, turbulent, riotous, wild, violent.

tune NOUN = **melody**, air, song.

tunnel NOUN = **underpass**, subway; burrow. VERB = **dig**, burrow, mine, drill.

turbulent ADJ **1** = **tempestuous**, stormy, rough, choppy, wild. **2** = **rowdy**, unruly, disorderly, restless, agitated, wild, violent.

turmoil NOUN = **agitation**, ferment, confusion, disorder, upheaval, chaos, pandemonium, bedlam, tumult.

turn VERB **1** = **rotate**, revolve, circle, roll, spin, wheel, whirl, twirl, gyrate, swivel, pivot. **2** = **aim**, point, level, direct, train. **3** = **become**, grow, get, go. NOUN **1** = **rotation**, revolution, circle, spin, whirl, twirl, gyration, swivel. **2** = **turning**, bend, corner; junction. **3** = **opportunity**, chance; stint, spell, time; try, attempt, go.

twilight NOUN = **dusk**, sunset, nightfall; [Scottish]

gloaming.

twin NOUN = **double**, lookalike, image, duplicate, clone; [inf] spitting image, dead ringer.

twinge NOUN = **pain**, spasm, pang, ache, throb; cramp, stitch.

twist VERB **1** = **contort**, misshape, deform, distort. **2** = **wrench**, turn, sprain, rick. **3** = **wind**, curve, swerve, bend, zigzag, meander, snake. **4** = **distort**, pervert, misinterpret, garble, misrepresent, falsify, change, alter.

two-faced ADJ = **hypocritical**, insincere, deceitful, duplicitous, false, untrustworthy, disloyal.

type NOUN = **kind**, sort, variety, form, class, classification, category, group, order, set, genre, strain, species, genus, ilk.

typical ADJ **1** = **representative**, classic, quintessential, archetypal, model, stereotypical. **2** = **normal**, average, ordinary, standard, regular, routine, run-of-the-mill, conventional, unremarkable, unexceptional.

typify VERB = **epitomize**, exemplify, characterize, personify, represent, embody.

tyrannical ADJ = **despotic**, autocratic, dictatorial, authoritarian, high-handed, oppressive, domineering, harsh, strict, severe, cruel.

tyrant NOUN = **despot**, autocrat, dictator, martinet, slave-driver, hard taskmaster, bully.

Uu

ubiquitous ADJ = **everywhere**, omnipresent, pervasive, universal.

ugly ADJ = **unattractive**, plain, hideous, ill-favoured, unsightly, unprepossessing;

misshapen, deformed.

ultimate ADJ = **last**, final, concluding, terminal, end.

umpire NOUN = **adjudicator**, arbitrator, judge, referee.

unacceptable ADJ = **unsatisfactory**, intolerable, objectionable, offensive, undesirable, disagreeable, distasteful, improper.

unanimous ADJ = **in agreement**, of one mind, in harmony, in accord, united.

unavoidable ADJ = **inescapable**, inevitable, inexorable, ineluctable, predestined, necessary, compulsory, required, obligatory, mandatory.

unaware ADJ = **unknowing**, unconscious, ignorant, heedless, unmindful, oblivious, uninformed, unenlightened, unwitting; [inf] in the dark.

unbelievable ADJ = **beyond belief**, incredible, unconvincing, far-fetched, implausible, improbable, inconceivable, unthinkable, unimaginable.

uncertain ADJ
1 = **unknown**, undetermined, unsettled, in the balance. 2 = **unsure**, doubtful, dubious, undecided, irresolute, hesitant, wavering, vacillating, ambivalent, in two minds.

uncivilized ADJ
1 = **barbarous**, primitive, savage, wild. 2 = **uncouth**, coarse, rough, boorish, vulgar, philistine, uneducated, unrefined, unsophisticated.

uncomfortable ADJ = **uneasy**, ill at ease, nervous, tense, edgy, self-conscious, awkward, embarrassed.

uncompromising ADJ = **inflexible**, unbending, unyielding, hard-line, determined, obstinate, obdurate, tenacious, inexorable, intransigent, intractable.

unconditional ADJ = **complete**, total, entire, full, absolute, utter, unequivocal, unquestioning, unlimited.

unconscious ADJ
1 = **comatose**, knocked out; [inf] out cold.

2 = **unaware**, heedless, ignorant, oblivious.

3 = **unintentional**, unintended, unthinking, unwitting, inadvertent.

unconventional ADJ = **unorthodox**, irregular, unusual, uncommon, unwonted, out of the ordinary, atypical, singular, individualistic, different, original, idiosyncratic, nonconformist, eccentric, extraordinary, bohemian, odd, strange.

uncouth ADJ = **rough**, coarse, uncivilized, uncultured, uncultivated, unrefined, unsophisticated, crude, loutish, boorish, oafish, rude, impolite, discourteous, bad-mannered, ill-bred, vulgar.

unctuous ADJ see **sycophantic**.

undergo VERB = **experience**, sustain, endure, bear, be subjected to, stand, withstand, weather.

underhand ADJ = **deceitful**, dishonest, dishonourable; devious, sneaky, furtive, covert.

undermine VERB = **weaken**, impair, damage, injure, threaten, subvert, sabotage.

underprivileged ADJ = **disadvantaged**, deprived, in need, needy, poor, impoverished.

understand VERB
1 = **comprehend**, apprehend, grasp, see, take in, follow, fathom; [inf] get the hang of, figure out. **2** = **appreciate**, recognize, accept, sympathize, empathize. **3** = **gather**, hear, be informed, learn, believe.

understanding NOUN
1 = **comprehension**, apprehension, grasp, appreciation.
2 = **compassion**, sympathy, empathy, sensitivity, insight.
3 = **agreement**, arrangement, bargain, pact, deal. ADJ = **compassionate**, sympathetic, sensitive, considerate, kind, thoughtful, tolerant, patient.

understate VERB = **downplay**, play down, make light of, minimize.

undertake VERB = **take on**,

set about, tackle, begin, start, commence, embark on, attempt, try.

undisguised ADJ = **open**, obvious, evident, patent, manifest, transparent, overt, unmistakable.

undoubted ADJ = **undisputed**, unquestioned, not in doubt, not in question, certain, unquestionable, indubitable, irrefutable, incontrovertible.

undue ADJ = **unwarranted**, unjustified, unreasonable, inappropriate; excessive, immoderate, disproportionate.

uneasy ADJ = **ill at ease**, troubled, perturbed, worried, anxious, apprehensive, agitated, nervous, on edge, edgy, restless, unsettled, uncomfortable, awkward; [inf] jittery.

unemotional ADJ = **undemonstrative**, passionless, cold, frigid, cool, unfeeling, reserved, restrained, unresponsive, unexcitable, impassive.

unemployed ADJ = **jobless**, out of work, redundant, laid off; [inf] on the dole.

unequal ADJ **1** = **different**, dissimilar, unlike, unalike, disparate, varying, variable. **2** = **unfair**, unjust, inequitable, uneven, one-sided, ill-matched.

unequivocal ADJ = **unambiguous**, clear, clear-cut, plain, explicit, unqualified, categorical, direct, straightforward, blunt.

uneven ADJ **1** = **rough**, bumpy, lumpy, potholed. **2** = **irregular** asymmetrical, unbalanced, lopsided.

uneventful ADJ = **unexciting**, uninteresting, monotonous, boring, dull, tedious, routine, ordinary, run-of-the-mill, everyday.

unexpected ADJ = **unforeseen**, unanticipated, unpredicted, sudden, abrupt, surprising, out of the blue.

unfair ADJ = **unjust**, inequitable, partisan, prejudiced, biased, one-sided; undeserved, unmerited, uncalled-for, unreasonable, unjustifiable.

unfaithful ADJ **1** = **disloyal**,

faithless, perfidious, treacherous, traitorous. 2 = **adulterous**; [inf] two-timing.

unfashionable ADJ = **out of fashion**, old-fashioned, outmoded, outdated, dated, passé, square.

unfortunate ADJ = **unlucky**, out of luck, luckless, ill-starred, ill-fated, star-crossed, hapless, wretched, poor.

unfriendly ADJ = **hostile**, antagonistic, uncongenial, unsociable, inhospitable, aloof, cold, cool, frosty, distant.

unhappy ADJ = **sad**, miserable, sorrowful, dejected, despondent, disconsolate, down, downcast, dispirited, depressed, melancholy, blue, gloomy, glum, mournful, woebegone.

unhealthy ADJ = **in poor health**, unwell, ill, ailing, sick, sickly, poorly, infirm.

uniform ADJ 1 = **constant**, consistent, invariable, unvarying, unchanging, steady, stable, regular, even. 2 = **same**, like, identical, similar, equal. NOUN = **livery**, regalia, dress, costume.

unimportant ADJ = **insignificant**, inconsequential, of no account, immaterial, irrelevant, minor, slight, trivial, petty.

uninhibited ADJ = **unselfconscious**, free and easy, relaxed, unrestrained, outgoing, extrovert.

unintentional ADJ = **unintended**, accidental, inadvertent, unplanned, unpremeditated, involuntary, unwitting.

uninterested ADJ see **indifferent**.

uninterrupted ADJ = **unbroken**, continuous, continual, constant, steady, sustained.

union NOUN 1 = **joining**, junction, merger, fusion, amalgamation, blend, combination, synthesis, coalition. 2 = **association**, league, consortium, syndicate, guild, confederation, federation.

unique ADJ = **only**, single, sole, lone, solitary, exclusive.

unit NOUN = **component**, part, element, constituent, subdivision, segment, module, item.

unite VERB 1 = **join**, unify, link, connect, combine, amalgamate, fuse, blend, mix, merge. 2 = **join forces**, band together, cooperate, collaborate.

unity NOUN = **agreement**, harmony, accord, unanimity, consensus, togetherness, solidarity.

universal ADJ = **general**, all-inclusive, all-embracing, comprehensive, across the board, worldwide, global, widespread, common, ubiquitous.

unkempt ADJ = **untidy**, dishevelled, disordered, tousled, rumpled, windblown, scruffy.

unkind ADJ = **mean**, spiteful, malicious, malevolent, unsympathetic, unfeeling, callous, hard-hearted, heartless, uncharitable, nasty.

unknown ADJ = **unidentified**, unnamed, nameless, anonymous, incognito, unheard of, obscure.

unlikely ADJ = **improbable**, doubtful, dubious, implausible, unconvincing, incredible, unbelievable.

unlimited ADJ 1 = **unrestricted**, unconstrained, unrestrained, uncontrolled, unchecked, untrammelled. 2 = **limitless**, boundless, inexhaustible, immeasurable, untold, incalculable, infinite.

unlucky see **unfortunate**.

unnatural ADJ 1 = **unusual**, abnormal, strange, queer, odd, bizarre. 2 = **affected**, artificial, feigned, false, contrived, studied, strained, forced.

unnecessary ADJ = **needless**, unneeded, inessential, uncalled for, gratuitous, dispensable, expendable, redundant, unwanted.

unpleasant ADJ = **disagreeable**, unpalatable, unsavoury, unappetizing, objectionable, obnoxious, disgusting, repugnant, revolting, nasty.

unpopular ADJ = **disliked**, friendless, unloved, unwanted, unwelcome, rejected, out of favour.

unpredictable ADJ = **erratic**, capricious,

mercurial, volatile,
unstable, unreliable.

unpretentious ADJ
= **simple**, plain, modest,
ordinary, unassuming,
unaffected, natural,
straightforward.

unrealistic ADJ
= **impractical**,
impracticable,
unworkable,
unreasonable, irrational,
illogical, improbable,
fanciful, silly, foolish.

unreasonable ADJ
= **unacceptable**,
outrageous, preposterous,
irrational, illogical;
excessive, immoderate,
undue, inordinate,
disproportionate.

unreliable ADJ
= **undependable**,
irresponsible,
untrustworthy, erratic,
fickle, unpredictable.

unrest NOUN
= **dissatisfaction**,
discontent; dissent,
discord, strife, protest,
rebellion, uprising,
disturbance, trouble.

unruly ADJ = **disorderly**,
undisciplined,
disobedient,
obstreperous, recalcitrant,
refractory, uncontrollable,

wild, wilful, wayward.

unsavoury ADJ
= **unpleasant**,
disagreeable, unpalatable,
distasteful, nasty,
disgusting; disreputable,
degenerate, dishonest,
dishonourable, immoral.

unscrupulous ADJ
= **unprincipled**, unethical,
amoral, immoral,
shameless, corrupt,
dishonest, dishonourable,
devious.

unselfish ADJ = **altruistic**,
selfless, self-sacrificing,
kind, generous,
charitable, public-
spirited, philanthropic.

unsophisticated ADJ
= **unworldly**, naive, simple,
innocent, inexperienced,
childlike, artless,
guileless, ingenuous,
natural, unaffected,
unpretentious.

unsuccessful ADJ
= **failed**, vain, unavailing,
futile, useless, abortive,
ineffective, fruitless,
unproductive,
unprofitable.

unsuitable ADJ
= **inappropriate**, inapt,
inapposite, unfitting, out
of place, unacceptable,
unbecoming, unseemly,

indecorous.

unsure ADJ see **uncertain**
(2).

untidy ADJ = **disordered**, in
disarray, messy,
disarranged, disorganized,
chaotic, cluttered,
muddled, jumbled, topsy-
turvy, at sixes and sevens,
higgledy-piggledy.

unusual ADJ
1 = **uncommon**, atypical,
abnormal, singular, odd,
strange, curious, queer,
bizarre, weird, surprising,
unexpected, different,
unconventional,
unwonted, unorthodox,
irregular.
2 = **extraordinary**,
exceptional, singular,
rare, remarkable,
outstanding.

unwarranted ADJ
= **unjustifiable**,
unjustified, indefensible,
inexcusable, unforgivable,
unpardonable, uncalled-
for, gratuitous.

unwieldy ADJ
= **cumbersome**,
unmanageable, awkward,
clumsy, hefty, bulky.

unwilling ADJ = **reluctant**,
disinclined,
unenthusiastic, grudging,
averse, loath.

upheaval NOUN
= **disruption**, disturbance,
disorder, confusion,
turmoil, chaos.

uphold VERB = **support**,
back, stand by, champion,
defend, maintain, sustain.

upright ADJ 1 = **erect**, on
end, vertical,
perpendicular; rampant.
2 = **honest**, honourable,
upstanding, decent,
respectable, worthy, good,
virtuous, righteous, law-
abiding, moral.

uproar NOUN = **tumult**,
turmoil, disorder,
confusion, commotion,
mayhem, pandemonium,
bedlam, din, noise,
clamour, hubbub, racket.

upset VERB 1 = **overturn**,
knock/push over, upend,
tip over, topple, capsize.
2 = **disturb**, unsettle,
dismay, disquiet, trouble,
worry, agitate, fluster,
distress, hurt, grieve.

up to date ADJ = **modern**,
contemporary, present-
day, new, state-of-the-art,
fashionable, voguish.

urbane ADJ = **suave**,
debonair, sophisticated,
smooth, worldly,
cultivated, cultured,
polished.

urge VERB 1 = **encourage**, exhort, press, enjoin, implore, entreat, appeal, beg, plead; egg on, spur, push. 2 = **advise**, recommend, counsel, advocate, suggest. NOUN = **desire**, need, compulsion, longing, yearning, wish; impulse.

urgent ADJ = **imperative**, vital, crucial, critical, top-priority, acute, pressing, serious, grave.

use VERB 1 = **make use of**, utilize, employ, work, operate, wield, ply, avail yourself of. 2 = **consume**, get through, exhaust, deplete, expend, spend. NOUN = **usefulness**, good, advantage, benefit, service, help, gain, profit, avail; purpose, point.

useful ADJ 1 = **of use**, functional, utilitarian, of service, practical, convenient. 2 = **beneficial**, advantageous, helpful, worthwhile, profitable, rewarding, productive, valuable.

useless ADJ = **vain**, in vain, to no avail, unavailing, unsuccessful, futile, fruitless, unprofitable, unproductive.

usual ADJ = **habitual**, customary, accustomed, wonted, normal, regular, routine, everyday, established, set, familiar, typical, ordinary, average, standard, stock.

usually ADV = **generally**, as a rule, normally, by and large, in the main, mainly, mostly, for the most part, on the whole.

usurp VERB = **take over**, seize, commandeer.

utilitarian ADJ = **practical**, functional, useful, serviceable.

utter VERB = **voice**, say, pronounce, express, enunciate, articulate, verbalize, vocalize.

utterance NOUN = **remark**, word, comment, statement, observation, pronouncement.

Vv

vacancy NOUN = **opening**, position, post, job, opportunity.

vacant ADJ
1 = **unoccupied**, unfilled, free, empty, available, uninhabited, untenanted.
2 = **blank**, expressionless, glassy, emotionless; vacuous, inane.

vacate VERB = **leave**, quit, move out of, evacuate.

vacillate VERB = **dither**, shilly-shally, waver, hesitate, equivocate; [inf] hum and haw.

vacuum NOUN = **emptiness**, void, empty space, nothingness.

vagary NOUN = **change**, variation, quirk, caprice, whim, fancy.

vagrant NOUN = **tramp**, beggar, itinerant, nomad, vagabond.

vague ADJ 1 = **indistinct**, indeterminate, ill-defined, unclear, nebulous, amorphous, shadowy, hazy, fuzzy, blurry. 2 = **imprecise**, inexact, loose, generalized, ambiguous, hazy, woolly.

vain ADJ 1 = **conceited**, narcissistic, self-admiring, proud, arrogant, boastful, cocky. 2 = **unsuccessful**, futile, useless, unavailing, to no avail, ineffective, fruitless, unproductive, abortive.

valid ADJ = **sound**, well founded, reasonable, logical, justifiable, defensible, bona fide; effective, cogent, powerful, convincing, credible, forceful.

validate VERB = **ratify**, legalize, legitimize, authorize, sanction, warrant, approve, endorse.

valley NOUN = **dale**, dell, vale; [Scottish] glen.

valuable ADJ 1 = **costly**, expensive, priceless, precious. 2 = **useful**, helpful, beneficial, advantageous, worthwhile.

value NOUN 1 = **cost**, price. 2 = **worth**, usefulness, advantage, benefit, gain, profit, good, avail; importance, significance. VERB = **rate highly**, appreciate, esteem, think highly of, set store by, respect; prize, cherish, treasure.

vanguard NOUN = **advance guard**, forefront, front, front line, van.

vanish VERB see **disappear**.

vanity NOUN = **conceit**, narcissism, self-love, pride, arrogance, boastfulness.

variation NOUN = **change**, alteration, modification; difference, dissimilarity.

varied ADJ = **diverse**, assorted, miscellaneous, mixed, heterogeneous.

variety NOUN 1 = **variation**, diversification, diversity, change, difference. 2 = **assortment**, selection, miscellany, range, mixture, medley. 3 see **sort**.

various ADJ = **varying**, diverse, different, differing, varied, assorted, sundry, mixed, miscellaneous, heterogeneous.

vary VERB 1 = **differ**, be different, be dissimilar.

2 = **change**, alter, fluctuate.

vault NOUN = **cellar**, basement; crypt, tomb. VERB = **jump**, leap, spring, bound.

veer VERB = **turn**, swerve, swing, sheer, wheel.

vehement ADJ = **passionate**, ardent, impassioned, fervent, strong, forceful, powerful, intense, zealous.

veil VERB = **hide**, conceal, cover, mask, screen.

vein NOUN 1 = **blood vessel**, capillary. 2 = **lode**, seam, stratum. 3 = **streak**, stripe, line, thread.

veneer NOUN 1 = **facing**, covering, coat, finish. 2 = **facade**, false front, show, appearance, semblance, guise, mask, pretence.

venerable ADJ = **venerated**, respected, revered, honoured, esteemed, hallowed.

veneration NOUN = **respect**, reverence, worship, adoration, honour, esteem.

vengeance NOUN = **revenge**, retribution, retaliation, reprisal, an eye for an eye.

venomous ADJ
= **poisonous**, toxic, lethal, deadly, fatal.

vent NOUN = **opening**, outlet, aperture, hole, duct, flue. VERB = **give vent to**, express, air, utter, voice, verbalize.

ventilate VERB = **air**, aerate, oxygenate, freshen.

venture NOUN = **enterprise**, undertaking, project, scheme, gamble.

verbal ADJ = **oral**, spoken, said, stated; unwritten.

verbatim ADJ = **word for word**, literal, exact, faithful, precise.

verbose ADJ = **wordy**, loquacious, garrulous, voluble; long-winded, prolix, lengthy, tautological.

verdict NOUN = **decision**, judgement, adjudication, finding, conclusion, ruling.

verge NOUN = **edge**, border, margin, rim, brink, boundary, perimeter. VERB (**verge on**) = **approach**, border on, be close to.

verify VERB = **confirm**, substantiate, prove, corroborate, attest to, testify to, validate, authenticate.

versatile ADJ = **adaptable**, flexible, resourceful; adjustable, handy, multi-purpose, all-purpose.

verse NOUN 1 = **stanza**, canto, couplet. 2 = **poem**, lyric, sonnet, ode, ballad.

version NOUN 1 = **account**, report, story, rendering, interpretation, understanding, reading, impression. 2 = **variant**, form, type, kind, sort.

verve NOUN = **enthusiasm**, vigour, energy, vitality, vivacity, liveliness, animation, spirit, life, brio, fervour, gusto, passion.

very ADV = **extremely**, exceedingly, exceptionally, uncommonly, unusually, decidedly, particularly, eminently, remarkably, really, truly, awfully, terribly, jolly.

vessel NOUN 1 = **ship**, boat, craft, barque.
2 = **container**, receptacle.

veto VERB = **reject**, turn down, prohibit, forbid, proscribe, disallow, embargo, ban. NOUN = **rejection**, prohibition, proscription, embargo, ban.

viable ADJ = **workable**, feasible, practicable, practical, possible.

vibrant ADJ = **lively**, energetic, spirited, animated, sparkling, vivacious, dynamic.

vibrate VERB = **shake**, oscillate, pulsate, tremble, quiver, throb; resonate, resound, reverberate, ring.

vicarious ADJ = **indirect**, second-hand, surrogate, at one remove.

vice NOUN 1 = **sin**, sinfulness, wrong, wrongdoing, wickedness, immorality, iniquity, evil, corruption, depravity, degeneracy. 2 = **failing**, flaw, fault, defect, weakness, shortcoming.

vicinity NOUN = **surrounding area**, neighbourhood, locality, area, district, region, environs, precincts.

vicious ADJ = **fierce**, ferocious, savage, dangerous, violent, brutal, cruel, inhuman, barbarous, barbaric, fiendish, sadistic.

victimize VERB = **persecute**, terrorize, pick on, discriminate against.

victor NOUN = **winner**, champion, conqueror.

victorious ADJ = **conquering**, triumphant, winning, successful, prize-winning, top, first.

vie VERB = **compete**, contend, contest, struggle, strive.

view NOUN 1 = **sight**, field/ range of vision, vision, eyeshot. 2 = **outlook**, prospect, scene, spectacle, vista, panorama, landscape. 3 = **point of view**, viewpoint, attitude, opinion, belief, way of thinking, thought, idea, feeling, sentiment. VERB = **look at**, watch, observe, contemplate, regard, survey, inspect, scrutinize.

vigilant ADJ = **watchful**, on the lookout, observant, sharp-eyed, eagle-eyed, attentive, alert, on your guard, careful, wary.

vigorous ADJ 1 = **robust**, healthy, strong, fit, tough. 2 = **energetic**, lively, spry, active, spirited, sprightly, vibrant, full of life.

vigour NOUN see **verve**.

vile ADJ = **foul**, nasty, horrid, horrible,

offensive, obnoxious, odious, repulsive, repellent, revolting, repugnant, disgusting, loathsome, hateful, nauseating, sickening, dreadful, abominable, monstrous.

vilify VERB = **defame**, run down, revile, denigrate, disparage, speak ill of, cast aspersions on, malign, slander, libel.

villain NOUN = **rogue**, scoundrel, blackguard, wretch, cad, reprobate, wrongdoer, miscreant.

vindicate VERB = **acquit**, clear, absolve, exonerate.

vindictive ADJ = **vengeful**, revengeful, avenging, unforgiving, resentful, spiteful, rancorous, venomous, malicious, malevolent.

vintage ADJ = **classic**, ageless, enduring, prime, choice, select, superior.

violate VERB 1 = **break**, breach, infringe, contravene, transgress, disobey, disregard. 2 = **desecrate**, profane, defile.

violence NOUN = **force**, brute force, roughness, ferocity, brutality, savagery.

violent ADJ 1 = **brutal**, vicious, destructive, savage, fierce, ferocious, bloodthirsty, homicidal, murderous. 2 = **strong**, powerful, uncontrolled, unrestrained, unbridled, uncontrollable, ungovernable, wild, passionate, intense, extreme, vehement.

virtue NOUN 1 = **goodness**, righteousness, morality, integrity, rectitude, honesty, honour, probity, decency, respectability. 2 = **good point**, asset, advantage, merit, strength.

virtuous ADJ 1 = **good**, righteous, moral, ethical, upright, upstanding, honest, honourable, incorruptible, decent, respectable. 2 = **virginal**, celibate, pure, chaste.

virulent ADJ 1 = **poisonous**, toxic, venomous, deadly, lethal, fatal. 2 = **hostile**, spiteful, venomous, vicious, vindictive, malicious, malevolent, vitriolic, bitter, rancorous, scathing.

visible ADJ = **perceptible**, apparent, evident,

noticeable, recognizable, manifest, plain, clear, obvious, patent, unmistakable, distinct.

vision NOUN 1 = **sight**, eyesight. 2 = **apparition**, dream, hallucination, mirage, illusion.

visionary ADJ = **idealistic**, impractical, unrealistic, utopian, romantic, quixotic; inspired, imaginative, creative. NOUN = **mystic**, seer, prophet; dreamer, daydreamer, idealist, romantic, fantasist.

visualize VERB = **envisage**, conjure up, picture, envision, imagine.

vital ADJ 1 = **essential**, necessary, indispensable, key, imperative, critical, crucial, all-important. 2 = **lively**, animated, spirited, vivacious, vibrant, dynamic, energetic, vigorous.

vitality NOUN = **life**, liveliness, animation, spirit, spiritedness, vivacity, vibrancy, zest, dynamism, energy, vigour.

vivacious ADJ = **lively**, full of life, animated, effervescent, bubbly, ebullient, sparkling, spirited, high-spirited, vibrant, dynamic, vital.

vivid ADJ 1 = **strong**, intense, colourful, rich, glowing, bright, brilliant, clear. 2 = **graphic**, dramatic, striking, lively, stirring, powerful, realistic, memorable.

vocation NOUN = **profession**, calling, life's work, occupation, career, métier, trade, craft, job.

voice VERB = **put into words**, express, utter, articulate, vocalize, air, give vent to.

void ADJ 1 = **empty**, emptied, vacant, bare, clear, free, unfilled. 2 = **null and void**, invalid, ineffective, non-viable, useless, worthless.

volatile ADJ 1 = **capricious**, mercurial, unpredictable, changeable, inconstant, erratic, unstable. 2 = **explosive**, charged, tense, strained.

voluble ADJ = **talkative**, loquacious, garrulous, chatty; eloquent, forthcoming, fluent, glib.

volume NOUN 1 = **book**, publication, tome. 2 = **space**, bulk, capacity.

3 = loudness, sound, amplification.

voluminous ADJ = **capacious**, roomy, ample, full, big, billowing.

voluntary ADJ = **of your own free will**, of your own accord; optional, discretionary, elective, non-compulsory.

voluptuous ADJ **1 = hedonistic**, sybaritic, epicurean, self-indulgent, sensual. **2 = curvy**, shapely, full-figured, buxom, curvaceous.

voracious ADJ **1 = greedy**, gluttonous, ravenous. **2 = insatiable**, compulsive, enthusiastic, eager.

vote NOUN = **ballot**, poll, election, referendum, plebiscite.

vouch VERB (**vouch for**) = **attest to**, bear witness to, answer for, be responsible for, guarantee.

vow VERB = **swear**, pledge, promise, undertake, give your word, commit yourself.

voyage NOUN = **journey**, trip, expedition, crossing, cruise, passage.

vulgar ADJ **1 = rude**, indecent, indecorous, indelicate, crude, coarse, offensive, off colour, ribald, bawdy, obscene, salacious, smutty, dirty, filthy; [inf] raunchy. **2 = tasteless**, crass, tawdry, ostentatious, showy, flashy, gaudy.

vulnerable ADJ = **exposed**, unprotected, unguarded, open to attack, defenceless, helpless, weak.

wad NOUN **1 = pad**, lump, mass, ball, plug. **2 = bundle**, roll.

wag VERB = **swing**, swish, shake, twitch, wave, wiggle, waggle.

wage NOUN = **pay**, salary, earnings, payment, fee, remuneration, stipend, emolument.

wager NOUN = **bet**, gamble, stake; [inf] flutter. VERB

= **bet**, gamble, lay odds, put money on, speculate.

wail VERB = **howl**, bawl, yowl, weep, cry, sob, moan, whine, lament.

wait VERB = **stay**, remain, rest, stop, linger; delay, hold back, bide your time, hang fire, mark time; [inf] hang around, sit tight, hold your horses. NOUN = **delay**, hold-up, interruption, interval.

waive VERB = **relinquish**, renounce, give up, abandon, surrender, yield, forgo.

wake[1] VERB 1 = **awake**, awaken, waken, wake up, stir, come to, get up; [formal] arise. 2 = **rouse**, evoke, stir up, activate, stimulate. NOUN = **vigil**, watch; funeral.

wake[2] NOUN = **wash**, backwash, slipstream, trail, path.

walk VERB 1 = **stroll**, saunter, amble, plod, trudge, hike, tramp, trek, march, stride, step. 2 = **go on/by foot**, go on/by Shanks's pony. 3 = **accompany**, escort, see, take. 4 (**walk out on**) = **desert**, abandon, forsake, leave, leave in the lurch, run away from, throw over, jilt; [inf] chuck, dump. NOUN 1 = **stroll**, saunter, promenade, ramble, hike, tramp, march, airing; [dated] constitutional. 2 = **path**, pathway, footpath, track, avenue, walkway, promenade, pavement.

wall NOUN 1 = **partition**, screen, divider, separator. 2 = **barrier**, barricade, obstacle.

wallet NOUN = **purse**, notecase; [US] pocketbook, billfold.

wallow VERB 1 = **loll around**, lie around, roll around, splash around. 2 = **luxuriate**, bask, indulge (yourself), delight, revel, glory; enjoy.

wan ADJ = **pale**, pallid, ashen, white; anaemic, colourless, bloodless, waxen, washed out, pasty, peaky.

wand NOUN = **baton**, stick, staff, bar, rod.

wander VERB 1 = **stroll**, saunter, walk, ramble, roam, meander, rove, range, drift; [inf] mosey, mooch. 2 = **stray**, depart, diverge, veer, swerve, deviate, digress.

wanderer NOUN = **traveller**, rambler, itinerant, nomad, bird of passage, rolling stone, drifter.

wane VERB = **decrease**, decline, diminish, dwindle, shrink, taper off, subside, sink, ebb, dim, fade away, vanish, die out, peter out.

want VERB 1 = **desire**, wish for, long for, hope for, yearn for, pine for, fancy, crave, hanker after, hunger for, thirst for, lust after, covet, need; [inf] have a yen for. 2 = **need**, be in need of, require, call for, demand, cry out for. NOUN 1 = **lack**, absence, unavailability; dearth, deficiency, inadequacy, insufficiency, paucity, shortage, scarcity. 2 = **need**, privation, poverty, destitution, penury. 3 = **wish**, desire, longing, yearning, fancy, craving, hankering, hunger, thirst.

wanting ADJ = **deficient**, inadequate, lacking, insufficient.

wanton ADJ 1 = **deliberate**, unprovoked, wilful, malicious, spiteful, wicked, arbitrary, unjustified, needless, unnecessary, uncalled for, gratuitous, senseless, pointless. 2 = **promiscuous**, immoral, shameless, fast, lascivious, licentious, libertine, dissolute; [dated] loose, of easy virtue.

war NOUN = **warfare**, hostilities, combat, fighting, struggle, armed conflict, battle, fight, campaign.

ward NOUN 1 = **room**, department, unit, area. 2 = **district**, constituency, division, quarter, zone, parish. 3 = **charge**, dependant, protégé. VERB (**ward off**) = **fend off**, stave off, parry, avert, deflect, repel, repulse.

warder NOUN = **prison officer**, guard, warden, jailer, gaoler; [inf] screw.

warehouse NOUN = **store**, storehouse, depot, depository, stockroom.

wares PLURAL NOUN = **goods**, products, commodities, merchandise, produce, stuff, stock.

warlike ADJ = **aggressive**, belligerent, bellicose, pugnacious, combative, militaristic, militant, martial.

warm ADJ **1** = **heated**, tepid, lukewarm. **2** = **sunny**, balmy. **3** = **kind**, friendly, affable, amiable, genial, cordial, sympathetic, affectionate, loving, tender, caring, charitable, sincere, genuine.

warn VERB **1** = **inform**, notify, give notice, tell, let know, forewarn; [inf] tip off, put wise. **2** = **advise**, exhort, urge, counsel, caution.

warning NOUN **1** = **information**, notification, notice, word, forewarning; [inf] tip-off. **2** = **advice**, exhortation, counselling, caution. **3** = **omen**, foretoken, token, augury, signal, sign.

warrant NOUN = **authorization**, consent, sanction, permission, licence. VERB = **justify**, vindicate, excuse, account for, be a reason for.

wary ADJ = **careful**, cautious, circumspect, chary, suspicious, distrustful, leery, on your guard, on the alert, attentive, heedful, watchful.

wash VERB **1** = **wash yourself**, bath, bathe, shower. **2** = **clean**, cleanse, sponge, scrub, launder, shampoo. **3** = **splash**, dash, break, beat. NOUN = **bath**, shower, ablutions; clean, cleaning.

waste VERB = **squander**, dissipate, fritter away, misspend, misuse, throw away, go through; [inf] blow. NOUN **1** = **squandering**, dissipation, misuse, prodigality. **2** = **rubbish**, refuse, debris, dross, dregs, leavings, garbage, trash. ADJ **1** = **leftover**, unused, superfluous, unwanted, worthless, useless. **2** = **desert**, barren, uncultivated, unproductive, arid, bare, desolate, uninhabited, unpopulated, wild, bleak, cheerless.

wasteful ADJ = **extravagant**, prodigal, profligate, thriftless, spendthrift, lavish.

watch VERB **1** = **look at**, observe, view, eye, gaze at, stare at, contemplate, behold, inspect, scrutinize, survey, scan, examine. **2** = **keep watch**

on, keep in sight, spy on; [inf] keep tabs on. **3 = mind**, take care of, look after, supervise, superintend, tend, guard, protect, keep an eye on. NOUN **1 = wristwatch**, pocket watch, timepiece, chronometer, stopwatch. **2 = guard**, vigil.

watchful ADJ **= vigilant**, alert, observant, attentive, heedful, sharp-eyed, eagle-eyed, wary, circumspect.

water NOUN **1** Adam's ale, H_2O. **2** sea, river, lake, loch, pool, reservoir. VERB **1 = sprinkle**, moisten, dampen, wet, douse, hose, spray, drench, saturate, flood. **2** (**water down**) **= dilute**, thin, weaken, adulterate.

waterfall NOUN **= falls**, cascade, cataract.

watertight ADJ **1 = waterproof**, impermeable. **2 = incontrovertible**, indisputable, foolproof, unassailable, impregnable, flawless.

watery ADJ **1 = liquid**, liquefied, fluid, aqueous. **2 = wet**, damp, moist, sodden, soggy, squelchy, saturated, waterlogged, marshy, boggy. **3 = thin**, runny, weak, diluted, watered down.

wave NOUN **1 = breaker**, roller, ripple, billow, white horse, swell, surf. **2 = curl**, undulation, kink. **3 = spate**, surge, upsurge, rush outbreak, rash. VERB **1 = shake**, move up and down, waggle, wag. **2 = gesture**, gesticulate, signal, sign, beckon, indicate. **3 = ripple**, undulate, stir, flutter, flap, sway, swing.

waver VERB **1 = falter**, flicker, wobble. **2 = hesitate**, be indecisive, dither, equivocate, hem and haw, vacillate; [inf] shilly-shally, pussyfoot around.

wavy ADJ **= curly**, undulating, squiggly, rippled, curving, winding.

way NOUN **1 = method**, means, course of action, process, procedure, technique, system, plan, scheme, manner, mode, modus operandi. **2 = habit**, custom, wont, practice, conduct, behaviour, manner, style, nature, disposition, characteristic, trait, attribute, mannerism, peculiarity, idiosyncrasy. 3 = **direction**, route, course, path.

waylay VERB = **ambush**, attack, lie in wait for, hold up; accost, intercept.

wayward ADJ = **wilful**, self-willed, headstrong, stubborn, obstinate, perverse, contrary, uncooperative, refractory, recalcitrant, unruly, ungovernable, unmanageable, incorrigible, disobedient.

weak ADJ 1 = **frail**, fragile, delicate, feeble, infirm, sickly, debilitated, incapacitated, puny. 2 = **unconvincing**, untenable, unsatisfactory, feeble, flimsy, lame.

weaken VERB 1 = **enfeeble**, debilitate, incapacitate, sap, enervate, tire, exhaust, wear out. 2 = **decrease**, dwindle, diminish, let up, abate, lessen, ease up.

weakling NOUN = **milksop**, namby-pamby, coward; [inf] wimp, sissy, drip, doormat.

weakness NOUN 1 = **frailty**, fragility, delicacy, feebleness, infirmity, debility, incapacity, indisposition, enervation, fatigue. 2 = **cowardliness**, spinelessness, timidity, impotence. 3 = **fault**, flaw, weak point, failing, defect, shortcoming, imperfection, Achilles' heel.

wealth NOUN 1 = **affluence**, riches, fortune, means, assets, possessions, resources, funds, money, cash, capital, treasure, property, holdings, wherewithal. 2 = **abundance**, profusion, plethora, mine, cornucopia.

wealthy ADJ = **rich**, affluent, well off, well-to-do, moneyed, prosperous, of means, of substance; [inf] well heeled, rolling in it, loaded.

wear VERB 1 = **have on**, be dressed in, be clothed in, sport. 2 = **erode**, corrode, abrade. 3 (**wear out**) = **fatigue**, tire, weary, exhaust, drain, sap, prostrate, enervate. 4 (**wear off**) = **fade**, diminish, dwindle, decrease, lessen, disappear, subside, ebb.

weary ADJ = **tired**, fatigued, exhausted, drained, worn out, spent, enervated, prostrate; [inf] dead beat, dog-tired, knackered.

weather VERB = **survive**, come through, ride out, withstand, surmount, overcome, resist.

weave VERB 1 = **entwine**, interlace, intertwine, twist, braid, plait.
2 = **invent**, make up, fabricate, construct, create, contrive.

web NOUN = **lacework**, mesh, lattice, latticework, net, netting.

wed VERB = **marry**, get married, become man and wife; [inf] get hitched, tie the knot.

wedding NOUN = **marriage**, nuptials.

wedge VERB = **squeeze**, cram, jam, thrust, stuff, ram, force.

weep VERB = **cry**, sob, wail, snivel, whimper, lament, grieve, mourn, keen; [inf] blubber, blub.

weigh VERB (**weigh up**) = **consider**, contemplate, think over, mull over, ponder, deliberate over, muse on, reflect on.

weight NOUN 1 = **heaviness**, load, poundage, tonnage, avoirdupois. 2 = **burden**, load, onus, millstone, albatross, trouble, worry, strain. 3 = **influence**, force, importance, significance, consequence, value, substance; [inf] clout.

weird ADJ 1 = **uncanny**, eerie, unnatural, unearthly, ghostly, strange, queer, mysterious; [inf] spooky, creepy. 2 = **bizarre**, outlandish, eccentric, odd, strange, peculiar, queer, freakish, offbeat.

welcome NOUN = **greeting**, salutation, reception. VERB 1 = **greet**, receive, meet, usher in. 2 = **approve of**, be pleased by, embrace. ADJ = **pleasing**, agreeable, gratifying, cheering; wanted, appreciated, popular, desirable.

welfare NOUN = **well-being**, health, happiness, comfort, security, prosperity, success, fortune.

well¹ ADJ 1 = **healthy**, fit, strong, robust, hale and hearty, thriving.
2 = **satisfactory**, all right, fine; [inf] OK.

well² NOUN **1** = **spring**, borehole, waterhole. **2** = **source**, supply, wellspring, fount, reservoir, mine.

well built ADJ = **sturdy**, burly, strapping, strong, muscular, brawny, hefty; [inf] husky, beefy.

well off ADJ = **wealthy**, rich, well-to-do, moneyed, affluent, prosperous, of means, of substance; [inf] well heeled, rolling in it, made of money, loaded, quids in, filthy rich.

wet ADJ **1** = **damp**, moist, soaked, drenched, saturated, sopping, dripping, soggy, waterlogged. **2** = **rainy**, raining, pouring, showery, drizzling, damp. VERB = **dampen**, damp, moisten, sprinkle, spray, douse.

wharf NOUN = **quay**, pier, jetty, dock, landing stage.

wheeze VERB = **gasp**, rasp, whistle, hiss, cough.

whim NOUN = **impulse**, desire, urge, notion, fancy, caprice, vagary, inclination.

whimper VERB = **whine**, cry, sob, sniffle, snivel, moan.

whimsical ADJ **1** = **fanciful**, playful, mischievous, waggish, quaint. **2** = **capricious**, fickle, volatile, changeable, unpredictable.

whine VERB = **whimper**, cry, wail, moan; [inf] grizzle.

whip VERB = **flog**, lash, scourge, flagellate, cane, thrash, beat, belt, tan the hide of. NOUN = **lash**, scourge, cat-o'-nine-tails, crop.

whirl VERB = **spin**, rotate, revolve, wheel, turn, circle, twirl, swirl, gyrate.

whirlpool NOUN = **eddy**, vortex, maelstrom.

whirlwind NOUN = **tornado**, hurricane, typhoon. ADJ = **rapid**, swift, quick, speedy, headlong.

whisper VERB = **murmur**, mutter, speak softly. NOUN = **murmur**, mutter, hushed tone, undertone.

white ADJ = **pale**, wan, pallid, ashen, bloodless, waxen, pasty, peaky.

whole ADJ **1** = **entire**, complete, full, unabridged, uncut. **2** = **intact**, in one piece, undamaged, unharmed, unhurt.

wholehearted ADJ
= **unreserved**, unqualified, complete, full, total, committed, emphatic, enthusiastic.

wholesale ADJ
= **extensive**, widespread, wide-ranging, indiscriminate, mass, total, comprehensive.

wholesome ADJ
1 = **nutritious**, nourishing, healthy, good. 2 = **moral**, ethical, uplifting, edifying, respectable, innocent, clean.

wholly ADV = **completely**, totally, fully, entirely, utterly, thoroughly, in every respect.

wicked ADJ = **evil**, sinful, immoral, bad, wrong, villainous, base, vile, foul, corrupt, iniquitous, nefarious, heinous, abhorrent, monstrous, atrocious, abominable, despicable, hateful, odious, criminal, lawless, dastardly.

wide ADJ 1 = **broad**, extensive, spacious.
2 = **extensive**, broad, large, vast, wide-ranging, comprehensive, catholic.

widen VERB = **broaden**, expand, extend, enlarge, increase; dilate.

widespread ADJ
= **general**, extensive, universal, common, prevalent, rife, pervasive.

width NOUN 1 = **breadth**, broadness, span, diameter. 2 = **scope**, breadth, range, extent, extensiveness.

wield VERB 1 = **brandish**, flourish, wave, swing, use, ply. 2 = **exercise**, exert, have, hold, possess.

wild ADJ 1 = **untamed**, undomesticated, feral, savage, fierce, ferocious.
2 = **uncultivated**, native, indigenous. 3 = **primitive**, uncivilized; savage, barbarous. 4 = **stormy**, tempestuous, turbulent, blustery, squally.
5 = **uncontrolled**, unrestrained, out of control, undisciplined, rowdy, unruly, riotous, disorderly.

wilful ADJ 1 = **deliberate**, intentional, conscious, premeditated, planned, calculated.
2 = **headstrong**, obstinate, stubborn, pig-headed, self-willed, recalcitrant, uncooperative.

will NOUN 1 = **volition**,

choice, option, decision, prerogative. **2** = **desire**, wish, preference, inclination.

3 = **determination**, will power, resolution, resolve, single-mindedness, doggedness, tenacity.

willing ADJ = **prepared**, ready, disposed, minded, happy, glad; [inf] game.

willingly ADV = **voluntarily**, of your own free will, of your own accord, readily, gladly, happily.

wilt VERB = **droop**, sag, wither, shrivel; languish.

wily ADJ = **shrewd**, clever, sharp, astute, canny; cunning, crafty, artful, sly.

win VERB **1** = **come first**, be victorious, carry the day, succeed, triumph, prevail. **2** = **secure**, gain, pick up, carry off; [inf] land, bag.

wind[1] NOUN = **breeze**, air current, gust; gale, hurricane; [literary] zephyr.

wind[2] VERB = **twist (and turn)**, curve, bend, loop, snake, zigzag.

windy ADJ = **breezy**, blowy, blustery, gusty; stormy, wild, tempestuous.

wink VERB **1** = **blink**, flutter, bat. **2** = **sparkle**, twinkle, shine, flash, glitter, gleam.

winner NOUN = **victor**, champion, conqueror.

winning ADJ **1** = **victorious**, successful, triumphant, conquering. **2** = **engaging**, charming, endearing, sweet, cute, disarming, winsome, fetching.

wintry ADJ = **cold**, chilly, icy, freezing, frosty, snowy, glacial, bleak, bitter.

wipe VERB = **rub**, mop, sponge, swab; clean, dry.

wiry ADJ **1** = **sinewy**, tough, athletic; lean, spare, thin. **2** = **coarse**, rough; curly.

wisdom NOUN = **sagacity**, intelligence, knowledge, discernment, perception, insight, sense, common sense, shrewdness, astuteness, prudence, judiciousness.

wise ADJ = **sage**, sagacious, clever, intelligent, learned, knowledgeable, discerning, perceptive, insightful, sensible, prudent, judicious, shrewd, canny, astute, smart.

wish NOUN = **desire**, longing, hope, yearning, craving, hunger, thirst, hankering, want, aspiration, inclination, urge, whim. VERB = **desire**, want, long for, hope for, yearn for, fancy, crave, hunger for, thirst for, lust after, covet, set your heart on, hanker after, have a yen for.

wishy-washy ADJ
1 = **feeble**, weak, ineffectual, effete, spineless, weak-kneed.
2 = **watery**, weak; bland, tasteless, flavourless, insipid.

wistful ADJ = **nostalgic**, yearning, longing; plaintive, regretful, rueful, forlorn, melancholy; pensive, reflective.

wit NOUN 1 = **wittiness**, humour, drollery; repartee, badinage, banter, raillery.
2 = **comedian**, humorist, wag, comic; [inf] card.

witch NOUN = **sorceress**, enchantress, hex.

witchcraft NOUN = **sorcery**, (black) magic, witchery, wizardry, the occult.

withdraw VERB 1 = **remove**, extract, take away, take out, pull out. 2 = **retract**, take back, unsay.

3 = **leave**, pull out, retreat, depart.

withdrawn ADJ
= **reserved**, quiet, uncommunicative, introverted, unsociable, inhibited; shy, timid, retiring.

wither VERB = **shrivel**, dry up/out, wilt, droop, die.

withhold VERB 1 = **hold back**, keep back, retain, refuse to give.
2 = **suppress**, repress, restrain, check, control.

withstand VERB = **resist**, hold out against, endure, weather, survive, stand, tolerate, bear.

witness NOUN
= **eyewitness**, observer, spectator, onlooker; bystander. VERB = **see**, observe, view, watch; be present at, attend.

witticism NOUN = **joke**, quip, jest, pun, bon mot; [inf] wisecrack, crack, one-liner.

witty ADJ = **amusing**, funny, humorous, droll, facetious, waggish, comic, sparkling, scintillating.

wizard NOUN = **sorcerer**, warlock, magician, magus.

wizened ADJ = **wrinkled**,

lined, gnarled, withered, shrivelled, weather-beaten, shrunken.

wobble VERB = **rock**, teeter, sway, see-saw, shake.

woe NOUN 1 = **misery**, sorrow, distress wretchedness, sadness, unhappiness, grief, anguish, pain, suffering, despair, gloom, melancholy. 2 (**woes**) = **troubles**, problems, misfortunes, trials, tribulations, difficulties.

woman NOUN 1 = **lady**, girl, female; [inf] bird, chick; [US inf] dame. 2 = **girlfriend**, sweetheart, partner, lover; wife, spouse.

wonder NOUN 1 = **awe**, admiration, fascination; surprise, astonishment, amazement. 2 = **marvel**, phenomenon, miracle, spectacle, beauty. VERB = **ponder**, think, speculate, conjecture, muse, reflect, ask yourself.

wonderful ADJ = **marvellous**, magnificent, superb, excellent, glorious, lovely; [inf] super, fantastic, great, terrific, tremendous, sensational, fabulous, incredible, awesome, brilliant.

wood NOUN 1 = **forest**, woodland, trees; copse, coppice, grove. 2 = **timber**, logs, planks; [US] lumber.

woolly ADJ 1 = **woollen**, wool. 2 = **fleecy**, fluffy, shaggy. 3 = **vague**, hazy, unclear, imprecise, confused, muddled.

word NOUN 1 = **term**, expression, name. 2 = **promise**, word of honour, pledge, assurance, guarantee, undertaking, vow, oath. 3 = **news**, information, communication, message, report. VERB = **phrase**, express, couch, put.

wordy ADJ = **long-winded**, verbose, prolix, rambling; garrulous, voluble.

work NOUN 1 = **labour**, toil, slog, effort, exertion, sweat, drudgery, industry; [literary] travail. 2 = **task**, job, duty, assignment; chore. 3 = **employment**, occupation; job, profession, career, trade, vocation, calling. VERB 1 = **be employed**, have a job, earn your living. 2 = **toil**, labour, slog, exert yourself, slave; [inf] plug away. 3 = **function**, go, operate, run. **4 = operate**, use, control, handle, manipulate.

worker NOUN = **employee**, hand, workman, labourer, operative; wage-earner.

workmanship NOUN = **craftsmanship**, craft, artistry, art, handiwork; expertise, skill.

workshop NOUN
1 = **factory**, works, plant.
2 = **workroom**, studio, atelier.

world NOUN 1 = **earth**, globe, planet. 2 = **sphere**, society, milieu, realm, domain, province.

worldly ADJ 1 = **earthly**, terrestrial, temporal, secular, material, carnal, fleshly, corporeal, physical.
2 = **sophisticated**, worldly-wise, urbane, experienced, knowing, cosmopolitan.

worn ADJ 1 = **shabby**, worn out, threadbare, tattered, in tatters, ragged, frayed.
2 = **haggard**, drawn, strained, careworn; weary, tired.

worried ADJ = **anxious**, perturbed, troubled, bothered, distressed, concerned, upset, distraught, uneasy, fretful, agitated, nervous, edgy, on edge, tense, apprehensive, fearful, afraid, frightened; [inf] uptight.

worry VERB 1 = **fret**, brood, be anxious. 2 = **trouble**, disturb, bother, distress, upset, concern, disquiet, unsettle. NOUN 1 = **anxiety**, perturbation, distress, concern, unease, disquiet, fretfulness, agitation, edginess, apprehension.
2 = **nuisance**, pest, trial, trouble, problem, headache.

worsen VERB 1 = **aggravate**, exacerbate, intensify, increase, heighten.
2 = **deteriorate**, degenerate, decline, slide; [inf] go downhill.

worship NOUN = **reverence**, veneration, homage, honour, adoration, devotion, praise, glorification, exaltation.
VERB 1 = **revere**, venerate, pay homage to, honour, adore, praise, pray to, glorify, exalt. 2 = **adore**, idolize, hero-worship, lionize.

worth NOUN 1 = **value**, price, cost. 2 = **benefit**, value, use, advantage, virtue, service, gain, profit, help.

worthless ADJ
1 = **valueless**, cheap, shoddy, gimcrack.
2 = **useless**, no use, ineffective, fruitless, unavailing, pointless.
3 = **good-for-nothing**, ne'er-do-well, useless, feckless.

worthwhile ADJ
= **valuable**, useful, of use, beneficial, advantageous, helpful, profitable, productive, constructive.

worthy ADJ = **virtuous**, good, moral, upright, upstanding, righteous, honest, principled, decent, honourable, respectable, reputable.

wound NOUN = **injury**, lesion, cut, graze, scratch, gash, laceration. VERB = **injure**, hurt, cut, graze, scratch, gash, lacerate, tear, puncture, slash.

wrap VERB = **swathe**, envelop, enfold, swaddle, cloak.

wrath NOUN = **anger**, rage, fury, outrage, annoyance, exasperation.

wreathe VERB 1 = **encircle**, surround; garland, festoon, adorn, deck,

decorate. 2 = **spiral**, twist, wind, coil, curl.

wreck NOUN 1 = **shipwreck**, sunken ship.
2 = **wreckage**, debris, remains, ruins. VERB
1 = **demolish**, smash up, damage, destroy, write off; vandalize. 2 = **ruin**, destroy, devastate, shatter, undo, spoil, dash.

wrench VERB = **twist**, pull, tug, yank, wrest, jerk, tear, force.

wretched ADJ = **miserable**, unhappy, sad, broken-hearted, sorrowful, distressed, desolate, dejected, despairing, depressed, melancholy, gloomy, mournful, woebegone, doleful, forlorn, abject.

wriggle VERB = **squirm**, twist, writhe, wiggle, flail; snake, worm, slither.

wring VERB 1 = **twist**, squeeze. 2 = **extract**, force, exact, wrest, wrench.

wrinkle NOUN = **crease**, fold, pucker, furrow, ridge, line, crinkle, crow's foot.

write VERB 1 = **write down**, put in writing, jot down, note, record, list, inscribe, scribble, scrawl.

2 = **compose**, draft, pen, dash off.

writer NOUN = **author**, wordsmith, penman, novelist, essayist, biographer, journalist, columnist, scriptwriter; [inf] hack, pen-pusher.

writhe VERB = **squirm**, twist and turn, toss and turn, wriggle, thrash, flail, struggle.

writing NOUN

1 = **handwriting**, hand, penmanship, script, calligraphy; scribble, scrawl. 2 = **works**, oeuvre, books, publications.

wrong ADJ 1 = **incorrect**, inaccurate, in error, erroneous, mistaken, inexact, wide of the mark, off target; [inf] off beam. 2 = **illegal**, unlawful, illicit, criminal, dishonest, unethical, immoral, bad, wicked, sinful, blameworthy; [inf] crooked. 3 = **inappropriate**, unsuitable, inapt, inapposite, undesirable, infelicitous. 4 = **amiss**, awry, out of order, faulty, defective. NOUN

1 = **immorality**, sin, sinfulness, wickedness, crime, villainy, wrongdoing. 2 = **misdeed**, offence, crime, transgression, sin. VERB

1 = **ill-use**, mistreat, abuse, harm, hurt. 2 = **malign**, misrepresent, impugn, defame, slander, libel.

wrongdoer NOUN

= **offender**, lawbreaker, criminal, delinquent, culprit, villain, malefactor, miscreant, sinner.

wrongful ADJ = **unfair**, unjust, improper, unjustified, unwarranted, unlawful, illegal.

wry ADJ 1 = **ironic**, sardonic, mocking, sarcastic, dry, droll, witty. 2 = **twisted**, contorted, crooked.

Yy

yearly ADJ = **annual**, once a year, every year, per annum.

yearn VERB = **long**, pine, crave, desire, wish for, hanker after, ache, hunger for, thirst for.

yell VERB = **shout**, cry out, howl, scream, shriek, screech, roar, bawl; [inf] holler.

yen NOUN = **hankering**, desire, wish, fancy, longing, craving, hunger, thirst.

yield VERB 1 = **produce**, provide, supply, give, return, bring in, earn. 2 = **give up**, surrender, relinquish, part with, cede. 3 = **admit defeat**, surrender, capitulate, submit, give in/up.

yokel NOUN = **rustic**, peasant, country bumpkin, provincial; [US] [inf] hillbilly.

young ADJ 1 = **youthful**, juvenile, junior, adolescent. 2 = **new**, recent, undeveloped, fledgling, in the making.

youngster NOUN = **child**, youth, juvenile, teenager, adolescent, boy, girl, lad, lass; [inf] kid.

youth NOUN 1 = **young days**, teens, adolescence, boyhood, girlhood, childhood. 2 = **boy**, lad, youngster, juvenile, teenager, adolescent; [inf] kid.

youthful ADJ = **young**, active, vigorous, spry, sprightly; boyish, girlish.

Zz

zeal NOUN = **passion**, energy, enthusiasm, commitment, ardour, fervour, eagerness, keenness, gusto; fanaticism.

zealous ADJ = **ardent**, fervent, fervid, passionate, enthusiastic, eager, keen, energetic; fanatical.

zenith NOUN = **highest point**, height, top, peak, pinnacle.

zero NOUN = **nought**, nothing, naught, nil, 0; [inf] zilch.

zest NOUN = **relish**, appetite, enjoyment, gusto, enthusiasm, eagerness, energy.

zone NOUN = **area**, sector, section, belt, district, region, province.